STUDY GUIDE AND SELF-EXAMINATION REVIEW

FOR KAPLAN AND SADOCK'S

Synopsis of Psychiatry

SIXTH  EDITION

Senior Contributing Editor

Robert Cancro, M.D., Med.D.Sc.

Professor and Chairman, Department of Psychiatry, New York University School of Medicine; Director, Department of Psychiatry, Tisch Hospital, the University Hospital of New York University Medical Center, New York, New York; Director, Nathan S. Kline Institute for Psychiatric Research, Orangeburg, New York

Contributing Editors

James C. Edmondson, M.D., Ph.D.

Clinical Assistant Professor of Neurology, Department of Neurology, College of Medicine, State University of New York Health Science Center at Brooklyn; Assistant Attending, Department of Neurology, Brooklyn Hospital Center; Assistant Attending, Department of Neurology, Long Island College Hospital, Brooklyn, New York

Myrl Manley, M.D.

Associate Professor of Clinical Psychiatry and Director of Medical Student Education, New York University School of Medicine, New York, New York

Caroly S. Pataki, M.D.

Assistant Clinical Professor of Psychiatry and Associate Director of Training and Education for Child and Adolescent Psychiatry, University of California at Los Angeles School of Medicine; Attending Psychiatrist, UCLA Neuropsychiatric Institute, Los Angeles, California

Virginia A. Sadock, M.D.

Clinical Professor of Psychiatry and Director, Program in Human Sexuality and Sex Therapy, Department of Psychiatry, New York University School of Medicine; Attending Psychiatrist, Tisch Hospital, the University Hospital of the New York University Medical Center; Attending Psychiatrist, Bellevue Hospital Center, New York, New York

STUDY GUIDE AND SELF-EXAMINATION REVIEW

FOR KAPLAN AND SADOCK'S

Synopsis of Psychiatry

SIXTH  EDITION

Harold I. Kaplan, M.D.

Professor of Psychiatry,
New York University School of Medicine
Attending Psychiatrist, Tisch Hospital, the University Hospital
of the New York University Medical Center
Attending Psychiatrist, Bellevue Hospital
Consultant Psychiatrist, Lenox Hill Hospital
New York, New York

Benjamin J. Sadock, M.D.

Professor and Vice Chairman,
Department of Psychiatry, New York University School of Medicine
Attending Psychiatrist, Tisch Hospital, the University Hospital
of the New York University Medical Center
Attending Psychiatrist, Bellevue Hospital
Consultant Psychiatrist, Lenox Hill Hospital
New York, New York

Williams & Wilkins

A WAVERLY COMPANY

BALTIMORE • PHILADELPHIA • LONDON • PARIS • BANGKOK
BUENOS AIRES • HONG KONG • MUNICH • SYDNEY • TOKYO • WROCLAW

Editor: Kathleen Courtney Millet
Managing Editor: Keith Rhett Murphy
Marketing Manager: Daniell Griffin
Production Editor: Bill Cady
Design Coordinator: Mario Fernandez

351 West Camden Street
Baltimore, Maryland 21201-2436 USA

Rose Tree Corporate Center
1400 North Providence Road
Building II, Suite 5025
Media, Pennsylvania 19063-2043 USA

Printed in the United States of America
First Edition, 1983
Second Edition, 1985
Third Edition, 1989
Fourth Edition, 1991
Fifth Edition, 1994

Library of Congress Cataloging-in-Publication Data
Kaplan, Harold I., 1927–
Study guide and self-examination review for Kaplan and Sadock's synopsis of psychiatry / Harold I. Kaplan, Benjamin J. Sadock.— 6th ed.
p. cm.
Study guide to: Kaplan and Sadock's synopsis of psychiatry / Harold I. Kaplan, Benjamin J. Sadock. 8th ed. 1997.
Includes bibliographical references and index.
ISBN 0-683-30591-3
1. Mental illness—Examinations, questions, etc. 2. Psychiatry—Examinations, questions, etc. I. Sadock, Benjamin J., 1933– II. Kaplan, Harold I., 1927– Kaplan and Sadock's synopsis of psychiatry. III. Title.
[DNLM: 1. Mental Disorders examination questions. 2. Psychiatry examination questions. WM 140 K17k 1997 Suppl.]
RC454.K35 1998
616.89′0076—dc21
DNLM/DLC
for Library of Congress 98-14746
CIP

To purchase additional copies of this book, call our customer service department at **(800) 638-0672** or fax orders to **(800) 447-8438.** For other book services, including chapter reprints and large quantity sales, ask for the Special Sales department.

Canadian customers should call **(800) 665-1148** or fax us at **(800) 665-0103.** For all other calls originating outside of the United States, please call **(410) 528-4223** or fax us at **(410) 528-8550.**

Visit Williams & Wilkins on the Internet: **http://www.wwilkins.com** or contact our customer service department at **custserv@wwilkins.com.** Williams & Wilkins customer service representatives are available from 8:30 am to 6:00 pm, EST, Monday through Friday, for telephone access.

98 99 00 01 02
1 2 3 4 5 6 7 8 9 10

Dedicated to
Nancy Barrett Kaplan
and
Virgina Alcott Sadock
and
to the memory of
Harold Irwin Kaplan, M.D.
(1927–1998)

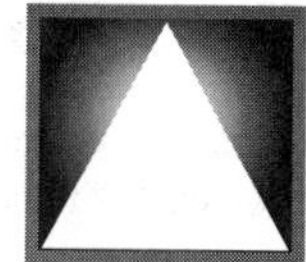

Preface

This edition of *Study Guide and Self-Examination Review for Kaplan and Sadock's Synopsis of Psychiatry* is being published simultaneously with the most recent 8th edition of *Kaplan and Sadock's Synopsis of Psychiatry*. They are designed to complement one another. *Study Guide* is keyed to the 8th edition of *Kaplan and Sadock's Synopsis* and is written to meet the needs of medical students, psychiatrists, neurologists, primary care and other nonpsychiatric physicians, and mental health professionals from all fields—psychology, social work, nursing—who require a review of the behavioral sciences and clinical psychiatry. *Study Guide* is designed especially to help those preparing for examinations, such as the United States Medical Licensing Examination (USMLE) and the examination in psychiatry of the American Board of Psychiatry and Neurology (ABPN). It also provides an excellent learning experience in psychiatry, allowing the student to review and integrate new areas from *Synopsis*.

The first *Study Guide*, published in 1983, contained 905 questions. To each subsequent edition, the authors have added new and different questions and modified and updated material from earlier editions. This *Study Guide* contains 1612 questions, including a specially prepared section on case studies. Questions are consistent with the format used by the USMLE, and their allocation has been carefully weighted with subjects of both clinical and theoretical importance taken into account.

Case Studies

A new section of never-before-published accounts of actual patients has been added to this edition. Each case history includes questions and a discussion of diagnosis, differential diagnosis, treatment strategies, and other related topics. The cases are from the authors' and other clinicians' experiences, including many derived from the medical student and psychiatric resident teaching services of the New York University Medical Center and Bellevue Hospital. In keeping with the *Principles of Medical Ethics With Annotation Especially Applicable to Psychiatry*, published by the American Psychiatric Association, each case history has been suitably disguised to safeguard patient confidentiality without altering material to provide less than a complete portrayal of the patient's actual condition.

This new section of the case studies will be of value to students preparing for examinations that increasingly use case examples (such as the USMLE); to those mental health professionals who may not be exposed to similar cases in their day-to-day work; to primary care physicians, who are often on the front lines of psychiatry; and to psychiatrists who wish to test their clinical acumen or who wish to learn more about complex diagnostic and treatment decisions.

KAPLAN AND SADOCK TEACHING SYSTEM

Study Guide forms one part of a comprehensive system developed by the authors to facilitate the teaching of psychiatry and the behavioral sciences. At the head of the system is *Comprehensive Textbook of Psychiatry,* which is global in depth and scope; it is designed for and used by psychiatrists, behavioral scientists, and all other workers in the mental health field. *Kaplan and Sadock's Synopsis of Psychiatry* is a relatively brief, highly modified, original, and current version useful for medical students, psychiatric residents, practicing psychiatrists, and other mental health professionals. The *Concise Textbook of Clinical Psychiatry,* dervied from *Synopsis,* emphasizes clinical psychiatry and includes extensive case studies useful for practitioners from all mental health fields. Other parts of the system are the pocket handbooks: *Pocket Handbook of Clinical Psychiatry, Pocket Handbook of Psychiatric Drug Treatment, Pocket Handbook of Emergency Psychiatric Medicine, and Pocket Handbook of Primary Care Psychiatry.* These books cover the diagnosis and the treatment of mental disorders, psychopharmacology, psychiatric emergencies, and primary care psychiatry, respectively, and are compactly designed and concisely written to be carried in the pocket by clinical clerks and practicing physicians, whatever their specialty, to provide a quick reference. Finally, *Comprehensive Glossary of Psychiatry and Psychology* provides simply written definitions for psychiatrists and other physicians, psychologists, students, other mental health professionals, and the general public. Taken together, these books create a multiple approach to the teaching, study, and learning of psychiatry.

HOW TO USE THIS BOOK

Because this is a study guide, each chapter begins with an introduction that directs students to areas of special significance used in their studying. The authors have prepared lists of helpful hints—now expanded and in alphabetical order—that present key terms and concepts essential to a basic knowledge of psychiatry. Students should be able to define and discuss each of the terms in depth as preparation for examinations.

The chapter, ''Objective Examinations in Psychiatry,'' will provide the student with helpful hints on how to take examinations. If the student understands how questions are constructed, their chances of answering correctly are greatly improved. This book defines distractors (wrong answers) as well as correct answers in each discussion.

To use this book most effectively, the student should attempt to answer all the questions in a particular chapter. By allowing about a minute for each answer, the student can approximate the time constraints of an actual written examination. The answers should then be verified by referring to the corresponding answer section in each chapter. Pay particular attention to the discussion of the wrong answers. The page numbers provided in the answers indicate a major discussion of the topic in *Kaplan and Sadock's Synopsis of Psychiatry.* The student can then refer to the appropriate pages of the book for an extensive and definitive discussion of the material.

ACKNOWLEDGEMENTS

We wish to thank Robert J. Campbell, M.D., and his publisher, Oxford University Press, for granting us permission to derive some of the definitions used in this text from his book, *Psychiatric Dictionary.* In the preparation of this edition, we have been fortunate to enlist the assistance of James C. Edmondson, M.D., Ph.D., who served as contributing editor for the sections on biological and psychopharmacologic psychiatry, Myrl Manley, M.D., who served as contributing editor for the section on case studies, and Caroly Pataki, M.D., who served as contributing editor for the section on child psychiatry. We thank them for their help.

We also thank John Emperio, M.D., and Rebecca Adams for their valuable assistance. Victoria Sadock, M.D., Peter Kaplan, M.D., Phillip Kaplan, M.D., James Sadock, and Jennifer Kaplan also helped. Justin Hollingsworth, Margaret Cuzzolino, Jennifer Peters, Linda Kenevich, and Sandhya Seshan played key roles in assisting us in all aspects of our work. We thank Ann Farkas for her help in editing this text. We wish to thank the following students of the New York University School of Medicine for their assistance: Greg Dakin, Peter Canoll, Rick Harada, John Harpel, Sue Hart, Chris Lascarides, Jeff Miner, Paul Modlinger, Stephen Russell, Mimi Ton, and Gena Zelman.

We want to extend special thanks to Virgina A. Sadock, M.D., Clinical Professor of Psychiatry and Director of Graduate Education in Human Sexuality and Sex Therapy at the New York University School of Medicine, who served as contributing editor and played an important role in planning and implementation. She worked on every editorial decision and assisted the authors throughout, as she has done in all our books.

Robert Cancro, M.D., Professor and Chairman of the Department of Psychiatry at New York University Medical Center, participated as senior contributing editor of this edition. He is also senior contributing editor of both *Kaplan and Sadock's Synopsis of Psychiatry* and the *Comprehensive Textbook of Psychiatry.* Dr. Cancro's support, encouragement, and inspiration have been of inestimable value. He is a personal friend, and it is our privilege to be associated with this outstanding clinician, researcher, and educator.

Finally, we want to thank our publishers, Williams & Wilkins, for their coorperation in every aspect of this book.

HIK
BJS

New York University Medical Center
New York, NY
January 15, 1998

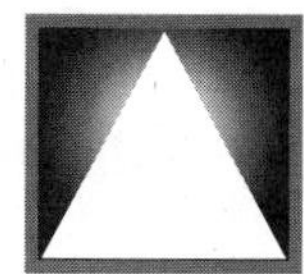

Contents

1

The Doctor–Patient Relationship and Interviewing Techniques

The doctor–patient relationship is the keystone of the practice of medicine. The relationship implies that an understanding and trust exist between them. With rapport, the patient feels that the doctor accepts him or her and recognizes both assets and liabilities.

Failure of the physician or therapist to establish good rapport accounts for much of his or her ineffectiveness in the care of patients. If a doctor dislikes a patient, there is the likelihood of being ineffective. If, however, the physician can handle the resentful patient with equanimity, the patient may become loyal and cooperative.

The reaction of the patient toward the doctor is apt to be a repetition of the attitude toward parents, teachers, or other authoritative persons who have figured importantly in the patient's past. Both individual experiences and cultural attitudes affect reactions of patients. It is desirable for the physician to have as much understanding as possible of the patient's subculture.

As a protective defensive pattern, a doctor or therapist may assume a habitual attitude toward all patients. Such rigidity is frequently inappropriate to the particular patient and situation. The doctor must avoid sidestepping issues that are important to the patient but that he or she finds boring or difficult to deal with.

When a therapist can convey to the patient that he or she is receptive to hearing about any subject, discussion is facilitated. It is then easier for the patient to talk about topics that are commonly embarrassing or disturbing.

To some degree, the ability to establish rapport with any patient and to manage particularly difficult patients is a product of the physician's ability to establish empathic and responsive relationships with people in general. That ability is based on the physician's innate capacity for self-knowledge and interpersonal sensitivity.

The doctor–patient relationship is an essential basis for practicing medicine, yet the subject is often neglected in medical training. To improve both the patients' and the doctors' perceptions of this relationship, it is necessary for students to learn the problems that lead to poor interactions and the productive factors that lead to good ones. The art of medicine has always been considered a skill at establishing rapport with patients and an ability to deal with difficult patients. Making explicit the facets of this art allows doctors to exercise their capacities with the greatest expertise.

To that end, this chapter covers in some detail such topics as transference, countertransference, compliance, interviewing techniques, and the management of difficult patients. Students should review Chapter 1 in *Kaplan and Sadock's Synopsis VIII* and then test their knowledge of the subject by studying the questions and answers provided below.

HELPFUL HINTS

The key terms listed below should be known by the student as they apply to the doctor–patient relationship and to interviewing techniques.

- ▶ active versus passive patients
- ▶ aggression and counteraggression
- ▶ authority figures
- ▶ belligerent patient
- ▶ biopsychosocial
- ▶ biopsychosocial model
- ▶ closed-ended questions
- ▶ compliance
- ▶ compliance versus noncompliance
- ▶ confrontation
- ▶ countertransference
- ▶ cultural attitudes
- ▶ defensive attitudes
- ▶ distortion
- ▶ early social pressures
- ▶ emotional reactions
- ▶ emotionally charged statements
- ▶ empathy
- ▶ George Engel
- ▶ "good patients"
- ▶ humor
- ▶ identification
- ▶ illness behavior
- ▶ individual experience
- ▶ insight
- ▶ listening
- ▶ misperception
- ▶ misrepresentation
- ▶ mutual participation
- ▶ open-ended questions
- ▶ overcompensatory anger
- ▶ personality
- ▶ psychodynamics
- ▶ rapport
- ▶ reflection
- ▶ self-monitoring
- ▶ sick role
- ▶ socioeconomic background
- ▶ sublimation
- ▶ therapeutic limitations
- ▶ transference
- ▶ unconscious guilt
- ▶ unresolved conflicts

▲ QUESTIONS

DIRECTIONS: Each of the incomplete statements or questions below is followed by five suggested completions or responses. Select the *one* that is *best* in each case.

1.1 The skills of active listening, which are the cornerstones of communication within the doctor–patient relationship, are the abilities of the physician to

A. comprehend the underlying meaning of the patient's spoken words while not overlooking the literal interpretation
B. formulate a differential diagnosis while taking the patient's history
C. understand both what the patient and the physician are saying and the undercurrents of unspoken feelings between the two
D. clarify what the patient relates without being paternalistic
E. evaluate the effect that transference is having on the doctor–patient relationship

1.2 Which of the following statements accurately describes the symptom-oriented approaches to psychiatric interviews?

A. Identifying a patient's course of illness is of interest.
B. A clinician can help a patient confront his or her innermost fears.
C. A patient's behavioral pattern can be clarified by interpreting unconscious anxieties.
D. Identifying symptoms can help psychiatrists to understand a patient's unconscious conflicts.
E. Symptoms are usually seen as symbolic.

1.3 The interviewing techniques that help a psychiatrist to obtain information include which of the following?

A. Asking questions such as "What do you mean by depressed?"
B. Asking questions that introduce topics as the interview proceeds.
C. Studying the patient's appearance and behavior to assess psychopathology.
D. Asking open-ended questions such as "How are you eating and sleeping?"
E. All of the above.

1.4 All of the following statements about confidentiality are correct *except*

A. Medical students may have access to a patient's record.
B. A physician should clarify confidentiality issues with a patient.
C. A clinician must warn a person toward whom a patient may violently act out.
D. Family members are sometimes informed about a patient's problems.
E. Information cannot be released to an insurance company without the patient's consent.

1.5 A person's attitude to illness may be affected by which one or more of the following factors?

A. Culture
B. Personality type
C. Family relationships
D. Socioeconomic status
E. All of the above

1.6 If a patient threatens to sue a clinician unless the clinician provides an immediate solution to the patient's disorder, the clinician's best response would be to

A. ask a colleague to join the clinician in the interview
B. try to turn the patient's attention to another subject
C. assure the patient that the clinician can provide a cure
D. discuss with the patient the uncertainty of treating any clinical disorder
E. inform the patient that in this situation the clinician finds it necessary to transfer the patient to another clinician's care

1.7 Of the following interview techniques, which is the most helpful for establishing a good rapport?

A. Taking notes
B. Using a private office
C. Maintaining eye contact
D. Listening to the patient without interrupting
E. Pursuing and responding to the patient's emotional concerns

1.8 Which of the following statements best describes the nature of both medical and psychiatric doctor–patient encounters?

A. Treatment is empirical.
B. The etiology of many symptoms is unknown.
C. Clinicians accurately predict patients' responses to treatment.
D. Diagnosing and assessing governs the initial phase of a first interview.
E. Treatment involves complexities such as a patient's relationship with family and friends.

1.9 At the beginning of her appointment, a patient wants to discuss her perception of why she fell ill, but the physician wants to know the chronology of her symptoms. The physician should

A. allow the patient to finish her discussion
B. politely interrupt the patient and continue with closed-ended questions
C. inform her that time is of the essence
D. inform her that an extra charge will be made if more time is needed for the appointment
E. immediately discuss how compliance will be affected by her perceptions

DIRECTIONS: Each set of lettered headings below is followed by a list of numbered statements. For each numbered statement, select the *best* lettered heading. Each heading can be used once, more than once, or not at all.

Questions 1.10–1.14

A. Active–passive model
B. Teacher–student model
C. Mutual participation model
D. Friendship model

1.10 A patient is admitted to the hospital with a sudden onset of altered mental status when he is found thrashing about in his bed. After a workup, a physician restrains him to perform a lumbar puncture.
1.11 A 64-year-old woman with diabetes mellitus visits her physician after repeatedly drawing high blood glucose levels during home monitoring.
1.12 After a patient's recovery from her illness, her physician continues to phone and visit her and declares his love for her.
1.13 Three days after abdominal surgery, a 32-year-old man has mild basal rales by auscultation. His surgeon tells him to ambulate.
1.14 The doctor of a 16-year-old girl with persistent lower abdominal pro
go for a lower gastro

Questions 1.15–1.18

A. Transference
B. Countertransferen

1.15 "That patient is one
in years; he's very g
1.16 "Doc, I've been lyin
going to give me sor
make me feel better?"
1.17 "No doctor ever liste
you're no exception."
1.18 "As your surgeon, ju
eration, and I'll make

Questions 1.19–1.20

A. Content of the inte
B. Process of the inte

1.19 "Doc, I've had diarrhe
1.20 The patient taps his fo
mentions the need for

Questions 1.21–1.25

A. Sick role
B. Illness behavior

1.21 A patient's reactions to the experience of being sick
1.22 The societal attribute conveyed to a sick person
1.23 A person receiving worker's compensation for pneumoconiosis
1.24 A defendant declared incompetent to stand trial
1.25 A person with influenza who stays in bed all day

Questions 1.26–1.30

A. Reflection
B. Summation
C. Compliance
D. Facilitation
E. Confrontation

1.26 The physician says, "Let's review what you've told me."
1.27 The degree to which the patient carries out the physician's clinical recommendations
1.28 An empathetic response meant to reassure the patient to know that the physician is listening to the
t's concerns and understands them
l and nonverbal cues that encourage the pa-
o keep talking
to point out to a patient something that the
ian thinks the patient is not paying attention
nissing, or is in some way denying

.31–1.35

trionic patients
ulsive patients
cissistic patients
lingering patients
ervigilant patients

as if superior to everyone around them
en seductive and flirtatious
usly feign illness for some clear secondary

difficult time delaying gratification
ical, evasive, and suspicious

ANSWERS

The Doctor–Patient Relationship and Interviewing Techniques

1.1 The answer is C (*Synopsis VIII,* page 1).
All the responses are partially correct, but only C covers both essential parts of active listening in the doctor–patient relationship.

One of the supreme tasks of any medical training center is to help the physician acquire skills of *active listening both to what the patient and the physician are saying and to the undercurrents of unspoken feelings between the two.* A physician who is continually monitoring not only the content of the interaction (what the patient and the physician say) but also the process (what the patient or the physician may not say but conveys in a variety of other ways) is a physician who realizes that communication between two people occurs on several levels at once. A physician who is sensitive to the effects that history, culture, environment, and psychology have on the doctor–patient relationship is a physician who is working with a multifaceted patient, not a disease syndrome. When the art and the technique of active listening are not emphasized, respected, and conveyed, physicians fail to be trained in the rudiments of establishing a relationship with their patients, and patient care is the inevitable loser.

The other responses contain only part of the equation needed for active listening. The doctor needs to comprehend and interpret what the patient is saying but that is not the major first task. A *differential diagnosis* is important, but the patient should not be looked on solely as a disease entity, nor should a differential diagnosis be formulated before a complete history is taken.

Clarification is an important technique used in the interviewing process. Through clarification, the physician attempts to get details from the patient about what the patient has already said. For example, the physician may say: "You're feeling depressed. When is it that you feel most depressed?" But clarification is not the physician's major task.

Transference is defined as the set of expectations, beliefs, and emotional responses that a patient brings to the doctor–patient relationship. This, too, is not the physician's major initial task, although it is an important part of understanding the patient.

1.2 The answer is A (*Synopsis VIII,* page 1).
Identifying *a patient's course of illness* is a symptom-oriented approach. There are two major goals of psychiatric interviewing: to recognize the psychological details of behavior and to clarify symptoms. Insight-oriented approaches emphasize eliciting and interpreting unconscious conflicts, anxieties, and defenses, whereas symptom-oriented approaches emphasize classifying patients' dysfunctions according to specific diagnostic categories.

In fact, psychiatrists would probably use both approaches, switching back and forth or combining the two, rather than applying only one or the other. Both ways of understanding patients are necessary for gathering information about the complexities of psychiatric disorders. Identifying a patient's *course of illness, behavioral patterns, and identifying symptoms* is a symptom-oriented approach. In insight-oriented psychiatry, the study of *unconscious conflicts, anxiety, symbols, and fears* is the major focus.

1.3 The answer is E (all) (*Synopsis VIII,* pages 2–3).
An open-ended question like "*What do you mean by* depressed?" encourages a patient to speak voluminously and freely, uninfluenced by possible concerns about what the patient thinks the doctor expects to hear. Such questions can help to further the doctor–patient relationship. *Questions that introduce topics* during the course of the interview help the patient to explore as yet untouched areas and also communicate the questioner's interest and expertise. A *patient's appearance and behavior* obviously offer many clues to psychopathology: A patient may be neatly dressed or in disarray, may appear nervous or withdrawn, or may sit quietly or pace excitedly. All these factors help to give the clinician a picture of the patient. Questions such as "*How are you sleeping and eating?*" (an open-ended question) have the advantage of not directing the patient's response. Closed-end questions that invite a short answer and that structure a patient's reply are also helpful interview techniques, although they should probably not be used extensively as opening questions.

Ending the interview with a confirmation of the clinician's attitude of genuine concern and interest helps to reinforce doctor–patient rapport and allows the patient to leave with a feeling that the clinician understands the patient. This technique does not, however, necessarily add any information to that already gained in the interview.

1.4 The answer is C (*Synopsis VIII,* page 12).
A clinician must warn a person who, to judge from the clinician's interaction with a patient, is likely to be violently harmed by the patient. Clinicians, however, do not warn anyone about whom a patient speaks disparagingly, if the clinician is not convinced that the patient intends to harm this person.

Physicians should explain to patients the nature of doctor–patient confidentiality, point out the instances in which the doctor must disclose information about the patient, and *clarify confidentiality issues* that a patient may raise. As part of the discussion of confidentiality, the clinician should inform the patient that no information will be *released to an insurance company without the patient's consent* and that, in teaching hospitals and other institutions, *medical students* and other medical staff *may have access to a patient's record,* although again only with the patient's consent. A clinician may inform *family members about a patient's problems* if the clinician thinks that family members can help alleviate the problems or if informing the family is otherwise in the patient's best interests.

1.5 The answer is E (*Synopsis VIII,* page 2).
All the factors listed in the question, as well as many others, may affect a person's attitude toward illness. For instance, the myriad effects of age on illness attitudes are obvious: An older

person may view an illness at the end of life with peaceful acceptance, whereas at a younger age, this person might take aggressive action against the illness. *Culture,* as well as ethnic attitudes about dependence behavior, can shape the way people ask for medical help and also whether they seek help at all. *Family relationships* and *personality type* can similarly influence attitudes toward illness. Clinicians must be aware of these factors and must assess a patient's illness behavior by asking specific questions, such as "What do you call your problem?" A high *socioeconomic status* may allow a person to seek treatment for a disorder that a person of low socioeconomic status may not be able to afford to attend to.

1.6 The answer is D (*Synopsis VIII,* page 3).
The clinician's best approach would be to honestly discuss *the uncertainty of treating any clinical disorder* with the patient and to assure the patient that the clinician will do everything possible to help the patient but that life has no guarantees. The patient will probably find this answer more helpful than a false promise that *the clinician can provide a cure.* Turning *the patient's attention to another subject* can suggest to the patient that the clinician does not take the patient seriously.

If the clinician tries to understand the patient's threat and to interpret the unsaid feelings behind it—usually anxiety—their discussion may have satisfactory results. If, however, the doctor senses that this is not the case, transferring *the patient to another clinician's care* should be considered.

The clinician would not *ask a colleague to join* the interview unless the clinician thought that the patient was dangerous.

1.7 The answer is E (*Synopsis VIII,* pages 5–6).
An important feature of establishing a good doctor–patient relationship is the ability to make the patient aware that the clinician is genuinely interested in and empathic with the patient's unspoken anxieties; an experienced interviewer can sense and elicit a *patient's emotional concerns.* Although early in the interview the clinician hopes to elicit as much information as possible and thus allows the patient to talk at length, it may sometimes be necessary to interrupt to focus the patient on another area or to obtain more specific information about an aspect of the patient's problem. Therefore, a clinician would not always listen to the patient *without interrupting.* A comfortable *private office* is an ideal setting for a first interview, but when such an office is unavailable, the interview is not canceled. An experienced clinician can establish a good relationship with a patient almost anywhere; the clinician's ability to communicate respect, interest, and genuine concern is more important than the setting.

During the first interview, a clinician usually takes notes for the patient's record, but not so obsessively that rapport is disturbed; in addition to recording needed information, *taking notes* lets the clinician demonstrate that what the patient says is worth paying attention to. Nevertheless, note taking is not essential for establishing a good doctor–patient relationship, and a clinician need not take notes if there is a good reason not to, such as the patient's discomfort with the procedure.

Although *to maintain eye contact* without forcing the issue is an important clinical tool to help a patient feel that the clinician is paying attention and is taking the patient seriously, using the technique is not more important than establishing empathy with the patient's concerns.

1.8. The answer is D (*Synopsis VIII,* page 3).
The most important function of both medical and psychiatric interviews is devoted to *diagnosing and assessing* the patient's disorder; however, in both fields, diagnosis cannot *accurately predict* all *patients' responses to treatment* even after correct assessment. Each patient is unique, and most psychiatric disorders are amenable to treatment—psychotherapy, medication, or both.

In psychiatry, *the etiology of many symptoms* is more likely to be unknown than is the case in other areas of medicine; psychiatric treatment is thus more often *empirical* than would be true for most medical disorders. In medical interviews, doctors would probably be less concerned with *complexities such as a patient's relationships with family and friends,* whereas such relationships are of great importance in psychiatric interviews.

1.9 The answer is A (*Synopsis VIII,* pages 6–7).
The early part of the interview is generally the most open-ended, in that the physician allows patients to speak as much as possible in their own words by asking open-ended questions and allows them to *finish.* An example of an open-ended question is, "Can you tell me more about that?" That type of questioning is important to establish rapport, which is the first step in an interview. In one survey of 700 patients, the patients substantially agreed that physicians do not have the time or the inclination to listen and to consider the patient's feelings, that physicians do not have enough knowledge of the emotional problems and socioeconomic background of the patient's family, and that physicians increase the patient's fear by giving explanations in technical language. Psychosocial and economic factors exert a profound influence on human relationships, so the physician should have as much understanding as possible of the patient's subculture.

Ekkehard Othmer and Sieglinde Othmer defined the development of rapport as encompassing six strategies: (1) putting the patient and the interviewer at ease, (2) finding the pain and expressing compassion, (3) evaluating the patient's insight and becoming an ally, (4) showing expertise, (5) establishing authority as a physician and a therapist, and (6) balancing the roles of empathic listener, expert, and authority. Interviewing any patient involves a fine balance between allowing the patient's story to unfold at will and obtaining the necessary data for diagnosis and treatment. Most experts on interviewing agree that the ideal interview is one in which the interviewer begins with broad open-ended questions, continues by becoming specific, and closes with detailed direct questions. Although closed-ended questions are valuable during the interview, they are generally not used at the start of the interview. A *closed-ended* or directive question is one that asks for specific information and that does not allow the patient many options in answering. Too many closed-ended questions, especially in the early part of the interview, can lead to a restriction of the patient's responses.

If the patient states that he or she has been feeling depressed, a closed-ended question might be, "Your mother died recently, didn't she?" That question can be answered only by a "yes" or a "no," and the mother's death may or may not be the reason the patient is depressed. More information is likely to be obtained if the physician responds with, "Can you tell me more about what you're feeling and what you think may be causing your depression?" That is an open-ended question. Sometimes directive questions are necessary to obtain important data, but, if they are used too often, the patient may think that information is to be given only in response to direct questioning by the physician.

As for *time* and *charges,* physicians should inform patients about their fee policies but should not interrupt patients to state such policies. Instead, those areas of business should ideally be dealt with before the initial visit, so that an ongoing relationship with a patient can be established. The matter of fees must be openly discussed from the beginning: the physician's charges, whether the physician is willing to accept insurance company payments directly (known as assignments), the policy concerning payment for missed appointments, and whether the physician is part of a managed care plan. Discussing those questions and any other questions about fees at the beginning of the relationship between the physician and the patient can minimize misunderstandings later.

A discussion of compliance with a medical plan is important, but it is premature to discuss compliance early in the interview. Furthermore, *compliance,* which is the degree to which the patient carries out clinical recommendations by the treating physician, is a two-way street. Studies have shown that noncompliance is associated with physicians who are perceived as rejecting and unfriendly. Noncompliance is also associated with asking a patient for information without giving any feedback and with failing to explain a diagnosis or the cause of the presenting symptoms. A physician who is aware of the patient's belief system, feelings, and habits and who enlists the patient in establishing a treatment regimen increases compliant behavior.

Answers 1.10–1.14

1.10 The answer is A (*Synopsis VIII,* page 2).

1.11 The answer is C (*Synopsis VIII,* page 2–3).

1.12 The answer is D (*Synopsis VIII,* page 3).

1.13 The answer is B (*Synopsis VIII,* page 2).

1.14 The answer is B (*Synopsis VIII,* page 2).
The doctor–patient relationship has a number of potential models. Often, neither the physician nor the patient is fully conscious of choosing one or another model. The models most often derive from the personalities, expectations, and needs of both the physician and the patient. The fact that their personalities, expectations, and needs are largely unspoken and may be different for the physician and the patient may lead to miscommunication and disappointment for both participants in the relationship. The physician must be consciously aware of which model is operating with which patient and must be able to shift models, depending on the particular needs of specific patients and on the treatment requirements of specific clinical situations. Models of the doctor–patient relationship include the active-passive model, the teacher–student (or parent–child or guidance–cooperation) model, the mutual participation model, and the friendship (or socially intimate) model.

The *active–passive model* implies the complete passivity of the patient and the taking over by the physician that necessarily results. In that model, patients assume virtually no responsibility for their own care and take no part in treatment. The model is appropriate when a patient is unconscious, immobilized, or delirious. The sudden onset of the patient's altered mental status can be a potentially life-threatening situation. Possible causes of the suddenly altered mental status are trauma, vascular disorders, brain tumors, meningitis, encephalitis, and toxicological, metabolic, endocrine, and psychiatric disorders. For some patients with an altered mental status, a *lumbar puncture* is necessary and should be performed, as long as increased intracranial pressure, which can cause brainstem herniation, is not suspected. A computed tomographic (CT) scan or an eye examination that checks for papilledema may aid in the assessment before a lumbar puncture is performed.

In the *teacher–student model* the physician's dominance is assumed and emphasized. The physician is paternalistic and controlling; the patient is essentially dependent and accepting. That model is often observed *after surgery* and before such diagnostic tests as a *GI series.*

The *mutual participation model* implies equality between the physician and the patient; both participants in the relationship require and depend on each other's input. The need for a doctor–patient relationship based on a model of mutual, active participation is most obvious in the treatment of such chronic illnesses as renal failure and *diabetes,* in which a patient's knowledge and acceptance of treatment procedures are critical to the success of the treatment. The model may also be effective in subtle situations—for example, in pneumonia.

The *friendship model* of the doctor–patient relationship is generally considered dysfunctional if not unethical. It is most often prompted by an underlying psychological problem in the physician, who may have an emotional need to turn the care of the patient into a relationship of mutual sharing of personal information and *love.* The model often involves a blurring of boundaries between professionalism and intimacy and an indeterminate perpetuation of the relationship, rather than an appropriate ending.

Answers 1.15–1.18

1.15 The answer is B (*Synopsis VIII,* pages 7–8).

1.16 The answer is A (*Synopsis VIII,* page 7).

1.17 The answer is A (*Synopsis VIII,* pages 6–7).

1.18 The answer is B (*Synopsis VIII,* pages 7–8).
Transference is generally defined as the set of expectations, beliefs, and emotional responses that a patient brings to the doctor–patient relationship. They are not necessarily based on who the physician is or how the physician acts in reality; rather, they are based on persistent experiences the patient has had with other important figures throughout life.

Patients' attitudes toward a physician are apt to be repetitions of their attitudes toward authority figures. A patient's attitude may range from one of realistic basic trust, with the expectation that the physician will have the patient's best interest at heart, through one of overidealization and even eroticized fantasy to one of basic mistrust, with the expectation that the physician will be contemptuous and potentially abusive. A patient may expect the physician to do something—for example, prescribe *medicine* or perform surgery—and can accept the physician's care as sufficient and competent only if those actions occur. Inherent in that attitude is the patient's role as a passive recipient in relation to the physician's role as an active bestower of help. Another patient may be active and expect to participate fully in treatment and, correspondingly, feels at odds with a physician who does not want patient participation and does not *listen.* A patient in whom those expectations are established feels uncomfortable if the physician has different expectations.

Just as patients bring transferential attitudes to the doctor–patient relationship, physicians often have countertransferential reactions to their patients. *Countertransference* may take the form of negative feelings that are disruptive to the doctor–patient relationship, but it may also encompass disproportionately positive, idealizing, or even eroticized reactions. Just as patients have expectations of physicians—for example, competence, lack of exploitation, objectivity, comfort, and relief—physicians often have unconscious or unspoken expectations of patients. Most commonly, patients are thought of as good patients if their expressed severity of symptoms correlates with an overtly diagnosable biological disorder, if they do not seek second opinions, if they *listen* and are generally nonchallenging about the treatment, if they are emotionally controlled, and if they are *grateful.* If those expectations are not met, the patient may be blamed and experienced as unlikable, unworkable, or bad.

The physician must understand such complex interpersonal factors as transference and countertransference to establish a genuine rapport with a patient. The failure of the physician to establish good rapport with the patient accounts for much of the ineffectiveness in care. The presence of rapport implies that understanding and trust between the physician and the patient are present. Differences in social, intellectual, and educational status can interfere seriously with rapport. Understanding or not understanding the patient's beliefs, use of language, and attitudes toward illness influences the character of the physician's examination and treatment.

Answers 1.19–1.20

1.19 The answer is A (*Synopsis VIII,* page 9).

1.20 The answer is B (*Synopsis VIII,* page 9).
The *content of an interview* is literally what is said between the physician and the patient: the topics discussed—for example, *diarrhea.* The *process of the interview* is what occurs nonverbally between the physician and the patient: what is happening in the interview beneath the verbal surface. Process involves feelings and reactions that are unacknowledged or unconscious. For example, patients may use body language to express feelings they cannot express verbally—*tapping foot* or nervous tearing at a paper tissue in the face of an apparently calm outward demeanor. Patients may shift the interview away from the anxiety-provoking subject onto a neutral topic without realizing that they are doing so. A patient may return again and again to a particular topic, regardless of what direction the interview appeared to be taking. Trivial remarks and apparently casual asides may reveal serious underlying concerns—for example, "Oh, by the way, a neighbor of mine tells me that he knows someone with the same symptoms as my son, and that person has cancer."

Answers 1.21–1.25

1.21 The answer is B (*Synopsis VIII,* page 2).

1.22 The answer is A (*Synopsis VIII,* page 2).

1.23 The answer is A (*Synopsis VIII,* page 2).

1.24 The answer is A (*Synopsis VIII,* page 2).

1.25 The answer is B (*Synopsis VIII,* page 2).
Illness behavior is the term used to describe a *patient's reactions to the experience of being sick.* Patients react to illness in various ways, depending on their habitual modes of thinking, feeling, and behaving. For example, one *patient with influenza may stay in bed all day;* another person with influenza may insist on going to work or may sit in a chair in front of the television set all day. Influenza is caused by a virus that annually results in significant mortality. Its symptoms are the abrupt onset of headaches, fever, chills, and myalgia accompanied by respiratory tract symptoms, particularly a cough and a sore throat.

> Edward Suchman described five stages of illness behavior: (1) the symptom-experience stage, in which a decision is made that something is wrong; (2) the assumption-of-the-sick-role stage, in which a decision is made that one is sick and needs professional care; (3) the medical-care-contact stage, in which a decision is made to seek professional care; (4) the dependent-patient-role stage, in which a decision is made to transfer control to the physician and to follow the prescribed treatment; and (5) the recovery or rehabilitation stage, in which a decision is made to give up the patient role.

The *sick role* is the role that *society attributes* to sick persons because they are ill. The characteristics of the sick role include such factors as being excused from certain responsibilities and being expected to want to obtain help to get well.

Being excused from certain responsibilities is the essence of *worker's compensation.* Some patients who worked in coal mines developed black lung or pneumoconiosis. At times, that condition prevented them from working and made them eligible for compensation. Pneumoconiosis is caused by the deposition of coal dust around the bronchioles. Another example of the sick role is the declaration that a defendant is *incompetent to stand trial.* The Supreme Court of the United States has stated that the prohibition against trying someone who is mentally incompetent is fundamental to the United States system of justice. Accordingly, in *Dusky v. United States,* the Court approved a test of competence that seeks to ascertain whether a criminal defendant has sufficient present ability to consult with his or her lawyer with a reasonable degree of rational understanding and whether he or she has a rational as well as factual understanding of the proceedings against him or her.

Answers 1.26–1.30

1.26 The answer is B (*Synopsis VIII,* page 10).

1.27 The answer is C (*Synopsis VIII,* pages 11–12).

1.28 The answer is A (*Synopsis VIII,* pages 9–10).

1.29 The answer is D (*Synopsis VIII,* page 10).

1.30 The answer is E (*Synopsis VIII,* page 10).
Many techniques are used during the interviewing process. In *summation,* the physician periodically takes a moment to briefly summarize what the patient has said thus far. Doing so assures both the patient and the physician that the information the physician has heard is the same as what the patient has actually said. For example, the physician may say, "*Let's review what you've told me.*"

Compliance, also known as adherence, is the degree to which a patient carries out the physician's clinical recommendations. *Examples of compliance include keeping appointments, entering into and completing a treatment program, taking medications correctly, and following recommended changes in behavior or diet.* Compliance behavior depends on the specific clinical situation, the nature of the illness, and the treatment program. In general, about one third of all patients comply with the treatment regimen, one third sometimes comply with certain aspects of treatment, and one third never comply with the treatment regimen. An overall figure assessed from a number of studies indicates that 54 percent of patients comply with the treatment regimen at any given time. One study found that up to 50 percent of hypertensive patients do not follow up at all with the treatment regimen and that 50 percent of those who do follow the regimen leave treatment within 1 year.

In the technique of *reflection,* the physician repeats to the patient in a supportive manner something that the patient has said. The purpose of reflection is twofold: to make sure that the physician has correctly understood what the patient is trying to say and to let the patient know that the physician is listening to what is being said. It is *an empathic response meant to reassure the patient that the physician is listening to the patient's concerns and understands them.* For example, if the patient is speaking about fears of dying and the effects of talking about those fears with the family, the physician may say, "It seems that you're concerned about becoming a burden to your family." That reflection is not an exact repetition of what the patient said but, rather, a paraphrase that indicates that the physician has perceived what the patient was trying to say.

In *facilitation,* the physician helps the patient continue by providing both *verbal and nonverbal cues that encourage the patient to keep talking.* Nodding one's head, leaning forward in one's seat and saying, "Yes, and then . . ." or "Uh-huh, go on" are all examples of facilitation.

The technique of *confrontation* is meant to point out to a patient something that the physician thinks the patient is not paying attention to, is missing, or is in some way denying. Confrontation must be done in a skillful way, so that the patient is not forced to become hostile and defensive. The confrontation is meant to help the patient face whatever needs to be faced in a direct but respectful way. For example, the physician may confront the patient with the need to lose weight. Or a patient who has just made a suicidal gesture but is telling the physician that it was not serious may be confronted with the statement, "What you have done may not have killed you, but it's telling me that you are in serious trouble right now and that you need help so that you don't try suicide again."

Answers 1.31–1.35

1.31 The answer is C (*Synopsis VIII,* page 14).

1.32 The answer is A (*Synopsis VIII,* page 14).

1.33 The answer is D (*Synopsis VIII,* page 15).

1.34 The answer is B (*Synopsis VIII,* page 14).

1.35 The answer is E (*Synopsis VIII,* page 14).
Some patients create undue stress if they are not treated effectively. Inherent in the treatment of all such patients is the physician's understanding of the covert emotions, fears, and conflicts that the patient's overt behavior represents. An appropriate understanding of what is hidden behind a particular patient's difficult behavior can lead the physician away from responding with anger, contempt, or anxiety and toward responding with helpful interventions.

Narcissistic patients act as though they were superior to everyone around them, including the physician. They have a tremendous need to appear perfect and are contemptuous of others, whom they perceive to be imperfect. They may be rude, abrupt, arrogant, or demeaning. They may initially overidealize the physician in their need to have their physician be as perfect as they are, but the overidealization may quickly turn to disdain when they discover that the physician is human. Underneath their surface arrogance, narcissistic patients often feel inadequate, helpless, and empty, and they fear that others will see through them.

Histrionic patients are often seductive and flirtatious with physicians out of an unconscious need for reassurance that they are still attractive, despite their illness, and out of fear that they will not be taken seriously unless they are found to be sexually desirable. They often appear overly emotional and intimate in their interactions with physicians. The physician needs to be calm, reassuring, firm, and nonflirtatious. The patients do not really want to seduce the physician, but they may not know any other way to get what they feel they need.

Sociopathic patients are often malingering patients. They consciously feign illness for some clear secondary gain (for example, to obtain drugs, to get a bed for the night, or to hide out from people pursuing them). Obviously, they sometimes do get sick, just as nonsociopathic people do; when they are sick, they need to be cared for in the same ways that others are cared for. The physician must treat them with respect but with a heightened sense of vigilance.

Sociopathic patients are those described in psychiatric terminology as having antisocial personality disorder; they do not appear to experience appropriate guilt and, in fact, may not even be consciously aware of what it means to be guilty. On the surface they may appear charming, socially adept, and intelligent, but they have over many years perfected the behavior they know to be appropriate, and they perform almost as an actor would. They often have histories of criminal acts, and they get by in the world through lying and manipulation. They are often self-destructive, harming not only others but themselves, in perhaps an unacknowledged expression of self-punishment.

Impulsive patients have a difficult time delaying gratification and may demand that their discomfort be eliminated immediately. They are easily frustrated and may become petulant or even angry and aggressive if they do not get what they want as soon as they want it. The patients may impulsively do something self-destructive if they feel thwarted by their physician and may appear manipulative and attention-seeking. They may fear that they will never get what they need from others and, thus, must act in an inappropriately aggressive way. They can be particularly difficult patients for any physician to treat; the physician must set firm limits at the outset, defining clearly acceptable and unacceptable behavior. The patients must be treated with respect and care but must be held responsible for their actions.

Hypervigilant patients are often paranoid patients who fear that people want to hurt them and are out to do them harm. The patients may misperceive cues in their environment to the degree that they see conspiracies in neutral events. *They are critical, evasive, and suspicious.* They are often called grievance seekers because they tend to blame others for everything bad that happens in their lives. They are extremely mistrustful and may question everything that the physician says needs to be done. The physician must remain somewhat formal, albeit always respectful and courteous, as expressions of warmth and empathy are often viewed with suspicion (''What does he want from me?''). As with obsessive patients, the physician should be prepared to explain in detail every decision and planned procedure and should react nondefensively to the patients' suspicions.

2

Human Development Throughout the Life Cycle

Developmental theorists believe that each phase in a person's life must be built on the preceding phase and that early phases of life must be successfully developed for a person to form a healthy, stable adult character. Thus, each person's developmental history can be retrieved from an understanding of the person's current functioning.

To fully understand a person's functioning, whether he or she is healthy or disturbed, psychiatrists must comprehend developmental theory. This process entails understanding the unfolding of normal human development as well as the ways that a person can stumble away from the normal path. Physicians who have studied developmental theory are well equipped to deal with patients who are difficult, particularly those who act irrationally. These physicians can appreciate the missteps in development that have led to current problems.

The theorists discussed in Chapter 2 approached developmental theory from different perspectives, which, when combined, offer a complex view of people's physical, intellectual, and psychological growth.

Jean Piaget concentrated on the cognitive development of children and offered striking evidence of the evolution of thought at different ages. Sigmund Freud focused on the psychosexual aspect of development through adolescence and opened the door to profound discoveries about the nature of infantile sexuality and its relation to the unconscious and to adult behavior. Erik Erikson provided a psychosocial developmental perspective, expanding on the discoveries of Freud to include characteristic maturational crises that correlate with the issues confronted psychosexually. Margaret Mahler described development in terms of the separation-individuation process and the development of object constancy, which emphasize the issues of both attachment and autonomy in development.

When all these theories are considered together, a dynamic and vibrant picture of the growing human organism emerges. More recent theorists, such as Daniel Levinson and Theodore Lidz, have contributed to the understanding of what is confronted and worked through in the course of the life cycle. The student who understands the basic tenets of different life-cycle theories and how they interrelate has not only a clear image of normal development but also a more lucid sense of dysfunctional development; knowing what can go wrong in early phases of development helps clarify different forms of psychopathology later in life. For instance, the student who understands Mahler's normative theories of the development of object constancy has a richer understanding of the dynamic causes of personality disorders. An even deeper dynamic understanding of these disorders is possible if the student is also aware of the potential points of dysfunction in cognitive, psychosexual, and psychosocial development.

In addition to developmental theories, Chapter 2 provides many perspectives on the human cycle through old age, along with a discussion of death, grief, mourning, and bereavement.

Reviewing Chapter 2 in *Kaplan and Sadock's Synopsis VIII* and then studying the questions and answers below provide useful knowledge of the subject.

HELPFUL HINTS

The student should be aware of the following theories, theorists, and developmental stages as they relate to human development throughout the life cycle.

- abortion
- adolescent homosexuality
- adoption
- adultery
- affectional bond
- age 30 transition
- age-related cell changes
- ageism
- Alexander Leighton
- alimony
- anal personality
- Anna Freud
- Arnold Gesell
- attachment
- autonomous ego functions
- average life expectancy
- bereavement
- bereavement in children
- Bernice Neugarten
- biological landmarks of aging
- birth order
- body image
- bonding
- brain dead
- burnout
- Carl Jung
- castration anxiety
- characteristics of thought:
  - concrete operations
  - formal operations
  - preoperational phase
  - sensorimotor phase (object permanence)

- climacterium
- cognitive decline
- concepts of normality as health, utopia, average, and process; psychoanalytic concepts
- contraception
- core identity
- crushes
- cults
- custody
- Dame Cicely Saunders
- Daniel Levinson
- Daniel Offer
- death and children
- death criteria
- delayed, inhibited, and denied grief
- dependence
- developmental landmarks
- developmental tasks
- divorce
- DNR
- dreams in children
- drug effects and hazards
- dual-career families
- effects of divorce
- ego ideal
- egocentrism
- Electra complex
- Elisabeth Kübler-Ross
- empty-nest syndrome
- epigenetic principle
- Erik Erikson
    - eight psychosocial stages
- ethology
- euthanasia
- failure to thrive
- family planning
- family size
- fathers and attachment
- feeding and infant care
- fetal development
- formal operations and morality
- foster parents
- gender expectations
- gender identity
- generativity
- genetic counseling
    - principles and conditions
- George Vaillant
- geriatric period
- grief:
    - anticipatory
    - pathological
    - versus depression
- handicaps
- Harry Stack Sullivan
- Harry Harlow
- Heinz Hartmann
- hormones
- hospice
- identification
- identity
- identity diffusion
- imagery and drawings
- imaginary companions
- imprinting
- inborn errors of metabolism
- integrity
- intimacy
- Jean Piaget
- John Bowlby's stages of bereavement
- Karl Abraham
- language development
- learning problems
- life cycle
- linkage objects
- living wills
- Madonna complex
- Margaret Mahler
    - infant-developmental stages
- marriage
- Masters and Johnson
- masturbation
- maternal behavior
- maternal neglect
- Melanie Klein
- menarche
- midlife crisis
- middle age
- mourning
- *Mourning and Melancholia*
- mutuality
- negativism
- neural organization of infancy
- normal autistic and normal symbiotic phases
- normative crisis
- Oedipus complex
- oppositionalism
- oral, anal, phallic, and latency phases
- pain management
- parental fit
- parental-right doctrine
- parenthood
- peer group
- penis envy
- perinatal complications
- play and pretend
- postpartum mood disorders and psychosis
- pregnancy:
    - marriage and alternative lifestyle
    - sexuality and prenatal diagnosis
    - teenage
- pregnancy and childbirth
- primary and secondary sex characteristics
- pseudodementia
- psychosexual moratorium
- puberty
- racism, prejudice
- reactions to authority
- religious behavior
- remarriage
- René Spitz
- retirement
- Roy Grinker
- school adjustment, behavior, refusal
- self-blame
- senility
- separation
- separation-individuation process:
    - differentiation
    - practicing
    - rapprochement
    - consolidation
- sex in the aged
- sibling and parental death
- sibling rivalry
- single-parent home
- smiling
- social and community psychiatry
- social deprivation syndromes (anaclitic depression-hospitalism)
- socially decisive stage
- somnambulism
- spacing of children
- spouse and child abuse
- stepparents and siblings
- stranger and separation anxiety
- stress reaction
- suicide in the aged
- superego
- surrogate mother
- survivor guilt
- temperament
- thanatology
- Thomas Szasz
- toilet training
- uncomplicated bereavement
- vasomotor instability
- vocation and unemployment
- worthlessness

▲ QUESTIONS

DIRECTIONS: Each of the statements or questions below is followed by five suggested responses or completions. Select the *one* that is *best* in each case.

2.1 The stage of formal operations, according to the theories of Jean Piaget, is characterized by the ability

A. to think abstractly
B. to reason deductively
C. to define concepts
D. to understand symbols
E. all of the above

2.2 All of the following statements about hormonal changes in adolescence are true *except*

A. Sex hormones correspond to bodily changes.
B. Luteinizing hormones may be higher in adolescence than in adulthood.
C. Androgen level correlates with libido in boys.
D. Hormones have as much influence on first episode of coitus in girls as they do in boys.
E. Estradiol can influence behavior in adolescent girls.

2.3 Optimal mental health may be best defined as

A. the absence of symptoms
B. the end result of interacting systems
C. the middle range of a bell-shaped curve
D. optimal functioning that blends diverse mental elements
E. all of the above

2.4 Which of the following statements about pregnancy is correct?

A. The risk of abuse decreases during pregnancy.
B. A majority of all women in the United States receive prenatal care.
C. The U.S. infant mortality rate is markedly lower than that in Canada and Japan.
D. Lamaze classes held during pregnancy encourage expectant women to develop their stomach muscles.
E. Ultrasound scanning can reveal a pregnant uterus as early as 4 weeks after a woman's last menstrual period.

2.5 All of the following statements about adolescent risk-taking behavior are correct *except*

A. Peer pressure can encourage teenagers to take risks.
B. Risk-taking behavior may have a genetic disposition.
C. Sexual diseases may result from promiscuous sexual behavior.
D. Self-destructive tendencies can encourage teenagers to take risks.
E. Vehicular accidents account for about 60 percent of adolescent deaths.

2.6 Good adult adjustment despite a high-risk childhood may be associated with

A. social support
B. high intelligence
C. structured upbringing
D. ability to bounce back
E. all of the above

2.7 All of the following statements about aging are correct *except*

A. A healthy mental attitude may slow the aging of cells.
B. Aging is caused by a genetically determined life span for cells.
C. Neurons in the central nervous system show signs of degeneration with age.
D. Changes in DNA caused by environmental pollution can appear in aging cells.
E. Genetic factors can cause common disorders of old age, such as heart disease and cancer.

2.8 All of the following factors shape human emotional and psychological growth in the developing child *except*

A. speech
B. arborization
C. social environment
D. physical maturation
E. increase in number of brain neurons

2.9 All of the following statements about the developing fetus are correct *except*

A. Most disorders in developing fetuses are multifactorial.
B. Uterine contractions can delay fetal development.
C. The Moro reflex appears at 25 weeks.
D. Tay-Sachs disease is a disorder that can be detected in prenatal testing.
E. The fetus can suck on its fingers.

2.10 According to Stella Chess and Alexander Thomas' study of the range of normal infant developmental patterns, which of the following statements is *not* correct?

A. Irritable infants may make mothers impatient.
B. Calm infants may make mothers feel rewarded.
C. Easy children make up 40 percent of all children.
D. Difficult children make up 20 percent of all children.
E. Difficult children cause parental anxiety.

2.11 Infancy is said to end when a child is able to

A. creep
B. stand without assistance
C. control his or her anal sphincter completely
D. climb stairs
E. speak

2.12 In an infant, social smiling is elicited preferentially by the mother at age

A. under 4 weeks
B. 4 to 8 weeks
C. 8 to 12 weeks
D. 3 to 4 months
E. more than 4 months

2.13 The main characteristic of Margaret Mahler's differentiation subphase is

A. separation anxiety
B. stranger anxiety
C. rapprochement
D. castration anxiety
E. none of the above

2.14 During pregnancy, sexual behavior may change because of

A. physiological changes in the woman
B. psychological factors in the woman
C. psychological factors in the man
D. fear, on the part of either partner, of harming the developing fetus
E. all the above

2.15 During pregnancy

A. maternal deaths have resulted from forcibly blowing air into the vagina during cunnilingus
B. sexual intercourse is prohibited by most obstetricians
C. if the husband has an extramarital affair, it usually occurs in the first trimester of his wife's pregnancy
D. psychological attachment to the fetus in utero rarely develops
E. 75 percent of Native-American mothers do not receive prenatal care during their first trimester

2.16 Pseudocyesis

A. is a presumptive sign of pregnancy seen in the first trimester
B. is a synonym for couvade
C. is a condition in which the patient has signs and symptoms of pregnancy but in reality is not pregnant
D. is associated with chronic, persistent, and frequent vomiting that leads to ketoacidosis, weight loss, and dehydration
E. is the repeated ingestion of nonnutritious substances

2.17 Statistics show that

A. 80 percent of all medical expenses incurred by the aged are covered by Medicare
B. of those persons who voluntarily retire, very few reenter the work force within the next 2 years
C. most nursing home care costs are covered by Medicare
D. 75 percent of the aged have incomes below $10,000
E. fewer than 40 percent of men over 60 are still sexually active

2.18 A person who is dying

A. should rarely have narcotics liberally dispensed
B. is legally allowed in some states to request a physician-assisted death
C. may have hospice care covered by Medicare if the patient's physician states that the patient has a life expectancy of six months or less
D. follows a fixed sequence of responses toward the impending death
E. may have a major depressive disorder, which is considered a normal reaction under the circumstances

2.19 Infants are born with

A. the Moro reflex
B. the rooting reflex
C. the Babinski reflex
D. endogenous smiling
E. all the above

2.20 An infant can differentiate

A. sweet-tasting sugar
B. the sour taste of lemon
C. the smell of bananas
D. the smell of rotten eggs
E. all the above

2.21 Normal adolescence is marked by

A. episodes of depression
B. occasional delinquent acts
C. the dissolution of intense ties to parents
D. vulnerability to crisis
E. all the above

2.22 The defense mechanisms used by the average 50-year-old man or woman include all of the following *except*

A. dissociation
B. repression
C. sublimation
D. altruism
E. splitting

2.23 The percentage of people between the ages of 65 and 85 living in nursing homes is

A. 5 percent
B. 10 percent
C. 15 percent
D. 20 percent
E. more than 25 percent

2.24 A child is generally able to conceptualize the true meaning of death by age

A. 3 years
B. 5 years
C. 7 years
D. 10 years
E. 13 years

2.25 Patients, on being told that they have a fatal illness, may respond with

A. denial
B. anger
C. bargaining
D. depression
E. all the above

DIRECTIONS: Each group of questions below consists of five lettered headings followed by a list of numbered words or statements. For each numbered word or statement, select the *one* lettered heading that is most closely associated with it. Each lettered heading may be selected once, more than once, or not at all.

Questions 2.26–2.30

A. 4 weeks
B. 16 weeks
C. 28 weeks
D. 40 weeks
E. 12 months

2.26 Grasping and manipulation
2.27 Ocular control
2.28 Verbalization of two or more words
2.29 Standing with slight support
2.30 Sitting alone

Questions 2.31–2.34

A. Child development has four stages: oral, anal, phallic, and latency.
B. There are eight stages of developmental potentials from birth to old age.
C. Cognitive development has four stages through which infants progress in predetermined stages.
D. Social interaction is vital at each stage of life, and personality is influenced by the quality of interactions.
E. External factors are important in human growth, and personality develops as a person comes to realize who he or she is.

2.31 Erik Erikson
2.32 Sigmund Freud
2.33 Carl Jung
2.34 Harry Stack Sullivan

Questions 2.35–2.39

A. Distress
B. Shame
C. Anger
D. Sadness
E. Guilt

2.35 Birth
2.36 3 to 4 months
2.37 8 to 9 months
2.38 12 to 18 months
2.39 3 to 4 years

Questions 2.40–2.44

A. 18 months
B. 2 years
C. 3 years
D. 4 years
E. 6 years

2.40 Copies a triangle
2.41 Copies a cross
2.42 Walks up stairs with one hand held
2.43 Puts on shoes
2.44 Refers to self by name

Questions 2.45–2.49

A. Birth to 6 months
B. 7 to 11 months
C. 12 to 18 months
D. 54 months on
E. None of the above

2.45 Plays at making sounds and babbles
2.46 Plays language games (pat-a-cake, peekaboo)
2.47 Understands up to 150 words and uses up to 20 words
2.48 Speech is 100 percent intelligible
2.49 Uses language to tell stories and share ideas

DIRECTIONS: The lettered headings below are followed by a list of numbered phrases. For each numbered phrase, select

A. if the item is associated with *A only*
B. if the item is associated with *B only*
C. if the item is associated with *both A and B*
D. if the item is associated with *neither A nor B*

Questions 2.50–2.53

A. Normal grief
B. Major depressive disorder
C. Both
D. Neither

2.50 Marked preoccupation with worthlessness
2.51 Psychomotor retardation or agitation
2.52 Weight loss
2.53 Suicide attempts

ANSWERS

Human Development Throughout the Life Cycle

2.1 The answer is E (all) (*Synopsis VIII,* pages 142–143).
The stage of formal operations is characterized by the young (11 years through adolescence) person's ability to think *abstractly,* to reason *deductively,* and to *define concepts.* This stage is so named because the person's thinking operates in a formal, highly logical, systematic, and *symbolic* manner. This stage is also characterized by skills in dealing with permutations and combinations; the young person can grasp the concept of probabilities. The adolescent attempts to deal with all possible relations and hypotheses to explain data and events. During this stage, language use is complex, follows formal rules of logic, and is grammatically correct. Abstract thinking is shown by the adolescent's interest in a variety of issues: philosophy, religion, ethics, and politics.

2.2 The answer is D (*Synopsis VIII,* pages 43–44).
Sexual intercourse in girls is determined almost entirely by psychosocial factors; hormones have much less influence on girls than on boys. Sex hormones increase slowly throughout adolescence and *correspond to bodily changes.* Follicle-stimulating hormone (FSH) and luteinizing hormone (LH) also increase throughout adolescence, but *LH is frequently elevated above adult values* between ages 17 and 18. LH levels characteristic of adult functioning begin in late adolescence. From age 16 to 17, a large increase seems to occur in average testosterone levels, which then decrease to stabilize at the adult level. Testosterone is the hormone responsible for the masculinization of boys, and estradiol is the hormone responsible for the feminization of girls.

2.3 The answer is E (all) (*Synopsis VIII,* pages 18–19).
Optimal mental health, or normality, is a complex concept that has been defined in many ways. The concept is best understood as a combination of all the features listed in the question. *The absence of symptoms* refers to mental health in terms of a lack of mental illness, whereas *the end result of interacting systems* describes mental health in positive terms as the product of mental systems acting in accord with one another. Mental health is statistically described as *the middle range of a bell-shaped curve;* in this sense, normality refers to a group, not to a single person. *Optimal functioning that blends diverse mental elements* applies to a healthy person's harmonious mental behavior.

2.4 The answer is B (*Synopsis VIII,* page 21).
Although the percentage of women who obtain prenatal care varies among ethnic groups, *a majority of all women in the United States receive prenatal care.* Despite this encouraging statistic, however, *the U.S. infant mortality rate* is higher than in Japan and Canada, both of which enjoy markedly lower rates than that in the United States.

An expectant mother's *risk of abuse* actually increases during pregnancy, when stress at the prospect of a new baby can produce a violent reaction in men who do not welcome the coming changes.

Lamaze classes held during pregnancy do not encourage prospective mothers to develop their stomach muscles; these classes teach women relaxation and deep breathing techniques to enable them to participate in the events of giving birth. *Ultrasound scanning reveals a pregnant uterus as early as 4 weeks after* fertilization, not after the end of a woman's last menstrual period.

2.5 The answer is E (all) (*Synopsis VIII,* pages 45–46).
Vehicular accidents account for about 40, not 60, percent of adolescent deaths, still a significant amount, which can be attributed to some teenagers' propensity for accident-prone behavior. *Acquired immunodeficiency syndrome (AIDS)* and other sexually transmitted diseases are among the risks faced by adolescents who engage in promiscuous sexual activity. Even teenagers who receive adequate education about the nature of sexually transmitted diseases and who understand the alternatives to exposure to these diseases still engage in unprotected sexual activity.

Peer pressure, a powerful stimulus to teenagers who are forming strong relationships outside the family, can encourage adolescents to engage in activities that may symbolize rebellion against family standards and compliance with the standards of groups to whom they want to belong. Other pressures can encourage risk-taking behavior: a need to establish self-identity; *a self-destructive tendency* that is masked by omnipotent fantasies; and a mental disorder that leads to delinquency or academic problems.

Recent studies have shown that *risk-taking behavior may have a genetic disposition.* This finding may offer still one more explanation of the tendency toward such adolescent behavior, as well as of the fact that some teenagers rebel less strenuously, or not at all, compared to others.

2.6 The answer is E (all) (*Synopsis VIII,* pages 47–48).
Workers have studied the reasons that some, but not all, adults who had undergone high-risk childhood experiences have shown good adjustment in maturity. These adults were able to overcome their earlier problems because of the factors listed in the question: *social support, high intelligence, structured upbringing,* and *the ability to bounce back.* A strong network of friends, siblings, and coworkers can offer support and security to these people, and an interest in self-understanding may encourage them to work on their difficulties in life. A family that offered a person a sense of structure and a set of standards accustoms the person to see life as orderly and rational, not chaotic and random. Children who meet adversities resiliently and struggle to overcome them are more likely to be well-adjusted adults.

2.7 The answer is A (*Synopsis VIII,* page 60).
A healthy mental attitude toward aging can help a person to lead a longer, better life than might otherwise be the case. A person who eats wisely, exercises, and has frequent checkups may avoid or ameliorate many disorders of aging, but mental attitude alone cannot slow cell aging.

Although the complex phenomenon that constitutes aging is not completely understood, scientists have discovered that the life span of cells is *genetically determined;* after a number of divisions, cells wear out. It has also been found that *neurons in the central nervous system show signs of degeneration with age;* this degeneration may explain many symptoms of aging, such as memory loss, loss of hearing and vision, and loss of physical flexibility.

Changes in DNA caused by environmental pollution can appear in aging cells; other factors, such as radiation, chemicals, and food, can also damage DNA, which prevents cells from correctly reproducing themselves. *Genetic factors can cause common disorders of old age:* heart disease and cancer, for instance, often occur among older people.

2.8 The answer is E (*Synopsis VIII,* pages 17–18).
An *increase in the number of brain neurons* does not occur; infants are born with all the neurons they will ever have. Emotional and psychological growth in humans does not depend on an increase in the number of brain neurons but in many other factors. *Physical maturation* is an important consideration: The brain grows and develops during infancy, and physical development of the body affects, and is regulated by, the brain.

Arborization, the growth of neurons throughout the brain in treelike patterns, also affects emotional growth and allows various areas of the brain to assume their mature forms. *Speech,* or human communication in some form, is an important factor in emotional and psychological growth; through communication interaction with and feedback from the outer world allow a child to learn, for instance, to speak the language of the environment.

The importance of *the social environment* in human growth is maximized in infants whose parents frequently interact with them. Such children are stimulated to grow and learn much more than are infants who are dutifully tended or ignored.

2.9 The answer is B (*Synopsis VIII,* pages 28–30).
Most disorders in developing fetuses are not genetic but multifactorial and have a global impact, compared to postnatal disorders. *Uterine contractions,* rather than delaying fetal development, are thought to contribute to fetal development by gently stimulating the fetus.

The Moro reflex indeed appears in a fetus at 25 weeks but is a burrowing reflex rather than a response to loud noise. Fetuses do respond to loud noises but are more likely to do so by a gross muscular reaction than by a burrowing reflex. *Tay-Sachs disease* can be detected by prenatal testing; the disease is an inborn metabolic error. The fetus (defined at 8 weeks of gestation) can suck on its *fingers* and toes.

2.10 The answer is D (*Synopsis VIII,* page 36).
Chess and Thomas studied the range of normal infant developmental patterns from noisy to quiet and concluded that many of their characteristics were inborn rather than produced through environmental interaction. They established the idea of parental fit—the nature of mother–child interaction: The better the fit, the better the relationship between the two. One result of their study was the finding that *easy children make up 40 percent of all children.* They also noted that *difficult children make up* 10 percent, not 20 percent, of all children. *Irritable infants may make mothers impatient,* and *calm infants may give mothers a sense of reward,* but Chess and Thomas studied normal developmental patterns and were not concerned with results such as these, which have to do with the impact of infants' personalities on the family. Difficult children create *anxiety in the parent.*

2.11 The answer is E (*Synopsis VIII,* page 33).
Infancy is considered to end when the child is able to *speak.* It is the period from birth until about 18 months of age. During the first month of life, the infant is termed a neonate or newborn. The child *creeps* at 40 weeks, *stands without assistance* at 52 weeks, develops meaningful speech and language at 15 months, *climbs stairs* at 2 years, and *controls his or her anal sphincter completely* at 3 years. There are normal variations in these figures among children.

2.12 The answer is B (*Synopsis VIII,* pages 28–29).
Arnold Gesell, a developmental psychologist and physician, described developmental schedules that outline the qualitative sequence of motor, adaptive, language, and personal-social behavior of the child from the age of 4 weeks to 6 years. Gesell's approach is normative; he viewed development as the unfolding of a genetically determined sequence. According to his schedules, at birth, all infants have a repertoire of reflex behaviors—breathing, crying, and swallowing. By 1 to 2 weeks of age, the infant smiles. The response is endogenously determined, as evidenced by smiling in blind infants. By 2 to 4 weeks of age, visual fixation and following are evident. By *4 to 8 weeks,* social smiling is elicited preferentially by the face or the voice of the caretaker.

2.13 The answer is B (*Synopsis VIII,* page 36).
Margaret S. Mahler (1897–1985) was a Hungarian-born psychoanalyst who practiced in the United States and who studied early childhood object relations. She described the separation-individuation process, resulting in a person's subjective sense of separateness and the development of an inner object constancy. The separation-individuation phase of development begins in the fourth or fifth month of life and is completed by the age of 3 years.

As described by Mahler, the characteristic anxiety during the differentiation subphase of separation-individuation is *stranger anxiety.* The infant has begun to develop an alert sensorium and has begun to compare what is and what is not mother. The subphase occurs between 5 and 10 months of age. A fear of strangers is first noted in infants at 26 weeks of age but does not fully develop until about 8 months. Unlike babies exposed to a variety of caretakers, babies who have only one caretaker are likely to have stranger anxiety. But, unlike stranger anxiety, which can occur even when the infant is in its mother's arms, *separation anxiety*—which is seen between 10 and 16 months, during the practicing subphase—is precipitated by the separation from the person to whom the infant is attached. The practicing subphase marks the beginning of upright locomotion, which gives the child a new perspective and a mood of elation, the "love affair with the world." The infant learns to separate as it begins to crawl and to move away from its mother but continues to look back and to return frequently to its mother as home base. Between the ages of 16 and 24 months, the *rapprochement* subphase occurs, with the characteristic event being the rapprochement crisis, during which the infant's struggle becomes one between wanting to be soothed by its mother and not wanting to accept her help. The symbol of rapprochement is the child standing on the threshold of a door in helpless frustration, not knowing which way to turn.

Castration anxiety, as described by Sigmund Freud, is a characteristic anxiety that arises during the oedipal phase of development, ages 3 to 5 years, concerning a fantasized loss or an injury to the genitalia.

2.14 The answer is E (all) (*Synopsis VIII,* page 20).

During pregnancy, a couple's sexual activity may increase or decrease. *Physiological changes in the woman,* including pelvic vasocongestion, help some women become more sexually responsive than before pregnancy, but symptoms such as nausea, vomiting, and fatigue lead some women to less frequent sexual activity. *Psychological factors in the woman* and *psychological factors in the man* may affect sexual behavior. Women may exhibit increased interest in sex because of the resolution of their ambivalent feelings regarding birth control. Alternatively, a woman may associate pregnancy as an asexual period, or she may feel unattractive because of the changes in her body proportions.

Psychological factors similarly affect men. Some men find their pregnant partners attractive; others find their partners ugly or become fearful of defiling a pregnant woman. The Madonna complex is exhibited by some men who view the pregnant woman as sacred.

Fear, on the part of either partner, of harming the developing fetus during coitus is common and may be caused by misinformation. The physician can reassure the couple that most obstetricians advise the couple to abstain from sex only in the last 4 to 6 weeks of pregnancy, if at all.

2.15 The answer is A (*Synopsis VIII,* page 20).

During pregnancy, *maternal deaths have resulted from forcibly blowing air into the vagina during cunnilingus.* Presumably, air emboli entered the placental-maternal circulation. Cunnilingus should be interdicted during pregnancy.

However, *sexual intercourse is not prohibited by most obstetricians.* Some suggest that sexual intercourse cease 4 to 6 weeks antepartum. If bleeding occurs early in pregnancy, it is usually, although not invariably, followed by a spontaneous abortion. In those cases, the obstetrician prohibits coitus on a temporary basis as a therapeutic measure.

Some couples, on their own, stop having sexual intercourse during pregnancy. Either the man or the woman may erroneously regard intercourse as potentially harmful to the developing fetus and as something to be avoided for that reason.

If *the husband has an extramarital affair, it usually occurs during the last trimester, not the first* trimester, of his wife's pregnancy.

Psychological attachment to the fetus begins in utero; by the beginning of the second trimester, most women have a mental picture of the infant. The fetus is viewed as a separate being, even before being born, and is endowed with a prenatal personality. According to psychoanalytic theorists, the child-to-be is a blank screen on which the mother projects her hopes and fears. In rare instances, those projections account for postpartum pathological states, such as the mother's wanting to harm the infant, who is viewed as a hated part of herself. Normally, however, giving birth to a child fulfills a woman's basic need to create and nurture life.

Prenatal care should begin before conception, so that the prospective mother's health can be assessed. The mother can be examined to ensure fetal health and survival, and information about the use of substances (including the interdiction of alcohol, tobacco, and coffee), exercise, and diet can be provided. Mothers who are under stress have a greater than usual risk of miscarriage, premature birth, and other complications. The risk of postpartum depression is increased if there is a history of depression in the mother or her family or if the mother had a previous postpartum psychiatric illness.

According to the U.S. Department of Health and Human Services, 21 percent of white mothers, 39.6 percent of black mothers, 40.5 percent of Hispanic mothers, and *42.1 percent, not 75 percent, of Native American mothers, receive no prenatal care during the first trimester.* Mexican Americans, Native Americans, Alaskan natives, and African Americans are the four ethnic groups who are least likely to receive prenatal care.

2.16 The answer is C (*Synopsis VIII,* page 21).

Pseudocyesis is a rare condition in which a patient *who is not pregnant has the signs and symptoms of pregnancy*—such as abdominal distention, breast enlargement, pigmentation, cessation of menses, and morning sickness. Pseudocyesis was first reported by Hippocrates; Mary Tudor, queen of England (1516–1558), allegedly had two episodes of pseudocyesis; and Sigmund Freud's patient Anna O. also suffered from pseudocyesis.

Pseudocyesis can occur at any age, and it has been reported in both men and women. Male pseudocyesis is different from *couvade,* which occurs in some primitive cultures; in couvade, the father takes to his bed during or shortly after the birth of his child, as though he himself had given birth to the child. The incidence of pseudocyesis has decreased over the past 50 years. It may be viewed as a somatoform disorder related to conversion disorder. Unconscious mechanisms may include the restitution of a lost object or conflicts over gender role and generativity. The term ''somatic compliance'' is used to indicate that the body undergoes genuine physiological changes in response to unconscious needs and conflicts. Thus, pseudocyesis is not *a presumptive sign of pregnancy seen in the first trimester,* although patients with pseudocyesis may have presumptive signs of pregnancy. The first presumptive sign of pregnancy is the absence of menses for 1 week. Other presumptive signs are breast engorgement and tenderness, changes in breast size and shape, nausea with or without vomiting (morning sickness), frequent urination, and fatigue.

Some patients during pregnancy may exhibit hyperemesis gravidarum, *vomiting that is chronic, persistent, and frequent and that leads to ketoacidosis, weight loss, and dehydration.* Maternal or fetal death may ensue. The cause is unknown. Preexisting hepatorenal disease may predispose to the condition. Women with a history of anorexia nervosa or bulimia nervosa may be at risk. In some subcultures, most notably among African-American women in the rural South, pica is seen in some pregnant women. Pica *is the repeated ingestion of nonnutritious substances, such as dirt, clay, starch, sand, and feces.*

2.17 The answer is D (*Synopsis VIII,* pages 61–64).
The economics of old age is of paramount importance to the aged themselves and to the society at large. In the United States, about *75 percent of the aged have incomes below $10,000,* and only about 10 percent have incomes above $20,000. About 3.5 million persons over age 65 live below the poverty line. Those over age 85 have the lowest incomes. Women make up the largest single group of the elderly poor and are twice as likely as men to be poor. Black elderly women over 65 are 5 times more likely to be poor than are white elderly women.

Medicare (Title 18) provides both hospital and medical insurance for those over age 65. About 150 million bills are reimbursed under the Medicare program each year, but only about *40 (not 80) percent of all medical expenses incurred by the aged are covered by Medicare.* The rest is paid by private insurance, state insurance, or personal funds. Some services—such as outpatient psychiatric treatment, skilled nursing care, physical rehabilitation, and preventive physical examinations—are covered minimally or not at all.

Many aged patients who are infirm require institutional care. Although only 5 percent of the aged are institutionalized in nursing homes at any one time, about 35 percent of the aged require care in a long-term facility at some time during their lives. Elderly nursing home residents are mainly widowed women, and about 50 percent are over age 85. *Nursing home care costs are not covered by Medicare,* and they range from $20,000 to $40,000 a year. About 20,000 long-term nursing care institutions are available in the United States—not enough to meet the need.

As for retirement, many elderly persons view it as a time for the pursuit of leisure and for freedom from the responsibility of previous working commitments. For others, it is a time of stress, especially if retirement results in economic problems or a loss of self-esteem. Ideally, employment after age 65 should be a matter of choice. With the passage of the Age Discrimination in Employment Act of 1967 and its amendments, forced retirement at age 70 has been virtually eliminated in the private sector, and it is not legal in federal employment. *Of those persons who voluntarily retire, a majority, not very few, reenter the work force within 2 years.* They do so for a variety of reasons—negative reactions to being retired, feelings of being unproductive, economic hardship, and loneliness.

Far more than 40 percent of men over 60 are still sexually active. In fact, an estimated 70 percent of men and 20 percent of women over age 60 are sexually active. Sexual activity is usually limited by the absence of an available partner. Longitudinal studies have found that the sex drive does not decrease as men and women age; some report an increase in sex drive. William Masters and Virginia Johnson reported sexual functioning of persons in their 80s.

2.18 The answer is C (*Synopsis VIII,* page 73).
A person who is dying *may have hospice care covered by Medicare* if the patient's physician states that the patient has a life expectancy of 6 months or less. In one study by C. M. Parkes, however, predictions concerning the length of survival for patients referred to a hospice did not correlate with the actual length of survival. Physicians were able to state only that patients with incurable cancer would die within a relatively short time and could not be more precise than that. Unfortunately, current federal regulations do not provide for financing hospital care once federally sponsored hospice care has begun; thus, a patient who enters a hospice will not be insured on reentry to a hospital if the need arises.

Other factors need to be considered in caring for the dying patient. Pain management should be vigorous in the terminally ill. A dying patient needs to function as effectively as possible. Doing so is made relatively easy when the patient is free of pain. The physician should use *narcotics as liberally as they are needed and tolerated,* so that the patient can attend to any business with a minimum of discomfort. The risk of dependence on narcotics used for pain management is minimal.

Currently, *no laws in any state explicitly allow physician-assisted death.* Oregon passed a law allowing physician-assisted suicide, which is being reviewed by the U.S. Supreme Court. Some states, such as Michigan, have passed laws strictly forbidding euthanasia in response to the actions of Jack Kevorkian, a doctor who has openly participated in euthanasia. The ethical and legal issues surrounding active and passive deprivation of life in severely ill patients are controversial.

Euthanasia, the act of killing a hopelessly ill or injured person for reasons of mercy, may take one of two forms, either direct (active) or indirect (passive). Either form may be voluntary or nonvoluntary. In view of the technological advances that prolong life, coupled with limitations on resources required to sustain human life of acceptable quality, society will probably move increasingly in the direction of designing a legal framework within which euthanasia can be clarified.

A number of researchers have studied reactions to death. One of the earliest and most useful organizations of reactions to impending death came from the psychiatrist and thanatologist Elisabeth Kübler-Ross. Seldom does any dying patient follow a *fixed sequence of responses* that can be clearly identified; no established sequence is applicable to all patients. However, the following five stages proposed by Kübler-Ross are widely encountered: stage 1, shock and denial; stage 2, anger; stage 3, bargaining; stage 4, depression; and stage 5, acceptance.

In the fourth stage, patients show clinical signs of depression—withdrawal, psychomotor retardation, sleep disturbances, hopelessness, and, possibly, suicidal ideation. The depression may be a reaction to the effects of the illness on their lives (for example, the loss of jobs, economic hardship, helplessness, hopelessness, and isolation from friends and family), or it may be in anticipation of the loss of life that will eventually occur. If a major depressive disorder with vegetative signs and suicidal ideation develops, treatment with antidepressant medication or electroconvulsive therapy (ECT) may be indicated. All persons feel some degree of sadness at the prospect of their own deaths, and normal sadness does not require biological intervention. However, *major depressive disorder is not a normal reaction* to impending death. A person who suffers from major depressive disorder may be unable to sustain hope. Hope can alter longevity and can enhance the dignity and the quality of the patient's life.

2.19 The answer is E (all) (*Synopsis VIII,* pages 32–34).
Infants are born with a number of reflexes, many of which were once needed for survival. Experts assume that the genes carry messages for those reflexes. Among the reflexes are the *Moro reflex,* flexion of the extremities when startled; the *rooting reflex,* turning toward the touch when the cheek is stroked; and the Babinski reflex, spreading of the toes with an upgoing big toe when the sole is stroked.

Infants are also born with the innate reflex pattern, *endogenous smiling,* which is unintentional and is unrelated to outside stimuli.

2.20 The answer is E (all) (*Synopsis VIII,* pages 34–36).
Infants are able to differentiate among various sensations. Babies as young as 12 hours old gurgle with satisfaction when *sweet-tasting sugar* water is placed on the tongue, and they grimace at *the sour taste of lemon* juice. Infants smile at *the smell of bananas* and protest at *the smell of rotten eggs.* At 8 weeks of age, they can differentiate between the shapes of objects and colors. Stereoscopic vision begins to develop at 3 months of age.

2.21 The answer is E (all) (*Synopsis VIII,* pages 42–45).
Early adolescence (12 to 15 years) is marked by increased anxiety and *episodes of depression,* acting-out behavior, and *occasional delinquent acts.* Teenagers, for example, obtain about 300,000 legal abortions and give birth to about 600,000 babies each year. They have a diminution in sustained interest and creativity; there is also *a dissolution of intense ties* to siblings, parents, and parental surrogates. Middle adolescence (14 to 18 years) is marked by efforts to master simple issues concerned with object relationships. The late adolescent phase (17 to 21 years), which is marked by the resolution of the separation-individuation tasks of adolescence, is characterized by *vulnerability to crisis,* particularly with respect to personal identity.

If adolescence does not proceed normally, the teenager may have an identity problem, which is characterized by a chaotic sense of self and a loss of the sense of personal sameness, usually involving a social role conflict as perceived by the person. Such conflict occurs when adolescents feel unwilling or unable to accept or adopt the roles they believe are expected of them by society. The identity problem is often manifested by isolation, withdrawal, rebelliousness, negativism, and extremism.

2.22 The answer is E (*Synopsis VIII,* pages 227, 660).
According to Melanie Klein, *splitting* is not a defense mechanism but an ego mechanism in which the object is perceived as either all good or all bad; it is a mechanism used against ambivalent feelings toward the object. It is also used by children and by patients in borderline states. A 50-year-old person is in midlife, which is marked by the use of certain defense mechanisms. The defenses that dominate during those years are dissociation, repression, sublimation, and altruism. *Dissociation* is an unconscious defense mechanisms involving the segregation of any group of mental or behavioral processes from the rest of the person's psychic activity. It may entail the separation of an idea from its accompanying emotional tone, as seen in dissociative disorders.

Repression is an unconscious defense mechanism in which unacceptable mental contents are banished or kept out of consciousness. A term introduced by Sigmund Freud, it is important in both normal psychological development and in neurotic and psychotic symptom formation. *Sublimation* is an unconscious defense mechanism in which the energy associated with unacceptable impulses or drives is diverted into personally and socially acceptable channels. Unlike other defense mechanisms, sublimation offers some minimal gratification of the instinctual drive or impulse. *Altruism* is a regard for and dedication to the welfare of others. In psychiatry the term is closely linked with ethics and morals. Freud recognized altruism as the only basis for the development of community interest; Eugen Bleuler equated it with morality.

2.23 The answer is A (*Synopsis VIII,* page 64).
More than 25 million Americans are over age 65, and, although a myth persists that most elderly people live in nursing homes, only *5 percent* of persons between the ages of 65 and 85 are so institutionalized. With increasing age, however, the rate of institutionalization does increase. Over the age of 85, about 20 percent of people live in nursing homes.

2.24 The answer is D (*Synopsis VIII,* pages 44–45).
By the age of *10 years,* a child is able to conceptualize the true meaning of death—something that may happen to the child and to the parent. At that time, the child shows a great tendency for logical exploration to dominate fantasy and shows an increased understanding of feelings and interactions in relationships. The child has well-developed capacities for empathy, love, and compassion, as well as emerging capacities for sadness and love in the context of concrete rules. As opposed to parents in some other parts of the world, middle-class adults in the United States tend to shield children from a knowledge of death. The air of mystery with which death is surrounded in such instances may unintentionally create irrational fears in children. Attending funerals is recommended for children if the adults present are trustworthy and reasonably composed. A funeral may act as an introduction to the adult world of crises and tribulations, on the way to a full transition to other phases of development.

The preschool child under age 5 years is beginning to be aware of death not in the abstract sense but as a separation similar to sleep. Between the ages of 5 and 10 years, the child shows a developing sense of inevitable human mortality; the child first fears that the parents may die and that the child will be abandoned. Discussing death with an inquiring child requires simplicity and candor. Adults are cautioned not to invent answers when they have none. Basically, death must be conveyed as a natural event that cannot be avoided but that causes pain because it separates people who love each other.

2.25 The answer is E (all) (*Synopsis VIII,* pages 66–67).
Elisabeth Kübler-Ross described five psychological stages that a dying person may experience on being told of the prognosis. Although Kübler-Ross presented the five stages in the sequential order of denial, anger, bargaining, depression, and acceptance, she did not intend that order to be taken literally. From

her work with dying patients, she recognized that the experience of those stages was fluid and individual; one person may initially react with anger, then denial, then depression, then anger again; another person may respond with immediate acceptance, whereas another may never experience the acceptance stage.

Kübler-Ross's description of those stages has been important to the understanding of the emotional life of a dying person. *Denial* is the first stage, when a patient may first appear dazed and then refuse to believe the diagnosis. *Anger* is often characterized by the response "Why me?" The *bargaining* stage occurs when the patient attempts to negotiate with the physician, friends, or even God by promising to fulfill certain bargains in return for a cure. *Depression* may result as a reaction to the reality of impending death or to the debilitating effects of illness. Acceptance is the stage when a patient is able to come to terms with the inevitability of death and with the losses associated with death. In that stage, a patient may be able to talk about death and to face the unknown.

Answers 2.26–2.30

2.26 The answer is B (*Synopsis VIII,* page 29).

2.27 The answer is A (*Synopsis VIII,* page 29).

2.28 The answer is E (*Synopsis VIII,* page 29).

2.29 The answer is E (*Synopsis VIII,* page 29).

2.30 The answer is C (*Synopsis VIII,* page 29).
Most of the developmental landmarks are readily observed. Growth is so rapid during infancy that developmental landmarks are measured in terms of weeks. Examples of some major developmental events and their approximate time of appearance are *ocular control, 4 weeks; grasping and manipulation, 16 weeks; sitting alone, 28 weeks;* creeping, poking, and ability to say one word, 40 weeks; *standing with slight support,* cooperation in dressing, and *verbalization of two or more words, 12 months;* and the use of words in phrases, 18 months.

Answers 2.31–2.34

2.31 The answer is B (*Synopsis VIII,* page 16).

2.32 The answer is A (*Synopsis VIII,* pages 16).

2.33 The answer is E (*Synopsis VIII,* pages 16).

2.34 The answer is D (*Synopsis VIII,* page 16).
Erik Erikson's epigenetic developmental sequence was composed of eight stages *from birth to old age.* Erikson's early stages coincided with those of Freud, but Erikson thought that people developed throughout life, not only in infancy, in predetermined stages. According to his theory, each stage had to be concluded effectively if not perfectly for the following stage to develop satisfactorily.

Sigmund Freud established the idea of *four stages of child development.* Most later workers drew on his ideas and either incorporated them, changed them, or rebelled against them. In contrast to Freud's theory of predetermined stages of development, Carl Jung's theory stressed that *external factors are important in human growth.* Jung was interested in problems of identity and maintained that personality develops as a person comes to realize who he or she is. Harry Stack Sullivan also stressed the importance of external factors in personality development and believed that *social interaction is vital at each stage of the life cycle.* According to Sullivan, the better the quality of the interactions, the healthier the development of the personality.

The unmatched statement describes the theory of Jean Piaget, whose work in *cognitive development* posited *four stages through which infants progress by predetermined steps.*

> These workers depended largely on observations of their patients and on anecdotal evidence. Large-scale, carefully conducted studies of human development have begun to be carried out in recent years. Today, workers find these studies, and recent discoveries about biological implications of human psychology, more relevant for research and treatment than are the theories of earlier scientists.

Answers 2.35–2.39

2.35 The answer is A (*Synopsis VIII,* page 35).

2.36 The answer is C (*Synopsis VIII,* page 35).

2.37 The answer is D (*Synopsis VIII,* page 35).

2.38 The answer is B (*Synopsis VIII,* page 35).

2.39 The answer is E (*Synopsis VIII,* page 35).
Mood or general emotional tone is an internal judgment based on the way children look and behave, as well as on their content of speech. During the first 12 months, mood is highly variable and is intimately related to internal states, such as hunger. Toward the second third of the first year, mood is also related to external social cues. When the child is internally comfortable, a sense of interest and pleasure in the world and in the primary caretakers should prevail. From 3 to 5 years, Sigmund Freud's oedipal phase and Erik Erikson's psychosocial crisis of initiative versus guilt prevail; thus, the child is capable of experiencing the complex emotions of jealousy and envy, as well as a growing sense of separation and security. At *birth,* the infant can experience *distress;* at *3 to 4 months, anger;* at *8 to 9 months,* fear and *sadness;* at *12 to 18 months, shame;* and at *3 to 4 years, guilt.*

Answers 2.40–2.44

2.40 The answer is E (*Synopsis VIII,* page 29).

2.41 The answer is D (*Synopsis VIII,* page 29).

2.42 The answer is A (*Synopsis VIII,* page 29).

2.43 The answer is C (*Synopsis VIII,* page 29).

2.44 The answer is B (*Synopsis VIII,* page 29).
To understand normal development, one must take a comprehensive approach and have an internal map of the age-expected norms for various aspects of human development. The areas of neuromotor, cognitive, and language milestones have many empirical normative data. The normal child is able to accomplish specific tasks at certain ages. For example, a *cross* can be copied at *4 years,* a square can be copied at 5 years, and a

triangle can be copied at *6 years.* At *18 months,* children can *walk up the stairs with one hand held,* at *2 years,* they can *refer to themselves by name,* and at *3 years* they can *put on their shoes.* Some children may be able to perform a task at an earlier or later age and still fall within the normal range. Other landmarks of normal behavioral development are listed in Table 2.1.

Answers 2.45–2.49

2.45 The answer is A (*Synopsis VIII,* page 29).

2.46 The answer is B (*Synopsis VIII,* page 29).

2.47 The answer is C (*Synopsis VIII,* page 29).

2.48 The answer is D (*Synopsis VIII,* page 29).

2.49 The answer is D (*Synopsis VIII,* page 29).
Language development occurs in well-delineated stages. At *birth to 6 months,* the child *plays at making sounds and babbles;* at *7 to 11 months,* the child *plays language games (pat-a-cake and peekaboo)*; at *12 to 18 months,* the child *uses up to 20 words and understands up to 150 words;* and from *54 months on,* the child's *speech is 100 percent intelligible,* and the child *uses language to tell stories and share ideas.*

Answers 2.50–2.53

2.50 The answer is B (*Synopsis VIII,* page 33).

2.51 The answer is C (*Synopsis VIII,* page 33).

2.52 The answer is C (*Synopsis VIII,* page 33).

2.53 The answer is B (*Synopsis VIII,* page 33).
Although depression as a symptom may occur as a prominent feature of normal bereavement, as well as of a depressive disorder, and although both conditions may be precipitated by a loss, some features differentiate grief from major depressive disorder. The full depressive syndrome may occur in complicated bereavement, although *marked preoccupation with worthlessness,* extended functional impairment, and marked psychomotor retardation are more often observed in *major depressive disorder.* Sadness, crying, and tension expressed as *psychomotor retardation or agitation* may be seen in *both* normal grief and major depressive disorder. Decreased appetite with *weight loss,* decreased libido, and withdrawal may be found in *both* conditions. The grief-stricken person, however, shows shifts of mood from sadness to a normal state within a reasonably short time and increasingly finds enjoyment in life as the loss recedes. A key aspect of the distinction between major depressive disorder and *normal grief* is similar to Sigmund Freud's original distinction between mourning and melancholy; that is, in normal grief a person does not show the marked lowering of self-esteem and the sense of personal badness that may be of delusional proportions in major depressive disorder, which may also give rise to *suicide attempts.*

Table 2.1
Landmarks of Normal Behavioral Development

Age	Motor and Sensory Behavior	Adaptive Behavior	Personal and Social Behavior
Under 4 weeks	Makes alternating crawling movements Moves head laterally when placed in prone position	Responds to sound of rattle and bell Regards moving objects momentarily	Quiets when picked up Impassive face
16 weeks	Symmetrical postures predominate Holds head balanced Head lifted 90 degrees when prone on forearm Visual accommodation	Follows a slowly moving object well Arms activate on sight of dangling object	Spontaneous social smile (exogenous) Aware of strange situations
28 weeks	Sits steadily, leaning forward on hands Bounces actively when placed in standing position	One-hand approach and grasp of toy Bangs and shakes rattle Transfers toys	Takes feet to mouth Pats mirror image Starts to imitate mother's sounds and actions
40 weeks	Sits alone with good coordination Creeps Pulls self to standing position Points with index finger	Matches two objects at midline Attempts to imitate scribble	Separation anxiety manifest when taken away from mother Responds to social play, such as pat-a-cake and peekaboo Feeds self cracker and holds own bottle
52 weeks	Walks with one hand held Stands alone briefly	Seeks novelty	Cooperates in dressing

Adapted from Arnold Gesell, M.D., and Stella Chess, M.D.

3 

The Brain and Behavior

An eclectic approach to understanding human behavior requires a thorough grounding in neuroanatomy, neurochemistry, neurophysiology, and behavioral genetics. Students of clinical psychiatry should be familiar with the gross and fine structure of the brain, the principles of chemical neurotransmission and the major classes of neurotransmitters, the full array of neuroimaging techniques, and the premises and possibilities of a molecular genetic analysis of behavior. An integration of these disciplines has led to emerging insights into the biological basis of behavior, and students who wish to understand and eventually contribute to current trends in psychiatric research must understand basic scientific methods in detail. A recent explosion of data from psychopharmacology, functional neuroimaging, and human molecular genetics has promoted a reexamination of many basic assumptions about the origins of psychopathology, and psychiatrists at all levels should be able to examine new claims rigorously and critically by applying their understanding of neuroscientific methods.

Behavioral neuroanatomy includes the ultrastructure of individual brain cells, the details of synaptic connectivity, the functional organization of the brain, and the behavioral consequences of pathological processes in the nervous system. Students should appreciate the vast functional diversity of brain cells and their organization into discrete functional units. These units include columns of cortical cells that share responses and basic multicellular units of highly repetitive structures such as the olfactory bulb, cerebellum, and hippocampus. Although the brain has been subdivided in many ways, students should be aware of Brodmann's cytoarchitectural classification as well as other, simpler schemata that recognize the brainstem and diencephalon (arousal and attention), the posterior cortex (sensory processing and associations), and the frontal cortex (executive functions) as three functional blocks. The basal ganglia, limbic structures, hypothalamus, and the four lobes of the cerebral cortex and their subdivisions are of particular importance to psychiatrists.

Students should know the classical syndromes of lobar dysfunction and should appreciate that most complex behaviors are the consequences of activating combinations of brain regions. They should understand the neuroanatomy of the sensory and motor systems and should be able to provide examples of how synaptic connectivity may be modified during development and in adulthood. Cerebral cortical lesions produce aphasias, apraxias, and visuoperceptive disorders; damage to the limbic system causes behavioral signs and memory dysfunction; and disruption of the basal ganglia produces movement disorders. The subdivisions of the prefrontal cortex should be familiar to students, since neuroimaging techniques are increasingly implicating prefrontal functions in both normal and abnormal behaviors. The location of the brainstem nuclei for the biogenic amine neurotransmitters and the widespread distribution of their axonal projections are of central importance to clinical psychopharmacology: These networks are the sites of action for most current psychotherapeutic drugs. Students should understand the stages of brain development, including cell birth, migration, elaboration of dendrites and axons, and onset of synaptic activity, and should know the ways in which development may deviate from normal.

Students must have a detailed understanding of the structure and function of the main components of neurotransmission and of the ways chemical and electrical signals interact in neurons. They must have a working knowledge of action potentials, voltage- and ligand-gated ion channels, second messengers, and the life cycle of neurotransmitters. They should clearly understand the presynaptic, synaptic, and postsynaptic machinery, which mediates the finest gradations of thought, along with the anatomy of serotonergic, noradrenergic, dopaminergic, and cholinergic projections. They must appreciate the contributions of the excitatory neurotransmitters, including glutamate; the inhibitory neurotransmitters, including γ-aminobutyric acid (GABA); the monoamine neurotransmitters, including serotonin, dopamine, norepinephrine, epinephrine, histamine, and acetylcholine; the peptide neurotransmitters, including the endorphins and enkephalins; and the other classes of neurotransmitters, including gases and arachidonates. The interplay between the nervous system and the endocrine and immune systems, as well as the influence of biological rhythms, are all important aspects of study. Students should be able to discuss critically the dopamine hypothesis of schizophrenia, the biogenic amine hypothesis of mood disorders, and the GABA and biogenic amine hypothesis of anxiety. They should also be able to associate specific drugs with one or more of the major neurotransmitter systems.

Students should be familiar with the physical principles, clinical and research indications, and limitations of the major neuroimaging methods, including magnetic resonance imaging (MRI), computed tomography (CT), magnetic resonance spectroscopy (MRS), single photon emission computed tomography (SPECT), proton emission tomography (PET), function MRI (fMRI), electroencephalography (EEG), magnetoencephalography (MEG), and event-related potentials (ERP). These methods are being applied with increasing frequency to the analysis of psychiatric conditions, and psychiatrists at all levels must understand neuroimaging studies and evaluate findings carefully. Emerging concepts include decreased frontal lobe metabolism in patients with schizophrenia, decreased right frontal lobe activity in attention-deficit/hyperactivity disorder, and complementary influences of the right and left prefrontal cortices on mood. Activation of the left prefrontal cortex may elevate mood, and activation of the right prefrontal cortex may depress mood.

Students must understand all levels of regulation of gene expression, DNA replication, messenger RNA synthesis and translation into protein, and the consequences of mutations in each of these steps. They should recognize the importance of assembling a complete pedigree in efforts to isolate genes for specific traits. Among the challenges of this area is deciphering the relative contributions of environmental influences (nurture) and genetic factors (nature) to isolate the genetic component. Also, the importance of twin and adoption studies should be understood. Students must know that the inherent limitations of the clinical definitions of psychiatric disorders represent the major impediment to efforts to identify genes responsible for behaviors. Students should be familiar with the candidate gene approach and with the methods used to evaluate a candidate gene, both in animals and in people.

Students should review Chapter 3 in Kaplan and Sadock's *Synopsis VIII* and then test their knowledge of the subject by studying the following questions and answers.

HELPFUL HINTS

The following items, including their structure and function and their relations with mental disorders and drugs, should be familiar to students.

- aphasia: Broca's, Wernicke's, conduction, global, transcortical motor, transcortical sensory, anomic, mixed transcortical
- apraxias: limb-kinetic, ideomotor; ideational
- basal ganglia and cerebellum and clinical syndromes
- behavioral neuroanatomy: arousal and attention, memory, language, emotions
- biological rhythms
- cytoarchitectonics and cortical columns
- development of cortical networks; plasticity
- dopamine and serotonin hypothesis of schizophrenia
- electrophysiology: membranes and charge; ion channels, action potentials, chemical neurotransmission
- epilepsy: complex partial seizures, temporal lobe epilepsy, TLE personality, déjà vu
- frontal, parietal, temporal and occipital lobes and clinical syndromes
- GABA and serotonin hypothesis of anxiety disorders
- glutamate, GABA, glycine, dopamine, norepinephrine, epinephrine, serotonin, acetylcholine, histamine, opioids, substance P, neurotensin, cholecystokinin, somatostatin, vasopressin, oxytocin, neuropeptide Y
- inheritance patterns: autosomal dominant, autosomal recessive, sex-linked
- ligand-gated ion channel; G protein-coupled receptor; second messenger
- limbic system: amygdala, hippocampus, Papez circuit
- molecular genetics: pedigree, positional cloning, candidate gene, mutations
- neuroimaging: CT, MRI, MRS, fMRI, SPECT, PET, EEG, MEG, TMS, EP, ERP
- neurons and glial cells
- neurotransmitters: biogenic amines, amino acids, peptides, nucleotides, gases, eicosanoids, anandamides
- norepinephrine and serotonin hypothesis of mood disorders
- organization of sensory and motor systems; hemispheric lateralization
- psychoneuroendocrinology: hormones and hormone receptors, adrenal axis, thyroid axis, growth hormone, estrogens
- psychoneuroimmunology: placebo effect, cancer, infection, AIDS
- synapses: presynaptic membrane, synaptic compartment, postsynaptic membrane

▲ QUESTIONS

DIRECTIONS: Each of the following questions or incomplete statements is followed by five suggested responses or completions. Select the *one* that is *best* in each case.

3.1 Which of the following statements about the neurotransmitters is accurate?

A. Glutamate is an inhibitory amino acid.
B. Phencyclidine (PCP) acts at the level of the GABA receptors.
C. Peptide neurotransmitters are made in the cell body of the neuron.
D. Serotonin is synthesized from the amino acid precursor tyrosine.
E. The nigrostriatal tract is a serotonergic tract.

3.2 The one advantage of computed tomography (CT) over magnetic resonance imaging (MRI) in psychiatric clinical practice is

A. CT has superior resolution.
B. CT can distinguish between white matter and gray matter.
C. CT has the ability to take thinner slices through the brain than does MRI.
D. CT is superior in detecting calcified brain lesions.
E. CT avoids exposing patients to radiation.

3.3 The image-resolution level of both positron emission tomography (PET) and single photon emission computed tomography (SPECT) is affected by

A. the Compton effect
B. signal attenuation
C. anatomical resolution
D. partial volume effect
E. all the above

3.4 The pedigree chart in Figure 3.1 shows a particular type of genetic inheritance known as

A. dominant
B. Y linked
C. X linked
D. recessive
E. none of the above

3.5 The dietary amino acid precursor of serotonin is

A. neurotensin
B. phenylalanine
C. glycine
D. tryptophan
E. tyramine

3.6 Enkephalins are which of the following?

A. Opioid-like peptides
B. Cholinergic agents
C. Dopamine-blocking agents
D. Serotonin-specific reuptake inhibitors
E. Tricyclic drugs

3.7 The velocity of conduction of the nerve action potential is increased because of the

A. axon hillock
B. myelin sheath
C. voltage-sensitive potassium channels
D. sodium-potassium ATPase
E. chloride conductance

3.8 Which of the following features is *least* likely to represent isolated injury to the dorsolateral prefrontal cortex?

A. Deficiencies in planning and monitoring
B. Inability to use foresight and feedback
C. Echolalia
D. Mood disorders
E. Akinetic mutism

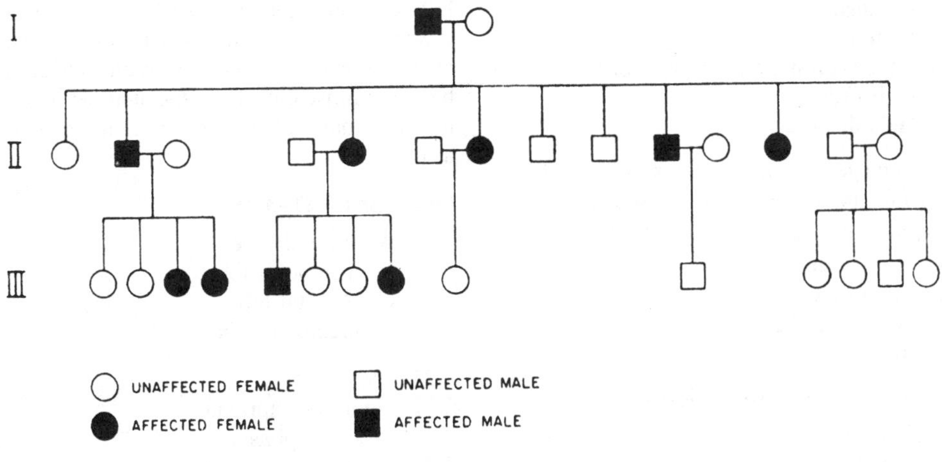

FIGURE 3.1
Pedigree chart.

3.9 Abnormalities of the gating of intended motor acts in Tourette's syndrome, Parkinson's disease, Huntington's disease, and obsessive-compulsive disorder are due to dysfunction of which of the basal ganglia?

A. Caudate
B. Putamen
C. Globus pallidus
D. Substantia nigra
E. Subthalamic nucleus

3.10 γ-Aminobutyric acid (GABA) is degraded by

A. glutamic acid decarboxylase (GAD)
B. GABA transporter
C. GABA transaminase (GABA-T)
D. monoamine oxidase (MAO)
E. tryptophan hydroxylase

3.11 Techniques that reflect regional brain activity by measuring neuronal activity rather than blood flow include

A. xenon-133 (^{133}Xe) single proton emission computed tomography (SPECT)
B. fluorine-18 [^{18}F]-fluorodeoxyglucose (FDG) positron emission tomography (PET)
C. technetium-99 (^{99}Tc) hexamethylpropyleneamine oxime (HMPAO) SPECT
D. nitrogen-13 (^{13}N) PET
E. functional magnetic resonance imaging (fMRI)

3.12 The functional neuroimaging technique with the best temporal resolution is

A. single proton emission computed tomography (SPECT)
B. positron emission tomography (PET)
C. electroencephalography (EEG)
D. magnetoencephalography (MEG)
E. functional magnetic resonance imaging (fMRI)

3.13 The psychiatric diagnosis for which there appears to be the strongest genetic hereditary component is

A. bipolar I disorder
B. schizophrenia
C. attention-deficit/hyperactivity disorder
D. autistic disorder
E. Tourette's disorder

3.14 Which language function shows sexual dimorphism in functional neuroimaging studies?

A. Phonological processing
B. Lexical processing
C. Generation of words
D. Auditory comprehension
E. Repetition

3.15 Word deafness results from a lesion of

A. Broca's area
B. left parietal cortex
C. striate cortex
D. splenium of the corpus callosum
E. inferior colliculus

3.16 Temporal lobe epilepsy is likely to be associated with each of the following *except*

A. fear
B. hyposexuality
C. hypermetamorphosis
D. viscosity
E. aggression

3.17 Activation of which neurotransmitter receptor is best associated with a decrease in anxiety?

A. Dopamine type 2 (D_2)
B. β-Adrenergic type 1 (β_1)
C. Nicotinic acetylcholine
D. Serotonin type 1_A (5-HT_{1A})
E. *N*-Methyl-D-aspartate (NMDA) glutamate

3.18 Which neurotransmitter is degraded in the synaptic cleft?

A. Acetylcholine
B. γ-Aminobutyric acid (GABA)
C. Dopamine
D. Serotonin
E. Norepinephrine

3.19 Which neurotransmitter is *not* derived from tyrosine?

A. Epinephrine
B. Dihydroxyphenylalanine (DOPA)
C. Dopamine
D. Serotonin
E. Norepinephrine

3.20 The fibers of which primary sensory system do not pass through the thalamus?

A. Auditory
B. Nociceptive somatosensory
C. Olfactory
D. Proprioceptive somatosensory
E. Visual

DIRECTIONS: Each set of lettered headings below is followed by a list of numbered words or statements. For each numbered word or statement, select the *one* lettered heading most closely associated with it. Each lettered heading may be selected once, more than once, or not at all.

Questions 3.21–3.25

A. Frontal lobe
B. Temporal lobe
C. Parietal lobe
D. Occipital lobe

3.21 Alexia
3.22 Ideomotor apraxia
3.23 Broca's aphasia
3.24 Klüver-Bucy syndrome
3.25 Wernicke's aphasia

Questions 3.26–3.28

A. Gerstmann syndrome
B. Anton's syndrome
C. Balint's syndrome

3.26 Cortical blindness and the denial of blindness
3.27 Optic ataxia, loss of panoramic vision, and supranuclear gaze palsy
3.28 Agraphia, acalculia, right-left disorientation, and finger agnosia

Questions 3.29–3.33

A. Acetylcholine
B. Dopamine
C. Glycine
D. Norepinephrine
E. Serotonin

3.29 Median and dorsal raphe nuclei
3.30 Locus ceruleus
3.31 Nucleus basalis of Meynert
3.32 Substantia nigra
3.33 Spinal cord

DIRECTIONS: The lettered headings below are followed by a list of numbered phrases. For each numbered phrase, select

A. if the item is associated with A only
B. if the item is associated with B only
C. if the item is associated with both A and B
D. if the item is associated with neither A nor B

Questions 3.34–3.37

A. Computed tomography (CT)
B. Magnetic resonance imaging (MRI)
C. Both
D. Neither

3.34 Uses X-ray photons
3.35 Differs in attenuation by the density of the structure
3.36 Is able to discriminate gray matter and white matter
3.37 Differs in attenuation by proton density

ANSWERS

The Brain and Behavior

3.1 The answer is C (*Synopsis VIII*, pages 106–109).

The three major types of neurotransmitters in the brain are the amino acids, the biogenic amines, and the peptides. Peptides differ from the other two major types of neurotransmitters in that only *peptides are made in the cell body,* where the genetic information for making them resides. Peptide neurotransmitters are usually first synthesized as long forms called preprohormones and are further processed during their transport to the axon terminals. First, the preprohormones are cleaved to make prohormones; then the prohormones are cleaved to make the final hormones.

The two major amino acid neurotransmitters are γ-aminobutyric acid (GABA) and glutamate. GABA is an inhibitory amino acid, and *glutamate is an excitatory amino acid.* An important drug of abuse, *phencyclidine (PCP) acts at the level of the glutamate receptors, not the GABA receptors.*

The six biogenic amine neurotransmitters are dopamine, norepinephrine, epinephrine, serotonin, acetylcholine, and histamine (Fig. 3.2). Dopamine, epinephrine, and norepinephrine are all synthesized from the same amino acid precursor, tyrosine, and are classified as a group as the catecholamines. *Serotonin is not synthesized from the amino acid precursor tyrosine.* It is synthesized from the amino acid precursor tryptophan and is the only indolamine in the group. Serotonin is also known as 5-hydroxytryptamine (5-HT); therefore, the abbreviation for serotonin is often written as 5-HT. A common feature of all the biogenic amine neurotransmitters is that they are synthesized in the axon terminal. *The nigrostriatal tract,* the mesolimbic-mesocortical tract, and the tuberoinfundibular tract are *dopaminergic tracts, not serotonergic tracts.* The nigrostriatal tract projects from its cell bodies in the substantia nigra to the corpus striatum. When the dopamine receptors at the end of this tract are blocked by classic antipsychotic drugs, the parkinsonian side effects of these drugs are the result. In Parkinson's disease the nigrostriatal tract degenerates, and the motor symptoms of the disease result. Because of the significant association between Parkinson's disease and depression, the nigrostriatal tract may somehow be involved with the control of mood, in addition to its classic role in motor control.

The mesolimbic-mesocortical tract projects from its cell bodies in the ventral tegmental area (which lies adjacent to the substantia nigra) to most areas of the cerebral cortex and the limbic system. Because the tract projects to the limbic system and the neocortex, the tract may be involved in mediating the antipsychotic effects of antipsychotic drugs.

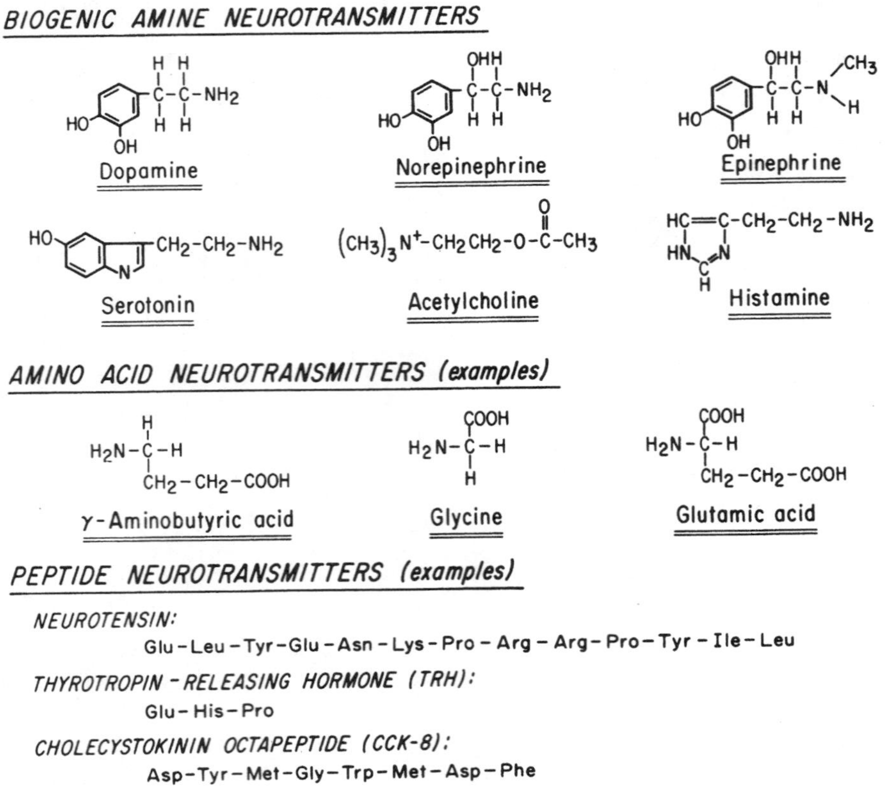

BIOGENIC AMINE NEUROTRANSMITTERS

Dopamine

Norepinephrine

Epinephrine

Serotonin

$(CH_3)_3N^+{-}CH_2CH_2{-}O{-}\overset{O}{\overset{\|}{C}}{-}CH_3$

Acetylcholine

Histamine

AMINO ACID NEUROTRANSMITTERS (examples)

γ-Aminobutyric acid

Glycine

Glutamic acid

PEPTIDE NEUROTRANSMITTERS (examples)

NEUROTENSIN:

Glu-Leu-Tyr-Glu-Asn-Lys-Pro-Arg-Arg-Pro-Tyr-Ile-Leu

THYROTROPIN-RELEASING HORMONE (TRH):

Glu-His-Pro

CHOLECYSTOKININ OCTAPEPTIDE (CCK-8):

Asp-Tyr-Met-Gly-Trp-Met-Asp-Phe

FIGURE 3.2
Three classes of neurotransmitters.

The cell bodies of the tuberoinfundibular tract are in the arcuate nucleus and the periventricular area of the hypothalamus and project to the infundibulum and the anterior pituitary. Dopamine acts as a release-inhibiting factor in the tract by inhibiting the release of prolactin from the anterior pituitary. Patients who take antipsychotic drugs have elevated prolactin levels because the blockade of dopamine receptors in the tract eliminates the inhibitory effect of dopamine.

3.2 The answer is D (*Synopsis VIII,* page 124).
One reason to order a computed tomography (CT) scan in preference to a magnetic resonance imaging (MRI) scan is that CT is superior in detecting calcified brain lesions. Whether to order a CT or a more expensive MRI is one of the common clinical questions in psychiatric practice. The resolution of both techniques is under 1 mm, but *MRI has the capability of taking thinner slices through the brain, does have superior resolution,* and *can better distinguish between white matter and gray matter.* CT is based on X-ray technology; MRI utilizes magnetic fields. Therefore, *MRI, not CT, avoids exposing patients to radiation.*

3.3 The answer is E (*Synopsis VIII,* page 131).
Four major factors affect the resolution level of both PET and SPECT: the Compton effect, signal attenuation, anatomical resolution, and partial volume effect.

The emitted photons in both positron emission tomography (PET) and single photon emission computed tomography (SPECT) are diverted from a straight path by the tissues through which they pass. This effect of the tissue is called the *Compton effect;* it limits the anatomical resolution of both PET and SPECT.

Not only are the photons diverted from their straight path by the tissue, but the energy of the photons is dissipated by bone, air, fluid, and brain tissue. In fact, the most carefully done PET and SPECT studies use prestudy CT examinations to correct for variable *signal attenuations* caused by differences in patients' head sizes.

A common term used in describing the *anatomical resolution* for both PET and SPECT is *full width at half maximum* (FWHM), which refers to the width of the curve of distribution for the signal at 50 percent of the maximal signal. In PET studies, FWHM is about 5 to 6 mm; in SPECT studies, FWHM is about 8 to 9 mm. This difference reflects the better resolution of the PET technique compared with the SPECT technique.

In both PET and SPECT, areas of interest within the slice are selected, but the signal from each area of interest also has an effect on neighboring areas of interest, an effect called *partial volume effect.* In some studies of SPECT and PET, the investigators use various computer modeling programs to subtract the energy contribution of neighboring areas from the areas of interest.

3.4 The answer is A (*Synopsis VIII,* page 136).
The *dominant* mode of inheritance, in which each child of an affected parent has a 50 percent chance of receiving a particular gene, is shown in Figure 3.1. The pedigree chart is that of a family affected by Huntington's disease.

For traits determined by single genes, three common inheritance patterns are recognized. Autosomal dominant transmission means that of the two copies of the gene in the cell nucleus, only one needs be mutated to produce the clinical trait. Autosomal *recessive* transmission indicates that the trait is seen only if both copies are mutated. Thus a parent with an autosomal recessive trait passes it to a child only if the other parent also passes on the mutant gene. *X-linked* recessive transmission applies when the gene is on the unpaired X chromosome and is thus the only copy of the gene in the nucleus. An X-linked recessive trait is seen in males, who have only one X chromosome, whereas females are carriers without the clinical trait, since they have a second, normal X chromosome. A gene may, in theory, also be *Y linked* if it is located on the Y (male) chromosome.

3.5 The answer is D (*Synopsis VIII,* pages 115–116).
Tryptophan is the dietary amino acid precursor of serotonin. It is hydroxylated by the enzyme tryptophan hydroxylase to form 5-hydroxytryptophan; 5-hydroxytryptophan is decarboxylated to serotonin. Serotonin is destroyed by reuptake into the presynaptic terminal and subsequent metabolism by monoamine oxidase (MAO), which oxidatively deaminates it to 5-hydroxyindoleacetic acid (5-HIAA).

Neurotensin is a neurotransmitter and an amino acid peptide that can lower blood pressure; it acts as an analgesic when injected directly into the brain. *Phenylalanine* is an amino acid in proteins. *Glycine,* an amino acid, functions as an inhibitory neurotransmitter in the spinal cord.

Tyramine is a sympathomimetic amine whose action is similar to that of epinephrine. It is present in ripe cheese, herring, and other foods. Because of the danger of adrenergic potentiation, tyramine-containing substances must be avoided by patients on monoamine oxidase inhibitors (MAOIs).

3.6 The answer is A (*Synopsis VIII,* pages 117–118).
Enkephalins are *opioid-like peptides* that are found in many parts of the brain and that bind to specific receptor sites. They are opioid-like because they decrease pain perception. They also serve as neurotransmitters.

Cholinergic agents are drugs that cause the liberation of acetylcholine. *Dopamine-blocking agents* are drugs, such as the antipsychotic haloperidol (Haldol), that block dopamine receptors on postsynaptic neurons; thus they effectively decrease the functional levels of the neurotransmitter dopamine. Dopamine blockers are most often used to treat psychotic patients whose psychosis is related to a hyperdopaminergic state.

The two major classes of antidepressant drugs are the *serotonin-specific reuptake inhibitors (SSRIs)* and the *tricyclic drugs.* SSRIs increase synaptic serotonin activity by inhibiting the reuptake of serotonin into the presynaptic terminal through the serotonin transporter. The tricyclic drugs are potent inhibitors of the reuptake inactivation mechanism of catecholamine and serotonin neurons. The ability of tricyclic drugs to inhibit the reuptake process results in a functional increase of such neurotransmitters as norepinephrine and serotonin and leads to the medication's antidepressant activity.

3.7 The answer is B (*Synopsis VIII,* page 101).
The increase in nerve conduction velocity that accounts for the rapid processing capabilities of the brain is due to the presence of *myelin sheaths,* which encircle larger axons. Myelin is a highly hydrophobic substance that completely prevents the

passage of ions. It is laid down along the axon in segments that are separated by gaps of bare axonal membrane, called nodes of Ranvier. The local changes in membrane charge constituting the action potential occur at the nodes of Ranvier and then jump over the myelin segment to the next node of Ranvier. For a given distance of axon, for example, the presence of myelin segments reduces the number of times the action potential must trigger neighboring voltage-gated ion channels to conduct an impulse along this distance of axon. The nerve conduction velocity may therefore increase to as high as 65 meters per second in large, myelinated fibers. The *axon hillock* is the segment of the axon located immediately adjacent to the cell body. When the membrane potential rises above the firing threshold, typically −55 to −50 mV, because of the actions of the dendritic ion channels, an action potential is generated. The axon hillock thus initiates but does not influence the rate of conduction of the action potential. During the action potential, the polarity of the membrane goes from negative to positive because of the actions of sodium and calcium channels. Calcium ion entry activates *voltage-sensitive potassium channels* that carry an outgoing flow of potassium ions involved in arresting the action potential. The activation of these potassium channels results in the afterhyperpolarization of the membrane after an action potential. During the afterhyperpolarization, the inside of the membrane is even more negatively charged than it was at baseline. The afterhyperpolarization contributes to the refractory period of a neuron after an action potential; during this period, another action potential cannot be generated. The principal ion pump, which generates the resting potential of the membrane, is the energy-requiring *sodium-potassium adenosine triphosphatase (ATPase)* ion exchange pump. Ion pumps and ion channels maintain a gradient of cations: Potassium ions are 15 to 20 times more concentrated inside neurons, and sodium ions are 8 to 15 times less concentrated inside neurons with respect to the extracellular space. Inhibitory neurotransmitters open chloride channels to allow *chloride conductance,* which hyperpolarizes the membrane and decreases the likelihood of the generation of an action potential.

3.8 The answer is E (*Synopsis VIII,* page 95).
The frontal lobes constitute a category unto themselves, the region that determines how the brain acts on its knowledge. There are four subdivisions of the frontal lobes. The first three, the motor strip, the supplemental motor area, and Broca's area, are components of the motor and language systems. The fourth, the most anterior division, is the prefrontal cortex. In the prefrontal cortex there are three regions, lesions of which produce distinct syndromes, the orbitofrontal, the dorsolateral, and the medial. *Akinetic mutism* is characteristic of injury to the medial region, especially the anterior cingulate gyrus, which normally appears to initiate a wide range of activities. Ablation of the medial region may produce a profound apathy characterized by limited spontaneous movement, gesture, and speech. In the extreme, there may be a state of akinetic mutism.

The remaining choices are typical features of damage to the dorsolateral region, which appears to be the executive headquarters of the brain. Lesions in the dorsolateral region lead to *deficiencies of planning, monitoring,* flexibility, and motivation. There may be an *inability to use foresight and feedback.* Patients are unable to maintain goal directedness, focus, and sustained effort, and they appear inattentive and undermotivated. They cannot plan novel cognitive activity and exhibit a tendency to linger on a trivial thought. They may merely echo the question of the examiner *(echolalia)* and react primarily to the details of environmental stimuli. In other words, they "miss the forest for the trees." On formal neuropsychological testing, however, they may exhibit intact memory, language, and visuospatial skills, which are functions of the occipital, temporal, and parietal lobes, respectively. Dorsolateral frontal lobe injury may also produce *mood disorders.*

Damage to the orbitofrontal region causes disinhibition, irritability, lability, euphoria, and a lack of remorse. Insight and judgment are impaired, and patients are distractible. These features are reminiscent of the fourth edition of *Diagnostic and Statistical Manual of Mental Disorders* (DSM-IV) diagnoses of antisocial personality disorder, intermittent explosive disorder, and episodic dyscontrol syndrome. The orbitofrontal syndrome may also produce a state of "pseudopsychopathy."

The prefrontal lobe syndromes are most commonly produced by trauma, infarction, tumors, lobotomy, multiple sclerosis, or Pick's disease. Unilateral frontal lobe lesions may go largely unnoticed because the remaining intact lobe can compensate with high efficiency.

3.9 The answer is A (*Synopsis VIII,* page 87).
The *caudate* nucleus plays an important role in the modulation of motor acts. Anatomical and functional neuroimaging studies have correlated decreased activation of the caudate with obsessive-compulsive behavior. When functioning properly, the caudate nucleus acts as a gatekeeper to allow the motor system to perform only goal-directed acts. When it fails to perform its gatekeeper function, extraneous acts are performed as in obsessive-compulsive disorder or in the tic disorders, such as Tourette's syndrome. Overactivity of the striatum because of lack of dopaminergic inhibition, for example, in parkinsonian conditions, results in bradykinesia, an inability to initiate movements. The caudate, in particular, shrinks dramatically in Huntington's chorea. This disorder is characterized by rigidity, on which are gradually superimposed choreiform or dancing movements. The *putamen* may be viewed as an anatomically and physiologically comparable structure to the caudate, although its function is less well known than that of the caudate. The caudate and putamen are collectively known as the corpus striatum, which harbors components of both motor and association systems.

The *globus pallidus* contains two parts, which are linked in series. In cross section, the internal and external parts of the globus pallidus are nested in the concavity of the putamen. The globus pallidus receives input from the corpus striatum and projects fibers to the thalamus. This structure may be severely damaged in Wilson's disease and in carbon monoxide poisoning, disorders that give rise to dystonic posturing and flapping movements of the arms and legs.

The *substantia nigra* is named the "black substance" because of its appearance to the naked eye, an appearance caused by melanin pigment. It has two parts, one of which is equivalent to the globus pallidus interna. The other part degenerates in Parkinson's disease. Degeneration of dopaminergic nigrostriatal fibers diminishes the inhibitory effects of the substantia nigra on the caudate and allows the caudate to oversuppress intended movements, seen clinically as bradykinesia. Parkinsonism is characterized by rigidity and tremor and is associated with depression in over 30 percent of cases.

Lesions in the *subthalamic nucleus* yield ballistic movements, sudden limb jerks of such velocity that they are compared to projectiles.

Taken in sum, the nuclei of the basal ganglia appear capable of initiating and maintaining the full range of useful movements. It has been speculated that the nuclei serve to configure the activity of the overlying motor cortex to fit the purposes of the association areas. They appear to integrate proprioceptive feedback to maintain an intended movement.

3.10 The answer is C (*Synopsis VIII,* page 110).
γ-Aminobutyric acid (GABA) is metabolized by mitochondrial-associated *GABA transaminase (GABA-T),* which is located in both neurons and glial cells. GABA is synthesized from glutamate by the rate-limiting enzyme *glutamic acid decarboxylase (GAD),* which requires pyridoxine (vitamin B_6) as a cofactor. Once released into the synaptic cleft, GABA is taken up by a specific *GABA transporter* into the presynaptic neuron and adjacent glia, where it is metabolized by GABA-T. Tiagabine, which inhibits the GABA transporter, and vigabatrin (Sabril), which inhibits GABA-T, both raise the effective levels of GABA, and both exhibit anticonvulsant activity.

Monoamine oxidases (MAOs) degrade biogenic amine neurotransmitters rather than GABA. MAOs are attached to the outer mitochondrial membrane and appear in two forms. MAO_A metabolizes norepinephrine and serotonin, and its inhibition by MAO inhibitors is associated with an elevation in mood. MAO_B metabolizes dopamine, and its inhibitors are used clinically as treatment for Parkinson's disease.

Tryptophan hydroxylase synthesizes serotonin from its precursor, the amino acid tryptophan. The availability of tryptophan is the rate-limiting function, and the enzyme tryptophan hydroxylase is not rate limiting. Therefore, dietary variations in tryptophan can measurably affect serotonin levels in the brain.

3.11 The answer is B (*Synopsis VIII,* pages 128–131).
Fluorine-18 [^{18}F]-fluorodeoxyglucose (FDG) is an analogue that the brain cannot metabolize. Glucose is by far the predominant energy source available to brain cells, and its utilization is therefore a highly sensitive indicator of the rate of brain metabolism. Thus, the brain regions with the highest metabolic rate and the highest blood flow take up the most FDG but are unable to metabolize and excrete the usual metabolic products. The concentration of ^{18}F builds up in these neurons and is detected by the PET camera. FDG PET therefore measures glucose metabolism.

Each of the other choices measures blood flow rather than metabolism. Blood flow generally is proportional to brain metabolism and may be measured by a wider variety of clinical techniques. *Xenon-133* is a noble gas that is inhaled directly and is detected by SPECT scanners. The xenon quickly enters the blood and is distributed to areas of the brain as a function of regional blood flow. It may therefore be referred to as the regional cerebral blood flow (rCBF) technique. Because of technical factors, xenon SPECT can measure blood flow only on the surface of the brain. This limitation is important because many mental tasks require communication between the cortex and subcortical structures, and the latter activity is missed by xenon SPECT. Assessment of blood flow over the whole brain with SPECT requires the injectable tracers, *technetium-99 (^{99}Tc) d,l-hexamethylpropyleneamine oxime (HMPAO* [Ceretec]*)* or iodoamphetamine (Spectamine). These radiotracers are highly lipophilic, cross the blood–brain barrier rapidly, and enter cells. Once inside a cell, the ligands are enzymatically converted to charged ions, which remain trapped in the cell. Thus, over time, the tracers are concentrated in areas of relatively higher blood flow. Although blood flow is usually assumed to be the major variable tested in HMPAO SPECT, local variations in the permeability of the blood–brain barrier and in the enzymatic conversion of the ligands in cells also contribute to regional differences in signal levels. In *nitrogen-13 (^{13}N) PET,* the radioactive nitrogen isotope (^{13}N) is usually linked to another molecule that is distributed into cells as a function of blood flow.

Functional MRI (fMRI) detects blood flow by measuring local levels of oxygenated hemoglobin. Although neuronal metabolism extracts more oxygen in active areas of the brain, the net effect of neuronal activity is to raise the local amount of oxygenated hemoglobin. This change can be detected essentially in real time with the T2* sequence. The T2* sequence thus detects which brain regions are functionally active. The volume of brain in which blood flow increases exceeds the volume of activated neurons by about 1 to 2 cm, a limit to the resolution of the technique. Thus, two tasks that activate clusters of neurons that are 5 mm apart, such as recognizing two different faces, yield overlapping signals on fMRI and therefore may be indistinguishable by this technique. fMRI is useful to localize neuronal activity to a particular lobe or subcortical nucleus and has even been able to localize activity to a single gyrus. The method detects tissue perfusion, but not neuronal metabolism. The great advantage of fMRI over PET and SPECT is that no radioactive isotopes are administered. Subjects can perform a variety of tasks, both experimental and control, in the same imaging session, a result less readily obtained with PET or SPECT. Generally, a routine T1 MRI image is obtained; then the T2* images are superimposed to allow the most precise localization.

3.12 The answer is D (*Synopsis VIII,* pages 133–134).
Magnetoencephalography (MEG) offers the best temporal resolution of any technique currently available but also has the lowest spatial resolution. MEG detects minute changes in the magnetic fields surrounding neurons; it uses supercooled magnetic detectors, called single superconducting quantum interference devices (SQUIDs), which operate near absolute zero temperature. MEG is the superior technique for detection of activity deep in the brain, in that magnetic fields are less attenuated than are electrical fields by the skull and scalp tissues. The fields registered by MEG are tiny, and recordings require careful shielding and extensive computerized computational algorithms for optimal localization in the brain.

Single photon emission computed tomography (SPECT) and *positron emission tomography (PET)* have the least temporal resolution; both require the accumulation of radioactive compounds inside neurons, the emissions of which are detected by arrays of scintillation counters. The accumulation of data takes from 2 to 60 minutes. Once the radiotracer has been inhaled or injected, it must decay to undetectable levels before readministration, which may take 10 minutes in the case of ^{15}O, up to several hours for many commonly used tracers, or up to several days for ^{133}Xe. *Electroencephalography (EEG)* detects the brain's electrical activity, and data acquisition is rapid. The temporal resolution of EEG is almost identical to that of MEG, on the order of milliseconds. *Functional magnetic resonance imaging (fMRI)* permits acquisitions of an image in as little as 200 ms, though typically it may require a full second. The spatial resolution of fMRI is far superior to that of EEG or MEG, and because it measures only naturally occurring variations in cerebral blood flow, there is no obligatory delay before acquisition of additional images.

3.13 The answer is E (*Synopsis VIII,* page 136).
Many major psychiatric disorders have been shown to have a strong hereditary predisposition. *Tourette's disorder,* also called Tourette's syndrome, shows the most convincing genetic association. Several family pedigrees for the disorder have been constructed in which its transmission is consistent with an autosomal dominant mode of genetic inheritance, with penetrance, or efficiency of expression, of 99 percent in males and 70 percent in females. These data lead to the reasonable assumption that linkage analysis should find the risk of inheriting the disorder to be associated with a single dominant genetic locus. Yet linkage analysis on several large pedigrees has thus far failed to find a single locus responsible for even a minority of the genetic variation. This finding has raised the possibility that the phenotype of the disorder may be a final common pathway for the expression of the effects of several different genes.

The presence of *schizophrenia* in a first-degree relative raises the risk of schizophrenia in a given individual to a 10 percent chance, far in excess of the 1 percent risk to the general population. Moreover, monozygotic twins display a nearly 50 percent concordance rate for schizophrenia. Similarly, *bipolar I disorder* and major depressive disorder exhibit familial clustering; first-degree relatives are 8 to 18 times more likely to have a mood disorder than is the general population, and monozygotic twins show a 33 to 90 percent concordance rate. Schizophrenia and bipolar I disorder also appear to be multigenic conditions, and their expression seems significantly influenced by environmental factors.

The inheritance of *attention-deficit/hyperactivity disorder* and *autistic disorder* generally do not fit a single gene model, and most cases are sporadic.

3.14 The answer is A (*Synopsis VIII,* pages 92–93, 127).
A recent analysis of the cortical localization of the processing of language, in which male and female volunteers were studied with functional magnetic resonance imaging (fMRI) while they performed tasks that drew on various aspects of language processing, revealed an unexpected sexual dimorphism for *phonological processing* (the determination of whether two words rhyme). This function activates the inferior frontal gyrus (IFG). In males, only the left IFG is activated, whereas in females, both the left and right IFGs are activated during phonological processing. The neurobiological basis of this sexual dimorphism is unknown, although in the hypothalamus and the basal forebrain of animals, sexually dimorphic brain development has been shown to be influenced by hormonal factors as well as by early rearing experiences. The functional significance of sexual dimorphism for phonological processing has not been determined.

Each of the other choices refers to an area, usually of the left hemisphere, that is identical in men and women. *Lexical processing,* the determination of whether a sound is a word, occurs in the left temporal lobe. *Generation of words* occurs in Broca's area at the inferior part of the posterior border of the frontal lobe. Lesions of this area lead to Broca's aphasia, in which comprehension is preserved, but subjects cannot generate fluent speech. The speech of people with Broca's aphasia is telegraphic and circumlocutory, but syntactical sentence structure retains its logic. *Auditory comprehension* occurs in Wernicke's area, which is located in the planum temporale, a triangular patch of cortex located on the superior surface of the dominant temporal lobe. There is hemispheric asymmetry of the planum temporale in most right-handed people, with the left planum temporale being larger than the right. The degree of hemispheric asymmetry of the planum temporale is partially under hormonal control, and this phenomenon may explain the fact that planum temporale is aberrantly symmetrical (a finding associated with left-handedness) more often in males than in females. Variants of the asymmetry of the planum temporale occur in less than 5 percent of the population. *Repetition* is disrupted by injury to the arcuate fasciculus, a bundle of nerve fibers that connect Wernicke's area with Broca's area.

3.15 The answer is B (*Synopsis VIII,* page 84).
Extraction of sonic features is achieved through a combination of mechanical and neural fitters. The representation of sound is roughly tonotopic in the primary auditory cortex, whereas vowels and consonants are extracted from the auditory input in higher language association areas, especially Wernicke's area in the left parietal lobe. The syndrome of word deafness may occur because of damage to the *left parietal cortex,* but it may also be due to injury of the superior left temporal lobe. It is characterized by intact hearing for voices but an inability to recognize speech and is thought to result from a disconnection of Wernicke's area from the parietal language association areas. A rare, complementary syndrome, auditory sound agnosia, is defined as the inability to recognize nonverbal sounds, such as a horn or a cat's meow, in the presence of intact hearing and speech recognition. The syndrome is thought to be the right hemisphere correlate of pure word deafness. *Broca's area* is involved in the generation rather than the comprehension of words.

The *striate cortex* in the occipital lobe is also called the primary visual cortex. It receives visual input from the lateral geniculate nucleus of the thalamus and contains cells that extract the presence and orientation of lines from the visual environment. Lesions of the striate cortex cause cortical blindness. The corpus callosum is a collection of white matter fibers that connect the two hemispheres. It is divided into the genu, the body, and the splenium. The *splenium of the corpus callosum* is the most posterior part and carries fibers involved in higher visual processing. Lesions of the splenium may cause problems with reading and writing (alexia with or without agraphia). The *inferior colliculus,* located in the dorsal midbrain, is a relay station for auditory input between the lateral lemniscus and the medial geniculate bodies. All auditory input passes through the inferior colliculus on its way to the cortex. Because of bilateral representations, a lesion to the inferior colliculus is not likely to cause clinically significant losses.

3.16 The answer is C (*Synopsis VIII,* pages 93–94).
In the hemispheres, the temporal and frontal lobes play a prominent role in emotion. The temporal lobe exhibits a high frequency of epileptic foci, and temporal lobe epilepsy (TLE) has presented an interesting model for the temporal lobe's role in behavior. Studies of epilepsy analyze abnormally excessive brain activation, rather than deficits in activity, which are analyzed in classical lesional studies. TLE is of particular interest to psychiatrists because temporal lobe seizures may often manifest bizarre behavior without the classical grand mal shaking movements caused by seizures in the motor cortex. A proposed TLE personality would be characterized by *hyposexuality,* emotional intensity, and a perseverative approach to interactions, termed *viscosity.* Patients with left TLE may generate references to personal destiny and philosophical themes and may display a humorless approach to life. In contrast, patients with right TLE may display excessive emotionality, ranging from elation to sadness. Although TLE patients may display excessive *aggression* between seizures, the seizure itself may produce *fear.*

The inverse of a TLE personality appears in patients with bilateral injury to the temporal lobes, following head trauma or herpes simplex encephalitis. This lesion resembles that described in the Klüver-Bucy syndrome, an experimental model of temporal lobe ablation in monkeys. Behavior in the Klüver-Bucy syndrome consists of hypersexuality, placidity, a tendency to explore the environment with the mouth, inability to recognize the emotional significance of visual stimuli, and constantly shifting attention, called *hypermetamorphosis.* In contrast to the aggression–fear spectrum sometimes seen in TLE patients, complete experimental ablation of the temporal lobes appears to produce a uniform, bland reaction to the environment, possibly due to inability to access memories.

3.17 The answer is D (*Synopsis VIII,* page 116).
Seven types of serotonin receptors—5-HT_1 through 5-HT_7—are now recognized, and there are numerous subtypes, in all a total of 14 distinct receptors. The diversity of serotonin receptors has initiated a significant effort to study the distribution of serotonin receptor subtypes in pathological states and to design subtype-specific drugs that may be of particular therapeutic benefit in specific conditions. For example, buspirone (BuSpar), a clinically effective antianxiety agent, is a potent *serotonin type* 1_A *(5-*HT_{1A}*)* agonist, and other 5-HT_{1A} agonists are being developed for the treatment of anxiety and depression. In contrast, antidepressant efficacy is associated with inhibition of the 5-HT_{2A} receptor. Activation of the central benzodiazepine receptors also reduces anxiety.

There are five subtypes of dopamine receptors, which can be divided into two groups. In the first group, the D_1 and D_5 receptors stimulate the formulation of cyclic adenosine monophosphate (cAMP) by activating the stimulatory G protein, Gs. The second group of dopamine receptors is made up of the D_2, D_3, and D_4 receptors. The *dopamine type 2 (*D_2*)* receptor inhibits the formation of cAMP by activating the inhibitory G protein, G_i, and some data indicate that the D_3 and D_4 receptors act similarly. One of the differences among the D_2, D_3, and D_4 receptors is their differential distribution. The D_2 receptor is prominent in the striatum (caudate nucleus and putamen), the D_3 receptor is especially concentrated in the nucleus accumbens in addition to other regions, and the D_4 receptor is especially concentrated in the frontal cortex in addition to other regions. Activation of the striatal D_2 receptors inhibits the role of the caudate nucleus to regulate the expression of the intended motor acts and leads to tics or other extraneous movements.

The two broad groups of adrenergic and noradrenergic receptors, often just referred to as adrenergic receptors, are the α-adrenergic receptors and the β-adrenergic receptors. There are four types of α_1 receptors (α_{1a}, α_{1b}, α_{1c}, and α_{1d}), three types of α_2 receptors (α_{2a}, α_{2b}, and α_{2c}), one type of α_3 receptor, and three types of β receptors (β_1, β_2, and β_3). Although the field is changing rapidly, all α_1 receptors seem to be linked to the phosphoinositol turnover system; α_2 receptors seem to inhibit the formation of cAMP; and β receptors seem to stimulate the formation of cAMP. The β_1 and β_2 receptors regulate the function of nearly every organ in the body, often in antagonism to the effects of the α-adrenergic receptors. Activation of the *β-adrenergic type 1 (*β_1*)* receptors increases heart rate and may contribute to the palpitations associated with anxiety states.

The two major subtypes of cholinergic receptors are muscarinic and nicotinic. There are five recognized types of muscarinic receptors with various effects on phosphoinositol turnover, cAMP and cyclic guanosine monophosphate (cGMP) production, and potassium ion channel activity. Muscarinic receptors are antagonized by atropine and by the anticholinergic drugs. The *nicotinic acetylcholine* receptors are ligand-gated ion channels, the receptor site of which is directly on the ion channel itself. The nicotinic receptor is actually made up of four subunits (α, β, γ, and δ). Nicotinic receptors can vary in the number of each of these subunits; thus, there is a multitude of subtypes of nicotinic receptors, based on the specific configuration of the subunits. Nicotinic receptor activation stimulates several central nervous system (CNS) regions. Potentiation of nicotinic acetylcholine neurotransmission is an approved therapeutic modality for treatment of dementia of the Alzheimer's type.

There are five major types of glutamate receptors. The *N-methyl-D-aspartate (NMDA) glutamate* receptor is the best understood and most complex of the receptors because it may play an essential role in learning and memory as well as psychopathology. The other four receptor types are therefore referred to as the non–NMDA glutamate receptors. The NMDA receptor allows the passage of sodium, potassium, and calcium. It opens only when it is bound by two molecules of glutamate and a molecule of glycine at the same time as the membrane in which it sits is depolarized to a potential less negative than -65 mV, which allows the magnesium ion that normally blocks the ion pore to fall off. As most cells that respond to glutamate display both NMDA and non–NMDA receptors, the initial depolarization response is mediated by the non–NMDA receptors until the membrane potential rises above -65 mV, at which time the NMDA receptors open. The requirement of simultaneous membrane depolarization and glutamate receptor occupancy for activation of NMDA-mediated calcium flux has piqued interest in the receptor as the essential feature of the cellular mechanism of memory. In this model, a prolonged set of temporally coordinated stimuli is required for NMDA receptor opening, which uniquely triggers a cascade in intracellular events, leading to the expression of a certain set of genes, among other things; this action in turn reinforces and stabilizes the synapses responsible for the initial receptor activation. Thus, a physical change in the synaptic relations results from a specific pattern of receptor stimulation. At this time there are no clinically useful drugs that directly influence NMDA receptor activation.

3.18 The answer is A (*Synopsis VIII,* page 117).
Acetylcholine is rapidly degraded in the synaptic cleft by acetylcholinesterase. Inhibitors of acetylcholinesterase potentiate cholinergic neurotransmission and are used clinically to improve cognitive and memory functions in dementia of the Alzheimer's type.

Each of the other neurotransmitters listed is inactivated either by being taken up into cells by specific transporter molecules or by diffusing away from the synapse. *γ-Aminobutyric acid (GABA)* is taken up by neurons or nonneuronal cells and is degraded by GABA transaminase, which is associated with mitochondria. *Dopamine, serotonin, and norepinephrine* are taken up into presynaptic cells by transporters, where they are degraded by monoamine oxidases (MAOs), which are attached to the outer mitochondrial membrane. MAO_A metabolizes norepinephrine and serotonin, and its inhibition by MAOIs is associated with an elevation in mood. MAO_B metabolizes dopamine. Dopamine and norepinephrine that diffuse into the postsynaptic cell are alternatively degraded by catechol-*O*-methyltransferase (COMT).

3.19 The answer is D (*Synopsis VIII,* pages 113–116).
Each of these neurotransmitters is synthesized in the axonal terminal. *Serotonin* is an indolamine, and its precursor amino acid is tryptophan. The availability of tryptophan is the rate-limiting function, and the enzyme tryptophan hydroxylase is not rate limiting. Therefore, dietary variations in tryptophan can measurably affect serotonin levels in the brain. For example, tryptophan depletion causes irritability and hunger, whereas tryptophan supplementation may induce sleep, relieve anxiety, and increase a sense of well-being.

Dopamine, norepinephrine, and *epinephrine* are endogenous catecholamines that are synthesized from the amino acid tyrosine. The rate-limiting enzymatic step in the synthesis of the catecholamines is tyrosine hydroxylase. Therefore, unlike the case for serotonin, dietary changes in tyrosine levels do not influence the synthesis of catecholamines. Tyrosine hydroxylase is a phosphoprotein—that is, subject to regulation by a range of protein kinases and protein phosphatases. Tyrosine hydroxylase transforms tyrosine into 3,4-*dihydroxyphenylalanine (DOPA).* Because it is past the rate-limiting synthetic step, DOPA may be administrated orally to increase the rate of synthesis of its product, dopamine. DOPA is used for this purpose to treat Parkinson's disease. In neurons that release norepinephrine, the enzyme dopamine β-carboxylase converts dopamine to norepinephrine; neurons that release dopamine lack this enzyme. In neurons that release epinephrine, the enzyme phenylethanolamine-*N*-methyltransferase (PNMT) converts norepinephrine into epinephrine. Neurons that release either dopamine or norepinephrine do not have PNMT.

3.20 The answer is C (*Synopsis VIII,* page 85).
Volatile chemical cues, or odorants, enter the nose, are solubilized in the nasal mucus, and bind to odorant receptors displayed on the surface of the sensory neurons of the *olfactory* epithelium. Odorant binding generates neural impulses, which travel along the axons of the sensory nerves through the cribriform plate to the olfactory bulb. The central projections of fibers from the olfactory bulb do not pass through the thalamus but project directly to the frontal lobe and the limbic system, especially the pyriform cortex. The connections to the limbic system (amygdala, hippocampus, pyriform cortex) are important because olfactory cues stimulate strong emotional responses and may evoke powerful memories.

Auditory stimuli cause the tympanic membrane to vibrate, and these vibrations are transmitted to the ossicles (malleus, incus, and stapes) and thereby to the fluid of the cochlear spiral, called endolymph. Vibration of the endolymph moves cilia on hair cells, which generate neural impulses. Neural impulses from the hair cells travel to the brain in a tonotopic arrangement in the fibers of the cochlear nerve. They enter the brainstem cochlear nuclei, are relayed through the lateral lemniscus to the inferior colliculi, and then travel to the medial geniculate nucleus (MGN) of the thalamus. MGN neurons project to the primary auditory cortex in the posterior temporal lobe. Dichotic listening tests, in which different stimuli are presented to each ear simultaneously, demonstrate that most input from one ear activates the contralateral auditory cortex and that the left hemisphere tends to be dominant for auditory processing.

All *somatosensory* fibers project to and synapse in the thalamus. The thalamic neurons preserve the somatotopic representation by projecting fibers to the somatosensory cortex, located immediately posterior to the sylvian fissure in the parietal lobe (Brodmann areas 1, 2, and 3 [*Synopsis VIII,* Fig. 3.1–4]). Although there is much overlap, several bands of cortex roughly parallel to the sylvian fissure separate the main somatosensory modalities. In each band is the sensory homunculus, the culmination of the careful somatotopic segregation of the sensory fibers at lower levels.

Visual images enter the eye and stimulate the photoreceptor cells. The receptor molecules change conformation in response to light and trigger an intracellular cascade that generates neural impulses. An exact, point-to-point visuotopic projection, from the halves of each retina that respond to the same half of the visual field, travels to the lateral geniculate nucleus (LGN) of the thalamus. The optic tracts project from the LGN to the primary visual cortex at the posterior pole of the occipital lobe. In the visual cortex of each hemisphere, the input from each eye is segregated into ocular dominance columns: radial columns of cortex that are activated by input from only one eye are adjacent to columns that respond only to input from the other eye.

Answers 3.21–3.25

3.21 The answer is D (*Synopsis VIII,* page 84).

3.22 The answers are A and C (*Synopsis VIII,* page 88).

3.23 The answer is A (*Synopsis VIII,* page 92).

3.24 The answer is B (*Synopsis VIII,* page 93).

3.25 The answer is B (*Synopsis VIII,* page 92).

Alexia is loss of the ability to read. Reading comprehension and reading aloud can be independently impaired. Reading involves the primary and secondary visual cortices, located in the occipital lobe. Alexia should be distinguished from dyslexia, which is a developmental problem in reading. *Alexia* is due to an *occipital lobe* lesion.

Ideomotor apraxia is loss of the ability to perform simple tasks (for example, hitting a nail with a hammer) on request by an examiner. However, a patient may be able to perform the identical task in its usual context (for example, hanging a picture on a wall). *Ideomotor apraxia* can be produced by lesions in the supplementary motor area of the *frontal lobe* dominant inferior *parietal lobe,* or the corpus callosum. The supplementary motor area contains neurons that drive complex motor acts by stimulating a specific set of neurons in the primary motor cortex. Lesions of the neurons of the supplementary motor area may interfere with the performance of simple tasks. The association cortices for auditory input are contained in the parietal lobes, and in ideomotor apraxia these receptive language areas are disconnected from the motor execution areas. Disconnection of command and execution areas across hemispheres may also result from lesions of the corpus callosum.

Broca's aphasia is due to a lesion in the *frontal lobe.* Aphasia is an acquired disorder of language (comprehension, word choice, expression, syntax) that is not due to dysarthria (a dysfunction of the muscles necessary for speech production). Broca's aphasia is produced by a lesion in Broca's area (Brodmann's area 44 in the frontal lobe), which is involved in the motor production of speech. Broca's aphasia is also called anterior aphasia, motor aphasia, and expressive aphasia. Comprehension is unimpaired, but patients' speech is telegraphic and agrammatical.

Klüver-Bucy syndrome is produced by a bilateral *temporal lobe* lesion that affects the part of the limbic system located in the temporal lobes. The limbic system was originally proposed as an anatomical substrate for the emotions. Subsequently, it has become clear that memory is a major function of the limbic system. The symptoms of Klüver-Bucy syndrome include placidity, apathy, hypersexuality, and visual and auditory agnosia. Amnesia, aphasia, dementia, and seizures may also occur in people with the syndrome.

Wernicke's aphasia is due to a lesion in the *temporal lobe.* Wernicke's area (Brodmann's area 22 in the superior temporal gyrus) is involved in the comprehension of speech. Wernicke's aphasia is also called posterior aphasia, fluent aphasia, and receptive aphasia. Patients with Wernicke's aphasia have a characteristically fluent but incoherent speech because they are unable to comprehend their own language or that of others. There may be paraphasic errors and neologisms in which words contain novel and erroneous combinations of vowels and consonants.

Answers 3.26–3.28

3.26 The answer is B (*Synopsis VIII,* page 84).

3.27 The answer is C (*Synopsis VIII,* page 84).

3.28 The answer is A (*Synopsis VIII,* page 84).
The occipital lobe is the primary sensory cortex for visual input, and lesions of the lobe result in various visual symptoms. *Anton's syndrome* is associated with bilateral occlusion of the posterior cerebral arteries, resulting in *cortical blindness and the denial of blindness.* The most common causes are hypoxic injury, stroke, metabolic encephalopathy, migraine, herniation caused by lesions, trauma, and leukodystrophy. *Balint's syndrome* is caused by bilateral occipital lesions and is characterized by *optic ataxia* (abnormal visual guidance of limb movements), *loss of panoramic vision, and supranuclear gaze paralysis.*

Gerstmann syndrome has been attributed to lesions of the dominant parietal lobe. The syndrome includes *agraphia,* calculation difficulties *(acalculia), right-left disorientation, and finger agnosia.*

Answers 3.29–3.33

3.29 The answer is E (*Synopsis VIII,* page 115).

3.30 The answer is D (*Synopsis VIII,* page 113).

3.31 The answer is A (*Synopsis VIII,* pages 116–117).

3.32 The answer is B (*Synopsis VIII,* page 111).

3.33 The answer is C (*Synopsis VIII,* pages 110–111).
The major site of serotonergic cell bodies is in the upper pons and the midbrain—specifically, the *median and dorsal raphe nuclei*—but also the caudal locus ceruleus, the area postrema, and the interpeduncular area. These neurons project to the basal ganglia, the limbic system, and the cerebral cortex.

The major concentration of noradrenergic (and adrenergic) cell bodies that project upward in the brain is in the compact *locus ceruleus* in the pons. The axons of these neurons project through the medial forebrain bundle to the cerebral cortex, the limbic system, the thalamus, and the hypothalamus.

A group of cholinergic neurons in the *nucleus basalis of Meynert* project to the cortex and the limbic system. Additional cholinergic neurons in the reticular system project to the cerebral cortex, the limbic system, the hypothalamus, and the thalamus. Some patients with dementia of the Alzheimer's type or Down's syndrome appear to have degeneration of the neurons in the nucleus basalis of Meynert.

The three most important dopaminergic tracts for psychiatry are the nigrostriatal tract, the mesolimbic-mesocortical tract, and the tuberoinfundibular tract. The nigrostriatal tract projects from its cell bodies in the *substantia nigra* to the corpus striatum. When the dopamine (D_2) receptors at the end of this tract are blocked by classic antipsychotic drugs, parkinsonian side effects emerge. In Parkinson's disease the nigrostriatal tract degenerates and results in the motor symptoms of the disease. Because of the significant association between Parkinson's disease and depression, the nigrostriatal tract may somehow be involved with the control of mood, in addition to its classic role in motor control.

The mesolimbic-mesocortical tract projects from its cell bodies in the ventral tegmental area (VTA), which lies adjacent to the substantia nigra, to most areas of the cerebral cortex and the limbic system. Because it projects to the limbic system and the neocortex, the tract may be involved in mediating the antipsychotic effects of antipsychotic drugs.

The cell bodies of the tuberoinfundibular tract are in the arcuate nucleus and the periventricular area of the hypothalamus and project to the infundibulum and the anterior pituitary. Dopamine acts as a release-inhibiting factor in the tract by inhibiting the release of prolactin from the anterior pituitary. Patients who take typical antipsychotic drugs often have roughly threefold elevated prolactin levels because the blockade of dopamine receptors in the tract eliminates the inhibitory effect of dopamine.

The receptor for the inhibitory amino acid neurotransmitter glycine is a chloride ion channel similar in general structure and function to the GABA receptors. It is present in highest quantities in the *spinal cord.* Mutations in the glycine receptor cause a rare neurological condition called hyperekplexia, which is characterized by an exaggerated, that is, poorly inhibited, startle response.

Answers 3.34–3.37

3.34 The answer is A *(Synopsis VIII,* page 124).

3.35 The answer is A *(Synopsis VIII,* page 124).

3.36 The answer is C *(Synopsis VIII,* pages 124–126).

3.37 The answer is B (*Synopsis VIII,* pages 124–126).
Computed tomography (CT) is based on the same physical principles as a skull X-ray—that is, the measurement of the attenuation of *X-ray photons* that have been passed through the brain. The *attenuation differs according to the density of the structure.* X-ray photons are attenuated less by low-density tissues such as cerebrospinal fluid (CSF) than by high-density tissues such as bone. The image of low-density tissues appears black, and the image of high-density tissues appears white. The major differences between CT and a skull X-ray are CT's application of X-ray photon detectors and computers in lieu of X-ray film. The CT image can be enhanced by the use of iodinated contrast materials that are injected into the blood circulation and that cause a high attenuation of the X-ray photons and thus appear white in the image. The use of contrast materials can help radiologists detect certain tumors, infections, and cerebrovascular diseases.

Magnetic resonance imaging (MRI) produces brain images that look much like CT scans but that have an increased in-focus appearance and are *better able to discriminate gray matter and white matter.* The ability to discriminate gray matter and white matter and other subtle differences in the brain tissue makes MRI good for such lesions as those in multiple sclerosis. Multiple sclerosis is characterized by diffuse multifocal lesions in the white matter of the CNS and by a course with typical exacerbations and remissions. MRI is performed by placing a patient in a long, tubelike structure that contains powerful magnets. MRI *detects attenuation by measuring proton density.* Once the patient is in the magnetic field, all the patient's hydrogen-containing molecules (especially water) line up in parallel and antiparallel arrays and move in a symmetrical fashion around their axes in a movement called precession. This orderly arrangement and movement are interrupted by radiofrequency pulses from the MRI device. The radiofrequency pulses cause the molecules to flip 90 or 180 degrees from their axes; the magnetic field results in the release of electromagnetic energy that is detected by the MRI equipment. These data, which are essentially measurements of hydrogen nuclei densities, are then relayed into the computer, which processes the information into images of the brain.

4

Contributions of the Psychosocial Sciences to Human Behavior

The understanding of human behavior has been enriched by research in many fields of study: psychology, biology, anthropology, ethology, sociology, and epidemiology among them. In the area of psychosocial sciences, both theories and researchers have been responsible for outstanding contributions.

Developed by psychologists, learning theory is an important basis for behavior therapy in both its operant and clinical conditioning aspects. Those who work with aggressive patients have benefited from research into the biological, social, and psychological factors in aggressive behavior. Anthropological studies have shown that although some issues in human behavior and development are unique to a single culture, other issues are common in many cultures and some are universal. Social science methods have helped to develop studies of health care socioeconomics and have led to plans for possible revamping of health care systems.

Among psychosocial science theorists, Jean Piaget (1896–1980) and John Bowlby (1907–1990) have been major contributors to ideas of human development. Piaget studied infants' cognitive development and established a theoretical framework that has influenced many psychologists. Although Piaget's work has sometimes been criticized, he drew researchers' attention to the importance of examining infants' evolving cognitive capacities. Bowlby's theories of attachment and human relationships have been significant paradigms for discussing children's development, both normal and abnormal. Ethologists such as Harry Harlow have also enriched the study of human behavior by demonstrating that animal behavior can illuminate human developmental factors.

This chapter also covers public psychiatry and preventive psychiatry, aspects of the field that deal with organized programs for the promotion of mental health and the treatment of mental illness.

With regard to the socioeconomics of health care in all medicine, the student needs to be aware of the availability of health care delivery systems and of the major health problems that are the focus of both government and commercial insurance programs. The effect of managed care and the emergence of for-profit Health Maintenance Organizations (HMOs) have had a major impact on the field of medicine. Because of arbitrary decisions made by HMOs, such as "drive-through deliveries" and "one-day mastectomies," the federal government has increased its oversight of HMOs, and many laws are being enacted to insure that doctors maintain control of the medical decision-making process.

The student should study Chapter 4 in *Kaplan and Sadock's Synopsis VIII.* The questions and answers in this chapter will help students test their knowledge of the subject.

HELPFUL HINTS

The student should know the following terms, theoreticians, and concepts.

- abstract thinking
- accommodation
- acculturation
- adaptation
- aggression
- Mary Ainsworth
- anaclitic depression
- anxiety hierarchy
- *Aplysia*
- assimilation
- attachment
- attachment phases
- aversive stimuli
- basic study design
- behavior disorders
- Ruth Benedict
- bias
- biostatistics
- bonding
- John Bowlby
- catharsis
- chronic stress
- CMHC
- cognitive dissonance
- cognitive strategies
- cognitive triad
- concrete operations
- contact comfort
- cross-cultural studies and syndromes: amok, latah, windigo, piblokto, curandero, esperitismo, voodoo
- culture-bound syndromes
- deductive reasoning
- deinstitutionalization
- deviation, significance
- DIS
- double-blind method
- drift hypothesis
- egocentric
- epidemiology
- epigenesis
- escape and avoidance conditioning
- ethology
- experimental neurosis
- extinction
- family types, studies
- Faris and Dunham
- fixed and variable ratios
- formal operations
- frequency
- frustration-aggression hypothesis
- genetic epistemology

- ▶ Harry Harlow
- ▶ health care providers
- ▶ Hollingshead and Redlich
- ▶ Holmes and Rahe
- ▶ hospitalism
- ▶ hospitals: beds, admissions, length of stay
- ▶ Clark L. Hull
- ▶ illness behavior
- ▶ imprinting
- ▶ incidence
- ▶ indirect surveys
- ▶ inductive reasoning
- ▶ information processing
- ▶ inhibition
- ▶ insurance
- ▶ Eric Kandel
- ▶ learned helplessness
- ▶ learning theory
- ▶ Alexander Leighton
- ▶ H. S. Liddell
- ▶ lifetime expectancy
- ▶ Konrad Lorenz
- ▶ Margaret Mead
- ▶ Midtown Manhattan study
- ▶ monotropic
- ▶ Monroe County study
- ▶ mortality trends
- ▶ motivation
- ▶ national character
- ▶ New Haven study
- ▶ NIMH ECA
- ▶ normative
- ▶ object permanence
- ▶ operant behavior
- ▶ operant and classical conditioning
- ▶ organization
- ▶ Ivan Petrovich Pavlov
- ▶ phenomenalistic causality
- ▶ Jean Piaget
- ▶ positive and negative reinforcement
- ▶ preattachment stage
- ▶ Premack's principle
- ▶ preoperational stage
- ▶ prevalence
- ▶ primary and secondary reward conditioning
- ▶ primary, secondary, and tertiary prevention
- ▶ protest-despair-detachment
- ▶ punishment
- ▶ randomization
- ▶ reciprocal determinism
- ▶ reciprocal inhibition
- ▶ reliability
- ▶ resource holding potential
- ▶ respondent behavior
- ▶ risk factors
- ▶ roles of women
- ▶ scheme
- ▶ segregation hypothesis
- ▶ Hans Selye
- ▶ sensorimotor stage
- ▶ sensory deprivation
- ▶ separation anxiety
- ▶ set
- ▶ B. F. Skinner
- ▶ social causation and selection theory
- ▶ social class and mental disorders
- ▶ social isolation and separation
- ▶ social learning
- ▶ sociobiology
- ▶ René Spitz
- ▶ Stirling County study
- ▶ strange situation
- ▶ stranger anxiety
- ▶ surrogate mother
- ▶ syllogistic reasoning
- ▶ symbolization
- ▶ systematic desensitization
- ▶ tension-reduction theory
- ▶ therapeutic community
- ▶ therapist monkeys
- ▶ Nikolaas Tinbergen
- ▶ type I and type II errors
- ▶ use of controls
- ▶ validity
- ▶ variation, average
- ▶ vulnerability theory
- ▶ John B. Watson
- ▶ Joseph Wolpe

▲ QUESTIONS

DIRECTIONS: Each of the questions or incomplete statements below is followed by five suggested responses or completions. Select the *one* that is *best* in each case.

4.1 Jean Piaget's theory of cognitive development states

A. Children are egocentric during the stage of concrete operations.
B. Imminent justice is the belief that punishment for bad deeds is inevitable.
C. Object permanence is developed during the stage of preoperational thought.
D. Symbolization is the endowing of physical events and objects with lifelike psychological attributes.
E. The most important sign that children have proceeded from the stage of preoperational thought to the stage of formal operations is the achievement of conservation and reversibility.

4.2 The attachment theory states

A. Infants are generally polytropic in their attachments.
B. Attachment occurs instantaneously between the mother and the child.
C. Attachment is synonymous with bonding.
D. Attachment disorders may lead to a failure to thrive.
E. Separation anxiety is most common when an infant is 5 months old.

4.3 In operant conditioning

A. continuous reinforcement is the reinforcement schedule least susceptible to extinction
B. negative reinforcement is a type of punishment
C. the process is related to trial-and-error learning
D. shaping occurs when responses are coincidentally paired to a reinforcer
E. respondent behavior is independent of a stimulus

4.4 Cross-cultural studies

A. are free from experimental bias
B. show that depression is not a universally expressed symptom
C. show that incest is not a universal taboo
D. show that schizophrenic persons are universally stigmatized as social outcasts
E. show that the nuclear family of mother, father, and children is a universal unit

4.5 All of the following statements correctly describe aspects of attachment theory *except*

A. The theory is applicable to behavior in all stages of life.
B. John Bowlby proposed a darwinian evolutionary basis for the theory.
C. Harry Harlow's experiments with monkeys were relevant to the theory.
D. Bonding refers to an infant's relying on the mother as a source of security.
E. Signal indicators are infants' signs of distress that trigger a mother's behavioral response.

4.6 Which of the following terms does *not* refer to operant conditioning?

A. Programming
B. Escape learning
C. Aversive control
D. Avoidance learning
E. Cognitive dissonance

4.7 Which of the following features is *not* characteristic of aggressive behavior?

A. It usually occurs among family members.
B. It can generally be predicted on the basis of previous behavior.
C. It may occur as a result of a head injury in a child with abusive parents.
D. It is sometimes thought to have social, environmental, or situational determinants.
E. Its probability increases as a person becomes more psychologically decompensated.

4.8 Certain universals relevant to psychiatry can be documented cross-culturally. These cultural universals include all of the following *except*

A. bulimia
B. anxiety
C. an incest taboo
D. smiling as a greeting
E. gender differences in social roles

4.9 According to Piaget, an important process that develops during the stage of concrete operations is the

A. ability to reason about reasoning or thinking
B. ability to make and follow rules
C. ability to distinguish between the ideal self and the real self
D. use of phenomenological causality as a mode of thinking
E. attainment of object permanence

4.10 John Bowlby's stages of bereavement include

A. protest
B. yearning
C. despair
D. reorganization
E. all the above

4.11 The final stage in Piaget's theory of cognitive development is

A. formal operations
B. sensorimotor
C. preoperational thought
D. concrete operations
E. epigenesis

4.12 The development of object permanence is associated with the

A. latency stage
B. sensorimotor stage
C. preattachment stage
D. stage of concrete operations
E. stage of formal operations

4.13 Children in Piaget's stage of preoperational thought characteristically display

A. intuitive thinking
B. egocentric thinking
C. magical thinking
D. animistic thinking
E. all the above

4.14 Attachment to a mothering figure is

A. a reciprocal affectionate relationship
B. developed during the first year of life
C. dependent on the intensity, the quality, and the amount of the time spent together
D. an instinctive behavior pattern
E. all the above

4.15 Predictive validity is

A. the extent to which knowledge that a person has a particular mental disorder is useful in predicting the future course of the illness
B. related to management and treatment
C. relevant to the specificity with which patients with bipolar I disorder improve when treated with lithium
D. the basis on which Emil Kraepelin differentiated manic-depressive psychosis from dementia precox
E. all the above

4.16 The increased frequency of aggressive behavior in abnormal children has been correlated with all of the following *except*

A. brain injury
B. faulty identification models
C. cultural environment
D. violence in movies
E. curiosity

4.17 Which of the following statements best describes the long-term effects of 6 months of total social isolation in monkeys?

A. They rarely exhibit aggression against age-mates who are more physically adept than they are.
B. They are able to make a remarkable social adjustment through the development of play.
C. They are totally unresponsive to the new physical and social world with which they are presented.
D. They are both abnormally aggressive and abnormally fearful.
E. They assume postures that are bizarre and schizoid.

4.18 Figure 4.1 depicts an experiment that interferes with normal social interactions among monkeys. *A* and *B* represent the two sequential stages that occur when the infant is separated from its mother. The stages are protest (*A*) and

A. yearning
B. resolution
C. despair
D. acceptance
E. none of the above

4.19 In a study of induced anaclitic depression in monkeys, Harry Harlow found

A. At initial separation, the rhesus infants exhibited a protest stage.
B. The protest stage changed to despair.
C. Play was almost abolished during a 3-week period of maternal separation, but resumed rapidly after maternal reunion.
D. Monkeys tested showed a nearly complete picture of anaclitic depression.
E. All the above statements are true.

4.20 To provide information regarding a planned modification of circumstances designed to lower the incidence of disease in a given population, experimenters most often use

A. preventive trials
B. community prevention
C. primary prevention
D. secondary prevention
E. tertiary prevention

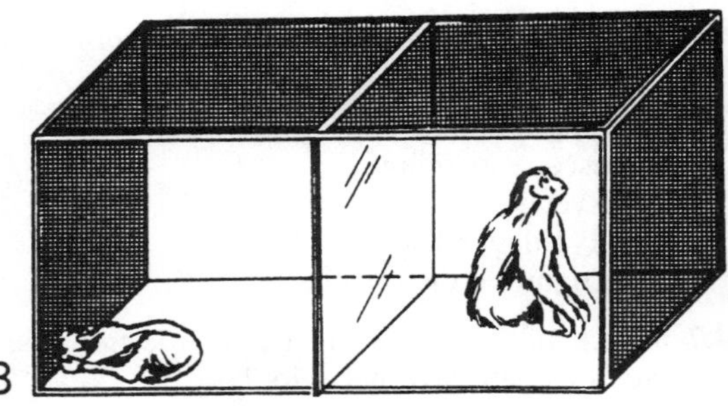

FIGURE 4.1
Two stages that occur when the infant is separated from its mother.

4.21 Prevalence is the

A. proportion of a population that has a condition at one moment in time
B. ratio of persons who acquire a disorder during a year's time
C. risk of acquiring a condition at some time
D. standard deviation
E. rate of first admissions to a hospital for a disorder

4.22 In the Stirling County study by Alexander Leighton, all of the following were found *except*

A. Only about 20 percent of the population were free of psychiatric symptoms.
B. Men showed more mental disorders than did women.
C. Psychophysiological symptoms were found in more than 50 percent of the population.
D. Mental disorders increased with age.
E. Mental health was related to economic status.

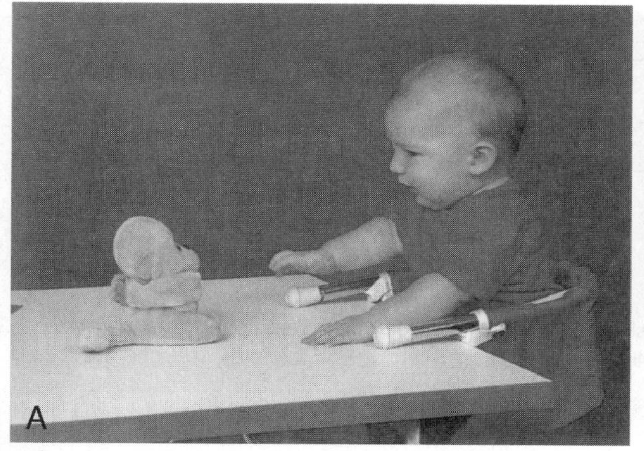

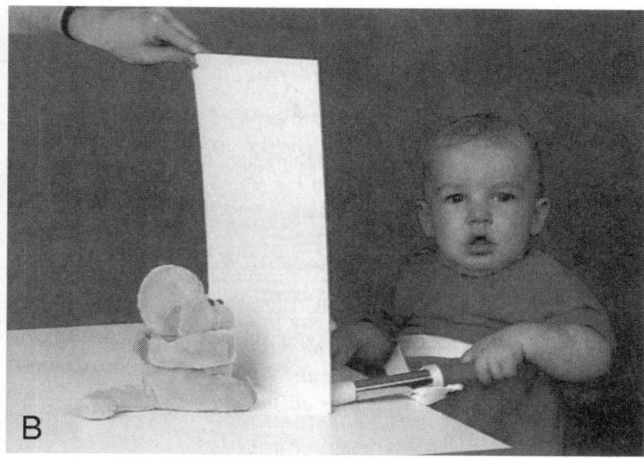

FIGURE 4.2
Reprinted with permission from Dworetzky JP: *Psychology,* ed 3, p 359. West Publishing Company, St. Paul, MN, 1988.

4.23 Which of the following statements applies ways in which hospitals are organized in the United States?

A. The state mental hospital system has about 100,000 beds.
B. Investor-owned hospitals are increasing in importance nationally.
C. Department of Veterans Affairs (VA) hospitals are usually affiliated with medical schools.
D. In special hospitals, 70 percent of the facility must be designated for the treatment of a single condition.
E. All the above statements are true.

4.24 In the infant portrayed in Figure 4.2, when the toy disappears from the infant's view, the infant acts as though the toy is no longer present. The infant's behavior illustrates which of the following concepts?

A. Symbolization
B. Reversibility
C. Object permanence
D. Conservation
E. Egocentrism

4.25 This infant's stage of development portrayed in Figure 4.2 is characterized by

A. animistic thinking
B. semiotic function
C. phenomenalistic causality
D. egocentric thought
E. none of the above

4.26 A child who answers correctly that Figure 4.3*B* contains the same quantity of fluid as Figure 4.3*A*

A. is most likely to be in the stage of preoperational thought
B. is demonstrating achievement of reversibility
C. is demonstrating achievement of objective permanence
D. is most likely 4 to 5 years of age
E. is demonstrating achievement of conservation

FIGURE 4.3
Reprinted with permission from Lefrancois GR: *Of Children: An Introduction to Child Development,* p 305. Wadsworth, Belmont, CA, 1973.

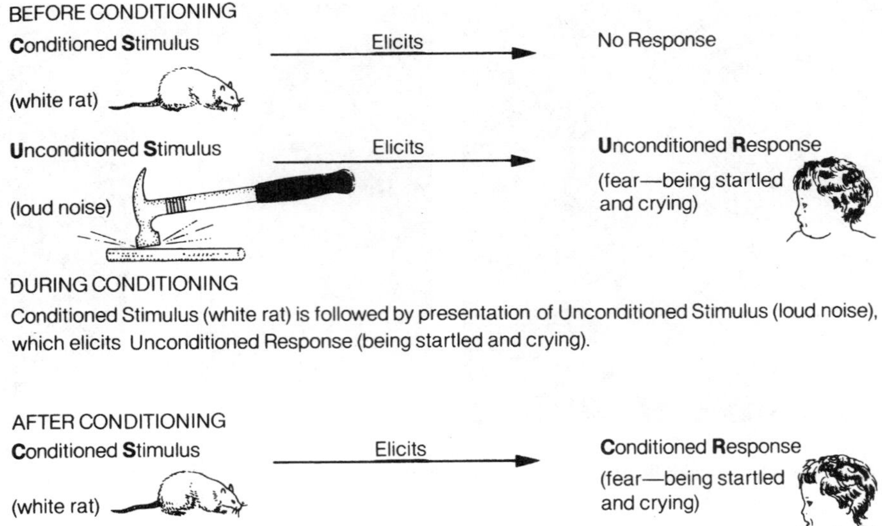

FIGURE 4.4
Reprinted with permission from Dworetzky JP: *Psychology,* ed 3, p 195. West Publishing Company, St. Paul, MN, 1988.

4.27 The child in this paradigm of classical conditioning shown in Figure 4.4 is conditioned to respond fearfully to a rat and subsequently responds fearfully to similar furry objects (a rabbit or a dog) but not to other dissimilar objects. This behavior is an example of

A. sensitization
B. stimulus generalization
C. discrimination
D. extinction
E. reinforcement

4.28 With regard to Figure 4.5, which of the following statements is *true?*

A. A teenager mowing the lawn to avoid parental complaints is an example of negative reinforcement.
B. A patient with anorexia nervosa eating and gaining weight to be discharged from the hospital is an example of positive reinforcement.
C. An animal jumping off a grid to escape a painful shock is an example of punishment.
D. The figure illustrates the principles of classical conditioning.
E. All of the above are true.

DIRECTIONS: Each set of lettered headings below is followed by a list of numbered phrases. For each numbered phrase, select

A. if the item is associated with *A only*
B. if the item is associated with *B only*
C. if the item is associated with *both A and B*
D. if the item is associated with *neither A nor B*

Questions 4.29–4.32

A. Health maintenance organization (HMO)
B. Preferred provider organization (PPO)
C. Both
D. Neither

4.29 Requires of members a prepayment or capitation fee to cover health care services
4.30 Uses a prospective payment system
4.31 Is equivalent to a health systems agency
4.32 Arranges health services at lower than usual rates for its members

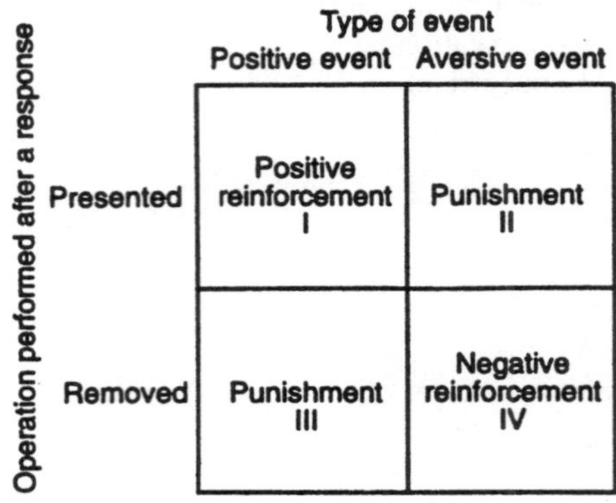

FIGURE 4.5
Reprinted with permission from Kazdin AE: *Behavior Modification in Applied Settings,* ed 2. Dorsey Press, Homewood, IL, 1983.

Questions 4.33–4.37

A. Lower class
B. Upper middle class
C. Both
D. Neither

4.33 More able to delay gratification
4.34 Seek health care earlier
4.35 See pregnancy as a time of crisis
4.36 Longer hospital stays
4.37 Low contraceptive use

DIRECTIONS: Each set of lettered headings below is followed by a list of numbered words or phrases. For each numbered word or phrase, select the *one* lettered heading that is most closely associated with it. Each lettered heading may be selected once, more than once, or not at all.

Questions 4.38–4.41

A. Ivan Petrovich Pavlov
B. Eric Kandel
C. Konrad Lorenz
D. Harry Harlow

4.38 Imprinting
4.39 Surrogate mother
4.40 Experimental neurosis
4.41 *Aplysia*

Questions 4.42–4.46

A. Magical thinking
B. Thinking about thoughts
C. Object permanence
D. Symbolic thought
E. Cause and effect

4.42 9 to 12 months
4.43 18 to 24 months
4.44 2 to 7 years
4.45 7 to 11 years
4.46 11 years through adolescence

DIRECTIONS: Match the items in Figure 4.6 with the correct lettered heading below.

Questions 4.47–4.51

A. Conservation of substance
B. Conservation of length
C. Conservation of numbers
D. Conservation of space
E. Conservation of liquid

4.47 Item I
4.48 Item II
4.49 Item III
4.50 Item IV
4.51 Item V

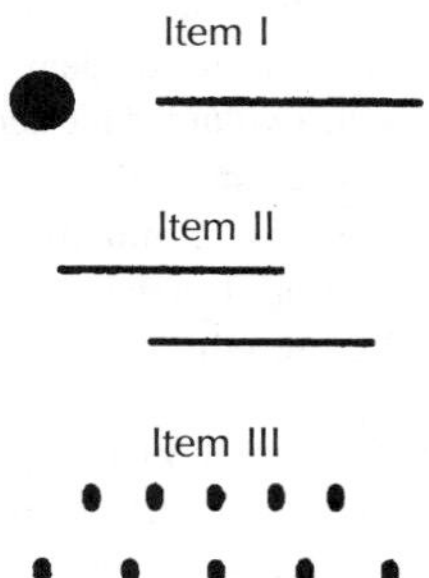

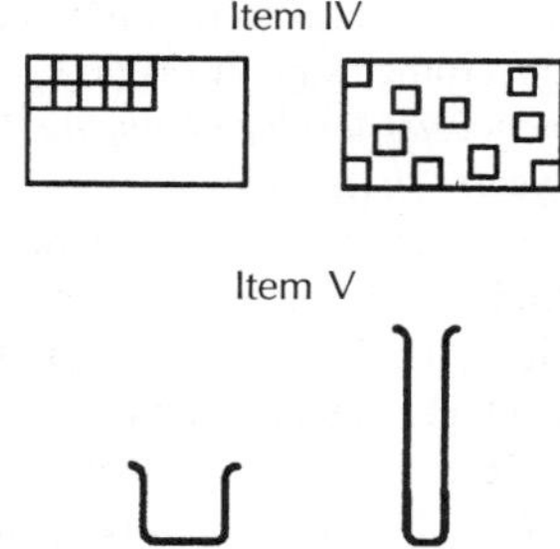

FIGURE 4.6
Tests for Piaget's theory of conservation. Reprinted with permission from Lefrancois GR: *Of Children: An Introduction to Child Development,* p 305. Wadsworth, Belmont, CA, 1973.

ANSWERS

Contributions of the Psychosocial Sciences to Human Behavior

4.1 The answer is B (*Synopsis VIII,* page 140).

Jean Piaget described four major stages leading to the capacity for adult thought. Each stage is a prerequisite for the one that follows. However, the rate at which children move through the stages varies with each child's native endowment and environmental circumstances. The four stages are (1) the sensorimotor stage, (2) the stage of preoperational thought, (3) the stage of concrete operations, and (4) the stage of formal operations.

Children in the preoperational stage of thought (2 to 7 years of age) have a sense of *imminent justice, the belief that punishment for bad deeds is inevitable.* However, children in the preoperational stage are unable to deal with moral dilemmas, even though they have a sense of what is good and what is bad. For example, when asked, "Who is more guilty: the person who breaks one dish on purpose or the person who breaks 10 dishes by accident?" the young child usually answers that the person who breaks 10 dishes by accident is more guilty because more dishes are broken.

Children are egocentric during the stage of preoperational thought, *not the stage of concrete operations.* They see themselves as the center of the universe, they have a limited point of view, and they are unable to take the role of another person. The children are unable to modify their behavior for someone else. For example, children are not being negativistic when they do not listen to commands to be quiet because their brother has to study. Their egocentric thinking prevents an understanding of their brother's point of view.

Object permanence is developed during the sensorimotor stage (birth to 2 years), *not during the preoperational stage.* Object permanence is the critical achievement in the sensorimotor stage. It tends to develop between 18 months and 2 years of age, and it marks the transition from the sensorimotor stage to the stage of preoperational thought. Through object permanence the child can understand that objects have an existence independent of the child's involvement with them. Infants learn to differentiate themselves from the world and are able to maintain a mental image of an object, even though it is not present and visible. If an object is dropped in front of infants, they learn to look down to the ground to search for the object; that is, they behave as though the object has a reality outside themselves.

Object permanence is achieved through the process of symbolization. At about 18 months, infants begin to develop mental symbols and to use words. Symbolization is the ability of an infant to create a visual image of a ball or a mental symbol of the word "ball" to stand for the real object. Such mental representations allow children to operate on new conceptual levels. Thus, *symbolization is not the endowing of physical events and objects with lifelike psychological attributes.* Such animistic thinking is seen in children already in the stage of preoperational thought.

During the stage of concrete operations (7 to 11 years), the child operates and acts on the concrete, real, and perceivable world of objects and events. Egocentric thought is replaced by operational thought, which involves attending to and dealing with a wide array of information outside the child. A child in the stage of concrete operations can see things from someone else's perspective.

The most important sign that children have proceeded from the stage of preoperational thought to the stage of concrete operations, not formal operations, is the achievement of conservation and reversibility. Conservation is the ability to recognize that, even though the shape and the form of objects change, the objects maintain other characteristics that enable them to be recognized as the same. For example, if a ball of clay is rolled into a long and thin sausage shape, the child in the stage of concrete operations recognizes that the same amount of clay is in the two forms. In the stage of preoperational thought, the child declares that more clay is in the sausage-shaped form because it is longer. Reversibility is the capacity to understand the relation between things, to understand that one thing can turn into another and back again—for example, ice and water.

The most important sign that children are in the stage of formal operations (11 years through the end of adolescence) is that they have the ability to think abstractly, to reason deductively, and to define concepts. The stage of formal operations is so named because the person's thinking operates in a formal, logical, systematic, and symbolic manner. The stage is also characterized by skills in dealing with permutations and combinations; the young person can grasp the concept of probabilities. The adolescent attempts to deal with all possible relations and hypotheses to explain data and events. During the stage of formal operations, language use is complex, follows formal rules of logic, and is grammatically correct. Abstract thinking is shown by the adolescent's interest in a variety of issues: philosophy, religion, ethics, and politics.

4.2 The answer is D (*Synopsis VIII,* pages 144–147).

Attachment disorders are characterized by biopsychosocial pathology that results from maternal deprivation, a lack of care by and interaction with the infant's mother or caretaker. Psychosocial dwarfism, separation anxiety disorder, avoidant personality disorder, depressive disorders, delinquency, learning disorders, borderline intelligence, and *failure to thrive* have been traced to negative attachment experiences. Failure to thrive results in the infant's being unable to maintain viability outside a hospital setting. When maternal care is deficient because the mother is mentally ill, because the child is institutionalized for a long time, or because the primary object of attachment dies, the child suffers emotional damage.

John Bowlby formulated a theory that normal attachment is crucial to healthy development. According to Bowlby, attachment occurs when the infant has a warm, intimate, and continuous relationship with its mother and both mother and infant find satisfaction and enjoyment. *Infants are generally monotropic, not polytropic, in their attachments,* but multiple attachments may also occur; attachment may be directed toward the father or a surrogate. *Attachment does not occur spontaneously between the mother and the child;* it is a gradually developing phenomenon. Attachment results in one person's wanting to be with a preferred person, who is perceived as stronger, wiser, and able to reduce anxiety or distress. Attachment produces a feeling of security in the infant. It is a process that is facilitated by interaction between the mother and the infant. The amount of time together is less important than the amount of activity between the two.

Attachment is not synonymous with bonding; they are different phenomena. Bonding concerns the mother's feelings for her infant and differs from attachment because a mother does not normally rely on her infant as a source of security, a requirement of attachment behavior. A great deal of research on the bonding of a mother to her infant reveals that it occurs when they have skin-to-skin contact or other types of contact, such as voice and eye contact.

Separation from the attachment person may or may not produce intense anxiety, depending on the child's developmental level and the current phase of attachment. Separation anxiety is an anxiety response, expressed as tearfulness or irritability, in a child who is isolated or separated from its mother or caretaker. *Separation anxiety is most common when an infant is 10 to 18 months of age (not 5 months),* and it disappears generally by the end of the third year.

4.3 The answer is C (*Synopsis VIII,* pages 149–150).
B. F. Skinner (1904–1990) proposed a theory of learning and behavior known as operant or instrumental conditioning. In operant conditioning the subject is active and behaves in a way that produces a reward—that is, learning occurs as a consequence of action.

The process is related to trial-and-error learning, as described by the American psychologist Edward L. Thorndike (1874–1949). In trial-and-error learning, one attempts to solve a problem by trying out a variety of actions until one action proves successful; a freely moving organism behaves in a way that is instrumental in producing a reward. For example, a cat in a Thorndike puzzle box must learn to lift a latch to escape from the box. Operant conditioning is sometimes called instrumental conditioning for that reason. Thorndike's law of effect states that certain responses are reinforced by reward, and the organism learns from those experiences.

In operant conditioning, the experimenter can vary the schedule of reward or reinforcement given to a behavioral pattern—a process known as programming. The intervals between reinforcements may be fixed (for example, every third response is rewarded) or variable (for example, sometimes the third response is rewarded; at other times, the sixth response is rewarded). A continuous reinforcement (also known as contingency reinforcement or management) schedule, in which every response is reinforced, leads to the most rapid acquisition of a behavior. However, *continuous reinforcement is the reinforcement schedule most susceptible to extinction.* Extinction occurs when a desired response no longer occurs.

Negative reinforcement is not punishment. Punishment is an aversive stimulus (for example, a slap) that is presented specifically to weaken or suppress an undesired response. Punishment reduces the probability that a response will recur. In learning theory, the punishment delivered is always contingent on performance, and its use reduces the frequency of the behavior being punished. Negative reinforcement is the process by which a response that leads to the removal of an aversive event increases that response. For example, a teenager mows the lawn to avoid parental complaints, and an animal jumps off a grid to escape a painful shock. Any behavior that enables one to avoid or escape a punishing consequence is strengthened.

Shaping involves changing behavior in a deliberate and predetermined way. By reinforcing those responses that are in the desired direction, the experimenter shapes the subject's behavior. If the experimenter wants to train a seal to ring a bell with its nose, the experimenter can give a food reinforcement as the animal's random behavior brings its nose near the bell. *Shaping does not occur when responses are coincidentally paired to a reinforcer.* When that occurs, it is called adventitious reinforcement. Adventitious reinforcement may have clinical implications on the development of phobias and other behaviors.

In formulating his theory of operant conditioning, Skinner described two types of behavior: (1) respondent behavior, which results from known stimuli (for example, the knee jerk reflex to patellar stimulation) and (2) operant behavior, which is independent of a stimulus (for example, the random movements of an infant or the aimless movements of a laboratory rat in a cage). Thus, *operant behavior, not respondent behavior, is independent of a stimulus.*

4.4 The answer is E (*Synopsis VIII,* pages 169–170).
Cross-cultural studies examine and compare various cultures along a number of parameters: attitudes, beliefs, expectations, memories, opinions, roles, stereotypes, prejudices, and values. Usually, the cultures studied use differing languages and have differing political organizations.

The nuclear family of mother, father, and children is a universal unit in all cultures. The extended family—in which grandparents, parents, children, and other relatives all live under the same roof—is no longer common in the United States, but it is still prevalent in less industrialized cultures. In the United States, more than 85 percent of the men and women between the ages 35 and 45 are husbands or wives in a nuclear family.

Cross-cultural studies *are not free from experimental bias;* in fact, they are subject to extreme bias because of problems in translation and other areas of information gathering. Questions have to be asked in ways that are clearly understood by the group under study. One of the best known cross-cultural studies, *Psychiatric Disorder among the Yoruba* by Alexander Leighton, was his attempt to replicate in Nigeria the Stirling County study he had conducted in Canada. The study was criticized because not only did it fail to distinguish psychophysiological symptoms from those associated with infections, parasites, and nutritional diseases, but also it assumed that the indicators of sociocultural disintegration in Stirling County could be used among the Yoruba. All cultures are relative; that is, each must be examined within the context of its own language, customs, and beliefs.

Nevertheless, some generalizations can be made about cross-cultural or comparative psychiatry. Certain symptoms exist in all societies; anxiety, mania, thought disorder, suicidal ideation, somatization, paranoia (persecutory delusions), and *depression are universally expressed symptoms.* Although various labels may be applied in various cultures, recognition of deviant behavior and agreement that conditions are treatable (whether by the psychiatrist in one culture or the shaman in another) are universal.

Some universals are observed in various cultures: (1) Smiling is a social greeting exhibited by all normal members of every known society. (2) Homicide and *incest are universal taboos.* (3) Gender role differences go beyond reproduction. (4) Males are more aggressive than females. (5) Strong attachments and fear of separation and of strangers appear in the second half of the first year of life.

Cross-cultural studies have also found that schizophrenia exists among all groups and is constant across cultures. The differences occur in the perception and the treatment of schizophrenia cross-culturally.

Schizophrenic persons are not universally stigmatized as social outcasts; in some cultures, they are integrated into the society.

4.5 The answer is D (Synopsis VIII, pages 146–147).
Attachment (not bonding) refers to an infant's relying on the mother as a source of security. Bonding refers to parents' feelings toward their infants. Although the two are often used synonymously, the words have distinct meanings in attachment theory, and *bonding* should not be used in place of *attachment.*

Attachment *theory is applicable to behavior in all stages of life;* people usually expand their social relationships to friends, marriage partners, coworkers, and other people during life. The success of these relationships is often associated with the success of earliest attachments during infancy, and disturbances in mother–child interactions may be reflected in dysfunctional attachments throughout life.

John Bowlby's *darwinian evolutionary basis* for the theory specifies that adults instinctively behave in a protective manner toward helpless infants to ensure their survival. Thus, attachment theory reflects an innate mechanism that appears not only in humans but in other primates and mammals.

Harry Harlow's experiments with monkeys showed that monkeys raised in isolation grew into isolated animals who were unable to mate and who performed poorly as parents. Thus, proper socialization in infancy is necessary for monkeys (and by extension humans) to develop healthy emotional and behavioral responses in later life.

Signal indicators are infants' signs of distress that trigger a mother's behavioral response. Mothers or other caretakers normally respond to an infant's crying, cooing, and smiling. A mother's voice and body contact can often soothe a crying infant. Thus, signal indicators reinforce attachment between mother and child.

4.6 The answer is E (*Synopsis VIII,* page 154).
Cognitive dissonance does not refer to operant conditioning but is a term describing incongruity or disharmony among a person's beliefs and behavior. When dissonance increases, a person generally changes ways of thinking or behaving to reestablish harmony. All the other terms refer to operant conditioning.

Programming refers to varying the schedule of reinforcements to a behavioral pattern in operant conditioning. *Escape learning* refers to one type of learning in negative reinforcement; for instance, an animal learns to jump off an electric grid whenever it is charged. In *aversive control,* an animal learns to change its behavior to avoid a noxious stimulus. *Avoidance learning* is a step beyond escape learning. In avoidance learning, an animal on an electric grid learns to avoid a shock by pushing a lever when a light comes on.

4.7 The answer is B (*Synopsis VIII,* pages 154–160).
Aggressive behavior cannot *generally be predicted on the basis of previous behavior,* unless that behavior is also aggressive. Predicting aggressive behavior in a person is difficult and is usually done after a pattern has been established. So many factors combine to cause such behavior in a person that it is often wise to avoid making predictions about the person's future actions.

Nevertheless, certain characteristics of aggressive behavior are apparent. When people, whether healthy or mentally ill, act aggressively, their actions *usually occur among family members* or other familiar people; aggressive behavior is less likely to occur toward strangers. A 1986 survey of death row inmates carried out by Dorothy Lewis showed that every inmate had a history of *head injury* as a child, injury often inflicted by *abusive parents.* Although studies have shown a link between early physical abuse, especially abuse that included head injuries, and later aggressive behavior, the linkage is still uncertain.

Aggressiveness characteristically has social, environmental, or situational determinants. Frustration sometimes, but not always, results in aggression, as do direct provocation by others and exposure to aggressive models. Environmental determinants of aggression can include air pollution, crowding, and noise; situational determinants can include physiological or sexual arousal and pain. In all these cases, only some people react with aggression, whereas others react differently; several factors, not just one, may be necessary to produce aggressive acts.

The probability of aggression *increases as a person becomes more psychologically decompensated.* Increased aggressive impulses and diminished control can produce violent acts; people often have violent thoughts or fantasies but do not act them out as long as they can control their thoughts.

4.8 The answer is A (*Synopsis VIII,* pages 170–171).
All the listed factors relevant to psychiatry can be documented cross-culturally except for *bulimia,* which is a disorder apparently limited to Western cultures. *Anxiety* is one of several symptoms that have been documented cross-culturally; other symptoms include mania, depression, suicidal ideation, paranoia, and thought disorder. These symptoms may be variously named in various societies, but they are generally considered instances of deviant or disordered behavior.

Across cultures, *smiling as a greeting* is universal, as is recognition of *gender differences in social roles.* Although role allocation by gender may differ from society to society, men and women play distinct roles that are not limited to reproduction. *Incest taboos* are also cultural universals. In one society, the taboo may apply to uncle–niece marriage, and in another society, to brother–sister marriage, which may be sanctioned in still a third society. Nevertheless, there are rules preventing intermarriage among certain blood relatives almost everywhere. Although the rules are not always adhered to, societies have severe sanctions against breaking the taboos, including death or exile.

4.9 The answer is B (*Synopsis VIII,* page 142).
The *ability to make and follow rules* occurs during the stage of concrete operations. At that time, syllogistic or deductive reasoning occurs, and children learn to engage in a form of deductive reasoning that allows them to begin to acquire and abide by rules.

The *ability to reason about reasoning or thinking* occurs during the stage of formal operations, as does the *ability to distinguish between the ideal self and the real self.* The *use of phenomenological causality as a mode of thinking* is seen during the stage of preoperational thought. The *attainment of object permanence* occurs during the sensorimotor stage.

An overview of the major developmental stages of the life cycle is presented in Table 4.1.

4.10 The answer is E (all) (*Synopsis VIII,* page 147).
John Bowlby is best known for his theory of attachment, which has influenced the understanding of normal and abnormal child development. Bowlby identified specific stages that occur in children who are separated from their mothers, comparing those phases to mourning and bereavement in adults.

Stage 1, called *protest,* is characterized by outbursts of distress, fear, or anger. Stage 2 is characterized by *yearning* and searching for the lost figure. That stage may last for several months or even years and is marked by preoccupation with the lost person to the point that the griever actually believes that the person is present. Stage 3 occurs as a result of a gradual recognition and integration of the reality of the loss, leading to a sense of disorganization and *despair.* In that stage, the person may be restless and aimless and make only ineffective and inefficient efforts to resume normal patterns of living. Stage 4 is the final stage, in which, ideally, the person begins to resolve grief and to *reorganize,* with a gradual recession of the grief and a replacement with cherished memories. Those stages are not discrete, and persons show tremendous variability. In general, normal grief resolves within 1 or 2 years as the person experiences the calendar year at least once without the lost person.

4.11 The answer is A (*Synopsis VIII,* page 142).
The final developmental stage that Piaget defined is the period of *formal operations* (from about 11 to about 15 years of age). The child develops true abstract thought during that time and is able to make hypotheses and test them logically.

The critical achievement of the *sensorimotor* stage (birth to 2 years) is the construction of object concepts. Objects and one's sense of their permanence are constructed during the first year or so of life by the progressive coordination of sensorimotor schemata—elementary concepts—that result from the infant's actions on the world and from its growing mental abilities and motor skills.

During the stage of *preoperational thought* (2 to 5 years), children begin to give evidence of having attained a new level of mental functioning. The evidence is shown not only in the child's language but also in its play, dreams, and imitative behavior. Those behaviors are symbolic. They are processes by which the child re-presents objects and activities in their absence. The attainment of object permanence, which involves representation by means of visual images, marks the transition from sensorimotor to preoperational or intuitive intelligence.

Toward the age of 5 or 6, children give evidence of having attained another level of mental structures that Piaget called *concrete operations.* Those operations enable children to engage in syllogistic reasoning, which permits them to acquire and to follow rules. In addition, concrete operations enable young people to construct unit concepts (a unit, such as a number, is both like and different from every other number) and thus to quantify their experience. That period of development is characterized by the construction of the lawful world.

Epigenesis is a term introduced by Erik Erikson to refer to the stages of ego and social development during the various stages of the life cycle.

4.12 The answer is B (*Synopsis VIII,* pages 140–141).
The critical cognitive achievement of *Piaget's sensorimotor stage* of development (birth to 2 years) is the construction of object concepts. The most important of those concepts is object permanence, and its attainment heralds the end of the sensorimotor period. To adults, objects have an existence independent of their immediate experience; a person or an object continues to exist even when it is not immediately present. That capacity is not innate, nor is it simply learned. A sense of object permanence is constructed during the first year or so of life, as the infant becomes progressively more coordinated—visually, motorically, and mentally.

The *latency stage* was described by Sigmund Freud as a stage of relative quiescence of the sexual drive; the latency stage occurs after the resolution of the Oedipus complex and extends until pubescence. The *preattachment stage* is a concept of John Bowlby's; it refers to the period during the first 2 to 3 months of life. Piaget's *stage of concrete operations* is characterized by deductive or syllogistic reasoning and encompasses the years between 7 and 11. The *stage of formal operations* is characterized by the attainment of abstract thought and extends from the age of 11 through the end of adolescence.

4.13 The answer is E (all) (*Synopsis VIII,* pages 141–142).
Piaget's stage of preoperational thought coincides in time with Sigmund Freud's oedipal phase and Erik Erikson's phase of initiative versus guilt. It is characterized by *intuitive,* as opposed to logical, *thinking* and transductive reasoning. Preoperational children display *egocentric thinking,* believing themselves to be the center of the universe, and they assume that whatever they are thinking or talking about is automatically—in fact, *magically*—understood by the other. The children are also observed to engage in thinking that is *animistic* and phenomenalistic. Animistic thinking is characterized by the endowment of inanimate objects with lifelike attributes (for example, "The chair hates me," "The moon is running"). Phenomenalistic causality is the belief that events that occur in close temporal proximity cause one another (for example, thinking bad thoughts about the mother caused the mother to get sick) and is another term for magical thinking. When adults regress under stress, they can return to the stage of preoperational thought.

4.14 The answer is E (all) (*Synopsis VIII,* pages 144–145).
John Bowlby was concerned with the concept of attachment, its development, and the consequences of its disruption.

Table 4.1
Life Cycle in Development Stages

Age (yr)	Epigenetic Stages of Erikson	Psychosexual Stages of Freud	Stages of Cognitive Development of Piaget	Major Emotional and Developmental Disorders
0–1	Trust vs. mistrust: Basic feelings of being cared for by outer-providers	Oral (merges into oral sadistic)	Sensorimotor: Infant moves from an indifferent stage to awareness of self and the outside world. Object permanence developed (birth to 2 yr).	Rumination, pylorospasm. Stranger anxiety at 8 months, infantile autism, failure to thrive
1–3	Autonomy vs. shame, doubt (begins at 18 mo): Rebellion, clean-dirty issues, compulsive behavior	Anal (divided into anal-explusive and anal-retentive)		Sleep disturbances, pica, negativism, temper tantrums, toilet-training problems. Night terrors, separation anxiety, phobias
3–7	Initiative vs. guilt: Competitiveness develops, self-confidence emerges	Phallic (includes urethral eroticism and Oedipus – Electra complex)	Preoperational thought: A prelogical period in which thinking is based on what child wants, not what is (3–7 yr)	Somnambulism. School phobias, encopresis, enuresis, reading disorder, gender identity disorders. Tic disorders
7–13	Industry vs. inferiority: Peer relations important, risk-taking behavior begins	Latency	Concrete operations: Child appears rational and able to conceptualize shapes and sizes of observed objects (7–13 yr)	Psychosomatic disorders, personality disorders, neurotic disorders, antisocial behavioral patterns, anorexia nervosa, bulimia nervosa
13–18	Identity vs. role diffusion: Develops sense of self, role model important	Genital phase	Formal operations: Person is able to abstract and can deal with external reality. Can conceptualize in adult manner and evaluate logically. Ideals develop (12 or 13 yr through adulthood)	Suicidal peak in adolescents, schizophrenia, identity crisis
Early adulthood	Intimacy vs. isolation: Love relationships, group affiliations important	Genital phase consolidation		Anxiety states. Bipolar I disorder
Middle adulthood	Generativity vs. self-absorption or stagnation: Contributing to future generations, acceptance of accomplishments	Maturity		Midlife crisis. Dysthymic disorder
Late adulthood	Integrity vs. despair: Learning to accept death, maintaining personal values			Highest suicide rates, cognitive disorders

Bowlby defined attachment as the *reciprocal affectionate relationship* between the infant and the primary caretaker that is gradually *developed during the first year of life.* The development of attachment between the infant and the caretaker is *dependent on the intensity, the quality, and the amount of time spent together.*

Bowlby believed that early separation and disruption of attachment have persistent and irreversible effects on personality and intelligence. He pointed to the overt and dynamic similarities between withdrawn, depressed behavior in infants and young children separated from the primary caretaker and mourning behavior in adults. He viewed attachment to a mothering figure as *an instinctive behavior pattern* and hypothesized that smiling increases the infant's chances of survival, as it makes the infant more appealing to the mother. He further suggested that smiling has been favorably selected in evolutionary terms and that infants without a strong smiling response have a higher than usual mortality rate.

4.15 The answer is E (all) (*Synopsis VIII,* page 142).
Validity is the degree to which a test measures what it claims to measure and the degree to which an experimental design yields data truly applicable to the phenomenon under investigation. Predictive validity is one type of validity used to judge the classification of a mental disorder. The validity of mental disorder classification is the extent to which the entire classification and each of its specific diagnostic categories achieve the purposes of communication, control, and comprehension. Predictive validity is also *the extent to which knowledge that a person has a particular mental disorder is useful in predicting the future course of the illness,* complications, and response to treatment. Predictive validity is directly related to management and treatment; thus, it is *relevant to the specificity with which patients with bipolar I disorder improve when treated with lithium,* whereas patients with depressive disorders do not. Predictive validity is *the basis on which Emil Kraepelin differentiated manic-depressive psychosis from dementia precox* because, in dementia precox deterioration occurred, whereas in manic-depressive psychosis the patient did not deteriorate.

4.16 The answer is E (*Synopsis VIII,* pages 154–158).
Curiosity and aggression show no correlation. In the normal child, aggression can be effectively understood in terms of the motives—for example, defense and mastery—for which aggressiveness is a suitable mediator. Its increased frequency in abnormal children can be correlated with defects in the organism, as in the case of *brain injury,* or with distortions in the child's environment, as in the case of *faulty identification models.* Moreover, the frequency of the display of aggressive behavior is a function of the child's *cultural environment.* Aggressive fantasy materials—*violence in movies,* crime comics, and television—rather than affording catharsis for instinctual aggressiveness, generate the very tensions they profess to release.

A central issue is the meaning to be ascribed to the term "aggression." If a boy is observed taking apart a watch, that behavior may be aggressive—if, for example, the watch belongs to the child's father, and the father has just punished him. However, if the watch is an old one in his stock of toys, the boy's motive may be curiosity about its mechanism, especially if he takes delight in reassembling it. If he strikes another child, that act may be motivated by aggression if the victim is the baby sister his parents have just embraced. Or the blow may be defensive if the victim has made a threatening gesture or has tried to seize the boy's favorite toy. Homely anecdotes make the point, but documented experimental examples of aggressive children are also available: children emulating adult models, children systematically subjected to frustration, and children watching films or television of aggressive behavior—all of whom show predictable increases in aggressiveness.

4.17 The answer is D (*Synopsis VIII,* pages 165–166).
The long-term effects of 6 months of total social isolation produce adolescent monkeys that *are both abnormally aggressive and abnormally fearful.* The isolates *exhibit aggression against age-mates who are more physically adept than they.*

Infant monkeys that survive a 3-month, rather than a 6-month, total social isolation can *make a remarkable social adjustment through the development of play.* When allowed to interact with equal-age normally reared monkeys, the isolates play effectively within a week.

Monkeys totally isolated for a 12-month period *are totally unresponsive to the new physical and social world with which they are presented.* Those isolates are devoid of social play and strong emotion. Totally isolated monkeys exhibit a depressive-type posture, including self-clutch, rocking, and depressive huddling. Partially isolated monkeys assume, with increasing frequency, *postures that are bizarre and schizoid,* such as extreme stereotypy and sitting at the front of the cage and staring vacantly into space.

4.18 The answer is C (*Synopsis VIII,* pages 165–166).
The initial reaction of the infant monkey to separation from mother is the strongly emotional protest stage, which is characterized by upset and continuous agitation on the part of the infant. When the separation is prolonged beyond 2 or 3 weeks, the infant's behavior changes to reflect the onset of the *despair* stage, in which the deprived monkey engages in less than usual activity, little or no play, and occasional crying. There is a parallel here to separation among humans and the occurrence of grief that is sometimes reflected in initial protest and later in despair.

Yearning is an urgent longing that is sometimes felt toward the deceased. *Resolution* is similar to C. M. Parkes' stage of reorganization in which a person comes to accept the loss of a loved one.

Acceptance is the final stage to impending death described by Elisabeth Kübler-Ross and is the recognition that death is universal.

4.19 The answer is E (all) (*Synopsis VIII,* page 165).
Harlow's study showed that, *at initial separation, the rhesus infants exhibited a protest stage* which included aggressive attempts to regain maternal contact, plaintive vocalization, and a persistent pattern of nondirected behavior. *The protest stage changed to despair* during the subsequent 48 hours. The most dramatic indicator of the despair stage was the almost total suppression of play. Associated with the suppression was a marked decrease in vocalization and movement. *Play was almost abolished during the three-week period of maternal separation, but resumed rapidly after maternal reunion.* The separated monkey infants typically reattached to the monkey mother vigorously and rapidly when the separation phase ended. In contrast, John Bowlby noted that, when many human children are reunited with their mothers, their responses are often those of rejection, termed by Bowlby the detachment stage.

In Harlow's study of monkeys, the age chosen to begin experimental maternal deprivation was 6 months, which was the age at which play appeared to be maximally matured. The separation was obtained by physically preventing the infant monkeys from being able to touch their mothers or to return from their play area into the home area, where their mothers could be seen. All *monkeys tested showed a nearly complete picture of human anaclitic depression.* Anaclitic depression is the term used by René Spitz for the syndrome shown by infants who are separated from their mothers for long periods of time. In Spitz's series, the reaction occurred in children who were 6 to 8 months old at the time of the separation, which continued for a practically unbroken period of 3 months.

4.20 The answer is A (*Synopsis VIII,* pages 177–178).
Planned *preventive trials* determine whether a planned modification of circumstances actually lowers the incidence of disease. The trials provide more information than any other method about the causes of disease.

A form of preventive trial occurs when a major reform is introduced with the intent of preventing a specific form of disorder. The trial cannot be designed to include a control group because the reform involves the reorganization of all the mental health services of a community to effect *community prevention.*

Encompassed within the scope of prevention in psychiatry are measures to prevent mental disorders *(primary prevention);* measures to limit the severity of illness, as through early case finding and treatment *(secondary prevention);* and measures to reduce disability after a patient has a disorder *(tertiary prevention).* An example of primary prevention is prenatal parent training groups, an example of secondary prevention is psychotherapy, and an example of tertiary prevention is social skills rehabilitation training of schizophrenic patients.

4.21 The answer is A (*Synopsis VIII,* page 174).
Prevalence is the *proportion of a population that has a condition at one moment in time.* The *ratio of persons who acquire a disorder during a year's time* (new cases) is called the annual incidence. In a stable situation, the prevalence is approximately equal to the annual incidence times the average duration, measured in years, of the condition. The *risk of acquiring a condition at some time* in the future is the accumulation of age-specific annual incidence rates over a period of time.

Standard deviation (SD) is a statistical measure of variability within a set of values so defined that, for a normal distribution, about 68 percent of the values fall within one SD of the mean, and about 95 percent lie within two SDs of the mean. It is sometimes represented by Σ, the Greek letter sigma.

The *rate of first admissions to a hospital for a disorder* is the ratio of all first admissions to an average general hospital during a particular year.

4.22 The answer is B (*Synopsis VIII,* page 184).
Alexander Leighton headed a psychiatric epidemiological study of Stirling County in Canada. The Stirling County study found that *women showed more mental disorders than did men* and that *only about 20 percent of the population were free of psychiatric symptoms.* In terms of symptom categories, *psychophysiological symptoms were found in 66 percent* of the men and 71 percent of the women. Neurosis was found in 44 percent of the men and 64 percent of the women. Age was found to be a factor; *mental disorders increased with age.* The study also disclosed that *mental health was related to economic status.*

4.23 The answer is E (all) (*Synopsis VIII,* pages 185–186).
Hospitals are organized in a variety of ways in the United States. *The state mental hospital system has about 100,000 beds.* State psychiatric hospitals have been markedly reduced in population since the 1960s and the 1970s, when deinstitutionalization and effective somatic therapies combined to focus on the outpatient treatment of mentally ill persons. *Investor-owned hospitals* are for-profit hospitals and *are increasing in importance. Department of Veterans Affairs (VA) hospitals are usually affiliated with medical schools* and with the U.S. Department of Defense, Public Health Service, and other entities. In *special hospitals, 70 percent of the facility must be designated for the treatment of a single condition* (not including substance-abuse or other mental disorders). Table 4.2 summarizes some aspects of hospital organization.

4.24 The answer is C (*Synopsis VIII,* page 141).
The infant is in what Piaget described as the sensorimotor stage of cognitive development (birth to 2 years). The critical achievement of this period is the development of *objective permanence.* That term relates to the child's ability to understand that objects have an existence independent of the child's involvement with them. Once object permanence is achieved, infants are able to maintain a mental image of an object, even though it is not present and visible. The sensorimotor stage is also characterized by development of *symbolization,* a process in which infants begin to develop mental symbols and to use words. *Reversibility* and *conversation* are both achieved during the stage of concrete operations (7 to 11 years). Reversibility is the capacity to understand the relation between things, to understand that one thing can turn into another and back again, for example, ice and water. Conservation is the ability to recognize that, even though the shape and form of objects may change, the objects still maintain or conserve the other characteristics that enable them to be recognized as the same. *Egocentrism* is a feature of the stage of preoperational thought (2 to 7 years) and refers to children's view of themselves as the center of the universe and inability to take on the role of another person.

4.25 The answer is E (*Synopsis VIII,* page 142).
The concepts listed (A–D) are all associated with the stage of preoperational thought (2 to 7 years) and are not characteristic of this infant's stage of cognitive development. *Animistic thinking* is the tendency to endow physical events and objects with lifelike psychologic attributes, such as feelings and intentions. *Semiotic function* is the ability to represent something—such as an object, event, or conceptual scheme—with a signifier, which serves a representative function (for example, language, mental image, symbolic gesture). *Phenomenalistic causality* is a type of magical thinking in which events that occur together are thought to cause one another (for example, thunder causes lightning). *Egocentric thought* is described previously.

Table 4.2
Aspects of Hospital Organization

Criteria	Voluntary Hospital	Investor-Owned Hospital	State Mental Hospital System	Municipal Hospital System	Federal Hospital System	Special Hospital
Patient population	All illnesses	All illnesses, although hospital may specialize	Mental illness	All illnesses	All illnesses	70% of facility must be for single diagnosis
Profit orientation	Nonprofit	For profit	Nonprofit	Nonprofit	Nonprofit	For profit or nonprofit
Ownership	Private management board	Private corporation; may be owned by medical doctors	State	City government	Federal government	Private or public
Affiliation	1,200 church-affiliated; privately owned or university-sponsored	May be owned by large chains such as Humana Corporation, Columbia/HCA	Free-standing or affiliated with various medical schools	Voluntary teaching hospitals and medical schools	Department of Defense; Public Health Service, Coast Guard, Prison, Merchant Marine, Indian Health Service; Department of Veterans Affairs (VA)	Optional affiliation with medical schools
Other	Provide bulk of care in US	Increasing in importance nationally; must be monitored financially to avoid fraud	Deinstitutionalization—number of patients has been reduced	Most physicians at municipal hospitals are employed by their affiliated medical school	VA hospitals usually have affiliations with medical schools	Less regulated than other types of hospitals

Notes: (1) To be designated a teaching hospital, a hospital must offer at least four types of approved residencies, clinical experiences for medical students, and an affiliation with a medical school. (2) Short-term hospitals have an average patient stay of less than 30 days; long-term hospitals, an average of longer duration. (3) Special hospitals include obstetrics and gynecology; eye, ear, nose, and throat. They do not include psychiatric hospitals or substance abuse hospitals.

4.26 The answer is E (*Synopsis VIII,* pages 142–143).
The child is demonstrating achievement of conservation, which is characteristic of the *stage of concrete operations* (age 7 to 11 years) in Piaget's stages of cognitive development.

Conservation is the ability to recognize that, even though the shape and the form of objects may change, the objects still maintain or conserve the other characteristics that enable them to be recognized as the same. Conservation of liquids (demonstrated in Fig. 4.3) is achieved approximately at 6 to 7 years of age.

Conservation is not a feature of the *stage of preoperational thought,* which is characterized by thinking that is based on what the child wants, not what is, from age 3 to 7 years. At *4 to 5 years of age* the child would be in the stage of preoperational thought. *Reversibility* is the capacity to understand the relationship between things. *Object permanence* is the knowledge that objects have an existence independent of the child's involvement with them.

4.27 The answer is B (*Synopsis VIII,* page 153).
All of the terms (A–E) are concepts used in learning theory. Stimulus generalization is the process whereby a conditioned response is transferred from one stimulus to another similar stimulus, such as from a rat (in this example) to a rabbit or a dog.

Sensitization is the process by which pairing the eliciting stimulus with a painful stimulus results is a stronger, more sensitive response. After sensitization to a sound, for example, one startles more easily upon hearing that sound than before being sensitized.

Discrimination is the process of recognizing and responding to the differences between similar stimuli. A child, for example, learns to discriminate four-legged animals (the common stimulus) into dogs, cats, cows, and other quadrupeds.

Extinction occurs when the conditioned stimulus is constantly repeated without the unconditioned stimulus until the response evoked by the conditioned stimulus gradually weakens and eventually disappears.

Reinforcement is a term used in operant conditioning. Positive reinforcement refers to the process by which certain consequences of behavior increase the probability that the behavior will occur again. Negative reinforcement describes the process by which behavior that leads to the removal of an unpleasant event strengthens that behavior.

4.28 The answer is A (*Synopsis VIII,* page 150).
The figure illustrates the principal procedures of operant conditioning (not classical conditioning). In the case of *operant conditioning,* learning is thought to occur as a result of the consequences of one's actions and the resultant effect on the environment. In *classical conditioning,* in contrast, learning is thought to take place as the result of the contiguity of environmental events; when events occur closely together in time, persons will probably come to associate the two.

In operant conditioning, *positive reinforcement* is the process by which certain consequences of a response increase the probability that the response will occur again. Food, water, praise, and money, as well as substances such as opium, cocaine, and nicotine, all may serve as positive reinforcers.

Negative reinforcement is the process by which a response that leads to the removal of an aversive event increases that response. A teenager mowing the lawn to avoid parental complaints or an animal jumping off a grid to escape painful shock are both examples of negative reinforcement. Any behavior that enables one to avoid or escape a punishing consequence is strengthened; therefore, a patient with anorexia nervosa, eating and gaining weight in order to get out of the hospital, is also an example of negative reinforcement.

Negative reinforcement is not punishment. *Punishment* is an aversive stimulus (for example, a slap) that is presented specifically to weaken or suppress an undesired response. Punishment reduces the probability that a response will occur.

Answers 4.29–4.32

4.29 The answer is A (*Synopsis VIII,* pages 188–189).

4.30 The answer is C (*Synopsis VIII,* pages 188–189).

4.31 The answer is D (*Synopsis VIII,* pages 188–189).

4.32 The answer is B (*Synopsis VIII,* pages 188–189).
A *health maintenance organization (HMO)* is an organized system providing comprehensive (both inpatient and outpatient) health care in all specialties, including psychiatry. *Members* voluntarily *pay a prepayment or capitation fee to cover all health care services* for a fixed period of time (a month or a year). By using a capitation or prospective payment method, the HMO is assuming a dominant role in United States health care. The HMO is popular because it decreases health care costs by limiting the number of new hospitalizations and by discharging patients from the hospital earlier than usual. The emphasis on prevention and health promotion and on performing as much diagnosis and therapy as possible on an outpatient basis also helps control expenses.

Both the HMO and the preferred provider organization (PPO) use a prospective payment system. In the PPO, however, a corporation or an insurance company makes an agreement with a particular group of community hospitals and doctors to *supply health services at a lower than usual rate for its members.* Patients who enroll in a PPO select their physicians from among the list of participating doctors, which includes both specialists and primary care physicians. Inpatient care is provided at the designated hospital that the patient chooses. There are about 1000 PPOs in the United States at this time.

Neither the HMO nor the PPO *is equivalent to a health systems agency.* Health systems agencies (HSAs) are nonprofit organizations mandated by the federal government and set up on a statewide basis. HSAs promote or limit the development of health services and facilities, depending on the needs of a particular locality or state. They are made up of consumers and have considerable power in medicine. HSAs control capital expenditures and, therefore, the availability of health resources. In each state, HSAs develop both long-term and short-term goals and plans, approve health care proposals requesting federal funding, review existing facilities and services, and suggest future construction and renovation projects on the basis of their findings.

Answers 4.33–4.37

4.33 The answer is B (*Synopsis VIII,* pages 181–184).

4.34 The answer is B (*Synopsis VIII,* pages 181–184).

4.35 The answer is A (*Synopsis VIII,* pages 181–184).

4.36 The answer is A (*Synopsis VIII,* pages 181–184).

4.37 The answer is A (*Synopsis VIII,* pages 181–184).
A person's socioeconomic status is not based solely on income but includes such factors as education, occupation, and lifestyle. The socioeconomic status of the patient influences atti-

tudes toward physical and mental health, as listed in Table 4.3. For example, *upper middle class* persons are *more able to delay gratification* than lower class persons and *seek health care earlier* than lower class persons. Lower class persons often *see pregnancy as a time of crisis,* have *longer hospital stays* than upper middle class persons, and have *low contraceptive use.*

Table 4.3
Attitudes Toward Health Issues

Lower Class	Upper Middle Class
Look for immediate solutions	More able to delay gratification
Negative view on life	More positive view of life
Low contraceptive use	High contraceptive use
Seek health care later	Seek health care earlier
Longer hospital stays	Shorter hospital stays
See pregnancy as a time of crisis	See pregnancy as a normal event

Answers 4.38–4.41

4.38 The answer is C (*Synopsis VIII,* page 162).

4.39 The answer is D (*Synopsis VIII,* page 165).

4.40 The answer is A (*Synopsis VIII,* page 163).

4.41 The answer is B (*Synopsis VIII,* page 153).
Imprinting has been described as the process by which certain stimuli become capable of eliciting certain innate behavior patterns during a critical period of an animal's behavioral development. The phenomenon is associated with *Konrad Lorenz,* who in 1935 demonstrated that the first moving object (in that case, Lorenz himself) a duckling sees during a critical period shortly after hatching is thereafter regarded and reacted to as the mother duck.

Harry Harlow is associated with the concept of the *surrogate mother* from his experiments in the 1950s with rhesus monkeys. Harlow designed a series of experiments in which infant monkeys were separated from their mothers during the earliest weeks of life. He found that the infant monkeys, if given the choice between a wire surrogate mother and a cloth-covered surrogate mother, chose the cloth-covered surrogates even if the wire surrogates provided food.

Ivan Petrovich Pavlov coined the term *"experimental neurosis"* to describe disorganized behavior that appears in the experimental subject (in Pavlov's case, dogs) in response to an inability to master the experimental situation. Pavlov described extremely agitated behavior in his dogs when they were unable to discriminate between sounds of similar pitch or test objects of similar shapes.

Eric Kandel contributed to the knowledge of the neurophysiology of learning. He demonstrated in the study of the snail *Aplysia* that synaptic connections are altered as a result of learning.

Answers 4.42–4.45

4.42 The answer is C (*Synopsis VIII,* page 141).

4.43 The answer is D (*Synopsis VIII,* page 141).

4.44 The answer is A (*Synopsis VIII,* pages 141–142).

4.45 The answer is E (*Synopsis VIII,* page 142).

4.46 The answer is B (*Synopsis VIII,* pages 142–143).
During Piaget's sensorimotor stage of development, the child develops *object permanence.* By *9 to 12 months,* the child has the ability to retain an object in its mind when the object is no longer in view. At that time, peekaboo becomes a game joyfully played with the child.

The end of the sensorimotor stage is marked by the attainment of *symbolic thought* by the child of *18 to 24 months* of age. With the acquisition of symbolic thought, the whole world of symbolic play is open to the child.

Ages *2 through 7 years* mark the years of preoperational thought, the stage of prelogical thinking. The child believes in imminent justice—that a bad deed will inevitably be punished. The child also believes in *magical thinking,* the idea that thoughts or wishes—good or bad—can come true. Magical thinking has positive and negative repercussions. After some ill has befallen a loved one, for example, the child may blame himself or herself because of "bad" wishes. Happily, some children believe they are gaining a new sibling because they have wished for it, and they can view a new baby as a present.

Ages 7 to 11 years are the years of concrete operations. The child is able to understand classifications and *cause and effect.* At that time the child is also able to take another's point of view, and in games children can take turns and follow rules.

The stage of formal operations is entered at about age *11 years through adolescence.* It is the time of the acquisition of abstract logic. In addition to being able to hypothesize and make deductions, the young person can comprehend probabilities and can now *think about thoughts.*

4.47 The answer is A (*Synopsis VIII,* page 143).

4.48 The answer is B (*Synopsis VIII,* page 143).

4.49 The answer is C (*Synopsis VIII,* page 143).

4.50 The answer is E (*Synopsis VIII,* page 143).

4.51 The answer is D (*Synopsis VIII,* page 143).
Conservation is the ability to recognize that, even though the shape and the form of objects may change, the objects still maintain or conserve other characteristics that enable them to be recognized as the same. It occurs between 7 and 11 years of age. In Figure 4.6, Item I is *conservation of substance.* One of the balls is deformed, and the subject is asked whether the balls still contain equal amounts. Item II is *conservation of length.* One of the sticks is to the right of the other, and the subject is asked whether they are the same length. Item III is *conservation of numbers.* The elongated line has the same numbers as the contracted row. Item IV is *conservation of space.* The experimenter scatters the blocks over one of the sheets and is asked if they are the same amount. Item V is *conservation of liquid.* Both containers can contain the same amount of liquid.

5

Psychology and Psychiatry: Psychometric and Neuropsychological Testing

Clinical psychologists perform testing on psychiatric patients, but psychiatrists must be familiar with the available tests and must understand what areas each test evaluates and each test's validity, reliability, and implications.

To work up and treat psychiatric patients, psychometric and neuropsychological testing is widely used. Evaluating intelligence, personality, and cognitive functioning with psychometric testing (objective or projective, individual or group) can help psychiatrists to diagnose and treat patients. Neuropsychological testing of various areas of functioning (memory, reasoning, mood, visual-spatial orientation) can evaluate disturbances in thought and behavior produced by injury or abnormal development.

A significant and increasingly sophisticated area of neuropsychological testing concentrates on neuroanatomical localization of mental deficits. Both clinicians and researchers can use such tests to learn, for instance, the area of a patient's brain associated with the ability to speak words correctly or to understand a spoken word. In addition to its use in cognitive and amnestic disorders, neuropsychological testing is important in mood disorders associated with insults to the brain—for example, tumors and strokes—and in schizophrenia. As this area expands and grows, neuropsychiatric testing can produce even more spectacular results.

Chapter 5 in *Kaplan and Sadock's Synopsis VIII* covers both psychological and neuropsychiatric testing. Students should review that chapter and then study the questions and answers below.

HELPFUL HINTS

The psychological terms and tests listed here should be defined and memorized.

- abstract reasoning
- accurate profile
- attention
- attention-deficit/hyperactivity disorder
- average IQ
- battery tests
- behavioral flexibility
- bell-shaped curve
- Bender Visual Motor Gestalt test
- Alfred Binet
- catastrophic reaction
- clang association
- classification of intelligence
- coping phase
- DAPT
- dementia
- dressing apraxia
- DSS
- dysgraphia
- dyslexia
- EEG abnormalities
- Eysenck personality inventory
- fluency
- full-scale IQ
- Gestalt psychology
- Halstead-Reitan
- House-Tree-Person test
- individual and group tests
- inferred diagnosis
- intelligence quotient (IQ)
- interrogation procedure
- learning disability
- Luria-Nebraska Neuropsychological Battery (LNNB)
- manual dexterity
- maturational levels
- memory: immediate, recent, recent past, remote
- memory—left versus right hemisphere disease
- mental age
- mental status cognitive tasks
- MMPI
- motivational aspects of behavior
- Henry Murray and Christiana Morgan
- neuropsychiatric tests
- objective tests
- organic dysfunction
- orientation
- performance subtests
- perseveration
- personality functioning
- personality testing
- primary assets and weaknesses
- prognosis
- projective tests
- prosody
- psychodynamic formulations
- Raven's Progressive Matrices
- reaction times
- recall phase
- reliability
- representational
- Rorschach test
- response sets
- scatter pattern
- SCT
- Shipley Abstraction test

- ▶ standardization
- ▶ Stanford-Binet
- ▶ stimulus words
- ▶ TAT
- ▶ temporal orientation
- ▶ test behavior
- ▶ validity
- ▶ verbal subtests
- ▶ visual-object agnosia
- ▶ WAIS
- ▶ Wechsler Adult Intelligence Scale
- ▶ Wechsler Memory Scale
- ▶ WISC
- ▶ word-association technique
- ▶ WPPSI

▲ QUESTIONS

DIRECTIONS: Each of the incomplete statements below is followed by five suggested completions. Select the *one* that is *best* in each case.

5.1 The Minnesota Multiphasic Personality Inventory (MMPI) is most correctly described as

A. composed of 200 questions
B. generally used as a good diagnostic tool
C. the most widely used personality assessment instrument
D. a good indication of a subject's disorder when the person scores high on one particular clinical scale
E. in the form of 10 clinical scales, each of which was derived empirically from heterogeneous groups

5.2 In the assessment of personality

A. the Thematic Apperception Test (TAT) requires the patient to construct or create stories about pictures
B. in the Rorschach test, lack of attention to detail is common in paranoid and obsessive subjects
C. tests using a projective approach are interpreted against a set of normative data
D. the word-association technique is no longer used
E. the Minnesota Multiphasic Personality Inventory (MMPI) uses a projective approach

5.3 In the field of memory

A. a nonverbal visual task is a poor assessor of immediate memory
B. recent memory can be tested by digit-span tasks
C. episodic memory is memory for knowledge and facts
D. the Wechsler Memory Scale yields a memory quotient
E. semantic memory and implicit memory decline with age

5.4 An intelligence quotient (IQ) of 100 corresponds to intellectual ability for the general population in the

A. 20th percentile
B. 25th percentile
C. 40th percentile
D. 50th percentile
E. 65th percentile

5.5 The first sign of beginning cerebral disease often is impairment in

A. remote memory
B. long-term memory
C. immediate memory
D. recent memory
E. none of the above

5.6 The most likely diagnosis for a 43-year-old college professor who drew Figure 5.1 on the Draw-a-Person Test (DAPT) is

A. obsessive-compulsive personality disorder
B. dysthymic disorder
C. brain damage
D. conversion disorder
E. bipolar I disorder, most recent episode manic

5.7 In the assessment of intelligence

A. the highest divisor in the intelligence quotient (IQ) formula is 25
B. the IQ is a measure of future potential
C. the Stanford-Binet test is the most widely used intelligence test
D. the average or normal range of IQ is 70 to 100
E. intelligence levels are based on the assumption that intellectual abilities are normally distributed

FIGURE 5.1
Drawing done on the Draw-a-Person Test (DAPT).

5.8 The Bender Visual Motor Gestalt test is administered to test

A. maturation levels in children
B. organic dysfunction
C. loss of function
D. visual and motor coordination
E. all of the above

5.9 In interpreting the Thematic Apperception Test (TAT), the examiner considers

A. many areas of the patient's functioning
B. with whom the patient identifies
C. all the figures
D. motivational aspects of behavior
E. all of the above

5.10 After taking the Wechsler Adult Intelligence Scale (WAIS), a patient showed that poor concentration and attention had adversely influenced the answers on one of the subtests. Select the letter of the WAIS subtest that screened the patient for these symptoms.

A. Arithmetic
B. Block design
C. Digit symbol
D. Comprehension
E. Picture completion

5.11 Which of the following items is evidence of brain damage in children?

A. No behavior deficit
B. Motor impersistence
C. Relatively high level of intelligence
D. Normal language
E. Absence of attention-deficit/hyperactivity disorder

DIRECTIONS: Each group of questions below consists of lettered headings followed by a list of numbered statements. For each numbered statement, select the *one* lettered heading that is most closely associated with it. Each lettered heading may be selected once, more than once, or not at all.

Questions 5.12–5.18

A. Bender Visual Motor Gestalt test
B. Shipley Abstraction test
C. Raven's Progressive Matrices
D. Wechsler Adult Intelligence Scale (WAIS)
E. Minnesota Multiphasic Personality Inventory (MMPI)
F. Thematic Apperception Test (TAT)
G. None of the above

5.12 A test of visuomotor coordination
5.13 A multiple-choice pictorial display
5.14 Impaired performance associated with poor visuoconstructive ability
5.15 The patient being asked to construct stories
5.16 Eleven subtests, six verbal and five performance, yielding a verbal IQ, a performance IQ, and a full-scale IQ
5.17 The self-report inventory consisting of over 500 statements to which the person has to respond with "True" or "False"
5.18 A series of sentence stems, such as "I like . . . ," that patients are asked to complete in their own words

Questions 5.19–5.23

A. Rorschach test
B. Luria-Nebraska Neuropsychological Battery
C. Halstead-Reitan Battery of Neurological Tests
D. Stanford-Binet
E. None of the above

5.19 Consists of 10 tests, including the trail-making test and the critical flicker frequency test
5.20 Is extremely sensitive in identifying discrete forms of brain damage, such as dyslexia
5.21 Consists of 120 items, plus several alternative tests, applicable to the ages between 2 years and adulthood
5.22 Furnishes a description of the dynamic forces of personality through an analysis of the person's responses
5.23 A test of diffuse cerebral dysfunction to which normal children by the age of 7 years respond negatively

Questions 5.24–5.28

A. Frontal lobes
B. Dominant temporal lobe
C. Nondominant parietal lobe
D. Dominant parietal lobe
E. Occipital lobes

5.24 The loss of gestalt, the loss of symmetry, and the distortion of figures
5.25 Patient not able to name a camouflaged object but able to name it when it is not camouflaged
5.26 Two or more errors or two or more 7-second delays in carrying out tasks of right-left orientation
5.27 Any improper letter sequence in spelling "earth" backward
5.28 Patient not able to name common objects

Questions 5.29–5.32

A. Wechsler Adult Intelligence Scale (WAIS)
B. Wechsler Intelligence Scale for Children (WISC)
C. Wechsler Preschool and Primary Scale of Intelligence (WPPSI)
D. All the above
E. None of the above

5.29 A scale for children ages 6 through 16 years
5.30 A scale for children ages 4 to 6½ years
5.31 Educational background affects the information and vocabulary segments
5.32 Assesses children from 8 weeks to 2½ years of age

Questions 5.33–5.36

A. Beck Depression Inventory
B. Hamilton Depression Rating Scale
C. Brief Psychiatric Rating Scale

5.33 Self-administered
5.34 Emphasizes subjective mood and thoughts
5.35 Emphasizes neurovegetative symptoms
5.36 Provides a global pathology index

Questions 5.37–5.39

A. Short-term memory loss
B. Signs of organic dysfunction
C. Korsakoff's syndrome
D. Posterior right-hemisphere lesion
E. Damage to frontal lobes or caudate

5.37 Wechsler Memory Scale
5.38 Wisconsin Card Sorting Test
5.39 Benton Visual Retention Test

ANSWERS

Psychology and Psychiatry: Psychometric and Neuropsychological Testing

5.1 The answer is C (*Synopsis VIII,* pages 195).

The MMPI is composed of over 500 statements, not *200 questions.* It is the *most* widely used test. Although the test was initially thought to be a *diagnostic tool,* workers now use the inventory to interpret the patterning of the entire profile obtained from the clinical scales. Researchers have identified personality correlates of various configurations produced on the inventory, which can serve as diagnostic aids. Therefore, *a good indication of a subject's disorder* is not a single high score on one scale; the complete results are examined for an interpretation, and at least two of the highest scores are used to arrive at a diagnosis. The inventory is in the form of clinical scales, but these scales were derived from *homogeneous* criterion groups of psychiatric patients, not from heterogeneous groups of people.

5.2 The answer is A (*Synopsis VIII,* pages 193, 197–198).

The Thematic Apperception Test (TAT) requires the patient to construct or create stories about pictures. It is a projective personality test that consists of 30 pictures and one blank card. Although most of the pictures depict people and all are representational, each picture is ambiguous. Generally, the TAT is more useful as a technique for inferring motivational aspects of behavior than as a basis for making a diagnosis.

The Rorschach test, another projective personality test, consists of a standard set of 10 inkblots that serve as stimuli for associations. The cards are shown to the patient in a particular order. The examiner keeps a record of the patient's verbatim response, initial reaction time, and total time spent on each card. After the completion of the free-association phase, the examiner conducts an inquiry phase to determine important aspects of each response that are crucial to its scoring. An overattention to detail, not a *lack of attention to detail, is common in paranoid and obsessive subjects.* Projective tests are essentially idiographic. *Tests using a projective approach are not interpreted against a set of normative data.* Typically, the interpretation is based on a theory of human behavior and personality; each person is assumed to have certain needs, characteristics, defenses, and other qualities that become apparent through the testing process.

The word-association technique is still used, primarily by psychodynamically oriented psychiatrists. In the technique, devised by Carl Gustav Jung, stimulus words are presented to patients, who respond to them with the first word that comes to mind. After the initial administration of the list, some clinicians repeat the list, asking the patient to respond with the same words used previously. Discrepancies between the two administrations of the list may reveal association difficulties.

The Minnesota Multiphasic Personality Inventory (MMPI) uses an objective approach, not a projective approach, to personality assessment. The objective approach is characterized by reliance on structured, standardized measurement devices—that is, straightforward test stimuli, such as direct questions regarding the subjects' opinions of themselves, and unambiguous instructions regarding the completion of the test. The MMPI is a self-report inventory that is the most widely used and most thoroughly researched of the objective personality assessment instruments. The test consists of more than 500 statements—such as, "I worry about sex matters," "I sometimes tease animals," and "I believe I am being plotted against"—to which the subject must respond with "true" or "false." The MMPI gives scores on 10 standard clinical scales, each of which was derived empirically (that is, homogeneous criterion groups of psychiatric patients were used in developing the scales). The items for each scale were selected for their ability to separate medical and psychiatric patients from normal controls. Various researchers have identified numerous personality correlates of various MMPI scales as the basis for core interpretive statements.

5.3 The answer is D (*Synopsis VIII,* page 200).

Memory is a comprehensive term that covers the retention of all types of material over various periods of time and that involves diverse forms of response. The Wechsler Memory Scale (WMS) is the most widely used memory test battery for adults. It is a composite of verbal paired-associate retention, paragraph retention, visual memory for designs, orientation, digit span, rote recall of the alphabet, and counting backward. *The Wechsler Memory Scale yields a memory quotient* (MQ), which is corrected for age and generally approximates the Wechsler Adult Intelligence Scale (WAIS) IQ.

Immediate (or short-term) memory is the reproduction, recognition, or recall of perceived material within 30 seconds of presentation. It is most often assessed by digit repetition and reversal (auditory) tests and memory-for-designs (visual) tests. Both an auditory-verbal task, such as digit span or memory for words or sentences, and a nonverbal visual task, such as memory for designs or for objects or faces, are good assessors of the patient's immediate memory. Patients can also be asked to listen to a standardized story and to repeat the story as they heard it. Patients with lesions of the right hemisphere of the brain are likely to show more severe defects on visual nonverbal tasks than on auditory verbal tasks. Conversely, patients with left hemisphere lesions, including patients who are not aphasic, are likely to show severe deficits on the auditory verbal tests, with variable performance on the visual nonverbal tasks.

Recent memory cannot be tested by digit-span tasks, as can immediate memory. Recent memory concerns events over the past few hours or days; it can be tested by asking patients what they had for breakfast and who visited them in the hospital.

Other types of memory that theorists have described include episodic memory, semantic memory, and implicit memory. Episodic memory is memory for specific events, such as a telephone message. *Episodic memory is not memory for knowledge and facts;* that is semantic memory. An example of semantic memory is knowing who was the first President of the United States. *Semantic memory and implicit memory do not decline with age;* persons continue to accumulate information over a lifetime. Episodic memory shows a minimal decline with aging that may relate to impaired frontal lobe functioning.

5.4 The answer is D (*Synopsis VIII,* page 193).
An intelligence quotient (IQ) of 100 corresponds to the *50th percentile* in intellectual ability for the general population. Modern psychological testing began in the first decade of the 20th century when Alfred Binet (1857–1911), a French psychologist, developed the first intelligence scale to separate the mentally defective (who were to be given special education) from the rest of the children (whose school progress was to be accelerated).

5.5 The answer is D (*Synopsis VIII,* page 200).
Impairment in *recent memory,* the inability to recall the past several hours or days, is a prominent behavioral deficit in brain-damaged patients and is often the first sign of beginning cerebral disease. Recent memory is also known as short-term memory. *Remote memory,* also known as *long-term memory,* consists of childhood data or important events known to have occurred when the patient was young or free of illness. *Immediate memory* is memory after 5 seconds and is the ability to repeat four to seven digits forward and backward. Patients with unimpaired memory can usually recall six or seven digits backward.

Memory is based on three essential processes: (1) registration, the ability to establish a record of an experience; (2) retention, the persistence or permanence of a registered experience; and (3) recall, the ability to arouse and repeat in consciousness a previously registered experience. A good memory involves the capacity to register swiftly and accurately, to retain for long periods of time, and to recall promptly. Memory is usually evaluated from the view of recent memory and remote memory.

5.6 The answer is C (*Synopsis VIII,* page 199).
The most likely diagnosis for the 43-year-old college professor who drew Figure 5.1 on the Draw-a-Person Test (DAPT) is *brain damage.* Brain-damaged patients often have a great deal of trouble projecting their images of the body into a figure drawing. Experience with the drawing technique allows for recognition of differences in drawings by brain-damaged patients from drawings by patients with other disorders. The DAPT should be used with other psychological tests to confirm the diagnosis. Deficiencies that accompany brain malfunctioning are frequently highlighted by means of psychological tests. Occasionally they are most apparent in areas ordinarily conceptualized as intellectual—in memory ability, arithmetical skills, and the analysis of visual designs. At other times they are most apparent in graphomotor productions, such as the DAPT, in which such distortions as difficulties in spatial orientation, fragmentation, and oversimplification of the figures can occur.

Obsessive-compulsive personality disorder patients in general pay attention to details of anatomy and clothing and show long, continuous lines; *dysthymic disorder* patients may draw small sizes, heavy lines, few details, and dejected facial expressions; patients with *conversion disorder* may show exaggeration, emphasis, or, conversely, negligence of body parts involved in the conversion symptom; persons with *bipolar I disorder, most recent episode manic,* may draw large, colorful figures with exaggerated features, sometimes filling the whole page.

5.7 The answer is E (*Synopsis VIII,* pages 194–197).
Intelligence levels are based on the assumption that intellectual abilities are normally distributed (in a bell-shaped curve) throughout the population. Intelligence can be defined as a person's ability to assimilate factual knowledge, recall either recent or remote events, reason logically, manipulate concepts (either numbers or words), translate the abstract to the literal and the literal to the abstract, analyze and synthesize forms, and deal meaningfully and accurately with problems and priorities deemed important in a particular setting. In 1905 Alfred Binet introduced the concept of the mental age (MA), which is the average intellectual level at a particular age. The intelligence quotient (IQ) is the ratio of MA over CA (chronological age) multiplied by 100 to do away with the decimal point; it is represented by the following equation:

$$\frac{\text{MA}}{\text{CA}} \times 100 = \text{IQ}$$

When the chronological age and the mental age are equal, the IQ is 100—that is, average. Because it is impossible to measure increments of intellectual power past the age of 15 by available intelligence tests, *the highest divisor in the IQ formula is 15, not 25.*

As measured by most intelligence tests, IQ is an interpretation or a classification of a total test score in relation to norms established by a group. *IQ is a measure of present functioning ability, not of future potential.* Under ordinary circumstances, the IQ is stable throughout life, but there is no certainty about its predictive properties.

The Wechsler Adult Intelligence Scale (WAIS), not the *Stanford-Binet test, is the most widely used intelligence test* in clinical practice today. The WAIS was constructed by David Wechsler at New York University Medical Center and Bellevue Psychiatric Hospital. It comprises 11 subtests—6 verbal subtests and 5 performance subtests—yielding a verbal IQ, a performance IQ, and a combined or full-scale IQ. The verbal IQ, the performance IQ, and the full-scale IQ are determined by the use of separate tables for each of the seven age groups (from 16 to 64 years) on which the test was standardized.

The average or normal range of IQ is 90 to 110, not 70 to 100. IQ scores of 120 and higher are considered superior. According to the American Association of Mental Deficiency (AAMD) and the fourth edition of *Diagnostic and Statistical Manual of Mental Disorders* (DSM-IV), mental retardation is defined as an IQ of 70 or below, which is found in the lowest 2.2 percent of the population. Consequently, 2 of every 100 persons have IQ scores consistent with mental retardation, which can range from mild to profound.

Table 5.1 presents the DSM-IV classification of intelligence by IQ range.

5.8 The answer is E (all) (*Synopsis VIII,* page 201).
The Bender Visual Motor Gestalt test, devised by the American neuropsychiatrist Lauretta Bender in 1938, is a technique that consists of nine figures that are copied by the subject (Fig. 5.2). It is administered as a means of evaluating *maturation levels in children* and *organic dysfunction.* Its chief applica-

Table 5.1
Classification of Intelligence by IQ Range

Classification	IQ Range
Profound mental retardation (MR)[a]	Below 20 or 25
Severe MR[a]	20–25 to 35–40
Moderate MR[a]	35–40 to 50–55
Mild MR[a]	50–55 to about 70
Borderline	70–79
Dull normal	80–90
Normal	90–110
Bright normal	110–120
Superior	120–130
Very Superior	130 and above

[a] According to the fourth edition of *Diagnostic and Statistical Manual of Mental Disorders* (DSM-IV).

tions are to determine retardation, *loss of function,* and organic brain defects in children and adults. The designs are presented one at a time to the subject, who is asked to copy them onto a sheet of paper. The subject then is asked to copy the designs from memory (Figs. 5.3 and 5.4); thus, the Bender designs can be used as a test of both *visual-motor coordination* and immediate visual memory.

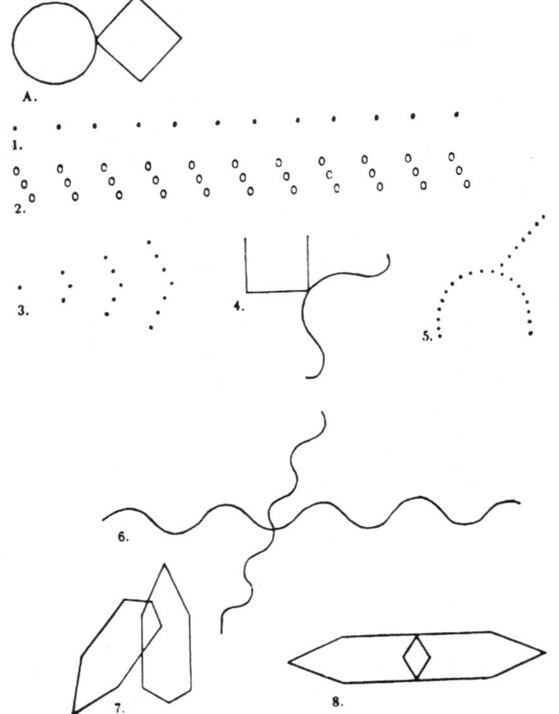

FIGURE 5.2
Test figures from the Bender Visual Motor Gestalt test, adapted from Max Wertheimer. Reprinted with permission from Bender L: *A Visual Motor Gestalt Test and Its Clinical Use,* p 33. American Orthopsychiatric Association, New York, 1938.

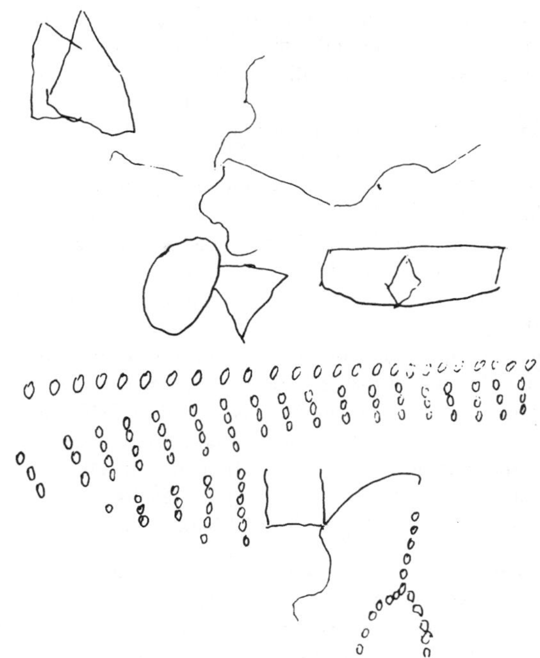

FIGURE 5.3
Bender Visual Motor Gestalt test drawings of a 57-year-old, brain-damaged woman.

5.9 The answer is E (all) (*Synopsis VIII,* pages 197–198).
The Thematic Apperception Test (TAT) was introduced by Henry A. Murray in 1943 as a new way of interpreting stories made up by the patient about pictures representing human beings of both sexes and varying ages, alone or in a group, and in a variety of surroundings and interactions. Originally, the test's chief usefulness was seen as revealing drives of which the patient was unaware. However, the test revealed conscious tendencies, as well as unconscious tendencies. Its aim expanded to include the study of *many areas of the patient's functioning,* including personality traits, emotions, neurotic defenses, conflicts, intellectual level, ambitions, attitudes toward parental figures, and psychopathology. The patient is shown one picture at a time and is asked to tell a complete story, including the interactions occurring, the events leading up to those interactions, the thoughts and feelings of the figures, and the outcome. In interpreting the TAT, the examiner, among other factors, notes *with whom the patient identifies* and as-

FIGURE 5.4
Bender Visual Motor Gestalt test recall by the 57-year-old brain-damaged patient who drew Figure 5.3.

sumes that *all the figures* may represent varying aspects of the patient being projected onto the ambiguous scenes and interactions; drives or attitudes that the patient considers as negative may, for instance, be projected onto the figures that are apparently most unlike the patient. The TAT appears to be most useful in helping the examiner infer *motivational aspects of behavior,* as opposed to providing a clear-cut and definitive diagnosis. As with all projective tests, there are disagreements about the value of the TAT; for example, investigators have failed to duplicate exactly the studies they set out to check, and a sufficiently comprehensive, clear, and formalized basis for the interpretations of TAT results are still lacking. Psychologists and other workers who believe that projective tests are useful maintain that any measure of potential behavior is valuable. Experienced clinical psychologists (who are most likely to administer and interpret a useful TAT) generally agree about the difficulty in acquiring sufficient skill and experience for satisfactory interpretations of TAT results. It is easy to learn how to administer the test but hard to interpret it well.

5.10 The answer is A (*Synopsis VIII,* pages 194–195).
The *Arithmetic* subtest showed that the patient's ability to do simple arithmetic was adversely influenced by poor attention and concentration. The *Block design* subtest requires a subject to arrange a series of pictures to tell a story. This process tests performance and cognitive styles. The *Digit symbol* subtest requires a subject to match digits and symbols in as little time as possible, as a test of performance. The *Comprehension* subtest reveals a subject's ability to adhere to social consequences and to understand social judgments, when the subject answers questions about how people should behave. On the *Picture completion* subtest, a subject must complete a picture with a missing part. Visuospatial defects appear when errors are made on this procedure.

5.11 The answer is B (*Synopsis VIII,* page 204).
Motor impersistence often occurs in children with brain damage. Other evidence of brain damage in children can be a *low level of intelligence* compared to peers, *gross maldevelopment of language,* and *attention-deficit/hyperactivity disorder.* If the brain damage occurred when the child was very young, *no behavior deficit* may be apparent.

Answers 5.12–5.18

5.12 The answer is A (*Synopsis VIII,* pages 201–203).

5.13 The answer is C (*Synopsis VIII,* pages 199–204).

5.14 The answer is C (*Synopsis VIII,* pages 199–204).

5.15 The answer is F (*Synopsis VIII,* pages 197–198).

5.16 The answer is D (*Synopsis VIII,* pages 194–195).

5.17 The answer is E (*Synopsis VIII,* pages 195–196).

5.18 The answer is G (*Synopsis VIII,* pages 199–204).
The Bender Visual Motor Gestalt test is a test of visuomotor coordination that is useful for both children and adults. The test material consists of nine designs adapted from those used by Max Wertheimer in his studies in Gestalt psychology. Each design is printed against a white background on a separate card. Patients are given unlined paper and asked to copy each design with the card in front of them. There is no time limit. That phase of the test is highly structured and does not investigate memory function because the cards remain in front of the patients. Many clinicians then remove the cards and, after an interval of 45 to 60 seconds, ask the patients to reproduce as many of the designs as they can from memory. That recall phase not only investigates visual memory but also presents a less structured situation because patients must rely essentially on their own resources. Comparing the patient's functioning under the two conditions is often helpful. The Bender Visual Motor Gestalt test is probably used most frequently with adults as a screening device for signs of organic dysfunction. Evaluation of the protocol depends on the form of the reproduced figures and on their relation to one another and to the whole spatial background.

Raven's Progressive Matrices requires the patient to select from *a multiple-choice pictorial display* the stimulus that completes a design in which a part is omitted. The difficulty of the discrimination increases over trials in the lengthy test. A briefer, less difficult version (Color Matrices) is especially useful for patients who are unable to complete the standard test, which can require 30 to 45 minutes. *Impaired performance is associated with poor visuoconstructive ability* and with posterior lesions of either cerebral hemisphere, but receptive language deficit may contribute to poor performance in patients with dominant-hemisphere damage.

The *Shipley Abstraction* test requires the patient to complete logical sequences; it assesses the patient's capacity to think abstractly. Because performance on a test of that type is related to educational background, an accompanying vocabulary test is also given to the patient, and a comparison is made between the patient's performances on the two tests. A low abstraction score in relation to vocabulary level is interpreted as reflecting an impairment in conceptual thinking.

The *Thematic Apperception Test (TAT)* consists of a series of 20 pictures of ambiguous figures and events and one blank card. Most patients are shown 10 pictures, the choice of pictures generally depending on the examiner's wish to clarify specific conflict areas. *The patient is asked to construct stories* based on the pictures. With the blank card, the patient has to imagine a scene first and then tell a story about it. The patient is asked to relate the story with a beginning, a middle, and an end. That projective test elicits information regarding a broad spectrum of psychological functioning, including needs, attitudes, and motives. Scoring of the TAT is not standardized. Although scoring systems exist, test interpretation is typically impressionistic and informal. The patient's stories are examined for recurrent themes to provide evidence of mood, conflict, interpersonal relationships, and areas of strengths and weaknesses.

The *Wechsler Adult Intelligence Scale (WAIS)* is an intelligence test designed for persons 16 years old or older. It is the best standardized and most widely used intelligence test in clinical practice today. The scale is designed for individual administration and consists of *11 subtests, 6 verbal and 5 performance, yielding a verbal IQ, a performance IQ, and a full-scale IQ.* Norms are provided for each of the tests, thus eliciting an IQ for the verbal test group, for the nonverbal performance test group, and for the entire scale. The subtests are information, comprehension, arithmetic, similarities, digit span, vocabulary, picture completion, block design, picture arrangement, object assembly, and digit symbol. A person's IQ score indicates the degree of deviation of the person's intellectual capacity from the average.

The *Minnesota Multiphasic Personality Inventory (MMPI),* introduced in 1943 and revised (MMPI-2) in 1990, is the most widely used and most thoroughly researched of the objective personality assessment instruments. The inventory is easy to administer and requires little time or effort on the part of the examiner, as the persons evaluate themselves. *The self-report inventory consists of over 500 statements to which the person has to respond with "True" or "False."* The statements pertain to many personality aspects, such as physiological functions, habits, attitudes, and psychopathology, and the persons are asked to report whether the statements apply to them. The MMPI gives scores on 10 standard clinical scales, each of which was derived from homogeneous-criteria groups of psychiatric patients. Each scale was validated by studying various diagnostic groups to determine whether the scale items truly differentiated between normal controls and medical or psychiatric patients.

The Sentence Completion Test (SCT) is composed of *a series of sentence stems, such as "I like . . . ," that patients are asked to complete in their own words* with the first words that come to mind. The test is designed to tap a patient's conscious associations to areas of functioning in which the examiner may be interested—for instance, responses that are highly emotional, repetitive, humorous, bland, or only factually informative.

Answers 5.19–5.23

5.19 The answer is C (*Synopsis VIII,* page 204).

5.20 The answer is B (*Synopsis VIII,* page 204).

5.21 The answer is D (*Synopsis VIII,* page 204).

5.22 The answer is A (*Synopsis VIII,* page 197).

5.23 The answer is E (*Synopsis VIII,* page 204).
Various neuropsychiatric tests, including the Halstead-Reitan and the Luria-Nebraska batteries, are sometimes useful in bringing to light subtle organic dysfunctions that are undetected in standard psychiatric, psychological, and even neurological assessments. The *Halstead-Reitan Battery of Neuropsychological Tests consists of 10 tests, including the trail making test and the critical flicker frequency test.* It was developed in an attempt to improve the reliability of the criteria used to diagnose brain damage. Assessment data were gathered on a group of patients with left-hemisphere injury, right-hemisphere injury, and global involvement. The trail making test is a test of visuomotor perception and motor speed, and the critical flicker frequency test (noting when a flickering light becomes steady) tests visual perception.

The *Luria-Nebraska Neuropsychological Battery (LNNB) is extremely sensitive in identifying discrete forms of brain damage, such as dyslexia* (an impairment in the ability to read) and dyscalculia (an inability to perform arithmetical operations), rather than more global forms.

The *Stanford-Binet Intelligence Scale* is one of the tests most frequently used in the individual examination of children. It *consists of 120 items, plus several alternative tests, applicable to the ages between 2 years and adulthood.* The tests have a variety of graded difficulties, both verbal and performance, designed to assess such functions as memory, free association, orientation, language comprehension, knowledge of common objects, abstract thinking, and the use of judgment and reasoning.

The *Rorschach test* is a psychological test consisting of 10 inkblots that the person is asked to look at and interpret. It *furnishes a description of the dynamic forces of personality through an analysis of the person's responses.*

The face-hand test, devised by Lauretta Bender, is *a test of diffuse cerebral dysfunction to which normal children by the age of 7 years respond negatively.* The person, whose eyes are closed, is touched simultaneously on the cheek and the hand; retesting is done with the person's eyes open. The results are considered positive if the person fails consistently to identify both stimuli within 10 trials.

Answers 5.24–5.28

5.24 The answer is C (*Synopsis VIII,* pages 201–202).

5.25 The answer is E (*Synopsis VIII,* pages 201–202).

5.26 The answer is D (*Synopsis VIII,* pages 201–202).

5.27 The answer is A (*Synopsis VIII,* pages 201–202).

5.28 The answer is B (*Synopsis VIII,* pages 201–202).
Numerous mental status cognitive tasks are available to test and localize various brain dysfunctions. Construction apraxia—*the loss of gestalt, the loss of symmetry, and the distortion of figures*—seen in the task of copying the outline of simple objects, is localized to the *nondominant parietal lobe.* Dysfunction of the *occipital lobes* is suggested when a *patient cannot name a camouflaged object but can name it when it is not camouflaged. Two or more errors or two or more 7-second delays in carrying out tasks of right-left orientation* (for example, place left hand to right ear, right elbow to right knee) are localized to dysfunction of the *dominant parietal lobe.* A dysfunction in concentration is thought to be localized to the *frontal lobes* and can be tested by eliciting *any improper letter sequence in spelling "earth" backward.* In anomia the *patient cannot name common objects* (for example, watch, key); the impairment is localized to the *dominant temporal lobe.*

Answers 5.29–5.32

5.29 The answer is B (*Synopsis VIII,* page 194).

5.30 The answer is C (*Synopsis VIII,* page 194).

5.31 The answer is D (*Synopsis VIII,* page 194).

5.32 The answer is E (*Synopsis VIII,* page 194).
The *Wechsler Adult Intelligence Scale (WAIS)* was originally designed in 1939; it has gone through several revisions since then. It is the test most often used to determine IQ in the average adult. *A scale for children ages 6 through 16 years* has been devised—the *Wechsler Intelligence Scale for Children (WISC)*—and *a scale for children ages 4 to 6½ years—the Wechsler Preschool and Primary Scale of Intelligence (WPPSI).* The WISC is an individual test that, like the WAIS, provides separate verbal and performance IQs, based on separate sets of tests, and a full-scale IQ; it requires a highly trained examiner. The WPPSI, devised in 1967, an individual test, extended the range of assessment downward in age. In

practice, the WAIS, the WISC, or the WPPSI is used as part of a battery of psychological tests.

Educational background affects the information and vocabulary segments of the scales and must be taken into account when evaluating a subject's scores on *all the tests.*

The Bayley Infant Scale of Development *assesses children from 8 weeks to 2½ years of age.* The test examines both motor and social functioning. The developmental quotient (DQ) obtained is based on standardized norms for the child's age.

Answers 5.33–5.36

5.33 The answer is A (*Synopsis VIII,* page 196).

5.34 The answer is A (*Synopsis VIII,* page 196).

5.35 The answer is B (*Synopsis VIII,* page 196).

5.36 The answer is C (*Synopsis VIII,* page 196).
The *Beck Depression Inventory* is a *self-administered* scale. It *emphasizes subjective mood and thoughts* within the framework of Aaron Beck's cognitive theory of depression. The scale has been criticized because it puts little emphasis on the neurovegetative symptoms of depression.

The *Hamilton Depression Rating Scale* is administered by the examiner. The patient is rated on signs and symptoms of depression, including psychomotor retardation, changes in sleep and appetite, and weight loss. The scale *emphasizes neurovegetative symptoms* and has been criticized for giving little attention to the affective and cognitive changes that may occur in patients with major depressive disorder.

The *Brief Psychiatric Rating Scale provides a global pathology index.* The scale, filled out by the examiner after the interview, screens for a wide range of psychiatric symptoms, including somatic concerns, anxiety, disorganization, guilt, tension, grandiosity, hostility, and suspiciousness. Because the scale covers many symptoms, it is best used as a barometer of a patient's global pathology and improvement during treatment.

5.37 The answer is C (*Synopsis VIII,* page 200).

5.38 The answer is E (*Synopsis VIII,* page 200).

5.39 The answer is A (*Synopsis VIII,* page 200).
The *Wechsler Memory Scale* screens for verbal and visual memory and yields a memory quotient. The results can reveal whether a subject has *amnestic Korsakoff's syndrome. The Wisconsin Card Sorting Test* assesses a person's abstract reasoning ability and flexibility in problem solving. The results can reveal whether a person has damage to the frontal lobes or to the caudate.

The *Benton Visual Retention Test* screens for *short-term memory loss.*

Signs of organic dysfunction may be screened for by the Bender Visual Motor Gestalt test. *Posterior right-hemisphere lesions* can be revealed through a Facial Recognition Test.

6 

Theories of Personality and Psychopathology

Psychoanalytic theory is a major foundation of psychiatric research and practice, and of all the thinkers who have contributed to understanding the human mind, Sigmund Freud (1856–1939) takes first place. The founder of psychoanalysis some 100 years ago, Freud's basic hypotheses, such as the unconscious and the major role of childhood in adult thought and behavior, are central to psychiatry today. Some modern theorists have based their own theories on elaborations and expansions of Freud's work; others have rejected Freud's concepts and have developed hypotheses challenging him. All workers in psychiatry, however, begin with a thorough knowledge of Freud's contributions.

Various schools of modern personality theory include ego psychology, object relations theory, self psychology, and the interpersonal school. Workers in each school have usually drawn their psychoanalytic techniques from their specific perspectives of personality development. Psychologists with widely differing viewpoints, who have concerned themselves with personality development, include Alfred Adler (1870–1937), Erik Erikson (1902–1994), Karen Horney (1885–1952), Carl Gustav Jung (1875–1961), Melanie Klein (1882–1960), and Harry Stack Sullivan (1892–1949). An understanding of these and other approaches is necessary to appreciate the various theories of personality structure, development, and treatment. Finally, the term ''personality'' is used in different ways by different theorists. Generally, it refers to a person's characteristic and enduring behavioral interactions with people and his or her environment. It reflects one's individual adjustment to life.

Students should review Chapter 6 in *Kaplan and Sadock's Synopsis VIII* and should study the questions and answers below.

HELPFUL HINTS

The student should know the various theorists, their schools of thought, and their theories.

- Karl Abraham
- abreaction
- acting out
- Alfred Adler
- Franz Alexander
- Gordon Allport
- analytical process
- attention cathexis
- Michael Balint
- behaviorism
- Eric Berne
- Wilfred Bion
- Joseph Breuer
- cathexis
- Raymond Cattell
- character traits
- condensation
- conflict
- conscious
- day's residue
- defense mechanisms
- displacement
- dream work
- ego functions
- ego ideal
- ego psychology
- Erik Erikson
- Eros and Thanatos
- Ronald Fairbairn
- Sandor Ferenczi
- Anna Freud
- free association
- Erich Fromm
- fundamental rule
- Kurt Goldstein
- Heinz Hartmann
- hypnosis
- hysterical phenomena
- infantile sexuality
- instinctual drives
- interpretation
- Carl Gustav Jung
- Karen Horney
- Søren Kierkegaard
- Melanie Klein
- Heinz Kohut
- Kurt Lewin
- latent dream
- libido
- libido and instinct theories
- manifest dream
- Abraham Maslow
- Adolph Meyer
- multiple self-organizations
- Gardner Murphy
- Henry Murray
- narcissism
- narcissistic, immature, neurotic, and mature defenses
- nocturnal sensory stimuli
- object constancy
- object relations
- parapraxes
- Frederick S. Perls
- preconscious
- preconscious system
- pregenital
- primary and secondary gains
- primary autonomous functions
- primary process
- psychic determinism
- psychoanalytic theory
- psychodynamic thinking
- psychoneurosis
- psychosexual development
- Sandor Rado
- Otto Rank
- reality principle
- reality testing
- regression
- Wilhelm Reich
- repetition compulsion
- repression
- resistance

- secondary process
- secondary revision
- signal anxiety
- structural model
- *Studies on Hysteria*
- Harry Stack Sullivan
- symbolic representation
- symbolism
- synthetic functions of the ego
- talking cure
- *The Ego and the Id*
- *The Interpretation of Dreams*
- *The Trauma of the Birth*
- topographic theory
- transference
- unconscious motivation
- Donald Winnicott
- wish fulfillment
- working through

▲ QUESTIONS

DIRECTIONS: Each of the questions or incomplete statements below is followed by five suggested responses or completions. Select the *one* that is *best* in each case.

6.1 All of the following statements correctly describe the theories of Erik Erikson *except*

A. Erikson described eight stages of human life cycles.
B. Erikson's stage 6, intimacy versus isolation, refers to young adulthood and later.
C. Erikson's stages do not extend beyond age 70.
D. Erikson described a corresponding zone for each of Sigmund Freud's three psychosexual stages.
E. Erikson described one developmental stage of childhood in terms similar to those of Piaget's stage of object permanence.

6.2 All of the following statements correctly describe the work of Sigmund Freud *except*

A. An important innovation of Freud's was his emphasis on infant sexuality.
B. Freud considered dreams to have two levels of content: manifest and latent.
C. In Freud's tripartite model of the mind, each entity is distinguished by its function.
D. Anna O. had many hysterical symptoms associated with her father's illness and death and was treated by Freud.
E. Freud's work on conflicts stressed the importance of working through them to ameliorate psychic disturbances.

6.3 Donald Winnicott's contributions to the British school of object relations theory included hypotheses of all of the following *except*

A. a true self
B. a traditional space
C. a transitional object
D. a holding environment
E. a good-enough mother

6.4 All of the following early psychoanalysts studied with Sigmund Freud *except*

A. Carl Jung
B. Alfred Adler
C. Karl Abraham
D. Frederick Perls
E. Sándor Ferenczi

6.5 According to Carl Gustav Jung, archetypes are

A. instinctual patterns
B. expressed in representational images
C. expressed in mythological images
D. organizational units of the personality
E. all the above

6.6 According to Alfred Adler, the helplessness of the infant accounts for

A. feelings of inferiority
B. a need to strive for superiority
C. fantasied organic or psychological deficits
D. compensatory strivings
E. all the above

6.7 Masculine protest is

A. a universal human tendency
B. a move from a female or passive role
C. a concept introduced by Alfred Adler
D. an extension of Adler's ideas about organ inferiority
E. all of the above

6.8 According to Harry Stack Sullivan, anxiety is characterized by

A. feelings of disapproval from a significant adult
B. an interpersonal context
C. somatic symptoms
D. restriction of functioning
E. all of the above

6.9 The fundamental rule of psychoanalysis is

A. resistance and repression
B. psychic determinism
C. abreaction
D. free association
E. the concept of the unconscious

6.10 Which of the following statements about dreams is true as described by Freud?

A. Dreams are the conscious expression of an unconscious fantasy.
B. Dreams represent wish-fulfillment activity.
C. Latent dream content derives from the repressed part of the id.
D. Sensory impressions may play a role in initiating a dream.
E. All of the above statements are true.

6.11 Autonomous functions of the ego include all of the following *except*

A. perception
B. language
C. motor development
D. repression
E. intelligence

6.12 A male office worker steals supplies from the office and, when confronted with the evidence, states: ''Well, everybody does it, and you can't fire me. I quit.'' Which of the following defense mechanisms is he using?

A. Denial and rationalization
B. Rationalization and identification with the aggressor
C. Identification and undoing
D. Projection and identification with the aggressor
E. Intellectualization and denial

6.13 Which of the following statements about dreams is *not* true?

A. Dreams have a definite but disguised meaning.
B. Dreams are considered a normal manifestation of unconscious activity.
C. Dreams represent unconscious wishes.
D. The core meaning of the dream is expressed by its manifest content.
E. Nocturnal sensory stimuli may be incorporated into the dream.

6.14 The major defense mechanism used in phobia is

A. projection
B. identification
C. displacement
D. undoing
E. reaction formation

6.15 Mature defenses, according to George Vaillant, include

A. altruism
B. controlling
C. intellectualization
D. rationalization
E. all of the above

6.16 Isolation, the defense mechanism involving the separation of an idea or memory from its attached feeling tone, is found most clearly in

A. obsessive-compulsive disorder
B. anxiety disorders
C. pain disorder
D. dissociative disorders
E. dysthymic disorder

6.17 Psychobiology is best characterized by which of the following concepts?

A. Analysis of the ego through the interpretation of defense mechanisms
B. Biographical study and common-sense understanding of patients
C. Primary understanding of the biological and biochemical origins and treatment of mental illness
D. Emphasis on genetic factors in mental illness and the use of drugs in psychiatry
E. Psychological factors affecting physical illness

6.18 Alienation from the self is a concept developed by

A. Sigmund Freud
B. Harry Stack Sullivan
C. Eric Berne
D. Karen Horney
E. Alfred Adler

6.19 The term ''habit training'' was coined by

A. Adolf Meyer
B. Carl Gustav Jung
C. Otto Rank
D. B. F. Skinner
E. Joseph Wolpe

6.20 The self-system concerns Harry Stack Sullivan's concept of the

A. unconscious
B. personality
C. libido
D. defense mechanisms
E. Oedipus complex

6.21 Erik Erikson used the term ''generativity versus stagnation'' to describe the conflict occurring in

A. childhood
B. adolescence
C. young adulthood
D. middle adulthood
E. late adulthood

6.22 Consistent and affectionate maternal behavior during infancy provides the child with a continuing sense of

A. trust
B. autonomy
C. initiative
D. industry
E. identity

6.23 The stage of industry versus inferiority is characterized by

A. eagerness and curiosity
B. self-indulgence
C. expanded desires
D. confidence in one's ability to use adult materials
E. preoccupation with one's appearance

6.24 Erik Erikson's stage of generativity versus stagnation is characterized by

A. interests outside the home
B. establishing and guiding the next generation
C. self-absorption
D. bettering society
E. all of the above

6.25 According to Sigmund Freud's structural theory of the mind, the psychic apparatus is divided into

A. id, ego, and superego
B. ego, unconscious, and id
C. superego, ego, and unconscious
D. unconscious, conscious, and preconscious
E. none of the above

6.26 According to Sigmund Freud, which of the following does *not* explain why a man falls in love with a particular type of woman?

A. She resembles the man's idealized self-image.
B. She resembles someone who took care of him when he was a boy.
C. She provides him with narcissistic gratification.
D. There is a sexual resemblance between them.
E. All of the above.

6.27 In the structural theory of the mind

A. the superego controls the delay and the modulation of drive expression
B. the superego is the executive organ of the psyche
C. the superego's activities occur unconsciously to a large extent
D. the reality principle and the pleasure principle are aspects of id functioning
E. the id operates under the domination of secondary process

6.28 In Carl Gustav Jung's psychoanalytic school

A. the collective unconscious is a collection of impulses of the id and the ego
B. archetypes contribute to complexes
C. the male part of the self is called the persona
D. individuation is a process that is completed in childhood
E. an emphasis is placed on infantile sexuality

6.29 In Erik Erikson's descriptions of the stages of the life cycle

A. the stage of industry versus inferiority corresponds to Freud's phallic-oedipal stage
B. the stage of identity versus role diffusion corresponds to Freud's latency stage
C. the stage of autonomy versus shame and doubt corresponds to Freud's anal stage
D. generativity can occur only if a person has or raises a child
E. the stage of integrity versus despair occurs from late adolescence through the early middle years

6.30 Which of the following statements applies to the unconscious?

A. Its elements are inaccessible to consciousness.
B. It is characterized by primary process thinking.
C. It is closely related to the pleasure principle.
D. It is closely related to the instincts.
E. All of the above statements are true.

6.31 All of the following statements regarding the unconscious system are true *except*

A. It is characterized by secondary process thinking.
B. Its contents can become conscious only by passing through the preconscious.
C. Its content is limited to wishes that are seeking fulfillment.
D. It disregards logical connections and permits contradictory ideas to exist simultaneously.
E. Its memories are divorced from connections with verbal symbols.

DIRECTIONS: Each group of questions below consists of lettered headings followed by a list of numbered words or statements. For each numbered word or statement, select the *one* lettered heading that is most closely associated with it. Each lettered heading may be selected once, more than once, or not at all.

Questions 6.32–6.36

A. Rationalization
B. Projection
C. Denial
D. Reaction formation
E. Sublimation

6.32 A 45-year-old man who is having problems at work begins to complain that his boss ''has it in for me.''
6.33 A 34-year-old married woman who finds herself strongly attracted to a friend of her husband's is nasty to that friend.
6.34 A 35-year-old gambler loses $500 at the race track but says that he is not upset because ''I would have spent the money on something else anyway.''
6.35 A 42-year-old man is discharged from a cardiac intensive care unit after suffering a severe myocardial infarction, but he continues to smoke two packs of cigarettes a day.
6.36 A 30-year-old man finds his greatest source of relaxation by going to watch football games.

Questions 6.37–6.41

A. Franz Alexander
B. Donald Winnicott
C. Karen Horney
D. Melanie Klein
E. Heinz Kohut

6.37 Introduced the concept of the transitional object
6.38 Believed that oedipal strivings are experienced during the first year of life and that, during the first year, gratifying experiences with the good breast reinforce basic trust
6.39 Emphasized cultural factors and disturbances in interpersonal and intrapsychic development
6.40 Introduced the concept of the corrective emotional experience
6.41 Expanded Sigmund Freud's concept of narcissism; theories are known as self psychology

Questions 6.42–6.46

A. Shadow
B. Anima
C. Animus
D. Persona
E. Collective unconscious

6.42 Face presented to the outside world
6.43 Another person of the same sex as the dreamer
6.44 A man's undeveloped femininity
6.45 A woman's undeveloped masculinity
6.46 Mythological ideas and primitive projections

Questions 6.47–6.51

A. Harry Stack Sullivan
B. Abraham Maslow
C. Wilhelm Reich
D. Kurt Lewin
E. Frederick S. Perls

6.47 ''Group dynamics''
6.48 Peak experience
6.49 Participant observer
6.50 Character formation and character types
6.51 Gestalt therapy

Questions 6.52–6.56

A. Basic trust versus basic mistrust
B. Integrity versus despair
C. Initiative versus guilt
D. Intimacy versus isolation
E. Identity versus role diffusion

6.52 Infancy
6.53 Early childhood
6.54 Puberty and adolescence
6.55 Early adulthood
6.56 Late adulthood

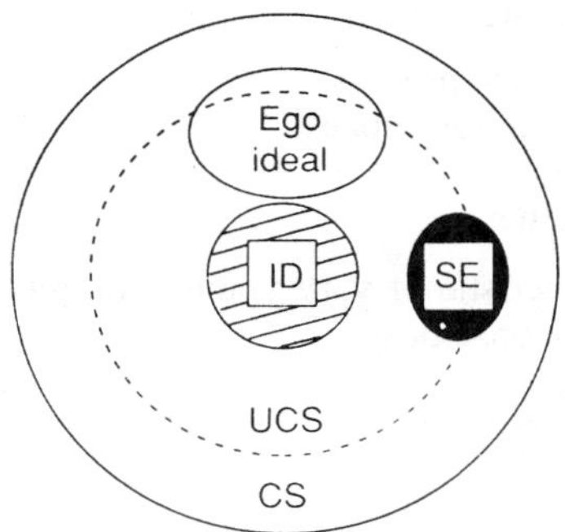

FIGURE 6.1
Freudian topology of the psychic apparatus. Reprinted with permission from Kaplan HI, Sadock BJ, editors: *Comprehensive Textbook of Psychiatry,* ed 6, p 490. Baltimore, Williams & Wilkins, 1995.

6.57 Based on Freud's structural model of the psychic apparatus, represented in Figure 6.1, select the lettered item (*A* to *C*) that *best* matches the function described for each of the numbered items (*1* to *5*) below. Each lettered item may be used once, more than once, or not at all.

A. Ego
B. Superego
C. Id

1. Delays and modifies drive expression through defense mechanisms
2. Reservoir of unorganized instinctual drives
3. Provides ongoing scrutiny of a person's behavior, thoughts, and feelings
4. Functions include logical and abstract thinking and verbal expression
5. Establishes and maintains a person's moral conscience

DIRECTIONS: Each set of lettered headings on the next page is followed by a list of numbered words or phrases. For each numbered word or phrase, select

A. if the item is associated with *A only*
B. if the item is associated with *B only*
C. if the item is associated with *both A and B*
D. if the item is associated with *neither A nor B*

Questions 6.58–6.62

A. Primary process
B. Secondary process
C. Both
D. Neither

6.58 Characteristic of very young children
6.59 The unconscious
6.60 The id
6.61 The preconscious
6.62 The ego

Questions 6.63–6.67

A. Topographic theory
B. Structural theory
C. Both
D. Neither

6.63 Set forth by Sigmund Freud in *The Interpretation of Dreams* in 1900
6.64 Presented in *The Ego and the Id* in 1923
6.65 Unconscious, preconscious, and conscious
6.66 Id, ego, and superego
6.67 First systematic and comprehensive study of the defenses used by the ego

ANSWERS

Theories of Personality and Psychopathology

6.1 The answer is C (*Synopsis VIII,* pages 233–239).
Erikson's stage integrity versus despair begins at age 65 and continues throughout life. A person in a state of despair is fearful of death. This endpoint of the life cycle requires preparation and the feeling of having lived a productive and worthwhile life.

Erikson described eight stages of human life cycles, ranging from 1 year to over 65 years. Each stage is marked by a crisis, which, if successfully mastered, allows a person to move on to the next stage. *Erikson's stage 6 refers to young adulthood and later,* from 21 to 40 years. This stage, called intimacy versus isolation, is characterized by successful fulfillment of the usual elements of this period: love, intimacy, and productivity.

Erikson described a corresponding zone for each of Freud's three psychosexual stages: oral, anal, and phallic. Each zone has a specific pattern of behavior associated with it. Erikson, however, emphasized that ego development is not only a result of intrapsychic energies but also of interactions between a child and society. *Erikson described one developmental stage of childhood in terms similar to those of Piaget's stage of object permanence.* In stage 1, basic trust versus basic mistrust, a healthy infant learns to let the mother go out of sight without experiencing fear or anger, a phenomenon related to Piaget's idea that an infant at this time can maintain a mental image of a person or an object although the image is not always visible.

6.2 The answer is D (*Synopsis VIII,* page 207).
Anna O., who *had many hysterical symptoms associated with her father's illness and death, was treated by Josef Breuer,* not by Sigmund Freud. Freud, a friend of Breuer, was interested in Breuer's treatment of Anna O. and investigated the reasons for symptoms appearing in patients with hysteria. His studies were a contributing factor to his developing psychoanalysis.

Freud's *emphasis of infant sexuality* was a major tenet of psychoanalytic theory, although many people found the idea difficult to accept. In Freud's concept of infantile sexuality, based on the notion that physical pleasure was not only genital, children from birth through puberty struggled to deal with erotic feelings and activities and with social reactions to these pleasures. *Freud considered dreams to have two levels of content.* The manifest level is recalled by dreamers; the latent content is unconscious. *Dream work* enabled latent content to be made conscious, or manifest, so that a person's conflicts could be worked through.

In Freud's tripartite model of the mind, each entity—id, ego, and superego—is distinguished by its function. The id is a reservoir of unorganized instinctual drives; the ego, which is conscious, preconscious, and unconscious, functions with logical, abstract thinking and with verbal expression; the superego functions as a conscience composed of ideals internalized from parents.

Freud's work on conflicts presumed that they occurred between instincts and external reality or between internal agencies. When conflicts have not been consciously examined and worked through, they are repressed from consciousness or otherwise defended against and become a basis for neurotic development.

6.3 The answer is B (*Synopsis VIII,* pages 218, 233).
A traditional space is not a term referring to one of Winnicott's concepts; the correct term is *transitional space,* the area in which a transitional object—the link to the mother—functions. This space, according to Winnicott, is a source of art, creativity, and metaphysical beliefs.

Donald Winnicott, a major figure in the British school of object relations theory, created several concepts of child development, including *a true self* (which emerges in a healthy environment), *a holding environment* (the context in which a true self emerges), *a good-enough mother* (one who provides adequate responses to her infant in a holding environment), and *a transitional object* (a pacifier or blanket, which substitutes for a mother as an infant matures).

6.4 The answer is D (*Synopsis VIII,* pages 223–234).
Frederick Perls did not work with Sigmund Freud. Rather, he was one of the creators of Gestalt theory in Germany. According to Perls, Gestalt therapy emphasizes a patient's current life experiences and not the ''there and then'' of Freudian psychoanalysis.

Carl Jung, although he later broke with Freud over the latter's ideas of infantile sexuality, initially was one of Freud's disciples. After breaking with Freud, Jung created a concept of the unconscious that included the collective unconscious, a reservoir of humans' common, shared myths and symbols in the form of archetypes or images with universal meanings. *Alfred Adler,* another early disciple of Freud, became estranged because of Freud's stress of sexuality in neurosis. Adler emphasized the role of aggression, which he saw as more important than sexuality, and coined the term *inferiority complex* to describe a universal, innate sense of inadequacy.

Karl Abraham, the first psychoanalyst in Germany, was an early disciple of Freud. Abraham elaborated Freud's stages of psychosexual development and linked each stage to a specific syndrome. He also developed a psychoanalytic view of depression, which he described as a fixation at the oral stage. *Sándor Ferenczi,* who was influenced by Freud's ideas early in his career and who was psychoanalyzed by Freud, later developed his own method of analysis, in which analysts were to love their patients to compensate them for the lack of love they had received from their parents.

6.5 The answer is E (all) (*Synopsis VIII,* page 227).
Carl Gustav Jung believed archetypes to be *instinctual patterns.* All psychic energy is transmitted in forms of experience, behavior, and emotion, which are *expressed in representational* or *expressed in mythological images.* Thus, the archetypes represent the basic motivations and drives that become *organizational units of the personality.*

6.6 The answer is E (all) (*Synopsis VIII,* pages 223–224).
According to Alfred Adler, infants are born with certain *feelings of inferiority.* As a result, they have *a need to strive for superiority,* perfection, and totality. Adler classified those strivings under the heading of the inferiority complex, which comprises the newborns' feelings secondary to their real or *fantasied organic or psychological deficits. Compensatory strivings* are the person's attempts to overcome feelings of inferiority.

6.7 The answer is E (all) (*Synopsis VIII,* page 223).
Masculine protest, the *universal human tendency* to *move from a female or passive role* to a masculine or active role, *is a concept introduced by Alfred Adler.* The doctrine is *an extension of Adler's ideas about organ inferiority.* Adler regarded that concept as the main force in neuroticism. It represents the distorted perception of sex differences caused by the striving for superiority. If it takes an active force in women, they attempt from an early age to usurp the male position. They become aggressive in manner, adopt masculine habits, and endeavor to domineer everyone about them. The masculine protest in a male indicates that he never fully recovered from an infantile doubt about his masculinity. He strives for an ideal masculinity, invariably perceived as the self-possession of freedom and power.

6.8 The answer is E (all) (*Synopsis VIII,* pages 232–233).
As with other concepts developed by Harry Stack Sullivan, he saw anxiety as an interpersonal phenomenon that is defined as the response to *feelings of disapproval from a significant adult.* Therefore, it occurs only in *an interpersonal context,* even if the other person is not real but only a fantasied image.

Feelings of disapproval can be communicated and interpreted by the person in several ways, sometimes false. A distressing feeling, such as anxiety, is accompanied by *somatic symptoms* and psychological feelings of doom, which the person cannot tolerate for long.

Sullivan viewed the development of personality as a process of learning to cope with anxiety by using adaptive maneuvers and defense techniques designed to gain approval from significant people in one's life. When a person feels that the anxiety is becoming too widespread, he or she tries to limit opportunities for the further development of such anxiety. Such limitation results in *restriction of functioning* that includes only those patterns of activity that are familiar and well-established.

6.9 The answer is D (*Synopsis VIII,* pages 206–210).
Free association is known as the fundamental rule of psychoanalysis. The use of free association in psychoanalysis evolved gradually from 1892 to 1895. Sigmund Freud began to encourage his patients to verbalize, without reservation or censorship, the passing thoughts in their minds. The conflicts that emerge while fulfilling the task of free association constitute *resistance,* which was first defined by Freud as the reluctance of his patients to recount significant memories. Later, Freud realized that resistance was often the result of an unconscious *repression* of conflictual material; the repression led to an active exclusion of painful or anxiety-producing feelings from consciousness. Freud thought that repression was at the core of all symptom formation.

Psychic determinism is the concept that actions as adults can be understood as the end result of a chain of psychological events that have a well-defined cause and effect.

Abreaction is a process in which a memory of a traumatic experience is released from repression and brought into consciousness. As the patient is able to express the affect associated with the memory, the affect is discharged, and the symptoms disappear.

The concept of the unconscious was one of Freud's most important contributions—first used to define mental material not in the field of awareness and, later, to designate a topographic area of the mind where psychic material is not readily accessible to conscious awareness.

6.10 The answer is E (all) (*Synopsis VIII,* pages 210–211).
The Interpretation of Dreams, published in 1900, is generally considered to be one of Sigmund Freud's most important contributions to the field. The book includes much of the data derived from his clinical experience with patients and the insights gained from his self-analysis and free association to his own dreams. On the basis of that evidence, Freud concluded that *dreams are the conscious expression of an unconscious fantasy* or wish. Freud maintained that *dreams represent wish-fulfillment activities,* albeit disguised and distorted through such mechanisms as symbolism, displacement, and condensation. Dream analysis yields material that has been repressed by the ego's defensive activities. The dream, as it is consciously recalled and experienced, is termed the manifest dream, and its various elements are termed the manifest dream content; the unconscious thoughts and wishes that make up the core meaning of the dream are described as the latent dream content. *Latent dream content derives from the repressed part of the id* and includes such categories as nocturnal sensory stimuli and the day's residue. Nocturnal sensory stimuli, such as pain or thirst, are *sensory impressions that may play a role in initiating a dream.* Repressed id impulses are wishes that have their origin in oedipal and preoedipal phases of development. The day's residue comprises thoughts and ideas connected with the activities of the dreamer's waking life.

6.11 The answer is D (*Synopsis VIII,* pages 209–212).
Repression is a mechanism of defense employed by the ego to help mediate conflict between the ego, superego, and the id. It is not considered an autonomous ego function. Repression is defined as an unconscious defense mechanism in which unacceptable mental contents are banished or kept out of consciousness.

Autonomous ego functions are based on rudimentary apparatuses that are present at birth. They develop outside the conflict with the id. Heinz Hartmann included *perception,* intuition, comprehension, thinking, *language,* some phases of *motor development,* learning, and *intelligence* among the functions of that conflict-free sphere.

6.12 The answer is B (*Synopsis VIII,* pages 220–221).
The office worker is controlling guilt feelings by *rationalization,* a process that involves justifying unacceptable and irrational behavior by a plausible but invalid excuse. By turning from the victim role (the one who is fired) to the active role (firing himself), the worker is identifying with his boss, whom he views as an aggressor. *Identification with the aggressor is*

a process by which persons incorporate the mental image of someone who is a source of frustration. A primitive defense, it operates in the interest and service of the developing ego.

Denial is a defense mechanism in which the existence of unpleasant realities is disavowed. The person keeps out of conscious awareness any aspects of either internal or external reality that, if acknowledged, would produce anxiety.

Identification is a defense mechanism by which persons pattern themselves after another person; in the process, the self is permanently altered. *Undoing* is a defense mechanism by which a person symbolically acts out in reverse something unacceptable that has already been done or against which the ego must defend itself. A primitive defense mechanism, undoing is a form of magical expiatory action. Repetitive in nature, it is commonly observed in obsessive-compulsive disorder.

Projection is an unconscious defense mechanism in which a person attributes to another those generally unconscious ideas, thoughts, feelings, and impulses that are personally undesirable or unacceptable. Projection protects the person from anxiety arising from an inner conflict. By externalizing whatever is unacceptable, persons deal with it as a situation apart from themselves.

Intellectualization is a defense mechanism in which reasoning or logic is used in an attempt to avoid confrontation with an objectionable impulse and to defend against anxiety. It is also known as brooding compulsion and thinking compulsion.

The most common defense mechanisms are listed and defined in Table 6.1.

6.13 The answer is D (*Synopsis VIII,* pages 210–211).
According to Sigmund Freud, the manifest dream is the dream itself as reported by the dreamer. *The core meaning of the dream is not expressed by its manifest content.* However, in the process of analyzing the manifest dream, the psychoanalyst obtains information concerning the patient that would otherwise be inaccessible. That information behind the dream is termed the latent dream-thoughts. The technique by which the latent dream-thoughts are derived from the manifest dream is called dream interpretation. The process by which the latent dream-thoughts become the manifest dream in the dreamer's mental life is called the dream work.

Freud first became aware of the significance of dreams in therapy when he realized that, in the process of free association, his patients frequently described their dreams of the night before or of years past. He then discovered that the *dreams have a definite but disguised meaning.* He also found that encouraging his patients to free-associate to dream fragments was more productive than their associations to real-life events; free-associating to dreams facilitated the disclosure of the patients' unconscious memories and fantasies.

In *The Interpretation of Dreams*, Freud concluded that a dream, like a neurotic symptom, is the conscious expression of an unconscious fantasy or wish that is not readily accessible in waking life. Although *dreams are considered a normal manifestation of unconscious activity,* they also bear some resemblance to the pathological thoughts of psychotic patients in the waking state. *Dreams represent unconscious wishes* or thoughts disguised through symbolization and other distorting mechanisms.

Nocturnal sensory stimuli may be incorporated into the dream and can be interpreted through free association.

6.14 The answer is C (*Synopsis VIII,* pages 220–221).
A phobia is an abnormal fear reaction caused by a paralyzing conflict resulting from an increase of sexual excitation attached to an unconscious object. The fear is avoided by *displacement;* the conflict is displaced onto an object or situation outside the ego system. Displacement transfers an emotion from the original idea to which it was attached to another idea or object.

Projection is a defense mechanism in which thoughts, feelings, and impulses that are undesirable are transferred to another person. *Identification* is a defense mechanism by which persons pattern themselves after another person. *Undoing* is an unconscious defense mechanism by which a person symbolically acts out in reverse something unacceptable. *Reaction formation* is an unconscious defense mechanism in which a person develops a socialized attitude or interest that is the direct antithesis of some infantile wish.

6.15 The answer is A (*Synopsis VIII,* page 221).
George Vaillant's mature defenses (Table 6.1) include *altruism,* anticipation, asceticism, humor, sublimation, and suppression. In the 1970s he published his 30-year follow-up study of people who had gone to Harvard in the 1930s. He delineated the psychological characteristics he considered essential to mental health in this group, including descriptions of defense mechanisms he thought to be healthy and those he thought to be more psychopathological. Vaillant classified four types of defenses: (1) narcissistic defenses, which are characteristic of young children and psychotic adults; (2) immature defenses, which are characteristic of adolescents and are also seen in psychopathological states, such as depression; (3) neurotic defenses, which may be seen in adults under stress; and (4) mature defenses, which are characteristic of adult functioning. At times, some of the defensive categories overlap; for instance, neurotic defenses may be seen in normally healthy, mature adults. *Controlling, intellectualization,* and *rationalization* are characterized by Vaillant as among the neurotic defenses.

Altruism is a regard for the intents and needs of others. Controlling is the excessive attempt to manage or regulate events or objects in the environment in the interest of minimizing anxiety and solving internal conflicts. Intellectualization represents the attempt to avoid unacceptable feelings by escaping from emotions into a world of intellectual concepts and words. Rationalization is justification, making a thing appear reasonable that otherwise would be regarded as irrational.

6.16 The answer is A (*Synopsis VIII,* pages 219–222).
Obsessive-compulsive disorder comes about as a result of the separation of affects from ideas or behavior by the defense mechanisms of undoing and isolation, by regression to the anal-sadistic level, or by turning the impulses against the self. To defend against a painful idea in the unconscious, the person displaces the affect onto some other indirectly associated idea, one more tolerable that, in turn, becomes invested with an inordinate quantity of affect.

Anxiety disorders are disorders in which anxiety is the most prominent disturbance or in which the patients experience anxiety if they resist giving in to their symptoms. The anxiety

Table 6.1
Defense Mechanisms

Acting out. An action rather than a verbal response to an unconscious instinctual drive or impulse that brings about the temporary partial relief of inner tension. Relief is attained by reacting to a present situation as if it were the situation that originally gave rise to the drive or impulse. An immature defense.

Altruism. Regard for and dedication to the welfare of others. The term was originated by Auguste Comte (1798–1857), a French philosopher. In psychiatry the term is closely linked with ethics and morals. Sigmund Freud recognized altruism as the only basis for the development of community interest. Eugen Bleuler equated it with morality. A mature defense.

Anticipation. The act of dealing with, doing, foreseeing, or experiencing beforehand. Anticipation is characteristic of the ego and is necessary for the judgment and planning of suitable later action. Anticipation depends on reality testing—by trying in an active manner and in small doses what may happen to one passively and in unknown doses. The testing affords the possibility of judging reality and is an important factor in the development of the ability to tolerate tensions. A mature defense.

Asceticism. A mode of life characterized by rigor, self-denial, and mortification of the flesh. Asceticism is seen typically as a phase in puberty, when it indicates a fear of sexuality and a simultaneous defense against sexuality. Asceticism is also seen as an extreme type of masochistic character disorder, in which almost all activity is forbidden because it represents intolerable instinctual demands. In such cases the very act of mortifying may become a distorted expression of the blocked sexuality and may produce masochistic pleasure. Examples are eccentrics who devote their lives to the combating of some particular evil that unconsciously may represent their own instinctual demands. A mature defense.

Blocking. The involuntary cessation of thought processes or speech because of unconscious emotional factors. It is also known as thought deprivation. An immature defense.

Controlling. The excessive attempt to manage or regulate events or objects in the environment in the interest of minimizing anxiety and solving internal conflicts. A neurotic defense.

Denial. A mechanism in which the existence of unpleasant realities is disavowed. The mechanism keeps out of conscious awareness any aspects of external reality that, if acknowledged, would produce anxiety. A narcissistic defense.

Displacement. A mechanism by which the emotional component of an unacceptable idea or object is transferred to a more acceptable one. A neurotic defense.

Dissociation. A mechanism involving the segregation of any group of mental or behavioral processes from the rest of the person's psychic activity. It may entail the separation of an idea from its accompanying emotional tone, as seen in dissociative disorders. A neurotic defense.

Distortion. A misrepresentation of reality. It is based on unconsciously determined motives. A narcissistic defense.

Externalization. A general term, correlative to internalization, for the tendency to perceive in the external world and in external objects components of one's own personality, including instinctual impulses, conflicts, moods, attitudes, and styles of thinking. It is a more general term than projection, which is defined by its derivation, form, and correlation with specific introjects. A neurotic defense.

Humor. The overt expression of feelings without personal discomfort or immobilization and without unpleasant effects on others. Humor allows one to bear, yet focus on, what is too terrible to be borne, in contrast to wit, which always involves distraction or displacement away from the affective issues. A mature defense.

Hypochondriasis. An exaggerated concern about one's physical health. The concern is not based on real organic pathology. An immature defense.

Identification. A mechanism by which one patterns oneself after another person. In the process, the self may be permanently altered. An immature defense.

Identification with the aggressor. A process by which one incorporates within oneself the mental image of a person who represents a source of frustration. The classic example of the defense occurs toward the end of the oedipal stage, when a boy, whose main source of love and gratification is his mother, identifies with his father. The father represents the source of frustration, being the powerful rival for the mother; the child cannot master or run away from his father, so he is obliged to identify with his father. An immature defense.

Incorporation. A mechanism in which the psychic representation of another person or aspects of another person are assimilated into oneself through a figurative process of symbolic oral ingestion. It represents a special form of introjection and is the earliest mechanism of identification.

Inhibition. The depression or arrest of a function; suppression or diminution of outgoing influences from a reflex center. The sexual impulse, for example, may be inhibited because of psychological repression. A neurotic defense.

Intellectualization. A mechanism in which reasoning or logic is used in an attempt to avoid confrontation with an objectionable impulse and thus defends against anxiety. It is also known as brooding compulsion and thinking compulsion. A neurotic defense.

Introjection. The unconscious, symbolic internalization of a psychic representation of a hated or loved external object with the goal of establishing closeness to the object and its constant presence. In the case of a loved object, anxiety consequent to separation or tension arising out of ambivalence toward the object is diminished; in the case of a feared or hated object, internalization of its malicious or aggressive characteristics serves to avoid anxiety by symbolically putting those characteristics under one's own control. An immature defense.

Isolation. In psychoanalysis a mechanism involving the separation of an idea or memory from its attached feeling tone. Unacceptable ideational content is thereby rendered free of its disturbing or unpleasant emotional charge. A neurotic defense.

Passive-aggressive behavior. The showing of aggressive feelings in passive ways, such as through obstructionism, pouting, and stubbornness. An immature defense.

Primitive idealization. Viewing external objects as either all good or all bad and as unrealistically endowed with great power. Most commonly, the all-good object is seen as omnipotent or ideal, and the badness in the all-bad object is greatly inflated. A narcissistic defense.

Table 6.1 *(continued)*

Projection. An unconscious mechanism in which one attributes to another the idea, thoughts, feelings, and impulses that are unacceptable to oneself. Projection protects a person from anxiety arising from an inner conflict. By externalizing whatever is unacceptable, one deals with it as a situation apart from oneself. A narcissistic and immature defense.

Projective identification. Depositing unwanted aspects of the self into another person and feeling at one with the object of the projection. The extruded aspects are modified by and recovered from the recipient. The defense allows one to distance and make oneself understood by exerting pressure on another person to experience feelings similar to one's own. A narcissistic defense.

Rationalization. A mechanism in which irrational or unacceptable behavior, motives, or feelings are logically justified or made consciously tolerable by plausible means. A neurotic defense.

Reaction formation. An unconscious defense mechanism in which a person develops a socialized attitude or interest that is the direct antithesis of some infantile wish or impulse in the unconscious. One of the earliest and most stable defense mechanisms, it is closely related to repression; both are defenses against impulses or urges that are unacceptable to the ego. A neurotic defense.

Regression. A mechanism in which a person undergoes a partial or total return to early patterns of adaptation. Regression is observed in many psychiatric conditions, particularly schizophrenia. An immature defense.

Repression. A mechanism in which unacceptable mental contents are banished or kept out of consciousness. A term introduced by Sigmund Freud, it is important in both normal psychological development and in neurotic and psychotic symptom formation. Freud recognized two kinds of repression: (1) repression proper—the repressed material was once in the conscious domain, (2) primal repression—the repressed material was never in the conscious realm. A neurotic defense.

Schizoid fantasy. The tendency to use fantasy and to indulge in autistic retreat for the purpose of conflict resolution and gratification. An immature defense.

Sexualization. The endowing of an object or function with sexual significance that it did not previously have or that it possesses to a small degree; it is used to ward off anxieties connected with prohibitive impulses. A neurotic defense.

Somatization. The defense conversion of psychic derivatives into bodily symptoms; a tendency to react with somatic rather than psychic manifestations. Infantile somatic responses are replaced by thought and affect during development (desomatization); regression to early somatic forms of response (resomatization) may result from unresolved conflicts and may play an important role in psychological reactions. An immature defense.

Splitting. Dividing external objects into all good and all bad, accompanied by the abrupt shifting of an object from one extreme category to the other. Sudden and complete reversals of feelings and conceptualizations about a person may occur. The extreme repetitive oscillation between contradictory self-concepts is another manifestation of the mechanism. A narcissistic defense.

Sublimation. A mechanism in which the energy associated with unacceptable impulses or drives is diverted into personally and socially acceptable channels. Unlike other defense mechanisms, sublimation offers some minimal gratification of the instinctual drive or impulse. A mature defense.

Substitution. A mechanism in which a person replaces an unacceptable wish, drive, emotion, or goal with one that is acceptable. A neurotic defense.

Suppression. A conscious act of controlling and inhibiting an unacceptable impulse, emotion, or idea. Suppression is differentiated from repression in that repression is an unconscious process. A mature defense.

Symbolization. A mechanism by which one idea or object comes to stand for another because of some common aspect or quality in both. Symbolization is based on similarity and association. The symbols formed protect the person from the anxiety that may be attached to the original idea or object. A mature defense.

Turning against the self. Changing an unacceptable impulse aimed at others by redirecting it against oneself. An immature defense.

Undoing. A mechanism by which a person symbolically acts out in reverse something unacceptable that has already been done or against which the ego must defend itself. A primitive defense mechanism, undoing is a form of magical action. Repetitive in nature, it is commonly observed in persons with obsessive-compulsive disorder. A neurotic defense.

Table compiled from Sigmund Freud, Anna Freud, E. Semrad, W. W. Meissner, and George Vaillant. Narcissistic defenses: used by children and psychotics; immature defenses: used by adolescents and in depressive disorders and obsessive-compulsive disorder; neurotic defenses: used by adults under stress and in obsessive-compulsive disorder and somatoform disorders; mature defenses: used by normal adults.

disorders include phobias, obsessive-compulsive disorder, posttraumatic stress disorder, and panic disorder.

Pain disorder is a disorder characterized by the complaint of pain. The pain may vary with intensity and duration and may range from a slight disturbance of the patient's social or occupational functioning to total incapacity and the need for hospitalization.

Dissociative disorders are characterized by a sudden, temporary alteration in consciousness, identity, or motor behavior. The dissociative disorders include dissociative amnesia, dissociative fugue, dissociative identity disorder, and depersonalization disorder.

Dysthymic disorder is a mood disorder characterized by depression.

6.17 The answer is B (*Synopsis VIII,* page 229).

Psychobiology, a term introduced by Adolf Meyer, emphasizes the importance of *biographical study and common-sense understanding of patients.* The immediate goal is to identify motives or indications for the psychiatric examination. In identifying important details of the patient's life history through a biographical study, the clinician records the most obvious related personality items, factors, and reactions. In addition, the clinician should study the patient's physical, neurological, genetic, and social status variables and the correlations between those variables and personality factors. The clinician should also formulate a differential diagnosis and a therapeutic schedule for each case.

Analysis of the ego through the interpretation of defense mechanisms is a concept used in psychoanalysis. A *primary understanding of the biological and biochemical origins and treatment of mental illness,* the *emphasis on genetic factors in mental illness, and the use of drugs in psychiatry* are concepts used in psychopharmacology. *Psychological factors affecting physical illness* are concerns in psychosomatic medicine.

6.18 The answer is D (*Synopsis VIII,* pages 226–227).
Alienation from the self is a concept developed by *Karen Horney* to describe the various neurotic mechanisms—such as distorted self-image, self-hatred, and estrangement of one's own feelings—that combine to lead to alienation. Such alienation of one's own feelings is characteristic of obsessive-compulsive disorder. Certain organs and body areas and even the entire body are often perceived as if they did not belong to the person or as if they were different from the usual. Some manifestations are objectively observable; others are subjective and subtle.

Sigmund Freud developed psychoanalysis; *Harry Stack Sullivan* conceptualized the interpersonal theory of psychiatry; *Eric Berne* developed transactional analysis; and *Alfred Adler* is best known for his concept of the inferiority complex.

6.19 The answer is A (*Synopsis VIII,* page 229).
Adolf Meyer used the term ''habit training'' to explain the process of therapy by which the main goal is to aid patients' adjustment by helping them to modify unhealthy adaptations. In the process of habit trainings, the psychiatrist always emphasizes patients' current life situations by using a variety of techniques, such as guidance, suggestion, reeducation, and direction.

Carl Gustav Jung developed the school known as analytic psychology. *Otto Rank* focused on the analytic aspects of what he called the birth trauma. *B. F. Skinner* and *Joseph Wolpe* are known for their work in learning theory and behavior therapy, respectively.

6.20 The answer is B (*Synopsis VIII,* pages 232–233).
Harry Stack Sullivan's self-system concerns the concept of the *personality.* The self-system reflects maternal and paternal attitudes and any accumulated sets of experiences that begin in infancy and continue for a long time.

The *unconscious* is the topographic division of the mind in which the psychic material is not readily accessible to conscious awareness by ordinary means. Its existence may be manifested in symptom formation, in dreams, or under the influence of drugs.

The *libido* is the psychic energy associated with the sexual drive or life instinct. *Defense mechanisms* are unconscious processes acting to relieve conflict and anxiety arising from one's impulses and drives.

The *Oedipus complex* is the constellation of feelings, impulses, and conflicts in the developing child that concern sexual impulses and attraction toward the opposite-sex parent and aggressive, hostile, or envious feelings toward the same-sex parent. Real or fantasied threats from the same-sex parent result in the repression of those feelings. The development of the Oedipus complex coincides with the phallic phase of psychosexual development. One of Freud's most important concepts, the term was originally applied only to boys. The female analogue of the Oedipus complex is called the Electra complex, a term attributed to Carl Jung used to describe unresolved developmental conflicts influencing a woman's relationships with men.

6.21 The answer is D (*Synopsis VIII,* pages 233–234).
Erik Erikson accepted Sigmund Freud's theory of infantile sexuality, but Erikson also saw the developmental potential of all stages of life. In each of Erikson's eight stages, a maturational crisis arises. During *middle adulthood,* each person has the opportunity to become generative, productive through contributions to society, or to become stagnant, preoccupied only with one's own well-being. Erikson used the terms ''basic trust versus basic mistrust,'' ''autonomy versus shame and doubt,'' ''initiative versus guilt,'' and ''industry versus inferiority'' to describe conflicts occurring in *childhood;* the term ''identity versus role diffusion'' to describe the conflict occurring during *adolescence;* ''intimacy versus isolation'' to describe the conflict occurring in *young adulthood;* and ''integrity versus despair'' to describe the conflict occurring in *late adulthood.* Erikson's stages are outlined in Table 6.2.

6.22 The answer is A (*Synopsis VIII,* pages 233–234).
According to Erik Erikson, the development of what he termed basic *trust* is a result of consistent and affectionate maternal behavior during infancy. The infant is extremely sensitive to the mother; both the overt and the subtle aspects of maternal behavior profoundly affect the infant. The infant's dependence on others is total, a fact that has important psychological effects.

Autonomy is children's ability to control their muscles, their impulses, themselves, and ultimately their environment. *Initiative* provides the freedom and the opportunity for children to begin motor-play gymnastics and intellectual questioning of those around them. During the period of *industry,* children learn to reason deductively; they are concerned with the details of how things are made, how they work, and what they do. *Identity* is a sense of who one is, where one has been, and where one is going.

6.23 The answer is D (*Synopsis VIII,* page 236).
The stage of industry versus inferiority, which runs from ages 6 to 11, is characterized by *confidence in one's ability to use adult materials.* During this period of latency, the child is learning, waiting, and practicing to be a provider.

Eagerness and curiosity are characteristics of the stage of initiative versus guilt. In the stage of intimacy versus isolation, young adults either become *self-indulgent* and self-interested or share themselves in intense, long-term relationships. In the stage of initiative versus guilt, children develop a division between their *expanded desires* and their exuberance at unlimited growth. *Preoccupation with one's appearance* is a characteristic of the stage of identity versus role diffusion.

6.24 The answer is E (all) (*Synopsis VIII,* pages 233–239).
The stage of generativity versus stagnation spans the middle years of life. Generativity is characterized by *interests outside the home,* by *establishing and guiding the oncoming generation,* and by *bettering society.* Even a childless couple or person can be generative. However, when adults live only to sat-

Table 6.2
Erik Erikson's Stages of the Life Cycle

Stage 1. Basic Trust versus Basic Mistrust
(birth to about 1 year)
- Corresponds to the oral psychosexual stage
- Trust is shown by ease of feeding, depth of sleep, bowel relaxation
- Depends on consistency and sameness of experiences provided by caretaker or outerprovider
- Second six months: teething and biting move the infant from getting to taking
- Weaning leads to nostalgia for the lost paradise
- If basic trust is strong, the child maintains a hopeful attitude and develops self-confidence
- Oral zone is associated with the mode of being satisfied

Stage 2. Autonomy versus Shame and Doubt
(about 1 to 3 years)
- Corresponds to the muscular-anal stage
- Biologically includes learning to walk, feed self, talk
- Need for outer control and firmness of caretaker before development of autonomy
- Shame occurs when the child is overtly self-conscious through negative exposure and punishment
- Self-doubt can evolve if the parents overtly shame the child, e.g., about elimination
- Anal zone is associated with the mode of holding on and letting go.

Stage 3. Initiative versus Guilt
(3 to 5 years)
- Corresponds to the phallic psychosexual stage
- Initiative arises in relation to tasks for the sake of activity, both motor and intellectual
- Guilt may arise over goals contemplated (especially aggressive goals)
- Desire to mimic adult world; involvement in oedipal struggle leads to resolution through social role identification
- Sibling rivalry is frequent
- Phallic zone is associated with the mode of competition and aggression

Stage 4. Industry versus Inferiority
(6 to 11 years)
- Corresponds to the latency psychosexual stage
- Child is busy building, creating, accomplishing
- Child receives systematic instruction and fundamentals of technology
- Danger of a sense of inadequacy and inferiority if the child despairs of tools, skills, and status among peers
- Socially decisive age
- No dominant zone or mode

Stage 5. Identity versus Role Diffusion
(11 years through the end of adolescence)
- Struggle to develop ego identity (sense of inner sameness and continuity)
- Preoccupation with appearance, hero worship, ideology
- Group identity (with peers) develops
- Danger of role confusion, doubts about sexual and vocational identity
- Psychosexual moratorium, stage between morality learned by the child and the ethics developed by the adult
- No dominant zone or mode

Stage 6. Intimacy versus Isolation
(21 to 40 years)
- Tasks are to love and to work
- Intimacy is characterized by self-abandonment, mutuality of sexual orgasm, intense friendship, attachments that are lifelong
- Isolation is marked by separation from others and by the view that others are dangerous
- General sense of productivity
- No dominant zone or mode

Stage 7. Generativity versus Stagnation
(40 to 65 years)
- Generativity includes raising children, guiding new generation, creativity, altruism
- Stagnation is not prevented by having a child; the parent must provide nurturance and love
- Self-concern, isolation, and the absence of intimacy are characteristic of stagnation
- No dominant zone or mode

Stage 8. Integrity versus Despair
(over 65 years)
- Integrity is a sense of satisfaction that life has been productive and worthwhile
- Despair is a loss of hope that produces misanthropy and disgust
- Persons in the state of despair are fearful of death
- An acceptance of one's place in the life cycle is characteristic of integrity

isfy their day-to-day personal needs and to acquire comforts and entertainment for themselves, they become immersed in *self-absorption.*

6.25 The answer is A (*Synopsis VIII,* pages 217–218).
According to Sigmund Freud's structural theory of the mind, the psychic apparatus is divided into three provinces: *id, ego, and superego.* The id is the locus of the instinctual drives. It is under the domination of the primary process; therefore, it operates in accordance with the pleasure principle, without regard for reality. The ego is a more coherent organization whose task it is to avoid unpleasure and pain by opposing or regulating the discharge of instinctual drives to conform with the demands of the external world. In addition, the discharge of id impulses is opposed or regulated by the superego, which contains the internalized moral values and influence of the parental images.

The *unconscious* is the topographical division of the mind in which the psychic material is not readily accessible to conscious awareness by ordinary means. Its existence may be manifested in symptom formation, in dreams, or under the influence of psychoactive substances. The theories about the conscious, preconscious, and unconscious divisions of the psychiatric apparatus predated by many years Freud's structural hypotheses. The conscious, according to Freud, refers to that portion of mental functioning within the realm of awareness at all times. The preconscious includes all mental contents that are not in immediate awareness but that can be consciously recalled with effort.

6.26 The answer is D (*Synopsis VIII,* pages 207–223).
Sigmund Freud's concept of *sexual resemblance* does not explain why a man falls in love with a particular type of woman. Sexual resemblance pertains to homosexual love.

A man may choose a particular type of woman in adult life because *she resembles the man's idealized self-image* or his fantasied self-image or because *she resembles someone who took care of him when he was a boy.* Persons who have an intense degree of self-love, especially certain beautiful women, have, according to Freud, an appeal over and above their esthetic attraction. Such women *provide narcissistic gratification* that their lovers were forced to give up in the process of turning toward object love (love for another).

6.27 The answer is C (*Synopsis VIII,* pages 217–218).
In *The Ego and the Id,* published in 1923, Sigmund Freud developed the tripartite structural model of ego, id, and superego. This model of the psychic apparatus, which is the cornerstone of ego psychology, represented a transition for Freud from his topographical model of the mind (conscious, preconscious, and unconscious). The three provinces of id, ego, and superego are distinguished by their varying functions.

The superego's activities occur unconsciously to a large extent. It establishes and maintains the person's moral conscience in the complex system of ideals and values internalized from one's parents. Freud viewed the superego as the heir to the Oedipus complex. In other words, the child internalizes the parental values and standards around the age of 5 or 6 years. The superego then serves as an agency that provides ongoing scrutiny of the person's behavior, thoughts, and feelings. It makes comparisons with expected standards of behavior and offers approval or disapproval.

The superego does not control the delay and the modulation of drive expression. The delay and the modulation of drive expression is achieved by the ego. *The ego, not the superego, is the executive organ of the psyche,* through the mechanisms of defense available to it and through mobility, perception, and contact with reality. According to Freud, the ego spans all three topographical dimension of conscious, preconscious, and unconscious. Logical and abstract thinking and verbal expression are associated with its conscious and preconscious functions. Defense mechanisms reside in its unconscious domain.

Freud also believed that the ego brings influences from the external world to bear on the id, and the ego simultaneously substitutes the reality principle for the pleasure principle. Thus, in Freud's view, both *the reality principle and the pleasure principle are aspects of ego functioning, not id functioning.* The id, according to Freud, harbors the innate, biological, instinctual drives; it is the source of libido and follows the pleasure principle. Secondary process is the form of thinking that is logical, organized, and reality-oriented.

6.28 The answer is B (*Synopsis VIII,* page 227).
According to Carl Gustav Jung's psychoanalytic school, known as analytical psychology, *archetypes contribute to complexes.* That occurs because complexes, which are feeling-toned ideas, develop as a result of personal experiences interacting with archetypal imagery. Archetypes are representational images and confirmations that have universal meanings. Archetypal figures exist for the mother, the father, the child, and the hero, among others. Thus, a mother complex is determined not only by the mother-child interaction but also by the conflict between archetypal expectations and actual experiences with the real woman who functions in a motherly role.

Archetypes are a part of Jung's concept of the collective unconscious, which consists of all humankind's common and shared mythological and symbolic past. *The collective unconscious is not a collection of the impulses of the id and the ego.*

The persona is the mask covering the personality; it is what the person presents to the outside world. The persona may become fixed, so that the real person is hidden even from the person. *The male part of the self is called the animus, not the persona.*

The aim of Jungian treatment is to bring about an adequate adaptation to reality, which involves fulfilling one's creative potentialities. The ultimate goal is to achieve *individuation, a process that continues throughout life* in which persons develop unique senses of their own identities. This developmental process may lead persons down new paths that may differ from their previous directions in life.

In analytical psychology, *an emphasis is not placed on infantile sexuality.*

6.29 The answer is C (*Synopsis VIII,* pages 234–237).
Erik Erikson described eight stages of the life cycle (Table 6.2). The stages are marked by one or more internal crises, which are defined as turning points—periods when the person is in a state of increased vulnerability. Ideally, the crisis is mastered successfully, and the person gains strength and is able to move on to the next stage.

In Erikson's stage of autonomy versus shame and doubt (about 1 to 3 years), autonomy concerns children's sense of mastery over themselves and over their drives and impulses. Toddlers gain a sense of their separateness from others. "I," "you," "me," and "mine" are common words used by children during that period. Children have a choice of holding on or letting go, of being cooperative or stubborn. *The stage of autonomy versus shame and doubt corresponds with Freud's anal stage* of development. For Erikson, it is the time for the child either to retain feces (holding in) or to eliminate feces (letting go); both behaviors have an effect on the mother.

The stage of initiative versus guilt (3 to 5 years), not *the stage of industry versus inferiority, corresponds to Freud's phallic-oedipal stage.* The stage of industry versus inferiority (6 to 11 years) *corresponds to Freud's latency period.* Industry, the ability to work and acquire adult skills, is the keynote of the stage. Children learn that they are able to make things and, most important, able to master and complete a task. A sense of inadequacy and inferiority, the potential negative outcome of the stage, results from several sources: children may be discriminated against in school; children may be told that they are inferior; children may be overprotected at home or excessively dependent on the emotional support of their families; children may compare themselves unfavorably with the same-sex parent. Good teachers and good parents who encourage children to value diligence and productivity and to persevere in difficult enterprises are bulwarks against a sense of inferiority.

The stage of identity versus role diffusion (11 years through the end of adolescence) *corresponds to Freud's phallic stage, not the latency stage.* According to Erikson, developing a sense of identity is the main task of the period, which coincides with puberty and adolescence. Identity is defined as the characteristics that establish who persons are and where they are going. Healthy identity is built on success in passing through the earlier stages. How successful the adolescents have been in attaining trust, autonomy, initiative, and industry has much to do with developing a sense of identity. Identifying with either healthy parents or parent surrogates facilitates the process. Failure to negotiate the stage leaves the adolescent without a solid identity; the person suffers from role diffusion or identity confusion, characterized by not having a sense of self and by confusion about one's place in the world.

The stage of intimacy versus isolation (21 to 40 years) extends from late adolescence through early middle age. Erikson pointed out that an important psychosocial conflict can arise during the stage; as in previous stages, success or failure depends on how well the groundwork has been laid in earlier periods and on how the young adult interacts with the environment. Erikson quoted Freud's view that a normal person must be able to love and work *(lieben und arbeiten).* Similarly, Erikson believes that meaningful work, procreation, and recreation within a loving relationship represents utopia.

The stage of generativity versus stagnation (40 to 65 years) occurs during the decades that span the middle years of life. *Generativity can occur even if a person has not had or raised a child.* Generativity also includes a vital interest outside the home in establishing and guiding the oncoming generation or in improving society. Childless people can be generative if they develop a sense of altruism and creativity. Most persons, if able, want to continue their personalities and energies in the production and care of offspring. Wanting or having children, however, does not ensure generativity. Parents need to have achieved successful identities themselves to be truly generative. Stagnation is a barren state. The inability to transcend the lack of creativity is dangerous because the person is not able to accept the eventuality of not being and the idea that death is inescapably a part of life.

The stage of integrity versus despair occurs in old age—not in late adolescence through the early middle years. It is Erikson's eighth stage of the life cycle. The stage (over 65 years) is described as the conflict between the sense of satisfaction that one feels in reflecting on a life productively lived and the sense that life has had little purpose or meaning. Integrity allows for an acceptance of one's place in the life cycle and of the knowledge that one's life is one's own responsibility. There is an acceptance of who one's parents are or were and an understanding of how they lived their lives.

Without the conviction that one's life has been meaningful and that one has made a contribution, either by producing happy children or by giving to the next generation, the elderly person fears death and has a sense of despair or disgust.

6.30 The answer is E (all) (*Synopsis VIII,* pages 210–212). Ordinarily, the repressed ideas and affects of the unconscious *are inaccessible to consciousness* because of the censorship or repression imposed by the preconscious. Those repressed elements may attain the level of consciousness when the censor is overpowered (as in neurotic symptom formation), relaxes (as in dream states), or is fooled (as by jokes).

The unconscious is associated with the form of mental activity that Freud called the primary process or *primary process thinking.* Characteristically seen in infancy and dreams, the primary process is marked by primitive, prelogical thinking and by the tendency to seek immediate discharge and gratification of instinctual demands. Consequently, the unconscious is also *closely related to the pleasure principle,* the principle by which the id seeks immediate tension reduction by direct or fantasied gratification. Similarly, the id also contains the mental representatives and derivatives of the *instinctual drives,* particularly those of the sexual instinct.

6.31 The answer is A (*Synopsis VIII,* page 212).
The unconscious system is the dynamic one; its mental contents and processes are kept out of conscious awareness through the force of censorship or repression. Key features of the unconscious include the following:

1. The unconscious is closely related to instinctual drives, characterized by Freud as sexual and self-preservative in nature.
2. *The content of the unconscious is limited to wishes that are seeking fulfillment.*
3. *The unconscious system is characterized by primary process thinking,* not secondary process thinking, which is associated with the preconscious. Primary process thinking is governed by the pleasure principle and *disregards logical connections, represents wishes as fulfillments, and permits contradictory ideas to exist simultaneously.*
4. *Memories in the unconscious have been divorced from their connections with verbal symbols.*
5. *The contents of the unconscious can become conscious only by passing through the preconscious,* where censors are empowered, allowing the elements to enter into consciousness.

Answers 6.32–6.36

6.32 The answer is B (*Synopsis VIII,* page 220).

6.33 The answer is D (*Synopsis VIII,* page 221).

6.34 The answer is A (*Synopsis VIII,* page 221).

6.35 The answer is C (*Synopsis VIII,* page 220).

6.36 The answer is E (*Synopsis VIII,* page 221).
Projection is an unconscious defense mechanism in which a person attributes to another those generally unconscious ideas, thoughts, feelings, and impulses that are personally undesirable or unacceptable. Projection protects the person from anxiety arising from an inner conflict. By externalizing whatever is unacceptable, persons deal with it as a situation apart from themselves.

Reaction formation is an unconscious defense mechanism in which a person develops a socialized attitude or interest that is the direct antithesis of some infantile wish or impulse that the person harbors either consciously or unconsciously. One of the earliest and most unstable defense mechanisms, it is closely related to repression; both are defenses against impulses or urges that are unacceptable to the ego.

Rationalization is an unconscious defense mechanism in which irrational or unacceptable behavior, motives, or feelings are logically justified or made consciously tolerable by plausible means. Ernest Jones introduced the term.

Denial is a defense mechanism in which the existence of unpleasant realities is disavowed. The term refers to a keeping out of conscious awareness any aspects of either internal or external reality that, if acknowledged, would produce anxiety.

Sublimation is an unconscious defense mechanism in which the energy associated with unacceptable impulses or drives is diverted into personally and socially acceptable channels. Unlike other defense mechanisms, sublimation offers some minimal gratification of the instinctual drive or impulse.

Answers 6.37–6.41

6.37 The answer is B (*Synopsis VIII,* page 218).

6.38 The answer is D (*Synopsis VIII,* page 228).

6.39 The answer is C (*Synopsis VIII,* pages 226–227).

6.40 The answer is A (*Synopsis VIII,* page 224).

6.41 The answer is E (*Synopsis VIII,* page 228).
Donald Winnicott (1897–1971) was an influential contributor to object relations theory. He focused on the conditions that make it possible for a child to develop awareness as a separate person. One of the conditions is the provision of an environment termed "good-enough mothering." Good-enough mothering enables the child to be nurtured in a nonimpinging environment that permits the emergence of the true self. Winnicott *introduced the concept of the transitional object,* something that helps the child gradually shift from subjectivity to external reality. Such a possession, usually blankets or a soft toy, exists in an intermediate realm as a substitute for the mother and as one of the first objects a child begins to recognize as separate from the self.

Melanie Klein (1882–1960) modified psychoanalytic theory, particularly in its application to infants and very young children. In contrast to orthodox psychoanalytic theory, which postulates the development of the superego during the fourth year of life, Klein's theory maintains that a primitive superego is formed during the first and second years. Klein further believed that aggressive, rather than sexual, drives are preeminent during the earliest stages of development. She deviated most sharply from classic psychoanalytic theory in her formulations concerning the Oedipus complex. She *believed that oedipal strivings are experienced during the first year of life,* as opposed to the classic formulation of its occurring between the ages of 3 and 5. She also believed that, *during the first year, gratifying experiences with the good breast reinforce basic trust* and that frustrating experiences can lead to a depressive position.

Karen Horney (1885–1952) was an American psychiatrist who ascribed great importance to the influence of sociocultural factors on individual development. She raised questions about the existence of immutable instinctual drives and developmental phases or sexual conflict as the root of neurosis while recognizing the importance of sexual drives. Rather than focusing on such concepts as the Oedipus complex, Horney *emphasized cultural factors and disturbances in interpersonal and intrapsychic development* as the cause of neuroses in general.

Franz Alexander (1891–1964) founded the Chicago Institute for Psychoanalysis. He *introduced the concept of the corrective emotional experience.* The therapist, who is supportive, enables the patient to master past traumas and to modify the effects of those traumas. Alexander was also a major influence in the field of psychosomatic medicine.

Heinz Kohut (1913–1981) *expanded Sigmund Freud's concept of narcissism.* In *The Analysis of the Self* (1971), Kohut wrote about a large group of patients suffering from narcissistic personality disorder whom he believed to be analyzable but who did not develop typical transference neuroses in the classic sense. The conflict involves the relation between the self and archaic narcissistic objects. Those objects are the grandiose self and the idealized parent image, the reactivations of which constitute a threat to the patient's sense of integrity. Kohut's *theories are known as self psychology.*

Answers 6.42–6.46

6.42 The answer is D (*Synopsis VIII,* page 227).

6.43 The answer is A (*Synopsis VIII,* page 227).

6.44 The answer is B (*Synopsis VIII,* page 227).

6.45 The answer is C (*Synopsis VIII,* page 227).

6.46 The answer is E (*Synopsis VIII,* page 227).
With the term *persona,* Carl Gustav Jung denoted the disguised or masked attitude assumed by a person, in contrast to the deeply rooted personality components. Such persons put on a mask, corresponding to their conscious intentions, that makes up the *face presented to the outside world.* Through their identification with the persons, they deceive other people and often themselves as to their real character.

The *shadow* appears in dreams as *another person of the same sex as the dreamer.* According to Jung, one sees much in another person that does not belong to one's conscious psychology but that comes out from one's unconscious.

In Jung's terminology, anima and animus are archetypal representations of potentials that have not yet entered conscious awareness or become personalized. *Anima* is *a man's undeveloped femininity. Animus* is *a women's undeveloped masculinity.* Those concepts are universal basic human drives from which both conscious and unconscious individual qualities develop. Usually, they appear as unconscious images of persons of the opposite sex.

The *collective unconscious* is defined as the psychic contents outside the realm of awareness that are common to humankind in general. Jung, who introduced the term, believed that the collective unconscious is inherited and derived from the collective experience of the species. It transcends cultural differences and explains the analogy between ancient *mythological ideas and primitive projections* observed in some patients who have never been exposed to those ideas.

Answers 6.47–6.51

6.47 The answer is D (*Synopsis VIII,* page 229).

6.48 The answer is B (*Synopsis VIII,* page 229).

6.49 The answer is A (*Synopsis VIII,* pages 232–233).

6.50 The answer is C (*Synopsis VIII,* pages 230–231).

6.51 The answer is E (*Synopsis VIII,* page 230).
Kurt Lewin (1890–1947) adapted the field approach from physics into a concept called field theory. A field is the totality of coexisting parts that are mutually interdependent. Applying field theory to groups, Lewin coined the term *"group dynamics"* and believed that a group is greater than the sum of its parts.

Abraham Maslow (1908–1970) was a developer of the self-actualization theory, which focuses on the need to understand the totality of the person. A *peak experience,* according to that school of thought, is an episodic, brief occurrence in which the person suddenly experiences a powerful transcendental state of consciousness. The powerful experience occurs most often in psychologically healthy persons.

Harry Stack Sullivan (1892–1949) made basic contributions to psychodynamic theory with his emphasis on the cultural matrix of personality development. Sullivan defined psychiatry as the study of interpersonal relationships that are manifest in the observable behavior of persons. Those relationships can be observed inside the therapeutic situation; the process is greatly enhanced when the therapist is one of the participants. The transaction is then between the therapist, who is a *participant observer,* and a patient, whose life is disturbed or disordered.

Wilhelm Reich's (1897–1957) major contributions to psychoanalysis were in the areas of *character formation and character types.* Reich placed special emphasis on the influence of social forces in determining character structure, particularly on their repressive and inhibiting effects. Reich's basic concept was that character is a defensive structure, an armoring of the ego against instinctual forces within and the world without. It is the person's characteristic manner of dealing with threats. Reich described four major character types: hysterical, compulsive, narcissistic, and masochistic.

The evolution of *Gestalt therapy* is closely associated with the work of *Frederick S. Perls* (1893–1970), a European émigré trained in the psychoanalytic tradition. Although acknowledging its influences, Perls largely rejected the tenets of psychoanalysis and founded his own school of Gestalt therapy, borrowing the name from Gestalt theory. Gestalt theory proposes that the natural course of the biological and psychological development of the organism entails a full awareness of physical sensations and psychological needs. Perls believed that, as any form of self-control interferes with healthy functioning, modern civilization inevitably produces neurotic people; thus, the task of the therapist is to instruct the patient in discovering and experiencing the feelings and the needs repressed by society's demands.

Answers 6.52–6.56

6.52 The answer is A (*Synopsis VIII,* page 234).

6.53 The answer is C (*Synopsis VIII,* pages 235–236).

6.54 The answer is E (*Synopsis VIII,* page 236).

6.55 The answer is D (*Synopsis VIII,* page 237).

6.56 The answer is B (*Synopsis VIII,* page 237).
The first of Erik Erikson's developmental stages (*infancy*—birth to 1 year) is characterized by the first psychosocial crisis the infant must face, that of *basic trust versus basis mistrust.* The crisis takes place in the context of the intimate relationship between the infant and its mother. The infant's primary orientation to reality is erotic and centers on the mouth. The successful resolution of the stage includes a disposition to trust others, a basic trust in oneself, a capacity to entrust oneself, and a sense of self-confidence.

During *early childhood* (ages 3 to 5 years) the crisis addressed by the child *is initiative versus guilt.* As the child struggles to resolve the oedipal struggle, guilt may grow because of aggressive thoughts or wishes. Initiative arises as the child begins to desire to mimic the adult world and as the child finds enjoyment in productive activity.

The stage of *puberty and adolescence* (age 11 years through the end of adolescence) is characterized by *identity versus role diffusion,* during which the adolescent must begin to establish a future role in adult society. During that psychosocial crisis, the adolescent is peculiarly vulnerable to social and cultural influences.

Early adulthood (21 to 40 years) is characterized by *intimacy versus isolation.* The crisis is characterized by the need to establish the capacity to relate intimately and meaningfully with others in mutually satisfying and productive interactions. The failure to achieve a successful resolution of that crisis results in a sense of personal isolation. *Late adulthood* (65 and older) is characterized by *integrity versus despair.* The crisis implies and depends on the successful resolution of all the preceding crises of psychosocial growth. It entails the acceptance of oneself and of all the aspects of life and the integration of their elements into a stable pattern of living. The failure to achieve ego integration often results in a kind of despair and an unconscious fear of death. The person who fails that crisis lives in basic self-contempt.

A further explanation of Erikson's stages appears in Table 6.2.

6.57 The answers are: 1, A; 2, C; 3, B; 4, A; and 5, B (*Synopsis VIII,* pages 217–218).
The three provinces of Freud's structural model—id, ego, and superego—are distinguished by their different functions in the psychic apparatus. *Id* refers to a reservoir of unorganized instinctual drives. Operating under the domination of the primary process, the id lacks the capacity to delay or modify the instinctual drives with which the infant is born. *Ego* is the executive organ of the psyche and functions to delay and modify drive expression through defense mechanisms. Defense mechanisms reside in the unconscious domain of the ego, whereas logical and abstract thinking and verbal expression are associated with conscious and preconscious functions of the ego. *Superego* establishes and maintains the person's moral conscience on the basis of a complex system of ideals and values internalized from one's parents. The superego provides ongoing scrutiny of the person's behavior, thoughts, and feelings. It then makes comparisons with expected standards of behavior and offers approval or disapproval. While the superego dictates what one should *not* do, the ego-ideal (featured in the diagram), often regarded as a component of the superego, prescribes what one should do according to internalized standards and values.

Answers 6.58–6.62

6.58 The answer is A (*Synopsis VIII,* pages 228–229).

6.59 The answer is A (*Synopsis VIII,* pages 228–229).

6.60 The answer is A (*Synopsis VIII,* page 217).

6.61 The answer is B (*Synopsis VIII,* page 211).

6.62 The answer is B (*Synopsis VIII,* pages 217–218).
Primary process was Sigmund Freud's term for the laws that govern unconscious processes. It is a type of thinking *characteristic of very young children, the unconscious, the id,* and dreams. Primary process is characterized by an absence of negatives, conditionals, and other qualifying conjunctions; by a lack of any sense of time; and by the use of allusion, condensation, and symbols. It is primitive, prelogical thinking marked by the tendency to seek immediate discharge and gratification of instinctual drives.

Secondary process was Freud's term for the laws that regulate events in *the preconscious and the ego.* It is a form of thinking that uses judgment, intelligence, logic, and reality testing; it helps the ego block the tendency of the instincts toward immediate discharge.

Answers 6.63–6.67

6.63 The answer is A (*Synopsis VIII,* page 210).

6.64 The answer is B (*Synopsis VIII,* page 217).

6.65 The answer is A (*Synopsis VIII,* page 210).

6.66 The answer is B (*Synopsis VIII,* page 217).

6.67 The answer is D (*Synopsis VIII,* pages 210–217).
The *topographic theory,* as *set forth by Sigmund Freud in* The Interpretation of Dreams *in 1900,* represented an attempt to divide the mind into three regions—*unconscious, preconscious, and conscious*—which were differentiated by their relation to consciousness. In general, all psychic material not in the immediate field of awareness—such as primitive drives, repressed desires, and memories—is in the unconscious. The preconscious includes all mental contents that are not in immediate awareness but can be consciously recalled with effort, in contrast to the unconscious, whose elements are barred from consciousness by some intrapsychic force, such as repression. The conscious is that portion of mental functioning that is within the realm of awareness at all times.

The *structural theory* of the mind was *presented in* The Ego and the Id *in 1923.* It represented a shift from the topographic model. Only when Freud discovered that not all unconscious processes can be relegated to the instincts (for example, that certain aspects of mental functioning associated with the ego and superego are unconscious) did he turn to the study of those structural components. From a structural viewpoint, the psychic apparatus is divided into three provinces—*id, ego, and superego.* Each is a particular aspect of human mental functioning and is not an empirically demonstrable phenomenon. The ego controls the apparatus of voluntary movement, perception, and contact with reality; through mechanisms of defense the ego is the inhibitor of primary instinctual drives. Freud conceived of the ego as an organized, problem-solving agent. Freud's concept of the id is as a completely unorganized, primordial reservoir of energy derived from the instincts; it is under the domination of the primary process. The id is not synonymous with the unconscious, as the structural viewpoint demonstrates that certain ego functions (for example, defenses against demands of the id) and aspects of the superego operate unconsciously. The discharge of id impulses is further regulated by the superego, which contains the internalized moral values and influence of the parental images—the conscience. The superego is the last of the structural components to develop; it results from the resolution of the Oedipus complex. Essentially, neurotic conflict can be explained structurally as a conflict between ego forces and id forces. Most often, the superego is involved in the conflict by aligning itself with the ego and imposing demands in the form of guilt. Occasionally, the superego may be allied with the id against the ego.

Sigmund Freud coined the idea of defense functions in 1894 and believed that defense mechanisms serve to keep conflictual ideation out of consciousness. However, the *first systematic and comprehensive study of the defenses used by the ego* was presented in Anna Freud's 1936 book, *The Ego and the Mechanisms of Defense,* which marked the beginning of ego psychology.

7 

Clinical Examination of the Psychiatric Patient

Learning about a patient during the first interview and interpreting the results of the various tests and examinations conducted before a patient can be treated are as vital to psychiatric practice as is a thorough knowledge of psychiatric theory. Making a reliable, accurate diagnosis is a skill that can be sharpened by a psychiatrist's learning about a patient's genetic, psychological, biological, developmental, and social history. To develop interviewing skills that encourage patients to trust and confide in them, psychiatrists must convey a genuine concern, empathy, and respect for patients.

Psychiatrists often deal with patients whose thinking is chaotic or who act violently; they must be able to reach these patients as effectively as they can interact with those who are moderately disturbed. Skilled interviewers are flexible and may change their interviewing techniques to suit different patients; they may also alter their approach as they learn more about a patient. Nevertheless, appropriate diagnosis and treatment require psychiatrists to have a standard by which they organize interviews and obtain the necessary data. For instance, a psychiatric history must provide objective data about a patient's chief complaint, history of illnesses, family history, and so on.

A mental status examination allows clinicians to obtain information about a patient's behavior, thought, and cognitive abilities; the examiner records such features as a patient's appearance, mood, speech, impulse control, and insight. Medical and laboratory evaluations are also helpful for supporting a specific diagnosis and treatment. Psychiatrists must be familiar with the wide array of laboratory tests available to them; these procedures can rule out medical disorders that may be associated with psychiatric signs and symptoms and may even help to make or confirm a diagnosis of a particular mental disorder. In ordering tests, there should be clinical evidence that it is warranted. For example, the use of psychotherapeutic drug serum levels should not be done as a matter of routine. In evidence based medicine, a specific drug level might be indicated in a nonresponder to help clarify the situation. In the clinical setting, the best guide is to ask whether a specific test result will affect diagnosis and treatment. If the answer is affirmative, then ordering the test is probably justified.

Chapter 7 of *Kaplan and Sadock's Synopsis VIII* will help the student answer the following questions.

HELPFUL HINTS

The student should know these terms, especially the acronyms and laboratory tests.

- ▶ adulthood
- ▶ AER
- ▶ antipsychotics
- ▶ appearance, behavior, attitude, and speech
- ▶ appropriateness
- ▶ BEAM
- ▶ BUN
- ▶ carbamazepine
- ▶ catecholamines
- ▶ chief complaint
- ▶ clang associations
- ▶ concentration, memory, and intelligence
- ▶ consciousness and orientation
- ▶ countertransference
- ▶ CSF
- ▶ CT
- ▶ current social situation
- ▶ cyclic antidepressants
- ▶ data
- ▶ dreams, fantasies, and value systems
- ▶ DSM-IV and Axes I–V
- ▶ DST
- ▶ early, middle, and late childhood history
- ▶ EEG
- ▶ family history
- ▶ history of present illness; previous illnesses
- ▶ initial interview and greeting
- ▶ judgment and insight
- ▶ LFT
- ▶ lithium
- ▶ marital and military history
- ▶ medical history
- ▶ mental status examination
- ▶ mood, feelings, and affect
- ▶ MRI
- ▶ neologisms
- ▶ NMR
- ▶ note taking
- ▶ occupational and educational history
- ▶ paraphasia
- ▶ patient questions
- ▶ perception
- ▶ PET
- ▶ polysomnography
- ▶ preliminary and personal identification
- ▶ prenatal history
- ▶ prognosis
- ▶ psychiatric history
- ▶ psychiatric report
- ▶ psychodynamic formulation
- ▶ psychosexual history
- ▶ punning
- ▶ rapport
- ▶ rCBF
- ▶ reliability

- religious background
- resistance
- sensorium and cognition
- sexuality
- social activity
- SSEP
- stress interview
- style
- subsequent interviews
- TFTs
- therapeutic alliance
- thought process
- transference
- treatment plan
- *Treponema pallidum*
- TRH
- TSH
- uncovering feelings
- using patient's words
- VDRL
- VEP
- word salad

▲QUESTIONS

DIRECTIONS: Each of the questions or incomplete statements below is followed by five suggested responses or completions. Select the *one* that is *best* in each case.

7.1 All of the following statements about interviewing situations are correct *except*

A. Depressed patients may not always realize that waking during the night is a symptom related to depression.
B. Violent patients should be interviewed in restraints and with at least one other person in attendance.
C. Interviews with family members must be carefully handled to preserve good doctor–patient relationships.
D. Depressed patients should be questioned in some detail about thoughts or plans that indicate increased risk of suicide.
E. Delusional patients should be asked such questions as "Have you ever thought that people are against you?" or "Do you have any special powers?"

7.2 Which of the following elements is *not* part of the mental status examination?

A. A description of the patient's speech
B. A description of the patient's judgment
C. A description of the patient's appearance
D. A description of the patient's sexual attitudes
E. A description of the patient's visuospatial ability

7.3 In the mental status examination

A. the patient's mood can be described as normal, blunted, constricted, or flat
B. hallucinations and illusions are disturbances in the patient's thought process
C. asking a patient to spell the word "world" backward is designed to measure visuospatial ability
D. the highest level of insight is true emotional insight
E. blocking is an attitude assumed by the patient to stop the interview

7.4 In a psychiatric evaluation, a complete medical history may reveal

A. polyuria, polydipsia, and diarrhea, which are signs of lithium toxicity
B. exposure to lead, which can produce anxiety disorders
C. dyspnea and breathlessness, which may occur in manic episodes
D. a hearing impairment, which is commonly associated with impulse control disorders
E. glaucoma, which contraindicates the use of antihistaminic drugs

7.5 Hypothyroidism

A. may present with symptoms of mania
B. may be caused by lithium
C. is found in 40 percent of all patients with depressive disorders
D. does not occur in neonates
E. may be assayed through urinalysis

7.6 Patients receiving

A. benzodiazepines need weekly assessments of their magnesium blood levels
B. clozapine need to be assessed for drug-induced anemia
C. lithium must have their serum drug levels monitored regularly
D. trazodone have reported no serious adverse effects
E. monoamine oxidase inhibitors (MAOIs) need to avoid foods containing glucose

7.7 Each of the following statements is true *except*

A. Sodium lactate provokes panic attacks in a majority of patients with panic disorder.
B. Sodium lactate can trigger flashbacks in patients with posttraumatic stress disorder.
C. Hyperventilation is as sensitive as lactate provocation in inducing panic attacks.
D. Panic attacks triggered by sodium lactate are not inhibited by propranolol.
E. Panic attacks triggered by sodium lactate are inhibited by alprazolam.

7.8 If a patient receiving clozapine shows a white blood count (WBC) of 2000 per cc, the clinician should

A. increase the dosage of clozapine at once
B. terminate any antibiotic therapy
C. place the patient in protective isolation in a medical unit
D. monitor the patient's WBC every 10 days
E. institute weekly complete blood count (CBC) tests with differential

7.9 An abnormal finding on a dexamethasone-suppression test (DST) means that the patient may have

A. a good response to electroconvulsive therapy (ECT)
B. a good response to cyclic drugs
C. disseminated cancer
D. received high-dosage benzodiazepine treatment
E. all of the above

7.10 Thyroid function tests are of use in clinical psychiatric practice because

A. up to 10 percent of patients with depression have thyroid disease
B. hypothyroidism may be a side effect of lithium
C. hypothyroidism may present as mental retardation
D. a blunted thyrotropin-releasing hormone (TRH) stimulation test is associated with depressive disorders
E. all of the above

7.11 A 43-year-old woman with progressive systemic lupus erythematosus has been responding poorly to treatment. She appears to be depressed, and her physician is concerned that she may commit suicide. The best treatment strategy is for the physician to

A. avoid further questioning of the patient
B. reassure the patient that she will get well
C. ask directly about any suicidal thoughts
D. request psychiatric hospitalization
E. immediately put the patient on high-dosage antidepressant medication

7.12 The first sign of beginning cerebral disease is impairment of

A. immediate memory
B. recent memory
C. long-term memory
D. remote memory
E. none of the above

7.13 A stress interview is characterized by

A. the use of the Social Readjustment Rating Scale
B. intimidation of the psychiatrist by the patient
C. confrontation of the patient by the psychiatrist
D. the destructive effect it has on the patient's psyche
E. anxiety in both the physician and the patient

7.14 Asking patients what they would do if they received someone else's mail among their own is an example of a test of

A. intelligence
B. abstract thinking
C. insight
D. judgment
E. cognition

7.15 The medication most commonly used in the drug-assisted psychiatric interview is

A. diazepam
B. meprobamate
C. amobarbital
D. chloral hydrate
E. phenothiazine

7.16 The reaction of the patient toward the psychiatrist may be affected by

A. the psychiatrist's attitude
B. previous experiences with physicians
C. the patient's view of authority figures in childhood
D. the patient's cultural background
E. all of the above

7.17 Which of the following substances has been implicated in mood disorders with seasonal pattern?

A. Luteotropic hormone (LTH)
B. Gonadotropin-releasing hormone (GnRH)
C. Testosterone
D. Estrogen
E. Melatonin

7.18 A 23-year-old heterosexual man, during his first meeting with a female psychiatrist, suddenly states, "All women are whores, and I'm wasting my time talking with you." The patient gives a history of having had long-term sexual relationships with two women over the previous 4 years, relationships that he says were enjoyable. He describes normal feelings of intimacy toward his present partner. The treating physician's best response is

A. "You are expressing latent homosexual impulses."
B. "Those feelings are oedipal in nature."
C. "Your feelings of hostility toward women will make it impossible for us to work together."
D. "Why do you have those feelings?"
E. "You're bringing on feelings of fear in me."

7.19 A good test for recent memory is to ask patients

A. their date of birth
B. what they had to eat for their last meal
C. the name of the hospital they are in
D. to subtract 7 from 100
E. who is the President of the United States

7.20 A favorable therapeutic window is associated with

A. imipramine
B. nortriptyline
C. desipramine
D. amitriptyline
E. all of the above

7.21 In a psychiatric interview

A. the psychiatrist may have to medicate a violent patient before taking a history
B. a violent patient should be interviewed alone to establish a doctor-patient relationship
C. delusions should be directly challenged
D. the psychiatrist must not ask depressed patients if they have suicidal thoughts
E. the psychiatrist should have a seat higher than the patient's seat

DIRECTIONS: Each group of questions below consists of lettered headings followed by a list of numbered phrases. For each numbered phrase, select the *best* lettered heading. Each heading may be used once, more than once, or not at all.

Questions 7.22–7.26

A. Serum ammonia
B. Cortisone
C. Copper
D. Creatinine
E. Platelet count

7.22 Increased in hepatic encephalopathy
7.23 Elevated in Wilson's disease
7.24 Decreased by carbamazepine
7.25 Pretreatment workup for lithium therapy
7.26 Increased in response to stress

Questions 7.27–7.31

A. Elevated level of 5-HIAA
B. Decreased level of 5-HIAA

7.27 Carcinoid tumors
7.28 Phenothiazine medications
7.29 Aggressive behavior
7.30 High banana intake
7.31 Suicidal patients

Questions 7.32–7.36

A. Hyperthyroidism
B. Hypothyroidism
C. Porphyria
D. Hepatolenticular degeneration
E. Pancreatic carcinoma

7.32 Jaundice, sense of imminent doom
7.33 Dry skin, myxedema madness
7.34 Kayser-Fleischer rings, brain damage
7.35 Abdominal crises, mood swings
7.36 Tremor, anxiety, and hyperactivity

ANSWERS

Clinical Examination of the Psychiatric Patient

7.1 The answer is B (*Synopsis VIII,* pages 240–241).
Violent patients need not always be interviewed in restraints. With a patient whose reality testing is not severely impaired, a clinician may consider it safe, for the patient and others, to remove restraints. Restraints should be removed slowly and, as restraints are loosened, the patient should be observed; as long as the patient remains calm and seems relieved, the restraints can be removed. Sometimes restraints are left on a patient until a clinician establishes rapport. If a patient again becomes agitated, the decision to remove restraints must be reexamined and medication may have to be given intramuscularly. With or without restraints, a patient who is potentially violent should not be left alone with a clinician; another person, a security guard or other physician, should always be present.

Depressed patients may not always realize that waking during the night is a symptom related to depression. Thus, an interviewer must ask these patients specific questions to elicit relevant information, as well as to overcome the hopelessness that overwhelms them. *Interviews with family members* must be carefully handled to preserve good doctor–patient relationships. These interviews are often difficult; family members may be so close to the patient that they are too anxious to provide objective data, or they may not realize the sort of information the interviewer needs them to supply. A psychiatrist must be sensitive to all the dimensions of family interviewing; a poor relationship with a patient's spouse or family members can destroy the doctor's relationship with the patient.

Depressed patients should be questioned in some detail about thoughts or plans that indicate the risk of suicide. Even when no risk is apparent, a psychiatrist cannot overlook the possibility and must take steps to protect the patient against suicidal impulses and behavior.

Delusional patients should be asked questions whose answers can reveal the nature of the delusions and their effect on a patient. Clinicians should not challenge a delusion or try to argue a patient out of a belief but should express understanding of the patient's belief. A clinician can state that he or she does not believe that the delusion is true but must also emphasize the desire to help the patient understand and eventually overcome the delusion.

7.2 The answer is D (*Synopsis VIII,* pages 250–251).
A description of the patient's sexual attitudes is not part of a mental status examination; this topic is part of the psychiatric history obtained during the first part of the interview. A mental status examination focuses on the interviewer's observations of the patient, and these observations can change from hour to hour.

The mental status examination is a description of a patient's appearance, speech, actions, and thoughts during an interview. Thus, the examination includes descriptions of *the patient's speech, judgment, appearance,* and *visuospatial ability.* The last is tested by asking the patient to copy a figure, such as a clock or pentagon.

7.3 The answer is D (*Synopsis VIII,* pages 250–251).
The mental status examination provides the sum total of the examiner's observations and impressions of the psychiatric patient at the time of the interview. Part of the mental status examination includes an assessment of insight. Insight is patients' degree of awareness and understanding that they are ill. *The highest level of insight is true emotional insight,* which occurs when patients' awareness of their own motives and deep feelings leads to changes in their personality or behavior patterns. Other levels of insight include (1) complete denial of illness; (2) slight awareness of being sick and needing help but denying it at the same time; (3) awareness of being sick but blaming it on others, on external factors, or on organic factors; (4) awareness that illness is caused by something unknown in the patient; and (5) intellectual insight—that is, admission that the patient is ill and that symptoms or failures in social adjustment are caused by the patient's own irrational feelings or disturbances but no application of that knowledge to future experiences.

Mood, affect, thought content, thought process, perception, sensorium, and cognition are also assessed in the mental status examination. *The patient's affect, not mood, can be described as normal, blunted, constricted, or flat.* Affect may be defined as the patient's present emotional responsiveness. Affect is what the examiner infers from the patient's facial expression, including the amount and the range of the patient's expressive behavior. In the normal range of affect, the patient shows a variation in facial expression, tone of voice, use of the hands, and body movements. When affect is constricted, the patient has a clear reduction in the range and the intensity of expression. In blunted affect, the patient's emotional expression is further reduced. To diagnose flat affect, the clinician should find virtually no signs of affective expression, the patient's voice should be monotonous, and the patient's face should be immobile.

Mood is defined as a pervasive and sustained emotion that colors the person's perception of the world. It is the patient's subjective view of his or her emotional state described as sad, depressed, or elated, and not as blurred or flat.

Hallucinations and illusions are perceptual disturbances, not disturbances in the patient's thought process. An illusion is a misperception or misinterpretation of real external sensory stimuli. A hallucination is a false sensory perception not associated with real external stimuli; hallucinations indicate a psychotic disturbance only when they are associated with an impairment in reality testing.

Asking a patient to spell the word "world" backward is designed to measure attention, not visuospatial ability. Attention can also be assessed by calculations and by asking the patient to name five things that start with a particular letter. Visuospatial ability is assessed by asking the patient to copy a figure, such as a clock face or interlocking pentagons.

Blocking is not an attitude assumed by the patient to stop the interview. It is a disturbance in thought process, an interruption of the patient's train of thought before an idea has been completed. The patient may indicate an inability to recall what was being said or intended to be said.

7.4 The answer is A (*Synopsis VIII,* page 270).
The presenting symptoms of some physical illnesses may be psychiatric signs or symptoms, and some symptoms may be caused by medications given to treat mental disorders or by a mental disorder itself. For example, *polyuria, polydipsia, and diarrhea are signs of lithium toxicity.*

Exposure to mercury may result in complaints suggesting a psychosis, and *exposure to lead,* as in smelting, *may produce cognitive disorders, not anxiety disorders.* Imbibing moonshine with a high lead content can also lead to cognitive disorders and brain damage.

Dyspnea and breathlessness may occur in depressive disorders. Those symptoms do not occur in manic episodes.

A hearing impairment is commonly associated with delusional disorders, not impulse control disorders.

A history of *glaucoma contraindicates drugs with anticholinergic adverse effects, not the use of antihistaminic* drugs (for example, diphenhydramine [Benadryl]).

7.5 The answer is B (*Synopsis VIII,* page 256).
Hypothyroidism and, occasionally, hyperthyroidism may be caused by lithium (Eskalith). Patients taking lithium must have their thyroid function monitored.

Hypothyroidism *does not present with symptoms of mania,* but it may present with symptoms of depression. In some studies, up to 10 percent of all patients who reported depression and associated fatigue had incipient hypothyroid disease. Other signs and symptoms common to both depression and hypothyroidism include weakness, stiffness, poor appetite, constipation, menstrual irregularities, slowed speech, apathy, impaired memory, hallucinations, and delusions. *Up to 10 percent, not 40 percent, of all patients with depressive disorders* have some thyroid illness.

Hypothyroidism does occur in neonates. It can lead to cretinism, in which the child suffers from stunted growth and mental retardation. Because the condition is preventable if it is diagnosed at birth, thyroid function tests are included in neonatal screening.

Hypothyroidism *cannot be assessed through urinalysis.* However, several thyroid function tests are available, including tests for thyroxine (T_4) by competitive protein binding (T_4D) and by radioimmunoassay (T_4RIA) involving a specific antigen-antibody reaction. More than 90 percent of T_4 is bound to serum protein and exerts feedback control on thyroid-stimulating hormone (TSH) secretion. Other thyroid measures include the free T_4 index (FT_4T), triiodothyronine uptake, and total serum triiodothyronine measured by radioimmunoassay (T_3RIA). The thyrotropin-releasing hormone (TRH) stimulation test is indicated in patients who have marginally abnormal thyroid test results with suspected subclinical hypothyroidism, which may account for clinical depression. The test is also used for patients with possible lithium-induced hypothyroidism. The procedure entails an intravenous injection of 500 mg of TRH, which produces a sharp rise in serum TSH when measured after 15, 30, 60, and 90 minutes. An increase in serum TSH of from 5 to 25 μIU/mL above the baseline is normal. An increase of less than 7 μIU/mL is considered a blunted response, which may correlate with a diagnosis of a depressive disorder.

7.6 The answer is C (*Synopsis VIII,* pages 260–261).
Patients receiving *lithium must have their serum drug levels monitored regularly* because there is a narrow therapeutic range beyond which cardiac, renal, and central nervous system (CNS) problems can occur. Blood is drawn 8 to 12 hours after the last dose of lithium, usually in the morning after the bedtime dose. The serum level should be measured at least twice a week while the patient is being stabilized, and blood may be drawn monthly thereafter.

Patients taking *benzodiazepines do not need weekly assessments of their magnesium blood levels.* However, benzodiazepines metabolized in the liver by oxidation have their half-lives increased by impaired hepatic function. Baseline liver function tests (LFTs) are indicated in patients with suspected liver damage. Urine testing for benzodiazepines is used routinely in cases of substance abuse.

Because of the risk of agranulocytosis (1 to 2 percent), patients who are being treated with the antipsychotic clozapine (Clozaril) must have a baseline white blood count (WBC) and differential count before the initiation of treatment, a WBC every week throughout treatment, and a WBC for 4 weeks after the discontinuation of clozapine. Clozapine does not affect red blood cells; therefore, patients receiving *clozapine do not need to be assessed for drug-induced anemia.*

Patients receiving trazodone (Desyrel) have reported serious side effects. Trazodone, an antidepressant unrelated to cyclic drugs, has been reported to cause ventricular arrhythmias and priapism (painful, persistent erections), mild leukopenia, and neutropenia.

Patients taking *monoamine oxidase inhibitors (MAOIs) need to avoid foods containing tyramine, not glucose.* Tyramine-containing foods pose the danger of a hypertensive crisis. A baseline normal blood pressure (BP) must be recorded, and the BP must be monitored during treatment. MAOIs may also cause orthostatic hypotension as a direct drug side effect unrelated to the diet. Other than their potential for causing an elevated BP when taken with certain foods, MAOIs are relatively free of other adverse effects.

7.7 The answer is C (*Synopsis VIII,* page 262).
Even though hyperventilation can trigger panic attacks in predisposed persons, *hyperventilation is not as sensitive as lactate provocation in inducing panic attacks. Sodium lactate provokes panic attacks* in a majority (up to 72 percent) of patients with panic disorder. Therefore, lactate provocation is used to confirm a diagnosis of panic disorder. *Sodium lactate can also trigger flashbacks in patients with posttraumatic stress disorder.* Carbon dioxide (CO_2) inhalation also precipitates panic attacks in those so predisposed. *Panic attacks triggered by sodium lactate are not inhibited by* peripherally acting β-blockers, such as *propranolol* (Inderal), but are *inhibited by alprazolam* (Xanax) and tricyclic drugs.

7.8 The answer is C (*Synopsis VIII,* page 260).
A patient who shows a white blood count of 2000 while taking clozapine (Clozaril) is at high risk for agranulocytosis. If agranulocytosis develops (that is, if the WBC is less than 1000) and there is evidence of severe infection (for example, skin ulcerations), the patient should be placed in *protective isolation on a medical unit.* The clinician should *stop the administration of clozapine at once,* not increase the dosage of

clozapine. The patient may or may not have clinical symptoms, such as fever and sore throat. *Even if the patient does have such symptoms, antibiotic therapy* may be necessary. Depending on the severity of the condition, the physician should *monitor patients' WBC every 2 days, not 10 days,* or institute *daily, not weekly, CBC tests* with differential.

Table 7.1 summarizes the treatment of patients with reduced WBCs.

7.9 The answer is E (all) (*Synopsis VIII,* pages 256–257).
The dexamethasone-suppression test can be used to confirm a diagnostic impression of major depressive disorder with melancholic features. In such depressions, the test result is abnormal in many cases, meaning that there is nonsuppression of endogenous cortisol production after exogenous steroid ingestion. Nonsuppression, a positive finding, indicates a hyperactive hypothalamic-pituitary-adrenal axis. The test is sometimes used to predict which patients will have *a good response to* somatic treatments, such as *electroconvulsive therapy (ECT)* and *cyclic drugs.* The clinician needs to be aware that false-positive findings can result from several factors, such as *disseminated cancer.* A false-negative finding can occur in patients who have *received high-dosage benzodiazepine treatment.* In a false-negative result, a diseased person has a normal finding. In a false-positive result, a nondiseased person has an abnormal finding.

7.10 The answer is E (all) (*Synopsis VIII,* page 256).
Thyroid function tests are of use in clinical psychiatric practice for several reasons. For instance, *up to 10 percent of patients with depression have thyroid disease,* and *hypothyroidism may be a side effect of lithium;* hyperthyroidism may also occur, but less often. In children, *hypothyroidism may present as mental retardation* or as delayed development. Neonatal hypothyroidism can result in mental retardation, which is preventable with early diagnosis and treatment. *A blurred thyrotropin-releasing hormone (TRH) stimulation test is associated with depressive disorders.* The test consists of giving the patient an intravenous injection of 500 mg TRH, which normally produces a rise in plasma TSH.

7.11 The answer is C (*Synopsis VIII,* page 256).
Patients with chronic illnesses and deteriorating health often become depressed. The physician must take any suicidal ideation seriously and must carefully evaluate all depressed patients for suicidal risk. Most patients who have suicidal ideation feel better after their physicians *ask directly about any suicidal thoughts.* The risk for suicide does not increase with direct questioning about suicide. *The physician should not avoid further questioning of the patient.* The physician must have a clear picture of the patient's psychiatric status to decide on an appropriate therapeutic plan. *Reassurance, hospitalization,* and *antidepressant medication* should not be used unless indicated.

7.12 The answer is B (*Synopsis VIII,* pages 252–253).
Memory impairment, most notably in *recent* or short-term *memory,* is usually the first sign of beginning cerebral disease. Memory is a process by which anything that is experienced or learned is established as a record in the central nervous system, where it persists with a variable degree of permanence and can be recollected or retrieved from storage at will. *Immediate* memory is the reproduction, recognition, or recall of perceived material after a period of 10 seconds or less has elapsed after the initial presentation. *Recent memory* covers a time period from a few hours to a few weeks after the initial presentation. *Long-term memory or remote memory* is the reproduction, recognition, or recall of experiences or information from the distant past. That function is usually not disturbed early in cerebral disease.

7.13 The answer is C (*Synopsis VIII,* pages 268–274).
The stress interview is a type of interview characterized by *confrontation of the patient by the psychiatrist* and by the avoidance of the usual ways of reducing anxiety during the session. Such interviews may be useful in diagnosis, but their repeated use is generally contraindicated in the course of psychotherapy. One situation in which the stress interview may be used is with patients who are monotonously repetitious or who show insufficient emotionality for motivation. Apathy, indifference, and emotional blunting are not conducive to a discussion of personality problems. In patients with such reactions, stimulation of their emotions can be constructive. The patients may require probing, challenging, or confrontation to arouse feelings that further their understanding.

The Social Readjustment Rating Scale, devised by Thomas H. Holmes, quantifies life events, assigning a point value to life changes that require adaptation. Research indicates a critical level at which too many of those events happening to a person during 1 year puts the person at great risk for illness.

The stress interview is not related to *intimidation of* any kind, nor should it be *destructive. Anxiety* may be present *in both the physician and the patient* during any initial interview.

7.14 The answer is D (*Synopsis VIII,* page 254).
Asking patients what they would do if they received someone else's mail among their own is a test of *judgment.* Judgment involves the process of evaluating choices within the framework of a given value system for the purpose of deciding on an appropriate course of action. The response that one would hand a misdirected letter back to the letter carrier or drop it into a mailbox reflects appropriate judgment. *Intelligence* is the ability to learn and the capacity to apply what one has learned. *Abstract thinking* is the ability to shift voluntarily from one aspect of a situation to another, to keep in mind simultaneously various aspects of a situation, and to think or to perform symbolically. *Insight* is the power or act of seeing into and recognizing the objective reality of a situation. *Cognition* involves the perceptual and intellectual level of mental functioning.

7.15 The answer is C (*Synopsis VIII,* page 262).
Amobarbital (Amytal) is the drug most commonly used in the drug-assisted psychiatric interview. It can be of use with patients who have difficulty in expressing themselves freely or who are suppressing anxiety-provoking material. In narcotherapy, regularly scheduled interviews use amobarbital as an adjunctive agent. However, the benzodiazepines—for example, *diazepam* (valium)— are just as effective as the barbiturates in drug-assisted interviewing and are less dangerous.

Meprobamate, diazepam, and *chloral hydrate* are antianxiety agents used as sedatives or hypnotics. The *phenothiazines* are antipsychotics used in the treatment of schizophrenia.

Table 7.1
Clinical Management of Patients with Reduced White Blood Cell Count (WBC), Leukopenia, and Agranulocytosis

Problem Phase	WBC Findings	Clinical Findings	Treatment Plan
Reduced WBC	WBC reveals a significant drop (even if WBC is still in normal range). "Significant drop" = (1) drop of more than 3,000 cells from prior test or (2) three or more consecutive drops in WBC	No symptoms of infection	1. Monitor patient closely 2. Institute twice-weekly CBC tests with differentials if deemed appropriate by attending physician 3. Clozapine therapy may continue
Mild leukopenia	WBC = 3,000–3,500	Patient may or may not show clinical symptoms, such as lethargy, fever, sore throat, weakness	1. Monitor patient closely 2. Institute a minimum of twice-weekly CBC tests with differentials 3. Clozapine therapy may continue
Leukopenia or granulocytopenia	WBC = 2,000–3,000 or granulocytes = 1,000–1,500	Patient may or may not show clinical symptoms, such as fever, fore throat, lethargy, weakness	1. Interrupt clozapine at once 2. Institute daily CBC tests with differentials 3. Increase surveillance, consider hospitalization 4. Clozapine therapy may be reinstituted after normalization of WBC
Agranulocytosis	WBC less than 2,000 or granulocytes less than 1,000	The patient may or may not show clinical symptoms, such as fever, sore throat, lethargy, weakness	1. Discontinue clozapine at once 2. Place patient in protective isolation in a medical unit with modern facilities 3. Consider a bone marrow specimen to determine if progenitor cells are being suppressed 4. Monitor patient every 2 days until WBC and differential counts return to normal (about 2 weeks) 5. Avoid use of concomitant medications with bone marrow-suppressing potential
Agranulocytosis (with complications)	WBC less than 2,000 or granulocytes less than 1,000	Definite evidence of infection, such as fever, sore throat, lethargy, weakness, malaise, skin ulcerations	6. Consult with hematologist or other specialist to determine appropriate antibiotic regimen 7. Start appropriate therapy; monitor closely
Recovery	WBC more than 4,000 and granulocytes more than 2,000	No symptoms of infection	1. Once-weekly CBC with differential counts for 4 consecutive normal values 2. Clozapine must not be restarted

Reprinted with permission of Sandoz Pharmaceuticals Corporation and MacKinnon A, Yudofsky SC: *Principles of Psychiatric Evaluation,* p 118. Lippincott, Philadelphia, 1991.

7.16 The answer is E (all) (*Synopsis VIII,* pages 740–755). The reaction of patients toward the psychiatrist is influenced by *the psychiatrist's attitude,* style, and orientation. If patients believe that they will lose their psychiatrist's respect as they expose their problems, they may be unwilling to disclose such material. If, in their *previous experiences with physicians* (psychiatric or nonpsychiatric), patients felt ridiculed or that their problems were minimized, those experiences influence what they do or do not tell the psychiatrist.

Transference is a process in which patients unconsciously and inappropriately displace onto persons in their current life those patterns of behavior and emotional reactions that originated in childhood. *The patient's view of authority figures in childhood* influences reactions to the psychiatrist. Differences in the social, educational, and intellectual backgrounds of each patient and the psychiatrist may also interfere with the development of rapport. It is an obvious advantage for the psychiatrist to acquire as much understanding and familiarity as possible with *the patient's cultural background.*

7.17 The answer is E (*Synopsis VIII,* page 258). *Melatonin* from the pineal gland has been implicated in mood disorders with seasonal pattern. Melatonin's exact mechanism of action is unknown, but its production is stimulated in the dark, and it may affect the sleep-wake cycle. Melatonin is synthesized from serotonin, an active neurotransmitter. Decreased nocturnal secretion of melatonin has been associated with depression. A number of other substances also affect behavior, and some known endocrine diseases (for example, Cushing's disease) have associated psychiatric signs. Symptoms of anxiety or depression may be explained in some patients by changes in endocrine function or homeostasis.

Luteotropic hormone (LTH) is an anterior pituitary hormone whose action maintains the function of the corpus luteum.

Gonadotropin-releasing hormone (GnRH), produced by the hypothalamus, increases the pituitary secretion of luteotropic hormone (LTH) and the follicle-stimulating hormone (FSH). GnRH is secreted in a pulsatile manner that is critical for the control of LTH and FSH from the pituitary. GnRH also acts as a neurotransmitter whose exact function is unknown.

Testosterone is the hormone responsible for the secondary sex characteristics in men. A decreased testosterone level has been associated with erectile dysfunction and depression. Testosterone is formed in greatest quantities by the interstitial cells of the testes, but it is also formed in small amounts by the ovaries and the adrenal cortex.

Estrogen is produced by the granulosa cells in the ovaries, and it is responsible for pubertal changes in girls. Exogenous estrogen replacement therapy has been associated with depression.

7.18 The answer is D (*Synopsis VIII,* pages 240–255).
The physician should try to encourage the patient to express his angry feelings to get to the causes of those hostile thoughts. Asking *"Why do you have those feelings"* allows the physician to plan a treatment program that will deal with the patient's feelings during the course of therapy.

Saying *"You are expressing latent homosexual impulses"* is premature and may be inaccurate. It is an inappropriate interpretation and may have nothing to do with the patient's personal experiences with women. It may also cause the patient to reject the physician's attempt to interact with him. Saying *"Those feelings are oedipal in nature"* is also premature. And saying *"Your feelings of hostility toward women will make it impossible for us to work together"* provides the ultimate therapeutic rejection to the patient and only further reinforces the patient's problems. It is totally inappropriate during the first psychiatric interview for the treating physician to discuss her countertransference fears with the patient by saying *"You're bringing on feelings of fear in me."*

7.19 The answer is B (*Synopsis VIII,* page 253).
Recent memory is the ability to remember what has been experienced within the past few hours, days, or weeks. It is assessed by asking patients to describe how they spent the last 24 hours, such as *what they had to eat for their last meal.*

Remote memory or long-term memory is the ability to remember events in the distant past. Memory for the remote past can be evaluated by inquiring about important dates in patients' lives, such as *their date of birth.* The answers must be verifiable.

To test patients' orientation to place, one can inquire whether patients know where they are—for instance, *the name of the hospital they are in.* Concentration may be tested by asking the patient *to subtract 7 from 100* serially. If the patient cannot do that task, the clinician must determine whether anxiety or some disturbance of mood or consciousness seems to be responsible for the difficulty.

To test a patient's general knowledge or fund of information, one can ask *who is the President of the United States.* The interviewer must ask questions that have some relevance to the patient's educational and cultural background.

7.20 The answer is E (all) (*Synopsis VIII,* page 260).
A favorable therapeutic window—that is, the range within which a drug is most effective—is associated with all the drugs listed. Blood levels should be tested routinely when using *imipramine* (Tofranil), *nortriptyline* (Pamelor), or *desipramine* (Norpramin) in the treatment of depressive disorders. Taking blood levels may also be of use in patients with poor responses at normal dosage ranges and in high-risk patients when there is an urgent need to know whether a therapeutic or toxic plasma level of the drug has been reached. Blood level tests should also include the measurement of active metabolites (for example, imipramine is converted to desipramine, and *amitriptyline* [Elavil] is converted to nortriptyline).

7.21 The answer is A (*Synopsis VIII,* pages 241–243).
Psychiatrists often encounter violent patients in a hospital setting. Frequently, the police bring a patient into the emergency room in some type of physical restraint (for example, handcuffs). The psychiatrist must establish whether effective verbal contact can be made with the patient or whether the patient's sense of reality is so impaired that effective interviewing is impossible. If impaired reality testing is an issue, *the psychiatrist may have to medicate a violent patient before taking a history.*

With or without restraints, *a violent patient should not be interviewed alone to establish a doctor-patient relationship.* At least one other person should always be present; in some situations that other person should be a security guard or a police officer. Other precautions include leaving the interview room's door open and sitting between the patient and the door, so that the interviewer has unrestricted access to an exit should it become necessary. The psychiatrist must make it clear, in a firm but nonangry manner, that the patient may say or feel anything but is not free to act in a violent way.

Delusions should never be directly challenged. Delusions are fixed false ideas that may be thought of as a patient's defensive and self-protective, albeit maladaptive, strategy against overwhelming anxiety, low self-esteem, and confusion. Challenging a delusion by insisting that it is not true or possible only increases the patient's anxiety and often leads the patient to defend the belief desperately. However, clinicians should not pretend that they believe the patient's delusion. Often, the best approach is for clinicians to indicate that they understand that the patient believes the delusion to be true but that they do not hold the same belief.

Being mindful of the possibility of suicide is imperative when interviewing any depressed patient, even if a suicidal risk is not apparent. *The psychiatrist must ask depressed patients if they have suicidal thoughts.* Doing so does not make patients feel worse. Instead, many patients are relieved to talk about their suicidal ideas. The psychiatrist should ask specifically, "Are you suicidal now?" or "Do you have plans to take your own life?" A suicide note, a family history of suicide, or previous suicidal behavior by the patient increases the risk for suicide. Evidence of impulsivity or of pervasive pessimism about the future also places patients at risk. If the psychiatrist decides that the patient is in imminent risk for suicidal behavior, the patient must be hospitalized or otherwise protected.

The way chairs are arranged in the psychiatrist's office affects the interview. *The psychiatrist should not have a seat higher than the patient's seat.* Both chairs should be about the same height, so that neither person looks down on the other. Most psychiatrists place the chairs without any furniture between the clinician and the patient. If the room contains several chairs, the psychiatrist indicates his or her own chair and then allows patients to choose the chairs in which they feel most comfortable.

Answers 7.22–7.26

7.22 The answer is A (*Synopsis VIII,* page 264).

7.23 The answer is C (*Synopsis VIII,* page 265).

7.24 The answer is E (*Synopsis VIII,* page 267).

7.25 The answer is D (*Synopsis VIII,* page 265).

7.26 The answer is B (*Synopsis VIII,* page 265).
Hepatic encephalopathy is associated with *increased serum ammonia* caused by chronic liver disease. The psychiatric signs of hepatic encephalopathy include personality changes, impaired consciousness, agitation, a musty sweet breath odor, and fetor hepaticus.

Wilson's disease is associated with an *elevated* level of *copper* caused by a disturbance in copper metabolism. The rare disease is transmitted in an autosomal recessive fashion.

Carbamazepine (Tegretol) is used in psychiatry as a mood stabilizer in bipolar I disorder. The most serious potential adverse effect is agranulocytosis, including a *decrease in platelet count.*

Lithium (Eskalith) is used in the treatment of manic episodes of bipolar I disorder. A side effect is polyuria secondary to decreased resorption of fluid from the distal tubule of the kidneys. *Creatinine* clearance is a good gauge of the patient's renal function and is part of the *pretreatment workup for lithium therapy.*

Stress is a physical or psychological event that produces strain or upsets physiological equilibrium (homeostasis). *Stress* is associated with *increased cortisone.*

Answers 7.27–7.31

7.27 The answer is A (*Synopsis VIII,* page 266).

7.28 The answer is A (*Synopsis VIII,* page 266).

7.29 The answer is B (*Synopsis VIII,* page 266).

7.30 The answer is A (*Synopsis VIII,* page 266).

7.31 The answer is B (*Synopsis VIII,* page 266).
The serotonin metabolite 5-hydroxyindoleacetic acid *(5-HIAA)* is *elevated* in the urine of patients with *carcinoid tumors* and at times in patients who take *phenothiazine medications* and in persons who eat foods high in L-tryptophan, the chemical precursor of serotonin (for example, walnuts, *bananas,* and avocados). The amount of 5-HIAA in cerebrospinal fluid is *decreased* in some persons who display *aggressive behavior* and in *suicidal patients* who have committed suicide in particularly violent ways.

Answers 7.32–7.36

7.32 The answer is E (*Synopsis VIII,* pages 258–259).

7.33 The answer is B (*Synopsis VIII,* page 256).

7.34 The answer is D (*Synopsis VIII,* page 256).

7.35 The answer is C (*Synopsis VIII,* pages 258–259).

7.36 The answer is A (*Synopsis VIII,* page 256).
The clinician should be aware of the many medical problems that may present as psychiatric symptoms. For example, *tremor, anxiety, and hyperactivity* are often associated with *hyperthyroidism; dry skin* and *myxedema madness* (which may mimic schizophrenia) are associated with *hypothyroidism; abdominal crisis* and *mood swings* are associated with *porphyria; Kayser-Fleischer rings* and *brain damage* are associated with *hepatolenticular degeneration (Wilson's disease);* and *jaundice* and a *sense of imminent doom* are associated with *pancreatic carcinoma.*

Table 7.2 gives some examples of medical problems that may present as psychiatric symptoms.

Table 7.2
Medical Problems That May Present as Psychiatric Symptoms

Medical Problem	Sex and Age Prevalence	Common Medical Symptoms	Psychiatric Symptoms and Complaints	Impaired Performance and Behavior	Diagnostic Problems
Hyperthyroidism (thyrotoxicosis)	Females 3:1, 30 to 50	*Tremor,* sweating, loss of weight and strength	*Anxiety* if rapid onset; depression if slow onset	Occasional *hyperactivity* or grandiose behavior	Long lead time; a rapid onset resembles anxiety attack
Hypothyroidism (myxedema)	Females 5:1, 30 to 50	Puffy face, *dry skin,* cold intolerance	Anxiety with irritability, thought disorder, somatic delusions, hallucinations	*Myxedema madness;* delusional, paranoid belligerent behavior	Madness may mimic schizophrenia; mental status is clear, even during most disturbed behavior
Porphyria—acute intermittent type	Females, 20 to 40	*Abdominal crises,* paresthesias, weakness	Anxiety—sudden onset, severe *mood swings*	Extremes of excitement or withdrawal; emotional or angry outbursts	Patients often have truly abnormal life styles; crises resemble conversion disorder or anxiety attacks
Hepatolenticular degeneration (Wilson's disease)	Males 2:1; adolescence	Liver and extrapyramidal symptoms, *Kayser-Fleischer rings*	Moods swings—sudden and changeable; anger—explosive	Eventual *brain damage* with memory and IQ loss; combativeness	In late teens, disorder may resemble adolescent storm, incorrigibility, or schizophrenia
Pancreatic carcinoma	Males 3:1, 50 to 70	Weight loss, abdominal pain, weakness, *jaundice*	Depression, *sense of imminent doom* but without severe guilt	Loss of drive and motivation	Long lead time; exact age and symptoms of involutional depression

8 Typical Signs and Symptoms of Psychiatric Illness Defined

Psychiatrists must master a new language to describe their observations of mental phenomena; to do this, they must be able to recognize and define behavioral and emotional signs (objective findings observed by clinicians) and symptoms (patients' subjective descriptions). Many psychiatric conditions are syndromes (several signs and symptoms occurring together as an observable condition) rather than specific disorders. To communicate with other clinicians and to diagnose, treat, and predict pathophysiology, psychiatrists must be expert at recognizing psychiatric signs and symptoms.

What sign is usually associated with a patient's hearing voices speaking to him or her? What symptoms are associated with a patient's finding fault with others' imperfections? Psychiatrists must understand and answer these and many other questions when they interview, diagnose, and treat their patients.

Clinicians, however, should not rely only on signs and symptoms as the means for diagnosing mental disorders. Although certain clusters are commonly associated with certain disorders, human feelings and behavior are too complex to be reduced to a list of signs and symptoms.

Psychological symptoms can be ego-syntonic or ego-dystonic; that is, they can be experienced either as acceptable and compatible or as unacceptable and alien. In general usage, the terms ''signs'' and ''symptoms'' tend to be used interchangeably. It is especially difficult to maintain the distinction of psychiatry. A patient may not report any symptoms (that is, the symptoms are ego-syntonic), but others believe the patient's behavior is strange, and that strange behavior constitutes the signs of illness. Conversely, a patient experiencing hallucinations may vigorously describe what he or she seems to be hearing (that is, the symptoms are ego-dystonic), but there are no observable signs of hallucinatory activity. Unlike certain medical conditions, psychiatric disorders have few, if any, signs or symptoms that are pathognomonic. Moreover, physical disease may first present with psychiatric symptoms, thereby compounding the difficult task of making an accurate diagnosis. A syndrome is a group of symptoms that occur together and constitute a recognizable condition, and the term ''syndrome'' is less specific than ''disorder'' or ''disease.'' Most psychiatric disorders are, in reality, syndromes.

Psychiatrists must also be familiar with signs and symptoms of medical disorders beyond those that are mental. Organic pathology often underlies psychiatric signs and symptoms, and mental disorders can sometimes be expressed in organic terms. A thorough understanding of interconnected signs and symptoms is crucial for appropriate diagnoses and treatments.

Students should study Chapter 8 of *Kaplan and Sadock's Synopsis VIII* and then assess their level of knowledge of the subject by studying the questions and answers below.

HELPFUL HINTS

The student should be able to define and categorize the signs and symptoms and other terms listed below.

- affect and mood
- aggression
- agnosias
- anxiety
- aphasic disturbances
- *cerea flexibilitas*
- coma
- déjà vu
- *déjà pensé*
- *déjà entendu*
- delirium
- delusion
- dementia
- depersonalization
- disorientation
- distractibility
- disturbances in the form and the content of thought
- disturbances in speech
- disturbances of conation
- disturbances of consciousness and attention
- disturbances of intelligence
- disturbances of memory
- disturbances of perception, both those caused by brain diseases and those associated with psychological phenomena
- *folie à deux*
- hypnosis
- illusions
- insight and judgment
- *jamais vu*
- noesis
- panic
- phobias
- pseudodementia
- stereotypy
- synesthesia

▲ QUESTIONS

DIRECTIONS: Each of the incomplete statements below is followed by five suggested completions. Select the *one* that is *best* in each case.

8.1 Overactivity, an impulse to repeat an act, includes all of the following *except*

A. tic
B. ataxia
C. akathisia
D. satyriasis
E. catalepsy

8.2 All of the following are general disturbances in the form or process of thinking *except*

A. stereotypy
B. blocking
C. derailment
D. word salad
E. incoherence

8.3 A medical student begins to fall asleep in class and is startled awake, thinking that the student's name was called; in reality, it was not. That is an example of

A. hypnagogic hallucination
B. hypnopompic hallucination
C. illusion
D. synesthesia
E. dissociation

8.4 A 27-year-old man comes to the emergency room reporting having his thoughts controlled by the CIA. Such thinking is

A. dereistic
B. magical
C. depersonalized
D. obsessional
E. delirious

8.5 A psychiatric patient who, although coherent, never gets to the point has a disturbance in the form of thought called

A. word salad
B. circumstantiality
C. tangentiality
D. verbigeration
E. blocking

8.6 A 26-year-old man believes that the Mafia and his brother are putting horrible thoughts into his head. That is an example of

A. thought broadcasting
B. delusion of reference
C. nihilistic delusion
D. thought insertion
E. pseudologia phantastica

8.7 Loss of normal speech melody is known as

A. stuttering
B. stammering
C. aphonia
D. dysprosody
E. dyslexia

8.8 Perceptual disturbances include all of the following *except*

A. hallucinations
B. hypnagogic experiences
C. echolalia
D. depersonalization
E. derealization

8.9 Asking a patient to interpret a proverb is used as a way of assessing

A. judgment
B. impulse control
C. abstract thinking
D. insight
E. intelligence

DIRECTIONS: Each group of questions below consists of lettered headings followed by a list of numbered phrases or statements. For each numbered phrase or statement, select the *one* lettered heading that is most associated with it. Each lettered heading may be selected once, more than once, or not at all.

Questions 8.10–8.14

A. Stupor
B. Delirium
C. Coma
D. Somnolence
E. Dreamlike state

8.10 Profound degree of unconsciousness
8.11 Lack of reaction to and an unawareness of one's surroundings
8.12 Restless, confused, and disoriented
8.13 Synonym for complex partial seizure or psychomotor epilepsy
8.14 Abnormal drowsiness

Questions 8.15–8.19

A. Anhedonia
B. Euphoria
C. Alexithymia
D. Euthymia
E. Expansive mood

8.15 "I don't know how I feel; I just can't say."
8.16 "I have no sex drive and no appetite; I just don't feel like doing anything."
8.17 "You can't keep me on this ward; I have to submit my plans for the country to the President."
8.18 "I feel fine—basically happy."
8.19 "I feel better today than I ever have in my life."

Questions 8.20–8.24

A. Echopraxia
B. Catalepsy
C. Cataplexy
D. Stereotypy
E. Tic

8.20 Weakness and temporary loss of muscle tone precipitated by emotional states
8.21 General term for an immobile position that is constantly maintained
8.22 Involuntary, spasmodic motor movement
8.23 Repetitive, fixed pattern of physical action or speech
8.24 Pathological imitation of another person's movements

Questions 8.25–8.29

A. Loosening of associations
B. Flight of ideas
C. Clang association
D. Blocking
E. Neologism

8.25 "I was gigglifying not just tempifying; you know what I mean."
8.26 "I was grocery training; but, when I ride the grocery, I drive the food everywhere on top of lollipops."
8.27 "Cain and Abel—they were cannibals. You see brothers kill brothers—that is laudable. If you ask me, though, never name your son Huxtibal. OK."
8.28 Patient: "I never wanted. . . ." Physician: "Go on. What were you saying?" Patient: "I don't know."
8.29 "Tired, mired, schmired, wired."

Questions 8.30–8.34

A. Delusion
B. Obsession
C. Compulsion
D. Phobia
E. Overvalued idea

8.30 Pathological need to act on a feeling
8.31 Pathological persistence of an irresistible thought or feeling
8.32 Fixed, false belief based on incorrect inferences about external reality
8.33 Unreasonable, sustained false belief that is not fixed
8.34 Persistent, irrational, exaggerated dread of some specific type of stimulus or situation

Questions 8.35–8.38

A. Broca's (motor) aphasia
B. Sensory aphasia
C. Nominal aphasia
D. Global aphasia
E. Syntactical aphasia

8.35 Difficulty in finding the correct names for objects
8.36 Loss of the ability to comprehend the meaning of words
8.37 Loss of the ability to speak
8.38 Inability to arrange words in a proper sequence

Questions 8.39–8.42

A. Dysdiadochokinesia
B. Astereognosis
C. Visual agnosia
D. Autotopagnosia
E. Simultanagnosia

8.39 Inability to recognize a body part as one's own
8.40 Inability to distinguish by touch between a quarter and a dime
8.41 Inability to perform rapid alternating movements
8.42 Inability to recognize objects or people

Questions 8.43–8.46

A. Déjà vu
B. *Déjà entendu*
C. *Déjà pensé*
D. *Jamais vu*
E. Confabulation

8.43 Illusion of auditory recognition
8.44 Regarding a new thought as a repetition of a previous thought
8.45 Feeling of unfamiliarity with a familiar situation
8.46 Regarding a new situation as a repetition of a previous experience

Questions 8.47–8.50

A. Synesthesia
B. Paramnesia
C. Hypermnesia
D. Eidetic images
E. Lethologica

8.47 Exaggerated degree of retention and recall
8.48 Temporary inability to remember a name
8.49 Confusion of facts and fantasies
8.50 Sensations that accompany sensations of another modality

Questions 8.51–8.55

A. Insight
B. Abstract thinking
C. Concrete thinking
D. Pseudodementia
E. Dementia

8.51 A 70-year-old woman can no longer remember her children's names.
8.52 A severely depressed 36-year-old man can no longer balance his checkbook, something he had done for years.
8.53 "People in glass houses shouldn't throw stones" means that the glass will break if a stone hits it.
8.54 "A rolling stone gathers no moss" means that you cannot form solid friendships or foundations if you are never in one place.

8.55 A 45-year-old man with alcohol dependence states that he will die if he continues to drink alcohol as he does.

Questions 8.56–8.59

A. Anxiety
B. Ambivalence
C. Guilt
D. Abreaction

8.56 Coexistence of two opposing impulses
8.57 Emotional discharge after recalling a painful experience
8.58 Feeling of apprehension
8.59 Emotion resulting from doing something perceived as wrong

Questions 8.60–8.64

A. Tangentiality
B. Anosognosia
C. Dysprosody
D. Erotomania
E. Nominal aphasia

8.60 Associated with denial of physical disorder
8.61 Person never gets to the point
8.62 Disturbance in language output
8.63 Disordered rhythm of speech
8.64 Disturbance in content of thought

ANSWERS

Typical Signs and Symptoms of Psychiatric Illness Defined

8.1 The answer is E (*Synopsis VIII,* page 280).
Catalepsy, or catatonia, is characterized by waxy rigidity of the limbs. There is also a lack of response to stimuli, as well as mutism and inactivity. *Overactivity* is abnormally active motor behavior that often expresses aspects of the psyche, including impulses, motivations, wishes, drives, instincts, and cravings. *Tic,* an involuntary, spasmodic motor movement; *ataxia,* a failure of muscular coordination or an irregularity of muscular action; and *akathisia,* a subjective feeling of muscular tension, are varieties of overactivity; *satyriasis,* a man's excessive and compulsive need for sex, is a type of compulsion or disorder, an uncontrollable impulse to repeat an action.

8.2 The answer is A (*Synopsis VIII,* page 280).
All of the terms except *stereotypy* involve disturbances in thinking. *Blocking* is an abrupt interruption in thinking; *derailment* is a deviation in the train of thought. *Word salad* refers to an incoherent mixture of words and phrases; *incoherence* is incomprehensible thought. *Stereotypy* is the continuous mechanical repetition of physical activity.

8.3 The answer is A (*Synopsis VIII,* pages 251, 284).
The phenomenon of the student who begins to fall asleep in class but is startled awake, thinking that the student's name was called, although it was not, is an example of a *hypnagogic hallucination.* A hypnagogic hallucination is a false sensory perception that occurs while the person is falling asleep; it is generally considered nonpathological. In contrast, a *hypnopompic hallucination* is a false sensory perception that occurs while the person's awakening from sleep; it, too, is generally considered nonpathological. An *illusion* is a misperception or a misinterpretation of real external sensory stimuli. *Synesthesia* is a sensation or hallucination caused by another sensation (for example, a sound is experienced as being seen, or a visual experience is seemingly heard). *Dissociation* is a defense mechanism. It is a temporary but drastic modification of a person's character or sense of personal identity to avoid emotional distress.

8.4 The answer is A (*Synopsis VIII,* page 282).
The patient in the emergency room who reports having his thoughts controlled by the CIA was using *dereistic* thinking—that is, thinking not concordant with logic or experience. *Magical* thinking is a form of thought found in Jean Piaget's stage of preoperational thought in children, in which thoughts and words assume power (for example, they can cause or prevent events). *Depersonalized* thinking is characterized by the sensation of unreality concerning oneself, parts of oneself, or one's environment that occurs under extreme stress or fatigue. *Obsessional* thinking is a disturbance in the content of thought. It is a pathological persistence of an irresistible thought or feeling that cannot be eliminated from consciousness by logical effort. A person who is *delirious* suffers from a disturbance of consciousness and is usually bewildered, restless, confused, and disoriented.

8.5 The answer is C (*Synopsis VIII,* pages 252, 282).
Tangentiality is the inability to have a goal-directed association of thoughts. The patient never gets from the desired point to the desired goal. *Word salad* is an incoherent mixture of words and phrases. *Circumstantiality* is indirect speech that is delayed in reaching the point but eventually gets there. Circumstantiality is characterized by an overinclusion of details and parenthetical remarks. *Verbigeration* is a meaningless repetition of specific words or phrases. *Blocking* is an abrupt interruption in the train of thinking before a thought or idea is finished. After a brief pause, the person indicates no recall of what was being said or what was going to be said. It is also known as thought deprivation.

8.6 The answer is D (*Synopsis VIII,* pages 244, 283).
All the lettered completions are examples of specific disturbances in the content of thought. *Thought insertion* is a type of delusion of control in which persons feel that thoughts are being implanted in their minds by other people or forces. *Thought broadcasting* is a delusion of control in which persons feel that their thoughts can be heard by others, as though the thoughts were being broadcast into the air.

Delusions are false beliefs based on incorrect inferences about external reality that are not consistent with the patient's intelligence or cultural background and that cannot be corrected by reasoning. A *delusion of reference* is a false belief that the behavior of others refers to oneself and that events, objects, or other people have a particular and unusual significance, usually negative. The delusion is derived from an idea of reference in which one falsely feels that one is being talked about by others (for example, a belief that people on television or the radio are talking to or about the patient). A *nihilistic delusion* is a false feeling that oneself, others, or the world is nonexisting or ending.

Pseudologia phantastica is a type of lying in which persons appear to believe in the reality of their fantasies and, therefore, act on them. It is associated with Munchausen syndrome, which is a repeated feigning of illness.

8.7 The answer is D (*Synopsis VIII,* page 284).
Loss of normal speech melody is known as *dysprosody.* A disturbance in speech inflection and rhythm results in a monotonous and halting speech pattern, which occasionally suggests a foreign accent. It can be the result of a brain disease, such as Parkinson's disease, or it can be a psychological defensive mechanism (seen in some people with schizophrenia). As a psychological device, it can serve the function of maintaining a safe distance in social encounters.

Stuttering is a speech disorder characterized by repetitions or prolongations of sound syllables and words and by hesitations or pauses that disrupt the flow of speech. It is also known as *stammering. Aphonia* is a loss of one's voice. *Dyslexia* is a specific learning disability involving a reading impairment that is unrelated to the person's intelligence.

8.8 The answer is C (*Synopsis VIII,* pages 282, 1215).
A disturbance in perception is a disturbance in the mental process by which data—intellectual, sensory, and emotional—are

organized. Through perception, people are capable of making sense out of the many stimuli that bombard them. Perceptual disturbances do not include *echolalia,* which is the repetition of another's words or phrases. Echolalia is a disturbance of thought form and communication. Examples of perceptual disturbances are *hallucinations,* which are false sensory perceptions without concrete external stimuli. Common hallucinations involve sights or sounds, although any of the senses may be involved, and *hypnagogic experiences,* which are hallucinations that occur just before falling asleep. Other disturbances of perception include *depersonalization,* which is the sensation of unreality concerning oneself or one's environment, and *derealization,* which is the feeling of changed reality or the feeling that one's surroundings have changed.

8.9 The answer is C (*Synopsis VIII,* pages 254, 286).
Asking a patient to interpret a proverb is generally used as a way of assessing whether the person has the capacity for *abstract thought.* Abstract thinking, as opposed to concrete thinking, is characterized primarily by the ability to shift voluntarily from one aspect of a situation to another, to keep in mind simultaneously various aspects of a situation, and to think symbolically. Concrete thinking is characterized by an inability to conceptualize beyond immediate experience or beyond actual things and events. Psychopathologically, it is most characteristic of persons with schizophrenia or organic brain disorders.

Judgment, the patient's ability to comprehend the meaning of events and to appreciate the consequences of actions, is often tested by asking how the patient would act in certain standard circumstances; for example, if the patient smelled smoke in a crowded movie theater. *Impulse control* is the ability to control acting on a wish to discharge energy in a manner that is, at the moment, felt to be dangerous, inappropriate, or otherwise ill-advised. *Insight* is a conscious understanding of forces that have led to a particular feeling, action, or situation. *Intelligence* is the capacity for learning, recalling, integrating, and applying knowledge and experience.

Answers 8.10–8.14

8.10 The answer is C (*Synopsis VIII,* page 275).

8.11 The answer is A (*Synopsis VIII,* page 275).

8.12 The answer is B (*Synopsis VIII,* pages 275, 320–321).

8.13 The answer is E (*Synopsis VIII,* page 275).

8.14 The answer is D (*Synopsis VIII,* page 275).
Consciousness is a person's state of awareness. The lettered responses represent varying degrees of disturbances in consciousness. The most *profound degree of unconsciousness* is *coma. Stupor* is a *lack of reaction to and an unawareness of one's surroundings.* Stupor is caused by intoxication, infection, and a host of other sources. *Delirium* is a bewildered, *restless, confused, and disoriented* state associated with fear and hallucinations. Delirium may be caused by many of the same sources resulting in stupor. Someone who suffers a certain kind of *complex partial seizure called psychomotor epilepsy* is said to suffer from a *dreamlike state.* The seizures usually arise from the temporal lobe—limbic cortex region; during the attack, memory and consciousness are either impaired or lost. Temporal lobe seizures may also produce a preseizure aura with feelings of *déjà vu, jamais vu,* micropsia, macropsia, or dreaminess. *Somnolence* is *abnormal drowsiness;* it may be seen in such conditions as narcolepsy and sleep apnea.

Answers 8.15–8.19

8.15 The answer is C (*Synopsis VIII,* page 279).

8.16 The answer is A (*Synopsis VIII,* pages 279, 480).

8.17 The answer is E (*Synopsis VIII,* pages 250, 279).

8.18 The answer is D (*Synopsis VIII,* page 279).

8.19 The answer is B (*Synopsis VIII,* page 279).
Alexithymia is difficulty in describing or becoming aware of one's emotions or moods. *Anhedonia* is a loss of interest in and withdrawal from all regular and pleasurable activities; the condition is most often associated with depression. Persons in an *expansive mood* express their feelings without restraint and frequently with an overestimation of the person's significance or importance; this condition is often seen in patients who are manic. Someone who shows a normal range of mood, implying an absence of depressed or elevated mood, is said to be displaying *euthymia. Euphoria* is an intense elation with feelings of grandeur.

Answers 8.20–8.24

8.20 The answer is C (*Synopsis VIII,* page 280).

8.21 The answer is B (*Synopsis VIII,* page 280).

8.22 The answer is E (*Synopsis VIII,* pages 280, 1215–1216).

8.23 The answer is D (*Synopsis VIII,* page 280).

8.24 The answer is A (*Synopsis VIII,* page 280).
Cataplexy is a *weakness and temporary loss of muscle tone precipitated by* a variety of *emotional states. Catalepsy* is a *general term for an immobile position that is constantly maintained* and is seen in certain types of schizophrenia. A *tic* is an *involuntary, spasmodic motor movement;* it is seen in such conditions as Tourette's disorder. A type of motor behavior with a *repetitive, fixed pattern of physical action or speech* is called *stereotypy. Echopraxia* is a *pathological imitation of another person's movements.*

Answers 8.25–8.29

8.25 The answer is E (*Synopsis VIII,* pages 252, 282).

8.26 The answer is A (*Synopsis VIII,* pages 252, 282).

8.27 The answer is B (*Synopsis VIII,* pages 251, 282).

8.28 The answer is D (*Synopsis VIII,* pages 252, 282).

8.29 The answer is C (*Synopsis VIII,* pages 252, 282).
All the lettered responses are examples of specific disturbances in form of thought. Most are seen in schizophrenic patients. *Neologisms* are new words created by the patient, often by combining syllables of other words, for idiosyncratic psychological reasons. *Loosening of associations* is a flow of thoughts in which ideas shift from one subject to another in completely unrelated ways. When the condition is severe, the patient's

speech may be incoherent. *Flight of ideas* is a rapid, continuous verbalization or play on words that produces a constant shifting from one idea to another; the ideas tend to be connected, and when the condition is not severe, a listener may be able to follow them; the thought disorder is most characteristic of someone in a manic state. *Blocking* is an abrupt interruption in a train of thinking before a thought or idea is finished; after a brief pause, the person indicates no recall of what was being said or what was going to be said. The condition is also known as thought deprivation. A person who is using *clang association* uses an association of words similar in sound but not in meaning; the words used have no logical connections and may include examples of rhyming and punning.

Answers 8.30–8.34

8.30 The answer is C (*Synopsis VIII,* pages 281, 283, 609).

8.31 The answer is B (*Synopsis VIII,* pages 283, 609).

8.32 The answer is A (*Synopsis VIII,* pages 252, 282).

8.33 The answer is E (*Synopsis VIII,* page 282).

8.34 The answer is D (*Synopsis VIII,* pages 283, 603).
The lettered headings are examples of specific disturbances in content of thought. A *compulsion* is a *pathological need to act on a feeling* that, if resisted, produces anxiety. An *obsession* is a *pathological persistence of an irresistible thought or feeling* that cannot be eliminated from consciousness by logical effort and is associated with anxiety; it is also termed rumination. A *delusion* is a *fixed, false belief, based on incorrect inferences about external reality,* that cannot be corrected by reasoning. A person who maintains an *unreasonable, sustained false belief that is not fixed* is said to have an *overvalued idea.* A *phobia* is a *persistent, irrational, exaggerated,* and invariably pathological *dread of some specific type of stimulus or situation;* the dread results in a compelling desire to avoid the stimulus.

Answers 8.35–8.38

8.35 The answer is C (*Synopsis VIII,* page 284).

8.36 The answer is B (*Synopsis VIII,* page 284).

8.37 The answer is A (*Synopsis VIII,* pages 89, 92, 1290–1291).

8.38 The answer is E (*Synopsis VIII,* pages 89, 92, 1290–1291).
Nominal aphasia, also known as anomia, is *difficulty in finding the correct names for objects.* A person who experiences an organic *loss of the ability to comprehend the meaning of words* suffers from *sensory aphasia;* speech is fluid and spontaneous but incoherent and nonsensical. A person who retains language comprehension but who suffers the *loss of the ability to speak* has *Broca's (motor) aphasia;* speech is halting, laborious, and inaccurate. *Syntactical aphasia* is the *inability to arrange words in a proper sequence. Global aphasia* is a combination of a grossly nonfluent aphasia and a severe fluent aphasia; the person has difficulty in both the comprehension and the production of language.

Answers 8.39–8.42

8.39 The answer is D (*Synopsis VIII,* page 285).

8.40 The answer is B (*Synopsis VIII,* pages 80, 285).

8.41 The answer is A (*Synopsis VIII,* pages 284–285).

8.42 The answer is C (*Synopsis VIII,* page 285).
The lettered responses are examples of cognitive disorders. *Autotopagnosia* is the *inability to recognize a body part as one's own;* it is also known as somatopagnosia. *Astereognosis* is the *inability to distinguish* objects *by touch,* such as a quarter and a dime. *Dysdiadochokinesia* is the *inability to perform rapid alternating movements;* it is usually a cerebellar dysfunction. *Visual agnosia* is the *inability to recognize objects or persons. Simultanagnosia* is the inability to comprehend more than one element of a visual scene at a time or to integrate the parts into a whole.

Answers 8.43–8.46

8.43 The answer is B (*Synopsis VIII,* page 285).

8.44 The answer is C (*Synopsis VIII,* page 285).

8.45 The answer is D (*Synopsis VIII,* page 285).

8.46 The answer is A (*Synopsis VIII,* pages 91, 285).
Déjà vu is *regarding a new situation as a repetition of a previous experience. Déjà entendu* is an *illusion of auditory recognition. Déjà pensé* is *regarding a new thought as a repetition of a previous thought. Jamais vu* is a *feeling of unfamiliarity with a familiar situation. Confabulation* is the unconscious filling in of memory by imagining experiences that have no basis in fact.

Answers 8.47–8.50

8.47 The answer is C (*Synopsis VIII,* page 285).

8.48 The answer is E (*Synopsis VIII,* page 285).

8.49 The answer is B (*Synopsis VIII,* page 285).

8.50 The answer is A (*Synopsis VIII,* page 284).
In *synesthesia* the patient experiences *sensations that accompany sensations of another modality;* for example, an auditory sensation is accompanied by or triggers a visual sensation, or a sound is experienced as being seen or accompanied by a visual experience. *Paramnesia* is a *confusion of facts and fantasies;* it lends to a falsification of memory by the distortion of real events by fantasies. *Hypermnesia* is an *exaggerated degree of retention and recall* or an ability to remember material that ordinarily is not retrievable. *Eidetic images,* also known as primary memory images, are visual memories of almost hallucinatory vividness. *Lethologica* is the *temporary inability to remember a name* or a proper noun.

Answers 8.51–8.55

8.51 The answer is E (*Synopsis VIII,* page 123).

8.52 The answer is D (*Synopsis VIII,* pages 340, 341).

8.53 The answer is C (*Synopsis VIII,* page 286).

8.54 The answer is B (*Synopsis VIII,* page 286).

8.55 The answer is A (*Synopsis VIII,* pages 254, 286).
Dementia is an organic and global deterioration of intellectual functioning without a clouding of consciousness. Dementia is caused by such illnesses as Alzheimer's disease, Huntington's disease, and acquired immune deficiency syndrome (AIDS). A depressed person may have clinical features that resemble a dementia but have no underlying organic condition. That is known as *pseudodementia. Concrete thinking* is one-dimensional thought. It results in the liberal use of metaphors without understanding the nuances of meaning. *Abstract thinking* is the ability to appreciate the nuances of meaning. People who think abstractly are capable of multidimensional thought and use metaphors and hypotheses appropriately.

Insight is the ability to understand the true cause and meaning of a situation. For example, a person with alcohol dependence may be cognizant of the cause-and-effect relation of alcohol on his life expectancy.

Answers 8.56–8.59

8.56 The answer is B (*Synopsis VIII,* page 280).

8.57 The answer is D (*Synopsis VIII,* pages 207, 280, 674).

8.58 The answer is A (*Synopsis VIII,* pages 279, 581).

8.59 The answer is C (*Synopsis VIII,* page 280).
Anxiety is a *feeling of apprehension* caused by anticipation of danger, which may be internal or external. *Ambivalence* is the *coexistence of two opposing impulses* toward the same thing in the same person at the same time. *Guilt* is an *emotion resulting from doing something perceived as wrong. Abreaction* is an *emotional discharge after recalling a painful experience.*

Answers 8.60–8.64

8.60 The answer is B (*Synopsis VIII,* pages 93, 285).

8.61 The answer is A (*Synopsis VIII,* pages 252, 282).

8.62 The answer is E (*Synopsis VIII,* page 284).

8.63 The answer is C (*Synopsis VIII,* page 284).

8.64 The answer is D (*Synopsis VIII,* pages 283, 516).
The many typical signs and symptoms of psychiatric illness that the student needs to be able to define and recognize include disturbances of consciousness, emotion, motor behavior, thinking, perception, memory, intelligence, insight, and judgment. Disturbances in the form of thought involve a disruption in the goal-directed flow of ideas and associations typical of the logical sequence of normal thinking. A formal thought disorder is a disturbance in the form, as opposed to the content, of thought. *Tangentiality* is a specific disorder in the form of thought that involves the patient's thinking in tangents that never return to the idea or question or origin; the *person never gets to the point.* Anosognosia is a disturbance associated with brain diseases of the nonlanguage sphere. *Anosognosia* is *associated with denial of a physical disorder.* The patient denies, suppresses, or is unable to recognize a physical disability. Aphasias are *disturbances in language output* and comprehension. They include motor (or Broca's) aphasia, which is characterized by difficulty in speaking, with comprehension intact; sensory (or Wernicke's) aphasia, which is characterized by impaired comprehension, with speech relatively fluent; and *nominal aphasia,* which is the defective use of words and the inability to name objects. *Dysprosody* is *disordered rhythm of speech* or the loss of normal speech melody; it may be caused by a frontal lesion that makes the patient's speech sound odd. *Erotomania,* also known as Clérembault's syndrome, is a delusional belief that another person is in love with the patient. It is an example of a *disturbance in content of thought.* Erotomania has been interpreted psychodynamically as a grandiose fantasy that defends against an underlying belief that the patient is unlovable.

9 

Classification in Psychiatry and Psychiatric Rating Scales

In psychiatric research and practice, workers use a standard language, which describes the real entities of their work, to document their observations, the data obtained from patients and family, the testing results, and diagnoses. Two classification systems are used: the 10th revision of *International Statistical Classification of Diseases and Related Health Problems* (ICD-10) and the 4th edition of *Diagnostic and Statistical Manual of Mental Disorders* (DSM-IV). ICD-10 was published by the World Health Organization in 1992 and is used in Europe; it will probably soon be used officially in the United States. Although similar to DSM-IV, ICD-10 includes disorders absent from DSM-IV and sometimes defines disorders appearing in both systems differently from DSM-IV.

DSM was first published in 1952 by the American Psychiatric Association; the most recent edition appeared in 1994. DSM-IV presents an atheoretical description of each disorder, as well as specific criteria for making a diagnosis, a description of essential and associated features for each disorder, and provisions for diagnostic uncertainties. The data are based on extensive field trials and clinical research so that the terms refer to specific clinical disorders like *anxiety or depression,* rather than vague expressions like *neurosis.*

Although the goal of classificatory standardization is critical to a valid and intellectually sophisticated practice of psychiatry, there are potential dangers. Foremost among these dangers is a simplistic approach to psychiatric diagnosis in which the patient loses any semblance of individuality or uniqueness and becomes merely a compilation of behavioral signs. Attention must be directed toward the humanistic and complex factors that contribute to the development of mental disorders and to the factors that lead to their resolution.

Chapter 9 in *Kaplan and Sadock's Synopsis VIII* addresses many of the issues in psychiatric classification. The questions below test the student's understanding of the issues.

HELPFUL HINTS

The student should be able to define the terms below, especially the diagnostic categories.

- age of onset
- agoraphobia
- alcohol delirium
- amnestic disorders
- associated and essential features
- atheoretical
- bipolar I disorder
- body dysmorphic disorder
- classification
- clinical syndromes
- cognitive disorders
- competence
- complications
- conversion disorder
- course
- delusional disorder
- dementia precox
- depersonalization disorder
- depressive disorders
- descriptive approach
- diagnostic criteria
- differential diagnosis
- disability determination
- dissociative disorders
- dissociative fugue
- dissociative identity disorder
- DSM-IV
- dysthymic disorder
- ego-dystonic and ego-syntonic
- familial pattern
- general medical conditions
- generalized anxiety disorder
- Global Assessment of Functioning Scale
- gross social norms
- highest level of functioning
- hypochondriasis
- ICD-10
- impairment
- Emil Kraepelin
- mood disorders
- multiaxial system
- obsessive-compulsive disorder
- panic disorder
- paraphilias
- partial and full remission
- personality disorders
- pervasive developmental disorders
- phobias
- posttraumatic stress disorder
- predictive validity
- predisposing factors
- premenstrual dysphoric disorder
- prevalence
- psychological factors affecting medical condition
- psychosis
- psychosocial and environmental stressors
- reality testing
- residual type
- schizophrenia
- severity-of-stress rating
- sex ratio
- sexual dysfunctions
- somatization disorder
- somatoform disorders
- validity and reliability

▲ QUESTIONS

DIRECTIONS: Each of the incomplete statements below is followed by five suggested completions. Select the *one* that is *best* in each case.

9.1 Bipolar affective disorder may be modified by each of the following *except*

A. current episode mixed
B. being currently in remission
C. current episode hypomanic
D. without symptoms of schizophrenia
E. current episode manic with psychotic symptoms

9.2 Dementia in Alzheimer's disease may be characterized by each of the following terms *except*

A. mixed type
B. atypical type
C. of acute onset
D. with late onset
E. with early onset

9.3 Which of the following represents a sexual preference disorder?

A. Voyeurism
B. Orgasmic dysfunction
C. Excessive sexual drive
D. Premature ejaculation
E. Erectile disorder

9.4 The fourth edition of *Diagnostic and Statistical Manual of Mental Disorders* (DSM-IV)

A. may not be used by Medicare in billing codes for reimbursement
B. provides the causes of the mental disorders
C. provides a list of treatment modalities for each disorder
D. is a multiaxial system
E. uses Axis I to list mental retardation

9.5 The term "psychotic"

A. applies to major and minor distortions of reality
B. is used in the presence of either delusions or hallucinations
C. has a precise meaning in current clinical and research practice
D. is not used in DSM-IV
E. is used to describe a person with a phobia

9.6 All of the following are classified as paraphilias *except*

A. fetishism
B. homosexuality
C. exhibitionism
D. sexual sadism
E. transvestic fetishism

9.7 The Social and Occupational Functioning Assessment Scale (SOFAS)

A. is scored independent of the person's psychological symptoms
B. does not include impairment in functioning that is caused by a general medical condition
C. may not be used to rate functioning at the time of the evaluation
D. may not be used to rate functioning of a past period
E. is included on Axis III

9.8 DSM-IV conditions that have been termed neurotic disorders in other classification systems include

A. anxiety disorders
B. somatoform disorders
C. dissociative disorders
D. dysthymic disorder
E. all of the above

DIRECTIONS: Each group of questions below consists of five lettered headings followed by a list of numbered phrases or statements. For each numbered phrase or statement, select the *one* lettered heading that is most closely associated with it. Each lettered heading may be selected once, more than once, or not at all.

Questions 9.9–9.10

A. Axis I
B. Axis II
C. Axis III
D. Axis IV
E. Axis V

9.9 Psychosocial and environmental problems
9.10 Global assessment of functioning

Questions 9.11–9.15

A. Paranoid personality disorder
B. Schizotypal personality disorder
C. Borderline personality disorder
D. Dependent personality disorder
E. Passive-aggressive personality disorder

9.11 Ideas of reference and magical thinking
9.12 Stubborn and procrastinates
9.13 Suspicious and hypervigilant
9.14 Impulsive and self-destructive
9.15 Clinging and subordinates own needs to those of others

Questions 9.16–9.20

A. Axis I
B. Axis II
C. Axis III
D. Axis IV
E. Axis V

9.16 Kidney failure
9.17 Borderline personality disorder
9.18 Mental retardation
9.19 Unemployment
9.20 Delusional disorder

ANSWERS

Classification in Psychiatry and Psychiatric Rating Scales

9.1 The answer is D (*Synopsis VIII,* pages 302, 552).
Without symptoms of schizophrenia refers to acute and transient psychotic disorders, not to bipolar affective disorder. The other four types—*current episode mixed, currently in remission, current episode hypomanic,* and *current episode manic with psychotic symptoms*—all refer to varieties of bipolar affective disorder.

9.2 The answer is C (*Synopsis VIII,* pages 288, 342).
Acute onset refers to vascular dementia, not to dementia in Alzheimer's disease, which has a slow onset. The other four types—*mixed, atypical, with late onset,* and *with early onset*—all refer to dementia in Alzheimer's disease.

9.3 The answer is A (*Synopsis VIII,* pages 289, 687–689).
Voyeurism is a disorder of sexual preference in which sexual excitement is obtained by observing nudity or sexual activity, whereas *orgasmic dysfunction, excessive sexual drive, premature ejaculation,* and *erectile disorder* are disorders of sexual dysfunction. Excessive sexual drive is characterized by insatiable fixed needs or desires. Orgasmic dysfunction is failure to achieve orgasm. Premature ejaculation is ejaculation occurring before or immediately after vaginal intromission. Erectile disorder is the inability to obtain an erection, especially one sufficiently turgid to achieve intromission.

9.4 The answer is D (*Synopsis VIII,* page 292).
The fourth edition of *Diagnostic and Statistical Manual of Mental Disorders* (DSM-IV) *is a multiaxial system* that contains five axes and evaluates the patient along several variables. Published in 1994, DSM-IV is the latest and most up-to-date classification of mental disorders.

DSM-IV correlates with the 10th revision of the World Health Organization's *International Statistical Classification of Diseases and Related Health Problems* (ICD-10), developed in 1992. Diagnostic systems used in the United States are compatible with ICD, and both *may be used by Medicare in billing codes for reimbursement.*

The approach in DSM-IV is atheoretical with regard to causes. Thus, DSM-IV describes the manifestations of the mental disorders; only rarely does DSM-IV attempt to *provide the causes of the mental disorders.*

DSM-IV does not *provide a list of treatment modalities for each disorder.* Nor does it mention management or controversial issues surrounding a particular diagnostic category. Clinical syndromes and other conditions that may be a focus of clinical attention are included on Axis I. DSM-IV does not *use Axis I to list mental retardation;* they are included on Axis II.

9.5 The answer is B (*Synopsis VIII,* pages 302–303).
The term "psychotic" *is used in the presence of either delusions or hallucinations;* patients do not have insight into their pathological nature. With gross impairment in reality testing, persons incorrectly evaluate the accuracy of their perceptions and thoughts and make incorrect inferences about external reality, even in the face of contrary evidence.

Psychosis *applies only to major distortions of reality;* it does not apply to minor distortions of reality that involve matters of relative judgment. For example, depressed patients who underestimate their achievements are not described as psychotic, whereas patients who believe that they have caused natural catastrophes are described as psychotic.

Although the traditional meaning of the term "psychotic" emphasized the loss of reality testing and the impairment of mental functioning—manifested by delusions, hallucinations, confusion, and impaired memory—two other meanings have evolved during the past 50 years. In the most common psychiatric use of the term, "psychotic" became synonymous with the severe impairment of social and personal functioning characterized by social withdrawal and the inability to perform the usual household and occupational roles. The other use of the term specifies the degree of ego regression as the criterion for psychotic illness. As a consequence of those multiple meanings, the term "psychotic" *does not have a precise meaning in current clinical and research practice. However, the term "psychotic" is used in DSM-IV.*

The term "neurotic," not "psychotic," is used to describe a person with a *phobia,* a persistent, irrational dread of a stimulus or a situation. The term is no longer used in DSM-IV, although "neurosis" is still found in the literature and in ICD-10. Neurosis has come to mean a chronic or recurrent nonpsychotic disorder characterized mainly by anxiety, which is experienced or expressed directly or is altered through defense mechanisms. Neurosis appears as a symptom, such as an obsession, a compulsion, a phobia, or a sexual dysfunction.

9.6 The answer is B (*Synopsis VIII,* pages 291, 700–702).
Paraphilias are conditions associated with (1) preference for the use of a nonhuman object for sexual arousal; (2) repetitive sexual activity with humans involving real or simulated suffering or humiliation; or (3) repetitive sexual activity with nonconsenting or inappropriate partners.

Homosexuality is not classified as a paraphilia. In December 1973, the Board of Trustees of the American Psychiatric Association voted to eliminate homosexuality as a mental disorder. The removal of homosexuality as a paraphilia was supported by the following rationale: The crucial issue in determining whether homosexuality should be regarded as a mental disorder is not the cause of the condition but its consequences and the definition of mental disorder. A significant proportion of homosexuals are satisfied with their sexual orientation, show no significant signs of manifest psychopathology, and are able to function socially and occupationally with no impairment. If one uses the criteria of distress or disability, homosexuality is not a mental disorder. If one uses the criterion of inherent disadvantage, it is not at all clear that homosexuality is a disadvantage in all cultures or subcultures.

In *fetishism,* sexual excitement is achieved by using an inanimate object, for example, a shoe or underwear. *Sexual sadism* is characterized by inflicting pain or humiliation on the sexual partner. In *transvestic fetishism,* sexual arousal is achieved by dressing in clothes of the opposite sex.

Table 9.1
Social and Occupational Functioning Assessment Scale (SOFAS)[a]

Consider social and occupational functioning on a continuum from excellent functioning to grossly impaired functioning. Include impairments in functioning due to physical limitations, as well as those due to mental impairments. To be counted, impairment must be a direct consequence of mental and physical health problems; the effects of lack of opportunity and other environmental limitations are not to be considered.

Code	(**Note:** Use intermediate codes when appropriate, eg, 45, 68, 72.)
100–91	Superior functioning in a wide range of activities.
90–81	Good functioning in all areas, occupationally and socially effective.
80–71	No more than a slight impairment in social, occupational, or school functioning (eg, infrequent interpersonal conflict, temporarily falling behind in schoolwork).
70–61	Some difficulty in social, occupational, or school functioning, but generally functioning well, has some meaningful interpersonal relationships.
60–51	Moderate difficulty in social, occupational, or school functioning (eg, few friends, conflicts with peers or coworkers).
50–41	Serious impairment in social, occupational, or school functioning (eg, no friends, unable to keep a job).
40–31	Major impairment in several areas, such as work or school, family relations (eg, depressed man avoids friends, neglects family, and is unable to work; child frequently beats up younger children, is defiant at home, and is failing at school).
30–21	Inability to function in almost all areas (eg, stays in bed all day; no job, home, or friends).
20–11	Occasionally fails to maintain minimal personal hygiene; unable to function independently.
10–1	Persistent inability to maintain minimal personal hygiene. Unable to function without harming self or others or without considerable external support (eg, nursing care and supervision).
0	Inadequate information.

Reprinted with permission from American Psychiatric Association: *Diagnostic and Statistical Manual of Mental Disorders,* ed 4. Copyright American Psychiatric Association, Washington, 1994.

[a] **Note:** The rating of overall psychological functioning on a scale of 0–100 was operationalized by Luborsky in the Health-Sickness Rating Scale (Luborsky L: Clinicians' judgments of mental health. Arch Gen Psychiatry *7:* 407, 1962). Spitzer and colleagues developed a revision of the Health-Sickness Rating Scale called the Global Assessment Scale (GAS) (Endicott J, Spitzer RL, Fleiss JL, et al: The Global Assessment Scale: A procedure for measuring overall severity of psychiatric disturbance. Arch Gen Psychiatry *33:* 766, 1976). The SOFAS is derived from the GAS and its development is described in Goldman HH, Skodol AE, Lave TR: Revising Axis V for DSM-IV: A review of measures of social functioning. Am J Psychiatry *149:* 1148, 1992.

9.7 The answer is A (*Synopsis VIII,* pages 298–299).

The Social and Occupational Functioning Assessment Scale (SOFAS) (Table 9.1) is a new scale included in a DSM-IV appendix. The scale differs from the Global Assessment of Functioning (GAF) Scale in that it focuses only on the person's level of social and occupational functioning. It is scored independent of the severity of the person's psychological symptoms. And, unlike the GAF scale, the SOFAS may include *impairment in functioning* that is caused by a general *medical condition.* The SOFAS may be used to rate functioning at the time of the evaluation, or *it may be used to rate functioning of a past period.* The SOFAS is included on Axis V, not Axis III.

9.8 The answer is E (all) (*Synopsis VIII,* page 302).

A neurosis is an ego-alien (ego-dystonic) nonorganic disorder in which reality testing is intact, anxiety is a major characteristic, and the use of various defense mechanisms plays a major role. As opposed to ICD-10, which contains a number of neurotic diagnostic classes, DSM-IV contains no diagnostic category of neuroses. However, several DSM-IV categories were termed neurotic disorders in the past, and many clinicians still use the term ''neurosis'' for those disorders. Those disorders include *anxiety disorders, somatoform disorders, dissociative disorders,* sexual and gender identity disorders, and *dysthymic disorder.*

Table 9.2
DSM-IV Axis IV: Psychosocial and Environmental Problems

Problems with primary support group—eg, death of a family member; health problems in family; disruption of family by separation, divorce, or estrangement; removal from the home; remarriage of parent; sexual or physical abuse; parental overprotection; neglect of child; inadequate discipline; discord with siblings; birth of a sibling

Problems related to the social environment—eg, death or loss of friend; social isolation; living alone; difficulty with acculturation; discrimination; adjustment to life-cycle transition (such as retirement)

Educational problems—eg, illiteracy; academic problems; discord with teachers or classmates; inadequate school environment

Occupational problems—eg,unemployment; threat of job loss; stressful work schedule; difficult work condition; job dissatisfaction; job change; discord with boss or coworkers

Housing problems—eg, homelessness; inadequate housing; unsafe neighborhood; discord with neighbors or landlord

Economic problems—eg, extreme poverty; inadequate finances; insufficient welfare support

Problems with access to health care services—eg, inadequate health care services; transportation to health care facilities unavailable; inadequate health insurance

Problems related to interaction with the legal system/crime—eg, arrest; incarceration; litigation; victim of crime

Other psychosocial problems—eg, exposure to disasters, war, other hostilities; discord with nonfamily caregivers (such as counselor, social worker, physician), unavailability of social service agencies.

Reprinted with permission from American Psychiatric Association: *Diagnostic and Statistical Manual of Mental Disorders,* ed 4. Copyright, American Psychiatric Association, Washington, 1994.

Answers 9.9–9.10

9.9 The answer is D (*Synopsis VIII,* page 302).

9.10 The answer is E (*Synopsis VIII,* page 302).
Axis IV is used to code the *psychosocial and environmental* problems that significantly contribute to the development or the exacerbation of the patient's disorder. The evaluation of stressors is based on the clinician's assessment of the stress that an average person with similar sociocultural values and circumstances would experience from the psychosocial stressors. That judgment considers the amount of change in the person's life caused by the stressor, the degree to which the event is desired and under the person's control, and the number of stressors. Stressors may be positive (for example, a job promotion) or negative (for example, the loss of a loved one). Information about stressors may be important in formulating a treatment plan that includes attempts to remove the psychosocial stressors or to help the patient cope with them. Table 9.2 presents the psychosocial and environmental problems listed in DSM-IV.

Axis V is the global assessment of functioning, in which the clinician judges the patient's overall level of functioning during a particular time period (for example, the patient's level of functioning at the time of the evaluation or the patient's highest level of functioning for at least a few months during the past year). Functioning is conceptualized as a composite of three major areas: social functioning, occupational functioning, and psychological functioning. The Global Assessment of Functioning (GAF) Scale, based on a continuum of mental health and mental illness, is a 100-point scale; 100 represents the highest level of functioning in all areas. Table 9.3 presents the Global Assessment of Functioning (GAF) Scale as it is published in DSM-IV.

Axis I consists of clinical disorders and other conditions

Table 9.3
DSM-IV Global Assessment of Functioning (GAF) Scale[a]

Consider psychological, social, and occupational functioning on a hypothetical continuum of mental health-illness. Do not include impairment in functioning due to physical (or environmental) limitations.

Code	(**Note:** Use intermediate codes when appropriate, eg, 45, 68, 72.)
100–91	**Superior functioning in a wide range of activities, life's problems never seem to get out of hand, is sought out by others because of his or her many positive qualities. No symptoms.**
90–81	**Absent or minimal symptoms** (eg, mild anxiety before an exam), **good functioning in all areas, interested and involved in a wide range of activities, socially effective, generally satisfied with life, no more than everyday problems or concerns** (eg, an occasional argument with family members).
80–71	**If symptoms are present, they are transient and expectable reactions to psychosocial stressors** (eg, difficulty concentrating after family argument); **no more than slight impairment in social, occupational, or school functioning** (eg, temporarily falling behind in school work).
70–61	**Some mild symptoms** (eg, depressed mood and mild insomnia) **OR some difficulty in social, occupational, or school functioning** (eg, occasional truancy, or theft within the household), **but generally functioning pretty well, has some meaningful interpersonal relationships.**
60–51	**Moderate symptoms** (eg, flat affect and circumstantial speech, occasional panic attacks) **OR moderate difficulty in social, occupational, or school functioning** (eg, few friends, conflicts with peers or coworkers).
50–41	**Serious symptoms** (eg, suicidal ideation, severe obsessional rituals, frequent shoplifting) **OR any serious impairment in social, occupational, or school functioning** (eg, no friends, unable to keep a job).
40–31	**Some impairment in reality testing or communication** (eg, speech is at times illogical, obscure, or irrelevant) **OR major impairment in several areas, such as work or school, family relations, judgment, thinking, or mood** (eg, depressed man avoids friends, neglects family, and is unable to work; child frequently beats up younger children, is defiant at home, and is failing at school).
30–21	**Behavior is considerably influenced by delusions or hallucinations OR serious impairment in communication or judgment** (eg, sometimes incoherent, acts grossly inappropriately, suicidal preoccupation) **OR inability to function in almost all areas** (eg, stays in bed all day; no job, home, or friends).
20–11	**Some danger of hurting self or others** (eg, suicide attempts without clear expectation of death; frequently violent; manic excitement) **OR occasionally fails to maintain minimal personal hygiene** (eg, smears feces) **OR gross impairment in communication** (eg, largely incoherent or mute).
10–1	**Persistent danger of severely hurting self or others** (eg, recurrent violence) **OR persistent inability to maintain minimal personal hygiene OR serious suicidal acts with clear expectation of death.**
0	Inadequate information.

Reprinted with permission from American Psychiatric Association: *Diagnostic and Statistical Manual of Mental Disorders,* ed 4. Copyright, American Psychiatric Association, Washington, 1994.

[a] The rating of overall psychological functioning on a scale of 0–100 was operationalized by Luborsky in the Health-Sickness Rating Scale (Luborsky L: Clinicians' judgments of mental health. Arch Gen Pscyhiatry *7:* 407, 1962). Spitzer and colleagues developed a revision of the Health-Sickness Rating Scale called the Global Assessment Scale (GAS) (Endicott J, Spitzer RL, Fleiss JL, Cohen J: The Global Assessment Scale: A procedure for measuring overall severity of psychiatric disturbance. Arch Gen Psychiatry *33:* 766, 1976). A modified version of the GAS was included in DSM-III-R as the Global Assessment of Functioning (GAF) Scale.

that may be a focus of clinical attention. *Axis II* consists of personality disorders and mental retardation. *Axis III* consists of physical disorders that may accompany the mental disorder, for example, diabetes.

Answers 9.11–9.15

9.11 The answer is B (*Synopsis VIII,* pages 776–777).

9.12 The answer is E (*Synopsis VIII,* page 775).

9.13 The answer is A (*Synopsis VIII,* page 776).

9.14 The answer is C (*Synopsis VIII,* page 775).

9.15 The answer is D (*Synopsis VIII,* page 777).
A person with *paranoid personality* disorder is suspicious, hypervigilant, secretive, and hypersensitive and has a generally restricted affect. A person with schizotypal personality disorder uses ideas of reference and magical thinking and may manifest an odd sense of speech, have recurrent depersonalization experiences or illusions, and be isolated and withdrawn. A person with *borderline personality* disorder is impulsive and self-destructive, shows patterns of unstable interpersonal relationships, and may make suicidal gestures. A person with *dependent personality* disorder is clinging and subordinates his or her own needs to the needs of others. Such a person is generally passive and finds it difficult to assume responsibility for major life duties. A person with *passive-aggressive personality* disorder is stubborn and procrastinates and shows long-standing social and occupational ineffectiveness.

Answers 9.16–9.20

9.16 The answer is C (*Synopsis VIII,* page 292).

9.17 The answer is B (*Synopsis VIII,* page 292).

9.18 The answer is B (*Synopsis VIII,* page 291).

9.19 The answer is D (*Synopsis VIII,* page 292).

9.20 The answer is A (*Synopsis VIII,* page 299).
DSM-IV uses a multiaxial scheme of classification consisting of five axes, each of which covers a different aspect of functioning. Each axis should be covered for each diagnosis. Axis I consists of all major clinical syndromes and other conditions that may be a focus of clinical attention. Examples include schizophrenia, mood disorders, and *delusional disorder.* Axis II consists of personality disorders, including *borderline personality disorder* and *mental retardation.* Axis III consists of general medical conditions. The condition may be causative (for example, *kidney failure* causing delirium), secondary (for example, acquired immune deficiency syndrome [AIDS] as a result of a substance-related disorder), or unrelated. Axis IV consists of psychosocial and environmental problems that are related to the current mental disorder. Examples include divorce, *unemployment,* and inadequate health insurance. Axis V is a global assessment of functioning in which the clinician evaluates the highest level of functioning by the patient in the past year. The Global Assessment of Functioning (GAF) Scale is a 100-point scale, with 100 representing the highest level of functioning in all areas.

10

Delirium, Dementia, and Amnestic and Other Cognitive Disorders and Mental Disorders Due to a General Medical Condition

The fourth edition of *Diagnostic and Statistical Manual of Mental Disorders* (DSM-IV) classifies three groups of disorders into a broad category that acknowledges the primary symptoms common to all, that is, impairments in cognition including, memory, judgment, and attention. Although other psychiatric disorders can include some cognitive impairment as a symptom, severe disturbance in cognitive function is the cardinal symptom in delirium, dementia, amnestic, and other cognitive disorders.

The hallmark of delirium is impairment of consciousness, usually with global defects in cognition. Delirium usually has a sudden onset, a brief course, and a rapid improvement when the cause is identified and treated. Psychiatrists need to be familiar with the many potential causes of delirium and how to differentiate between delirium and dementia.

Dementia is characterized by multiple impairments in cognitive functions without disturbances in consciousness. The cognitive functions that can be affected include general intelligence, learning and memory, language, problem solving, orientation, perception, attention and concentration, judgment, and social skills. The critical clinical points of dementia are the identification of the syndrome and the clinical workup of its cause. The disorder can be progressive or static, permanent or reversible. Clinicians need to be familiar with the most common types of dementia, in particular dementia of the Alzheimer's type and how it is distinguished from vascular dementia. They also need to know the principles of treatment, including the use of acetylcholinesterase inhibitors for Alzheimer's disease.

The amnestic disorders are characterized primarily by memory dysfunction that causes significant impairment in social or occupational functioning. The amnestic disorders are differentiated from the dissociative disorders (for example, dissociative amnesia, dissociative fugue) by the presumed or identified presence of a causally related general medical condition (for example, head trauma).

Many mental disorders are caused by a general medical condition. To make the diagnosis, the physician must find a medical cause that antedates the onset of the symptoms and that is known to be associated with the disorder. Thus, the physician needs to be aware of the possible psychiatric symptoms associated with a wide-ranging array of medical disorders. Symptoms of depression, mania, anxiety, psychosis, and changes in personality—all may be directly caused by such medical conditions as neurological, endocrine, systemic, inflammatory, and immune deficiency disorders.

The student should refer to Chapter 10 in *Kaplan and Sadock's Synopsis VIII.* The questions and answers below test the student's knowledge of the subject.

HELPFUL HINTS

The student should be able to define the signs, symptoms, and syndromes listed below.

- abstract attitude
- Addison's disease
- AIP
- ALS
- amnestic disorders
- anxiety disorder due to a general medical condition
- aphasia
- beriberi
- catastrophic reaction
- catatonic disorder due to a general medical condition
- cognition
- confabulation
- Creutzfeldt-Jakob disease
- Cushing's syndrome
- delirium:
  - black-patch
  - postoperative
- delusional disorder
- dementia:
  - Alzheimer's type
  - vascular
- diabetic ketoacidosis
- dissociative disorders
- Down's syndrome
- dysarthria
- encephalopathy:
  - hypoglycemic
  - hepatic
  - uremic
- epilepsy
- general paresis
- granulovacuolar degeneration

- hallucinations:
  - auditory, olfactory, and visual
  - hypnagogic and hypnopompic
  - tactile or haptic
  - lilliputian
- head trauma
- Huntington's disease
- intellectual functions
- intracranial neoplasms
- interictal manifestations
- kuru
- memory
- mood disorder due to a general medical condition
- multiple sclerosis
- neurofibrillary tangles
- normal aging
- normal pressure hydrocephalus
- orientation
- Parkinson's disease
- partial versus generalized seizures
- pellagra
- pernicious anemia
- personality change due to a general medical condition
- Pick's disease
- pseudobulbar palsy
- pseudodementia
- psychotic disorder due to general medical condition
- retrograde versus anterograde amnesia
- senile plaques
- sexual dysfunction due to a general medical condition
- short-term versus long-term memory loss
- SLE
- sleep disorder due to a general medical condition
- TIA
- transient global amnesia
- vertebrobasilar disease
- Wernicke-Korsakoff syndrome

▲ QUESTIONS

DIRECTIONS: Each of the questions or incomplete statements below is followed by five suggested responses or completions. Select the *one* that is *best* in each case.

10.1 The most common cause of delirium within 3 days postoperatively in a 40-year-old man is

A. stress of surgery
B. postoperative pain
C. pain medication
D. infection
E. delirium tremens

10.2 Inpatient cognitive tests that are helpful in the diagnosis of dementia include assessing

A. patients' ability to remember three objects after 5 minutes
B. patients' ability to remember place of birth or what happened yesterday
C. patients' fund of common information, such as past U.S. Presidents
D. patients' ability to find similarities and differences between related words
E. all of the above

10.3 Which of the following statements is true regarding personality change caused by a general medical condition?

A. Many patients exhibit low drive and initiative.
B. Emotions are typically labile and shallow.
C. True sadness and depression are uncommon.
D. The expression of impulses is characteristically disinhibited.
E. All of the above statements are true.

10.4 Delirium

A. has an insidious onset
B. rarely has associated neurological symptoms
C. generally causes a diffuse slowing of brain activity on an electroencephalogram (EEG)
D. generally has an underlying cause residing in the central nervous system
E. may be successfully treated with lithium

10.5 Common behavioral symptoms of multiple sclerosis include all of the following *except*

A. euphoria
B. depression
C. psychosis
D. personality changes
E. apathy

10.6 Korsakoff syndrome

A. is caused by folate deficiency
B. is equivalent to Wernicke's encephalopathy
C. is best treated with antipsychotic medications
D. often has confabulation as a prominent symptom
E. is a dissociative disorder

10.7 Which of the following drugs is best used to treat acute delirium?

A. Chlorpromazine (Thorazine)
B. Diazepam (Valium)
C. Haloperidol (Haldol)
D. Amobarbital (Amytal)
E. Physostigmine salicylate (Antilirium)

10.8 The incidence of delirium after open-heart and coronary-bypass surgery is

A. less than 10 percent
B. 20 percent
C. 30 percent
D. 40 percent
E. more than 50 percent

10.9 All of the following statements about the clinical differentiation of delirium and dementia are true *except*

A. The onset of delirium is sudden.
B. The duration of delirium is usually less than 1 month.
C. In delirium, symptoms worsen at night.
D. The sleep–wake cycle is disrupted in delirium.
E. Visual hallucinations and transient delusions are more common in dementia than in delirium.

10.10 The electroencephalogram (EEG) shown in Figure 10.1 is an example of

A. partial seizure
B. grand mal epilepsy
C. petit mal epilepsy or absence seizure
D. psychomotor epilepsy
E. none of the above

10.11 Patients with dementia

A. may show idiosyncratic responses to benzodiazepines
B. usually show equal impairment of short-term memory and long-term memory early in the course of the dementia
C. are believed to have a dopamine deficiency
D. often have an impairment of consciousness
E. usually have a marked disturbance of the sleep–wake cycle

10.12 The causes of delirium include

A. antihistamines
B. cerebral meningitis
C. hypoglycemia
D. urinary tract infection
E. all of the above

10.13 The diagnosis of vascular dementia is associated with

A. cerebrovascular disease
B. hypertension
C. a stepwise progression of focal motor symptoms
D. such personality changes as emotional lability and hypochondriasis
E. all of the above

10.14 Features of amnestic disorders include

A. an impairment of memory as the single or predominant cognitive defect
B. retrograde amnesia and anterograde amnesia
C. preservation of the ability for immediate recall
D. evidence of a specific causative medical or substance-related factor
E. all of the above

10.15 Amnestic disorders may be

A. transient
B. chronic
C. permanent
D. slowly progressive
E. all of the above

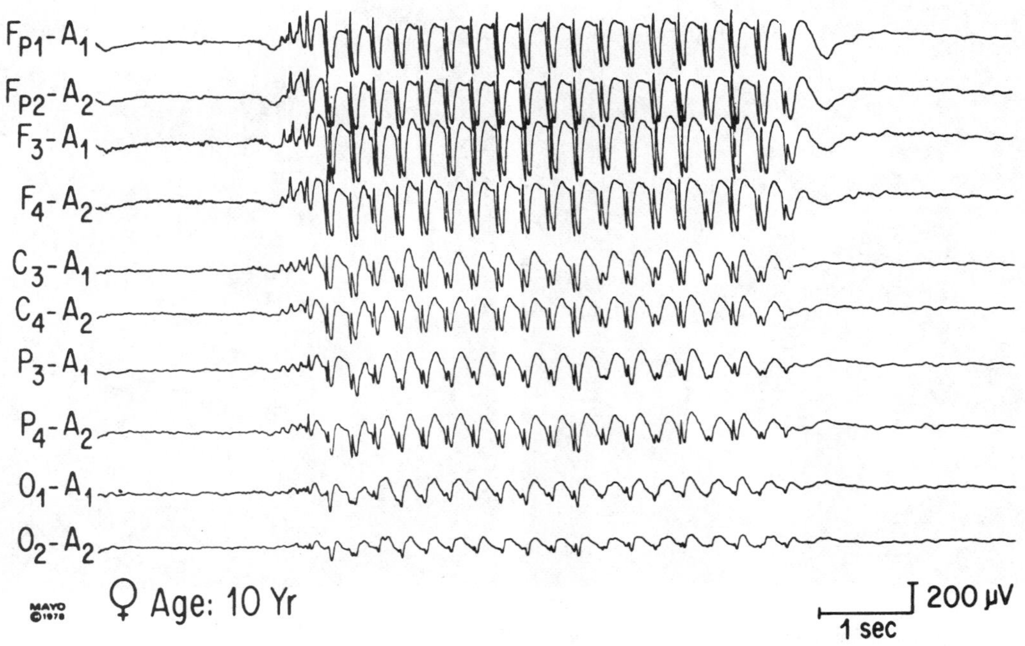

FIGURE 10.1
Electroencephalogram (EEG).

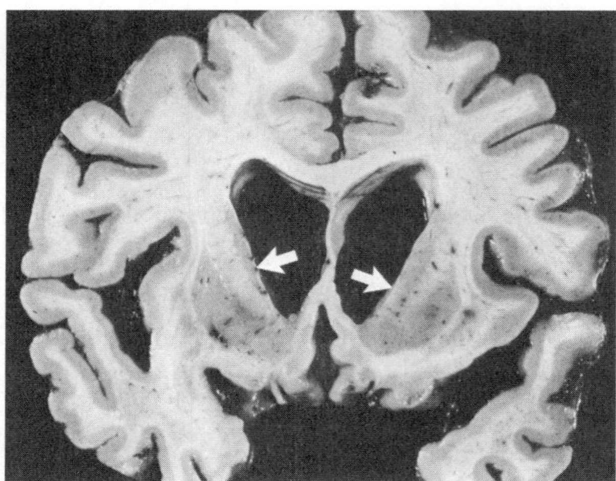

FIGURE 10.2

Reprinted with permission from Golden A, Powell DE, Jennings CD, editors: *Pathology: Understanding Human Disease,* ed 2, p 278. Williams & Wilkins, Baltimore, 1985.

10.16 A person with a complex partial seizure disorder

A. has no alteration in consciousness during the seizure
B. may exhibit a personality disturbance, such as religiosity
C. usually does not experience preictal events (auras)
D. usually displays a characteristic electroencephalogram (EEG) pattern
E. may have acute intermittent porphyria as the underlying cause

10.17 The gross neuropathology in Figure 10.2, demonstrating marked atrophy of the caudate nuclei *(arrows),* corresponds with a disorder characterized by which of the following manifestations?

A. Urinary incontinence, gait disturbance, progressive dementia
B. Confusion, ataxia, ophthalmoplegia
C. Psychomotor slowing, difficulty with complex tasks, choreiform movements
D. Memory impairment, aphasia, personality changes
E. Bradykinesia, rigidity, resting tremor

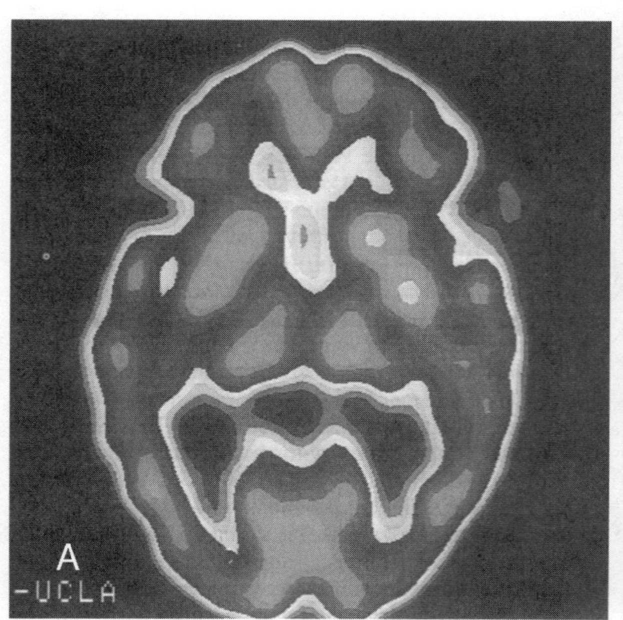

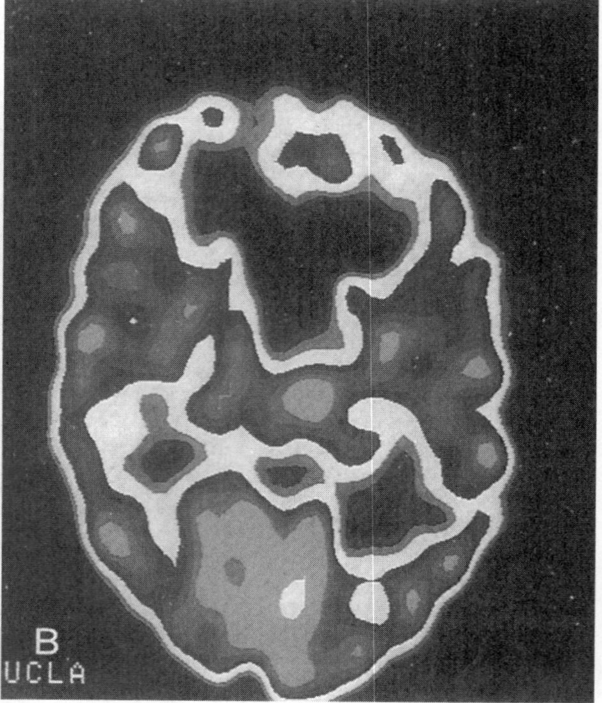

FIGURE 10.3

Reprinted with permission from Kaplan HI, Sadock BJ, editors: *Comprehensive Textbook of Psychiatry,* ed 6, pp 260, 263. Williams & Wilkins, Baltimore, 1995.

10.18 The SPECT image on the right in Figure 10.3 demonstrates an area of hypoperfusion (compared to normal on the left) in a patient showing behavioral disinhibition and features of Klüver-Bucy syndrome, with subsequent onset of dementia. The most likely diagnosis is

A. normal pressure hydrocephalus
B. pseudodementia
C. neurosyphilis
D. Pick's disease
E. progressive supranuclear palsy

10.19 The SPECT image in Figure 10.4, demonstrating a 50 percent reduction in blood flow in the posterior temporal-parietal cortex, is most consistent with the pathological changes found in which of the following?

A. Pick's disease
B. Huntington's disease
C. Normal pressure hydrocephalus
D. Alzheimer's disease
E. Parkinson's disease

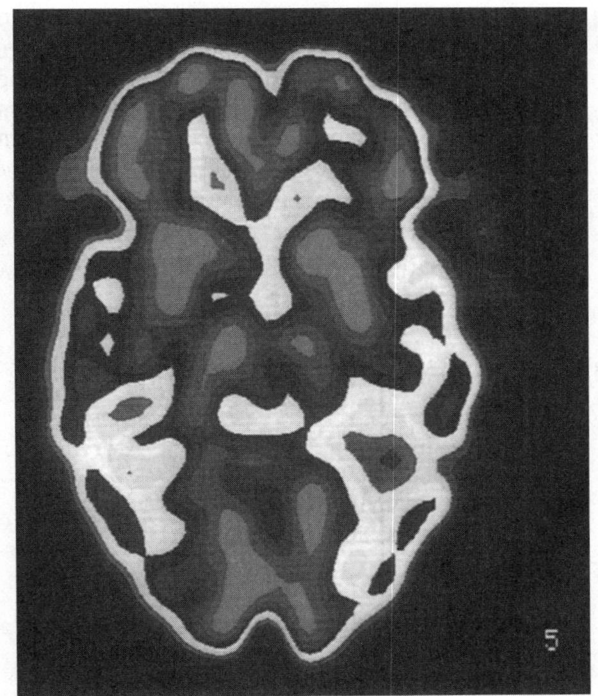

FIGURE 10.4

Reprinted with permission from Kaplan HI, Sadock BJ, editors: *Comprehensive Textbook of Psychiatry,* ed 6, p 262. Williams & Wilkins, Baltimore, 1995.

10.20 Microscopic examination of the gross pathological specimen shown in Figure 10.5 revealed, among other abnormalities, plaques composed of β/A_4 protein, a breakdown product of amyloid precursor protein. In life, the patient would have had

A. fluctuation of cognitive impairment during the course of the day
B. progressive memory impairment and aphasia
C. sudden onset of dementia with discrete, stepwise deterioration
D. marked variability in performance of tasks of similar difficulty
E. early and prominent loss of social skills

10.21 All of the following statements regarding the neuropathological specimen shown in Figure 10.6 are false *except*

A. A cholinergic deficit is implicated in the pathophysiology of the patient's disease.
B. The course of the patient's disease (from onset until death) was likely to have been under 6 months.
C. The patient's symptoms would have improved with L-dopa administration.
D. Motor dysfunction was the initial and predominant manifestation of this patient's disease.
E. The patient suffered from a treatable condition.

10.22 Microscopic examination of Figure 10.7 would be expected to reveal all of the following neuropathological changes *except*

A. neuronal loss in cortex and hippocampus
B. granulovacuolar degeneration of neurons
C. senile plaques
D. multiple lacunar infarcts involving the thalamus and internal capsule
E. neurofibrillary tangles

10.23 The coronal section depicted in Figure 10.8 reveals, adjacent to the lateral ventricles *(arrows),* large sharply demarcated plaques, as part of a chronic disease characterized pathologically by multiple areas of white matter inflammation, demyelination, and glial scarring. In addition to manifestations such as motor weakness, paresthesias, ataxia, and diplopia, common neuropsychiatric symptoms of this disorder include all of the following *except*

A. depression
B. psychosis
C. memory impairment
D. euphoric mood
E. personality changes

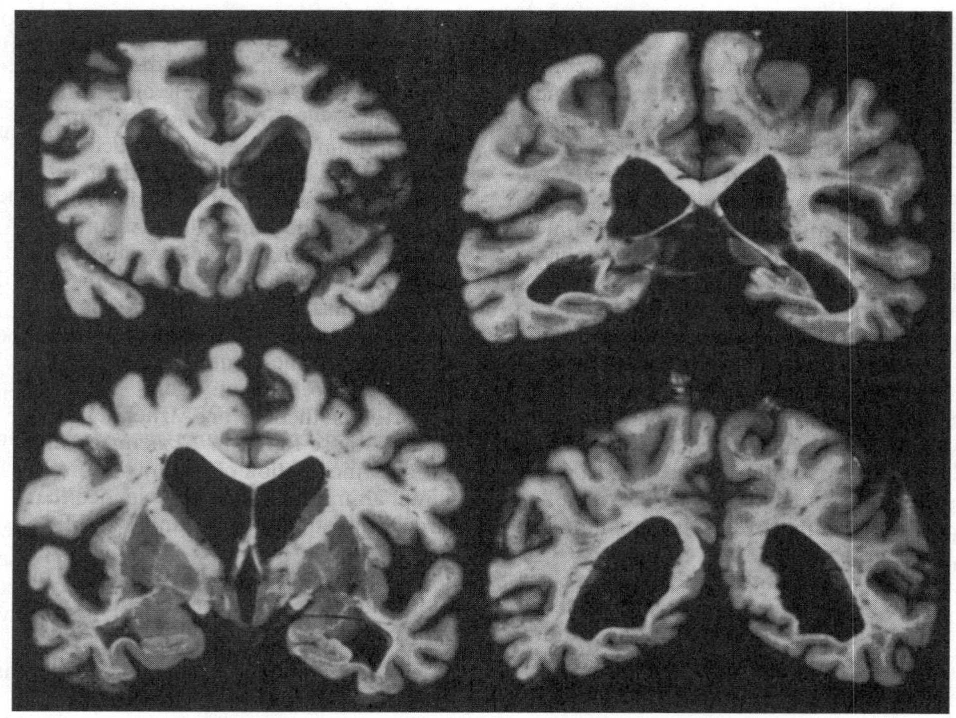

FIGURE 10.5
From Kaplan HI, Sadock BJ, editors: *Comprehensive Textbook of Psychiatry,* ed 4, p 863. Williams & Wilkins, Baltimore, 1985.

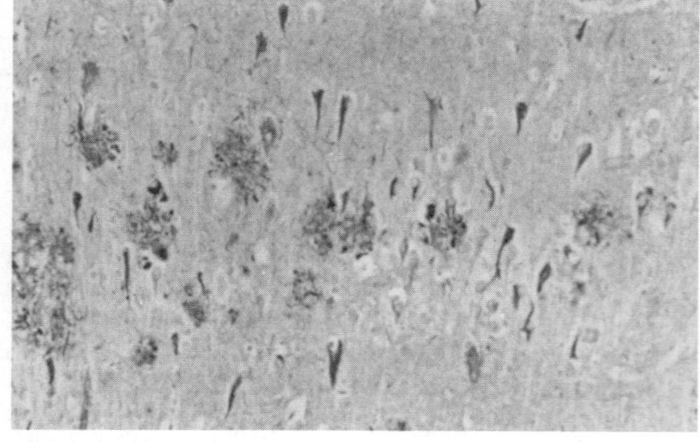

FIGURE 10.6
Reprinted with permission from Kaplan HI, Sadock BJ, editors: *Synopsis of Psychiatry,* ed 8, p 1294. Williams & Wilkins, Baltimore, 1998.

10.24a The gross neuropathology shown in Figure 10.9 shows depigmentation of the substantia nigra and locus ceruleus in a patient's diseased tissue on the left *(arrows),* with normal tissue shown on the right. Physical examination of this patient might have revealed all of the following *except*

A. sucking reflexes
B. positive Babinski signs
C. impairment of fine movements
D. intention tremor
E. cogwheel rigidity

10.24b The patient's disease commonly features

A. depression
B. apathy
C. dementia
D. intellectual impairment
E. all of the above

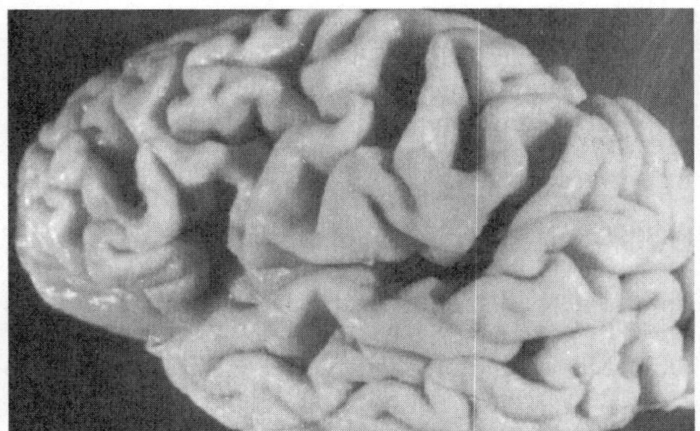

FIGURE 10.7

Reprinted with permission from Kaplan HI, Sadock BJ, editors: *Synopsis of Psychiatry,* ed 8, p 330. Williams & Wilkins, Baltimore, 1998.

DIRECTIONS: Each set of lettered headings below is followed by a list of numbered words or phrases. For each numbered word or phrase, select

A. if the item is associated with *A only*
B. if the item is associated with *B only*
C. if the item is associated with *both A and B*
D. if the item is associated with *neither A nor B*

Questions 10.25–10.29

A. Niacin deficiency
B. Thiamine deficiency
C. Both
D. Neither

10.25 Pellagra
10.26 Beriberi

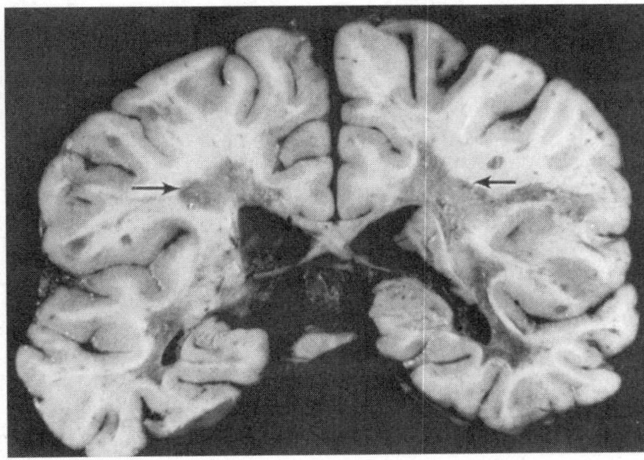

FIGURE 10.8

Reprinted with permission from Golden A, Powell DE, Jennings CD, editors: *Pathology: Understanding Human Disease,* ed 2, p 281. Williams & Wilkins, Baltimore, 1985.

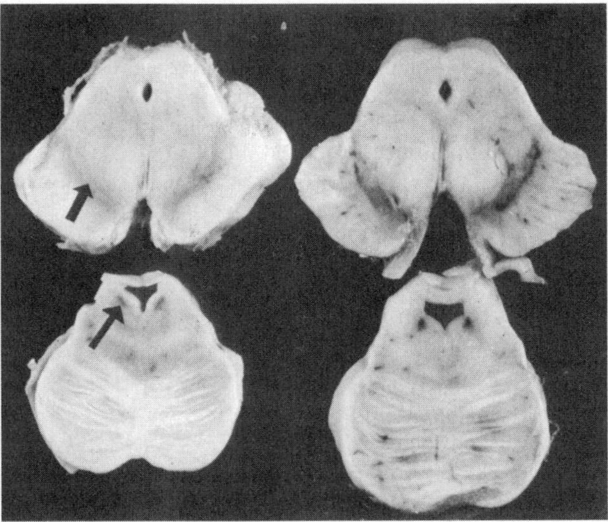

FIGURE 10.9

Reprinted with permission from Golden A, Powell DE, Jennings CD, editors: *Pathology: Understanding Human Disease,* ed 2, p 277. Williams & Wilkins, Baltimore, 1985.

10.27 Wernicke-Korsakoff syndrome
10.28 Apathy
10.29 Depression

Questions 10.30–10.39

A. Delirium
B. Dementia
C. Both
D. Neither

10.30 Sudden onset
10.31 Insidious onset
10.32 Clouding of consciousness
10.33 Reversible
10.34 Insight present
10.35 Hallucinations
10.36 Sundowning
10.37 Catastrophic reaction
10.38 High mortality rate
10.39 Decreased acetylcholine activity

Questions 10.40–10.45

A. Alzheimer's type
B. Pick's disease
C. Both
D. Neither

10.40 Unknown cause
10.41 Senile plaques and neurofibrillary changes
10.42 Lobar atrophy
10.43 Reversible
10.44 Tacrine (Cognex)
10.45 Donepezil (Aricept)

DIRECTIONS: Each group of questions below consists of lettered headings followed by a list of numbered phrases or statements. For each numbered phrase or statement, select the *one* lettered heading that is most closely associated with it. Each lettered heading may be used once, more than once, or not at all.

Questions 10.46–10.49

A. Lead poisoning
B. Manganese madness
C. Mercury poisoning
D. Thallium intoxication

10.46 Alopecia
10.47 Succimer (Chemet)
10.48 Mad Hatter syndrome
10.49 Masked facies

Questions 10.50–10.54

A. Creutzfeldt-Jakob disease
B. Normal pressure hydrocephalus
C. Neurosyphilis
D. Huntington's disease
E. Multiple sclerosis

10.50 Death occurring 15 to 20 years after the onset of the disease, with suicide being common
10.51 Slow virus, with death occurring within 2 years of the diagnosis
10.52 Manic syndrome with neurological signs in up to 20 percent of cases
10.53 Treatment of choice being a shunt
10.54 More prevalent in cold and temperate climates than in the tropics and subtropics

ANSWERS

Delirium, Dementia, and Amnestic and Other Cognitive Disorders and Mental Disorders Due to a General Medical Condition

10.1 The answer is E (*Synopsis VIII,* page 321).
The most common cause of delirium in this case is *delirium tremens* (called alcohol withdrawal delirium in DSM-IV). It is a medical emergency that results in mortality in about 20 percent of cases if left untreated. It occurs within 1 week after the person stops drinking. It usually develops on the third hospital day in a patient admitted for an unrelated condition (such as surgery) who has no access to alcohol and stops drinking suddenly. Another less common cause of postoperative delirium is *stress,* especially in major procedures such as cardiac or transplantation surgery. *Pain, pain medication,* and *infection* must also be considered in the postoperative period. *Infection* is commonly associated with high fever.

10.2 The answer is E (all) (*Synopsis VIII,* pages 318–320).
Dementia is characterized by a loss of cognitive and intellectual abilities that is severe enough to impair social or occupational performance. The diagnostic criteria for dementia include impairment in short-term memory and long-term memory, which means an inability to learn new information and to remember information that was known in the past. Patients' ability to remember *three objects after 5 minutes* can assess their short-term memory; patients' ability to remember *their place of birth or what happened yesterday* or patients' funds of common information, such as *past U.S. Presidents,* can test their long-term memory. Other criteria for the diagnosis of dementia include impairment of abstract thinking, which can be indicated by the patient's ability to find similarities and differences between *related words.*

10.3 The answer is E (all) (*Synopsis VIII,* pages 319–320).
In personality change due to a general medical condition, many patients *exhibit low drive and initiative.* Emotions are typically *labile and shallow,* with euphoria or apathy predominating. Apathy may lead one to assume the presence of a depressed mood, but *true sadness and depression are uncommon.* Temper outbursts may occur with little or no provocation, resulting in violent behavior; the expression of *impulses is characteristically disinhibited,* resulting in inappropriate jokes, a crude manner, improper sexual advances, or outright antisocial behavior. Evidence of some causative organic factors must antedate the onset of the syndrome. Table 10.1 lists the diagnostic criteria for personality change due to a general medical condition.

Table 10.1
DSM-IV Diagnostic Criteria for Personality Change Due to a General Medical Condition

A. A persistent personality disturbance that represents a change from the individual's previous characteristic personality pattern. (In children, the disturbance involves a marked deviation from normal development or a significant change in the child's usual behavior patterns lasting at least 1 year.)
B. There is evidence from the history, physical examination, or laboratory findings that the disturbance is the direct physiological consequence of a general medical condition.
C. The disturbance is not better accounted for by another mental disorder (including other mental disorders due to a general medical condition).
D. The disturbance does not occur exclusively during the course of a delirium and does not meet criteria for a dementia.
E. The disturbance causes clinically significant distress or impairment in social, occupational, or other important areas of functioning.

Specify type:
Labile type: if the predominant feature is affective lability
Disinhibited type: if the predominant feature is poor impulse control as evidenced by sexual indiscretions, etc.
Aggressive type: if the predominant feature is aggressive behavior
Apathetic type: if the predominant feature is marked apathy and indifference
Paranoid type: if the predominant feature is suspiciousness or paranoid ideation
Other type: If the predominant feature is not one of the above, eg, personality change associated with a seizure disorder
Combined type: if more than one feature predominantes in the clinical picture
Unspecified type

Coding note: Include the name of the general medical condition on Axis I, eg, personality change due to temporal lobe epilepsy; also code the general medical condition on Axis III.

Reprinted with permission from American Psychiatric Association: *Diagnostic and Statistical Manual of Mental Disorders,* ed 4. Copyright, American Psychiatric Association, Washington, 1994.

10.4 The answer is C (*Synopsis VIII,* page 324).
Delirium generally causes *a diffuse slowing of brain activity* on the electroencephalogram (EEG), which may be useful in differentiating delirium from depression and psychosis. The EEG of a delirious patient sometimes shows focal areas of hyperactivity. In rare cases, differentiating delirium related to epilepsy from delirium related to other causes may be difficult. In general, delirium has a sudden, not insidious, onset. Patients with delirium *commonly have associated neurological* symptoms, including dysphasia, tremor, asterixis, incoordination, and urinary incontinence. Delirium does not have an underlying cause residing in the central nervous system. *Delirium has many causes,* all of which result in a similar pattern of symptoms relating to the patient's level of consciousness and cognitive impairment. Most of the causes of delirium lie outside the central nervous system—for example, renal and hepatic failures. Delirium *cannot be successfully treated with lithium (Eskalith).* Patients with lithium serum concentrations greater than 1.5 mEq/L are at risk for delirium. Table 10.2 presents the diagnostic criteria for delirium due to a general medical condition.

10.5 The answer is C (*Synopsis VIII,* page 360).
Psychosis is a rare complication of multiple sclerosis (MS). The behavioral symptoms associated with MS are *euphoria*

Table 10.2
Diagnostic Criteria for Delirium Due to a General Medical Condition

A. Disturbance of consciousness (ie, reduced clarity of awareness of the environment) with reduced ability to focus, sustain, or shift attention.
B. A change in cognition (such as memory deficit, disorientation, language disturbance) or the development of a perceptual disturbance that is not better accounted for by a preexisting, established, or evolving dementia.
C. The disturbance develops over a short period of time (usually hours to days) and tends to fluctuate during the course of the day.
D. There is evidence from the history, physical examination, or laboratory findings that the disturbance is caused by the direct physiological consequences of a general medical condition.

Coding note: If delirium is superimposed on a preexisting dementia of the Alzheimer's type or vascular dementia, indicate the delirium by coding the appropriate subtype of the dementia, eg, dementia of the Alzheimer's type, with late onset, with delirium.

Coding note: Include the name of the general medical condition on Axis I, eg, delirium due to hepatic encephalopathy; also code the general medical condition on Axis III.

Reprinted with permission from American Psychiatric Association: *Diagnostic and Statistical Manual of Mental Disorders,* ed 4. Copyright, American Psychiatric Association, Washington, 1994.

and *personality changes.* About 25 percent of people with MS exhibit a euphoric mood that is not hypomanic in severity; rather, it is somewhat more cheerful than their situation warrants and not necessarily in character with their disposition before the onset of MS. About 10 percent of MS patients have a sustained and elevated mood, although it is not truly hypomanic in severity. *Depression* is common; it affects 25 to 50 percent of patients with MS and results in a higher rate of suicide than is seen in the general population. *Personality changes* are also common in MS patients; they affect 20 to 40 percent of patients and are often characterized by increased irritability or *apathy.*

10.6 The answer is D (*Synopsis VIII,* page 347).
Korsakoff's syndrome often has confabulation as a prominent symptom. Korsakoff's syndrome is the amnestic syndrome *caused by thiamine deficiency; it is not due to folate deficiency.* Folate deficiency may cause megaloblastic anemia. Thiamine deficiency is most commonly associated with the poor nutritional habits of persons with chronic alcohol abuse. Other causes of poor nutrition (for example, starvation), gastric carcinoma, hemodialysis, hyperemesis gravidarum, prolonged intravenous hyperalimentation, and gastric plication may also result in thiamine deficiency.

Korsakoff''s syndrome is *not equivalent to Wernicke's encephalopathy,* but the two conditions are often associated. Wernicke's encephalopathy is characterized by confusion, ataxia, and ophthalmoplegia. In patients with those thiamine deficiency-related symptoms, the neuropathological findings include hyperplasia of the small blood vessels with occasional hemorrhages, hypertrophy of astrocytes, and subtle changes in neuronal axons. Although the delirium clears up within a month or so, the amnestic syndrome either accompanies or follows untreated Wernicke's encephalopathy in about 85 percent of all cases.

Korsakoff's syndrome *is not best treated with antipsychotics* but rather with thiamine, whose deficiency is the underlying cause of the syndrome. The administration of thiamine is the best treatment because it may prevent the development of additional amnestic symptoms, but rarely is the treatment able to reverse severe amnestic symptoms once present. About a quarter to a third of all patients recover completely, and about a quarter of all patients have no improvement of their symptoms. Antipsychotics may be used to control the patient's agitated behavior. Korsakoff's syndrome *is not a dissociative disorder,* although differentiating the conditions may sometimes be difficult. Patients with dissociative disorders are more likely to have lost their orientation to self and may have more selective memory deficits than do patients with amnestic disorders. Dissociative disorders are also often associated with emotionally stressful life events involving money, the legal system, or troubled relationships.

10.7 The answer is C (*Synopsis VIII,* page 327).
The drug of choice for delirium is *haloperidol (Haldol),* a butyrophenone. Depending on the patient's age, weight, and physical condition, the initial dose may range from 2 to 10 mg intramuscularly, repeated in an hour if the patient remains agitated. As soon as the patient is calm, oral medication in liquid concentrate or tablet form should begin. Two daily oral doses should suffice, with two thirds of the dose being given at bedtime. To achieve the same therapeutic effect, the clinician should give an oral dose about 1.5 times higher than a parenteral dose. The effective total daily dosage of haloperidol may range from 5 to 50 mg for the majority of delirious patients.

Phenothiazines, such as *chlorpromazine (Thorazine),* should be avoided in delirious patients because those drugs are associated with significant anticholinergic activity. *Benzodiazepines* with long half-lives, such as diazepam (Valium), and barbiturates, such as amobarbital *(Amytal),* should be avoided unless they are being used as part of the treatment for the underlying disorder (for example, alcohol withdrawal). Sedatives can increase cognitive disorganization in delirious patients. When the delirium is due to anticholinergic toxicity, the use of *physostigmine salicylate* (Antilirium) 1 to 2 mg intravenously or intramuscularly, with repeated doses in 15 to 30 minutes, may be indicated; but it is not the first drug to be used in an acute delirium in which the cause has not been determined.

10.8 The answer is C (*Synopsis VIII,* pages 321–322).
The incidence of delirium after open-heart and coronary-bypass surgery is *about 30 percent.* Delirium is the psychiatric syndrome encountered most often by psychiatrists who are called to consult on patients in medical and surgical wards. Forty to 50 percent of patients who are recovering from surgery for hip fractures have an episode of delirium. An estimated 20 percent of patients with severe burns and 30 percent of patients with acquired immune deficiency syndrome (AIDS) have episodes of delirium while hospitalized.

10.9 The answer is E (*Synopsis VIII,* pages 326–327).
The distinction between delirium and dementia may be difficult or, at times, impossible to make, particularly during the

transition between delirium and dementia. *Visual hallucinations and transient delusions* are more common in delirium than in dementia. *The onset of delirium is generally sudden,* but prodromal symptoms (for example, daytime restlessness, anxiety, fearfulness, and hypersensitivity to light or sounds) may occur. The duration of delirium is usually *less than 1 month.* Also, in delirium, symptoms *worsen at night,* and *the sleep–wake cycle is disrupted.* Intellectual deterioration of more than 1 month is more likely in dementia than in delirium. Table 10.3 presents the frequency of clinical features of delirium contrasted with those of dementia.

10.10 The answer is C (*Synopsis VIII,* page 352).
Petit mal epilepsy or absence seizure is associated with a characteristic generalized, bilaterally synchronous, 3-hertz spike-and-wave pattern in the electroencephalogram (EEG) and is often easily induced by hyperventilation. Petit mal epilepsy occurs predominantly in children. It usually consists of simple absence attacks lasting 5 to 10 seconds, during which the patient has an abrupt alteration in awareness and responsiveness and an interruption in motor activity. The child often has a blank stare associated with an upward deviation of the eyes and some mild twitching movements of the eyes, eyelids, face, or extremities. Petit mal epilepsy is usually a fairly benign seizure disorder, often resolving after adolescence.

A *partial seizure* (also known as jacksonian epilepsy) is a type of epilepsy characterized by recurrent episodes of focal motor seizures. It begins with localized tonic or clonic contraction, increases in severity, spreads progressively through the entire body, and terminates in a generalized convulsion with loss of consciousness. *Grand mal epilepsy* is the major form of epilepsy. Gross tonic-clonic convulsive seizures are accompanied by loss of consciousness and, often, incontinence of stool or urine. *Psychomotor epilepsy* is a type of epilepsy characterized by recurrent behavior disturbances. Complex hallucinations or illusions, frequently gustatory or olfactory, often herald the onset of the seizure, which typically involves a state of impaired consciousness resembling a dream, during which paramnestic phenomena, such as *déjà vu* and *jamais vu,* are experienced and the patient exhibits repetitive, automatic, or semipurposeful behaviors. In rare instances, violent behavior may be prominent. The EEG reveals a localized seizure focus in the temporal lobe.

Table 10.3
Frequency of Clinical Features of Delirium Contrasted with Dementia

Feature	Delirium	Dementia
Impaired memory	+ + +	+ + +
Impaired thinking	+ + +	+ + +
Impaired judgment	+ + +	+ + +
Clouding of consciousness	+ + +	−
Major attention deficits	+ + +	+[a]
Fluctuation over course of a day	+ + +	+
Disorientation	+ + +	+ +[a]
Vivid perceptual disturbances	+ +	+
Incoherent speech	+ +	+[a]
Disrupted sleep–wake cycle	+ +	+[a]
Nocturnal exacerbation	+ +	+[a]
Insight	+ +[b]	+[b]
Sudden onset	+ +	−[c]

Adapted from Liston EH: Diagnosis and management of delirium in the elderly patient. Psychiatr Ann *14:* 117, 1984.
+ + +, always present; + +, usually present; +, occasionally present; −, usually absent.
[a] More frequent in advanced stages of dementia.
[b] Present during lucid intervals or on recovery from delirium; present during early stages of dementia.
[c] Onset may be sudden in some dementias, eg, vascular dementia, hypoxemia, certain reversible dementias.

10.11 The answer is A (*Synopsis VIII,* pages 345–346).
The clinician may prescribe benzodiazepines for insomnia and anxiety but must be aware that patients with dementia *may show idiosyncratic responses to benzodiazepines.* In such patients, benzodiazepines may precipitate agitated, aggressive, or psychotic behavior.

Patients with dementia *do not usually show equal impairment of short-term memory and long-term memory* early in the course of the dementia. Memory impairment is typically an early and prominent feature in dementias, especially in dementias involving the cortex, such as dementia of the Alzheimer's type. Early in the course of dementia, memory impairment is mild and is usually most marked for recent events, such as forgetting telephone numbers, conversations, and events of the day. As the dementia progresses, memory impairment becomes severe, and only the most highly learned information (for example, place of birth) is retained.

Patients with dementia *are not believed to have a dopamine deficiency.* The neurotransmitters most implicated in the pathophysiology of dementia are acetylcholine and norepinephrine, both of which are hypothesized to be hypoactive in dementia of the Alzheimer's type. Several studies have reported data consistent with the hypothesis that a specific degeneration of cholinergic neurons is present in the nucleus basalis of Meynert in patients with dementia of the Alzheimer's type. Additional support for the cholinergic deficit hypothesis comes from the observation that cholinergic antagonists, such as scopolamine and atropine, impair cognitive abilities, whereas acetylcholinesterase inhibitors, such as physostigmine, have been reported to enhance cognitive abilities. Patients with dementia do not have an impairment of consciousness. That symptom is characteristic of delirium, not dementia. Patients with dementia do not usually have a marked disturbance of the sleep–wake cycle. Such disturbances are characteristic of delirium, not dementia.

10.12 The answer is E (all) (*Synopsis VIII,* pages 320–324).
The syndrome of delirium is almost always due to identifiable systemic or cerebral disease or to drug intoxication or withdrawal. Examples include *antihistamine* intoxication, *cerebral meningitis, hypoglycemia,* and *urinary tract infection.* Delirium has many causes, including hypoglycemia, hypokalemia, migraine, and infectious mononucleosis. Other frequently encountered causes of delirium are listed in Table 10.4.

10.13 The answer is E (all) (*Synopsis VIII,* pages 330–331).
The diagnosis of vascular dementia is associated with *cerebrovascular disease.* The disorder affects small and medium cerebral vessels, producing multiple, widely spread cerebral lesions that result in a combination of neurological and psychiatric symptoms. Vascular dementia is also associated with *hypertension* and manifests *a stepwise progression* of focal,

Table 10.4
Common Causes of Delirium

Drug intoxication
- Anticholinergics
- Lithium
- Antiarrhythmics (eg, lidocaine)
- H_2-receptor blockers
- Sedative-hypnotics
- Alcohol

Drug withdrawal
- Alcohol
- Sedative-hypnotics

Tumor
- Primary cerebral

Trauma
- Cerebral contusion (as an example)
- Subdural hematoma

Infection
- Cerebral (eg, meningitis, encephalitis, HIV, syphilis)
- Systemic (eg, sepsis, urinary tract infection, pneumonia)

Cardiovascular
- Cerebrovascular (eg, infarcts, hemorrhage, vasculitis)
- Cardiovascular (eg, low-output states, congestive heart failure, shock)

Physiological or metabolic
- Hypoxemia, electrolyte disturbances, renal or hepatic failure, hypoglycemia or hyperglycemia, postictal states (as examples)

Endocrine
- Thyroid or glucocorticoid disturbances (as examples)

Nutritional
- Thiamine or vitamin B_{12} deficiency, pellagra (as examples)

Courtesy of Eric D. Caine, M.D., Hillel Grossman, M.D., and Jeffrey Lyness, M.D.

sometimes fluctuating, motor symptoms. Those symptoms are accompanied by dementia. The clinical description of the disorder includes a variety of symptoms, ranging from headaches, dizziness, and transient focal neurological symptoms to such *personality changes* as emotional lability and hypochondriasis. Table 10.5 gives the diagnostic criteria for vascular dementia.

Table 10.5
DSM-IV Diagnostic Criteria for Vascular Dementia

A. The development of multiple cognitive deficits manifested by both
   (1) memory impairment (impaired ability to learn new information or to recall previously learned information)
   (2) one (or more) of the following cognitive disturbances:
      (a) aphasia (language disturbance)
      (b) apraxia (impaired ability to carry out motor activities despite intact motor function)
      (c) agnosia (failure to recognize or identify objects despite intact sensory function)
      (d) disturbance in executive functioning (ie, planning, organizing, sequencing, abstracting)

B. The cognitive deficits in criteria A1 and A2 each cause significant impairment in social or occupational functioning and represent a significant decline from a previous level of functioning.

C. Focal neurological signs and symptoms (eg, exaggeration of deep tendon reflexes, extensor plantar response, pseudobulbar palsy, gait abnormalities, weakness of an extremity) or laboratory evidence indicative of cerebrovascular disease (eg, multiple infarctions involving cortex and underlying white matter) that are judged to be etiologically related to the disturbance.

D. The deficits do not occur exclusively during the course of a delirium.

Code based on predominant features:

With delirium: if delirium is superimposed on the dementia
With delusions: if delusions are the predominant feature
With depressed mood: if depressed mood (including presentations that meet full symptom criteria for a major depressive episode) is the predominant feature. A separate diagnosis of mood disorder due to general medical condition is not given.
Uncomplicated: if none of the above predominates in the current clinical presentation

Specify if:
With behavioral disturbance

Coding note: Also code cerebrovascular condition on Axis III.

10.14 The answer is E (all) (*Synopsis VIII,* pages 345–350). Amnestic disorders have an *impairment of memory* as the single or predominant cognitive defect. The memory pathology is of two types: *retrograde amnesia and anterograde amnesia.* Retrograde amnesia is the loss of memory of events that took place before the onset of the illness. Anterograde amnesia is the reduced ability to recall current events. Although short-term memory is impaired, the patient has *preservation of the ability for immediate recall,* as tested by digit span. Because a number of organic pathological factors and conditions can give rise to amnestic disorders, evidence of a *specific causative medical or substance-related factor* is required for the diagnosis. Table 10.6 gives the diagnostic criteria for amnestic disorder due to a general medical condition.

10.15 The answer is E (all) (*Synopsis VIII,* pages 345–350). The mode of onset, the course, and the prognosis of amnestic disorders depend on their causes. The syndrome may be *transient, chronic,* or *permanent,* and the outcome may be complete or partial recovery of memory function or an irreversible or even *slowly progressive* memory defect. The transient syndrome may result from a head injury, carbon monoxide poisoning, temporal lobe epilepsy, migraine, cardiac arrest, or electroconvulsive therapy. Chronic memory impairment may result from subarachnoid hemorrhage, cerebral infarction, or herpes simplex encephalitis. A slowly progressive disorder suggests a brain tumor or dementia of the Alzheimer's type. Table 10.7 lists the major causes of amnestic disorders.

10.16 The answer is B (*Synopsis VIII,* page 355). A person with a complex partial seizure disorder *may exhibit a personality disturbance,* such as religiosity. The most frequent psychiatric abnormalities reported in epileptic patients (especially patients with partial complex seizures of temporal lobe origin) are *personality disturbances.* In a person displaying *religiosity,* the religiosity may be striking and may be manifested not only by increased participation in overtly religious activities but also by unusual concern for moral and ethical issues, preoccupation with right and wrong, and heightened interest in global and philosophical concerns. The hyperreli-

Table 10.6
DSM-IV Diagnostic Criteria for Amnestic Disorder Due to a General Medical Condition

A. The development of memory impairment as manifested by impairment in the ability to learn new information or the inability to recall previously learned information.

B. The memory disturbance causes significant impairment in social or occupational functioning and represents a significant decline from a previous level of functioning.

C. The memory disturbance does not occur exclusively during the course of a delirium or a dementia.

D. There is evidence from the history, physical examination, or laboratory findings that the disturbance is the direct physiological consequence of a general medical condition (including physical trauma).

Specify if:

Transient: if memory impairment lasts for 1 month or less

Chronic: if memory impairment lasts for more than 1 month

Coding note: Include the name of the general medical condition on Axis I, eg, amnestic disorder due to head trauma; also code the general medical condition on Axis III (see Appendix G for codes).

Reprinted with permission from American Psychiatric Association: *Diagnostic and Statistical Manual of Mental Disorders,* ed 4. Copyright, American Psychiatric Association, Washington, 1994.

Table 10.7
Major Causes of Amnestic Disorders

Systemic medical conditions
- Thiamine deficiency (Korsakoff's syndrome)
- Hypoglycemia

Primary brain conditions
- Seizures
- Head trauma (closed and penetrating)
- Cerebral tumors (especially thalamic and temporal lobe)
- Cerebrovascular diseases (especially thalamic and temporal lobe)
- Surgical procedures on the brain
- Encephalitis due to herpes simplex
- Hypoxia (including nonfatal hanging attempts and carbon monoxide poisoning)
- Transient global amnesia
- Electroconvulsive therapy
- Multiple sclerosis

Substance-related causes
- Alcohol use disorders
- Neurotoxins
- Benzodiazepines (and other sedative-hypnotics)
- Many over-the-counter preparations

gious features can sometimes seem like the prodromal symptoms of schizophrenia and can result in a diagnostic problem in an adolescent or a young adult.

Partial seizures are classified as complex if they are associated with alterations in consciousness during the seizure episode. Thus, a person with a complex partial seizure disorder always has an alteration in consciousness during the seizure.

The person also experiences *preictal events (auras).* Preictal events in complex partial seizures include autonomic sensations (for example, fullness in the stomach, blushing, and changes in respiration), cognitive sensations (for example, déjà vu, *jamais vu,* forced thinking, and dreamy states), affective states (for example, fear, panic, depression, and elation), and, classically, automatisms (for example, lip smacking, rubbing, and chewing).

A person with a complex partial seizure disorder does not display a characteristic electroencephalogram (EEG) pattern. On the contrary, multiple normal EEGs are often obtained from a patient with complex partial seizures; therefore, normal EEGs cannot be used to exclude a diagnosis of complex partial seizures. The use of long-term EEG recordings (usually 24 to 72 hours) can help the clinician detect a seizure focus in some patients. Only in petit mal epilepsy does one see a characteristic EEG pattern of 3-per-second spike-and-wave activity.

Acute intermittent porphyria is not the underlying cause of complex partial seizures. The porphyrias are disorders of heme biosynthesis, resulting in the excessive accumulation of porphyrins. However, a disease that may lead to the development of complex partial seizures is herpes simplex encephalitis.

10.17 The answer is C (*Synopsis VIII,* pages 329–330).
The neuropathology is consistent with that found in Huntington's disease, which involves atrophy of the caudate nuclei and putamen. Huntington's disease is an autosomal dominant disorder characterized by choreiform movements and by subcortical dementia, which may present with psychomotor slowing and difficulty with complex tasks.

Urinary incontinence, gait disturbance, and progressive dementia are characteristic of normal pressure hydrocephalus. *Confusion, ataxia and ophthalmoplegia* are characteristic of Wernicke's encephalopathy, a disorder caused by deficiency of thiamine (vitamin B_1) as seen in chronic alcoholism. *Memory impairment, aphasia, and personality changes* are characteristic of dementia, such as dementia of the Alzheimer's type and vascular dementia. *Bradykinesia, resting tremor and rigidity* are characteristic of Parkinson's disease.

10.18 The answer is D (*Synopsis VIII,* page 361).
Pick's disease is characterized by a preponderance of atrophy in the frontal and anterior temporal lobes, *seen as frontal,* sparing the temporal-parietal regions (in contrast to Alzheimer's disease, which mainly affects the temporal-parietal regions). Initial symptoms of Pick's disease often involve behavior and personality changes, with dementia symptoms occurring later. Common early symptoms include apathy and behavioral disinhibition, with some patients showing features of the Klüver-Bucy syndromes (hypersexuality, placidity, hyperorality).

Normal pressure hydrocephalus often appears as global cerebral hypoperfusion on SPECT and is characterized by urinary incontinence, gait disturbance, and progressive dementia. *Neurosyphilis* appears 10 to 15 years after the primary Treponema infection and generally affects the frontal lobes, resulting in personality changes, impaired judgment, irritability, and decreased care for self with later development of dementia and tremor. *Pseudodementia* refers to clinical features resembling a dementia not caused by an organic condition, most often caused by depression. *Progressive supranuclear palsy* is a heterogeneous deterioration involving the brainstem, basal ganglia, and cerebellum, with nuchal dystonia and dementia.

10.19 The answer is D (*Synopsis VIII,* pages 328–330).
Parietal-temporal hypoperfusion on SPECT imaging is consistent with the distribution of pathology found in *Alzheimer's disease.*

In contrast, *Pick's disease* is characterized by a preponderance of atrophy in the frontotemporal regions and appears on SPECT imaging as frontal hypoperfusion. The neuropathology in *Huntington's disease* involves atrophy of the caudate and putamen, which is visualized on SPECT as hypoperfusion of the caudate regions. Patients with *normal pressure hydrocephalus* often demonstrate global cerebral hypoperfusion on SPECT imaging and do not show the Alzheimer's pattern of selective parietal-temporal changes. The neuropathology of *Parkinson's disease* involves degeneration of subcortical structures, primarily the substantia nigra but also the globus pallidus, caudate, and putamen.

10.20 The answer is B (*Synopsis VIII,* page 329).
The patient suffered from Alzheimer's disease. Pathological examination of the brain tissue is the only means by which this diagnosis can be established with certainty. As shown in the photograph, the classic gross neuroanatomical observation of the brain from a patient with Alzheimer's disease is diffuse cerebral atrophy with dilation of ventricles and widening of the cortical sulci. Senile plaques composed of β/A_4 protein (a breakdown product of amyloid precursor protein) is a classic and pathognomonic microscopic finding. Other neuropathologic changes in Alzheimer's disease include neurofibrillary tangles, synaptic loss, and granulovacuolar degeneration of neurons.

The DSM-IV diagnostic criteria for dementia of the Alzheimer's type (DAT) emphasize the presence of memory impairment and the associated presence of at least one other symptom of cognitive decline (aphasia, apraxia, agnosia, or abnormal executive functioning). *The sudden onset of dementia with discrete, stepwise deterioration* is characteristic of vascular dementia rather than DAT, which is characterized by insidious onset and slow progression of symptoms over 8 to 10 years. *Fluctuation of cognitive impairment during the course of the day* is characteristic of delirium rather than dementia. Although both delirium and dementia involve cognitive impairment, the changes in dementia are more stable over time and do not fluctuate over the course of a day. The differential diagnosis of dementia includes depression-related cognitive dysfunction, referred to as pseudodementia. *Early and prominent loss of social skills* and *marked variability in performance of tasks of similar difficulty* are characteristic of pseudodementia rather than dementia. Patients with dementia often retain social skills and show consistently poor performance tasks of similar difficulty.

10.21 The answer is A (*Synopsis VIII,* page 329).
Figure 10.6 shows the microscopic appearance of the hippocampus from a patient with Alzheimer's disease, showing large numbers of neurofibrillary tangles and senile plaques. Although neurofibrillary tangles are not unique to Alzheimer's disease, senile plaques (also referred to as amyloid plaques) are much more indicative of Alzheimer's. The *neurotransmitter acetylcholine and norepinephrine are among the factors implicated in the pathophysiology of Alzheimer's disease, both of which are hypothesized to be hypoactive.*

The course of Alzheimer's is characteristically one of gradual decline over 8 to 10 years; *disease progression of less than 6 months would not be expected.* The mean survival of patients with Alzheimer's disease is approximately 8 years, with a range of 1 to 20 years. *Cognitive dysfunction, rather than motor dysfunction, is the initial and predominant manifestation of Alzheimer's disease.* Memory impairment is accompanied by such deficits as aphasia, apraxia, agnosia, and disturbances in executive functioning. The general sequence of deficits is memory, language, and visuospatial functions. *Dementia of Alzheimer's type has no known prevention or cure.* Treatment is palliative, and medication may be helpful in managing agitation and behavior disturbances. *L-Dopa is a medication used in the treatment of Parkinson's disease.*

10.22 The answer is D (*Synopsis VIII,* pages 329–330).
Figure 10.7 illustrates the classic gross neuroanatomical appearance of a brain from a patient with Alzheimer's disease: diffuse atrophy with flattened cortical sulci. The classic and pathognomonic microscopic findings in Alzheimer's disease are *senile (amyloid) plaques, neurofibrillary tangles, neuronal loss (particularly in the cortex and hippocampus), synaptic loss, and granulovacuolar degeneration of neurons.*

Multiple lacunar infarcts are characteristic of vascular dementia rather than dementia of the Alzheimer's type.

10.23 The answer is B (*Synopsis VIII,* page 360).
The neuropathology is consistent with multiple sclerosis (MS), the most common demyelinating disorder. Pathologically, multiple sclerosis consists of multifocal demyelination, producing irregularly shaped areas (plaques) of demyelination with sharp borders. In addition to multiple exacerbations and remissions of neurological deficits, MS often features behavioral symptoms including *depression, personality changes, and euphoric mood, as well as cognitive impairment.* Memory is the most commonly affected cognitive function. *Psychosis* is a rare complication of MS.

10.24a The answer is D (*Synopsis VIII,* pages 331, 352).

10.24b The answer is E (*Synopsis VIII,* pages 331, 352).
The neuropathology is consistent with Parkinson's disease, which results from a loss of cells in the substantia nigra, a decrease in the concentration of dopamine, and a degeneration of dopaminergic tracts. The major finding on observation of gross neuropathology is depigmentation of the substantia nigra and locus ceruleus.

Parkinson's disease is a progressive disease of late adult life with characteristic symptoms of *bradykinesia, rigidity, and tremor at rest (no intention tremor, which is characteristic of cerebellar dysfunction).* Physical examination of a patient with Parkinson's disease reveals an *impairment of fine movements, cogwheel rigidity, sucking reflexes, positive Babinski signs, and other evidence of pyramidal tract involvement.*

Apathy, intellectual impairment, depression, and dementia are commonly seen in Parkinson's disease. The prevalence of *depression* in Parkinson's disease has been reported to be between 40 to 60 percent, whereas *dementia* is present in 30 to 60 percent.

Answers 10.25–10.29

10.25 The answer is A (*Synopsis VIII,* page 363).

10.26 The answer is B (*Synopsis VIII,* page 363).

10.27 The answer is B (*Synopsis VIII,* page 363).

10.28 The answer is D (*Synopsis VIII,* page 363).

10.29 The answer is D (*Synopsis VIII,* page 363).
Dietary insufficiency of niacin and its precursor, tryptophan, is associated with *pellagra,* a nutritional deficiency disease of global importance. Pellagra is associated with alcohol abuse, vegetarian diets, and extreme poverty and starvation.

Thiamine (vitamin B_1) deficiency leads to *beriberi,* characterized mainly by cardiovascular and nutritional changes, and the *Wernicke-Korsakoff syndrome.* The psychiatric symptoms of both disorders can include *apathy,* irritability, and *depression.*

Answers 10.30–10.39

10.30 The answer is A (*Synopsis VIII,* page 322).

10.31 The answer is B (*Synopsis VIII,* page 328).

10.32 The answer is A (*Synopsis VIII,* pages 322, 328).

10.33 The answer is C (*Synopsis VIII,* pages 328, 330).

10.34 The answer is D (*Synopsis VIII,* page 320).

10.35 The answer is C (*Synopsis VIII,* page 330).

10.36 The answer is C (*Synopsis VIII,* pages 328, 339–340).

10.37 The answer is B (*Synopsis VIII,* pages 331, 333).

10.38 The answer is A (*Synopsis VIII,* pages 322, 328).

10.39 The answer is C (*Synopsis VIII,* page 334).
The differentiation between delirium and dementia can be difficult. Several clinical features help in the differentiation. In contrast to the *sudden onset* of delirium, dementia usually has an *insidious onset.* Although both conditions include cognitive impairment, the changes in dementia are relatively stable over time and do not fluctuate over the course of a day, for example. A patient with dementia is usually alert; a patient with delirium has episodes of *clouding of consciousness.* Both delirium and dementia are *reversible,* although delirium has a better chance of reversing if treatment is timely. *Insight,* defined as the awareness that one is mentally ill, is absent in both conditions. *Hallucinations* can occur in both conditions and must be differentiated from those that occur in schizophrenia. In general, the hallucinations of schizophrenic patients are more constant and better formed than are the hallucinations of delirious patients. *Sundowning* is observed in both demented and delirious patients. Sundowning is characterized by drowsiness, confusion, ataxia, and accidental falls just about bedtime. Kurt Goldstein described a *catastrophic reaction* in demented patients; it is marked by agitation secondary to the subjective awareness of one's intellectual deficits under stressful circumstances. The presence of delirium is a bad prognostic sign. Patients with delirium have a *high mortality rate.* The 3-month mortality rate of patients who have an episode of delirium is estimated to be 23 to 33 percent; the 1-year mortality rate may be as high as 50 percent. The major neurotransmitter hypothesized to be involved in delirium and dementia is acetylcholine. Several types of studies of delirium and dementia have shown a correlation between *decreased acetylcholine activity* in the brain and both delirium and dementia.

Answers 10.40–10.45

10.40 The answer is C (*Synopsis VIII,* pages 328–331).

10.41 The answer is A (*Synopsis VIII,* pages 328–330).

10.42 The answer is B (*Synopsis VIII,* page 331).

10.43 The answer is D (*Synopsis VIII,* pages 328–330).

10.44 The answer is A (*Synopsis VIII,* pages 328–330).

10.45 The answer is A (*Synopsis VIII,* pages 328–330).
Alzheimer's disease and dementia of the Alzheimer's type are characterized by a severe loss of intellectual function with an unknown cause. The specific lesions found in Alzheimer's disease include senile plaques and neurofibrillary changes. *Pick's disease* is a rare form of dementia that has an unknown cause.

Pick's disease is distinctive in that it is characterized by lobar atrophy. The frontal and temporal lobes are usually the most seriously affected, the occipital lobes are less affected, and the parietal lobes are still less affected. The neurofibrillary changes and senile plaques that characterize Alzheimer's disease are absent. Neither dementia of the Alzheimer's type nor Pick's disease is *reversible.* Treatment is generally supportive, and pharmacological treatments are used for specific symptoms. *Tacrine (Cognex)* and *donepezil (Aricept)* are acetylcholinesterase inhibitors used to treat dementia of the Alzheimer's type. However, the drugs do not prevent the neurological degeneration of Alzheimer's disease.

Answers 10.46–10.49

10.46 The answer is D (*Synopsis VIII,* pages 363–364).

10.47 The answer is A (*Synopsis VIII,* page 363).

10.48 The answer is C (*Synopsis VIII,* page 363).

10.49 The answer is B (*Synopsis VIII,* page 363).
In acute *mercury poisoning,* the central nervous system symptoms of lethargy and restlessness may occur, but the primary symptoms are secondary to severe gastrointestinal irritation, with bloody stools, diarrhea, and vomiting leading to circulatory collapse because of dehydration. Mad Hatter syndrome, named for the *Mad Hatter* in *Alice's Adventures in Wonderland,* is a parody of the madness resulting from the inhalation of mercury nitrate vapors; mercury nitrate was used in the past in the processing of felt hats.

Early intoxication with *manganese* produces manganese madness, with symptoms of headache, irritability, joint pains, and somnolence. Lesions involving the basal ganglia and pyramidal system result in gait impairment, rigidity, monotonous or whispering speech, tremors of the extremities and tongue, masked facies (manganese mask), micrographia, dystonia, dysarthria, and loss of equilibrium.

Thallium intoxication initially causes severe pains in the legs, as well as diarrhea and vomiting. Within a week, delirium, convulsions, cranial nerve palsies, blindness, choreiform movements, and coma may occur. Behavioral changes include paranoid thinking and depression, with suicidal tendencies. Alopecia is a common and important diagnostic clue.

Chronic lead poisoning occurs when the amount of lead ingested exceeds the ability to eliminate it. Toxic symptoms appear after several months. Treatment should be instituted as rapidly as possible, even without laboratory confirmation, because of the high mortality. The treatment of choice to facilitate lead excretion is the oral administration of *succimer (Chemet)* every 8 hours for 5 days. Each dose is 10 mg/kg or 350 mg/m^2. An additional 2 weeks of twice-daily dosages completes a 19-day course of therapy.

Answers 10.50–10.54

10.50 The answer is D (*Synopsis VIII,* pages 331, 339).

10.51 The answer is A (*Synopsis VIII,* page 361).

10.52 The answer is C (*Synopsis VIII,* page 361).

10.53 The answer is B (*Synopsis VIII,* pages 359–360).

10.54 The answer is E (*Synopsis VIII,* page 360).

Huntington's disease, inherited in an autosomal dominant pattern, leads to major atrophy of the brain with extensive degeneration of the caudate nucleus. The onset is usually insidious and most commonly begins in late middle life. The course is one of gradual progression; death occurs 15 to 20 years after the onset of the disease, and suicide is common.

Creutzfeldt-Jakob disease is a rare degenerative brain disease caused by a slow virus, with death occurring within 2 years of the diagnosis. A computed tomography (CT) scan shows cerebellar and cortical atrophy.

Neurosyphilis (also known as general paresis) is a chronic dementia and psychosis caused by the tertiary form of syphilis that affects the brain. The presenting symptoms include a manic syndrome with neurological signs in up to 20 percent of cases.

Normal pressure hydrocephalus is associated with enlarged ventricles and normal cerebrospinal fluid (CSF) pressure. The characteristic signs include dementia, a gait disturbance, and urinary incontinence. The treatment of choice is a shunt of the CSF from the ventricular space to either the atrium or the peritoneal space. Reversal of the dementia and associated signs is sometimes dramatic after treatment.

Multiple sclerosis is characterized by diffuse multifocal lesions in the white matter of the central nervous system (CNS). Its clinical course is characterized by exacerbations and remissions. It has no known specific cause, although research has focused on slow viral infections and autoimmune disturbances. Multiple sclerosis is much more prevalent in cold and temperate climates than in the tropics and subtropics, is more common in women than in men, and is predominantly a disease of young adults.

11

Neuropsychiatric Aspects of Human Immunodeficiency Virus (HIV) Infection and Acquired Immune Deficiency Syndrome (AIDS)

The psychiatrist plays an important role in the diagnosis and treatment of HIV-positive persons and those with AIDS. Many such patients develop neuropsychiatric disorders as the first manifestations of illness of which the psychiatrist must be aware.

The management of such patients is extraordinarily complex. Major psychodynamic themes for HIV-infected patients involve self-blame, self-esteem, and issues regarding death. The psychiatrist can help patients deal with feelings of guilt about behaviors that contributed to the development of AIDS. Some AIDS patients feel that they are being punished for a deviant lifestyle. Difficult health care decisions, such as whether to participate in an experimental drug trial, and terminal care and life-support systems may have to be made with the help of the psychiatrist. Major practical themes for the patients involve employment, medical benefits, life insurance, career plans, and relationships with families and friends. The entire range of psychotherapeutic approaches may be appropriate for patients with HIV-related disorders.

The homosexual community has provided a significant support system for HIV-infected people, particularly homosexual and bisexual persons. Public education campaigns within that community have resulted in significant (more than 50 percent) reductions in the highest-risk sexual practices. That educational program has also helped intravenous drug users, who are also at risk, and the heterosexual community as well.

All physicians, regardless of specialty, must be comfortable discussing the issues of AIDS and HIV infection with their patients and must be able to provide accurate information to questions from patients and their families.

The reader is referred to Chapter 11 in *Kaplan and Sadock's Synopsis VIII.* Students can assess their knowledge by studying the questions and answers that follow.

HELPFUL HINTS

The following terms should be known by the student.

- AIDS dementia complex
- AIDS in children
- astrocytes
- AZT
- *Candida albicans*
- CNS infections
- confidentiality
- ddI
- ELISA
- false-positives
- HIV encephalopathy
- HIV-1 and HIV-2
- institutional care
- Kaposi's sarcoma
- neuropsychiatric syndromes
- *Pneumocystis carinii* pneumonia
- pretest and posttest counseling
- psychopharmacology
- psychotherapy
- retrovirus
- seropositive
- T4 lymphocytes
- transmission
- tuberculosis
- Western blot analysis
- worried well

▲ QUESTIONS

DIRECTIONS: Each of the questions or incomplete statements below is followed by five suggested responses or completions. Select the *one* that is *best* in each case.

11.1 All of the following statements about psychotherapy with HIV-infected patients are true *except*

A. The patient must feel that the therapist is not judging past or present behaviors.
B. Therapists must acknowledge to themselves their predetermined attitudes toward sexual orientation.
C. Issues regarding the therapist's own past behaviors and eventual death may give rise to countertransference issues.
D. Seeing many HIV-infected patients in a short time is less stressful to therapists than seeing a small number of HIV-infected patients over a long period.
E. Mental health care workers often help patients deal with legal matters.

11.2 The major exception to an approach of confidentiality and restricted disclosure about a patient's HIV status is

A. employers
B. coworkers
C. friends
D. sexual partners
E. family members

11.3 Which of the following pharmacological regimens is not indicated for treating HIV infection and AIDS?

A. Ritonavir (Norvir) and saquinavir (Invirase)
B. Ritonavir (Norvir), didanosine (Videx), and zidovudine (Retrovir)
C. Zalcitabine (Hivid), saquinavir, and zidovudine
E. Didanosine and zidovudine
E. Lamivudine (Epivir) and indinavir (Crixivan)

11.4 The human immunodeficiency virus (HIV)

A. is a deoxyribonucleic acid (DNA) retrovirus
B. is not present in the tears of infected persons
C. cannot be transmitted through breast feeding
D. has infected 10 million people worldwide
E. does not infect glial cells within the central nervous system (CNS)

11.5 In persons infected by HIV

A. seroconversion usually occurs 2 weeks after infection
B. the estimated length of time from infection to the development of AIDS is 5 years
C. 10 percent have neuropsychiatric complications
D. the T4 lymphocyte count usually falls to abnormal levels during the asymptomatic period
E. the majority are infected by HIV type 2 (HIV-2)

11.6 Statistics regarding HIV and AIDS reveal that

A. the number of HIV-infected men is growing 4 times faster than the number of HIV-infected women
B. more women are infected by HIV through heterosexual intercourse than through intravenous (IV) substance use
C. New York, Los Angeles, San Francisco, and Miami account for 30 percent of all AIDS cases in the United States
D. not every state in the United States has reported cases of AIDS
E. more than 3 million persons in the United States are HIV positive

11.7 In tests for HIV

A. assays usually detect the presence of viral proteins
B. the enzyme-linked immunosorbent assay (ELISA) is used to confirm positive test results of the Western blot analysis
C. the results cannot be shared with other members of a medical treatment team
D. pretest counseling should not inquire why a person desires HIV testing
E. a person may have a true negative result, even if the person is infected by HIV

11.8 In the treatment of HIV and HIV-related disorders

A. azidothymidine (AZT) acts by inhibiting the adherence of glycoprotein-120 (GP-120) to the CD4 receptor on T4 lymphocytes
B. AZT has caused increased neuropsychiatric symptoms
C. patients taking haloperidol (Haldol) have decreased sensitivity to the drug's extrapyramidal effects
D. the entire range of psychotherapeutic approaches may be appropriate
E. pentamidine is used prophylactically to guard against the development of *Cryptosporidium* infection

11.9 Diseases affecting the central nervous system (CNS) in patients with AIDS include

A. atypical aseptic meningitis
B. *Candida albicans* abscess
C. primary CNS lymphoma
D. cerebrovascular infarction
E. all of the above

11.10 All of the following statements about the serum test for HIV are true *except*

A. False-positive results occur in about 1 percent of persons tested.
B. The Western blot analysis is less likely to give a false-positive result than is the enzyme-linked immunosorbent assay (ELISA).
C. A person should be notified immediately if the result of the ELISA is positive.
D. Blood banks must exclude sera that are ELISA-positive.
E. About 1 million Americans are seropositive to HIV.

11.11 Which of the following drugs should be chosen for a HIV-infected patient with depression and cognitive impairment, such as delirium?

A. Amitriptyline (Elavil)
B. Clomipramine (Anafranil)
C. Sertraline (Zoloft)
D. Trimipramine (Surmontil)
E. Thioridazine (Mellaril)

11.12 In the psychotherapy for a homosexual AIDS patient

A. therapy with the patient's lover is unwarranted
B. a discussion of safe-sex practices is not necessary
C. such issues as terminal care and life-support systems should be avoided
D. the psychiatrist can help the patient deal with feelings of guilt
E. the patient should be advised not to come out to the family

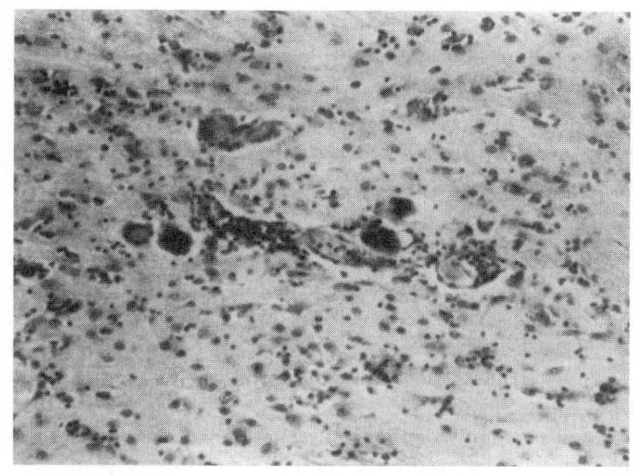

FIGURE 11.1
Reprinted with permission from Pajeau AK, Roman GC: HIV encephalopathy and dementia. Psychiatr Clin North Am *15:* 461, 1992.

11.13a The multinucleated giant cells shown in Figure 11.1 are part of a neuropathological picture that includes diffuse astrocytosis, microglial nodules, and white matter vacuolation and demyelination in this HIV-positive patient. This neuropathology is consistent with a diagnosis of

A. *Toxoplasma gondii* infection
B. primary central nervous system (CNS) lymphoma
C. HIV encephalopathy
D. metastatic Kaposi's sarcoma
E. cryptococcal meningitis

11.13b Clinical symptoms associated with this patient's diagnosis include all of the following *except*

A. early-onset aphasia
B. mood and personality changes
C. hyperreflexia and paraparesis
D. psychomotor slowing
E. problems with memory and concentration

ANSWERS

Neuropsychiatric Aspects of Human Immunodeficiency Virus (HIV) Infection and Acquired Immune Deficiency Syndrome (AIDS)

11.1 The answer is D (*Synopsis VIII,* page 374).
Countertransference issues and the burnout of therapists who treat many HIV-infected patients are two key issues to evaluate regularly. For some psychotherapists who have practices with many HIV-infected patients, professional burnout can hinder their effectiveness. Some studies have found that seeing many HIV-infected patients in a short period of time is *more, not less, stressful* to therapists than seeing a small number of HIV-infected patients over a long period. The assessment of HIV-infected patients should include a sexual and substance-abuse history, a psychiatric history, and an evaluation of the support systems available to the patient. However, *the patients must feel that the therapist is not judging past or present behaviors.* A sense of trust and empathy can often be encouraged by the therapist's asking specific, well-informed, and straightforward questions about the patient's sexual or substance-using culture. *Therapists must acknowledge to themselves their predetermined attitudes toward sexual orientation* and substance abuse so that those attitudes do not interfere with the treatment of the patient. Furthermore, *issues regarding the therapist's own past behaviors and eventual death may give rise to countertransference issues.*

Mental health care workers often help patients deal with legal matters, such as making a will and taking care of hospital and other medical expenses. The resolution of such matters is of such practical importance that it is often well worth the time of the mental health workers to make sure that those matters are addressed satisfactorily.

11.2 The answer is D (*Synopsis VIII,* page 369).
Confidentiality is a key issue in serum testing. The major exception to restriction of disclosure is the need to notify potential and past *sexual partners* or intravenous (IV) substance partners. The results of an HIV test can also be shared with other members of a medical team. Patients should be advised against too readily disclosing the result of HIV testing to *employers, coworkers, friends,* and *family members,* because the information could result in discrimination in employment, housing, and insurance.

11.3 The answer is A (*Synopsis VIII,* pages 372–373).
Zidovudine (previously called azidothymidine [AZT]) is an inhibitor of reverse transcriptase. It was for many years a primary medication for HIV-infected patients, having been shown to slow the course of the disease and prolong survival in some patients. However, polydrug therapy for the treatment of HIV infection has replaced single-drug therapy. The nucleoside analogues and the protease inhibitors are the two classes of drugs commonly used (Table 11.1). However, the protease inhibitors are always used in combination with one or more nucleosides; protease inhibitors, such as *ritonavir (Norvir) and saquinavir (Invirase),* should not be used alone.

Some studies indicate that triple-drug therapy with two nucleosides and one protease inhibitor—for example, *ritonavir, didanosine (Videx), and zidovudine*—is the most potent antiretroviral treatment available. In one study of HIV-infected patients, treatment with *zalcitabine, saquinavir, and zidovudine* reduced HIV-1 replication and increased CD4+ cell counts. Double treatment with two nucleosides—for example, *didanosine and indinavir*—or with one nucleoside analogue and one protease inhibitor—for example, *lamivudine* (*Epivir*) *and indinavir* (*Crixivan*)—may also be effective.

Table 11.1
Selected Drugs for HIV Infection

Class/Generic Name	Trade Name	Typical Daily Dosage (mg/day)
Nucleoside analogue transcriptase inhibitors		
Didanosine	Videx	400
Lamivudine	Epivir	300
Stavudine	Zerit	80
Zalcitabine	Hivid	2.25
Zidovudine	Retrovir	600
Nonnucleoside transcriptase inhibitors		
Delavirdine	Rescriptor	1,200
Viviratine	Viramune	400
Protease inhibitors		
Indinavir	Crixivan	2,400
Ritonavir	Norvir	1,200
Saquinavir	Invirase	1,800

11.4 The answer is D (*Synopsis VIII,* page 367).
At the end of 1993, the World Health Organization (WHO) estimated that HIV *has infected 10 million people worldwide.* HIV *is not a deoxyribonucleic acid* (*DNA*) *retrovirus;* rather, it is a ribonucleic acid (RNA) retrovirus that was isolated and identified in 1983. HIV is present in the blood, the semen, and cervical and vaginal secretions; to a small extent, HIV *is present in the tears,* breast milk, and cerebrospinal fluid *of infected persons.* HIV *can be transmitted through breast feeding;* children can also be infected in utero when their mothers are HIV-positive. Once a person is infected by HIV, the virus targets primarily CD4+ lymphocytes, which are also called T4 (helper) lymphocytes. HIV *infects glial cells within the central nervous system* (*CNS*), particularly astrocytes. Astrocytes are glial cells, the nonneuronal cellular elements found on the CNS that are believed to carry out important metabolic functions.

11.5 The answer is D (*Synopsis VIII,* pages 365–366).
The T4 lymphocyte count usually falls to abnormal levels during the asymptomatic period of HIV infection. The normal values are greater than 1,000/mm^3, and grossly abnormal values can be fewer than 200/mm^3.

Seroconversion is the change after infection with HIV from a negative HIV antibody test result to a positive HIV antibody test result. *Seroconversion usually occurs 6 to 12 weeks after infection.* In rare cases, seroconversion can take 6 to 12 months. *The estimated length of time from infection to the development of AIDS is 8 to 11 years,* although that time is gradually increasing because of the early implementation of treatment. At least *50 percent* of HIV-infected patients *have neuropsychiatric complications,* which may be the first signs of the disease in about 10 percent of patients. Two types of HIV have been identified, HIV type 1 (HIV-1) and HIV type 2 (HIV-2). *The majority* of HIV-positive patients *are infected by HIV-1.* However, HIV-2 infection seems to be increasing in Africa.

11.6 The answer is B (*Synopsis VIII,* pages 365–366).
Current statistics reveal that *more women are infected by HIV through heterosexual intercourse than through intravenous (IV) substance use.* That finding is the opposite of what was found in years past.

The ratio of men to women who are infected by HIV is estimated to be 6 to 1, but *the number of HIV-infected women is growing 4 times faster than the number of HIV-infected men,* not vice versa. Although the geographic distribution is heavily skewed toward large urban centers—for example, *the cities of New York, Los Angeles, San Francisco, and Miami account for more than 50 percent of all AIDS cases in the United States—every state in the United States has reported cases of AIDS.* At the end of 1995, *more than 320,000 deaths in the United States had been caused by AIDS;* 510,000 cases of AIDS were reported. At present 1 million people in the United States are infected with HIV. By the year 2000, 30 million to 40 million people worldwide will be infected with HIV.

11.7 The answer is E (*Synopsis VIII,* page 367).
A person may have a true negative result, even if the person is infected by HIV, if the test takes place after infection but before seroconversion. *Assays do not usually detect the presence of viral proteins. The enzyme-linked immunosorbent assay (ELISA) is not used to confirm positive test results of the Western blot analysis.* Rather, the ELISA is used as an initial screening test because it is less expensive than the Western blot analysis and more easily used to screen a large number of samples. The ELISA is sensitive and reasonably specific; although it is unlikely to report a false-negative result, it may indicate a false-positive result. For that reason, positive results from an ELISA are confirmed by using the more expensive and cumbersome Western blot analysis, which is sensitive and specific.

Confidentiality is a key issue in serum testing. No persons should be given HIV tests without their prior knowledge and consent, although various jurisdictions and organizations (for example, the military) now require HIV testing for all its inhabitants or members. *The results can be shared with other members of a medical treatment team* but should be provided to no one else.

Any person who wants to be tested should probably be tested, although *pretest counseling should inquire why a person desires HIV testing* to detect unspoken concerns and motivations that may merit psychotherapeutic intervention.

11.8 The answer is D (*Synopsis VIII,* pages 366–368).
The entire range of psychotherapeutic approaches may be appropriate in the treatment of HIV and HIV-related disorders. Treatment with *AZT does not cause increased neuropsychiatric symptoms;* rather, it prevents or reverses the neuropsychiatric symptoms associated with HIV encephalopathy. Although dopamine receptor antagonists such as haloperidol (Haldol) may be required for control of agitation, they should be used in as low a dosage as possible because *patients taking haloperidol have increased sensitivity to the drug's extrapyramidal effects.* Also, the prophylactic use of aerosolized pentamidine (NebuPent) and of trimethoprim (Bactrim) and sulfamethoxazole (Gantanol) against the development of *Pneumocystis carinii* is now in common practice. Aerosolized *pentamidine is not used prophylactically to guard against the development of* Cryptosporidium, which causes intermittent or severe watery diarrhea, primarily in HIV-positive homosexual men. No treatment is available.

11.9 The answer is E (all) (*Synopsis VIII,* page 369).
Most of the infections secondary to HIV involvement of the central nervous system (CNS) are viral or fungal. *Atypical aseptic meningitis,* Candida albicans *abscess, primary CNS lymphoma,* and *cerebrovascular infarction* can all affect a patient with AIDS. Table 11.2 lists the most common diseases affecting the CNS in patients with AIDS.

11.10 The answer is C (*Synopsis VIII,* page 367).
A *person should not be notified immediately if the result of the ELISA is positive* until a confirmatory test, such as the

Table 11.2
Diseases Affecting the CNS in Patients with AIDS

Primary viral diseases
HIV encephalopathy
Atypical aseptic meningitis
Vacuolar myelopathy
Secondary viruses (encephalitis, myelitis, retinitis, vasculitis)
Cytomegalovirus
Herpes simplex virus types 1 and 2
Herpes varicella-zoster virus
Papovavirus (PML)
Nonviral infections (encephalitis, meningitis, abscess)
Toxoplasma gondii
Cryptococcus neoformans
Candida albicans
Histoplasma capsulatum
Aspergillus fumigatus
Coccidioides immitis
Acremonium albamensis
Rhizopus species
Mycobacterium avium-intracellulare
Mycobacterium tuberculosis hominis
Mycobacterium kansasii
Listeria monocytogenes
Nocardia asteroides
Neoplasms
Primary CNS lymphoma
Metastatic systemic lymphoma
Metastatic Kaposi's sarcoma
Cerebrovascular diseases
Infarction
Hemorrhage
Vasculitis
Complications of systemic therapy

Reprinted with permission from Beckett A: The neurobiology of human immunodeficiency virus infection. In *American Psychiatric Press Review of Psychiatry,* vol 9, A Tasman, SM Goldfinger, CA Kaufman, editors, p 595. Copyright, American Psychiatric Press, Washington, 1990.

Western blot analysis, is conducted. The serum test used to detect HIV is the enzyme-linked immunosorbent assay (ELISA). *False-positive results* (nondiseased persons with abnormal test results) *occur in about 1 percent of persons tested* with ELISA. If an ELISA result is suspected of being incorrect, the serum can be subjected to a *Western blot analysis,* which *is less likely to give a false-positive* or false-negative *result* (diseased person with normal test result) *than is the ELISA.* However, *blood banks must exclude sera that are ELISA-positive. About 1 million Americans are seropositive to HIV.*

11.11 The answer is C (*Synopsis VIII,* pages 372–373).
Antidepressants (Table 11.3), particularly those with few anticholinergic effects, are beneficial in treating depression due to HIV disease. Anticholinergic drugs should be avoided in patients with delirium or other cognitive impairment to prevent atropine psychosis.

Sertraline (*Zoloft*) and fluoxetine (Prozac) are two serotonin-specific reuptake inhibitors that have no anticholinergic effects. *Clomipramine* (*Anafranil*), *amitriptyline (Elavil)*, and *trimipramine* (*Surmontil*) are three tricyclic drugs with very high anticholinergic effects; *thioridazine (Mellaril)* is a dopamine receptor antagonist approved in the United States for depression with severe anxiety or agitation. However, this is an outdated indication for the drug because of the availability of drugs with superior efficacy and safety profiles. Thioridazine also has high anticholinergic effects.

11.12 The answer is D (*Synopsis VIII,* page 373).
Psychotherapy with a homosexual AIDS patient requires great flexibility. *The psychiatrist can help the patient deal with feelings of guilt* regarding behaviors that contributed to AIDS and that are disapproved of by segments of society, for example, the feeling that he or she is being punished for a deviant lifestyle. *Therapy with the patient's lover is warranted* in many cases. *A discussion of safe-sex practices,* such as using condoms in anal sex, *is necessary.* Difficult health care decisions and *such issues as terminal care and life-support systems should be explored.* The treatment of homosexuals and bisexuals with AIDS often involves both helping *the patient to come out to the family* (that is, telling the family that the patient is homosexual) and dealing with the possible issues of rejection, guilt, shame, and anger.

11.13a The answer is C (*Synopsis VIII,* page 370).
The neuropathology described for this patient is consistent with a diagnosis of HIV encephalopathy. HIV enters the CNS, where it infects primarily glial cells, particularly astrocytes. The virus is also harbored within immune cells in the CNS. The neuropathology of *HIV encephalopathy is* characterized by multinucleated giant cells, microglial nodules, diffuse astrocytosis, perivascular lymphocyte cuffing, cortical atrophy, and white matter vacuolation and demyelination.

Table 11.3
Comparison of Drugs Used to Treat Depression and Their Anticholinergic Effects

Drug	Anticholinergic Effects
Trazodone	None
Moclobemide	Minimal
Nefazodone	Minimal
Venlafaxine	Minimal
Bupropion	None
Mirtazapine	Moderate
Serotonin-specific reuptake inhibitors	
Fluoxetine	None
Sertraline	None
Fluvoxamine	Minimal
Paroxetine	Low
Tricyclics	
Desipramine	Low
Doxepine	Moderate
Imipramine	Moderate
Nortriptyline	Moderate
Protriptyline	Moderate
Trimipramine	High
Amitriptyline	Very high
Clomipramine	Very high
Tetracyclics	
Amoxapine	Low
Maprotiline	Moderate

11.13b The answer is A (*Synopsis VIII,* page 370).
HIV encephalopathy is a subacute encephalitis that results in a progressive subcortical dementia without focal neurological signs. *The major differentiating feature between subcortical dementia and cortical dementia is the absence of classical cortical symptoms* (*for example, aphasia*) *until late in the illness.* Patients with HIV encephalitis or their friends usually notice *subtle mood and personality changes, problems with memory and concentration, and some psychomotor slowing.* The presence of motor symptoms may also suggest a diagnosis of HIV encephalopathy. Motor symptoms associated with subcortical dementia include *hyperreflexia,* spastic or ataxic gait, *paraparesis,* and increased muscle tone.

12

Substance-Related Disorders

The phenomenon of substance abuse has many implications for brain research, clinical psychiatry, and society in general. Substances can cause neuropsychiatric symptoms that are indistinguishable from those of common psychiatric disorders with no known causes (for example, schizophrenia and mood disorders). That observation can then be taken to suggest that psychiatric disorders and disorders involving the use of brain-altering substances are related. If the depressive symptoms seen in some persons who have not taken a brain-altering substance are indistinguishable from the depressive symptoms in a person who has taken a brain-altering substance, there may be some brain-based commonality between substance-taking behavior and depression. The fact that brain-altering substances exist is a fundamental clue regarding how the brain works in both normal and abnormal states.

It is important to be clear about the definition of addiction, dependence, abuse, tolerance, cross-tolerance, intoxication, and withdrawal. The term ''addiction'' has essentially been replaced by the term ''dependence.'' Dependence implies a psychological and physical reliance on a substance that leads to substance-seeking behavior, an inability to stop using the substance, an increasing tolerance to its effects, and a deterioration in physical and mental health as a result of continued use of the substance.

Tolerance is the need for increased amounts of the substance to achieve the desired effect. Tolerance to one substance may develop as the result of exposure to another, a phenomenon termed cross-tolerance. Alcohol and benzodiazepines are cross-tolerant. Tolerance varies widely among persons and can differ because of ethnic background. Substance abuse is a pattern of use that may or may not result in substance dependence. Intoxication results from abuse and withdrawal results from dependence. Both intoxication and withdrawal have syndromes unique to the particular substance involved.

Some specific relationships exist between mood and anxiety symptoms and certain substances of abuse (for example, cocaine, amphetamines, and benzodiazepines). However, it is often difficult to determine whether a patient who is anxious or depressed is self-medicating with substances or has caused the mood symptoms by using substances. In many patients it is a vicious cycle, with the mood symptoms and the substance abuse interacting, so that each exacerbates the other.

For each of the specific substance-related disorders, the clinician must know its definition, epidemiology, and clinical features.

Students are referred to Chapter 12 in *Kaplan and Sadock's Synopsis VIII* to prepare for the questions and answers below that assess their knowledge of the subject.

HELPFUL HINTS

The student should know each of the terms below and the fourth-edition *Diagnostic and Statistical Manual of Mental Disorders* (DSM-IV) diagnostic criteria.

- ▶ AA
- ▶ abuse
- ▶ addiction
- ▶ AIDS
- ▶ Al-Anon
- ▶ alcohol delirium
- ▶ alcohol psychotic disorder
- ▶ alcohol withdrawal
- ▶ amotivational syndrome
- ▶ amphetamine
- ▶ anabolic
- ▶ anabolic steroids
- ▶ anticholinergic side effects
- ▶ arylcyclohexylamine
- ▶ belladonna alkaloids
- ▶ blackouts
- ▶ caffeine
- ▶ cocaine delirium
- ▶ cocaine intoxication and withdrawal
- ▶ cocaine psychotic disorder
- ▶ comorbidity
- ▶ cross-tolerance
- ▶ DEA
- ▶ delta alcohol dependence
- ▶ dementia
- ▶ dispositional tolerance
- ▶ disulfiram
- ▶ DMT
- ▶ DOM
- ▶ DPT
- ▶ DTS
- ▶ dual diagnosis
- ▶ fetal alcohol syndrome
- ▶ flashback
- ▶ gamma alcohol dependence
- ▶ hallucinogen
- ▶ hallucinogen persisting perception disorder
- ▶ idiosyncratic alcohol intoxication
- ▶ inhalant intoxication
- ▶ ketamine
- ▶ Korsakoff's and Wernicke's syndromes
- ▶ LAMM

- ▶ LSD
- ▶ MDMA
- ▶ methadone withdrawal
- ▶ miosis
- ▶ misuse
- ▶ MPTP-induced parkinsonism
- ▶ mydriasis
- ▶ nicotine receptor
- ▶ NIDA
- ▶ nitrous oxide
- ▶ opiate
- ▶ opioid
- ▶ opioid antagonists
- ▶ opioid intoxication
- ▶ opioid withdrawal
- ▶ pathological alcohol use
- ▶ patterns of pathological use
- ▶ PCP
- ▶ persisting amnestic disorder
- ▶ persisting dementia
- ▶ physical dependence
- ▶ psychedelics
- ▶ psychoactive
- ▶ psychological dependence
- ▶ RFLP
- ▶ ''roid'' rage
- ▶ sedative-hypnotic-anxiolytic
- ▶ STP alcohol intoxication; blood levels
- ▶ substance abuse
- ▶ substance dependence
- ▶ sympathomimetic signs
- ▶ THC
- ▶ tolerance
- ▶ type I alcoholism
- ▶ type II alcoholism
- ▶ volatile hydrocarbons
- ▶ WHO
- ▶ WHO definitions
- ▶ withdrawal

▲ QUESTIONS

DIRECTIONS: Each of the questions or incomplete statements below is followed by five suggested responses or completions. Select the *one* that is *best* in each case.

12.1 In 1996, voters in California approved referenda allowing physicians to prescribe

A. methamphetamine
B. lysergic acid diethylamide
C. marijuana
D. heroin
E. all of the above

12.2 All of the following are considered to be psychoactive substances *except*

A. chlorpromazine
B. cocaine
C. nicotine
D. caffeine
E. morphine

12.3 According to U.S. health surveys, what is the estimate of the number of people who use an illicit drug each month?

A. 1 million to 5 million
B. 5 million to 10 million
C. 10 million to 15 million
D. 15 million to 20 million
E. More than 20 million

12.4 Which of the following is the most common illicitly used drug in the United States?

A. Cocaine
B. Amphetamine
C. Marijuana
D. Heroin
E. Codeine

12.5 Match the lettered blood alcohol level with the appropriate numbered item.

A. 0.05 percent
B. 0.10 percent
C. 0.15 percent
D. 0.20 percent
E. 0.50 percent

1. Legal intoxication in most states
2. Judgment impaired
3. Clumsy voluntary motor action
4. Coma
5. Confusion or stupor

12.6 Match the lettered headings with the appropriate numbered phrases.

A. Alcohol dehydrogenase
B. Aldehyde dehydrogenase
C. Both
D. Neither

1. Involved in alcohol metabolism
2. Converts alcohol into acetaldehyde
3. Inhibited by disulfiram (Antabuse)
4. Converts acetaldehyde into acetic acid
5. Decreased in Asian people

12.7 The effects of alcohol on the cardiovascular system include all of the following *except*

A. increased risk of myocardial infarction
B. decreased cardiac output
C. increased heart rate
D. increased incidence of esophageal cancer
E. increased level of estradiol in women

12.8 All of the following statements about seizures associated with alcohol withdrawal are true *except*

A. They are tonic-clonic in character.
B. They usually recur after 3 to 6 hours after the first seizure.
C. They often progress to status epilepticus.
D. They do not respond to anticonvulsants.
E. They may be associated with hypomagnesemia.

12.9 Anabolic steroids

A. have legitimate medical use
B. are used illegally by more than 1 million people in the United States
C. can produce euphoria
D. may be associated with violent outbursts
E. all of the above

12.10 All of the following statements about dehydroepiandrosterone (DHEA) are false *except*

A. DHEA is a regulated drug.
B. DHEA is a precursor of serotonin.
C. DHEA can decrease low-density lipoproteins.
D. DHEA produces reversible gynecomastia in men.
E. DHEA has addictive potential.

12.11 The highest comorbidity of psychiatric disorders is associated with abuse of which of the following substances?

A. Marijuana
B. Diazepam
C. Organic solvents
D. Opioids
E. None of the above

12.12 The most common dual diagnosis (comorbidity) associated with substance abuse is

A. major depressive disorder
B. another substance
C. antisocial personality disorder
D. anxiety disorder
E. dysthymic disorder

12.13 In a person with an alcohol-related disorder

A. alcohol withdrawal delirium should be treated with antipsychotics
B. the most common hallucinations during alcohol withdrawal are visual
C. the person loses consciousness during a blackout
D. idiosyncratic alcohol intoxication usually occurs after excessive alcohol consumption
E. a classic sign of alcohol withdrawal is tremulousness

12.14 Amphetamines

A. have their primary effects mediated through the cholinergic system
B. do not cause substance dependence
C. are used in the treatment of obesity
D. cause an intoxication syndrome easily distinguished from cocaine intoxication
E. are not associated with adverse physical effects

12.15 Cannabis

A. has its euphoric effect a few hours after smoking it
B. can have a profound effect on the user's respiratory rate
C. may induce a short-lived anxiety state
D. depresses the user's sensitivity to external stimuli
E. intoxication does not impair motor skills

12.16 Cocaine

A. competitively blocks dopamine reuptake by the dopamine transporter
B. does not lead to physiological dependence
C. -induced psychotic disorders are most common in those who snort cocaine
D. had been used by 40 percent of the United States population since 1991
E. is no longer used as a local anesthetic

12.17 Hallucinogens

A. cause physical dependence
B. cause withdrawal symptoms characterized by increased fatigue and somnolence
C. are associated with a phenomenon known as flashback
D. cause perceptions to become blunted
E. have a number of medical uses

12.18 The lifetime use of inhalants is highest in

A. young adults aged 18 to 25 years
B. adults aged 26 to 34 years
C. youths aged 12 to 17 years
D. adults 40 to 65 years old
E. adults over the age of 65

12.19 Adverse effects on the brain that have been associated with long-term inhalant use include all the following *except*

A. rhabdomyolysis
B. brain atrophy
C. decreased intelligence quotient (IQ)
D. electroencephalographic (EEG) changes
E. decreased cerebral blood flow

12.20 Acute phencyclidine (PCP) intoxication is *not* treated with

A. diazepam (Valium)
B. cranberry juice
C. phentolamine (Regitine)
D. phenothiazines
E. all of the above

12.21 All the following are associated with caffeine withdrawal symptoms *except*

A. headaches
B. nervousness
C. hallucinations
D. depression
E. insomnia

12.22 Which of the following statements about opioid abuse and opioid dependence is *true*?

A. About a fourth of all Americans with opioid dependence live in the New York City area.
B. About 500,000 persons with opioid dependence are in the United States.
C. An estimated 2 percent of the United States population have used heroin.
D. The male-to-female ratio of persons with opioid dependence is 1 to 1.
E. Most users of opiates and opioids started to use substances in their late 20s to mid-30s.

12.23 Which of the following drugs is an opioid antagonist?

A. Naloxone
B. Naltrexone
C. Nalorphine
D. Apomorphine
E. All of the above

12.24 The heroin behavior syndrome includes

A. depression
B. fear of failure
C. low self-esteem
D. need for immediate gratification
E. all of the above

12.25 The symptoms of benzodiazepine withdrawal include

A. dysphoria
B. intolerance for bright lights
C. nausea
D. muscle twitching
E. all of the above

12.26 The SPECT image (Fig. 12.1) shows multifocal areas of hypoperfusion in a patient with chronic substance abuse. The patient's ischemic cerebrovascular disorder is most likely precipitated by which of the following substances?

A. PCP
B. Cocaine
C. Heroin
D. Cannabis
E. Barbiturates

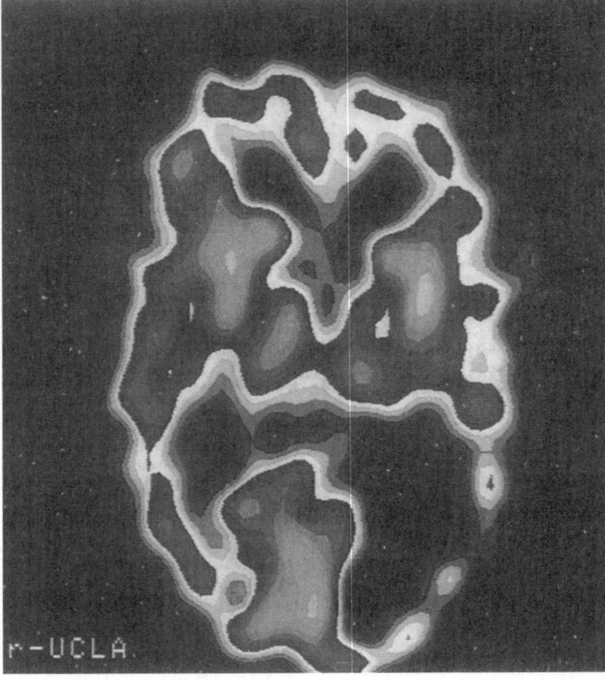

FIGURE 12.1
Reprinted with permission from Kaplan HI, Sadock BJ, editors: *Comprehensive Textbook of Psychiatry,* ed 6, p 268. Williams & Wilkins, Baltimore, 1995.

Questions 12.27–12.28

An 18-year-old high school senior was brought to the emergency room by police after being picked up wandering in traffic on the Triborough Bridge. He was angry, agitated, and aggressive, and he talked of various people who were deliberately trying to confuse him by giving him misleading directions. His story was rambling and disjointed, but he admitted to the police that he had been using speed. In the emergency room he had difficulty focusing his attention and had to ask that questions be repeated. He was disoriented as to time and place and was unable to repeat the names of three objects after five minutes. His family gave a history of the patient's regular use of pep pills over the previous 2 years, during which time he was frequently high and did poorly in school.

12.27 Which of the following would *not* be a clinical effect of amphetamine intoxication in this patient?

A. Increased libido
B. Formication
C. Delirium
D. Catatonia
E. All of the above

12.28 The abrupt discontinuation of amphetamine in this patient would produce

A. fatigue
B. dysphoria
C. nightmares
D. agitation
E. all of the above

12.29 The patient is a 20-year-old man who was brought to the hospital, trussed in ropes, by his four brothers. It was his seventh hospitalization in the past 2 years, each for similar behavior. One of his brothers reported that he "came home crazy" late one night, threw a chair through a window, tore a gas heater off the wall, and ran into the street. The family called the police, who apprehended him shortly thereafter as he stood, naked, directing traffic at a busy intersection. He assaulted the arresting officers, escaped, and ran home screaming threats at his family. There his brothers were able to subdue him.

On admission, the patient was observed to be agitated, his mood fluctuating between anger and fear. He had slurred speech, and he staggered when he walked. He remained extremely violent and disorganized for the first several days of his hospitalization; then he began having longer and longer lucid intervals, still interspersed with sudden, unpredictable periods during which his speech was slurred, he displayed great suspiciousness, and he assumed a fierce expression and clenched his fists.

After calming down, the patient denied ever having been violent or acting in an unusual way ("I'm a peaceable man") and said that he could not remember how he got to the hospital. He admitted to using alcohol and marijuana socially but denied phencyclidine (PCP) use except once, experimentally, 3 years previously. Nevertheless, blood and urine tests were positive for PCP, and a brother said that "he gets dusted every day."

After 3 weeks of hospitalization, the patient was released, still sullen, watchful, and quick to remark sarcastically on the smallest infringement of the respect due him. He was mostly quiet and isolated from others but was easily provoked to fury. His family reported that "this is as good as he gets now." He lived and ate most of his meals at home and kept himself physically clean, but mostly he lay around the house, did no housework, and had not held a job for nearly 2 years. The family did not know how he got his spending money or how he spent his time outside the hospital.

Which of the following diagnoses does not apply in this case?

A. Substance intoxication
B. Phencyclidine-induced psychotic disorder, with hallucinations
C. Substance dependence
D. Hallucinogen persisting perception disorder
E. All of the above

12.30 A 55-year-old man with a long history of alcohol dependence was admitted to a medical ward. At the time of admission, he was noted to have alcohol on his breath. Two days after admission he became acutely agitated and reported hearing other patients calling him homosexual. He appeared to be alert and well-oriented. The patient was probably exhibiting symptoms of

A. schizophrenia
B. delirium tremens (alcohol withdrawal)
C. alcohol-induced psychotic disorder, with hallucinations
D. pathological intoxication (idiosyncratic alcohol intoxication)
E. methanol intoxication

12.31 A 20-year-old man was seen in the emergency room in a severely agitated state. He was labile emotionally, appeared to be frightened and markedly anxious, and showed slurred speech and dysarthria. According to a friend, the patient took angel dust about an hour before being seen in the emergency room. The reaction the patient was having was probably

A. caused by phencyclidine (PCP)
B. spontaneously cleared within 48 hours
C. diagnosed by urine testing for PCP
D. accompanied by violent acts
E. all of the above

DIRECTIONS: Each set of lettered headings is followed by a list of numbered words or phrases. For each numbered word or phrase, select

A. if the item is associated with *A only*
B. if the item is associated with *B only*
C. if the item is associated with *both A and B*
D. if the item is associated with *neither A nor B*

Questions 12.32–12.35

A. Alcohol withdrawal delirium
B. Alcohol-induced psychotic disorder with hallucinations
C. Both
D. Neither

12.32 Withdrawal seizures

12.33 Auditory hallucinations

12.34 Clear sensorium

12.35 Benzodiazepines

Questions 12.36–12.40

A. Intoxication
B. Withdrawal
C. Both
D. Neither

12.36 Follows the recent ingestion and the presence in the body of a substance

12.37 Follows the cessation or the reduction of the intake of a substance

12.38 Is a substance-specific syndrome

12.39 Has a clinical picture that may correspond to one of the cognitive disorders

12.40 Requires maladaptive behavior as an essential diagnostic criterion

Questions 12.41–12.45

A. Benzodiazepines
B. Barbiturates
C. Both
D. Neither

12.41 Cause rapid eye movement (REM) sleep suppression

12.42 Have symptoms of withdrawal that usually appear within 3 days

12.43 Are associated with high suicide potential

12.44 Are clinically used as muscle relaxants

12.45 Are antipsychotics

DIRECTIONS: The questions below consist of lettered headings followed by a list of numbered words or phrases. For each numbered word or phrase, select the *one* lettered heading that is most closely associated with it. Each lettered heading may be selected once, more than once, or not at all.

A. γ-Aminobutyric acid (GABA) receptor system
B. Opioid receptor system
C. Glutamate receptor system
D. Adenosine receptor system
E. Acetylcholine receptor system

12.46 Ethanol

12.47 Phenobarbital

12.48 Diazepam

12.49 Heroin

12.50 Phencyclidine (PCP)

12.51 Caffeine

12.52 Nicotine

ANSWERS

Substance-Related Disorders

12.1 The answer is C (*Synopsis VIII,* page 419).
In 1996, voters in California approved referenda allowing physicians to prescribe *marijuana* for medical purposes, including treatment of nausea secondary to antineoplastic agents, to stimulate appetite in cachectic patients, and to relieve intraocular pressure in glaucoma. *Heroin* and *lysergic acid diethylamide* have no medical use and cannot be prescribed. *Methamphetamine* is a controlled substance that physicians may prescribe, primarily as an anorectic agent.

12.2 The answer is A (*Synopsis VIII,* pages 376–377).
Chlorpromazine is a dopamine receptor antagonist that is psychotropic, not psychoactive. Psychoactive drugs are substances that are addictive or drugs that are used for recreational purposes or to produce an altered state of consciousness. They may be legal (*nicotine*) or illegal (*cocaine*). The concept includes organic solvents, which may be ingested either on purpose or by accident and which have brain-altering properties.

12.3 The answer is C (*Synopsis VIII,* page 378)
In 1995, an estimated *12.8 million* people in the United States were current illicit drug users and had used an illicit drug in the month preceding the interview. This figure represents no change from 1994, when the estimate was 12.6 million. The number of illicit drug users was at its highest level, 25 million, in 1979.

Between 1994 and 1995, there was a continuing increase, from 8.2 percent to 10.9 percent, in the rate of past-month illicit drug use among adolescents. This rate had doubled since 1992. Significant increases in past-month marijuana use (from 6 percent to 8.2 percent), cocaine use (from 0.3 percent to 0.8 percent), and hallucinogen use (from 1.1 percent to 1.7 percent) occurred among adolescents between 1994 and 1995.

12.4 The answer is C (*Synopsis VIII,* page 416).
Marijuana is the most common illicit drug, used by 77 percent of current illicit drug users. Approximately 57 percent of current illicit drug users used marijuana only; 20 percent used marijuana and another illicit drug, and the remaining 23 percent used only an illicit drug other than marijuana in the past month. An estimated 5.6 million people (2.6 percent of the U.S. population) were current users of illicit drugs other than marijuana and hashish.

12.5 The answers are: 1, C; 2, A; 3, B; 4, E; and 5, D (*Synopsis VIII,* pages 395–407).
At a level of *0.05 percent* alcohol in the blood, thought, judgment, and restraint are loosened and sometimes disrupted. At a concentration of *0.1 percent,* voluntary motor actions usually become perceptibly clumsy. In most states, legal intoxication ranges from *0.1 to 0.15 percent* blood alcohol level. At *0.2 percent* the function of the entire motor area of the brain is measurably depressed; the parts of the brain that control emotional behavior are also affected. At *0.3 percent* a person is commonly confused or may become stuporous; at *0.4 to 0.5 percent* the person falls into a coma. At higher levels, the primitive centers of the brain that control breathing and heart rate are affected, and death ensues. People with long-term histories of alcohol abuse, however, can tolerate much higher concentrations of alcohol than can alcohol-naive people; their alcohol tolerance may cause them to appear less intoxicated than they really are.

12.6 The answers are: 1, C; 2, A; 3, B; 4, B; and 5, C (*Synopsis VIII,* pages 395–407).
Alcohol is metabolized by two enzymes: *alcohol dehydrogenase* (ADH) and *aldehyde dehydrogenase.* ADH catalyzes the conversion of alcohol into acetaldehyde, which is a toxic compound, and aldehyde dehydrogenase catalyzes the conversion of acetaldehyde into acetic acid. Aldehyde dehydrogenase is inhibited by disulfiram (Antabuse), often used in the treatment of alcohol-related disorders. Some studies have shown that women have a lower ADH blood content than do men; this fact may account for women's tendency to become more intoxicated than do men after drinking the same amount of alcohol. The decreased function of alcohol-metabolizing enzymes in some Asian people can also lead to easy intoxication and toxic symptoms.

About 90 percent of absorbed alcohol is metabolized through oxidation in the liver; the remaining 10 percent is excreted unchanged by the kidney and the lungs. The rate of oxidation by the liver is constant and independent of the body's energy requirements. The body is capable of metabolizing at 15 mg/dL an hour, the range of 10 to 34 mg/dL an hour. Stated another way, the average person oxidizes three fourths of an ounce of 40 percent (80 proof) alcohol in an hour. In people with a history of alcohol consumption, an upregulation of the necessary enzymes results in fast metabolism of alcohol.

12.7 The answer is B (*Synopsis VIII,* pages 391–393).
Alcohol *increases, not decreases, the cardiac output* among alcoholics and among people who do not drink on a regular basis. A significant intake of alcohol has been associated with increased blood pressure, dysregulation of lipoproteins and triglycerides, and increased risk of myocardial infarctions and cerebrovascular diseases. Alcohol has been shown to affect the hearts of people who do not usually drink: it increases the heart rate and the myocardial oxygen consumption. Evidence indicates that alcohol intake can adversely affect the hematopoietic system and can increase the incidence of cancer, particularly head, neck, *esophageal,* stomach, hepatic, colonic, and lung cancer. Acute intoxication may also be associated with hypoglycemia, which, when unrecognized, may be responsible for some of the sudden deaths of people who are intoxicated. Muscle weakness is another side effect of alcoholism. Recent evidence shows that alcohol intake raises the blood concentration of *estradiol* in women. The increase in estradiol correlates with the blood alcohol level.

12.8 The answer is C (*Synopsis VIII,* pages 399–402).
Status epilepticus is *relatively rare (not common), occurring in fewer than 3 percent of all patients.* Seizures associated with alcohol withdrawal are stereotyped, generalized, and *tonic-clo-*

nic in character. Patients often have *more than one* seizure 3 to 6 hours after the first seizure. Although anticonvulsant medications are not required routinely for the management of alcohol withdrawal seizures, the cause of the seizures is difficult to establish when a patient is first assessed in the emergency room; thus, many patients with withdrawal seizures *receive anticonvulsant medications,* which are discontinued once the cause of the seizures is recognized. Seizure activity in patients with known alcohol abuse histories should still prompt clinicians to consider other causative factors, such as head injuries, CNS infections, CNS neoplasms, and other cerebrovascular diseases; long-term severe alcohol abuse can result in hypoglycemia, hyponatremia, and *hypomagnesemia,* all of which can also be associated with seizures.

12.9 The answer is E (all) (*Synopsis VIII,* pages 454–455). Anabolic steroids are schedule III drugs and therefore are subject to the same regulatory dispensing requirements as narcotics. Although anabolic steroids have *legitimate medical use,* they are illegally used primarily by men to enhance their physical performance and appearance as measured by muscle bulk, muscle definition, and athletic prowess.

A estimated *1 million people* in the United States have used illegal steroids at least once. Users are primarily middle class and white. Male users of anabolic steroids outnumber female users approximately 50 to 1; about half the users started before the age of 16. The highest use was among 18 to 25 year olds, with 26 to 34 year olds having the next highest rate of use. Estimates for the rate of use in body builders have ranged up to 50 to 80 percent.

Anabolic steroids may initially induce *euphoria* and hyperactivity, but after relatively short periods the use can become associated with increased anger, arousal, irritability, hostility, anxiety, somatization, and depression (especially during periods of not using steroids). There is a correlation between steroid abuse and *violence,* so-called *roid rage* in the parlance of users. Steroid abusers with no record of sociopathy or violence have committed murders and other violent crimes.

12.10 The answer is E (*Synopsis VIII,* page 455). DHEA is an adrenal androgen marketed as a food supplement and sold over the counter in health food stores. It is *not approved* by the FDA or regulated by it.

DHEA is a steroid precursor of both androgens and estrogens (*not of serotonin*), and persons taking the substance report an increase in physical and psychological well-being. The adverse effects of the drug are hirsutism and *nonreversible gynecomastia in men.* Because DHEA is available in health food stores and may have *addictive potential,* increased reports of misuse and adverse effects should be expected.

12.11 The answer is D (*Synopsis VIII,* page 438). In general, the most potent and dangerous substances have the highest comorbidity rates of psychiatric disorders. Among *marijuana, diazepam, organic solvents,* and opioids, it is the last, *opioids,* that are most closely associated with psychiatric disorders. Opioids are the *most potent substances* of abuse throughout recorded history.

12.12 The answer is B (*Synopsis VIII,* page 442). Comorbidity (also known as dual diagnosis) is the diagnosis of two or more psychiatric disorders in a single patient. The most common comorbidity involves two substances of abuse, usually alcohol and *another substance.* Other psychiatric diagnoses commonly associated with substance abuse are *antisocial personality disorder,* phobias (and other *anxiety* disorders), *major depressive disorder,* and *dysthymic disorder.*

12.13 The answer is E (*Synopsis VIII,* pages 399–401). In the diagnostic criteria for alcohol withdrawal in the fourth edition of *Diagnostic and Statistical Manual of Mental Disorders* (DSM-IV) (Table 12.1), *a classic sign of alcohol withdrawal is tremulousness.* Tremulousness (commonly called the shakes or jitters) develops 6 to 8 hours after the cessation of drinking. The tremor of alcohol withdrawal can be similar to physiological tremor, with a continuous tremor of great amplitude and faster than 8 Hz, or to familial tremor, with bursts of tremor slower than 8 Hz.

Alcohol withdrawal delirium should not be treated with antipsychotics, which may reduce the seizure threshold in the patient. The best treatment for alcohol withdrawal delirium is prevention. Patients who are withdrawing from alcohol who exhibit any withdrawal phenomena should receive a benzodiazepine, such as 25 to 50 mg of chlordiazepoxide (Librium) every 2 to 4 hours until they seem to be out of danger. Once the delirium appears, however, 50 to 100 mg of chlordiazepoxide should be given every 4 hours orally, or intravenous lorazepam (Ativan) should be used if oral medication is not possible (Table 12.2).

The most common hallucinations during alcohol withdrawal are auditory, usually voices. The voices are characteristically maligning, reproachful, or threatening, although some patients report that the voices are pleasant and nondisruptive.

Table 12.1
DSM-IV Diagnostic Criteria for Alcohol Withdrawal

A. Cessation of (or reduction in) alcohol use that has been heavy and prolonged.

B. Two (or more) of the following, developing within several hours to a few days after criterion A:
   (1) autonomic hyperactivity (eg, sweating or pulse rate greater than 100)
   (2) increased hand tremor
   (3) insomnia
   (4) nausea and vomiting
   (5) transient visual, tactile, or auditory hallucinations or illusions
   (6) psychomotor agitation
   (7) anxiety
   (8) grand mal seizures

C. The symptoms in criterion B cause clinically significant distress or impairment in social, occupational, or other important areas of functioning.

D. The symptoms are not due to a general medical condition and not better accounted for by another mental disorder.

Specify if:
With perceptual disturbances

Table 12.2
Drug Therapy for Alcohol Intoxication and Withdrawal

Clinical Problem	Drug	Route	Dosage	Comment
Tremulousness and mild to moderate agitation	Chlordiazepoxide	Oral	25–100 mg every 4–6 hr	Initial dose can be repeated every 2 hr until patient is calm; subsequent doses must be individualized and titrated
	Diazepam	Oral	5–20 mg every 4–6 hr	
Hallucinosis	Lorazepam	Oral	2–10 mg every 4–6 hr	
Extreme agitation	Chlordiazepoxide	Intravenous	0.5 mg/kg at 12.5 mg/min	Give until patient is calm; subsequent doses must be individualized and titrated
Withdrawal seizures	Diazepam	Intravenous	0.15 mg/kg at 2.5 mg/min	
Delirium tremens	Lorazepam	Intravenous	0.1 mg/kg at 2.0 mg/min	

Adapted from Koch-Weser J, Sellers EM, Kalan H: Alcohol Intoxication and withdrawal. N Engl J Med *294:* 757, 1976.

Blackouts are not included in the DSM-IV diagnostic classification of alcohol use disorders (Table 12.3).

A *person does not lose consciousness during a blackout.* Instead, the person experiences anterograde amnesia, which can be distressing because the person may fear that he or she has unknowingly harmed someone or behaved imprudently while intoxicated.

Idiosyncratic alcohol intoxication (previously referred to as pathological intoxication) *does not usually occur after excessive alcohol consumption.* Instead, it is a severe behavioral syndrome that develops rapidly after the person consumes a small amount of alcohol that in most people has minimal behavioral effects. Idiosyncratic alcohol intoxication is an example of an alcohol use disorder not otherwise specified (Table 12.4).

Table 12.3
DSM-IV Alcohol-Related Disorders

Alcohol use disorders

Alcohol dependence
Alcohol abuse

Alcohol-induced disorders

Alcohol intoxication
Alcohol withdrawal
Specify if: With perceptual disturbances
Alcohol intoxication delirium
Alcohol withdrawal delirium
Alcohol-induced persisting dementia
Alcohol-induced persisting amnestic disorder
Alcohol-induced psychotic disorder, with delusions
Specify if: With onset during intoxication/with onset during withdrawal
Alcohol-induced psychotic disorder, with hallucinations
Specify if: With onset during intoxication/with onset during withdrawal
Alcohol-induced mood disorder
Specify if: With onset during intoxication/with onset during withdrawal
Alcohol-induced anxiety disorder
Specify if: With onset during intoxication/with onset during withdrawal
Alcohol-induced sexual dysfunction
Specify if: With onset during intoxication
Alcohol-induced sleep disorder
Specify if: With onset during intoxication/with onset during withdrawal
Alcohol-related disorder not otherwise specified

12.14 The answer is C (*Synopsis VIII,* pages 407–412).
Amphetamines *are used in the treatment of obesity,* although their safety and efficacy for that indication are controversial. They are also used for attention-deficit/hyperactivity disorder, narcolepsy, and some depressive disorders.

Amphetamines do not have their primary effects mediated through the cholinergic system. Instead, they cause the release of catecholamines, particularly dopamine, from presynaptic terminals. The designer amphetamines (for example, MDMA, 3,4-methylenedioxymethamphetamine; MDEA, ethylmethylenedioxyamphetamine; MMDA, methoxymethylenedioxyamphetamine; and DOM, dimethoxymethylamphetamine) also cause the release of serotonin.

Table 12.4
DSM-IV Diagnostic Criteria for Alcohol-Related Disorder Not Otherwise Specified

The alcohol-related disorder not otherwise specified category is for disorders associated with the use of alcohol that are not classifiable as alcohol dependence, alcohol abuse, alcohol intoxication, alcohol withdrawal, alcohol intoxication delirium, alcohol withdrawal delirium, alcohol-induced persisting dementia, alcohol-induced persisting amnestic disorder, alcohol-induced psychotic disorder, alcohol-induced mood disorder, alcohol-induced anxiety disorder, alcohol-induced sexual dysfunction, or alcohol-induced sleep disorder.

Amphetamines *do cause substance dependence* (Table 12.5). Amphetamine dependence can result in a rapid down spiral of a person's abilities to cope with work-related and family-related obligations and stresses. An amphetamine-abusing person requires increasingly high doses of amphetamine to obtain the usual high, and physical signs of amphetamine abuse (for example, decreased weight and paranoid ideas) almost always develop with continued abuse. Table 12.6 lists the diagnostic criteria for substance abuse.

Amphetamines *cause an intoxication syndrome that is not easily distinguished from cocaine intoxication.* Table 12.7 presents the diagnostic criteria for amphetamine intoxication. Amphetamines *are associated with adverse physical effects.* Cerebrovascular, cardiac, and gastrointestinal effects are among the most serious adverse effects associated with amphetamine abuse. The specific life-threatening conditions include myocardial infarction, severe hypertension, cerebrovascular disease, and ischemic colitis. A continuum of neurological symptoms, from twitching to tetany to seizures to coma and death, is associated with increasingly high amphetamine doses. The less than life-threatening adverse effects include flushing, pallor, cyanosis, fever, headache, tachycardia, palpitations, nausea, vomiting, bruxism (teeth grinding), shortness of breath, tremor, and ataxia.

Table 12.5
DSM-IV Diagnostic Criteria for Substance Dependence

A maladaptive pattern of substance use, leading to clinically significant impairment or distress, as manifested by three (or more) of the following, occurring at any time in the same 12-month period:

(1) tolerance, as defined by either of the following:
  (a) need for markedly increased amounts of the substance to achieve intoxication or desired effect
  (b) markedly diminished effect with continued use of the same amount of the substance
(2) withdrawal, as manifested by either of the following:
  (a) the characteristic withdrawal syndrome for the substance (refer to criteria A and B of the criteria sets for withdrawal from the specific substances)
  (b) The same (or closely related) substance is taken to relieve or avoid withdrawal symptoms
(3) the substance is often taken in larger amounts or over a longer period than was intended
(4) there is a persistent desire or unsuccessful efforts to cut down or control substance use
(5) a great deal of time is spent in activities necessary to obtain the substance (eg, visiting multiple doctors or driving long distances), use the substance (eg, chain-smoking), or recover from its effects
(6) important social, occupational, or recreational activities given up or reduced because of substance use
(7) the substance use is continued despite knowledge of having a persistent or recurrent physical or psychological problem that is likely to have been caused or exacerbated by the substance (eg, current cocaine use despite recognition of cocaine-induced depression, or continued drinking despite recognition that an ulcer was made worse by alcohol consumption)

Table 12.6
DSM-IV Diagnostic Criteria for Substance Abuse

A. A maladaptive pattern of substance use leading to clinically significant impairment or distress, as manifested by one (or more) of the following, occurring within a 12-month period:
  (1) recurrent substance use resulting in a failure to fulfill major role obligations at work, school, or home (eg, repeated absences or poor work performance related to substance use; substance-related absences, suspensions, or expulsions from school; neglect of children or household)
  (2) recurrent substance use in situations in which it is physically hazardous (eg, driving an automobile or operating a machine when impaired by substance use)
  (3) recurrent substance-related legal problems (eg, arrests for substance-related disorderly conduct)
  (4) continued substance use despite having persistent or recurrent social or interpersonal problems caused or exacerbated by the effects of the substance (eg, arguments with spouse about consequences of intoxication, physical fights)
B. The symptoms above never met the criteria for substance dependence for this class of substance

Table 12.7
DSM-IV Diagnostic Criteria for Amphetamine Intoxication

A. Recent use of amphetamine or a related substance (e.g., methylphenidate).
B. Clinically significant maladaptive behavioral or psychological changes (eg, euphoria or affective blunting; changes in sociability; hypervigilance; interpersonal sensitivity; anxiety, tension, or anger; stereotyped behaviors; impaired judgment; or impaired social or occupational functioning) developing during, or shortly after, use of amphetamine or a related substance.
C. Two (or more) of the following, developing during, or shortly after, use of amphetamine or related substance:
  (1) tachycardia or bradycardia
  (2) pupillary dilation
  (3) elevated or lowered blood pressure
  (4) perspiration or chills
  (5) nausea or vomiting
  (6) evidence of weight loss
  (7) psychomotor agitation or retardation
  (8) muscular weakness, respiratory depression, chest pain, or cardiac arrhythmias
  (9) confusion, seizures, dyskinesias, dystonias, or coma
D. The symptoms are not due to a general medical condition and not better accounted for by another mental disorder.

Specify if:
With perceptual disturbances

Table 12.8
DSM-IV Diagnostic Criteria for Substance-Induced Anxiety Disorder

A. Prominent anxiety, panic attacks, obsessions or compulsions predominate in the clinical picture.

B. There is evidence from the history, physical examination, or laboratory findings of either (1) or (2):
   (1) the symptoms in criterion A developed during, or within 1 month of, substance intoxication or withdrawal
   (2) medical use is etiologically related to the disturbance

C. The disturbance is not better accounted for by an anxiety disorder that is not substance induced. Evidence that the symptoms are better accounted for by an anxiety disorder that is not substance induced might include the following: the symptoms precede the onset of the substance use (or medication use); the symptoms persist for a substantial period of time (eg, about a month) after the cessation of acute withdrawal or severe intoxication or are substantially in excess of what would be expected given the type or amount of the substance used or the duration of use; or there is other evidence suggesting the existence of an independent non–substance-induced anxiety disorder (eg, a history of recurrent non–substance-related panic episodes).

D. The disturbance does not occur exclusively during the course of a delirium.

E. The disturbance causes clinically significant distress or impairment in social, occupational, or other important areas of functioning.

Note: This diagnosis should be made instead of a diagnosis of substance intoxication or substance withdrawal only when the anxiety symptoms are in excess of those usually associated with the intoxication or withdrawal syndrome and when the anxiety symptoms are sufficiently severe to warrant independent clinical attention.

Code: [Specific substance]-induced anxiety disorder (Alcohol; amphetamine [or amphetamine-like substance]; caffeine; cannabis; cocaine; hallucinogen; inhalant; phencyclidine [or phencyclidine-like substance]; sedative, hypnotic, or anxiolytic; other [or unknown] substance)

Specify if:
With generalized anxiety: if excessive anxiety or worry about a number of events or activities predominates in the clinical presentation
With panic attacks: if panic attacks predominate in the clinical presentation
With obsessive-compulsive symptoms: if obsessions or compulsions predominate in the clinical presentation
With phobic symptoms: if phobic symptoms predominate in the clinical presentation

Specify if:
With onset during intoxication: if the criteria are met for intoxication with the substance and the symptoms develop during the intoxication syndrome
With onset during withdrawal: if criteria are met for withdrawal from the substance and the symptoms develop during, or shortly after, a withdrawal syndrome

Reprinted with permission from American Psychiatric Association: *Diagnostic and Statistical Manual of Mental Disorders,* ed 4. Copyright, American Psychiatric Association, Washington, 1994.

Table 12.9
DSM-IV Diagnostic Criteria for Cannabis Intoxication

A. Recent use of cannabis.

B. Clinically significant maladaptive behavioral or psychological changes (eg, impaired motor coordination, euphoria, anxiety, sensation of slowed time, impaired judgment, social withdrawal) that developed during, or shortly after, cannabis use.

C. Two (or more) of the following signs, developing with 2 hours of cannabis use:
   (1) conjunctival injection
   (2) increased appetite
   (3) dry mouth
   (4) tachycardia

D. The symptoms are not due to a general medical condition and are not better accounted for by another mental disorder.

Specify if:
With perceptual disturbances

Reprinted with permission from American Psychiatric Association: *Diagnostic and Statistical Manual of Mental Disorders,* ed 4. Copyright, American Psychiatric Association, Washington, 1994.

12.15 The answer is C (*Synopsis VIII,* page 418).
Cannabis *may induce a short-lived anxiety state,* diagnosed as cannabis-induced anxiety disorder (Table 12.8). Panic attacks may be induced, based on ill-defined and disorganized fears. The appearance of anxiety symptoms is correlated with the dose and is the most frequent adverse reaction to the moderate use of smoked cannabis. Inexperienced users are much more likely to experience anxiety symptoms than are experienced users. When cannabis is smoked, *its euphoric effects appear within minutes,* peak in about 30 minutes, and last 2 to 4 hours. Some of the motor and cognitive effects last 5 to 12 hours. Cannabis does *not have an effect on the user's respiratory rate.* Probably for that reason, no case of death caused by cannabis intoxication has been clearly documented. Cannabis use commonly *heightens the user's sensitivity to external stimuli,* reveals new details, makes colors seem brighter and richer than in the past, and subjectively slows down the appreciation of time. In high doses, the user may also experience depersonalization and derealization. Cannabis *intoxication* (Table 12.9) *does impair motor skills,* and the impairment remains after the subjective euphoriant effects have resolved. For 8 to 12 hours after using cannabis, the impairment of motor skills interferes with the operation of motor vehicles and other heavy machinery. Moreover, those effects are additive to those of alcohol, which is commonly used in combination with cannabis.

12.16 The answer is A (*Synopsis VIII,* pages 420–421).
Cocaine *competitively blocks dopamine reuptake by the dopamine transporter.* This primary pharmacodynamic effect is believed to be related to cocaine's behavioral effects, including elation, euphoria, heightened self-esteem, and perceived improvement on mental and physical tasks. Table 12.10 presents the diagnostic criteria for cocaine intoxication. Cocaine *does lead to physiological dependence,* although cocaine withdrawal (Table 12.11) is mild compared with the effects of withdrawal from opiates and opioids. A psychological dependence on cocaine can develop after a single use because of its potency as

Table 12.10
DSM-IV Diagnostic Criteria for Cocaine Intoxication

A. Recent use of cocaine.
B. Clinically significant maladaptive behavioral or psychological changes (eg, euphoria or affective blunting; changes in sociability; hypervigilance; interpersonal sensitivity; anxiety, tension, or anger; stereotyped behaviors; impaired judgment; or impaired social or occupational functioning) that developed during, or shortly after, use of cocaine.
C. Two (or more) of the following, developing during, or shortly after, use:
  (1) tachycardia or bradycardia
  (2) pupillary dilation
  (3) elevated or lowered blood pressure
  (4) perspiration or chills
  (5) nausea or vomiting
  (6) evidence of weight loss
  (7) psychomotor agitation or retardation
  (8) muscular weakness, respiratory depression, chest pain, or cardiac arrhythmias
  (9) confusion, seizures, dyskinesias, dystonias, or coma
D. The symptoms are not due to a general medical condition and are not better accounted for by another mental disorder.

Specify if:
With perceptual disturbances

Reprinted with permission from American Psychiatric Association: *Diagnostic and Statistical Manual of Mental Disorders,* ed 4. Copyright, American Psychiatric Association, Washington, 1994.

a positive reinforcer of behavior. Cocaine-*induced psychotic disorders are most common in intravenous* (*IV*) users and crack users, *not in those who snort cocaine.* The National Institute of Drug Abuse (NIDA) reported that cocaine *had been used by 12 percent, not 40 percent, of the United States population since 1991.* The highest use was in the 18- to 25-year-old age group; 18 percent of them had used cocaine at least once, and 2 percent were current users. In that age group, 3.8 percent had used crack at least once. Although cocaine use is highest among the unemployed, cocaine is also used by highly educated persons in high socioeconomic groups. Cocaine use among males is twice as frequent as cocaine use among females.

Despite its reputation as the most addictive commonly abused substance and one of the most dangerous, cocaine does have some important medical applications. Cocaine *is still used as a local anesthetic,* especially for eye, nose, and throat surgery, for which its vasoconstrictive effects are helpful.

12.17 The answer is C (*Synopsis VIII,* page 428).
Hallucinogens *are associated with a phenomenon known as flashback,* which involves hallucinogenic symptoms that appear long after the ingestion of a hallucinogen. The syndrome is diagnosed as hallucinogen persisting perception disorder (Table 12.12).

Hallucinogens *do not cause physical dependence.* However, a user may experience a psychological dependence on the insight-inducing experiences seemingly associated with hallucinogen use. Hallucinogens *do not cause withdrawal symptoms.*

Hallucinogens *do not cause perceptions to become blurred.* Rather, perceptions become unusually brilliant and intense.

Table 12.11
DSM-IV Diagnostic Criteria for Cocaine Withdrawal

A. Cessation of (or reduction in) cocaine use that has been heavy and prolonged.
B. Dysphoric mood and two (or more) of the following physiological changes, developing within a few hours to several days after criterion A:
  (1) fatigue
  (2) vivid, unpleasant dreams
  (3) insomnia or hypersomnia
  (4) increased appetite
  (5) psychomotor retardation or agitation
C. The symptoms in criterion B cause clinically significant distress or impairment in social, occupational, or other important areas of functioning.
D. The symptoms are not due to a general medical condition and are not better accounted for by another mental disorder.

Reprinted with permission from American Psychiatric Association: *Diagnostic and Statistical Manual of Mental Disorders,* ed 4. Copyright, American Psychiatric Association, Washington, 1994.

Colors and textures seem to be richer than in the past, contours sharpened, music more emotionally profound, and smells and tastes heightened. Synesthesia is common; colors may be heard or sounds seen. Table 12.13 lists the diagnostic criteria for hallucinogen intoxication.

Hallucinogens *have no medical uses.*

12.18 The answer is A (*Synopsis VIII,* page 430).
According to the National Institute of Drug Abuse (NIDA), *young adults aged 18 to 25 years* make up the largest group to have used inhalants in their lifetimes; 10.9 percent of that age group have used inhalants. Among the *adults aged 26 to 34 years,* 9.2 percent have used inhalants; 7 percent of *youths aged 12 to 17 years* have used inhalants, and only 2.5 percent of adults over 35, including *adults 40 to 65 years old,* have used inhalants. Inhalant use is minimal in *adults over the age of 65.*

Table 12.12
DSM-IV Diagnostic Criteria for Hallucinogen Persisting Perception Disorder (Flashbacks)

A. The reexperience, following cessation of use of a hallucinogen, of one or more of the perceptual symptoms that were experienced while intoxicated with the hallucinogen (eg, geometric hallucinations, false perceptions of movement in the peripheral visual fields, flashes of color, intensified colors, trails of images of moving objects, positive afterimages, halos around objects, macropsia, and micropsia).
B. The symptoms in criterion A cause clinically significant distress or impairment in social, occupational, or other important areas of functioning.
C. The symptoms are not due to a general medical condition (eg, anatomical lesions and infections of the brain, visual epilepsies) and are not better accounted for by another mental disorder (eg, delirium, dementia, schizophrenia) or hypnopompic hallucinations.

Reprinted with permission from American Psychiatric Association: *Diagnostic and Statistical Manual of Mental Disorders,* ed 4. Copyright, American Psychiatric Association, Washington, 1994.

Table 12.13
DSM-IV Diagnostic Criteria for Hallucinogen Intoxication

A. Recent use of a hallucinogen.
B. Clinically significant maladaptive behavioral or psychological changes (eg, marked anxiety or depression, ideas of reference, fear of losing one's mind, paranoid ideation, impaired judgment, or impaired social or occupational functioning) that developed during, or shortly after, hallucinogen use.
C. Perceptual changes occurring in a state of full wakefulness and alertness (eg, subjective intensification of perceptions, depersonalization, derealization, illusions, hallucinations, synesthesias) that developed during, or shortly after, hallucinogen use.
D. Two (or more) of the following signs, developing during, or shortly after, hallucinogen use:
   (1) pupillary dilation
   (2) tachycardia
   (3) sweating
   (4) palpitations
   (5) blurring of vision
   (6) tremors
   (7) incoordination
E. The symptoms are not due to a general medical condition and are not better accounted for by another mental disorder.

12.19 The answer is A (*Synopsis VIII,* pages 430–432).
Rhabdomyolysis does not affect the brain. It is a potentially fatal disease that entails destruction of skeletal muscles. It is a reported adverse effect of inhalant use that if not fatal, results in permanent muscle damage.

The combination of organic solvents and high concentrations of copper, zinc, and heavy metals has been associated with the development of *brain atrophy,* temporal lobe epilepsy, *decreased intelligence quotient* (*IQ*), and a variety of *electroencephalographic* (*EEG*) *changes.* Several studies of house painters and factory workers who have been exposed to solvents for long periods have found evidence of brain atrophy on computed tomography (CT) scans and *decreased cerebral blood flow.*

12.20 The answer is D (*Synopsis VIII,* page 446).
Phenothiazines are not used in the treatment of acute phencyclidine (PCP) intoxication because they have anticholinergic effects that may potentiate the adverse effects of PCP, such as seizures. *Diazepam* (*Valium*) is useful in reducing agitation. If agitation is severe, however, the antipsychotic haloperidol (Haldol) may have to be used. *Cranberry juice* is used to acidify the urine and to promote the elimination of the drug. Ammonium chloride or ascorbic acid also serves the same purpose. *Phentolamine* (*Regitine*) is a hypotensive agent that may be needed to deal with severe hypertensive crises produced by PCP.

12.21 The answer is C (*Synopsis VIII,* page 414).
Hallucinations are false sensory perceptions occurring in the absence of any relevant external stimulation of the sensory modality involved. Hallucinations do not occur during caffeine withdrawal.

According to laboratory experiments, the symptom of caffeine withdrawal most often reported is *headaches.* In nonlaboratory settings, as many as one third of the moderate and high caffeine consumers suffer that symptom if their daily caffeine intake is interrupted. The headaches, which seem to be remarkably consistent in different persons, are described as generalized and throbbing, proceeding from lethargy to a sense of cerebral fullness to a full-blown headache. They occur about 18 hours after the discontinuation of habitual caffeine intake and respond best to a renewed elevation of caffeine plasma levels, perhaps explaining why many tension headache–prone persons prefer over-the-counter analgesics that contain caffeine.

Other caffeine withdrawal symptoms include *nervousness,* a vague feeling of *depression,* drowsiness and lethargy, rhinorrhea, a disinclination to work, occasional yawning, nausea, and *insomnia* or sleep disturbances. Few recent reports have emphasized depression as a central feature of caffeinism. Surveys of psychiatric patients, however, revealed that the highest caffeine consumers (ingesting more than 750 mg daily) reported significantly high scores on the Beck Depression Inventory. Caffeine toxicity may induce psychosis in susceptible persons or exacerbate thinking disruptions in patients with diagnoses of schizophrenia.

In DSM-IV, caffeine withdrawal appears in an appendix of DSM-IV (Table 12.14) and is an example of caffeine use disorder not otherwise specified (Table 12.15).

12.22 The answer is B (*Synopsis VIII,* pages 436–437).
About 500,000 persons with opioid dependence are in the United States. About half of them live in the New York City area. In 1991, an estimated 1.3 percent of the United States population had used heroin at least once. The male-to-female ratio of persons with opioid dependence is about 3 to 1. Typically, *users of opiates and opioids started to use substances in their teens and early 20s, not their late 20s to mid-30s.* Currently, most persons with opioid dependence are in their 30s and 40s. Opioid-related disorders are listed in Table 12.16.

12.23 The answer is E (all) (*Synopsis VIII,* page 436).
Opioid antagonists block or antagonize the effects of opiates

Table 12.14
DSM-IV Research Criteria for Caffeine Withdrawal

A. Prolonged daily use of caffeine.
B. Abrupt cessation of caffeine use, or reduction in the amount of caffeine used, closely followed by headache and one (or more) of the following symptoms:
   (1) marked fatigue or drowsiness
   (2) marked anxiety or depression
   (3) nausea or vomiting
C. The symptoms in criterion B cause clinically significant distress or impairment in social, occupational, or other important areas of functioning.
D. The symptoms are not due to the direct physiological effects of a general medical condition (eg, migraine, viral illness) and are not better accounted for by another mental disorder.

Table 12.15
DSM-IV Diagnostic Criteria for Caffeine-Related Disorder Not Otherwise Specified

The caffeine-related disorder not otherwise specified category is for disorders associated with the use of caffeine that are not classifiable as caffeine intoxication, caffeine-induced anxiety disorder, or caffeine-induced sleep disorder. An example is caffeine withdrawal.

and opioids. Unlike methadone, they do not in themselves exert narcotic effects and do not cause dependence. The antagonists include the following drugs: *naloxone,* which is used in the treatment of opiate and opioid overdose because it reverses the effects of narcotics; *naltrexone,* which is the longest-acting (72 hours) antagonist; *nalorphine,* levallorphan, and *apomorphine.*

12.24 The answer is E (all) (*Synopsis VIII,* page 438).
Some consistent behavior patterns seem to be especially pronounced in adolescents with opioid dependence. Those patterns have been called the heroin behavior syndrome: underlying *depression,* often of an agitated type and frequently accompanied by anxiety symptoms; impulsiveness expressed by a passive-aggressive orientation; *fear of failure;* use of heroin as an antianxiety agent to mask feelings of *low self-esteem,* hopelessness, and aggression; limited coping strategies and low frustration tolerance, accompanied by the *need for immediate gratification;* sensitivity to substance contingencies, with a keen awareness of the relation between good feelings and the act of substance taking; feelings of behavioral impotence counteracted by momentary control over the life situation by means of substances; and disturbances in social and interpersonal relationships with peers maintained by mutual substance experiences.

12.25 The answer is E (all) (*Synopsis VIII,* page 449).
The severity of the withdrawal syndrome associated with the benzodiazepines varies significantly according to the average dose and the duration of use. However, a mild withdrawal syndrome can follow even short-term use of relatively low doses of benzodiazepines. A significant withdrawal syndrome is likely to occur at the cessation of dosages in the 40 mg a day range for diazepam, for example, although 10 to 20 mg a day, taken for a month, can also result in a withdrawal syndrome when the drug is stopped. The onset of withdrawal symptoms usually occurs 2 to 3 days after the cessation of use, but with long-acting drugs, such as diazepam, the latency before onset may be 5 or 6 days.

The symptoms of benzodiazepine withdrawal include anxiety, *dysphoria, intolerance for bright lights* and loud noises, *nausea,* sweating, *muscle twitching,* and sometimes seizures (generally at dosages of 50 mg a day or more of diazepam).

Table 12.17 lists the diagnostic criteria for sedative, hypnotic, or anxiolytic withdrawal.

12.26 The answer is B (*Synopsis VIII,* page 380).
The development of an ischemic cerebrovascular disorder is an adverse effect of *cocaine abuse.* The most common cerebrovascular diseases associated with cocaine use are nonhemorrhagic cerebral infarctions. When hemorrhagic infarctions do occur, they can include subarachnoid hemorrhages. Other adverse effects of cocaine use include seizures, myocardial infarction, and arrhythmias.

Table 12.16
DSM-IV Opioid-Related Disorders

Opioid use disorders
Opioid dependence
Opioid abuse
Opioid-induced disorders
Opioid intoxication
  Specify if: With perceptual disturbances
Opioid withdrawal
Opioid intoxication delirium
Opioid-induced psychotic disorder, with delusions
  Specify if: With onset during intoxication
Opioid-induced psychotic disorder, with hallucinations
  Specify if: With onset during intoxication
Opioid-induced mood disorder
  Specify if: With onset during intoxication
Opioid-induced sexual dysfunction
  Specify if: With onset during intoxication
Opioid-induced sleep disorder
  Specify if: With onset during intoxication/with onset during withdrawal
Opioid-related disorder not otherwise specified

Table 12.17
DSM-IV Diagnostic Criteria for Sedative, Hypnotic, or Anxiolytic Withdrawal

A. Cessation of (or reduction in) sedative, hypnotic, or anxiolytic use that has been heavy and prolonged.
B. Two (or more) of the following, developing within several hours to a few days after criterion A:
   (1) autonomic hyperactivity (eg, sweating or pulse rate greater than 100)
   (2) increased hand tremor
   (3) insomnia
   (4) nausea or vomiting
   (5) transient visual, tactile, or auditory hallucinations or illusions
   (6) psychomotor agitation
   (7) anxiety
   (8) grand mal seizures
C. The symptoms in criterion B cause clinically significant distress or impairment in social, occupational, or other important areas of functioning.
D. The symptoms are not due to a general medical condition and are not better accounted for by another mental disorder.

Specify if:
  With perceptual disturbances

12.27 The answer is D (*Synopsis VIII,* pages 409–410). *Catatonia* is not a clinical effect of amphetamine intoxication. When amphetamine is taken intravenously, the user experiences a characteristic rush of well-being and euphoria. Intoxication with high doses can lead to transient ideas of reference, paranoid ideation, *increased libido,* tinnitus, hearing one's name being called, and *formication* (tactile sensation of bugs crawling on the skin). Stereotyped movements may occur. *Delirium* (Table 12.18) with episodes of violence and substance-induced psychotic disorder (Table 12.19) may also be seen.

12.28 The answer is E (all) (*Synopsis VIII,* page 409). Abrupt discontinuation of an amphetamine results in a letdown or crash characterized by the onset of *fatigue, dysphoria, nightmares,* and *agitation.* According to DSM-IV, the syndrome may develop within a few hours to several days after the cessation of heavy amphetamine use. The withdrawal dysphoria may be treated with antidepressant medication. The agitation of the immediate letdown syndrome responds to diazepam (Valium). The diagnostic criteria for amphetamine (or related substance) withdrawal are listed in Table 12.20.

12.29 The answer is D (*Synopsis VIII,* pages 426–429). *Hallucinogen persisting perception disorder* (Table 12.12) does not apply in this case. This disorder is characterized by the reexperiencing of the signs and symptoms of hallucinogen intoxication after having stopped the drug. The patient is mostly quiet and isolated and shows no loss of contact with reality or perceptual distortions unrelated to hallucinogen ingestion.

On the basis of the information given in the case of the 20-year-old man, the patient showed agitation, fluctuating mood, suspiciousness, and disorientation after the ingestion of a substance. Therefore, a general diagnosis of *substance intoxication* (Table 12.21) can apply. The substance, identified as phencyclidine (PCP), is an arylcyclohexylamine, a class of drugs (similar to hallucinogens) that produce hallucinations, loss of contact with reality, and other changes in thinking and feeling. PCP is a potent drug that may be taken orally, intravenously, or by sniffing. The disorder is diagnosed specifically as PCP

Table 12.18 DSM-IV Diagnostic Criteria for Substance Withdrawal Delirium

A. Disturbance of consciousness (eg, reduced clarity of awareness of the environment) with reduced ability to focus, sustain, or shift attention.

B. A change in cognition (such as memory deficit, disorientation, language disturbance) or the development of a perceptual disturbance that is not better accounted for by a preexisting, established, or evolving dementia.

C. The disturbance develops over a short period of time (usually hours to days) and tends to fluctuate during the course of the day.

D. There is evidence from the history, physical examination, or laboratory findings that the symptoms in criteria A and B developed during, or shortly after, a withdrawal syndrome.

Note: This diagnosis should be made instead of a diagnosis of substance withdrawal only when the cognitive symptoms are in excess of those usually associated with the withdrawal syndrome and when the symptoms are sufficiently severe to warrant independent clinical attention.

Code: [Specific substance] withdrawal delirium (Alcohol; sedative, hypnotic, or anxiolytic; other [or unknown] substance)

Reprinted with permission from American Psychiatric Association: *Diagnostic and Statistical Manual of Mental Disorders,* ed 4. Copyright, American Psychiatric Association, Washington, 1994.

Table 12.19 DSM-IV Diagnostic Criteria for Substance-Induced Psychotic Disorder

A. Prominent hallucinations or delusions. **Note:** Do not include hallucinations if the person has insight that they are substance induced.

B. There is evidence from the history, phsyical examination, or laboratory findings of either (1) or (2):
   (1) the symptoms in criterion A developed during, or within a month of, substance intoxication or withdrawal
   (2) medication use is etiologically related to the disturbance

C. The disturbance is not better accounted for by a psychotic disorder that is not substance induced. Evidence that the symptoms are better accounted for by a psychotic disorder that is not substance induced might include the following: the symptoms precede the onset of the use (or medication use); the symptoms persist for a substantial period of time (eg, about a month) after the cessation of acute withdrawal or severe intoxication, or are substantially in excess of what would be expected given the type or amount of the substance used or the duration of use; or there is other evidence that suggests the existence of an independent non–substance-induced psychotic disorder (eg, a history of recurrent non–substance-related episodes).

D. The disturbance does not occur exclusively during the course of a delirium.

Note: This diagnosis should be made instead of a diagnosis of substance intoxication or substance withdrawal only when the symptoms are in excess of those usually associated with the intoxication or withdrawal syndrome and when the symptoms are sufficiently severe to warrant independent clinical attention.

Code: [Specific substance]-induced psychotic disorder (Alcohol, with delusions; alcohol, with hallucinations; amphetamine [or amphetamine-like substance], with delusions; amphetamine [or amphetamine-like substance], with hallucinations; cannabis, with delusions; cannabis, with hallucinations; cocaine, with delusions; cocaine, with hallucinations; hallucinogen, with delusions; hallucinogen, with hallucinations; inhalant, with delusions; inhalant, with hallucinations; opioid, with delusions; opioid, with hallucinations; phencyclidine [or phencyclidine-like substance], with delusions; phencyclidine [or phencyclidine-like substance], with hallucinations; sedative, hypnotic or anxiolytic, with delusions; sedative, hypnotic or anxiolytic, with hallucinations, other [or unknown] substance, with delusions; other [or unknown] subtance, with hallucinations)

Specify if:
With onset during intoxication: if criteria are met for intoxication with the substance and the symptoms develop during the intoxication syndrome
With onset during withdrawal: if criteria are met for withdrawal from the substance and the symptoms develop during, or shortly after, a withdrawal syndrome

Reprinted with permission from American Psychiatric Association: *Diagnostic and Statistical Manual of Mental Disorders,* ed 4. Copyright, American Psychiatric Association, Washington, 1994.

Table 12.20
DSM-IV Diagnostic Criteria for Amphetamine Withdrawal

A. Cessation of (or reduction in) amphetamine (or related substance) use which has been heavy and prolonged.
B. Dysphoric mood and two (or more) of the following physiological changes, developing within a few hours to several days after criterion A:
   (1) fatigue
   (2) vivid, unpleasant dreams
   (3) insomnia or hypersomnia
   (4) increased appetite
   (5) psychomotor retardation or agitation
C. The symptoms in criterion B cause clinically significant distress or impairment in social, occupational, or other important areas of functioning.
D. The symptoms are not due to a general medical condition and not better accounted for by another mental disorder.

Table 12.21
DSM-IV Diagnostic Criteria for Substance Intoxication

A. The development of a reversible substance-specific syndrome due to recent ingestion of (or exposure to) a substance. **Note:** Different substances may produce similar or identical syndromes.
B. Clinically significant maladaptive behavioral or psychological changes that are due to the effect of the substance on the central nervous system (eg, belligerence, mood lability, cognitive impairment, impaired judgment, impaired social or occupational functioning) and develop during or shortly after use of the substance.
C. The symptoms are not due to a general medical condition and are not better accounted for by another mental disorder.

intoxication (Table 12.22). A patient who is found naked, directing traffic, screaming threats, and displaying great suspiciousness can be presumed to be suffering from delusions, hallucinations, or both, and a diagnosis of *phencyclidine-induced psychotic disorder, with hallucinations,* can be made (Table 12.19). A history of the regular use of PCP with resultant impairment of functioning allows for a diagnosis of *substance dependence* (Table 12.5).

12.30 The answer is C (*Synopsis VIII,* pages 400–401).
The usual case of *alcohol-induced psychotic disorder, with hallucinations,* differs from *schizophrenia* by the temporal relation to alcohol withdrawal, the short-lived course, and the absence of a history of schizophrenia. Alcohol-induced psychotic disorder, with hallucinations, is usually manifested primarily by auditory hallucinations, sometimes accompanied by delusions, in the absence of symptoms of a mood disorder or a cognitive disorder.

Delirium tremens (DTs), another reaction to withdrawal from alcohol, usually occurs 72 to 96 hours after the cessation of heavy drinking. A distinctive characteristic is marked autonomic hyperactivity (tachycardia, fever, hyperhidrosis, and dilated pupils).

Pathological intoxication (called *idiosyncratic alcohol intoxication* in DSM-IV) is a syndrome of marked intoxication with subsequent amnesia for the period of intoxication. It is produced by the ingestion of an amount of alcohol insufficient to induce intoxication in most people. *Methanol intoxication* does not cause hallucinations but does cause blindness.

12.31 The answer is E (all) (*Synopsis VIII,* pages 444–446).
The patient was having a reaction *caused by phencyclidine (PCP),* which is known as angel dust. Reactions are related to the dose taken. Less than 5 mg of PCP is considered a low dose, and doses above 10 mg are considered high. Experienced users report that the effects of 2 to 3 mg of smoked PCP begin within 5 minutes and plateau within half an hour. Reactions are sometimes *spontaneously cleared within 48 hours.* PCP can be *diagnosed by urine testing.* The patient's reaction may be *accompanied by violent acts.*

Answers 12.32–12.35

12.32 The answer is A (*Synopsis VIII,* page 401).

12.33 The answer is C (*Synopsis VIII,* pages 399–403).

12.34 The answer is B (*Synopsis VIII,* page 401).

12.35 The answer is C (*Synopsis VIII,* pages 399–403).
Withdrawal seizures commonly precede the development of *alcohol withdrawal delirium,* but the delirium can also appear unheralded. The essential feature of the syndrome is delirium

Table 12.22
DSM-IV Diagnostic Criteria for Phencyclidine Intoxication

A. Recent use of phencyclidine (or a related substance).
B. Clinically significant maladaptive behavioral changes (eg, belligerence, assaultiveness, impulsiveness, unpredictability, psychomotor agitation, impaired judgment, or impaired social or occupational functioning) that developed during, or shortly after, use of phencyclidine.
C. Within an hour (less when smoked, "snorted," or used intravenously), two (or more) of the following signs:
   (1) vertical or horizontal nystagmus
   (2) hypertension or tachycardia
   (3) numbness or diminished responsiveness to pain
   (4) ataxia
   (5) dysarthria
   (6) muscle rigidity
   (7) seizures or coma
   (8) hyperacusis
D. The symptoms are not due to a general medical condition and are not better accounted for by another mental disorder.

Specify if:
With perceptual disturbances

that occurs within 1 week after the person stops drinking or reduces the intake of alcohol. In addition to the symptoms of delirium, the features include (1) autonomic hyperactivity, such as tachycardia, diaphoresis, fever, anxiety, insomnia, and hypertension; (2) perceptual distortions, which are most frequently visual or *auditory hallucinations;* and (3) fluctuating levels of psychomotor activity, ranging from hyperexcitability to lethargy. The best treatment for alcohol withdrawal delirium is its prevention. Patients who are withdrawing from alcohol and who exhibit any withdrawal phenomena should receive a *benzodiazepine,* such as 25 to 50 mg of chlordiazepoxide (Librium) every 2 to 4 hours until they seem to be out of danger. Once the delirium appears, however, 50 to 100 mg of chlordiazepoxide should be given every 4 hours orally, or intravenous lorazepam (Ativan) should be used if oral medication is not possible.

In *alcohol-induced psychotic disorder, with hallucinations,* the patient may have *auditory hallucinations,* usually voices, but they are often unstructured. The voices are characteristically maligning, reproachful, or threatening, although some patients report that the voices are pleasant and nondisruptive. The hallucinations usually last less than a week, although during that week impaired reality testing is common. After the episode, most patients realize the hallucinatory nature of the symptoms. The hallucinations are differentiated from alcohol withdrawal delirium by the presence of a *clear sensorium* in patients with alcohol-induced psychotic disorder, with hallucinations.

Answers 12.36–12.40

12.36 The answer is A (*Synopsis VIII,* page 376).

12.37 The answer is B (*Synopsis VIII,* page 376).

12.38 The answer is C (*Synopsis VIII,* page 376).

12.39 The answer is D (*Synopsis VIII,* page 376).

12.40 The answer is A (*Synopsis VIII,* page 376).
Intoxication is a syndrome that *follows the recent ingestion and the presence in the body of a substance.* Withdrawal is the state that *follows the cessation or the reduction of the intake of a substance.* Both withdrawal and intoxication *are substance-specific syndromes. The clinical picture* in withdrawal and intoxication *does not correspond to any cognitive disorder. Maladaptive behavior is an essential diagnostic criterion* only for intoxication. The diagnostic criteria for substance withdrawal are listed in Table 12.23, and the diagnostic criteria for substance intoxication are listed in Table 12.21.

Answers 12.41–12.45

12.41 The answer is B (*Synopsis VIII,* pages 447–450).

12.42 The answer is C (*Synopsis VIII,* pages 447–450).

12.43 The answer is B (*Synopsis VIII,* pages 447–450).

12.44 The answer is A (*Synopsis VIII,* pages 447–450).

12.45 The answer is D (*Synopsis VIII,* pages 447–450).
Barbiturates *cause rapid eye movement (REM) sleep suppression.* An abrupt withdrawal of a barbiturate will cause a marked increase or rebound in REM sleep. *Symptoms of withdrawal* from both benzodiazepines and barbiturates *usually appear within three days.* Barbiturates have a *high suicide potential.* Virtually no cases of successful suicide have occurred in patients taking benzodiazepines by themselves. In addition to treating anxiety, benzodiazepines are used in alcohol detoxification, for anesthetic induction, *as muscle relaxants,* and as anticonvulsants. Neither benzodiazepines nor barbiturates are *antipsychotics,* which are used to treat schizophrenia.

Table 12.23
DSM-IV Diagnostic Criteria for Substance Withdrawal

A. The development of a substance-specific syndrome due to the cessation of (or reduction in) substance use that has been heavy and prolonged.

B. The substance-specific syndrome causes clinically significant distress or impairment in social, occupational, or other important areas of functioning.

C. The symptoms are not due to a general medical condition and are not better accounted for by another mental disorder.

Reprinted with permission from American Psychiatric Association: *Diagnostic and Statistical Manual of Mental Disorders,* ed 4. Copyright, American Psychiatric Association, Washington, 1994.

Answers 12.46–12.52

12.46 The answer is A (*Synopsis VIII,* page 388).

12.47 The answer is A (*Synopsis VIII,* page 388).

12.48 The answer is A (*Synopsis VIII,* page 388).

12.49 The answer is B (*Synopsis VIII,* page 388).

12.50 The answer is C (*Synopsis VIII,* page 388).

12.51 The answer is D (*Synopsis VIII,* page 388).

12.52 The answer is E (*Synopsis VIII,* page 388).
Ethanol acts on the γ-aminobutyric acid (GABA) receptor system and has effects on noradrenergic neurons in the locus ceruleus and on the dopaminergic neurons of the ventral tegmental area. Barbiturates, such as *phenobarbital,* also act primarily on the GABA system, specifically on the GABA receptor complex, which includes a binding site for the inhibitory amino acid GABA, a regulatory site that binds benzodiazepines, and a chloride ion channel. The binding of the barbiturate results in the facilitation of chloride ion influx into the neuron, making the neuron more negatively charged and less likely to be stimulated.

Diazepam (Valium), a benzodiazepine, affects the GABA receptor complex by binding to the site for benzodiazepines. When diazepam or another benzodiazepine binds to that site, the chloride ions flow through the channel, resulting in inhibition of the neuron. The benzodiazepine antagonist flumazenil (Mazicon) reverses the effects of benzodiazepines.

Opiates such as *heroin* bind to specific sites in the brain labeled opioid receptors. Changes in the number or the sensitivity of the opiate receptors may occur as the result of continuous exposure to an opiate, producing dependence on the substance. The activity of adrenergic neurons in the locus ceruleus also decreases with long-term use.

Phencyclidine (*PCP*) binds to specific receptor sites located in the ion channel associated with the receptor for glutamate, an excitatory amino acid. Tolerance to PCP does not occur.

The leading theory regarding a mechanism of action for *caffeine* involves antagonism of the adenosine receptors. Adenosine appears to function as a neuromodulator, possibly as a neurotransmitter in the brain. Caffeine may also affect dopaminergic systems and adrenergic systems.

Nicotine is believed to exert its effects on the central nervous system through the nicotinic receptors, one subclass of *acetylcholine receptors*. Nicotine affects the nicotinic receptors in the receptor-gated ion channels of the receptor system.

13 

Schizophrenia

Although schizophrenia is a well-known mental disorder, it is not simple to define and diagnose. Schizophrenia is now thought to be made up of a spectrum of disorders with similar symptoms and signs but with many different causes. Patients with this spectrum of disorders can function at varying levels, show varying responses to medications, and have varying prognoses. People usually succumb to schizophrenia as young adults; the disorder, which is generally lifelong, affects people's interactions, emotional experiences, and cognitive processes.

Emil Kraepelin, Eugen Bleuler, Karl Jaspers, and Kurt Schneider were among the early workers in Europe whose observations contributed to current ideas about the criteria for schizophrenia. Although the complexities involved in studying the brain have made it difficult to delineate the many causes of schizophrenia, these causes are thought to include insults of infectious, genetic, neurochemical, or traumatic nature affecting the frontal lobes, limbic system, or basal ganglia. All of the various causes produce similar signs and symptoms of hallucinations, delusions, and loosening of associations; the various expressions of these symptoms seem to depend on which part of the brain is most affected by the insult.

Among the many biological theories about the causes of schizophrenia, one of the most useful is the stress–diathesis model, according to which an underlying diathesis must be present for a disorder to be manifested. This model reveals the intricate interactions among the disorder's biological, psychological, and environmental factors. Even when subject to the most severe stresses, people without a specific diathesis (infectious, genetic, and so on) never develop schizophrenia. Such people may become anxious, depressed, manic, or disordered in personality, but never schizophrenic. Minimal stress, however, can provoke people with an underlying diathesis to manifest schizophrenia, and they may thereafter have a schizophrenic reaction to any biological or psychological stress.

An important area of study in the biological theories of schizophrenia is the strengths and weaknesses of the dopamine hypothesis. Students must understand the workings of the dopamine system, the pathways and areas of the brain in which dopamine acts, and the significance of dopamine's role in signs, symptoms, medication responses, and side effects. Neurochemical studies and positron emission tomography (PET) scan data for the dopamine system must also be familiar to students. The recent expansion of this hypothesis to include serotonin, based on the therapeutic success of the serotonin-dopamine antagonist drugs, should be known.

Treatment of schizophrenia is as complex as the disorder itself. Physicians must be thoroughly aware of psychopharmacology and psychosocial interventions; they must know the medications that treat schizophrenic symptoms and the side effects of the medications. The mechanisms affected by medications must be familiar to students: neural pathways, neurotransmitters, and areas of the brain. When traditional treatments fail, students must be able to recall the alternative medication plans that can be used.

Many workers consider that optimal psychosocial treatments can reduce the number of patients' relapses, the frequency and length of their hospitalizations, and the amounts of their medications. Students must understand the various modalities, such as supportive psychotherapy, family therapy, partial hospitalization, and day treatment, and must understand which options are useful for which patients. Diagnosis and treatment of schizophrenia demand physicians' and health workers' best efforts.

Students are referred to Chapter 13 in *Kaplan and Sadock's Synopsis VIII* and should then study the questions and answers below.

HELPFUL HINTS

The following names and terms, including the schizophrenic signs and symptoms listed, should be studied and the definitions memorized.

- antipsychotics
- autistic disorder
- Gregory Bateson
- Eugen Bleuler
- *bouffée délirante*
- brain imaging—CT, PET, MRI
- catatonic type
- delusions
- *dementia precox*
- disorganized type
- dopamine hypothesis
- double bind
- downward-drift hypothesis
- ECT
- ego boundaries
- electrophysiology—EEG
- flat affect and blunted affect
- *forme fruste*
- fundamental and accessory symptoms
- genetic hypothesis
- hallucinations
- impulse control, suicide, and homicide
- Karl Jaspers
- Karl Kahlbaum
- Emil Kraepelin
- Gabriel Langfeldt
- mesocortical and mesolimbic tracts
- Adolf Meyer
- Benedict Morel
- neurotransmitters and neurodegeneration
- orientation, memory, judgment, and insight
- paranoia
- paranoid type

- paraphrenia
- projective testing
- psychoanalytic and learning theories
- psychoimmunology and psychoendocrinology
- psychosocial treatments
- residual type
- RFLPs
- schizoaffective disorder
- Kurt Schneider
- seasonality of birth
- serotonin hypothesis
- social causation hypothesis
- soft signs
- Harry Stack Sullivan
- tardive dyskinesia
- thought disorders
- undifferentiated type

▲ QUESTIONS

DIRECTIONS: Each of the questions or incomplete statements below is followed by five suggested responses or completions. Select the *one* that is *best* in each case.

13.1 Which of the following lettered choices best describes the discussion of the category of schizophrenia in the fourth edition of *Diagnostic and Statistical Manual of Mental Disorders* (DSM-IV)?

A. All of the disorders discussed under the classification of schizophrenia have psychotic symptoms as the defining feature.
B. Shared psychotic disorder is a disturbance in which a person mimes the condition of another person with an established delusion.
C. The term *psychotic* refers exclusively to delusions and prominent hallucinations, which occur without insight into their pathological nature.
D. Delusional disorder is characterized by at least 6 months of nonbizarre delusions without other active-phase symptoms of schizophrenia.
E. Schizophreniform disorder has symptoms similar to those of schizophrenia, except that the disturbance lasts only 12 months and there must be a decline in functioning.

13.2 Which of the following lettered choices best describes the schizophrenic condition?

A. Disturbances of volition are prominent in paranoid schizophrenia.
B. Hebephrenic schizophrenia is often first diagnosed in patients about the age of 40.
C. Clear consciousness, with certain cognitive defects, is typical of schizophrenic disorders.
D. Most delusional disorders are unrelated to schizophrenia.
E. In postschizophrenic depression, symptoms may be intrinsically related to schizophrenia or may be a psychological reaction to it.

13.3 Which of the following lettered choices correctly describes other aspects related to schizophrenia?

A. Abrupt-onset psychotic disorders are associated with a poor outcome.
B. Mood-incongruent hallucinations or delusions are a characteristic of schizoaffective disorders.
C. In acute-onset psychotic disorders, a change from a state without psychotic features to a clearly abnormal psychotic state occurs in 4 weeks or less.
D. Persistent delusional disorders are characterized by long-standing delusions and other symptoms that workers consider to be related to schizophrenia.
E. Schizotypal disorder is characterized by eccentric behavior and thought and affect anomalies similar to those in schizophrenia, but no definite schizophrenic changes ever occur.

13.4 Which of the following lettered choices best describes a characteristic of the epidemiology of schizophrenia?

A. Schizophrenic patients occupy about 50 percent of all hospital beds.
B. Some regions of the world have an unusually high prevalence of schizophrenia.
C. Female patients with schizophrenia are more likely to commit suicide than are male patients.
D. In the Northern Hemisphere, schizophrenia occurs more often among people born from July to September than in those born in the other months.
E. Reproduction rates among people with schizophrenia are typically higher than those among the general population.

13.5 An 18-year-old female high school student was admitted for the first time to the psychiatry service because she had not spoken or eaten for 3 days. According to her parents, she had been a normal teenager, with good grades and friends, until about a year previously, when she began to stay at home alone in her room, and seemed preoccupied and less animated than in the past. About 6 months before her admission, she began to refuse to go to school, and her grades went down. About a month later, she started to talk incoherently, speaking gibberish about spirits, magic, the devil—concepts that were totally foreign to her background. For the week preceding admission to the hospital, she had stared into space, immobile, allowing herself only to be moved from her bed to a chair or from one room to another. The least likely diagnosis is

A. schizophreniform disorder
B. brief psychotic disorder
C. a mood disorder
D. schizophrenia
E. delusional disorder

13.6 A patient has been brought into the emergency room by the police for striking an elderly woman in his apartment building. He complained that the woman he struck was a "bitch" and that she and "the others" deserved more than that for what they put him through. The patient had recently been fired from his job as an investment counselor, which he had held for 7 months. At work he was getting an increasing number of distracting "signals" from coworkers and he had become more and more suspicious and withdrawn. At that time he first reported hearing voices. Soon thereafter he was hospitalized for the first time at the age of 24. In the treatment of this patient's condition

A. long-term hospitalization would be less effective than short-term hospitalization
B. psychotherapy would have little effect on other treatments
C. the minimum length of an antipsychotic trial should be 2 weeks
D. electroconvulsive therapy (ECT) would be harmful
E. risperidone is indicated

13.7 Investigations into the cause of schizophrenia have revealed that

A. no significant abnormalities appear in the evoked potentials in schizophrenic patients
B. monozygotic twins who are reared by adoptive parents have schizophrenia at the same rate as their siblings
C. a specific family pattern plays a causative role in the development of schizophrenia
D. the efficacy and potency of most antipsychotics correlate with their ability to act primarily as antagonists of the dopamine type 1 (D_1) receptor
E. a particular defective chromosomal site has been found in all schizophrenic patients

13.8 Epidemiological studies of schizophrenia have found all of the following *except*

A. Schizophrenic patients occupy 50 percent of all mental hospital beds.
B. The peak age of onset for schizophrenia is the same for men and women.
C. Schizophrenia is equally prevalent among men and women.
D. Approximately 50 percent of schizophrenic patients attempt to commit suicide at least once in their lifetime.
E. The lifetime prevalence is usually between 1 and 1.5 percent of the population.

13.9 Hospital records suggest that for the past 100 years the incidence of schizophrenia in the United States has probably

A. increased greatly
B. increased slightly
C. decreased greatly
D. decreased slightly
E. remained unchanged

13.10 The mortality rate among schizophrenic patients

A. is higher than the rate for normal persons
B. is lower than the rate for normal persons
C. is the same as the rate for normal persons
D. has never been studied
E. is the same as the rate for patients with phobias

13.11 All of the following statements are factors that can increase the risk of schizophrenia *except*

A. having a schizophrenic family member
B. having a history of temporal lobe epilepsy
C. having low levels of monoamine oxidase, type B, in blood platelets
D. having previously attempted suicide
E. having a deviant course of personality maturation and development

13.12 Simple schizophrenia is characterized by

A. an insidious loss of drive and ambition
B. persistent hallucinations
C. persistent delusions
D. a desire for social and work-related situations
E. all of the above

13.13 A schizophrenic patient who cuts off his penis is said to be suffering from

A. penis envy
B. castration complex
C. the Van Gogh syndrome
D. *bouffée délirante*
E. homosexual panic

13.14 A schizophrenic patient who feels a burning sensation in the brain is said to be experiencing a

A. delusional feeling
B. gustatory hallucination
C. cenesthetic hallucination
D. haptic hallucination
E. hypnopompic hallucination

13.15 A relapse in schizophrenia is most closely related to

A. the natural course of the illness
B. noncompliance in taking medicine
C. whether or not the patient is working
D. physical therapy
E. individual psychotherapy

13.16 Which of the following symptoms must be present in order to make a diagnosis of schizophrenia?

A. Thought broadcasting
B. Hallucinations
C. Flat affect
D. Disorganized behavior
E. All of the above

13.17 The majority of computed tomographic (CT) studies of patients with schizophrenia have reported

A. enlarged lateral and third ventricles in 10 to 50 percent of patients
B. cortical atrophy in 10 to 35 percent of patients
C. atrophy of the cerebellar vermis
D. findings that are not artifacts of treatment
E. all of the above

13.18 In general, pooled studies show concordance rates for schizophrenia in monozygotic twins of

A. 0.1 percent
B. 5 percent
C. 25 percent
D. 40 percent
E. 50 percent

13.19 Paraphrenia is sometimes used as a synonym for

A. latent schizophrenia
B. simple deteriorative disorder (simple schizophrenia)
C. catatonic schizophrenia
D. hebephrenic schizophrenia
E. delusional disorder

13.20 The most common type of schizophrenic hallucination is

A. tactile
B. visual
C. auditory
D. gustatory
E. olfactory

13.21 A 33-year-old male psychiatric inpatient put on his dark sunglasses whenever he met with his doctor. He stated that doing so made it impossible for the doctor to control his thoughts. The patient was exhibiting

A. social withdrawal
B. hypervigilance
C. fragmentation of thinking
D. delusional thinking
E. magical thinking

13.22 The schizophrenic patient shown in Figure 13.1 has the characteristic posture known as

A. catalepsy
B. mannerism
C. cataplexy
D. perseveration
E. none of the above

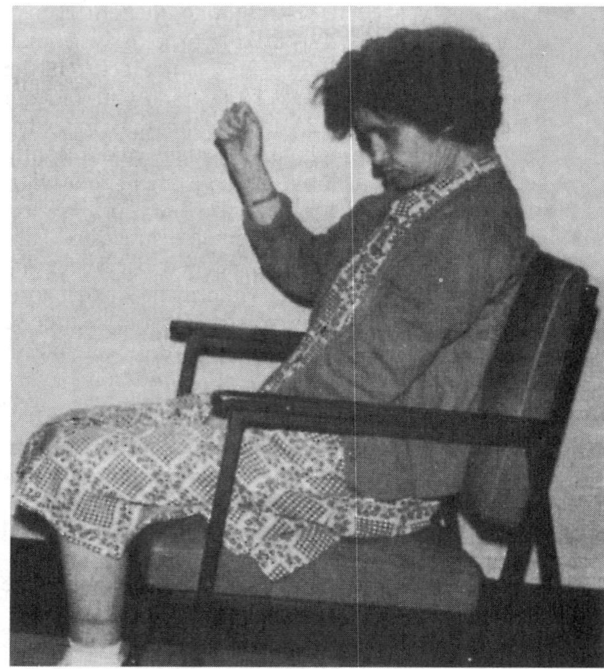

FIGURE 13.1
Courtesy of Heinz E. Lehmann, M.D.

13.23 Features weighing toward a good prognosis in schizophrenia include all of the following *except*

A. depression
B. a family history of mood disorders
C. paranoid features
D. undifferentiated or disorganized features
E. an undulating course

13.24 Thought disorders in schizophrenia are characterized by

A. delusions
B. loss of ego boundaries
C. sexual confusion
D. looseness of associations
E. all of the above

13.25 Clozapine (Clozaril)

A. is an appropriate first-line drug for the treatment of schizophrenia
B. is associated with a 10 to 20 percent incidence of agranulocytosis
C. requires monthly monitoring of blood chemistry
D. has not been associated with extrapyramidal side effects
E. is believed to exert its therapeutic effect mainly by blocking dopamine receptors

13.26 Electrophysiological studies of persons with schizophrenia show

A. decreased alpha activity
B. spikes in the limbic area that correlate with psychotic behavior
C. increased frontal lobe slow-wave activity
D. increased parietal lobe fast-wave activity
E. all of the above

Questions 13.27–13.28

A 40-year-old man is brought to the hospital, his 12th admission, by his mother, because she is afraid of him. He is dressed in a ragged overcoat, bedroom slippers, and a baseball cap, and wears several medals around his neck. His affect ranges from anger at his mother (''She feeds me shit . . . what comes out of other people's rectums'') to a giggling, obsequious seductiveness toward his interviewer. His speech and manner have a childlike quality, and he walks with a mincing step and exaggerated hip movements. His mother reports that he stopped taking his medication about a month ago and has since begun to hear voices and to look and act more bizarrely. His spontaneous speech is often incoherent and marked by frequent rhyming and clang associations. His first hospitalization occurred after he dropped out of school at age 16, and since that time he has never been able to attend school or hold a job. [Reprinted with permission from Spitzer RL, editor: *DSM-IV Casebook.* American Psychiatric Press, Washington, 1994.]

13.27 As described, the patient's condition is best diagnosed as

A. schizophrenia, paranoid type
B. schizophrenia, disorganized type
C. schizophrenia, catatonic type
D. schizophrenia, undifferentiated type
E. schizophrenia, residual type

13.28 Which of the following neuroleptics is a serotonin-dopamine antagonist (SDA) that would lessen the need for antiparkinsonian medication in this patient?

A. Haloperidol
B. Fluphenazine
C. Trifluoperazine
D. Risperidone
E. Pimozide

13.29 A 23-year-old schizophrenic patient is under your care. Two months after you have placed him on medication, haloperidol, the patient's family begins to complain that he has recently begun to drool and that when he walks he has a shuffling gait. They also state that the patient seems to have a tremor around his mouth and appears to be indifferent to his surroundings. All of the following treatments could improve the patient's condition *except*

A. starting the patient on an anticholinergic agent
B. decreasing the dosage of haloperidol
C. giving the patient diphenhydramine
D. switching the patient to risperidone
E. adding an antidepressant

13.30 Figure 13.2 illustrates a patient's fragmented, abstract, and overly inclusive thinking and preoccupation with religious idealogies and mathematical proofs. The patient's schema demonstrates a disorder of

A. perception
B. judgment
C. affect
D. sensorium
E. thought

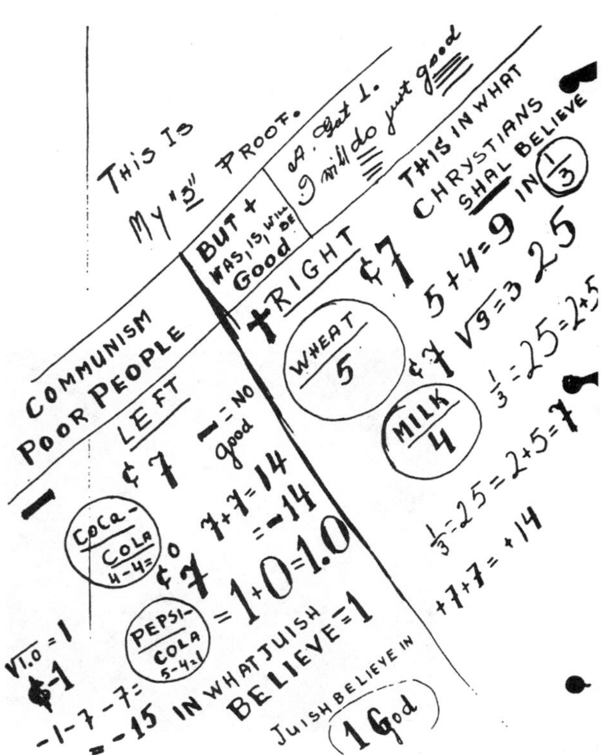

FIGURE 13.2
Courtesy of Heinz E. Lehmann, M.D.

13.31 The magnetic resonance images shown in Figure 13.3 demonstrate a difference in lateral ventricular size in monozygotic twins discordant for schizophrenia. *Panel 1A* shows normal lateral ventricles; *Panel 1B* shows abnormal lateral ventricles. With regard to the ventricular size in schizophrenia, which of the following statements is *true*?

A. Ventricular enlargement is a pathognomonic finding in schizophrenia.
B. Ventricular changes in schizophrenia are likely to be specific for the pathophysiological processes underlying this disorder.
C. Patients with schizophrenia invariably demonstrate significant enlargement of the lateral ventricles.
D. All of the above statements are true.
E. None of the above statements are true.

13.32 All of the following statements regarding the patient shown in Figure 13.1 are true *except*

A. The patient might also be expected to exhibit mutism.
B. The patient suffers a marked disturbance in motor function as a manifestation of her disorder.
C. A history of a young onset of illness is associated with a relatively good prognosis for this patient.
D. The patient might also be expected to exhibit echolalia or echopraxia.
E. An absence of precipitating factors for the patient's disorder is associated with a relatively poor prognosis.

DIRECTIONS: Each group of questions consists of lettered headings followed by a list of numbered words or statements. For each numbered word or statement, select the *one* lettered heading that is most closely associated with it. Each lettered heading may be selected once, more than once, or not at all.

Questions 13.33–13.37

A. Eugen Bleuler
B. Benedict Morel
C. Karl Kahlbaum
D. Ewald Hecker
E. Gabriel Langfeldt

13.33 *Démence précoce*
13.34 Schizophrenia
13.35 Catatonia
13.36 Hebephrenia
13.37 Schizophreniform psychosis

Questions 13.38–13.41

A. Eugen Bleuler
B. Emil Kraepelin

13.38 Latinized the term *démence précoce*
13.39 Classified patients as being afflicted with manic-depressive psychoses, dementia precox, or paranoia
13.40 Coined the term schizophrenia
13.41 Described the four As of schizophrenia—associations, autism, affect, and ambivalence

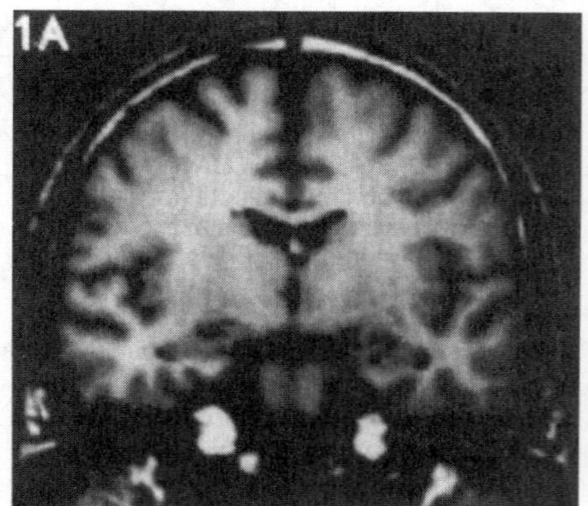

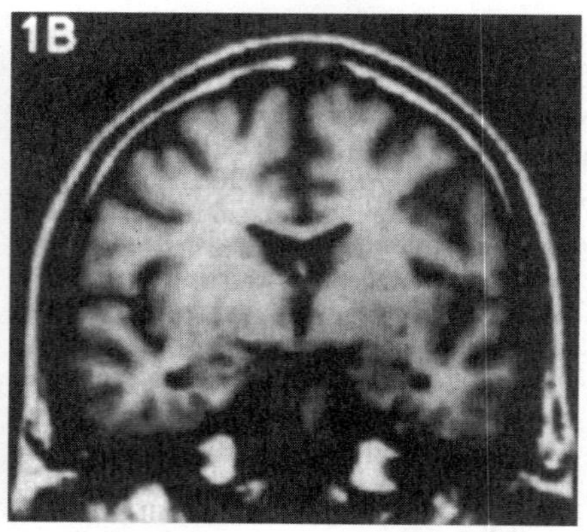

FIGURE 13.3

Reprinted with permission from Suddath RL, Christison GW, Torrey EF, Casanova MF, Weinberger DR: Anatomical abnormalities in the brains of monozygotic twins discordant for schizophrenia. N Engl J Med *322:* 789, 1990.

Questions 13.42–13.46

A. Incoherence
B. Neologism
C. Mutism
D. Echolalia
E. Verbigeration

13.42 Functional inhibition of speech
13.43 New expression or word
13.44 Empty or obscure language
13.45 Repeating of the same words the questioner has asked
13.46 Senseless repetition of the same words or phrases

Questions 13.47–13.52

A. Schneiderian first-rank symptom
B. Schneiderian second-rank symptom

13.47 Sudden delusional ideas
13.48 Perplexity
13.49 Audible thoughts
13.50 Voices commenting
13.51 Thought withdrawal
13.52 The experience of having one's thoughts controlled

ANSWERS

Schizophrenia

13.1 The answer is A (*Synopsis VIII,* pages 456, 466–467, 473).
According to the fourth edition of *Diagnostic and Statistical Manual of Mental Disorders* (DSM-IV), all of the disorders discussed under the category of schizophrenia *have psychotic symptoms as the defining feature.*

According to DSM-IV, *shared psychotic disorder* is a disturbance in which a person with an established delusion causes another person to develop the same delusion; the latter person does not mime the disorder but actually develops it. DSM-IV defines the term *psychotic* in several ways and discusses not only the narrowest sense—*delusions and prominent hallucinations that occur without insight into their pathological nature*—but also incorporates a variety of other meanings and applies most of them to various aspects of the disorders discussed under schizophrenia.

DSM-IV describes *delusional disorder* as characterized by at least 1 month, not 6 months, of nonbizarre delusions. *Schizophreniform disorder,* as discussed in DSM-IV, lasts 1 to 6 months, not 12 months.

13.2 The answer is E (*Synopsis VIII,* pages 473–475).
Patients with schizophrenia may get depressed. Whether depressive symptoms of schizophrenic depression are *intrinsically related to schizophrenia or* are *a psychological reaction to it* is uncertain and immaterial to the diagnosis of the disorder. Patients with paranoid schizophrenia have *disturbances of volition* as well as of affect and speech. *Hebephrenic schizophrenia is often first diagnosed in patients* between the ages of 15 and 25 years, not about the age of 40.

Clear consciousness and intellectual capacity are said to be maintained in patients with schizophrenic disorders, although *cognitive defects* may evolve in time. *Delusional disorders* are *probably unrelated to schizophrenia.* There is no history of family illness in delusional disorder.

13.3 The answer is E (*Synopsis VIII,* page 473).
Schizotypal disorder is characterized by eccentric behavior and changes in thought and affect similar to those that occur in schizophrenia, but no definite schizophrenic anomalies such as delusions or hallucinations occur. Occasionally the disorder evolves into overt schizophrenia.

Abrupt-onset psychotic disorders are associated with a good outcome; the more abrupt the onset (within 48 hours or less), the better the outcome. *Mood-incongruent hallucinations or delusions* in mood disorders may occur in but are not sufficient to justify a diagnosis of schizoaffective disorder.

In acute-onset psychotic disorder, the defining feature is early onset, which must occur within 2 weeks, not in 4 weeks or less. *Persistent delusional disorders* are probably heterogeneous, and they are not considered related to schizophrenia.

13.4 The answer is B (*Synopsis VIII,* page 458).
An important epidemiological factor in schizophrenia is that *some regions of the world have an unusually high prevalence* of the disorder. Certain researchers have interpreted this geographic inequity as supporting an infective cause for schizophrenia, whereas others emphasize genetic factors.

Schizophrenic patients occupy 50 percent of mental hospital beds, not of all hospital beds.

Female patients with schizophrenia are no more likely to commit suicide than are male patients; the risk factors are equal.

There is a difference in prevalence of schizophrenia according to season, but *in the Northern Hemisphere, schizophrenia occurs more often among people born from* January to April, not from July to September. The latter time range refers to seasonal preference for the disorder in the Southern Hemisphere. *Reproduction rates among people with schizophrenia* have been rising in recent years because of newly introduced medications and changes in laws and policies about hospitalization and community-based care. The fertility rate among people with schizophrenia, however, is only approaching the rate for the general population and does not exceed it.

13.5 The answer is E (*Synopsis VIII,* page 484).
The least likely diagnosis in the 18-year-old female high school student is *delusional disorder,* based on the clinical presentation. In delusional disorder, one expects nonbizarre delusions to be present but only in the absence of other symptoms of schizophrenia, such as incoherence and prominent hallucinations. The patient's presenting symptoms point more toward incoherence and disorganization, which are not characteristic of delusional disorder.

The most likely diagnosis is *schizophrenia,* based on the presence of delusions about supernatural phenomena, incoherence, and catatonic symptoms—for example, allowing herself to be passively moved. The diagnostic criteria for schizophrenia are listed in Table 13.1.

Her symptoms had been noted for about a year. That fact rules out *schizophreniform disorder,* which is diagnosed when the criteria for schizophrenia have been met but the symptoms have been present for at least 1 month but less than 6 months. *Brief psychotic disorder* is diagnosed when symptoms have been present for at least a day but less than a month.

The differential diagnosis of schizophrenia and *a mood disorder* can be difficult. In the case presented, the patient's mood was not reported to be disturbed.

13.6 The answer is E (*Synopsis VIII,* pages 485–486).
Based on the clinical presentation, this patient is best diagnosed as schizophrenic, paranoid type. *Risperidone* is of use for these types of patients. The available data indicate that risperidone is an effective antipsychotic that is not associated with the development or exacerbation of tardive dyskinesia, a movement disorder that develops after the prolonged use of antipsychotic medications.

The minimum length of an antipsychotic trial is usually 4 to 6 weeks, not 2 weeks. If the trial is unsuccessful, a different antipsychotic, usually from a different class, can be tried.

Electroconvulsive therapy (ECT) is not harmful to schizophrenic patients. Although ECT is much less effective than antipsychotics, it may be indicated for catatonic patients and for patients who for some reason cannot take antipsychotics.

Table 13.1
DSM-IV Diagnostic Criteria for Schizophrenia

A. *Characteristic symptoms:* Two (or more) of the following, each present for a significant portion of time during a 1-month period (or less if successfully treated):
   (1) delusions
   (2) hallucinations
   (3) disorganized speech (eg, frequent derailment or incoherence)
   (4) grossly disorganized or catatonic behavior
   (5) negative symptoms, ie, affective flattening, alogia, or avolition

   Note: Only one criterion A symptom is required if delusions are bizarre or hallucinations consist of a voice keeping up a running commentary on the person's behavior or thoughts, or two or more voices conversing with each other.

B. *Social/occupational dysfunction:* For a significant portion of the time since the onset of the disturbance, one or more major areas of functioning such as work, interpersonal relations, or self-care, are markedly below the level achieved prior to the onset (or when the onset is in childhood or adolescence, failure to achieve expected level of interpersonal, academic, or occupational achievement).

C. *Duration:* Continuous signs of the disturbance persist for at least 6 months. This 6-month period must include at least 1 month of symptoms that meet criterion A (ie, active-phase symptoms), and may include periods of prodromal or residual symptoms. During these prodromal or residual periods, the signs of the disturbance may be manifested by only negative symptoms or two or more symptoms listed in criterion A present in an attenuated form (eg, odd beliefs, unusual perceptual experiences).

D. *Schizoaffective and mood disorder exclusion:* Schizoaffective disorder and mood disorder with psychotic features have been ruled out because either (1) no major depressive, manic, or mixed episodes have occurred concurrently with the active-phase symptoms; or (2) if mood episodes have occurred during active-phase symptoms, their total duration has been brief relative to the duration of the active and residual periods.

E. *Substance/general medical condition exclusion:* The disturbance is not due to the direct physiological effects of a substance (eg, a drug of abuse, a medication) or a general medical condition.

F. *Relationship to a pervasive developmental disorder:* If there is a history of autistic disorder or another pervasive developmental disorder, the additional diagnosis of schizophrenia is made only if prominent delusions or hallucinations are also present for at least a month (or less if successfully treated).

Classification of longitudinal course (can be applied only after at least 1 year has elapsed since the initial onset of active-phase symptoms):

Episodic with interepisode residual symptoms (episodes are defined by the reemergence of prominent psychotic symptoms); *also specify if:* **with prominent negative symptoms**
Episodic with no interepisode residual symptoms
Continuous (prominent psychotic symptoms are present throughout the period of observation); *also specify if:* **with prominent negative symptoms**
Single episode in partial remission; *also specify if:* **with prominent negative symptoms**
Single episode in full remission
Other or unspecified pattern

Hospitalization decreases stress on patients and helps them structure their daily activities. The length of hospitalization depends on the severity of the patient's illness and the availability of outpatient treatment facilities. Research has shown that *short-term hospitalization* (4 to 6 weeks) *is just as effective as long-term hospitalization* and that hospitals with active behavioral approaches are more effective than custodial institutions and insight-oriented therapeutic communities.

Psychotherapeutic interventions would have an effect on aiding other treatments. Studies have provided data that therapy is helpful and is additive to the effects of pharmacological treatment.

13.7 The answer is B (*Synopsis VIII,* pages 459–460, 464–465).

The cause of schizophrenia is not known. However, a wide range of genetic studies strongly suggest a genetic component to the inheritance of schizophrenia. *Monozygotic twins have the highest concordance rate for schizophrenia.* The studies of adopted monozygotic twins show that twins who are reared by adoptive parents have schizophrenia at the same rate as their twin siblings raised by their biological parents. That finding suggests that the genetic influence outweighs the environmental influence. In further support of the genetic basis is the observation that the more severe the schizophrenia, the more likely the twins are to be concordant for the disorder.

Nevertheless, *a particular genetic defect has not been found in all schizophrenic patients.* Many associations between particular chromosomal sites and schizophrenia have been reported in the literature since the widespread application of the techniques of molecular biology. More than half of the chromosomes have been associated with schizophrenia in those various reports, but the long arms of chromosomes 5, 11, 18, and 22; the short arms of chromosomes 6, 8, and 19; and the X chromosome have been the most commonly reported. At this time, the literature is best summarized as indicating a potentially heterogeneous genetic basis for schizophrenia.

The research literature also report that *a large number of abnormalities appear in the evoked potentials in schizophrenic patients.* The P300, so far the most studied, is defined as a large positive evoked-potential wave that occurs about 300 milliseconds after a sensory stimulus is detected. The major source of the P300 wave may be in the limbic system structures of the medial temporal lobes. In schizophrenic patients the P300 has been reported to be statistically smaller and later than in comparison groups.

Except for the serotonin-dopamine antagonists, *the efficacy and the potency of most antipsychotics correlate with their ability to act as antagonists of the dopamine type 2 (D_2) (not type 1) receptor.*

No well-controlled evidence indicates that any *specific family pattern plays a causative role in the development of schizophrenia.* Some schizophrenic patients do come from dysfunctional families, just as many persons who are not psychiatrically ill come from dysfunctional families.

13.8 The answer is B (*Synopsis VIII,* pages 457–458).

Men have an earlier onset of schizophrenia than do women. The peak ages of onset for men are 15 to 25; for women the peak ages are 25 to 35. However, *schizophrenia is equally prevalent in men and women.*

Schizophrenic patients occupy about 50 percent of all mental hospital beds.

Suicide is a common cause of death among schizophrenic patients. *About 50 percent of all patients with schizophrenia attempt suicide at least once in their lifetimes,* and 10 to 15 percent of schizophrenic patients die by suicide during a 20-year follow-up period.

The lifetime prevalence of schizophrenia is usually between 1 and 1.5 percent of the population. Consistent with that range, the National Institute of Mental Health (NIMH)-sponsored Epidemiologic Catchment Area (ECA) study reported a lifetime prevalence of 1.3 percent.

13.9 The answer is E (*Synopsis VIII,* page 459).
Hospital records suggest that the incidence of schizophrenia in the United States has probably *remained unchanged* for the past 100 years and possibly throughout the entire history of the country, despite tremendous socioeconomic and population changes.

13.10 The answer is A (*Synopsis VIII,* page 458).
The mortality rate among schizophrenic patients *is higher than the rate for normal persons.* The reasons for the high rate are not readily explainable.

13.11 The answer is D (*Synopsis VIII,* pages 458, 481–482).
Having previously attempted suicide does not increase the risk for developing schizophrenia. At least 50 percent of schizophrenic patients attempt suicide once in their lifetime. *Having a schizophrenic family member,* especially having one or two schizophrenic parents and a monozygotic twin who is schizophrenic, *increases the risk for schizophrenia.* Other risk factors include (1) having lived through a difficult obstetrical delivery, presumably with trauma to the brain; (2) having, for unknown reasons, *a deviant course of personality maturation and development* that has produced an excessively shy, daydreaming, withdrawn, friendless child; an excessively compliant, good, or dependent child; a child with idiosyncratic thought processes; a child who is particularly sensitive to separation; a child who is destructive, violent, incorrigible, and prone to truancy; or an anhedonic child; (3) having a parent who is overpossessive, hostile, or incapable of defining the child's needs or who has paranoid attitudes and formal disturbances of thinking; (4) *having low levels of monoamine oxidase, type B, in the blood platelets;* (5) having abnormal pursuit eye movements; (6) having taken a variety of drugs—particularly lysergic acid diethylamide (LSD), amphetamines, cannabis, cocaine, and phencyclidine; and (7) *having a history of temporal lobe epilepsy,* Huntington's disease, homocystinuria, folic acid deficiency, and the adult form of metachromatic leukodystrophy.

None of those risk factors invariably occurs in schizophrenic patients; they may occur in various combinations. Not everyone who ingests psychotomimetic drugs later becomes schizophrenic. Not every schizophrenic patient has abnormal pursuit eye movements, and some well relatives of schizophrenic patients may also have abnormal pursuit eye movements.

13.12 The answer is A (*Synopsis VIII,* pages 472–473).
The diagnosis of simple schizophrenia was used during a period when schizophrenia had a broad diagnostic conceptualization. Simple schizophrenia was characterized by a gradual, *insidious loss of drive and ambition.* Patients with the disorder were usually not overtly psychotic, nor did they always experience *persistent hallucinations* or *delusions.* The primary symptom is the patient's loss of *desire for social and work-related situations.* The syndrome may reflect depression, a phobia, dementia, or an exacerbation of personality traits. The clinician should be sure that the patient truly meets the diagnostic criteria for schizophrenia before making that diagnosis. In spite of those reservations, simple schizophrenia (now called simple deteriorative disorder) has reappeared as a diagnostic category in an appendix of DSM-IV.

13.13 The answer is C (*Synopsis VIII,* pages 639, 734, 880).
Dramatic self-mutilation in schizophrenic patients—for example, the gouging out of an eye or the cutting off of the penis—has been called *the Van Gogh syndrome* after the artist who cut off his ear during a psychotic episode. It sometimes is the expression of dysmorphophobic delusions, the irrational conviction that a serious bodily defect exists, or some other complex unconscious mechanism.

Penis envy is Sigmund Freud's concept that the woman envies the man for his possession of a penis. In psychoanalytic theory, *castration complex* is a group of unconscious thoughts and motives that are related to the fear of losing the genitalia, usually as punishment for forbidden sexual desires. *Bouffée délirante* is a term used in France and is considered a diagnostic category in its own right, not a type of schizophrenia. The criteria are similar to those for schizophrenia, but the symptoms must be present for less than 3 months, thereby approximating the diagnosis of schizophreniform disorder. French psychiatrists report that about 40 percent of patients with the diagnosis are later classified as having schizophrenia.

Homosexual panic is the sudden onset of severe anxiety precipitated by the unconscious fear or conflict that one may be a homosexual or act out homosexual impulses.

13.14 The answer is C (*Synopsis VIII,* page 480).
A person with schizophrenia often experiences a *cenesthetic hallucination,* a sensation of an altered state in body organs without any special receptor apparatus to explain the sensation—for example, a burning sensation in the brain, a pushing sensation in the abdominal blood vessels, or a cutting sensation in the bone marrow.

A *delusional feeling* is a feeling of false belief, based on an incorrect inference about external reality. A *gustatory hallucination* involves primarily taste. A tactile or *haptic hallucination* involves the sense of touch (for example, formication—the feeling of bugs crawling under the skin). A *hypnopompic hallucination* is a hallucination that occurs as one awakes.

13.15 The answer is B (*Synopsis VIII,* page 486).
Noncompliance in taking medication after the first episode of schizophrenia is related to a subsequent relapse. Patients who do not take their medications as prescribed have a higher than usual relapse rate.

The risk of personality deterioration increases with each schizophrenic relapse. Schizophrenic recoveries are often called remissions because many of the patients later relapse. With each schizophrenic episode, the patient has an increased probability of some permanent personality damage. *The nat-*

ural course of the illness, however, does not inevitably lead to intellectual deterioration or relapse. *Whether or not the patient is working, physical therapy,* and *individual psychotherapy* do not influence relapse as much as does medication.

13.16 The answer is E (all) (*Synopsis VIII,* pages 466–467). To make a diagnosis of schizophrenia, the psychiatrist must find at least one of the following symptoms: delusions (for example, *thought broadcasting*), *hallucinations,* disorganized speech, negative symptoms (for example, *flat affect*), and catatonic or grossly *disorganized behavior.*

13.17 The answer is E (all) (*Synopsis VIII,* pages 462–463). The majority of computed tomographic (CT) studies of patients with schizophrenia have reported *enlarged lateral and third ventricles in 10 to 50 percent of patients* and *cortical atrophy in 10 to 35 percent of patients.* Controlled studies have also revealed *atrophy of the cerebellar vermis,* decreased radiodensity of brain parenchyma, and reversals of the normal brain asymmetries. Those *findings are not artifacts of treatment* and are not progressive or reversible. The enlargement of the ventricles seems to be present at the time of diagnosis, before the use of medication. Some studies have correlated the presence of CT scan findings with the presence of negative or deficit symptoms (for example, social isolation), neuropsychological impairment, frequent motor side effects from antipsychotics, and a poor premorbid adjustment.

13.18 The answer is E (*Synopsis VIII,* pages 459–460). In general, pooled studies show concordance rates of about *50 percent* in monozygotic twins.

13.19 The answer is E (*Synopsis VIII,* page 472). Paraphrenia is not listed in DSM-IV as a diagnostic entity; it does, however, appear in the 10th revision of *International Statistical Classification of Diseases and Related Health Problems* (ICD-10). Paraphrenia is sometimes used as a synonym for *delusional disorder.* The term may also be used for a progressively deteriorating course of illness with schizophrenic features; at present, however, it has no precise meaning in the United States.

In paranoid schizophrenia there is a deterioration and splitting off of many of the psychic functions, whereas in paraphrenia the delusions are logical, at least on the surface. *Latent schizophrenia* is a form of schizophrenia in which, despite the existence of fundamental symptoms, no clear-cut psychotic episode or gross break with reality has occurred. It is not a term used in DSM-IV. In *simple deteriorative disorder (simple schizophrenia)* an insidious psychic impoverishment affects the emotions, the intellect, and the will. Chronic dissatisfaction or complete indifference to reality is characteristic, and the simple schizophrenic patient is isolated, estranged, and asocial. *Catatonic schizophrenia* is a state characterized by muscular rigidity and immobility. *Hebephrenic schizophrenia* is a complex of symptoms characterized by wild or silly behavior or mannerisms, an inappropriate affect, frequent hypochondriacal complaints, and delusions and hallucinations that are transient and unsystematized.

13.20 The answer is C (*Synopsis VIII,* page 480). The most common schizophrenic hallucination is *auditory,* particularly the hearing of voices. Characteristically, two or more voices talk about the patient in the third person. Frequently, the voices address the patient, comment on the patient's activities and what is going on around that person, or are threatening or obscene and very disturbing to the patient. Many schizophrenic patients hear their own thoughts. When they are reading silently, for example, they may be disturbed by hearing every word they are reading clearly spoken to them.

The second most common schizophrenic hallucination is *visual.* When visual hallucinations occur in schizophrenia, they are usually seen nearby, clearly defined, in color, life-size, in three dimensions, and moving. Visual hallucinations almost never occur by themselves but always in combination with hallucinations in one of the other sensory modalities.

Tactile, gustatory, and *olfactory* hallucinations are less common than visual hallucinations.

13.21 The answer is D (*Synopsis VIII,* pages 480–481). The male psychiatric inpatient was exhibiting symptoms of *delusional thinking.* He believed that the doctor could control his thoughts.

Social withdrawal is a pathological retreat from interpersonal contact and social involvement. It is an extreme decrease of intellectual and emotional interest in the environment. It may be seen in schizophrenia and depression. *Hypervigilance* is the continual scanning of the environment for signs of threat. It is most often seen in paranoid disorders. *Fragmentation of thinking* is a disturbance in association characterized by loosening, in which basic concepts become vague and incoherent and the thinking processes become so confused that they cannot result in a complete idea or action. It is a form of thinking often associated with schizophrenia. *Magical thinking* is a notion that thinking something is either the same thing as doing it or may cause it to happen. It is commonly experienced in dreams, in certain mental disorders, and by children.

13.22 The answer is A (*Synopsis VIII,* page 479). *Catalepsy* is a condition in which a person maintains the body position in which it has been placed. The position can be maintained for long periods, even though it may appear to be uncomfortable. The condition is also known as waxy flexibility and *cerea flexibilitas.*

A *mannerism* is a stereotyped gesture or expression that is peculiar to a given person. *Cataplexy* is the temporary sudden loss of muscle tone, causing weakness and immobilization. It can be precipitated by a variety of emotional states, and it is often followed by sleep. *Perseveration,* which is speech rather than motor behavior, consists of the patient's giving the same verbal response to various questions.

13.23 The answer is D (*Synopsis VIII,* page 468). Poor prognostic features in schizophrenia include a family history of schizophrenia, poor premorbid social, sexual, and work histories, and *undifferentiated or disorganized features.* Features weighting toward a good prognosis in schizophrenia include mood symptoms (especially *depression*), *a family history of mood disorders, paranoid features,* and *an undulating course.* Table 13.2 presents a summary of the factors used to assess prognosis in schizophrenia.

13.24 The answer is E (all) (*Synopsis VIII,* pages 480–481). Disordered thought is characteristic of schizophrenia. Thought disorders may be divided into disorders of content, form, and

Table 13.2
Features Weighting Toward Good Prognosis and Poor Prognosis in Schizophrenia

Good Prognosis	Poor Prognosis
Late onset	Early onset
Obvious precipitating factors	No precipitating factors
Sudden onset	Insidious onset
Good premorbid social, sexual, and work histories	Poor premorbid social, sexual, and work histories
Mood disorder symptoms (especially depressive disorders)	Withdrawn, autistic behavior
Married	Single, divorced, or widowed
Family history of mood disorders	Family history of schizophrenia
Good support systems	Poor support symptoms
Positive symptoms	Negative symptoms
	Neurological signs and symptoms
	History of perinatal trauma
	No remissions in 3 years
	Many relapses
	History of assaultiveness

process. Disorders of content reflect ideas, beliefs, and interpretations of stimuli. *Delusions* are the most obvious examples of disorder of thought content. The delusions may be persecutory, grandiose, religious, or somatic. *Loss of ego boundaries* is the patient's lack of a clear sense of where the patient's own body, mind, and influence end and where those of other animate and inanimate objects begin. For example, the content of thought may include ideas of reference that other people, persons on television, or newspaper items are making reference to the patient. Other symptoms include a sense of fusion with outside objects (for example, a tree or another person) or a sense of disintegration. Given that state of mind, patients with schizophrenia may have *sexual confusion* and doubts as to what sex they are or what their sexual orientation is. Disorders in thought form or process reflect how thoughts are conveyed. *Looseness of associations,* a disorder of thought form, was once thought to be pathognomonic for schizophrenia; however, that form of thought may be seen in other psychotic states as well. It is characterized by thoughts that are connected to each other by meanings known only to the patient and conveyed in a manner that is diffuse, unfocused, illogical, and even incoherent.

13.25 The answer is D (*Synopsis VIII,* pages 485–486).
Clozapine (Clozaril) *has not been associated with extrapyramidal side effects* or tardive dyskinesia. It is an antipsychotic medication that is appropriate in the treatment of schizophrenic patients who have not responded to first-line dopamine receptor antagonists or who have tardive dyskinesia. It *is not an appropriate first-line drug for the treatment of schizophrenia.* Clozapine *has been associated with a 1 to 2 percent (not 10 to 20 percent) incidence of agranulocytosis* and thus *requires weekly, not monthly, monitoring of blood chemistries.* Clozapine *is believed to exert its therapeutic effect by blocking serotonin type 2 (5-HT$_2$) and, secondarily, dopamine receptors.*

13.26 The answer is E (all) (*Synopsis VIII,* page 464).
Electrophysiological studies of schizophrenia patients include electroencephalogram (EEG) studies. Those studies indicate a higher than usual number of patients with abnormal recordings, increased sensitivity (for example, frequent spike activity) to activation procedures (for example, sleep deprivation), *decreased alpha activity,* increased theta and delta activity, possibly more epileptiform activity, and possibly more left-sided abnormalities. Evoked potential studies have generally shown increased amplitude of early components and decreased amplitude of late components. That difference may indicate that although schizophrenia patients are more sensitive to sensory stimulation than other persons, they compensate for that increased sensitivity by blunting their processing of the information at higher cortical levels.

Other central nervous system (CNS) electrophysiological investigations include depth electrodes and quantitative EEG (QEEG). One study reported that schizophrenic patients showed *spikes in the limbic area that correlate with psychotic behavior;* however, no control subjects were examined. QEEG studies of schizophrenia show *increased frontal lobe slow-wave activity* and *increased parietal lobe fast-wave activity.*

13.27 The answer is B (*Synopsis VIII,* page 469).
The patient's condition is best diagnosed as *schizophrenia, disorganized type,* characterized by a marked regression to primitive, disinhibited, and unorganized behavior and by the absence of symptoms that meet the criteria for the catatonic type. The onset is usually early, before age 25. Disorganized patients are usually active but in an aimless, nonconstructive manner. Their thought disorder is pronounced, with symptoms such as marked loosening of associations, and their contact with reality is poor. Their personal appearance is sloppy, and their social behavior is strange. Their emotional responses are inappropriate, and they often burst out laughing without any apparent reason. Incongruous grinning and grimacing are common in disorganized patients whose behavior is best described as silly or fatuous.

Schizophrenia, paranoid type is marked by preoccupation with delusions or auditory hallucinations. However, for that diagnosis to be made, there must be no disorganized speech or behavior, both of which are present in this case.

Schizophrenia, catatonic type, although common several decades ago, is now rare in Europe and North America. The classic feature of the catatonic type is a marked disturbance in motor function, which may involve stupor, negativism, rigidity, excitement, or posturing. Sometimes the patient shows a rapid alteration between extremes of excitement and stupor. Associated features include stereotypies, mannerisms, and waxy flexibility. Mutism is particularly common.

Frequently, patients who are clearly schizophrenic cannot be easily fitted into one of the other types. The fourth edition of *Diagnostic and Statistical Manual of Mental Disorders* (DSM-IV) diagnoses their condition as *schizophrenia, undifferentiated type.*

Schizophrenia, residual type is characterized by the presence of continuing evidence of the schizophrenic disturbance and the absence of a complete set of active symptoms. Emotional blunting, social withdrawal, eccentric behavior, illogical thinking, and mild loosening of associations are common in the residual type. If delusions or hallucinations are present, they are not prominent and are not accompanied by strong affect. Table 13.3 lists the diagnostic criteria for the schizophrenia subtypes.

13.28 The answer is D (*Synopsis VIII,* pages 1069–1071). *Risperidone* is chemically distinct from all other antipsychotics. In addition to its significant affinity for the dopamine (D_2) receptors, risperidone is a potent antagonist of serotonin type 2 ($5\text{-}HT_2$) receptors. Drugs of this class are referred to as serotonin-dopamine antagonists (SDAs). In addition to risperidone, this group includes clozapine, olanzapine, sertindole, quetiapine, and ziprasidone.

13.29 The answer is E (*Synopsis VIII,* page 1035). *Adding an antidepressant* may increase the levels of the antipsychotics within the patient, leading to a worsening of neuroleptic-induced parkinsonism. For this reason, drug interactions have to be carefully monitored.

13.30 The answer is E (*Synopsis VIII,* pages 480–481). The items listed (A to E) are components of the mental status examination. This schizophrenic patient exhibits a *disorder of thought,* specifically, a disorder of thought content. Often observed in schizophrenia, disorders of thought are divided into disorders of thought content, thought form, and thought process. Disorders of *thought content* reflect the patient's ideas, beliefs, and interpretations of stimuli. Delusions are the most obvious examples of a disorder of thought content. Patients (such as the patient in this example) may have an intense and consuming preoccupation with esoteric, abstract, symbolic, psychological, or philosophical ideas (as reflected in the patient's drawing). Disorders of *thought form* are objectively observable in patient's spoken and written language; they may include looseness of associations, derailment, incoherence, tangentiality, circumstantiality, and word salad. Disorders in *thought process* concern the way ideas and language are formulated; they may include flight ideas, thought blocking, perseveration, and impaired attention.

Disorders of *perception* include hallucinations (auditory, visual, olfactory, tactile, gustatory), illusions, feelings of unreality, déjà vu, and hypnopompic or hypnagogic experiences.

Judgment refers to the ability to understand relationships between facts and to draw conclusions. For example, does the patient understand the likely outcome of his or her behavior, and is he or she influenced by that understanding?

Affect may be defined as the patient's present emotional responsiveness. Affect is what the examiner infers from the patient's facial expression, and it may or may not be congruent with mood. Affect is described as being within normal range, constricted, blunted, or flat.

Table 13.3
DSM-IV Diagnostic Criteria for Schizophrenia Subtypes

Paranoid type
A type of schizophrenia in which the following criteria are met:

A. Preoccupation with one or more delusions or frequent auditory hallucinations.
B. None of the following is prominent: disorganized speech, disorganized or catatonic behavior, or flat or inappropriate affect or catatonic behavior.

Disorganized type
A type of schizophrenia in which the following criteria are met:

A. All of the following are prominent:
   (1) disorganized speech
   (2) disorganized behavior
   (3) flat or inappropriate affect
B. The criteria are not met for catatonic type.

Catatonic type
A type of schizophrenia in which the clinical picture is dominated by at least two of the following:

(1) motoric immobility as evidenced by catalepsy (including waxy flexibility) or stupor
(2) excessive motor activity (that is apparently purposeless and not influenced by external stimuli)
(3) extreme negativism (an apparently motiveless resistance to all instructions or maintenance of a rigid posture against attempts to be moved) or mutism
(4) peculiarities of voluntary movement as evidenced by posturing (voluntary assumption of inappropriate or bizarre postures), stereotyped movements, prominent mannerisms, or prominent grimacing
(5) echolalia or echopraxia

Undifferentiated type
A type of schizophrenia in which symptoms that meet criterion A are present, but the criteria are not met for the paranoid, catatonic, or disorganized type.

Residual type
A type of schizophrenia in which the following criteria are met:

A. Absence of prominent delusions, hallucinations, disorganized speech, and grossly disorganized or catatonic behavior.
B. There is continuing evidence of the disturbance, as indicated by the presence of negative symptoms or two or more symptoms listed in criterion A for schizophrenia, present in an attenuated form (eg, odd beliefs, unusual perceptual experiences).

Reprinted with permission from American Psychiatric Association: *Diagnostic and Statistical Manual of Mental Disorders,* ed. 4, Copyright, American Psychiatric Association, Washington, 1994.

13.31 The answer is E (*Synopsis VIII,* pages 462–463). Magnetic resonance imaging (MRI) studies have consistently shown that the brains of schizophrenic patients have lateral and third ventricular enlargement and some degree of reduction in cortical volume, as shown in *Panel 1B.* Those findings can be interpreted as consistent with the presence of less than usual brain tissue in affected patients; whether that decrease is due to abnormal development or to degeneration remains undetermined.

However, the abnormalities reported in MRI studies of schizophrenic patients have also been reported in other neuropsychiatric conditions, including mood disorders, alcohol-related disorders, and dementias. Thus, those changes are not likely to be pathognomonic for the pathological processes underlying schizophrenia. Although the enlarged ventricles in schizophrenic patients can be shown when groups of patients and controls are used, the difference between affected and unaffected persons is variable and usually small.

One of the most important MRI studies examined monozygotic twins who were discordant with schizophrenia. The study found that virtually all of the affected twins had larger cerebral ventricles than did the nonaffected twins, although most of the affected twins had cerebral ventricles within a normal range.

13.32 The answer is C (*Synopsis VIII,* pages 479–480).
The patient shown in Figure 13.1 is suffering from schizophrenia. The patient's stony facial expression and mobility (waxy flexibility) are characteristic of the catatonic subtype of schizophrenia. The classic feature of the catatonic schizophrenic is a *marked disturbance in motor function,* which may involve stupor, negativism, rigidity, or posturing. *Mutism* is particularly common in these patients. The clinical picture of the catatonic type of schizophrenia may also include *echolalia,* the involuntary repetition of a word or sentence just spoken by another person, and *echopraxia,* the involuntary imitation of movements made by another.

The DSM-IV subtypes of schizophrenia, which include the paranoid, disorganized, catatonic, undifferentiated, and residual subtypes, are not closely correlated with differentiations of prognosis. Such differentiations can best be done by looking at specific predictors of prognosis. *Among the predictors, a history of young onset and the absence of precipitating factors are both associated with a poor prognosis.*

Table 13.4
Kurt Schnedier's Diagnostic Criteria for Schizophrenia

1. First-rank symptoms
   a. Audible thoughts
   b. Voices arguing or discussing or both
   c. Voices commenting
   d. Somatic passivity experiences
   e. Thought withdrawal and other experiences of influenced thought
   f. Thought broadcasting
   g. Delusional perceptions
   h. All other experiences involving volition, made affects, and made impulses
2. Second-rank symptoms
   a. Other disorders of perception
   b. Sudden delusional ideas
   c. Perplexity
   d. Depressive and euphoric mood changes
   e. Feelings of emotional impoverishment
   f. "... and several others as well"

Answers 13.33–13.37

13.33 The answer is B (*Synopsis VIII,* page 456).

13.34 The answer is A (*Synopsis VIII,* page 456).

13.35 The answer is C (*Synopsis VIII,* page 456).

13.36 The answer is D (*Synopsis VIII,* page 456).

13.37 The answer is E (*Synopsis VIII,* page 456–457).
Key people in the history of schizophrenia include *Eugen Bleuler* (Swiss, 1857–1939), who coined the term *schizophrenia; Benedict Morel* (French, 1809–1873), who used the term *démence précoce* for deteriorated patients whose illnesses began in adolescence; *Karl Kahlbaum* (German, 1828–1899), who described symptoms of *catatonia; Ewald Hecker* (German, 1843–1909), who wrote about the extremely bizarre behavior of *hebephrenia,* and *Gabriel Langfeldt* (Norwegian, 1895–1900), who distinguished two groups of schizophrenias—process (nuclear) schizophrenia and the *schizophreniform psychosis.* Process schizophrenia has an insidious onset and a deteriorating course; schizophreniform psychosis has typical schizophrenic characteristics, but the patient has a relatively well-integrated premorbid personality with a sudden onset of illness and a good prognosis.

Answers 13.38–13.41

13.38 The answer is B (*Synopsis VIII,* page 456).

13.39 The answer is B (*Synopsis VIII,* page 456).

13.40 The answer is A (*Synopsis VIII,* page 456).

13.41 The answer is A (*Synopsis VIII,* pages 456–457).
Emil Kraepelin (1856–1926) *latinized the term* démence précoce *to dementia precox,* a term that emphasized a distinct cognitive process (dementia) and the early onset (precox) that is characteristic of the disorder. Kraepelin *classified patients as being afflicted with manic-depressive psychoses, dementia precox, or paranoia.*

Eugen Bleuler (1857–1939) *coined the term "schizophrenia"* and *described the four As of schizophrenia: Associations* are loose; ideas have *autistic* qualities with meanings only the patient can understand; *affect* is restricted or flat; and the patient has conscious *ambivalent* feelings about almost everything.

Answers 13.42–13.46

13.42 The answer is C (*Synopsis VIII,* pages 469, 483).

13.43 The answer is B (*Synopsis VIII,* page 483).

13.44 The answer is A (*Synopsis VIII,* page 483).

13.45 The answer is D (*Synopsis VIII,* page 483).

13.46 The answer is E (*Synopsis VIII,* page 483).
Incoherence results from the use of *empty or obscure language.* A *neologism* is a *new expression or word. Mutism* is the *functional inhibition of speech. Echolalia* is the *repeating of the same words the questioner has used. Verbigeration* is the *senseless repetition of the same words or phrases.* It may go on for days.

Answers 13.47–13.52

13.47 The answer is B (*Synopsis VIII,* pages 457, 476).

13.48 The answer is B (*Synopsis VIII,* pages 457, 476).

13.49 The answer is A (*Synopsis VIII,* pages 457, 476).

13.50 The answer is A (*Synopsis VIII,* pages 457, 476).

13.51 The answer is A (*Synopsis VIII,* pages 457, 476).

13.52 The answer is A (*Synopsis VIII,* pages 457, 476).
Kurt Schneider (1887–1967) described a number of *first-rank symptoms* of schizophrenia that are considered of pragmatic

value in making the diagnosis of schizophrenia, although they are not specific to the disease. The symptoms include *audible thoughts,* hearing one's thoughts aloud; *voices* or auditory hallucinations *commenting* on the patient's behavior; *thought withdrawal,* the removal of the patient's thoughts by others; and *the experience of having one's thoughts controlled.* Schneider pointed out that schizophrenia can be diagnosed by *second rank symptoms* when accompanied by a typical clinical presentation. Second-rank symptoms include *sudden delusional ideas, perplexity,* and feelings of emotional impoverishment. Schneider's diagnostic criteria for schizophrenia are listed in Table 13.4.

14

Other Psychotic Disorders

Other psychotic disorders include a variety of conditions, such as schizophreniform disorder, schizoaffective disorder, delusional disorder, brief psychotic disorder, and shared psychotic disorder. These disorders are classified in the fourth edition of *Diagnostic and Statistical Manual of Mental Disorders* (DSM-IV) as psychotic disorders that do not meet the diagnostic criteria for schizophrenia or for mood disorders with psychotic features. The disorders are diverse and wide ranging; their main common factor is the presence of psychotic symptoms, which arise from many causes.

Postpartum psychosis is included in this group, and doctors should be familiar with its serious potential. In postpartum psychosis, new mothers undergo depression and delusions and may have thoughts of harming their infants or themselves.

Among the other disorders in this classification, schizophreniform disorder is similar to schizophrenia except for the shorter duration of symptoms, which are present for at least 1 but less than 6 months. Schizoaffective disorder, by contrast, shows symptoms of both schizophrenia and a mood disorder. In delusional disorder, a patient has nonbizarre delusions, no hallucinations, and a generally intact personality. Brief psychotic disorder has symptoms similar to schizophrenia but lasts at least 1 day and less than 1 month. In shared psychotic disorder, often called *folie à deux,* a person closely attached to another person with an established delusion develops a similar delusion.

Students should read Chapter 14 in Kaplan and Sadock's *Synopsis VIII* and test their knowledge with the following questions and answers.

HELPFUL HINTS

Students should know the psychotic syndromes and other terms listed here.

- age of onset
- amok
- antipsychotic drugs:
  - clozapine
  - dopamine receptor antagonists
- Arctic hysteria
- atypical psychoses
- autoscopic psychosis
- *bouffée délirante*
- brief psychotic disorder
- Norman Cameron
- Capgras's syndrome
- Clérambault's syndrome
- Cotard's syndrome
- course
- culture-bound syndromes
- Cushing's syndrome
- delusional disorder
- delusions
- denial
- differential diagnosis
- double insanity
- EEG and CT scan
- erotomania
- family studies
- *folie à deux*
- Fregoli's syndrome
- Ganser's syndrome
- good-prognosis schizophrenia
- homicide
- ICD-10
- incidence
- inclusion and exclusion criteria
- koro
- Gabriel Langfeldt
- lifetime prevalence
- limbic system and basal ganglia
- lithium
- lycanthropy
- marital status
- mental status examination
- neuroendocrine function
- neurological conditions
- neuropsychological testing
- nihilistic delusion
- paranoia
- paranoid pseudocommunity
- paranoid states
- paraphrenia
- passive person and dominant person
- piblokto
- postpartum blues
- postpartum psychosis
- prognostic variables
- projection
- psychodynamic formulation
- psychosis of association
- psychotherapy
- psychotic disorder not otherwise specified
- reaction formation
- reduplicative paramnesia
- schizoaffective disorder
- schizophreniform disorder
- Daniel Paul Schreber
- SES
- shared psychotic disorder
- significant stressor
- suicidal incidence
- *suk-yeong*
- TRH stimulation test
- wihtigo psychosis

▲ QUESTIONS

DIRECTIONS: For each of the three numbered statements below, choose the most appropriate response from the following five lettered terms.

A. Koro
B. Amok
C. *Boufée délirante*
D. Schizoaffective disorder
E. Schizophreniform disorder

14.1 It occurs mainly in China.
14.2 Symptoms last less than 3 months.
14.3 Symptoms last at least 1 month but less than 6 months.

DIRECTIONS: Each of the questions or incomplete statement below is followed by five suggested responses or completions. Select the *one* that is *best* in each case.

14.4 Hallucinations in a patient with a substance-induced psychotic disorder can take all of the following forms. Which are least likely to occur?

A. Religious songs
B. Bugs crawling on the skin
C. Noxious or unpleasant odors
D. Scenes of tiny human figures
E. Voices telling the patient to commit suicide

14.5 Which of the following statements best describes a clinical feature of postpartum depression?

A. Patient is hysterical.
B. Patient has insomnia.
C. Patient claims to feel healthy.
D. Patient wants to leave hospital.
E. Patient's beginning to nurse causes symptoms.

14.6 Which of the following choices does *not* correctly describe a type of delusional behavior?

A. Mixed
B. Somatic
C. Atypical
D. Grandiose
E. Unspecified

14.7 Erotomania, the delusional disorder in which the person makes repeated efforts to contact the object of the delusion, through letter, phone call, and stalking, is also referred to as

A. Cotard's syndrome
B. Clérambault's syndrome
C. Fregoli's syndrome
D. Ganser's syndrome
E. Capgras's syndrome

14.8 A successful 34-year-old interior designer was brought to a clinic by her 37-year-old husband, an attorney. The husband lamented that for the past 3 years his wife had made increasingly shrill accusations that he was unfaithful to her. He declared that he had done everything in his power to convince her of his innocence, but there was no shaking her conviction. An examination of the facts revealed no evidence that the man had been unfaithful. When his wife was asked what her evidence was, she became vague and mysterious, declaring that she could tell such things by a far-away look in his eyes.

The patient experienced no hallucinations; her speech was well-organized; she interpreted proverbs with no difficulty; she seemed to have a good command of current events and generally displayed no difficulty in thinking, aside from her conviction of her husband's infidelity. She described herself as having a generally full life, with a few close friends and no problems except those centering on her experiences of unhappiness in the marriage. The husband reported that his wife was respected for her skills but that she had had difficulties for most of her life in close relationships with friends. She had lost a number of friends because of her apparent intolerance of differences in opinion. The patient reported that she did not want to leave the marriage, nor did she want her husband to leave her; instead, she was furious about his "injustice" and demanded that it be confessed and redeemed.

The patient's condition is best diagnosed as

A. schizophrenia, paranoid type
B. delusional disorder, jealous type
C. schizophreniform disorder
D. schizoaffective disorder, depressive type
E. delusional disorder, persecutory type

14.9 Delusional disorder

A. involves bizarre delusions
B. has a prevalence in the United States of 5 percent
C. may lead to the development of a pseudocommunity
D. has a mean age of onset in the early 20s
E. of the somatic type is the most common

14.10 Schizoaffective disorder patients

A. tend to have a deteriorating course
B. do not usually respond to lithium
C. may exhibit symptoms of schizophrenia and a mood disorder in an alternating fashion
D. tend to have a worse prognosis than do patients with schizophrenia
E. have a suicide rate of at least 50 percent

14.11 Ms. B. was a 43-year-old married woman who entered the hospital in 1968 with a chief complaint of being concerned about her sex problem; she stated that she needed hypnotism to find out what was wrong with her sexual drive. Her husband supplied the history; he complained that she had had many extramarital affairs, with many different men, throughout their married life. He insisted that in one 2-week period she had had as many as 100 sexual experiences with men outside the marriage. The patient agreed with that assessment of her behavior but would not speak of the experiences, saying that she blocked the memories out. She denied any particular interest in sexuality but said that apparently she felt a compulsive drive to go out and seek activity despite her lack of interest.

The patient had been married to her husband for more than 20 years. He was clearly the dominant partner in the marriage. The patient was fearful of his frequent jealous rages, and apparently it was he who suggested that she enter the hospital to receive hypnotherapy. The patient maintained that she could not explain why she sought out other men, that she really did not want to do it. Her husband stated that on occasion he had tracked her down, and when he found her, she acted as though she did not know him. She confirmed that statement and said she believed it was because the episodes of her sexual promiscuity were blotted out by amnesia.

When the examining physician indicated that he questioned the reality of the woman's sexual adventures, her husband became furious and accused the physician and a ward attendant of having sexual relations with his wife.

Neither an amobarbital (Amytal) interview nor considerable psychotherapy with the wife was able to clear the blocked-out memory of periods of sexual activities. The patient did admit to a memory of having had two extramarital relationships in the past, one 20 years before her admission to the hospital and the other just a year before her admission. She stated that the last one had actually been planned by her husband and that he was in the same house at the time. She continued to believe that she had actually had countless extramarital sexual experiences, although she remembered only two of them.

On the basis of the woman's history, the most likely diagnosis is

A. amnestic disorder
B. dissociative amnesia
C. schizophrenia
D. shared psychotic disorder
E. brief psychotic disorder

14.12 A 45-year-old single woman was taken to the hospital by her parents. Over the preceding year, the patient had begun to believe that her parents and state government officials were involved in a plan to get her to give away a piece of land she owned in the country. She began accusing the officials of putting substances in her food that damaged her hair and caused her to have receding gums. She wrote numerous letters to federal officials complaining of those events, yet all the while she worked efficiently at her job of examining income tax forms. She had had no previous contact with mental health professionals. The mental status examination revealed no hallucinations, incoherence, or loosening of associations.

The most likely diagnosis is

A. schizophrenia, paranoid type
B. schizophreniform disorder
C. delusional disorder
D. a mood disorder with psychotic features
E. paranoid personality disorder

14.13 True statements concerning brief psychotic disorder include all the following *except*

A. The stressor must be of sufficient severity to cause significant stress to any person in the same socioeconomic and cultural class.
B. Many patients also have preexisting personality disorders.
C. Prodromal symptoms appear before the onset of the precipitating stressor.
D. Mood disorders may be common in the relatives of affected probands.
E. Good prognostic features include a severe precipitating stressor, acute onset, and confusion or perplexity during psychosis.

14.14 Which of the following statements applies to schizoaffective disorders?

A. The patient does not present with a mixture of psychotic and mood disorder features.
B. Mood-congruent delusions and hallucinations are part of the clinical picture.
C. The diagnosis can be made if the patient is suffering from a cognitive disorder.
D. Delusions of control and auditory hallucinations are common features.
E. All of the above statements are true.

14.15 The major treatment methods used for schizoaffective disorder are all the following *except*

A. psychoanalysis
B. antipsychotic agents
C. tricyclic drugs
D. antimanic drugs
E. electroconvulsive therapy

14.16 Which of the following combinations best characterizes the occurrence of mental disorders among the relatives of patients with schizoaffective disorder?

A. A frequency of schizophrenia comparable to that seen among the relatives of schizophrenic patients and a frequency of mood disorders greater than that expected for the general population
B. A frequency of schizophrenia less than that seen in the general population and a frequency of mood disorders greater than that expected for the relatives of patients with mood disorders
C. A frequency of schizoaffective disorder greater than that seen in the general population and a frequency of mood disorders less than that seen among the relatives of patients with mood disorders
D. A frequency of schizophrenia less than that seen in the relatives of schizophrenic patients and a frequency of mood disorders comparable to that seen in the relatives of patients with mood disorders
E. A frequency of schizoaffective disorder comparable with that of the general population and a frequency of schizophrenia greater than that of the general population

14.17 The main defense mechanism used in shared psychotic disorder is

A. projection
B. regression
C. reaction formation
D. displacement
E. identification with the aggressor

14.18 Most studies of normal pregnant women indicate that the percentage who report the ''blues'' in the early postpartum period is about

A. 10 percent
B. 25 percent
C. 50 percent
D. 75 percent
E. 100 percent

14.19 All of the following are true statements about postpartum psychosis *except*

A. The risk is increased if the patient had a recent mood disorder.
B. Hallucinations involve voices telling the patient to kill her baby.
C. It is found in 1 to 2 per 1,000 deliveries.
D. Symptoms generally last up to 12 weeks after delivery.
E. Delusional material may involve the idea that the baby is dead.

14.20 In schizoaffective disorder, all of the following variables indicate a poor prognosis *except*

A. depressive type
B. no precipitating factor
C. a predominance of psychotic symptoms
D. bipolar type
E. early onset

14.21 Examples of atypical psychoses include

A. Capgras's syndrome
B. Cotard's syndrome
C. postpartum psychosis
D. koro
E. all of the above

14.22 According to the fourth edition of *Diagnostic and Statistical Manual of Mental Disorders* (DSM-IV), postpartum psychosis is best classified as

A. an anxiety disorder
B. a psychotic disorder not otherwise specified
C. a mood disorder
D. schizophrenia
E. a personality disorder

14.23 True statements concerning the treatment of shared psychotic disorder include all of the following *except*

A. Recovery rates have been reported to be as low as 10 percent.
B. The submissive person commonly requires treatment with antipsychotic drugs.
C. Psychotherapy for nondelusional members of the patient's family should be undertaken.
D. Separation of the submissive person from the dominant person is the primary intervention.
E. The submissive person and the dominant person usually move back together after treatment.

14.24 Shared psychotic disorder occurs most frequently among

A. women
B. low socioeconomic groups
C. the deaf
D. members of the same family
E. all of the above

14.25 Delusional disorder

A. is less common than schizophrenia
B. is caused by frontal lobe lesions
C. is an early stage of schizophrenia
D. usually begins by age 20
E. is more common in men than in women

14.26 The characteristic feature of conjugal paranoia is

A. somatic delusion
B. idea of reference
C. delusion of grandeur
D. delusion of infidelity
E. delusion of persecution

14.27 Which of the following statements is correct?

A. The delusions of schizophrenia, paranoid type, tend to be bizarre and fragmented, in contrast to the better-organized delusions of delusional disorder.
B. In the few patients who have hallucinations in conjunction with delusional disorder, the hallucinations are associated with the delusions, whereas hallucinations in schizophrenia are not necessarily connected with the delusions.
C. In paranoid patients with a depressed affect, the affect is secondary to the delusional system, whereas in depressed patients the delusions are secondary to the depression.
D. Delusions seen in cognitive disorders are characterized by forgetfulness and disorientation, whereas delusional disorder is characterized by intact orientation and memory.
E. All of the above statements are true.

14.28 A 17-year-old high school junior was brought to the emergency room by her distraught mother, who was at a loss to understand her daughter's behavior. Two days earlier, the patient's father had been buried; he had died of a sudden myocardial infarction earlier in the week. The patient had become wildly agitated at the cemetery, screaming uncontrollably and needing to be restrained by relatives. She was inconsolable at home, sat rocking in a corner, and talked about a devil that had come to claim her soul. Before her father's death, her mother reported, she was a "typical teenager, popular, a very good student, but sometimes prone to overreacting." The girl had no previous psychiatric history.

The most likely diagnosis is

A. grief
B. brief psychotic disorder
C. schizophrenia
D. substance intoxication
E. delusional disorder

14.29 Which of the following statements regarding delusional disorder in immigrants is true?

A. The development of delusional disorder is aggravated by the immigrant's appearance and mannerisms.
B. Uncertainty in the new environment tends to increase isolation.
C. The incidence of delusional disorder in immigrants is about 3 times as high as that among native-born American patients.
D. The increased incidence of delusional disorders in immigrants may be due to an increased immigration of persons with unstable personalities.
E. All of the above statements are true.

DIRECTIONS: Each group of questions below consists of lettered headings followed by a list of numbered words or statements. For each numbered word or statement, select the *one* lettered heading that is most closely associated with it. Each lettered heading may be selected once, more than once, or not at all.

Questions 14.30–14.32

A. Schizophreniform disorder
B. Brief psychotic disorder
C. Simple deteriorative disorder

14.30 Schizophrenic symptoms last at least 1 day but no more than 1 month.
14.31 It is characterized as the progressive development of symptoms of social withdrawal and other deficit symptoms of schizophrenia.
14.32 Schizophrenic symptoms last at least 1 month but less than 6 months.

Questions 14.33–14.35

A. Amok
B. Koro
C. Wihtigo

14.33 There is a delusion that the person's penis is shrinking and may disappear.
14.34 Affected persons believe that they may be transformed into a giant monster that eats human flesh.
14.35 In sudden, unprovoked outbursts of wild rage, affected persons attack anything in their path.

Questions 14.36–14.40

A. Delusions of guilt and somatic delusions
B. Delusions secondary to perceptual disturbances
C. Grandiose delusions
D. Bizarre delusions of being controlled
E. Delusions of jealousy and persecution

14.36 Delusional disorder
14.37 Schizophrenia
14.38 Mania
14.39 Depressive disorders
14.40 Cognitive disorders

Questions 14.41–14.45

A. Paranoid personality disorder
B. Delusional disorder
C. Schizophrenia
D. Manic episode
E. Major depressive episode

14.41 Psychomotor retardation
14.42 Thought broadcasting
14.43 Easy distractibility with an elevated, expansive, or irritable mood
14.44 Persecutory or grandiose delusions
14.45 Suspiciousness and mistrust of people

ANSWERS

Other Psychotic Disorders

Answers 14.1–14.3

14.1 The answer is A (*Synopsis VIII,* page 498).

14.2 The answer is C (*Synopsis VIII,* page 522).

14.3 The answer is E (*Synopsis VIII,* pages 504–508).
Koro, which occurs in Southeast Asia and in *China,* is a syndrome in which a patient has the delusion that his penis is shrinking and may disappear into his abdomen and that death may ultimately result. *Amok,* a Malayan word, is the name of a syndrome characterized by sudden, unprovoked outbursts of wild rage. Those affected indiscriminately run about and attack whatever or whoever they encounter. Afterward, the person is exhausted, has forgotten the outburst, and may commit suicide. A syndrome similar to amok is sometimes described in the United States, where it is usually a symptom of schizophrenia, a bipolar disorder, a mood disorder, or a general medical condition.

Bouffée délirante is a French diagnostic term for a disorder similar to schizophrenia but whose *symptoms last less than 3 months.* The diagnosis is similar to that of the DSM-IV category for *schizophreniform disorder,* a disorder like schizophrenia whose *symptoms last at least 1 month but less than 6 months.*

Schizoaffective disorder has elements of schizophrenia and mood disorders.

14.4 The answer is C (*Synopsis VIII,* pages 493–494).
Auditory hallucinations are common in patients with substance-induced psychotic disorders. However, hearing *religious songs* is not a usual occurrence. In alcohol-related hallucinations, for example, *voices telling the patients to commit suicide* often occur, and clinicians should be aware that patients may act on such hallucinations.

Cocaine use can lead to tactile hallucinations, such as feelings of *bugs crawling on the skin.* Visual hallucinations in substance-induced disorders can include *scenes of tiny figures,* human or animal.

Olfactory hallucinations are not uncommon in temporal lobe epilepsy, but hallucinations of *noxious or unpleasant odors* do not usually occur in patients with a substance-induced psychotic disorder.

14.5 The answer is B (*Synopsis VIII,* pages 500–501).
The clinical features of postpartum depression include complaints of fatigue, *insomnia,* and restlessness, with periods of tearfulness, but *patients* are not *hysterical.* These symptoms begin within days of delivery but can appear as late as within 8 weeks of delivery; *a patient's beginning to nurse* does not *bring on symptoms.*

After the initial symptoms, patients may experience suspiciousness and confusion and may show irrational concern about their infants' health. A patient might feel unwilling to take care of the baby and may even want to harm the baby as well as herself. *Patients* do not *claim to feel healthy* and generally do not *want to leave hospital.*

14.6 The answer is C (*Synopsis VIII,* pages 512–517).
Atypical does not refer to a type of delusional behavior, which is classified into specific categories. *Somatic, grandiose,* and *nihilistic* do, however, refer to types of delusional behavior, which are based on the prominent delusional theme. Persecutory delusions are the most common type, followed by grandiose.

14.7 The answer is B (*Synopsis VIII,* page 517)
Erotomania, the delusional disorder in which the person makes repeated efforts to contact the object of the delusion, through letters, phone calls, gifts, visits, surveillance, and even stalking, is also called *Clérambault's syndrome.* Most patients with erotomania are women. In forensic samples in which harm is done to another person, most are men. In *Cotard's syndrome,* patients may believe that they have lost everything: possessions, strength, and even bodily organs. *Fregoli's syndrome* is the delusion that a persecutor is taking on a variety of faces, like an actor. *Ganser's syndrome* is the voluntary production of severe psychiatric symptoms, sometimes described as the giving of approximate answers. *Capgras's syndrome* is the delusion that familiar people have been replaced by identical impostors.

14.8 The answer is B (*Synopsis VIII,* page 517).
The patient's condition is best diagnosed as *delusional disorder, jealous type* (Table 14.1). Although not all complaints of infidelity are unfounded, in this case the evidence supported the idea that the wife's jealousy was delusional. Delusional jealousy may be seen in schizophrenia, but in the absence of the characteristic psychotic symptoms of schizophrenia, such as bizarre delusions, hallucinations, and disorganized speech, it is a symptom of delusional disorder. As is commonly the case in delusional disorder, the woman's impairment because of her delusion did not affect her daily functioning apart from her relationship with her husband.

The patient's condition cannot be diagnosed as *schizophrenia, paranoid type,* because of the absence of the characteristic psychotic symptoms of schizophrenia, such as bizarre delusions and hallucinations. Furthermore, the woman showed no evidence since the onset of the disturbance of a deterioration of functioning in the areas of work, self-care, and other interpersonal relationships not involved in the delusion. A person with *schizophreniform disorder* (Table 14.2) has symptoms identical to those of schizophrenia except that the symptoms last at least 1 month but less than 6 months; in schizophrenia, the symptoms must be present for at least 6 months. The patient's condition cannot be diagnosed as *schizoaffective disorder, depressive type* (Table 14.3) because she showed no evidence of schizophrenia or a major depressive episode. In *delusional disorder, persecutory type,* the delusion usually involves a single theme or a series of connected themes, such as being conspired against, cheated, spied on, followed, poisoned or drugged, maliciously maligned, harassed, or obstructed in the pursuit of long-term goals. The patient in this question did not have such a delusion.

14.9 The answer is C (*Synopsis VIII,* page 514).
Delusional disorder *may lead to the development of a pseudocommunity.* Elaboration of the delusion to include imagined

Table 14.1
DSM-IV Diagnostic Criteria for Delusional Disorder

A. Nonbizarre delusions (ie, involving situations that occur in real life, such as being followed, poisoned, infected, loved at a distance, or deceived by one's spouse or lover, or having a disease) of at least 1 month's duration.

B. Criterion A for schizophrenia has never been met. **Note:** Tactile and olfactory hallucinations may be present in delusional disorder if they are related to the delusional theme.

C. Apart from the impact of the delusion(s) or its ramifications, functioning is not markedly impaired and behavior is not obviously odd or bizarre.

D. If mood episodes have occurred concurrently with delusions, their total duration has been brief relative to the duration of the delusional periods.

E. The disturbance is not due to the direct physiological effects of a substance (eg, a drug of abuse, a medication) or a general medical condition.

Specify type (the following types are assigned based on the predominant delusional theme):

Erotomanic type: delusions that another person, usually of higher status, is in love with the individual
Grandiose type: delusions of inflated worth, power, knowledge, identity, or special relationship to a deity or famous person
Jealous type: delusions that the individual's sexual partner is unfaithful
Persecutory type: delusions that the person (or someone to whom the person is close) is being malevolently treated in some way
Somatic type: delusions that the person has some physical defect or general medical condition
Mixed type: delusions characteristic of more than one of the above types but no one theme predominates.
Unspecified type

Reprinted with permission from American Psychiatric Association: *Diagnostic and Statistical Manual of Mental Disorders,* ed 4. Copyright, American Psychiatric Association, Washington, 1994.

persons and the attribution of malevolent motivations to both real and imagined people results in the organization of the pseudocommunity—that is, a perceived community of plotters. That delusional entity hypothetically binds together projected fears and wishes to justify the patient's aggression and to provide a tangible target for the patient's hostilities.

Delusional disorder, unlike schizophrenia, does not involve bizarre delusions that are impossible. For example, patients with delusional disorder may feel that they are being followed by the Federal Bureau of Investigation, which is possible; schizophrenia patients may feel that they are being controlled by Martians, which is impossible.

Delusional disorder has a prevalence *in the United States of 0.025 to 0.03 percent.* Thus, delusional disorder is much rarer than schizophrenia, which has a prevalence of about 1 percent, and the mood disorders, which have a prevalence of about 5 percent. Many persons with delusional beliefs do not talk about them, so the prevalence may be higher.

Delusional disorder *has a mean age of onset of about 40 years,* but the range for the age of onset runs from 18 to the 90s. Delusional disorder *of the somatic type is not the most common.* The persecutory type is the most common.

Table 14.2
DSM-IV Diagnostic Criteria for Schizophreniform Disorder

A. Criteria A, D, and E of schizophrenia are met.

B. An episode of the disorder (including prodromal, active, and residual phases) lasts at least 1 month but less than 6 months. (When the diagnosis must be made without waiting for recovery, it should be qualified as "provisional.")

Specify if:

Without good prognostic features
With good prognostic features as evidenced by two (or more) of the following:
(1) onset of prominent psychotic symptoms within 4 weeks of the first noticeable change in usual behavior or functioning
(2) confusion or perplexity at the height of the psychotic episode
(3) good premorbid social and occupational functioning
(4) absence of blunted or flat affect

Reprinted with permission from American Psychiatric Association: *Diagnostic and Statistical Manual of Mental Disorders,* ed 4. Copyright, American Psychiatric Association, Washington, 1994.

14.10 The answer is C (*Synopsis VIII,* pages 508–512).
Schizoaffective disorder patients *may exhibit symptoms of schizophrenia and a mood disorder in an alternating fashion.* As a group, schizoaffective disorder patients *tend to have a nondeteriorating course* and *usually respond to lithium.* Also as a group, schizoaffective disorder patients tend to *have a better prognosis than do patients with schizophrenia* and a worse prognosis than do patients with mood disorders. Schizoaffective disorder patients *have a suicide rate of 10 percent, not 50 percent.*

14.11 The answer is D (*Synopsis VIII,* pages 496–497).
The most likely diagnosis in the case of the 43-year-old

Table 14.3
DSM-IV Diagnostic Criteria for Schizoaffective Disorder

A. An uninterrupted period of illness during which, at some time, there is either a major depressive episode, a manic episode, or a mixed episode concurrent with symptoms that meet criterion A for schizophrenia.
Note: The major depressive episode must include criterion A1: depressed mood.

B. During the same period of illness, there have been delusions or hallucinations for at least 2 weeks in the absence of prominent mood symptoms.

C. Symptoms that meet criteria for a mood episode are present for a substantial portion of the total duration of the active and residual periods of the illness.

D. The disturbance is not due to the direct physiological effects of a substance (eg, a drug of abuse, a medication) or a general medical condition.

Specify type:

Bipolar type: if the disturbance includes a manic or a mixed episode (or a manic or a mixed episode and major depressive episodes)
Depressive type: if the disturbance only includes major depressive episodes

Reprinted with permission from American Psychiatric Association: *Diagnostic and Statistical Manual of Mental Disorders,* ed 4. Copyright, American Psychiatric Association, Washington, 1994.

woman is *shared psychotic disorder* (Table 14.4). This disorder occurs when the delusional system of the patient has developed out of a close relationship with another person who has a previously established delusion. The disorder has been popularly known as *folie à deux*. Shared psychotic disorder is characterized by a passive person who absorbs the more dominant person's delusion. The delusion is often something in the realm of possibility, not as bizarre as the delusions often seen in schizophrenia.

In the case described, one's first impression is that an *amnestic disorder* or *dissociative amnesia* should be considered. However, the woman was not suffering from a lack of memory of events as much as the husband was suffering from persecutory delusions that his wife was unfaithful, and his wife had accepted that delusion. She adopted his persecutory delusion and did not really have any kind of amnesia. She showed none of the essential features of *schizophrenia* (bizarre delusions, hallucinations, or incoherence), and the essential criteria for *brief psychotic disorder* (the sudden onset of a florid psychosis immediately after a significant psychosocial stressor and lasting less than 1 month) were not present.

Table 14.4
DSM-IV Diagnostic Criteria for Shared Psychotic Disorder

A. A delusion develops in an individual in the context of a close relationship with another person(s), who has an already established delusion.
B. The delusion is similar in content to that of the person who already has the established delusion.
C. The disturbance is not better accounted for by another psychotic disorder (eg, schizophrenia) or a mood disorder with psychotic features and is not due to the direct physiological effects of a substance (eg, a drug of abuse, a medication) or a general medical condition.

Reprinted with permission from American Psychiatric Association: *Diagnostic and Statistical Manual of Mental Disorders,* ed 4. Copyright, American Psychiatric Association, Washington, 1994.

14.12 The answer is C (*Synopsis VIII,* pages 512–517).
On the basis of the information given, the most likely diagnosis in the case described is *delusional disorder.* The central features are the nonbizarre delusions involving situations that occur in real life—such as being followed, poisoned, and deceived—of at least 1 month's duration. The age of onset for delusional disorder is usually between 40 and 55. Intellectual and occupational functioning is usually satisfactory, whereas social and marital functioning is often impaired. The diagnosis is made only when no organic factor can be found that has initiated or maintained the disorder.

By definition, delusional disorder patients do not have prominent or sustained hallucinations, and the nonbizarre quality of the delusions cited—for example, substances put in her food—rule out *schizophrenia, paranoid type,* and *schizophreniform disorder.* In addition, as compared with schizophrenia, delusional disorder usually produces less impairment in daily functioning. Another consideration in the diagnostic criteria of schizophreniform disorder is the specification that the episode lasts less than 6 months (the patient described had symptoms over 1 year). The differential diagnosis with *mood disorders with psychotic features* can be difficult, as the psychotic features associated with mood disorders often involve nonbizarre delusions, and prominent hallucinations are unusual. The differential diagnosis depends on the relation of the mood disturbance and the delusions. In a major depression with psychotic features, the onset of the depressed mood usually antedates the appearance of psychosis and is present after the psychosis remits. Also, the depressive symptoms are usually prominent and severe. If depressive symptoms occur in delusional disorder, they occur after the onset of the delusions, are usually mild, and often remit while the delusional symptoms persist. In *paranoid personality disorder* there are no delusions, although there is suspiciousness and mistrust.

14.13 The answer is C (*Synopsis VIII,* pages 520–522).
No prodromal symptoms appear before the onset of the precipitating stressor in brief psychotic disorder. A significant stressor may be a causative factor for brief psychotic disorder, and *the stressor must be of sufficient severity to cause significant stress to any person in the same socioeconomic and cultural class.* However, *many patients also have preexisting personality disorders.* Although schizophrenia has not been found to be common in the relatives of persons with brief psychotic disorder, *mood disorders may be common in the relatives of affected probands. Good prognostic features include a severe precipitating stressor, acute onset, and confusion or perplexity during the psychosis.* Table 14.5 lists the diagnostic criteria for brief psychotic disorder.

14.14 The answer is B (*Synopsis VIII,* pages 508–512).
In schizoaffective disorder, *delusions and hallucinations are part of the clinical feature, and their content is congruent with the mood,* not mood incongruent. *The patient presents with a mixture of psychotic and mood disorder features.* The diagnosis of schizoaffective disorder *should not be made if the patient is suffering from a cognitive disorder.* Psychotic symptoms are common in schizoaffective disorders. In general, if mood-incongruent delusions and *auditory hallucinations* occur, that suggests schizophrenia.

14.15 The answer is A (*Synopsis VIII,* pages 508–512).
Since schizoaffective disorder includes (Table 14.3) psychotic symptoms that are part of the criterion list for schizophrenia, it follows that *psychoanalysis,* which is not effective in psychotic disorders, is not the treatment of choice. Rather, psychopharmacological or biological treatments are indicated, perhaps ideally in conjunction with some form of supportive psychotherapy.

Most patients with schizoaffective disorder require hospitalization because of their psychotic and mood disorder features or their risk for suicide. *Antipsychotic agents* (such as the phenothiazines and butyrophenones), *tricyclic drugs, antimanic drugs* (such as lithium [Eskalith]), and *electroconvulsive therapy* (ECT) are the major treatment methods used.

14.16 The answer is D (*Synopsis VIII,* pages 508–512).
The occurrence of mental disorders among the relatives of patients with schizoaffective disorder includes an increased risk of schizoaffective disorder, *a frequency of schizophrenia less than that seen in the relatives of schizophrenic patients, and a frequency of mood disorders comparable with that seen in the relatives of patients with mood disorders* but greater than

Table 14.5 DSM-IV Diagnostic Criteria for Brief Psychotic Disorder

A. Presence of one (or more) of the following symptoms:
   (1) delusions
   (2) hallucinations
   (3) disorganized speech (eg, frequent derailment or incoherence)
   (4) grossly disorganized or catatonic behavior

   Note: Do not include a symptom if it is a culturally sanctioned response pattern.

B. Duration of an episode of the disturbance is at least 1 day but less than 1 month, with eventual full return to premorbid level of functioning.

C. The disturbance is not better accounted for by a mood disorder with psychotic features, schizoaffective disorder, or schizophrenia and is not due to the direct physiological effects of a substance (eg, a drug of abuse, a medication) or a general medical condition.

Specify if:

With marked stressor(s) (brief reactive psychosis): if symptoms occur shortly after and apparently in response to events that, singly or together, would be markedly stressful to almost anyone in similar circumstances in the person's culture

Without marked stressor(s): if pscyhotic symptoms do not occur shortly after, or are not apparently in response to events that, singly or together, would be markedly stressful to almost anyone in similar circumstances in the person's culture

With postpartum onset: if onset within 4 weeks postpartum

Reprinted with permission from American Psychiatric Association: *Diagnostic and Statistical Manual of Mental Disorders,* ed 4. Copyright, American Psychiatric Association, Washington, 1994.

Table 14.6 DSM-IV Diagnostic Criteria for Psychotic Disorder Not Otherwise Specified

This category includes psychotic symptomatology (ie, delusions, hallucinations, disorganized speech, grossly disorganized or catatonic behavior) about which there is inadequate information to make a specific diagnosis or about which there is contradictory information, or disorders with psychotic symptoms that do not meet the criteria for any specific psychotic disorder.

Examples include:

1. Postpartum psychosis that does not meet criteria for mood disorder with psychotic features, brief psychotic disorder, psychotic disorder due to a general medical condition, or substance-induced psychotic disorder
2. Psychotic symptoms that have lasted for less than 1 month but that have not yet remitted, so that the criteria for brief psychotic disorder are not met
3. Persistent auditory hallucinations in the absence of any other features
4. Persistent nonbizarre delusions with periods of overlapping mood episodes that have been present for a substantial portion of the delusional disturbance
5. Situations in which the clinician has concluded that a psychotic disorder is present, but is unable to determine whether it is primary, due to a general medical condition, or substance induced

Reprinted with permission from American Psychiatric Association: *Diagnostic and Statistical Manual of Mental Disorders,* ed 4. Copyright, American Psychiatric Association, Washington, 1994.

that expected for the general population. In fact, most of the ill relatives of patients with schizoaffective disorders suffer from uncomplicated mood disorders.

14.17 The answer is E (*Synopsis VIII,* pages 496–497).
The main defense mechanism used in shared psychotic disorder is *identification with the aggressor.* The aggressor is the dominant member of the two persons who share the psychosis. The initiator of the psychosis is usually the sicker of the two, often a person with schizophrenia, paranoid type, on whom the other person is dependent. Identification with the aggressor is an unconscious process by which persons incorporate within themselves the mental image of a person who represents a source of frustration in the outside world. A primitive defense, it operates in the interest and the service of the developing ego.

Projection is an unconscious defense mechanism in which a person attributes to another generally unconscious ideas, thoughts, feelings, and impulses that are personally undesirable or unacceptable. By externalizing whatever is unacceptable, such persons deal with it as a situation apart from themselves. *Regression* is an unconscious defense mechanism in which a person undergoes a partial or total return to early patterns of adaptation. Regression is observed in many psychiatric conditions, particularly schizophrenia. *Reaction formation* is an unconscious defense mechanism in which a person has an attitude or interest that is the direct antithesis of some unacceptable wish or impulse that the person harbors. *Displacement* is an unconscious defense mechanism by which the emotional component of an unacceptable idea or object is transferred to a more acceptable component.

14.18 The answer is C (*Synopsis VIII,* pages 500–501).
Postpartum psychosis should not be confused with postpartum "blues," a normal condition that occurs in about *50 percent* of women after childbirth. The "blues" are self-limited, last only a few days, and are characterized by tearfulness, fatigue, anxiety, and irritability that begin shortly after childbirth and lessen in severity each day postpartum. Postpartum psychosis is characterized by agitation, severe depression, and thoughts of infanticide.

14.19 The answer is D (*Synopsis VIII,* pages 500–501).
The symptoms for postpartum psychosis do not last up to 12 weeks after delivery; rather, the condition usually resolves within 2 months. *It is found in 1 to 2 per 1,000 deliveries. The risk is increased if the patient or the patient's mother had a previous postpartum illness or mood disorder.* The symptoms are usually experienced within days of delivery, and almost always within the first 8 weeks after giving birth. The patient begins to complain of insomnia, restlessness, and fatigue, and she shows lability of mood with tearfulness. Later symptoms include suspiciousness, confusion, incoherence, irrational statements, and obsessive concerns about the baby's health. *Delusional material may involve the idea that the baby is dead* or defective. The birth may be denied, or ideas of persecution, influence, or perversity may be expressed. *Hallucinations may involve voices telling the patient to kill her baby.* Postpartum

psychosis is a psychiatric emergency. In one study, 5 percent of patients killed themselves, and 4 percent killed the baby. Postpartum psychosis is not to be confused with postpartum "blues."

14.20 The answer is D (*Synopsis VIII,* pages 508–512).
The course and the prognosis of schizoaffective disorder are variable. As a group, patients with this disorder have a prognosis intermediate between patients with schizophrenia and patients with mood disorders. Schizoaffective disorder, *bipolar type,* is associated with a good prognosis. A poor prognosis is associated with the *depressive type* of schizoaffective disorder. A poor prognosis is also associated with the following variables: *no precipitating factor, a predominance of psychotic symptoms, early* or insidious *onset,* a poor premorbid history, and a positive family history of schizophrenia.

14.21 The answer is E (all) (*Synopsis VIII,* pages 498, 500–501).
Examples of atypical psychoses include *Capgras's syndrome, Cotard's syndrome, postpartum psychosis,* and *koro.* In general, they are rare, exotic, and unusual mental disorders: (1) syndromes that occur only at a particular time, for example, during the menses or postpartum; (2) syndromes that are restricted to a specific cultural setting, that is, culture-bound syndromes; (3) psychoses with unusual features, such as persistent auditory hallucinations; (4) syndromes that seem to belong to a well-known diagnostic entity but that show some features that cannot be reconciled with the generally accepted typical characteristics of that diagnostic category; and (5) psychoses about which information is inadequate to make a specific diagnosis.

Capgras's syndrome is characterized by the delusional conviction that other persons in the environment are not their real selves but are doubles who, like impostors, assume the roles of the persons they impersonate and behave like them.

In Cotard's syndrome, patients complain of having lost not only possessions, status, and strength but also the heart, blood, and intestines. The world outside is often reduced to nothingness.

Postpartum psychosis is a syndrome that occurs after childbirth and is characterized by delusions and severe depression. Thoughts of wanting to harm the newborn infant or oneself are common and represent a real danger. Most patients with this disorder have an underlying mental illness—most commonly a bipolar disorder; less commonly, schizophrenia. A few cases result from a cognitive disorder associated with perinatal events. Women with a history of schizophrenia or a mood disorder should be classified as having a recurrence of those disorders, rather than an atypical psychosis.

Koro is a culture-bound syndrome characterized by a patient's desperate fear that his penis is shrinking and may disappear into his abdomen. The syndrome is found in Southeast Asia and in China.

In the fourth edition of *Diagnostic and Statistical Manual of Mental Disorders* (DSM-IV), atypical psychoses are classified as psychotic disorders not otherwise specified (Table 14.6).

14.22 The answer is B (*Synopsis VIII,* page 500).
According to DSM-IV, postpartum psychosis is classified as a psychotic disorder not otherwise specified when no other psychotic disorder can be diagnosed. An *anxiety disorder* is a disorder in which anxiety is the most prominent disturbance or in which the patients experience anxiety if they resist giving in to their symptoms. A *mood disorder* is a mental disorder in which disturbance of mood is the primary characteristic; disturbances in thinking and behavior are secondary characteristics. *Schizophrenia* is a psychotic mental disorder characterized by disturbances in thinking, mood, and behavior. A *personality disorder* is a mental disorder characterized by inflexible, deeply ingrained, maladaptive patterns of adjustment to life that cause significant impairments of adaptive functioning.

14.23 The answer is C (*Synopsis VIII,* pages 496–497).
Psychotherapy for nondelusional *members of the patient's family is not necessary.* Clinical reports vary, but recovery rates have been reported to be *as low as 10 percent.* The submissive person often *requires treatment with antipsychotic drugs,* as does the dominant person. *Separation* of the submissive person from the dominant person is the primary intervention. The submissive person and the dominant person usually *move back together* after treatment.

14.24 The answer is E (all) (*Synopsis VIII,* pages 496–497).
Shared psychotic disorder is rare but is more common in *women* than in men. Persons in all socioeconomic classes may be affected, although it may be most common in *low socioeconomic groups.* Patients with physical disabilities, such as *the deaf,* are also at increased risk because of the dependent relationships that may develop among them. More than 95 percent of all cases involve two *members of the same family.* About a third of the cases involve two sisters; another third involve a husband and a wife or a mother and a child. Two brothers, a brother and a sister, and a father and a child have also been reported.

14.25 The answer is A (*Synopsis VIII,* pages 512–513).
Delusional disorder *is less common than schizophrenia.* Its prevalence in the United States is estimated to be 0.03 percent—in contrast with schizophrenia, 1 percent, and mood disorders, 5 percent.

The neuropsychiatric approach to delusional disorder derives from the observation that delusions are a common symptom in many neurological conditions, particularly those involving the limbic systems and the basal ganglia. No evidence indicates that the disorder *is caused by frontal lobe lesions.* Long-term follow-up of patients with delusional disorder has found that their diagnoses are rarely revised as schizophrenia or mood disorders; hence, delusional disorder *is not an early stage of schizophrenia* or mood disorders. Moreover, delusional disorder has a later onset than does schizophrenia or mood disorders. The mean age of onset is 40 years; the disorder *does not usually begin by age 20.* The disorder *is slightly more common in women than in men.*

14.26 The answer is D (*Synopsis VIII,* page 517).
The main feature of conjugal paranoia is the *delusion of infidelity,* or the Othello syndrome. Small bits of "evidence," such as disarrayed clothing and spots on the sheets, may be collected and used to justify the delusion. Delusional disorder, jealous type, is the diagnosis.

The characteristic feature of a *somatic delusion* is that the body is perceived to be disturbed or disordered in all or individual organs or parts. An *idea of reference* is a preoccupation with the idea that the actions of other persons relate to oneself. The characteristic feature of a *delusion of grandeur* is an exaggerated concept of one's importance, power, knowledge, or identity. A *delusion of persecution* involves the pathological belief that one is being attacked, harassed, cheated, or conjured against.

14.27 The answer is E (all) (*Synopsis VIII,* pages 512–520). *The delusions of schizophrenia, paranoid type, tend to be bizarre and fragmented,* in contrast to the better-organized delusions of delusional disorder. In the few patients who have hallucinations in conjunction with delusional disorder, *the hallucinations are associated with the delusions,* whereas hallucinations in schizophrenia are not necessarily connected with the delusions. In paranoid patients with a depressed affect *the affect is secondary to the delusional system,* whereas in depressed patients the delusions are secondary to the depression. *Delusions seen in cognitive disorders are characterized by forgetfulness and disorientation,* whereas delusional disorder is characterized by intact orientation and memory.

14.28 The answer is B (*Synopsis VIII,* pages 520–522). The sudden onset of a florid psychotic episode immediately after a marked psychosocial stressor, such as the death of a loved one, in the absence of increasing psychopathology before the stressor indicates the diagnosis of *brief psychotic disorder. Grief* is an expected and normal reaction to the loss of a loved one. The girl's reaction, however, was not only more severe than would be expected (wildly agitated, screaming) but also involved psychotic symptoms (the devil). Typically, the psychotic symptoms in brief psychotic disorder last for more than a day but no more than a month. In *schizophrenia* the symptoms last for at least 6 months. *Substance intoxication* can mimic brief psychotic disorder, but the case presented shows no evidence of substance use. *Delusional disorder* presents with nonbizarre delusions of at least 1 month's duration, with otherwise apparently normal behavior.

14.29 The answer is E (all) (*Synopsis VIII,* pages 512–520). The development of suspiciousness and paranoid ideas is commonly found in immigrants. Surrounded by strange people whose ways of emotional reaction are much different, *the development of delusional disorder is aggravated by the immigrant's appearance and mannerisms,* which often become objects of contempt or ridicule. Uncertainty in the new *environment tends to increase isolation.* The incidence of *delusional disorder* in immigrants is about 3 times as high as that among native-born American patients. *The increased incidence of delusional disorder in immigrants may be due to an increased immigration of persons with unstable personalities.*

Answers 14.30–14.32

14.30 The answer is B (*Synopsis VIII,* pages 520–523).

14.31 The answer is C (*Synopsis VIII,* page 495).

14.32 The answer is A (*Synopsis VIII,* page 504). *Schizophreniform disorder* is identical in every respect to schizophrenia except that its *symptoms last at least 1 month but less than 6 months.* Patients with schizophreniform disorder return to their baseline level of functioning once the disorder has resolved. In contrast, for a patient to meet the diagnostic criteria for schizophrenia, the symptoms must have been present for at least 6 months. *Brief psychotic disorder* is characterized primarily by the *fact that the schizophrenic symptoms last at least 1 day but less than 1 month.*

Simple deteriorative disorder, still a controversial diagnostic category, is characterized as the progressive development of symptoms of social withdrawal and other symptoms similar to the deficit symptoms of schizophrenia (Table 14.7).

Answers 14.33–14.35

14.33 The answer is B (*Synopsis VIII,* page 498).

14.34 The answer is C (*Synopsis VIII,* page 499).

14.35 The answer is A (*Synopsis VIII,* page 498). The Malayan word *amok* means to engage furiously in battle. The amok syndrome consists of a *sudden, unprovoked outburst of wild rage in which affected persons attack anything in their path.* Savage homicidal attack is generally preceded by a period of preoccupation, brooding, and mild depression. After the attack, the person feels exhausted, has no memory of the attack, and commonly commits suicide.

Koro is characterized by the *delusion that the person's penis is shrinking and may disappear* into his abdomen and that he may die. The koro syndrome occurs among the people of Southeast Asia and in China, where it is known as *suk-yeong.* A corresponding disorder in women involves complaints of the shrinkage of the vulva, the labia, and the breasts.

Wihtigo or windigo psychosis is a psychiatric disorder confined to the Cree, Ojibwa, and Salteaux Indians of North America. *Affected persons believe that they may be transformed into a giant monster that eats human flesh.* During times of starvation, affected persons may have the delusion that they have been transformed into a wihtigo, and they may feel and express a craving for human flesh. Because of the person's belief in witchcraft and in the possibility of such a

Table 14.7
DSM-IV Research Criteria for Simple Deteriorative Disorder

A. Progressive development over a period of at least a year of all of the following:
   (1) marked decline in occupational or academic functioning
   (2) gradual appearance and deepening of negative symptoms such as affective flattening, alogia, and avolition
   (3) poor interpersonal rapport, social isolation, or social withdrawal
B. Criterion A for schizophrenia has never been met.
C. The symptoms are not better accounted for by schizotypal or schizoid personality disorder, a psychotic disorder, a mood disorder, an anxiety disorder, a dementia, or mental retardation and are not due to the direct physiological effects of a substance or a general medical condition.

transformation, symptoms concerning the alimentary tract, such as loss of appetite and nausea from trivial causes, may sometimes cause the person to become greatly excited for fear of being transformed into a wihtigo.

Answers 14.36–14.40

14.36 The answer is E (*Synopsis VIII,* page 517).

14.37 The answer is D (*Synopsis VIII,* pages 512–515).

14.38 The answer is C (*Synopsis VIII,* page 516).

14.39 The answer is A (*Synopsis VIII,* page 517).

14.40 The answer is B (*Synopsis VIII,* pages 512–515).
In *delusional disorder, delusions of jealousy and persecution* are most commonly found. In *schizophrenia, bizarre delusions of being controlled* and delusions of persecution can occur. In *mania, grandiose delusions* are seen. In *depressive disorders, delusions of guilt and somatic delusions* may occur. In *cognitive disorders,* such as dementia, *delusions secondary to perceptual disturbances* are evident.

Answers 14.41–14.45

14.41 The answer is E (*Synopsis VIII,* pages 492–496).

14.42 The answer is C (*Synopsis VIII,* pages 492–496).

14.43 The answer is D (*Synopsis VIII,* pages 492–496).

14.44 The answer is B (*Synopsis VIII,* pages 512–518).

14.45 The answer is A (*Synopsis VIII,* pages 492–496).
Psychomotor retardation is a general slowing of mental and physical activity. It is often a sign of a *major depressive episode,* which is characterized by feelings of sadness, loneliness, despair, low self-esteem, and self-reproach. *Thought broadcasting* is the feeling that one's thoughts are being broadcast or projected into the environment. Such feelings are encountered in *schizophrenia.*

A patient in a *manic episode* is *easily distracted with an elevated, expansive, or irritable mood* with pressured speech and hyperactivity.

Delusional disorder is characterized by *persecutory or grandiose delusions* and related disturbances in mood, thought, and behavior.

The essential feature of *paranoid personality disorder* is a long-standing *suspiciousness and mistrust of people.* Patients with this disorder are hypersensitive and continually alert for environmental clues that will validate their original prejudicial ideas.

15

Mood Disorders

In the fourth edition of *Diagnostic and Statistical Manual of Mental Disorders* (DSM-IV), mood disorders refer to disturbances predominantly of mood. Mood *episodes* include major depressive episode, manic episode, and hypomanic episode. *Mood disorders* comprise a long list of disorders, including depressive disorders (major depressive disorder, dysthymic disorder, depressive disorder not otherwise specified), bipolar disorders (bipolar I disorder, bipolar II disorder, cyclothymic disorder, bipolar disorder not otherwise specified), and other mood disorders (mood disorder due to a general medical condition, substance-induced mood disorder, and mood disorder not otherwise specified). There are also many specifiers to describe the most recent mood episode, such as mild, moderate, severe without psychotic features, severe with psychotic features, and so on.

Two major mood disorders are major depressive disorder and bipolar I disorder. In DSM-IV, the former is characterized by one or more major depressive episodes, which consist of at least 2 weeks of depressed mood or loss of interest accompanied by at least four additional symptoms of depression. The latter is characterized by one or more manic or mixed episodes, usually accompanied by major depressive episodes.

Because the experience of mood is subjective, clinicians must be able to differentiate between normal and abnormal ranges of mood. People experiencing mood disorders cannot control their moods; their signs and symptoms arise from both psychological and biological dysregulation. The degree of disturbance can vary and can affect thought process, thought content, activity level, cognitive ability, speech, and social functioning. Mood disorders are common; the lifetime prevalence of major depressive disorder is about 10 percent for women and 6 percent for men; for bipolar I disorder, about 1 percent, similar to the lifetime prevalence of schizophrenia. Only about half of those with major depressive disorder receive medical and psychiatric attention; their symptoms are often dismissed as reactions to stress or instances of self-indulgence. Those with bipolar I disorder are more likely to receive medical treatment.

Although the specific causes of mood disorders are unknown, the relevant factors are thought to be a complex interaction of biological, genetic, and psychosocial elements. Many studies have implicated biogenic amine dysregulations, including norepinephrine, serotonin, dopamine, and γ-aminobutyric acid (GABA). Neuroendocrine dysregulations focus on the adrenal, thyroid, and growth hormone axes. Investigators have also studied abnormalities in the sleep cycle, regulation of circadian rhythms, and seizurelike phenomena in the temporal lobes.

There is evidence of complex genetic inheritance, particularly for the transmission of bipolar I disorder, which is one of the most genetically determined disorders in psychiatry. About 50 percent of people with bipolar I disorder have at least one parent with a mood disorder. If one parent has bipolar I disorder, there is a 25 percent chance that a child will have a mood disorder. If both parents have bipolar I disorder, there is a 50 to 75 percent chance that a child will have a mood disorder. Implicated psychosocial factors include loss, both real and symbolic; family dynamics; conflicts; and stress, particularly for the first episodes of mood disorders. It has been suggested that the stress associated with the first episode may produce long-lasting changes in brain tissue.

Clinicians must be familiar with all of the diagnostic categories of mood disorders and with the complex and varied treatment strategies, largely based on a biopsychosocial approach. They must know which one and which combinations of a wide range of drugs are effective and which other treatments, such as electroconvulsive therapy (ECT), can be helpful.

Students are referred to Chapter 15 in *Kaplan and Sadock's Synopsis VIII* to study in depth the material addressed in the questions and answers below.

HELPFUL HINTS

The student should know the following terms that relate to mood disorders.

- affect
- age-dependent symptoms
- amphetamine
- antipsychotics
- atypical features
- biogenic amines
- bipolar I disorder
- bipolar II disorder
- carbamazepine
- catatonic features
- clinical management
- cognitive, behavioral, family, and psychoanalytic therapies
- cognitive theories
- cyclothymic disorder
- depression rating scales
- depressive equivalent

- ▶ differential diagnosis
- ▶ double depression
- ▶ dysthymic (early and late onset) disorder
- ▶ ECT
- ▶ euthymic
- ▶ *folie à double forme*
- ▶ *folie circulaire*
- ▶ *forme fruste*
- ▶ GABA
- ▶ genetic studies
- ▶ GH
- ▶ 5-HT
- ▶ hypomania
- ▶ hypothalamus
- ▶ incidence and prevalence
- ▶ Karl Kahlbaum
- ▶ Heinz Kohut
- ▶ Emil Kraepelin
- ▶ learned helplessness
- ▶ LH, FSH
- ▶ life events and stress
- ▶ lithium
- ▶ major depressive disorder
- ▶ mania
- ▶ MAOIs
- ▶ melancholic features
- ▶ melatonin
- ▶ mild depressive disorder
- ▶ mood
- ▶ mood-congruent and mood-incongruent psychotic fear
- ▶ norepinephrine
- ▶ phototherapy
- ▶ postpartum onset
- ▶ premenstrual dysphoric disorder
- ▶ premorbid factors
- ▶ pseudodementia
- ▶ rapid cycling
- ▶ REM latency, density
- ▶ RFLP
- ▶ seasonal pattern
- ▶ sex ratios of disorders
- ▶ SSRI
- ▶ suicide
- ▶ T3
- ▶ thymoleptics
- ▶ TSH, TRH
- ▶ vegetative functions

▲ QUESTIONS

DIRECTIONS: From the following list of lettered choices, select the most appropriate feature, as described in DSM-IV, to associate with each disorder in questions 15.1 to 15.3.

A. Dysphoria
B. Brain tumor
C. Suicidal behavior
D. Multiple sclerosis
E. Obsessive rumination

15.1 Manic episode
15.2 Mixed episode
15.3 Major depressive episode

DIRECTIONS: From the following list of lettered lifetime prevalence criteria, select the correct percentage, as given in DSM-IV, for each disorder in questions 15.4 to 15.6.

A. Lifetime prevalence is about 6 percent.
B. Lifetime prevalence is about 0.5 percent.
C. Lifetime prevalence is 0.4 to 1.6 percent.
D. Lifetime prevalence is about 3 to 5 percent.
E. Lifetime prevalence is about 0.4 to 1 percent.

15.4 Bipolar I disorder
15.5 Bipolar II disorder
15.6 Cyclothymic disorder

DIRECTIONS: Each of the questions or incomplete statements below is followed by five suggested responses or completions. Select the *one* that is *best* in each case.

15.7 Major depressive disorder

A. may have catatonic symptoms
B. cannot have psychotic features as part of its symptoms
C. has its mean age of onset at 60 years
D. cannot have its onset in childhood
E. has a lifetime prevalence of 1 percent

15.8 In the treatment of a patient with a depressive disorder

A. tricyclic drugs are not lethal when taken at overdose levels
B. antidepressants do not have sexual adverse effects
C. monoamine oxidase inhibitors (MAOIs) are chosen as first-line drugs more often than are serotonin-specific reuptake inhibitors (SSRIs)
D. antidepressants alone are effective in the treatment of major depressive episode with psychotic features
E. a drug trial of adequate dosage can be considered unsuccessful if the patient does not respond favorably in 4 weeks

15.9 All of the following statements about patients with bipolar I disorder are true *except*

A. They have a poorer prognosis than do patients with major depressive disorder.
B. They have bizarre and mood-incongruent delusions and hallucinations when manic.
C. About 75 percent of female patients have had a manic episode before exhibiting their first depressive disorder.
D. Only 50 to 60 percent of these patients achieve significant control of their symptoms with lithium.
E. When manic, they may be emotionally labile and not easily interrupted while they are speaking.

15.10 Dysthymic disorder

A. cannot coexist with major depressive disorder
B. usually has an abrupt onset
C. is synonymous with minor depressive disorder
D. has not shown successful treatment with antidepressants
E. is common among unmarried and young persons

15.11 Which of the following is helpful in the differential diagnosis and the formulation of a treatment plan for a patient with a mood disorder?

A. Family history of psychiatric illness
B. Knowledge of the type of psychiatric medication used in the past
C. Medical problems
D. Past or present substance abuse
E. All of the above

15.12 The defense mechanism most commonly used in depression is

A. projection
B. introjection
C. sublimation
D. undoing
E. altruism

15.13 A 24-year-old single female copy editor was presented at a case conference 2 weeks after her first psychiatric hospitalization. Her hospital admission followed an accident in which she wrecked her car while driving at high speed late at night when she was feeling energetic and thought that "sleep was a waste of time." The episode began while she was on vacation, when she felt high and on the verge of a great romance. She apparently took off all her clothes and ran naked through the woods. On the day of her hospital admission, she reported hearing voices telling her that her father and the emergency room staff were emissaries of the devil, out to get her for no reason that she could understand.

At the case conference, she was calm and cooperative and talked of the voices she had heard in the past, which she now acknowledged had not been real. She realized that she had an illness but was still irritated at being hospitalized. She was receiving lithium, 2,100 mg a day and had a blood level of 1 mEq/L.

The most likely diagnosis is

A. bipolar I disorder, most recent episode manic, with mood-incongruent psychotic features
B. bipolar I disorder, most recent episode manic, with mood-congruent psychotic features
C. bipolar I disorder, most recent episode mixed, with mood-congruent psychotic features
D. bipolar I disorder, most recent episode depressed, with mood-congruent psychotic features
E. cyclothymic disorder

15.14 Vegetative signs in depression include all the following *except*

A. weight loss
B. abnormal menses
C. obsessive rumination
D. decreased libido
E. fatigability

15.15 The percentage of depressed patients who eventually commit suicide is estimated to be

A. 0.5 percent
B. 5 percent
C. 15 percent
D. 25 percent
E. 35 percent

15.16 All of the following statements about bipolar I disorder are true *except*

A. Bipolar I disorder most often starts with depression.
B. About 10 to 20 percent of patients experience only manic episodes.
C. An untreated manic episode lasts about 3 months.
D. As the illness progresses, the amount of time between episodes often increases.
E. Rapid cycling is much more common in women than in men.

15.17 According to the fourth edition of *Diagnostic and Statistical Manual of Mental Disorders* (DSM-IV), the course specifier "with seasonal pattern" can be applied to

A. dysthymic disorder
B. cyclothymic disorder
C. major depressive disorder, single episode
D. bipolar II disorder
E. all of the above

15.18 Life events are

A. a possible factor in the onset and the timing of a specific episode of depression
B. most associated with the development of depression in later life when a parent is lost before age 11
C. most associated with the onset of a depressive episode when a spouse is lost
D. not significantly related to the onset and the timing of a specific episode of mania
E. all of the above

15.19 Of the following neurological diseases, which is most often associated with depression?

A. Epilepsy
B. Brain tumor
C. Parkinson's disease
D. Dementia of the Alzheimer's type
E. Huntington's disease

15.20 A 59-year-old married attorney with a promising practice, two daughters, and a good marriage was noticed by his wife to be ''not functioning properly'' during the previous 2 months. He called his office frequently, telling his partners that he was ill, while actually he could not get out of bed in the mornings. His colleagues were concerned about his frequent cancellation of appointments and his change in behavior. He stopped taking pride in his appearance, lost his appetite for food and his interest in sex, and was sleeping many hours each day. He told his wife that he was unsure whether he wanted to go on living. He had no history of alcohol or other drug use. He had had a thorough physical examination 3 months earlier and was told that he was in good health.

Which of the following is the most likely diagnosis?

A. Bipolar I disorder
B. Major depressive disorder
C. Generalized anxiety disorder
D. Schizophrenia
E. None of the above

Questions 15.21–15.22

A 25-year-old junior executive was referred to a health service because he had been drinking excessively over the previous 2 weeks. The patient reported that he had been ''down'' for about a month, cried frequently, and had no interest in sex or work. His history revealed that he had suffered those down periods for several years; but he also described himself as having experienced periods of elation during which he was gregarious, productive, and optimistic. During those times, he said, he did not drink at all. The young man also stated that the behavior had been present on and off since he was about 15 years old.

15.21 The patient was suffering from

A. major depressive disorder
B. bipolar I disorder
C. cyclothymic disorder
D. dysthymic disorder
E. bipolar II disorder

15.22 If the patient was treated with a tricyclic antidepressant (TCA), which of the following is *least likely* to result?

A. Tachycardia, flattened T waves, and prolonged QT intervals
B. Delusions and hallucinations
C. Excessive involvement in pleasurable activities with a high potential for painful consequences
D. Myoclonic twitches and tremors of the tongue
E. A hypomanic state

15.23 A 40-year-old man was taken to the psychiatric emergency room after becoming involved in a fist fight at a bar. He was speaking rapidly, jumping from one thought to another in response to simple, specific questions (for example, ''When did you come to New York?'' ''I came to New York, the Big Apple, it's rotten to the core, no matter how you slice it, I sliced a bagel this morning for breakfast. . .''). The patient described experiencing his thoughts as racing. He was unable to explain how he got into the fight other than to say that the other person was jealous of the patient's obvious sexual prowess, the patient having declared that he had slept with at least 100 women. He made allusions to his father as being God, and he stated that he had not slept in 3 days. ''I don't need it,'' he said. The patient's speech was full of amusing puns, jokes, and plays on words.

Associated findings consistent with the patient's probable diagnosis include all of the following *except*

A. emotional lability
B. hallucinations
C. flight of ideas
D. nocturnal electroencephalographic (EEG) changes
E. mood-incongruent delusions

15.24 Cyclothymic disorder is considered an attenuated form of bipolar I disorder because of

A. a similarity of symptoms in the two disorders
B. the significant number of cyclothymic patients who eventually have bipolar I disorder
C. the two disorders' favorable response to lithium
D. a hypomanic response to tricyclic drugs among cyclothymic disorder patients
E. all of the above

15.25 The lifetime prevalence of dysthymic disorder is

A. 5 cases per 1,000 persons
B. 10 cases per 1,000 persons
C. 20 cases per 1,000 persons
D. 35 cases per 1,000 persons
E. 45 cases per 1,000 persons

15.26 Which of the following symptoms is incompatible with dysthymic disorder?

A. Weight change
B. Sleep difficulty
C. Delusions
D. Decreased sexual performance
E. Suicidal ideas

15.27 Age-associated features of major depressive disorder include

A. separation anxiety
B. antisocial behavior
C. running away
D. pseudodementia
E. All of the above

15.28 The course of major depressive disorder usually includes all of the following *except*

A. an untreated episode of depression lasting 6 to 13 months
B. a treated episode of depression lasting about 3 months
C. the return of symptoms after the withdrawal of antidepressants before 3 months have elapsed
D. an average of five to six episodes over a 20-year period
E. progression to bipolar II disorder

15.29 A manic episode is differentiated from a schizophrenic episode by

A. quality of mood
B. psychomotor activity
C. speed of onset
D. family history
E. all of the above

15.30 Which of the following medications may produce depressive symptoms?

A. Analgesics
B. Antibacterials
C. Antipsychotics
D. Antihypertensives
E. All of the above

15.31 L-Tryptophan

A. is the amino acid precursor to dopamine
B. has been used as an adjuvant to both antidepressants and lithium
C. has been used as stimulant
D. has not been associated with any serious side effects
E. is all of the above

15.32 Drugs that may precipitate mania include all of the following *except*

A. bromocriptine
B. isoniazid
C. propranolol
D. cimetidine
D. disulfiram
E. all of the above

15.33 Major depressive disorder

A. is more common in men than in women
B. peaks in women after age 55
C. shows no conclusive evidence for any difference between blacks and whites
D. is highest in the poor
E. is characterized by all of the above

15.34 Figure 15.1 illustrates the suppression of plasma cortisol in a patient before (*solid line*) and 6 weeks after (*dashed line*) initiation of treatment with a drug, where plasma cortisol above 5 mg/dL indicates nonsuppression. All of the following statements regarding this test are true *except*

A. The test helps confirm the diagnosis of major depressive disorder.
B. A positive test is indicated by suppression of plasma cortisol to levels below 5 mg/dL.
C. Normalization of test results is not an indication to stop drug treatment.
D. False-positive and false-negative results are common.
E. Suppression of cortisol indicates normal functioning of the hypothalamic-adrenal-pituitary axis.

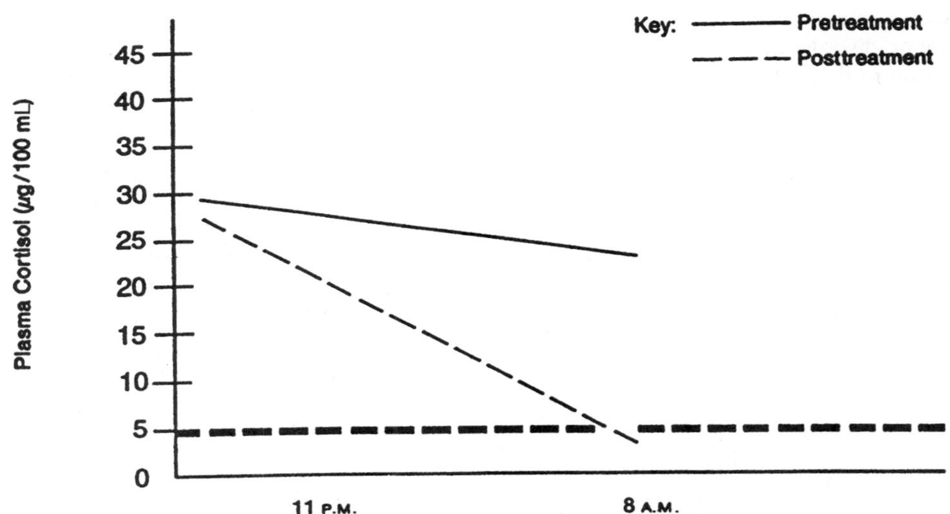

FIGURE 15.1
Reprinted with permission from MacKinnon A, Yudofsky SC: *Principles of the Psychiatric Evaluation.* Lippincott, Philadelphia, 1991.

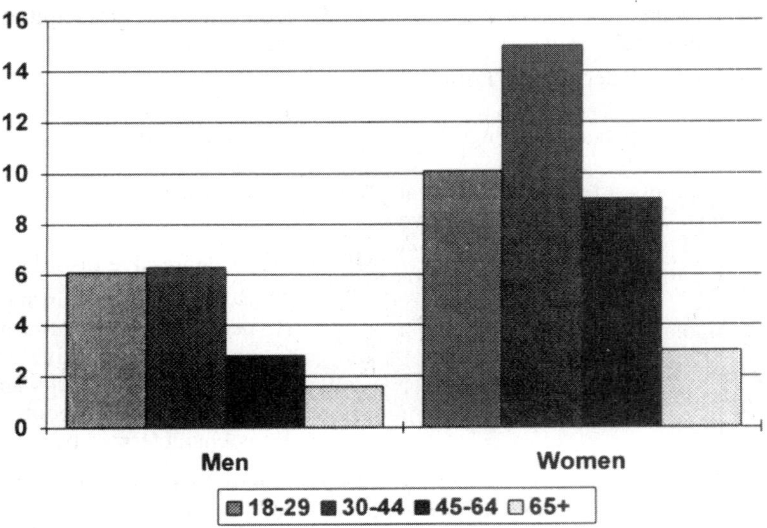

FIGURE 15.2
Data derived from the Epidemiologic Catchment Area study.

15.35 Figure 15.2 depicts the distribution, according to age and sex, of which of the following?

A. Incidence of anorexia nervosa
B. Prevalence of mood disorders
C. Incidence of obsessive-compulsive disorder
D. Prevalence of schizophrenia
E. Incidence of somatization disorder

15.36 The patient shown in Figure 15.3*A* suffers from an episode of illness characterized by loss of energy, decreased interest and pleasure in most activities, sleep and appetite disturbance, and feelings of worthlessness. Figure 15.3*B* shows the same patient in recovery, 2 months later, after treatment with amitriptyline. The differential diagnosis of a patient with these symptoms might include

A. substance-related disorders
B. psychotic disorders
C. somatoform disorders
D. anxiety disorders
E. all of the above

15.37 A 37-year-old white man comes to your office at the urging of his wife. A few years earlier he had an asymptomatic thyroid mass removed, which was followed by dramatic mood changes a month later. The patient would experience 25 days of remarkable energy, hyperactivity, and euphoria, followed by 5 days of depression during which he slept a lot and felt he could hardly move. That rapid pattern of alternating periods of elation and depression, apparently with few "normal" days, repeated itself continuously to the present time. The patient denies any drug use and states that his last batch of hospital tests revealed some evidence of thyroid hypofunctioning but that he was without clinical signs of thyroid disease. The patient also states that he has been minimally cooperative and noncompliant with several medications that were prescribed for him, including lithium, neuroleptics, and antidepressants.

The correct first-line treatment for this patient's disorder is

A. lithium
B. electroconvulsive therapy (ECT)
C. valproate or carbamazepine
D. tricyclic antidepressants
E. clozapine (Clozaril)

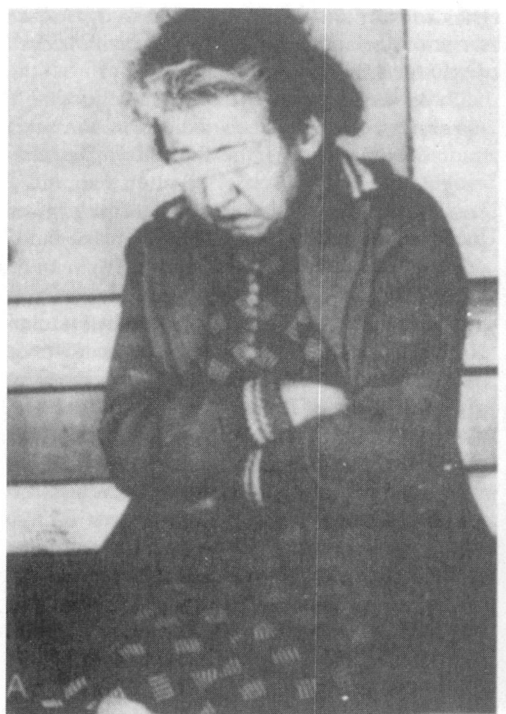

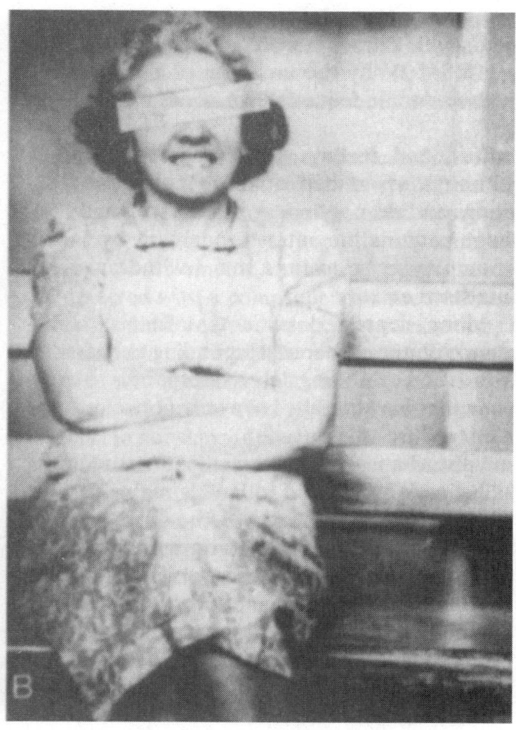

FIGURE 15.3
Courtesy of Heinz E. Lehmann, M.D.

DIRECTIONS: Each set of lettered headings below is followed by a list of phrases or statements. For each numbered phrase or statement, select

A. if the item is associated with *A only*
B. if the item is associated with *B only*
C. if the item is associated with *both A and B*
D. if the item is associated with *neither A nor B*

Questions 15.38–15.40

A. Minor depressive disorder
B. Recurrent brief depressive disorder
C. Both
D. Neither

15.38 Symptoms meet most of the diagnostic criteria for major depressive disorder.
15.39 Symptoms are equal in duration but fewer in number than those in major depressive disorder.
15.40 Treatment may include the use of antidepressants.

Questions 15.41–15.45

A. Mood-incongruent delusion
B. Mood-congruent delusion
C. Both
D. Neither

15.41 A 52-year-old suicidal man believes that he is the new Messiah.
15.42 A 45-year-old elated man believes that he has been reincarnated as a millionaire.
15.43 A 12-year-old boy thinks that he hears voices telling him to jump out the window.
15.44 A 25-year-old depressed woman thinks that she has committed terrible crimes.
15.45 A 30-year-old depressed woman believes that she is the Virgin Mary.

Questions 15.46–15.49

A. Major depressive disorder, recurrent
B. Dysthymic disorder
C. Both
D. Neither

15.46 Episodic periods of depression
15.47 Family history of mood disorders, decreased rapid eye movement latency, and therapeutic response to antidepressants
15.48 DSM-IV–defined subtypes based on onset before and after age 21
15.49 Possible psychotic symptoms

Questions 15.50–15.55

A. Dysthymic disorder
B. Cyclothymic disorder
C. Both
D. Neither

15.50 Treatment with antidepressants leading to hypomanic symptoms
15.51 Delusions and hallucinations
15.52 Favorable response to lithium
15.53 Alcohol abuse
15.54 Sexual promiscuity
15.55 Confusion with substance abuse

Questions 15.56–15.57

A. Cyclothymic disorder
B. Bipolar II disorder
C. Both
D. Neither

15.56 Characterized by episodes of hypomanic-like symptoms and periods of mild depression
15.57 Characterized by major depressive episodes and hypomanic episodes

ANSWERS

Mood Disorders

15.1 The answer is C (*Synopsis VIII,* pages 553–554, 557).
A manic episode is a period of abnormally and persistently elevated, expansive, or irritable mood. The period lasts at least 1 week (or less if hospitalization is required). The mood disturbance must be accompanied by at least three other symptoms such as inflated self-esteem, decreased need for sleep, distractibility, increased involvement in goal-directed activities or psychomotor agitation, and excessive involvement in pleasurable activities with a high possibility of painful consequences. *Suicidal behavior* is one of several features associated with a manic episode; others include resistance to accepting the idea of mental illness, impulsive travel, change in appearance to a flashy style, gambling and antisocial behaviors, disregard for ethical concerns, and hostility and combativeness toward others.

15.2 The answer is A (*Synopsis VIII,* page 553).
A mixed episode is a period of at least 1 week during which criteria for both a manic and a major depressive episode are met. Thus the person experiences rapidly alternating moods accompanied by both manic and depressive symptoms, such as agitation, insomnia, appetite dysregulation, psychotic features, and suicidal thinking. The disturbance must be severe enough to markedly impair a person's social or occupational functioning or to require hospitalization, or it must be characterized by psychotic features. Associated features of a mixed episode resemble those of manic and major depressive episodes. Patients are disorganized in thinking and behavior and experience more *dysphoria* than do patients in manic episodes.

15.3 The answer is E (*Synopsis VIII,* pages 544–546).
A major depressive episode is a period of at least 2 weeks during which a person is either depressed or loses interest or pleasure in most activities. To be diagnosed with a major depressive episode, a person must have at least four other symptoms such as changes in appetite or weight, sleep, and psychomotor activity; decreased energy; feelings of worthlessness or guilt; difficulty thinking or making decisions; or recurrent thoughts of death or suicide plans or attempts. *Obsessive rumination* is one of many features associated with a major depressive episode. Other features include tearfulness, irritability, brooding, anxiety, phobias, worry over physical health, and complaints of pain.

15.4 The answer is C (*Synopsis VIII,* pages 525, 546–548).
Bipolar I disorder is characterized by one or more manic or mixed episodes and sometimes by one or more major depressive episodes. People with this disorder have a rate of suicide that may be as high as 10 to 15 percent. Child or spouse abuse or other violent behavior can occur during severe manic episodes or in patients whose disorders show psychotic features. Other problems include antisocial behavior, occupational failure, and divorce. The *lifetime prevalence* of bipolar I disorder *is 0.4 to 1.6 percent.*

15.5 The answer is B (*Synopsis VIII,* pages 525, 548).
Bipolar II disorder is characterized by one or more major depressive episodes accompanied by at least one hypomanic episode. The presence of a manic or mixed disorder precludes the diagnosis of bipolar II disorder. People with bipolar II disorder are at significant risk for suicide, which occurs in 10 to 15 percent of those with this disorder. Associated features similar to those of bipolar I disorder include occupational failure and divorce. This disorder may be more common in women than in men. *Lifetime prevalence* of bipolar II disorder *is about 0.5 percent.*

15.6 The answer is E (*Synopsis VIII,* pages 525, 578–580).
Cyclothymic disorder is a chronic fluctuating mood disturbance with many periods of hypomanic and depressive symptoms. The hypomanic symptoms are too few and not severe, pervasive, or long-lasting enough to satisfy the criteria for a manic episode, and the depressive symptoms are too few and not severe, pervasive, or long-lasting enough to satisfy the criteria for a major depressive episode. Although some people function well during some periods of hypomania, there is usually a significant level of impairment or distress in social, occupational, or other important areas of functioning. The disorder apparently occurs at the same rate in both women and men, on the basis of community sampling, but women seek treatment more than do men. *The lifetime prevalence rate* of cyclothymic disorder *is about 0.4 to 1 percent.*

15.7 The answer is A (*Synopsis VIII,* pages 550–551).
Major depressive disorder *may have catatonic features;* in fact, the fourth edition of *Diagnostic and Statistical Manual of Mental Disorders* (DSM-IV) includes catatonic features as an additional symptom feature that can be used to describe patients with various mood disorders. Table 15.1 lists the criteria for cross-sectional symptom features.

Major depressive disorder *can have psychotic features as part of its symptoms.* The presence of psychotic features in major depressive disorder reflects severe disease and indicates a poor prognosis. The psychotic symptoms themselves are often categorized as either mood-congruent—that is, in harmony with mood disorder ("I deserve to be punished because I am so bad")—or mood-incongruent—that is, not in harmony with the mood disorder ("I am a hero"). The criteria for catatonic features appear in Table 15.2.

The *mean age of onset* for major depressive disorder is about *40 years, not 60 years;* 50 percent of patients have an onset between the ages of 20 and 50. Major depressive disorder *can have its onset in childhood,* although that is unusual. A later onset is associated with the absence of a family history of mood disorders, antisocial personality disorder, and alcohol abuse.

Major depressive disorder *has a lifetime prevalence of about 6 percent, not 1 percent.*

15.8 The answer is E (*Synopsis VIII,* page 567).
The most common clinical mistake leading to an unsuccessful trial of an antidepressant drug is the use of too low a dosage for too short a time. Unless adverse events prevent it, *a drug trial of adequate dosage can be considered unsuccessful if the patient does not respond favorably in 4 weeks.*

Table 15.1
DSM-IV Criteria for Severity/Psychotic/Remission Specifiers for Current (or Most Recent) Major Depressive Episode

Note: Code in fifth digit. Can be applied to the most recent major depressive episode in major depressive disorder and to a major depressive episode in bipolar I or II disorder only if it is the most recent type of mood episode.

Mild: Few, if any, symptoms in excess of those required to make the diagnosis and symptoms result in only minor impairment in occupational functioning or in usual social activities or relationships with others.

Moderate: Symptoms or functional impairment between "mild" and "severe."

Severe without psychotic features: Several symptoms in excess of those required to make the diagnosis, **and** symptoms markedly interfere with occupational functioning or with usual social activities or relationships with others.

Severe with psychotic features: Delusions or hallucinations. If possible, specify whether the psychotic features are mood-congruent or mood-incongruent:

Mood-congruent psychotic features: Delusions or hallucinations whose content is entirely consistent with the typical depressive themes of personal inadequacy, guilt, disease, death, nihilism, or deserved punishment.

Mood-Incongruent psychotic features: Delusions or hallucinations whose content does not involve typical depressive themes of personal inadequacy, guilt, disease, death, nihilism, or deserved punishment. Included here are such symptoms as persecutory delusions (not directly related to depressive themes), thought insertion, thought broadcasting, and delusions of control.

In partial remission Intermediate between "in full remission" and "mild," **and** no previous dysthymic disorder. (If the major depressive episode was superimposed on dysthymic disorder, the diagnosis of dysthymic disorder alone is given once the full criteria for a major depressive episode are no longer met).

In full remission: During the past 2 months no significant signs or symptoms of the disturbance were present.

Unspecified.

Reprinted with permission from American Psychiatric Association: *Diagnostic and Statistical Manual of Mental Disorders,* ed 4. Copyright, American Psychiatric Association, Washington, 1994.

Tricyclic drugs may be lethal when taken in overdose levels. Tricyclic and tetracyclic drugs are by far the most lethal of the antidepressants; the serotonin-specific reuptake inhibitors (SSRIs), bupropion (Wellbutrin), trazodone (Desyrel) and the monoamine oxidase inhibitors (MAOIs) are much safer, although even those drugs can be lethal when taken in combination with alcohol or other substances.

Antidepressants do have sexual adverse effects. Almost all of the antidepressants, except bupropion, have been associated with decreased libido, erectile dysfunction, or anorgasmia. The serotonergic drugs are probably more closely associated with sexual adverse effects than are the noradrenergic compounds.

The MAOIs are usually not chosen as first-line drugs more often than are SSRIs because of the association with tyramine-induced hypertensive crises, which are caused when a patient taking conventional MAOIs ingests certain drugs or foods with a high tyramine content. Although that adverse interaction can be avoided by the patient's following simple dietary guidelines, the potentially life-threatening nature of a hypertensive crisis and the need for dietary restrictions limit the acceptability of MAOIs.

Table 15.2
DSM-IV Criteria for Catatonic Features Specifier

Specify if:

With catatonic features (can be applied to the current or most recent major depressive episode, manic episode, or mixed episode in major depressive disorder, bipolar I disorder, or bipolar II disorder)

The clinical picture is dominated by at least two of the following:

(1) motoric immobility as evidenced by catalepsy (including waxy flexibility) or stupor
(2) excessive motor activity (that is apparently purposeless and not influenced by external stimuli)
(3) extreme negativism (an apparently motiveless resistance to all instructions or maintenance of a rigid posture against attempts to be moved) or mutism
(4) peculiarities of voluntary movement as evidenced by posturing (voluntary assumption of inappropriate or bizarre postures), stereotyped movements, prominent mannerisms, or prominent grimacing
(5) echolalia or echopraxia

Reprinted with permission from American Psychiatric Association: *Diagnostic and Statistical Manual of Mental Disorders,* ed 4. Copyright, American Psychiatric Association, Washington, 1994.

Antidepressants alone are not effective in the treatment of major depressive episodes with psychotic features. One exception may be amoxapine (Asendin), an antidepressant closely related to loxapine (Loxitane), an antipsychotic. The usual practice, however, is to use a combination of an antidepressant and an antipsychotic.

15.9 The answer is C (*Synopsis VIII,* pages 560–561).

Patients with bipolar I disorder *usually have had a depressive episode* (Table 15.3) *before exhibiting their first manic episode* (Table 15.4). That has been found true 75 percent of the time in women and 67 percent of the time in men. Most patients experience both depressive and manic episodes, although 10 to 20 percent experience only manic episodes.

Patients with bipolar I disorder *have a poorer prognosis than do patients with major depressive disorder.* About 40 to 50 percent of bipolar I disorder patients may have a second manic episode within 2 years of the first episode. Although lithium (Eskalith) prophylaxis improves the course and the prognosis of bipolar I disorder, probably *only 50 to 60 percent of patients achieve significant control of their symptoms with lithium.*

Patients may be emotionally labile when manic, switching from laughter to irritability to depression in minutes or hours. Patients *are not easily interrupted while they are speaking when manic,* and they are often intrusive nuisances to those around them. Patients *do have bizarre and mood-incongruent delusions and hallucinations when manic.*

15.10 The answer is E (*Synopsis VIII,* page 574).

Dysthymic disorder *is common among unmarried and young persons* and among persons with low incomes. Moreover, dysthymic disorder *can coexist with major depressive disorders,*

Table 15.3
DSM-IV Criteria for Major Depressive Episode

A. Five (or more) of the following symptoms have been present during the same 2-week period and represent a change from previous functioning; at least one of the symptoms is either (1) depressed mood or (2) loss of interest or pleasure
Note: Do not include symptoms that are clearly due to a general medical condition, or mood-incongruent delusions or hallucinations.
   (1) depressed mood most of the day, nearly every day, as indicated by either subjective report (eg, feels sad or empty) or observation made by others (eg, appears tearful). **Note:** In children and adolescents, can be irritable mood.
   (2) markedly diminished interest or pleasure in all, or almost all, activities most of the day, nearly every day (as indicated by either subjective account or observation made by others)
   (3) significant weight loss when not dieting or weight gain (eg, a change of more than 5% of body weight in a month), or decrease or increase in appetite nearly every day. **Note:** In children, consider failure to make expected weight gains.
   (4) insomnia or hypersomnia nearly every day
   (5) psychomotor agitation or retardation nearly every day (observable by others, not merely subjective feelings of restlessness or being slowed down)
   (6) fatigue or loss of energy nearly every day
   (7) feelings of worthlessness or excessive or inappropriate guilt (which may be delusional) nearly every day (not merely self-reproach or guilt about being sick)
   (8) diminished ability to think or concentrate, or indecisiveness, nearly every day (either by subjective account or as observed by others)
   (9) recurrent thoughts of death (not just fear of dying), recurrent suicidal ideation without a specific plan, or a suicide attempt or a specific plan for committing suicide

B. The symptoms do not meet criteria for a mixed episode.

C. The symptoms cause clinically significant distress or impairment in social, occupational, or other important areas of functioning.

D. The symptoms are not due to the direct physiological effects of a substance (eg, a drug of abuse, a medication) or a general medical condition (eg, hypothyroidism).

E. The symptoms are not better accounted for by bereavement, ie, after the loss of a loved one, the symptoms persist for longer than 2 months or are characterized by marked functional impairment, morbid preoccupation with worthlessness, suicidal ideation, psychotic symptoms, or psychomotor retardation.

Table 15.4
DSM-IV Criteria for Manic Episode

A. A distinct period of abnormally and persistently elevated, expansive, or irritable mood, lasting at least 1 week (or any duration if hospitalization is necessary).

B. During the period of mood disturbance, three (or more) of the following symptoms have persisted (four if the mood is only irritable) and have been present to a significant degree:
   (1) inflated self-esteem or grandiosity
   (2) decreased need for sleep (eg, feels rested after only 3 hours of sleep)
   (3) more talkative than usual or pressure to keep talking
   (4) flight of ideas or subjective experience that thoughts are racing
   (5) distractibility (ie, attention too easily drawn to unimportant or irrelevant external stimuli)
   (6) increase in goal-directed activity (either socially, at work or school, or sexually) or psychomotor agitation
   (7) excessive involvement in pleasurable activities that have a high potential for painful consequences (eg, engaging in unrestrained buying sprees, sexual indiscretions, or foolish business investments)

C. The symptoms do not meet criteria for a mixed episode.

D. The mood disturbance is sufficiently severe to cause marked impairment in occupational functioning or in usual social activities or relationships with others, or to necessitate hospitalization to prevent harm to self or others, or there are psychotic features.

E. The symptoms are not due to the direct physiological effects of a substance (eg, a drug of abuse, a medication, or other treatment) or a general medical condition (eg, hyperthyroidism).

Note: Maniclike episodes that are clearly caused by somatic antidepressant treatment (eg, medication, electroconvulsive therapy, light therapy) should not count toward a diagnosis of bipolar I disorder.

anxiety disorders (especially panic disorder), substance abuse, and probably borderline personality disorder. About 50 percent of dysthymic disorder patients *experience an insidious onset, not an abrupt onset,* of the symptoms before age 25.

Dysthymic disorder *is not synonymous with minor depressive disorder.* The difference between dysthymic disorder and minor depressive disorder is primarily the episodic nature of the symptoms in minor depressive disorder. Between episodes, patients with minor depressive disorder have a euthymic mood, whereas patients with dysthymic disorder have virtually no euthymic periods.

Dysthymic disorder *has shown successful treatment with antidepressants.* In general, however, monoamine oxidase inhibitors (MAOIs) may be more beneficial than tricyclic drugs. The relatively recent introduction of the well-tolerated serotonin-specific reuptake inhibitors (SSRIs) has led to their frequent use by patients with dysthymic disorder; preliminary reports indicate that the SSRIs may be the drugs of choice for this disorder. Similarly, initial reports indicate that bupropion may be an effective treatment for patients with dysthymic disorder.

15.11 The answer is E (all) (*Synopsis VIII,* pages 245–250).

A patient's history and *family history of psychiatric illness* can provide valuable information about the patient's clinical picture. Suicide in a parent, for example, increases the risk of suicide in the patient. If a patient has been depressed before, *knowledge of the type of medication used in the past* can provide the physician with a head start. Knowing whether the patient has ever had a period of mania or has had a recent severe emotional trauma is essential in making the correct diagnosis and formulating an effective treatment plan. For example, a history of a manic episode is indicative of bipolar I disorder. *Medical problems,* such as cancer of the pancreas, multiple sclerosis, and a space-occupying lesion of the brain, can produce depression. *Past or present substance abuse* is also important, since certain substances, such as alcohol and amphetamines, can mimic the clinical picture of depression.

15.12 The answer is B (*Synopsis VIII,* page 220).
In Sigmund Freud's structural theory, the *introjection* of the lost object into the ego leads to the typical depressive symptoms of a lack of energy available to the ego. The superego, unable to retaliate against the lost object externally, flails out at the psychic representation of the lost object, now internalized in the ego as an introject. When the ego overcomes or merges with the superego, energy previously bound in the depressive symptoms is released, and a mania supervenes with the typical symptoms of excess.

Projection is the unconscious defense mechanism in which a person attributes to another person those generally unconscious ideas, thoughts, feelings, and impulses that are personally undesirable or unacceptable. *Sublimation* is an unconscious defense mechanism in which the energy associated with unacceptable impulses or drives is diverted into personally and socially acceptable channels. *Undoing* is an unconscious defense mechanism by which a person symbolically acts out in reverse something unacceptable that has already been done or against which the ego must defend itself. *Altruism* is regard for and dedication to the welfare of others.

15.13 The answer is A (*Synopsis VIII,* pages 547–548).
In the case of the 24-year-old single female copy editor, the most likely diagnosis is *bipolar I disorder, most recent episode manic, with mood-incongruent psychotic features.* The patient exhibited the characteristic features of a manic episode: elevated mood (feeling high), increased energy, decreased need for sleep, and involvement in activities with a high potential for painful consequences (reckless driving). The reference to being on the verge of a great romance also suggested the presence of grandiosity. In DSM-IV the presence of a manic episode, even without a history of a depressive episode, is sufficient to make a diagnosis of bipolar I disorder, manic, as the familial history, course, and treatment response of unipolar mania are apparently the same as in disorders with both manic and major depressive episodes.

The presence of the persecutory delusions is noted by including "with psychotic features." Since the content of the delusions had no apparent connection with themes of either inflated worth, power, knowledge, identity, or a special relationship to a deity or famous person, the delusions were mood-incongruent. Since the psychotic features are mood-incongruent, *bipolar I disorder, most recent episode manic, with mood-congruent psychotic features,* is not warranted.

Bipolar I disorder, most recent episode mixed, with mood-congruent psychotic features involves the full symptomatic picture of both mania and depression intermixed or rapidly alternating every few days, with psychotic features congruent with manic and depressed moods. *Bipolar I disorder, most recent episode depressed, with mood-congruent psychotic features,* involves a current presentation of a major depressive episode in a previously manic patient. The mood-congruent psychotic features would involve depressive themes, such as guilt, poverty, nihilism, or somatic concerns.

Cyclothymic disorder is a chronic disorder of at least 2 years' duration, characterized by both hypomanic episodes and numerous periods of depressed mood or loss of interest or pleasure. In cyclothymia the patient shows no psychotic features, and the disorder is a less severe mood disorder than bipolar I disorder.

15.14 The answer is C (*Synopsis VIII,* page 280).
Obsessive rumination is a state of tension in which a patient has a persistent thought that serves no adaptive purpose. It is seen in depression but is more common in obsessive-compulsive disorder and is usually classified not as a vegetative sign but as a disorder of thought content. Vegetative signs usually refer to functions that relate to the autonomic nervous system, which provides innervation to the blood vessels, heart, glands, viscera, and smooth muscle. Signs that point toward a slowing of the organism rather than to a quickening are also known as vegetative (for example, decreased libido). Vegetative signs in depression include *weight loss, abnormal menses, decreased libido,* and *fatigability.*

15.15 The answer is C (*Synopsis VIII,* page 556).
Approximately two thirds of depressed patients have suicidal ideation, and about *15 percent* do eventually commit suicide.

15.16 The answer is D (*Synopsis VIII,* pages 560–561).
As the illness progresses, the amount of time between episodes often decreases, not increases. After approximately five episodes, however, the interepisode interval often stabilizes at about 6 to 9 months. *Bipolar I disorder most often starts with depression* (75 percent of the time in females, 67 percent in males). Most patients experience both depression and mania, although *about 10 to 20 percent of patients experience only manic episodes. An untreated manic episode lasts about 3 months;* therefore, it is unwise to discontinue drugs before that time. Some patients develop rapidly cycling bipolar I disorder episodes. *Rapid cycling is much more common in women than in men,* although it is not related temporally to the menstrual cycle. Rapid cycling may be associated with treatment with tricyclic drugs, and patients receiving those medications often respond to combination therapies of lithium and MAOIs.

15.17 The answer is D (*Synopsis VIII,* page 552).
According to DSM-IV, the specifier "with seasonal pattern" can be applied to bipolar I disorder, *bipolar II disorder,* and major depressive disorder, recurrent. According to DSM-IV, the specifier "with seasonal pattern" cannot be applied to *dysthymic disorder, cyclothymic disorder,* or *major depressive disorder, single episode.* The criteria for the seasonal pattern specifier are listed in Table 15.5.

15.18 The answer is E (all) (*Synopsis VIII,* page 543).
Some clinicians believe that life events play the primary or principal role in depression; others are more conservative, believing that life events are *a possible factor in the onset and the timing of a specific episode of depression.* However, the research data to support that relation are inconclusive. The most robust data indicate that life events are *most associated with the development of depression in later life when parent is lost before age 11.* The environmental stressor *most associated with the onset of an episode of depression is the loss of a spouse.* Although reasonable data suggest some relation

Table 15.5
DSM-IV Criteria for Seasonal Pattern Specifier

Specify if:
With seasonal pattern (can be applied to the pattern of major depressive episodes in bipolar I disorder, bipolar II disorder, or major depressive disorder, recurrent)

A. There has been a regular temporal relationship between the onset of major depressive episodes in bipolar I or bipolar II disorder or major depressive disorder, recurrent, and a particular time of the year (eg, regular appearance of the major depressive episode in the fall or winter)
Note: Do not include cases in which there is an obvious effect of seasonal-related psychosocial stressors (eg, regularly being unemployed every winter).
B. Full remissions (or a change from depression to mania or hypomania) also occurs at a characteristic time of the year (eg, depression disappears in the spring).
C. In the past 2 years, two major depressive episodes have occurred that demonstrate the temporal seasonal relationships defined in criteria A and B, and no nonseasonal major depressive episodes have occurred during that same period.
D. Seasonal major depressive episodes (as described above) substantially outnumber the nonseasonal major depressive episodes that may have occurred over the individual's lifetime.

Reprinted with permission from American Psychiatric Association: *Diagnostic and Statistical Manual of Mental Disorders,* ed 4. Copyright, American Psychiatric Association, Washington, 1994.

between life events and the onset of depression, life events *are not significantly related to the onset and the timing of a specific episode of mania.*

15.19 The answer is C (*Synopsis VIII,* pages 87, 542, 553, 557–558).
Parkinson's disease is most often associated with depression. Up to 90 percent of Parkinson's disease patients may have marked depressive symptoms that are not correlated with their degree of physical disability or age or duration of their illness. The symptoms of depression may be masked by the almost identical motor symptoms of Parkinson's disease. The depressive symptoms of Parkinson's disease often respond to antidepressant drugs or electroconvulsive therapy.

Other neurological diseases less often associated with depression are *epilepsy, brain tumors, dementia of the Alzheimer's type,* and *Huntington's disease.*

15.20 The answer is B (*Synopsis VIII,* page 544).
The most likely diagnosis is *major depressive disorder.* The patient had symptoms for 2 months, and according to DSM-IV, the minimal criterion for length of depression is 2 weeks. Other symptoms included loss of appetite, hypersomnia, loss of interest or pleasure in usual activities, decreased libido, loss of energy, and recurrent thoughts of death, suicidal ideation, and wishes to kill himself.

Bipolar I disorder, by definition, must involve an episode of mania—not seen in this case—either currently or in the past. *Generalized anxiety disorder* is ruled out by the absence of any prominent symptoms of anxiety. *Schizophrenia* is also ruled out because indications of psychotic symptoms, such as hallucinations, delusions, and disorganized thinking, were not present.

The diagnostic criteria for major depressive disorder, single episode, are listed in Table 15.6.

15.21 The answer is C (*Synopsis VIII,* pages 578–579).
The patient was suffering from *cyclothymic disorder* (Table 15.7); he had symptoms of both depression and hypomania. His down or depressed periods were marked by crying and loss of interest in sex and work, and his excessive use of alcohol during those times was a defense against depression and not the primary illness from which he suffered. When elated, the patient was gregarious, optimistic, and productive.

The essential feature of *major depressive disorder* is a severe dysphoric mood and persistent loss of interest or pleasure in all usual activities. Because of the patient's hypomanic episodes and mild depressive symptoms, major depressive disorder is ruled out.

Bipolar I disorder is characterized by severe alterations in mood that are usually episodic and recurrent. The patient in this case had mood changes similar to those seen in bipolar I disorder, but the mildness of his symptoms precluded the full diagnosis of bipolar I disorder.

A diagnosis of *dysthymic disorder* is excluded because the patient showed episodes of elated moods. In dysthymic disorder, the patient's mood is chronic depression; in adult patients, a 2-year history of such depression is required before the diagnosis can be made.

Bipolar II disorder is characterized by one or more major depressive episodes, at least one hypomanic episode, and no manic episodes. This patient had no major depressive episodes.

15.22 The answer is C (*Synopsis VIII,* pages 1104–1106).
Tricyclic drugs have cardiac, neurological, and physiological adverse effects. Cardiac effects include *tachycardia, flattened T waves, and prolonged QT intervals.* Neurological effects in-

Table 15.6
DSM-IV Diagnostic Criteria for Major Depressive Disorder, Single Episode

A. Presence of a major depressive episode.
B. The major depressive episode is not better accounted for by schizoaffective disorder, and is not superimposed on schizophrenia, schizophreniform disorder, delusional disorder, or psychotic disorder not otherwise specified.
C. There has never been a manic episode, a mixed episode, or a hypomanic episode. **Note:** This exclusion does not apply if all of the maniclike, mixedlike, or hypomanic-like episodes are substance or treatment induced or are due to the direct physiological effects of a general medical condition.

Specify (for current or most recent episode):
Severity/psychotic/remission specifiers
Chronic
With catatonic features
With melancholic features
With atypical features
With postpartum onset

Reprinted with permission from American Psychiatric Association: *Diagnostic and Statistical Manual of Mental Disorders,* ed 4. Copyright, American Psychiatric Association, Washington, 1994.

Table 15.7
DSM-IV Diagnostic Criteria for Cyclothymic Disorder

A. For at least 2 years, the presence of numerous periods with hypomanic symptoms and numerous periods with depressive symptoms that do not meet criteria for a major depressive episode. **Note:** In children and adolescents, the duration must be at least 1 year.

B. During the above 2-year period (1 year in children and adolescents), the person has not been without the symptoms in criterion A for more than 2 months at a time.

C. No major depressive episode, manic episode, or mixed episode has been present during the first 2 years of the disturbance.
Note: After the initial 2 years (1 year in children or adolescents) of cyclothymic disorder, there may be superimposed manic or mixed episodes (in which case both bipolar I disorder and cyclothymic disorder may be diagnosed) or major depressive episodes (in which case both bipolar II disorder and cyclothymic disorder may be diagnosed).

D. The symptoms in criterion A are not better accounted for by schizoaffective disorder and are not superimposed on schizophrenia, schizophreniform disorder, delusional disorder, or psychotic disorder not otherwise specified.

E. The symptoms are not due to the direct physiological effects of a substance (eg, a drug of abuse, a medication) or a general medical condition (eg, hyperthyroidism).

F. The symptoms cause clinically significant distress or impairment in social, occupational, or other important areas of functioning.

Reprinted with permission from American Psychiatric Association: *Diagnostic and Statistical Manual of Mental Disorders,* ed 4. Copyright, American Psychiatric Association, Washington, 1994.

clude *myoclonic twitches and tremors of the tongue.* Some patients may become *hypomanic* or develop *delusions and hallucinations,* but this is rare. The least likely effect would be *involvement in pleasurable activities with a high potential for painful consequences.* Such behavior, also known as risk-taking behavior, most often occurs in manic patients, certain adolescents, and adults with brain syndromes, particularly of the parietal lobe.

15.23 The answer is E (*Synopsis VIII,* pages 252, 282, 553). *Mood-incongruent delusions* are usually not part of bipolar disorder, which usually includes mood congruent delusions and hallucinations. Mood-incongruent delusions usually point to a diagnosis of schizophrenia. The patient was experiencing a manic episode, characterized by a predominantly elevated, expansive, or irritable mood. The mood may be characterized by *emotional lability,* with rapid shifts to brief depression from mania. The essential feature of a manic episode is a distinct period of intense psychophysiological activation with a number of accompanying symptoms, such as lack of judgment of the consequences of actions, pressure of speech, flight of ideas, inflated self-esteem, and at times hypersexuality. *Delusions* of grandiosity, *hallucinations,* and ideas of reference may also be present. *Nocturnal electroencephalographic* (EEG) changes in mania include a decreased total sleep time, a decreased percentage of dream time, and an increased dream latency. Those findings have been interpreted as indicating that circadian rhythm activities are delayed in mania because the activity of the intrinsic pacemaker is increased. In DSM-IV the diagnosis of a manic episode requires not a specific duration, such as 3 days, but rather only a distinct period of abnormally and persistently disordered mood. Table 15.9 lists the DSM-IV criteria for a manic episode.

15.24 The answer is E (all) (*Synopsis VIII,* pages 578–579). Although the manifestations of cyclothymic disorder are usually insufficiently severe to meet the diagnostic criteria for bipolar I disorder, certain similarities have led to a consensus that cyclothymic disorder is an attenuated form of bipolar I disorder. Those similarities include a *similarity of symptoms in the two disorders,* a *significant number of cyclothymic patients who eventually have bipolar I disorder,* and pharmacological similarities—notably *favorable response to lithium in both disorders* and frequently *a hypomanic response to tricyclic drugs among cyclothymic disorder patients.*

15.25 The answer is E (*Synopsis VIII,* pages 1247–1248). The lifetime prevalence of dysthymic disorder has been reported by a number of studies to be *45 cases per 1,000 persons.*

15.26 The answer is C (*Synopsis VIII,* page 576). The presence of *delusions* and hallucinations is inconsistent with the diagnosis of dysthymic disorder. Among the associated symptoms are those commonly associated with depressive episodes, including poor appetite, *weight change, sleep difficulty* (particularly early morning wakening), loss of energy, fatigability, psychomotor retardation, loss of interest or pleasure in activities, decreased sexual drive, *decreased sexual performance,* feelings of guilt and self-reproach, obsessive preoccupation with health, complaints of difficulty in thinking,

Table 15.8
DSM-IV Diagnostic Criteria for Bipolar Disorder, Most Recent Episode Mixed

A. Currently (or most recently) in a mixed episode.

B. There has previously been at least one major depressive episode, manic episode, or mixed episode.

C. The mood episodes in criteria A and B are not better accounted for by schizoaffective disorder and are not superimposed on schizophrenia, schizophreniform disorder, delusional disorder, or psychotic disorder not otherwise specified.

Specify (for current or most recent episode):
Severity/psychotic/remission specifiers
With catatonic features
With postpartum onset

Specify:
Longitudinal course specifiers (with and without interepisode recovery)
With seasonal pattern (applies only to the pattern of major depressive episodes)
With rapid cycling

Reprinted with permission from American Psychiatric Association: *Diagnostic and Statistical Manual of Mental Disorders,* ed 4. Copyright, American Psychiatric Association, Washington, 1994.

Table 15.9
DSM-IV Diagnostic Criteria for Dysthymic Disorder

A. Depressed mood for most of the day, for more days than not, as indicated either by subjective account or observation by others, for at least 2 years. **Note:** In children and adolescents, mood can be irritable and duration must be at least 1 year.

B. Presence, while depressed, of two (or more) of the following:
(1) poor appetite or overeating
(2) insomnia or hypersomnia
(3) low energy or fatigue
(4) low self-esteem
(5) poor concentration or difficulty making decisions
(6) feelings of hopelessness

C. During the 2-year period (1 year for children or adolescents) of the disturbance, the person has never been without the symptoms in criteria A and B for more than 2 months at a time.

D. No major depressive episode has been present during the first 2 years of the disturbance (1 year for children and adolescents); ie, the disturbance is not better accounted for by chronic major depressive disorder, or major depressive disorder, in partial remission.
Note: There may have been a previous major depressive episode, provided there was a full remission (no significant signs or symptoms for 2 months) before development of the dysthymic disorder. In addition, after the initial 2 years (1 year in children or adolescents) of dysthymic disorder, there may be superimposed episodes of major depressive disorder, in which case both diagnoses may be given when the criteria are met for a major depressive episode.

E. There has never been a manic episode, a mixed episode, or a hypomanic episode, and criteria have never been met for cyclothymic disorder.

F. The disturbance does not occur exclusively during the course of a chronic psychotic disorder, such as schizophrenia or delusional disorder.

G. The symptoms are not due to the indirect physiological effects of a substance (eg, a drug of abuse, a medication) or a general medical condition (eg, hypothyroidism).

H. The symptoms cause clinically significant distress or impairment in social, occupational, or other important areas of functioning.

Specify if:
Early onset: if onset is before age 21 years
Late onset: if onset is age 21 years or older

Specify (for most recent 2 years of dysthymic disorder):
With atypical features

Reprinted with permission from American Psychiatric Association: *Diagnostic and Statistical Manual of Mental Disorders*, ed 4. Copyright, American Psychiatric Association, Washington, 1994.

indecisiveness, *suicidal ideas,* feelings of helplessness and hopelessness, and pessimism. The diagnostic criteria for dysthymic disorder are listed in Table 15.9.

15.27 The answer is E (all) (*Synopsis VIII,* page 553).
Excessive clinging to parents and school phobia, both of which reflect *separation anxiety,* may be symptoms of depression in children. In latency and in early adolescent boys especially, negative and *antisocial behavior* may occur (depressive equivalents). Sexual acting out, truancy, and *running away* are seen in older boys and girls. In the elderly, *pseudodementia*—that is, depression presenting primarily as a loss of intellectual functioning—must be carefully differentiated from true dementia caused by a medical condition.

15.28 The answer is E (*Synopsis VIII,* pages 553–555).
The course of major depressive disorder by definition does not include *bipolar II disorder,* but it usually includes *an untreated episode of depression lasting 6 to 13 months, a treated episode of depression lasting about 3 months, the return of symptoms after the withdrawal of antidepressants before 3 months have elapsed,* and *an average of five to six episodes over a 20-year period.*

15.29 The answer is E (all) (*Synopsis VIII,* pages 553–554).
Although differentiating between a manic episode and a schizophrenic episode can be difficult, the clinical guidelines include the following: (1) *quality of mood:* merriment, elation, and infectiousness of mood are much more common in mania than in schizophrenia; (2) *psychomotor activity:* the combination of an elated mood, rapid or pressured speech, and hyperactivity heavily weighs toward a diagnosis of mania, although hyperactivity can also occur in schizophrenia; (3) *speed of onset:* the onset in mania, as opposed to schizophrenia, is often more rapid, being a marked change from previous behavior; and (4) *family history:* half of bipolar I disorder patients have a family history of a mood disorder; schizophrenic patients do not have as high a correlation.

15.30 The answer is E (all) (*Synopsis VIII,* pages 567–569).
Many substances used to treat somatic illnesses may trigger depressive symptoms. Commonly prescribed medications associated with depressive symptoms include *analgesics* (for example, ibuprofen [Advil]), *antibacterials* (for example, ampicillin), *antipsychotics* (for example, phenothiazines), and *antihypertensives* (for example, propranolol [Inderal]). Certain substances used to treat medical disorders may also trigger a manic response. The most commonly encountered manic response is to steroids. In some cases spontaneous manic and depressive episodes originated some years later in patients whose first illness episode seemed to be triggered by the medical use of steroids. Other drugs are also known to have the potential for initiating a manic syndrome, including amphetamines and tricyclic drugs (for example, imipramine [Tofranil], amitriptyline [Elavil, Endep]). Table 15.10 lists drugs that can cause depression.

15.31 The answer is B (*Synopsis VIII,* page 571).
L-Tryptophan, the amino acid precursor to serotonin, *has been used as an adjuvant to both antidepressants and lithium* in the treatment of bipolar I disorder. Tyrosine *is the amino acid precursor to dopamine.* L-Tryptophan has also been used alone as a hypnotic and an antidepressant. L-Tryptophan and L-tryptophan-containing products have been recalled in the United States because L-tryptophan *has been associated with eosinophilia-myalgia syndrome.* The symptoms include fatigue, myalgia, shortness of breath, rashes, and swelling of the extremities. Congestive heart failure and death can also occur. Although several studies have shown that L-tryptophan is an efficacious adjuvant in the treatment of mood disorders, it

Table 15.10
Pharmacological Causes of Depressive Symptoms

Analgesics and anti-inflammatory drugs Ibuprofen Indomethacin Opiates Phenacetin	Antineoplastics C-Asparaginase Azathioprine (AZT) 6-Azauridine Bleomycin Trimethoprim Vincristine
Antibacterials and antifungals Ampicillin Cycloserine Ethionamide Griseofulvin Metronidazole Nalidixic acid Nitrofurantoin Streptomycin Sulfamethoxazole Sulfonamides Tetracycline	Neurological and psychiatric drugs Amantadine Antipsychotics (butyrophenones, phenothiazines, oxyindoles) Baclofen Bromocriptine Carbamazepine Levodopa Phenytoin Sedatives and hypnotics (barbiturates, benzodiazepines, chloral hydrate)
Antihypertensives and cardiac drugs Alphamethyldopa Bethanidine β-Blockers (propranolol) Clonidine Digitalis Guanabenz acetate Guanethidine Hydralazine Lidocaine Prazosin Procainamide Rescinnamine Reserpine Veratrum	Steroids and hormones Corticosteroids (including ACTH) Danazol Oral contraceptives Prednisone Triamcinolone Miscellaneous Acetazolamide Choline Cimetidine Cyproheptadine Diphenoxylate Disulfiram Methysergide Stimulants (amphetamines, fenfluramine)

ACTH, adrenocorticotropic hormone.

should not be used for any purpose until the problem with eosinophilia-myalgia syndrome is resolved. Current evidence points to a contaminant in the manufacturing process.

15.32 The answer is C (*Synopsis VIII*, pages 531–532).
Propranolol (a β-blocker) is an antihypertensive and may actually cause depressive symptoms. Many pharmacological agents, such as *bromocriptine* (Parlodel), *isoniazid* (Nydrazid), *cimetidine* (Tagamet), and *disulfiram* (Antabuse), may precipitate mania, as can antidepressant treatment or withdrawal. Table 15.11 lists drugs associated with manic symptoms.

15.33 The answer is C (*Synopsis VIII*, pages 538–539).
Major depressive disorder *shows no conclusive evidence for any difference between blacks and whites,* even though more blacks than whites are hospitalized for major depressive disorder. This disorder *is twice as common in women as in men,* and it *peaks in women between the ages of 35 and 45.* Major depressive disorder shows no pattern in social class; it *is not highest in the poor.*

15.34 The answer is B (*Synopsis VIII*, pages 539–541).
The dexamethasone-suppression test (DST) is used to help *confirm a diagnostic impression of major depressive disorder.* The patient is given 1 mg of dexamethasone by mouth at 11 P.M., and plasma cortisol is measured at 8 A.M., 4 P.M., and 11 P.M. *Plasma cortisol above 5 μg/dL (known as nonsuppression) is considered abnormal (that is, positive). Suppression of cortisol indicates that the hypothalamic-adrenal-pituitary axis is functioning properly.* The DST can be used to follow the response of a depressed person to treatment. *Normalization of DST,* however, is not an indication to stop antidepressant treatment, because the DST may normalize before the depression resolves. The problems associated with the DST include varying reports of sensitivity and specificity; *false-positive and false-negative results are common.*

Table 15.11
Drugs Associated with Manic Symptoms

Amphetamines
Baclofen
Bromide
Bromocriptine
Captopril
Cimetidine
Cocaine
Corticosteroids (including ACTH)
Cyclosporine
Disulfiram
Hallucinogens (intoxication and flashbacks)
Hydralazine
Isoniazid
Levodopa
Methylphenidate
Metrizamide (following myelography)
Opiates and opioids
Procarbazine
Procyclidine

ACTH, adrenocorticotropic hormone.

15.35 The answer is B (*Synopsis VIII*, pages 171–173).
The graph depicts the lifetime *prevalence of mood disorder. Anorexia nervosa* occurs 10 to 20 times more often in females than in males, and the most common age of onset of anorexia nervosa is the mid-teenage years.

Regarding *obsessive-compulsive disorder,* men and women are equally likely to be affected (however, adolescent boys are more commonly affected than adolescent girls). The mean age of onset is about 20 years, and about two-thirds of patients have the onset of symptoms before age 25. *Schizophrenia* is equally prevalent among men and women, with the peak ages of onset for men 15 to 25 and women 25 to 35. Women with *somatization disorder* outnumber men 5 to 20 times. Somatization disorder is defined as beginning before age 30; it most often begins during a person's teens.

15.36 The answer is E (*Synopsis VIII*, pages 544, 555–556).
The patient's symptoms are consistent with those found in major depressive disorder (Table 15.3).

The differential diagnosis of a patient with depressive symptoms should include consideration of *substance-related disorders, psychotic disorders, somatoform disorders, anxiety disorders,* eating disorders, and adjustment disorders, all of which are commonly associated with depressive symptoms.

15.37 The answer is C (*Synopsis VIII*, pages 571–572).
The treatment of bipolar I disorder has been changed by the

many studies that have demonstrated the efficacy of two anticonvulsants—*carbamazepine* and *valproate* (Depakene)—in the treatment of manic episodes and in the prophylaxis of manic and depressive episodes in bipolar I disorder. Although the data in support of the efficacy of *lithium* are numerous, sufficient data have accumulated to warrant the use of the two anticonvulsants as first-line treatments of bipolar I disorder. Such a decision should be based primarily on the compatibility between the patient and the relevant side effects of the drugs. The long-term treatment of bipolar I disorder is an indication for those anticonvulsants, but the initial stages of manic episodes often require the addition of drugs with potent sedative effects. Drugs commonly used at the initiation of therapy for bipolar I disorder include clonazepam (Klonopin) (1 mg every 4 to 6 hours), lorazepam (Ativan) (2 mg every 4 to 6 hours), and haloperidol (Haldol) (5 mg every 2 to 4 hours). The physician should taper those medications and discontinue them as soon as the initial phase of the manic episode has subsided and the effects of lithium, carbamazepine, or valproate are beginning to be seen clinically.

The patient in this case was *noncompliant* with lithium, neuroleptics, and antidepressants; that is a further indication to try valproate or carbamazepine. In addition, obtaining a history of why the patient was noncompliant is helpful. Some patients cannot tolerate anticholinergic symptoms, which are most likely with *tricyclic antidepressants.*

Answers 15.38–15.40

15.38 The answer is B (*Synopsis VIII,* pages 527–528).

15.39 The answer is A (*Synopsis VIII,* page 526).

15.40 The answer is C (*Synopsis VIII,* pages 526–528).
Recurrent brief depressive disorder (Table 15.12) is characterized by multiple, relatively brief (less than 2 weeks) episodes of depressive *symptoms* that *meet most of the diagnostic criteria for major depressive disorder.* The clinical features of recurrent brief depressive disorder are almost identical to those of major depressive disorder. One subtle difference is that the lives of patients with recurrent brief depressive disorder may seem more disrupted or chaotic because of the frequent changes in their moods when compared with the lives of patients with major depressive disorder, whose depressive episodes occur at a measured pace.

The treatment of patients with recurrent brief depressive disorder should be similar to the treatment of patients with major depressive disorder. The main treatments should be psychotherapy (insight-oriented psychotherapy, cognitive therapy, interpersonal therapy, or behavior therapy). *Treatment may include the use of antidepressants.*

In *minor depressive disorder the symptoms are equal in duration but fewer in number than those in major depressive disorder* (Table 15.13). The treatment of minor depressive disorder can include psychotherapy or pharmacotherapy or both. *Treatment may include the use of antidepressants.*

Answers 15.41–15.45

15.41 The answer is A (*Synopsis VIII,* pages 282, 547, 549).

15.42 The answer is B (*Synopsis VIII,* pages 282, 547, 549).

15.43 The answer is D (*Synopsis VIII,* pages 282, 547, 549).

Table 15.12
DSM-IV Research Criteria for Recurrent Brief Depressive Disorder

A. Criteria, except for duration, are met for a major depressive episode.
B. The depressive periods in criterion A last at least 2 days but less than 2 weeks.
C. The depressive periods occur at least once a month for 12 consecutive months and are not associated with the menstrual cycle.
D. The periods of depressed mood cause clinically significant distress or impairment in social, occupational, or other important areas of functioning.
E. The symptoms are not due to the direct physiological effects of a substance (ie, a drug of abuse, a medication) or a general medical condition (eg, hypothyroidism).
F. There has never been a major depressive episode, and criteria are not met for dysthymic disorder.
G. There has never been a manic episode, a mixed episode, or a hypomanic episode, and criteria are not met for cyclothymic disorder. **Note:** This exclusion does not apply if all of the maniclike, mixedlike, or hypomanic-like episodes are substance or treatment induced.
H. The mood disturbance does not occur exclusively during schizophrenia, schizophreniform disorder, schizoaffective disorder, delusional disorder, or psychotic disorder not otherwise specified.

15.44 The answer is B (*Synopsis VIII,* pages 282, 547, 549).

15.45 The answer is A (*Synopsis VIII,* pages 282, 547, 549).
A mood-incongruent delusion is characterized by content that is not consistent with the patient's mood. Thus, a depressed patient who has delusions of inflated worth, power, identity or a special relationship to a deity or a famous person has a mood-incongruent delusion, as in the cases of *a suicidal man who believes that he is the Messiah* and *a 30-year-old depressed woman who believes that she is the Virgin Mary. Mood-congruent delusions* are those that are consistent with the patient's mood. *An elated man who believes that he has been reincarnated as a millionaire* and *a depressed woman who thinks that she has committed terrible crimes* are suffering from mood-congruent delusions. The *boy who thinks that he hears voices* is experiencing a hallucination, and hallucinations can also be described as either mood-congruent or mood-incongruent.

Answers 15.46–15.49

15.46 The answer is A (*Synopsis VIII,* pages 567–571).

15.47 The answer is C (*Synopsis VIII,* page 574).

15.48 The answer is B (*Synopsis VIII,* page 575).

15.49 The answer is A (*Synopsis VIII,* page 549).
Dysthymic disorder does not include patients who have *episodic periods of depression.* By definition, dysthymic disorder symptoms do not occur exclusively during the course of a chronic psychotic disorder; dysthymic disorder *does not have psychotic symptoms.* Dysthymic disorder has nonpsychotic

Table 15.13
DSM-IV Research Criteria for Minor Depressive Disorder

A. A mood disturbance, defined as follows:
  (1) at least two (but less than five) of the following symptoms have been present during the same 2-week period and represent a change from previous functioning; at least one of the symptoms is either (a) or (b):
    (a) depressed mood most of the day, nearly every day, as indicated by either subjective report (eg, feels sad or empty) or observation made by others (eg, appears tearful). **Note:** In children and adolescents, can be irritable mood.
    (b) markedly diminished interest of pleasure in all, or almost all, activities most of the day, nearly every day (as indicated by either subjective account or observation made by others).
    (c) significant weight loss when not dieting or weight gain (eg, a change of more than 5% of body weight in a month), or decrease or increase in appetite nearly every day. **Note:** In children, consider failure to make expected weight gains.
    (d) insomnia or hypersomnia nearly every day
    (e) psychomotor agitation or retardation nearly every day (observable by others, not merely subjective feelings of restlessness or being slowed down)
    (f) fatigue or loss of energy nearly every day
    (g) feelings of worthlessness or excessive or inappropriate guilt (which may be delusional) nearly every day (not merely self-reproach or guilt about being sick)
    (h) diminished ability to think or concentrate, or indecisiveness, nearly every day (either by subjective account or as observed by others)
    (i) recurrent thoughts of death (not just fear of dying), recurrent suicidal ideation without a specific plan, or a suicide attempt or a specific plan for committing suicide
  (2) the symptoms cause clinically significant distress or impairment in social, occupational, or other important areas of functioning
  (3) the symptoms are not due to the direct physiological effects of a substance (eg, a drug of abuse, a medication) or a general medical condition (eg, hypothyroidism)
  (4) the symptoms are not better accounted for by bereavement (ie, a normal reaction to the death of a loved one)

B. There has never been a major depressive episode, and criteria are not met for dysthymic disorder.

C. There has never been a manic episode, a mixed episode, or a hypomanic episode, and criteria are not met for cyclothymic disorder. **Note:** This exclusion does not apply if all of the maniclike, mixedlike or hypomanic-like episodes are substance or treatment induced.

D. The mood disturbance does not occur exclusively during schizophrenia, schizophreniform disorder, schizoaffective disorder, delusional disorder, or psychotic disorder not otherwise specified.

Reprinted with permission from American Psychiatric Association: *Diagnostic and Statistical Manual of Mental Disorders,* ed 4. Copyright, American Psychiatric Association, Washington, 1994.

signs and symptoms of depression that meet specific diagnostic criteria, but do not meet the diagnostic criteria for major depressive disorder. About 5 to 10 percent of patients with *major depressive disorder have psychotic symptoms,* including both delusions and hallucinations. *Major depressive disorder, recurrent,* is characterized by *episodic periods of depression. Many patients* with major depressive disorder and some patients with dysthymic disorder *have a positive family history of mood disorders, decreased rapid eye movement latency, and a positive therapeutic response to antidepressants. DSM-IV defines subtypes of dysthymic disorder based on onset before and after age 21.* Table 15.9 lists the diagnostic criteria for dysthymic disorder.

Answers 15.50–15.55

15.50 The answer is B (*Synopsis VIII,* page 580).

15.51 The answer is D (*Synopsis VIII,* pages 574–580).

15.52 The answer is B (*Synopsis VIII,* page 580).

15.53 The answer is C (*Synopsis VIII,* pages 576, 579).

15.54 The answer is B (*Synopsis VIII,* page 578).

15.55 The answer is C (*Synopsis VIII,* pages 576–579).
In cyclothymic disorder, *treatment with antidepressants may lead to hypomanic symptoms* and patients may have a *favorable response to lithium.* During the hypomanic phase of cyclothymia, *sexual promiscuity* may be seen. With regard to *alcohol abuse,* 25 to 50 percent of persons with alcohol abuse have dysthymic disorder, and mood swings, such as those seen in cyclothymic disorder, have also been described as part of the mood disorder related to alcohol abuse. Both dysthymic disorder and cyclothymic disorder may be *confused with substance abuse.* Steroids, amphetamines, barbiturates, and central nervous system (CNS) depressants produce depression after periods of heavy use, and mood swings may be associated with the ingestion of steroids, cocaine, amphetamines, and hallucinogens. *Delusions and hallucinations* are, by definition, *inconsistent with the diagnosis of both dysthymic disorder and cyclothymic disorder.*

Answers 15.56–15.57

15.56 The answer is A (*Synopsis VIII,* page 578).

15.57 The answer is B (*Synopsis VIII,* page 572).
Cyclothymic disorder is *characterized by episodes of hypomanic-like symptoms* (Table 15.14) *and periods of mild depression.* In DSM-IV, cyclothymic disorder is differentiated from *bipolar II disorder,* which is *characterized by major depressive episodes and hypomanic episodes* (Table 15.15).

Table 15.14
DSM-IV Criteria for Hypomanic Episode

A. A distinct period of persistently elevated, expansive, or irritable mood, lasting throughout at least 4 days, that is clearly different from the usual nondepressed mood.

B. During the period of mood disturbance, three (or more) of the following symptoms have persisted (four if the mood is only irritable) and have been present to a significant degree:
  (1) inflated self-esteem or grandiosity
  (2) decreased need for sleep (eg, feels rested after only 3 hours of sleep)
  (3) more talkative than usual or pressure to keep talking
  (4) flight of ideas or subjective experience that thoughts are racing
  (5) distractibility (ie, attention too easily drawn to unimportant or irrelevant external stimuli)
  (6) increase in goal-directed activity (either socially, at work or school, or sexually) or psychomotor agitation
  (7) excessive involvement in pleasurable activities that have a high potential for painful consequences (eg, the person engages in unrestrained buying sprees, sexual indiscretions, or foolish business investments)

C. The episode is associated with an unequivocal change in functioning that is uncharacteristic of the person when not symptomatic.

D. The disturbance in mood and the change in functioning are observable by others.

E. The episode is not severe enough to cause marked impairment in social or occupational functioning, or to necessitate hospitalization, and there are no psychotic features.

F. The symptoms are not due to the direct physiological effects of a substance (eg, a drug of abuse, a medication, or other treatment) or a general medical condition (eg, hyperthyroidism).

Note: Hypomanic-like episodes that are clearly caused by somatic antidepressant treatment (eg, medication, electroconvulsive therapy, light therapy) should not count toward a diagnosis of bipolar II disorder.

Table 15.15
DSM-IV Diagnostic Criteria for Bipolar II Disorder

A. Presence (or history) of one or more major depressive episodes.
B. Presence (or history) of at least one hypomanic episode.
C. There has never been a manic episode or a mixed episode.
D. The mood symptoms in criteria A and B are not better accounted for by schizoaffective disorder and are not superimposed on schizophrenia, schizophreniform disorder, delusional disorder, or psychotic disorder not otherwise specified.
E. The symptoms cause clinically significant distress or impairment in social, occupational, or other important areas of functioning.

Specify current or most recent episode:
  Hypomanic: if currently (or most recently) in a hypomanic episode
  Depressed: if currently (or most recently) in a major depressive episode

Specify (for current or most recent major depressive episode only if it is the most recent type of mood episode):
  Severity/psychotic/remission specifiers. Note: Fifth-digit codes cannot be used here because the code for bipolar II disorder already uses the fifth digit.
  Chronic
  With catatonic features
  With melancholic features
  With atypical features
  With postpartum onset

Specify:
  Longitudinal course specifiers (with and without interepisode recovery)
  With seasonal pattern (applies only to the pattern of major depressive episodes)
  With rapid cycling

16

Anxiety Disorders

The fourth edition of *Diagnostic and Statistical Manual of Mental Disorders* (DSM-IV) lists several anxiety disorders: panic attack, agoraphobia, panic disorder without agoraphobia, panic disorder with agoraphobia, agoraphobia without history of panic disorder, specific phobia, social phobia, obsessive-compulsive disorder, posttraumatic stress disorder, acute stress disorder, generalized anxiety disorder, anxiety disorder due to a general medical condition, substance-induced anxiety disorder, and anxiety disorder not otherwise specified. The criteria for panic attack and agoraphobia are discussed separately, as both occur along with some of the anxiety disorders.

Feelings of anxiety can range from normal to pathological, from adaptive to maladaptive. This familiar emotion arises from a person's perception and interpretation of genuine external stress and from a biological reaction to internal changes. Although anxiety can be almost entirely either psychological or biological, it is generally produced by a complex interplay of psychology, temperament, environment, conditioning, and biology.

The psychological theories of the causes of anxiety spring from the three major schools: psychoanalytic, behavioral, and existential. The biological theories of the causes of anxiety, which are presently of great interest to investigators, focus on the autonomic nervous system, the role of specific neurotransmitters, and the ways that anxiolytic drugs affect these transmitters. Brain-imaging techniques such as positron emission tomography (PET), magnetic resonance imaging (MRI), and single photon emission computed tomography (SPECT) have indicated that cerebral pathology may be associated with anxiety disorders in some patients. Study of neuroanatomical areas such as the locus ceruleus and the raphe nuclei and their projections to the limbic system and cerebral cortex have also engaged the attention of researchers.

By studying Chapter 16 in *Kaplan and Sadock's Synopsis VIII,* students will be able to test their knowledge of anxiety disorders with the questions and answers below.

HELPFUL HINTS

The student should know the following names, cases, terms, and acronyms related to anxiety disorders.

- acute stress disorder
- adrenergic
- aggression
- ambivalence
- anticipatory anxiety
- anxiety
- *Aplysia*
- aversive conditioning
- benzodiazepines
- cerebral cortex
- cleanliness
- clomipramine (Anafranil)
- conflict
- counterphobic attitude
- Jacob M. DaCosta
- Charles Darwin
- dopamine
- ego-dystonic
- fear
- Otto Fenichel
- flooding
- Sigmund Freud
- GABA
- generalized anxiety disorder
- hypnosis
- imipramine (Tofranil)
- implosion
- isolation
- lactate infusion
- limbic system
- Little Albert
- Little Hans
- magical thinking
- MHPG
- MMPI, Rorschach
- norepinephrine
- numbing
- obsessive-compulsive disorder
- panic attack
- panic disorder
- PET
- phobias:
  - agoraphobia
  - social
  - specific
- posttraumatic stress disorder
- propranolol (Inderal)
- reaction formation
- repression
- secondary gain
- serotonin
- shell shock
- sleep EEG studies
- soldier's heart
- stress
- systematic desensitization
- thought stopping
- time-limited psychotherapy
- trauma
- undoing
- John B. Watson
- Joseph Wolpe

▲ QUESTIONS

DIRECTIONS: Each of the incomplete statements below is followed by five suggested completions. Select the *one* that is *best* in each case.

Questions 16.1–16.2

An 8-year-old boy is brought to your office. He is described as being obsessed with cleanliness and neatness. Currently he has no friends because he refuses to visit them, feeling that their houses are "dirty"; he gets upset when another child touches him. He is always checking whether he is doing things the way they "should" be done. He becomes very agitated and anxious about this. He has to get up at least 2 hours before leaving for school each day to give himself time to get ready. Recently he woke up at 1:30 A.M. to prepare for school. [Reprinted with permission from Spitzer RL, editor: *DSM-IV Casebook.* American Psychiatric Press, Washington, 1994.]

16.1 What is the most likely diagnosis for the patient?

A. Generalized anxiety disorder
B. Agoraphobia
C. Panic disorder
D. Obsessive-compulsive disorder
E. Social phobia

16.2 An adult patient with this diagnosis might exhibit all of the following brain-imaging findings *except*

A. abnormalities in frontal lobes, cingulum, and basal ganglia
B. decreased caudate volumes bilaterally compared with normal controls
C. lower metabolic rates in basal ganglia and white matter than in normal controls
D. longer mean T1 relaxation times in the frontal cortex than normal controls
E. significantly more gray matter and less white matter than normal controls

DIRECTIONS: For each of the three numbered statements that follow, select the most appropriate of the lettered choices.

A. Agoraphobia
B. Panic disorder
C. Acute stress disorder
D. Acute stress reaction
E. Posttraumatic stress disorder

16.3 This diagnosis appears only in DSM-IV.
16.4 This diagnosis appears only in ICD-10.
16.5 This diagnosis appears in both DSM-IV and ICD-10, but the onset of symptoms is differently defined in each case.

DIRECTIONS: For each of the following numbered questions, select the most appropriate response from among the lettered choices.

16.6 Which of the following choices most accurately describes the role of serotonin in obsessive-compulsive disorder?

A. Serotonin is involved in the cause.
B. Serotonergic drugs are an ineffective treatment.
C. Dysregulation of serotonin is involved in the symptom formation.
D. Measures of platelet binding sites of titrated imipramine are abnormally low.
E. Measures of serotonin metabolites in cerebrospinal fluid are abnormally high.

16.7 Which of the following does *not* correctly refer to the causation of generalized anxiety disorder?

A. Flumazenil can induce anxiety.
B. Antihypertensives such as reserpine and methyldopa can precipitate generalized anxiety disorder.
C. Benzodiazepine receptor agonists may reduce symptoms of anxiety in generalized anxiety disorder.
D. About 25 percent of first-degree relatives of patients with generalized anxiety disorder are also affected.
E. The case of Little Hans was the first presentation of Sigmund Freud's psychological theory of anxiety.

DIRECTIONS: Each of the incomplete statements below is followed by five suggested completions. Select the *one* that is *best* in each case.

16.8 Anxiety

A. is associated with the awareness of being nervous or frightened
B. may occur without physiological sensations
C. is a response to a known external threat
D. tends to sharpen concentration
E. tends to increase recall

16.9 The most common form of phobia is

A. photophobia
B. thanatophobia
C. acrophobia
D. agoraphobia
E. nyctophobia

16.10 The obsessive-compulsive disorder patient who tries to resist carrying out the compulsion generally experiences

A. anxiety
B. hypochondriasis
C. somatization disorder
D. dissociation
E. ambivalence

16.11 Sigmund Freud postulated that the defense mechanisms necessary in phobias are

A. repression, displacement, and avoidance
B. regression, condensation, and projection
C. regression, repression, and isolation
D. repression, projection, and displacement
E. regression, condensation, and dissociation

16.12 All of the following may be used effectively in the treatment of phobias *except*

A. diazepam
B. chlordiazepoxide
C. imipramine
D. hypnosis
E. chlorpromazine

16.13 Therapy for phobias may include all of the following *except*

A. propranolol (Inderal)
B. systematic desensitization
C. phenelzine (Nardil)
D. flooding
E. counterphobic attitudes

16.14 Posttraumatic stress disorder is associated with all of the following *except*

A. a psychologically abnormal reaction to stress
B. reexperiencing of the trauma through dreams
C. biological vulnerability
D. emotional numbing
E. decreased rapid eye movement (REM) latency

16.15 Medications used to treat posttraumatic stress disorder include

A. amitriptyline
B. imipramine
C. phenelzine
D. clonidine
E. all of the above

16.16 In acute stress disorder the symptoms

A. must last for a minimum of 2 days
B. can last for a maximum of 8 weeks
C. must occur within 1 year of the trauma
D. must occur within 6 months of the trauma
E. must occur within 2 months of the trauma

16.17 Unexpected panic attacks are required for the diagnosis of

A. panic disorder
B. social phobia
C. specific phobia
D. generalized anxiety disorder
E. all of the above

16.18 The symptoms of a panic attack can include all of the following *except*

A. derealization
B. chest pain
C. fear of going crazy
D. sweating
E. delusions

DIRECTIONS: Each set of lettered headings below is followed by a list of numbered words or phrases. For each numbered word or phrase, select

A. if the item is associated with *A only*
B. if the item is associated with *B only*
C. if the item is associated with *both A and B*
D. if the item is associated with *neither A nor B*

Questions 16.19–16.24

A. Obsessions
B. Compulsions
C. Both
D. Neither

16.19 Idea or impulse intruding insistently and persistently into awareness
16.20 Ego-alien
16.21 Patient feels a strong desire to resist
16.22 Ideas or sensations
16.23 Acts or behaviors
16.24 Ego-syntonic

Questions 16.25–16.28

A. Little Hans
B. Little Albert
C. Both
D. Neither

16.25 Fear of horses
16.26 Castration anxiety
16.27 Conditioned response
16.28 Fear of rabbits

Questions 16.29–16.33

A. Panic disorder without agoraphobia
B. Generalized anxiety disorder
C. Both
D. Neither

16.29 Discrete and episodic
16.30 Chronic and persistent
16.31 Dizziness and paresthesias
16.32 Other psychiatric symptoms present
16.33 Obvious physical evidence of respiratory alkalosis

DIRECTIONS: Each group of questions below consists of lettered headings followed by a list of numbered statements. For each numbered statement, select the *one* lettered heading that is most closely associated with it. Each lettered heading may be used once, more than once, or not at all.

Questions 16.34–16.37

A. Psychoanalytic theories of anxiety
B. Behavioral theories of anxiety
C. Existential theories of anxiety

16.34 Anxiety is a conditioned response to specific environmental stimuli.
16.35 Persons become aware of a profound nothingness in their lives.
16.36 Anxiety is a signal to the ego that an unacceptable drive is pressing for conscious representation.
16.37 Treatment is usually with some form of desensitization to the anxiogenic stimulus.

Questions 16.38–16.40

A. Norepinephrine
B. Serotonin
C. γ-Aminobutyric acid (GABA)

16.38 The cell bodies of the neurotransmitter's neurons are localized primarily to the locus ceruleus.
16.39 Benzodiazepines enhance the neurotransmitter's effects at its receptors.
16.40 The cell bodies of the neurotransmitter's neurons are localized primarily to the raphe nuclei.

Questions 16.41–16.46

A. Generalized anxiety disorder
B. Obsessive-compulsive disorder
C. Specific phobia
D. Social phobia
E. Posttraumatic stress disorder

16.41 Fear of flying
16.42 Fear of public speaking
16.43 Isolation, undoing, and reaction formation
16.44 Shell shock
16.45 Buspirone a drug of choice
16.46 Possibility of associated Tourette's disorder

Questions 16.47–16.51

A. Walter Cannon
B. James Lange
C. Otto Rank
D. Harry Stack Sullivan
E. Melanie Klein

16.47 Trauma of birth
16.48 Transmission of maternal anxiety
16.49 Adrenal release of epinephrine
16.50 Anxiety in response to peripheral phenomena
16.51 Primitive superego anxiety

ANSWERS

Anxiety Disorders

16.1 The answer is D (*Synopsis VIII,* pages 609–617).
The most likely diagnosis for the patient is *obsessive-compulsive disorder.* The patient exhibits compulsions, performing behaviors hours ahead of leaving for school. The obsessions are not verbalized here, but the compulsions that they generate are time consuming and interfere with the patient's social relationships. The patient does not show any signs of anxiety that are chronic and persistent, as is seen in *generalized anxiety disorder. Agoraphobia* is a dread of open spaces, which is also not present in this patient. *Panic disorder* is not present in this patient, because the patient shows no concern for recurrent unexpected panic attacks, which are common to this disorder. Situationally bound panic attacks, such as the fear of speaking in public, are characteristic of *social phobia* and not witnessed in the patient.

16.2 The answer is C (*Synopsis VIII,* pages 609–617).
The patient's diagnosis is obsessive-compulsive disorder (OCD). Brain-imaging studies of OCD patients using positron emission testing (PET) have found *abnormalities in frontal lobes, cingulum, and basal* ganglia. PET scans have shown *higher levels of metabolism* and blood flows to those areas in OCD patients than in controls. Volumetric computed tomography (CT) scans have shown *decreased caudate volumes bilaterally in OCD patients* compared with controls. Morphometric magnetic resonance imaging (MMRI) has revealed that *OCD patients have significantly more gray matter and less white matter* than normal controls. MRI has also shown *longer mean T1 relaxation times in the frontal cortex in OCD patients* than is seen in normal controls. Please refer to *Synopsis VIII,* p. 610, Figure 16.4–1.

Answers 16.3–16.5

16.3 The answer is C (*Synopsis VIII,* page 585).

16.4 The answer is D (*Synopsis VIII,* page 592).

16.5 The answer is E (*Synopsis VIII,* pages 585, 592).
Agoraphobia and *panic disorder* are discussed in both DSM-IV and ICD-10 (the 10th revision of *International Statistical Classification of Diseases and Related Health Problems*). Agoraphobia is characterized by an anxiety about being in places outside the home where escape is difficult or where help is unavailable. These situations are avoided with marked distress, and the disorder is not better accounted for by another diagnosis. Panic disorder entails a period of intense fear or discomfort, in which the diagnostic symptoms develop and reach a peak within 10 minutes. Panic disorder may occur with or without agoraphobia.

In DSM-IV, *acute stress disorder* is characterized by symptoms like those of posttraumatic stress disorder occurring immediately after a traumatic event. In ICD-10, *acute stress reaction* is described as a severe transient disorder that develops in immediate response to exceptional physical or mental stress and that usually subsides in hours or days. Thus the two conditions, although differently named, are similar.

The diagnosis of posttraumatic stress disorder *appears in both DSM-IV* and *ICD-10, but the onset of symptoms is defined differently.* According to DSM-IV, posttraumatic stress disorder develops after a person experiences an event involving a serious threat to personal integrity or witnesses or learns about such an event that occurred to another. The disorder may be described as ''with delayed onset'' when at least 6 months has passed between the traumatic event and the appearance of the symptoms; other such qualifiers are ''acute'' and ''chronic.'' According to ICD-10, posttraumatic stress disorder is a delayed or protracted (or both) response to a stressful event or situation of a threatening or catastrophic nature, which can occur in almost anyone. The onset follows the trauma with a latency of a few weeks to months but rarely of more than 6 months.

16.6 The answer is C (*Synopsis VIII,* pages 609–617).
Clinical trials of drugs have supported the hypothesis that *dysregulation of serotonin is involved in the symptom formation* of obsessions and compulsions. Data show that *serotonergic drugs are* an effective, not *an ineffective treatment,* but it is unclear whether *serotonin is involved in the cause* of obsessive-compulsive disorder.

Clinical studies have shown that *measures of platelet binding sites of imipramine* and of *serotonin metabolites in cerebrospinal fluid are* variable, neither *abnormally low* nor *abnormally high.*

16.7 The answer is B (*Synopsis VIII,* page 627).
Antihypertensives such as reserpine and methyldopa can precipitate substance-induced mood disorder, not generalized anxiety disorder.

In generalized anxiety disorder, *benzodiazepine receptor agonists may reduce symptoms of anxiety,* and *flumazenil,* a benzodiazepine receptor antagonist, *can induce anxiety.*

A study has shown a correlation between the disorder and major depressive disorder in women. A genetic component has also been discovered in generalized anxiety disorder*: About 25 percent of first-degree relatives of patients with the disorder are also affected.* Male relatives may have an alcohol-use disorder.

Freud's 1909 *case of Little Hans was the first presentation of his psychological theory of anxiety;* before then, Freud had ascribed a physiological cause to anxiety. Contemporary schools of thought suggest that the disorder arises from an incorrectly perceived danger or that anxiety is a symptom of unresolved unconscious conflicts.

16.8 The answer is A (*Synopsis VIII,* pages 585–587).
Anxiety *is associated with the awareness of being nervous or frightened* and with *physiological sensations,* such as palpitations and sweating. Anxiety *is not a response to a known external threat.* Anxiety adversely affects thinking, perception, and learning. It *tends to lower, not sharpen, concentration,* and it *tends to reduce, not increase, recall.*

16.9 The answer is D (*Synopsis VIII,* page 594).
Agoraphobia, a dread of open spaces, seems to be one of the

most common forms of phobia, constituting some 60 percent of all phobias. The diagnostic criteria for agoraphobia without history of panic disorder are listed in Table 16.1, and the diagnostic criteria for panic disorder with agoraphobia are listed in Table 16.2. *Photophobia* usually means an organically determined hypersensitivity to light (as in many acute infectious diseases with conjunctivitis) that results in severe pain and marked tearing when the patient is exposed to very strong light. Photophobia can also be defined as a neurotic fear or avoidance of light. *Thanatophobia* is the fear of death. *Acrophobia* is the fear of high places. *Nyctophobia* is the fear of night or darkness.

16.10 The answer is A (*Synopsis VIII,* page 611).
If the obsessive-compulsive disorder patient tries to resist carrying out the compulsion, the patient generally experiences *anxiety. Hypochondriasis* is a somatoform disorder characterized by excessive, morbid anxiety about one's health. *Somatization disorder* is a somatoform disorder characterized by recurrent and multiple physical complaints with no apparent physical cause. *Dissociation* is an unconscious defense mechanism involving the segregation of any group of mental or behavioral processes from the rest of the person's psychic activity. It may entail the separation of an idea from its accompanying emotional tone, as seen in dissociative disorders. *Ambivalence* is strong and often overwhelming simultaneous contrasting attitudes, ideas, feelings, and drives toward an object, person, or goal.

Table 16.2
DSM-IV Diagnostic Criteria for Panic Disorder with Agoraphobia

A. Both (1) and (2):
   (1) recurrent unexpected panic attacks
   (2) at least one of the attacks has been followed by 1 month (or more) of one (or more) of the following:
      (a) persistent concern about having additional attacks
      (b) worry about the implications of the attack or its consequences (eg, losing control, having a heart attack, "going crazy")
      (c) a significant change in behavior related to the attacks
B. The presence of agoraphobia
C. The panic attacks are not due to the direct physiological effects of a substance (eg, a drug of abuse, a medication) or a general medical condition (eg, hyperthyroidism).
D. The panic attacks are not better accounted for by another mental disorder, such as social phobia (eg, occurring on exposure to feared social situations), specific phobia (eg, on exposure to a specific phobia situation), obsessive-compulsive disorder (eg, on exposure to dirt in someone with an obsession about contamination), posttraumatic stress disorder (eg, in response to stimuli associated with a severe stressor), or separation anxiety disorder (eg, in response to being away from home or close relatives).

16.11 The answer is A (*Synopsis VIII,* pages 581–583).
Sigmund Freud viewed phobias as resulting from conflicts centered on an unresolved childhood oedipal situation. In the adult, because the sexual drive continues to have a strong incestuous coloring, its arousal tends to arouse anxiety that is characteristically a fear of castration. The anxiety then alerts the ego to exert *repression* to keep the drive away from conscious representation and discharge. Because repression is not entirely successful in its function, the ego must call on auxiliary defenses. In phobic patients, the defenses, arising genetically from an earlier phobic response during the initial childhood period of the oedipal conflict, involves primarily the use of *displacement*—that is, the sexual conflict is transposed or displaced from the person who evoked the conflict to a seemingly unimportant, irrelevant object or situation, which has the power to arouse the entire constellation of affects, including anxiety. The phobic object or situation thus selected has a direct associative connection with the primary source of the conflict and has thus come naturally to symbolize it. Furthermore, the situation or object is usually such that the patient is able to keep out of its way and by the additional defense mechanism of *avoidance,* to escape suffering from serious anxiety.

Regression is an unconscious defense mechanism in which a person undergoes a partial or total return to early patterns of adaptation. *Condensation* is a mental process in which one symbol stands for a number of components. *Projection* is an unconscious defense mechanism in which persons attribute to another person generally unconscious ideas, thoughts, feelings, and impulses that are undesirable or unacceptable in themselves. Projection protects persons from anxiety arising from an inner conflict. By externalizing whatever is unacceptable, persons deal with it as a situation apart from themselves. In psychoanalysis, *isolation* is a defense mechanism involving the separation of an idea or memory from its attached feeling tone. Unacceptable ideational content is thereby rendered free of its disturbing or unpleasant emotional charge. *Dissociation* is an unconscious defense mechanism involving the segregation of any group of mental or behavioral processes from the rest of the person's psychic activity.

Table 16.1
DSM-IV Diagnostic Criteria for Agoraphobia Without History of Panic Disorder

A. The presence of agoraphobia related to fear of developing paniclike symptoms (eg, dizziness or diarrhea).
B. Criteria have never been met for panic disorder.
C. The disturbance is not due to the direct physiological effects of a substance (eg, a drug of abuse, a medication) or a general medical condition.
D. If an associated general medical condition is present, the fear described in criterion A is clearly in excess of that usually associated with the condition.

16.12 The answer is E (*Synopsis VIII,* pages 608–609).
Chlorpromazine (Thorazine) is a phenothiazine derivative used primarily as an antipsychotic agent and in the treatment of nausea and vomiting. It is not used in phobias.

Diazepam (Valium) and *chlordiazepoxide* (Librium) may be useful in decreasing symptoms of anxiety. They should be prescribed with caution for patients who have a history suggesting a tendency for psychological or physical dependence on substances. *Imipramine* (Tofranil) may be useful in decreasing phobic or depressive symptoms. All of these drugs should be used with caution in patients suffering from posttraumatic stress disorder after accidents that have led to serious physical illness. Imipramine in particular may precipitate symptoms of delirium in patients suffering from serious medical illness.

Hypnosis is useful not only in enhancing the suggestion that is a part of the therapist's generally supportive approach but in directly combating the anxiety arising from the phobic situation. The psychiatrist can teach patients the techniques of autohypnosis, through which they can achieve a degree of relaxation that will enable them to tolerate the phobic situation when they must face it. Patients who cannot be hypnotized may be taught techniques of muscle relaxation. Some clinicians find that serotonin-specific receptor inhibitors (SSRIs), such as paroxetine (Paxil) and fluoxetine (Prozac), are also useful in treating phobias.

16.13 The answer is E (*Synopsis VIII,* pages 602, 608).
A *counterphobic attitude* is not a therapy for phobias. Many activities may mask phobic anxiety, which can be hidden behind attitudes and behavior patterns that represent a denial, either that the dreaded object or situation is dangerous or that one is afraid of it. Basic to this phenomenon is a reversal of the situation in which one is the passive victim of external circumstances to a position of attempting actively to confront and master what one fears. The counterphobic person seeks out situations of danger and rushes enthusiastically toward them. The devotee of dangerous sports, such as parachute jumping, rock climbing, bungee jumping, and parasailing, may be exhibiting counterphobic behavior. Such patterns may be secondary to phobic anxieties or may be used as a normal means of dealing with a realistically dangerous situation.

Both behavioral and pharmacological techniques have been

Table 16.3
DSM-IV Diagnostic Criteria for Posttraumatic Stress Disorder

A. The person has been exposed to a traumatic event in which both of the following have been present:
   (1) the person experienced, witnessed, or was confronted with an event or events that involved actual or threatened death or serious injury, or a threat to the physical integrity of self or others
   (2) the person's response involved intense fear, helplessness, or horror. **Note:** In children, this may be expressed instead by disorganized or agitated behavior

B. The traumatic event is persistently reexperienced in one (or more) of the following ways:
   (1) recurrent and intrusive distressing recollections of the event, including images, thoughts, or perceptions. **Note:** In young children, repetitive play may occur in which themes or aspects of the trauma are expressed.
   (2) recurrent distressing dreams of the event. **Note:** In children, there may be frightening dreams without recognizable content.
   (3) acting or feeling as if the traumatic event were recurring (includes a sense of reliving the experience, illusions, hallucinations, and dissociative flashback episodes, including those that occur upon awakening or when intoxicated) **Note:** In young children, trauma-specific reenactment may occur.
   (4) intense psychological distress at exposure to internal or external cues that symbolize or resemble an aspect of the traumatic event
   (5) physiologic reactivity on exposure to internal or external cues that symbolize or resemble an aspect of the traumatic event

C. Persistent avoidance of stimuli associated with the trauma and numbing of general responsiveness (not present before the trauma), as indicated by three (or more) of the following:
   (1) efforts to avoid thoughts, feelings, or conversations associated with the trauma
   (2) efforts to avoid activities, places, or people that arouse recollections of the trauma
   (3) inability to recall an important aspect of the trauma
   (4) markedly diminished interest or participation in significant activities
   (5) feeling of detachment or estrangement from others
   (6) restricted range of affect (eg, unable to have loving feelings)
   (7) sense of a foreshortened future (eg, does not expect to have a career, marriage, children, or a normal life span)

D. Persistent symptoms of increased arousal (not present before the trauma), as indicated by two (or more) of the following:
   (1) difficulty falling or staying asleep
   (2) irritability or outbursts of anger
   (3) difficulty concentrating
   (4) hypervigilance
   (5) exaggerated startle response

E. Duration of the disturbance (symptoms in criteria B, C, and D) is more than 1 month.

F. The disturbance causes clinically significant distress or impairment in social, occupational, or other important areas of functioning.

Specify if:
Acute: if duration of symptoms is less than 3 months
Chronic: if duration of symptoms is 3 months or more

Specify if:
With delayed onset: if onset of symptoms is at least 6 months after the stressor

Reprinted with permission from American Psychiatric Association: *Diagnostic and Statistical Manual of Mental Disorders,* ed 4. Copyright, American Psychiatric Association, Washington, 1994.

used in treating phobias. The most common behavioral technique is *systematic desensitization,* in which the patient is exposed serially to a predetermined list of anxiety-provoking stimuli graded in a hierarchy from the least frightening to the most frightening. Patients are taught to self-induce a state of relaxation in the face of each anxiety-provoking stimulus. In *flooding,* patients are exposed to the phobic stimulus (actual [in vivo] or through imagery) for as long as they can tolerate the fear until they reach a point at which they can no longer feel it. The social phobia of stage fright in performers has been effectively treated with such β-adrenergic antagonists as *propranolol (Inderal),* which blocks the physiological signs of anxiety (for example, tachycardia). *Phenelzine (Nardil),* a monoamine oxidase inhibitor, is also useful in treating social phobia.

16.14 The answer is A (*Synopsis VIII,* pages 617–623). Posttraumatic stress disorder is not associated with a *psychologically abnormal reaction to stress.* The stress that precipitates posttraumatic stress disorder is generally outside the range of usual human experiences, such as earthquakes, flood, or war (Tables 16.3 and 16.4). It is also a stress that would distress anyone. The fact that a person finds the stressor disagreeable is not a sign of being psychologically abnormal. Each person has his or her threshold for developing symptoms of posttraumatic stress disorder; that threshold is based on the character traits of the person, *biological vulnerability,* and the nature of the stressor. Research on the biological theories of posttraumatic stress disorder have found labile autonomic nervous system reactions to stress, *decreased rapid eye movement (REM) latency* periods, and increased endogenous opioid secretion. The major associated features are the *reexperiencing of the trauma through dreams* and waking thoughts; *emotional numbing* to other life experiences, including relationships; and associated symptoms of autonomic instability, depression, and cognitive difficulties, such as poor concentration.

Table 16.4
Syndromes Associated with Toxic Exposure[a]

Syndrome	Characteristics	Possible Toxins
1	Impaired cognition	Insect repellant containing *N,N'*-diethylmetatoluamide (DEET[b]) absorbed through skin
2	Confusion ataxia	Exposure to chemical weapons, eg, sarin
3	Arthromyo-neuropathy	Insect repellant containing DEET[b] in combination with oral pyridostigmine[c]

[a] The three syndromes involve a relatively small group (N = 249) of veterans and are based on self-reported descriptions and selection. Data are from R. W. Haley and T. L. Kurt.
[b] DEET is a carbomate compound used as an insect repellant. Concentrations above 30 percent DEET are neurotoxic in children. The military repellant contained 75 percent. (DEET is available in 100 percent concentrations as an unregulated over-the-counter preparation usually sold in sports stores.)
[c] Most U.S. troops took low-dose pyridostigmine (Mestinon, 30 mg every 8 hours) for about 5 days in 1991 to protect against exposure to the nerve agent soman.

16.15 The answer is E (all) (*Synopsis VIII,* pages 617–623). Tricyclic drugs, especially *amitriptyline* (Elavil) and *imipramine* (Tofranil), and the monoamine oxidase inhibitor *phenelzine* (Nardil) are the drugs most often used to treat posttraumatic stress disorder. They are indicated particularly when depression or panic symptoms are present. Increasing numbers of clinicians report therapeutic success with *clonidine* (Catapres), and a few reports suggest that propranolol (Inderal) may be an effective treatment. Antipsychotic medications may be necessary for brief periods during treatment if behavior is particularly agitated.

16.16 The answer is A (*Synopsis VIII,* pages 617–623). In acute stress disorder (Table 16.5) the symptoms *must last for a minimum of 2 days,* can last for a maximum of 4 weeks (not 8 weeks), and *must occur within 4 weeks (not 1 year, 6 months, or 2 months) of the trauma.*

16.17 The answer is A (*Synopsis VIII,* pages 596–601). Unexpected panic attacks are required for the diagnosis of *panic disorder,* but panic attacks (Table 16.6) can occur in several anxiety disorders. The clinician must consider the context of the panic attack when making a diagnosis. Panic attacks can be divided into two types: (1) unexpected panic attacks, which are not associated with a situational trigger, and (2) situationally bound panic attacks, which occur immediately after exposure in a situational trigger or in anticipation of the situational trigger. Situationally bound panic attacks are most characteristic of *social phobia* and *specific phobia.* In *generalized anxiety disorder* the anxiety cannot be about having a panic attack.

16.18 The answer is E (*Synopsis VIII,* pages 596–601). *Delusions* are not a symptom of panic attacks. The symptoms of a panic attack can include *sweating, chest pain, derealization* (feelings of unreality), and *fear of going crazy.* Table 16.6 lists all of the symptoms of panic attack in the diagnostic criteria of the fourth edition of *Diagnostic and Statistical Manual of Mental Disorders* (DSM-IV).

Answers 16.19–16.24

16.19 The answer is C (*Synopsis VIII,* pages 609–617).

16.20 The answer is C (*Synopsis VIII,* pages 609–617).

16.21 The answer is C (*Synopsis VIII,* pages 609–617).

16.22 The answer is A (*Synopsis VIII,* pages 609–617).

16.23 The answer is B (*Synopsis VIII,* pages 609–617).

16.24 The answer is D (*Synopsis VIII,* pages 609–617). Obsessions and compulsions have certain features in common: (1) *an idea or an impulse intrudes insistently and persistently into awareness;* (2) a feeling of anxious dread accompanies the central manifestation and frequently leads the person to take countermeasures against the initial idea or impulse; (3) the obsession or compulsion is *ego-alien;* that is, it is experienced as being foreign to the person's experience of himself or herself as a psychological being; (4) the person recognizes the obsession or compulsion as absurd and irrational; and (5) *the person feels a strong desire to resist them. Obsessions* are

Table 16.5 DSM-IV Diagnostic Criteria for Acute Stress Disorder

A. The person has been exposed to a traumatic event in which both of the following were present:
   (1) the person has experienced, witnessed, or was confronted with an event or events that involved actual or threatened death or serious injury, or a threat to the physical integrity of self or others.
   (2) the person's response involved intense fear, helplessness, or horror

B. Either while experiencing or after experiencing the distressing event, the individual has three (or more) of the following dissociative symptoms:
   (1) a subjective sense of numbing, detachment, or absence of emotional responsiveness
   (2) a reduction in awareness of his or her surroundings (eg, "being in a daze")
   (3) derealization
   (4) depersonalization
   (5) dissociative amnesia (ie, inability to recall an important aspect of the trauma)

C. The traumatic event is persistently reexperienced in at least one of the following ways: recurrent images, thoughts, dreams, illusions, flashback episodes, or a sense of reliving the experience; or distress on exposure to reminders of the traumatic event.

D. Marked avoidance of stimuli that arouse recollections of the trauma (eg, thoughts, feelings, conversations, activities, places, people).

E. Marked symptoms of anxiety or increased arousal (eg, difficulty sleeping, irritability, poor concentration, hypervigilance, exaggerated startle response, motor restlessness).

F. The disturbance causes clinically significant distress or impairment in social, occupational, or other important areas of functioning or impairs the individual's ability to pursue some necessary task, such as obtaining necessary assistance or mobilizing personal resources by telling family members about the traumatic experience.

G. The disturbance lasts for a minimum of 2 days and a maximum of 4 weeks and occurs within 4 weeks of the traumatic event.

H. The disturbance is not due to the direct physiological effects of a substance (eg, a drug of abuse, a medication) or a general medical condition, is not better accounted for by brief psychotic disorder, and is not merely an exacerbation of a preexisting Axis I or Axis II disorder.

thoughts, feelings, *ideas, or sensations. Compulsions* are *acts or behaviors. Neither* obsessions nor compulsions *are ego-syntonic.* A patient with obsessive-compulsive disorder recognizes the irrationality of the obsession, which means that both the obsession and the compulsion are ego-dystonic.

Answers 16.25–16.28

16.25 The answer is A (*Synopsis VIII,* page 605).

16.26 The answer is A (*Synopsis VIII,* page 605).

16.27 The answer is B (*Synopsis VIII,* page 604).

Table 16.6 DSM-IV Criteria for Panic Attack

Note: A panic attack is not a codable disorder. Code the specific diagnosis in which the panic attack occurs (eg, panic disorder with agoraphobia).

A discrete period of intense fear or discomfort, in which four (or more) of the following symptoms developed abruptly and reached a peak within 10 minutes:
   (1) palpitations, pounding heart, or accelerated heart rate
   (2) sweating
   (3) trembling or shaking
   (4) sensations of shortness of breath or smothering
   (5) feeling of choking
   (6) chest pain or discomfort
   (7) nausea or abdominal distress
   (8) feeling dizzy, unsteady, lightheaded, or faint
   (9) derealization (feelings of unreality) or depersonalization (being detached from oneself)
   (10) fear of losing control or going crazy
   (11) fear of dying
   (12) paresthesias (numbness or tingling sensations)
   (13) chills or hot flashes

16.28 The answer is B (*Synopsis VIII,* page 604).
In Sigmund Freud's case history of *Little Hans,* a 5-year-old boy who had a *fear of horses,* Hans's fear of horses represented *castration anxiety,* a displaced fear that his penis would be cut off by his father.

In 1920 John B. Watson recounted his experiences with Little Albert, an infant with a phobia about rabbits. Unlike Freud's Little Hans, who showed his symptoms in the natural course of his maturation, Little Albert's difficulties were the direct result of the scientific experiments of two psychologists, who used techniques that had successfully induced *conditioned responses* in laboratory animals. They produced a loud noise paired with the rabbit, so that a *fear of rabbits* was elicited in Little Albert.

Answers 16.29–16.33

16.29 The answer is A (*Synopsis VIII,* pages 601–602).

16.30 The answer is B (*Synopsis VIII,* pages 623–627).

16.31 The answer is C (*Synopsis VIII,* pages 601–602, 623–627).

16.32 The answer is D (*Synopsis VIII,* pages 601–602, 623–627).

16.33 The answer is A (*Synopsis VIII,* pages 601–602).
Panic disorder is characterized by *discrete and episodic* attacks of anxiety, whereas generalized anxiety disorder is characterized by anxiety that is *chronic and persistent.* Such symptoms as *dizziness, paresthesia,* restlessness, and palpitations are seen in both types of anxiety. The classifications of panic disorder without agoraphobia (Table 16.7) and generalized anxiety disorder (Table 16.8) are reserved for patients in whom *other psychiatric symptoms,* such as obsessions and phobias, *are ab-*

Table 16.7
DSM-IV Diagnostic Criteria for Panic Disorder Without Agoraphobia

A. Both (1) and (2):
   (1) recurrent unexpected panic attacks
   (2) at least one of the attacks has been followed by at least 1 month of one (or more) of the following:
      (a) persistent concern about having additional attacks
      (b) worry about the implications of the attack or its consequences (eg, losing control, having a heart attack, "going crazy")
      (c) a significant change in behavior related to the attacks
B. Absence of agoraphobia
C. The panic attacks are not due to the direct physiological effects of a substance (eg, a drug of abuse, a medication) or a general medical condition (eg, hyperthyroidism).
D. The panic attacks are not better accounted for by another mental disorder, such as social phobia (eg, occurring on exposure to feared social situations), specific phobia (eg, on exposure to a specific phobic situation), obsessive-compulsive disorder (eg, on exposure to dirt in someone with an obsession about contamination), posttraumatic stress disorder (eg, in response to stimuli associated with a severe stressor), or separation anxiety disorder (eg, in response to being away from home or close relatives).

sent. Hyperventilation may be seen in both types of anxiety disorder, but only in panic disorder without agoraphobia is sufficient carbon dioxide blown off to bring on *obvious evidence of respiratory alkalosis,* such as muscle twitching and tetany.

Answers 16.34–16.37

16.34 The answer is B (*Synopsis VIII,* pages 581–585).

16.35 The answer is C (*Synopsis VIII,* pages 581–585).

16.36 The answer is A (*Synopsis VIII,* pages 581–585).

16.37 The answer is B (*Synopsis VIII,* pages 581–585). Three major schools of psychological theory—psychoanalytic, behavioral, and existential—have contributed theories regarding the causes of anxiety. Within the *psychoanalytic* school of thought, Sigmund Freud proposed that *anxiety is a signal to the ego that an unacceptable drive is pressing for conscious representation and discharge. Behavioral* theories state that *anxiety is a conditioned response to specific environmental stimuli.* In a model of classic conditioning, a person who does not have any food allergies may become sick after eating contaminated shellfish in a restaurant. Subsequent exposures to shellfish may cause that person to feel sick. Through generalization, such a person may come to distrust all food prepared by others.

Treatment is usually with some form of desensitization to the anxiogenic stimulus, coupled with cognitive psychotherapeutic approaches. In *existential* theories of anxiety, *persons become aware of a profound nothingness in their lives,* feelings that may be even more profoundly discomforting than an acceptance of their inevitable death. Anxiety is the person's response to that vast void.

Table 16.8
DSM-IV Diagnostic Criteria for Generalized Anxiety Disorder

A. Excessive anxiety and worry (apprehensive expectation), occurring more days than not for at least 6 months, about a number of events or activities (such as work or school performance).
B. The person finds it difficult to control the worry.
C. The anxiety and worry are associated with three (or more) of the following six symptoms (with at least some symptoms present for more days than not for the past 6 months). **Note:** only one item is required for children.
   (1) restlessness or feeling keyed up or on edge
   (2) being easily fatigued
   (3) difficulty concentrating or mind going blank
   (4) irritability
   (5) muscle tension
   (6) sleep disturbance (difficulty falling or staying asleep, or restless unsatisfying sleep)
D. The focus of the anxiety and worry is not confined to features of an Axis I disorder, eg, the anxiety or worry is not about having a panic attack (as in panic disorder), being embarrassed in public (as in social phobia), being contaminated (as in obsessive-compulsive disorder), being away from home or close relatives (as in separation anxiety disorder), gaining weight (as in anorexia nervosa), having multiple physical complaints (as in somatization disorder), or having a serious illness (as in hypochondriasis), and the anxiety and worry do not occur exclusively during posttraumatic stress disorder.
E. The anxiety, worry, or physical symptoms cause clinically significant distress or impairment in social, occupational, or other important areas of functioning.
F. The disturbance is not due to the direct physiological effects of a substance (eg, a drug of abuse, a medication) or a general medical condition (eg, hyperthyroidism) and does not occur exclusively during a mood disorder, a psychotic disorder, or a pervasive developmental disorder.

Answers 16.38–16.40

16.38 The answer is A (*Synopsis VIII,* page 584).

16.39 The answer is C (*Synopsis VIII,* page 584).

16.40 The answer is B (*Synopsis VIII,* pages 584–585). The three major neurotransmitters associated with anxiety are norepinephrine, serotonin, and γ-aminobutyric acid (GABA). The general theory regarding the role of *norepinephrine* in anxiety disorders is that affected patients may have a poorly regulated noradrenergic system that has occasional bursts of activity. In that system *the cell bodies of the neurotransmitter's neurons are localized primarily to the locus ceruleus* in the rostral pons, and they project their axons to the cerebral cortex, the limbic system, the brainstem, and the spinal cord. Experiments in primates have shown that stimulation of the locus ceruleus produces a fear response.

The interest in *serotonin* was initially motivated by the observation that serotonergic antidepressants have therapeutic effects in some anxiety disorders—for example, clomipramine (Anafranil) in obsessive-compulsive disorder. The effectiveness of buspirone (BuSpar), a serotonergic type 1A ($5\text{-}HT_{1A}$) receptor agonist in the treatment of anxiety disorders also suggests the possibility of an association between serotonin and anxiety. *The cell bodies of most of the serotonergic neurons are in the raphe nuclei* in the rostral brainstem, especially the amygdala and the hippocampus, and the hypothalamus.

The role of *GABA* in anxiety disorders is most strongly supported by the undisputed efficacy of *benzodiazepines, which enhance the activity of GABA at the $GABA_A$ receptor* in the treatment of some types of anxiety disorders.

Answers 16.41–16.46

16.41 The answer is C (*Synopsis VIII*, page 603).

Table 16.9
DSM-IV Diagnostic Criteria for Specific Phobia

A. Marked and persistent fear that is excessive or unreasonable, cued by the presence of anticipation of a specific object or situation (eg, flying, heights, animals, receiving an injection, seeing blood).

B. Exposure to the phobic stimulus almost invariably provokes an immediate anxiety response, which may take the form of a situationally bound or situationally predisposed panic attack. **Note:** In children, the anxiety may be expressed by crying, tantrums, freezing, or clinging.

C. The person recognizes that the fear is excessive or unreasonable. **Note:** In children, this feature may be absent.

D. The phobic situation(s) is avoided or else endured with intense anxiety or distress.

E. The avoidance, anxious anticipation, or distress in the feared situation(s) interferes significantly with the person's normal routine, occupational (or academic) functioning, or with social activities or relationships, or there is marked distress about having the phobia.

F. In individuals under age 18 years, the duration is at least 6 months.

G. The anxiety, panic attacks, or phobic avoidance associated with the specific object or situation are not better accounted for by another mental disorder, such as obsessive-compulsive disorder (eg, fear of dirt in someone with an obsession about contamination), posttraumatic stress disorder (eg, avoidance of stimuli associated with a severe stressor), separation anxiety disorder (eg, avoidance of school), social phobia (eg, avoidance of social situations because of fear of embarrassment), panic disorder with agoraphobia, or agoraphobia without history of panic disorder.

Specify type:

Animal type
Natural environment type (eg, heights, storms, water)
Blood-injection-injury type
Situational type (eg, planes, elevators, enclosed places)
Other type (eg, phobic avoidance of situations that may lead to choking, vomiting, or contracting an illness; in children, avoidance of loud sounds or costumed characters)

16.42 The answer is D (*Synopsis VIII*, page 603).

16.43 The answer is B (*Synopsis VIII*, pages 609–617).

16.44 The answer is E (*Synopsis VIII*, pages 617–623).

16.45 The answer is A (*Synopsis VIII*, pages 623–627).

16.46 The answer is B (*Synopsis VIII*, pages 609–617). Excessive *fear of flying* is an example of a *specific phobia* (Table 16.9). *Fear of public speaking* is an example of a *social phobia* (Table 16.10).

Sigmund Freud described three major psychological defense mechanisms that determine the form and the quality of *obsessive-compulsive disorder: isolation, undoing, and reac-*

Table 16.10
DSM-IV Diagnostic Criteria for Social Phobia

A. A marked and persistent fear of one or more social or performance situations in which the person is exposed to unfamiliar people or to possible scrutiny by others. The individual fears that he or she will act in a way (or show anxiety symptoms) that will be humiliating or embarrassing. **Note:** In children, there must be evidence of the capacity for age-appropriate social relationships with familiar people and the anxiety must occur in peer settings, not just in interactions with adults.

B. Exposure to the feared social situation almost invariably provokes anxiety, which may take the form of a situationally bound or situationally predisposed panic attack. **Note:** In children, the anxiety may be expressed by crying, tantrums, freezing, or shrinking from social situations with unfamiliar people.

C. The person recognizes that the fear is excessive or unreasonable. **Note:** In children, this feature may be absent.

D. The feared social or performance situations are avoided or else are endured with intense anxiety or distress.

E. The avoidance, anxious anticipation, or distress in the feared social or performance situation(s) interferes significantly with the person's normal routine, occupational (academic) functioning, or social activities or relationships, or there is marked distress about having the phobia.

F. In individuals under age 18 years, the duration is at least 6 months.

G. The fear or avoidance is not due to the direct physiological effects of a substance (eg, a drug of abuse, a medication) or a general medical condition and is not better accounted for by another mental disorder (eg, panic disorder with or without agoraphobia, separation anxiety disorder, body dysmorphic disorder, a pervasive developmental disorder, or schizoid personality disorder).

H. If a general medical condition or another mental disorder is present, the fear in criterion A is unrelated to it, eg, the fear is not of stuttering, trembling in Parkinson's disease, or exhibiting abnormal eating behavior in anorexia nervosa or bulimia nervosa.

Specify if:

Generalized: if the fears include most social situations (also consider the additional diagnosis of avoidant personality disorder)

Table 16.11
DSM-IV Diagnostic Criteria for Obsessive-Compulsive Disorder

A. Either obsessions or compulsions:
Obsessions as defined by (1), (2), (3), and (4):
(1) recurrent and persistent thoughts, impulses, or images that are experienced, at some time during the disturbance, as intrusive and inappropriate and that cause marked anxiety or distress
(2) the thoughts, impulses, or images are not simply excessive worries about real-life problems
(3) the person attempts to ignore or suppress such thoughts, impulses, or images, or to neutralize them with some other thought or action
(4) the person recognizes that the obsessional thoughts, impulses, or images are a product of his or her own mind (not imposed from without as in thought insertion)
Compulsions as defined by (1) and (2):
(1) repetitive behaviors (eg, hand washing, ordering, checking) or mental acts (eg, praying, counting, repeating words silently) that the person feels driven to perform in response to an obsession, or according to rules that must be applied rigidly
(2) the behaviors or mental acts are aimed at preventing or reducing distress or preventing some dreaded event or situation; however, these behaviors or mental acts either are not connected in a realistic way with what they are designed to neutralize or prevent or are clearly excessive

B. At some point during the course of the disorder, the person has recognized that the obsessions or compulsions are excessive or unreasonable. **Note:** This does not apply to children.

C. The obsessions or compulsions cause marked distress, are time consuming (take more than 1 hour a day), or significantly interfere with the person's normal routine, occupational (or academic) functioning, or usual social activities or relationships.

D. If another Axis I disorder is present, the content of the obsessions or compulsions is not restricted to it (eg, preoccupation with food in the presence of an eating disorder; hair pulling in the presence of trichotillomania, concern with appearance in the presence of body dysmorphic disorder; preoccupation with drugs in the presence of a substance use disorder; preoccupation with having a serious illness in the presence of hypochondriasis; preoccupation with sexual urges or fantasies in the presence of a paraphilia; or guilty ruminations in the presence of major depressive disorder).

E. The disturbance is not due to the direct physiological effects of a substance (eg, a drug of abuse, a medication) or a general medical condition.

Specify if:
With poor insight: if, for most of the time during the current episode, the person does not recognize that the obsessions and compulsions are excessive or unreasonable

Reprinted with permission from American Psychiatric Association: *Diagnostic and Statistical Manual of Mental Disorders,* ed 4. Copyright, American Psychiatric Association, Washington, 1994.

tion formation. Isolation is a defense mechanism in which the affect and the impulse of which it is a derivative are separated from the ideational component and are pushed out of consciousness. Undoing is a compulsive act that is performed in an attempt to prevent or undo the consequences that the patient irrationally anticipates from a frightening obsessional thought or impulse. Reaction formation involves manifest patterns of behavior and consciously experienced attitudes that are exactly the opposite of the underlying impulses.

In World War I, *posttraumatic stress disorder* was called *shell shock* and was hypothesized to result from brain trauma caused by the explosion of shells. The psychiatric morbidity associated with Vietnam War veterans brought the concept of posttraumatic stress disorder into full fruition as it is known today (Table 16.3). The Gulf War syndrome may be a type of posttraumatic disorder precipitated by exposure to toxins (Table 16.4).

Buspirone is a drug of choice in *generalized anxiety disorder.* The drug is most likely effective in 60 to 80 percent of patients with the disorder. Data indicate that buspirone is more effective in reducing the cognitive symptoms of generalized anxiety disorder than in reducing the somatic symptoms.

Patients with *obsessive-compulsive disorder* (Table 16.11) *may have associated Tourette's disorder.* The characteristic symptoms of Tourette's disorder are motor and vocal tics that occur frequently and virtually every day. About 90 percent of Tourette's disorder patients have compulsive symptoms, and as many as two thirds meet the diagnostic criteria for obsessive-compulsive disorder.

Answers 16.47–16.51

16.47 The answer is C (*Synopsis VIII,* pages 623–627).

16.48 The answer is D (*Synopsis VIII,* pages 623–627).

16.49 The answer is A (*Synopsis VIII,* pages 623–627).

16.50 The answer is B (*Synopsis VIII,* pages 623–627).

16.51 The answer is E (*Synopsis VIII,* pages 623–627).
Otto Rank traced the genesis of all anxiety to the processes associated with the *trauma of birth. Harry Stack Sullivan* placed emphasis on the early relationship between the mother and the child and the importance of the *transmission of maternal anxiety* to the infant. *Melanie Klein* wrote that anxiety becomes fear of persecutory objects and later, through reintroduction of aggression in the form of internalized bad objects, the fear of outer and inner persecutors. Inner persecutors constitute the origin of *primitive superego anxiety. Walter Cannon* demonstrated that cats exposed to barking dogs exhibited behavioral and physiological signs of fear associated with the *adrenal release of epinephrine.* The *James Lange* theory is that subjective *anxiety* is a *response to peripheral phenomena.*

17

Somatoform Disorders

According to the fourth edition of *Diagnostic and Statistical Manual of Mental Disorders* (DSM-IV), somatoform disorders are characterized by physical symptoms that suggest a general medical condition and that are not explained by a general medical condition, by the effects of a substance, or by another mental disorder. DSM-IV lists several varieties: somatization disorder, conversion disorder, hypochondriasis, body dysmorphic disorder, and pain disorder, as well as undifferentiated somatoform disorder and somatoform disorder not otherwise specified.

Diagnosing a somatoform disorder presents clinicians with difficulties. Patients may be thought to be malingering, lying, or creating factitious disorders, but this is not the case; their symptoms, although without medical justification, are genuine and often severe. Before diagnosing a somatoform disorder, clinicians must rule out any medical disorders; patients must thus undergo thorough medical and neurological examinations and tests to eliminate a medical cause of onset, intensity, and duration of the physical complaint. Some patients do indeed have nonpsychiatric medical disorders; these do not always account for the symptoms of a somatoform disorder, although the medical disorders must be diagnosed and treated.

Somatoform disorders occur most commonly in women, except for hypochondriasis, which affects both sexes equally. These disorders may be associated with other mental disorders, such as anxiety and depressive disorders. Some somatoform disorders are chronic; others are episodic. In all cases signs and symptoms are exacerbated by psychological stress.

Treatment involves biological and psychological strategies, including behavioral treatments, psychodynamic or insight-oriented treatments, and psychopharmacological treatments. Other underlying mental and physical disorders must be diagnosed and treated before the somatoform disorders themselves. The symptoms of somatoform disorders have powerful unconscious meanings for patients, and patients must explore and understand the psychodynamics involved. Pharmacotherapy can include tricyclic and tetracyclic drugs, monoamine oxidase inhibitors, serotonin-specific reuptake inhibitors, and dopamine receptor antagonists. Students must know the medications that are effective with the specific somatoform disorders.

Students should study Chapter 17 in *Kaplan and Sadock's Synopsis VIII* and the following questions and answers.

HELPFUL HINTS

The student should be able to define the somatoform disorder terms listed below.

- amobarbital (Amytal) interview
- anorexia nervosa
- antidepressants
- antisocial personality disorder
- astasia-abasia
- biofeedback
- body dysmorphic disorder
- Briquet's syndrome
- conversion blindness
- conversion disorder
- depression
- dysmorphophobia
- endorphins
- generalized anxiety disorder
- hemianesthesia
- hypochondriasis
- identification
- instinctual impulse
- *la belle indifférence*
- major depressive disorder
- pain disorder
- pimozide (Orap)
- primary gain and secondary gain
- pseudocyesis
- secondary symptoms
- somatization disorder
- somatoform disorder not otherwise specified
- somatosensory input
- stocking-and-glove anesthesia
- symbolization and projection
- undifferentiated somatoform disorder
- undoing

▲ QUESTIONS

DIRECTIONS: Each of the questions or incomplete statements below is followed by five suggested responses or completions. Select the *one* that is *best* in each case.

17.1 According to DSM-IV, a patient with conversion disorder would typically have

A. feigned symptoms
B. sexual dysfunction
C. *la belle indifférence*
D. an urban background
E. symptom onset after age 50

17.2 A characteristic of hypochondriacal disorder is

A. Onset is after age 50.
B. Women are more commonly afflicted.
C. Patients emphasize signs and symptoms.
D. Patients use excessive amounts of drugs.
E. Patients seek diagnosis of their condition.

17.3 Factors affecting the etiology of somatization disorder can include

A. alcohol addiction
B. abnormal serotonin regulation
C. a family history of mental retardation
D. a genetic cause in 50 percent of cases
E. symbolic meanings

17.4 Which of the following is *not* characteristic of body dysmorphic disorder?

A. Slightly more women than men are affected by the disorder.
B. The most common anatomical preoccupation is with the breasts.
C. Sigmund Freud's history of the Wolf-Man was an early description.
D. Serotonin-specific drugs have been found to be more effective than surgery.
E. At least 50 percent of college students were found to be preoccupied with their appearance.

17.5 A 29-year-old mother of two children requested medical clearance for impending surgery for cysts in her breasts. She described the cysts as rapidly enlarging and unbearably painful. While drawing attention to her breasts, she said: "They're so large and so tender to the touch. And I just can't have relations. Forget that."

She also had disabling back pain that spread up and down her spine and that made her legs give out on her suddenly, causing her to fall. When discussing that symptom, she winced visibly and said: "Oh, there it goes; my back keeps clicking. The pain is so severe it affects me with my kids. Pain like that will make anyone into a beast." (She had previously been suspected of child abuse.) She also complained of dyspnea and a dry cough that prevented her walking uphill.

Her medical history began at menarche with dysmenorrhea and menorrhagia. At 18 she had exploratory surgery for a possible ovarian cyst and later underwent another operation for suspected abdominal adhesions. She also had a history of recurrent urinary tract symptoms, although no organisms were ever clearly documented, and she had normal findings after a workup for "an enlarged thyroid." At various times she had received the diagnoses of spastic colon, migraine, and endometriosis.

Two marriages, both to alcoholic and abusive men, had ended in divorce. She had lost several clerical jobs because of excessive absences. During the periods when she felt worst, she spent most of the day at home in a bathrobe while her relatives cared for her children. She had a history of opioid dependence and claimed that she began using analgesics for her back pain and then "I overdid it."

The physical examination at the time of her medical visit revealed inconsistencies in the breast tissue but no frank masses, and the mammography findings were normal.

The patient is probably suffering from

A. hypochondriasis
B. conversion disorder
C. pain disorder
D. somatization disorder
E. body dysmorphic disorder

17.6 A 38-year-old married woman had complained of nervousness since childhood. She also said she was sickly since her youth, with a succession of physical problems doctors often indicated were caused by her nerves or depression. She, however, believed that she had a physical problem that had not yet been discovered by the doctors. Besides nervousness, she had chest pain and had been told by a variety of medical consultants that she had a nervous heart. She also consulted doctors for abdominal pain and had been told she had a spastic colon. She had seen chiropractors and osteopaths for backaches, for pains in her extremities, and for anesthesia of her fingertips. Three months previously, she was vomiting and had chest pain and abdominal pain, and she was admitted to a hospital for a hysterectomy. Since the hysterectomy, she had had repeated anxiety attacks, fainting spells that she claimed were associated with unconsciousness, vomiting, food intolerance, weakness, and fatigue. She had been hospitalized several times for medical workups for vomiting, colitis, vomiting of blood, and chest pain. She had had a surgical procedure for an abscess of the throat. She said she felt depressed but thought that it was all because her "hormones were not straightened out." She was still looking for a medical explanation for her physical and psychological problems.

The most likely diagnosis is

A. somatization disorder
B. conversion disorder
C. hypochondriasis
D. dysthymic disorder
E. none of the above

17.7 The treatment of hypochondriasis is characterized by

A. resistance to psychotherapy
B. better response to group psychotherapy than to individual therapy
C. frequent physical examinations
D. treatment of any underlying psychiatric disorder
E. all of the above

17.8 Which of the following statements about conversion disorder is most accurate?

A. The inability to speak is intentionally produced in a conversion disorder.
B. Conversion disorder is most common among patients in a high socioeconomic group.
C. Psychoanalytic theory holds that the major defense mechanism in conversion disorder is suppression.
D. Mutism is one of the most common symptoms of conversion disorder.
E. *La belle indifférence* is a necessary component in making the diagnosis of conversion disorder.

17.9 Characteristic behavioral features in patients with conversion disorder include

A. somatic compliance
B. *la belle indifférence*
C. autonomic dysfunction
D. sexual disturbances
E. all of the above

17.10 The most accurate statement regarding hypochondriasis is

A. Patients with hypochondriasis usually believe that they have multiple diseases.
B. Hypochondriasis may be the result of an unconscious desire to assume the sick role.
C. The patient's belief that a particular disease is present can have delusional intensity.
D. More men than women are affected by hypochondriasis.
E. The incidence of hypochondriasis is affected by educational level and marital status.

17.11 Characteristic signs of conversion disorder include all of the following *except*

A. astasia-abasia
B. stocking-and-glove anesthesia
C. hemianesthesia of the body beginning precisely at the midline
D. normal reflexes
E. cogwheel rigidity

17.12 A third-year medical student returned to the student health services for the third time thinking he had ulcerative colitis. After a thorough medical workup, he was told that no organic disease was present. Despite that reassurance, the student continued to test his stool for blood and continued to believe that his doctors had missed the correct diagnosis. The student is exhibiting

A. depersonalization
B. phobia
C. conversion disorder
D. bulimia nervosa
E. hypochondriasis

17.13 In body dysmorphic disorder

A. plastic surgery is usually beneficial
B. a comorbid diagnosis is unusual
C. anorexia nervosa may also be diagnosed
D. some 50 percent of patients may attempt suicide
E. serotonin-specific drugs are effective in reducing the symptoms

17.14 A patient with somatization disorder

A. presents the initial physical complaints after age 30
B. has had physical symptoms for 3 months
C. has complained of symptoms not explained by a known medical condition
D. usually experiences minimal impairment in social or occupational functioning
E. may have a false belief of being pregnant and objective signs of pregnancy, such as decreased menstrual flow or amenorrhea

17.15 All of the following are classified as somatoform disorders *except*

A. conversion disorder
B. hypochondriasis
C. somatization disorder
D. Munchausen syndrome
E. body dysmorphic disorder

17.16 Medical disorders to be considered in a differential diagnosis of somatization disorder include

A. multiple sclerosis
B. systemic lupus erythematosus
C. acute intermittent porphyria
D. hyperparathyroidism
E. all of the above

17.17 Hypochondriasis enables patients to provide themselves with all of the following *except*

A. various secondary gains
B. protection from their sense of guilt
C. gratification of their dependence needs
D. denial of the pain of low self-esteem
E. verification of their delusional beliefs

17.18 The most accurate statement regarding pain disorder is

A. Peak ages of onset are in the second and third decades.
B. First-degree relatives of patients have an increased likelihood of having the same disorder.
C. It is least common in persons with blue-collar occupations.
D. It is diagnosed equally among men and women.
E. Depressive disorders are no more common in patients with pain disorder than in the general public.

DIRECTIONS: The questions below consist of lettered headings followed by a list of numbered words or phrases. For each numbered word or phrase, select the *one* lettered heading that is most closely associated with it. Each heading may be used once, more than once, or not at all.

Questions 17.19–17.22

A. Conversion disorder
B. Pain disorder
C. Somatization disorder

17.19 *La belle indifférence*
17.20 Alexithymia
17.21 Briquet's syndrome
17.22 Astasia-abasia

DIRECTIONS: Each set of lettered headings below is followed by a list of numbered phrases. For each numbered phrase, select

A. if the item is associated with *A only*
B. if the item is associated with *B only*
C. if the item is associated with *both A and B*
D. if the item is associated with *neither A nor B*

Questions 17.23–17.27

A. Somatization disorder
B. Pain disorder
C. Both
D. Neither

17.23 Affects women more than men
17.24 Most often begins during a person's teens
17.25 Responds to antidepressants
17.26 May involve serotonin in its pathophysiology
17.27 Is commonly associated with anorexia nervosa

Questions 17.28–17.31

A. Autonomic arousal disorder
B. Neurasthenia
C. Both
D. Neither

17.28 The symptom pattern seen in undifferentiated somatoform disorder
17.29 Complaints involving the cardiovascular, respiratory, or gastrointestinal system
17.30 Complaints of mental and physical fatigue
17.31 Symptoms caused by a tick bite

Questions 17.32–17.37

A. Hypochondriasis
B. Somatization disorder
C. Both
D. Neither

17.32 Is found approximately equally in men and women
17.33 Has peak incidence during the 40s or 50s
17.34 Is likely to have a hysterical cognitive and interpersonal style
17.35 Includes disease conviction or disease fear
17.36 Is associated with anhedonia
17.37 May include hallucinations

ANSWERS

Somatoform Disorders

17.1 The answer is C (*Synopsis VIII,* pages 636, 638).
In conversion disorder, a patient has symptoms or deficits that affect voluntary motor or sensory functions and that suggest a neurological or other general medical condition. Psychological factors are thought to be connected with the symptom or deficit, which is usually preceded by conflict or other stress. The disorder is ruled out if the symptoms or deficits can be explained by a medical condition, by the effects of a substance, or by cultural standards. It is ruled out if the symptoms are limited to pain or sexual dysfunction, occur only during somatization disorder, or are better accounted for by another mental disorder. To diagnose conversion disorder, a clinician must establish that a patient is in marked distress and that important areas of functioning are impaired.

La belle indifférence, a lack of concern about symptoms, can occur with conversion disorder, although other patients may exhibit their symptoms dramatically or histrionically. In conversion disorder, there is no question of *feigned symptoms;* patients do not intentionally produce symptoms to obtain certain benefits.

Sexual dysfunction may appear in conversion disorder, but it cannot be the only symptom. *An urban background* is less likely than a rural one; it occurs more commonly among rural populations, people of lower socioeconomic status, and those less familiar with medical and psychological ideas.

Symptom onset after age 50 is unlikely. Although it has been reported in the ninth decade, onset generally occurs from late childhood to early adulthood, rarely before the age of 10 years or after the age of 35 years. When conversion disorder seems to appear in a patient of middle or old age, there is probably an occult neurological or other general medical condition. The onset is usually acute, and the symptoms typically do not last long. Recurrence, however, is common; it occurs within 1 year in one fifth to one quarter of people; a single recurrence predicts future episodes.

17.2 The answer is E (*Synopsis VIII,* page 638).
Whereas in somatization disorder *patients emphasize signs and symptoms,* in hypochondriacal disorder *patients seek a diagnosis of their condition.* As they are concerned about a serious, progressive disease affecting them, patients ask doctors to investigate the nature of the underlying disease rather than asking for treatment, as would patients with somatization disorder. Hypochondriacal patients manifest persistent somatic complaints, usually in only one or two organ systems. They may identify the disorder but waver in their certainty about its presence.

Although *patients* with somatization disorder *use excessive amounts of drugs,* those with hypochondriacal disorder are fearful of drugs and their adverse effects; they generally seek reassurance by visiting different physicians. These patients may be depressed and anxious, and these symptoms may also warrant treatment.

Women are not *more commonly affected* than are men; in contrast to the other somatoform disorders, hypochondriasis occurs equally in both sexes. It has no special familial characteristics, unlike somatization disorder. *The onset is* not *after age 50;* in fact, hypochondriasis rarely first occurs after this age.

17.3 The answer is E (*Synopsis VIII,* pages 629–632).
Although the cause of somatization disorder is unknown, psychological factors in its causation are thought to involve *symbolic meanings.* Symptoms can be understood as a desire to avoid obligations, to express strong emotions, or to symbolize a feeling or belief. A psychoanalytic interpretation involves the notion that symptoms substitute for repressed instincts. Behavioral perspectives on somatization disorder emphasize parental teaching and example and ethnic mores. Some patients from unstable homes have been physically abused.

Alcohol addiction, abnormal serotonin regulation, and *a family history of mental retardation* are not considered to play any direct part in somatization disorder. Studies have suggested, however, that patients show attention and cognitive impairments that produce faulty perception of somatosensory inputs. There is also some evidence from brain-imaging studies that the frontal lobes and nondominant hemisphere show decreased metabolism in these patients. Although no studies have yet confirmed the hypothesis, it has been suggested that abnormal regulation of the cytokine system may produce some symptoms of somatoform disorders.

A genetic cause is not indicated *in 50 percent of patients,* but genetic data show that transmission has genetic components in some cases. It tends to run in families and occurs in 10 to 20 percent of first-degree female relatives of patients with somatization disorder. First-degree male relatives in these families are prone to substance abuse and antisocial personality disorder.

17.4 The answer is B (*Synopsis VIII,* page 639).
Body dysmorphic disorder is a preoccupation with an imagined bodily defect or an exaggerated distortion of a minor defect. The concern must cause a person significant distress or impair his or her functioning. Although the disorder is poorly studied and the cause is unknown, it is known that *the most common anatomical preoccupation is* not *with the breasts,* but with facial features, such as the nose. The specific area of concern may change from time to time, however; one study showed that patients focused on four body regions during the course of the disorder.

Emil Kraepelin recognized it as a compulsive disorder more than a century ago, and Pierre Janet also wrote about it. *Sigmund Freud's history of the Wolf-Man was an early description* of body dysmorphic disorder; the Wolf-Man was excessively concerned about his nose. This disorder was not mentioned in United States diagnostic criteria until 1980.

Slightly more women than men are affected by body dysmorphic disorder, whose most common age of onset is between 15 and 20 years. Affected patients are likely to be unmarried and to have other mental disorders. One study found that *at least 50 percent of college students were preoccupied with their appearance* and that in 25 percent of students feelings and functioning were significantly affected. In a society in which plastic surgery is commonly advertised and discussed, a less than perfect appearance can come to be seen as a disability or disorder to be repaired, particularly when a person's livelihood is believed to depend on youth and facial beauty. People thus seek medical or surgical help to address their concerns; nevertheless, surgical, dental, and other medical procedures almost never succeed in overcoming the disorder. Data indicate that *serotonin-specific drugs are more effective than surgery* in reducing symptoms in at least 50 percent of patients. Coexisting mental disorders should also receive appropriate pharmacotherapy and psychotherapy.

17.5 The answer is D (*Synopsis VIII,* pages 629–635).
The patient is probably suffering from *somatization disorder,* since she fits the diagnostic criteria listed in Table 17.1. The patient complained of at least four pain symptoms (breast, back, urinary, and migraine), two gastrointestinal symptoms (spastic colon and adhesions), one sexual symptom ("can't have relations"), and one pseudoneurological symptom (falling)—none of which is completely explained by physical or laboratory examinations. In addition, her symptoms had their onset before age 30.

Hypochondriasis is characterized by the false belief that one has a specific disease; in contrast, somatization disorder is characterized by concern with many symptoms. The symptoms of *conversion disorder* are limited to one or two neurological symptoms, rather than the wide-ranging symptoms of somatization disorder. *Pain disorder* is limited to one or two complaints of pain symptoms.

Body dysmorphic disorder is not distinguished by any type of symptoms. Instead, body dysmorphic disorder entails the preoccupation with an imagined defect in appearance. No such preoccupation was found in the patient described.

17.6 The answer is A (*Synopsis VIII,* pages 629–635).
Nearly all of the physical symptoms that the patient described were apparently without an organic basis. That suggested a somatoform disorder, and the large number of symptoms involving multiple organ systems suggested *somatization disorder.* She had symptoms relating to the gastrointestinal, cardiovascular, pulmonary, neurological, and gynecological systems, which meet the criteria for that diagnosis. *Conversion disorder* was ruled out because the patient's symptoms were not limited to the sensorimotor areas alone; they covered a far broader range. *Hypochondriasis* is distinguished from somatization disorder in that it includes the fear of disease and bodily preoccupation. In *dysthymic disorder,* patients show cognitive (slow thinking), behavioral (early morning awakening, lethargy), and mood (depression or suicidal ideation) symptoms.

17.7 The answer is E (all) (*Synopsis VIII,* page 639).
In the treatment of hypochondriasis, most *patients are resistant to psychotherapy.* Some hypochondriacal patients accept psychiatric treatment if it takes place in a medical setting and focuses on stress reduction and education in coping with chronic illness. Such *patients may respond better to group psychotherapy than to individual therapy,* perhaps because the group provides the social support and the social interaction that the patients need. Individual insight-oriented traditional psychotherapy for primary hypochondriasis is generally not successful. *Frequent physical examinations* should be performed; they reassure patients that they are not being abandoned by their physicians and that their complaints are being taken seriously. Invasive diagnostic and therapeutic procedures, however, should be undertaken only on the basis of objective evidence. When possible, the clinician should refrain from treating equivocal or incidental findings. Pharmacotherapy alleviates hypochondriacal symptoms only when the patient has an underlying drug-sensitive condition, such as an anxiety disorder or a major depressive disorder. When hypochondriasis is secondary to some other primary mental disorder, the *underlying psychiatric disorder* should be treated in its own right. When hypochondriasis is a transient situational reaction, patients must be helped to cope with the stress without reinforcing their illness behavior and their use of the sick role as solutions to their problems.

Table 17.1
DSM-IV Diagnostic Criteria for Somatization Disorder

A. A history of many physical complaints beginning before age 30 years that occur over a period of several years and result in treatment being sought or significant impairment in social, occupational, or other important areas of functioning.

B. Each of the following criteria must have been met, with individual symptoms occurring at any time during the course of the disturbance:
   (1) *four pain symptoms:* a history of pain related to at least four different sites or functions (eg, head, abdomen, back, joints, extremities, chest, rectum, during menstruation, during sexual intercourse, or during urination)
   (2) *two gastrointestinal symptoms:* a history of at least two gastrointestinal symptoms other than pain (eg, nausea, bloating, vomiting other than during pregnancy, diarrhea, or intolerance of several different foods)
   (3) *one sexual symptom:* a history of at least one sexual or reproductive symptom other than pain (eg, sexual indifference, erectile or ejaculatory dysfunction, irregular menses, excessive menstrual bleeding, vomiting throughout pregnancy)
   (4) *one pseudoneurologic symptoms:* a history of at least one symptom or deficit suggesting a neurological condition not limited to pain (conversion symptoms such as impaired coordination or balance, paralysis or localized weakness, difficulty swallowing or lump in throat, aphonia, urinary retention, hallucinations, loss of touch or pain sensation, double vision, blindness, deafness, seizures; dissociative symptoms such as amnesia; or loss of consciousness other than fainting)

C. Either (1) or (2):
   (1) after appropriate investigation, each of the symptoms in criterion B cannot be fully explained by a known general medical condition or the direct effects of a substance (eg, the effects of injury, medication, drugs, or alcohol)
   (2) when there is a related general medical condition, the physical complaints or resulting social or occupational impairment are in excess of what would be expected from the history, physical examination, or laboratory findings.

D. The symptoms are not intentionally feigned or produced (as in factitious disorder or malingering).

Reprinted with permission from American Psychiatric Association: *Diagnostic and Statistical Manual of Mental Disorders,* ed 4. Copyright, American Psychiatric Association, Washington, 1994.

17.8 The answer is D (*Synopsis VIII,* page 635).

Mutism is one of the most common symptoms of conversion disorder. Other common symptoms are paralysis and blindness. Conversion disorder may be most commonly associated with passive-aggressive, dependent, antisocial, and histrionic personality disorders. Symptoms of depressive disorders and anxiety disorders often accompany the symptoms of conversion disorder, and affected patients are at risk for suicide.

The inability to speak is not intentionally produced in a conversion disorder. If the symptoms are under conscious voluntary control, malingering and factitious disorders must be considered. A factitious disorder is produced or feigned for the sole purpose of assuming the patient role. Malingering is motivated by some secondary gain (for example, money or shelter). In both of those disorders, the patient's history is usually more inconsistent and contradictory than is the conversion disorder patient's history.

Conversion disorder is most common among patients in a low socioeconomic group, rural populations, little-educated persons, those with low intelligence quotients (IQs), and military personnel who have been exposed to combat.

Psychoanalytic theory holds that the major defense mechanism in conversion disorder is repression, not suppression. Suppression is the conscious or semiconscious act of inhibiting an impulse or idea. Repression is the active process of keeping out of consciousness ideas and impulses that are unacceptable to the patient. The conflict is between an instinctual impulse (for example, aggressive or sexual) and the prohibitions against its expression. The symptoms allow the partial expression of the forbidden wish or urge but disguise it, so that the patients need not consciously confront their unacceptable impulses. The conversion disorder symptoms also enable the patients to communicate that they need special consideration and special treatment. Such symptoms may function as a nonverbal means of controlling or manipulating others.

La belle indifférence, the patient's inappropriately cavalier attitude toward a serious symptom, is not always an accurate measure of whether a patient has conversion disorder, and so *la belle indifférence is not a necessary component in making the diagnosis of conversion disorder.* Table 17.2 lists the diagnostic criteria for conversion disorder.

Table 17.2
DSM-IV Diagnostic Criteria for Conversion Disorder

A. One or more symptoms or deficits affecting voluntary motor or sensory function that suggest a neurological or other general medical condition.
B. Psychological factors are judged to be associated with the symptom or deficit because the initiation or exacerbation of the symptom or deficit is preceded by conflicts or other stressors.
C. The symptom or deficit is not intentionally produced or feigned (as in factitious disorder or malingering).
D. The symptom or deficit cannot, after appropriate investigation, be fully explained by a general medical condition, or by the direct effects of a substance, or as a culturally sanctioned behavior or experience.
E. The symptom or deficit causes clinically significant distress or impairment in social, occupational, or other important areas of functioning or warrants medical evaluation.
F. The symptom or deficit is not limited to pain or sexual dysfunction, does not occur exclusively during the course of somatization disorder, and is not better accounted for by another mental disorder.

Specify type of symptom or deficit:
With motor symptom or deficit
With sensory symptom or deficit
With seizures or convulsions
With mixed presentation

17.9 The answer is E (all) (*Synopsis VIII,* pages 635–639).

A characteristic behavioral feature in patients with conversion disorder is what the French authors of the 19th century called *la belle indifférence.* Despite what appear to be the most extensive and crippling disturbances in function, the patient may be completely unconcerned and may not spontaneously mention such disturbances, which often results in their being overlooked. Unless specifically searched for, *la belle indifférence* is a calm mental attitude of acquiescence and complacency directed specifically at the physical symptom. It may not always be present, however.

Somatic compliance is the degree to which a person's physical structure coincides with his or her psychological mechanisms of defense in the symptomatic expression of a conflict. In conversion symptoms, for instance, an objectionable impulse such as anger is condensed into a definite physical function such as paralysis of an arm. The ability of the affected part or function of the body to reflect the conflict is its somatic compliance.

Autonomic dysfunctions may be reflected in various visceral symptoms, such as anorexia, vomiting, hiccoughs, and other abdominal complaints, which are considered a part of the classical syndrome of conversion disorders. Sensory disturbances—anesthesias and paresthesias in particular—are also typical of the physical symptoms of hysterical neurosis.

A history of *sexual disturbances*—especially impotence, anorgasmia, and a lack of desire—is frequently seen along with conversion symptoms. According to psychoanalytic theory, conversion disorder has been linked to a psychosexual conflict arising from the failure to relinquish oedipal ties and to rid the normal adult libido of its incestuous ties.

17.10 The answer is B (*Synopsis VIII,* page 637).

A number of theories attempt to explain the cause of hypochondriasis. One theory is that *hypochondriasis is the result of an unconscious desire to assume the sick role* by a person facing seemingly insurmountable and insolvable problems. The sick role offers a way out, because the sick patient is allowed to avoid unpleasant obligations and to postpone unwelcome challenges and is excused from usually expected duties. The diagnostic criteria for hypochondriasis (Table 17.3) require that patients be preoccupied with the false belief that they have a serious disease and that the false belief be based on a misinterpretation of physical signs or sensations. *Patients with hypochondriasis usually believe that they have a specific disease, not multiple diseases. The patient's belief that a particular disease is present is not of delusional intensity.* If it were of such intensity, a delusional disorder, somatic type, would be

Table 17.3
DSM-IV Diagnostic Criteria for Hypochondriasis

A. Preoccupation with fears of having, or the idea that one has, a serious disease based on the person's misinterpretation of bodily symptoms.
B. The preoccupation persists despite appropriate medical evaluation and reassurance.
C. The belief in criterion A is not of delusional intensity (as in delusional disorder, somatic type) and is not restricted to a circumscribed concern about appearance (as in body dysmorphic disorder).
D. The preoccupation causes clinically significant distress or impairment in social, occupational, or other important areas of functioning.
E. The duration of the disturbance is at least 6 months.
F. The preoccupation is not better accounted for by generalized anxiety disorder, obsessive-compulsive disorder, panic disorder, a major depressive episode, separation anxiety, or another somatoform disorder.

Specify if:
With poor insight: if, for most of the time during the current episode, the person does not recognize that the concern about having a serious illness is excessive or unreasonable

diagnosed, since delusion is a fixed false idea. *Men are not affected by hypochondriasis more than women;* in fact, men and women are equally affected. *The incidence of hypochondriasis is not affected by educational level or marital status.* Hypochondriacs are usually reassured by a normal physical examination; delusional persons are not.

17.11 The answer is E (*Synopsis VIII,* pages 634–639). *Cogwheel rigidity* is an organic sign secondary to disorders of the basal ganglia and not a sign of conversion disorder. In conversion disorder, anesthesia and paresthesia, especially of the extremities, are common. All sensory modalities are involved, and the distribution of the disturbance is inconsistent with that of either central or peripheral neurological disease. Thus, one sees the characteristic *stocking-and-glove anesthesia* of the hands or feet or *hemianesthesia of the body beginning precisely at the midline.* Motor symptoms include abnormal movements and gait disturbance, which is often a wildly ataxic, staggering gait accompanied by gross, irregular, jerky truncal movements and thrashing and waving arms (also known as *astasia-abasia*). *Normal reflexes* are seen. The patient shows no fasciculations or muscle atrophy, and electromyography findings are normal.

17.12 The answer is E (*Synopsis VIII,* pages 634–639). In *hypochondriasis,* patients have an unrealistic interpretation of physical signs or sensations as abnormal, leading to a preoccupation with the fear or belief of having a disease. *Depersonalization* is a nonspecific syndrome in which patients feel that they have lost their personal identity. As a result, they experience themselves as strange or unreal. It can be seen in schizophrenia, depersonalization disorder, and schizotypal personality disorder. A *phobia* is a persistent, pathological, unrealistic, intense fear of an object or situation. The phobic person may realize that the fear is irrational but is nonetheless unable to dispel it. In *conversion disorder* the anxiety that stems from an intrapsychic conflict is converted and expressed in a symbolic somatic symptom. In *bulimia nervosa* a large amount of food is ingested in a short period of time, usually less than 2 hours, and the patient then compensates by such maneuvers as self-induced vomiting.

17.13 The answer is E (*Synopsis VIII,* pages 640–641). *Serotonin-specific drugs* such as clomipramine (Anafranil) and fluoxetine (Prozac) *are effective in reducing the symptoms* in at least 50 percent of patients with body dysmorphic disorder. In any patient with a coexisting mental disorder or an anxiety disorder, the coexisting disorder should be treated with the appropriate pharmacotherapy and psychotherapy. How long treatment should be continued when the symptoms of body dysmorphic disorder have remitted is unknown. *Plastic surgery is not usually beneficial* in the treatment of patients with body dysmorphic disorder. In fact, surgical, dermatological, dental, and other medical procedures to address the alleged defects rarely satisfy the patient.

A comorbid diagnosis is not unusual. Body dysmorphic disorder commonly coexists with other mental disorders. One study found that more than 90 percent of body dysmorphic disorder patients had experienced a major depressive episode in their lifetimes, about 70 percent had had an anxiety disorder, and about 30 percent had a psychotic disorder. However, *anorexia nervosa should not be diagnosed* along with body dysmorphic disorder, since distortions of body image occur in anorexia nervosa, gender identity disorders, and some specific types of brain damage (for example, neglect syndromes).

The effects of body dysmorphic disorder on a person's life can be significant. Almost all affected patients avoid social and occupational exposure. As many as a third of the patients may be housebound by their concern about being ridiculed for their alleged deformities, and as many as *20 percent, not 50 percent, of patients attempt suicide.*

The diagnostic criteria for body dysmorphic disorder are listed in Table 17.4.

17.14 The answer is C (*Synopsis VIII,* pages 629–635). During the course of somatization disorder, the patient *has complained of* pain, gastrointestinal, sexual, and pseudoneurological symptoms that are *not explained by a known medical*

Table 17.4
DSM-IV Diagnostic Criteria for Body Dysmorphic Disorder

A. Preoccupation with an imagined defect in appearance. If a slight physical anomaly is present, the person's concern is markedly excessive.
B. The preoccupation causes clinically significant distress or impairment in social, occupational, or other important areas of functioning.
C. The preoccupation is not better accounted for by another mental disorder (eg, dissatisfaction with body shape and size in anorexia nervosa).

condition. In addition, the patient *presents the initial physical complaints before, not after, age 30.* The patient *has had physical symptoms for years, not just 3 months.* The patient has had interpersonal problems and tremendous psychological distress and *usually experiences significant, not minimal, impairment in social or occupational functioning.* A patient who has *a false belief of being pregnant* and objective signs of pregnancy, such as decreased menstrual flow or amenorrhea, does not have somatization disorder. Instead, the patient has pseudocyesis, a somatoform disorder not otherwise specified (Table 17.5).

17.15 The answer is D (*Synopsis VIII,* page 644).
Munchausen syndrome is categorized as a factitious disorder with predominantly physical signs and symptoms; the essential feature is the ability of patients to present physical symptoms so well that they are able to gain admission to and stay in hospitals. The symptom production in somatoform disorders is not intentional. *Conversion disorder* is a condition in which psychological factors are judged to be causatively related to a loss or an alteration of physical functioning. *Hypochondriasis* is preoccupation with the fear of having a serious disease. *Somatization disorder* is a chronic, polysymptomatic disorder that begins early in life. *Body dysmorphic disorder* is characterized by preoccupation with some imagined defect in one's appearance.

17.16 The answer is E (all) (*Synopsis VIII,* pages 629–637).
The clinician must always rule out organic causes for the patient's symptoms. Medical disorders that present with nonspecific, transient abnormalities pose the greatest diagnostic difficulty in the differential diagnosis of somatization disorder. The disorders to be considered include *multiple sclerosis, systemic lupus erythematosus, acute intermittent porphyria,* and *hyperparathyroidism.* In addition, the onset of many somatic symptoms late in life must be presumed to be caused by a medical illness until testing rules it out.

Table 17.5
DSM-IV Diagnostic Criteria for Somatoform Disorder Not Otherwise Specified

This category includes disorders with somatoform symptoms that do not meet the criteria for any specific somatoform disorder. Examples include

1. Pseudocyesis: a false belief of being pregnant that is associated with objective signs of pregnancy, which may include abdominal enlargement (although the umbilicus does not become everted), reduced menstrual flow, amenorrhea, subjective sensation of fetal movement, nausea, breast engorgement and secretions, and labor pains at the expected date of delivery. Endocrine changes may be present, but the syndrome cannot be explained by a general medical condition that causes endocrine changes (eg, a hormone-secreting tumor).
2. A disorder involving nonpsychotic hypochondriacal symptoms of less than 6 months' duration
3. A disorder involving unexplained physical complaints (eg, fatigue or body weakness) of less than 6 months' duration that are not due to another mental disorder.

17.17 The answer is E (*Synopsis VIII,* pages 637–639).
Patients with hypochondriasis *do not have beliefs of delusional proportions* and therefore, by definition, do not require verification of them. Investigators see hypochondriacal symptoms as playing a primarily defensive role in the psychic economy. For Harry Stack Sullivan they represented a protective activity that enabled the patient to *deny the pain of low self-esteem.* In other words, persons can substitute an image of themselves as physically ill or deficient for the far more devastating view of themselves as worthless human beings. Hypochondriasis also enables patients to *gratify their dependence needs, protect themselves from their sense of guilt,* and provide themselves with *various secondary gains.* The obvious advantage that persons gain from their illness is secondary gain, such as gifts, attention, and release from responsibility.

17.18 The answer is B (*Synopsis VIII,* pages 641–644).
The most accurate statement about pain disorder is that *first-degree relatives of pain disorder patients have an increased likelihood of having the same disorder,* thus indicting the possibility of genetic inheritance or behavioral mechanisms in the transmission of the disorder. Pain disorder is in fact *diagnosed twice as frequently in women as in men.* The *peak ages of onset are in the fourth and fifth decades,* when the tolerance for pain declines. Pain disorder is *most common in persons with blue-collar occupations,* perhaps because of increased job-related injuries. *Depressive disorders, anxiety disorders, and substance abuse are also more common in families of pain disorder patients* than in the general population.

Answers 17.19–17.22

17.19 The answer is A (*Synopsis VIII,* page 638).

17.20 The answer is B (*Synopsis VIII,* pages 641–644).

17.21 The answer is C (*Synopsis VIII,* page 629).

17.22 The answer is A (*Synopsis VIII,* page 635).
La belle indifférence is a psychological symptom often associated with *conversion disorder. La belle indifférence* is the patient's inappropriately cavalier attitude toward a serious symptom. The bland indifference may be lacking in some conversion disorder patients. *Alexithymia* is the inability to articulate internal feelings that is often associated with *pain disorder.* Some patients who are unable to articulate their internal feelings do so by the body's expressing them in the form of a pain disorder. Patients who experience aches and pains in their bodies without identifiable physical causes may be symbolically expressing an intrapsychic conflict through the body. Table 17.6 lists the diagnostic criteria for pain disorder.

Briquet's syndrome is a synonym for *somatization disorder.* In 1859 Paul Briquet, a French physician, observed the multiplicity of the symptoms and affected organ symptoms and commented on the usually chronic course of the disorder. Somatization disorder became the standard name in 1980. *Astasia-abasia* is gait disturbance seen in *conversion disorder.* A wildly ataxic, staggering gait is accompanied by gross, irregular, jerky truncal movements and thrashing and waving arm movements. Patients with the symptoms rarely fall, and if they do, are generally not injured.

Answers 17.23–17.27

17.23 The answer is C (*Synopsis VIII,* pages 632, 641).

Table 17.6
DSM-IV Diagnostic Criteria for Pain Disorder

A. Pain in one or more anatomical sites is the predominant focus of the clinical presentation and is of sufficient severity to warrant clinical attention.

B. The pain causes clinically significant distress or impairment in social, occupational, or other important areas of functioning.

C. Psychological factors are judged to have an important role in the onset, severity, exacerbation, or maintenance of the pain.

D. The symptom or deficit is not intentionally produced or feigned (as in factitious disorder or malingering).

E. The pain is not better accounted for by a mood, anxiety, or psychotic disorder and does not meet criteria for dyspareunia.

Code as follows:

Pain disorder associated with psychological factors: psychological factors are judged to have a major role in the onset, severity, exacerbation, or maintenance of the pain. (If a general medical condition is present, it does not have a major role in the onset, severity, exacerbation, or maintenance of the pain.) This type of pain disorder is not diagnosed if criteria are also met for somatization disorder.

Specify if:
Acute duration of less than 6 months
Chronic duration of 6 months or longer

Pain disorder associated with both psychological factors and a general medical condition: both psychological factors and a general medical condition are judged to have important roles in the onset, severity, exacerbation, or maintenance of the pain. The associated general medical condition or anatomical site of the pain (see below) is coded on Axis III.

Specify if:
Acute duration of less than 6 months
Chronic duration of 6 months or longer

Note: The following is not considered to be a mental disorder and is included here to facilitate differential diagnosis.

Pain disorder associated with a general medical condition: a general medical condition has a major role in the onset, severity, exacerbation, or maintenance of the pain. (If psychological factors are present, they are not judged to have a major role in the onset, severity, exacerbation, or maintenance of the pain.) The diagnostic code for the pain is selected based on the associated general medical condition if one has been established or on the anatomical location of the pain if the underlying general medical condition is not yet clearly established—for example, low back, sciatic, pelvic, headache, facial, chest, joint, bone, abdominal, breast, renal, ear, eye, throat, tooth, and urinary.

17.24 The answer is A (*Synopsis VIII*, pages 629–632).

17.25 The answer is C (*Synopsis VIII*, pages 634–643).

17.26 The answer is B (*Synopsis VIII*, page 643).

17.27 The answer is D (*Synopsis VIII*, pages 629–634, 641–644).
Both somatization disorder and pain disorder affect *women more than men.* Somatization disorder has a 5 to 1 female-to-male ratio. The lifetime prevalence of somatization disorder among women in the general population may be 1 to 2 percent. Pain disorder is diagnosed twice as commonly in women as in men. Somatization disorder is defined as beginning before age 30, and it *most often begins during a person's teens.* As for pain disorder, the peak of onset is in the fourth and fifth decades, perhaps because the tolerance for pain decreases with age.

Antidepressants, such as fluoxetine (Prozac), sertraline (Zoloft), and clomipramine (Anafranil), *are effective* in the treatment of pain disorder and somatization disorder. *Serotonin may be involved in the pathophysiology of pain disorder.* It is probably the main neurotransmitter in the descending inhibitory pathways. Endorphins also play a role in the central nervous system modulation of pain. *Anorexia nervosa is not commonly associated with either pain disorder or somatization disorder.* Anorexia nervosa is an eating disorder that presents a dramatic picture of self-starvation, peculiar attitudes toward food, weight loss (leading to the maintenance of the patient's body weight at least 15 percent below that expected), and an intense fear of weight gain.

Answers 17.28–17.31

17.28 The answer is C (*Synopsis VIII*, page 644).

17.29 The answer is A (*Synopsis VIII*, page 644).

17.30 The answer is B (*Synopsis VIII*, page 644).

17.31 The answer is D (*Synopsis VIII*, page 644).
Both *autonomic arousal disorder and neurasthenia* are *symptom patterns seen in patients with undifferentiated somatoform disorder* (Table 17.7). In *autonomic arousal disorder,* patients are affected with somatoform disorder symptoms that are limited to bodily functions innervated by the autonomic nervous system. Such patients have *complaints involving the cardiovascular, respiratory, gastrointestinal,* urogenital, and dermatological *systems.* Other patients have *complaints of mental and physical fatigue,* physical weakness and exhaustion, and the inability to perform many everyday activities because of their symptoms. That syndrome is often referred to as *neurasthenia. Neither autonomic arousal disorder nor neurasthenia* has *symptoms caused by a tick bite.* Tick bites are the cause of Lyme disease.

Answers 17.32–17.37

17.32 The answer is A (*Synopsis VIII*, page 637).

17.33 The answer is A (*Synopsis VIII*, pages 637–640).

17.34 The answer is B (*Synopsis VIII*, pages 629–634).

17.35 The answer is A (*Synopsis VIII*, pages 637–640).

17.36 The answer is C (*Synopsis VIII*, pages 629–634, 637–640).

17.37 The answer is D (*Synopsis VIII*, pages 629–634, 637–640).
Hypochondriasis, which is an excessive concern about disease and a preoccupation with one's health, *is found approximately equally in men and women.* Somatization disorder, which is a

Table 17.7
DSM-IV Diagnostic Criteria for Undifferentiated Somatoform Disorder

A. One or more physical complaints (eg, fatigue, loss of appetite, gastrointestinal or urinary complaints)
B. Either (1) or (2):
 (1) after appropriate investigation, the symptoms cannot be fully explained by a known general medical condition or the direct effects of a substance (eg, the effects of injury, medication, drugs, or alcohol)
 (2) when there is a related general medical condition, the physical complaints or resulting social or occupational impairment is in excess of what would be expected from the history, physical examination, or laboratory findings
C. The symptoms cause clinically significant distress or impairment in social, occupational, or other important areas of functioning.
D. The duration of the disturbance is at least 6 months.
E. The disturbance is not better accounted for by another mental disorder (eg, another somatoform disorder, sexual dysfunction, mood disorder, anxiety disorder, sleep disorder, or psychotic disorder).
F. The symptom is not intentionally produced or feigned (as in factitious disorder or malingering).

chronic syndrome of multiple somatic symptoms that cannot be explained medically, is much more common in women than in men. The *peak incidence* of hypochondriasis is thought to occur *during the 40s or 50s,* whereas somatization disorder begins before age 30. *Somatization disorder* patients are *likely to have a hysterical cognitive and interpersonal style,* as opposed to obsessional hypochondriac patients. Somatization disorder does not *include disease conviction or disease fear,* as does hypochondriasis. *Anhedonia* (the inability to experience pleasure) is a sign of depression but may be present in both hypochondriasis and somatization disorders. *Hallucinations are not present* in either disorder.

18

Neurasthenia and Chronic Fatigue Syndrome

Neurasthenia is classified as a neurotic disorder in the 10th revision of *International Statistical Classification of Diseases and Related Health Problems* (ICD-10). In the United States the disorder is categorized as an undifferentiated somatoform disorder in the fourth edition of *Diagnostic and Statistical Manual of Mental Disorders* (DSM-IV). Students must understand the causes and symptoms of neurasthenia not only in the United States but also in Europe and Asia, especially in China and other areas of Asia, where it is most commonly diagnosed.

The difficulties of investigating neurasthenia stem from its occurrence with other conditions and from the fact that it has not been much studied on its own. The major symptoms—fatigue and heightened concern over bodily symptoms—commonly appear among those who are socially and economically deprived, although neurasthenia is not more prevalent among this group.

George Miller Beard, an American neuropsychiatrist who introduced the term in the 1860s, postulated a ''nervous diathesis'' theory for neurasthenia. Sigmund Freud, who was familiar with neurasthenia, instead considered it a result of disturbed sexual functioning. Psychoanalysts after Freud thought of neurasthenia as a reaction to unconscious feelings such as rejection and low self-esteem. The modern hypothesis is probably most similar to Beard's; it holds that prolonged stress lowers the levels of neurotransmitters, which when depleted, cause symptoms of depression or anxiety. In fact, many neuroendocrine dysregulations have been reported in patients with mood and anxiety disorders. Students must be thoroughly acquainted with these abnormalities as well as the normal functioning of the neuroendocrine systems to diagnose and treat neurasthenia.

Chronic fatigue syndrome was identified by the U.S. Centers for Disease Control and Prevention (CDC) in 1988, and the disorder is classified in ICD-10, under the heading of Malaise and Fatigue, as an ill-defined condition of unknown etiology. Its incidence is not known but is estimated to be 1 per 1,000. Chronic fatigue syndrome is observed primarily in young adults and occurs twice as often in women as in men.

Chronic fatigue syndrome is difficult to diagnose because it lacks any pathognomonic features. Clinicians must discover as many signs and symptoms as possible to facilitate diagnosis, and they must also be aware of many other conditions that might cause a patient's distress. The 1994 CDC guidelines for chronic fatigue syndrome are a good source for its clinical features. Treatment is largely supportive, and as yet no effective medical treatment has been identified. Psychiatric treatment can help.

Students should read Chapter 18 in Kaplan and Sadock's *Synopsis of Psychiatry VIII* and should pay close attention to the case examples. The following questions and answers allow students to test their knowledge of the material.

HELPFUL HINTS

Students should know the terms listed here.

- asthenia
- autonomic nervous system
- George Miller Beard
- CDC guidelines
- Centers for Disease Control and Prevention (CDC)
- chronic fatigue syndrome
- chronic stress
- depletion hypothesis
- endocrine disorders
- environmental components
- epidemiology
- Epstein-Barr herpesvirus
- etiology
- flulike illness
- growing pains
- ICD-10 classification
- immune abnormalities
- incidence and prevalence
- insight-oriented psychotherapy
- methylphenidate (Ritalin)
- nervous diathesis
- nervous exhaustion
- neurasthenia
- neuroendocrine dysregulations
- pathognomonic features
- spontaneous recovery
- supportive treatment
- treatment options
- undifferentiated somatoform disorder
- unspecified disability

▲ QUESTIONS

DIRECTIONS: Each of the questions or statements below is followed by five lettered responses or completions. Select the *one* that is most appropriate in each case.

18.1 George Miller Beard considered neurasthenia to be caused by

A. disability
B. chronic fatigue
C. stored nutrients
D. "discharged battery"
E. nervous exhaustion

18.2 All of the following are components of Beard's nervous diathesis theory *except*

A. specific vulnerability
B. biological component
C. drain on nervous energy
D. psychological component
E. disturbed sexual functioning

18.3 Neuroendocrine dysregulations occurring in patients with mood and anxiety disorders include all of the following *except*

A. low serotonin levels
B. increased testosterone levels
C. low neuronal dopamine activity
D. decreased basal levels of luteinizing hormone
E. decreased basal levels of follicle-stimulating hormone

18.4 The 1994 CDC guidelines for chronic fatigue syndrome include

A. nausea
B. arthritis
C. sleep disturbance
D. infected lymph nodes
E. chronic fatigue for at least 3 months

18.5 All of the following statements correctly describe current approaches in treating neurasthenia *except*

A. Psychiatric intervention is helpful.
B. Clinicians must recognize objective symptoms.
C. Patients must recognize environmental stresses.
D. Somatic symptoms must be treated when possible.
E. Benzodiazepines are useful drugs for long-term treatment.

18.6 The symptoms of neurasthenia include all of the following *except*

A. paresthesia
B. tachycardia
C. migraine headaches
D. physical aches and pains
E. chronic weakness and fatigue

ANSWERS

Neurasthenia and Chronic Fatigue Syndrome

18.1 The answer is E (*Synopsis VIII,* page 646).
George Beard considered neurasthenia to be caused by *nervous exhaustion,* the depletion of the nerve cell's *''stored nutrient''* and that stress caused such depletion.

Neurasthenia is indeed characterized by *chronic fatigue and disability,* but these symptoms are distinct from the cause. As described by Arthur Noyes, it is a situation in which ''the nervous system is drained of its energy in the manner of a partially *discharged battery* of low voltage,'' a description that refers to symptoms as well as to cause.

18.2 The answer is E (*Synopsis VIII,* page 646).
Freud, not Beard, ascribed neurasthenia to *disturbed sexual functioning.* Freud agreed with Beard that stress was involved but thought that the stress was produced by the inadequate discharge of sexual energy, which occurred when masturbation replaced normal intercourse. Beard's theory required that a person with a *specific vulnerability* be acted on by a stressful environmental influence. This stress could be *biological* (such as an infection) or *psychological* (such as the death of a loved one). The resulting *drain on nervous energy* produced the disorder. Beard's theory is similar to the contemporary depletion hypothesis, although the latter uses modern research on depletion of brain amines to explain the symptoms of the disorder.

18.3 The answer is B (*Synopsis VIII,* pages 646–647).
Neuroendocrine dysregulations in people with mood and anxiety disorders do not include *increased testosterone levels.* On the contrary, testosterone levels are decreased, and testosterone replacement is sometimes attempted. Long-term treatment with testosterone, however, can have serious adverse affects such as prostate cancer. All of the other lettered choices have been reported in mood and anxiety disorders: *Low serotonin levels* occur in depressive disorder; *low neuronal dopamine activity* is found in depression. *Decreased basal levels of luteinizing hormone* and *of follicle-stimulating hormone* are additional neuroendocrine abnormalities. These hormones are also altered during prolonged stress states and presumably in neurasthenia as well.

18.4 The answer is C (*Synopsis VIII,* pages 650–651).
Sleep disturbance is one of the 1994 CDC guidelines for chronic fatigue syndrome. *Nausea* and *arthritis* are not included as symptoms among these guidelines (Table 18.1). Tender or enlarged *lymph nodes,* not *infected lymph nodes,* are a symptom of chronic fatigue syndrome. The first guideline for the disorder is *chronic fatigue for at least* 6, not *3, months.* Other guidelines include impaired memory or concentration, muscle pain, arthralgias, headache, and postexertional malaise.

Table 18.1
1994 U.S. Centers for Disease Control and Prevention (CDC) Criteria for Chronic Fatigue Syndrome

A. Severe unexplained fatigue for over 6 months that is:
  (1) of a new or definite onset
  (2) not due to continuing exertion
  (3) not resolved by rest
  (4) functionally impairing

B. The presence of four or more of the following new symptoms:
  (1) impaired memory or concentration
  (2) sore throat
  (3) tender lymph nodes
  (4) muscle pain
  (5) pain in several joints
  (6) new pattern of headaches
  (7) unrefreshing sleep
  (8) postexertional malaise lasting more than 24 hours

18.5 The answer is E (*Synopsis VIII,* pages 651–653).
Benzodiazepines are not useful drugs for long-term treatment of neurasthenia. Physicians should be careful when prescribing drugs for this disorder; patients may misuse them and become dependent. As benzodiazepines have the potential for abuse, they must be used only briefly and with careful supervision, for anxiety, phobias, or insomnia. *Psychotherapeutic intervention* is helpful during treatment for neurasthenia. Along with medications, *patients must recognize environmental stresses* that help to produce the disorder, the coping mechanisms with which they deal with the stresses, and the interaction between mind and body. Without insight-oriented psychotherapy, neurasthenia may well continue without improvement. *Clinicians must recognize objective symptoms;* this concept is of primary importance in treating neurasthenia. Patients' symptoms are not imaginary, and *somatic symptoms must be treated.* They are produced by emotions that influence the autonomic nervous system, which in turn affects bodily functions. Stress can produce structural change in organ systems; in some cases the results can be life threatening.

18.6 The answer is C (*Synopsis VIII,* pages 650–651).
Although *headache* is one of the symptoms of neurasthenia, specifically *migraine headaches* are not. All other listed choices—*paresthesia, tachycardia, physical aches and pains,* and *chronic weakness and fatigue*—are symptoms of neurasthenia. There are many more symptoms, such as difficulty in concentrating, dizziness, indigestion, constipation and diarrhea, palpitations, excess sweating, chills, noise or light intolerance, flushing, insomnia, and tremors. The similarity between the signs and symptoms reported by patients with neurasthenia and those with chronic fatigue syndrome are apparent when comparing Table 18.2 and Table 18.3.

Table 18.2
Signs and Symptoms Reported by Patients with Neurasthenia

General fatigue	Flatulence	Pessimism
Exhaustion	Palpitations	Chronic worry
General anxiety	Extrasystole	Fear of disease
Difficulty concentrating	Tachycardia	Irritability
Physical aches and pains	Excess sweating	Feelings of hopelessness
Dizziness	Flushing of skin	Dry mouth or hypersalivation
Headache	Sexual dysfunction, eg, erectile disorder, anorgasmia	Arthralgias
Intolerance of noise (hyperacusis) or bright lights	Dysmenorrhea	Heat insensitivity
Chills	Paresthesia	Dysphagia
Indigestion	Insomnia	Pruritus
Constipation or diarrhea	Poor memory	Tremors
		Back pain

Table 18.3
Signs and Symptosm Reported by Patients with Chronic Fatigue Syndrome

Fatigue or exhaustion	Diarrhea	Insomnia
Headache	Constipation	Fever or sensation of fever
Malaise	Bloating	Chills
Short-term memory loss	Panic attacks	Night sweats
Muscle pain	Eye pain	Weight gain
Difficulty concentrating	Scratchiness in eyes	Allergies
Joint pain	Blurring of vision	Chemical sensitivities
Depression	Double vision	Palpitations
Abdominal pain	Sensitivity to bright lights	Shortness of breath
Lymph node pain	Numbness and/or tingling in extremities	Flushing rash of the face and cheeks
Sore throat	Fainting spells	Swelling of the extremities or eyelids
Lack of restful sleep	Light-headedness	Burning on urination
Muscle weakness	Dizziness	Sexual dysfunction
Bitter or metallic taste	Clumsiness	Hair loss
Balance disturbance		

Adapted from Bell DS: *The Doctor's Guide to Chronic Fatigue Syndrome: Understanding, Treating, and Living with CFIDS*, pp 10–11. Addison-Wesley, Reading, MA, 1995.

19

Factitious Disorders

According to the fourth edition of *Diagnostic and Statistical Manual of Mental Disorders* (DSM-IV), factitious disorders are characterized by intentionally produced physical or psychological signs or symptoms to assume a sick role. Patients with factitious disorders have no external incentive, such as avoiding legal responsibility or collecting disability. Patients' motivation for such behavior is obscure, but the disorder is best described as illness behavior and the sick role.

Factitious disorders occur most often among health care workers and other people with extensive experience with illness or hospitalization during their early years. It is speculated that the disorder aims to unconsciously master the serious illness by reliving the experience. Patients with a factitious disorder may also have symptoms of borderline personality disorder.

The DSM-IV categories for the disorder include predominantly physical signs and symptoms, predominantly psychological signs and symptoms, both physical and psychological signs and symptoms, and factitious disorder not otherwise specified. Patients with factitious disorder with predominantly physical signs and symptoms may have multiple scars from previous surgeries; they may complain of hematoma, abdominal pain, fever, seizures, and many other symptoms. Patients commonly visit many hospitals and seek admission for different symptoms.

Patients with factitious disorder with predominantly psychological signs and symptoms are difficult to diagnose. The symptoms can include hallucinations, depression, dissociated states, and bereavement, which may involve stories of violent deaths. In factitious disorder by proxy, one person intentionally produces physical signs or symptoms in another person who is under the first person's care. Commonly, a mother convinces medical personnel that her child is ill by giving false information and even by inducing injury or illness in the child.

Students should review Chapter 19 in *Kaplan and Sadock's Synopsis VIII* and should then study the questions and answers below to test their knowledge of the area.

HELPFUL HINTS

The student should be able to define each of these terms.

- approximate answers
- as-if personality
- Briquet's syndrome
- factitious disorder:
  - by proxy
  - not otherwise specified
  - with predominantly physical signs and symptoms
  - with predominantly psychological signs and symptoms
- Ganser's syndrome
- gridiron abdomen
- malingering
- Munchausen syndrome
- pseudologia phantastica
- pseudomalingering
- regression
- schizophrenia
- somatoform disorders
- substance abuse
- symbolization
- unmasking ceremony

▲ QUESTIONS

DIRECTIONS: Each of the incomplete statements below is followed by five suggested completions. Select the *one* that is *best* in each case.

19.1 A 22-year-old male ambulance driver who complained of severe abdominal pain and tenderness was admitted to the hospital through the emergency room. The patient demanded an appendectomy. When test after test returned with a negative result, the patient grew abusive and threatening. A likely diagnosis is

A. malingering
B. hypochondriasis
C. Ganser's syndrome
D. Briquet's syndrome
E. Munchausen syndrome

19.2 Which of the following is *not* involved in a case of factitious disorder by proxy?

A. A false medical history
B. A history of drug abuse
C. The alteration of records
D. The contamination of lab samples
E. The induction of injury in the patient

19.3 Which of the following does *not* correctly describe pseudologia phantastica?

A. A patient distorts the medical history.
B. A listener's interest reinforces the symptom.
C. A patient is pleased by a listener's attention.
D. A patient pretends to be a fearless war hero.
E. A patient gives conflicting accounts of family background.

19.4 Factors in the etiology of factious disorders can include which of the following?

A. Patients were adopted.
B. Patients have hearing problems.
C. Patients have cognitive disorders.
D. Patients come from one-parent families.
E. Patients were abused or deprived in childhood.

19.5 Patients with factitious disorders

A. do not intentionally produce signs of medical or mental disorders
B. use the facsimile of genuine illness for secondary gains
C. do not seek out painful procedures
D. usually had a family of origin with either an absent father or a rejecting mother
E. are easily engaged in exploratory psychotherapy

19.6 In patients suspected of having a factitious disorder

A. emphasis should be placed on securing information from any available friend or relative
B. the examiner should ask pointed questions to reveal the false nature of the illness
C. their intelligence quotients (IQs) are usually below average
D. there is evidence of a formal thought disorder
E. their tolerance to frustration is usually high

19.7 The differential diagnosis of a factitious disorder includes

A. somatization disorder
B. hypochondriasis
C. antisocial personality disorder
D. malingering
E. all of the above

19.8 Factitious disorders

A. usually begin in childhood
B. are best treated with psychoactive drugs
C. usually have a good prognosis
D. are synonymous with Ganser's syndrome
E. may occur by proxy

19.9 Patients with factitious disorders

A. do not usually gain admission to a hospital
B. may take anticoagulants to simulate bleeding disorders
C. are usually easy to manage in the hospital
D. do not display symptoms of pseudologia phantastica
E. usually receive the codiagnosis of schizotypal personality disorder

Questions 19.10–19.11

19.10 A 29-year-old female laboratory technician was admitted to the medical service through the emergency room because of bloody urine. The patient said that she was being treated for lupus erythematosus by a physician in a different city. She also mentioned that she had had von Willebrand's disease (a rare hereditary blood disorder) as a child. On the third day of her hospitalization, a medical student told the resident that she had seen the patient several weeks before at a different hospital, where the patient had been admitted for the same problem. A search of the patient's belongings revealed a cache of anticoagulant medication. When confronted with the evidence, she refused to discuss the matter and hurriedly signed out of the hospital against medical advice.

The best diagnosis is

A. somatoform disorder
B. malingering
C. factitious disorder with predominantly physical signs and symptoms
D. factitious disorder with psychological symptoms
E. antisocial personality disorder

19.11 A leading predisposing factor in the development of factitious disorder with predominantly physical signs and symptoms is employment as a

A. teacher
B. health care worker
C. police officer
D. banker
E. waitress

Questions 19.12–19.14

19.12 Factitious disorder with predominantly physical signs and symptoms is synonymous with all of the following *except*

A. hospital addiction
B. Munchausen syndrome
C. professional patient syndrome
D. Briquet's syndrome
E. polysurgical addiction

19.13 All of the following apply to factitious disorder with predominantly physical signs and symptoms *except*

A. It is frequently seen in patients with a family history of serious illness or disability.
B. It is often used as a method to obtain disability payments.
C. It is under voluntary control, but most patients deny the voluntary production of the illness.
D. It is frequently seen in persons employed in health care jobs.
E. It is occasionally seen in patients with a grudge against the medical profession.

19.14 Persons displaying a factitious disorder are often characterized by

A. a history of being exposed to genuine illness in a family member
B. employment in a health-related field
C. a history of early parental rejection
D. a tendency to view the physician as a loving parent
E. all of the above

19.15 You are asked by the court to evaluate a 21-year-old man arrested in a robbery because his lawyer raised the issue of his competence to stand trial. During the interview the man appears calm and in control, sits slouched in the chair, and has good eye contact. His affect shows a good range. His thought processes are logical, sequential, and spontaneous even when he describes many difficulties with his thinking. He seems guarded in his answers, particularly to questions about his psychological symptoms.

He claims to have precognition on occasion, knowing, for instance, what is going to be served for lunch in the jail; that people hear his thoughts, as if broadcast on the radio; and that he does not like narcotics because Jean Dixon doesn't like narcotics either, and she is in control of his thoughts. He states that he has seen a vision of General Lee in his cell and that his current incarceration is a mission in which he is attempting to be an undercover agent for the police, although none of the local police realize this. Despite the overtly psychotic nature of these thoughts as described, the patient does not seem to be really engaged in the ideas; he seems to be simply reciting a list of what appears to be crazy rather than recounting actual experiences and beliefs.

Which of the following is the most likely diagnosis?

A. Malingering
B. Schizophrenia, paranoid type
C. Factitious disorder with predominantly psychological symptoms
D. Delusional disorder
E. Capgras's syndrome

ANSWERS

Factitious Disorders

19.1 The answer is E (*Synopsis VIII,* page 656).

Munchausen syndrome is another name for factitious disorder with predominantly physical signs and symptoms. Munchausen syndrome was named after Baron von Münchhausen, an 18th century German traveler and raconteur. Other names are hospital addiction, polysurgical addiction, and professional patient syndrome. A primary feature of this disorder is a patient's ability to present physical symptoms so well that he or she gains admission to a hospital. A patient may feign symptoms of a severe disorder with which he or she is familiar and may also give a history good enough to deceive a skilled clinician. The patient usually demands surgery or other treatment and can become abusive when negative test results threaten to reveal the factitious behavior. As these features are similar to the ambulance driver's behavior, a diagnosis of Munchausen syndrome is justified.

Malingering, by contrast, is a voluntary production of false or exaggerated physical or psychological symptoms, which arise from an external motivation to avoid difficult situations, to receive some sort of compensation, or to retaliate when he or she feels guilty or has suffered a loss. Malingering is differentiated from factitious disorders primarily because of its clearly definable goal.

Hypochondriasis, a person's concern or preoccupation with disease, is a genuine feeling and is not voluntarily produced. *Ganser's syndrome* is a controversial condition that occurs most often among prison inmates. Those with Ganser's syndrome respond to simple questions with amazingly incorrect answers. In DSM-IV, Ganser's syndrome is classified as a dissociative disorder not otherwise specified. In *Briquet's syndrome,* or somatization disorder, the symptoms are not voluntarily produced, hospitalization is not frequent, and patients do not seek to undergo numerous mutilating procedures.

19.2 The answer is B (*Synopsis VIII,* pages 657).

A history of drug abuse has no connection with factitious disorder by proxy. In this disorder, one person intentionally produces signs and symptoms in another person who is under the first person's care, often a mother and a child. The mother may give *a false medical history* and can be responsible for *the alteration of* medical *records, the contamination of lab samples,* and *the induction of injury in the patient.* The only apparent reason for such behavior is for the caretaker to indirectly assume the sick role.

19.3 The answer is D (*Synopsis VIII,* pages 283, 655).

Although a patient who *pretends to be a fearless war hero* may well have a factitious disorder of the physical type, imposture is distinct from pseudologia phantastica. Patients may assume the identity of a famous or prestigious person or may claim to be related to someone special.

In pseudologia phantastica, limited factual material is mixed with extensive, colorful fantasies: *A patient distorts the medical history* and can also *give conflicting accounts of family background.* Because the *patient is pleased by a listener's attention,* the *listener's interest can reinforce the symptom.*

19.4 The answer is E (*Synopsis VIII,* page 654).

Factors in the etiology of factitious disorders can include *patients being abused or deprived* in childhood, a situation that called for frequent hospitalizations. Escape from home might have come to be desired, and patients might have learned to seek loving and caring treatment from hospital workers rather than from rejecting or absent parents and siblings. Factitious disorders are thought to be a form of repetition compulsion—a repetition of the basic conflict of needing and seeking acceptance, which is not expected to be forthcoming; patients transform hospital staff into rejecting parents.

The other factors, *hearing problems, cognitive disorders, coming from one-parent families, or being adopted,* have no direct influence on the etiology of factitious disorders.

19.5 The answer is D (*Synopsis VIII,* page 654).

Anecdotal case reports of patients with factitious disorders indicate that many of the patients suffered childhood abuse or deprivation, resulting in frequent hospitalizations during early development and that the patient *usually had a family of origin with either an absent father or a rejecting mother.* In such circumstances, an inpatient stay may have been regarded as an escape from a fragmented home situation, and the patient may have found the series of caretakers (such as doctors, nurses, and hospital workers) as loving and caring.

In factitious disorders, patients *do intentionally produce signs of medical or mental disorders* and misrepresent their histories and symptoms. The only apparent objective of the behavior is to assume the role of a patient. Patients also *use the facsimile of genuine illness to re-create the desired positive parent-child bond, not for secondary gains. Patients may seek out painful procedures,* such as surgical operations and invasive diagnostic tests. Those patients may have masochistic personalities in which pain serves as punishment for past sins, imagined or real.

Given the intentionally deceptive nature of factitious disorders, patients *are difficult to engage in exploratory psychotherapy.* They may insist that their symptoms are physical and, therefore, that psychological treatment is useless. The diagnostic criteria for factitious disorder in the fourth edition of *Diagnostic and Statistical Manual of Mental Disorders* (DSM-IV) are given in Table 19.1.

19.6 The answer is A (*Synopsis VIII,* pages 654–655).

In patients suspected of having factitious disorder, *emphasis should be placed on securing information from any available friend, relative,* or other informant, because interviews with reliable outside sources often reveal the false nature of the patient's illness. Although it is time-consuming and tedious, verifying all of the facts presented by the patient concerning prior hospitalizations and medical care is essential.

The examiner should not ask accusatory or *pointed questions to reveal the false nature of the illness.* Such questions may provoke truculence, evasion, or flight from the hospital. There may be a danger of provoking frank psychosis if vigorous confrontation is used; in some instances the feigned ill-

Table 19.1
DSM-IV Diagnostic Criteria for Factitious Disorder

A. Intentional production or feigning of physical or psychological signs or symptoms.
B. The motivation for the behavior is to assume the sick role.
C. External incentives for the behavior (such as economic gain, avoiding legal responsibility, or improving physical well-being, as in malingering) are absent.

Code based on type:

With predominantly psychological signs and symptoms: if psychological signs and symptoms predominate in the clinical presentation

With predominantly physical signs and symptoms: if physical signs and symptoms predominate in the clinical presentation

With combined psychological and physical signs and symptoms: if both psychological and physical signs and symptoms are present but neither predominate in the clinical presentation

Table 19.2
DSM-IV Diagnostic Criteria for Factitious Disorder by Proxy

A. Intentional production or feigning of physical or psychological signs or symptoms in another person who is under the individual's care.
B. The motivation for the perpetrator's behavior is to assume the sick role by proxy.
C. External incentives for the behavior (such as economic gain) are absent.
D. The behavior is not better accounted for by another mental disorder.

ness serves an adaptive function and is a desperate attempt to ward off further disintegration.

Certain features are overrepresented in patients with factitious disorder. For example, *their intelligence quotients (IQs) are usually normal or above average; there is an absence of a formal thought disorder;* the patients have a poor sense of identity, including confusion over sexual identity, and poor sexual adjustment; *their tolerance to frustration is usually low;* and they have strong dependence needs and narcissism.

19.7 The answer is E (all) (*Synopsis VIII,* pages 657–658).
A factitious disorder is differentiated from *somatization disorder* (Briquet's syndrome) by the voluntary production of factitious symptoms, the extreme course of multiple hospitalizations, and the patient's seeming willingness to undergo an extraordinary number of mutilating procedures.

Hypochondriasis differs from factitious disorder in that the hypochondriacal patient does not voluntarily initiate the production of symptoms, and hypochondriasis typically has a later age of onset. As is the case with somatization disorder, patients with hypochondriasis do not usually submit to potentially mutilating procedures.

Because of their pathological lying, lack of close relationships with others, hostile and manipulative manner, and associated substance and criminal history, factitious disorder patients are often classified as having *antisocial personality disorder;* however, persons with antisocial personality disorder do not usually volunteer for invasive procedures or resort to a way of life marked by repeated or long-term hospitalizations.

Factitious disorders must be distinguished from *malingering.* Malingerers have an obvious, recognizable environmental goal in producing signs and symptoms. They may seek hospitalization to secure financial compensation, evade the police, avoid work, or merely obtain free bed and board for the night; but they always have some apparent end for their behavior.

19.8 The answer is E (*Synopsis VIII,* pages 656–657).
Factitious disorders *may occur by proxy* (Table 19.2); such disorders are classified as factitious disorder not otherwise specified (Table 19.3).

Factitious disorders *usually begin in early adult life,* although they may appear during childhood or adolescence. The onset of the disorder or of discrete episodes of treatment seeking may follow a real illness, loss, rejection, or abandonment. Usually, the patient or a close relative had a hospitalization in childhood or early adolescence for a genuine physical illness. Thereafter, a long pattern of successive hospitalizations unfolds, beginning insidiously.

Factitious disorders *are not best treated with psychoactive drugs.* No specific psychiatric therapy has been effective in treating factitious disorders. Although no adequate data are available about the ultimate outcome for the patients, a few of them probably die as a result of needless medication, instrumentation, or surgery. They *usually have a poor prognosis.*

Factitious disorders *are not synonymous with Ganser's syndrome,* a controversial condition most typically associated with prison inmates. It is characterized by the use of approximate answers. Ganser's syndrome may be a variant of malingering, in that the patients avoid punishment or responsibility for their actions. Ganser's syndrome is classified as a dissociative disorder not otherwise specified.

19.9 The answer is B (*Synopsis VIII,* page 656).
Patients with factitious disorder *may take anticoagulants to simulate bleeding disorders.* The patients are able to present physical or psychological symptoms so well that they *are usually able to gain admission to a hospital.* They continue to be

Table 19.3
DSM-IV Diagnostic Criteria for Factitious Disorder Not Otherwise Specified

This category includes disorders with factitious symptoms that do not meet the criteria for factitious disorder. An example is factitious disorder by proxy: the intentional production or feigning of physical or psychological signs or symptoms in another person who is under the individual's care for the purpose of indirectly assuming the sick role.

demanding and difficult and so *are not easy to manage in the hospital.* They may *display symptoms of pseudologia phantastica,* in which limited factual material is mixed with extensive and colorful fantasies. Patients with factitious disorders *do not usually receive the codiagnosis of schizotypal personality disorder.* However, many such patients have the poor identity formation and the disturbed self-image that are characteristic of someone with borderline personality disorder.

19.10 The answer is C (*Synopsis VIII,* page 656).
The best diagnosis is *factitious disorder with predominantly physical signs and symptoms.* The unusual circumstances, such as the woman's possession of anticoagulants (taken to simulate bleeding disorders), her history of repeated hospitalizations, and her leaving the hospital when confronted, strongly suggest that her symptoms were under voluntary control and were not genuine symptoms of a physical disorder. The differential diagnoses to consider are malingering, somatoform disorder, and factitious disorders.

In *somatoform disorders* the production of symptoms is unconscious and involuntary; in the case presented the symptom production appeared to be under voluntary control. In *malingering* the patients have obvious environmental goals in producing their symptoms; from what is known in this case, it appears that the patient had no goal other than that of assuming the role of a patient. Since the feigned symptoms were physical (bloody urine), the diagnosis of *factitious disorder with predominantly psychological signs and symptoms* is ruled out. Because of pathological lying, a hostile and manipulative manner, and lack of close relationships with others, many factitious disorder patients also receive the diagnosis of *antisocial personality disorder.* However, persons with antisocial personality disorder rarely volunteer for invasive procedures or resort to hospitalization as a way of life, as the woman described did. Not enough information is available to determine whether the woman had a personality disorder.

19.11 The answer is B (*Synopsis VIII,* page 654).
Employment as a *health care worker* is considered a leading predisposing factor in the development of factitious disorder with predominantly physical signs and symptoms; nurses make up one of the largest risk groups. In the case presented, the patient was a laboratory technician.

Employment as a *teacher, police officer, banker, or waitress* is not a predisposing factor in the development of factitious disorders.

19.12 The answer is D (*Synopsis VIII,* pages 657–658).
Briquet's syndrome (somatization disorder) *is not synonymous with factitious disorder with predominantly physical signs and symptoms.* A factitious disorder is differentiated from Briquet's syndrome by the voluntary production of factitious symptoms, the extreme course of multiple hospitalizations, and the patient's seeming willingness to undergo an extraordinary number of mutilating procedures. Factitious disorder with predominantly physical signs and symptoms has been designated by a variety of labels, the best known of which is *Munchausen syndrome,* named for Baron von Münchhausen. A German who lived in the 18th century, he wrote many fantastic travel and adventure stories and wandered from tavern to tavern, telling tall tales. Patients who suffer from Munchausen syndrome wander from hospital to hospital, where they manage to be admitted because of the dramatic stories they tell about being dangerously ill. Baron von Münchhausen never underwent any operations and was not known to be concerned about illness. Other names for the disorder are *hospital addiction, polysurgical addiction,* and *professional patient syndrome;* sometimes the patients are called hospital hoboes.

19.13 The answer is B (*Synopsis VIII,* page 656).
The essential feature of factitious disorder with predominantly physical signs and symptoms is the patient's plausible presentation of physical symptoms that are apparently *under voluntary control,* but *the patient often denies the voluntary production of the illness.* This disorder, *also known as Munchausen syndrome,* is *frequently seen in patients with a family history of serious illness or disability* and is *frequently seen in persons employed in health care jobs.* Factitious disorder with predominantly physical signs and symptoms is *not often used as a method to obtain disability payments.* In fact, if the patient's goal was to get disability payments, the diagnosis of *malingering* would be made.

19.14 The answer is E (all) (*Synopsis VIII,* pages 654–655).
A frequent occurrence in the histories of factitious disorder patients is a personal history of serious illness or disability *or a history of being exposed to genuine illness in a family member* or significant extrafamilial figure. Prior or current *employment in a health-related field* as a nurse, laboratory technician, ambulance driver, or physician is so common that it suggests inclusion as a clinical feature and a causal factor. Consistent with the concept of poor identity formation is the observation that the patients vacillate between two separate roles—a health professional and a patient—with momentary confusion as to which role is being played at the time.

Psychological models of factitious disorders generally emphasize the causal significance of *a history of parental rejection.* The usual history reveals that one or both parents are experienced as rejecting figures who are unable to form close relationships.

The patients have *a tendency to view the physician as a loving parent,* a potential source of the sought-for love, and person who will fulfill their unmet dependence needs.

19.15 The answer is A (*Synopsis VIII,* page 658).
Malingering is the most likely diagnosis based on the clinical presentation. The man's mental status examination is apparently normal; there are no disorganized thoughts, or loosening of associations. The patient claims a variety of unrelated bizarre beliefs, presenting responses in a manner that is inconsistent with the disorganization of psychological functioning that would be expected if the symptoms were genuine. In this case the "psychotic" symptoms are under voluntary control, and since there is external incentive (avoiding prosecution) and no evidence of an intrapsychic need to maintain a sick role, the diagnosis of *factitious disorder with predominantly psychotic features* is ruled out. The patient expresses no paranoid feelings, as would be seen in *schizophrenia, paranoid types.* His delusions lack conviction and are therefore not indicative of the unshakable beliefs in a *delusional disorder. Capgras's syndrome,* the delusion that familiar people have been replaced by identical impostors, is not seen here.

20

Dissociative Disorders

In the fourth edition of *Diagnostic and Statistical Manual of Mental Disorders* (DSM-IV), dissociative disorders are described as a disruption of the usually integrated consciousness, memory, identity, or perception of the environment. This category includes the following: dissociative amnesia, dissociative fugue, dissociative identity disorder, depersonalization disorder, and dissociative disorder not otherwise specified.

Normal people may have dissociative experiences, one of which is under hypnosis. People who are mentally healthy, however, feel that they have integrated thoughts, emotions, and actions, as if they are a single person with a single self. In dissociative disorders, this sense of being an integrated personality is lacking, usually as a defense against trauma. In a dissociative defensive reaction, people remove themselves from traumatic experiences and delay confronting the effects of the trauma. When people experience pathological dissociative states, they have often been physically or sexually abused as children or have undergone other traumatic crises such as war or a natural disaster. Before diagnosing a dissociative disorder, however, clinicians must ascertain that no underlying organic condition has caused the state.

Students should study Chapter 20 in *Kaplan and Sadock's Synopsis of Psychiatry VIII* and test their knowledge using the questions and answers that follow.

HELPFUL HINTS

The terms below relate to dissociative disorders and should be defined.

- anterograde amnesia
- approximate answers
- automatic writing
- brainwashing
- coercive persuasion
- continuous amnesia
- crystal gazing
- denial
- depersonalization
- derealization disorder
- dissociation
- dissociative amnesia
- dissociative fugue
- dissociative identity disorder
- dissociative trance
- dominant personality
- double orientation
- doubling
- epidemiology of dissociative disorders
- Ganser's syndrome
- hemidepersonalization
- highway hypnosis
- Korsakoff's syndrome
- localized amnesia
- malingering
- paramnesia
- possession state
- reduplicative paramnesia
- retrograde amnesia
- secondary gain
- selective amnesia
- sleepwalking disorder
- temporal lobe functions
- transient global amnesia
- wandering

▲ QUESTIONS

DIRECTIONS: Each of these questions or incomplete statements is followed by five suggested responses or completions. Select the *one* that is *best* in each case.

20.1 Which response does *not* apply to dissociative identity disorder?

A. Researchers cannot agree about the incidence of the disorder.
B. The most common secondary personality is childlike or a child.
C. Children with the disorder often express other personalities as invisible playmates.
D. Until the early 19th century, patients with this disorder were thought to be possessed.
E. In this most severe form of dissociative disorder, many people show nothing unusual on a mental status examination.

20.2 A patient who seems out of touch with the environment and who has amnesia for immediate past experience is likely to have

A. dementia
B. dissociative fugue
C. localized amnesia
D. generalized amnesia
E. sleepwalking disorder

20.3 Causes for the symptom of depersonalization do *not* include

A. epilepsy
B. brain tumor
C. derealization
D. hyperventilation
E. anxiety disorders

20.4 Dissociative trance disorder can include all of the following *except*

A. automatic writing
B. airplane pilot hypnosis
C. possession by a spirit or deity
D. dementia of the Alzheimer's type
E. amnesia after trauma in children

20.5 DSM-IV includes dissociative symptoms in the criteria for all but which of the following mental disorders?

A. Conversion disorder
B. Acute stress disorder
C. Somatization disorder
D. Posttraumatic stress disorder
E. Obsessive-compulsive disorder

20.6 Transient global amnesia is differentiated from dissociative amnesia by

A. the presence of anterograde amnesia in dissociative amnesia
B. the greater upset in patients with transient global amnesia
C. the loss of personal identity in patients with transient global amnesia
D. the older age of the dissociative amnesia patient
E. the absence of a psychological stressor in dissociative amnesia

20.7 The cause of dissociative identity disorder has been attributed to all of the following *except*

A. generalized environmental factors
B. specific traumatic life event
C. the absence of existing support
D. an inborn biological tendency
E. encephalitis

20.8 Each of the following statements about dissociative identity disorder is true *except*

A. The transition from one personality to another is often sudden and dramatic.
B. The patient generally has amnesia for the existence of the other personalities.
C. Each personality has a characteristic behavioral pattern.
D. The host personality rarely seeks treatment.
E. The personalities may be of both sexes.

20.9 Depersonalization disorder is characterized by

A. impaired reality testing
B. ego-dystonic symptoms
C. occurrence in the late decades of life
D. gradual onset
E. a brief course and a good prognosis

20.10 Clinical features of dissociative amnesia include

A. some precipitating emotional trauma
B. abrupt onset
C. awareness of the memory loss
D. retaining the capacity to learn new information
E. all of the above

20.11 All of the following are true statements about dissociative fugue *except*

A. It is a rare type of dissociative disorder.
B. It is not characterized by behavior that appears extraordinary to others.
C. It is characterized by a lack of awareness of the loss of memory.
D. It is usually a long-lasting state.
E. Recovery is spontaneous and rapid.

20.12 Dissociative amnesia is

A. most common during periods of war and during natural disasters
B. the least common type of dissociative disorder
C. most common in elderly adults
D. more common in men than in women
E. all of the above

20.13 Patients predisposed to dissociative fugue include those with all of the following *except*

A. mood disorders
B. schizophrenia
C. histrionic personality disorders
D. heavy alcohol abuse
E. borderline personality disorders

20.14 The differential diagnosis of dissociative amnesia includes

A. transient global amnesia
B. alcohol persisting amnestic disorder
C. postconcussion amnesia
D. epilepsy
E. all of the above

20.15 Signs of dissociative identity disorder include

A. reports by the patient of being recognized by people whom the patient does not know
B. the use of the word "we" by the patient to refer to himself or herself
C. reports by the patient of time distortions and lapses
D. changes in behavior reported by a reliable observer
E. all of the above

20.16 Dissociative identity disorder is

A. most common in early childhood
B. not nearly as rare as it once was thought to be
C. much more frequent in men than in women
D. not common in first-degree relatives of persons with the disorder

20.17 Dissociative disorders include all of the following *except*

A. amnestic disorders
B. dissociative identity disorder
C. depersonalization disorder
D. Ganser's syndrome
E. dissociative trance disorder

20.18 Which of these statements regarding the prognosis of dissociative identity disorder is *incorrect*?

A. Recovery is possible and generally complete.
B. The earlier the onset of dissociative identity disorder, the worse the prognosis is.
C. The level of impairment is determined by the number and type of various personalities.
D. Individual personalities may have their own separate mental disorders.
E. One or more of the personalities may function relatively well.

DIRECTIONS: These lettered headings are followed by a list of numbered phrases. For each numbered phrase, select

A. if the item is associated with *A only*
B. if the item is associated with *B only*
C. if the item is associated with *both A and B*
D. if the item is associated with *neither A nor B*

Questions 20.19–20.22

A. Dissociation
B. Splitting
C. Both
D. Neither

20.19 Separation of mental contents
20.20 Defense mechanism
20.21 Impaired impulse control
20.22 Impaired memory

DIRECTIONS: The lettered headings below are followed by a list of numbered statements. For each numbered statement, select the *one* lettered heading that is most closely associated with it. Each lettered heading may be selected once, more than once, or not at all.

Questions 20.23–20.26

A. Dissociative amnesia
B. Dissociative fugue
C. Dissociative identity disorder
D. Depersonalization disorder

20.23 A 25-year-old man comes to the emergency room and cannot remember his name.
20.24 A 35-year-old man states that his body feels unreal, not attached to him.
20.25 A 16-year-old girl is found in another city far from her home and does not recall how she got there.
20.26 A 30-year-old woman suddenly has a new child-like voice in the interview.

ANSWERS

Dissociative Disorders

20.1 The answer is C (*Synopsis VIII,* pages 660, 666, 669). *Children with the disorder* (Table 20.1) do not *express other personalities as invisible playmates.* In children, the symptoms usually appear trancelike, with depressive disorder symptoms, periods of amnesia, hallucinatory voices, and suicidal or self-injurious behavior. Although the disorder is more common in women than men, affected children are more likely to be boys than girls. The earlier the onset of dissociative identity disorder, the worse the prognosis.

The most common secondary personality is childlike or a child. The personalities can be of both sexes, of various races and ages, and of differing family backgrounds. The personalities are often different, even opposites: One may be extroverted, the other withdrawn.

Researchers cannot agree about the incidence of the disorder. Some researchers think that the condition is extremely rare, and others believe that it is greatly underrecognized. Studies have reported that 0.5 to 2 percent of psychiatric hospital admissions meet the diagnosis for dissociative identity disorder and that about 5 percent of all psychiatric patients have this disorder. Women outnumber men by 90 to 100 percent, but many workers believe that men enter the criminal justice system rather than the mental health system and so are underreported.

Until the early 19th century, patients with this disorder were thought to be possessed. In the early 1800s, Benjamin Rush described the disorder on the basis of clinical reports of others. Later, Jean-Martin Charcot and Pierre Janet described the disorder, and Sigmund Freud and Eugen Bleuler recognized the symptoms.

In this most severe form of dissociative disorder, people often show nothing usual on a mental status examination. They may, however, give evidence of a possible amnesia for varying times. The multiple personalities may be discovered only after many interviews or contacts with a patient. Approximately 60 percent of patients exhibit alternate personalities only occasionally; another 20 percent have rare episodes and are able to cover the switches.

20.2 The answer is E (*Synopsis VIII,* pages 664–665). Patients with *sleepwalking disorder,* classified in DSM-IV as a type of sleep disorder, often behave like someone in a dissociative state. They appear out of touch with their environment and preoccupied with a private world; they may act emotionally upset and speak excitedly and incomprehensibly. When the episode has ended, patients have amnesia for it. By contrast, patients with *localized* or *generalized amnesia* do not seem out of touch with the environment and do not appear to be dreaming; to observers, they seem to act normally and are alert both before and after amnesia appears.

Dissociative fugue (Table 20.2) is similar to dissociative amnesia, but in dissociative fugue patients' behavior seems more integrated with their amnesia than it is for patients with dissociative amnesia. Patients with dissociative fugue travel away from home or work and forget their name, occupation, and other aspects of their identity. Patients often take on a new identity and profession.

When patients with *dementia* have symptoms of amnesia, the dementia is often advanced, and the amnesia does not give way to a clear memory. Social awareness and ability to perform complex activities are also diminished, and personality is affected.

20.3 The answer is C (*Synopsis VIII,* pages 670–672). *Derealization* is perceiving objects in the external world as strange and unreal. Depersonalization (Table 20.3), by contrast, refers to a person's feeling of strangeness and unreality for his or her own self or body. Thus these two terms refer to different phenomena, and derealization is not a symptom of depersonalization.

All the other responses, *epilepsy, brain tumor, hyperventilation,* and *anxiety disorders,* and many other factors as well

Table 20.1
DSM-IV Diagnostic Criteria for Dissociative Identity Disorder

A. The presence of two or more distinct identities or personality states (each with its own relatively enduring pattern of perceiving, relating to, and thinking about the environment and self).

B. At least two of these identities or personality states recurrently take control of the person's behavior.

C. Inability to recall important personal information that is too extensive to be explained by ordinary forgetfulness.

D. The disturbance is not due to the direct effects of a substance (eg, blackouts or chaotic behavior during alcohol intoxication) or a general medical condition (eg, complex partial seizures). **Note:** In children, the symptoms are not attributable to imaginary playmates or other fantasy play.

Reprinted with permission from American Psychiatric Association: *Diagnostic and Statistical Manual of Mental Disorders,* ed 4. Copyright, American Psychiatric Association, Washington, 1994.

Table 20.2
DSM-IV Diagnostic Criteria for Dissociative Fugue

A. The predominant disturbance is sudden, unexpected travel away from home or one's customary place of work, with inability to recall one's past.

B. Confusion about personal identity or assumption of new identity (partial or complete).

C. The disturbance does not occur exclusively during the course of dissociative identity disorder and is not due to the direct physiological effects of a substance (eg, a drug of abuse, a medication) or a general medical condition (eg, temporal lobe epilepsy).

D. The symptoms cause clinically significant distress or impairment in social, occupational, or other important areas of functioning.

Reprinted with permission from American Psychiatric Association: *Diagnostic and Statistical Manual of Mental Disorders,* ed 4. Copyright, American Psychiatric Association, Washington, 1994.

Table 20.3
DSM-IV Diagnostic Criteria for Depersonalization Disorder

A. Persistent or recurrent experiences of feeling detached from, and as if one is an outside observer of, one's mental processes or body (eg, feeling like one is in a dream).
B. During the depersonalization experience, reality testing remains intact.
C. The depersonalization causes clinically significant distress or impairment in social, occupational, or other important areas of functioning.
D. The depersonalization experience does not occur exclusively during the course of another mental disorder, such as schizophrenia, panic disorder, acute stress disorder, or another dissociative disorder, and is not due to the direct physiological effects of a substance (eg, a drug of abuse, a medication) or a general medical condition (eg, temporal lobe epilepsy).

can cause symptoms of depersonalization. Thus clinicians should diagnose depersonalization disorder only when depersonalization is the predominating symptom. Many patients with depressive disorders and schizophrenia have symptoms of depersonalization, and clinicians should consider these common mental disorders before diagnosing depersonalization disorder. A history, a mental status examination, inquiry into substance use, and neurological evaluation should help to eliminate causes other than depersonalization disorder.

20.4 The answer is D (*Synopsis VIII,* pages 661, 673–674).
Dementia of the Alzheimer's type is not included in dissociative trance disorder, in which patients have single or episodic alternations in consciousness that are limited to particular locations or cultures.

Trance states and possession are altered states of consciousness that are not well understood as forms of dissociation. Both DSM-IV and ICD-10 (the 10th revision of *International Statistical Classification of Diseases and Related Health Problems*) include criteria for dissociative trance disorder. *Automatic writing* and crystal gazing are examples of trance states. In automatic writing, the dissociation affects only the arm and hand that write the message, of which the writer is usually unaware; this phenomenon is sometimes said to reflect the writer's unconscious thoughts and feelings rather than a message from a spirit or deity. Crystal gazing can produce a trance in which visual hallucinations occur.

Airplane pilot hypnosis, like highway hypnosis, is a phenomenon related to trance states and is produced by moving at high speeds through a monotonous environment with little distraction or visual stimulation. The operator may fixate on a single object such as a dial on the instrument panel and may have visual hallucinations; people in this condition are in grave danger of accidents.

Possession by a spirit or deity, for instance during a seance, can occur during a trance state. A person's customary sense of identity is taken over by a spirit, deity, or other power, that speaks through the possessed figure. Spirit possession is an accepted belief in some cultures and it can occur during a religious or spiritual ceremony, but dissociative trance disorder is not diagnosed unless the condition is not a broadly accepted cultural practice.

Amnesia after trauma in children can be associated with trancelike states, especially when a child has been physically or sexually abused.

20.5 The answer is E (*Synopsis VIII,* pages 660–675).
DSM-IV does not include dissociative symptoms in the criteria for *obsessive-compulsive disorder. Conversion disorder, acute stress disorder, somatization disorder,* and *posttraumatic stress disorder* all include dissociative symptoms in their criteria as given in DSM-IV. A diagnosis of dissociative disorder is not given if the symptoms occur exclusively during the course of one of these disorders. DSM-IV notes that neurological or other medical conditions should be considered before diagnosing conversion disorder.

20.6 The answer is B (*Synopsis VIII,* pages 664–665).
Transient global amnesia can be differentiated from dissociative amnesia in several ways, for example, the *greater upset* in patients with transient global amnesia than in those with dissociative amnesia; the presence of anterograde amnesia in transient global amnesia but not in dissociative amnesia; the *loss of personal identity* in patients with dissociative amnesia but not in transient global amnesia; *the older age* of the transient global amnesia patient than the dissociative disorder patient; and the presence of a *psychological stressor* in dissociative amnesia but not in transient global amnesia.

20.7 The answer is E (*Synopsis VIII,* pages 666–667).
Dissociative identity disorder *has not been attributed to encephalitis.* Encephalitis is an inflammation of the brain. The cause of dissociative identity disorder is unknown, although the histories of the patients invariably involve a traumatic event, most often in childhood. In general, four types of causative factors have been identified: (1) *a specific traumatic life event,* (2) *an inborn biological or psychological tendency* for the disorder to develop, (3) *generalized environmental factors,* and (4) *the absence of external support.* The traumatic event is usually childhood physical or sexual abuse, commonly incestuous. Other traumatic events may include the death of a close relative or friend during childhood and witnessing a trauma or a death.

20.8 The answer is D (*Synopsis VIII,* pages 667–668).
In dissociative identity disorder, *the host personality is usually the one who seeks treatment. The transition from one personality to another is often sudden and dramatic. The patient generally has amnesia for the existence of the other personalities* and for the events that took place when another personality was dominant. *Each personality has a characteristic behavioral pattern. The personalities may be of both sexes,* of various races and ages, and from families different from the patient's family of origin. The most common subordinate personality is childlike. Often, the personalities are disparate and may even be opposites.

20.9 The answer is B (*Synopsis VIII,* page 670).
Depersonalization disorder is characterized by *ego-dystonic symptoms*—that is, symptoms at variance with the ego. However, the person maintains *intact reality testing;* he or she is aware of the disturbances. Depersonalization *rarely occurs in*

the late decades of life; it most often starts between the ages of 15 and 30 years. In the large majority of patients, the symptoms first appear suddenly; only a few patients report a *gradual onset.* A few follow-up studies indicate that in more than half the cases, depersonalization disorder tends to have *a long-term course and a poor prognosis.* Table 20.3 lists the diagnostic criteria for depersonalization disorder.

20.10 The answer is E (all) (*Synopsis VIII,* page 663).
Although some episodes of amnesia occur spontaneously, the history usually reveals *some precipitating emotional trauma* charged with painful emotions and psychological conflict. The disorder usually has *an abrupt onset,* and the patient usually has an *awareness of the memory loss. Retaining the capacity to learn new information* is another clinical feature. Table 20.4 lists the diagnostic criteria for dissociative amnesia.

20.11 The answer is D (*Synopsis VIII,* page 666).
A dissociative fugue is *usually brief,* hours to days. Generally, *recovery is spontaneous and rapid,* and recurrences are rare. Dissociative fugue is considered *rare,* and like dissociative amnesia, it occurs most often during wartime, after natural disasters, and as a result of personal crises with intense conflict. Dissociative fugue is *characterized by a lack of awareness of the loss of memory but not by behavior that appears extraordinary to others.* Table 20.2 lists the diagnostic criteria for dissociative fugue.

20.12 The answer is A (*Synopsis VIII,* page 662).
Dissociative amnesia is *most common during periods of war and during natural disasters.* It is *the most common type of dissociative disorder, occurs most often in adolescents and young adults, and is more common in women than in men.*

20.13 The answer is B (*Synopsis VIII,* page 665).
Schizophrenia does not predispose patients to dissociative fugue state. *Heavy alcohol abuse* may predispose a person to dissociative fugue, but the cause is thought to be basically psychological. The essential motivating factor appears to be a desire to withdraw from emotionally painful experiences. Patients with *mood disorders* and certain personality disorders (for example, *borderline, schizoid,* and histrionic *personality disorders*) are predisposed to dissociative fugue.

20.14 The answer is E (all) (*Synopsis VIII,* pages 662–664).
The differential diagnosis of dissociative amnesia includes dissociative mental disorders in which the patient experiences a memory disturbance, especially *transient global amnesia.* In *alcohol persisting amnestic disorder,* short-term memory loss occurs. In *postconcussion amnesia,* the memory disturbance follows head trauma, is often retrograde, and usually does not extend beyond one week. *Epilepsy* leads to sudden memory impairment associated with motor and electroencephalogram abnormalities. A history of an aura, head trauma, or incontinence helps in the diagnosis.

20.15 The answer is E (all) (*Synopsis VI,* pages 667–668).
Dissociative identity disorder (formerly called multiple personality disorder) may be misdiagnosed as a schizophrenic disorder or a personality disorder. The clinician should listen for specific features suggestive of the disorder. Signs of the disorder include reports by the patient of *being recognized* by people whom the patient does not know, *the use of the word "we"* by the patient to refer to himself or herself, reports by the patient of *time distortions and lapses,* and *changes in behavior* reported by a reliable observer. Table 20.5 lists the signs of multiplicity.

20.16 The answer is B (*Synopsis VIII,* page 667).
Recent reports on dissociative identity disorder suggest that it is *not nearly as rare as it was once thought to be.* It is *most common in late adolescence and young adult life, not childhood,* and is *much more frequent in women than in men.* Several studies have indicated that it is *more common in first-*

Table 20.4
DSM-IV Diagnostic Criteria for Dissociative Amnesia

A. The predominant disturbance is one or more episodes of inability to recall important personal information, usually of a traumatic or stressful nature, that is too extensive to be explained by ordinary forgetfulness.

B. The disturbance does not occur exclusively during the course of dissociative identity disorder, dissociative fugue, posttraumatic stress disorder, acute stress disorder, or somatization disorder and is not due to the direct physiological effects of a substance (eg, a drug of abuse, a medication) or a neurological or other general medical condition (eg, amnestic disorder due to head trauma).

C. The symptoms cause clinically significant distress or impairment in social, occupational, or other important areas of functioning.

Reprinted with permission from American Psychiatric Association: *Diagnostic and Statistical Manual of Mental Disorders,* ed 4. Copyright, American Psychiatric Association, Washington, 1994.

Table 20.5
Signs of Multiplicity

1. Reports of time distortions, lapses, and discontinuities
2. Being told of behavioral episodes by others that are not remembered by the patient
3. Being recognized by others or called by another name by people whom the patient does not recognize
4. Notable changes in the patient's behavior reported by a reliable observer; the patient may call himself or herself by a different name or refer to himself or herself in the third person
5. Other personalities are elicited under hypnosis or during amobarbital interviews
6. Use of the word "we" in the course of an interview
7. Discovery of writings, drawings, or other productions or objects (identification cards, clothing, etc.) among the patient's personal belongings that are not recognized or cannot be accounted for
8. Headaches
9. Hearing voices originating from within and not identified as separate
10. History of severe emotional or physical trauma as a child (usually before the age of 5 years)

Reprinted with permission from Cummings JL: Dissociative states, depersonalization, multiple personality, episodic memory lapses. In *Clinical Neuropsychiatry,* JL Cummings, editor, p 122. Grune & Stratton, Orlando, 1985.

degree relatives of persons with the disorder than in the general population. It is classified as *a dissociative disorder.*

20.17 The answer is A (*Synopsis VIII,* page 660).
The *amnestic disorders* are classified with the cognitive disorders (for example, dementias), not the dissociative disorders. The dissociative disorders are dissociative amnesia, dissociative fugue, *dissociative identity disorder, depersonalization disorder,* and dissociative disorder not otherwise specified. *Ganser's syndrome* is listed in the fourth edition of *Diagnostic and Statistical Manual of Mental Disorders* (DSM-IV) as an example of dissociative disorder not otherwise specified (Table 20.6). In Ganser's syndrome, patients give approximate answers to questions (for example, 2 + 2 = 5). Another example of dissociative disorder not otherwise specified is *dissociative trance disorder* (Table 20.7).

20.18 The answer is A (*Synopsis VIII,* page 669)
In dissociative identity disorder, *while recovery is possible, it is generally incomplete.* This is considered the most severe and chronic of the dissociative disorders. The *earlier the onset of dissociative identity disorder, the worse the prognosis is.* The *level of impairment* ranges from moderate to severe and *is determined by variables such as the number, the type, and the chronicity of the various personalities.* The *individual personalities may have their own separate mental disorders;* mood disorders, personality disorders, and other distinctive disorders are most common. *One or more of the personalities may function relatively well,* while others function marginally.

Answers 20.19–20.22

20.19 The answer is C (*Synopsis VIII,* page 660).

20.20 The answer is C (*Synopsis VIII,* page 660).

20.21 The answer is B (*Synopsis VIII,* page 660).

20.22 The answer is A (*Synopsis VIII,* page 660).
Dissociation and *splitting* have both similarities and differences. Both involve an active compartmentalization and *separation of mental contents.* Both are used as *defense mechanisms* to ward off unpleasant affects associated with the integration of contradictory parts of the self. They differ to some extent in the nature of the ego functions that are affected. With splitting, anxiety tolerance and *impulse control are impaired.* In dissociation, *memory* and consciousness are *affected.*

Table 20.6
DSM-IV Diagnostic Criteria for Dissociative Disorder Not Otherwise Specified

This category is included for disorders in which the predominant feature is a dissociative symptom (ie, a disruption in the usually integrated functions of consciousness, memory, identity, or perception of the environment) that does not meet the criteria for any specific dissociative disorder. Examples include

1. Clinical presentation similar to dissociative identity disorder that fail to meet full criteria for this disorder. Examples include presentation in which a) there are not two or more distinct personality states, or b) amnesia for important personal information does not occur.
2. Derealization unaccompanied by depersonalization in adults.
3. States of dissociation that occur in individuals who have been subjected to periods of prolonged and intense coercive persuasion (eg, brainwashing, thought reform, or indoctrination while a captive).
4. Dissociative trance disorder: single or episodic disturbances in the state of consciousness, identity, or memory that are indigenous to particular locations and cultures. Dissociative trance involves narrowing of awareness of immediate surroundings or stereotyped behaviors or movements that are experienced as being beyond one's control. Possession trance involves replacement of the customary sense of personal identity by a new identity, attributed to the influence of a spirit, power, deity, or other person, and associated with stereotyped "involuntary" movements or amnesia. Examples include *amok* (Indonesia), *bebainan* (Indonesia), *latah* (Malaysia), *pibloktoq* (Arctic), *ataque de nervios* (Latin America), and possession (India). The dissociative or trance disorder is not a normal part of a broadly accepted collective cultural or religious practice.
5. Loss of consciousness, stupor, or coma not attributable to a general medical condition.
6. Ganser's syndrome: the giving of approximate answers to questions (eg, "2 plus 2 equals 5") when not associated with dissociative amnesia or dissociative fugue.

Reprinted with permission from American Psychiatric Association: *Diagnostic and Statistical Manual of Mental Disorders,* ed 4. Copyright, American Psychiatric Association, Washington, 1994.

Table 20.7
DSM-IV Research Criteria for Dissociative Trance Disorder

A. Either (1) or (2):
   (1) trance, ie, temporary marked alteration in the state of consciousness or loss of customary sense of personal identity without replacement by an alternative identity, associated with at least one of the following:
      (a) narrowing of awareness of immediate surroundings, or unusually narrow and selective focusing on environmental stimuli
      (b) stereotyped behaviors or movements that are experienced as being beyond one's control
   (2) possession trance, a single or episodic alteration in the state of consciousness characterized by the replacement of customary sense of personal identity by a new identity. This is attributed to the influence of a spirit, power, deity, or other person, as evidenced by one (or more) of the following:
      (a) stereotyped and culturally determined behaviors or movements that are experienced as being controlled by the possessing agent
      (b) full or partial amnesia for the event
B. The trance or possession trance state is not accepted as a normal part of a collective cultural or religious practice.
C. The trance or possession trance state causes clinically significant distress or impairment in social, occupational, or other important areas of functioning.
D. The trance or possession trance state does not occur exclusively during the course of a psychotic disorder (including mood disorder with psychotic features and brief psychotic disorder) or dissociative identity disorder and is not due to the direct physiological effects of a substance or general medical condition.

Reprinted with permission from American Psychiatric Association: *Diagnostic and Statistical Manual of Mental Disorders,* ed 4. Copyright, American Psychiatric Association, Washington, 1994.

Answers 20.23–20.26

20.23 The answer is A (*Synopsis VIII,* page 662).

20.24 The answer is D (*Synopsis VIII,* page 670).

20.25 The answer is B (*Synopsis VIII,* page 665).

20.26 The answer is C (*Synopsis VIII,* page 666).
Dissociative amnesia (Table 20.4), as in the case of the man who *cannot remember his name,* is characterized by inability to remember information, usually related to a stressful or traumatic event, that cannot be explained by ordinary forgetfulness, the ingestion of substances, or a general medical condition. *Dissociative fugue,* as in the case of the girl who *is found in another city far from her home,* is characterized by sudden and unexpected travel away from home or work, associated with an inability to recall one's past and confusion about one's personal identity or the adoption of a new identity. *Dissociative identity disorder,* as in the case of the woman who *suddenly has a new childlike voice in the interview,* is characterized by the presence of two or more distinct personalities within a single person; dissociative identity disorder is generally considered the most severe and chronic of the dissociative disorders. *Depersonalization disorder,* as in the case of the man who *states that his body feels unreal,* is characterized by recurrent or persistent feelings of detachment from one's body or mind.

21 Human Sexuality

Normal sexual behavior is largely in the eye of the beholder; abnormal sexual behavior is destructive and compulsive, cannot be directed toward a partner, and causes a person to be overwhelmed by guilt or anxiety.

Several terms that describe human sexuality are often wrongly defined and misused: sexual identity, gender identity, sexual orientation, and sexual behavior. These terms, which refer to factors that affect people's growth, development, and functioning, are called psychosexual factors. Sexual identity is a person's biological sexual characteristics, including genes, external and internal genitalia, hormonal makeup, and secondary sex characteristics. Gender identity is a person's sense of masculinity or femininity. Sexual orientation describes the object of a person's sexual impulses: heterosexual, bisexual, or homosexual. Sexual behavior is a physiological experience triggered by psychological and physical stimuli.

In the fourth edition of *Diagnostic and Statistical Manual of Mental Disorders* (DSM-IV), sexual and gender identity disorders consist of sexual dysfunctions, paraphilias, gender identity disorders, and sexual disorder not otherwise specified. Sexual dysfunctions refer to disturbed sexual desire and psychophysiological changes in the sexual response cycle. Paraphilias are characterized by recurrent sexual urges or fantasies involving unusual objects, activities, or situations. In gender identity disorders, people have strong cross-gender identification and discomfort with their own assigned sex. Sexual disorder not otherwise specified describes sexual dysfunction not classifiable in any other category.

Clinicians should not only understand the various disorders but should distinguish between experimentation and a genuine disorder. A sexual disorder is typically pervasive, recurrent, or compulsive and not an isolated event.

Students are referred to Chapter 21 in *Kaplan and Sadock's Synopsis VIII* to expand their knowledge about normal sexuality and sexual dysfunctions and paraphilias. The following questions and answers can then be addressed.

HELPFUL HINTS

The student should know the following terms and their definitions.

- anorgasmia
- autoerotic asphyxiation
- biogenic versus psychogenic
- bisexuality
- castration
- clitoral versus vaginal orgasm
- coming out
- coprophilia
- cystometric examination
- desensitization therapy
- Don Juanism
- dual-sex therapy
- dyspareunia
- erection and ejaculation
- excitement
- exhibitionism
- female orgasmic disorder
- female sexual arousal disorder
- fetishism
- frotteurism
- FSH
- gender role
- heterosexuality
- HIV, AIDS
- homosexuality
- hymenectomy
- hypoactive sexual desire disorder
- hypoxyphilia
- incest
- infertility
- intimacy
- Alfred Kinsey
- male erectile disorder
- male orgasmic disorder
- William Masters and Virginia Johnson
- masturbation
- moral masochism
- necrophilia
- nocturnal penile tumescence
- orgasm
- orgasm disorders
- orgasmic anhedonia
- paraphilias
- pedophilia
- penile arteriography
- Peyronie's disease
- phases of sexual response
- postcoital dysphoria
- postcoital headache
- premature ejaculation
- prosthetic devices
- psychosexual stages
- rape (male and female)
- refractory period
- resolution
- retarded ejaculation
- retrograde ejaculation
- satyriasis
- scatalogia
- sensate focus
- sexual arousal disorders
- sexual aversion disorder
- sexual desire disorders
- sexual dysfunction not otherwise specified
- sexual identity and gender identity
- sexual masochism and sexual sadism
- sexual orientation distress
- sexual pain disorders
- spectatoring
- spouse abuse

- squeeze technique
- statutory rape
- steal phenomenon
- sterilization
- stop-start technique
- sympathetic and parasympathetic nervous systems
- telephone scatologia
- transvestic fetishism
- tumescence and detumescence
- unconsummated marriage
- urophilia
- vagina dentata
- vaginismus
- vaginoplasty
- voyeurism
- zoophilia

▲ QUESTIONS

DIRECTIONS: Each of the questions or incomplete statements below is followed by five suggested responses or completions. Select the *one* that is *best* in each case.

21.1 According to DSM-IV, which of the following is *not* a possible type of diagnosis for sexual dysfunction?

A. Relational
B. Induced by a substance
C. Not otherwise specified
D. Due to combined factors
E. Due to a general medical disorder

21.2 Which of the following substances has *not* been associated with sexual dysfunction?

A. Cocaine
B. Levodopa
C. Trazodone
D. Amoxapine
E. Antihistamines

21.3 Which of the following is *not* a disorder of sexual preference?

A. Fetishism
B. Voyeurism
C. Frotteurism
D. Necrophilia
E. Transsexualism

21.4 Which of the following conditions is classified as a psychological or behavioral disorder associated with sexual development or orientation?

A. Transvestism
B. Exhibitionism
C. Gender identity disorder
D. Sexual relationship disorder
E. All of the above

21.5 Which of the following is *not* an intersexual disorder?

A. Hypoxyphilia
B. Turner's syndrome
C. Klinefelter's syndrome
D. 5α-Reductase deficiency
E. 17-Hydroxysteroid dehydrogenase deficiency

21.6 Homosexuality

A. is listed in the fourth edition of *Diagnostic and Statistical Manual of Mental Disorders* (DSM-IV) as a mental disorder
B. among men has a prevalence of 15 percent
C. was perceived by Sigmund Freud as a mental illness
D. is socially stigmatized less for women than for men
E. does not have a genetic or biological component

21.7 Male erectile disorder is

A. sometimes situational
B. the chief complaint in fewer than 25 percent of all men presenting with sexual disorders
C. universal in aging men
D. organic in cause
E. all of the above

21.8 Masturbation

A. is not common in infancy and childhood
B. leads to a decrease in sexual potency
C. is common among married couples
D. usually results in orgasmic anhedonia
E. is not associated with autoerotic asphyxiation

21.9 Paraphilias

A. are usually not distressing to the person with the disorder
B. are found equally among men and women
C. according to the classic psychoanalytic model, are due to a failure to complete the process of genital adjustment
D. with an early age of onset are associated with a good prognosis
E. such as pedophilia usually involve vaginal or anal penetration of the victim

21.10 Figure 21.1 shows a man with gynecomastia and small testes. He has positive Barr bodies and an XXY karyotype. The most likely diagnosis is

A. androgen insensitivity
B. Klinefelter's syndrome
C. Turner's syndrome
D. hermaphroditism
E. Cushing's syndrome

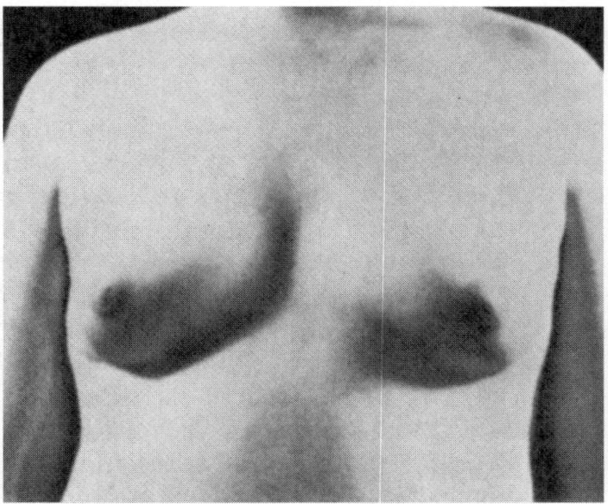
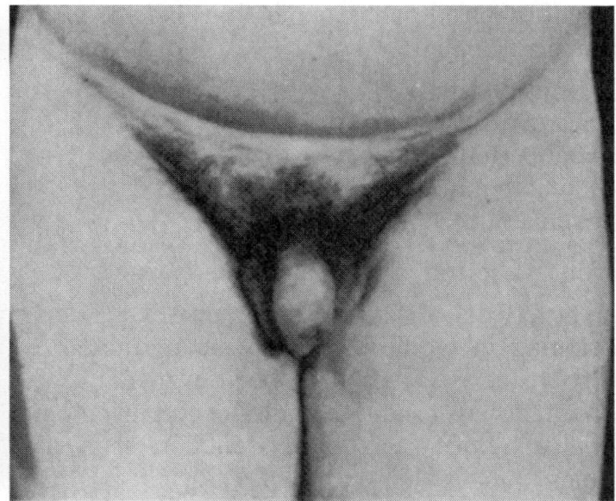

FIGURE 21.1
Courtesy of Robert B. Greenblatt, M.D., and Virginia P. McNamara, M.D.

21.11 Which of the following statements about fetishism is *false*?

A. A fetish is an inanimate object that is used as the preferred or necessary adjunct to sexual arousal.
B. A fetish is integrated into sexual activity with a human partner.
C. A fetish is a device that may function as a hedge against separation anxiety.
D. A fetish is a device with magical phallic qualities that is used to ward off castration anxiety.
E. Fetishism is a disorder found equally in males and females.

21.12 Which of the following has been associated with male erectile disorder due to a general medical condition?

A. Mumps
B. Atherosclerosis
C. Klinefelter's syndrome
D. Multiple sclerosis
E. All of the above

21.13 Orgasm is characterized by all of the following *except*

A. involuntary contractions of the anal sphincter
B. carpopedal spasm
C. absence of contractions of the uterus
D. blood pressure rise
E. slight clouding of consciousness

21.14 A married man with a chief complaint of premature ejaculation is best treated with

A. antianxiety agents
B. psychoanalysis
C. squeeze technique
D. cognitive therapy
E. none of the above

21.15 Autoerotic asphyxiation is most commonly associated with

A. adolescent girls
B. middle-aged men
C. a heightened intensity of orgasm
D. adolescent boys
E. no other mental disorder

21.16 Measures used to help differentiate organically caused impotence from functional impotence include

A. monitoring of nocturnal penile tumescence
B. glucose tolerance tests
C. follicle-stimulating hormone (FSH) determinations
D. testosterone level tests
E. all of the above

21.17 Which of the following statements about sexual masochism is *false*?

A. The most common finding is that the person with sexual masochism is unable to take the opposite role of the sexual sadist with arousal and pleasure.
B. The essential feature is sexual excitement produced by the person's own suffering.
C. Masochistic sexual fantasies are likely to have been present in childhood.
D. It is usually chronic.
E. Self-mutilation, if it occurs, is likely to be recurrent.

21.18 Premature ejaculation

A. is associated with stress
B. results from negative cultural conditioning
C. occurs most frequently among college-educated men
D. is caused by medical factors
E. all of the above

21.19 Which of the following medications is *least likely* to impair ejaculation?

A. Amitriptyline
B. Spironolactone
C. Haloperidol
D. Phentolamine
E. Fluoxetine

21.20 Which of the following statements is true?

A. The effects of various drugs on sexual functioning in women have not been studied as extensively as they have been in men.
B. Women are less vulnerable to pharmacologically induced sexual dysfunction than are men.
C. Phenelzine decreases libido in some women.
D. Sexual dysfunction associated with the use of a drug disappears when the drug is discontinued.
E. All of the above statements are true.

21.21 Male orgasmic disorder is

A. also called retarded ejaculation
B. less common than premature ejaculation
C. sometimes a result of prostate surgery
D. sometimes caused by antihypertensive drugs
E. characterized by all of the above

21.22 Which of the following surgical procedures may be used in treating sexual dysfunctions?

A. Insertion of a penile prosthesis
B. Penile revascularization
C. Hymenectomy
D. Vaginoplasty
E. All of the above

21.23 Which of the following statements regarding homosexuality are *false*?

A. Same-sex fantasies in children aged 3 to 5 years can be recovered from homosexuals.
B. It was viewed by Freud as an arrest of psychosexual development.
C. Chromosome studies have been able to differentiate homosexuals from heterosexuals.
D. Female couples appear to have more enduring monogamous relationships than male couples.
E. Prenatal hormones appear to play a role in the sexual organization of the central nervous system.

21.24 On biopsy of gonadal structures in the patient shown in Figure 21.2, an abdominal ovary and scrotal testis were found. The most likely diagnosis is

A. androgen insensitivity syndrome
B. pseudohermaphroditism
C. Klinefelter's syndrome
D. true hermaphroditism
E. adrenogenital syndrome

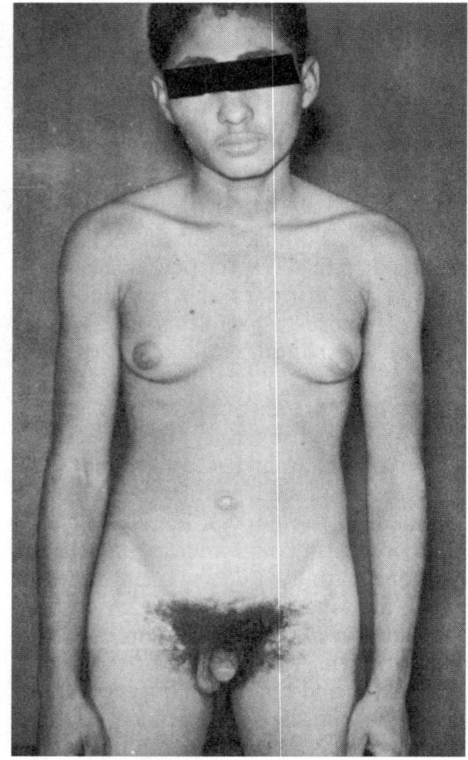

FIGURE 21.2
Courtesy of Robert B. Greenblatt, M.D., and Virginia P. McNamara, M.D.

21.25 The patient in Figure 21.3 has an XX genotype and a diagnosis of congenital adrenal hyperplasia. All of the following statements regarding her condition are true *except*

A. It is the most common female intersex disorder.
B. Patients have no uterus and a short, blind vagina.
C. The condition results from excess fetal androgens.
D. Clitoral enlargement and adolescent hirsutism are characteristic.
E. All of the above statements are true.

21.26a Figure 21.4 shows a phenotypic woman with an XY karyotype. The most likely diagnosis is

A. pseudohermaphroditism
B. testicular feminization syndrome
C. Turner's syndrome
D. adrenogenital syndrome
E. true hermaphroditism

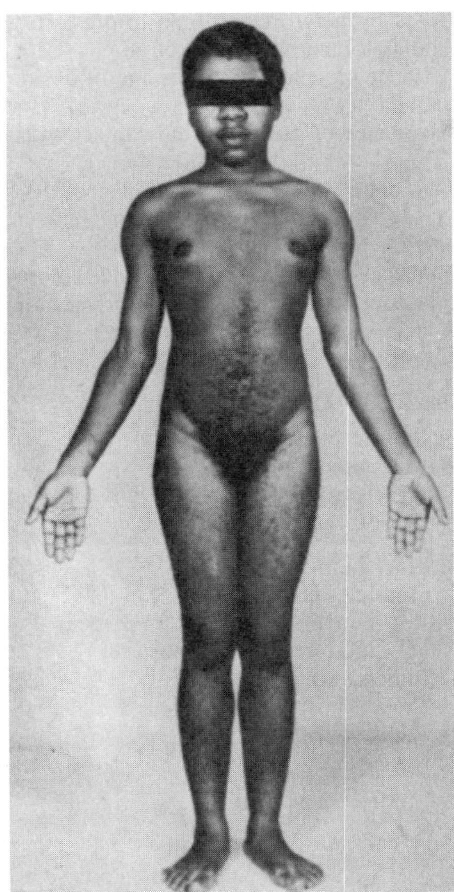

FIGURE 21.3
Courtesy of Robert B. Greenblatt, M.D., and Virginia P. McNamara, M.D.

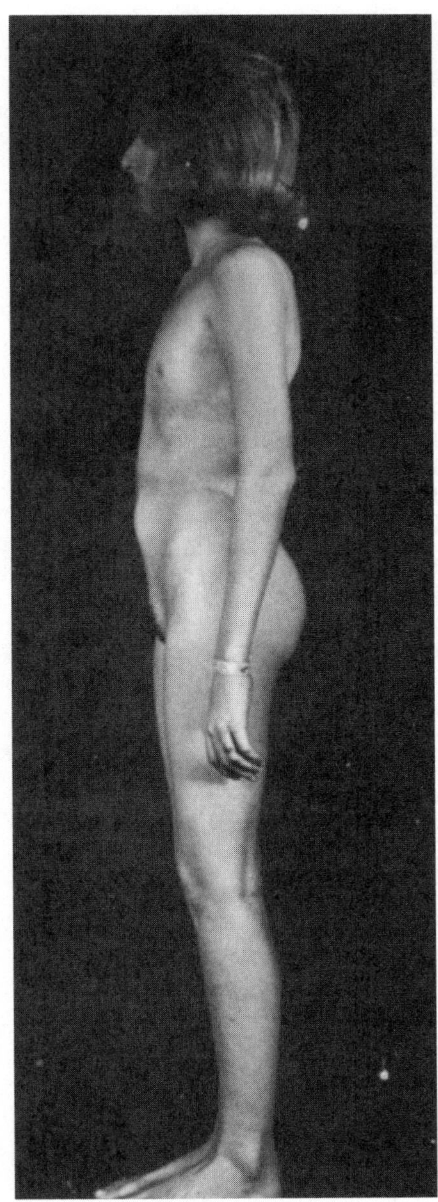

FIGURE 21.4
Courtesy of Robert B. Greenblatt, M.D., and Virginia P. McNamara, M.D.

21.26b This patient's condition results from

A. insufficient androgen production
B. testicular agenesis
C. inability of target tissues to respond to androgens
D. excess estrogen production
E. pituitary dysfunction

21.26c Which of the following statements regarding the patient's condition is *false*?

A. Secondary sex characteristics at puberty are female.
B. Internal sexual organs are minimal or absent at birth.
C. The condition is an X-linked recessive trait.
D. External genitalia appear ambiguous at birth.
E. Patients are born with cryptorchid testes.

DIRECTIONS: Each group of questions below consists of lettered headings followed by a list of numbered words or phrases. For each numbered word or phrase, select the *one* lettered heading that is most closely associated with it. Each lettered heading may be used once, more than once, or not at all.

Questions 21.27–21.37

A. Fetishism
B. Voyeurism
C. Frotteurism
D. Exhibitionism
E. Sexual masochism
F. Sexual sadism
G. Transvestic fetishism
H. Hypoactive sexual desire disorder
I. Sexual aversion disorder
J. Dyspareunia
K. Vaginismus

21.27 Observing people who are naked or engaging in sexual activity
21.28 Rubbing up against a fully clothed woman to achieve orgasm
21.29 Sexual focus on objects intimately associated with the human body
21.30 Urges by heterosexual men to dress in women's clothes for purposes of arousal
21.31 Absence of sexual fantasies and of desire for sexual activity
21.32 Avoidance of genital sexual contact with a sexual partner
21.33 Involuntary muscle contraction
21.34 Persistent genital pain occurring before, during, or after intercourse
21.35 Fantasies involving harm to others
21.36 Fantasies involving the act of being humiliated
21.37 Recurrent urge to expose one's genitals to a stranger

Questions 21.38–21.42

A. Desire phase
B. Excitement phase
C. Orgasm phase
D. Resolution phase

21.38 Vaginal lubrication
21.39 Orgasmic platform
21.40 Testes increase in size by 50 percent
21.41 Slight clouding of consciousness
21.42 Detumescence

ANSWERS

Human Sexuality

21.1 The answer is A (*Synopsis VIII,* pages 684–700).
This question requires the student to understand classification. If another clinical condition such as a *relational* problem is associated with sexual dysfunctioning, the two disorders should be separately diagnosed, according to DSM-IV.

All of the other choices are categories of diagnosis for sexual dysfunction. Sexual dysfunction that is *substance induced* is diagnosed when the dysfunction is exclusively caused by a drug, a medication, or a toxic exposure. Sexual dysfunction *due to a general medical condition* is diagnosed when the disorder is exclusively caused by the effects of the specific condition. A diagnosis of sexual dysfunction *due to combined factors* applies to a disorder that combines psychological factors and either a medical condition or a substance, so that no one etiology is clear. Sexual dysfunction *not otherwise specified* refers to a disorder that cannot be clearly ascribed to psychological factors, a medical condition, or substance use.

21.2 The answer is B (*Synopsis VIII,* pages 694–696).
Levodopa, an indirectly acting dopamine agonist, is not listed in DSM-IV as a substance associated with sexual dysfunction. All of the other responses are noted in DSM-IV. Intoxication with *cocaine* and alcohol, among other substances, produces sexual dysfunction. Prescribed medications of *antihistamines,* antidepressants, and antiepileptics, among others, can cause arousal and orgasmic disorders as well as decreased sexual interest. *Trazodone* is one of the substances associated with priapism, and *amoxapine* is one of the substances associated with painful orgasm. Still other substances implicated in sexual dysfunction include antihypertensives, anxiolytics, hypnotics, sedatives, amphetamines, and anabolic steroids.

21.3 The answer is E (*Synopsis VIII,* pages 703, 705, 706).
Transsexualism is described as a gender identity disorder that is characterized by a desire to live and be accepted as a member of the opposite sex, rather than a disorder of sexual preference. In transsexualism, a person feels uncomfortable about his or her own anatomic sex and wishes to undergo treatments to change the body to the preferred sex.

The other choices all refer to disorders of sexual preferences. *Fetishism* is a reliance on a nonliving object as a stimulus for sexual arousal and gratification. Many fetishes are extensions of the human body, such as shoes or articles of clothing; others have a particular texture such as leather or plastic. When fetishes are used, they need not always be primary but may simply enhance sexual excitement.

In *voyeurism,* a person feels impelled to look at people engaging in sexual activity or other intimate behavior, such as undressing. *Frotteurism* is a desire to seek sexual stimulation by rubbing against people in crowded places, such as on a subway. *Necrophilia* refers to a desire to be near dead bodies or to have an impulse to have sex with a dead body.

21.4 The answer is E (all) (*Synopsis VIII,* pages 677–678, 702, 703).
Sexual relationship disorder is a gender identity abnormality that produces difficulties in relationships with sexual partners. Other disorders in this category include sexual maturation disorder, in which people are uncertain about their gender identity or sexual orientation, and ego-dystonic sexual orientation, in which people wish for a different gender identity or sexual preference because of associated psychological and behavioral disorders.

Transvestism, transsexualism, and gender identity disorder of childhood are classified as *gender identity disorders,* a category rather than a specific disorder. *Exhibitionism,* voyeurism, pedophilia, and fetishism are classified as sexual preference disorders, also a category rather than a specific disorder. Transvestism is a desire to wear clothes of the opposite sex and to enjoy temporary membership in the opposite sex, without any wish for permanent sex change. Exhibitionism is a tendency to expose the genitalia to people in public places, without any desire for closer contact. Some people experience this tendency only during periods of stress.

21.5 The answer is A (*Synopsis VIII,* page 707).
Intersexual disorders include several syndromes that produce gross anatomical or physiological aspects of the opposite sex. *Hypoxyphilia* is not an intersexual disorder but rather a desire to experience an altered state of consciousness during orgasm by producing hypoxia with drugs.

Turner's syndrome results from the absence of a second female sex chromosome (XO). The infants are usually assigned as females because of their female-looking genitals. In *Klinefelter's syndrome,* the genotype is XXY; infants have a male habitus with a small penis and rudimentary testes caused by low androgen production. They are usually assigned as males. *5α-Reductase deficiency* and *17-hydroxysteroid dehydrogenase deficiency* are types of enzymatic defects in the XY genotype resulting in congenital interruption of dihydrotestosterone and testosterone production, respectively. As a result, infants have a female habitus and ambiguous genitals. They are usually assigned as females because of their female-looking genitalia.

21.6 The answer is D (*Synopsis VIII,* page 682).
Homosexuality is socially stigmatized less for women than for men. Homosexual male couples are therefore more likely to be subjected to civil and social discrimination than are homosexual female couples.

Homosexuality *is not listed in the fourth edition of DSM-IV as a mental disorder.* In 1973, homosexuality was eliminated as a diagnostic category by the American Psychiatric Association and was removed from *Diagnostic and Statistical Manual of Mental Disorders.* Doing so was the result of the view that homosexuality is an alternative lifestyle, rather than a mental disorder, and that it occurs with some regularity as a variant of human sexuality. As David Hawkins wrote, "The presence of homosexuality does not appear to be a matter of choice; the expression of it is a matter of choice." However, if a person persistently finds his or her homosexuality markedly distressing, that person may be classified as having a sexual disorder not otherwise specified.

Although no sex surveys are wholly reliable, a 1988 survey

Table 21.1
Estimates of Homosexual Behavior

Country	Sample	Findings
Canada	5,514 first-year college students under age 25	98% heterosexual 1% bisexual 1% homosexual
Norway	6,155 adults, ages 18–26	3.5% of males and 3% of females reported past homosexual experiences
France	20,055 adults	Lifetime homosexual experience: 4.1% for men and 2.6% for women
Denmark	3,178 adults, ages 18–59	Fewer than 1% of men exclusively homosexual
Britain	18,876 adults, ages 16–59	6.1% of men reported past homosexual experiences

Data reported by *The Wall Street Journal* (March 31, 1993) and *The New York Times* (April 15, 1993) from research studies on homosexual behavior.

by the U.S. Bureau of the Census concluded that homosexuality among men has a *prevalence of 2 to 3 percent, not 15 percent.* In 1993 the Alan Guttmacher Institute found that the percentage of men reporting exclusively homosexual activity in the previous year was 1 percent and that 2 percent reported a lifetime history of homosexual experiences. Other estimates of homosexual behavior are given in Table 21.1.

Homosexuality *was perceived by Sigmund Freud as an arrest of psychosexual development, not a mental illness.* Recent studies indicate that homosexuality *may have a genetic or biological component.* In some studies homosexual men reportedly exhibited lower levels of circulatory androgen than did heterosexual men. And women with hyperadrenocorticalism become bisexual or homosexual in greater proportion than does the general population. In addition, genetic studies have found a higher incidence of homosexual concordance among monozygotic twins than among dizygotic twins, which suggests a genetic predisposition; but chromosome studies have been unable to differentiate homosexuals from heterosexuals. Male homosexuals also show a familial distribution; homosexual men have more brothers who are homosexual than do heterosexual men.

21.7 The answer is A (*Synopsis VIII,* pages 687–688).
Male erectile disorder (Table 21.2) is *sometimes situational.* In situational male erectile disorder the man is able to have coitus in certain circumstances but not in others; for example, a man may function effectively with a prostitute but be impotent with his wife.

Male erectile disorder is *the chief complaint in more than 50 (not 25) percent of all men presenting with sexual disorders.* The incidence increases with age. However, male erectile disorder is *not universal in aging men;* having an available sex partner is closely related to continuing potency, as is a history of consistent sexual activity. Male erectile disorder may be *organic or psychological in cause* or a combination of both, but most cases have a psychological cause.

21.8 The answer is C (*Synopsis VIII,* page 681).
Masturbation *is common among married couples;* Alfred Kinsey reported that it occurs, on average, once a month among married couples. Masturbation is a normal activity that is common in all stages of life, from infancy to old age. Longitudinal studies of development show that it *is common in infancy and childhood.* No scientific evidence supports myths generated by moral taboos, such as the myth that masturbation *leads to a decrease in sexual potency.* Masturbation *does not result in orgasmic anhedonia,* a condition in which the person has no physical sensation of orgasm, even though the physiological component (for example, ejaculation) remains intact.

Masturbation *is associated with autoerotic asphyxiation.* Some masturbatory practices involve masturbating while hanging oneself by the neck to heighten erotic sensations and the intensity of the orgasm through the mechanism of mild hypoxia. Although the persons intend to release themselves from the noose after orgasm, an estimated 500 to 1,000 persons a year accidentally kill themselves by hanging.

21.9 The answer is C (*Synopsis VIII,* pages 700–702).
Paraphilias, *according to the classic psychoanalytic model, are due to a failure to complete the process of genital adjustment.* However bizarre its manifestation, the paraphilia provides an outlet for the sexual and aggressive drives that would otherwise have been channeled into proper sexual behavior. Paraphilias *are usually distressing to the person with the disorder.* Paraphilias *are not found equally among men and women.* As usually defined, paraphilias seem to be largely male condi-

Table 21.2
DSM-IV Diagnostic Criteria for Male Erectile Disorder

A. Persistent or recurrent inability to attain, or to maintain until completion of the sexual activity, an adequate erection.
B. The disturbance causes marked distress or interpersonal difficulty.
C. The erectile dysfunction is not better accounted for by another Axis I disorder (other than a sexual dysfunction) and is not due exclusively to the direct physiological effects of a substance (eg, a drug of abuse, a medication) or a general medical condition.

Specify type:
Lifelong type
Acquired type

Specify type:
Generalized type
Situational type

Specify:
Due to psychological factors
Due to combined factors

Table 21.3
Frequency of Paraphiliac Acts Committed by Paraphilia Patients Seeking Outpatient Treatment

Diagnostic Category	Paraphilia Patients Seeking Outpatient Treatment (%)	Paraphiliac Acts per Paraphilia Patient[a]
Pedophilia	45	5
Exhibitionism	25	50
Voyeurism	12	17
Frotteurism	6	30
Sexual masochism	3	36
Transvestic fetishism	3	25
Sexual sadism	3	3
Fetishism	2	3
Zoophilia	1	2

Courtesy of Gene G. Abel, M.D.
[a] Median number.

tions. Paraphilias *with an early age of onset are associated with a poor prognosis,* as are paraphilias with a high frequency of the acts (Table 21.3), no guilt or shame about the acts, and substance abuse. Paraphilias *such as pedophilia* (Table 21.4) *usually do not involve vaginal or anal penetration of the victim.* The majority of child molestations involve genital fondling or oral sex.

21.10 The answer is B (*Synopsis VIII,* page 678).
Klinefelter's syndrome is a chromosomal abnormality in which an extra sex chromosome exists; instead of the normal 46, the affected child is born with 47 chromosomes. For example, there is an XXY pattern, instead of the usual XX or XY pairs. The persons affected are male in development, with small firm testes, eunuchoid habitus, variable gynecomastia and other signs of androgen deficiency, and elevated gonadotropin levels.

Table 21.4
DSM-IV Diagnostic Criteria for Pedophilia

A. Over a period of at least 6 months, recurrent, intense sexually arousing fantasies, sexual urges, or behaviors involving sexual activity with a prepubescent child or children (generally age 13 years or younger).

B. The fantasies, sexual urges, or behaviors cause clinically significant distress or impairment in social, occupational, or other important areas of functioning.

C. The person is at least age 16 years and at least 5 years older than the child or children in criterion A.
Note: Do not include an individual in late adolescence involved in an ongoing sexual relationship with a 12- or 13-year-old.

Specify if:
Sexually attracted to males
Sexually attracted to females
Sexually attracted to both

Specify if:
Limited to incest

Specify type:
Exclusive type (attracted only to children)
Nonexclusive type

Reprinted with permission from American Psychiatric Association: *Diagnostic and Statistical Manual of Mental Disorders,* ed 4. Copyright, American Psychiatric Association, Washington, 1994.

Androgen insensitivity is a congenital disorder resulting from an inability of target tissues to respond to androgen. *Turner's syndrome* is a chromosome disorder affecting girls. Instead of an XX sex chromosome, an XO sex chromosome exists, and the girl has a total of 45 chromosomes, rather than the usual 46. *Hermaphroditism* is a state in which a person has both female and male gonads, usually with one sex dominating. *Cushing's syndrome,* or hyperadrenocorticism, is named for an American neurosurgeon, Harvey W. Cushing (1869–1939). It is characterized by muscle wasting, obesity, osteoporosis, atrophy of the skin, and hypertension. Emotional lability is common, and frank psychoses are occasionally observed. Table 21.5 lists and describes intersexual disorders.

21.11 The answer is E (*Synopsis VIII,* page 703).
Fetishism is a disorder found almost exclusively in males. The essential feature of a fetish is *a nonliving object that is used as the preferred or necessary adjunct to sexual arousal.* Sexual activity may involve the fetish alone, or the fetish may be *integrated into sexual activities with a human partner.* In the absence of the fetish, the male may be impotent. According to psychoanalytic theory, the fetish *may function as a hedge against separation anxiety* from the love object and may be *used to ward off castration anxiety.* Table 21.6 lists the diagnostic criteria for fetishism.

21.12 The answer is E (all) (*Synopsis VIII,* pages 687–688).
The incidence of psychological as opposed to organic male erectile disorder has been the focus of many studies. Statistics indicate that 20 to 50 percent of men with erectile disorder have an organic basis for the disorder. Organic causes of male erectile disorder include *mumps, atherosclerosis, Klinefelter's syndrome, multiple sclerosis,* surgery, and many other medical conditions.

Mumps is an acute infectious and contagious disease caused by *Paramyxovirus;* it is characterized by inflammation and swelling of the parotid gland and sometimes of other glands, and occasionally there is inflammation of the testes, ovaries, pancreas, and meninges.

Atherosclerosis is characterized by irregularly distributed lipid deposits in the intima of large and medium-sized arteries. The deposits are associated with fibrosis and calcification and are almost always present to some degree in middle-aged and elderly adults. In its severe form, atherosclerosis may lead to arterial narrowing, and the following disorders can occur: angina pectoris, myocardial infarction, cerebrovascular disease, intermittent claudication, and gangrene of the lower extremities.

Klinefelter's syndrome is a chromosomal anomaly in which the person has an extra X chromosome. The affected person is male in development, with small firm testes, eunuchoid habitus, variable gynecomastia and other signs of androgen deficiency, and elevated gonadotropin levels.

Multiple sclerosis is one of the demyelinating diseases of the central nervous system and at least in temperate zones, one of the most common neurological disorders. It is characterized pathologically by swelling and then demyelination of the medullary sheath, which is followed by glial proliferation. The re-

Table 21.5
Classification of Intersexual Disorders[a]

Syndrome	Description
Virilizing adrenal hyperplasia (andrenogenital syndrome)	Results from excess androgens in a fetus with XX genotype; most common female intersex disorder; associated with enlarged clitoris, fused labia, hirsutism in adolescence
Turner's syndrome	Results from absence of second female sex chromosome (XO); associated with web neck, dwarfism, cubitus valgus; no sex hormones produced; infertile; usually assigned as females because of female-looking genitals
Klinefelter's syndrome	Genotype is XXY; male habitus presents with small penis and rudimentary testes because of low androgen production; weak libido; usually assigned as male
Androgen insensitivity (testicular-feminizing syndrome)	Congenital X-linked recessive disorder that results in inability of tissues to respond to androgens; external genitals look female and cryptorchid testes present; assigned as females, even though they have XY genotype; in extreme form patient has breasts, normal external genitals, short blind vagina, and absence of pubic and axillary hair
Enzymatic defects in XY genotype (eg, 5α-reductase deficiency, 17-hydroxysteroid dehydrogenase deficiency)	Congenital interruption in production of testosterone that produces ambiguous genitals and female habitus; usually assigned as female because of female-looking genitalia
Hermaphroditism	True hermaphrodite is rare and characterized by both testes and ovaries in same person (may be 46 XX or 46 XY)
Pseudohermaphroditism	Usually the result of endocrine or enzymatic defect (eg, adrenal hyperplasia) in persons with normal chromosomes; female pseudohermaphrodites have masculine-looking genitals but are XX; male pseudohermaphrodites have rudimentary testes and external genitals and are XY; assigned as males or females depending on morphology of genitals

[a] Intersexual disorders include a variety of syndromes that produce persons with gross anatomical or physiological aspects of the opposite sex.

sult is an irregular scattering of well-demarcated sclerotic plaques throughout the white and gray matter of the brain and spinal cord.

21.13 The answer is C (*Synopsis VIII,* pages 680–681).
In the woman, orgasm is characterized by 3 to 15 involuntary contractions of the lower third of the vagina and by *strong sustained contractions of the uterus,* flowing from the fundus downward to the cervix. Both men and women have *involuntary contractions of the anal sphincter.* Those and the other contractions during orgasm occur at intervals of 0.8 seconds. Other manifestations include voluntary and involuntary movements of the large muscle groups, including facial grimacing and *carpopedal spasm.* Systolic *blood pressure rises* 20 mm, diastolic blood pressure rises 40 mm, and the heart rate increases up to 160 beats a minute. Orgasm lasts 3 to 15 seconds and is associated with a *slight clouding of consciousness.*

Table 21.6
DSM-IV Diagnostic Criteria for Fetishism

A. Over a period of at least 6 months, recurrent, intense sexually arousing fantasies, sexual urges, or behaviors involving the use of nonliving objects (eg, female undergarments).
B. The fantasies, sexual urges, or behaviors cause clinically significant distress or impairment in social, occupational, or other important areas of functioning.
C. The fetish objects are not limited to articles of female clothing used in cross-dressing (as in transvestic fetishism) or devices designed for the purpose of tactile genital stimulation (eg, vibrator).

21.14 The answer is C (*Synopsis VIII,* pages 697–698).
A married man with a chief complaint of premature ejaculation is best treated with the *squeeze technique.* In that method the woman squeezes the coronal ridge of the erect penis just before ejaculation or the time of ejaculatory inevitability. That moment is signaled to the woman by the man in a manner previously agreed to, at which time the woman forcefully applies the squeeze technique. The erection subsides slightly, and ejaculation is postponed. Eventually, the threshold of ejaculatory inevitability is raised, and the condition thereby improves.

Even though premature ejaculation is accompanied by anxiety, drug therapy with *antianxiety agents* is not indicated. Positive results have been obtained using the side effects of fluoxetine (Prozac), which delays orgasm in some men. *Psychoanalysis* may reveal unconscious fears of women that contribute to premature ejaculation, but it is not the most effective therapy. Psychoanalysis can be used if the patient does not respond to the squeeze technique because of deep-seated psychological conflicts. *Cognitive therapy* is used as a treatment of depression and is of limited use as a primary treatment approach to any of the sexual disorders. If the patient has a depression secondary to the sexual disorder, however, cognitive therapy may be useful. Table 21.7 lists the diagnostic criteria for premature ejaculation.

21.15 The answer is D (*Synopsis VIII,* page 681).
Autoerotic asphyxiation is a masturbatory phenomenon most common among *adolescent boys,* not *adolescent girls* or *middle-aged men.* The practice involves hanging oneself by the neck while masturbating to induce hypoxia. Hypoxia does produce a slightly altered state of consciousness, but it does *not heighten the intensity of orgasm.* The practice is associated with *severe mental disorders.* Although death is accidental, an

Table 21.7
DSM-IV Diagnostic Criteria for Premature Ejaculation

A. Persistent or recurrent ejaculation with minimal sexual stimulation before, on, or shortly after penetration and before the person wishes it. The clinician must take into account factors that affect duration of the excitement phase, such as age, novelty of the sexual partner or situation, and recent frequency of sexual activity.

B. The disturbance causes marked distress or interpersonal difficulty.

C. The premature ejaculation is not due exclusively to the direct effects of a substance (eg, withdrawal form opioids).

Specify type:
Lifelong type
Acquired type

Specify type:
Generalized type
Situational type

Specify:
Due to psychological factors
Due to combined factors

estimated 500 to 1,000 deaths by hanging occur each year as a result of the masturbatory practice. Some apparent hanging suicides by adolescent boys are actually caused by autoerotic asphyxiation.

21.16 The answer is E (all) (*Synopsis VIII,* pages 687–688). A variety of measures are used to differentiate organically caused impotence from psychologically caused impotence. The *monitoring of nocturnal penile tumescence* is a noninvasive procedure; normally, erections occur during sleep and are associated with rapid eye movement (REM) sleep periods. Tumescence may be determined with a simple strain gauge. In most cases in which organic factors account for the impotence, the man has minimal or no nocturnal erections. Conversely, in most cases of psychologically caused or psychogenic impotence, erections do occur during REM sleep.

Other diagnostic tests that delineate organic bases of impotence include *glucose tolerance tests, follicle-stimulating hormone (FSH) determinations,* and *testosterone level tests.* The glucose tolerance curve measures the metabolism of glucose over a specific period and is useful in diagnosing diabetes, of which impotence may be a symptom. FSH is a hormone produced by the anterior pituitary that stimulates the secretion of estrogen from the ovarian follicle in the female; it is also responsible for the production of sperm from the testes in men. An abnormal finding suggests an organic cause for impotence. Testosterone is the male hormone produced by the interstitial cells of the testes. In the male, a low testosterone level produces a lack of desire as the chief complaint, which may be associated with impotence. If the measure of nocturnal penile tumescence is abnormal, indicating the possibility of organic impotence, a measure of plasma testosterone is indicated.

21.17 The answer is A (*Synopsis VIII,* page 704). Sexual masochism is *sexual excitement produced by the person's own suffering. Masochistic sexual fantasies are likely to have been present in childhood,* although the age of onset of overt masochistic activities with partners is variable. *The disorder is usually chronic,* and *self-mutilation, if it occurs, is likely to be recurrent.* The most common finding is that the person with sexual masochism is able to take the opposite role of the sexual sadist with arousal and pleasure. The diagnostic criteria for sexual masochism are listed in Table 21.8.

21.18 The answer is E (all) (*Synopsis VIII,* pages 689–690). In premature ejaculation, the man recurrently achieves orgasm and ejaculation before he wishes to. *Stress* clearly plays a role in exacerbating the condition; for example, in ongoing relationships, the partner has been found to have great influence on the premature ejaculator, and a stressful marriage exacerbates the disorder. Difficulty in ejaculatory control may also result from *negative cultural conditioning.* For example, men who experience most of their early sexual contacts with prostitutes who demand that the sexual act proceed quickly or in situations in which discovery would be embarrassing (the back seat of a car or the parental home) may become conditioned to achieve orgasm rapidly. Premature ejaculation is associated with *more frequency among college-educated men than among men with less education.* The condition is thought to be related to their concern for partner satisfaction, which may induce performance anxiety, or to their greater awareness of the availability of therapy. As with other sexual dysfunctions, premature ejaculation is not caused by *general medical factors exclusively.*

21.19 The answer is B (*Synopsis VIII,* pages 689–690). *Spironolactone* (Aldactone), an antihypertensive drug, is *the least likely medication to impair ejaculation. Amitriptyline* (Elavil) is a tricyclic antidepressant that occasionally causes impaired ejaculation. *Haloperidol* (Haldol), *phentolamine* (Regitine), and *fluoxetine* (Prozac) have all been shown to be implicated in impaired or delayed ejaculation.

21.20 The answer is E (all) (*Synopsis VIII,* pages 694–696). The effects of various drugs on sexual functioning in women have not been studied as extensively as they have been in men. In general, however, *women are less vulnerable* to pharmacologically induced sexual dysfunction than are men. Oral contraceptives are reported to decrease libido in some women, and the monoamine oxidase inhibitor *phenelzine* (Nardil) *decreases libido* in some women. Sexual dysfunction associated with the

Table 21.8
DSM-IV Diagnostic Criteria for Sexual Masochism

A. Over a period of at least 6 months, recurrent, intense sexually arousing fantasies, sexual urges, or behaviors involving the act (real, not stimulated) of being humiliated, beaten, bound, or otherwise made to suffer.

B. The fantasies, sexual urges, or behaviors cause clinically significant distress or impairment in social, occupational, or other important areas of functioning.

Table 21.9
Psychiatric Drugs Implicated in Female Orgasmic Disorder[a]

Amoxapine (Asendin)[b]
Clomipramine (Anafranil)[c]
Fluoxetine (Prozac)[d]
Imipramine (Tofranil)
Isocarboxazid (Marplan)[e]
Nortriptyline (Aventyl)[d]
Phenelzine (Nardil)[e]
Thioridazine (Mellaril)
Tranylcypromine (Parnate)[e]
Trifluoperazine (Stelazine)

Courtesy of Virginia A. Sadock, M.D.

[a] The interrelation between female sexual dysfunctions and pharmacological agents has been less extensively evaluated than have male reactions. Oral contraceptives are reported to decrease libido in some women, and some drugs with anticholinergic side effects may impair arousal and orgasm. Benzodiazepines have been reported to decrease libido, but in some patients the diminution of anxiety caused by those drugs enhances sexual function. Both increases and decreases in libido have been reported with psychoactive agents. It is difficult to separate those effects from the underlying condition or from improvement of the condition. Sexual dysfunction associated with the use of a drug disappears when the drug is discontinued.

[b] Bethanachol (Urecholine) can reverse the effects of amoxepine-induced anorgasmia.

[c] Clomipramine is also reported to increase arousal and orgasmic potential.

[d] Cyproheptadine (Periactin) reverses fluoxetine- and nortriptyline-induced anorgasmia.

[e] Monoamine oxidase inhibitor (MAOI)-induced anorgasmia may be a temporary reaction to the medication that disappears even though administration of the drug is continued.

Table 21.10
DSM-IV Diagnostic Criteria for Female Orgasmic Disorder

A. Persistent or recurrent delay in, or absence of, orgasm following a normal sexual excitement phase. Women exhibit wide variability in the type or intensity of stimulation that triggers orgasm. The diagnosis of female orgasmic disorder should be based on the clinician's judgment that the woman's orgasmic capacity is less than would be reasonable for her age, sexual experience, and the adequacy of sexual stimulation she receives.

B. The disturbance causes marked distress or interpersonal difficulty.

C. The orgasmic dysfunction is not better accounted for by another Axis I disorder (except another sexual dysfunction) and is not due exclusively to the direct physiological effects of a substance (eg, a drug of abuse, a medication) or a general medical condition.

Specify type:
Lifelong type
Acquired type

Specify type:
Generalized type
Situational type

Specify:
Due to psychological factors
Due to combined factors

Reprinted with permission from American Psychiatric Association: *Diagnostic and Statistical Manual of Mental Disorders,* ed 4. Copyright, American Psychiatric Association, Washington, 1994.

use of a drug *disappears* when the drug is discontinued. Psychiatric drugs implicated in female orgasmic disorder are listed in Table 21.9, and the diagnostic criteria for female orgasmic disorder are listed in Table 21.10.

21.21 The answer is E (all) (*Synopsis VIII,* page 689).
In male orgasmic disorder, which is *also called retarded ejaculation,* the man achieves climax during coitus with great difficulty, if at all. Male orgasmic disorder is *less common than premature ejaculation* and impotence. The problem is more common among men with obsessive-compulsive disorders than among other men. Male orgasmic disorder may have physiological causes and *is sometimes a result of prostate surgery.* It may also be associated with Parkinson's disease and other neurological disorders involving the lumbar or sacral sections of the spinal cord. It is *sometimes caused by antihypertensive drugs,* such as guanethidine (Ismelin) and methyldopa (Aldomet), and the phenothiazines. The diagnostic criteria for male orgasmic disorder are listed in Table 21.11.

21.22 The answer is E (all) (*Synopsis VIII,* page 699).
The *insertion of a penile prosthesis* in a man with inadequate erectile responses who is resistant to other treatment methods or who has organically caused deficiencies is sometimes effective. Some physicians use *penile revascularization* as a direct approach to treating erectile dysfunction attributable to vascular disorders. Such surgical procedures may be indicated in patients with corporal shunts, in which normally entrapped blood leaks from the corporal space, leading to inadequate erections.

Among the surgical approaches to female dysfunctions are *hymenectomy* (excision of the hymen) in dyspareunia or in the treatment of an unconsummated marriage because of hymenal obstruction. *Vaginoplasty* (plastic surgery involving the vagina) in multiparous women complaining of lessened vaginal sensations is sometimes used.

21.23 The answer is C (*Synopsis VIII,* pages 682–683).
Studies have shown that genetic predisposition does exist in homosexuality, but *chromosome studies have been unable to differentiate homosexuals from heterosexuals.* Sigmund Freud viewed homosexuality as an *arrest of psychosexual development.* Richard Isay has described *same-sex fantasies in children aged 3 to 5 years that can be recovered from homosexuals* and that occur at about the same ages when heterosexuals have opposite-sex fantasies. It has also been found that *female couples appear to have more enduring monogamous or primary relationships* than male couples. *Prenatal hormones do appear to play a role* in the sexual organization of the central nervous system.

21.24 The answer is D (*Synopsis VIII,* page 678).
True hermaphroditism is the presence in one individual of both ovarian and testicular tissue; it is a rare condition. *Pseudohermaphroditism,* or false hermaphroditism, is a state in which the individual has unambiguous gonadal sex (for example, possessing either ovaries or testes) but has ambiguous external genitalia. *Androgen insensitivity syndrome* is a congenital X-linked recessive trait disorder that results in an inability of

Table 21.11 DSM-IV Diagnostic Criteria for Male Orgasmic Disorder

A. Persistent or recurrent delay in, or absence of, orgasm following a normal sexual excitement phase during sexual activity that the clinician, taking into account the person's age, judges to be adequate in focus, intensity, and duration.

B. The disturbance causes marked distress or interpersonal difficulty

C. The orgasmic dysfunction is not better accounted for by another Axis I disorder (except another sexual dysfunction) and is not due exclusively to the direct physiological effects of a substance (eg, a drug of abuse, a medication) or a general medical condition.

Specify type:
Lifelong type
Acquired type

Specify type:
Generalized type
Situational type

Specify:
Due to psychological factors
Due to combined factors

Reprinted with permission from American Psychiatric Association: *Diagnostic and Statistical Manual of Mental Disorders,* ed 4. Copyright, American Psychiatric Association, Washington, 1994.

target tissues to respond to androgens. The syndrome is characterized by female genitalia and cryptorchid testes. Patients are assigned as females even though they have an XY genotype. *Klinefelter's syndrome* is a chromosomal anomaly with XXY sex chromosome constitution, characterized by a male habitus presenting with a small penis and rudimentary testis because of low androgen production. *Adrenogenital syndrome,* also known as congenital virilizing adrenal hyperplasia, results from excess androgens in a fetus with an XX genotype, causing androgenization of the external genitals.

21.25 The answer is B (*Synopsis VIII,* page 678).
Congenital virilizing adrenal hyperplasia, also known as adrenogenital syndrome, *the most common female intersex disorder,* results from *excess androgens* in a fetus with XX genotype. The syndrome is characterized by androgenization of the external genitals, ranging from mild *clitoral enlargement* to external genitals that look like a normal scrotal sac, testes, and a penis; but *hidden behind those external genitals are a vagina and uterus.* The patients are otherwise normally female.

21.26a The answer is B (*Synopsis VIII,* page 678).

21.26b The answer is C (*Synopsis VIII,* page 678).

21.26c The answer is D (*Synopsis VIII,* page 678).
The phenotypic female with XY karyotype has *androgen insensitivity syndrome,* also known as *testicular feminization syndrome,* a congenital X-linked recessive trait disorder that results in an inability of target tissues to respond to a mutant allele on androgens. Because it is X-linked recessive, the person needs only one X chromosome. In an XX genotype, the person would carry the gene but not express it phenotypically. The infant at birth appears to be an *unremarkable girl,* although she is later found to have cryptorchid testes, which produce the testosterone to which the tissues do not respond, and *minimal or absent internal sexual organs.* Secondary sex characteristics *at puberty are female* because of the small but sufficient amounts of estrogens typically produced by the testes. The patients invariably sense themselves as female and are feminine.

True hermaphroditism is the presence in one individual of both ovarian and testicular tissue. *Pseudohermaphroditism* is a state in which the individual has an unambiguous gonadal sex (for example, possessing either ovaries or testes) but has ambiguous external genitalia. *Turner's syndrome* is a chromosomal anomaly with only a single X chromosome (XO genotype), resulting in absence (agenesis) or minimal development (dysgenesis) of the gonads and no significant production of sex hormones. *Adrenogenital syndrome* results from excess androgens in a fetus with an XX genotype, causing androgenization of the external genitals.

Answers 21.27–21.37

21.27 The answer is B (*Synopsis VIII,* page 705).

21.28 The answer is C (*Synopsis VIII,* page 703).

21.29 The answer is A (*Synopsis VIII,* page 703).

21.30 The answer is G (*Synopsis VIII,* pages 705–706).

21.31 The answer is H (*Synopsis VIII,* page 687).

21.32 The answer is I (*Synopsis VIII,* page 687).

21.33 The answer is K (*Synopsis VIII,* pages 690–691).

21.34 The answer is J (*Synopsis VIII,* page 690).

21.35 The answer is F (*Synopsis VIII,* page 705).

21.36 The answer is E (*Synopsis VIII,* page 704).

21.37 The answer is D (*Synopsis VIII,* page 702).
In *fetishism* the *sexual focus is on objects* (such as shoes, gloves, pantyhose, and stockings) *that are intimately associated with the human body.* The particular fetish is linked to someone closely involved with the patient during childhood and has some quality associated with that loved, needed, or even traumatizing person. *Voyeurism* is the recurrent preoccupation with fantasies and acts that involve *observing people who are naked or engaging in sexual activity* (Table 21.12). It is also known as scopophilia. Masturbation to orgasm usually occurs during or after the event.

Table 21.12 DSM-IV Diagnostic Criteria for Voyeurism

A. Over a period of at least 6 months, recurrent, intense sexually arousing fantasies, sexual urges, or behaviors involving the act of observing an unsuspecting person who is naked, in the process of disrobing, or engaging in sexual activity.

B. The fantasies, sexual urges, or behaviors cause clinically significant distress or impairment in social, occupational, or other important areas of functioning.

Reprinted with permission from American Psychiatric Association: *Diagnostic and Statistical Manual of Mental Disorders,* ed 4. Copyright, American Psychiatric Association, Washington, 1994.

Table 21.13
DSM-IV Diagnostic Criteria for Frotteurism

A. Over a period of at least 6 months, recurrent, intense sexually arousing fantasies, sexual urges, or behaviors involving touching and rubbing against a nonconsenting person.

B. The fantasies, sexual urges, or behaviors cause clinically significant distress or impairment in social, occupational, or other important areas of functioning.

Table 21.15
DSM-IV Diagnostic Criteria for Sexual Sadism

A. Over a period of at least 6 months, recurrent, intense sexually arousing fantasies, sexual urges, or behaviors involving acts (real, not simulated) in which the psychological or physical suffering (including humiliation) of the victim is sexually exciting to the person.

B. The fantasies, sexual urges, or behaviors cause clinically significant distress or impairment in social, occupational, or other important areas of functioning.

Frotteurism is usually characterized by the male's *rubbing up against a fully clothed woman to achieve orgasm* (Table 21.13). The acts usually occur in crowded places, particularly subways and buses. *Exhibitionism* is the *recurrent urge to expose one's genitals to a stranger* or an unsuspecting person (Table 21.14). Sexual excitement occurs in anticipation of the exposure, and orgasm is brought about by masturbation during or after the event.

Persons with *sexual masochism* have a recurrent preoccupation with sexual urges and *fantasies involving the act of being humiliated,* beaten, bound, or otherwise made to suffer (Table 21.8). Persons with *sexual sadism* (Table 21.15) have *fantasies involving harm to others.* According to psychoanalytic theory, sexual sadism is a defense against fears of castration—the persons with sexual sadism do to others what they fear will happen to them. Pleasure is derived from expressing the aggressive instinct.

Transvestic fetishism is marked by fantasies and sexual *urges by heterosexual men to dress in female clothes for purposes of arousal* and as an adjunct to masturbation or coitus (Table 21.16). Transvestic fetishism typically begins in childhood or early adolescence. As years pass, some men with transvestic fetishism want to dress and live permanently as women. Such persons are classified as persons with transvestic fetishism with gender dysphoria.

Sexual desire disorders are divided into two classes: *hypoactive sexual desire disorder,* characterized by a deficiency or the *absence of sexual fantasies and of desire for sexual activity* (Table 21.17), and *sexual aversion disorder,* characterized by an aversion to and *avoidance of genital sexual contact with a sexual partner* (Table 21.18). Hypoactive sexual desire disorder is more common than sexual aversion disorder. An estimated 20 percent of the total population have hypoactive sexual desire disorder.

Dyspareunia is recurrent or *persistent genital pain occurring before, during, or after intercourse* in either the man or the woman. Dyspareunia should not be diagnosed when an organic basis for the pain is found or when, in a woman, it is caused exclusively by vaginismus or by a lack of lubrication (Table 21.19).

Vaginismus is an *involuntary muscle constriction* of the outer third of the vagina that interferes with penile insertion and intercourse (Table 21.20).

Answers 21.38–21.42

21.38 The answer is B (*Synopsis VIII,* page 680).

21.39 The answer is B (*Synopsis VIII,* page 680).

21.40 The answer is B (*Synopsis VIII,* page 680).

21.41 The answer is C (*Synopsis VIII,* pages 680–681).

21.42 The answer is D (*Synopsis VIII,* page 681).
The fourth edition of *Diagnostic and Statistical Manual of Mental Disorders* (DSM-IV) defines a four-phase sexual response cycle: phase 1, desire; phase 2, excitement; phase 3, orgasm; phase 4, resolution.

The *desire phase* is distinct from any phase identified solely through physiology, and it reflects the psychiatrist's funda-

Table 21.14
DSM-IV Diagnostic Criteria for Exhibitionism

A. Over a period of at least 6 months, recurrent, intense sexually arousing fantasies, sexual urges, or behaviors involving the exposure of one's genitals to an unsuspecting stranger.

B. The fantasies, sexual urges, or behaviors cause clinically significant distress or impairment in social, occupational, or other important areas of functioning.

Table 21.16
DSM-IV Diagnostic Criteria for Transvestic Fetishism

A. Over a period of at least 6 months, in a heterosexual male, recurrent, intense sexually arousing fantasies, sexual urges, or behaviors involving cross-dressing.

B. The fantasies, sexual urges, or behaviors cause clinically significant distress or impairment in social, occupational, or other important areas of functioning.

Specify if:

With gender dysphoria: if the person has persistent discomfort with gender role or identity.

Table 21.17
DSM-IV Diagnostic Criteria for Hypoactive Sexual Desire Disorder

A. Persistently or recurrently deficient (or absent) sexual fantasies and desire for sexual activity. The judgment of deficiency or absence is made by the clinician, taking into account factors that affect sexual functioning, such as age and the context of the person's life.

B. The disturbance causes marked distress or interpersonal difficulty.

C. The sexual dysfunction is not better accounted for by another Axis I disorder (except another sexual dysfunction) and is not due exclusively to the direct physiological effects of a substance (eg, a drug of abuse, a medication) or a general medical condition.

Specify type:
Lifelong type
Acquired type

Specify type:
Generalized type
Situational type

Specify:
Due to psychological factors
Due to combined factors

Table 21.18
DSM-IV Diagnostic Criteria for Sexual Aversion Disorder

A. Persistently or recurrent aversion to, and avoidance of, all (or almost all) genital sexual contact with a sexual partner.

B. The disturbance causes marked distress or interpersonal difficulty.

C. The sexual dysfunction is not better accounted for by another Axis 1 disorder (except another sexual dysfunction).

Specify type:
Lifelong type
Acquired type

Specify type:
Generalized type
Situational type

Specify:
Due to psychological factors
Due to combined factors

Table 21.19
DSM-IV Diagnostic Criteria for Dyspareunia

A. Recurrent or persistent genital pain associated with sexual intercourse in either a male or a female.

B. The disturbance causes marked distress or interpersonal difficulty.

C. The disturbance is not caused exclusively by vaginismus or lack of lubrication, is not better accounted for by another Axis I disorder (except another sexual dysfunction) and is not due exclusively to the direct physiological effects of a substance (eg, a drug of abuse, a medication) or a general medical condition.

Specify type:
Lifelong type
Acquired type

Specify type:
Generalized type
Situational type

Specify:
Due to psychological factors
Due to combined factors

Table 21.20
DSM-IV Diagnostic Criteria for Vaginismus

A. Recurrent or persistent involuntary spasm of the musculature of the outer third of the vagina that interferes with sexual intercourse.

B. The disturbance causes marked distress or interpersonal difficulty.

C. The disturbance is not better accounted for by another Axis I disorder (eg, somatization disorder) and is not due exclusively to the direct physiological effects of a general medical condition.

Specify type:
Lifelong type
Acquired type

Specify type:
Generalized type
Situational type

Specify:
Due to psychological factors
Due to combined factors

Table 21.21
Male Sexual Response Cycle

Organ	Excitement Phase	Orgasmic Phase	Resolution Phase
	Lasts several minutes to several hours; heightened excitement before orgasm, 30 seconds to 3 minutes	3 to 15 seconds	10 to 15 minutes; if no orgasm, ½ to 1 day
Skin	Just before orgasm: sexual flush inconsistently appears; maculopapular rash originates on abdomen and spreads to anterior chest wall, face, and neck and can include shoulders and forearms	Well-developed flush	Flush disappears in reverse order of appearance; inconsistently appearing film of perspiration on soles of feet and palms of hands
Penis	Erection in 10 to 30 seconds caused by vasocongestion of erectile bodies of corpus cavernosa of shaft; loss of erection may occur with introduction of asexual stimulus, loud noise; with heightened excitement, size of glans and diameter of penile shaft increase further	Ejaculation: emission phase marked by three to four contractions of 0.8 second of vas, seminal vesicles, prostate; ejaculation proper marked by contractions of 0.8 second of urethra and ejaculatory spurt of 12 to 20 inches at age 18, decreasing with age to seepage at 70	Erection: partial involution in 5 to 10 seconds with variable refractory period; full detumescence in 5 to 30 minutes
Scrotum and testes	Tightening and lifting of scrotal sac and elevation of testes; with heightened excitement, 50% increase in size of testes over unstimulated state and flattening against perineum, signaling impending ejaculation	No change	Decrease to baseline size because of loss of vasocongestion; testicular and scrotal descent within 5 to 30 minutes after orgasm; involution may take several hours if no orgasmic release takes place
Cowper's glands	2 to 3 drops of mucoid fluid that contain viable sperm are secreted during heightened excitement	No change	No change
Other	Breasts: inconsistent nipple erection with heightened excitement before orgasm Myotonia: semispastic contractions of facial, abdominal, and intercostal muscles Tachycardia: up to 175 a minute Blood pressure: rise in systolic 20 to 80 mm; in diastolic 10 to 40 mm Respiration: increased	Loss of voluntary muscular control Rectum: rhythmical contractions of sphincter Heart rate: up to 180 beats a minute Blood pressure: up to 40 to 100 mm systolic; 20 to 50 mm diastolic Respiration: up to 40 respirations a minute	Return to baseline state in 5 to 10 minutes

Courtesy of Virginia A. Sadock, M.D.

Table 21.22
Female Sexual Response Cycle

Organ	Excitement Phase	Orgasmic Phase	Resolution Phase
	Lasts several minutes to several hours; heightened excitement before orgasm, 30 seconds to 3 minutes	3 to 15 seconds	10 to 15 minutes; if no orgasm, ½ to 1 day
Skin	Just before orgasm: sexual flush inconsistently appears; maculopapular rash originates on abdomen and spreads to anterior chest wall, face, and neck; can include shoulders and forearms	Well-developed flush	Flush disappears in reverse order of appearance; inconsistently appearing film of perspiration on soles of feet and palms of hands
Breasts	Nipple erection in two thirds of women, venous congestion and areolar enlargement; size increases to one fourth over normal	Breasts may become tremulous	Return to normal in about ½ hour
Clitoris	Enlargement in diameter of glans and shaft; just before orgasm, shaft retracts into prepuce	No change	Shaft returns to normal position in 5 to 10 seconds; detumescence in 5 to 30 minutes; if no orgasm, detumescence takes several hours
Labia majora	Nullipara: elevate and flatten against perineum Multipara: congestion and edema	No change	Nullipara: increase to normal size in 1 to 2 minutes Multipara: decrease to normal size in 10 to 15 minutes
Labia minora	Size increase two to three times over normal; change to pink, red, deep red before orgasm	Contractions of proximal labia minora	Return to normal within 5 minutes
Vagina	Color change to dark purple; vaginal transudate appears 10 to 30 seconds after arousal; elongation and ballooning of vagina; lower third of vagina constricts before orgasm	3 to 15 contractions of lower third of vagina at intervals of 0.8 second	Ejaculate forms seminal pool in upper two thirds of vagina; congestion disappears in seconds or, if no orgasm, in 20 to 30 minutes
Uterus	Ascends into false pelvis; laborlike contractions begin in heightened excitement just before orgasm	Contractions throughout orgasm	Contractions cease, and uterus descends to normal position
Other	Myotonia A few drops of mucoid secretion from Bartholin's glands during heightened excitement Cervix swells slightly and is passively elevated with uterus	Loss of voluntary muscular control Rectum: rhythmical contractions of sphincter Hyperventilation and tachycardia	Return to baseline status in seconds to minutes Cervix color and size return to normal, and cervix descends into seminal pool

Courtesy of Virginia A. Sadock, M.D.

mental concern with motivations, drives, and personality. It is characterized by sexual fantasies and the desire to have sexual activity. The *excitement phase* is brought on by psychological stimulation (fantasy or the presence of a love object) or physiological stimulation (stroking or kissing) or a combination of the two. It consists of a subjective sense of pleasure. The excitement phase is characterized by penile tumescence leading to erection in the man and by *vaginal lubrication* in the woman. Initial excitement may last several minutes to several hours. With continued stimulation, the woman's vaginal barrel shows a characteristic constriction along the outer third, known as the *orgasmic platform*, and the man's *testes increase in size 50 percent and elevate.*

The *orgasm phase* consists of a peaking of sexual pleasure, with the release of sexual tension and the rhythmic contraction of the perineal muscles and the pelvic reproductive organs. A subjective sense of ejaculatory inevitability triggers the man's orgasm. The forceful emission of semen follows. The male orgasm is also associated with four to five rhythmic spasms of the prostate, seminal vesicles, vas, and urethra. In the woman, orgasm is characterized by 3 to 15 involuntary contractions of the lower third of the vagina and by strong sustained contractions of the uterus, flowing from the fundus downward to the cervix. Blood pressure rises 20 to 40 mm (both systolic and diastolic), and the heart rate increases up to 160 beats a minute. Orgasm lasts 3 to 25 seconds and is associated with a *slight clouding of consciousness.*

The *resolution phase* consists of the disgorgement of blood from the genitalia *(detumescence),* and that detumescence brings the body back to its resting state. If orgasm occurs, resolution is rapid; if it does not occur, resolution may take 2 to 6 hours and may be associated with irritability and discomfort. Tables 21.21 and 21.22 describe the male and female sexual response cycles.

22 Gender Identity Disorders

The fourth edition of *Diagnostic and Statistical Manual of Mental Disorders* (DSM-IV) describes gender identity disorder as having two components: a strong cross-gender identification and a persistent sense of discomfort with or inappropriateness of the person's own sex. That is, a person wants or claims to be of the opposite sex and does not accept the fact of his or her own sex. The person must be experiencing significant stress or have impaired social, occupational, or other functioning.

In discussing gender identity disorders, the terms *sexual orientation, gender role,* and *gender identity* must be well understood. Sexual orientation refers to the object of a person's choice: heterosexual, homosexual, or bisexual. Gender role describes a person's inner sense of masculinity or femininity, which is reflected in his or her behavior. Gender identity is a person's inner conviction of being male or female. A person with a gender identity disorder thus experiences persistent distress that his or her assigned gender is wrong.

Gender identity disorders have been reported to occur more often in males than in females, but it is unclear whether the reports reflect a genuine disparity or a greater sensitivity about the presence of the disorder in boys. Studies on the role of prenatal hormones on feminization or masculinization of the brain organization are controversial, and the causes of gender identity disorder are not yet known. Researchers generally focus on psychosocial and postnatal factors that influence the development of gender identity. These factors can include the quality of the mother–child relationship, the father's role, the effects of child abuse, and a child's reactions to a mother's death, absence, or emotional distance.

Students must be familiar with the DSM-IV criteria for the disorder and must ascertain that patients have an intense, persistent discomfort with their assigned sex. These disorders do not apply to people who behave unconventionally as far as male-female social stereotypes are concerned, but they do refer to those with a deep disgust toward their genitals and secondary sex characteristics and with an all-consuming need to belong to the opposite sex.

Studying Chapter 22 in *Kaplan and Sadock's Synopsis VIII* will prepare students to test their knowledge with the questions and answers that follow.

HELPFUL HINTS

The student should know the gender identity syndromes and terms listed below.

- ▶ adrenogenital syndrome
- ▶ agenesis
- ▶ ambiguous genitals
- ▶ androgen insensitivity syndrome
- ▶ asexual
- ▶ assigned sex
- ▶ Barr chromatin body
- ▶ bisexuality
- ▶ buccal smear
- ▶ cross-dressing
- ▶ cross-gender
- ▶ cryptorchid testis
- ▶ dysgenesis
- ▶ gender confusion
- ▶ gender identity
- ▶ gender identity disorder not otherwise specified
- ▶ gender role
- ▶ genotype
- ▶ hermaphroditism
- ▶ heterosexual orientation
- ▶ homosexual orientation
- ▶ intersex conditions
- ▶ Klinefelter's syndrome
- ▶ male habitus
- ▶ phenotype
- ▶ pseudohermaphroditism
- ▶ sex of rearing
- ▶ sex steroids
- ▶ testicular feminization syndrome
- ▶ transsexualism
- ▶ transvestic fetishism
- ▶ Turner's syndrome
- ▶ virilized genitals
- ▶ X-linked

▲ QUESTIONS

DIRECTIONS: For each group of numbered conditions, select the most appropriate of the following lettered responses.

Questions 22.1–22.3

A. Asperger's syndrome
B. DaCosta's syndrome
C. Klinefelter's syndrome
D. Adrenogenital syndrome
E. Androgen insensitivity syndrome

22.1 Congenital virilizing adrenal hyperplasia
22.2 Testicular feminization syndrome
22.3 XXY genotype

DIRECTIONS: Select the most appropriate response to the following questions.

22.4 Which of the following conditions is *not* a gender identity disorder not otherwise specified, as classified in DSM-IV?

A. Gender dysphoria
B. Tourette's syndrome
C. Cross-dressing behavior
D. Castration preoccupation
E. Cross-gender identification

22.5 Which of the following terms best expresses the anatomical characteristics that indicate whether one is male or female?

A. Gender identity
B. Gender role
C. Sex identity
D. Sexual orientation
E. Transsexual

DIRECTIONS: Each of these incomplete statements is followed by five suggested completions. Select the *one* that is *best* in each case.

22.6 Persons with gender identity disorder

A. usually try to maintain the gender role assigned by biological sex
B. are usually adults
C. usually assert that they will grow up to be members of the opposite sex
D. usually desire sex-change operations
E. usually achieve sexual excitement when cross-dressing

22.7 A boy with gender identity disorder

A. usually begins to display signs of the disorder after age 9
B. experiences sexual excitement when he cross-dresses
C. has boys as his preferred playmates
D. is treated with testosterone
E. may say that his penis or testes are disgusting

22.8 Girls with gender identity disorder in childhood

A. regularly have male companions
B. may refuse to urinate in a sitting position
C. may assert that they have or will grow a penis
D. give up masculine behavior by adolescence
E. are characterized by all the above

22.9 Which of the following statements does *not* apply to the treatment of gender identity disorder?

A. Adult patients generally enter psychotherapy to learn how to deal with their disorder, not to alter it.
B. Before sex-reassignment surgery, patients must go through a trial of cross-gender living for at least 3 months.
C. A one-to-one play relationship is used with boys in which adults role-model masculine behavior.
D. Hormonal therapy is not required as a preceding event in sex-reassignment surgery.
E. During hormonal treatments, both males and females need to be watched for hepatic dysfunction and thromboembolic phenomena.

DIRECTIONS: Each group of questions below consists of lettered headings followed by a list of numbered statements or descriptions. For each numbered statement or description, select the *one* lettered heading that is most closely associated with it. Each heading can be used once, more than once, or not at all.

Questions 22.10–22.13

A. Sexual identity
B. Sexual orientation
C. Gender identity
D. Gender role

22.10 Anatomical and physiological characteristics that indicate whether one is male or female
22.11 Reflects the inner sense of oneself as being male or female
22.12 The image of maleness versus femaleness that is communicated to others
22.13 A person's erotic-response tendency toward men or women or both

Questions 22.14–22.17

A 25-year-old patient called Charles requested a sex-change operation. Charles had for 3 years lived socially and been employed as a man. For the past 2 years, Charles had been the housemate, economic provider, and husband-equivalent of a bisexual woman who had fled from a bad marriage. Her two young children regarded Charles as their stepfather, and they had a strong affectionate bond.

In social appearance the patient passed as a not very virile man whose sexual development in puberty could be conjectured to have been delayed or hormonally deficient. Charles's voice was pitched low but was not baritone. Charles wore bulky clothing to camouflage tightly bound, flattened breasts. A strap-on penis produced a masculine-looking bulge in the pants; it was so constructed that in case of social necessity, it could be used as a urinary conduit in the standing position. Without success the patient had tried to obtain a mastectomy so that in summer only a T-shirt could be worn while working outdoors as a heavy construction machine operator. Charles had also been unsuccessful in trying to get a prescription for testosterone to produce male secondary sex characteristics and to suppress menses. The patient wanted a hysterectomy and an oophorectomy and looked forward to obtaining a successful phalloplasty.

The patient's history was straightforward in its account of progressive recognition in adolescence of being able to fall in love only with a woman, following a tomboyish childhood that had finally consolidated into the transsexual role and identity.

A physical examination revealed normal female anatomy, which the patient found personally repulsive, incongruous, and a source of continual distress. The endocrine laboratory results were within normal limits for a woman.

A. Gender identity
B. Gender role
C. Sexual identity
D. Sexual orientation

22.14 Charles recognized in adolescence that she could fall in love only with a woman.

22.15 Charles was regarded by the two young children of her housemate as their stepfather.

22.16 The physical examination revealed normal female anatomy, and the endocrine laboratory results were within normal limits for a woman.

22.17 In a subsequent interview, Charles stated that she viewed herself as a man.

Questions 22.18–22.22

A. Klinefelter's syndrome
B. Turner's syndrome
C. Congenital virilizing adrenal hyperplasia
D. True hermaphroditism
E. Androgen insensitivity syndrome

22.18 A 17-year-old girl presented to a clinic with primary amenorrhea and no development of secondary sex characteristics. She was short in stature and had a webbed neck.

22.19 A baby was born with ambiguous external genitalia. Further evaluation revealed that both ovaries and testes were present.

22.20 A baby was born with ambiguous external genitalia. Further evaluation revealed that ovaries, a vagina, and a uterus were normal and intact. No testes were found.

22.21 A buccal smear from a phenotypically female patient revealed that the patient was XY. A further workup revealed undescended testes.

22.22 A tall, thin man who presented for infertility problems was found to be XXY.

ANSWERS

Gender Identity Disorders

22.1 The answer is D (*Synopsis VIII,* page 714).
Congenital virilizing adrenal hyperplasia, also known as *adrenogenital syndrome,* results from an excess amount of androgen acting on the fetus. In females, the condition can cause androgenization of the external genitals ranging from clitoral enlargement to a normal-looking scrotal sac, testes, and penis; a vagina and a uterus may be hidden behind the external genitalia. If the genitals look male, the infant may be reared as a boy, who will have a sense of maleness. A hermaphroditic identity can result when parents are uncertain about the sex. Infants raised as girls have a heterosexual orientation but display a more intense tomboy quality than that of a control group. Thus the gender identity reflects rearing practices, but androgens may help determine behavior.

22.2 The answer is E (*Synopsis VIII,* pages 714–715).
Testicular feminization syndrome, also known as *androgen insensitivity syndrome,* is a congenital X-linked recessive trait that arises from the inability of target tissues to respond to androgens. Because the tissues remain in their female resting state, the central nervous system is not organized as masculine. At birth such infants appear female but later are found to have cryptorchid testes, which produce the testosterone to which the tissues do not respond, and minimal or absent internal sexual organs. At puberty, the secondary sex characteristics are female, and the patients are feminine and feel themselves to be female.

22.3 The answer is C (*Synopsis VIII,* page 714).
Persons with *Klinefelter's syndrome* usually have an *XXY genotype;* the habitus is male, under the influence of the Y chromosome, but the effect is weakened by the second X chromosome. Such persons are born with a penis and small, infertile testes; in adolescence they may develop gynecomastia and other feminine-appearing contours. Sex assignment and rearing should lead to a clear sense of maleness, but many of those with Klinefelter's syndrome have gender disturbances ranging from transsexualism to an intermittent desire to wear women's clothes. Because of lessened androgen production, patients' central nervous system organization might not have been completed, and many such patients have varying psychopathology.

Asperger's disorder is characterized by abnormalities of social interaction typical of autism along with a stereotyped, restricted repertoire of interests and activities. Some cases may be mild varieties of autism. Unlike those with autism, patients with Asperger's disorder show little or no delay in language or cognitive development; they may, however, be clumsy in their movements. The condition occurs in a ratio of about 8 boys to 1 girl. The abnormalities, which usually last into adulthood, seem little affected by environmental factors.

DaCosta's syndrome is a somatoform autonomic dysfunction in which patients seem to have a physical disorder of the heart or cardiovascular system, which is largely under autonomic control. Neither of the two types of symptoms concerns a physical disorder. The first type is complaints based on objective signs of autonomic arousal such as palpitations. The second is subjective and nonspecific and may consist of fleeting aches and other sensations. The combination of autonomic involvement, additional nonspecific subjective complaints, and persistent referral to the heart or cardiovascular system as the cause define the typical clinical picture.

DaCosta's syndrome is not included in DSM-IV. The concept of irritable heart syndrome was described in Civil War soldiers by Jacob Mendes DaCosta, and the syndrome included many psychic and somatic symptoms now assigned to panic disorder. DaCosta's syndrome is also called psychogenic cardiac nondisease, a disorder in which patients complain of symptoms of heart disease without any physical evidence. There are many other names for it, including neurocirculatory asthenia, effort syndrome, cardiac neurosis, and hyperkinetic heart syndrome.

22.4 The answer is B (*Synopsis VIII,* pages 714–716).
Tourette's syndrome is a tic disorder unrelated to gender identity disorders. The remaining responses refer to gender identity disorders in general as well as to gender identity disorder not otherwise specified.

Gender dysphoria, a general symptom of gender identity disorders, describes a person's discomfort with or distaste for his or her own sex and the desire to belong to the opposite sex. *Cross-dressing behavior* is also a symptom of gender identity disorder not otherwise specified; it occurs transiently and in association with stressful situations. *Castration preoccupation* without a desire to acquire the sex characteristics of the other sex occurs in gender identity disorder not otherwise specified, and *cross-gender identification* refers to the tendency in all gender identity disorders for a person to want to be or to believe that he or she is of the opposite sex.

22.5 The answer is C (*Synopsis VIII,* page 711).
Sexual identity is the best term used to express the anatomical and physiological characteristics that indicate whether one is male or female, for example, a penis or vagina. *Gender identity* is a psychological state that reflects the inner sense of oneself as being male or female. *Gender role* is the external behavioral pattern that reflects the person's inner sense of gender identity. *Sexual orientation* is the person's erotic-response tendency, for example homosexual, heterosexual, bisexual; it takes into account one's object choice (men or women) and fantasy life. *Transsexuals* are persistently preoccupied with getting rid of primary and secondary sex characteristics and with acquiring the sex characteristics of the other sex, and wish to dress and live as a member of the other sex.

22.6 The answer is C (*Synopsis VIII,* page 712).
Persons with gender identity disorder *usually assert that they will grow up to be members of the opposite sex.* The essential feature of gender identity disorder is a persistent and intense distress about their assigned sex and the desire to be the other sex or an insistence that they are the other sex. Therefore, they *do not usually try to maintain the gender role assigned by*

biological sex. The patients may be *adults* or children. Table 22.1 lists the diagnostic criteria for gender identity disorder.

The desire for sex-reassignment surgery occurs in fewer than 10 percent of gender identity disorder patients. Therefore, they *do not usually desire sex-change operations.* Persons who *achieve sexual excitement when cross-dressing* are given the diagnosis of transvestic fetishism, not gender identity disorder. The cross-dressing in gender identity disorder does not usually cause sexual excitement.

22.7 The answer is E (*Synopsis VIII,* pages 712–713).
A boy with gender identity disorder *may say that his penis or testes are disgusting* and that he would be better off without them. Persons with this disorder *usually begin to display signs of the disorder before age 4,* although it may present at any age. Cross-dressing may be part of the disorder, but boys *do not experience sexual excitement when they cross-dress.* A boy with a gender identity disorder is usually preoccupied with female stereotypical activities and usually *has girls as his preferred playmates, not boys.* Gender identity disorder *is not treated with testosterone.*

22.8 The answer is E (all) (*Synopsis VIII,* page 712).
Girls with gender identity disorder in childhood *regularly have male companions* and an avid interest in sports and rough-and-tumble play; they show no interest in dolls and playing house. In a few cases a girl with this disorder *may refuse to urinate in a sitting position, may assert that she has or will grow a penis,* does not want to grow breasts or menstruate, and asserts that she will grow up to become a man. Most girls *give up masculine behavior by adolescence.*

22.9 The answer is D (*Synopsis VIII,* pages 718–719).
Hormone treatment is required and must be received by patients for about a year prior to sex-reassignment surgery, with estradiol and progesterone in male-to-female changes and testosterone in female-to-male changes. Many transsexuals like the changes in their bodies that occur as a result of that treatment, and some stop at that point. Another requirement before sex reassignment surgery is that patients *must go through a trial of cross-gender living for at least 3 months* and sometimes up to one year. *Adult patients* generally do *enter psychotherapy to learn how to deal with their disorder,* not to alter it. In boys with gender identity disorder, a *one-to-one play relationship is used,* in which *adults or peers role-model masculine behavior. During hormonal treatments,* both males and females need to be watched for *hepatic dysfunction and thromboembolic phenomena.*

Table 22.1
DSM-IV Diagnostic Criteria for Gender Identity Disorder

A. A strong and persistent cross-gender identification (not merely a desire for any perceived cultural advantages of being the other sex).
In children, the disturbance is manifested by four (or more) of the following:
(1) repeatedly stated desire to be, or insistence that he or she is, the other sex
(2) in boys, preference for cross-dressing or simulating female attire; in girls, insistence on wearing only stereotypical masculine clothing
(3) strong and persistent preferences for cross-sex roles in make-believe play or persistent fantasies of being the other sex
(4) intense desire to participate in the stereotypical games and pastimes of the other sex
(5) strong preference for playmates of the other sex

In adolescents and adults, the disturbance is manifested by symptoms such as a stated desire to be the other sex, frequent passing as the other sex, desire to live or be treated as the other sex, or the conviction that one has the typical feelings and reactions of the other sex.

B. Persistent discomfort with his or her sex or sense of inappropriateness in the gender role of that sex.
In children, the disturbance is manifested by any of the following: in boys, assertion that his penis or testes are disgusting or will disappear or assertion that it would be better not to have a penis, or aversion toward rough-and-tumble play and rejection of male stereotypical toys, games, and activities; in girls, rejection of urinating in a sitting position, assertion that she has or will grow a penis, or assertion that she does not want to grow breasts or menstruate, or marked aversion toward normative feminine clothing.
In adolescents and adults, the disturbance is manifested by symptoms such as preoccupation with getting rid of one's primary and secondary sex characteristics (eg, request for hormones, surgery, or other procedures to physically alter sexual characteristics to simulate the other sex) or belief that one was born the wrong sex.

C. The disturbance is not concurrent with a physical intersex condition.

D. The disturbance causes clinically significant distress or impairment in social, occupational, or other important areas of functioning.

Code based on current age:
Gender identity disorder in childhood
Gender identity disorder in adolescents or adults

Specify if (for sexually mature individuals):
Sexually attracted to males
Sexually attracted to females
Sexually attracted to both
Sexually attracted to neither

Reprinted with permission from American Psychiatric Association: *Diagnostic and Statistical Manual of Mental Disorders,* ed 4. Copyright, American Psychiatric Association, Washington, 1994.

Answers 22.10–22.13

22.10 The answer is A (*Synopsis VIII,* page 711).

22.11 The answer is C (*Synopsis VIII,* pages 711–712).

22.12 The answer is D (*Synopsis VIII,* page 711).

22.13 The answer is B (*Synopsis VIII,* page 714).
Sexual identity (also known as biological sex), is strictly limited to the *anatomical and physiological characteristics that indicate whether one is male or female.*

Sexual orientation is a *person's erotic-response tendency toward men or women or both.* Sexual orientation takes into account one's object choice (man or woman) and one's fantasy life—for example, erotic fantasies about men or women or both.

Gender identity is a psychological state that *reflects the inner sense of oneself as being male or female.* Gender identity is based on culturally determined sets of attitudes, behavior patterns, and other attributes usually associated with masculinity or femininity. The person with a healthy gender identity is able to say with certainty, "I am male" or "I am female."

Gender role is the external behavioral pattern that reflects the person's inner sense of gender identity. It is a public declaration of gender; it is *the image of maleness versus femaleness that is communicated to others.*

Answers 22.14–22.17

22.14 The answer is D (*Synopsis VIII,* page 714).

22.15 The answer is B (*Synopsis VIII,* page 711).

22.16 The answer is C (*Synopsis VIII,* page 711).

22.17 The answer is A (*Synopsis VIII,* pages 711– 712).
When *Charles stated that she viewed herself as a man,* that was a statement of her *gender identity. Since Charles was regarded by the two young children of her housemate as their stepfather,* that revealed her masculine *gender role.* Charles's *sexual identity* was confirmed when *the physical examination revealed normal female anatomy, and the endocrine laboratory results were within normal limits for a woman.* Charles's expressed *sexual orientation* was toward the same sex, as was shown when she stated that she *recognized in adolescence that she could fall in love only with a woman.*

Answers 22.18–22.22

22.18 The answer is B (*Synopsis VIII,* page 714).

22.19 The answer is D (*Synopsis VIII,* page 717).

22.20 The answer is C (*Synopsis VIII,* page 714).

22.21 The answer is E (*Synopsis VIII,* pages 714, 716).

22.22 The answer is A (*Synopsis VIII,* page 714).
In *Turner's syndrome,* one sex chromosome is missing (XO). The result is an absence (agenesis) or minimal development (dysgenesis) of the gonads; no significant sex hormones, male or female, are produced in fetal life or postnatally. The sexual tissues remain in a female resting state. Because the second X chromosome, which seems to be responsible for full femaleness, is missing, the girls have an incomplete sexual anatomy and, lacking adequate estrogens, have *amenorrhea* and *develop no secondary sex characteristics* without treatment. They often have other stigmata, such as *webbed neck,* low posterior hairline margin, *short stature,* and cubitus valgus. The infant is born with normal-appearing female external genitals and so is unequivocally assigned to the female sex and is so reared. All the children develop as unremarkably feminine, heterosexually oriented girls.

True hermaphroditism is characterized by the presence of *both ovaries and testes* in the same person. The *genitals' appearance at birth* determines the sex assignment, and the core gender identity is male, female, or hermaphroditic, depending on the family's conviction about the child's sex. Usually, a panel of experts determine the sex of rearing; they base their decision on buccal smears, chromosome studies, and parental wishes.

Congenital virilizing adrenal hyperplasia results from an excess of androgen acting on the fetus. When the condition occurs in girls, excessive fetal androgens from the adrenal gland cause *ambiguous external genitals,* ranging from mild clitoral enlargement to external genitals that look like a normal scrotal sac, testes, and a penis; but they also have *ovaries, a vagina, and a uterus.*

Androgen insensitivity syndrome, a congenital X-linked recessive trait disorder, results from an inability of the target tissues to respond to androgens. Unable to respond, the fetal tissues remain in their female resting state, and the central nervous system is not organized as masculine. The infant at birth appears to be female, although she is later found to have *undescended testes,* which produce the testosterone to which the tissues do not respond, and minimal or absent internal sexual organs. Secondary sex characteristics at puberty are female because of the small but sufficient amounts of estrogens typically produced by the testes. The patients invariably sense themselves to be female and are feminine. They are clinically considered to be female. Androgen insensitivity syndrome is diagnosed as a gender identity disorder not otherwise specified (Table 22.2).

In *Klinefelter's syndrome* the person (usually *XXY*) has a male habitus, under the influence of the Y chromosome, but the effect is weakened by the second X chromosome. Although the patient is born with a penis and testes, the testes are small and infertile, and the penis may also be small. Beginning in adolescence, some patients develop gynecomastia and other feminine-appearing contours. Their sexual desire is usually weak. Sex assignment and rearing should lead to a clear sense of maleness, but the patients often have gender disturbances, ranging from transsexualism to an intermittent desire to put on women's clothes. As a result of lessened androgen production, the fetal hypogonadal state in some patients seems to have interfered with the completion of the central nervous system organization that should underlie masculine behavior. In fact, patients may have any of a wide variety of psychopathology, ranging from emotional instability to mental retardation.

Table 22.2
DSM-IV Diagnostic Criteria for Gender Identity Disorder Not Otherwise Specified

This category is included for coding disorders in gender identity that are not classifiable as a specific gender identity disorder. Examples include

1. Intersex conditions (eg, androgen insensitivity syndrome or congenital adrenal hyperplasia) and gender dysphoria
2. Transient, stress-related cross-dressing behavior
3. Persistent preoccupation with castration or penectomy without a desire to acquire the sex characteristics of the other sex

Reprinted with permission from American Psychiatric Association: *Diagnostic and Statistical Manual of Mental Disorders,* ed 4. Copyright, American Psychiatric Association, Washington, 1994.

23 

Eating Disorders

In the fourth edition of *Diagnostic and Statistical Manual of Mental Disorders* (DSM-IV), eating disorders are defined as severe disturbances in eating behavior, including anorexia nervosa and bulimia nervosa. In anorexia nervosa, a person refuses to maintain a minimally normal body weight, fears gaining weight, and has a disturbed perception of his or her body shape or size. In bulimia nervosa, a person engages in binge eating and inappropriate compensatory methods to prevent weight gain.

These disorders usually occur in young women in midteenage years; they are most common in highly developed countries. Bulimia nervosa is more frequently found than anorexia nervosa. Researchers have investigated social, psychological, and biological factors as causes of eating disorders. Patients tend to be high achievers or perfectionists, who struggle with internal and external expectations and with issues of autonomy and control. Both disorders tend to occur in families with a history of depression. Serotonin and norepinephrine transmitters have been implicated in the disorders, as have endogenous opiates and endorphins.

Although treatments for the two disorders differ somewhat, there is usually a combination of individual, group, and family therapy and pharmacotherapy. Patients may be hospitalized if their health has been severely compromised; eating disorders, if pursued to an extreme, can be fatal.

Students should study Chapter 23 of *Kaplan and Sadock's Synopsis VIII.* They can then test their knowledge by studying the questions and answers that follow.

HELPFUL HINTS

The student should know and be able to define these terms.

- ACTH
- amenorrhea
- anorexia nervosa
- aversive conditioning
- binge eating
- borderline personality disorder
- bulimia nervosa
- cyproheptadine (Periactin)
- denial
- eating disorder not otherwise specified
- ECT
- edema
- fluoxetine
- geophagia
- hyperphagia
- hypersexuality
- hypersomnia
- hypokalemic alkalosis
- hypothermia
- imipramine (Tofranil)
- Kleine-Levin syndrome
- Klüver-Bucy–like syndrome
- lanugo
- LH
- MHPG
- obsessive-compulsive disorder
- postbinge anguish
- pyloric stenosis
- self-stimulation
- ST segment depression
- T waves

▲ QUESTIONS

DIRECTIONS: Select the most appropriate lettered response for each of the following numbered questions or statements.

23.1 According to DSM-IV, patients with anorexia nervosa develop signs and symptoms usually attributable to starvation. These signs and symptoms include all of the following *except*

A. lanugo
B. seizures
C. amenorrhea
D. hypotension
E. bradycardia

23.2 According to DSM-IV, which of the following laboratory findings is *not* associated with anorexia nervosa?

A. Arrhythmias
B. Thrombocytopenia
C. Metabolic alkalosis
D. Elevated liver function tests
E. Increased ventricular–brain ratio

23.3 Which of the following features can be associated with bulimia nervosa?

A. Undeveloped breasts
B. Abnormal insulin secretion
C. Widespread endocrine disorder
D. A previous episode of anorexia nervosa
E. Body weight at least 15 percent below normal

23.4 In the classification schema, which of the following should be coded with overeating associated with other psychological disturbances?

A. Obesity-caused dieting anxiety
B. Obesity reactive to bereavement
C. Obesity-caused dieting depression
D. Obesity caused by long-term medication
E. Obesity as a cause of psychological disturbance

23.5 The cachetic patient shown in Figure 23.1 has a history of depressed feeling, obsessive ruminations, and intense fear of becoming overweight. The patient is most likely suffering from

A. schizophrenia
B. bulimia nervosa
C. major depressive disorder
D. anorexia nervosa
E. somatization disorder

DIRECTIONS: Each of the incomplete statements below is followed by five suggested completions. Select the *one* that is *best* in each case.

23.6 Studies of anorexia nervosa have found that

A. the most common age of onset is the late 20s
B. good sexual adjustment is frequently described
C. most patients are interested in psychiatric treatment
D. sisters of anorexia nervosa patients are not likely to be afflicted
E. compulsive stealing, usually of candy and laxatives, is common

23.7 A person with anorexia nervosa

A. disproportionately consumes foods high in carbohydrates
B. usually retains her menstrual period
C. may not also have somatization disorder
D. may have either the restricting type or the binge eating–purging type
E. rarely has a family history of other mental disorders

23.8 Patients with bulimia nervosa

A. experience a postbinge euphoria
B. are usually underweight
C. usually do not induce vomiting
D. feel a lack of control of their eating during binge episodes
E. usually describe their parents as loving and accepting

23.9 Anorexia nervosa occurs

A. 10 to 20 times more often in females than in males
B. 5 times more often in males than in females
C. in 4 percent of adolescent girls
D. predominantly in the upper economic classes
E. with greatest frequency among young women in professions associated with food preparation

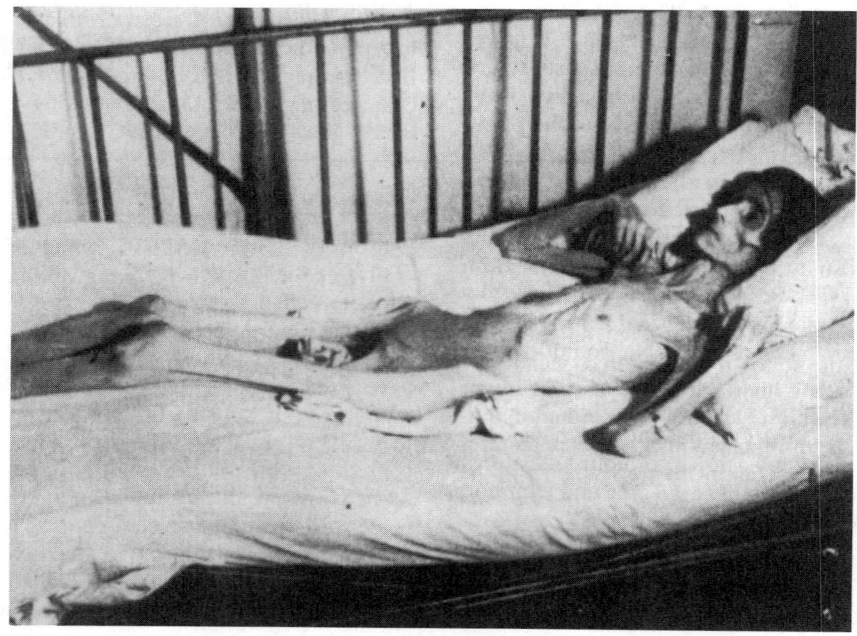

FIGURE 23.1
Courtesy of Katherine Halmi, M.D.

23.10 The patient in Figure 23.1 has rejected all food and has lost more than 30 percent of her original body weight. No physical illness has been found to account for the weight loss. One may also expect to find

A. an intense fear of becoming fat
B. denial of emaciation by the patient
C. feelings of hunger
D. a warm, seductive, and passive father
E. all of the above

23.11 Anorexia nervosa has a mortality rate of up to

A. 1 percent
B. 18 percent
C. 30 percent
D. 42 percent
E. 50 percent

23.12 Anorexia nervosa is characterized by all the following *except*

A. self-imposed dietary limitations
B. weight loss
C. normal menses
D. intense fear of gaining weight
E. disturbed body image

23.13 Characteristics of binge-eating disorder include

A. recurrent episodes of binge eating
B. inappropriate compensatory behaviors characteristic of bulimia nervosa
C. binge eating that occurs at least twice a week for less than 6 months
D. fixation on body weight
E. all of the above

23.14 All of the following treatments have shown some success in the treatment of anorexia nervosa *except*

A. cyproheptadine
B. amitriptyline
C. chlorpromazine
D. imipramine
E. electroconvulsive therapy (ECT)

Questions 23.15–23.16

Mary was a gaunt 15-year-old high school student evaluated at the insistence of her parents, who were concerned about her weight loss. She was 5 feet 3 inches tall and had reached her greatest weight, 100 pounds, a year earlier. Shortly thereafter she decided to lose weight to be more attractive. She felt chubby and thought she would be more appealing if she were thinner. She first eliminated all carbohydrate-rich foods and gradually increased her dieting until she was eating only a few vegetables a day. She also started a vigorous exercise program. Within 6 months, she was down to 80 pounds. She then became preoccupied with food and started to collect recipes from magazines to prepare gourmet meals for her family. She had difficulty in sleeping and was irritable and depressed, having several crying spells every day. Her menses started the previous year, but she had had only a few normal periods.

Mary had always had high grades in school and had spent a great deal of time studying. She had never been active socially and had never dated. She was conscientious and perfectionistic in everything she undertook. She had never been away from home as long as a week. Her father was a business manager. Her mother was a housewife who for the past 2 years had had a problem with hypoglycemia and had been on a low-carbohydrate diet.

During the interview, Mary said she felt fat, even though she weighed only 80 pounds, and she described a fear of losing control and eating so much food that she would become obese. She did not feel she was ill and thought that hospitalization was unnecessary.

23.15 The diagnosis of anorexia nervosa can be made on the basis of Mary's

A. 20-pound weight loss
B. feeling fat at a weight of 80 pounds and a height of 5 feet 3 inches
C. having had only a few normal periods
D. fear of becoming obese
E. all of the above

23.16 Features associated with anorexia nervosa include

A. normal hair structure and distribution
B. the fact that 7 to 9 percent of those affected are male
C. onset between the ages of 10 and 30
D. mortality rates of 20 to 25 percent
E. all of the above

DIRECTIONS: The questions below consist of lettered headings followed by a list of numbered phrases. For each numbered phrase, select

A. if the item is associated with *A only*
B. if the item is associated with *B only*
C. if the item is associated with *both A and B*
D. if the item is associated with *neither A nor B*

Questions 23.17–23.24

A. Anorexia nervosa
B. Bulimia nervosa
C. Both
D. Neither

23.17 Must have missed at least three consecutive menstrual periods
23.18 May engage in binge eating and purging behaviors
23.19 Preoccupied with weight, food, and body shape
23.20 Continued sexual activity in most patients
23.21 Denies symptoms and resists treatment
23.22 Body weight of less than 85 percent of the patient's normal weight
23.23 Tricyclic drugs successfully used
23.24 Usually experiences loss of appetite

ANSWERS

Eating Disorders

23.1 The answer is B (*Synopsis VIII,* pages 722, 724).
Of the signs and symptoms of starvation found in patients with anorexia nervosa, *seizures* is not one, but *lanugo, amenorrhea, hypotension,* and *bradycardia* are. Lanugo is a fine body hair that sometimes develops on the trunks of patients with this disorder. Amenorrhea, hypotension, and bradycardia are other common symptoms of anorexia nervosa, as are emaciation, constipation, abdominal pain, yellowing of the skin, and hypertrophy of the salivary glands.

23.2 The answer is C (*Synopsis VIII,* pages 720–727).
According to DSM-IV, *metabolic alkalosis* (elevated serum bicarbonate) is a symptom of bulimia nervosa caused by the loss of stomach acid through vomiting. *Arrhythmias,* although rare, and sinus bradycardia are findings discovered on electrocardiography. *Thrombocytopenia* is occasionally seen in blood work of patients with anorexia. *Elevated liver function tests* are common results, and patients often show an *increased ventricular–brain ratio* in brain imaging.

23.3 The answer is D (*Synopsis VIII,* page 727).
A previous episode of anorexia nervosa is often a symptom of bulimia nervosa. This episode may have been fully or only moderately expressed.

Undeveloped breasts, abnormal insulin secretion, widespread endocrine disorder, and *body weight at least 15 percent below normal* are all associated with anorexia nervosa, not bulimia nervosa.

23.4 The answer is B (*Synopsis VIII,* page 734).
Obesity reactive to bereavement is classified as overeating associated with other psychological disturbances, a subtype of eating disorders. Such obesity is a result of overeating that is indulged in as a reaction to stress such as an accident, surgical operation, or the death of a loved one. This reactive obesity is especially common in those inclined to gain weight.

Obesity-caused dieting anxiety or *obesity-caused dieting depression* should be coded first according to the symptoms of the appropriate mental disorder, then as an other eating disorder, and finally as a specific type of obesity, but not as overeating associated with other psychological disturbances.

Obesity caused by long-term medication should be coded as a drug-induced obesity, with an additional code to identify the drug. Such obesity can arise from long-term treatment with neuroleptic antidepressants, among other medications.

Obesity as a cause of psychological disturbance should be coded as other mood disorders, mixed anxiety and depressive disorder, or neurotic disorder, unspecified, in addition to a code specifying the type of obesity. Such obesity can make people sensitive about their appearance and can cause them to lack confidence in personal relationships.

23.5 The answer is D (*Synopsis VIII,* pages 720–727).
The patient is suffering from *anorexia nervosa.* As described in the DSM-IV, the diagnostic criteria for anorexia nervosa include a refusal to maintain body weight at or above a minimally normal weight for age and height (for example, weight loss leading to maintenance of body weight less than 85% of that expected), and an intense fear of gaining weight or becoming fat, even though underweight (see Table 23.1 for complete criteria). The patient's dramatic weight loss and history of intense fear of gaining weight make anorexia nervosa the most likely diagnosis.

Anorexia nervosa must be differentiated from *bulimia nervosa,* a disorder in which episodic binge eating—followed by depressive moods, self-deprecating thoughts, and often self-induced vomiting—occurs while patients maintain their weight in the normal range. Furthermore, in bulimia nervosa, the patient seldom has a 15 percent weight loss.

Although patients with *schizophrenia* may have delusions about food and bizarre eating habits, patients with schizophrenia are rarely preoccupied with a fear of becoming obese and do not have the entire syndrome of anorexia nervosa. Although *depressive disorders* have several features in common with anorexia nervosa, such as depressed feeling, crying spells, and obsessive ruminations, the two disorders are distinguished by several features, including that patients with depression have no intense fear of gaining weight or disturbance of body image.

Weight fluctuations, vomiting, and peculiar food handling may occur in *somatization disorder.* Generally, however, the weight loss in somatization disorder is not as severe as that in

Table 23.1
DSM-IV Diagnostic Criteria for Anorexia Nervosa

A. Refusal to maintain body weight at or above a minimally normal weight for age and height (eg, weight loss leading to maintenance of body weight less than 85% of that expected; or failure to make expected weight gain during period of growth, leading to body weight less than 85% of that expected).
B. Intense fear of gaining weight or becoming fat, even though underweight.
C. Disturbance in the way in which one's body weight or shape is experienced, undue influence of body weight or shape on self-evaluation, or denial of the seriousness of the current low body weight.
D. In postmenarchal females, amenorrhea, ie, the absence of at least three consecutive menstrual cycles. (A woman is considered to have amenorrhea if her periods occur only following hormone, eg, estrogen, administration.)

Specify type:
Restricting type: during the current episode of anorexia nervosa, the person has not regularly engaged in binge-eating or purging behavior (ie, self-induced vomiting or the misuse of laxatives, diuretics, or enemas)
Binge eating–purging type: during the current episode of anorexia nervosa, the person has regularly engaged in binge-eating or purging behavior (ie, self-induced vomiting or the misuse of laxatives, diuretics, or enemas)

anorexia nervosa, nor does the patient with somatization disorder express a morbid fear of becoming overweight, as is common in the anorexia nervosa patient.

23.6 The answer is E (*Synopsis VIII,* pages 721–722). *Compulsive stealing, usually of candy and laxatives, is common.* The *most common age of onset is between the ages of 13 and 20 years.* In few patients does the disorder develop in the late 20s. *Poor sexual adjustment is frequently described* in patients with the disorder. Many adolescent anorexia nervosa patients have delayed psychosocial sexual development, and adults often have a markedly decreased interest in sex. *Most patients are uninterested in psychiatric treatment* and even resistant to it; they are brought to a doctor's office unwillingly by agonizing relatives or friends. The patients rarely accept the recommendation of hospitalization without arguing and criticizing the program being offered. The intense fear of gaining weight undoubtedly contributes to the patients' lack of interest and even resistance to therapy. *Sisters of anorexia nervosa patients are likely to be afflicted,* but that association may reflect social influences more than genetic factors.

23.7 The answer is D (*Synopsis VIII,* pages 720–721). A person with anorexia nervosa *may have either the restricting type or the binge eating–purging type.* Persons with the restricting type limit their food selection, take in as few calories as possible, and commonly have obsessive-compulsive traits with respect to food and other matters. However, they do not regularly engage in binge eating or purging behavior (for example, self-induced vomiting or the misuse of laxatives or diuretics) during the episode of anorexia nervosa. Persons with the binge eating–purging type do regularly engage in binge eating or purging behavior during the episode of anorexia nervosa. Regardless of type, persons with anorexia nervosa *disproportionately decrease their consumption of foods high in carbohydrates* and fats.

For anorexia nervosa to be diagnosed (Table 23.1), a woman who is postmenarchal must have missed at least three consecutive menstrual periods. Thus, a woman with anorexia nervosa *does not retain her menstrual period.*

Weight fluctuations, vomiting, and peculiar food handling may occur in somatization disorder. On rare occasions a patient fulfills the diagnostic criteria for both somatization disorder and anorexia nervosa; in such a case both diagnoses should be made. Therefore, patients with anorexia nervosa *may also have somatization disorder.* A patient with anorexia nervosa *is likely to have a family history of other mental disorders,* such as depressive disorders, alcohol use disorder, and eating disorders.

23.8 The answer is D (*Synopsis VIII,* pages 727–728). Patients with bulimia nervosa (Table 23.2) *feel a lack of control of their eating during binge episodes.* The binge eating is often followed by feelings of guilt, depression, or self-disgust. Bulimia nervosa patients *do not experience a postbinge euphoria.* Unlike anorexia nervosa patients, those with bulimia nervosa *are not usually underweight.* Patients with bulimia nervosa *usually induce vomiting* by sticking a finger down the throat, although some patients are able to vomit at will. Bulimia nervosa patients usually *describe their parents as neglectful and rejecting, not loving and accepting.*

Table 23.2
DSM-IV Diagnostic Criteria for Bulimia Nervosa

A. Recurrent episodes of binge eating. An episode of binge eating is characterized by both of the following:
   (1) eating, in a discrete period of time (eg, within any 2-hour period), an amount of food that is definitely larger than most people would eat during a similar period of time and under similar circumstances
   (2) A sense of lack of control over eating during the episode (eg, a feeling that one cannot stop eating or control what or how much one is eating)
B. Recurrent inappropriate compensatory behavior in order to prevent weight gain, such as self-induced vomiting; misuse of laxatives, diuretics, enemas, or other medications; fasting; or excessive exercise.
C. The binge eating and inappropriate compensatory behaviors both occur, on average, at least twice a week for 3 months.
D. Self-evaluation is unduly influenced by body shape and weight.
E. The disturbance does not occur exclusively during episodes of anorexia nervosa.

Specify type:
Purging type: during the current episode of bulimia nervosa, the person has regularly engaged in self-induced vomiting or the misuse of laxatives, diuretics, or enemas
Nonpurging type: during the current episode of bulimia nervosa, the person has used other inappropriate compensatory behaviors, such as fasting or excessive exercise, but has not regularly engaged in self-induced vomiting or the misuse of laxatives, diuretics, or enemas

23.9 The answer is A (*Synopsis VIII,* page 720). Anorexia nervosa occurs *10 to 20 times more often in females than in males.* Anorexia nervosa is estimated to occur *in about 0.5 percent of adolescent girls.* Although the disorder was initially reported *predominantly in the upper economic classes,* recent epidemiological surveys do not show that distribution. The disorder may be seen *with greatest frequency among young women in professions that require thinness,* such as modeling and ballet, *not in professions associated with food preparation.*

23.10 The answer is E (all) (*Synopsis VIII,* pages 720–727). The patient is suffering from anorexia nervosa, which is characterized by a weight loss leading to the maintenance of body weight less than 85 percent of that expected. Anorexia nervosa patients have *an intense fear of becoming fat,* a disturbance of body image, and amenorrhea. Patients *deny that they are emaciated,* and they *do not lose their feelings of hunger* but steadfastly refuse to eat.

Psychodynamic theories in anorexia nervosa postulate that the patients reject, through starvation, a wish to be pregnant and have fantasies of oral impregnation. Other dynamic formulations have included a dependent relationship with *a warm, seductive, and passive father* and guilt over aggression toward an ambivalently regarded mother.

23.11 The answer is B (*Synopsis VIII,* page 725). Studies have shown that anorexia nervosa has a range of mortality rates from 5 percent to *18 percent.*

23.12 The answer is C (*Synopsis VIII,* pages 720–727).
Anorexia nervosa is characterized in women by *amenorrhea, not normal menses.* It is also characterized by *self-imposed dietary limitations,* behavior directed toward losing weight, peculiar patterns of handling food, *weight loss, intense fear of gaining weight, and disturbance of body image.*

23.13 The answer is A (*Synopsis VIII,* page 727).
Binge-eating disorder (Table 23.3) is characterized by *recurrent episodes of binge eating* in *the absence of the inappropriate compensatory behaviors characteristic of bulimia nervosa.* The binge eating *occurs,* on average, *at least twice a week for at least 6 months.* Patients with eating disorder are *not fixated on body weight.* Binge-eating disorder is an example of eating disorder not otherwise specified (Table 23.4).

23.14 The answer is C (*Synopsis VIII,* page 726)
Studies using *chlorpromazine* (Thorazine), clomipramine (Anafranil) and pimozide (Orap) have not yielded positive responses. *Cyproheptadine* (Periactin), a drug with antihistaminic and antiserotonergic properties has been used in the restricting type of anorexia nervosa. *Amitriptyline* (Elavil) has been reported to have some benefit in patients with anorexia nervosa, as have *imipramine* (Tofranil) and desipramine (Norpramin). There is some evidence that *electroconvulsive therapy* (ECT) is beneficial in certain cases of anorexia nervosa and major depressive disorder.

Table 23.4
DSM-IV Diagnostic Criteria for Eating Disorder Not Otherwise Specified

The eating disorder not otherwise specified category is for disorders of eating that do not meet the criteria for any specific eating disorder. Examples include

1. For females, all of the criteria for anorexia nervosa are met except the individual has regular menses.
2. All of the criteria for anorexia nervosa are met except that despite significant weight loss the individual's current weight is in the normal range.
3. All of the criteria for bulimia nervosa are met except that the binge eating and inappropriate compensatory mechanisms occur at a frequency of less than twice a week or for a duration of less than 3 months.
4. The regular use of inappropriate compensatory behavior by an individual of normal body weight after eating small amounts of food (eg, self-induced vomiting after the consumption of two cookies).
5. Repeatedly chewing and spitting out, but not swallowing, large amounts of food.
6. Binge-eating disorder: recurrent episodes of binge eating in the absence of the regular use of inappropriate compensatory behaviors characteristic of bulimia nervosa.

Table 23.3
DSM-IV Research Criteria for Binge-Eating Disorder

A. Recurrent episodes of binge eating. An episode of binge eating is characterized by both of the following:
   (1) eating, in a discrete period of time (eg, within any 2-hour period) an amount of food that is definitely larger than most people would eat in a similar period of time under similar circumstances
   (2) a sense of lack of control over eating during the episode (eg, a feeling that one cannot stop eating or control what or how much one is eating)
B. The binge-eating episodes are associated with three (or more) of the following:
   (1) eating much more rapidly than normal
   (2) eating until feeling uncomfortably full
   (3) eating large amounts of food when not feeling physically hungry
   (4) eating alone because of being embarrassed by how much one is eating
   (5) feeling disgusted with oneself, depressed, or feeling very guilty after overeating
C. Marked distress regarding binge eating is present.
D. The binge eating occurs, on average, at least 2 days a week for 6 months.
   Note: The method of determining frequency differs from that used for bulimia nervosa; future research should address whether the preferred method of setting a frequency threshold is counting the number of days on which binges occur or counting the number of episodes of binge eating.
E. The binge eating is not associated with the regular use of inappropriate compensatory behaviors (eg, purging, fasting, excessive exercise) and does not occur exclusively during the course of anorexia nervosa or bulimia nervosa.

23.15 The answer is E (all) (*Synopsis VIII,* pages 720–727).
The diagnosis of anorexia nervosa can be made on the basis of *Mary's 20-pound weight loss, her feeling fat at a weight of 80 pounds and a height of 5 feet 3 inches, her having had only a few normal periods,* and *her fear of becoming obese.*

23.16 The answer is C (*Synopsis VIII,* page 721).
Features associated with anorexia nervosa include *onset between the ages of 10 and 30, lanugo* (neonatal-like body hair), *mortality rates of 5 to 18 percent,* and *the fact that 4 to 6 percent of those affected are male.*

23.17–23.24

23.17 The answer is A (*Synopsis VIII,* page 720).

23.18 The answer is C (*Synopsis VIII,* pages 720, 727).

23.19 The answer is C (*Synopsis VIII,* pages 720, 727).

23.20 The answer is B (*Synopsis VIII,* page 728).

23.21 The answer is A (*Synopsis VIII,* page 723).

23.22 The answer is A (*Synopsis VIII,* page 720).

23.23 The answer is C (*Synopsis VIII,* pages 726, 730).

23.24 The answer is D (*Synopsis VIII,* pages 720–727, 727–731).
To meet the diagnostic criteria for *anorexia nervosa,* postmenarchal females *must have missed at least three consecutive menstrual periods.* Patients with anorexia nervosa are often secretive, *deny their symptoms, and resist treatment.* The di-

agnostic criteria include a persistent refusal to maintain body weight at or above a minimum expected weight (for example, loss of weight leading to a *body weight of less than 85 percent of the patient's expected weight*) or a failure to gain the expected weight during a period of growth, leading to a body weight less than 85 percent of the expected weight.

Most bulimia nervosa patients remain sexually active, in contrast to anorexia nervosa patients, who are not interested in sex. Antidepressant medications can reduce binge eating and purging independent of the presence of a mood disorder. Thus, for particularly difficult binge eating–purging cycles that are not responsive to psychotherapy alone, *tricyclic drugs have been successfully used. Both* bulimia nervosa patients and patients with the binge eating–purging type of anorexia nervosa *may engage in binge eating and purging behaviors. Both* persons with anorexia nervosa and persons with bulimia nervosa are excessively *preoccupied with weight, food, and body shape.*

Neither anorexia nervosa patients nor bulimia nervosa patients *experience loss of appetite.*

24

Normal Sleep and Sleep Disorders

Normal sleep is a recurrent state characterized by quiescence and higher response thresholds to external stimuli than in waking states. Sleep is thought to be crucial for thermoregulation and energy conservation and for maintaining the body's normal functions. Sleep deprivation is known to lead to ego disorganization, hallucinations, and delusions.

People's normal sleep patterns differ: Some people sleep less than 6 hours each night, whereas others require more than 9 hours to function adequately. Physical work and exercise, illness, pregnancy, mental stress, and increased mental activity can all increase a person's need for sleep.

Although people's natural body clocks follow a 25-hour cycle, external factors (the light–dark cycle, daily routines such as work, school, and meal times) shape the 24-hour clock. Biological rhythms also affect sleep: People sleep once or twice during each 24-hour cycle, a pattern that develops during the first 2 years of life. Sleep patterns during the daytime differ from those of the night; the psychological and behavioral effects of sleep differ as well. Even for people who do not work at night, interference with the body's rhythms can produce problems, a fact that is increasingly significant in today's global 24-hour-a-day economy.

As people sleep, their brain waves go through four stages. Stage 1, the lightest stage, is characterized by low-voltage regular activity at 3 to 7 cycles per second as recorded on an electroencephalogram (EEG). After a few seconds or minutes, stage 2 shows a pattern of spindle-shaped tracings at 12 to 14 cycles a second and slow triphasic waves called K complexes. In stage 3, delta waves (high-voltage activity at 0.5 to 2.5 cycles per second) appear and occupy less than 50 percent of the tracing. Delta waves occupy more than 50 percent of the record in stage 4.

Sleep has two physiological states: non–rapid eye movement (NREM) sleep and rapid eye movement (REM) sleep. NREM sleep, during which physiological functions are strongly reduced, is composed of stages 1 through 4. REM sleep, a qualitatively different sleep stage of low-voltage random fast activity with sawtooth waves, is characterized by highly active brain and physiological levels similar to the awake state. About 90 minutes after a person falls asleep, NREM sleep changes to the first REM episode. A shortening of this 90-minute latency is typical of disorders such as depression and narcolepsy. The first REM period is usually the shortest, less than 10 minutes; later periods last 15 to 40 minutes each. Most REM sleep occurs in the last third of the night, whereas most stage 4 sleep occurs in the first third.

Sleep disorders are so common that about a third of all people in the United States experience them at some time during their lives. Insomnia is the most common sleep disorder; others are hypersomnia, parasomnia, and sleep–wake schedule disturbances. Clinicians must be familiar with the complex nature of sleep and must be able to diagnose and treat the causes of the various disorders. Factors associated with increased prevalence of sleep disorders include female sex, mental and medical disorders, substance abuse, and advanced age.

In the fourth edition of *Diagnostic and Statistical Manual of Mental Disorders* (DSM-IV), sleep disorders are organized according to their etiology as primary sleep disorder (dyssomnias and parasomnias), sleep disorder related to another mental disorder, sleep disorder due to a general medical condition, and substance-induced sleep disorder. Primary sleep disorders are thought to arise from abnormalities in sleep–wake generating or timing mechanisms. Dyssomnias are abnormalities in the amount, quality, or timing of sleep, and parasomnias are abnormal or physiological events occurring in connection with sleep, sleep stages, or sleep–wake transition. A sleep disorder related to another mental disorder is often produced by a mood or anxiety disorder, whereas sleep disorder due to a general medical condition is a result of the physiological effects of the medical condition on the sleep–wake system. Finally, a substance-induced sleep disorder arises from use or recent discontinuation of use of a substance, which can include medications.

Students should review Chapter 24 in *Kaplan and Sadock's Synopsis VIII* before challenging their level of knowledge with the questions and answers that follow.

HELPFUL HINTS

The student should know and be able to define each of these terms.

- ▶ advanced sleep phase syndrome
- ▶ alveolar hypoventilation syndrome
- ▶ circadian rhythm sleep disorder
- ▶ delayed sleep phase syndrome
- ▶ dysesthesia
- ▶ dyssomnias
- ▶ EEG
- ▶ familial sleep paralysis
- ▶ hypersomnia
- ▶ idiopathic CNS hypersomnolence
- ▶ insomnia:
  - nonorganic
  - organic
  - persistent
  - primary
  - secondary
  - transient
- ▶ jactatio capitis nocturna
- ▶ K complexes
- ▶ Kleine-Levin syndrome
- ▶ melatonin
- ▶ microsleeps
- ▶ narcolepsy
- ▶ nightmare disorder
- ▶ nightmares
- ▶ normal sleep
- ▶ parasomnias
- ▶ paroxysmal nocturnal hemoglobinuria
- ▶ pavor nocturnus, incubus
- ▶ poikilothermic
- ▶ REM, NREM
- ▶ sleep apnea
- ▶ sleep deprivation, REM-deprived
- ▶ sleep drunkenness
- ▶ sleep paralysis, sleep attacks
- ▶ sleep-related abnormal swallowing syndrome
- ▶ sleep-related asthma
- ▶ sleep-related bruxism
- ▶ sleep-related cardiovascular symptoms
- ▶ sleep-related cluster headaches and chronic paroxysmal hemicrania
- ▶ sleep-related epileptic seizures
- ▶ sleep-related gastroesophageal reflux
- ▶ sleep-related (nocturnal) myoclonus syndrome
- ▶ sleep terror disorder
- ▶ sleepwalking disorder
- ▶ somniloquy
- ▶ somnolence
- ▶ L-tryptophan
- ▶ variable sleepers

▲ QUESTIONS

DIRECTIONS: Each of the questions or incomplete statements below is followed by five suggested responses or completions. Select the *one* that is *best* in each case.

24.1 Which of the following features is *not* typical of REM sleep?

A. Dreams are typically lucid and creative.
B. Polygraph measures show irregular patterns.
C. The resting muscle potential is lower in REM sleep than in a waking state.
D. Near-total paralysis of the postural muscles is present.
E. A condition of temperature regulation similar to that in reptiles occurs.

24.2 Which of the following statements does *not* correctly describe sleep regulation?

A. Melatonin secretion helps regulate the sleep–wake cycle.
B. Destruction of the dorsal raphe nucleus of the brainstem reduces sleep.
C. L-Tryptophan deficiency is associated with less time spent in NREM sleep.
D. REM sleep can be reduced by increased firing of noradrenergic neurons.
E. Disrupted REM sleep patterns in patients with depression show shortened REM latency.

24.3 Which of the following descriptions of insomnia is *incorrect*?

A. Insomnia can precede a psychotic episode.
B. Insomnia can be an outlet for discharging anxiety.
C. Persistent insomnia arises from a two-phase problem.
D. After a person is fired, he or she can experience brief insomnia.
E. Treatment with hypnotic medication should be of brief duration.

24.4 REM sleep with hypnagogic and hypnopompic hallucinations can be a symptom of which of the following disorders?

A. Narcolepsy
B. Primary insomnia
C. Primary hypersomnia
D. Sleep apnea syndrome
E. Circadian rhythm sleep disorder

24.5 Which of the following items characterizes nightmares but not sleep terrors?

A. The person is difficult to awaken.
B. The person may scream and cry out.
C. The person may have limited movement.
D. The phenomenon occurs at a specific time.
E. The person has only little memory of the event.

24.6 The characteristic electroencephalographic (EEG) patterns from a wakeful state to sleep are

A. regular activity, delta waves at 3 to 7 cycles a second, sleep spindles and K complexes
B. regular activity at 3 to 7 cycles a second, delta waves, sleep spindles and K complexes
C. regular activity, sleep spindles and K complexes, delta waves at 3 to 7 cycles a second
D. regular activity, delta waves, sleep spindles and K complexes at 3 to 7 cycles a second
E. regular activity at 3 to 7 cycles a second, sleep spindles and K complexes, delta waves

24.7 During rapid eye movement (REM) sleep

A. the pulse rate is typically 5 to 10 beats below the level of restful waking
B. a poikilothermic condition is present
C. frequent involuntary body movements are seen
D. dreams are typically lucid and purposeful
E. sleepwalking may occur

24.8 In the fourth edition of *Diagnostic and Statistical Manual of Mental Disorders* (DSM-IV) category of dyssomnias

A. psychotherapy has been useful in the treatment of primary insomnia
B. narcolepsy is a psychogenic disturbance
C. nasal continuous positive airway pressure is the treatment of choice for obstructive sleep apnea
D. Kleine-Levin syndrome has insomnia as a major symptom
E. sleep drunkenness results from sleep deprivation

24.9 Sleep apnea is

A. pure obstructive sleep apnea when airflow and respiratory effort cease
B. believed to be a benign condition
C. usually found in men in their early 30s
D. called pickwickian syndrome in obese patients
E. all of the above

24.10 A 40-year-old man who snores loudly while sleeping and at times seems to stop breathing is likely to be suffering from

A. narcolepsy
B. catalepsy
C. sleep apnea
D. Kleine-Levin syndrome
E. primary hypersomnia

24.11 An 11-year-old girl asked her mother to take her to a psychiatrist because she feared she was going crazy. Several times during the past 2 months she had awakened confused about where she was until she realized that she was on the living room couch or in her little sister's bed, even though she went to bed in her own room. When she woke up in her older brother's bedroom, she became concerned and felt guilty about it. Her younger sister said that she had seen the patient walking during the night, looking like "a zombie," that she did not answer when called, and that she had walked at night several times but usually went back to her bed. The patient feared she had amnesia because she had no memory of anything happening during the night.

Which of the following statements about the person's disorder is *false*?

A. Usually the disorder begins between the ages of 4 and 8 and peaks at age 12.
B. Patients often have vivid hallucinatory recollections of an emotionally traumatic event with no memory upon awakening.
C. There is no impairment in consciousness several minutes after awakening.
D. The disorder is more commonly seen in girls than in boys.
E. There is a tendency of the disorder to run in families.

24.12 Which of the following is involved in sleep and waking mechanisms?

A. Serotonin
B. Dopamine
C. Norepinephrine
D. Acetylcholine
E. All of the above

24.13 Hypersomnia related to an Axis I or Axis II disorder may be the result of

A. major depressive disorder
B. amphetamine withdrawal
C. alcohol intoxication
D. jet lag
E. all of the above

24.14 The symptoms of narcolepsy include all of the following *except*

A. catalepsy
B. daytime sleepiness
C. hallucinations
D. sleep paralysis
E. cataplexy

24.15 Hypersomnia is associated with

A. Kleine-Levin syndrome
B. trypanosomiasis
C. depression
D. amphetamine withdrawal
E. all of the above

24.16 All of the following disorders can take place during deep sleep (stages 3 and 4) *except*

A. enuresis
B. somnambulism
C. nightmare disorder
D. somniloquy
E. sleep terror disorder

24.17 Which of the following statements about the sleep stage histograms shown in Figure 24.1 is *true*?

A. *A* is characteristic of obstructive sleep apnea syndrome.
B. Both are normal.
C. *B* is characteristic of major depressive disorder.
D. *A* is characterized by an abnormal latency to REM sleep.
E. Both are within normal limits.

24.18 Figure 24.2 illustrates the stages of a patient's sleep pattern. Which of the following statements regarding this sleep pattern is *true*?

A. The sleep pattern is abnormal because of the shortened latency of REM sleep.
B. The sleep pattern represents human sleep between the ages of newborn and young adult.
C. The sleep pattern is consistent with that found in a patient with depression.
D. The sleep pattern is consistent with that found in a patient with narcolepsy.
E. The sleep pattern is normal.

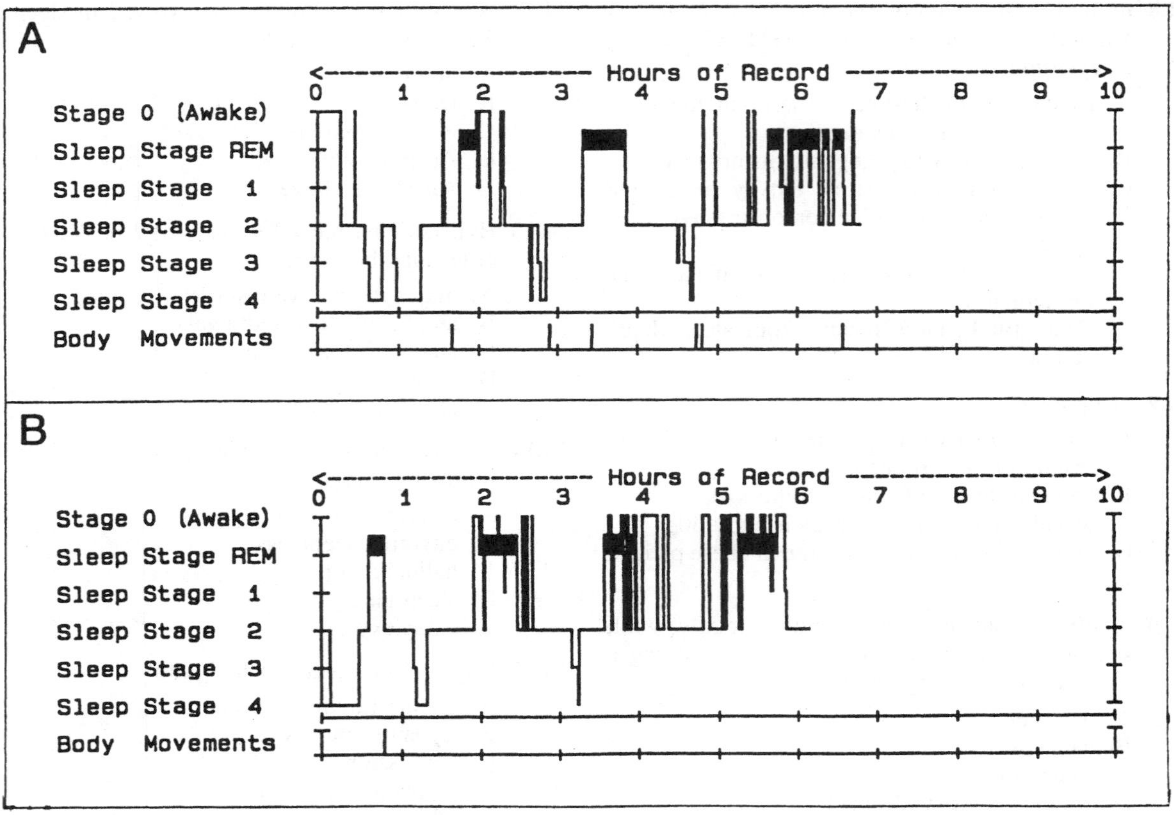

A
<------------------ Hours of Record ------------------>
0 1 2 3 4 5 6 7 8 9 10
Stage 0 (Awake)
Sleep Stage REM
Sleep Stage 1
Sleep Stage 2
Sleep Stage 3
Sleep Stage 4
Body Movements
B
<------------------ Hours of Record ------------------>
0 1 2 3 4 5 6 7 8 9 10
Stage 0 (Awake)
Sleep Stage REM
Sleep Stage 1
Sleep Stage 2
Sleep Stage 3
Sleep Stage 4
Body Movements

FIGURE 24.1
Reprinted with permission from Kaplan HI, Sadock BJ, editors: *Comprehensive Textbook of Psychiatry,* ed 6, p 1392. Williams & Wilkins, Baltimore, 1995.

Awake
Stage 1 and REM sleep
Stage 2 sleep
Delta sleep
Stage 1 sleep and REM sleep ( ) are graphed on the same level because their EEG patterns are very similar.
Time: Hours 1 2 3 4 5 6 7 8

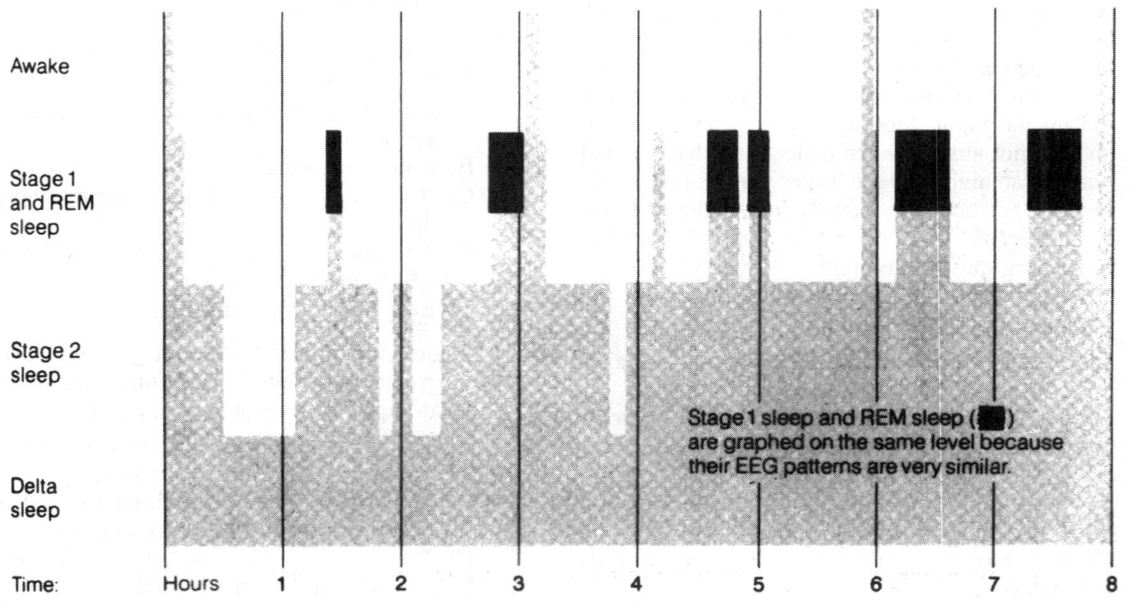

FIGURE 24.2
Reprinted with permission from Hauri P: *The Sleep Disorders,* p 8. Current Concepts. Upjohn, Kalamazoo, MI, 1982.

DIRECTIONS: Each group of questions below consists of lettered headings followed by a list of numbered words or phrases. For each numbered word or phrase, select the *one* lettered heading that is most closely associated with it. Each lettered heading may be selected once, more than once, or not at all.

Questions 24.19–24.21

A. Rapid eye movement (REM) sleep
B. Nonrapid eye movement (NREM) sleep

24.19 Sleep terror disorder
24.20 Nightmare disorder
24.21 Sleepwalking disorder

Questions 24.22–24.26

A. Sleep terror disorder
B. Nocturnal myoclonus
C. Jactatio capitis nocturnus
D. Sleep-related hemolysis
E. Sleep-related bruxism

24.22 Urge to move the legs
24.23 Brownish-red morning urine
24.24 Patient wakes up screaming
24.25 Head banging
24.26 Damage to the teeth

Questions 24.27–24.30

A. REM sleep
B. NREM sleep

24.27 Sleepwalking
24.28 Bed-wetting (enuresis)
24.29 Paroxysmal hemicrania
24.30 Erections

Questions 24.31–24.35

A. Nightmares
B. Night terrors

24.31 REM sleep
24.32 NREM sleep
24.33 Perseverative movements
24.34 Usually recalled in some detail
24.35 Usually followed by amnesia

ANSWERS

Normal Sleep and Sleep Disorders

24.1 The answer is A (*Synopsis VIII,* pages 737–739).
In REM sleep, *dreams are typically* abstract and surreal, not *lucid and creative.* People report dreaming 60 to 90 percent of the time during REM sleep. Dreaming also occurs during NREM sleep, but these dreams are lucid and purposeful.

During REM sleep, *polygraph measures show irregular patterns,* sometimes close to waking patterns. Aside from measures of muscle tone, physiological measures during REM periods could be inferred as those of a person in a waking state. Pulse, respiration, and blood pressure are all high during REM sleep, higher than during NREM sleep, and sometimes higher than during waking.

The resting muscle potential is lower in REM sleep than in a waking state. Near-total paralysis of the postural muscles is present during REM sleep, so that the body cannot move. This motor inhibition is sometimes thought to be associated with dreams of being unable to move. Also during REM sleep, *a condition of temperature regulation similar to that in reptiles occurs;* in this condition—poikilothermia—body temperature varies with the temperature of the environment.

24.2 The answer is C (*Synopsis VIII,* pages 739–740).
L-Tryptophan deficiency is associated with less time spent in REM sleep, not in *NREM sleep.* Ingestion of large amounts of L-tryptophan reduces sleep latency and nocturnal awakening.

Melatonin secretion helps regulate the sleep–wake cycle; melatonin secretion is inhibited by bright light, so that the lowest concentrations occur during the day. A circadian pacemaker in the hypothalamus may regulate melatonin secretion. *Destruction of the dorsal raphe nucleus* of *the brainstem reduces sleep,* as nearly all of the brain's serotonergic cell bodies are located here. *Reduced REM sleep can* also *be caused by increase firing of noradrenergic neurons.*

Disrupted REM sleep patterns in patients with depression show shortened REM latency. As compared with normal sleep patterns, those of people with depression also show an increased percentage of REM sleep and a shift of REM sleep from the last to the first half of the night.

24.3 The answer is C (*Synopsis VIII,* page 741).
Persistent insomnia does not arise from a two-phase problem. Rather, the disorder involves two separable but often related problems: somatized tension and anxiety and a conditioned associative response. *Insomnia can be an outlet for discharging anxiety.* Patients with persistent insomnia may experience insomnia but no anxiety, or they may complain of feelings or thoughts that keep them awake.

After a person is fired from a job, he or she can experience brief insomnia. Such insomnia is often associated with anxiety, either before or after a stressful experience. Brief insomnia is usually not serious, but *insomnia can precede a psychotic episode.* Specific treatment for brief insomnia is usually unnecessary, and *treatment with hypnotic medication should be of short duration.* Some symptoms, including a recurrence of the insomnia, are to be expected when medication is discontinued.

24.4 The answer is A (*Synopsis VIII,* pages 741–742).
Narcolepsy is a disorder of excessive daytime sleepiness and abnormal manifestations of REM sleep occurring daily for at least 3 months. The REM sleep includes hypnagogic and hypnopompic hallucinations, cataplexy, and sleep paralysis. The appearance of REM sleep within 10 minutes of sleep onset is also evidence of narcolepsy.

In *primary insomnia,* the chief complaint is difficulty falling asleep or staying asleep or sleep that is not restful; the complaint must be at least 1 month in duration. *Primary hypersomnia* is diagnosed when no other cause for excessive somnolence occurring for at least 1 month can be found. People may normally sleep for long or short periods, but those with hypersomnia do not enjoy the benefits of normal sleep.

In *sleep apnea syndrome,* airflow at the nose or mouth ceases for 10 seconds or more. In pure central sleep apnea, airflow and respiratory effort cease and begin again during arousals. In pure obstructive sleep apnea, airflow ceases, but respiratory effort increases during apneic periods. Sleep apnea can be dangerous and is thought to account for many unexplained deaths and for infants' crib deaths. It may also cause many pulmonary and cardiovascular deaths in adults and older people.

Circadian rhythm sleep disorder refers to several conditions in which there is a misalignment between desired and actual sleep periods. DSM-IV includes four types: delayed sleep phase, jet lag, shift work, and unspecified.

24.5 The answer is C (*Synopsis VIII,* pages 753–754).
Sleep terrors is a disorder that differs from nightmares, which are the common bad dreams. In nightmares, *the person may have limited movement* and probably does not cry out. Nightmares occur at any time during the night, the person is easy to arouse, and he or she easily remembers the event.

In contrast, a person with sleep terrors *is difficult to awaken* and *may scream and cry out. The person has only little memory of the event,* and *the phenomenon occurs at a specific time,* usually during the first third of nocturnal sleep. Each episode begins with a panicky scream and continues with intense anxiety and unconscious hyperactivity. Episodes are repeated, and each lasts 1 to 10 minutes.

24.6 The answer is E (*Synopsis VIII,* pages 737–739).
The characteristic electroencephalographic (EEG) changes from a wakeful state to sleep are *regular activity at 3 to 7 cycles a second, sleep spindles and K complexes, and delta waves.* The waking EEG is characterized by alpha waves of 8 to 12 cycles a second and low-voltage activity of mixed frequency. As the person falls asleep, alpha activity begins to disappear. Stage 1, considered the lightest stage of sleep, is characterized by low-voltage regular activity at 3 to 7 cycles a second. After a few seconds or minutes, that stage gives way to stage 2, a pattern showing frequent spindle-shaped tracings at 12 to 14 cycles a second (sleep spindles) and slow triphasic waves known as K complexes. Soon thereafter, delta waves—high-voltage activity at 0.5 to 2.5 cycles a second—make their appearance and occupy less than 50 percent of the tracing

(stage 3). Eventually, in stage 4, delta waves occupy more than 50 percent of the record. It is common practice to describe stages 3 and 4 as delta sleep or slow-wave sleep because of their characteristic appearance on the EEG record.

24.7 The answer is B (*Synopsis VIII,* pages 737–739). During rapid eye movement (REM) sleep *a poikilothermic condition is present.* Poikilothermia is a state in which body temperature varies with the temperature of the surrounding medium. In contrast, a homeothermic condition is present during wakefulness and nonrapid eye movement (NREM) sleep; in that condition the body temperature remains constant regardless of the temperature of the surrounding medium.

In REM sleep *the pulse rate is not typically 5 to 10 beats below the level of restful waking;* that is characteristic of NREM sleep. In fact, pulse, respiration, and blood pressure in humans are all high during REM sleep—much higher than during NREM sleep and often higher than during waking. Because of motor inhibition, *body movement is absent* during REM sleep. *Dreams* during REM sleep *are typically abstract and unreal.* Dreaming does occur during NREM sleep, but it is typically lucid and purposeful. *Sleepwalking does not occur* in REM sleep but does occur during stages 3 and 4 of NREM sleep. The diagnostic criteria for sleepwalking disorder are listed in Table 24.1.

24.8 The answer is C (*Synopsis VIII,* pages 744–753). *Nasal continuous positive airway pressure is the treatment of choice for obstructive sleep apnea.* Other procedures include weight loss, nasal surgery, tracheotomy, and uvulopalatoplasty. No medications are consistently effective in normalizing sleep in specific patients. *Psychotherapy has not been useful in the treatment of primary insomnia.* The condition is commonly treated with benzodiazepine hypnotics, chloral hydrate (Noctec), and other sedatives. Hypnotic drugs should be used with care. Various nonspecific measures—so-called sleep hygiene—can be helpful in improving sleep. Light therapy is also used.

Narcolepsy is *not psychogenic.* It is an abnormality of the sleep mechanisms—specifically, REM-inhibiting mechanisms. Psychological problems are secondary to narcolepsy. *Kleine-Levin syndrome does not have insomnia* as a major symptom: in fact, just the opposite is true. Kleine-Levin syndrome is a relatively rare condition consisting of recurrent periods of prolonged sleep (from which the patient may be aroused) with intervening periods of normal sleep and alert waking. *Sleep drunkenness* is an abnormal form of awakening in which the lack of a clear sensorium in the transition from sleep to full wakefulness is prolonged and exaggerated. *Sleep drunkenness does not result from sleep deprivation.* The diagnostic criteria for breathing-related sleep disorder are listed in Table 24.2. The diagnostic criteria for primary insomnia are listed in Table 24.3.

Table 24.1
DSM-IV Diagnostic Criteria for Sleepwalking Disorder

A. Repeated episodes of rising from bed during sleep and walking about, usually occurring during the first third of the major sleep episode.
B. While sleepwalking, the person has a blank, staring face, is relatively unresponsive to the efforts of others to communicate with him or her, and can be awakened only with great difficulty.
C. On awakening (either from the sleepwalking episode or the next morning), the person has amnesia for the episode.
D. Within several minutes after awakening from the sleepwalking episode, there is no impairment of mental activity or behavior (although there may initially be a short period of confusion or disorientation).
E. The sleepwalking causes clinically significant distress or impairment in social, occupational, or other important areas of functioning.
F. The disturbance is not due to the direct physiological effects of a substance (eg, a drug of abuse, a medication) or a general medical condition.

Table 24.2
DSM-IV Diagnostic Criteria for Breathing-Related Sleep Disorder

A. Sleep disruption, leading to excessive sleepiness or insomnia, that is judged to be due to a sleep-related breathing condition (eg, obstructive or central sleep apnea syndrome or central alveolar hypoventilation syndrome).
B. The disturbance is not better accounted for by another mental disorder and is not due to the direct physiological effects of a substance (eg, a drug of abuse, a medication) or another general medical condition (other than a breathing-related disorder).

Coding notes: Also code sleep-related breathing disorder on Axis III.

Table 24.3
DSM-IV Diagnostic Criteria for Primary Insomnia

A. The predominant complaint is difficulty initiating or maintaining sleep, or nonrestorative sleep, for at least 1 month.
B. The sleep disturbance (or associated daytime fatigue) causes clinically significant distress or impairment in social, occupational, or other important areas of functioning.
C. The sleep disturbance does not occur exclusively during the course of narcolepsy, breathing-related sleep disorder, circadian rhythm sleep disorder, or a parasomnia.
D. The disturbance does not occur exclusively during the course of another mental disorder (eg, major depressive disorder, generalized anxiety disorder, a delirium).
E. The disturbance is not due to the direct physiological effects of a substance (eg, a drug of abuse, a medication) or a general medical condition.

24.9 The answer is D (*Synopsis VIII,* page 750).
Sleep apnea, the cessation of airflow at the nose or the mouth, is called *pickwickian syndrome* in obese patients. It is pure *obstructive sleep apnea* when airflow ceases but respiratory effort increases during apneic periods because that combination indicates an obstruction in the airway and increasing efforts by the abdominal and thoracic muscles to force air past the obstruction. Sleep apnea is *not believed to be a benign condition*; in fact it can be dangerous and is thought to account for a number of unexplained deaths. Sleep apnea *is not usually found in men in their 30s*. The most characteristic picture is of middle-aged or elderly men who report tiredness and inability to stay awake in the daytime, sometimes associated with depression, mood changes, and daytime sleep attacks.

24.10 The answer is C (*Synopsis VIII,* page 750).
Sleep apnea is characterized by multiple apneas during sleep, loud snoring, and daytime sleepiness. *Narcolepsy* (Table 24.4) is a dyssomnia characterized by recurrent, brief, uncontrollable episodes of sleep. *Catalepsy* is a condition in which a person maintains the body position in which the body is placed. It is a symptom observed in severe cases of catatonic schizophrenia. It is also known as waxy flexibility and cerea flexibilitas. *Kleine-Levin syndrome* is a condition characterized by periodic episodes of hypersomnia and bulimia. Most often seen in adolescent boys, it eventually disappears spontaneously. *Primary hypersomnia* (Table 24.5) is characterized by excessive time spent sleeping. It is not related to narcolepsy.

24.11 The answer is D (*Synopsis VIII,* pages 754–755).
The patient's diagnosis is *sleepwalking disorder.* This disorder is *more commonly seen in boys than in girls.* Patients often have *vivid hallucinatory recollections* of emotionally traumatic events *with no memory upon awakening.* Sleepwalking disorder consists of a sequence of complex behaviors initiated in the first third of the night during deep nonrapid eye movement (NREM) sleep (stages 3 and 4). It consists of arising from bed during sleep and walking about, appearing unresponsive during the episode, amnestic for the sleepwalking on awakening, and *no impairment in consciousness several minutes* after awakening. Sleepwalking usually begins between ages 6 and 12 and *tends to run in families.* Table 24.1 lists the diagnostic criteria for sleepwalking disorder. Table 24.6 lists the diagnostic criteria for nightmare disorder.

24.12 The answer is E (all) (*Synopsis VIII,* pages 739–740).
The neurotransmitter most clearly involved in sleep and wak-

Table 24.4
DSM-IV Diagnostic Criteria for Narcolepsy

A. Irresistible attacks of refreshing sleep that occur daily over at least 3 months.
B. The presence of one or both of the following:
  (1) cataplexy (ie, brief episodes of sudden bilateral loss of muscle tone, most often in association with intense emotion)
  (2) recurrent intrusions of elements of rapid eye movement (REM) sleep into the transition between sleep and wakefulness, as manifested by either hypnopompic or hypnagogic hallucinations or sleep paralysis at the beginning or end of sleep episodes
C. The disturbance is not due to the direct physiological effects of a substance (eg, a drug of abuse, a medication) or another general medical condition.

Table 24.5
DSM-IV Diagnostic Criteria for Primary Hypersomnia

A. The predominant complaint is excessive sleepiness for at least 1 month (or less if recurrent) as evidenced by either prolonged sleep episodes or daytime sleep episodes that occur almost daily.
B. The excessive sleepiness causes clinically significant distress or impairment in social, occupational, or other important areas of functioning.
C. The excessive sleepiness is not better accounted for by insomnia and does not occur exclusively during the course of another sleep disorder (eg, narcolepsy, breathing-related sleep disorder, circadian rhythm sleep disorder, or a parasomnia) and cannot be accounted for by an inadequate amount of sleep.
D. The disturbance does not occur exclusively during the course of another mental disorder.
E. The disturbance is not due to the direct physiological effects of a substance (eg, a drug of abuse, a medication) or a general medical condition.

Specify if:
Recurrent: if there are periods of excessive sleepiness that last at least 3 days occurring several times a year for at least 2 years

Table 24.6
DSM-IV Diagnostic Criteria for Nightmare Disorder

A. Repeated awakenings from the major sleep period or naps with detailed recall of extended and extremely frightening dreams, usually involving threats to survival, security, or self-esteem. The awakenings generally occur during the second half of the sleep period.
B. On awakening from the frightening dream, the person rapidly becomes oriented and alert (in contrast to the confusion and disorientation seen in sleep terror disorder and some forms of epilepsy).
C. The dream experience, or the sleep disturbance resulting from the awakening, causes clinically significant distress or impairment in social, occupational, or other important areas of functioning.
D. The nightmares do not occur exclusively during the course of another mental disorder (eg, a delirium, posttraumatic stress disorder) and are not due to the direct physiological effects of a substance (eg, a drug of abuse, a medication) or a general medical condition.

ing mechanisms is brain *serotonin.* The administration of the serotonin precursor L-tryptophan induces sleep (reduces sleep latency) and tends to increase total sleep and to increase rapid eye movement (REM) sleep time without altering the states and stages of sleep.

Dopamine seems to be involved in sleep-waking mechanisms. Pharmacological methods of increasing brain dopamine tend to produce arousal and wakefulness, whereas dopamine blockers, such as pimozide (Orap) and the phenothiazines, tend to increase sleep time somewhat.

Norepinephrine may also be involved in the control of sleep. There seems to be an inverse relation between functional brain norepinephrine and REM sleep. Drugs and manipulations that increase the available brain norepinephrine produce a marked decrease in REM sleep, whereas reducing brain norepinephrine levels increases REM sleep. That action of norepinephrine almost certainly involves α-adrenergic receptors, because an α-blocker, such as phenoxybenzamine, increases REM sleep, but a β-blocker, such as propranolol (Inderal), has no effect. *Acetylcholine* is also involved in sleep. Physostigmine and similar cholinomimetric agents can trigger REM sleep in humans.

24.13 The answer is A (*Synopsis VIII,* pages 741–742). Hypersomnia related to an Axis I or Axis II disorder (Table 24.7) may be the result of *major depressive disorder.* Hypersomnia due to *amphetamine withdrawal* is diagnosed as substance-induced sleep disorder with onset during withdrawal, hypersomnia type (Table 24.8). Hypersomnia due to *alcohol intoxication* is diagnosed as substance-induced sleep disorder with onset during intoxication, hypersomnia type. Jet lag is diagnosed as circadian rhythm sleep disorder, *jet lag* type (Table 24.9).

24.14 The answer is A (*Synopsis VIII,* pages 748–749). *Catalepsy* is a condition in which a person maintains the body position in which it is placed. It is a symptom observed in

Table 24.7
DSM-IV Diagnostic Criteria for Hypersomnia Related to [Axis I or Axis II Disorder]

A. The predominant complaint is excessive sleepiness for at least 1 month as evidenced by either prolonged sleep episodes or daytime sleep episodes that occur almost daily.

B. The excessive sleepiness causes clinically significant distress or impairment in social, occupational, or other important areas of functioning.

C. The hypersomnia is judged to be related to another Axis I or Axis II disorder (eg, major depressive disorder, dysthymic disorder), but is sufficiently severe to warrant independent clinical attention.

D. The disturbance is not better accounted for by another sleep disorder (eg, narcolepsy, breathing-related sleep disorder, a parasomnia) or by an inadequate amount of sleep.

E. The disturbance is not due to the direct physiological effects of a substance (eg, a drug of abuse, a medication) or a general medical condition.

Reprinted with permission from American Psychiatric Association: *Diagnostic and Statistical Manual of Mental Disorders,* ed 4. Copyright, American Psychiatric Association, Washington, 1994.

Table 24.8
DSM-IV Diagnostic Criteria for Substance-Induced Sleep Disorder

A. A prominent disturbance in sleep that is sufficiently severe to warrant independent clinical attention.

B. There is evidence from the history, physical examination, or laboratory findings of either (1) or (2):
   (1) the symptoms in criterion A developed during, or within a month of, substance intoxication or withdrawal
   (2) medication use is etiologically related to the sleep disturbance

C. The disturbance is not better accounted for by a sleep disorder that is not substance induced. Evidence that the symptoms are better accounted for by a sleep disorder that is not substance induced might include the following: the symptoms precede the onset of the substance use (or medication use); the symptoms persist for a substantial period of time (eg, about a month) after the cessation of acute withdrawal or severe intoxication, or are substantially in excess of what would be expected given the type or amount of the substance used or the duration of use; or there is other evidence that suggests the existence of an independent non-substance-induced sleep disorder (eg, a history of recurrent non-substance-related episodes).

D. The disturbance does not occur exclusively during the course of a delirium.

E. The sleep disturbance causes clinically significant distress or impairment in social, occupational, or other important areas of functioning.

Note: This diagnosis should be made instead of a diagnosis of substance intoxication or substance withdrawal only when the sleep symptoms are in excess of those usually associated with the intoxication or withdrawal syndrome and when the symptoms are sufficiently severe to warrant independent clinical attention.

Code [specific substance]-induced sleep disorder: (alcohol; amphetamine; caffeine; cocaine; opioid; sedative, hypnotic, or anxiolytic; other [or unknown] substance)

Specify type:
- **Insomnia type:** if the predominant sleep disturbance is insomnia
- **Hypersomnia type:** if the predominant sleep disturbance is hypersomnia
- **Parasomnia type:** if the predominant sleep disturbance is a parasomnia
- **Mixed type:** if more than one sleep disturbance is present and none predominates

Specify if:
- **With onset during intoxication:** if the criteria are met for intoxication with the substance and the symptoms develop during the intoxication syndrome
- **With onset during withdrawal:** if criteria are met for withdrawal from the substance and the symptoms develop during, or shortly after, a withdrawal syndrome

Reprinted with permission from American Psychiatric Association: *Diagnostic and Statistical Manual of Mental Disorders,* ed 4. Copyright, American Psychiatric Association, Washington, 1994.

severe cases of catatonic schizophrenia. Excessive *daytime sleepiness* and naps and the accessory symptoms of *cataplexy, sleep paralysis,* and hypnagogic *hallucinations are* the classically recognized symptoms of narcolepsy. Patients generally first report the onset of daytime sleepiness before the accessory symptoms are noted.

The sleepiness may persist throughout the day, but more

Table 24.9
DSM-IV Diagnostic Criteria for Circadian Rhythm Sleep Disorder

A. A persistent or recurrent pattern of sleep disruption leading to excessive sleepiness or insomnia that is due to a mismatch between the sleep-wake schedule required by a person's environment and his or her circadian sleep-wake pattern
B. The sleep disturbance causes clinically significant distress or impairment in social, occupational, or other important areas of functioning.
C. The disturbance does not occur exclusively during the course of another sleep disorder or other mental disorder.
D. The disturbance is not due to the direct physiological effects of a substance (eg, a drug of abuse, a medication) or a general medical condition.

Specify type:
Delayed sleep phase type: a persistent pattern of late sleep onset and late awakening times, with an inability to fall asleep and awaken at a desired earlier time
Jet lag type: sleepiness and alertness that occur at an inappropriate time of day relative to local time, occurring after repeated travel across more than one time zone
Shift work type: insomnia during the major sleep period or excessive sleepiness during the major awake period associated with night shift work or frequently changing shift work
Unspecified type

Reprinted with permission from American Psychiatric Association: *Diagnostic and Statistical Manual of Mental Disorders,* ed 4. Copyright, American Psychiatric Association, Washington, 1994.

often it is periodic and may be relieved by a sleep attack or by a nap from which the patient characteristically awakens refreshed. Thus, there are often refractory periods of 2 or 3 hours of almost normal alertness. The sleep attacks are usually associated with characteristic times of the day, such as after meals, when some degree of sleepiness is quite normal. The attacks are typically irresistible and may even occur while eating, riding a bicycle, or actively conversing and also during sexual relations.

Cataplexy, which occurs in 67 to 95 percent of the cases, is paralysis or paresis of the antigravity muscles in the awake state. A cataplectic attack often begins during expressions of emotion, such as laughter, anger, and exhilaration. The attacks vary in intensity and frequency; they can consist of a weakening of the knees, a jaw drop, a head drop, or a sudden paralysis of all of the muscles of the body—except for the eyes and the diaphragm—leading to a complete collapse.

Sleep paralysis is a neurological phenomenon that is most likely due to a temporary dysfunction of the reticular activating system. It consists of brief episodes of an inability to move or speak when awake or asleep.

Hypnagogic hallucinations are vivid perceptual dreamlike experiences occurring at sleep onset. They occur in about 50 percent of the patients. The accompanying affect is usually fear or dread. The hallucinatory imagery is remembered best after a brief narcoleptic sleep attack, when it is often described as a dream.

24.15 The answer is E (all) (*Synopsis VIII,* pages 741–742). *Hypersomnia* manifests as excessive amounts of sleep and excessive daytime sleepiness (somnolence). In some situations both symptoms are present. *Kleine-Levin syndrome* is characterized by recurrent periods of hypersomnia, usually associated with hyperphagia, and also by periodic episodes of bulimia. The hypersomnia is characterized by prolonged sleep from which the patient cannot be aroused. Infectious causes of hypersomnolence as an isolated symptom are extremely rare or nonexistent at present in the United States, but they are common in Africa and have been seen at times in many parts of the world. The best-known such condition is *trypanosomiasis,* which produces sleeping sickness. Excessive sleep and *depression* are typical symptoms of *amphetamine withdrawal.* Withdrawal from other stimulant drugs, including caffeine, can produce similar effects. Table 24.10 lists some common causes

Table 24.10
Common Causes of Hypersomnia

Symptom	Chiefly Medical	Chiefly Psychiatric or Environmental
Excessive sleep (hypersomnia)	Kleine-Levin syndrome Menstrual-associated somnolence Metabolic or toxic conditions Encephalitic conditions Alcohol and depressant medications Withdrawal from stimulants	Depression (some) Avoidance reactions
Excessive daytime sleepiness	Narcolepsy and narcolepsy-like syndromes Sleep apneas Hypoventilation syndrome Hyperthyroidism and other metabolic and toxic conditions Alcohol and depressant medications Withdrawal from stimulants Sleep deprivation or insufficient sleep Any condition producing serious insomnia	Depression (some) Avoidance reactions Circadian rhythm sleep disorder

Courtesy of Ernest Hartmann, M.D.

of hypersomnia. As with insomnia, hypersomnia is associated with borderline conditions, situations that are hard to classify, and idiopathic cases.

24.16 The answer is C (*Synopsis VIII,* pages 737–739)
Nightmare disorder consists of repeated awakenings from long, frightening dreams. The awakening usually occurs during the second half of the sleep period, during rapid eye movement (REM) sleep. *Enuresis,* the involuntary loss of urine, can occur during all stages of sleep. *Somnambulism,* also known as sleep-walking disorder, takes place during the first third of the night during stages 3 and 4. *Sleep terror disorder* is characterized by terrified arousal in the first third of the night during deep NREM stages (stages 3 and 4). *Somniloquy*—talking in one's sleep—occurs in all stages of sleep but is more common in NREM stages.

24.17 The answer is C (*synopsis VIII,* page 738).
The sleep stage histograms demonstrate normal sleep in *A* and that found in a patient with major depressive disorder in *B. As shown in histogram* A, *REM sleep normally has a latency (time between sleep onset and first REM episode) of about 90 minutes. In contrast, REM latency is shortened to 60 minutes or less in major depressive disorder, as shown in histogram* B. Other findings in *B* consistent with major depressive disorder include disruption of sleep continuity and early morning awakenings.

Obstructive sleep apnea syndrome is characterized by repetitive episodes of upper airway obstruction that occur during sleep, usually associated with a reduction in blood oxygen saturation. Sleep is disturbed by frequent awakenings, while REM and slow wave (stages 3 and 4) sleep are nearly absent.

24.18 The answer is E (*Synopsis VIII,* page 739).
Figure 24.2 represents a normal sleep pattern of a young human adult. The periods of REM sleep shown are consistent with that found in a normal young adult, occurring every 90 to 100 minutes during the night, with most REM sleep occurring in the last third of the night.

Depressed patients, in contrast, experience shortened REM latency (60 minutes or less), an increased percentage of REM sleep (over the normal 25%), and a shift in REM distribution from most occurring in the last half (normal) to most occurring in the first half of the night (abnormal).

Narcolepsy is characterized by abnormal manifestations of REM sleep, including the appearance of REM sleep within 10 minutes of sleep onset (sleep onset REM periods), as well as hypnagogic and hypnopompic hallucinations, cataplexy and sleep paralysis.

Sleep patterns change over the life span. In the neonatal period, REM sleep occurs during more than 50 percent of total sleep time, whereas in young adulthood, REM sleep occurs during 25 percent of total sleep time. In addition, the EEG pattern of newborns goes from the alert state directly to the REM state without going through stages 1 through 4.

Answers 24.19–24.21

24.19 The answer is B (*Synopsis VIII,* page 755).

24.20 The answer is A (*Synopsis VIII,* pages 737–739).

24.21 The answer is B (*Synopsis VIII,* page 755).
Nightmare disorder is associated with rapid eye movement (REM) sleep. *Sleep terror disorder* and sleepwalking disorder are associated with non–rapid eye movement (NREM) sleep. The diagnostic criteria for nightmare disorder are listed in Table 24.6. The diagnostic criteria for sleep terror disorder are listed in Table 24.11.

Answers 24.22–24.26

24.22 The answer is B (*Synopsis VIII,* page 752).

24.23 The answer is D (*Synopsis VIII,* page 758).

24.24 The answer is A (*Synopsis VIII,* page 754).

24.25 The answer is C (*Synopsis VIII,* page 756).

24.26 The answer is E (*Synopsis VIII,* page 755).
Nocturnal myoclonus consists of highly stereotyped contractions of certain leg muscles during sleep. Though rarely painful, the syndrome causes an almost irresistible urge to move the legs, thus interfering with sleep. *Sleep-related hemolysis* (paroxysmal nocturnal hemoglobinuria) is a rare acquired chronic hemolytic anemia in which intravascular hemolysis results in hemoglobinemia and hemoglobinuria. Accelerated during sleep, the hemolysis and consequent hemoglobinuria color the morning urine a *brownish red.* Sleep-related hemolysis is diagnosed as sleep disorder due to a general medical condition (Table 24.12).

In *sleep terror disorder* (Table 24.11) the patient typically sits up in bed with a frightened expression and wakes up *screaming,* often with a feeling of intense terror; patients are often amnestic for the episode. Sleep-related *head banging (jactatio capitis nocturnus)* consists chiefly of rhythmic to-and-fro head rocking, less commonly of total body rocking, occurring just before or during sleep, rarely persisting into or occurring in deep non–rapid eye movement (NREM) sleep.

Table 24.11
DSM-IV Diagnostic Criteria for Sleep Terror Disorder

A. Recurrent episodes of abrupt awakening from sleep, usually occurring during the first third of the major sleep episode and beginning with a panicky scream.
B. Intense fear and signs of autonomic arousal, such as tachycardia, rapid breathing, and sweating, during each episode.
C. Relative unresponsiveness to efforts of others to comfort the person during the episode.
D. No detailed dream is recalled, and there is amnesia for the episode.
E. The episodes cause clinically significant distress or impairment in social, occupational, or other important areas of functioning.
F. The disturbance is not due to the direct physiological effects of a substance (eg, a drug of abuse, a medication) or a general medical condition.

Table 24.12
DSM-IV Diagnostic Criteria for Sleep Disorder Due to a General Medical Condition

A. A prominent disturbance in sleep that is sufficiently severe to warrant independent clinical attention.

B. There is evidence from the history, physical examination, or laboratory findings that the sleep disturbance is the direct physiological consequence of a general medical condition.

C. The disturbance is not better accounted for by another mental disorder (eg, an adjustment disorder in which the stressor is a serious medical illness).

D. The disturbance does not occur exclusively during the course of a delirium.

E. The disturbance does not meet the criteria for breathing-related sleep disorder or narcolepsy.

F. The sleep disturbance causes clinically significant distress or impairment in social, occupational, or other important areas of functioning.

Specify type:

Insomnia type: if the predominant sleep disturbance is insomnia

Hypersomnia type: if the predominant sleep disturbance is hypersomnia

Parasomnia type: if the predominant sleep disturbance is a parasomnia

Mixed type: if more than one sleep disturbance is present and none predominates

Coding note: Include the name of the general medical condition on Axis I, eg, sleep disorder due to chronic obstructive pulmonary disease insomnia type; also code the general medical condition on Axis III.

According to dentists, 5 to 10 percent of the population suffer from sleep-related *bruxism* (tooth grinding) severe enough to produce noticeable *damage to the teeth.* Although the condition often goes unnoticed by the sleeper, except for an occasional feeling of jaw ache in the morning, the bed partner and roommates are acutely cognizant of the situation, as they are repeatedly awakened by the sound.

Sleep-related head banging and sleep-related bruxism are diagnosed as parasomnia not otherwise specified (Table 24.13).

Answers 24.27–24.30

24.27 The answer is B (*Synopsis VIII,* pages 754–755).

24.28 The answer is B (*Synopsis VIII,* page 737).

24.29 The answer is A (*Synopsis VIII,* page 757).

24.30 The answer is A (*Synopsis VIII,* page 739).

Table 24.13
DSM-IV Diagnostic Criteria for Parasomnia Not Otherwise Specified

The parasomnia not otherwise specified category is for disturbances that are characterized by abnormal behavioral or physiological events during sleep or sleep-wake transitions, but that do not meet criteria for a more specific parasomnia. Examples include

1. REM sleep behavior disorder: motor activity, often of a violent nature, that arises during rapid eye movement (REM) sleep. Unlike sleepwalking, these episodes tend to occur later in the night and are associated with vivid dream recall.
2. Sleep paralysis: an inability to perform voluntary movement during the transition between wakefulness and sleep. The episodes may occur at sleep onset (hypnagogic) or with awakening (hypnopompic). The episodes are usually associated with extreme anxiety and, in some cases, fear of impending death. Sleep paralysis occurs commonly as an ancillary symptom of narcolepsy and, in such cases, should not be coded separately.
3. Situations in which the clinician has concluded that a parasomnia is present but is unable to determine whether it is primary, due to a general medical condition, or substance induced.

Sleepwalking occurs during the first third of the night during NREM sleep, stages 3 and 4. *Bed-wetting (enuresis),* a repetitive and inappropriate passage of urine during sleep, is usually associated with NREM sleep, stages 3 and 4. *Paroxysmal hemicrania* is a type of unilateral vascular headache that is exacerbated during sleep and that occurs only in association with REM sleep. Erections are associated with REM sleep. Almost every REM period is accompanied by a partial or full penile *erection* (or clitoral erection in women).

Answers 24.31–24.35

24.31 The answer is A (*Synopsis VIII,* page 753).

24.32 The answer is B (*Synopsis VIII,* page 754).

24.33 The answer is B (*Synopsis VIII,* page 754).

24.34 The answer is A (*Synopsis VIII,* page 753).

24.35 The answer is B (*Synopsis VIII,* page 754).
Night terrors must be clearly distinguished from nightmares. Nightmares occur during REM sleep and manifest with less intense anxiety than do night terrors. Nightmares are usually not forgotten and in fact are *usually recalled in some detail.* Night terrors occur during NREM sleep and manifest with severe anxiety, being heralded by a panicky scream. They are accompanied by disorientation and *perseverative movements* and are usually followed by *amnesia* for the event.

25

Impulse-Control Disorders Not Elsewhere Classified

In the fourth edition of *Diagnostic and Statistical Manual of Mental Disorders* (DSM-IV), impulse-control disorders not elsewhere classified include disorders not discussed in other sections of the manual. The disorders are characterized by failure to resist an impulse, drive, or temptation to perform an act that is harmful to the person or to others. A person with such a disorder usually feels a growing sense of tension before committing the act and afterward experiences pleasure. The disorders are intermittent explosive disorder, kleptomania, pyromania, pathological gambling, trichotillomania, and impulse-control disorder not otherwise specified.

In intermittent explosive disorder, episodes of aggressive impulses produce serious assaults or destruction of property. Kleptomania is characterized by failing to resist a desire to steal unneeded or worthless objects. A person with pyromania sets fires for pleasure or to relieve tension. Trichotillomania is recurrent pulling out of hair for pleasure or relief of tension; the result is noticeable hair loss. Impulse-control disorder not otherwise specified refers to disorders that do not meet the criteria for any other disorder in DSM-IV.

Psychosocial factors associated with impulse-control disorders include exposure to violence in the home, alcohol abuse, erratic sexual relationships, antisocial behavior, and parental figures with impulse-control problems. Researchers have extensively investigated biological factors in patients with impulse-control disorder, especially those who behave violently. Relevant factors include areas of the brain such as the limbic system, hormones such as testosterone, histories of head trauma, and the adult residue of childhood attention-deficit/hyperactivity disorder. There may be a correlation between cerebrospinal fluid (CSF) levels of 5-hydroxyindoleacetic acid (5-HIAA) and impulsive aggression: in some suicide victims, brainstem and CSF levels of 5-HIAA are decreased.

Each impulse-control disorder has its own epidemiology, causes, psychodynamic formulation, course, prognosis, and treatment. Each must be viewed individually, even though common threads are found in them. Students should study Chapter 25 in *Kaplan and Sadock's Synopsis VIII* and the questions and answers that follow.

HELPFUL HINTS

These terms relate to impulse-control disorders and should be defined by the student.

- ▶ alopecia
- ▶ anticonvulsants
- ▶ behavior therapy
- ▶ benzodiazepines
- ▶ biofeedback
- ▶ desperate stage
- ▶ enuresis
- ▶ epileptoid personality
- ▶ hydroxyzine hydrochloride
- ▶ hypnotherapy
- ▶ impulse-control disorder
- ▶ impulse-control disorder not otherwise specified
- ▶ intermittent explosive disorder
- ▶ kleptomania
- ▶ limbic system
- ▶ lithium
- ▶ lust angst
- ▶ multidetermined
- ▶ pathological gambling
- ▶ pleasure principle, reality principle
- ▶ progressive-loss stage
- ▶ psychodynamics
- ▶ pyromania
- ▶ testosterone
- ▶ trichophagy
- ▶ trichotillomania
- ▶ winning phase

▲ QUESTIONS

DIRECTIONS: For each of the three numbered disorders, choose the lettered selection most likely to be associated with it.

A. Absent father
B. Bulimia nervosa
C. Epileptoid personality
D. Major depressive disorder
E. Obsessive-compulsive disorder

25.1 Kleptomania
25.2 Pathological gambling
25.3 Intermittent explosive disorder

25.4 Which of the following selections *cannot* be associated with intermittent explosive disorder?

A. Patients may feel helpless before an episode.
B. The disorder usually grows less severe with age.
C. A predisposing factor in childhood is encephalitis.
D. Dopaminergic neurons mediate behavioral inhibition.
E. Neurological examination can show left-right ambivalence.

DIRECTIONS: Each of the questions or incomplete statements below is followed by five suggested responses or completions. Select the *one* that is *best* in each case.

25.5 Which of the following statements about impulse-control disorders is *not* true?

A. The patients cannot resist the temptation to perform the act.
B. The patients feel an increasing surge of tension before they commit the act.
C. The patients feel a burst of pleasure while committing the act.
D. The act is ego-syntonic.
E. After the act the patients rarely feel guilt or self-reproach.

25.6 Biological factors involved in the causes of impulse-control disorders include all the following *except*

A. limbic system
B. testosterone
C. tyrosine levels
D. temporal lobe epilepsy
E. mixed cerebral dominance

25.7 Which of the following drugs has been found to cause a paradoxical reaction of dyscontrol in some cases of impulse-control disorder?

A. Lithium
B. Phenytoin
C. Carbamazepine
D. Trazodone
E. Benzodiazepines

25.8 Which statement about trichotillomania is *false*?

A. The diagnosis should not be made if the hair pulling is the result of another mental disorder.
B. Pulling out hair causes gratification.
C. The disorder is more common in males than in females.
D. The most common site is the scalp.
E. Trichobezoars may result.

25.9 The estimated number of pathological gamblers in the United States is

A. fewer than 100,000
B. 250,000
C. 500,000
D. 750,000
E. 1 million or more

25.10 All of the following may be predisposing factors for the development of pathological gambling *except*

A. loss of a parent before the child is 15 years old
B. childhood enuresis
C. attention-deficit/hyperactivity disorder
D. inappropriate parental discipline
E. family emphasis on material symbols

25.11 Figure 25.1 shows a patient with an area of incomplete alopecia on the frontal and vertex scalp. The patient's alopecia is the result of recurrent pulling out of her own hair, a behavior associated with an increasing sense of tension immediately before pulling out the hair and a sense of relief and gratification while pulling out the hair. With regard to this patient's disorder, all of the following are true *except*

A. The behavior is recognized by the patient as undesirable.
B. The disorder is characterized by specific histopathological changes of the hair follicle.
C. The disorder is characterized by obsessive thought.
D. The disorder may be associated with mental retardation.

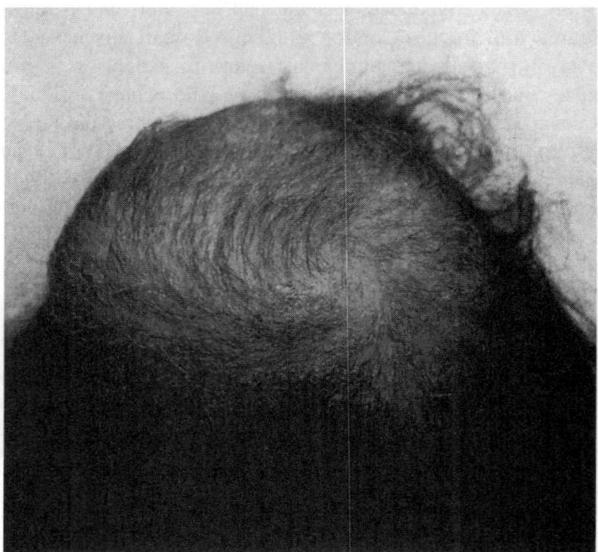

FIGURE 25.1

Reprinted with permission from Kaplan HI, Sadock BJ, editors: *Comprehensive Textbook of Psychiatry,* ed 6, p 1530. Williams & Wilkins, Baltimore, 1995.

DIRECTIONS: Each set of lettered headings below is followed by a list of numbered words or phrases. For each numbered word or phrase, select

A. if the item is associated with *A only*
B. if the item is associated with *B only*
C. if the item is associated with *both A and B*
D. if the item is associated with *neither A nor B*

Questions 25.12–25.18

A. Trichotillomania
B. Pyromania
C. Both
D. Neither

25.12 More common in females than in males
25.13 Onset generally in childhood
25.14 Sense of gratification or relief during the behavior
25.15 Treated with lithium
25.16 Associated with truancy
25.17 May be a response to an auditory hallucination
25.18 Associated with mental retardation

Questions 25.19–25.22

A. Intermittent explosive disorder
B. Kleptomania
C. Both
D. Neither

25.19 Greater prevalence among males than among females
25.20 Associated with organic brain disease
25.21 Treatment with carbamazepine (Tegretol)
25.22 May be due to antisocial personality disorder

ANSWERS

Impulse-Control Disorders Not Elsewhere Classified

25.1 The answer is B (*Synopsis VIII,* page 763).
Kleptomania frequently occurs as part of *bulimia nervosa* and other eating disorders and is often associated with mood disorders and obsessive-compulsive disorders. Nearly one quarter of patients with bulimia nervosa are said to meet the diagnostic criteria for kleptomania.

25.2 The answer is D (*Synopsis VIII,* page 766).
Pathological gambling is often associated with mood disorders, particularly *major depressive disorder*. The condition can also be associated with panic disorder, obsessive-compulsive disorder, and agoraphobia.

25.3 The answer is C (*Synopsis VIII,* page 761).
The typical outbursts of *intermittent explosive disorder* sometimes have a seizurelike quality called *epileptoid personality.* The outbursts are not typical of the patient, and an organic disease process may be present. Other features suggest an epileptoid state: the patient may experience an aura, and after the episode, a person may have changes in the sensorium or be hypersensitive to light and sound. *An absent father* has been noted in studies of patients with pyromania. *Obsessive-compulsive disorder* can be associated with several impulse-control disorders.

25.4 The answer is D (*Synopsis VIII,* page 761).
Serotonergic neurons, not *dopaminergic neurons, mediate behavioral inhibition.* Decreases in serotonergic transmission can reduce the effect of punishment as a deterrent of behavior, and the restoration of serotonin activity restores the behavioral effect of punishment. Researchers have suggested a connection between low levels of CSF 5-HIAA and impulsive behavior. Patients with intermittent explosive disorder are typically large, dependent men with a poor sense of masculine identity. *Patients may feel helpless before an episode. A predisposing factor in childhood is encephalitis,* as are perinatal trauma, minimal brain dysfunction, and hyperactivity. A patient's childhood was often violent and traumatic. *Neurological examination can show left-right ambivalence* and perceptual reversal. *The disorder usually grows less severe with age,* but heightened organic impairment can lead to frequent and severe episodes.

25.5 The answer is E (*Synopsis VIII,* page 769).
After the act the patients may feel guilt or self-reproach. Patients with impulse-control disorders share the following features: (1) *The patients cannot resist the temptation to perform an act* that is harmful to themselves or others. They may or may not consciously resist the impulse and may or may not plan the act. (2) *The patients feel an increasing sense of tension before they commit the act.* (3) *They feel a burst of pleasure while committing the act. The act is ego-syntonic* in that it is consonant with the patient's immediate conscious wishes.

25.6 The answer is C (*Synopsis VIII,* page 769).
Tyrosine levels have not been implicated in impulse-control disorders. Specific brain regions, such as the *limbic system,* are associated with impulsive and violent activity; other brain regions are associated with the inhibition of such behaviors. Certain hormones, especially *testosterone,* have been associated with violent and aggressive behavior. Some reports have described a relation between *temporal lobe epilepsy* and certain impulsive violent behaviors, an association of aggressive behavior in patients with histories of head trauma, increased numbers of emergency room visits, and other potential organic antecedents. A high incidence of *mixed cerebral dominance* may be found in some violent populations.

25.7 The answer is E (*Synopsis VIII,* page 769).
Anticonvulsants have long been used in treating explosive patients, with mixed results. *Phenothiazines* and antidepressants have been effective in some cases. *Benzodiazepines have been reported to produce a paradoxical reaction of dyscontrol in some cases. Lithium (Eskalith)* has been reported to be useful in generally lessening aggressive behavior, as have *carbamazepine (Tegretol)* and *phenytoin (Dilantin).* Propranolol (Inderal), buspirone (BuSpar), and *trazodone (Desyrel)* have also been effective in some cases. Reports increasingly indicate that fluoxetine (Prozac) and other serotonin-specific reuptake inhibitors are useful in reducing impulsivity and aggression.

25.8. The answer is C (*Synopsis VIII,* pages 767–768).
Trichotillomania *is apparently more common in females than in males. The diagnosis should not be made if the hair pulling is the result of another mental disorder* (for example, disorders manifesting delusions or hallucinations) or a general medical disorder (for example, a preexisting lesion of the skin). The diagnosis criteria are listed in Table 25.1. Before engaging in the behavior, trichotillomaniac patients experience an increasing sense of tension. *Pulling out hair causes a sense* of release or *gratification.* All areas of the body may be affected. *The most common site is the scalp.* Other areas involved are the eyebrows, eyelashes, and the beard; less commonly, the trunk, armpits, and the pubic area are involved. Trichophagy (hair

Table 25.1
DSM-IV Diagnostic Criteria for Trichotillomania

A. Recurrent pulling out of one's hair resulting in noticeable hair loss.
B. An increasing sense of tension immediately before pulling out the hair or when attempting to resist the behavior.
C. Pleasure, gratification, or relief when pulling out the hair.
D. The disturbance is not better accounted for by another mental disorder and is not due to a general medical condition (eg, a dermatological condition).
E. The disturbance causes clinically significant distress or impairment in social, occupational, or other important areas of functioning.

balls), mouthing of the hair, may follow the hair plucking. *Trichobezoars,* malnutrition, and intestinal obstruction result.

25.9 The answer is E (*Synopsis VIII,* pages 766–767). Estimates place the number of pathological gamblers in the United States at *1 million or more.* The disorder is thought to be more common in men than in women. Males whose fathers have the disorder and females whose mothers have the disorder are more likely to gamble pathologically than the population at large. The diagnostic criteria for pathological gambling are listed in Table 25.2.

25.10 The answer is B (*Synopsis VIII,* pages 766–767) *Childhood enuresis* is the involuntary loss of urine (sometimes the condition is seen as voluntary). It is not a predisposing factor for the development of pathological gambling. *Loss of a parent* by death, separation, divorce, or desertion before the child is 15 years old may be a predisposing factor. Other possible factors include *attention-deficit/hyperactivity disorder, inappropriate parental discipline, family emphasis on material symbols,* and a lack of family emphasis on saving, planning, and budgeting.

25.11 The answer is C (*Synopsis VIII,* pages 667–668). The patient suffers from trichotillomania. According to DSM-IV, the essential feature of trichotillomania is the recurrent pulling out of one's hair, resulting in noticeable hair loss. Other clinical symptoms include an increasing sense of tension before, and a sense of relief or gratification during, the act of pulling out the hair. *Trichotillomania generally begins in childhood or adolescence* and is apparently more common in females than in males. Associated disorders also include *obsessive-compulsive disorder* (OCD), obsessive-compulsive personality disorder, borderline personality disorder, and depressive disorders. Like OCD, *trichotillomania is commonly chronic and recognized by the patient as undesirable.* Unlike OCD patients, *patients with trichotillomania need not have obsessive thoughts,* and the compulsive activity is limited to one act—hair pulling. *Characteristic histopathological changes in the hair follicles* are demonstrated by biopsy and help distinguish trichotillomania from other causes of alopecia. It has no etiological relationship with *mental retardation.*

Table 25.2
DSM-IV Diagnostic Criteria for Pathological Gambling

A. Persistent and recurrent maladaptive gambling behavior as indicated by five (or more) of the following:
   (1) is preoccupied with gambling (eg, preoccupied with reliving past gambling experiences, handicapping or planning the next venture, or thinking of ways to get money with which to gamble)
   (2) needs to gamble with increasing amounts of money in order to achieve the desired excitement
   (3) has repeated unsuccessful efforts to control, cut back, or stop gambling
   (4) is restless or irritable when attempting to cut down or stop gambling
   (5) gambles as a way of escaping from problems or of relieving a dysphoric mood (eg, feelings of helplessness, guilt, anxiety, depression)
   (6) after losing money gambling, often returns another day to get even ("chasing" one's losses)
   (7) lies to family members, therapist, or others to conceal the extent of involvement with gambling
   (8) has committed illegal acts such as forgery, fraud, theft, or embezzlement to finance gambling
   (9) has jeopardized or lost a significant relationship, job, or educational or career opportunity because of gambling
   (10) relies on others to provide money to relieve a desperate financial situation caused by gambling

B. The gambling behavior is not better accounted for by a manic episode.

Reprinted with permission from American Psychiatric Association: *Diagnostic and Statistical Manual of Mental Disorders,* ed 4, Copyright, American Psychiatric Association, Washington, 1994.

Answers 25.12–25.18

25.12 The answer is A (*Synopsis VIII,* pages 767–768).

25.13 The answer is C (*Synopsis VIII,* pages 764, 766).

25.14 The answer is C (*Synopsis VIII,* pages 764, 768).

25.15 The answer is D (*Synopsis VIII,* pages 766–769).

25.16 The answer is B (*Synopsis VIII,* page 764).

25.17 The answer is D (*Synopsis VIII,* pages 764–765, 768).

25.18 The answer is C (*Synopsis VIII,* pages 764–765, 768). *Both* pyromania and trichotillomania have their *onset in childhood* and are characterized by a *sense of gratification or release during the act. Trichotillomania* is apparently *more common in females than in males.* People who set fires are more likely to be *moderately retarded* than people who do not set fires, and the inability to resist the impulse to pull out one's own hair may also be associated with *mental retardation. Pyromania* is associated with antisocial traits, such as *truancy,* running away from home, and delinquency. *Neither disorder* is *treated with lithium* (Eskalith), and *neither is a response to an auditory hallucination.* Table 25.3 lists the diagnostic cri-

Table 25.3
DSM-IV Diagnostic Criteria for Pyromania

A. Deliberate and purposeful fire setting on more than one occasion.

B. Tension or affective arousal before the act.

C. Fascination with, interest in, curiosity about, or attraction to fire and its situational contexts (eg, paraphernalia, uses, consequences).

D. Pleasure, gratification, or relief when setting fires, or when witnessing or participating in their aftermath.

E. The fire setting is not done for monetary gain, as an expression of sociopolitical ideology, to conceal criminal activity, to express anger or vengeance, to improve one's living circumstances, in response to a delusion or hallucination, or as a result of impaired judgment (eg, in dementia, mental retardation, substance intoxication).

F. The fire setting is not better accounted for by conduct disorder, a manic episode, or antisocial personality disorder.

Reprinted with permission from American Psychiatric Association: *Diagnostic and Statistical Manual of Mental Disorders,* ed 4, Copyright, American Psychiatric Association, Washington, 1994.

Table 25.4
DSM-IV Diagnostic Criteria for Kleptomania

A. Recurrent failure to resist impulses to steal objects not needed for personal use or for their monetary value.
B. Increasing sense of tension immediately before committing the theft.
C. Pleasure, gratification, or relief at the time of committing the theft.
D. The stealing is not committed to express anger or vengeance and is not in response to a delusion or hallucination.
E. The stealing is not better accounted for by conduct disorder, a manic episode, or antisocial personality disorder.

Table 25.5
DSM-IV Diagnostic Criteria for Intermittent Explosive Disorder

A. Several discrete episodes of failure to resist aggressive impulses that result in serious assaultive acts or destruction of property.
B. The degree of aggressiveness expressed during the episodes is grossly out of proportion to any precipitating psychosocial stressors.
C. The aggressive episodes are not better accounted for by another mental disorder (eg, antisocial personality disorder, borderline personality disorder, a psychotic disorder, a manic episode, conduct disorder, or attention-deficit/hyperactivity disorder) and are not due to the direct physiological effects of a substance (eg, a drug of abuse, a medication) or a general medical condition (eg, head trauma, Alzheimer's disease).

teria for pyromania. Table 25.1 lists the diagnostic criteria for trichotillomania.

Answers 25.19–25.22

25.19 The answer is A (*Synopsis VIII,* page 761).

25.20 The answer is C (*Synopsis VIII,* pages 762–763).

25.21 The answer is A (*Synopsis VIII,* page 763).

25.22 The answer is D (*Synopsis VIII,* pages 761–763). *Intermittent explosive disorder* is apparently very rare and appears to have a *greater prevalence among males than females. Kleptomania* is also rare, and the sex ratio is unknown. Most patients with intermittent explosive disorder are treated with a combined pharmacological and psychotherapeutic approach. Psychotherapy with violent patients is exceedingly difficult because of potential problems with countertransference and limit setting. Anticonvulsants, phenothiazines, and antidepressants have all been effective in some cases of intermittent explosive disorder, and studies have shown that both lithium and *carbamazepine* are useful in certain cases. Both disorders may be *associated with organic brain disease.* Lesions in the limbic system, for example, have been associated with violent behavior and loss of control of aggressive impulses. Kleptomania has also been associated with brain disease and mental retardation. *Neither* intermittent explosive disorder nor kleptomania can be diagnosed when impulsiveness, aggressiveness, or stealing is *due to antisocial personality disorder.* Table 25.4 lists the diagnostic criteria for kleptomania. Table 25.5 lists the diagnostic criteria for intermittent explosive disorder.

26

Adjustment Disorders

According to the fourth edition of *Diagnostic and Statistical Manual of Mental Disorders* (DSM-IV), the essential feature of an adjustment disorder is the development of clinically significant emotional or behavioral symptoms in response to a psychosocial stressor. The symptoms must develop within 3 months of the onset of the stress, and there must be marked distress or marked impairment in social or occupational functioning. The disorder must resolve within 6 months of the termination of the stressor, unless the symptoms occur in response to a chronic stressor or one with enduring consequences. The subtypes of adjustment disorders include with depressed mood, with anxiety, with mixed anxiety and depressed mood, with disturbance of conduct, with mixed disturbances of emotions and conduct, and unspecified.

Adjustment disorders are characterized by subjective distress, and the emotional disturbance interferes with the person's social functioning. All persons are vulnerable to stress; but that predisposition varies from one person to another.

Clinicians must be able to distinguish between the varieties of adjustment disorders and to differentiate adjustment disorders from other conditions. Treatment can include combined crisis-intervention strategies, insight-oriented psychotherapy, environmental and behavioral manipulations, and brief pharmacotherapy if indicated.

Students should study Chapter 26 in *Kaplan and Sadock's Synopsis VIII* and then test themselves with the following questions and answers.

HELPFUL HINTS

The student should know these terms and types (including case examples) of adjustment disorder.

- adjustment disorder:
  - with anxiety
  - with depressed mood
  - with disturbance of conduct
  - with mixed anxiety and depressed mood
  - with mixed disturbance of emotions and conduct
- bereavement
- good-enough mother
- maladaptive reaction
- mass catastrophes
- posttraumatic stress disorder
- psychosocial stressor
- recovery rate
- secondary gain
- severity of stress scale
- Donald Winnicott

▲ QUESTIONS

DIRECTIONS: Each of these statements or questions is followed by five suggested responses or completions. Select the *one* that is *best* in each case.

26.1 According to DSM-IV, which of the following conditions need *not* be considered when diagnosing adjustment disorder?

A. Bereavement
B. Panic disorder
C. Personality disorder
D. Acute stress disorder
E. Posttraumatic stress disorder

26.2 A 39-year-old divorced woman was referred for psychiatric evaluation after a brief hospitalization for complaints of intermittent numbness in her arms and the right side of her face. Extensive neurological evaluation revealed stenosis of the outlets of several cervical vertebrae; intermittently compromised nerve roots were thought to account for the physical symptoms. The patient, an artist who composed large structures from various work materials, was advised by her physicians to stop for the next several months all lifting, reaching, raising her arms, and other strenuous activities requisite to her work. She had felt despondent for more than 2 months, with episodes of tearfulness, anxiety, and increased irritability. She continued to supervise her assistants but was increasingly uninterested in work. She had no sleep or appetite change, but her libido was diminished. She was still able to enjoy music. The patient had no prior personal or familial history of a mood disorder.

The best diagnosis is

A. major depressive disorder
B. dysthymic disorder
C. adjustment disorder with depressed mood
D. adjustment disorder with anxiety
E. adjustment disorder, unspecified

26.3 For a diagnosis of adjustment disorder, the reaction to a psychosocial stressor must occur within

A. 1 week
B. 2 weeks
C. 1 month
D. 2 months
E. 3 months

26.4 Adjustment disorder

A. correlates with the severity of the stressor
B. occurs more often in males than in females
C. is a type of bereavement
D. usually requires years of treatment
E. occurs in all age groups

26.5 Adjustment disorder is

A. an exacerbation of a preexisting verbal disorder
B. a normal response to a nonspecific stressor
C. a normal response to a clearly identifiable event
D. a maladaptive reaction to an identifiable stressor
E. a type of brief psychotic disorder

26.6 Adjustment disorder may be associated with

A. beginning school
B. leaving home
C. getting married
D. becoming a parent
E. all of the above

26.7 All of the following affect vulnerability to adjustment disorder *except*

A. adolescence
B. a previous history of a personality disorder
C. poor mothering experiences
D. severity of the stress
E. genetic predisposition

26.8 In adjustment disorder

A. the severity of the stress is not always predictive of the severity of the disorder
B. premorbid cognitive disorder may increase vulnerability
C. specific developmental stages usually show no associations
D. personality traits do not play a role
E. all of the above are true

26.9 Regarding the treatment of an adjustment disorder, which of the following is *incorrect*?

A. Patients with clearly delineated stressors do not require psychotherapy, since their disorder will remit spontaneously.
B. Crisis intervention is a brief type of therapy that may involve the use of hospitalization to resolve the disorder.
C. A brief period of pharmacotherapy with antidepressants or antianxiety agents may benefit some patients.
D. Patients may attempt secondary gains through the use of the illness role.
E. Psychotherapy remains the treatment of choice for adjustment disorder.

26.10 From a psychodynamic viewpoint, persons are vulnerable to adjustment disorder if

A. they have lost a parent during adolescence
B. they have concurrent personality disorder
C. they use mature defense mechanisms
D. their parents were supportive and nurturing in early childhood
E. they are in childhood

DIRECTIONS: The lettered headings below are followed by a list of numbered phrases. For each numbered phrase, select

A. if the item is associated with *A only*
B. if the item is associated with *B only*
C. if the item is associated with *both A and B*
D. if the item is associated with *neither A nor B*

Questions 26.11–26.13

A. Posttraumatic stress disorder
B. Adjustment disorder
C. Both
D. Neither

26.11 Disorder is induced by stressors.
26.12 Stressors producing the disorder are expected to do so in the average human being.
26.13 Psychotherapy is usually not recommended.

ANSWERS

Adjustment Disorders

26.1 The answer is B (*Synopsis VIII,* page 773).
Panic disorder is not considered when diagnosing adjustment disorder. All of the other conditions—*bereavement, personality disorder, acute stress disorder,* and *posttraumatic stress disorder*—are possible diagnoses when considering adjustment disorder. To diagnose adjustment disorder, there must be an external stressor producing the symptoms, and the patient must show considerable social dysfunctioning. Panic disorder occurs without a stressor.

26.2 The answer is C (*Synopsis VIII,* page 771).
The best diagnosis for the case study of the 39-year-old woman is *adjustment disorder with depressed mood* (Table 26.1). The patient had stressors—a physical illness and the directive to minimize for several months the use of her arms. As a result, the patient was unable to continue her artistic endeavors, which were crucial to her sense of self. In response, she developed a depressive constellation with less than a full vegetative set of symptoms; therefore, *major depressive disorder* could not be diagnosed. *Dysthymic disorder* was ruled out because her depressive symptoms were episodic. *Adjustment disorder with anxiety* would be diagnosed if the patient had such complaints as palpitations, agitation, jitters, and other symptoms of anxiety. Although the patient's response was maladaptive, it was not atypical, which is required for a diagnosis of *adjustment disorder, unspecified.*

Table 26.1
DSM-IV Diagnostic Criteria for Adjustment Disorder

A. The development of emotional or behavioral symptoms in response to a identifiable stressor(s) occurring within 3 months of the onset of the stressor(s).

B. These symptoms or behaviors are clinically significant as evidenced by either of the following:
   (1) marked distress that is in excess of what would be expected from exposure to the stressor
   (2) significant impairment in social or occupational (academic) functioning

C. The stress-related disturbance does not meet the criteria for any specific Axis I disorder and is not merely an exacerbation of a preexisting Axis I or Axis II disorder.

D. Does not represent bereavement.

E. Once the stressor (or its consequences) has terminated, the symptoms do not persist for more than an additional 6 months.

Specify if:
Acute: if the disturbance lasts less than 6 months
Chronic: if the disturbance lasts for 6 months or longer

Adjustment Disorders are coded based on the subtype, which is selected according to the predominant symptoms. The specific stressor(s) can be specified on Axis IV.
With depressed mood
With anxiety
With mixed anxiety and depressed mood
With disturbance of conduct
With mixed disturbance of emotions and conduct
Unspecified

Reprinted with permission from American Psychiatric Associaton: *Diagnostic and Statistical Manual of Mental Disorders,* ed 4. Copyright, American Psychiatric Association, Washington, 1994.

26.3 The answer is E (*Synopsis VIII,* page 771).
According to the fourth edition of *Diagnosis and Statistical Manual of Mental Disorders* (DSM-IV), symptoms of adjustment disorder must occur within *3 months* of the onset of the stressor. If a longer time intervenes between the onset of the psychiatric symptoms and an identifiable psychosocial stressor, the clinician should not make a diagnosis of adjustment disorder. Symptoms can occur as early as *1 week, 2 weeks, 1 month,* or *2 months,* but DSM-IV allows more time between the stressor and the onset of the symptoms.

26.4 The answer is E (*Synopsis VIII,* page 770).
Adjustment disorder *occurs in all age groups.* It *does not always correlate with the severity of the stressor* and appears to *occur more often in females than in males.* Adjustment disorder *is not a type of bereavement.* The overall prognosis for a person with adjustment disorder is generally favorable with appropriate treatment. Most patients return to their previous level of functioning within 3 months and *do not require years of therapy.*

26.5 The answer is D (*Synopsis VIII,* page 770).
According to DSM-IV, adjustment disorder is *a maladaptive reaction to an identifiable stressor.* It is *not an exacerbation of a preexisting mental disorder.* The patient's response is to an identifiable stressor rather than to a nonspecific stressor. The response must be identified by significant impairment in social or occupational functioning or by symptoms that are in marked excess of a normal and expectable reaction to the stressor. Thus, adjustment disorder is *not a normal response to either a nonspecific stressor or to a clearly identifiable event.* Adjustment disorder is not *a type of brief psychotic disorder.* Even if a precipitant stressor can be identified, the diagnosis of brief psychotic disorder is assigned only if the patient shows evidence of psychotic thinking, speech, or behavior.

26.6 The answer is E (all) (*Synopsis VIII,* page 770).
Specific developmental stages—such as *beginning school, leaving home, getting married, becoming a parent,* failing to achieve occupational goals, the last child's leaving home, and retiring—are often associated with adjustment disorder.

26.7 The answer is E (*Synopsis VIII,* pages 770–771).
There have been *no studies showing genetic predisposition* as a condition that *affects vulnerability to adjustment disorders.* Each person has a particular threshold prior to developing the disorder, but all persons can develop an adjustment disorder given sufficient stressors. Vulnerability to adjustment disorder is affected by many factors. Persons with *a history of a personality disorder* or a cognitive disorder are susceptible. *The severity of the stressor* also increases vulnerability (for example, the loss of a young child is a greater stress than the loss of an aged parent.) Adjustment disorder may occur at any

age, but it is most common during *adolescence* and young adulthood. Vulnerability is increased by *poor mothering experiences.* Providing the infant with an environment in which anxiety is attended to appropriately enables the growing child to tolerate the frustrations in life. Vulnerability is also associated with the lack of a parent during infancy and childhood.

26.8 The answer is B (*Synopsis VIII,* pages 770–771).
In adjustment disorder, *premorbid cognitive disorders may increase vulnerability.* The severity of the stress is *not always predictive of the severity of the disorder.* Specific developmental stages *are often associated with adjustment disorder. Personality traits do play a role in adjustment disorder.*

26.9 The answer is A (*Synopsis VIII,* pages 773–774).
Regarding the treatment of an adjustment disorder, it is often believed that *patients with clearly delineated stressors do not require psychotherapy, since their disorder will remit spontaneously.* However, such thinking fails to consider that many persons exposed to the same stressor do not experience similar symptoms and that the response is pathological. Psychotherapy can help the person adapt to the stressor if it is not reversible or time-limited and can serve as a preventive intervention if the stressor does not remit. *Crisis intervention* is a brief type of therapy that may involve the use of hospitalization to resolve the disorder. A course of *brief pharmacotherapy* using antidepressants or antianxiety agents may benefit some patients if used especially in conjunction with psychotherapy. Patients may attempt *secondary gains* through the use of the illness role's capacity to remove them from responsibility. Psychotherapy remains *the treatment of choice for adjustment disorder.*

26.10 The answer is B (*Synopsis VIII,* page 770).
Persons who *have a concurrent personality disorder* or organic impairment are vulnerable to adjustment disorder. Vulnerability is also increased if *they lost a parent during infancy, not during adolescence.* Actual or perceived support from key relationships may mediate behavioral and emotional responses to stressors. Persons who use *mature defense mechanisms* are not vulnerable; they bounce back quickly from the stressor. Studies of trauma repeatedly indicate that if *parents were supportive and nurturing in early childhood,* traumatic incidents do not cause permanent psychological damage. No increased vulnerability to adjustment disorder is found *in childhood years;* adjustment disorder may occur at any age.

Answers 26.11–26.13

26.11 The answer is C (*Synopsis VIII,* pages 770, 773).

26.12 The answer is A (*Synopsis VIII,* page 773).

26.13 The answer is D (*Synopsis VIII,* pages 773–774).
Both adjustment disorder and posttraumatic stress disorder are *induced by stressors. Stressors producing posttraumatic stress disorder are expected to do so in the average human being.* The response to a stressor in adjustment disorder is beyond the normal, usual, or expected response to such a stressor. *Psychotherapy is the treatment of choice for both adjustment disorder and posttraumatic stress disorder.*

27 

Personality Disorders

The fourth edition of *Diagnostic and Statistical Manual of Mental Disorders* (DSM-IV) specifies 11 personality disorders, each of which is marked by an enduring, pervasive, and inflexible pattern of inner experience and behavior that deviates markedly from cultural expectations. Personality disorder has an onset in adolescence or early adulthood, is stable over time, and leads to distress or impairment. The DSM-IV categories include paranoid, schizoid, schizotypal, antisocial, borderline, histrionic, narcissistic, avoidant, dependent, and obsessive-compulsive personality disorders and personality disorder not otherwise specified.

Specific personality disorders are a condition of ingrained and enduring behavior patterns that manifest themselves as inflexible responses to a broad range of personal and social situations. These patterns are extreme or significant deviations from cultural norms; they are stable and often associated with subjective distress and problems in social functioning and performance.

Human personality refers to everything about a person's behavior, temperament, and psychology; it arises from a complex interaction of biology, development, and environment and is manifested in the ways a person behaves with himself or herself, with others, and with the world.

There is a wide range of personality variation, but people with healthy personalities are flexible and adaptive. A personality disorder reflects a breakdown somewhere in the complex process of personality formation—in biology, genetics, temperament, psychology, environment.

Stress can produce maladaptive or rigid reactions in everyone, but in a person with a personality disorder such reactions are sustained and pervasive. People with these disorders see the world around them as causing their distress, unhappiness, rage, or anxiety; they ignore and do not consciously experience their impaired capacity to get along with others and their inability to enjoy life. If they are aware of their own contribution to their unhappiness, they may be unable to change their patterns of behavior. Although these patterns are deeply maladaptive, they also protect people with personality disorders from their unconscious feelings of anxiety and depression, which might otherwise overwhelm them and make them unable to function at all.

In DSM-IV, the personality disorders are grouped into three clusters—A, B, and C—according to the predominant personality traits. Cluster A, for instance, includes paranoid, schizoid, and schizotypal personality disorders, all of which are manifested in odd, reclusive, eccentric behavior. Personality disorder not otherwise specified includes passive-aggressive and depressive personality disorders.

In addition to the psychodynamic factors in personality disorders, genetic factors also play a role. More people with schizotypal personality disorder are found in families of people with schizophrenia than in control groups, and borderline personality disorder often coexists with a mood disorder.

These disorders are difficult to treat because of the lifelong, inflexible patterns of functioning. Successful treatment includes psychotherapy, cognitive behavioral techniques, pharmacotherapy, and family, substance abuse, and group interventions.

Students are referred to Chapter 27 in *Kaplan and Sadock's Synopsis VIII* to prepare for the questions and answers in this chapter.

HELPFUL HINTS

The student should be able to define the terms that follow.

- acting out
- alloplastic
- ambulatory schizophrenia
- anal triad
- antisocial
- as-if personality
- autoplastic
- avoidant
- borderline
- Briquet's syndrome
- castration anxiety
- chaotic sexuality
- character armor
- Stella Chess, Alexander Thomas
- clusters A, B, and C
- counterprojection
- denied affect
- dependence
- dependent
- depressive
- dissociation
- ego-dystonic
- ego-syntonic
- emotionally unstable personality
- endorphins
- Erik Erikson
- extroversion
- fantasy
- free association
- goodness of fit
- histrionic
- hypochondriasis
- ideas of reference
- identity diffusion
- inferiority complex
- introversion
- isolation

- Carl Gustav Jung
- Heinz Kohut
- *la belle indifférence*
- macropsia
- magical thinking
- mask of sanity
- micropsychotic episodes
- narcissistic
- object choices
- obsessive-compulsive
- oral character
- organic personality disorder
- panambivalence
- pananxiety
- panphobia
- paranoid
- passive-aggressive
- platelet MAO
- projection
- psychotic character
- Wilhelm Reich
- repression
- saccadic movements
- Leopold von Sacher-Masoch
- Marquis de Sade
- sadistic personality
- sadomasochistic personality
- schizoid
- schizotypal
- secondary gain
- self-defeating personality
- splitting
- three Ps
- timid temperament
- turning anger against the self

▲ QUESTIONS

DIRECTIONS: For each of the numbered symptoms, choose the most appropriate of the following lettered disorders.

A. Paranoid personality disorder
B. Dependent personality disorder
C. Depressive personality disorder
D. Passive-aggressive personality disorder
E. Obsessive-compulsive personality disorder

27.1 A patient agrees with his mother when she tells the clinician of her son's incompetence.

27.2 A patient criticizes her family's spendthrift ways and sees her future as gloomy and hopeless.

27.3 A patient accuses his teacher of always grading him unfairly but later begs the teacher to raise a grade.

DIRECTIONS: For the following numbered question, select the most appropriate lettered response.

27.4 Which of the following symptoms is *least* typical of schizoid personality disorder?

A. Love of swimming
B. Painful social interactions
C. Obsession with computer games
D. Disinterest in sexual experiences
E. Apparently bland reaction to stress

DIRECTIONS: Each of these questions or incomplete statements is followed by five suggested responses or completions. Select the *one* that is *best* in each case.

27.5 A 21-year-old man was interviewed by a psychiatrist while he was being detained in jail awaiting trial for attempted robbery. The patient had a history of arrests for substance abuse, robbery, and assault and battery.

The patient's history revealed that he had been expelled from junior high school for truancy, fighting, and generally poor academic performance. After his theft of a car when he was 14 years old, he was placed in a juvenile detention center. Subsequently, he spent brief periods in a variety of institutions, from which he usually ran away. At times, his parents attempted to let him live at home, but he was disruptive and threatened them with physical harm. After one incident in which he threatened them with a knife, he was admitted to a psychiatric hospital, but he signed himself out against medical advice a day later.

The most likely diagnosis is

A. narcissistic personality disorder
B. borderline personality disorder
C. antisocial personality disorder
D. schizoid personality disorder
E. paranoid personality disorder

27.6 Which statement concerning antisocial personality disorder is *false*?

A. The prevalence of antisocial personality disorder is 3 percent in men and 1 percent in women.
B. A familial pattern is present.
C. The patients commonly show abnormalities in their electroencephalograms and soft neurological signs.
D. Antisocial personality disorder is synonymous with criminality.
E. The patients appear to lack a conscience.

27.7 Leon was a 45-year-old postal service employee who was evaluated at a clinic specializing in the treatment of depression. He claimed to have felt constantly depressed since the first grade, without a period of normal mood for more than a few days at a time. His depression was accompanied by lethargy, little or no interest or pleasure in anything, trouble in concentrating, and feelings of inadequacy, pessimism, and resentfulness. His only periods of normal mood occurred when he was home alone, listening to music or watching TV.

On further questioning, Leon revealed that he could never remember feeling comfortable socially. Even before kindergarten, if he was asked to speak in front of a group of family friends, his mind would go blank. He felt overwhelming anxiety at children's social functions, such as birthday parties, which he either avoided or attended in total silence. He could answer questions in class only if he wrote down the answers in advance; even then, he frequently mumbled and could not get the answer out. He met new children with his eyes lowered, fearing their scrutiny, expecting to feel humiliated and embarrassed. He was convinced that everyone around him thought he was dumb or a jerk.

During the past several years, he had tried several therapies to help him get over his shyness and depression. Leon had never experienced sudden anxiety or a panic attack in social situations or at other times. Rather, his anxiety gradually built to a constant level in anticipation of social situations. He had never experienced any psychotic symptoms.

The *best* diagnosis is

A. avoidant personality disorder
B. schizoid personality disorder
C. schizotypal personality disorder
D. social phobia
E. adjustment disorder with anxiety

27.8 Which of the following statements about borderline personality disorder is *false*?

A. Patients with borderline personality disorder have more relatives with mood disorders than do control groups.
B. Borderline personality disorder and mood disorders often coexist.
C. First-degree relatives of persons with borderline personality disorder show an increased prevalence of alcohol dependence.
D. Smooth-pursuit eye movements are abnormal in borderline personality disorder.
E. Monoamine oxidase inhibitors are used in the treatment of borderline personality disorder patients.

27.9 Adult patients with borderline personality disorder who pigeonhole people into all-good and all-bad categories are demonstrating which of the following mechanisms?

A. Undoing
B. Intellectualization
C. Projection
D. Splitting
E. Displacement

27.10 The defense mechanism most often associated with paranoid personality disorder is

A. hypochondriasis
B. splitting
C. isolation
D. projection
E. dissociation

27.11 A pervasive pattern of grandiosity, lack of empathy, and need for admiration suggests the diagnosis of which of the following personality disorders?

A. Schizotypal
B. Passive-aggressive
C. Borderline
D. Narcissistic
E. Paranoid

27.12 Which of the following is *not* characteristic of the dependent personality disorder?

A. More often diagnosed in men than in women
B. More common in youngest children of a sibship than in the older children
C. Pessimism
D. Marked lack of self-confidence
E. Getting others to assume responsibility for major areas of the patient's life

27.13 People who are prone to dependent personality disorder include all of the following *except*

A. men
B. younger children
C. persons with chronic physical illness in childhood
D. persons with a history of separation anxiety disorder
E. children of mothers with panic disorder

27.14 Sadomasochistic personality disorder is

A. not included in the fourth edition of *Diagnostic and Statistical Manual of Mental Disorders* (DSM-IV)
B. characterized by unconscious castration anxiety
C. characterized by severe guilt about sex
D. best treated with insight-oriented psychotherapy
E. all of the above

27.15 A 34-year-old single man who lives with his mother and works as an accountant is seeking treatment because he is very unhappy after having just broken up with his girlfriend. He feels trapped and forced to choose between his mother and his girlfriend, and because "blood is thicker than water," he has decided not to go against his mother's wishes. Nonetheless, he is angry at himself and at her and believes that she will never let him marry and is possessively hanging on to him. His mother wears the pants in the family and is a very domineering woman who is used to getting her way. He is afraid of disagreeing with his mother for fear that she will not be supportive of him and he will have to fend for himself. He feels that his own judgment is poor.

He has lived at home his whole life except for 1 year of college, from which he returned because of homesickness. Heterosexual adjustment has been normal except for his inability to leave his mother in favor of another woman.

Based on this patient's clinical presentation, what is the *least likely* diagnosis?

A. Adjustment disorder
B. Dependent personality disorder
C. Narcissistic personality disorder
D. Schizoid personality disorder
E. Borderline personality disorder

27.16 The same patient provides you with additional personal information. At his accounting job, he has on several occasions turned down promotions because he didn't want the responsibility of having to supervise other people or make independent decisions. He has worked for the same boss for 10 years, gets on well with him, and is in turn highly regarded as a dependable and unobtrusive worker. He has two very close friends whom he has had since early childhood. He has lunch with one of them every workday and feels lost if his friend is sick and misses a day.

He is the youngest of four children and the only boy. He was "babied and spoiled" by his mother and elder sisters. He had considerable separation anxiety as a child—he had difficulty falling asleep unless his mother stayed in the room, mild school refusal, and unbearable homesickness when he occasionally tried sleepovers.

Based on the additional information provided, what is the *most likely* diagnosis for this patient?

A. Adjustment disorder
B. Dependent personality disorder
C. Narcissistic personality disorder
D. Schizoid personality disorder
E. Borderline personality disorder

DIRECTIONS: Each group of questions consists of lettered headings followed by a list of numbered statements. For each numbered phrase or statement, select the *one* lettered heading that is most closely associated with it. Each lettered heading may be selected once, more than once, or not at all.

Questions 27.17–27.21

A. Schizoid personality disorder
B. Schizotypal personality disorder

27.17 Strikingly odd or eccentric behavior
27.18 Magical thinking
27.19 Ideas of reference
27.20 Formerly called latent schizophrenia
27.21 Suspiciousness or paranoid ideation

Questions 27.22–27.29

A. Dependent personality disorder
B. Organic personality disorder
C. Obsessive-compulsive personality disorder
D. Paranoid personality disorder
E. Histrionic personality disorder
F. Borderline personality disorder
G. Avoidant personality disorder
H. Antisocial personality disorder

27.22 Cognitive disturbances, suspiciousness, and paranoid ideation
27.23 Preoccupation with orderliness and perfectionism; rigidity and stubbornness
27.24 Feelings of helplessness when alone, difficulty in doing things on their own
27.25 Desire to be the center of attention, preoccupation with physical appearance
27.26 Unwillingness to get involved with people unless certain of being liked
27.27 Identity disturbance, impulsivity, and recurrent suicidal behavior
27.28 Reading of hidden demeaning or threatening meanings into benign events and comments
27.29 Apparent lack of remorse for their actions

ANSWERS

Personality Disorders

27.1 The answer is B (*Synopsis VIII,* pages 790–791).
People with *dependent personality disorder* have a pervasive need to be taken care of. This need leads to submissive behavior and fears of separation, a pattern that begins by early adulthood. The dependent behaviors are meant to elicit the desired caregiving, and patients feel unable to function on their own. People with this disorder need help from others for decisions of everyday life such as what to wear, where to live, what job to work at, and what people to know. Parents and spouses must take responsibility for such decisions, and because patients are often unable to disagree with those on whom they are dependent, they must accept others' words and actions even when they are negative. Thus *a patient can agree with his mother's poor evaluation* of himself to maintain the dependent relationship.

27.2 The answer is C (*Synopsis VIII,* pages 794–795).
People with *depressive personality disorder* exhibit a pervasive pattern of depressive thoughts and behaviors that begin by early adulthood and that include persistent feelings of gloominess, dejection, hopelessness, and unhappiness. Such people seem unable to enjoy life and may lack a sense of humor. They brood about the present and future and see their attitude as realistic rather than pessimistic. They judge others as harshly as they judge themselves, and by focusing on the negative rather than positive aspects of situations, they seem to close the door on life. Thus a patient with depressive personality disorder would *brood about her family's lack of thrift* and would see the future as bleakly as the present.

27.3 The answer is D (*Synopsis VIII,* pages 793–794).
People with *passive-aggressive personality disorder* show a pervasive pattern of negative attitudes and passive resistance to demands for adequate performance in social and occupational situations. The pattern begins in early adulthood and occurs in many contexts. Such people resent and resist demands to function at an expected level and may procrastinate, forget, and even intentionally fail tasks given by figures of authority. They blame their failures on others, feel cheated and unappreciated, and complain to and about others, but they can also beseech others to accept them. Thus a person with passive-aggressive personality disorder would be *likely to blame his teacher,* rather than his own poor performance, for his low grades and in the belief that a low grade was unfairly given, would ask the teacher to *improve the grade.*

Paranoid personality disorder is characterized by a pattern of distrust and suspiciousness toward others, who are thought to have evil intentions. *Obsessive-compulsive personality disorder* is a pattern of preoccupation with orderliness, perfectionism, and control. Neither of these disorders would apply to the symptoms described in the questions.

27.4 The answer is A (*Synopsis VIII,* pages 780–782).
People with schizoid personality disorder exhibit a pervasive pattern of detachment from social relationships and a restricted range of emotional expression. The pattern begins in early adulthood. Such people seem to lack a desire for close relationships and prefer to be alone. Their work and hobbies are almost always solitary. Because they do not especially enjoy the pleasures of sensory and bodily experiences, they are unlikely to have a *love of swimming.* They also show a *disinterest in sexual relationships.* Such people are likely to develop an *obsession with computer games.*

Painful social interactions are typical for such people because such situations may force them to reveal themselves. Generally they show an *apparently bland reaction to stress* and seem to cultivate a distance between themselves and the rest of the world.

27.5 The answer is C (*Synopsis VIII,* pages 784–785)
The most likely diagnosis is *antisocial personality disorder,* which is characterized by continual antisocial or criminal acts and an inability to conform to social norms that involves many aspects of the patient's adolescent and adult development. In the case of the 21-year-old man described, the many arrests for criminal acts, the aggressiveness, and the inability to maintain an enduring attachment to a sexual partner all suggest antisocial personality disorder. The fourth edition of *Diagnostics and Statistical Manual of Mental Disorders* (DSM-IV) requires evidence of conduct disorder before age 15 to make the diagnosis of antisocial personality disorder; in the case described, the history of truancy, expulsion from school, fighting, and thefts, all before age 15, confirms the diagnosis.

Narcissistic personality disorder is characterized by a heightened sense of self-importance, grandiose feelings of uniqueness, lack of empathy, and need for admiration. *Borderline personality disorder* is characterized by severely unstable mood, affect, behavior, object relations, and self-image. Antisocial personality disorder is frequently associated with narcissistic and borderline personality disorders. *Schizoid personality disorder* is diagnosed in patients with a lifelong pattern of social withdrawal. Such persons are often seen by others as eccentric, isolated, or lonely. *Paranoid personality disorder* is characterized by long-standing suspiciousness and mistrust of people in general and a tendency to interpret other people's actions as deliberately demeaning or threatening. The history provided in the case described does not justify the diagnosis of either schizoid personality disorder or paranoid personality disorder. Table 27.1 lists the diagnostic criteria for antisocial personality disorder.

27.6 The answer is D (*Synopsis VIII,* pages 782–783).
Antisocial personality disorder is characterized by continual antisocial or criminal acts, but it *is not synonymous with criminality.* Rather, it is a pattern of irresponsible and antisocial behavior that pervades the patient's adolescence and adulthood. *The prevalence of antisocial personality disorder is 3 percent in men and 1 percent in women. A familial pattern is present* in that it is 5 times more common among first-degree relatives of males with the disorder than among controls. A notable finding is a lack of remorse; that is, *the patients appear to lack a conscience.* The patients often *show abnormalities in*

Table 27.1
DSM-IV Diagnostic Criteria for Antisocial Personality Disorder

A. There is a pervasive pattern of disregard for and violation of the rights of others occurring since age 15 years, as indicated by three (or more) of the following:
   (1) failure to conform to social norms with respect to lawful behaviors as indicated by repeatedly performing acts that are grounds for arrest
   (2) deceitfulness, as indicated by repeated lying, use of aliases, or conning others for personal profit or pleasure
   (3) impulsivity or failure to plan ahead
   (4) irritability and aggressiveness, as indicated by repeated physical fights or assaults
   (5) reckless disregard for safety of self or others
   (6) consistent irresponsibility, as indicated by repeated failure to sustain consistent work behavior or honor financial obligations
   (7) lack of remorse, as indicated by being indifferent to or rationalizing having hurt, mistreated, or stolen from another

B. The individual is at least age 18 years.

C. There is evidence of conduct disorder with onset before age 15 years.

D. The occurrence of antisocial behavior is not exclusively during the course of schizophrenia or a manic episode.

Reprinted with permission from American Psychiatric Association: *Diagnostic and Statistical Manual of Mental Disorders,* ed 4. Copyright, American Psychiatric Association, Washington, 1994.

Table 27.2
DSM-IV Diagnostic Criteria for Avoidant Personality Disorder

A pervasive pattern of social inhibition, feelings of inadequacy, and hypersensitivity to negative evaluation, beginning by early adulthood and present in a variety of contexts, as indicated by four (or more) of the following:
   (1) avoids occupational activities that involve significant interpersonal contact because of fears of criticism, disapproval, or rejection
   (2) is unwilling to get involved with people unless certain of being liked
   (3) shows restraint within intimate relationships because of the fear of being shamed or ridiculed
   (4) is preoccupied with being critized or rejected in social situations
   (5) is inhibited in new interpersonal situations because of feelings of inadequacy
   (6) views self as socially inept, personally unappealing, or inferior to others
   (7) is unusually reluctant to take personal risks or to engage in any new activities because they may prove embarrassing

Reprinted with permission from American Psychiatric Association: *Diagnostic and Statistical Manual of Mental Disorders,* ed 4. Copyright, American Psychiatric Association, Washington, 1994.

their electroencephalograms and soft neurological signs suggestive of minimal brain damage in childhood.

27.7 The answer is A (*Synopsis VIII,* pages 789–790).
The best diagnosis is *avoidant personality disorder.* Although feeling constantly depressed caused him to seek treatment, the pervasive pattern of social avoidance, fear of criticism, and lack of close peer relationships was of equal importance. Persons with avoidant personality show an extreme sensitivity to rejection, which may lead to social withdrawal. They are not asocial but are shy and show a great desire for companionship; they need unusually strong guarantees of uncritical acceptance. In the case presented, the patient exhibited a long-standing pattern of difficulty in relating to others. Persons with *schizoid personality disorder* do not evince the same strong desire for affection and acceptance; they want to be alone. *Schizotypal personality disorder* is characterized by strikingly odd or strange behavior, magical thinking, peculiar ideas, ideas of reference, illusions, and derealization. The patient described did not exhibit those characteristics. *Social phobia* is an irrational fear of social or performance situations such as public speaking and eating in public. A social phobia is anxiety concerning socially identified situations, not relationships in general.

A person with a personality disorder can have a superimposed adjustment disorder, but only if the current episode includes new clinical features not characteristic of the person's personality. No evidence in the case described indicated that the anxiety was qualitatively different from what the patient always experienced in social situations. Thus, an additional diagnosis of *adjustment disorder with anxiety* is not made. The diagnostic criteria for avoidant personality disorder are listed in Table 27.2.

27.8 The answer is D (*Synopsis VIII,* pages 786–787).
Smooth pursuit eye movements are normal in borderline personality disorder. They are abnormal in schizophrenic patients and patients with schizotypal personality disorder.

Patients with borderline personality disorders have *more relatives with mood disorders* than do members of control groups, and *borderline personality disorder and mood disorder often coexist.* First-degree relatives of persons with borderline personality disorder show an *increased prevalence of alcohol dependence* and substance abuse. *Monoamine oxidase inhibitors* are used in the treatment of borderline personality disorder patients and have been effective in modulating affective instability and impulsivity in a number of patients. Table 27.3 lists the diagnostic criteria for borderline personality disorder.

27.9 The answer is D (*Synopsis VIII,* page 780).
Adult patients with borderline personality disorder distort their relationships by pigeonholing people into all-good and all-bad categories, a defense mechanism known as *splitting.* People are seen as either nurturant and attachment figures or hateful and sadistic persons who deprive the patients of security needs and threaten them with abandonment whenever they feel dependent.

Undoing is an unconscious defense mechanism by which a person symbolically acts out in reverse something unacceptable that has already been done or against which the ego must defend itself. A primitive defense mechanism, undoing is a form of magical expiatory action. Repetitive in nature, it is commonly observed in obsessive-compulsive disorder. *Intellectualization* is an unconscious defense mechanism in which reasoning or logic is used in an attempt to avoid confrontation with an objectionable impulse and thus defend against anxiety. It is also known as brooding compulsion and thinking compulsion. *Projection* is an unconscious defense mechanism in which persons attribute to another generally unconscious ideas,

Table 27.3
DSM-IV Diagnostic Criteria for Borderline Personality Disorder

A pervasive pattern of instability of interpersonal relationships, self-image, and affects and marked impulsivity beginning by early adulthood and present in a variety of contexts, as indicated by five (or more) of the following:

(1) frantic efforts to avoid real or imagined abandonment. **Note:** Do not include suicidal or self-mutilating behavior covered in criterion 5.
(2) a pattern of unstable and intense interpersonal relationships characterized by alternating between extremes of idealization and devaluation
(3) identity disturbance: markedly and persistently unstable self-image or sense of self
(4) impulsivity in at least two areas that are potentially self-damaging (eg, spending, sex, substance abuse, reckless driving, binge eating). **Note:** Do not include suicidal or self-mutilating behavior covered in criterion 5.
(5) recurrent suicidal behavior, gestures, or threats, or self-mutilating behavior
(6) affective instability due to a marked reactivity of mood (eg, intense episodic dysphoria, irritability, or anxiety usually lasting a few hours and only rarely more than a few days)
(7) chronic feelings of emptiness
(8) inappropriate, intense anger or difficulty controlling anger (eg, frequent displays of temper, constant anger, recurrent physical fights)
(9) transient, stress-related paranoid ideation or severe dissociative symptoms

Reprinted with permission from American Psychiatric Association: *Diagnostic and Statistical Manual of Mental Disorders,* ed 4. Copyright, American Psychiatric Association, Washington, 1994.

thoughts, feelings, and impulses that are personally undesirable or unacceptable. Projection protects persons from anxiety arising from an inner conflict. By externalizing whatever is unacceptable, persons deal with it as a situation apart from themselves. *Displacement* is an unconscious defense mechanism by which the emotional component of an unacceptable idea or object is transferred to a more acceptable one.

27.10 The answer is D (*Synopsis VIII,* page 780).
The defense mechanism most often associated with paranoid personality disorder is *projection.* The patients externalize their own emotions and attribute to others impulses and thoughts that they are unable to accept in themselves. Excessive fault finding, sensitivity to criticism, prejudice, and hypervigilance to injustice can all be understood as examples of projecting unacceptable impulses and thoughts onto others.

Hypochondriasis is a defense mechanism in some personality disorders, particularly in borderline, dependent, and passive-aggressive personality disorders. Hypochondriasis disguises reproach; that is, the hypochondriac complaint that others do not provide help often conceals bereavement, loneliness, or unacceptable aggressive impulses. The mechanism of hypochondriasis permits covert punishment of others with the patient's own pain and discomfort.

Splitting is used by patients with borderline personality disorder in particular. With splitting, the patient divides ambivalently regarded people, both past and present, into all-good or all-bad, rather than synthesizing and assimilating less-than-perfect caretakers.

Isolation is the defense mechanism characteristic of the orderly, controlled person, often labeled an obsessive-compulsive personality. Isolation allows the person to face painful situations without painful affect or emotion and thus to remain always in control.

Dissociation consists of a replacement of unpleasant affects with pleasant ones. It is most often seen in patients with histrionic personality disorder.

The diagnostic criteria for paranoid personality disorder are listed in Table 27.4.

27.11 The answer is D (*Synopsis VIII,* pages 788–789).
A pervasive pattern of grandiosity (in fantasy or behavior), lack of empathy, and need for admiration suggests the diagnosis of *narcissistic* personality disorder. The fantasies of narcissistic patients are of unlimited success, power, brilliance, beauty, and ideal love; their demands are for constant attention and admiration. Narcissistic personality disorder patients are indifferent to criticism or respond to it with feelings of rage or humiliation. Other common characteristics are a sense of entitlement, surprise and anger that people do not do what the patient wants, and interpersonal exploitiveness.

Schizotypal personality disorder is characterized by various eccentricities in communication or behavior, coupled with defects in the capacity to form social relationships. The term emphasizes a possible relation with schizophrenia. The manifestation of aggressive behavior in passive ways—such as obstructionism, pouting, stubbornness, and intentional inefficiency—typify *passive-aggressive* personality disorder. *Borderline* personality disorder is marked by instability of

Table 27.4
DSM-IV Diagnostic Criteria for Paranoid Personality Disorder

A. A pervasive distrust and suspiciousness of others such that their motives are interpreted as malevolent, beginning by early adulthood and present in a variety of contexts, as indicated by four (or more) of the following:
   (1) suspects, without sufficient basis, that others are exploiting, harming, or deceiving him or her
   (2) is preoccupied with unjustified doubts about the loyalty or trustworthiness of friends or associates
   (3) is reluctant to confide in others because of unwarranted fear that the information will be used maliciously against him or her
   (4) reads hidden demeaning or threatening meanings into benign remarks or events
   (5) persistently bears grudges, eg, is unforgiving of insults, injuries, or slights
   (6) perceives attacks on his or her character or reputation that are not apparent to others and is quick to react angrily or to counterattack
   (7) has recurrent suspicions, without justification, regarding fidelity of spouse or sexual partner

B. Does not occur exclusively during the course of schizophrenia, a mood disorder with psychotic features, or another psychotic disorder and is not due to the direct physiological effects of a general medical condition.

   Note: If criteria are met prior to the onset of schizophrenia, add "premorbid," eg, "paranoid personality disorder (premorbid)."

Reprinted with permission from American Psychiatric Association: *Diagnostic and Statistical Manual of Mental Disorders,* ed 4. Copyright, American Psychiatric Association, Washington, 1994.

mood, interpersonal relationships, and self-image. *Paranoid* personality disorder is characterized by rigidity, hypersensitivity, unwarranted suspicion, jealousy, envy, an exaggerated sense of self-importance, and a tendency to blame and ascribe evil motives to others.

Table 27.5 lists the diagnostic criteria for narcissistic personality disorder.

27.12 The answer is A (*Synopsis VIII,* pages 790–791). Dependent personality disorder is *more often diagnosed in women than in men.* It is *more common in the youngest children of a sibship than in the older children.*

Pessimism, marked lack of self-confidence, passivity, and fears about expressing sexual and aggressive feelings characterize the behavior of the person with dependent personality disorder. *Getting others to assume responsibility for major areas of the patient's life* is characteristic. The diagnostic criteria for dependent personality disorder are listed in Table 27.6.

27.13 The answer is A (*Synopsis VIII,* pages 790–791). People who are prone to dependent personality disorder include *women (who are more commonly affected than men), younger children,* and *persons with chronic physical illness in childhood.* Some workers believe that *a history of separation anxiety disorder* predisposes to the development of dependent personality disorder. Separation anxiety disorder has its onset before the age of 18 and is characterized by excessive anxiety concerning separation from people to whom the child is attached. Separation anxiety disorder itself may be frequent in *children of mothers with panic disorder,* and that factor may predispose to the development of dependent personality disorder.

Table 27.5
DSM-IV Diagnostic Criteria for Narcissistic Personality Disorder

A pervasive pattern of grandiosity (in fantasy or behavior), need for admiration, and lack of empathy, beginning by early adulthood and present in a variety of contexts, as indicated by five (or more) of the following:

(1) has a grandiose sense of self-importance (eg, exaggerates achievements and talents, expects to be recognized as superior without commensurate achievements)
(2) is preoccupied with fantasies of unlimited success, power, brillance, beauty, or ideal love
(3) believes that he or she is "special" and unique and can only be understood by, or should associate with, other special or high-status people (or institutions)
(4) requires excessive admiration
(5) has a sense of entitlement, ie, unreasonable expectations of especially favorable treatment or automatic compliance with his or her expectations
(6) is interpersonally exploitative, ie, takes advantage of others to achieve his or her own ends
(7) lacks empathy: is unwilling to recognize or identify with the feelings and needs of others
(8) is often envious of others or believes that others are envious of him or her
(9) shows arrogant, haughty behaviors or attitudes

Table 27.6
DSM-IV Diagnostic Criteria for Dependent Personality Disorder

A pervasive and excessive need to be taken care of that leads to submissive and clinging behavior and fears of separation, beginning by early adulthood and present in a variety of contexts, as indicated by five (or more) of the following:

(1) has difficulty making everyday decisions without an excessive amount of advice and reassurance from others
(2) needs others to assume responsibility for most major areas of his or her life
(3) has difficulty expressing disagreement with others because of fear of loss of support or approval. **Note:** Do not include realistic fears of retribution
(4) has difficulty initiating projects or doing things on his or her own (because of a lack of self-confidence in judgment or abilities rather than a lack of motivation or energy)
(5) goes to excessive lengths to obtain nurturance and support from others, to the point of volunteering to do things that are unpleasant
(6) feels uncomfortable or helpless when alone because of exaggerated fears of being unable to care for himself or herself
(7) urgently seeks another relationship as a source of care and support when a close relationship ends
(8) is unrealistically preoccupied with fears of being left to take care of himself or herself

27.14 The answer is E (all) (*Synopsis VIII,* page 795). Sadomasochistic personality disorder is characterized by elements of sadism, masochism or a combination of the two. Although *not included in DSM-IV,* it is clinically interesting.

Sigmund Freud believed that sadists warded off *unconscious castration anxiety* and were able to achieve sexual pleasure only when they were able to do to others what they feared would be done to them. Freud believed that masochists' ability to achieve orgasm is disturbed by anxiety and *severe guilt about sex* that are alleviated by their own suffering and punishment. Clinical observations indicate that elements of both sadistic and masochistic behavior are usually present in the same person. *Treatment with insight-oriented psychotherapy,* including psychoanalysis, has been effective in some cases. As a result of therapy, the patient becomes aware of the need for self-punishment secondary to excessive unconscious guilt and also comes to recognize repressed aggressive impulses that have their origins in early childhood.

27.15 The answer is C (*Synopsis VIII,* pages 788–789). The *least likely diagnosis is narcissistic personality disorder* because the patient exhibits no signs of a heightened sense of self importance, grandiose feelings of uniqueness, lack of empathy, and need for admiration. *Adjustment disorder* is a more likely diagnosis based on the patient's mood from his recent break-up with his girlfriend. *Dependent personality disorder* is a possible diagnosis because the patient shows a lack of self-confidence, and has difficulty expressing disagreement with others because of fear of loss of support or approval. *Schizoid personality disorder* is another possibility based on the patient's seemingly lifelong pattern of social withdrawal. Finally, *borderline personality disorder* is considered because the patient shows unstable mood and self-image.

27.16 The answer is B *(Synopsis VIII,* pages 790–791). Based on the additional information provided, *dependent personality disorder* is the most likely diagnosis for this patient. The patient states he turned down promotions at work to avoid the responsibility of supervising others and to avoid making independent decisions. The patient feels uncomfortable or helpless when alone because of exaggerated fear of being unable to care for himself. The patient exhibits no *narcissistic traits. Adjustment disorder* cannot be applied to this patient's case, because his symptoms are lifelong symptoms, and not just causally related to his recent break-up. The patient does not wish to be alone, as seen in *schizoid personality disorder,* and in fact, desires affection and acceptance. He shows no signs of impulsivity, recurrent suicidal behavior, or chronic feelings of emptiness, as seen in *borderline personality disorder.*

Answers 27.17–27.21

27.17 The answer is B (*Synopsis VIII,* page 783).

27.18 The answer is B (*Synopsis VIII,* page 783).

27.19 The answer is B (*Synopsis VIII,* page 783).

27.20 The answer is B (*Synopsis VIII,* page 784).

27.21 The answer is B (*Synopsis VIII,* pages 783–784). Unlike schizoid personality disorder (Table 27.7), *schizotypal personality disorder* (Table 27.8) manifests with *strikingly odd or eccentric behavior. Magical thinking, ideas of reference,* illusions, and derealization are common; their presence formerly led to defining this disorder as borderline, *or latent schizophrenia. Suspiciousness or paranoid ideation* occurs in schizotypal personality disorder, not schizoid personality disorder.

Table 27.8
DSM-IV Diagnostic Criteria for Schizotypal Personality Disorder

A. A pervasive pattern of social and interpersonal deficits marked by acute discomfort with, and reduced capacity for, close relationships as well as by cognitive or perceptual distortions and eccentricities of behavior, beginning by early adulthood and present in a variety of contexts, as indicated by five (or more) of the following:
  (1) ideas of reference (including delusions of reference)
  (2) odd beliefs or magical thinking that influence behavior and are inconsistent with subcultural norms (eg, superstitiousness, belief in clairvoyance, telepathy, or "sixth sense"; in children and adolescents, bizarre fantasies or preoccupations)
  (3) unusual perceptual experiences, including bodily illusions
  (4) odd thinking and speech (eg, vague, circumstantial, metaphorical, overelaborate, or stereotyped)
  (5) suspiciousness or paranoid ideation
  (6) inappropriate or constricted affect
  (7) behavior or appearance that is odd, eccentric, or peculiar
  (8) lack of close friends or confidants other than first-degree relatives
  (9) excessive social anxiety that does not diminish with familiarity and tends to be associated with paranoid fears rather than negative judgments about self

B. Does not occur exclusively during the course of schizophrenia, a mood disorder with psychotic features, another psychotic disorder, or a pervasive developmental disorder.

Note: If criteria are met prior to the onset of schizophrenia, add "premorbid," eg, "schizotypal personality disorder (premorbid)."

Table 27.7
DSM-IV Diagnostic Criteria for Schizoid Personality Disorder

A. A pervasive pattern of detachment from social relationships and a restricted range of expression of emotions in interpersonal settings, beginning by early adulthood and present in a variety of contexts, as indicated by four (or more) of the following:
  (1) neither desires nor enjoys close relationships, including being part of a family
  (2) almost always chooses solitary activities
  (3) has little, if any, interest in having sexual experiences with another person
  (4) takes pleasure in few, in any, activities
  (5) lacks close friends or confidants other than first-degree relatives
  (6) appears indifferent to the praise or criticism of others
  (7) shows emotional coldness, detachment, or flattened affectivity

B. Does not occur exclusively during the course of schizophrenia, a mood disorder with psychotic features, another psychotic disorder, or a pervasive developmental disorder and is not due to the direct physiological effects of a general medical condition.

Note: If criteria are met prior to the onset of schizophrenia, add "premorbid," eg, "schizoid personality disorder (premorbid)."

Answers 27.22–27.29

27.22 The answer is B (*Synopsis VIII,* page 790).

27.23 The answer is C (*Synopsis VIII,* page 791).

27.24 The answer is A (*Synopsis VIII,* page 790).

27.25 The answer is E (*Synopsis VIII,* pages 787–788).

27.26 The answer is G (*Synopsis VIII,* page 789).

27.27 The answer is F (*Synopsis VIII,* page 786).

27.28 The answer is D (*Synopsis VIII,* page 781).

27.29 The answer is H (*Synopsis VIII,* page 785). *Organic personality disorder* (Table 27.9) is characterized by *cognitive disturbances, suspiciousness, and paranoid ideation.* In the 10th revision of *International Statistical Classification of Diseases and Related Health Problems* (ICD-10), it is classified with personality and behavioral disorders due to brain disease, damage, and dysfunction.

Table 27.9
ICD-10 Diagnostic Criteria for Organic Personality Disorder

This disorder is characterized by a significant alteration of the habitual patterns of premorbid behavior. The expression of emotions, needs, and impulses is particularly affected. Cognitive functions may be defective mainly or even exclusively in the areas of planning and anticipating the likely personal and social consequences, as in the so-called frontal lobe syndrome. However, it is now known that this syndrome occurs not only with frontal lobe lesions but also with lesions to other circumscribed areas of the brain.

Diagnostic guidelines
In addition to an established history or other evidence of brain disease, damage, or dysfunction, a definitive diagnosis requires the presence of two or more of the following features:

(a) consistently reduced ability to persevere with goal-directed activities, especially those involving longer periods of time and postponed gratification;
(b) altered emotional behavior, characterized by emotional lability, shallow and unwarranted cheerfulness (euphoria, inappropriate jocularity), and easy change to irritability or short-lived outbursts of anger and aggression; In some instances apathy may be a more prominent feature;
(c) expression of needs and impulses without consideration of consequences or social convention (the patient may engage in dissocial acts, such as stealing, inappropriate sexual advances, or voracious eating, or may exhibit disregard for personal hygiene);
(d) cognitive disturbances, in the form of suspiciousness or paranoid ideation, and/or excessive preoccupation with a single, usually abstract, theme (eg, religion, "right" and "wrong");
(e) marked alteration of the rate and flow of language production, with features such as circumstantiality, overinclusiveness, viscosity, and hypergraphia;
(f) altered sexual behavior (hyposexuality or change of sexual preference).

Reprinted with permission from World Health Organization: *The ICD-10 Classification of Mental and Behavioural Disorders: Clinical Disorders and Diagnostic Guidelines.* Copyright, World Health Organization, Geneva, 1992.

Patients with *obsessive-compulsive personality disorder* (Table 27.10) are *preoccupied with orderliness and perfectionism and are rigid and stubborn.* In ICD-10 it is called anankastic personality disorder. In *dependent personality disorder patients feel helpless when alone and have difficulty in doing things on their own.* Patients with *histrionic personality disorder* (Table 27.11) *want to be the center of attention* and are *preoccupied with physical appearance.* Patients with *avoidant personality disorder* are *unwilling to get involved with people unless certain of being liked.* In ICD-10 this is called anxious personality disorder. *Borderline personality disorder* is characterized by *identity disturbance, impulsivity, and recurrent suicidal behavior.* In ICD-10 the disorder is called emotionally unstable personality disorder. Patients with *paranoid personality disorder read hidden demeaning or threatening meanings into benign events and comments.* Antisocial personalities lack a conscience or superego and have no *remorse* for their actions.

Table 27.10
DSM-IV Diagnostic Criteria for Obsessive-Compulsive Personality Disorder

A pervasive pattern of preoccupation with orderliness, perfectionism, and mental and interpersonal control, at the expense of flexibility, openness, and efficiency, beginning by early adulthood and present in a variety of contexts, as indicated by four (or more) of the following:

(1) is preoccupied with details, rules, lists, order, organization, or schedules to the extent that the major point of the activity is lost
(2) shows perfectionism that interferes with task completion (eg, is unable to complete a project because his or her own overly strict standards are not met)
(3) is excessively devoted to work and productivity to the exclusion of leisure activities and friendships (not accounted for by obvious economic necessity)
(4) is overconscientious, scrupulous, and inflexible about matters of morality, ethics, or values (not accounted for by cultural or religious identification)
(5) is unable to discard worn-out or worthless objects even when they have no sentimental value
(6) is reluctant to delegate tasks or to work with others unless they submit to exactly his or her way of doing things
(7) adopts a miserly spending style toward both self and others; money is viewed as something to be hoarded for future catastrophes
(8) shows rigidity and stubbornness

Reprinted with permission from American Psychiatric Association: *Diagnostic and Statistical Manual of Mental Disorders,* ed 4. Copyright, American Psychiatric Association, Washington, 1994.

Table 27.11
DSM-IV Diagnostic Criteria for Histrionic Personality Disorder

A pervasive pattern of excessive emotionality and attention seeking, beginning by early adulthood and present in a variety of contexts, as indicated by five (or more) of the following:

(1) is uncomfortable in situations in which he or she is not the center of attention
(2) interaction with others is often characterized by inappropriate sexually seductive or provocative behavior
(3) displays rapidly shifting and shallow expression of emotions
(4) consistently uses physical appearances to draw attention to self
(5) has a style of speech that is excessively impressionistic and lacking in detail
(6) shows self-dramatization, theatricality, and exaggerated expression of emotion
(7) is suggestible, ie, easily influenced by others or circumstances
(8) considers relationships to be more intimate than they actually are

Reprinted with permission from American Psychiatric Association: *Diagnostic and Statistical Manual of Mental Disorders,* ed 4. Copyright, American Psychiatric Association, Washington, 1994.

28 

Psychological Factors Affecting Medical Condition

The fourth edition of *Diagnostic and Statistical Manual of Mental Disorders* (DSM-IV) describes psychological factors affecting medical condition as characterized by one or more specific psychological or behavioral factors that adversely affect a general medical condition. These factors can affect a medical condition by influencing its course, interfering with its treatment, constituting an additional health risk, or precipitating the symptoms. Almost all medical conditions seen by clinicians have associated psychological or behavioral factors, which can affect the course of these conditions. DSM-IV reserves the category of psychological factors affecting medical condition for situations in which the psychological factors have a significant effect on the course or outcome of the medical condition or place the patient at significantly higher risk for an adverse outcome. There must be a close temporal correlation between the psychological factors and the course of the medical condition even when direct causality cannot be shown. DSM-IV gives five choices for the nature of the psychological factor: mental disorder, psychological symptoms, personality traits or coping styles, maladaptive health behaviors, and unspecified psychological factors. DSM-IV diagnostic criteria exclude somatoform disorders and physical complaints associated with substance-related disorders or specific mental disorders.

The subtle and complex relation between mind and body is far from understood, and the precise ways that psychological factors affect medical conditions are unknown. The answer is probably a combination of interactions, including a person's genetic and biological vulnerability, personality and psychological resilience, and general health, as well as the nature of the stress. Although the nature of the reactions that produce disease is under inquiry, the psychological factors in some disorders are well known. Disorders of the cardiovascular system, the respiratory system, the musculoskeletal system, the endocrine system, and the immune system have been investigated, and headaches, chronic pain, cocaine abuse, and dermatological disorders have also been studied for their associations with psychological factors.

The work of consultation-liaison psychiatrists addresses the needs of patients with psychological factors affecting their physical condition. Acting as consultants for medical doctors, consultation-liaison psychiatrists help to identify mental disorders and psychological responses to medical illnesses. They take note of a patient's way of coping with illness and recommend the most effective therapeutic intervention in each case. Consultation-liaison psychiatrists are called on for cases of suicidal ideation, agitation, hallucination, sleep disorders, disorientation, noncompliance, and disorders with no apparent organic basis. They may work in intensive care units, hemodialysis units, and surgical units.

The psychiatrist who deals with a patient's psychological problems works together with the medical specialist who handles the nonpsychiatric aspect's of a patient's disorder. The psychiatrist may offer psychodynamic psychotherapy, cognitive therapy, behavior therapy, and pharmacotherapy.

Students are referred to Chapter 28 in *Kaplan and Sadock's Synopsis VIII* for detailed information on the topic. After studying Chapter 28, students will be prepared to address the questions and answers that follow.

HELPFUL HINTS

These terms relating to psychophysiological medicine should be defined.

- ▶ AIDS
- ▶ Franz Alexander
- ▶ alexithymia
- ▶ allergic disorders
- ▶ analgesia
- ▶ atopic
- ▶ autoimmune diseases
- ▶ behavior modification deconditioning program
- ▶ biofeedback
- ▶ bronchial asthma
- ▶ bulimia nervosa and anorexia nervosa
- ▶ C-L psychiatry
- ▶ cardiac arrhythmias
- ▶ cell-mediated immunity
- ▶ chronic pain
- ▶ climacteric
- ▶ command hallucination
- ▶ compulsive personality traits
- ▶ congestive heart failure
- ▶ conversion disorder
- ▶ coronary artery disease
- ▶ crisis intervention
- ▶ Jacob DaCosta
- ▶ diabetes mellitus
- ▶ dialysis dementia
- ▶ Flanders Dunbar
- ▶ dysmenorrhea
- ▶ dysthymic disorder
- ▶ essential hypertension
- ▶ Meyer Friedman and Roy Rosenman
- ▶ general adaptation syndrome
- ▶ giving up-given up concept

- gun-barrel vision
- hay fever
- hemodialysis units
- Thomas Holmes and Richard Rahe
- hormonal personality factors
- humoral immunity
- hyperhidrosis
- hyperthyroidism
- hyperventilation syndrome
- hypochondriasis
- ICUs
- idiopathic amenorrhea
- IgM and IgA
- immediate and delayed hypersensitivity
- immune disorders
- immune response
- life-change units
- low back pain
- menopausal distress
- migraine
- myxedema madness
- neurocirculatory asthenia
- obesity
- obsessional personalities
- organ transplantation
- pain clinics
- pain threshold and perception
- pancreatic carcinoma
- peptic ulcer
- personality types
- pheochromocytoma
- PMS
- postcardiotomy delirium
- premenstrual dysphoric disorder
- propranolol (Inderal)
- pruritus
- psyche and soma
- psychogenic cardiac nondisease
- psychophysiological
- psychosomatic
- relaxation therapy
- rheumatoid arthritis
- Hans Selye
- skin disorders
- social readjustment rating scale
- somatization disorder
- specific versus nonspecific stress
- specificity hypothesis
- surgical patients
- systemic lupus erythematosus
- tension headaches
- thyrotoxicosis
- type A and type B personalities
- ulcerative colitis
- undermedication
- vasomotor syncope
- vasovagal attack
- Wilson's disease

▲ QUESTIONS

DIRECTIONS: Each of the questions or incomplete statements below is followed by five responses or completions. Select the *one* that is *best* in each case.

28.1 A major advance in the revised fourth edition of *Diagnostic and Statistical Manual of Mental Disorders* (DSM-IV) in regard to the diagnostic criteria for psychological factors affecting medical condition is that DSM-IV allows for emphasis on

A. environmental stimuli
B. psychological stimuli
C. somatoform disorders
D. conversion disorder
E. all of the above

28.2 A decrease in T lymphocytes has been reported in all of the following *except*

A. bereavement
B. caretakers of patients with dementia of the Alzheimer's type
C. women who are having extramarital affairs
D. nonpsychotic inpatients
E. medical students during final examinations

28.3 Which of the following statements about the relative importance of various stresses is *false*?

A. Divorce is a greater stress than marriage.
B. Marital separation is a greater stress than pregnancy.
C. Retirement from work is a greater stress than major illness.
D. In-law troubles are a greater stress than trouble with the boss.
E. Changing to a new school is a greater stress than going on vacation.

28.4 The major worker in the application of psychoanalytic concepts to the study of psychosomatic disorders was

A. George Mahl
B. Harold Wolff
C. Franz Alexander
D. Robert Ader
E. Meyer Friedman

28.5 Dialysis dementia is characterized by all of the following *except*

A. disorientation
B. loss of memory
C. seizures
D. dystonias
E. delusions

28.6 Which of the following statements about psychoneuroimmunology is *true*?

A. Immunological reactivity is not affected by hypnosis.
B. Lymphocytes cannot produce neurotransmitters.
C. The immune system is affected by conditioning.
D. Growth hormone does not affect immunity.
E. Marijuana does not affect the immune system.

28.7 Therapies that are considered alternatives to standard psychotherapy include all of the following *except*

A. acupuncture
B. cognitive therapy
C. homeopathy
D. ozone therapy
E. chiropractic

28.8 The percentage of cancer patients who later have mental disorders is

A. 1 to 10 percent
B. 15 to 20 percent
C. 25 to 30 percent
D. 35 to 40 percent
E. 45 to 50 percent

28.9 A highly emetogenic anticancer agent is

A. cisplatin
B. doxorubicin
C. vincristine
D. vinblastine
E. bleomycin

28.10 Symptoms of mood disorder and psychotic disorder are found most often with the use of

A. hexamethylmelamine
B. steroids
C. interferon
D. hydroxyurea
E. L-asparaginase

28.11 A patient presenting with mood disturbances, psychoses, fever, photosensitivity, butterfly rash, and joint pains is *most likely* to be given a diagnosis of

A. acute intermittent porphyria
B. hypoparathyroidism
C. systemic lupus erythematosus
D. hepatic encephalopathy
E. pheochromocytoma

28.12 Which of the following statements about common consultation-liaison problems is *false*?

A. Agitation is often associated with cognitive disorders and withdrawal from drugs.
B. In a disoriented patient, delirium must be differentiated from dementia.
C. Negative transference to a doctor is the most common cause of noncompliance.
D. In a hospital the most common cause of hallucinations is schizophrenia.
E. A major high-risk factor for men over 45 in a hospital is suicide.

28.13 In the psychotherapeutic treatment of patients with psychosomatic disorders, the most difficult problem is patients'

A. resistance to entering psychotherapy
B. erotic transference to the psychotherapist
C. positive response to the interpretation of the physiological meaning of their symptoms
D. recognition of the psychological correlation with their physiological symptoms
E. none of the above

28.14 Acute cerebellar syndrome with ataxia is a common complication of chemotherapy with

A. methotrexate
B. 5-fluorouracil
C. cisplatin
D. misonidazole
E. intrathecal thiotepa

28.15 Disorders in which autoimmune diseases have been implicated include all of the following *except*

A. Graves' disease
B. rheumatoid arthritis
C. peptic ulcer
D. regional ileitis
E. pernicious anemia

28.16 The giving up–given up concept in psychology is associated with

A. Arthur Schmale
B. Walter Cannon
C. Jurgen Ruesch
D. Hans Selye
E. Flanders Dunbar

28.17 Phantom limb occurs after leg amputation in what percentage of patients?

A. 98 percent
B. 90 percent
C. 80 percent
D. 50 percent
E. 10 percent

28.18 The most common symptom associated with chronic headaches is

A. depression
B. hallucinations
C. perseveration
D. memory disturbance
E. altered body image

28.19 The most common cause of time lost from work in this country is

A. hypochondriasis
B. low back pain
C. angina pectoris
D. gout
E. dental pain

28.20 The number of patients who go to a physician with headaches as their main complaint has been estimated to be

A. fewer than 10 percent
B. 10 to 20 percent
C. 20 to 30 percent
D. 30 to 40 percent
E. more than 50 percent

28.21 A psychosis associated with hypothyroidism is called

A. hypothyroid crisis
B. schizophrenia, paranoid type
C. bipolar I disorder
D. myxedema madness
E. delirium

28.22 The scratching of the skin in generalized pruritus is often said to represent

A. aggression turned against the self
B. poor body image
C. anal sadism
D. orality
E. orgasm

28.23 Correct statements about persons with asthma include which of the following?

A. They are overly dependent on their mothers.
B. Attacks follow episodes of frustration.
C. Poor impulse control may be seen.
D. Attacks often follow separation from parents or parental figures.
E. All of the above statements are correct.

28.24 Which of the following may be associated with a complaint of chronic pain?

A. Depression
B. Mourning
C. Psychosis
D. Delusions
E. All of the above

28.25 In evaluating patients with complaints of chronic pain of whatever cause, the physician must be alert to

A. the patient's use of an over-the-counter medication
B. alcohol dependence
C. withdrawal symptoms during the evaluation
D. an underlying medical illness
E. all of the above

28.26 Factors associated with a risk for obesity include

A. socioeconomic status
B. social mobility
C. age
D. sex
E. all of the above

28.27 A 53-year-old male patient is found to have an occipital lobe tumor. He would be *least likely* to exhibit which of the following symptoms and complaints?

A. Paranoid delusions
B. Visual hallucinations
C. Headache
D. Papilledema
E. Homonymous hemianopsia

DIRECTIONS: The questions below consist of five lettered headings followed by a list of numbered phrases. For each numbered item, select the *one* lettered heading that is most closely associated with it. Each lettered heading may be selected once, more than once, or not at all.

Questions 28.28–28.32

A. Wilson's disease
B. Pheochromocytoma
C. Systemic lupus erythematosus
D. Acquired immune deficiency syndrome (AIDS)
E. Pancreatic cancer

28.28 Dementia syndrome with global impairment and seropositivity
28.29 Resemblance to steroid psychosis
28.30 Explosive anger and labile mood
28.31 Symptoms of a classic panic attack
28.32 Sense of imminent doom

ANSWERS

Psychological Factors Affecting Medical Condition

28.1 The answer is B (*Synopsis VIII,* page 797).
A major advance in the fourth edition of *Diagnostic and Statistical Manual of Mental Disorders* (DSM-IV) from the third edition (DSM-III-R) is that DSM-IV allows clinicians to specify the *psychological stimuli* that affect the patient's medical condition. In DSM-III-R, psychologically meaningful *environmental stimuli* were temporally related to the physical disorder. Excluded in DSM-III-R were *somatoform disorders,* such as *conversion disorder,* in which the physical symptoms are not based on organic pathology. The DSM-IV emphasis on psychological factors permits a wide range of psychological stimuli to be noted (for example, personality traits, maladaptive health behaviors). Table 28.1 lists the DSM-IV diagnostic criteria for psychological factors affecting medical condition.

Table 28.1
DSM-IV Diagnostic Criteria for Psychological Factors Affecting Medical Condition

A. A general medical condition (coded on Axis III) is present.

B. Psychological factors adversely affect the general medical condition in one of the following ways:
   (1) the factors have influenced the course of the general medical condition as shown by a close temporal association between the psychological factors and the development or exacerbation of, or delayed recovery from, the general medical condition
   (2) the factors interfere with the treatment of the general medical condition
   (3) the factors constitute additional health risks for the individual
   (4) stress-related physiologic responses precipitate or exacerbate symptoms of the general medical condition

Choose name based on the nature of the psychological factors (if more than one factor is present, indicate the most prominent):

Mental disorder affecting medical condition (eg, an Axis I disorder such as major depressive disorder delaying recovery from a myocardial infarction)

Psychological symptoms affecting medical condition (eg, depressive symptoms delaying recovery from surgery; anxiety exacerbating asthma)

Personality traits or coping style affecting medical condition (eg, pathological denial of the need for surgery in a patient with cancer; hostile, pressured behavior contributing to cardiovascular disease)

Maladaptive health behaviors affecting medical condition (eg, overeating; lack of exercise, unsafe sex)

Stress-related physiological response affecting medical condition (eg, stress-related exacerbations of ulcer, hypertension, arrhythmia, or tension headache)

Other or unspecified psychological factors affecting medical condition (eg, interpersonal, cultural, or religious factors)

Reprinted with permission from American Psychiatric Association: *Diagnostic and Statistical Manual of Mental Disorders,* ed 4. Copyright, American Psychiatric Association, Washington, 1994.

28.2 The answer is C (*Synopsis VIII,* pages 811–812).
There are no studies on the T cells of *women who are having extramarital affairs.* Investigators have found a decrease in lymphocytic response in *bereavement* (conjugal and anticipatory), the *caretakers of patients with dementia of the Alzheimer's type,* in *nonpsychotic inpatients,* in resident physicians, in *medical students during final examinations,* in women who were separated or divorced, in the elderly with no social support, and in the unemployed.

28.3 The answer is C (*Synopsis VIII,* page 799).
Stressful situations are weighted in the social readjustment rating scale of Thomas Holmes and Richard Rahe. (Table 28.2). According to the scale, retirement from work is not as stressful as major illness. *Divorce* is a greater stress than marriage. *Marital* separation is a greater stress than pregnancy. *In-law troubles* are a greater stress than trouble with the boss. And *changing to a new school* is a greater stress than going on vacation.

28.4 The answer is C (*Synopsis VIII,* page 802).
Franz Alexander applied psychoanalytic concepts to the study of peptic ulcers, bronchial asthma, and essential hypertension. He studied specific repressed unconscious conflicts associated with those diseases. *George Mahl* was an experimental animal psychologist who studied ulcer development in animals. He concluded that chronic anxiety caused by any conflict is causally important. *Harold Wolff* and Stewart Wolf attempted to correlate life stress with physiological protective human responses. *Robert Ader* studied the immune response and psychoneuroimmunology in psychosomatic disorders. *Meyer Friedman* correlated personality types (type A and type B) with certain psychosomatic disorders, such as coronary heart disease.

28.5 The answer is E (*Synopsis VIII,* pages 823–824).
Delusions are not usually a characteristic of dialysis dementia. Dialysis dementia is a rare condition characterized by *loss of memory, disorientation, dystonias, and seizures.* The dementia occurs in patients who have been receiving dialysis treatment for many years. The cause is unknown.

28.6 The answer is C (*Synopsis VIII,* page 811).
The immune system is affected by *conditioning.* According to Ader, immunological reactivity is affected *by hypnosis, lymphocytes* can produce neurotransmitters, *growth hormone* does affect immunity, and *marijuana* does affect the immune system. Robert Ader has summarized the psychoneuroimmunology factors (Table 28.3).

28.7 The answer is B (*Synopsis VIII,* page 807).
Cognitive therapy is considered standard psychotherapy. It is based on the theory that behavior is secondary to the way in which persons think about themselves and their roles in the world. Maladaptive behavior is secondary to ingrained stereotyped thoughts that can lead to cognitive distortions or errors in thinking. The therapy is aimed at correcting those cognitive distortions and the self-defeating behaviors that result from them. It is especially useful in treating depressive disorders.

Table 28.2
Social Readjustment Rating Scale

Life Event	Mean Value
1. Death of spouse	100
2. Divorce	73
3. Marital separation from mate	65
4. Detention in jail or other institution	63
5. Death of a close family member	63
6. Major personal injury or illness	53
7. Marriage	50
8. Being fired at work	47
9. Marital reconcilation with mate	45
10. Retirement from work	45
11. Major change in the health or behavior of a family member	44
12. Pregnancy	40
13. Sexual difficulties	39
14. Gaining a new family member (through birth, adoption, oldster moving in, etc.)	39
15. Major business readjustment (merger, reorganization, bankruptcy, etc.)	39
16. Major change in financial state (a lot worse off or a lot better off than usual)	38
17. Death of a close friend	37
18. Changing to a different line of work	36
19. Major change in the number of arguments with spouse (either a lot more or a lot less than usual regarding child rearing, personal habits, etc.)	35
20. Taking on a mortgage greater than $10,000 (purchasing a home, business, etc.)[a]	31
21. Foreclosure on a mortgage or loan	30
22. Major change in responsibilities at work (promotion, demotion, lateral transfer)	29
23. Son or daughter leaving home (marriage, attending college, etc.)	29
24. In-law troubles	29
25. Outstanding personal achievement	28
26. Wife beginning or ceasing work outside the home	26
27. Beginning or ceasing formal schooling	26
28. Major change in living conditions (building a new home, remodeling, deterioration of home or neighborhood)	25
29. Revision of personal habits (dress, manners, associations, etc.)	24
30. Troubles with the boss	23
31. Major change in working hours or conditions	20
32. Change in residence	20
33. Changing to a new school	20
34. Major change in usual type or amount of recreation	19
35. Major change in church activities (a lot more or a lot less than usual)	19
36. Major change in social activities (clubs, dancing, movies, visiting, etc.)	18
37. Taking on a mortgage or loan less than $10,000 (purchasing a car, TV, freezer, etc.)	17
38. Major change in sleeping habits (a lot more or a lot less sleep or change in part of day when asleep)	16
39. Major change in number of family get-togethers (a lot more or a lot less than usual)	15
40. Major change in eating habits (a lot more or a lot less food intake or very different meal hours or surroundings)	15
41. Vacation	15
42. Christmas	12
43. Minor violations of the law (traffic tickets, jaywalking, disturbing the peace, etc.)	11

Reprinted with permission from Holmes T: Life situations, emotions, and disease. Psychosom Med *19:* 747, 1978.

[a] This figure no longer has any relevance in the light of inflation; what is significant is the total amount of debt from all sources.

Table 28.3
Summary of Psychoneuroimmunology Factors by Robert Ader

Nerve endings have been found in the tissues of the immune system. The central nervous system is linked to both the bone marrow and the thymus, where immune system cells are produced and developed, and to the spleen and the lymph nodes, where those cells are stored.

Changes in the central nervous system (the brain and the spinal cord) alter immune responses, and triggering an immune response alters central nevous sytem activity. Animal experiments dating back to the 1960s show that damage to different parts of the brain's hypothalamus can either suppress or enhance the allergic-type response. Recently, researchers have found that inducing an immune response causes nerve cells in the hypothalamus to become more active and that the brain cell anxiety peaks at precisely the same time that levels of antibodies are at their highest. Apparently, the brain monitors immunological changes closely.

Changes in hormone and neurotransmitter levels alter immune responses, and vice versa. The stress hormones generally suppress immune responses. But other hormones, such as growth hormone, also seem to affect immunity. Conversely, when experimental animals are immunized, they show changes in various hormone levels.

Lymphocytes are chemically responsive to hormones and neurotransmitters. Immune system cells have receptors—molecular structures on the surface of their cells—that are responsive to endorphins, stress hormones, and a wide range of other hormones.

Lymphocytes can produce hormones and neurotransmitters. When an animal is infected with a virus, lymphocytes produce minuscle amounts of many of the same substances produced by the pituitary gland.

Activated lymphocytes—cells actively involved in an immune response—produce substances that can be perceived by the central nervous system. The interleukins and interferons—chemicals that immune system cells use to talk to each other—can also trigger receptors on cells in the brain, more evidence that the immune system and the nervous system speak the same chemical language.

Psychosocial factors may alter the susceptibility to or the progression of autoimmune disease, infectious disease, and cancer. Evidence for those connections comes from many researchers.

Immunological reactivity may be influenced by stress. Chronic or intense stress, in particular, generally makes immune system cells less responsive to a challenge.

Immunological reactivity can be influenced by hypnosis. In a typical study, both of a subject's arms are exposed to a chemical that normally causes an allergic reaction. But the subject is told, under hypnosis, that only one arm will show the response—and that, in fact, is often what happens.

Immunological reactivity can be modified by classical conditioning. As Ader's own key experiments showed, the immune system can learn to react in certain ways as a conditioned response.

Psychoactive drugs and drugs of abuse influence immune function. A range of drugs that affect the nervous system—including alcohol, marijuana, cocaine, heroin, and nicotine have all been shown to affect the immune response, generally suppressing it. Some psychiatric drugs, such as lithium (prescribed for bipolar I disorder), also modulate the immune system.

Adapted from Goleman D, Guerin J: *Mind Body Medicine.* Consumer Reports, Yonkers, NY, 1993.

Table 28.4
Suicide Vulnerability Factors in Cancer Patients

Depression and hopelessness
Poorly controlled pain
Mild delirium (disinhibition)
Feeling of loss of control
Exhaustion
Anxiety
Preexisting psychopathology (substance abuse, character pathology, major psychiatric disorder)
Acute family problems
Threats or history of prior attempts at suicide
Positive family history of suicide
Other usually described risk factors in psychiatric patients

Reprinted with permission from Breitbart W: Suicide in cancer patients. Oncology *1*: 49, 1987.

Table 28.5
Emetogenic Potential of Some Commonly Used Anticancer Agents

Highly emetogenic	Cisplatin Dacarbazine Streptozocin Actinomycin Nitrogen mustard
Moderately emetogenic	Doxorubicin Daunorubicin Cyclophosphamide Nitrosoureas Mitomycin-C Procarbazine
Minimally emetogenic	Vincristine Vinblastine 5-Fluorouracil Bleomycin

Courtesy of Marguerite S. Lederberg, M.D., and Jimmie C. Holland, M.D.

Acupuncture is the use of needles to stimulate areas that are supposed to have neural connections with specific organs and body functions. In *homeopathy,* medication is based on the premise that disease can be cured with diluted doses of various substances. *Ozone therapy* is the introduction of ozone gas into the bloodstream as a way to fight disease. *Chiropractic* is the manipulation or subluxation of the spinal vertebrae to relieve back problems and other ailments.

28.8 The answer is E (*Synopsis VIII,* page 813).
About *50 percent* of cancer patients later have mental disorders; 68 percent of these disorders are adjustment disorder; 15 percent of those with psychiatric symptoms have major depressive disorder, and 8 percent have delirium. Although cancer patients may express suicidal wishes, the actual suicide incidence is only 1.4 to 1.9 times that of the general population. Vulnerability to suicide is increased by the factors listed in Table 28.4.

28.9 The answer is A (*Synopsis VIII,* page 814).
Cisplatin (Platinol) is highly emetogenic. *Doxorubicin* (Adriamycin) is moderately emetogenic, and *vincristine* (Oncovin), *vinblastine* (Velban), and *bleomycin* (Blenoxane) are minimally emetogenic. Table 28.5 summarizes the emetogenic problems with various chemotherapeutic agents.

28.10 The answer is B (*Synopsis VIII,* page 814).
Steroids produce marked alterations of the patient's mental status, particularly from mania to depression—even to a suicidal degree. Dacarbazine produces depression and suicide, especially when used with *hexamethylmelamine*. *Interferon* produces anxiety and depression with suicidal ideation. Hallucinations have been reported with *hydroxyurea*. *L-Asparaginase* produces reversible depression. Table 28.6 lists chemotherapy agents with mood and psychotic symptoms.

28.11 The answer is C (*Synopsis VIII,* pages 797–802).
Although the psychological symptoms are similar in all of the conditions listed, a medical workup would reveal that fever, photosensitivity, butterfly rash, and joint pains are diagnostic of *systemic lupus erythematosus.*

In *acute intermittent porphyria,* abdominal pain, fever, peripheral neuropathy, and elevated porphobilinogen are significant. In *hypoparathyroidism* the patient has constipation, polydipsia, and nausea with increased calcium and variable parathyroid hormone (PTH) levels. In *hepatic encephalopathy* the patient has asterixis, spider angioma, and abnormal liver function test results. In *pheochromocytoma* the patient has paroxysmal hypertension, headache, elevated vanillylmandelic acid (VMA), and tachycardia.

28.12 The answer is D (*Synopsis VIII,* pages 818–822).
In a hospital the most common cause of *hallucinations* is not schizophrenia but delirium tremens. *Agitation* is often associated with cognitive disorders and withdrawal from drugs. In a disoriented patient, *delirium must be differentiated from dementia. Negative transference* to a doctor is the most common cause of noncompliance. And a major high-risk factor for men over 45 in a hospital is *suicide.* Table 28.7 presents common consultation-liaison problems encountered in hospital practice.

28.13 The answer is A (*Synopsis VIII,* page 827).
The most difficult problem in the treatment of psychosomati-

Table 28.6
Chemotherapy Agents with Mood and Psychotic Symptoms

Dacarbazine: depression and suicide reported, especially when used with hexamethylamine
Vinblastine: frequent reversible depression
Vincristine: 5 percent incidence of hallucinations; depression noted
L-Asparaginase: reversible depression noted
Procarbazine: MAOI; concurrent tricyclic drugs are contraindicated; associated with mania and depression; potentiates alcohol, barbiturates, phenothiazines
Hydroxyurea: hallucinations reported
Interferon: anxiety, depression with suicidal ideation common at doses above 40 million units
Steroids: frequent alterations of mental state ranging from emotional lability through mania or severe, suicidal depression to frank psychosis

Courtesy of Marguette B. Loderberg, M.D., and Jimmie C. Holland, M.D.

Table 28.7
Common Consultation-Liaison Problems

Reason for Consultation	Comments
Suicide attempt or threat	High-risk factors are men over 45, no social support, alcohol dependence, previous attempt, incapacitating medical illness with pain, and suicidal ideation. If risk is present, transfer to psychiatric unit or start 24-hour nursing care.
Depression	Suicidal risks must be assessed in every depressed patient (see above); presence of cognitive defects in depression may cause diagnostic dilemma with dementia; check for history of substance abuse or depressant drugs (eg, reserpine, propranolol); use antidepressants cautiously in cardiac patients because of conduction side effects, orthostatic hypotension.
Agitation	Often related to cognitive disorder, withdrawal from drugs (eg, opioids, alcohol, sedative-hypnotics); haloperidol most useful drug for excessive agitation; use physical restraints with great caution; examine for command hallucinations or paranoid ideation to which patient is responding in agitated manner; rule out toxic reaction to medication.
Hallucinations	Most common cause in hospital is delirium tremens; onset 3 to 4 days after hospitalization. In intensive care units, check for sensory isolation; rule out brief psychotic disorder, schizophrenia, cognitive disorder. Treat with antipsychotic medication.
Sleep disorder	Common cause is pain; early morning awakening associated with depression; difficulty in falling asleep associated with anxiety. Use antianxiety or antidepressant agent, depending on cause. Those drugs have no analgesic effect, so prescribe adequate painkillers. Rule out early substance withdrawal.
No organic basis for symptoms	Rule out conversion disorder, somatization disorder, factitious disorder, and malingering; glove and stocking anesthesia with autonomic nervous system symptoms seen in conversion disorder; multiple body complaints seen in somatization disorder; wish to be hospitalized seen in factitious disorder; obvious secondary gain in malingering (e.g., compensation case).
Disorientation	Delirium versus dementia; review metabolic status, neurological findings, substance history. Prescribe small dose of antipsychotics for major agitation; benzodiazepines may worsen condition and cause sundowner syndrome (ataxia, confusion); modify environment so patient dose not experience sensory deprivation.
Noncompliance or refusal to consent to procedure	Explore relationship of patient and treating doctor; negative transference is most common cause of noncompliance; fears of medication or of procedure require education and reassurance. Refusal to give consent is issue of judgment; if impaired, patient can be declared incompetent but only by a judge; cognitive disorder is main cause of impaired judgment in hospitalized patients.

cally ill patients is *patients' resistance to entering psychotherapy* and to recognizing the psychological factors in their illness. Generally, clinicians have difficulty in forming a positive transference with the patients. *An erotic transference to the psychotherapist usually does not develop,* nor is it relevant to the treatment of their patients. The *patients usually react negatively to the interpretation of the physiological meaning of their symptoms* and *do not recognize the psychological correlation with their physiological symptoms.*

28.14 The answer is B (*Synopsis VIII,* page 814).
Acute cerebellar syndrome with ataxia is a common complication of chemotherapy with *5-fluorouracil* (Efudex). *Methotrexate* often produces encephalopathy. *Cisplatin* (Platinol) and *misonidazole* may manifest ototoxicity, and *intrathecal thiotepa* (Thioplex) produces myelopathy. Table 28.8 lists neurological complications of chemotherapy.

28.15 The answer is C (*Synopsis VIII,* page 812).
Peptic ulcer is not considered an autoimmune disease. Disorders in which an autoimmune component has been implicated include *Graves' disease,* Hashimoto's disease, *rheumatoid arthritis,* ulcerative colitis, *regional ileitis,* systemic lupus erythematosus, psoriasis, myasthenia gravis, and *pernicious anemia.*

28.16 The answer is A (*Synopsis VIII,* page 801).
Arthur Schmale developed the giving up–given up concept for psychosomatic disorders. It is associated with a feeling of learned helplessness. *Walter Cannon* showed that the physiological concomitants of certain conditions are mediated by the autonomic nervous system. *Jurgen Ruesch* emphasized the importance of the communication between people in the development of psychosomatic disorders. *Hans Selye* showed that under stress, a general adaption syndrome may produce physiological reactions that may eventuate in psychosomatic dis-

Table 28.8
Neurological Complications of Chemotherapy

Encephalopathy	Myelopathy
Methotrexate with radiotherapy	Intrathecal methotrexate
Hexamethylmelamine	Intrathecal cytarabine
5-Fluorouracil	Intrathecal thiotepa
Procarbazine	Neuropathy
Carmustine (BCNU) (intracarotid)	Vinca alkaloids[a]
Cisplatin (intracarotid)	Cisplatin
Cyclophosphamide	Procarbazine
5-Azacytidine	5-Azacytidine
Spirogermanium	Vasopressin 16
Misonidazole	VM-26
Cytarabine (high dose)	Misonidazole
L-Asparaginase	Methyl-G
Acute cerebellar syndrome, ataxia	Cytarabine
5-Fluorouracil	Ototoxicity
Cytarabine	Cisplatin
Procarbazine	Misonidazole
Hexamethylmelamine	

Adapted from Patchell RA, Posner JB: Neurologic complications of systemic cancer. In *Symposium on Neuro-oncology Neurologic Clinics,* NA Vick, DD Bigner, editors, vol 3, p 729. Saunders, Philadelphia, 1985.
[a] Also involve cranial nerves.

orders. *Flanders Dunbar* correlated specific conscious personality types with specific psychosomatic disorders.

28.17 The answer is A (*Synopsis VIII,* page 824).
Phantom limb occurs in *98 percent* of patients who have undergone leg amputation. The experience may last for years. Sometimes the sensation is painful, and a neuroma at the stump should be ruled out. The condition has no known cause or treatment and usually stops spontaneously.

28.18 The answer is A (*Synopsis VIII,* page 807).
The most common symptom associated with chronic headaches is *depression.* The depression apparently has no organic basis but rather is secondary to the stress of having to deal with a chronic illness. The converse is also true; that is, headaches may also be seen as the presenting symptom of depression.

Hallucinations (false sensory perceptions) and *perseveration* (verbal repetition of words or phrases) are typically seen in psychotic illnesses and cognitive disorders and are not associated with headaches. *Memory disturbance* is most often evidence of an organic dysfunction, toxic or otherwise, and is not typical of headaches. *Altered body image,* the idea that one's body is shaped differently than it really is, is seen in the eating disorders anorexia nervosa and bulimia nervosa.

28.19 The answer is B (*Synopsis VIII,* page 806).
Chronic *low back pain* is the most common cause of time lost from work in this country. *Hypochondriasis* is a somatoform disorder characterized by excessive, morbid anxiety about one's health. Hypochondriacal patients exhibit a predominant disturbance in which the physical symptoms or complaints are not explainable on the basis of demonstrable organic findings and are apparently linked to psychological factors. *Angina pectoris* is severe constricting pain in the chest that is usually caused by coronary artery disease. *Gout* is an inherited metabolic disorder most commonly occurring in men. It is characterized by an elevated blood uric acid level and recurrent acute arthritis of sudden onset, which leads to progressive and chronic arthritis. *Dental pain* is a general term referring to any pain in the mouth, teeth, or gums caused by various oral disorders.

28.20 The answer is B (*Synopsis VIII,* page 807).
Every year about 80 percent of the population are estimated to suffer from at least one headache, and *10 to 20 percent* of the population go to a physician with headaches as their primary complaint.

28.21 The answer is D (*Synopsis VIII,* page 819).
A high proportion of patients with adult onset of hypothyroidism show evidence of mental disturbance as part of the syndrome. *Myxedema madness* is a psychosis in which a wide range of organicity, from minimal to marked, may be manifest. It is often characterized by paranoid suspicions and auditory hallucinations.

Hypothyroid crisis is marked by a sudden reduction in thyroid function. *Schizophrenia, paranoid type,* is characterized by persecutory or grandiose delusions, often accompanied by hallucinations. *Bipolar disorder* is a mood disorder in which the patient exhibits both manic and depressive episodes. *Delirium* is an acute, reversible cognitive disorder characterized by confusion and some impairment of consciousness. It is generally associated with emotional lability, hallucinations or illusions, and inappropriate, impulsive, irrational, or violent behavior.

28.22 The answer is A (*Synopsis VIII,* page 817).
In generalized pruritus the rubbing of the skin represents *aggression turned against the self.* The emotions that most frequently lead to generalized psychogenic pruritus are repressed anger and repressed anxiety. An inordinate need for affection is a common characteristic of the patients. Frustration of that need elicits inhibited aggressiveness.

Body image is the conscious and unconscious perception of one's body at any particular time. One can perceive one's body image to be *poor,* good, or altered in some way. *Anal sadism* is the aggression, destructiveness, negativism, and externally directed rage that are typical components of the anal stage of development between the ages of 1 and 3. *Orality,* the earliest stage in psychosexual development, lasts through the first 18 months of life. During that period the oral zone is the center of the infant's needs, expression, and pleasurable erotic experiences. An *orgasm* is a sexual climax or peak psychophysiological reaction to sexual stimulation.

28.23 The answer is E (all) (*Synopsis VIII,* page 800).
Clinical research on asthmatic patients, especially children, has been guided by these main principles: (1) No single or uniform personality type has bronchial asthma. (2) Some asthmatic patients have strong unconscious wishes for protection and for being encompassed by another person; *they are overly dependent on their mothers.* Their wishes for protection sensitize some patients to separation from the mother. In other patients, the wish produces such an intense conflict that separation from the mother or her surrogate produces remission from asthmatic attacks. (3) The specific wishes for protection or envelopment are said to be caused by the mother's attitudes toward her asthmatic child. Studies of asthmatic children and their families, however, have shown that no single pattern of mother–child relationship obtains. The mother may be overprotective and oversolicitous of the child; perfectionistic and overambitious for the child; overtly domineering, punitive, or cruel to the child; or helpful and generative. Presumably, those attitudes both precede the illness and are responsible for the child's conflicts and failure to develop psychologically. There is, however, no proof of those assumptions. In fact, the attitude of the mother is probably related more to the child's social adjustment—his or her truancy or invalidism—than to the asthmatic attacks. (4) Asthmatic *attacks follow episodes of frustration* by the mother or some other person, or they are activated and produce conflict. In both instances, strong emotions are aroused. (5) Some adult asthmatic patients have various psychological conflicts other than the ones already described.

Many asthmatic children have age-inappropriate behaviors and traits, and *poor impulse control may be seen.* Some children may be seen as timid, babyish, and overly polite; others are tense, restless, rebellious, irritable, and explosive in their emotional outbursts. Asthmatic boys, in particular, tend to be passively dependent, timid, and immature, and at times they become irritable when frustrated. Asthmatic girls tend to depend on their fathers more than their mothers and try to be self-sufficient but are commonly chronically depressed. Asthmatic children are also dominated by a fear of losing parental support. They attempt to defend against that fear by a show of independence and maturity. Regardless of the quality of the parental attitudes, *attacks often follow separation from parents or parental figures.*

28.24 The answer is E (all) (*Synopsis VIII,* page 810).
A large number of emotional states and mental disorders may lead to chronic pain. *Patients* with *depression* are especially prone to chronic pain, and if a psychotic depression is present, the patients may have delusions of cancer or may use metaphors of decay and death to explain the chronic pain.

A *mourning* person may have pain similar to that experienced by the lost person as a means of identifying with and introjecting part of the person in an attempt to deny the loss. Patients with *psychosis* may have bizarre forms of pain that are attributed to some persecuting external force. Psychotic patients are also at risk for incorporating the pain of an organic illness—for example, myocardial infarction or perforated ulcer—into *delusions* and not seeking medical help.

28.25 The answer is E (all) (*Synopsis VIII,* pages 810–811).
Most chronic pain patients attempt to treat themselves before seeking medical help. Billions of dollars are spent annually by people seeking relief through *over-the-counter preparations* or other nonmedical means. Those persons often have *alcohol dependence* and other substance-related disorders. Therefore, the physician should be alert for substance toxicity (especially overmedication) and *withdrawal symptoms during the evaluation* and treatment of chronic pain patients. Explaining to the patient and family that sensitivity to pain may greatly increase during substance withdrawal may partially decrease anxiety and increase pain sensitivity caused by weaning. A physician should always remember that a psychiatric diagnosis does not preclude the existence of *an underlying medical illness.* Finally, the clinician should recognize that the patient's pain is not imaginary. It is real and cannot be ''willed away.''

28.26 The answer is E (all) (*Synopsis VIII,* pages 731–736).
The most striking influence on obesity is *socioeconomic status.* Obesity is 6 times more common among women of low status than among those of high status. A similar, although weaker, relationship is found among men. Obesity is also far more prevalent among lower-class children than it is among upper-class children; significant differences are already apparent by age 6. *Social mobility,* ethnic factors, and generation in the United States also influence the prevalence of obesity.

Age is the second major influence on obesity. There is a an increase in the prevalence of obesity between childhood and age 50; a threefold increase occurs between ages 20 and 50. At age 50, prevalence falls sharply, presumably because of the high mortality of obese persons from cardiovascular disease in the elderly. *Gender* also plays a role. *Women* show a higher prevalence of obesity than do men; the difference is particularly pronounced past age 50 because of the higher mortality rate among obese men after that age.

28.27 The answer is A (*Synopsis VIII,* page 819).
A patient with an occipital lobe tumor would be least likely to exhibit *paranoid delusions. Visual hallucinations, headache, papilledema, and homonymous hemianopsia* are all reported symptoms and complaints of occipital lobe tumors. Papilledema, edema of the optic disk, may be caused by increased intracranial pressure. Homonymous hemianopsia is blindness in the corresponding (right or left) field of vision of each eye.

Answers 28.28–28.32

28.28 The answer is D (*Synopsis VIII,* page 820).

28.29 The answer is C (*Synopsis VIII,* page 821).

28.30 The answer is A (*Synopsis VIII,* page 821).

28.31 The answer is B (*Synopsis VIII,* page 821).

28.32 The answer is E (*Synopsis VIII,* page 820).
Wilson's disease, hepatolenticular degeneration, is a familial disease of adolescence that tends to have a long-term course. Its cause is defective copper metabolism leading to excessive copper deposits in tissues. The earliest psychiatric symptoms are *explosive anger and labile mood*—sudden and rapid changes from one mood to another. As the illness progresses, eventual brain damage occurs with memory and intelligence quotient (IQ) loss. The lability and combativeness tend to persist even after the brain damage develops.

Pheochromocytoma is a tumor of the adrenal medulla that causes headaches, paroxysms of severe hypertension, and the physiological and psychological *symptoms of a classic panic attack*—intense anxiety, tremor, apprehension, dizziness, palpitations, and diaphoresis. The tumor tissue secretes catecholamines that are responsible for the symptoms.

Systemic lupus erythematosus is an autoimmune disorder in which the body makes antibodies against its own cells. The antibodies attack cells as if the cells were infectious agents, and depending on which cells are being attacked, give rise to various symptoms. Frequently, the arteries in the cerebrum are affected, causing a cerebral arteritis, which alters the blood flow to various parts of the brain. The decreased blood flow can give rise to psychotic symptoms, such as a thought disorder with paranoid delusions and hallucinations. The symptoms can *resemble steroid psychosis* or schizophrenia.

The diagnosis of *acquired immune deficiency syndrome (AIDS)* includes a *dementia syndrome with global impairment and seropositivity.* The dementia can be caused by the direct attack on the central nervous system by the human immunodeficiency virus (HIV) or by secondary infections, such as toxoplasmosis.

Although any chronic illness can give rise to depression, some diseases, such as *pancreatic cancer,* are more likely causes than are others. The depression of pancreatic cancer patients is often associated with a sense of imminent doom.

29 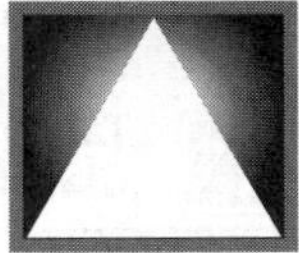

Alternative Medicine and Psychiatry

Alternative or complementary medicine has become increasingly popular in recent years. It may provide hope and, in rare cases, cure those with life-threatening illnesses. One in three people are estimated to use alternative medicine at some time for common ailments such as back problems and headaches. Many of the methods are untested and may do more harm than good. Physicians should keep an open mind, however, until such time as these methods are subject to controlled studies.

In 1991, the National Institutes of Health (NIH) established an Office of Alternative Medicine (OAM) to evaluate and scientifically explain many unrelated unorthodox therapeutic systems. In 1995, the OAM published a classification of alternative medical practices, listed in Table 29.1, but did not endorse any of the listed treatments. Many of the methods are effective through the power of suggestion.

Health maintenance organizations (HMOs) have approved many such therapies for reimbursement. Although HMOs claim to be responding to public pressure by financing alternative medical treatments, many experts see financial reasons as the actual motivation: Alternative practitioners receive lower fees than do physicians, and patients may sometimes refer themselves to these practitioners rather than asking a primary care physician for a referral. This practice may endanger the health of the general public by encouraging people to seek alternative treatment for disorders that require medical attention.

Students should study Chapter 29 in Kaplan and Sadock's *Synopsis VIII* and should familiarize themselves with Table 29.1 before answering the following questions.

HELPFUL HINTS

Students should know the following terms.

- ▶ acupressure
- ▶ acupuncture
- ▶ Alexander technique
- ▶ allopathy
- ▶ anthroposophically extended medicine
- ▶ aromatherapy
- ▶ Ayurveda
- ▶ Bates method
- ▶ bioenergetics
- ▶ biofeedback
- ▶ chelation therapy
- ▶ chiropractic
- ▶ color therapy
- ▶ complementary medicine
- ▶ dance therapy
- ▶ diet and nutrition
- ▶ environmental medicine
- ▶ Moshe Feldenkrais
- ▶ Max Gerson, M.D.
- ▶ Samuel Hahnemann, M.D.
- ▶ herbal medicine
- ▶ holistic medicine
- ▶ homeopathy
- ▶ hypnosis
- ▶ light therapy
- ▶ macrobiotics
- ▶ massage
- ▶ meditation
- ▶ moxibustion
- ▶ naturopathy
- ▶ Office of Alternative Medicine (OAM)
- ▶ osteopathy
- ▶ ozone therapy
- ▶ past life
- ▶ psychosomatic approach
- ▶ reflexology
- ▶ Reiki
- ▶ Ida Rolf
- ▶ scientific method
- ▶ shamanism
- ▶ sound therapy
- ▶ Rudolf Steiner

▲ QUESTIONS

DIRECTIONS: Each of the three incomplete statements below refers to one of the six lettered terms. Choose the most appropriate term for each statement.

A. Allopathy
B. Homeopathy
C. Osteopathy
D. Biomedicine
E. Technomedicine
F. Herbal medicine

29.1 The medicine taught in U.S. schools

29.2 Similar methods of practice to those of allopathy

29.3 A term coined by Samuel Hahnemann, M.D.

DIRECTIONS: Each of the questions or statements below is followed by five lettered responses. Select the *one* response that is most appropriate in each case.

Table 29.1
Classification of Alternative Medical Practices from the NIH Office of Alternative Medicine

Diet, Nutrition, Lifestyle Changes
Changes in lifestyle
Diet
Nutritional supplements
Gerson therapy
Macrobiotics
Megavitamin therapy

Mind/Body Control
Art therapy, relaxation techniques
Biofeedback
Counseling and prayer therapies
Dance therapy
Guided imagery
Humor therapy
Psychotherapy
Sound, music therapy
Support groups
Yoga, meditation

Alternative Systems of Medical Practice
Acupuncture
Anthroposophically extended medicine
Ayurveda
Community-based health care practices
Environmental medicine
Homeopathic medicine
Latin American rural practices
Native American
Natural products
Naturopathic medicine
Past life therapy
Shamanism
Tibetan medicine
Traditional Oriental medicine

Manual Healing
Acupressure
Alexander technique
Aromatherapy
Biofield therapeutics
Chiropractic medicine
Feldenkrais method
Massage therapy
Osteopathy
Reflexology
Rolfing
Therapeutic touch
Trager method
Zone therapy

Pharmacological and Biological Treatments
Antioxidizing agents
Cell treatment
Chelation therapy
Metabolic therapy
Oxidizing agents (ozone, hydrogen peroxide)

Bioelectromagnetic Applications
Blue light treatment and artificial lighting
Electroacupuncture
Electromagnetic fields
Electrostimulation and neuromagnetic stimulation devices
Magnetoresonance spectroscopy

Herbal Medicine
Echinacea (purple coneflower)
Ginkgo biloba extract
Ginger rhizome
Ginseng root
Wild chrysanthemum flower
Witch hazel
Yellowdock

This classification was developed by the ad hoc Advisory Panel to the Office of Alternative Medicine (OAM), National Institutes of Health (NIH), and further refined by the Workshop on Alternative Medicine as described in the report *Alternative Medicine: Expanding Medical Horizons.* This classification was designed to facilitate the grant review process and should not be considered definitive. This listing is not an endorsement and does not connote approval by the NIH.

29.4 All of the following correctly refer to biofeedback *except*

A. often helps relieve emotional stress
B. can reduce severity of tension headaches
C. teaches patients to lower their blood pressure
D. helps patients undergo surgery without anesthesia
E. an alternative medicine that has entered mainstream psychiatry

29.5 Which of the following correctly describes Asian medicine?

A. It includes Ayurveda and massage.
B. It rests on a basis of philosophy and logic.
C. It is widely practiced in Europe and the Middle East.
D. It sends Reiki to all areas of a patient's body that need healing.
E. A practitioner may go into a trance to determine the nature of a patient's ailment.

29.6 All of the following statements correctly describe acupressure, acupuncture, or both, *except*

A. balances yang and yin
B. uses pathways for chi
C. originated in Tibetan monasteries
D. corrects imbalances at about 350 points
E. mentioned in medical texts as early as 3000 B.C.

ANSWERS

Alternative Medicine and Psychiatry

29.1 The answer is A (*Synopsis VIII,* page 829).

29.2 The answer is C (*Synopsis VIII,* page 840).

29.3 The answer is B (*Synopsis VIII,* pages 829, 834, 838).
Allopathy, from the Greek *allos* (''other''), is the term for traditional medicine of the kind taught in U.S. medical schools. It is based on scientific method, the use of experiments to validate a theory or to determine the validity of a hypothesis. In allopathy, the body is a biological and physiological system, and disorders have causes that can be treated with medications, surgery, and other complex methods to produce cures. Other terms for traditional medicine are *biomedicine* and *technomedicine.* Allopathy refers to the use of medicine to counteract signs and symptoms of diseases; it remains the most prevalent form of medicine in the Western world.

Homeopathy was derived from the Greek *homos* (''same''); it refers to a form of medicine in which special medicinal remedies, different from allopathic remedies, are used. Homeopathic healing was developed in Germany in the early 1800s by Samuel Hahnemann, M.D., who coined the term *homeopathy.* It is based on the concept that the medicine whose effects in normal people most closely resemble the illness being treated is the one most likely to cure the illness. Traditional medical practitioners doubt the efficacy of homeopathic therapy because the substances used are highly dilute and undetectable by chemical methods and because no pharmacological studies have demonstrated the veracity of homeopathic medicine's claims. Although there are no more homeopathic medical schools in the United States, homeopathy is increasingly used in this country, in Europe, and throughout the world.

Osteopathy is similar to traditional medicine; doctors of osteopathy are licensed to practice in every state, are qualified to practice in every branch of clinical medicine, and take the same licensure examinations as do medical doctors. Their medical education is identical, except that doctors of osteopathy have additional training in musculoskeletal system disorders.

29.4 The answer is D (*Synopsis VIII,* page 828).
Biofeedback cannot help *patients undergo surgery without anesthesia.* The process can, however, *help relieve emotional stress, reduce severity of tension headaches,* and *teach patients to lower their blood pressure.* Biofeedback, along with hypnosis, is *an alternative medicine that has entered mainstream psychiatry.* Both biofeedback and hypnosis are tools used during psychiatric treatment.

29.5 The answer is B (*Synopsis VIII,* page 840).
Asian or Oriental medicine is a broad term covering traditional medicines of China, Korea, Japan, Vietnam, Tibet, and other Asian countries. Asian medicine is not *widely practiced in Europe and the Middle East.* Its techniques, first developed in China, include *massage,* acupuncture, herbology, and exercise. *Ayurveda* (''knowledge of life'') originated in India about 2000 B.C. Although it is similar to Chinese medicine in its beliefs about a vital force and balanced energy flow, Oriental medicine does not *include Ayurveda.*

Reiki, a Japanese practice believed to *send* energy *to all areas of a patient's body that need healing,* is also similar to beliefs in Chinese medicine. *Reiki,* however, is a Japanese term and refers to a Japanese form of treatment; in a strict sense, *Reiki* does not apply to Asian medicine in general. In Asian medicine, *a practitioner* does not *go into a trance to determine the nature of a patient's ailment.* This description refers to shamanism, a form of healing practiced in simple societies.

Asian or Oriental medicine is a coherent system of thought and practice developed long before ideas of Western medicine. It has been critically explored and tested by respected clinicians and physicians. Perhaps more than medicine in the Western world, Oriental medicine is rooted in *philosophy and logic* and is entwined with ancient habits of civilization.

29.6 The answer is C (*Synopsis VIII,* pages 829–830).
Both acupressure and acupuncture are Chinese healing techniques *mentioned in medical texts as early as 3000* B.C. These techniques did not *originate in Tibetan monasteries.* A tenet of Chinese medicine is the belief that vital energy flows throughout the human body, and both acupressure and acupuncture *use pathways for chi,* or vital energy, *to correct* energy *imbalances at about 350 points,* whose manipulation stimulates flow or removes blockages. These techniques also *balance yang and yin,* the opposing energy fields that can cause ill health when they are not in accord.

30

Relational Problems

Relational problems include patterns of interaction between or among members of a relational unit that are associated with significantly impaired functioning or symptoms among one or more members of the unit or impaired functioning of the unit itself. Although they can arise independently, relational problems can complicate or arise from the treatment of a mental disorder or medical condition. In this category the fourth edition of *Diagnostic and Statistical Manual of Mental Disorders* (DSM-IV) includes relational problems related to a mental disorder or general medical condition, parent–child relational problem, partner relational problem, sibling relational problem, and relational problem not otherwise specified. These categories are used when the focus of clinical attention is a pattern of impaired interaction associated with a mental disorder or general medical condition or an impaired interaction between parent and child, between partners, or between siblings.

An example of a relational problem related to a mental disorder or general medical condition might be found in a family who cares for a child with autism or a young couple who is responsible for a parent with dementia of the Alzheimer's type. An example of a parent–child relational problem might occur when divorced parents must deal with joint custody of a child or when a child must adjust to a new stepparent.

Students should study Chapter 30 in *Kaplan and Sadock's Synopsis VIII* and test their knowledge with the questions and answers that follow.

HELPFUL HINTS

The student should know these terms.

- birth of a child
- chronic illness
- dual-career families
- elderly abuse
- parent–child relational problem
- partner relational problem
- prejudice
- racism
- relational problem not otherwise specified
- relational problem related to a mental disorder or general medical condition
- religious bigotry
- role reversal
- sibling relational problem
- sibling rivalry
- stress relationship

▲ QUESTIONS

DIRECTIONS: Each of the questions or incomplete statements below is followed by five suggested responses or completions. Select the *one* that is *best* in each case.

30.1 When a child has a congenital defect such as deafness,

A. parents generally adapt quickly to the extra demands of the handicapped child
B. parent–child problems may arise with the unaffected siblings
C. money for hearing aids is provided by the government
D. divorce occurs in 80 percent of the families
E. the siblings are at an increased risk for childhood schizophrenia

30.2 Partner relational problems

A. may occur with a first episode of bipolar I disorder
B. rarely present after the birth of a child
C. have associated sibling relational problems
D. usually occur among the low socioeconomic group
E. are best handled through psychoanalysis

30.3 Which of the following statements about marital stress is *not* correct?

A. If the partners are from similar backgrounds, conflicts are not likely to arise.
B. The birth of a child often precipitates a problem.
C. Abortion is not generally included as a potential conflict in a seemingly healthy marriage.
D. Sexual dissatisfaction is involved in most cases of marital maladjustment.
E. Complaints of female orgasmic disorder or male orgasmic disorder are usually indicative of deeper problems.

DIRECTIONS: The questions below consist of lettered headings followed by a list of numbered statements. For each numbered statement, select the *one* lettered heading that is most closely associated with it. Each lettered heading may be used once, more than once, or not at all.

Questions 30.4–30.8

A. Relational problem related to a mental disorder or general medical condition
B. Parent–child relational problem
C. Partner relational problem
D. Sibling relational problem
E. Relational problem not otherwise specified

30.4 A man with multiple sclerosis resents being taken care of by his wife.

30.5 A 60-year-old married woman has problems with her neighbor; because of differences between the two, the police have been called numerous times; otherwise, the woman has many good friends.

30.6 The oldest daughter in a family of four siblings refuses to come home for any family gatherings if her oldest brother also comes home.

30.7 An adopted child continually feels that the family who adopted him pays more attention to their biological daughter than to him; he is becoming increasingly withdrawn and irritable.

30.8 An infant dies of sudden infant death syndrome (SIDS); the mother blames the father for lax parental supervision and is asking for a divorce.

ANSWERS

Relational Problems

30.1 The answer is B (*Synopsis VIII,* page 844).
When a child has a congenital defect such as deafness, the situation can stress the healthiest family, and *parent–child problems may arise with the unaffected siblings,* as well as the handicapped child. The unaffected siblings may be resented, preferred, or neglected because the ill child requires so much time and attention. *Parents generally do not adapt quickly to the extra demands of the handicapped child.* If the handicap is severe, it may place an economic burden on the family. *Money for hearing aids is not provided by the government* and is not included in managed care plans. No statistics report that *divorce occurs in 80 percent of the families* with handicapped children. *The siblings are not at an increased risk for childhood schizophrenia.*

30.2 The answer is A (*Synopsis VIII,* page 844).
A partner relational problem *may occur with a first episode of bipolar I disorder.* Bipolar I disorder is a mood disorder with alternating periods of mania and depression. A partner relational problem *may be precipitated by the birth of a child,* abortion or miscarriage, economic stresses, a move to a new area, episodes of illness, major career changes, and any situations that involve a significant change in marital roles. Illness in a child exerts the greatest strain on a marriage, and marriages in which a child has died through illness or an accident end in divorce more often than not. People with partner relational problems rarely *have associated sibling relational problems,* and partner relational problem does not *usually occur among the low socioeconomic group.* Socioeconomic status in itself does not predispose a person to partner relational problem. It can, however, be a problem if the partners are of different backgrounds and have been raised with different value systems. Partner relational problem *is best handled through marital therapy, not psychoanalysis.*

30.3 The answer is C (*Synopsis VIII,* pages 844–845).
Abortion is generally included as a potential conflict in a seemingly healthy marriage, as are economic stresses, moves to new areas, and unplanned pregnancies. *If the partners are from different backgrounds, conflicts are more likely to arise* than if they came from similar backgrounds. The areas of potential conflict that should be explored include sexual relations; attitudes toward contraception, childbearing, and child rearing; handling of money; relationships with in-laws; and attitudes toward social life.

Answers 30.4–30.8

30.4 The answer is A (*Synopsis VIII,* pages 843–844).

30.5 The answer is E (*Synopsis VIII,* page 845).

30.6 The answer is D (*Synopsis VIII,* page 845).

30.7 The answer is B (*Synopsis VIII,* page 844).

30.8 The answer is C (*Synopsis VIII,* page 844).
The man who resents being taken care of by his wife is classified as having *relational problem related to a mental disorder or general medical condition.* The 60-year-old woman who has problems with her neighbor is classified as having *relational problem not otherwise specified.* The classification of *sibling relational problem* is best for the daughter who refuses to attend family gatherings if her oldest brother is also present. Parent–child *relational problem* is the appropriate diagnosis for the adopted child in a family with a biological daughter. In the case of the marital discord, *partner relational problem* is related to the accidental death of the infant.

31

Problems Related to Abuse or Neglect

Problems relating to abuse or neglect include physical abuse of child, sexual abuse of child, neglect of a child, physical abuse of an adult, and sexual abuse of an adult. Child abuse occurs in all ethnic groups and at all socioeconomic levels. Abuse and neglect occur at extremely high levels in the United States and are implicated in many emotional problems and psychiatric syndromes. About 1 million cases of child abuse occur in the United States each year. Abuse and neglect lead to the deaths of 2,000 to 4,000 children annually in this country.

Abusive parents may themselves have been abused as children. Overcrowding, poverty, and other stressful living conditions can lead to child abuse, as can social isolation and parental substance abuse. Depression, severe personality disorders, or psychosis may affect parents' judgment and cause them to abuse their children. Children who are premature or mentally or physically handicapped or children who cry excessively or are extremely demanding may elicit abuse from their parents.

To diagnose child abuse, clinicians and other caretakers must be alert to suspicious signs and symptoms. Symmetric patterns of bruises and other marks, bruising, pain, or itching in the genital region, and recurrent urinary tract infections or vaginal discharges are all indicators of sexual abuse. Many abused children are withdrawn, anxious, aggressive, and precociously knowledgeable about sexual acts. Neglected children often fail to thrive; they may be malnourished, have poor skin hygiene and chronic infections, and show inappropriate social interaction. Treatment of abuse and neglect entails intervention with children and parents; the prognosis depends on the severity and nature of the abuse or neglect and the child's vulnerabilities.

Physical or sexual abuse of an adult is a problem whose awareness is growing. Spouse abuse is thought to occur in 12 million families in the United States. Although the problem is far from new, the emphasis on feminism and civil rights has spotlighted spousal abuse and has encouraged the creation of programs such as shelters where women and children can seek safety. There are estimated to be about 1.8 million battered wives in the United States. Although all racial and religious backgrounds and all socioeconomic levels are implicated, abuse is most likely to occur in families in which the husband uses alcohol, crack cocaine, or other substances of abuse. Family therapy in connection with social and legal agencies may be effective when the husband realizes that the wife intends to stay away until the husband seeks treatment. Some men are deterred by external controls, such as calling the police. Sexual abuse, or rape, is an act of aggression that happens to be expressed sexually. Rape is usually used to act out power or anger, not for the sake of the sexual encounter. Students should be familiar with the findings of recent research that categorizes male rapists into separate groups, with the psychological sequelae of rape, and with effective treatment strategies.

The various types of abuse are also a worldwide problem. In many countries abuse is rampant, far greater than in the United States. The World Health Organization tries to monitor the problem and has educational programs in third-world countries that are geared to lowering the incidence of abusive encounters that occur most often in that part of the world.

Students are referred to Chapter 31 and Chapter 54 in *Kaplan and Sadock's Synopsis VIII* and then to the questions and answers that follow to test their knowledge on the subject.

HELPFUL HINTS

Each of the following terms should be defined by the student.

- annual deaths
- child abuse
- child pornography
- cortisol
- cyclothymic disorder
- diagnosis of child abuse
- differential diagnosis
- dysthymic disorder
- environmental factors
- family characteristics
- functional impairment
- genetic factors
- hospitalization
- hypomania
- imipramine (Tofranil)
- incest:
  - father–daughter
  - mother–son
- irritable versus depressed mood
- learning disability
- low-birth-weight child
- major depressive disorder
- mania
- mood disorders
- physician's responsibility
- polysomnographic findings
- premature child
- prevention
- psychobiology
- psychopharmacology
- psychotherapy
- psychotic symptoms
- REM latency
- schizoaffective disorder
- secondary complications
- suicide
- treatment

▲QUESTIONS

DIRECTIONS: Each of the questions or incomplete statements below is followed by five suggested responses or completions. Select the *one* that is *best* in each case.

31.1 Which of the following statements about rape is *incorrect*?

A. Rapes are usually premeditated.
B. Rape most often occurs in a woman's own neighborhood.
C. Fifty percent of all rapes are perpetrated by close relatives of the victim.
D. The age range reported for rape cases in the United States is 15 months to 82 years.
E. According to the Federal Bureau of Investigation, more than 100,000 rapes are reported each year.

31.2 Which of the following features is *not* typical of father–daughter incest?

A. An overcrowded household
B. A father who abuses alcohol
C. An incapacitated or absent mother
D. A daughter who assumes a maternal role
E. Sexually inviting behavior on the part of the child

31.3 Spouse abuse is

A. carried out by men who tend to be independent and assertive
B. a recent phenomenon
C. least likely to occur when the woman is pregnant
D. directed at specific actions of the spouse
E. an act that is self-reinforcing

31.4 Incestuous behavior

A. occurs most often in families of high socioeconomic status
B. is easily hidden by economically stable families
C. is perpetrated by men and women equally
D. occurs with a daughter who was emotionally distant from her father throughout childhood
E. usually begins before the child is 5 years old

31.5 Which of the following statements is *true*?

A. About 10 percent of abused or neglected children were born prematurely or had low birth weight.
B. Many abused children are perceived by their parents as slow in development or mentally retarded.
C. More than 80 percent of abused children are living with single parents at the time of the abuse.
D. About 25 percent of abusing parents were abused by their own mothers or fathers.
E. All of the above statements are true.

31.6 The best way to establish a cause-and-effect relation between the type of mothering received and the symptoms of infant abuse is to show that

A. the child appears to be unduly afraid
B. the child shows evidence of repeated skin injuries
C. the child is undernourished
D. significant recovery occurs in the infant when the mothering is altered
E. the child is dressed inappropriately for the weather

31.7 The estimated number of deaths from child maltreatment throughout the country each year is

A. 1,000 to 1,500
B. 2,000 to 4,000
C. 5,000 to 6,000
D. 7,000 to 8,000
E. more than 10,000

31.8 Which of the following statements about incest is *true*?

A. About 15 million women in the United States have been the object of incestuous attacks.
B. One third of incest cases occur before the age of 9.
C. It is most frequently reported in families of low socioeconomic status.
D. Father–daughter incest is the most common type.
E. All of the above statements are true.

31.9 Rape is predominantly used to express power and anger in all of the following cases *except*

A. rape of elderly women
B. homosexual rape
C. rape of young children
D. statutory rape
E. date rape

31.10 Which of the following statements about rape is *false*?

A. About 10 to 25 percent of rapes are reported to authorities.
B. The greatest danger of rape exists for women aged 16 to 24.
C. Most men who commit rape are between 25 and 44 years of age.
D. Alcohol is involved in at least 75 percent of forcible rapes.
E. About 50 percent of rapes are committed by strangers.

DIRECTIONS: The questions below consist of lettered headings followed by a list of numbered phrases or statements. For each numbered phrase or statement, select

A. if the item is associated with *A only*
B. if the item is associated with *B only*
C. if the item is associated with *both A and B*
D. if the item is associated with *neither A nor B*

Questions 31.11–31.13

A. Battered child syndrome
B. Sexual abuse

31.11 Usually it is perpetrated by men.
31.12 Premature children are most vulnerable.
31.13 Hyperactivity is a risk factor for the victim.

ANSWERS

Problems Related to Abuse or Neglect

31.1 The answer is C (*Synopsis VIII,* pages 854–855).
About 10 percent, not *50 percent, of rapes are perpetrated by close relatives.* About half of rapes are committed by strangers and half by men known in varying degrees (but unrelated) to the victim. *Rapes are usually premeditated,* although rape often accompanies another crime such as mugging. A rapist frequently threatens a victim with his fists or a weapon and often harms her in nonsexual as well as sexual ways. *Rape most often occurs in a woman's own neighborhood.* It may take place inside or near her home. *The age range reported for rape cases in the United States is 15 months to 82 years. According to the Federal Bureau of Investigation, more than 100,000 rapes are reported each year.* The incidence is declining slightly.

31.2 The answer is E (*Synopsis VIII,* page 851).
Sexually inviting behavior on the part of the child is not typical in cases of father–daughter incest, although the perpetrator may claim that such was the case. Features of father–daughter incest include *an overcrowded household, a father who abuses alcohol, an incapacitated or absent mother,* and *a daughter who assumes a maternal role.*

31.3 The answer is E (*Synopsis VIII,* pages 853–854).
Spouse abuse is an *act that is self-reinforcing;* once a man has beaten his wife, he is likely to do so again. Abusive husbands *tend to be* immature, *dependent, and nonassertive* and to suffer from strong feelings of inadequacy. Spouse abuse is *not a recent phenomenon;* it is a problem of long standing that is *most likely to occur when the woman is pregnant;* 15 to 25 percent of pregnant women are physically abused while pregnant, and the abuse often results in birth defects. The *abuse is not directed at specific actions of the spouse.* Rather, impatient and impulsive abusive husbands physically displace aggression provoked by others onto their wives.

31.4 The answer is B (*Synopsis VIII,* page 851).
Incest is easily hidden by economically stable families. Incestuous behavior *does occur most often in families of low (not high) socioeconomic status.* Incestuous behavior *is usually perpetrated by men:* fathers, stepfathers, uncles, and older siblings. In father–daughter incest the *daughter frequently had a close relationship with her father throughout childhood* and may not be upset at first when he approaches her sexually. The incestuous behavior *usually begins when the daughter is 10 years old.*

31.5 The answer is B (*Synopsis VIII,* page 848).
More than 50 percent of abused or neglected children were born prematurely or had low birth weight. Many abused children are perceived by their parents as difficult, *slow in development or mentally retarded,* bad, selfish, or hard to discipline. More than 80 percent of abused children are living with *married parents* at the time of the abuse, and 90 percent of abusing parents were *abused by their own mothers or fathers.*

31.6 The answer is D (*Synopsis VIII,* page 853).
The only way to establish an unchallengeable cause-and-effect relation between the mothering received and the symptoms of infant abuse is to show that *significant recovery occurs in the infant when the mothering is altered.* That single criterion can make the diagnosis of maternal deprivation syndrome possible. Once made, this diagnosis calls for the development of a treatment plan based on immediate intervention and continued persistent surveillance. All markedly deprived infants should have an investigation of the social and environmental condition of the family and the psychological status of the mother to determine the factors responsible for inefficient mothering.

Child abuse and neglect may be suspected when several of the following factors are in evidence: the *child appears to be unduly afraid,* especially of the parents; the child is kept confined—as in a crib, playpen, or cage—for overlong periods of time; *the child shows evidence of repeated skin injuries;* the child's injuries are inappropriately treated in terms of bandages and medication; *the child is undernourished;* the child is given inappropriate food, drink, or medicine; *the child is dressed inappropriately for the weather;* the child shows evidence of overall poor care; the child cries often; and the child takes over the role of a parent and tries to be protective or to take care of the parent's needs.

31.7 The answer is B (*Synopsis VIII,* page 847).
The National Center on Child Abuse and Neglect in Washington, D.C., has estimated that there are more than 300,000 instances of child maltreatment reported to central registries throughout the country every year and *2,000 to 4,000* deaths from abuse annually.

31.8 The answer is E (all) (*Synopsis VIII,* page 851).
About 15 million women in the United States have been the object of incestuous attention, and *one-third of incest cases occur before the age of 9.* Incest is most frequently reported *in families of low socioeconomic status.* That finding may be the result of their families' greater than usual contact with welfare workers, public health personnel, law enforcement agents, and other reporting officials; it is not a true reflection of higher incidence in that demographic group. *Father–daughter* incest is the most common type.

31.9 The answer is D (*Synopsis VIII,* pages 854–855).
Statutory rape varies dramatically from the other kinds of rape in being nonassaultive and in being a sexual act, not a violent act. Statutory rape is intercourse that is unlawful because of the age of the participants. Intercourse is unlawful between a male older than 16 years of age and a female under the age of consent, which ranges from 14 to 21 years, depending on the jurisdiction.

Other types of rape—including *the rape of elderly women, homosexual rape, date or acquaintance rape,* and *the rape of young children*—are predominantly used to express power and anger. Studies of convicted rapists suggest that the crime is committed to relieve pent-up aggressive energy against persons of whom the rapist is in some awe. Although the awesome persons are usually men, the retaliatory violence is displaced toward women.

31.10 The answer is D *(Synopsis VIII,* page 854).
Alcohol is involved in about 35 percent, not 75 percent, of all forcible rapes. The greatest danger of rape exists for women age 16 to 24, although victims of rape can be any age. Most men who commit rape are *between the ages of 25 and 44 years old.* It has been estimated that *10 to 25 percent of rapes are reported* to authorities. *About 50 percent of rapes are committed by strangers,* and the remaining 50 percent are committed by men known to varying degrees by the victim.

Answers 31.11–31.13

31.11 The answer is B (*Synopsis VIII,* pages 854–855).

31.12 The answer is C (*Synopsis VIII,* pages 848, 854–855).

31.13 The answer is A (*Synopsis VIII,* pages 847–849).
Sexual abuse is usually *perpetrated by men,* although women acting in concert with men or alone have also been involved, especially in child pornography. *Premature children* are vulnerable to both battered child syndrome and sexual abuse. *Hyperactivity* is also a risk factor for the victim.

32

Additional Conditions That May Be a Focus of Clinical Attention

The fourth edition of *Diagnostic and Statistical Manual of Mental Disorders* (DSM-IV) lists 13 conditions that may be associated with mental disorders or may be early manifestations of mental disorders. These conditions are noncompliance with treatment, malingering, adult antisocial behavior, child or adolescent antisocial behavior, borderline intellectual functioning, age-related cognitive decline, bereavement, academic problem, occupational problem, identity problem, religious or spiritual problem, acculturation problem, and phase of life problem. Although these conditions are not true mental disorders, clinicians should ensure that patients with such conditions receive a thorough neuropsychiatric evaluation to determine whether there is an underlying mental disorder.

For example, normal bereavement after the loss of a loved one can lead to a depressive disorder that requires treatment. Symptoms of such a disorder include feelings of sadness, insomnia, poor appetite, and weight loss. The affected person may view the depression as normal, although he or she may seek treatment for an associated symptom such as insomnia. Features of a major depressive disorder that would probably not occur in normal bereavement include a morbid preoccupation with worthlessness, marked psychomotor retardation, prolonged and marked functional impairment, some hallucinatory experiences, thoughts of death not associated with the deceased person, and guilt not associated with the person's actions toward the deceased person.

Examples of occupational problem include job dissatisfaction and uncertainty about career choices. Adult antisocial behavior is characterized by illegal or immoral activities that usually begin in childhood and continue throughout a person's life. Examples include thievery, racketeering, and drug dealing. Such behavior may be influenced by genetic and social factors, and therapy seems to have little effect on lifelong behavior patterns. Both occupational problem and adult antisocial behavior must be diagnosed by excluding relevant mental disorders.

Malingering is the willful producing of false physical or psychological symptoms to avoid responsibilities or punishment; to receive free compensation, haven, or drugs; or to retaliate against a perceived loss, penalty, or feeling of guilt. The clearly definable goal distinguishes malingering from factitious disorders.

A phase of life problem is associated with a developmental phase or other life situation that is not part of a mental disorder. Such problems include starting school, beginning a new job, and getting divorced. Major life-cycle changes such as occur in marriage, occupation, and parenthood, are likely to precipitate this condition.

Noncompliance with treatment may be caused by discomforts associated with the treatment, the expense of treatment, personal values or religious or cultural beliefs about the treatment, or maladaptive personality traits. For this condition to be diagnosed, a person's problem must be severe enough to warrant clinical attention but must not be caused by a mental disorder.

Religious and spiritual problems include loss or questioning of faith, problems associated with converting to a new religion, and questioning of spiritual values not necessarily related to organized religion. Young people who join cults provide examples of such a problem.

An acculturation problem involves adjusting to a new culture. People are often vulnerable to stress during times of cultural transition, such as when they join the army or are transferred to another country as part of their occupation.

Age-related cognitive decline is an objectively identified decline in cognitive functions; the decline is the result of aging and is within normal limits for a person's age. People may have trouble remembering names or doctor appointments. This condition, like all those previously described, is diagnosed only when it is not attributable to a specific mental disorder or abnormal neurological condition. Students should study Chapter 32 in *Kaplan and Sadock's Synopsis VIII* before turning to the questions and answers that follow.

HELPFUL HINTS

The student should know the following words and terms.

- ▶ acculturation problem
- ▶ adherence
- ▶ adoption studies
- ▶ age-associated memory decline
- ▶ antisocial behavior
- ▶ bereavement
- ▶ brainwashing
- ▶ compliance
- ▶ conditioning
- ▶ coping mechanisms
- ▶ cults
- ▶ cultural transition
- ▶ culture shock
- ▶ doctor–patient match
- ▶ dual-career families
- ▶ emotional deprivation
- ▶ galvanic skin response
- ▶ job-related stress
- ▶ kleptomania
- ▶ malingering
- ▶ marital problems
- ▶ mature defense mechanisms
- ▶ medicolegal context of presentation
- ▶ noncompliance
- ▶ noncustodial parent
- ▶ normal grief
- ▶ occupational problem
- ▶ patient contract
- ▶ phase of life problem
- ▶ religious or spiritual problem
- ▶ sociopathic
- ▶ stress
- ▶ superego lacunae

▲ QUESTIONS

DIRECTIONS: Each of the questions or incomplete statements below is followed by five suggested responses or completions. Select the *one* that is *best* in each case.

32.1 Which of the following is *not* a symptom or sign of adult antisocial behavior?

A. Arrest record
B. Feelings of guilt
C. Substance abuse
D. Somatic complaints
E. Abnormal findings on an electroencephalogram (EEG)

32.2 Which of the following is *not* considered a mental disorder?

A. Factitious disorder
B. Antisocial personality disorder
C. Malingering
D. Hypochondriasis
E. Somatization disorder

32.3 Adult antisocial behavior

A. has been effectively treated by psychotherapy
B. can be diagnosed in the presence of a mental disorder
C. is not influenced by genetic factors
D. is not associated with the use and abuse of alcohol and other substances
E. must be distinguished from temporal lobe epilepsy in the differential diagnosis

32.4 Exit therapy is designed to help people

A. with adult antisocial behavior
B. with acculturation problems
C. who are involved in cults
D. with occupational problems
E. in bereavement

32.5 Bereavement

A. usually leads to a full depressive disorder
B. is the same cross-culturally in terms of duration
C. includes guilt about things other than actions taken or not taken at the time of the death
D. includes preoccupation with thoughts about the deceased, tearfulness, irritability, and insomnia
E. can involve hallucinatory experiences other than hearing or seeing the deceased

32.6 The field of occupational or industrial psychiatry has found that

A. overwhelming ambition can usually overcome poor education and training and lead to success
B. few corporations are willing to employ a husband and a wife in the same firm
C. some people may fear success because of their inability to tolerate envy from others
D. fathers and mothers use unpaid parental leaves equally
E. the transition from outside employment to homemaking is stress free

32.7 A person who malingers

A. often expresses subjective, ill-defined symptoms
B. should be confronted by the treating clinician
C. is usually found in settings with a preponderance of women
D. rarely seeks secondary gains
E. can achieve symptom relief by suggestion or hypnosis

32.8 Antisocial behavior is generally characterized by

A. lack of social charm and poor intelligence
B. heightened nervousness with neurotic manifestations
C. often successful suicide attempts
D. lack of remorse or shame
E. all of the above

32.9 Factors most often associated with job-related stress include all of the following *except*

A. not enough work
B. unclear work objectives
C. conflicting demands
D. feeling distracted by family problems
E. responsibility with authority over others

32.10 Which of the following conditions is motivated by the avoidance of responsibility?

A. Factitious disorder
B. Conversion disorder
C. Somatization disorder
D. Malingering
E. Body dysmorphic disorder

32.11 Occupational problems may arise from psychodynamic conflicts that include

A. problems with authority figures
B. competitive rivalries
C. pathological envy
D. fear of hostility from others
E. all of the above

32.12 In dual-career families

A. mothers are vulnerable to guilt and anxiety regarding their maternal role
B. mothers emphasize the importance of discipline
C. the parents assume equal responsibility for child rearing and homemaking
D. the children are likely to have academic difficulties and psychological problems
E. the divorce rate is higher than in single-career families

32.13 Which of the following statements involving women in the work force is *false*?

A. More than 50 percent of all mothers in the work force have preschool-age children.
B. Specific issues that should be addressed are provisions for child care or for the care of elderly parents.
C. Managers are more sensitive to crises in women employees' lives than in men employees' lives.
D. Ninety percent of women and girls alive today in the United States will have to work to support themselves.
E. Managers ignore the stress placed on a worker by the illness of a child.

DIRECTIONS: The questions below consist of lettered headings followed by a list of numbered phrases. For each numbered phrase, select

A. if the item is associated with *A only*
B. if the item is associated with *B only*
C. if the item is associated with *both A and B*
D. if the item is associated with *neither A nor B*

Questions 32.14–32.16

A. Adult antisocial behavior
B. Antisocial personality disorder
C. Both
D. Neither

32.14 Previous diagnosis of conduct disorder with onset before age 15
32.15 Mental disorder
32.16 Occurs more often in males than in females

ANSWERS

Additional Conditions That May Be a Focus of Clinical Attention

32.1 The answer is B (*Synopsis VIII,* pages 859–860).

Feelings of guilt are not a symptom of adult antisocial behavior; people with this condition tend not to feel guilt about their behavior, a factor that makes successful treatment difficult. Adults with antisocial behavior often have an *arrest record,* perhaps for thievery, drug dealing, or violence. *Substance abuse* is common, as is alcohol abuse; clinicians must take care to distinguish between antisocial behavior related to drug use from similar behavior that is unrelated to substance dependence. Many people with antisocial behavior have *somatic complaints,* and they may show *abnormal findings on an electroencephalogram (EEG).* Recurrently violent people commonly have sustained continued insults to the central nervous system beginning prenatally and continuing through childhood and adolescence as a result of parental alcohol and substance use and physical abuse. Temporal lobe epilepsy or encephalitis can contribute to adult antisocial behavior; an estimated 50 percent of aggressive criminals have abnormal EEG findings.

32.2 The answer is C (*Synopsis VIII,* pages 860–861).

Malingering is not considered a mental disorder; it is characterized by the voluntary production and presentation of false or grossly exaggerated physical or psychological symptoms. The patient always has an external motivation, which falls into one of three categories: (1) to avoid difficult or dangerous situations, responsibilities, or punishment; (2) to receive compensation, free hospital room and board, drugs, or haven from the police; and (3) to retaliate when the patient feels guilt or suffers a financial loss, legal penalty, or job loss.

Factitious disorder, antisocial personality disorder, hypochondriasis, and *somatization* disorder are all considered mental disorders. The presence of a clearly definable goal is the main factor that differentiates malingering from *factitious disorder. Antisocial personality disorder* requires evidence of conduct disorder that began before the age of 15. Hypochondriasis and somatization disorder are both somatoform disorders, which are characterized by physical symptoms that suggest physical disease, although no demonstrable organ pathology or pathophysiological mechanism can be identified. In *hypochondriasis* the patient is excessively concerned about disease and health. In *somatization disorder,* multiple somatic symptoms cannot be explained medically and are associated with psychosocial distress and medical help seeking. Table 32.1 lists malingering features usually not found in genuine illness.

Table 32.1
Malingering Features Usually Not Found in Genuine Illness

Symptoms are vague, ill-defined, overdramatized, and not in conformity with known clinical conditions.

The patient seeks addicting drugs, financial gain, the avoidance of onerous (eg, jail) or other unwanted conditions.

History, examination, and evaluative data do not elucidate complaints.

The patient is uncooperative and refuses to accept a clean bill of health or an encouraging prognosis.

The findings appear compatible with self-inflicted injuries.

History or records reveal multiple past episodes of injury or undiagnosed illness.

Records or test data appear to have been tampered with (eg, erasures, unprescribed substances in urine).

Courtesy of Arthur T. Meyerson, M.D.

32.3 The answer is E (*Synopsis VIII,* pages 859–860).

Adult antisocial behavior *must be distinguished from temporal lobe epilepsy in the differential diagnosis.* When a clear-cut diagnosis of temporal lobe epilepsy or encephalitis can be made, that may contribute to the adult antisocial behavior. Abnormal electroencephalogram (EEG) findings are prevalent among violent offenders. An estimated 50 percent of aggressive criminals have abnormal EEG findings.

Adult antisocial behavior has not been effectively treated by psychotherapy, and there have been no major breakthroughs with biological treatments, including the use of medications. More enthusiasm is found for the use of therapeutic communities and other forms of group treatment. Many adult criminals who are incarcerated and in institutional settings have shown some response to group therapy approaches.

Adult antisocial behavior *cannot be diagnosed in the presence of a mental disorder,* but it *is influenced by genetic factors.* A 60 percent concordance rate has been found in monozygotic twins and about a 30 percent concordance rate in dizygotic twins. Adoption studies show a high rate of antisocial behavior in the biological relatives of adoptees identified with antisocial behavior and a high incidence of antisocial behavior in the adopted-away offspring of those with antisocial behavior. Adult antisocial behavior *is associated with the use and abuse of alcohol and other substances.* Table 32.2 lists the major symptoms of adult antisocial behavior.

32.4 The answer is C (*Synopsis VIII,* page 862).

Exit therapy is designed to help people *who are involved in cults;* it works only if their lingering emotional ties to persons outside the cult can be mobilized. Most potential cult members are in their adolescence or otherwise struggling with establishing their own identities. The cult holds out the false promise of emotional well-being and purports to offer the sense of direction for which the persons are searching. Cult members are encouraged to proselytize and to draw new members into the group. They are often encouraged to break with family members and friends and to socialize only with other group members. Cults are invariably led by charismatic personalities, who are often ruthless in their quest for financial, sexual, and power gains and in their insistence on conformity to the cult's ideological belief system, which may have strong religious or quasi-religious overtones.

Table 32.2
Symptoms of Adult Antisocial Behavior

Life Area	Antisocial Patients with Significant Problems in Area (%)
Work problems	85
Marital problems	81
Financial dependence	79
Arrests	75
Alcohol abuse	72
School problems	71
Impulsiveness	67
Sexual behavior	64
Wild adolescence	62
Vagrancy	60
Belligerence	58
Social isolation	56
Military record (of those serving)	53
Lack of guilt	40
Somatic complaints	31
Use of aliases	29
Pathological lying	16
Substance abuse	15
Suicide attempts	11

Data from Robins L: *Deviant Children Grown Up: A Sociological and Psychiatric Study of Sociopathic Personality.* Williams & Wilkins, Baltimore, 1966.

Exit therapy is not designed to help people with adult antisocial behavior with acculturation or occupational *problems,* or in bereavement. *Adult antisocial behavior* has no clearly successful mode of treatment. *Occupational problems* may bring a person into contact with the mental health field, and psychotherapy may aid in working through some occupational problems.

32.5 The answer is D (*Synopsis VIII,* page 857).
Bereavement, a normal process, includes feelings of sadness, *preoccupation with thoughts about the deceased, tearfulness, irritability, insomnia,* and difficulties in concentrating and carrying out one's daily activities. Many of the symptoms are similar to those in major depressive disorder, but that diagnosis is generally not given unless the depressive symptoms persist 2 months after the loss. Bereavement *does not usually lead to a full depressive disorder.* In different cultures the length of bereavement varies, and so bereavement *is not the same cross-culturally in terms of duration.* Bereavement *does not include guilt about things other than actions taken or not taken at the time of the death, nor does it involve hallucinatory experiences other than hearing or seeing the deceased.* Those symptoms are indicative of a major depressive episode.

32.6 The answer is C (*Synopsis VIII,* pages 857–859).
Some people may fear success because of their inability to tolerate envy from others. Other people may suffer from a pathological envy of the success of others. And *overwhelming ambition cannot usually overcome poor education and training and lead to success.* In the past 25 years, major changes have occurred in the business world in the United States. Formerly, many businesses considered the employment of a husband and a wife taboo. That situation has changed. *Many corporations are now willing to employ a husband and a wife in the same firm.* The Family Leave Law allows 3 months of unpaid maternal and paternal leave to employees, both men and women. However, *fathers and mothers do not use unpaid parental leaves equally. The transition from outside employment to homemaking is not stress free.* Researchers have found that women are specifically at risk for stress when they leave outside employment for homemaking.

32.7 The answer is A (*Synopsis VIII,* pages 860–861).
A person who malingers *often expresses subjective, ill-defined symptoms*—for example, headache; pains in the patient's neck, lower back, chest, or abdomen; dizziness; vertigo; amnesia; anxiety; and depression—and the symptoms often have a family history, in all likelihood not organically based but extremely difficult to refute. A patient suspected of malingering should be thoroughly and objectively evaluated, and the physician should refrain from showing any suspicion. The patient *should not be confronted by the treating clinician.* If the clinician becomes angry (a common response to malingerers), a confrontation may occur, with two consequences: (1) The doctor–patient relationship is disrupted, and no further positive intervention is possible. (2) The patient is even more on guard, and obtaining proof of deception may become virtually impossible. Preserving the doctor–patient relationship is often essential to the diagnosis and long-term treatment of the patient. Careful evaluation usually reveals the relevant issue without the need for a confrontation.

Malingering *is usually found in settings with a preponderance of men,* such as the military, prisons, factories, and other industrial settings. The malingerer *always seeks secondary gains,* such as money, food, and shelter. The malingerer *cannot usually achieve symptom relief by suggestion or hypnosis.*

32.8 The answer is D (*Synopsis VIII,* pages 859–860).
Antisocial behavior is generally characterized by *lack of remorse or shame.* Other characteristics are a *superficial charm and good intelligence, an absence of nervousness and neurotic manifestations, and rarely successful suicide attempts.*

32.9 The answer is E (*Synopsis VIII,* pages 857–859).
Having *responsibility without (not with) authority over others* is a factor most often associated with job-related stress. Job-related stress is most likely to develop in the presence of *unclear work objectives, conflicting demands,* too much or *not enough work,* responsibility for the professional development of others, *feeling distracted by family problems,* and little control over decisions that affect them.

32.10 The answer is D (*Synopsis VIII,* pages 860–861).
Malingering, characterized by the voluntary production and presentation of false or grossly exaggerated physical or psychological symptoms, always has an external motivation, such as financial gain or the avoidance of responsibility. The presence of a clearly definable goal is the main factor that differentiates malingering from *factitious disorder.* Evidence of an intrapsychic need to maintain the sick role suggests factitious disorder.

Conversion disorder and *somatization disorder* do not show intention; the patient has no obvious, external incentives. Patients with *body dysmorphic disorder* believe that they are physically misshapen or defective in some way despite an objectively normal appearance. The clinical features of the disorder are not motivated by the prospect of financial gain.

32.11 The answer is E (all) (*Synopsis VIII,* pages 857–859). Occupational problems may arise from psychodynamic conflicts that include *problems with authority figures.* People with unresolved conflicts over *competitive rivalries* may experience great difficulty at work. They may suffer from a *pathological envy* of the success of others or *fear hostility from others.* Those conflicts are also present in other areas of the patient's life.

32.12 The answer is A (*Synopsis VIII,* page 858).
In dual-career families, defined as families in which both spouses have careers, *mothers are vulnerable to guilt and anxiety regarding their maternal role* and their relative lack of availability to their children. The *mothers* usually accept middle-class or upper-middle-class values that *emphasize the importance of psychological health and the individual development of the child, not discipline.* They espouse sophisticated child-rearing practices that use sensitivity and communication to impart values to the child, rather than punishment. Despite the high educational levels and the intellectual sophistication of the couples, *the women generally still assume the major responsibility for child rearing and homemaking.* The husbands do contribute more than in previous generations, but their help is frequently couched in the form of helping out their wives rather than as a fully shared, equal burden. No evidence suggests that *the children are likely to have academic difficulties and psychological problems* as a result of the familial arrangements. No evidence indicates that *the divorce rate is higher in dual career families than in single-career families.*

32.13 The answer is C (*Synopsis VIII,* page 858).
Studies reveal that managers are more sensitive to crises in men's than in women's lives. Managers respond to such major events as divorce and death of a family member but *ignore the stress placed on a worker by the illness of a child* or a school closing because of a snow day. *More than 50 percent of mothers* in the work force have preschool-age children. *Specific issues* that should be addressed are provisions for child care or for the care of elderly parents. *Ninety percent of women and girls alive today in the United States will have to work to support themselves* and probably one or two other people.

Answers 32.14–32.16

32.14 The answer is B (*Synopsis VIII,* pages 859–860).

32.15 The answer is B (*Synopsis VIII,* pages 859–860).

32.16 The answer is C (*Synopsis VIII,* pages 859–860).
The diagnosis of *antisocial personality disorder,* in contrast to *adult antisocial behavior,* requires evidence of preexisting psychopathology, such as *previous diagnosis of conduct disorder with onset before age 15,* and a long-standing pattern of irresponsible and antisocial behavior since the age of 15. Illegal behavior is not considered the equivalent of psychopathology and without evidence of preexisting psychological disturbance is not deemed secondary to antisocial personality disorder.

Adult antisocial behavior is not considered a *mental disorder,* but antisocial personality disorder is. Both adult antisocial behavior and antisocial personality disorder *occur more often in males than in females.* Familial patterns for both diagnostic classes have also been reported.

33 

Psychiatric Emergencies

A psychiatric emergency is a disturbance in thoughts, feelings, or actions for which immediate therapeutic intervention is necessary. In psychiatric emergencies, people may be severely disabled and unable to care for themselves or may be at risk for harming themselves or others. Psychiatric emergencies also arise when mental disorders impair people's judgment, impulse control, or reality testing.

Clinicians must be familiar with the common psychiatric diagnoses associated with emergencies. Suicide is the prototypical psychiatric emergency; emergencies are also associated with manic and depressive episodes in mood disorders, schizophrenia, alcohol and other substance dependence, borderline personality disorder, and toxic conditions. When interviewing patients in psychiatric emergencies, clinicians must consider protecting themselves, the patient, and others, and they must be knowledgeable about organic conditions that may cause the relevant symptoms. Clinicians must also be familiar with guidelines about the use of restraints, including pharmacological and chemical restraints.

Suicide, the most frequently encountered psychiatric emergency, is the eighth leading cause of death in the United States. Indicators for increased risk of suicide include factors such as age, sex, race, religion, marital status, occupation, physical and mental health, family history, current mental state, and history of suicidal behavior. Although a knowledge of the known risk factors can help clinicians predict and intervene in suicide, they must treat the patient, not the statistical risk.

Suicide tends to run in families, a fact that suggests psychodynamic and biological theories about its causes. Genetic influence in suicide can be deduced from twin and adoption studies of people who have committed suicide. Major depressive disorder, alcohol abuse, and schizophrenia are associated with higher than usual risk for suicide, but genetic transmission of a tendency toward impulsive behavior (associated with a deficiency in cerebral serotonin) may also be implicated.

Suicide may be differently perceived in different societies and among different cultural groups. Émile Durkheim described suicide types as egoistic, altruistic, and anomic. Egoistic suicides are those who are not strongly integrated into a social group. Unmarried people have a higher suicide rate than do married people; the rate of city dwellers exceeds that of the rural population; and Protestants have a higher suicide rate than do Roman Catholics. Altruistic suicide refers to those who act from excessive group integration, such as soldiers in battle or old people in Eskimo society. Anomic suicide applies to people whose social integration is disturbed or fragile, such as a person who suddenly loses a fortune or who faces exposure as a criminal.

Psychological factors in suicide include repressed aggression toward another according to Freud and powerful desires for revenge, atonement, oblivion, or rebirth according to contemporary psychiatrists. The group dynamics that underlie mass suicide are puzzling and little studied.

Clinicians must assess patients' suicide risk on the basis of clinical examination. High risk factors include age over 45 years, male sex, alcohol dependence, prior suicidal behavior, and previous psychiatric hospitalization. Clinicians should specifically ask patients whether they have contemplated suicide, and they should be concerned about signs indicating that such behavior is imminent. Most suicides among psychiatric patients are preventable.

To become knowledgeable about suicide and other psychiatric emergencies, students are referred to Chapter 33 in *Kaplan and Sadock's Synopsis VIII.* The following questions and answers can then be addressed.

HELPFUL HINTS

These terms relate to psychiatric emergencies and should be defined.

- ▶ acute intoxication
- ▶ adolescent suicide
- ▶ age of suicide
- ▶ akinetic mutism
- ▶ alcohol dependence
- ▶ alcohol withdrawal
- ▶ alkalosis
- ▶ amnesia
- ▶ anniversary suicide
- ▶ anorexia nervosa
- ▶ Aaron Beck
- ▶ blackout
- ▶ bulimia nervosa
- ▶ catatonic excitement
- ▶ catatonic stupor
- ▶ copycat suicide
- ▶ crisis listening post
- ▶ delirious state
- ▶ delirium
- ▶ dementia
- ▶ drugs and suicide
- ▶ DTs
- ▶ Émile Durkheim
- ▶ dysmenorrhea
- ▶ ECT
- ▶ exhaustion syndrome
- ▶ grief and bereavement
- ▶ headache
- ▶ 5-HIAA in CSF
- ▶ homosexual panic
- ▶ hyperthermia
- ▶ hypertoxic schizophrenia
- ▶ hyperventilation
- ▶ hypnosis
- ▶ hypothermia

- ▶ insomnia
- ▶ lethal catatonia
- ▶ Karl Menninger
- ▶ method
- ▶ miosis
- ▶ *Mourning and Melancholia*
- ▶ mydriasis
- ▶ nystagmus
- ▶ opioid withdrawal:
  - anxiolytic
  - hypnotic
  - sedative
- ▶ panic
- ▶ platelet MAO activity
- ▶ posttraumatic stress disorder mania
- ▶ premenstrual dysphoric disorder
- ▶ prevention center
- ▶ psychotic withdrawal
- ▶ suicidal depression
- ▶ suicidal thoughts
- ▶ suicidal threats
- ▶ suicide
  - altruistic
  - anomic
  - egoistic
- ▶ suicide belt
- ▶ suicide rate
- ▶ Thanatos
- ▶ Wernicke's encephalopathy
- ▶ Werther's syndrome

▲ QUESTIONS

DIRECTIONS: Each of these questions or incomplete statements is followed by five suggested responses or completions. Select the *one* that is *best* in each case.

33.1 Which of the following is *not* a sign or symptom that a patient is at serious risk for suicide?

A. A patient with lung cancer views life as hopeless.
B. A patient with mild depression has a new will drawn up.
C. A patient with schizophrenia hears voices ordering her to stab herself.
D. A patient with substance dependence states that his father and brother committed suicide.
E. A patient with severe depression describes a fantasy of taking an overdose of sleeping pills.

33.2 Which of the following is *not* a sign of impending violence?

A. A verbal threat
B. A rage disorder
C. Ecstasy intoxication
D. Excessive sleepiness
E. Catatonic excitement

33.3 Which of the following features does *not* suggest a medical cause of a mental disorder?

A. Acute onset
B. Gait disorder
C. Current mental illness
D. Loss of consciousness
E. Impaired concentration

DIRECTIONS: For each of the three numbered syndromes, select the letter of the most appropriate set of emergency manifestations.

Questions 33.4–33.6

A. Delirium, delusions
B. Delirium, mania, depression
C. Confusion, agitation, impulsivity
D. Alcohol stigmata, amnesia, confabulation
E. Mental confusion, oculomotor disturbances

33.4 Bromide intoxication
33.5 Korsakoff's syndrome
33.6 Alcohol persisting dementia

DIRECTIONS: Each of the questions or incomplete statements below is followed by five suggested responses or completions. Select the *one* that is *best* in each case.

33.7 The patient was a 25-year-old female graduate student in physical chemistry who was brought to the emergency room by her roommates, who found her sitting in her car with the motor running and the garage door closed. The patient had entered psychotherapy 2 years before, complaining of longstanding unhappiness, feelings of inadequacy, low self-esteem, chronic tiredness, and a generally pessimistic outlook on life. While she was in treatment, as before, periods of well-being were limited to a few weeks at a time. During the 2 months before her emergency room visit, she had become increasingly depressed, had had difficulty in falling asleep and trouble in concentrating, and had lost 10 pounds. The onset of those symptoms coincided with a rebuff she had received from a chemistry instructor to whom she had become attracted.

The treatment of the patient could include

A. hospitalization
B. outpatient treatment
C. antidepressants
D. electroconvulsive therapy
E. all of the above

33.8 Suicide rates

A. are equal among men and women
B. decrease with age
C. are higher among blacks than among whites
D. increase during December and other holiday periods
E. among Catholics are lower than the rates among Protestants and Jews

33.9 An increased risk for suicide is found in

A. patients with mood disorders
B. patients with schizophrenia
C. patients with alcohol dependence
D. patients with panic disorder
E. all of the above

33.10 For patients seen in psychiatric emergency rooms

A. haloperidol can be given only every 6 hours
B. electroconvulsive therapy (ECT) may be used to control psychotic violence
C. restraints are illegal in most states
D. cognitive psychotherapy is the treatment modality of choice
E. extrapyramidal emergencies are treated with antipsychotic medications

33.11 Suicide

A. is usually a random or pointless act
B. rates in the United States are at the high point of the national rates reported to the United Nations by the industrialized countries
C. accounts for about 30,000 deaths in the United States each year
D. does not run in families
E. is characterized by all of the above

33.12 Which of the following neurobiological findings is associated with suicide?

A. Increased 5-hydroxyindoleacetic acid (5-HIAA) levels in the cerebrospinal fluid (CSF)
B. Changes in the dopaminergic system
C. Serotonin deficiency
D. Increased levels of platelet monoamine oxidase (MAO)
E. Normal findings on electroencephalogram (EEG)

33.13 Which of the following statements about the predictability of suicide is *true*?

A. Of persons who eventually kill themselves, 50 percent give warnings of their intent.
B. Of persons who eventually kill themselves, 50 percent say openly that they want to die.
C. A patient who openly admits to a plan of suicidal action is at less risk for suicide than is a patient who has only vague ideas about suicide.
D. A patient who has been threatening suicide who becomes quiet and less agitated is at less risk for suicide than is a patient who remains agitated.
E. A previously suicidal patient who begins to show a positive response to the pharmacological treatment of depression is not at risk for suicide.

33.14 The psychodynamics of persons who commit suicide includes which of the following?

A. It is a means to a better life.
B. Someone is telling them to kill themselves.
C. It is a way to get revenge against a loved person.
D. It is a release from illness.
E. It is characterized by all of the above.

33.15 Suicide attempts may

A. provide a sense of mastery over a situation
B. represent a turning in of murderous rage
C. be part of an attempt at reunion
D. represent self-punishment
E. be characterized by all of the above

33.16 Among men, suicide peaks after age 45; among women, it peaks after age

A. 35
B. 40
C. 45
D. 50
E. 55

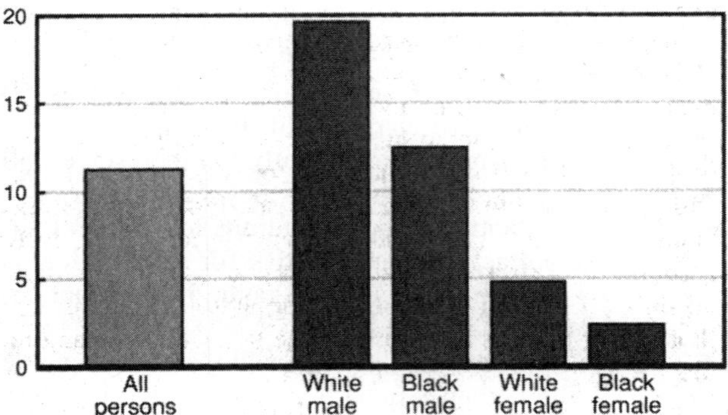

FIGURE 33.1

Reprinted with permission from National Center for Health Statistics: *Health, United States, 1991*. Public Health Service, Hyattsville, MD, 1992.

33.17 Figure 33.1 shows the U.S. distribution, according to race and sex, of which of the following?

A. The prevalence of schizophrenia
B. Rates of alcohol-related disorders
C. Rates of suicide attempts (successful and unsuccessful)
D. Death rates for suicide
E. Prevalence of bipolar disorder

DIRECTIONS: Each group of questions below consists of lettered headings followed by a list of numbered phrases or statements. For each numbered phrase or statement, select the *one* lettered heading that is most closely associated with it. Each lettered heading may be selected once, more than once, or not at all.

Questions 33.18–33.20

A. Émile Durkheim
B. Sigmund Freud
C. Karl Menninger

33.18 Divided suicide into three social categories: egoistic, altruistic, and anomic

33.19 Described three components of hostility in suicide: the wish to kill, the wish to be killed, and the wish to die

33.20 Wrote that suicide represents aggression turned inward

Questions 33.21–33.26

A. Opioids
B. Barbiturates
C. Phencyclidine (PCP)
D. Monoamine oxidase inhibitors (MAOIs)
E. Acetaminophen (Tylenol)

33.21 Hypertensive crisis can occur

33.22 Pinpoint pupils after overdose

33.23 Cross-tolerant with diazepam (Valium)

33.24 Treated with propranolol (Inderal)

33.25 Toxic interaction with meperidine hydrochloride (Demerol)

33.26 Phenothiazines contraindicated

ANSWERS

Psychiatric Emergencies

33.1 The answer is B (*Synopsis VIII,* pages 867–874).
Although having *a new will drawn up* might be a predictor of suicide in a person with severe depression, a mildly depressed person who takes such an action is at low risk for suicide.

The other choices, however, should all suggest to a clinician that a patient is at high risk of suicide: *A patient with lung cancer* who *views life as hopeless; a patient with schizophrenia* who *hears voices ordering her to stab herself; a patient with substance dependence* who has a family history of suicide; and *a patient with severe depression* who fantasizes about suicide. Other indications of high risk of suicide include age over 45 years, male sex, being divorced or widowed, being unemployed, having chaotic or conflicted family and personal relationships, being hypochondriacal, having a psychosis or severe personality disorder, having a strong wish to die, having available methods of suicide, having poor achievement and poor insight, and being socially isolated.

33.2 The answer is D (*Synopsis VIII,* pages 873–876).
Excessive sleepiness is not a sign of impending violence, but *a verbal threat, a rage disorder, intoxication* with ecstasy or another substance, and *catatonic excitement* are signs of impending violence. Other signs of violence include recent violent acts, including property violence, carrying weapons or objects that can be used as weapons such as a fork, progressive psychomotor agitation, having a brain disease with global or frontal lobe findings, and personality disorders.

In the face of such signs, clinicians must evaluate a patient's potential for acting violently. Most important is to consider the cause and then to institute appropriate treatment. Patients who need hospitalization (for example, those who have thought disorders with hallucinations commanding them to kill somebody) must be persuaded to accept treatment or must be certified, both to protect society from the violent behavior and to protect the patient. Not all psychiatric patients will act violently, and clinicians must assess each patient as a unique case. The strongest predictors of violence are excessive alcohol intake, a history of violent acts with arrests or criminal activity, and a history of childhood abuse.

33.3 The answer is C (*Synopsis VIII,* pages 865–866).
Current mental illness does not imply a necessary medical cause of the disorder. *Acute onset, gait disorder, loss of consciousness,* and *impaired concentration* are features that point to a medical cause of a mental disorder. Other indicators that a mental disorder has a physical cause include first episode, geriatric age, current medical illness or injury, nonauditory disturbances of perception, seizures, head injury, change in headache pattern or vision, diminished alertness, disorientation, memory impairment, speech or movement disorders, constructional apraxia, and catatonic features.

33.4 The answer is B (*Synopsis VIII,* page 879).
Delirium, mania, depression, and psychosis are manifestations of bromide intoxication. If a patient's serum levels are above 50 mg a day, bromide intake should be discontinued; if the patient is agitated, lorazepam (Ativan) may be given for sedation. For severe agitation or psychotic syndromes an antipsychotic dopamine receptor antagonist may be necessary.

33.5 The answer is D (*Synopsis VIII,* page 878).
Alcohol stigmata, amnesia, and *confabulation* are manifestations of Korsakoff's syndrome. Because this disorder has no effective treatment, the patient must often be institutionalized in a protective environment.

33.6 The answer is C (*Synopsis VIII,* page 878).
Confusion, agitation, and *impulsivity* are manifestations of alcohol persisting dementia. If the dementia has no other causes, the patient may have to be hospitalized; there is no effective treatment. *Delirium and delusions* are manifestations of cimetidine psychotic disorder. *Mental confusion, oculomotor disturbances,* and cerebellar ataxia are manifestations of Wernicke's encephalopathy.

33.7 The answer is E (all) (*Synopsis VIII,* pages 870–872).
The treatment of the depressed, suicidal 25-year-old female graduate student described in question 33.7 could include *hospitalization* or *outpatient treatment, antidepressants,* or *electroconvulsive therapy* (ECT). Whether to hospitalize the patient with suicidal ideation is a crucial clinical decision. Not all such patients require hospitalization; some may be treated as outpatients. Indications for hospitalization include the lack of a strong social support system, a history of impulsive behavior, and a suicidal plan of action. Most psychiatrists believe that the young woman described should be hospitalized because she had made a suicide attempt and so was clearly at increased risk. Other psychiatrists believe that they could treat the patient on an outpatient basis provided certain conditions were met, such as (1) reducing the patient's psychological pain by modifying her stressful environment through the aid of a friend, a relative, or her employer; (2) building realistic support by recognizing that the patient may have legitimate complaints and offering alternatives to suicide; (3) securing commitment on the part of the patient to agree to call when she reached a point beyond which she was uncertain of controlling further suicidal impulses; and (4) assuring commitment on the part of the psychiatrist to be available to the patient 24 hours a day. Also, if the patient is not to be hospitalized, the family must take the responsibility of being with the patient 24 hours a day until the risk has passed. Because it is difficult to meet many of those conditions, hospitalization is often the safest route.

Many depressed suicidal patients require treatment with antidepressants or ECT. The young woman described had a recent sustained and severely depressed mood that was associated with insomnia, trouble in concentrating, weight loss, and a suicide attempt. Those factors indicate a major depressive episode. There was also evidence of long-standing mild depressive symptoms (pessimism, feelings of inadequacy, and low energy level) that although insufficient to meet the diagnostic criteria for a major depressive episode, do meet the criteria for dysthymic disorder. With those clinical features, the indication for the use of antidepressants is clear; ECT may be necessary if the patient was unresponsive to antidepressants or so severely depressed and suicidal that she required faster-acting treatment than is possible with antidepressants. ECT is a safe and effective procedure that is being attacked by antipsychiatry forces in society.

33.8 The answer is E (*Synopsis VIII,* page 865).
Suicide rates *among Catholics are lower than the rates among Protestants and Jews.* A religion's degree of orthodoxy and integration may be a more accurate measure of risk for suicide than is religious affiliation.

Suicide rates *are not equal among men and women.* Men commit suicide more than 3 times as often as do women. Women, however, are 4 times as likely to attempt suicide as are men. The higher rate of completed suicide for men is related to the methods they use. Men use firearms, hanging, or jumping from high places. Women are likely to take an overdose of psychoactive substances or a poison, but they are beginning to use firearms more than previously. The use of guns has decreased as a method of suicide in states with gun control laws.

Suicide rates *increase with age.* The significance of the midlife crisis is underscored by suicide rates. Rates of 40 suicides per 100,000 population are found in men aged 65 and older. The elderly attempt suicide less often than do younger people but are successful more often. The elderly account for 25 percent of the suicides, although they make up only 10 percent of the total population. The rate for those 75 or older is more than 3 times the rate among the young.

Suicide rates *are higher among whites than among blacks.* In 1989 the suicide rate for white males (19.6 per 100,000 persons) was 1.6 times that for black males (12.5), 4 times that for white females (4.8), and 8.2 times that for black females (2.4). Among ghetto youth and certain Native American and Alaskan Indian groups, suicide rates have greatly exceeded the national rate. Suicide among immigrants is higher than in the native-born population. Two of every three suicides are white males. Contrary to popular belief, suicide rates *do not increase during December and other holiday periods.*

33.9 The answer is E (all) (*Synopsis VIII,* pages 864–868).
Patients with mood disorders are at greatest risk for suicide in both sexes. The age-adjusted suicide rates for patients suffering from mood disorders have been estimated to be 400 per 100,000 for male patients and 180 per 100,000 for female patients. The suicide risk is also high among *patients with schizophrenia;* up to 10 percent die by committing suicide. In the United States an estimated 4,000 schizophrenic patients commit suicide each year. *Patients with alcohol dependence* also are at high risk for committing suicide. Up to 15 percent of all alcohol-dependent persons commit suicide. Their suicide rate is estimated to be 270 per 100,000 a year; in the United States, between 7,000 and 13,000 alcohol-dependent persons are suicide victims each year. *Patients with panic disorder* also have an increased suicide risk. One study reported that such patients have a suicide rate more than 7 times the age-adjusted and sex-adjusted rate for the general population, but the rate is similar to that of other clinical psychiatric populations.

33.10 The answer is B (*Synopsis VIII,* page 871).
Electroconvulsive therapy (ECT) may be used to control psychotic violence. One or several ECT sessions within several hours usually end an episode of psychotic violence. However, haloperidol (Haldol) is one of the most useful emergency treatments of violent psychotic patients and is generally used instead of ECT. *Haloperidol may be given more than every 6 hours.* In some instances, haloperidol 5 to 10 mg every half hour to an hour is needed until a patient is stabilized. A contraindication to the use of haloperidol is that the patient has suffered a head injury, because the medication can confuse the clinical picture.

Restraints are not illegal in most states, and restraints should be applied when patients are so dangerous to themselves or to others that they pose a severe threat that cannot be controlled in any other way. Most often, patients in restraints quiet down after some time has elapsed. On a psychodynamic level, such patients may even welcome the control of their impulses that restraints provide. Table 33.1 lists the guidelines for the use of restraints.

In emergency room psychiatry, *no one form of psychotherapy is the treatment modality of choice.* In an emergency psychiatric intervention, all attempts are made to help patients maintain self-esteem. More than one form of psychotherapy is frequently used in emergency therapy. The emphasis is on how various psychiatric modalities act synergistically to enhance recovery.

Table 33.1
Use of Restraints

Preferably five or a minimum of four persons should be used to restrain the patient. Leather restraints are the safest and surest types of restraints.

Explain to the patient why he or she is going into restraints.

A staff member should always be visible and reassuring the patient who is being restrained. Reassurance helps alleviate the patient's fear of helplessness, impotence, and loss of control.

The patient should be restrained with legs spread-eagled and one arm restrained to one side and the other arm restrained over the patient's head.

Restraints should be placed so that intravenous fluids can be given if necessary.

The patient's head should be raised slightly to decrease the patient's feelings of vulnerability and to reduce the possibility of aspiration.

The restraints should be checked periodically for safety and comfort.

After the patient is in restraints, the clinician should begin treatment, using verbal intervention.

Even in restraints, a majority of patients still take antipsychotic medication in concentrated form.

After the patient is under control, one restraint at a time should be removed at 5-minute intervals until the patient has only two restraints on. Both of the remaining restraints should be removed at the same time, because it is inadvisable to keep a patient in only one restraint.

Always thoroughly document the reason for the restraints, the course of treatment, and the patient's response to treatment while in restraints.

Data are from Dubin WR, Weiss KJ: Emergency psychiatry. In *Psychiatry,* R Michaels, A Cooper, SB Guze, LL Judd, GL Klerman, AJ Solnit, AJ Sunkard, PJ Wilner, editors, vol 2. Lippincott, Philadelphia, 1991.

Extrapyramidal emergencies are not treated with antipsychotic medications. Extrapyramidal emergencies are usually the result of the adverse effects of antipsychotic medications. Patients in such emergencies usually respond to benztropine (Cogentin) 2 mg orally or intramuscularly (IM) or diphenhydramine (Benadryl) 50 mg IM or intravenously (IV). Some patients respond to diazepam (Valium) 5 to 10 mg orally or IV.

33.11 The answer is C (*Synopsis VIII,* page 864).
Suicide *accounts for about 30,000 deaths in the United States each year.* That figure is for completed suicides; the number of attempted suicides is estimated to be 8 to 10 times that number. Lost in the reporting are intentional misclassifications of the cause of death, accidents of undetermined cause, deaths through alcohol and other substance abuse, and consciously poor adherence to medical regimens for diabetes, obesity, and hypertension.

Suicide *rates in the United States are at the midpoint, not the high point, of the national rates reported to the United Nations by the industrialized countries.* Internationally, suicide rates range from highs of more than 25 per 100,000 people in Scandinavia, Switzerland, Germany, Austria, the eastern European countries (the suicide belt), and Japan to fewer than 10 per 100,000 in Spain, Italy, Ireland, Egypt, and the Netherlands.

Suicide is intentional self-inflicted death. Suicide *is not a random or pointless act.* On the contrary, it is a way out of a problem or a crisis that is invariably causing intense suffering. Suicide is associated with thwarted or unfulfilled needs, feelings of hopelessness and helplessness, ambivalent conflicts between survival and unbearable stress, a narrowing of perceived options, and a need for escape; the suicidal person sends out signals of distress.

Suicide *does run in families.* At all stages of the life cycle, a family history of suicide is present more often among persons who have attempted suicide than among those who have not. One major study found that the suicide risk for first-degree relatives of psychiatric patients was almost 8 times greater than for the relatives of controls. Furthermore, the suicide risk among the first-degree relatives of the psychiatric patients who had committed suicide was 4 times greater than among the relatives of patients who had not committed suicide.

33.12 The answer is C (*Synopsis VIII,* page 869).
A *serotonin deficiency,* as measured by *decreased (not increased) 5-hydroxyindoleacetic acid (5-HIAA) levels in the cerebbrospinal fluid (CSF),* has been found in some patients who attempted suicide. In addition, some postmortem studies have reported *changes in the noradrenergic system (not dopaminergic system). Decreased (not increased) levels of platelet monoamine oxidase (MAO)* have been discovered in some suicidal patients. When blood samples from normal volunteers were analyzed, it was found that those with the lowest level of MAO in their platelets had 8 times the prevalence of suicide in their families. *Abnormal findings on electroencephalograms (EEGs), not normal findings,* and ventricular enlargement have been found in a few studies of suicidal patients.

33.13 The answer is B (*Synopsis VIII,* page 870).
Of persons who eventually kill themselves, 50 percent say openly that they want to die, but 80 percent (not 50 percent) give warnings of their intent. *A patient who openly admits to a plan of action is at greater (not less) risk for suicide than is a patient who has only vague suicidal ideas about suicide. A patient who has been threatening suicide who becomes quiet and less agitated may be at increased (not less) risk,* as may be *a previously suicidal patient who begins to show a positive response to the pharmacological treatment of depression.* Such patients may still harbor suicidal thoughts, and because they are energized, they can carry out their plans. Depressed patients are most likely to commit suicide at the onset or at the end of a depressive episode. The risk of suicide also increases in the immediate period after discharge from inpatient psychiatric treatment.

33.14 The answer is E (all) (*Synopsis VIII,* page 864).
Shneidman and Farberow classified suicides into four groups: (1) patients who conceive of suicide as *a means to a better life;* (2) patients who commit suicide as a result of psychosis with associated delusions or hallucinations—for example, *someone is telling them to kill themselves;* (3) patients who commit suicide *to get revenge against a loved person;* and (4) patients who are old or infirm for whom suicide is *a release from illness.*

33.15 The answer is E (all) (*Synopsis VIII,* pages 864–870).
Suicide attempts and the possibility of suicide seem to *provide a sense of mastery over a situation* through the control of life and death. In many young, severely disturbed, and seriously suicidal patients, suicide *represents a turning in of murderous rage* that is far from repressed. The act of dying can be conceived of as *an attempt to reunite* with deceased parental figures or with wives, husbands, or siblings substituting as parents. Suicide attempts may also *represent self-punishment.*

33.16 The answer is E (*Synopsis VIII,* page 864).
Among women suicide peaks after age 55. Rates of 40 per 100,000 population are found in men age 65 and older; the elderly attempt suicide less often than do younger people but are successful more frequently, accounting for 25 percent of all completed suicides, although the elderly make up only 10 per cent of the total population. A decline in suicide in men begins between the ages 75 to 85. A peak risk among males is also found in late adolescence, when death by suicide is exceeded only by death attributed to accidents and cancer.

33.17 The answer is D (*Synopsis VIII,* page 865).
Figure 33.1 represents *death rates for suicide* in the United States according to race and sex. The rate of suicide among whites is nearly twice that among nonwhites, but the figures are being questioned, as the suicide rate among blacks is increasing. In 1989, the suicide rate for white males was 1.6 times that for black males, 4 times that for white females and 8.2 times that for black females. Two out of every three suicides are white males. Women are 4 times as likely to attempt suicide as are men, while overall, men commit suicide more than 3 times as often as do women.

Schizophrenia is equally prevalent in men and women. *Bipolar I disorder* also has a prevalence that is equal for men and women. The ratio of *alcohol-related disorder* diagnoses for men to women is about 2 to 1 or 3 to 1. Although the rate of alcohol-related disorders has traditionally been highest among young white men, evidence now indicates that young black men and young Hispanic men may have surpassed young white men in their rates of alcohol-related disorders.

Answers 33.18–33.20

33.18 The answer is A (*Synopsis VIII,* page 868).

33.19 The answer is C (*Synopsis VIII,* page 868).

33.20 The answer is B (*Synopsis VIII,* page 868).
The first major contribution to the study of the social and cultural influences on suicide was made at the end of the 19th century by the French sociologist *Émile Durkheim.* In an attempt to explain statistical patterns, Durkheim *divided suicides into three social categories: egoistic, altruistic, and anomic.* Egoistic suicide applies to those who are not strongly integrated into any social group. The lack of family integration can be used to explain why the unmarried are more vulnerable to suicide than are the married and why couples with children are the best-protected group of all. Rural communities have more social integration than do urban areas and thus less suicide. Protestantism is a less cohesive religion than Catholicism is, and so Protestants have a higher suicide rate than do Catholics. Altruistic suicide applies to those whose proneness to suicide stems from their excessive integration into a group, with suicide being the outgrowth of that integration—for example, the Japanese soldier who sacrifices his life in battle. Anomic suicide applies to persons whose integration into society is disturbed, depriving them of the customary norms of behavior. Anomie can explain why those whose economic situation has changed drastically are more vulnerable than they were before their change in fortune. Anomie also refers to social instability, with a breakdown of society's standards and values.

The first important psychological insight into suicide came from *Sigmund Freud.* In his paper "Mourning and Melancholia," Freud *wrote that suicide represents aggression turned inward* against an introjected, ambivalently cathected love object. Freud doubted that there would be a suicide without the repressed desire to kill someone else.

Building on Freud's concepts, *Karl Menninger* in *Man Against Himself* conceived of suicide as a retroflexed murder, inverted homicide as a result of the patient's anger toward another person, which is either turned inward or used as an excuse for punishment. He also described a self-directed death instinct (Freud's concept of Thanatos). He *described three components of hostility in suicide: the wish to kill, the wish to be killed, and the wish to die.*

Answers 33.21–33.26

33.21 The answer is D (*Synopsis VIII,* pages 866–872).

33.22 The answer is A (*Synopsis VIII,* pages 866–872).

33.23 The answer is B (*Synopsis VIII,* pages 866–872).

33.24 The answer is C (*Synopsis VIII,* pages 866–872).

33.25 The answer is D (*Synopsis VIII,* pages 866–872).

33.26 The answer is C (*Synopsis VIII,* pages 866–872).
Substance abuse is one of the many reasons for visits to psychiatric emergency rooms. Patients who take overdoses of *opioids* (for example, heroin) tend to be pale and cyanotic (a dark bluish or purplish coloration of the skin and mucous membranes), with *pinpoint pupils* and absent reflexes. After blood is drawn for a study of drug levels, those patients should be given intravenous naloxone hydrochloride (Narcan), a narcotic antagonist that reverses the opiate effects, including respiratory depression, within 2 minutes of the injection.

The use of barbiturates and anxiolytics is widespread, and withdrawal from sedative-hypnotic drugs is a common reason for psychiatric emergencies. The first symptom of withdrawal can start as soon as 8 hours after the last pill has been taken and may consist of anxiety, confusion, and ataxia. As withdrawal progresses, the patient may have seizures; occasionally, a psychotic state erupts, with hallucinations, panic, and disorientation. *Barbiturates* are *cross-tolerant with* all antianxiety agents, such as *diazepam (Valium).* In the treatment of sedative, hypnotic, or anxiolytic withdrawal, one must take into account the usual daily substance intake.

Phencyclidine (*PCP* or angel dust) is a common cause of psychotic drug-related hospital admissions. The presence of dissociative phenomena, nystagmus (ocular ataxia), muscular rigidity, and elevated blood pressure in a patient who is agitated, psychotic, or comatose strongly suggests PCP intoxication. In the treatment of PCP overdose, the patient should have gastric lavage to recover the drug, diazepam to reduce anxiety, an acidifying diuretic program consisting of ammonium chloride and furosemide (Lasix), which will enhance PCP excretion, and the treatment of hypertension with *propranolol (Inderal).* Acidification is not recommended with hepatic or renal failure or when barbiturate use is suspected. *Phenothiazines are contraindicated,* because muscle rigidity and seizures, side effects of PCP, can be exacerbated by phenothiazines, as can the anticholinergic effects of PCP.

Monoamine oxidase inhibitors (MAOIs) are useful in treating depression, but a *hypertensive crisis can occur* if the patients have eaten food with a high tyramine content while on their medication. Hypertensive crisis is characterized by severe occipital headaches, nausea, vomiting, sweating, photophobia, and dilated pupils. When a hypertensive crisis occurs, the MAOI should be discontinued, and therapy should be instituted to reduce blood pressure. Chlorpromazine (Thorazine) and phentolamine (Regitine) have both been found useful in those hypertensive crises. MAOIs have a *toxic interaction with meperidine hydrochloride (Demerol),* which can be fatal. When patients combine the two drugs, they become agitated, disoriented, cyanotic, hyperthermic, hypertensive, and tachycardic.

Acetaminophen (Tylenol) is an analgesic and antipyretic. Overdose with acetaminophen is characterized by fever, pancytopenia, hypoglycemic coma, renal failure, and liver damage. Treatment should begin with the induction of emesis or gastric lavage, followed by the administration of activated charcoal. Early treatment is critical to protect against hepatotoxicity.

34 Psychotherapies

The many theorists of psychiatry have developed a variety of treatments, each of which deals with an underlying constellation of forces thought to constitute a mental disturbance. Most clinicians are familiar with several kinds of psychiatric treatment. They may choose techniques from different psychiatric therapies to treat their patients, and they understand what therapy is indicated for a specific patient and how various therapies can work effectively together.

Psychoanalysis, psychoanalytic psychotherapy, and brief dynamic psychotherapies are all derived from the Freudian theory of the unconscious. In these therapies, clinicians help patients to gain insight into and to resolve their unconscious conflicts to change unsatisfactory, self-destructive, or painful behavior and to shape their lives to productive and creative ends. In contrast to psychoanalysis, psychoanalytic psychotherapy emphasizes exploring a patient's current life more than his or her past. Brief psychotherapy generally focuses on a specific problem. All of these therapies, which can include group psychotherapy, stress the importance of a person's gaining insight into the conflicts that hamper human growth.

Family and marital therapy, which is based on general systems theory, focuses on helping family members recognize covert patterns that maintain a possibly maladaptive homeostasis. Rather than identifying one family member as a patient to be treated, family therapists help to reveal faulty patterns of communication that sustain the patient's behavior. Family and marital therapists may work with a group or a single family member; no single approach is superior to another.

Behavior therapy focuses on removing a person's overt symptoms without exploring private experiences or inner conflicts. The basic tenet of this therapy is that maladaptive behavior is conditioned or learned and that various forms of deconditioning or unlearning are successful treatments. Behavior therapy is most often used to treat specific habits of reacting anxiously to nonthreatening stimuli, such as phobias and compulsions. The varieties of behavior therapy include systematic desensitization, graded exposure, flooding, participant modeling, assertiveness and social skills training, aversion therapy, and positive reinforcement.

Cognitive therapy is a short-term structured therapy that uses active collaboration between therapist and patient to achieve therapeutic goals. Cognitive therapy, individual or group, is used to treat depressive disorders and is used in obsessive-compulsive disorder, panic disorder, and somatoform disorders.

Biofeedback is a method of giving a person information about a usually unconscious physiological process so that the person can gain some control over it. For example, a person can learn to control tension headaches through relaxation exercises. Using biofeedback, people can also learn to control their skin temperature, blood pressure, and heart rate.

Hypnosis has been defined as a state in which a person responds to suggestions by experiencing altered perceptions, memory, mood, or behavior. Clinical hypnosis and therapeutic trance are thought to be extensions of processes such as daydreaming. Although it is sometimes considered an altered state of consciousness, no characteristic electroencephalogram (EEG) changes mark the state of hypnosis. Hypnotherapy can be used to increase relaxation so that a person can deal with a phobia. It has also been used, although not always successfully, to control obesity and substance-related disorders such as alcohol abuse and nicotine dependence.

Students should study Chapter 34 in *Kaplan and Sadock's Synopsis VIII* before turning to the questions and answers that follow.

HELPFUL HINTS

The names of the workers, their theories, and the therapy techniques should be known to the student.

- AA, GA, OA
- abreaction
- analyst incognito
- Anna O.
- assertiveness
- authority anxiety
- autogenic therapy
- aversive therapy
- Michael Balint
- Aaron Beck
- behavioral medicine
- bell and pad
- Hippolyte Bernheim
- Murray Bowen
- cognitive rehearsal
- cognitive triad of depression
- cohesion
- combined individual and group psychotherapy
- confidentiality
- countertransference
- crisis intervention
- crisis theory
- day's residue
- disorders of self-control
- disulfiram (Antabuse) therapy
- double and multiple double
- dyad
- early therapy

- ego psychology
- eye-roll sign
- H. J. Eysenck
- family group therapy
- family sculpting
- family systems
- family therapy
- flexible schemata
- flooding
- galvanic skin response
- genogram
- Gestalt group therapy
- graded exposure
- group psychotherapy
- guided imagery
- hierarchy construction
- homogeneous versus heterogeneous groups
- hypnosis
- hypnotic capacity and induction
- hysteria
- implosion
- indicated patient
- insight-oriented psychotherapy
- intellectualization, interpretation
- interpersonal psychotherapy
- Jacobson's exercise
- Daniel Malan
- mental imagery
- mirror technique
- Jacob Moreno
- operant conditioning
- parapraxes
- participant modeling
- patient–therapist encounter
- peer anxiety
- positive reinforcement
- psychodrama
- psychodynamic model
- psychotherapeutic focus
- psychotherapy
- reality testing
- reciprocal inhibition
- relaxation response
- resistance
- reward of desired behavior
- Carl Rogers
- role reversal
- rule of abstinence
- schemata
- Paul Schilder
- self-analysis
- self-help groups
- self-observation
- Peter Sifneos
- B. F. Skinner
- splitting
- structural model
- structural theory
- *Studies on Hysteria*
- supportive therapy
- systematic desensitization
- tabula rasa
- testing automatic thoughts
- token economy
- transactional group therapy
- transference, transference neurosis, negative triangulation
- universalization
- ventilation and catharsis

▲ QUESTIONS

DIRECTIONS: For each of the numbered therapies, select the lettered choice that most appropriately refers to it.

Questions 34.1–34.3

A. Reliance on the leader is high.
B. Negative transference feelings are analyzed.
C. Dreams are always analyzed and encouraged.
D. Socialization outside the group is encouraged.
E. The goal is extensive reconstruction of personality dynamics.

34.1 Supportive group therapy
34.2 Behavioral group therapy
34.3 Transactional group therapy

DIRECTIONS: Each of the questions or incomplete statements below is followed by five suggested responses or completions. Select the *one* that is *best* in each case.

34.4 Which of the following is *not* a psychotherapeutic intervention?

A. Affirmation
B. Verification
C. Clarification
D. Confrontation
E. Interpretation

34.5 Which of the following instances suggests that psychotherapy is contraindicated?

A. A person with superior intelligence
B. A person who is a close friend of the analyst
C. A person whose life situation cannot be modified
D. A person with an inability to form emotional attachments
E. A person who completely lacks remorse for past violent behavior

34.6 Patients with poor frustration tolerance and poor reality testing are best treated with

A. supportive psychotherapy
B. insight-oriented psychotherapy
C. expressive therapy
D. intensive psychoanalytic psychotherapy
E. all of the above

34.7 The most effective psychotherapeutic method for patients with pathological gambling is

A. activity groups
B. self-help groups
C. family therapy
D. psychodrama
E. individual therapy

34.8 The use of disulfiram (Antabuse) therapy in the treatment of alcohol abuse is an example of

A. relaxation training
B. graded exposure
C. aversion therapy
D. positive reinforcement
E. token economy

34.9 A patient with a fear of heights is brought to the top of a tall building and is required to remain there until the anxiety dissipates. That is an example of

A. graded exposure
B. participant modeling
C. aversion therapy
D. flooding
E. systematic desensitization

34.10 Which of the following conditions is *not* amenable to hypnosis?

A. Paranoia
B. Pruritus
C. Alcohol dependence
D. Obesity
E. Asthma

34.11 Systematic desensitization is applicable in the treatment of

A. obsessive-compulsive disorder
B. sexual disorders
C. stuttering
D. bronchial asthma
E. all of the above

34.12 The therapeutic factors in group therapy include

A. multiple transferences
B. collective transference
C. universalization
D. cohesion
E. all of the above

34.13 Patients who experience anxiety in group therapy include

A. patients who are fearful in the presence of authority
B. patients who have had destructive relationships with peers
C. patients who were isolated from peers
D. children without siblings
E. all of the above

34.14 Cotherapy in groups may be characterized by

A. each therapist's being as active as the other
B. neither therapist's being in a position of greater authority than the other
C. having a male therapist and a female therapist
D. replication of parental surrogates
E. all of the above

34.15 Which of the following methods is *not* used in biofeedback?

A. Electromyography
B. Electroencephalography
C. Galvanic skin response
D. Strain gauge
E. All of the above

34.16 The cognitive therapy approach includes

A. eliciting automatic thoughts
B. testing automatic thoughts
C. identifying maladaptive underlying assumptions
D. testing the validity of maladaptive assumptions
E. all of the above

DIRECTIONS: The questions below consist of five lettered headings followed by a list of numbered statements. For each numbered statement, select the *one* lettered heading that is most closely associated with it. Each lettered heading may be selected once, more than once, or not at all.

Questions 34.17–34.21

A. Biofeedback
B. Behavior therapy
C. Crisis intervention
D. Cognitive therapy
E. Hypnosis

34.17 Based on the principles of learning theory
34.18 Based on the concept that autonomic responses can be controlled through the process of operant or instrumental conditioning
34.19 Based on an underlying theoretical rationale that affect and behavior are largely determined by the way a person structures the world
34.20 Emphasizes not only immediate responses to an immediate situation but also long-term development of psychological adaptation aimed at preventing future problems
34.21 Has subjective experiential change as the essential feature

DIRECTIONS: The lettered headings below are followed by a list of numbered statements. For each numbered statement, select

A. if the item is associated with *A only*
B. if the item is associated with *B only*
C. if the item is associated with *both A and B*
D. if the item is associated with *neither A nor B*

Questions 34.22–34.25

A. Psychoanalytic psychotherapy
B. Psychoanalysis
C. Both
D. Neither

34.22 Has the patient lying on a couch
34.23 Uncovers and works through infantile conflicts
34.24 Takes as its focus the patient's current conflicts and current dynamic patterns
34.25 Uses free association and the analysis of the transference neurosis

ANSWERS

Psychotherapies

34.1 The answer is D (*Synopsis VIII,* pages 897–902).
In *supportive group therapy, socialization outside the group is encouraged.* Supportive group therapy is a short-term therapy with weekly sessions for about 6 months. This form of therapy is primarily indicated for those with psychotic and anxiety disorders. Patients discuss environmental factors, and therapists try to strengthen patients' existing defenses by actively advising them. Positive transference is encouraged to promote improved functioning; dreams are not analyzed, and no interpretations of unconscious conflicts are given. Reality testing is the major group process, and the therapy aims to improve patients' adaptation to the environment.

34.2 The answer is A (*Synopsis VIII,* pages 911–916).
In *behavioral group therapy, reliance on the leader is high.* This short-term therapy requires meetings 1 to 3 times weekly for about 6 months. Phobias, passivity, and sexual problems are dealt with. Patients discuss specific symptoms without focusing on causality; dream analysis is not used. Therapists aim to create new defenses and intervene actively in patients' discussions. Interpretation is not practiced. The major group processes are cohesion, reinforcement, and conditioning. The goal is relief of specific psychiatric symptoms.

34.3 The answer is B (*Synopsis VIII,* pages 897, 898).
In *transactional group therapy, negative transference feelings are analyzed.* This type of therapy can last 1 to 3 years, with sessions 1 to 3 times a week. The therapy is indicated for anxiety and psychotic disorders. Patients primarily discuss intragroup relationships and the here and now; past histories are rarely explored, and dreams are rarely analyzed. Therapists actively challenge patients' defenses and give personal responses to patients' behavior rather than advice. The major group processes are abreaction and reality testing. The goal is to alter patients' behavior through the mechanism of conscious control.

Dreams are always analyzed and encouraged in the psychoanalysis of groups, which has as a goal the *extensive reconstruction of personality dynamics.*

34.4 The answer is B (*Synopsis VIII,* pages 887–888).
Verification is not a psychotherapeutic intervention. *Affirmation* involves brief comments that support a patient's words or actions, such as "I see what you mean." In *clarification,* a therapist reformulates a patient's communication to express a coherent view of the content. Clarification helps patients articulate ideas that are difficult to put into words. *Confrontation* addresses something a patient does not want to accept or refers to a patient's avoidance or minimization. Confrontation need not be forceful or hostile and probably is more effective when phrased gently. *Interpretation* is considered a therapist's ultimate decisive instrument. When a therapist interprets something, he or she makes conscious that which was unconscious. Interpretation may associate a feeling, thought, behavior, or symptom with its unconscious significance.

34.5 The answer is C (*Synopsis VIII,* page 888).
A person whose life situation cannot be modified is a poor candidate for psychotherapy. Analysis can make life worse for such people, for example, by creating goals that they cannot fulfill because of external limitations. *A person with superior intelligence* is not necessarily a poor candidate for psychotherapy. *A person who is a close friend of the analyst* should choose another therapist for psychotherapy. Analysts should avoid working with friends, relatives, and acquaintances because such relationships can distort the transference and the therapists' objectivity. People *with an inability to form emotional attachments* and those who *completely lack remorse for past violent behavior* are probably unsuitable for analytically oriented psychotherapy. The absence of relatedness to others is thought to be the single most negative predictor of psychotherapy response. People with antisocial behavior may, however, benefit from some kinds of therapy, such as group therapy with other antisocial personalities. An inability to engage in therapy is seen as linked to sadistic cruelty, total absence of remorse, and lack of emotional attachment. People with characteristics such as antisocial personality behavior may also cause countertransference fears in therapists and thus may sabotage the analytic effort. A mildly retarded antisocial personality may lack the cognitive capacity to engage in analysis.

34.6 The answer is A (*Synopsis VIII,* page 902).
Patients with poor frustration tolerance and poor reality testing are best treated with *supportive psychotherapy.* Supportive psychotherapy (also called relationship-oriented psychotherapy) offers the patient support by an authority figure during a period of illness, turmoil, or temporary decompensation. It has the goal of restoring and strengthening the patient's defenses and integrating capacities that have been impaired. It provides a period of acceptance and dependence for a patient who is in need of help in dealing with guilt, shame, and anxiety and in meeting the frustrations or the external pressures that may be too great to handle. Supportive therapy uses a number of methods, either singly or in combination, including (1) warm, friendly, strong leadership; (2) gratification of dependency needs; (3) support in the ultimate development of legitimate independence; (4) help in the development of pleasurable sublimations (for example, hobbies); (5) adequate rest and diversion; (6) the removal of excessive external strain if possible; (7) hospitalization when indicated; (8) medication to alleviate symptoms; and (9) guidance and advice in dealing with current issues. It uses the techniques that help the patient feel secure, accepted, protected, encouraged, and safe and not anxious.

Insight-oriented psychotherapy (also called *expressive therapy* and *intensive psychoanalytic psychotherapy*) is not the best treatment for patients with poor frustration tolerance and poor reality testing. The psychiatrist's emphasis in insight-oriented therapy is on the value to patients of gaining a number of new insights into the current dynamics of their feelings, responses, behavior, and, especially, current relationships with other persons. Insight-oriented therapy is the treatment of choice for a

Table 34.1
Indications for Expressive or Supportive Emphasis in Psychotherapy

Insight-Oriented (Expressive)	Supportive
Strong motivation to understand	Significant ego defects of a long-term nature
Significant suffering	Severe life crisis
Ability to regress in the service of the ego	
Tolerance for frustration	Poor frustration tolerance
Capacity for insight (psychological mindedness)	Lack of psychological-mindedness
Intact reality testing	Poor reality testing
Meaningful object relations	Severely impaired object relations
Good impulse control	Poor impulse control
Ability to sustain work	Low intelligence
Capacity to think in terms of analogy and metaphor	Little capacity for self-observation
Reflective responses to trial interpretations	Organically based cognitive dysfunction
	Tenuous ability to form a therapeutic alliance

Reprinted with permission from Gabbard GO: *Psychodynamic Psychotherapy in Clinical Practice,* p 88. American Psychiatric Press, Washington, 1990.

patient who has adequate ego strength but who, for one reason or another, should not or cannot undergo psychoanalysis. Table 34.1 summarizes the indication for insight-oriented (expressive) therapy versus supportive therapy.

34.7 The answer is B (*Synopsis VIII,* page 902).
Self-help groups are the most effective psychotherapeutic method for patients with pathological gambling. Gamblers seldom come forward voluntarily for treatment. Legal difficulties, family pressures, or other psychiatric complaints are what bring the gamblers into treatment. Gamblers Anonymous (GA) was founded in 1957 and was modeled after Alcoholics Anonymous (AA); both GA and AA are self-help groups led and organized by nonprofessional group members. A distinguishing characteristic of the self-help group is its homogeneity. Members suffer from the same disorder, and they share their experiences—good and bad, successful and unsuccessful—with one another. By so doing, they educate one another, provide mutual support, and alleviate the sense of alienation that is usually felt by the person drawn to the group. Self-help groups emphasize cohesion.

Activity groups are a type of group therapy introduced and developed by S. R. Slavson and designed for children and young adolescents. Activity group therapy assumes that poor experiences have led to deficits in personality development of children; thus, corrective experiences in a therapeutic environment will modify them. Activity group therapy uses interview techniques, verbal explanations of fantasies, group play, work, and other communications. *Family therapy* is the treatment of more than one member of a family in the same session. Family relationships and processes are viewed as part of a family system, which has a stake in maintaining the status quo. The family believes that one or several family members are the source of all family problems. Family therapy may be helpful to pathological gamblers, in conjunction with GA. *Psychodrama* is a psychotherapy method originated by Jacob L. Moreno in which personality makeup, interpersonal relationships, conflicts, and emotional problems are expressed and explored through dramatization. The therapeutic dramatization of emotional problems includes the protagonist (patient), auxiliary egos (other group members), and the director (leader or therapist). *Individual therapy* is the traditional dyadic therapeutic technique, in which a psychotherapist treats one patient during a given therapeutic session. Individual therapy techniques are useful with some impulse disorders, but, in such disorders as pathological gambling, results are better when groups are composed of other gamblers who have mastered the problem.

34.8 The answer is C (*Synopsis VIII,* page 914).
The use of disulfiram (Antabuse) therapy in the treatment of alcohol abuse is an example of *aversion therapy.* The alcohol-free patient is given a daily dose of disulfiram, which produces severe physiological consequences if alcohol is ingested while it is in the system (for example, nausea, vomiting, hypertension, and epilepsy). Another type of aversion therapy is to make the alcohol-abusing patient vomit by adding an emetic to an alcoholic drink, which is then imbibed.

Relaxation training is a method in which the patient is taught to relax major muscle groups to relieve anxiety. *Graded exposure* teaches phobic patients to approach a feared object in small increments until the phobia is extinguished. In *positive reinforcement* a desirable behavioral response is followed by a reward, such as food, the avoidance of pain, or praise. The person repeats the behavior to receive the reward. In *token economy* a patient is rewarded with a token that is used to purchase luxury items or certain privileges. It is used on inpatient hospital wards to modify behavior.

34.9 The answer is D (*Synopsis VIII,* pages 912, 914).
Flooding is a technique in which, for example, a patient with a fear of heights is brought to the top of a tall building and is required to remain there until the anxiety dissipates. Flooding is based on the premise that escaping from an anxiety-provoking experience reinforces the anxiety through conditioning. Thus, if the person is not allowed to escape, anxiety can be extinguished, and the conditioned avoidance behavior can be prevented. In clinical situations, flooding consists of having the patient confront the anxiety-inducing object or situation at full intensity for prolonged periods of time, resulting in the patient's being flooded with anxiety. The confrontation may be done in imagination, but results are better when real-life situations are used.

In *graded exposure* the patient is exposed over a period of time to objects that cause increasing levels of anxiety. It is similar to flooding except that the phobic object or situation is approached through a series of small steps, rather than all at once. *Participant modeling* is based on imitation, whereby patients learn to confront a fearful situation or object by modeling themselves after the therapist. *Aversion therapy* involves the presentation of a noxious stimulus immediately after a specific behavioral response, leading to the response's being inhibited and extinguished. The negative stimulus (punishment) is paired with the undesired behavior, which is thereby suppressed. *Systematic desensitization,* like graded exposure, is based on the concept that a person can overcome maladaptive anxiety elicited by a situation or object by approaching the feared situation gradually and in a psychophysiological state that inhibits anxiety. The patient attains a state of complete relaxation and then is exposed to the anxiety-producing stimulus. The negative reaction of anxiety is inhibited by the relaxed state. Systematic desensitization differs from graded exposure in two respects: (1) systematic desensitization uses relaxation training, whereas graded exposure does not, and (2) systematic desensitization uses a graded list or hierarchy of anxiety-provoking scenes that the patient imagines, as opposed to graded exposure, in which the treatment is carried out in a real-life context.

34.10 The answer is A (*Synopsis VIII,* pages 916–917). *Paranoia* is not amenable to hypnosis, simply because paranoid patients are suspicious and usually avoid or resist efforts to be hypnotized. Any patient who has difficulty with basic trust or who has problems with giving up control is not a good candidate for hypnosis. However, a variety of conditions have been treated with varying degrees of success with hypnosis, including *pruritus, alcohol dependence, obesity, asthma,* substance-released disorders, smoking, warts, and chronic pain.

34.11 The answer is E (all) (*Synopsis VIII,* page 912). Systematic desensitization is applicable in the treatment of *obsessive-compulsive disorder, sexual disorders, stuttering, bronchial asthma,* and other conditions. Joseph Wolpe first described systematic desensitization, a behavioral technique in which the patient is trained in muscle relaxation; a hierarchy of anxiety-provoking thoughts or objects are paired with the relaxed state until the anxiety is systematically decreased and eliminated.

Obsessive-compulsive disorder (recurrent, intrusive mental events and behavior) is mediated by the anxiety elicited by specific objects or situations. Through systematic desensitization, the patient can be conditioned not to feel anxiety when around those objects or situations and thus to diminish the intensity of the obsessive-compulsive behavior. Desensitization has been used effectively with some stutterers by deconditioning the anxiety associated with a range of speaking situations. Some sexual disorders—such as male orgasmic disorder, female orgasmic disorder, and premature ejaculation—are amenable to desensitization therapy.

34.12 The answer is E (all) (*Synopsis VIII,* pages 897–899). Many factors account for therapeutic change in group therapy. *Multiple transferences* are possible because a variety of group members stand for people significant in a patient's past or current life situation. Group members may take the roles of wife, mother, father, siblings, and employer. The patient can then work through actual or fantasized conflicts with the surrogate figures to a successful resolution.

Collective transference is a member's pathological personification of the group as a single transferential figure, generally the mother or the father. It is a phenomenon unique to group therapy. The therapist attempts to encourage the patient to respond to members of the group as individuals and to differentiate them. *Universalization* is the process by which patients recognize that they are not alone in having an emotional problem. It is one of the most important processes in group therapy. *Cohesion* is a sense of ''we-ness,'' a sense of belonging. The members value the group, which engenders loyalty and friendliness among them. The members are willing to work together and take responsibility for one another in achieving their common goals. And they are willing to endure a certain degree of frustration to maintain the group's integrity. The more cohesion a group has, the more likely it is that it will have a successful outcome. Cohesion is considered the most important therapeutic factor in group therapy.

34.13 The answer is E (all) (*Synopsis VIII,* pages 897–899). Many patients experience anxiety when placed in a group or when group therapy is suggested. They include *patients who are fearful in the presence of authority figures*—real or projected persons in a position of power who are, transferentially, projected parents. *Patients who have destructive relationships with peers or who were isolated from peers* generally react negatively or with increased anxiety when placed in a group setting, as do *patient without siblings.*

34.14 The answer is E (all) (*Synopsis VIII,* page 903). Ideally, cotherapy in groups is characterized by *each therapist's being as active as the other, so that neither is in a position of greater authority than the other. Having a male therapist and a female therapist* can simulate the *replication of parental surrogates* in the group; if the two interact harmoniously, they can serve as a corrective emotional experience for the members. Even if the cotherapists are of the same sex, one often tends to be confrontative and interpretative and is seen as masculine, and the other tends to be evocative of feelings and is seen as feminine. Styles of leadership and the personality characteristics of the cotherapists, regardless of their genders, also elicit transferential reactions.

34.15 The answer is D (*Synopsis VIII,* pages 910–911). In *electromyography* (EMG) muscle fibers generate electrical potentials that can be measured on an electromyograph. Electrodes placed in or on a specific muscle group—for example, masseter, deltoid, or temporalis—can be monitored for relaxation training. In *electroencephalography* (EEG) the evoked potential of the EEG is monitored to determine relaxation. Alpha waves are generally indicative of meditative states, but wave frequency and amplitude are also measured. In *galvanic skin response* (GSR), skin conductance of electricity is measured as an indicator of autonomic nervous system activity. Stress increases electrical conduction and the GSR; conversely, relaxation is associated with lowered autonomic activity and changes in skin response. Similarly, skin temperature as a measure of peripheral vasoconstriction is decreased under stress and can be measured with thermistors (thermal feedback). A *strain gauge* is a device for measuring nocturnal penile tumescence that is used to determine whether erections occur during sleep. It has no biofeedback applications.

34.16 The answer is E (all) (*Synopsis VIII,* pages 919–924). The cognitive therapy approach includes four processes: (1) *eliciting automatic thoughts,* (2) *testing automatic thoughts,* (3) *identifying maladaptive underlying assumptions,* and (4) *testing the validity of maladaptive assumptions.* Automatic thoughts are cognitions that intervene between external events and the patient's emotional reaction to the event. An example of an automatic thought is the belief that ''everyone is going to laugh at me when they see how badly I bowl''—a thought that occurs to someone who has been asked to go bowling and responds negatively. The therapist, acting as a teacher, helps the patient test the validity of automatic thoughts. The goal is to encourage patients to reject inaccurate or exaggerated automatic thoughts after careful examination. Patients often blame themselves for things that go wrong that may well have been outside their control. The therapist reviews with the patient the entire situation and helps to reattribute the blame or cause of the unpleasant events. Generating alternative explanations for events is another way of undermining inaccurate and distorted automatic thoughts.

Answers 34.17–34.21

34.17 The answer is B (*Synopsis VIII,* page 911).

34.18 The answer is A (*Synopsis VIII,* page 910).

34.19 The answer is D (*Synopsis VIII,* page 919).

34.20 The answer is C (*Synopsis VIII,* page 897).

34.21 The answer is E (*Synopsis VIII,* page 916).
Behavior therapy is *based on the principles of learning theory*—in particular, operant and classical conditioning. Behavior therapy is most often directed at specific habits of reacting with anxiety to objectively nondangerous stimuli (for example, phobias, compulsions, psychophysiological reactions, and sexual dysfunctions).

Biofeedback provides information to a person regarding one or more physiological processes in an effort to enable the person to gain some element of voluntary control over bodily functions that normally operate outside consciousness. Biofeedback is *based on the concept that autonomic responses can be controlled through the process of operant or instrumental conditioning.* Physiological manifestations of anxiety or tension (for example, headaches, tachycardia, and pain) can be reduced by teaching the patient to be aware of the physiological differences between tension and relaxation. The teaching involves immediate feedback to the patient through visible or audible recordings of the patient's biological functioning during anxiety versus relaxation states; the procedure reinforces the patient's awareness of which state is present and helps the patient control it.

Cognitive therapy—according to its originator, Aaron Beck—is *based on an underlying theoretical rationale that affect and behavior* are *largely determined by the way a person structures the world.* A person's structuring of the world is based on cognitions (verbal or pictorial ideas available to consciousness), which are based on assumptions (schemata developed from previous experiences).

Crisis intervention, by definition, is a therapy limited by the parameters of whatever crisis has led the patient to the clinician. Crisis intervention is based on crisis theory, which *emphasizes not only immediate responses to an immediate situation but also long-term development of psychological adaptation aimed at preventing future problems.*

Hypnosis is a state or condition in which a person is able to respond to appropriate suggestions by experiencing alterations of perceptions, memory, or mood. The essential feature is subjective experiential change.

Answers 34.22–34.25

34.22 The answer is B (*Synopsis VIII,* page 887).

34.23 The answer is B (*Synopsis VIII,* page 887).

34.24 The answer is A (*Synopsis VIII,* page 890).

34.25 The answer is B (*Synopsis VIII,* page 887).
In *psychoanalysis the patient lies on a couch,* and the analyst sits behind, partially or totally outside the patient's field of vision. The couch helps the analyst produce the controlled regression that favors the emergence of repressed material. The patient's reclining position in the presence of an attentive analyst almost re-creates symbolically the early parent-child situation, which varies from patient to patient. The position also helps the patient focus on inner thoughts, feelings, and fantasies, which can then become the focus of free associations. Psychoanalysis *uncovers and works through infantile conflicts* and *uses free association and the analysis of transference neurosis. Psychoanalytic psychotherapy takes as its focus the patient's current conflicts and current dynamic patterns*—that is, the analysis of the patient's problems with other persons and with themselves. Psychoanalytic psychotherapy is characterized by interviewing and discussion techniques that infrequently use free association. And unlike psychoanalysis, psychoanalytic psychotherapy usually limits its work on transference to a discussion of the patient's reactions to the psychiatrist and others. The reaction to the psychiatrist is not interpreted to as great a degree as it is in psychoanalysis.

35 Biological Therapies

Psychopharmacological drugs provide today's clinicians with an essential therapeutic approach to psychiatric disorders. In the past 10 years, an explosion in the number of psychiatric drugs has greatly increased the range of patients that may benefit from drug treatment. Newer agents with safer profiles of adverse effects and effectiveness for a wider range of indications have begun to replace the traditional agents of the past 4 decades. For treatment of depression, the serotonin-specific reuptake inhibitors and the newer agents bupropion (Wellbutrin), venlafaxine (Effexor), nefazodone (Serzone), and mirtazapine (Remeron) offer several advantages over the tricyclic drugs and monoamine oxidase inhibitors. Patients with treatment-resistant depression may respond to augmentation strategies with lithium, thyroid hormone, or combinations of antidepressants. For treatment of schizophrenia and psychotic disorders, the serotonin-dopamine antagonists cause fewer extrapyramidal symptoms and appear to be more effective not only for positive symptoms but also for negative symptoms of psychosis than the dopamine receptor antagonists (the ''typical'' antipsychotics). For treatment of bipolar disorder, the options have been expanded beyond lithium to include the anticonvulsants valproic acid (Depakote) and carbamazepine (Tegretol), with several more anticonvulsants being tested. For the treatment of the spectrum of anxiety disorders, the serotonergic drugs—the selective serotonin-specific reuptake inhibitors (SSRIs) and clomipramine (Anafranil)—and to a lesser degree the other antianxiety agents—buspirone (BuSpar) and the β-adrenergic receptor antagonists—provide several advantages over the benzodiazepines and older sedatives. For treatment of attention-deficit/hyperactivity disorder, the sympathomimetics may provide one of the most dramatic responses of any of the psychiatric drugs. For treatment of addictions, disulfiram (Antabuse) continues to be used for alcoholism, naltrexone (ReVia) is a novel alternative to methadone for opioid addiction, and bupropion (Zyban) has been approved for smoking cessation. The serotonergic agents are effective for treatment of compulsive behaviors, including eating disorders and paraphilias. After years of intensive drug development, acetylcholinesterase inhibitors have emerged as the first agents approved for treatment of dementia of the Alzheimer's type.

In learning the psychiatric drugs, students should learn the biological mechanisms and the indications for each drug but should also note the profile of adverse effects, the drug–drug interactions, and how to manage the emergence of unwanted consequences. Although many of the newer agents cause fewer adverse effects than the older agents, for which elaborate accommodations were sometimes necessary, many patients continue to be treated with drugs that may cause disturbing, even life-threatening, complications. The management of medication-induced movement disorders with anticholinergics, amantadine, or substitution of a newer agent should be thoroughly understood. Prompt treatment of the neuroleptic malignant syndrome with supportive care, dantrolene (Dantrium), and dopamine agonists is associated with a favorable outcome. The sexual suppression of the SSRIs may be countered in some males with yohimbine (Yocon).

Electroconvulsive therapy (ECT) and other therapies, including transcranial magnetic stimulation, surgical procedures, alteration of light exposure, acupuncture, and dietary supplementation, continue to be refined. ECT is particularly important for many patients with severe depression who do not respond to drugs. The techniques of ECT have been tailored to a high degree, and it is a safe and effective therapy.

The therapeutic bond between the clinician and the patient is very important to the successful response to psychiatric drugs. Clinicians must complete a thorough diagnostic evaluation, including a medical evaluation as indicated, prior to offering psychiatric medications. Drug–drug interactions should be anticipated, and dietary restrictions should be clearly stated. The benefits and the adverse effects should be thoroughly explained, so that the patient can develop realistic expectations. A therapeutic end point should be agreed upon, and any changes in dosage are best made gradually, to limit an aversive reaction on the part of the patient.

Students should be aware of how investigational drugs are evaluated, including classification according to chemical structure; pharmacokinetics, including absorption, distribution, bioavailability, metabolism, and excretion; pharmacodynamics, including receptor affinities, dose–response curves, therapeutic indices, the development of tolerance, and withdrawal phenomena; therapeutic indications and what constitutes evidence of a significant beneficial effect; adverse effects; drug–drug interactions; and signs and symptoms of overdosage. Modification of dosages for special populations, such as children, older people, patients with suicide potential, and those with chronic and acute medical conditions, should be considered.

Students should read and understand Chapter 35 of *Kaplan and Sadock's Synopsis VIII* for an extensive discussion of each of the psychopharmacological and other biological therapies. The following questions may then be addressed.

HELPFUL HINTS

The student should know these terms and specific drugs.

- adrenergic blockade
- akathisia
- allergic dermatitis
- amantadine (Symmetrel)
- anticholinergic side effects
- antipsychotics
- apnea
- artificial hibernation
- atropine sulfate
- benzodiazepine receptor agonists and antagonists
- Lucio Bini
- biotransformation
- bipolar I disorder, bipolar II disorder
- BPH
- buspirone (BuSpar)
- John Cade
- carbon dioxide therapy
- cardiac effects
- catatonia
- Ugo Cerletti
- cholinergic rebound
- clomipramine (Anafranil)
- clonazepam (Klonopin)
- clonidine (Catapres)
- CNS depression
- combination drugs
- continuous sleep treatment
- CYP enzymes
- D_2 receptors
- DEA
- demethylation
- depot preparations
- distribution volume
- dopamine receptor antagonists
- dose–response curve
- downregulation of receptors
- drug-assisted interviewing
- drug holidays
- drug-induced mania
- drug intoxications
- dystonias
- eating disorders
- Ebstein's anomaly
- ECT
- ECT contraindications
- EEG, EMG
- electrolyte screen
- electrosleep therapy
- epileptogenic effects
- FDA
- fluoxetine (Prozac)
- fluvoxamine (Luvox)
- generalized anxiety disorder
- half-life
- haloperidol (Haldol)
- hematological effects
- hemodialysis
- hydroxylation and glucuronidation
- idiopathic psychosis
- impulse-control disorders
- informed consent
- insulin coma therapy
- jaundice
- light therapy
- lipid solubility
- MAOIs
- medication-induced movement disorders
- megadose therapy
- megavitamin therapy
- melatonin
- mesocortical
- mesolimbic
- metabolic enzymes
- metabolites
- Egas Moniz
- monoamine hypothesis
- movement disorders
- mute patients
- narcotherapy
- narrow-angle glaucoma
- neuroendocrine tests
- noncompliance
- noradrenergic, histaminic, cholinergic receptors
- obsessive-compulsive disorder
- oculogyric crisis
- orthomolecular therapy
- orthostatic (postural) hypotension
- overdose
- panic disorder with agoraphobia
- parkinsonian symptoms
- paroxetine (Paxil)
- pharmacodynamics
- pharmacokinetics
- phosphatidylinositol
- photosensitivity
- physostigmine
- pill-rolling tremor
- pilocarpine
- plasma levels
- positive and negative symptoms
- potency, high and low
- prolactin
- prophylactic treatment
- protein binding
- psychosurgery
- rabbit syndrome
- rapid neuroleptization
- *Rauwolfia serpentina*
- receptor blockade
- renal clearance
- retinitis pigmentosa
- retrograde ejaculation
- reuptake blockade
- schizoaffective disorder
- schizophrenia
- secondary depression
- secondary psychosis
- sertraline (Zoloft)
- side effect profile
- sleep deprivation
- SSRI
- status epilepticus
- stereotactic
- sudden death
- sympathomimetic
- tapering
- tardive dyskinesia
- TD_{50}
- teratogenic
- TFT
- therapeutic index
- therapeutic trial
- tonic, clonic phase
- tricyclic and tetracyclic drugs
- L-triiodothyronine
- triplicate prescription
- use in pregnancy
- Julius Wagner-Jauregg
- weight gain
- zeitgebers

▲ QUESTIONS

DIRECTIONS: Each of the questions or incomplete statements below is followed by five suggested responses or completions. Select the *one* that is *best* in each case.

35.1 Depressive episodes arising during lithium therapy may be due to any of the following *except*

A. the natural history of the illness
B. inadequate dosage
C. coexisting substance-related disorders
D. noncompliance with therapy
E. drug-induced hyperthyroidism

35.2 Donepezil should be used with caution in combination with

A. bethanechol
B. tricyclic antidepressants
C. haloperidol
D. digoxin
E. serotonin-specific reuptake inhibitors

35.3 Which of the following drugs or foods is *not* contraindicated for concurrent administration with triazolobenzodiazepines such as alprazolam (Xanax), based on inhibition of the hepatic enzyme cytochrome P450 (CYP) 3A4?

A. Cisapride (Propulsid)
B. Grapefruit juice
C. Nefazodone (Serzone)
D. Venlafaxine (Effexor)
E. All of the above

35.4 Carbamazepine affects each of the following organ systems *except*

A. dermatological
B. hematopoietic
C. hepatic
D. pulmonary
E. renal

35.5 Disulfiram (Antabuse) causes which of the following symptoms in patients who have *not* ingested alcohol?

A. Fatigue
B. Headache
C. Hypertension
D. Nausea
E. Vomiting

35.6 Which of the following dopamine receptor antagonists has more than 150 known metabolites?

A. Chlorpromazine (Thorazine)
B. Fluphenazine (Prolixin)
C. Haloperidol (Haldol)
D. Molindone (Moban)
E. Trifluoperazine (Stelazine)

35.7 Drugs that are effective for the treatment of akathisia include

A. haloperidol (Haldol) and thioridazine (Mellaril)
B. benztropine (Cogentin) and fluoxetine (Prozac)
C. propranolol (Inderal) and lorazepam (Ativan)
D. bupropion (Wellbutrin) and mirtazapine (Remeron)
E. risperidone (Risperdal) and pentobarbital (Nembutal)

35.8 Drugs approved by the U.S. Food and Drug Administration for the treatment of mild to moderate dementia of the Alzheimer's type include

A. antiamyloid drugs
B. membrane stabilizers
C. acetylcholinesterase inhibitors
D. nerve growth factors
E. calcium channel blockers

35.9 Which of the following is the most common adverse effect of valproate (Depakote)?

A. Ataxia
B. Nausea
C. Sedation
D. Vomiting
E. Weight gain

35.10 Which of the following interventions is considered an effective treatment for tardive dyskinesia?

A. Cessation of treatment with an antipsychotic drug
B. Increase in the dose of a dopamine receptor antagonist
C. Substitution of a serotonin-dopamine antagonist
D. Addition of an anticholinergic drug
E. No change in treatment

35.11 Dantrolene is a potentially effective treatment for each of the following disorders *except*

A. acute mania
B. catatonia
C. malignant hyperthermia
D. neuroleptic malignant syndrome
E. serotonin syndrome

35.12 Which of the following over-the-counter preparations may precipitate a disulfiram–alcohol reaction?

A. Aftershave lotions
B. Antihistamines
C. Aspirin
D. Petroleum jelly
E. Toothpaste

35.13 Which of the following drugs is *least* likely to calm an acutely agitated patient?

A. Clozapine (Clozaril)
B. Haloperidol (Haldol)
C. Olanzapine (Zyprexa)
D. Risperidone (Risperdal)
E. Thioridazine (Mellaril)

35.14 Data supporting the dopamine hypothesis of schizophrenia include each of the following *except*

A. correlation of a decrease in plasma concentrations of homovanillic acid with improvement in symptoms
B. PET scan data correlating D_2 receptor occupancy with antipsychotic efficacy
C. precipitation of psychosis with amphetamines
D. the clinical efficacy of clozapine (Clozaril)
E. correlation of D_2 receptor affinity with the clinical efficacy of dopamine receptor antagonists (Fig. 35.3.16–4 in *Synopsis VIII*)

35.15 Which of the following statements about dexfenfluramine (Redux) is *false*?

A. It may deplete brain serotonin stores.
B. It may inhibit reuptake of serotonin.
C. It may result in activation of serotonin 5-HT_{2c} receptors.
D. It triggers release of dopamine.
E. It triggers release of serotonin.

35.16 Which of the following antipsychotic drugs is *least* likely to cause tardive dyskinesia?

A. Clozapine (Clozaril)
B. Haloperidol (Haldol)
C. Olanzapine (Zyprexa)
D. Risperidone (Risperdal)
E. Sertindole (Serlect)

35.17 Serotonin-specific reuptake inhibitors are generally *not* considered as monotherapy for which of the following indications?

A. Attention-deficit/hyperactivity disorder
B. Premature ejaculation
C. Schizophrenia
D. Syncope
E. Trichotillomania

35.18 Which of the following statements about sympathomimetics is *correct*?

A. They are poorly absorbed from the gastrointestinal tract and therefore require high dosages to achieve a therapeutic effect.
B. The chemical structures of dextroamphetamine, methylphenidate, and pemoline are closely related.
C. Tolerance for the therapeutic effect in attention-deficit/hyperactivity disorder develops for dextroamphetamine and pemoline but not for methylphenidate, which is therefore the most frequently used agent for attention-deficit/hyperactivity disorder.
D. Use of sympathomimetics for treatment of depression is limited by concerns about abuse potential.
E. All sympathomimetics have exactly the same pharmacodynamic profile.

35.19 Valproate (Depakote) may increase the tremor caused by which of the following drugs?

A. Amitriptyline (Elavil)
B. Diazepam (Valium)
C. Gabapentin (Neurontin)
D. Lithium (Eskalith)
E. Warfarin (Coumadin)

35.20 Factors that may slow drug absorption include all of the following *except*

A. intravenous administration
B. gastrectomy
C. use of antacids
D. cirrhosis
E. use of anticholinergic agents

35.21 β-Adrenergic receptor antagonists are generally more effective than benzodiazepines for treatment of

A. panic disorder
B. generalized anxiety disorder
C. alcohol withdrawal
D. akathisia
E. psychogenic seizures

35.22 Data from well-controlled studies support the use of bromocriptine for which indication?

A. Hyperprolactinemia
B. Depression
C. Cocaine withdrawal
D. Bipolar disorder
E. Alcohol withdrawal

35.23 Factors that predict a better response to carbamazepine (Tegretol) than to lithium (Eskalith) in bipolar I disorder include each of the following *except*

A. comorbid seizure disorder
B. dysphoric mania
C. first episode of mania
D. negative family history
E. rapid cycling

35.24 Which of the following drugs has the fastest onset of action against acute mania?

A. Carbamazepine (Tegretol)
B. Haloperidol (Haldol)
C. Lithium (Eskalith)
D. Risperidone (Risperdal)
E. Valproate (Depakote)

35.25 Which of the following is the most common adverse effect of olanzapine (Zyprexa)?

A. Constipation
B. Orthostatic hypotension
C. Sedation
D. Tardive dyskinesia
E. Weight gain

35.26 Potential treatments for the sexual adverse effects of the serotonin-specific reuptake inhibitors include each of the following drugs *except*

A. amantadine (Symmetrel)
B. bromocriptine (Parlodel)
C. cyproheptadine (Periactin)
D. liothyronine (Cytomel)
E. yohimbine (Yocon)

35.27 Each of the following factors increases the likelihood of a therapeutic response to tricyclic drugs *except*

A. family history of depressive disorders
B. hypersomnolence
C. melancholic features
D. previous major depressive episodes
E. response to another antidepressant drug

35.28 Which of the following is the most important factor determining a successful response to treatment with naltrexone (ReVia)?

A. Abstinence from opioids during therapy
B. Dosage
C. Duration of therapeutic trials
D. Opioid-free state prior to use of naltrexone
E. Psychosocial factors

35.29 Metabolic modifications of drugs include all of the following *except*

A. oxidation
B. reduction
C. hydrolysis
D. lipid adduction
E. glucuronide conjugation

35.30 Anticholinergic drugs are indicated for treatment of all of the following *except*

A. neuroleptic-induced parkinsonism
B. Huntington's chorea
C. neuroleptic-induced acute dystonia
D. idiopathic Parkinson's disease
E. medication-induced postural tremor

35.31 Which of the following adverse effects is *not* usually associated with bromocriptine?

A. Dizziness
B. Headache
C. Nausea
D. Polyuria
E. Syncope

35.32 Well-controlled studies have supported the use of carbamazepine (Tegretol) for which of the following disorders?

A. Anorexia nervosa
B. Insomnia
C. Neuroleptic-induced parkinsonism
D. Schizophrenia
E. Social phobia

35.33 Which of the following dopamine receptor antagonists would probably be the safest to use for psychotic symptoms due to a brain tumor?

A. Chlorpromazine (Thorazine)
B. Fluphenazine (Prolixin)
C. Mesoridazine (Serentil)
D. Sulpiride (Dogmatil)
E. Thioridazine (Mellaril)

35.34 Levodopa is considered a first-line agent for which of the following indications?

A. Antipsychotic-induced parkinsonism
B. Cocaine abuse
C. Negative symptoms of schizophrenia
D. Neuroleptic malignant syndrome
E. None of the above

35.35 The most common adverse effects of sertindole (Serlect) include each of the following *except*

A. galactorrhea
B. nasal congestion
C. postural hypotension
D. tachycardia
E. weight gain

35.36 Which of the following antidepressants disrupts sleep continuity?

A. Fluoxetine (Prozac)
B. Nefazodone (Serzone)
C. Sertraline (Zoloft)
D. Trazodone (Desyrel)
E. None of the above

35.37 Which of the following tricyclic drugs is *least* associated with anticholinergic effects?

A. Amitriptyline (Elavil)
B. Clomipramine (Anafranil)
C. Desipramine (Norpramin)
D. Imipramine (Tofranil)
E. Trimipramine (Surmontil)

35.38 Lithium affects each of the following organ systems *except*

A. cardiovascular
B. central nervous system
C. hematopoietic
D. hepatic
E. thyroid

35.39 Which cytochrome P450 (CYP) enzyme has a polymorphism that renders it a poor metabolizer of fluoxetine and paroxetine?

A. 3A3/4
B. 2C19
C. 2C9/10
D. 1A2
E. 2D6

ANSWERS

Biological Therapies

35.1 The answer is E (*Synopsis VIII,* pages 941–942, 1046–1049).

When a depressive episode occurs in a patient already receiving maintenance lithium, the differential diagnosis should include lithium-induced *hypothyroidism* (not hyperthyroidism). Lithium affects thyroid function, causing a generally benign and often transient diminution in the concentrations of circulating thyroid hormones. Reports have attributed goiter (5 percent of patients), benign reversible exophthalmos, and hypothyroidism (7 to 9 percent of patients) to lithium treatment. About 50 percent of patients receiving long-term lithium treatment have an abnormal thyrotropin-releasing hormone (TRH) response, and about 30 percent have elevated levels of thyroid-stimulating hormone (TSH). If symptoms of hypothyroidism are present, treatment with levothyroxine (Synthroid) is indicated. Even in the absence of hypothyroid symptoms, some clinicians treat patients with elevated TSH levels with levothyroxine. In lithium-treated patients, TSH levels should be measured every 6 to 12 months.

Lithium has proved to be effective in both the short-term treatment and the prophylaxis of bipolar I disorder in about 70 to 80 percent of patients. Both manic and depressive episodes respond to lithium treatment alone. Lithium should also be considered for patients with severe cyclothymic disorder. About 80 percent of bipolar I disorder depressive patients respond to lithium treatment alone, thereby eliminating the risk of an antidepressant-induced manic episode. Other causes of depression in patients taking lithium include *substance abuse* and the *lack of compliance with the lithium therapy.* Because the *natural history of bipolar I disorder* is one of cycling between manic and depressive phases, a particular dose of lithium appropriate for the manic phase may be inadequate for the subsequent depressive phase, particularly in patients with mixed and dysphoric manic episodes (which may occur in as many as 40 percent of patients), rapid cycling, and coexisting substance-related disorders.

If a patient taking lithium develops depression, possible treatment approaches include increasing the lithium concentration (up to 1.2 mEq/L), adding supplemental thyroid hormone (such as 25 μg a day L-iodothyronine) even in the presence of normal findings on thyroid function tests, the judicious use of antidepressants, and electroconvulsive therapy (before which lithium should be discontinued to avoid complicating the cognitive assessment of the patient).

35.2 The answer is A (*Synopsis VIII,* pages 972–973).

Donepezil should be used cautiously with drugs that also possess cholinomimetic activity, such as succinylcholine or *bethanechol.* The coadministration of donepezil and drugs that have cholinergic antagonist activity (such as *tricyclic drugs*) is not necessarily dangerous but is probably counterproductive. Donepezil is highly protein-bound, but it does not displace other protein-bound drugs, such as furosemide, *digoxin,* or warfarin. Ketoconazole and quinidine inhibit donepezil metabolism in vitro, but the clinical significance of this observation is unclear. Although donepezil is not known to induce hepatic enzymes, its metabolism may be increased due to induction of CYP 2D6 and CYP 3A4 by phenytoin, carbamazepine, dexamethasone, rifampin, or phenobarbital. There are no known interactions between donepezil and *haloperidol* or *serotonin-specific reuptake inhibitors.*

35.3 The answer is D (*Synopsis VIII,* pages 934–935, 1081–1082).

Venlafaxine (Effexor) may be given with drugs such as alprazolam. An essential element of the ability of a chemical to act as a drug is that it can be metabolized by the body. Most psychotherapeutic drugs are oxidized by the hepatic cytochrome P450 (CYP) enzyme system.

The CYP genes may be induced by alcohol, certain drugs (barbiturates, anticonvulsants), or by smoking, which increases the metabolism of certain drugs and precarcinogens. Other agents may directly inhibit the enzymes and slow the metabolism of other drugs. In some cases, if one CYP enzyme is inhibited, once the precursor accumulates to a sufficiently high level within the cell, another CYP enzyme may begin to act. Cellular pathophysiology, such as that caused by viral hepatitis or cirrhosis, may also affect the efficiency of the CYP system. With the DNA sequence data available, several genetic polymorphisms in the CYP genes are now recognized, some of which are manifested in a decreased rate of metabolism. Patients with an inefficient version of a specific CYP enzyme are considered "poor metabolizers."

With respect to CYP 2D6, for which 7 percent of whites are poor metabolizers, tricyclic antidepressants, antipsychotics, and type 1C antiarrhythmics should be used cautiously or avoided with serotonin-specific reuptake inhibitors (SSRIs). Because of inhibition of the CYP 3A4 enzyme, *nefazodone, cisapride, grapefruit juice,* and fluoxetine should not be used with terfenadine (Seldane), astemizole (Hismanal), carbamazepine (Tegretol), or the triazolobenzodiazepines alprazolam (Xanax) and triazolam (Halcion). Inhibition of CYP 2C9/10 and CYP 2C19 warrants caution for the following combinations: fluoxetine plus phenytoin (Dilantin) and sertraline plus tolbutamide (Orinase). It is also important to consider the long half-lives of certain of the psychiatric drugs, especially fluoxetine, which may prolong their inhibition of the CYP enzymes. *Venlafaxine* does not have any clinically significant CYP interactions.

35.4 The answer is D (*Synopsis VIII,* pages 1008–1009).

Carbamazepine has no known effects on the *pulmonary* system. Besides the effects on the CNS, carbamazepine has its most significant effects on the *hematopoietic* system. Carbamazepine is associated with a benign and often transient decrease in the white blood cell count, with values usually remaining above 3,000. The decrease is thought to be due to the inhibition of the colony-stimulating factor in the bone marrow, an effect that can be reversed by the coadministration of lithium (Eskalith), which stimulates the colony-stimulating factor. The benign suppression of white blood cell production must be differentiated from the potentially fatal adverse effects of agranulocytosis, pancytopenia, and aplastic anemia.

As reflected by its use to treat diabetes insipidus, carbamazepine apparently has a vasopressin-like effect on the *renal* vasopressin receptor, sometimes causing the development of water intoxication or hyponatremia, particularly in elderly patients. That side effect can be treated with demeclocycline (Declomycin) or lithium. Another endocrine effect associated with carbamazepine is an increase in urinary free cortisol.

Carbamazepine induces several *hepatic* enzymes and may thus interfere with the metabolism of a variety of other drugs. The effects of carbamazepine on the cardiovascular system are minimal. It does decrease atrioventricular (A-V) conduction, so the use of carbamazepine is contraindicated in patients with A-V heart block.

Carbamazepine may cause a rash, which may be transient even if the drug is continued, but which rarely leads to serious and potentially life-threatening *dermatological* conditions. Other system-specific allergic reactions have been reported, and rarely, a lupuslike disorder has been associated with use of carbamazepine.

35.5 The answer is A (*Synopsis VIII,* pages 1018–1019).
Disulfiram (Antabuse) is used to ensure abstinence in the treatment of alcohol dependence. Its main effect is to produce a rapid and violently unpleasant reaction in a person who ingests even a small amount of alcohol while taking disulfiram. However, because of the risk of severe and even fatal disulfiram–alcohol reactions, disulfiram therapy is used less often today than previously.

The metabolism of ethanol proceeds through oxidation via alcohol dehydrogenase to the formation of acetaldehyde, which is further metabolized to acetyl coenzyme A by aldehyde dehydrogenase and other pathways. Disulfiram is an aldehyde dehydrogenase inhibitor that interferes with the metabolism of alcohol by producing a marked increase in blood acetaldehyde levels. The accumulation of acetaldehyde (to a level up to 10 times higher than occurs in the normal metabolism of alcohol) produces a wide array of unpleasant reactions called the disulfiram–alcohol reaction, characterized by the following signs and symptoms: *nausea, throbbing headache, vomiting, hypertension,* flushing, sweating, thirst, dyspnea, tachycardia, chest pain, vertigo, and blurred vision. The reaction occurs almost immediately after the ingestion of one alcoholic drink and may last up to 30 minutes. In extreme cases it is marked by respiratory depression, cardiovascular collapse, myocardial infarction, convulsions, and death.

The primary indication for disulfiram use is an aversive conditioning treatment for alcohol dependence. Either the fear of having a disulfiram–alcohol reaction or the memory of having had one is meant to condition the patient not to use alcohol. Some clinicians induce a disulfiram–alcohol reaction in patients at the beginning of therapy to convince the patients of the severe unpleasantness of the symptoms. However, that practice is not recommended, since a disulfiram–alcohol reaction can lead to cardiovascular collapse. It is usually sufficient to describe the severity and the unpleasantness of the disulfiram–alcohol reaction graphically to discourage the patient from imbibing alcohol. Disulfiram treatment should be combined with such treatments as psychotherapy, group therapy, and support groups like Alcoholics Anonymous (AA). The treatment of alcohol dependence requires careful monitoring; since a patient can simply decide not to take the disulfiram, compliance with the medication should be monitored if possible.

The adverse effects of disulfiram in the absence of alcohol consumption include *fatigue,* dermatitis, impotence, optic neuritis, a variety of mental changes, and hepatic damage. A metabolite of disulfiram inhibits dopamine hydroxylase, thus potentially exacerbating psychosis in patients with psychotic disorders.

35.6 The answer is A (*Synopsis VIII,* pages 1024–1026).
Chlorpromazine is notorious among psychopharmacologists for having more than 150 metabolites, some of which are active. The nonaliphatic phenothiazines, such as fluphenazine and *trifluoperazine,* the dihydroindole *molindone,* and the butyrophenone haloperidol, have few metabolites, and whether those metabolites are active remains controversial. The potential presence of active metabolites complicates the interpretation of plasma drug levels that report the presence of only the parent compound.

Peak plasma concentrations of dopamine receptor antagonists are usually reached 1 to 4 hours after oral administration and 30 to 60 minutes after parenteral administration. The half-lives of the butyrophenones and the diphenylbutylpiperidines are longer than for the phenothiazines, and the clinical effects are seen in the tendency of parkinsonism caused by the butyrophenones and the diphenylbutylpiperidines to linger longer than when parkinsonism is caused by other dopamine receptor antagonists. In addition, most dopamine receptor antagonist drugs have high binding to plasma proteins, volumes of distribution, and lipid solubilities. Dopamine receptor antagonist drugs are metabolized in the liver and reach steady-state plasma levels in 5 to 10 days. Some evidence indicates that after a few weeks of administration, chlorpromazine, thiothixene, and thioridazine induce metabolic enzymes, resulting in low plasma concentrations of the drugs.

Although the pharmacokinetic properties of the dopamine receptor antagonists vary widely (such as their half-lives range from 10 to 20 hours), the most important clinical generalization is that all of the antipsychotics currently available in the United States (with the exception of clozapine) can be given in one daily oral dose once the patient is in a stable condition and has adjusted to any adverse effects. Most dopamine receptor antagonists are incompletely absorbed after oral administration, although liquid preparations are absorbed more efficiently than are other forms. Many dopamine receptor antagonists are also available in parenteral forms that can be given intramuscularly in emergencies, resulting in a more rapid and more reliable attainment of therapeutic plasma concentrations than is possible with oral administration.

In the United States, two dopamine receptor antagonists, *haloperidol* and *fluphenazine,* are available in long-acting depot parenteral formulations that can be given once every 1 to 4 weeks, depending on the dose and the patient. The depot formulations of haloperidol and fluphenazine consist of esters of the parent compound mixed in sesame seed oil. The rate of entry of the drug into the body is determined by the rate at which the esterified drug diffuses out of the oil into the body;

then the esterified drug is rapidly hydrolyzed, releasing the active compound. Because of the long half-life of that formulation, it can take up to 6 months of treatment to reach steady-state plasma levels, indicating that oral therapy should perhaps be continued during the first month or so of depot antipsychotic treatment. The long half-life of the depot formulation also means that detectable concentrations of the antipsychotic are present long after the last administration of the drug.

35.7 The answer is C (*Synopsis VIII,* pages 959–960). *Akathisia*, one of the medication-induced movement disorders, is characterized by the subjective feelings of restlessness or the objective signs of restlessness or both. Examples include a sense of anxiety, an inability to relax, jitters, pacing, rocking motions while sitting, and the rapid alternation of sitting and standing. Akathisia can often be misdiagnosed as anxiety or as increased psychotic agitation. Middle-aged women are at increased risk for akathisia. Akathisia has been associated with the use of a wide range of psychiatric drugs, including antipsychotics, antidepressants, and sympathomimetics. Among the drugs known to cause akathisia are *bupropion, fluoxetine, haloperidol, mirtazapine, risperidone,* and *thioridazine.* Standard anticholinergic drugs—such as *benztropine*—are often ineffective in treating neuroleptic-induced acute akathisia. The first-line drug for akathisia is most commonly a β-adrenergic receptor antagonist—such as *propranolol.* However, several studies have found that benzodiazepines—such as *lorazepam*—are also effective in treating some cases of akathisia. *Pentobarbital* has no recognized role in treatment of akathisia.

The three basic steps in the treatment of akathisia are to reduce the psychotherapeutic medication dosage, to attempt treatment with appropriate drugs, and to consider changing the psychotherapeutic drug. Patients may be less likely to experience akathisia on low-potency neuroleptics—such as thioridazine (Mellaril)—than on high-potency neuroleptics—such as haloperidol (Haldol)—and the serotonin-dopamine antagonists are associated with a low but significant incidence of akathisia.

35.8 The answer is C (*Synopsis VIII,* pages 968–969). Only two drugs, donepezil (Aricept) and tacrine (Cognex), are FDA-approved for the treatment of the mild to moderate dementia of the Alzheimer's type. Both are *acetylcholinesterase inhibitors.* They reduce the intrasynaptic cleavage and inactivation of acetylcholine and thus potentiate cholinergic neurotransmission, which tends to produce a modest improvement in memory and goal-directed thought. Preliminary studies suggested the efficacy of physostigmine, an old acetylcholinesterase inhibitor; however, donepezil and tacrine have a longer half-life and a wider therapeutic window than physostigmine, which has not entered widespread use for this indication. These drugs are considered most useful for patients with mild to moderate memory loss, who nevertheless have enough of their basal forebrain cholinergic neurons to benefit from augmentation of cholinergic neurotransmission. Cognitive enhancers, such as the acetylcholinesterase inhibitors, are best used as part of a multifaceted approach to the relentless diminution in the basic skills of daily living that affects Alzheimer's patients and their families. Some data show that acetylcholinesterase inhibitors may allow patients to maintain nearly the same scores on cognition scales over several months, whereas control groups would be expected to worsen over the same period. However, the effect is always temporary, as there are no clinical studies to suggest that the drugs influence the underlying neurodegenerative condition.

Other pharmacological agents have been tested for treatment of dementia of the Alzheimer's type. The oldest putative cognition-enhancing drug is Hydergine, which was introduced in the 1940s. It is a mixture of four ergotoxine derivatives that have diverse effects on the central α-adrenergic, dopaminergic, and serotonergic systems. Several clinical trials of variable rigor have failed to demonstrate a clear benefit of Hydergine. Other treatment approaches are also beginning to be evaluated. These approaches fall under six broad categories: (1) agents affecting *amyloid deposition* directly; (2) agents that may *stabilize neuronal membranes* and therefore prolong neuronal life span; (3) estrogens and *nerve growth factors,* which provide trophic support to neurons, especially those in the basal forebrain; (4) antioxidants, *N*-methyl-D-aspartate (NMDA) receptor antagonists, *calcium channel blockers* (such as nimodipine), monoamine oxidase type B inhibitors, and other agents that may reduce excitotoxic cell death; (5) angiotensin-converting enzyme inhibitors; and (6) phosphodiesterase inhibitors.

35.9 The answer is B (*Synopsis VIII,* pages 1111–1113). Valproate treatment is generally well tolerated and safe, although a range of common mild adverse effects and serious and rare adverse effects have been associated with valproate treatment. The common adverse effects associated with valproate are those affecting the gastrointestinal system, such as *nausea* (25 percent of all patients treated), *vomiting* (5 percent of patients), and diarrhea. The gastrointestinal effects are generally most common in the first month of treatment but are also common when the treatment is with valproic acid or sodium valproate, rather than enteric-coated divalproex sodium (Depakote), especially the sprinkle formulation. Some clinicians have also treated gastrointestinal symptoms with histamine type 2 (H_2) receptor antagonists, such as cimetidine (Tagamet). Other common adverse effects, such as *sedation, ataxia,* dysarthria, and tremor, affect the nervous system. Valproate-induced tremor has been reported to respond well to treatment with β-adrenergic receptor antagonists. Treatment of the other neurological adverse effects usually requires lowering of the valproate dosage. *Weight gain* is a common adverse effect, especially in long-term treatment, and can best be treated by recommending a combination of a reasonable diet and moderate exercise. Hair loss has been reported to occur in 5 to 10 percent of all patients treated; rare cases of complete loss of body hair have been reported. Some clinicians have recommended treatment of valproate-associated hair loss with vitamin supplements that contain zinc and selenium. Another adverse effect that may occur in 5 to 40 percent of patients is a persistent elevation in liver transaminases to 3 times the upper limit of normal, which is usually asymptomatic and resolves after discontinuation of the drug. Other rare adverse events include effects on the hematopoietic system, including thrombocytopenia and platelet dysfunction, occurring most commonly at high dosages and resulting in the prolongation of bleeding times. Overdoses of valproate can lead to coma and death. There are reports that valproate-induced coma can be successfully treated with naloxone (Narcan) and reports that hemodialysis and hemoperfusion can be useful in the treatment of valproate overdoses.

The two most serious adverse effects of valproate treatment affect the pancreas and the liver. Rare cases of pancreatitis have been reported; they occur most often in the first 6 months of treatment, and the condition occasionally results in death. The most attention has been paid to an association between valproate and fatal hepatotoxicity. A result of that focus has been the identification of risk factors, including young age (less than 2 years), the use of multiple anticonvulsants, and the presence of neurological disorders, especially inborn errors of metabolism, in addition to epilepsy. The rate of fatal hepatotoxicity in patients who have been treated with only valproate is 0.85 per 100,000 patients; no patients over the age of 10 years are reported to have died of fatal hepatotoxicity. Therefore, the risk of that adverse reaction in adult psychiatric patients seems to be extremely low. Nevertheless, if symptoms of malaise, anorexia, nausea and vomiting, edema, and abdominal pain occur in a patient treated with valproate, the clinician must consider the possibility of severe hepatotoxicity. However, a modest change in liver function test results does not correlate with the development of serious hepatotoxicity.

Valproate should not be used by pregnant or nursing women. It has been associated with neural tube defects (such as spina bifida) in about 1 to 2 percent of women who took valproate during the first trimester of the pregnancy. Valproate is contraindicated in nursing mothers because it is excreted in breast milk. Clinicians should not administer it to patients with hepatic diseases.

35.10 The answer is C (*Synopsis VIII,* pages 960–961). Neuroleptic-induced tardive dyskinesia is a late-appearing disorder of involuntary choreoathetoid movements. The most common movements involve the orofacial region and the fingers and the toes. Athetoid movements of the head, the neck, and the hips are also present in seriously affected patients. In the most serious cases the patients may have irregularities in breathing and swallowing, resulting in aerophagia, belching, and grunting. The risk factors for tardive dyskinesia include long-term treatment with dopamine receptor antagonist (typical) neuroleptics, increasing age, female sex, the presence of a mood disorder, and the presence of a cognitive disorder. Although various treatments for tardive dyskinesia have not always been successful, the course of tardive dyskinesia is considered less relentless than was previously thought. The serotonin-dopamine antagonists are associated with an extremely low risk of the development of tardive dyskinesia and therefore present an effective treatment approach. *Substitution of a serotonin-dopamine antagonist* may limit the abnormal movements without worsening the progression of the dyskinesia. In contrast, patients with tardive dyskinesia frequently experience an exacerbation of their symptoms when the dopamine receptor antagonist is withheld; therefore, *cessation of treatment with an antipsychotic drug* usually worsens tardive dyskinesias. In addition, stopping the antipsychotic drug may precipitate psychosis. Conversely, *increasing the dose of a dopamine receptor antagonist* would likely suppress the dyskinesia temporarily, but could eventually lead to an even more severe case of tardive dyskinesia and is therefore not recommended. Most likely because tardive dyskinesia, unlike neuroleptic-induced parkinsonism, does not appear to result in a straightforward fashion from disruption of the nigrostriatal dopamine pathway, *addition of an anticholinergic drug* has not been found to be beneficial. Prior to the appearance of the antipsychotics in the 1950s, clinicians noted that 1 to 5 percent of psychiatric inpatients with schizophrenia developed movements resembling tardive dyskinesia, suggesting that not all cases of tardive dyskinesia are necessarily attributable to antipsychotics. This does not mean that tardive dyskinesia is a self-limited condition, however, and *specific changes in treatment are indicated.* The treatment is the same whether the tardive dyskinesia is spontaneous or drug induced.

35.11 The answer is A (*Synopsis VIII,* pages 1017–1018). Dantrolene (Dantrium) is a direct-acting skeletal muscle relaxant. The only indication for dantrolene in contemporary clinical psychiatry is as one of the potentially effective treatments for *neuroleptic malignant syndrome, catatonia,* and *serotonin syndrome.* It is also used to treat *malignant hyperthermia,* an adverse effect of general anesthesia that bears a clinical resemblance to neuroleptic malignant syndrome. Dantrolene has *no other uses in psychiatry.*

Dantrolene produces skeletal muscle relaxation by directly affecting the contractile response of the muscles at a site beyond the myoneural junction. Specifically, dantrolene dissociates excitation–contraction coupling by interfering with the release of calcium from the sarcoplasmic reticulum. The skeletal muscle relaxant effect is the basis of its efficacy in reducing the muscle destruction and hyperthermia associated with neuroleptic malignant syndrome.

The primary psychiatric indication for intravenous (IV) dantrolene is muscle rigidity in neuroleptic malignant syndrome. Dantrolene is almost always used in conjunction with appropriate supportive measures and a dopamine receptor agonist—such as bromocriptine (Parlodel). If all available case reports and studies are summarized, about 80 percent of all patients with neuroleptic malignant syndrome who received dantrolene apparently benefited clinically from the drug. Muscle relaxation and a general and dramatic improvement in symptoms can appear within minutes of IV administration, although in most cases the beneficial effects can take several hours to appear. Some evidence indicates that dantrolene treatment must be continued for some time, perhaps days to a week or more, to minimize the risk of the recurrence of symptoms, although the data for that clinical opinion are limited. Dantrolene has been used in efforts to treat other psychiatric conditions characterized by life-threatening muscle rigidity, such as catatonia and serotonin syndrome.

35.12 The answer is A (*Synopsis VIII,* pages 1018–1019). Patients who take disulfiram must be instructed that the ingestion of even the smallest amount of alcohol will bring on a disulfiram–alcohol reaction, with all of its unpleasant effects. In addition, the patient should be warned against ingesting any alcohol-containing preparations, such as cough drops, tonics of any kind, and alcohol-containing foods and sauces. Some reactions have occurred in men who used alcohol-based *aftershave lotions* and inhaled the fumes; therefore, precautions must be explicit and should include any topically applied preparations containing alcohol, such as perfume. Most, if not all, preparations of *antihistamines, aspirin, petroleum jelly,* and *toothpaste* do not contain alcohol.

Disulfiram should not be administered until the patient has abstained from alcohol for at least 12 hours. Patients should be warned that the disulfiram–alcohol reaction may occur as long as 1 or 2 weeks after the last dose of disulfiram. Patients should carry identification cards describing the disulfiram–alcohol reaction and listing the name and the telephone number of the physician to be called.

35.13 The answer is D (*Synopsis VIII,* page 1075).
Risperidone is less likely than *clozapine, olanzapine,* and the dopamine receptor antagonists, such as *haloperidol* and *thioridazine,* to produce a calming effect acutely or in the first few days of use. This is due to risperidone's lack of anticholinergic and antihistaminergic effects. If risperidone is chosen for an acutely psychotic patient, addition of a benzodiazepine or a high-potency dopamine receptor antagonist may be necessary in the first 1 to 2 weeks. The benefit of risperidone is usually noted within 4 weeks.

35.14 The answer is D (*Synopsis VIII,* pages 113, 460).
The dopamine hypothesis of schizophrenia grew from the observations that drugs that block dopamine receptors (such as haloperidol) have antipsychotic activity and drugs that stimulate dopamine activity (such as *amphetamine*) can, when given in high enough doses, induce psychotic symptoms in nonschizophrenic persons. The dopamine hypothesis remains the leading neurochemical hypothesis for schizophrenia, but room is being made for a role for serotonin, based on the therapeutic success of the serotonin-dopamine antagonists, such as clozapine. Schizophrenia is now thought to result from misregulation of both dopamine and serotonin function. It is likely that the theories will have to be reconceived several times in the near future as agents become available for modification of particular receptor subtypes. Clozapine has relatively low potency as a dopamine type 2 (D_2) receptor antagonist. Clozapine has much higher potency as an antagonist at D_1, D_3, and D_4, serotonin type 2 (5-HT_2), and noradrenergic α-receptors (especially α_1). Clozapine also has intermediate antagonist activity at muscarinic and histamine type 1 (H_1) receptors. *Clozapine is one of the most effective antipsychotic drugs,* and its unique pharmacodynamic profile has indicated that dopamine is not the only neurotransmitter system involved in the etiology of schizophrenia. In animal models, clozapine appears more active in the mesolimbic system than in the striatonigral system, which correlates with the lack of parkinsonian side effects.

Evidence in support of the dopamine hypothesis of schizophrenia is as follows. *The potency of dopamine receptor antagonist drugs to reduce psychotic symptoms is most closely correlated with the affinity of these drugs for D_2 receptors.* The mechanism of therapeutic action for dopamine receptor antagonist drugs is hypothesized to be through D_2 receptor antagonism, thus preventing endogenous dopamine from activating the receptors. Neuroanatomists have defined two major dopamine tracts, the mesolimbic to cortical (mostly frontal lobe) projection, and the substantia nigra to striatum projection. Studies using the *PET technique* in patients who were taking a variety of dopamine receptor antagonists in different dosages have produced data indicating that occupancy of about 60 percent of the D_2 receptors in the caudate-putamen is correlated with clinical response and that occupancy of more than 70 percent of the D_2 receptors is correlated with the development of extrapyramidal symptoms.

Another positive association between the clinical efficacy of dopamine receptor antagonists and their dopamine receptor activity is suggested by the effects of the drugs on the plasma concentrations of homovanillic acid, the major metabolite of dopamine. Several studies have reported that high pretreatment concentrations of plasma homovanillic acid are positively correlated with an increased likelihood of a favorable clinical response. Furthermore, a *decrease in plasma homovanillic acid concentrations early in the course of treatment is correlated with a favorable clinical response.*

35.15 The answer is D (*Synopsis VIII,* pages 1042–1044).
Unlike its relatives amphetamine and racemic fenfluramine (Pondimin), *dexfenfluramine does not appear to be associated with a facilitation of dopamine release from neurons.* The major short-term effect of fenfluramine and dexfenfluramine is to *release neuronal stores of serotonin.* Some data indicate that fenfluramine and dexfenfluramine are also *inhibitors of serotonin reuptake.* It is possible that *stimulation of serotonin 5-HT_{2c} receptors,* which results from increased synaptic concentrations of serotonin, may reduce the appetite. However, troubling questions remain about whether dexfenfluramine *may permanently deplete the brain of certain serotonin stores.* In 1997, both drugs were withdrawn from the market because they produced serious heart valve disorders in patients using these medications, which had wide use in the United States.

35.16 The answer is A (*Synopsis VIII,* pages 1071, 1077–1078).
Many clinicians are using *clozapine* in patients who are seriously ill or who have severe tardive dyskinesia or a particular sensitivity to the extrapyramidal side effects of standard antipsychotic drugs. Clozapine treatment suppresses the abnormal movements of tardive dyskinesia, as does treatment with conventional antipsychotics; but in contrast to conventional antipsychotics, clozapine does not appear to worsen the movement disorder. Clozapine has the lowest dopamine D_2 receptor antagonism of any of the antipsychotic drugs, which is the pharmacodynamic index that best correlates with the development of medication-induced tardive dyskinesia. Data from PET scanning show that 10 mg of haloperidol produces 80 percent occupancy of striatal D_2 receptors, whereas clinically effective doses of clozapine occupy only 40 to 50 percent of striatal D_2 receptors. Although antagonism of serotonin and dopamine receptors is emphasized in the name "serotonin-dopamine antagonists," it is not known which particular combination of receptor affinities is responsible for the effects of clozapine and other serotonin-dopamine antagonists.

Olanzapine probably poses the next lowest risk of tardive dyskinesia, followed by *risperidone.* A few case reports have emerged in which risperidone appeared to cause tardive dyskinesias. There are scant clinical data on the risk of tardive dyskinesia attributable to *sertindole.* High-potency dopamine receptor antagonists such as *haloperidol* appear most likely to cause tardive dyskinesia. It should be noted that in the pre-antipsychotic drug era, as many as 5 percent of patients with schizophrenia developed symptoms of tardive dyskinesia as part of the natural history of their disease.

35.17 The answer is C (*Synopsis VIII,* pages 1087–1088). There have been case reports of fluoxetine monotherapy for *schizophrenia,* although SSRIs are generally not considered for the treatment of psychotic symptoms. Other indications for which there is preliminary evidence of efficacy for the SSRIs are dysthymic disorder, borderline personality disorder, panic disorder, hypochondriasis, *trichotillomania,* elective mutism, *attention-deficit/hyperactivity disorder,* obsessional jealousy, *premature ejaculation,* body dysmorphic disorder, autistic disorder in children and adults, Asperger's syndrome, augmentation of anticonvulsant for bipolar disorder, Tourette's disorder, self-injurious behavior, paraphilias, aggression in schizophrenia, *syncope,* neuropathic (diabetic, postherpetic) and nonneuropathic chronic pain, migraine and tension types of headache, and fibromyalgia.

35.18 The answer is D (*Synopsis VIII,* pages 1092–1096). Many psychiatrists believe that amphetamine use has been overregulated by governmental authorities. Amphetamines and narcotics are listed as schedule II drugs by the U.S. Drug Enforcement Agency (DEA). In addition, in New York State, physicians must use triplicate prescriptions for such drugs; one copy is filed with a state government agency. Such mandates worry both patients and physicians about breaches in confidentiality, and physicians are concerned that their prescribing practices may be misinterpreted by official agencies. *Consequently, some physicians may withhold sympathomimetics, even from patients who may benefit from the medications, for example for treatment of depression, because of concern about potential for abuse.*

Dextroamphetamine and methylphenidate are structurally similar to each other and to amphetamine, and all three drugs are similar in structure to the catecholamines. *Pemoline has a different structure from the other three compounds* and differs in its speed of onset.

All three *sympathomimetics are well absorbed from the gastrointestinal tract.* Dextroamphetamine reaches peak plasma concentrations in 2 to 3 hours and has a half-life of about 6 hours, which necessitates multiple daily doses. Dextroamphetamine is partially metabolized in the liver and is partially excreted unchanged by the kidneys. Methylphenidate reaches peak plasma levels in 1 to 2 hours and has a short half-life of 2 to 3 hours, which necessitates multiple daily doses. A sustained-release formulation essentially doubles the effective half-life. Methylphenidate is completely metabolized by the liver. Pemoline reaches peak plasma concentrations in 2 to 4 hours and has a half-life of about 12 hours, allowing once-daily dosing. Pemoline is metabolized by the liver and is excreted unchanged by the kidneys.

Dextroamphetamine and methylphenidate are indirect-acting sympathomimetics, with the primary effect of causing the release of catecholamines from presynaptic neurons. Dextroamphetamine stimulates release of a cytoplasmic store of dopamine, whereas methylphenidate releases dopamine from long-term vesicular stores. Pemoline's strong CNS dopamine effects have not been fully characterized. *The pharmacodynamic profiles are therefore not identical.* Current data place equal emphasis on the role of dopamine and norepinephrine in the clinical effects of sympathomimetics. More recently, dysregulation of serotonin has been implicated in attention-deficit/hyperactivity disorder, and interest in the development of serotonergic drugs for attention-deficit/hyperactivity disorder has increased. The release of dopamine may have primary importance in the sympathomimetics' clinical effects, although recent data indicate that the release of norepinephrine may be more involved with the clinical effects than was previously thought. Dextroamphetamine and methylphenidate are also inhibitors of catecholamine reuptake and inhibitors of monoamine oxidase. The net result of those activities is believed to be the stimulation of several brain regions, particularly the ascending reticular activating system and areas of the striatum, which have recently been implicated in the pathophysiology of attention-deficit/hyperactivity disorder. The pharmacodynamics of pemoline are less well understood than are the pharmacodynamics of dextroamphetamine and methylphenidate.

The short-term use of the sympathomimetics induces a euphoric feeling; however, tolerance develops for both the euphoric feeling and the sympathomimetic activity. *Tolerance does not develop for the therapeutic effects in attention-deficit/hyperactivity disorder.*

35.19 The answer is D (*Synopsis VIII,* pages 1051–1052). Valproate is commonly coadministered with lithium and the antipsychotics. The only consistent drug interaction with *lithium* is the exacerbation of drug-induced tremors, which can usually be treated with β-adrenergic receptor antagonists or *gabapentin.* The combination of valproate and antipsychotics may result in increased sedation, as can be seen when valproate is added to any CNS depressant (such as alcohol), and increased severity of extrapyramidal symptoms, which usually respond to treatment with the usual antiparkinsonian drugs. The plasma concentrations of *diazepam, amitriptyline,* nortriptyline (Pamelor), and phenobarbital (Luminal) may be increased when those drugs are coadministered with valproate, and the plasma concentrations of phenytoin (Dilantin) and desipramine (Norpramin) may be decreased when phenytoin is combined with valproate. The plasma concentrations of valproate may be decreased when the drug is coadministered with carbamazepine and may be increased when coadministered with amitriptyline (Elavil) or fluoxetine (Prozac). Patients who are treated with anticoagulants, such as aspirin and *warfarin,* should also be monitored when valproate is initiated to assess the development of any undesired augmentation of the anticoagulation effects.

35.20 The answer is A (*Synopsis VIII,* page 934). *Intravenous administration* is the quickest route to achieve therapeutic blood levels; however, it also carries the highest risk of sudden and life-threatening adverse effects. A psychotherapeutic drug must first reach the blood on its way to the brain, unless it is directly administered into the cerebrospinal fluid or the brain. Orally administered drugs must dissolve in the fluid of the gastrointestinal (GI) tract before the body can absorb them. Drug tablets can be designed to disintegrate quickly or slowly, the absorption depending on the drug's concentration and lipid solubility and the GI tract's local pH, motility, and surface area. Depending on the drug's pK_a and the

GI tract's pH, the drug may be present in an ionized form that limits its lipid solubility. Omeprazole (Zofran), histamine H_2 receptor blockers, such as cimetidine (Tagamet) or ranitidine (Zantac), or *antacids* may reduce stomach acidity and interfere with drug solubility. Gastric and intestinal motility may be slowed by *anticholinergic drugs* or may be increased by dopamine receptor antagonists, such as metoclopramide (Reglan), which may influence the rate of drug absorption. *Gastrectomy* may also prevent conversion of a drug to an absorbable form because of the lack of an acidic environment. *Cirrhosis* may alter the splanchnic blood flow and slow the absorption of drugs. If the pharmacokinetic absorption factors are favorable, the drug may reach therapeutic blood concentrations quickly if it is administered intramuscularly. If a drug is coupled with an appropriate carrier molecule, intramuscular administration can sustain the drug's release over a long period. Some antipsychotic drugs are available in depot forms that allow the drug to be administered only once every 1 to 4 weeks.

35.21 The answer is D (*Synopsis VIII,* pages 944–945, 959–960, 975–976).
The use of the β-adrenergic receptor antagonists is best supported for neuroleptic-induced acute *akathisia,* lithium-induced postural tremor, and social phobia. The data on the use of those drugs as adjuncts to benzodiazepines for alcohol withdrawal and for the control of impulsive aggression or violence are also promising.

Neuroleptic-induced acute akathisia is recognized in the fourth edition of *Diagnostic and Statistical Manual of Mental Disorders* (DSM-IV) as one of the medication-induced movement disorders. Many studies have shown that β-adrenergic receptor antagonists can be effective in the treatment of neuroleptic-induced acute akathisia. The majority of clinicians and researchers believe that β-adrenergic receptor antagonists are more effective for this indication than are anticholinergics and benzodiazepines, although the relative efficacy of those agents may vary among patients. However, the clinician must realize that the β-adrenergic receptor antagonists are not effective in the treatment of such neuroleptic-induced movement disorders as acute dystonia and parkinsonism. Propranolol has been most studied for neuroleptic-induced acute akathisia, and at least one study has reported that a less lipophilic compound was not effective in the treatment of the disorder. There does not appear to be a clear superiority of β_1-selective versus nonselective agents for this indication.

Propranolol has been reported to be useful as an adjuvant to benzodiazepines but not as a sole agent in the treatment of *alcohol withdrawal.* One study used the following dose schedule: no propranolol for a pulse less than 50; 50 mg propranolol for a pulse between 50 and 79; and 100 mg propranolol for a pulse equal to or greater than 80. The patients who received propranolol and benzodiazepines had less severe withdrawal symptoms, more stable vital signs, and a shorter hospital stay than did the patients who received only benzodiazepines.

Propranolol has been well studied for the treatment of social phobia, primarily of the performance type (for example, disabling anxiety before a musical performance), but data are also available for their use in treatment of social phobia, *panic disorder,* posttraumatic stress disorder and *generalized anxiety disorder.* Use of β-adrenergic receptor antagonists for panic disorder, generalized anxiety disorder, and *psychogenic seizures* is less efficacious than the use of benzodiazepines or serotonin-specific reuptake inhibitors.

35.22 The answer is A (*Synopsis VIII,* pages 999–1000).
Bromocriptine is FDA approved as safe and effective for the treatment of *hyperprolactinemia.* Because most antipsychotic drugs act as potent antagonists of dopamine D_2 receptors, they cause an increase in prolactin release by blocking the inhibitory effects of endogenous dopamine in the pituitary. The increase in serum prolactin can result in amenorrhea, sexual dysfunction, and galactorrhea in women. Bromocriptine is an effective treatment because its dopamine agonist activity stimulates the D_2 receptors in the pituitary and inhibits prolactin release. In spite of the dopamine agonist activity of bromocriptine, its use does not appear to be associated with an exacerbation of psychotic symptoms. Bromocriptine is used in a dosage range of 5 to 15 mg a day for that indication.

The other established indication for bromocriptine is as part of a multimodal treatment for neuroleptic malignant syndrome. This is a potentially fatal syndrome of autonomic instability associated with the use of antipsychotics, such as haloperidol (Haldol). Because of the sporadic, unpredictable nature of neuroleptic malignant syndrome, most of the data regarding the effectiveness of bromocriptine in the condition come from case reports. Bromocriptine may be effective in neuroleptic malignant syndrome because its dopamine agonist activity reverses the effects of the dopamine antagonists on hypothalamic thermoregulatory function and peripheral muscle contraction.

Other less robust data support the use of bromocriptine for *cocaine withdrawal, depressive disorders, bipolar disorder,* antipsychotic-induced parkinsonism, antipsychotic-induced tardive dyskinesia, and *alcohol withdrawal.* The data in support of the use of bromocriptine in cocaine withdrawal come primarily from case reports and not well-controlled studies. Nevertheless, since there is no clearly superior treatment for cocaine withdrawal, a clinical trial of bromocriptine may be warranted in some patients. Bromocriptine has been used to treat both the withdrawal symptoms of cocaine and the long-term craving for cocaine.

35.23 The answer is C (*Synopsis VIII,* pages 1009, 1047).
Lithium is the most commonly used agent for treatment of a *first manic episode* because it is generally the most effective drug for this purpose. Almost two dozen well-controlled studies, however, have shown that carbamazepine is effective in the treatment of acute mania, with efficacy comparable to lithium and antipsychotics. About 10 studies have also shown that carbamazepine is effective in the prophylaxis of both manic and depressive episodes in bipolar I disorder when it is used for prophylactic treatment. Carbamazepine is an effective antimanic agent in 50 to 70 percent of all patients. Additional evidence from those studies indicates that carbamazepine may be effective in some patients who are not responsive to lithium, such as patients with *dysphoric mania, rapid cycling,* or a *negative family history of mood disorders.* However, a few clinical and basic science data indicate that some patients may experience a tolerance for the antimanic effects of carbamazepine. Because lithium toxicity may produce convulsions, carbamazepine may be a preferred drug for patients with *comorbid seizure disorders.*

35.24 The answer is B (*Synopsis VIII,* page 1027).
Dopamine receptor antagonists are often used in combination with antimanic drugs to treat psychosis or manic excitement in bipolar I disorder. Although *lithium, carbamazepine,* and *valproate* are the drugs of choice for that condition, these drugs generally have a slower onset of action than do dopamine receptor antagonists, such as *haloperidol,* in the treatment of the acute symptoms. Thus, the general practice is to use combination therapy at the initiation of treatment and to gradually withdraw the dopamine receptor antagonist after the antimanic agent has reached its onset of activity. *Risperidone* lacks the anticholinergic and antihistamine activities that contribute to the calming effects of the dopamine receptor antagonists, and it is not as effective as haloperidol for the treatment of acute mania.

35.25 The answer is C (*Synopsis VIII,* pages 1076–1077).
The most common adverse effect of olanzapine is *sedation,* which may occur in 30 percent of patients on the usual maintenance dose (10 mg/day). Therefore, patients who take olanzapine should exercise caution when driving or operating dangerous machinery. This side effect may be minimized by giving the dose before sleep. Olanzapine-associated seizures are seen in less than 1 percent of patients. The D_2 receptor antagonism of olanzapine causes a modest rise in prolactin levels for the duration of the therapy. This is a theoretical concern in patients with a history of breast cancer, a tumor that may be dependent on prolactin for growth, although there are no human data establishing such a connection. Dizziness, akathisia and nonaggressive objectionable behavior have also been reported at frequencies higher than those seen in placebo controls.

No cases of *tardive dyskinesia* have yet been reported in patients taking olanzapine, although experience is limited. No agranulocytosis was reported in more than 3100 patients taking olanzapine, including 29 who previously had clozapine-induced agranulocytosis.

If the initial dose of olanzapine is titrated up rapidly, fewer than 1 percent of patients may develop signs and symptoms of *orthostatic hypotension,* such as dizziness, tachycardia, and syncope. The risk of these effects may be minimized by limiting the starting dose to 5 mg a day, then increasing to the therapeutic range of 10 to 15 mg a day over a few weeks. In 2 percent of patients taking olanzapine, serum ALT (SGPT) elevations more than 3 times normal were seen. None of these patients developed jaundice. The levels returned to normal whether or not the drug was discontinued. These data suggest that olanzapine should be used with caution by patients with underlying liver disease. *Weight gain* and *constipation* have been significantly associated with olanzapine use.

35.26 The answer is D (*Synopsis VIII,* pages 1086–1087).
Serotonergic drugs may cause a reduction in libido, anorgasmia, inhibition of ejaculation, and/or impotence in up to 80 percent of patients. Many clinicians do not inquire about sexual adverse effects, yet these may be very troubling to patients. Some drugs that may be helpful in reducing these adverse effects are *amantadine, bromocriptine, cyproheptadine,* and *yohimbine.* Amantadine and bromocriptine have dopamine agonist effects; cyproheptadine is a serotonin antagonist; and yohimbine is an α_2-adrenergic antagonist that potentiates release of norepinephrine. Mirtazapine (Remeron), another α_2-adrenergic antagonist, and bupropion (Wellbutrin), an antidepressant with little serotonergic activity, are two antidepressants that are practically free of sexual adverse effects. *Liothyronine* is used as augmentation treatment for SSRI nonresponders, but it has no role in the treatment of sexual adverse effects. Thioridazine (Mellaril) is a dopamine receptor-antagonist that causes dose-related retrograde ejaculation.

35.27 The answer is B (*Synopsis VIII,* page 1104).
The sedative effects of tricyclic drugs make them a poor choice for patients with *hypersomnolence.* The treatment of a major depressive episode and the prophylactic treatment of major depressive disorder are the principal indications for using tricyclic and tetracyclic drugs. Tricyclic drugs are also effective in the treatment of depression in bipolar I disorder patients. *Melancholic features, prior major depressive episodes, response to another antidepressant drug,* and a *family history of depressive disorders* increase the likelihood of a therapeutic response. The treatment of a major depressive episode with psychotic features almost always requires the coadministration of an antipsychotic drug and an antidepressant.

Depression associated with a general medical disorder (secondary depression) may respond to tricyclic and tetracyclic drug treatment. The depression may occur in more than half of victims of cerebrovascular diseases and central nervous system (CNS) trauma. Depression is also strongly associated with dementias and movement disorders, such as Parkinson's disease. Depression associated with acquired immune deficiency syndrome (AIDS) may also respond to tricyclic drugs.

35.28 The answer is E (*Synopsis VIII,* pages 1064–1067).
The success of naltrexone drug and alcohol abstinence programs is more closely associated with *psychosocial factors,* such as educational level, motivation, family support, and continued behavioral therapy, than with factors associated directly with the use of naltrexone, such as *dosage* or *duration of therapeutic trials.*

Naltrexone is a pure opioid antagonist, effective in a once-a-day dose, that has improved the success of existing behavioral approaches to the treatment of opioid and alcohol addiction. Naltrexone appears to reduce or eliminate the drug craving that torments former addicts, by simply eliminating the subjective "high" associated with a return to drug abuse. *Abstinence from opioids during therapy* is therefore a secondary issue, because users do not experience the usual effects of opioids. Naltrexone must be initiated cautiously in individuals who may still be abusing opioids, because it may induce an acute withdrawal reaction, which may include life-threatening dehydration due to vomiting and diarrhea. It is therefore necessary to ensure an *opioid-free state prior to use of naltrexone.* Once in use, however, naltrexone may be started and stopped usually without physical consequence. This feature has unfortunately allowed many less motivated former addicts to withdraw from naltrexone treatment programs, which is an outcome in contrast to that usually seen in methadone programs, where stopping the drug precipitates an unpleasant withdrawal syndrome.

35.29 The answer is D (*Synopsis VIII,* pages 934–935).
Metabolism is synonymous with the term "biotransforma-

tion.'' The four major metabolic routes for drugs are *oxidation, reduction, hydrolysis,* and *conjugation. Lipid adduction,* or lipid peroxidation, is a consequence of formation of free radicals and is evidence of pathological stress in the cell. Although the usual result of metabolism is to produce inactive metabolites that are more readily excreted than are the parent compounds, many examples of active metabolites are produced from psychoactive drugs. The liver is the principal site of metabolism, and bile, feces, and urine are the major routes of excretion. Psychoactive drugs are also excreted in sweat, saliva, tears, and breast milk; therefore, mothers who are taking psychotherapeutic drugs should not breast-feed their children. Disease states and coadministered drugs can either raise or lower the blood concentrations of a psychoactive drug.

An essential element of the ability of a chemical to act as a drug is that it can be metabolized by the body. Most psychotherapeutic drugs are metabolized by the hepatic cytochrome P450 (CYP) enzyme system. This family of enzymes was named for its ability to absorb light at the wavelength of 450 nm. It is phylogenetically very old, arising at the time of the evolutionary divergence of plants and animals. The xenobiotic system, which oxidizes and inactivates foreign compounds, such as toxins and carcinogens, evolved from an even older system, the steroidogenic enzymes, which synthesizes components of the cellular membranes. The xenobiotic enzymes are responsible for the inactivation of plant toxins, and these are the enzymes that metabolize most psychiatric drugs, many of which were originally isolated from plants. Although these enzymes are distributed widely throughout the body, they act primarily in the endoplasmic reticulum of the hepatocytes and the cells of the intestine. In the past 10 years, a large family of human CYP enzymes has been molecularly cloned, and the gene sequences are known. This has permitted the categorization of the CYP enzymes into families and subfamilies. Members of separate families share at least 40 percent identity of the primary amino acid sequence, whereas members of a specific family share at least 55 percent amino acid identity. At least 27 families are recognized, but clinically relevant interactions have been attributed to members of only 3 families. A nomenclature has been established, in which the family is denoted by a numeral, the subfamily by a capital letter, and the individual member of the subfamily by a second number (such as 2D6 or, with a roman numeral, IID6).

35.30 The answer is B (*Synopsis VIII,* pages 978–980). Anticholinergics have not been shown to be effective for treatment of *Huntington's chorea.* In the clinical practice of psychiatry, the anticholinergic drugs and amantadine (Symmetrel), like the antihistamines, have their primary use as treatments for medication-induced movement disorders, particularly *neuroleptic-induced parkinsonism, neuroleptic-induced acute dystonia,* and *medication-induced postural tremor.* The anticholinergic drugs and amantadine may also be of limited use in the treatment of neuroleptic-induced acute akathisia. Before the introduction of levodopa (Larodopa), the anticholinergic drugs were commonly used in the treatment of *idiopathic Parkinson's disease.* The antiparkinsonian effects of amantadine, which was initially developed as an antiviral compound, were discovered when its use improved the parkinsonian symptoms of a patient who was being treated with amantadine for influenza A2.

All of the available anticholinergics and amantadine are equally effective in the treatment of parkinsonian symptoms, although the efficacy of amantadine may diminish in some patients within the first month of treatment. Amantadine may be more effective than the anticholinergics in the treatment of rigidity and tremor. Amantadine may also be the drug of choice if a clinician does not want to add more anticholinergic drugs to a patient's treatment regimen, particularly if a patient is taking an antipsychotic or an antidepressant with high anticholinergic activity—such as chlorpromazine (Thorazine) or amitriptyline (Elavil)—or is elderly and therefore at risk for anticholinergic adverse effects.

Neuroleptic-induced acute dystonia is most common in young men. The syndrome often occurs early in the course of treatment and is commonly associated with high-potency antipsychotics, such as haloperidol. The dystonia most commonly affects the muscles of the neck, the tongue, the face, and the back. Opisthotonos (involving the entire body) and oculogyric crises (involving the muscles of the eyes) are examples of specific dystonias. Dystonias are uncomfortable, sometimes painful, and often frightening to the patient. Although the onset is often sudden, onset in 3 to 6 hours may occur, often resulting in patients' complaining about having a thick tongue or difficulty in swallowing. Dystonic contractions can be powerful enough to dislocate joints, and laryngeal dystonias can result in suffocation if the patient is not treated immediately.

35.31 The answer is D (*Synopsis VIII,* pages 1000–1001). The adverse effects of bromocriptine tend to be severe at the initiation of treatment and with dosages of more than 20 mg a day. The most common side effects are *nausea, headache,* and *dizziness.* Less common gastrointestinal side effects include vomiting, abdominal cramps, and constipation. About 1 percent of patients have *syncopal episodes* 15 to 60 minutes after the first dose of the drug, although they can tolerate subsequent doses and dosage increases without syncope. Other patients, however, experience symptomatic orthostatic hypotension, for which they do not have tolerance with continued treatment. Other cardiovascular symptoms can include cardiac arrhythmias and an exacerbation of underlying angina. Rare psychiatric side effects can include hallucinations, delusions, confusion, and behavioral changes, although those symptoms are most common after long-term usage and in elderly patients. Bromocriptine should be used with caution in patients with hypertension, cardiovascular disease, and hepatic disease. Bromocriptine is not recommended for pregnant or breast-feeding patients. Less than 5 percent of bromocriptine is excreted in the urine, and it does not cause *polyuria.*

35.32 The answer is D (*Synopsis VIII,* pages 1009–1010). Several well-controlled studies have produced data indicating that carbamazepine is effective in the treatment of *schizophrenia* and schizoaffective disorder. Patients with positive symptoms (such as hallucinations) and few negative symptoms (such as anhedonia) may be likely to respond, as are patients who have impulsive aggressive outbursts as a symptom.

The available data indicate that carbamazepine is also an effective treatment for depression in some patients. About 25 to 33 percent of depressed patients respond to carbamazepine. That percentage is significantly smaller than the 60 to 70 percent response rate for standard antidepressants. Nevertheless, carbamazepine is an alternative drug for depressed patients who have not responded to conventional treatments, including electroconvulsive therapy (ECT), or who have a marked or rapid periodicity in their depressive episodes.

Several studies have reported that carbamazepine is effective in controlling impulsive, aggressive behavior in nonpsychotic patients of all ages from children to the elderly. Other drugs for impulse control disorders, particularly intermittent explosive disorder, include lithium, propranolol (Inderal), and antipsychotics. Because of the risk of serious adverse effects with carbamazepine, treatment with those other agents are warranted before initiating a trial with carbamazepine.

According to several studies, carbamazepine is as effective as the benzodiazepines in the control of symptoms associated with alcohol withdrawal. It may also assist in withdrawal from chronic benzodiazepine use, especially in seizure-prone patients. However, the lack of any advantage of carbamazepine over the benzodiazepines for alcohol withdrawal and the risk of adverse effects with carbamazepine limit the clinical usefulness of this application. Carbamazepine has not been shown to be useful in the treatment of *social phobia, insomnia, anorexia nervosa,* or *neuroleptic-induced parkinsonism.*

35.33 The answer is B (*Synopsis VIII,* pages 342–344, 1027–1028).

Secondary psychoses are psychotic syndromes that are associated with an identified organic cause, such as a brain tumor, a dementing disorder (such as dementia of the Alzheimer's type), or substance abuse. The dopamine receptor antagonist drugs are generally effective in the treatment of psychotic symptoms that are associated with those syndromes. The high-potency dopamine receptor antagonists, such as *fluphenazine,* are usually safer than the low-potency dopamine receptor antagonists, such as *chlorpromazine, mesoridazine, sulpiride,* and *thioridazine,* in such patients because of the high-potency drugs' lower cardiotoxic, epileptogenic, and anticholinergic activities. However, dopamine receptor antagonist drugs should not be used to treat withdrawal symptoms associated with ethanol or barbiturates because of the risk that such treatment will facilitate the development of withdrawal seizures. The drug of choice in such cases is usually a benzodiazepine. Agitation and psychosis associated with such neurological conditions as dementia of the Alzheimer's type are responsive to antipsychotic treatment; high-potency drugs and low dosages are generally preferable. Even with high-potency drugs, as many as 25 percent of elderly patients may experience episodes of hypotension. Low dosages of high-potency drugs, such as 0.5 to 5 mg a day of haloperidol, are usually sufficient for the treatment of those patients, although thioridazine 10 to 50 mg a day is also used because of its particularly potent sedative properties.

35.34 The answer is E (none) (*Synopsis VIII,* pages 1044–1046).

Within the field of clinical psychiatry, levodopa is not a primary therapy for any single indication; rather, levodopa is used as a second-line or third-line treatment for *antipsychotic-induced parkinsonism, neuroleptic malignant syndrome,* and in experimental use, for *cocaine abuse.* Skillful use of levodopa together with serotonin-dopamine antagonists, such as clozapine, has permitted more effective treatment of Parkinson's disease than with levodopa alone. Levodopa indirectly potentiates dopaminergic neurotransmission by increasing the synthesis of dopamine. Levodopa, given in combination with a peripheral inhibitor of dopa decarboxylase (such as carbidopa), is the most commonly used treatment for idiopathic Parkinson's disease and several other movement disorders. A commonly used commercially available combination of levodopa and carbidopa is Sinemet.

In psychiatry, anticholinergics, amantadine (Symmetrel), antihistamines, and bromocriptine (Parlodel) are more frequently used than is levodopa for the treatment of antipsychotic-induced parkinsonism, because the other drugs are equally effective and are associated with fewer side effects. Nonetheless, levodopa can be used to treat extrapyramidal symptoms, akinesia, and focal perioral tremors (sometimes called rabbit syndrome). Additional evidence, based on case reports and small studies, indicates that levodopa may be effective in the treatment of restless legs syndrome and tardive dyskinesia. Preliminary data indicate that levodopa may be effective in the treatment of the *negative symptoms of schizophrenia,* although that indication should be considered only in research settings. Levodopa has been used as one component of the treatment of neuroleptic malignant syndrome and as part of a multimodal cocaine detoxification program.

35.35 The answer is A (*Synopsis VIII,* pages 1078–1079).

Although sertindole is a potent dopamine D_2 receptor antagonist, little elevation of serum prolactin levels was seen in preclinical trials, and the drug would therefore not be expected to produce significant *galactorrhea.* The most common side effects of sertindole are *tachycardia, nasal congestion, postural hypotension,* dizziness, *weight gain,* nausea, reduced volume of ejaculation, and prolongation of the QT_c interval. There is evidence that sertindole causes few or no extrapyramidal effects. Although rarer with serotonin-dopamine antagonists, all antipsychotic drugs may cause neuroleptic malignant syndrome and tardive dyskinesia. Sertindole is not associated with sedation or adverse cognitive effects.

35.36 The answer is A (*Synopsis VIII,* pages 1087–1088).

Fluoxetine and paroxetine, but not *sertraline,* disrupt sleep continuity, and fluoxetine, sertraline, and paroxetine reduce rapid eye movement (REM) sleep. Some experts recommend the addition of *trazodone,* a highly sedating antidepressant, for the first several weeks of treatment with fluoxetine, until the full antidepressant and antianxiety effects appear. *Nefazodone* and trazodone are unusual among antidepressants in that they do not decrease but rather increase REM sleep, and they also improve sleep continuity. However, nefazodone is much less likely than trazodone to produce daytime sedation.

35.37 The answer is C (*Synopsis VIII,* pages 980–981, 1103–1104).

Clinicians should warn patients that anticholinergic effects of tricyclic drugs are common but that the patient may develop a tolerance for them with continued treatment. *Amitriptyline, imipramine, trimipramine, clomipramine,* and doxepin are the most anticholinergic drugs; amoxapine, nortriptyline, and maprotiline are less anticholinergic; and *desipramine* may be the least anticholinergic. Anticholinergic effects include dry mouth, constipation, blurred vision, and urinary retention. Sugarless gum, candy, or fluoride lozenges can alleviate the dry mouth. Bethanechol (Urecholine), 25 to 50 mg 3 or 4 times a day, may reduce urinary hesitancy and may be helpful in cases of impotence when the drug is taken 30 minutes before sexual intercourse. Narrow-angle glaucoma can also be aggravated by anticholinergic drugs, and the precipitation of glaucoma requires emergency treatment with a miotic agent. Tricyclic and tetracyclic drugs should be avoided in patients with glaucoma, and an SSRI should be substituted. Severe anticholinergic effects can lead to a CNS anticholinergic syndrome with confusion and delirium, especially if tricyclic and tetracyclic drugs are administered with antipsychotics or anticholinergic drugs. Some clinicians have used intramuscular (IM) or intravenous (IV) physostigmine (Antilirium) as a diagnostic tool to confirm the presence of anticholinergic delirium.

35.38 The answer is D (*Synopsis VIII,* pages 1047–1050). Lithium does not affect the *hepatic* system. The most common effects of lithium are on the *central nervous system, thyroid, heart,* kidneys, and *hematopoietic system.* Lithium impedes the release of thyroid hormone from the thyroid and can result in hypothyroidism or goiter; the disorder affects women more than men. Lithium also impairs sinus node function, which can result in heart block in susceptible persons. Lithium reduces the ability of the kidneys to concentrate urine. Although this effect is usually not clinically significant, the effect is not always reversible after the discontinuation of lithium. Pathological nonspecific interstitial fibrosis has been reported as a postmortem finding in some persons who were treated for a long time with lithium, but this is an unusual outcome. The major effect of lithium on the hematopoietic system is a clinically insignificant increase in leukocyte production.

The most common adverse effects of lithium treatment are gastric distress, weight gain, tremor, fatigue, and mild cognitive impairment. Gastrointestinal symptoms can include nausea, decreased appetite, vomiting, and diarrhea and can often be reduced by dividing the dosage, administering the lithium with food, or switching to another lithium preparation. Weight gain results from a poorly understood effect of lithium on carbohydrate metabolism. Weight gain can also result from lithium-induced edema. The only reasonable approach to weight gain is to encourage the patient to eat wisely and to engage in moderate exercise.

The most common adverse renal effect of lithium is polyuria with secondary polydipsia. The symptom is particularly a problem in 25 to 35 percent of patients who may have a urine output of more than 3 L a day (normal 1 to 2 L a day). The polyuria is a result of the lithium antagonism to the effects of antidiuretic hormone, the net effect of which is to decrease the resorption of fluid from the distal tubules of the kidneys. Polyuria may be significant enough to result in problems at work and in social settings, with associated insomnia, weight gain, and dehydration.

Lithium affects thyroid function, causing a generally benign and often transient diminution in the concentrations of circulating thyroid hormones. Reports have attributed goiter (5 percent of patients), benign reversible exophthalmos, and hypothyroidism (7 to 9 percent of patients) to lithium treatment. About 50 percent of patients receiving long-term lithium treatment have an abnormal thyrotropin-releasing hormone (TRH) response, and about 30 percent have elevated levels of thyroid-stimulating hormone (TSH). If symptoms of hypothyroidism are present, treatment with levothyroxine (Synthroid) is indicated. Even in the absence of hypothyroid symptoms, some clinicians treat patients with elevated TSH levels with levothyroxine. In lithium-treated patients, TSH levels should be measured every 6 to 12 months. Lithium-induced hypothyroidism should be considered when evaluating depressive episodes that emerge during lithium therapy.

The cardiac effects of lithium, which resemble those of hypokalemia on the electrocardiogram (ECG), are caused by the displacement of intracellular potassium by the lithium ion. The most common changes on the ECG are T wave flattening or inversion. The changes are benign and disappear after the lithium is excreted from the body. Nevertheless, baseline ECGs are essential and should be repeated annually.

35.39 The answer is E (*Synopsis VIII,* pages 935, 1090). The major differences among the available SSRIs lie primarily in their pharmacokinetic profiles, specifically their half-lives. *Paroxetine and fluoxetine* are metabolized in the liver by CYP *2D6,* which may indicate that clinicians should be careful in the coadministration of other drugs that are also metabolized by CYP 2D6. With respect to CYP 2D6, 7 percent of whites are poor metabolizers, which means that they have a genetic variant of the enzyme with a low efficiency of action. Because of this, toxic levels of unmetabolized drugs may build up, especially in the presence of other drugs that may compete for the limited capacity of the enzyme, such as tricyclic antidepressants, antipsychotics, and type 1C antiarrhythmics. These drugs should therefore be used cautiously or avoided with serotonin-specific reuptake inhibitors (SSRIs). Other clinically relevant drug–drug interactions due to the CYP enzymes have been described. Because of inhibition of the CYP *3A3/4* enzyme, fluvoxamine (Luvox), nefazodone, and fluoxetine should not be used with terfenadine (Seldane), astemizole (Hismanal), alprazolam (Xanax), triazolam (Halcion), or carbamazepine (Tegretol). Due to interactions with CYP *1A2,* fluvoxamine should not be used with theophylline (Slo-Bid, Theo-Dur) or clozapine. Inhibition of CYP *2C9/10* and CYP *2C19* warrants caution for the following combinations: fluoxetine plus phenytoin (Dilantin), sertraline plus tolbutamide (Orinase), and fluvoxamine plus warfarin (Coumadin). It is also important to consider the long half-lives of certain of the psychiatric drugs, especially fluoxetine, which may prolong their inhibition of the CYP enzymes. Fluoxetine has the longest half-life, 2 to 3 days; its active metabolite has a half-life of 7 to 9 days. The half-lives of the other SSRIs are much shorter, about 20 hours, and these SSRIs have no major active metabolites.

36 

Child Psychiatry: Assessment, Examination, and Psychological Testing

The psychiatric assessment of a child includes an integration of social, physical, and intellectual development; temperament; and evolution of psychiatric symptoms and disorders. A combination of clinical observations and comprehensive history, along with standardized tests of intellectual functioning, developmental level, and academic achievement, are often used to understand all of these dimensions.

A knowledge of normative child development is crucial in evaluating a child's interpersonal skills and in correctly interpreting historical information regarding fears and anxieties, temper tantrums, attention span, and many other anecdotes in the daily life of a child. The assessment process includes direct meetings with the child, the parents, and sometimes siblings. Pertinent information is also collected from teachers, pediatricians, and school counselors.

Very young children are usually seen with their parents, whereas adolescents are often seen alone in the initial session. Parents are generally better informants than their children regarding developmental milestones and the chronology of symptoms. Children are the best informants of their current mood status, presence or absence of perceptual distortions, and feelings regarding their family's functioning. Children under age 5 years are usually seen in a room that contains toys, dolls, or puppets, to aid evaluation of their developmental level and disclosure of feelings.

Physical appearance, activity level, parent–child interactions, and separation and reunion behaviors from parents are all vital parts of the mental status examination of children. Mannerisms, communication style, and language development must be observed. Temperament includes a variety of dimensions that characterize the way a child interacts with the environment and that mediate psychiatric symptoms. Categories that define a temperament include activity level, rhythmicity (regularity) of biological function, approach or withdrawal to new stimuli, adaptability to changes, threshold of responsiveness, intensity of reaction, quality of mood, attention span, and persistence. Three constellations of these categories seem to occur with some frequency:

1. *Easy temperament* characterizes a child who tends to adapt to changes without negativity, to approach new stimuli rather than withdraw, and to exhibit positive mood of moderate intensity and who seems to be internally regular with respect to sleep–wake cycle, hunger, and activity level.
2. *Difficult temperament* is characterized by irritability in response to change, intense and negative reactions, withdrawal from new stimuli, and biological irregularity with regard to sleep–wake cycle, hunger, and mood.
3. *Slow-to-warm-up temperament* includes the tendency to withdraw from new stimuli, slow adaptability to change, and frequent negative emotional reactions of low intensity. Children in this group are described as shy.

A comprehensive mental status examination that includes a great deal of observation as well as direct questioning is always a part of an assessment of a child or adolescent. Abnormal levels of physical activity and abnormal motor movements, speech, language, and cognition should be observed. Thought process, mood state, self-esteem, and affect are included. An assessment of self-destructive behaviors and suicidal ideation should always be included. It is important to note that children under the age of 4 years may not fully understand the notion of death or an absolute distinction between reality and make-believe. Children of average intelligence who are more than 4 years old should be able to understand these concepts.

Students should read the material in Chapter 36 in *Kaplan and Sadock's Synopsis VIII.* By studying the questions and answers below, they can assess their knowledge of the area.

HELPFUL HINTS

The student should memorize the following terms and their definitions.

- adaptive function
- attention span
- best-estimate diagnosis
- clinical interview
- cognitive function
- confidentiality
- developmental delay
- developmental milestones
- Draw-A-Person
- family functioning
- family psychiatric history
- intelligence quotient (IQ)
- judgment
- limit setting
- mental status examination
- minor physical anomaly
- motor activity level
- neurological soft signs
- psychological tests
- rapport
- separation and reunion
- social relatedness
- speech and language
- squiggle game
- structured interview
- suicidal ideation
- symbolic play
- temperament
- three wishes
- unstructured play

▲ QUESTIONS

DIRECTIONS: Each of these questions or incomplete statements is followed by five suggested responses or completions. Select the *one* that is *best* in each case.

36.1 The psychiatric assessment of a 3-year-old child includes all of the following *except*

A. using an unstructured playroom to observe symbolic play
B. directing questions to a doll or a puppet
C. playing peekaboo games
D. observing separation and reunion behavior with the child's parents
E. noting motor activity and activity level

36.2 Techniques that are helpful in eliciting information and feelings from a school-age child include all of the following *except*

A. asking the child to disclose three wishes
B. asking the child to draw a family
C. using Donald Winnicott's squiggle game
D. using only open-ended questions
E. using indirect commentary

36.3 All of the following are components of the mental status examination of a child *except*

A. parent–child interaction
B. the child's activity level
C. the child's social relatedness
D. the child's intelligence quotient (IQ)
E. mood and affect

36.4 The mental status examination of children includes

A. fantasies and inferred conflicts
B. judgment and insight
C. positive attributes
D. self-esteem
E. all of the above

36.5 The psychiatric assessment of adolescents includes

A. giving adolescents the choice of being seen first alone or having the parents present during the initial interview
B. seeing each parent in a separate interview to discern differences in their views of the child's problem
C. asking adolescents about sexual experiences and the use of drugs
D. sharing information with the parents with patient consent
E. all of the above

36.6 Hostility by an adolescent in the initial psychiatric interview may reflect all of the following *except*

A. a test of how much the clinician can be trusted
B. a defense against anxiety
C. borderline intellectual functioning
D. a transference phenomenon
E. depression

36.7 Countertransference phenomena include all of the following *except*

A. expectations that exceed the child's developmental level
B. identification with the child or the adolescent
C. ambivalent feelings toward the child's siblings
D. reactions by the child to the therapist as if the therapist were a parent
E. repeated arguing with the child or the adolescent

36.8 Which of the following statements about personality tests for children is *true*?

A. Personality tests and tests of ability have equal reliability and validity.
B. Both the Children's Apperception Test (CAT) and the Thematic Apperception Test (TAT) use pictures of people in situations.
C. The Rorschach test has not been developed for children or adolescents.
D. The Mooney Problem Check List is basically a checklist of personal problems.
E. All of the above statements are true.

36.9 During a psychiatric examination of a child, the psychiatrist should

A. encourage the child to sit quietly in a chair
B. avoid looking at the child
C. always have the parent in the same room with the child
D. use a conversational approach and encourage the child to take the initiative
E. all of the above

36.10 Figure 36.1 is part of a series of drawings used to test children for

A. depression
B. elation
C. frustration
D. anger
E. all of the above

DIRECTIONS: Each group of questions consists of lettered headings followed by a list of numbered phrases or statements. For each numbered phrase or statement, select the *one* lettered heading that is most closely associated with it. Each lettered heading may be selected once, more than once, or not at all.

Questions 36.11–36.13

A. Rorschach test
B. Blacky pictures
C. Toy tests and dolls

36.11 Bilaterally symmetrical inkblots
36.12 Reveals through play the child's attitudes toward the family, sibling rivalries, fears, aggressions, and conflicts

FIGURE 36.1
Courtesy of Saul Rosenzweig.

36.13 Cartoons of a small dog, its parents, and a sibling designed to elicit sexual conflicts

Questions 36.14–36.18

A. Vineland Adaptive Behavior Scales
B. Children's Apperception Test (CAT)
C. Wide-Range Achievement Test–Revised (WRAT-R)
D. Peabody Picture Vocabulary Test–Revised (PPVT-R)
E. Wechsler Intelligence Scale for Children–III (WISC-III)

36.14 Measures receptive word understanding, with resulting standard scores, percentiles, and age equivalents

36.15 Measures communication, daily living skills, socialization, and motor development, yielding a composite expressed in a standard score, percentiles, and age equivalents

36.16 Generates stories from picture cards of animals that reflect interpersonal functioning

36.17 Measures functioning in reading, spelling, and arithmetic, with resulting grade levels, percentiles, and standard scores

36.18 Measures verbal, performance, and full-scale ability, with scaled subtest scores permitting specific skill assessment

Questions 36.19–36.21

Which test would be helpful in the psychiatric evaluation of a child who presents with the described symptoms?

A. WISC-III
B. Child Behavior Checklist
C. Children's Apperception Test (CAT)

36.19 A 6-year-old is highly aggressive and becomes very angry when he doesn't get his way. He has always been prone to severe tantrums and has difficulty with his behavior and mood in school. At home, he is considered manageable, although he seems to have a short attention span. He seems to break new toys in a matter of minutes. He is unable to play with peers because of frequent fighting.

36.20 A 9-year-old is clingy with her mother and usually will not speak to strangers. She is willing to answer specific questions but not to describe her thoughts or feelings. When she is stressed, she tends to withdraw and become tearful. She seems to be unusually sensitive to criticism and will not join in a group activity.

36.21 A 7-year-old is reported to be unable to follow directions, is clumsy and slow, and has a poor vocabulary. Although he is friendly and good natured, he has been brutally picked on by peers, who say that he doesn't understand the rules of games. His teacher is also concerned about his comprehension.

36.22 Neurological soft signs include all of the following *except*

A. contralateral overflow movements
B. learning disabilities
C. asymmetry of gait
D. nystagmus
E. poor balance

36.23 Minor physical anomalies include all of the following *except*

A. multiple hair whorls
B. low-set ears
C. high-arched palate
D. partial syndactyly of several toes
E. Babinski reflex

ANSWERS

Child Psychiatry: Assessment, Examination, and Psychological Testing

36.1 The answer is C (*Synopsis VIII,* page 1129).
Playing peekaboo games is appropriate with infants of 18 months or younger, but children over 2 years of age should be able to engage in symbolic play with the examiner and with toys. Assessments of young children generally include *using an unstructured playroom to observe symbolic play.* Many young children reveal more in play than in conversation. Children under age 6 years often reveal information most easily if the examiner *directs questions to a doll or a puppet. Observing separation and reunion behavior with the child's parents* is part of the mental status examination, and assessments of very young children usually begin with their parents present, since young children may be frightened by the interview situation. *Noting motor behavior and activity level* is important in the assessment of young children.

36.2 The answer is D (*Synopsis VIII,* page 1129).
Open-ended questions can overwhelm a school-age child and result in withdrawal or a shrugging of the shoulders; multiple-choice questions and partially open-ended questions may elicit more information from a school-age child. Techniques that can structure and facilitate the disclosure of feelings include *asking the child to disclose three wishes.* If a child is not adept with verbal skills, *asking the child to draw a family* is often a way to break the ice. Games such as *Donald Winnicott's squiggle,* in which the examiner draws a curved line and then takes turns with the child in continuing the drawing, may also help open up communication with the child. *Using indirect commentary,* such as "I once knew a child about your age who felt very sad when he moved away from all his friends . . . ," helps elicit feelings from the child, although the clinician must be careful not to lead children into confirming what they think the clinician wants to hear.

36.3 The answer is D (*Synopsis VIII,* page 1128).
Although intelligence affects the mental status examination, the *child's intelligence quotient (IQ),* a numerical figure derived from a standardized assessment of the child's intellectual abilities, is not a component of the mental status examination. The mental status examination in a child includes *parent–child interaction, the child's activity level* and *social relatedness, mood, and affect.*

36.4 The answer is E (all) (*Synopsis VIII,* page 1131).
Included in the mental status examination of children (Table 36.1) is the evaluation of fantasies and inferred conflicts, judgment and insight, positive attributes, and self-esteem. *Fantasies and inferred conflicts* can be assessed by direct questioning about the child's dreams, drawings, doodles, or spontaneous play. *Judgment and insight* can be assessed by exploring what the child thinks caused the presenting problem, how upset the child appears to be about the problem, what the child thinks may help solve the problem, and how the child thinks the clinician can help. *Positive attributes* include physical health, attractive appearance, normal height and weight, normal vision and hearing, even temperament, normal intelligence, appropriate emotional responses, recognition of feelings and fantasies, a good command of language, and good academic and social performance at school. Low *self-esteem* is often indicated by such remarks as "I can't do that" or "I'm no good at anything."

Table 36.1
Mental Status Examination of Children

1. Physical appearance
2. Parent–child interaction
3. Separation and reunion
4. Orientation to time, place, and person
5. Speech and language
6. Mood
7. Affect
8. Thought process and content
9. Social relatedness
10. Motor behavior
11. Cognition
12. Memory
13 Judgment and insight

36.5 The answer is E (all) (*Synopsis VIII,* page 1129).
The psychiatric assessment of adolescents should include *giving adolescents the choice of being seen first alone or having the parents present during the initial interview.* In addition to seeing the parents together, the clinician should *see each parent in a separate interview to discern differences in their views of the problem.* Eventually, the clinician should *ask adolescents about sexual experiences and the use of drugs. Sharing information with the parents* is part of the assessment. The younger a child or adolescent is, the more information has to be shared with the parents.

36.6 The answer is C (*Synopsis VIII,* page 1129).
In the initial psychiatric interview, hostility by an adolescent *does not reflect borderline intellectual functioning.* The hostility is often *a test of how much the clinician can be trusted, a defense against anxiety, a transference phenomenon,* or evidence of a *depression.* In adolescents, poor academic performance, substance abuse, antisocial behavior, sexual promiscuity, truancy, and running away from home may all be symptoms of a depressive disorder. Transference phenomena involve reactions to the clinician that derive from unconscious feelings for childhood authority figures rather than from the real relationship with the clinician. That real relationship must also be examined, and the experienced clinician always asks whether the patient's reaction is justified.

36.7 The answer is D (*Synopsis VIII,* page 1129).
Reactions by the child to the therapist as if the therapist were a parent is an example of transference, not countertransference. In countertransference the therapist responds to the patient as if the patient were an important figure from the therapist's past. Examples of countertransference include (1) the

clinician's setting *expectations that exceed the child's developmental level;* (2) the regressive pull experienced by the clinician, causing the clinician's *identification with the child or the adolescent;* (3) *ambivalent feelings toward the child's siblings,* which may be due to residual feelings from the clinician's own childhood relationships; (4) *repeated arguing with the child or the adolescent,* which may suggest that the clinician has become enmeshed with the patient.

36.8 The answer is D (*Synopsis VIII,* pages 1133, 1135).
The Mooney Problem Check List is basically a checklist of personal problems. It is a self-report inventory, a series of questions concerning emotional problems, worries, interests, motives, values, and interpersonal traits. The major usefulness of personality inventories is in the screening and identifying of children in need of further evaluation. *Personality tests and tests of ability do not have equal reliability and validity.* Personality tests are much less satisfactory with regard to norms, reliability, and validity. *The Children's Apperception Test (CAT) is different from the adult Thematic Apperception Test (TAT)* in that *the TAT uses pictures of people, whereas the CAT uses pictures of animals* on the assumption that children respond more readily to animal characters than to people. *The Rorschach test,* one of the most widely used projective techniques, *has been developed for children* between the ages of 2 and 10 years *and for adolescents* between the ages of 10 and 17.

36.9 The answer is D (*Synopsis VIII,* page 1129).
During a psychiatric examination of a child, the psychiatrist should *use a conversational approach and encourage the child to take the initiative.* The psychiatrist should *not encourage the child to sit quietly in a chair* and should *not avoid looking the child.* Nor should the psychiatrist *always have the parent in the same room with the child.*

36.10 The answer is C (*Synopsis VIII,* page 1131).
Figure 36.1 is part of the Rosenzweig Picture-*Frustration* Study. The test presents a series of cartoons in which one person frustrates another. In the blank space provided, the child writes what the frustrated person replies. From that reply, the examiner determines the effect of frustration on the child; the effect can range from extreme passivity to extreme violence. The test is not used to measure *depression, elation,* or *anger.*

Answers 36.11–36.13

36.11 The answer is A (*Synopsis VIII,* page 1133).

36.12 The answer is C (*Synopsis VIII,* page 1129).

36.13 The answer is B (*Synopsis VIII,* page 1134).
One of the most widely used projective techniques is the *Rorschach test,* in which the subjects are shown a set of *bilaterally symmetrical inkblots* and asked to tell what they see or what the blot represents. Another projective test is the *Blacky Pictures,* in which *cartoons showing a small dog, its parents, and a sibling are designed to elicit sexual conflicts.* Drawings, *toy tests, and dolls* are used in other applications of projective methods. The objects are usually selected because of their associative value, often including dolls representing adults and children, bathroom and kitchen fixtures, and other household furnishings. Play with such articles is expected to *reveal the child's attitudes toward the family, sibling rivalries, fears, aggressions, and conflicts.* They are particularly useful in eliciting sexual abuse problems in children.

Answers 36.14–36.18

36.14 The answer is D (*Synopsis VIII,* page 1134).

36.15 The answer is A (*Synopsis VIII,* page 1134).

36.16 The answer is B (*Synopsis VIII,* page 1133).

36.17 The answer is C (*Synopsis VIII,* page 1134).

36.18 The answer is E (*Synopsis VIII,* page 1134).
The *Vineland Adaptive Behavior Scales are used to measure communication, daily living skills, socialization, and motor development, yielding a composite expressed in a standard score, percentiles, and age equivalents.* The scales are standardized for normal and mentally retarded people. A measure of adaptive function, as well as a standardized measure of intelligence, is a prerequisite when a diagnosis of mental retardation is being considered.

The *Children's Apperception Test (CAT)* is an adaptation for children of the Thematic Apperception Test (TAT). The CAT *generates stories from picture cards of animals that reflect interpersonal functioning.* The cards show ambiguous scenes related to family issues and relationships. The child is asked to describe what is happening and to tell a story about the outcome of the scene in the card. Animals are used because it was hypothesized that children respond more readily to animal images than to human figures.

The *Wide-Range Achievement Test–Revised (WRAT-R) measures functioning in reading, spelling, and arithmetic, with resulting grade levels, percentiles, and standard scores.* It can be used in children 5 years of age and older. It yields a score that is compared with the average expected score for the child's chronological age and grade level.

The *Peabody Picture Vocabulary Test–Revised (PPVT-R) measures receptive word understanding, with resulting standard scores; percentile and age equivalents* can be used for children 4 years of age and older. The *Wechsler Intelligence Scale for Children–III (WISC-III),* the most widely used test of intelligence for school-age children, *measures verbal, performance, and full-scale ability, with scaled subtest scores permitting specific skill assessment.* In a full-scale intelligence quotient (IQ), 70 to 80 indicates borderline intelligence, 80 to 90 indicates low-average intelligence, 90 to 109 indicates average intelligence, and 110 to 119 indicates high average intelligence. Table 36.2 lists some commonly used child and adolescent assessment instruments.

36.19 The answer is B (*Synopsis VIII,* page 1133).

36.20 The answer is C (*Synopsis VIII,* pages 1133, 1135).

36.21 The answer is A (*Synopsis VIII,* page 1133).
The *Child Behavior Checklist* can be very helpful in the evaluation of a 6-year-old child with multiple behavior problems, especially if the child presents with different symptoms in different settings, such as in school and home. The Child Behavior Checklist provides a broad range of symptoms that relate to academic and social competence. There is a parent version and a teacher version so that the reports of these two observers

Table 36.2
Commonly Used Child and Adolescent Assessment Instruments

Test	Ages or Grades	Comments and Data Generated
Intellectual Ability		
Wechsler Intelligence Scale for Children, 3rd edition (WISC-III) (Psychological Corporation)	6–16	Standard scores: verbal, performance, and full-scale IQ; scaled subtest scores permitting specific skill assessment
Wechsler Adult Intelligence Scale–Revised (WAIS-R) (Psychological Corporation)	16–adult	Same as WISC-R
Wechsler Preschool and Primary Scale of Intelligence (WPPSI) (Psychological Corporation)	4–6	Same as WISC-R
McCarthy Scales of Children's Abilities (MSCA) (Psychological Corporation)	2.6–8	Scores: general cognitive index (IQ equivalent), language, perceptual performance, quantitative memory and motor domain scores; percentiles
Kaufman Assessment Battery for Children (K-ABC) (American Guidance Service)	2.6–12.6	Well-grounded in theories of cognitive psychology and neuropsychology. Allows immediate comparison of intellectual capacity with acquired knowledge. Scores: mental processing composite (IQ equivalent); sequential and simultaneous processing and achievement standard scores; scaled mental processing and achievement subtest scores; age equivalents, percentiles
Stanford Binet Intelligence Scale, 4th edition (SB:FE) (Riverside Publishing Company)	2–23	Scores: IQ, verbal, abstract-visual, and quantitative reasoning; short-term memory; standard age
Peabody Picture Vocabulary Test–Revised (PPVT-R) (American Guidance Service)	4–adult	Measures receptive vocabulary acquisition. Standard scores, percentiles, age equivalents
Development		
Gesell Infant Scale	8 wk–3½ yr	Mostly motor development in the first year, with some social and language assessment
Bayley Infant Scale of Development	8 wk–2½ yr	Motor and social
Denver Developmental Screening Test	2 mo–6 yr	Screening
Yale Revised Developmental Schedule	4 wk–6 yr	Gross motor, fine motor, adaptive, personal-social, language
Achievement		
Woodcock-Johnson Psycho-Educational Battery (DLM/Teaching Resources)	K–12	Scores: reading and mathematics (mechanics and comprehension), written language, other academic achievement; grade and age scores, standard scores, percentiles
Wide-Range Achievement Test–Revised, Levels 1 and 2 (WRAT-R) (Jastak Associates)	Level 1: 5–11 Level 2: 12–75	Permits screening for deficits in reading, spelling, and arithmetic; grade levels, percentiles, stanines, standard scores
Kaufman Test of Educational Achievement, Brief and Comprehensive Forms (K-TEA) (American Guidance Service)	1–12	Standard scores: reading, mathematics, and spelling; grade and age equivalents, percentiles, stanines. Brief form sufficient for most clinical applications; comprehensive form allows error analysis and more detailed curriculum planning
Adaptive Behavior		
Vineland Adaptive Behavior Scales (American Guidance Service)	Normal: 0–19 Retarded: all ages	Standard scores: adaptive behavior composite and communication, daily living skills, socialization and motor domains; percentiles, age equivalents, developmental age scores. Separate standardization groups for normal, visually handicapped, hearing-impaired, emotionally disturbed, and retarded
Scales of Independent Behavior (DLM Teaching Resources)	Newborn–adult	Standard scores: four adaptive (motor, social interaction and communication, personal living, community living) and three maladaptive (internalized, asocial, and externalized) areas; general maladaptive index and broad independence cluster

Table 36.2 *(continued)*

Test	Ages or Grades	Comments and Data Generated
Projective		
Rorschach Inkblots (Huber, Haus; U.S. Distributor: Grune & Stratton)	3–adult	Special scoring systems. Most recently developed and increasingly universally accepted is Exner's (1974) Comprehensive System. Assesses perceptual accuracy, integration of affective and intellectual functioning, reality testing, and other psychological processes
Thematic Apperception Test (TAT) (Harvard University Press)	6–adult	Generates stories that are analyzed qualitatively. Assumed to provide especially rich data regarding interpersonal functioning
Machover Draw-A-Person (DAP) Test (Charles C Thomas)	3–adult	Qualitative analysis and hypothesis generation, especially regarding subject's feelings about self and significant others
Kinetic Family Drawing (KFD) (Brunner/Mazel)	3–adult	Qualitative analysis and hypothesis generation regarding a person's perception of family structure and sentient environment. Some objective scoring systems in existence
Rotter Incomplete Sentences Blank (Psychological Corporation)	Child, adolescent, and adult forms	Primarily qualitative analysis, although some objective scoring systems have been developed
Personality		
Minnesota Multiphasic Personality Inventory (MMPI) (University of Minnesota Press)	16–adult	Most widely used personality inventory. Standard scores: 3 validity scales and 14 clinical scales
Millon Adolescent Personality Inventory (MAPI) (National Computer Systems)	13–18	Standard scores for 20 scales grouped into three categories: personality styles, expressed concerns, behavioral correlates. Normed on adolescent population. Focuses on broad functional spectrum, not just problem areas
Children's Personality Questionnaire (Institute for Personality and Ability Testing)	8–12	Measures 14 primary personality traits, including emotional stability, self-concept level, excitability, and self-assurance. Generates combined broad trait patterns, including extroversion and anxiety
Neuropsychological		
Beery-Buktenika Developmental Test of Visual-Motor Integration (VMI) (Modern Curriculum Press)	2–16	Screening instrument for visual-motor deficits. Standard scores, age equivalents, percentiles
Benton Visual Retention Test (Psychological Corporation)	6–adult	Assesses presence of deficits in visual-figural memory. Mean scores by age
Bender Visual Motor Gestalt Test (American Orthopsychiatric Association)	5–adult	Assesses visual-motor deficits and visual-figural retention. Age equivalents
Reitan-Indiana Neuropsychological Test Battery for Children (Neuropsychology Press)	5–8	Cognitive and perceptual-motor tests for children with suspected brain damage
Halstead-Reitan Neuropsychological Test Battery for Older Children (Neuropsychology Press)	9–14	Same as Reitan-Indiana
Luria-Nebraska Neuropsychological Battery: Children's Revision (LNNB-C) (Western Psychological Services)	8–12	Sensory-motor, perceptual, and cognitive tests measuring 11 clinical and 2 additional domains of neuropsychological functioning. Provides standard scores

Reprinted with permission from Racusin GR, Moss NE: Psychological assessment of children and adolescents. In *Child and Adolescent Psychiatry: A Comprehensive Textbook,* M Lewis, editor, p 475. Williams & Wilkins, Baltimore, 1991. Adapted by Melvin Lewis, M.B.

may be compared. The child behavior checklist can help to systematically identify the problem symptoms related to mood, frustration tolerance, hyperactivity, oppositional behavior, and anxiety. For a child who has a variety of symptoms that spans many diagnostic categories, a broad rating scale can be very helpful.

The *Children's Apperception Test* consists of cards with pictures of animals in ambiguous situations that show scenes related to parent–child and sibling issues. The *child is asked to describe what is happening in the scenes.* Animals are felt to be less threatening to children who have difficulties speaking about emotional issues. For this 9-year-old girl who is inhibited and has difficulty disclosing her thoughts and feelings, the use of a projective but structured test such as the CAT can often be a conduit to helping these disclosures.

The *WISC-III (the Wechsler Intelligence Scale for Children–III) is the most widely used test of intellectual function. Used in children from 6 to 17 years old,* it provides information in a variety of verbal areas (vocabulary, similarities, general information, arithmetic, and comprehension), as well as testing abilities in the areas of performance (block design, picture completion, picture arrangement, object assembly, coding, and mazes). For a 7-year-old child who appears to be globally slow, unable to understand directions, follow rules, or comprehend the tasks in the classroom, a test of intellectual function is indicated. The WISC-III will yield a full-scale IQ, a verbal IQ, and a performance IQ.

36.22 The answer is B *(Synopsis VIII,* pages 1132–1133).
The term ''neurological soft signs'' was first used by Lauretta Bender in reference to nondiagnostic abnormalities that are seen in some children with schizophrenia. It is now evident that neurological soft signs do not indicate neurological disorders but are relatively common in children with a wide variety of developmental disabilities. Learning disabilities themselves are not neurological soft signs, although children with low intellectual function, learning disabilities, or brain damage are likely to show these signs. Soft signs refer to both behavioral findings, such as severe impulsivity or mood instability, and physical findings, such as persistence of infantile reflexes, *mild incoordination, poor balance, contralateral* overflow movements, asymmetry of gait, nystagmus, and mild choreiform movements. The Physical and Neurological Examination for Soft Signs (PANESS), an instrument that is used for children up to 15 years, consists of 15 medical questions and 43 physical tasks such as touching finger to nose and hopping tasks. Neurological soft signs are important but are not specific in making a psychiatric diagnosis.

36.23 The answer is E *(Synopsis VIII,* pages 1132–1133).
Minor physical anomalies or dysmorphic features are most frequently seen in children with developmental disabilities, speech and language disorders, learning disorders, and severe hyperactivity. As with neurological soft signs, they are rarely specific in determining a psychiatric diagnosis, but they are important to document in an examination of a child. Minor physical anomalies include *low-set ears, a high-arched palate,* epicanthal folds, hypertelorism, transverse palmar creases, *multiple hair whorls,* a large head, a furrowed tongue, *partial syndactyly of several toes,* and other facial asymmetries. The presence of the *Babinski reflex* is a neurological sign rather than a minor physical anomaly.

37 Mental Retardation

Mental retardation denotes global deficits in intellectual capacity and adaptive function below the average range. Mental retardation must be diagnosed before the age of 18 years, and the more severe the mental retardation, the more evident it is. Mental retardation is estimated to affect approximately 1 percent of the population. Mental retardation is about 1½ times as common in males as in females. There is an increasing body of scientific knowledge to explain the multiple etiologies that can produce mental retardation. These include hereditary syndromes, a variety of developmental abnormalities, and prenatal exposure to toxic substances. The degree of impairment by a toxic exposure depends on the timing and duration of an exposure as well as on the nature of the substance. In general, the more severe the mental retardation is, the higher probability that a cause can be identified. Among chromosomal and metabolic disorders, Down's syndrome, fragile X syndrome, and phenylketonuria (PKU) are most frequently identified. In addition to problems with adaptation to social and occupational limitations, persons with mental retardation have higher than average rates of many psychiatric disorders, including mood disorders, psychotic disorders, attentional disorders, and disruptive behavior disorders.

The fourth edition of *Diagnostic and Statistical Manual of Mental Disorders* (DSM-IV) divides mental retardation into four categories according to severity:

Mild: IQ 50–55 to approximately 70
Moderate: IQ 35–40 to 50–55
Severe: IQ 20–25 to 35–40
Profound: IQ below 20–25

Mental retardation, severity unspecified, is diagnosed when there is a strong presumption of mental retardation but the person is untestable by standard intelligence tests.

Down's syndrome can be the result of any of three chromosomal aberrations: (1) trisomy 21, the most common underlying abnormality, in which three of chromosome 21 are present; (2) nondisjunction, in which both normal and trisomic cells are found in various tissues (mosaicism); and (3) translocation, in which two chromosomes, usually 21 and 15, fuse; that aberration is usually inherited. Down's syndrome is diagnosed in a baby by noting its oblique palpebral fissures, small flattened skull, single palmar crease, high cheekbones, and protruding tongue. Many children and adolescents with Down's syndrome are characterized as sociable and good-natured; they tend to show a marked deterioration in language, memory, self-care skills, and problem-solving abilities after age 30 years.

Fragile X syndrome is the second most common single cause of mental retardation. It results from a mutation on the X chromosome at the fragile site. The fragile site is expressed in only some cells. The typical phenotype includes a large long head, short stature, hyperextensible joints, and macro-orchidism after puberty. Persons with fragile X syndrome have relatively strong skills in socialization, but their language is commonly characterized by perseverative speech, with abnormal modes of combining words into phrases. Persons with fragile X syndrome have higher than average rates of attention-deficit/hyperactivity disorder, learning disorders, and pervasive developmental disorders.

Prader-Willi syndrome is mental retardation postulated to be due to a small deletion on chromosome 15 manifested by compulsive eating, obesity, small stature, and hypogonadism. Children with Prader-Willi syndrome are commonly reported to be oppositional and defiant.

Prenatal noxious exposures, such as that resulting in fetal alcohol syndrome, can also result in mental retardation. In fetal alcohol syndrome, hypertelorism, microcephaly, short palpebral fissures, and inner epicanthal folds are present. Many children whose mothers consumed alcohol regularly during pregnancy have attention-deficit disorders and learning disorders whether or not they exhibit the facial dysmorphism of fetal alcohol syndrome.

Treatment of mental disorders in mentally retarded persons is generally the same as for persons who are not mentally retarded. However, the clinician should individualize the psychotherapy to make it appropriate for the patient's intellectual level. Students should study Chapter 37 in *Kaplan and Sadock's Synopsis VIII* and then address the questions and answers herein.

HELPFUL HINTS

The student should define these terms.

- AAMD
- adaptive functioning
- Bayley Infant Scale of Development
- borderline intellectual functioning
- Cattell Infant Scale
- chromosomal abnormality
- cri-du-chat syndrome
- Down's syndrome
- fragile X syndrome
- intelligence quotient (IQ)
- Lesch-Nyhan syndrome
- mental deficiency
- mental retardation
- neurofibrillary tangles
- neurofibromatosis
- nondysjunction
- PKU
- Prader-Willi syndrome
- prenatal exposure
- rubella
- Turner's syndrome
- Vineland Adaptive Behavior Scales
- WHO

▲ QUESTIONS

DIRECTIONS: For each of the following numbered syndromes, choose the correct lettered form of transmission. A lettered choice can be used once, more than once, or not at all.

Questions 37.1–37.4

A. Unknown
B. Trisomy 21
C. Autosomal dominant
D. Autosomal recessive
E. X-linked semidominant

37.1 Neurofibromatosis
37.2 Tuberous sclerosis
37.3 Crouzon's syndrome
37.4 Cockayne's syndrome

DIRECTIONS: Each of the questions or incomplete statements below is followed by five suggested responses or completions. Select the *one* that is *best* in each case.

37.5 Which type of chromosomal aberration does *not* occur in Down's syndrome?

A. Patients have only 45 chromosomes.
B. Patients have 46 chromosomes but have 3 of chromosome 21.
C. Patients have 47 chromosomes with an extra chromosome 21.
D. Patients have 46 chromosomes, but 2, usually 21 and 15, are fused.
E. Patients have mosaicism, with normal and trisomic cells in various tissues.

37.6 Which of the following mental disorders is seen with a greater frequency in mentally retarded persons than in the general population?

A. Autistic disorder
B. Schizophrenia
C. Depressive disorders
D. Stereotypic movement disorder
E. All of the above

37.7 Risk factors for psychopathology among mentally retarded persons include all of the following *except*

A. neurological impairments
B. genetic syndromes
C. family dysfunctions
D. borderline intellectual functioning
E. communication limitations

37.8 Children born to mothers affected with rubella may have

A. congenital heart disease
B. deafness
C. cataracts
D. microcephaly
E. all of the above

37.9 Profoundly retarded preschool-age children respond to

A. social and communicative skills training
B. training in self-help
C. motor development training
D. constant aid and supervision only
E. all of the above

37.10 The genetic finding most likely to be associated with advancing maternal age is

A. translocation between chromosome 14 and chromosome 21
B. mitotic nondisjunction of chromosome 21
C. partially trisomic karyotype
D. meiotic nondisjunction of chromosome 21
E. all of the above

37.11 Which of the following chromosomal abnormalities is most likely to cause mental retardation?

A. Fusion of chromosomes 21 and 15
B. XO (Turner's syndrome)
C. XXY (Klinefelter's syndrome)
D. Extra chromosome 21 (trisomy 21)
E. XXYY (Klinefelter's syndrome variation)

37.12 Mental retardation should be diagnosed when the intelligence quotient (IQ) is below

A. 20
B. 40
C. 70
D. 90
E. 100

37.13 Which of the following statements about mental retardation is *true*?

A. Idiopathic intellectual impairment is usually severe and associated with intelligence quotients (IQs) below 40.
B. Psychosocial deprivation is not believed to contribute to mental retardation.
C. Rubella is second only to syphilis as the major cause of congenital malformations and mental retardation attributable to maternal infection.
D. The prevalence of mental retardation at any one time is estimated to be about 1 percent of the general population.
E. All of the above statements are true.

37.14 Fragile X syndrome

A. has a phenotype that includes postpubertal micro-orchidism
B. affects only males
C. usually causes severe to profound mental retardation
D. is associated with schizoid personality disorder in adulthood
E. has a phenotype that includes a large head and large ears

37.15 The mentally retarded young child shown in Figure 37.1 demonstrates the characteristic facial features and high degree of social responsivity suggestive of which of the following etiologies?

A. Autosomal dominant inheritance
B. Prenatal substance exposure
C. Trisomy 21
D. Enzyme deficiency
E. Abnormality in sex chromosomes

37.16 Which of the following statements regarding the child with the karyotype shown in Figure 37.2 is *true*?

A. The father's karyotype is normal.
B. The child's physical phenotype is likely to include microcephaly.
C. The child's disorder is most likely the result of nondisjunction during mitosis.
D. The child's IQ is likely to be in the range of 70 to 90.
E. A minority of cases of the syndrome are the result of translocation involving fusion of two chromosomes.

37.17 The physical phenotype shown in Figure 37.3, including long facial contour, large anteverted ears, and macro-orchidism (not shown) in this young adult with mental retardation, is consistent with which of the following diagnoses?

A. Prader-Willi syndrome
B. Down's syndrome
C. Klinefelter's syndrome
D. Fetal alcohol syndrome
E. Fragile X syndrome

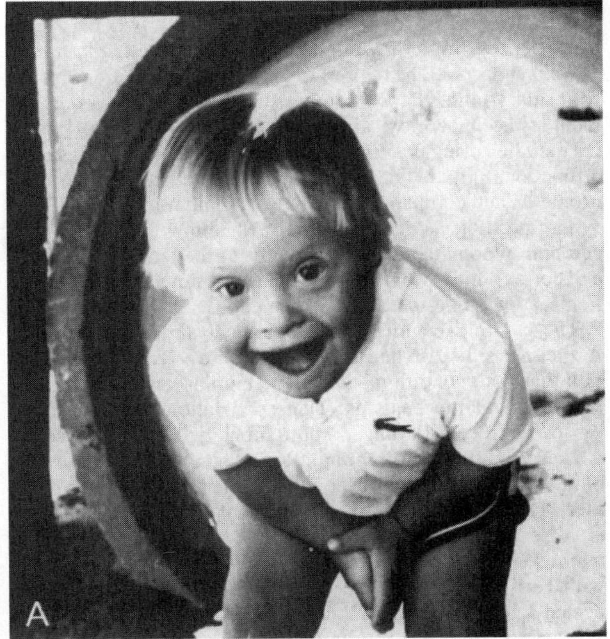

FIGURE 37.1
Courtesy of Ludwik S. Szymanski, M.D.

DIRECTIONS: Each group of questions consists of lettered headings followed by a list of numbered words or phrases. For each numbered word or phrase, select the *one* lettered heading that is most closely associated with it. Each lettered heading may be selected once, more than once, or not at all.

Questions 37.18–37.22

A. Fragile X syndrome
B. Prader-Willi syndrome
C. Down's syndrome
D. Fetal alcohol syndrome
E. Lesch-Nyhan syndrome

37.18 Compulsive eating behavior, obesity, hypogonadism, and small stature

37.19 Compulsive self-mutilation by biting of the mouth and the fingers

37.20 Microcephaly, hypertelorism, short palpebral fissures, attention-deficit/hyperactivity disorder, and learning disorders

37.21 Long head and ears, short stature, hyperextensible joints, postpubertal macro-orchidism, and a risk of pervasive developmental disorders

37.22 A marked deterioration in language, memory, self-care, and problem-solving abilities in the patient's 30s

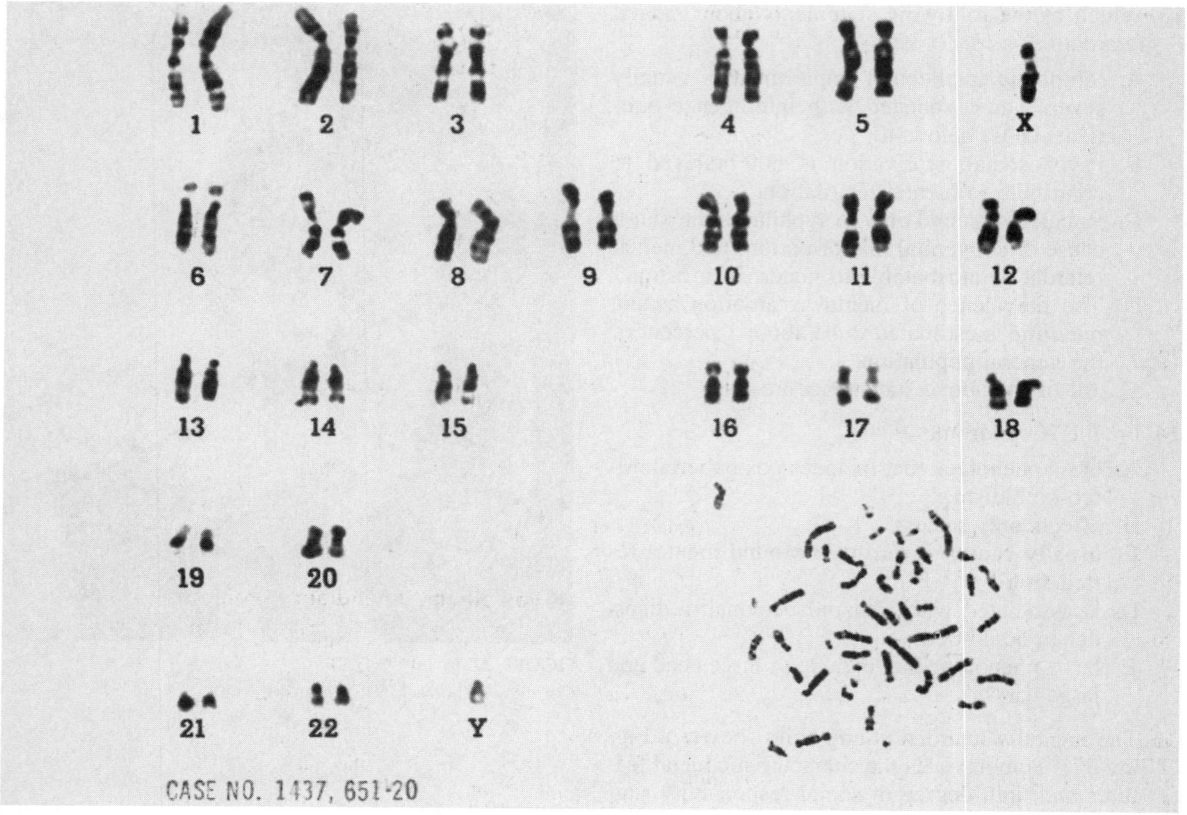

CASE NO. 1437, 651-20

FIGURE 37.2
Courtesy of the Department of Genetics, New York State Psychiatric Institute.

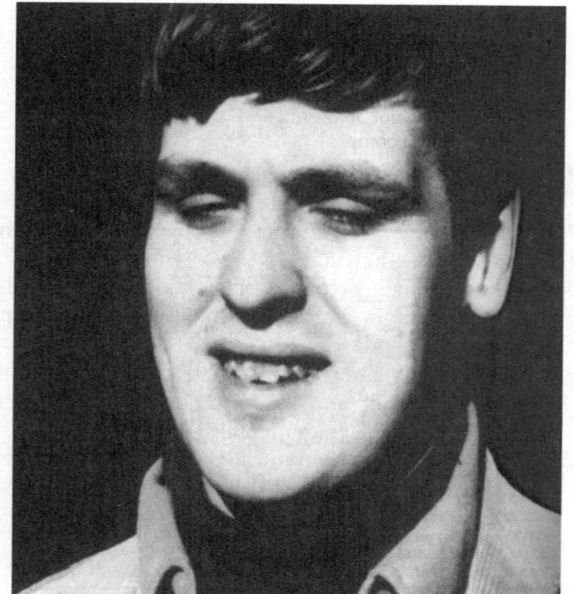

FIGURE 37.3
Courtesy of Ludwik S. Szymanski, M.D.

Questions 37.23–37.27

A. Phenylketonuria (PKU)
B. Rett's disorder
C. Acquired immune deficiency syndrome (AIDS)
D. Rubella
E. Cytomegalic inclusion disease

37.23 Mental retardation with cerebral calcifications, jaundice, microcephaly, and hepatosplenomegaly

37.24 Progressive encephalopathy and mental retardation

37.25 An X-linked mental retardation syndrome that is degenerative and affects only females

37.26 Mental retardation, eczema, vomiting, and seizures

37.27 Mental retardation, microcephaly, microphthalmia, congenital heart disease, deafness, and cataracts

Questions 37.28–37.32

A. Hyperglycinemia
B. Histidinemia
C. Homocystinuria
D. Oculocerebrorenal dystrophy
E. Cystathioninuria

37.28 Cataracts
37.29 Severe ketosis
37.30 Positive ferric chloride test result
37.31 Treatment with pyridoxine
37.32 Patients resembling those with Marfan's syndrome

DIRECTIONS: Match the lettered level of mental retardation with the appropriate skills.

Questions 37.33–37.36

A. Mild
B. Moderate
C. Severe
D. Profound

37.33 These persons can benefit from training in social and occupational skills and are unlikely to progress beyond the second grade academically.
37.34 Some motor and speech development may be present, but persons in this category will always need some self-help care.
37.35 Persons in this group can learn to communicate and can profit from systematic behavioral training, although they do not usually develop vocational competence.
37.36 Persons in this group can usually learn academic skills approximately up to the sixth grade by their late teens and may eventually develop enough vocational skills to support themselves.

DIRECTIONS: Match the lettered mode of transmission and deficit with the appropriate disorder.

Questions 37.37–37.40

A. Prader-Willi syndrome
B. Down's syndrome
C. Fragile X syndrome
D. Phenylketonuria (PKU)

37.37 Theorized to be due to a deletion in chromosome 15
37.38 Autosomal recessive transmission, phenylalanine hydroxylase deficiency
37.39 Nondisjunction, translocation, or trisomy involving chromosome 21
37.40 Due to a mutation on the X chromosome at Xq27.3

ANSWERS

Mental Retardation

37.1 The answer is C (*Synopsis VIII,* page 1144).
Neurofibromatosis may manifest itself in the form of neurofibromas, café au lait spots, and seizures; optic and acoustic gliomas and bone lesions may also be present. Its form of genetic transmission is *autosomal dominant.*

37.2 The answer is C (*Synopsis VIII,* page 1144).
Tuberous sclerosis manifests itself as seizures, intracranial calcification, pink to brownish skin lesions, and possibly bone lesions. Its form of transmission is *autosomal dominant.*

37.3 The answer is C (*Synopsis VIII,* page 1142).
In *Crouzon's syndrome,* or craniofacial dysostosis, proptosis with shallow orbits, maxillary hypoplasia, and craniosynostosis are apparent. Its form of transmission is *autosomal dominant.*

37.4 The answer is D (*Synopsis VIII,* page 1142).
Cockayne's syndrome is manifested by hypotrichosis, photosensitivity, thin skin, diminished subcutaneous fat, and impaired hearing. The craniofacial area may show pinched facies, sunken eyes, thin nose, prognathism, and retinal degeneration. Skeletal abnormalities include long limbs with large hands and feet and flexion deformities. Its form of transmission is *autosomal recessive.*

Cerebral gigantism, Noonan's syndrome, and Williams syndrome are examples of disorders whose form of transmission is *unknown.* Down's syndrome exhibits *trisomy 21.* Aarskog-Scott syndrome has an *X-linked semidominant* form of transmission.

37.5 The answer is A (*Synopsis VIII,* page 1140).
Persons who *have only 45 chromosomes* do not exhibit the Down's phenotype but are asymptomatic carriers (parents and siblings) of the inherited disorder of translocation. In Down's syndrome, *patients have 46 chromosomes but have 3 of chromosome 21; 2, usually 21 and 15, are fused. Patients have 47 chromosomes with an extra chromosome 21* in trisomy 21, the most common chromosomal aberration in Down's syndrome. A nondisjunction during meiosis is thought to cause the disorder. The mothers' karyotypes are normal. *Patients have mosaicism, with normal and trisomic cells in various tissues,* when nondisjunction occurs after fertilization.

37.6 The answer is E (all) (*Synopsis VIII,* pages 1137–1138).
Persons with severe mental retardation have especially high rates of *autistic disorder* and other pervasive developmental disorders. About 2 to 3 percent of mentally retarded persons meet the diagnostic criteria for *schizophrenia;* that figure is several times greater than the figure for the general population. Up to half of all mentally retarded persons have *depressive disorders,* according to structured interviews and rating scales given to samples. The prevalence of depressive disorders in mentally retarded persons is not known, but it appears to be higher than in the general population. *Stereotypic movement disorder is* known to occur at a high rate in certain mental retardation syndromes (for example, Lesch-Nyhan syndrome) and is more prevalent in mentally retarded persons than in the general population.

37.7 The answer is D (*Synopsis VIII,* pages 1137–1140).
Borderline intellectual functioning is defined as an IQ between 71 and 84. It is not a category of mental retardation but results in some limitations that can become a focus of psychiatric intervention. The risk of psychopathology increases with *neurological impairments,* such as seizure disorders. Increased neurological impairment is frequently present with severe mental retardation, which also presents a risk factor for psychopathology.

Various known *genetic syndromes* (for example, fragile X syndrome, Prader-Willi syndrome, and Down's syndrome) have predictable aberrant behavioral components. People with fragile X syndrome have high rates (up to 75 percent) of attention-deficit/hyperactivity disorder and language dysfunction. Prader-Willi syndrome is almost always associated with hyperphagia and obesity, often along with oppositional defiant disorder; temper tantrums, irritability, and poor socialization skills seem to characterize persons with the syndrome in adolescence. In Down's syndrome, language function is relatively weak compared with social skills and interpersonal engagement. A variety of mental disorders occur in persons with Down's syndrome, but pervasive developmental disorders are lower in that population than in other groups of mentally retarded persons.

Family dysfunctions, leading to an inability to provide a supportive home environment for mentally retarded persons, may exacerbate their already frustrating interactions with society. A lack of appropriate expectations and support may further increase vulnerability in a mentally retarded person, leading to an increase in anxiety, anger, dysphoria, and depression.

Communication limitations result in chronic frustration and may increase the negative self-image and poor self-esteem that many mentally retarded persons exhibit. Persons who have trouble communicating often withdraw and become isolated and depressed.

37.8 The answer is E (all) (*Synopsis VIII,* page 1146).
The children of mothers affected with rubella may present with a number of abnormalities, including *congenital heart disease,* mental retardation, *deafness, cataracts, microcephaly,* and microphthalmia. Timing is crucial, as the extent and the frequency of the complications are inversely related to the duration of pregnancy at the time of the maternal infection. When mothers are infected in the first trimester of pregnancy, 10 to 15 percent of the children are affected, but the incidence rises to almost 50 percent when the infection occurs in the first month of pregnancy. The situation is often complicated by subclinical forms of maternal infection, which often go undetected. Maternal rubella can be prevented by immunization.

37.9 The answer is D (*Synopsis VIII,* page 1150).
Profoundly retarded preschool-age children require nursing care that they are able to get with *constant aid and supervision only.* Children who have the capacity to respond to *social and*

communicative skills training are considered mildly retarded. Children who are able to profit from *training in self-help* and *motor development training* are categorized as moderately or mildly retarded.

37.10 The answer is D (*Synopsis VIII,* page 1140).
Meiotic nondisjunction of chromosome 21 not only produces the majority of cases of Down's syndrome—almost 85 percent—but also has been most closely linked to advancing maternal age. Paternal age has also been implicated as a factor in some studies.

Translocation events, by contrast, constitute only 5 percent of Down's syndrome cases. Furthermore, in many cases in which an asymptomatic parent carries the aberrant chromosome in the genotype, the incidence of Down's syndrome is obviously unrelated to parental age. If the *translocation* occurs *between chromosome 14 and chromosome 21* (14/21), the proband carries 46 chromosomes, including 2 normal 21 chromosomes, 1 normal 14 chromosome, and the 14/21 translocation, which carries parts of both chromosomes. Any asymptomatic parent or sibling who is a carrier of the translocation has only 45 chromosomes, missing 1 chromosome 21 and thus being spared the excessive genetic complement.

Mitotic nondisjunction of chromosome 21, which occurs in 1 percent of all Down's syndrome cases, occurs after fertilization of a presumably healthy ovum and may thus be considered independent of maternal age. *Partially trisomic karyotype* may refer to the mosaicism—some cells normal, others with trisomy 21—seen in mitotic nondisjunction or to the excessive complement of chromosome 21 produced by translocation. Neither case is as closely tied to maternal age as is meiotic nondisjunction.

37.11 The answer is D (*Synopsis VIII,* pages 1137–1139).
An *extra chromosome 21 (trisomy 21)* is the most common genetic abnormality found in Down's syndrome and the abnormality most likely to cause mental retardation. Abnormalities in autosomal chromosomes are, in general, associated with mental retardation. The chromosomal aberration represented by 46 chromosomes with *fusion of chromosomes 21 and 15* produces a type of Down's syndrome that unlike trisomy 21, is usually inherited. Aberrations in sex chromosomes are not always associated with mental retardation, for example, *XO (Turner's syndrome), XXY (Klinefelter's syndrome)* and *XXYY* and XXXY (*Klinefelter's syndrome variations*). Some children with Turner's syndrome have normal to superior intelligence.

In Turner's syndrome one sex chromosome is missing (XO). The result is an absence (agenesis) or minimal development (dysgenesis) of the gonads; no significant sex hormone, male or female, is produced in fetal life or postnatally. The sexual tissues thus retain a female resting state. Because the second X chromosome, which seems responsible for full femaleness, is missing, the affected girls are incomplete in their sexual anatomy and, lacking adequate estrogens, develop no secondary sex characteristics without treatment. They often have other stigmata, such as web neck.

In Klinefelter's syndrome, the person (usually XXY) has a male habitus, under the influence of the Y chromosome, but that effect is weakened by the presence of the second X chromosome. Although born with a penis and testes, the child has small and infertile testes, and the penis may also be small. In adolescence, some patients begin to show gynecomastia and other feminine-appearing contours.

37.12 The answer is C (*Synopsis VIII,* page 1137).
Mental retardation should be diagnosed when the intelligence quotient (IQ) falls below *70.* According to the fourth edition of *Diagnostic and Statistical Manual of Mental Disorders* (DSM-IV), the following classification of mental retardation is used: mild (IQ 50–55 to approximately 70), moderate (IQ 35–40 to 50–55), severe (IQ 20–25 to 35–40), and profound (IQ below 20 or 25). Table 37.1 lists the diagnostic criteria for mental retardation.

37.13 The answer is D (*Synopsis VIII,* page 1137).
The prevalence of mental retardation at any one time is estimated to be about 1 percent of the population. Persons with profound mental retardation—intelligence quotient (IQ) below 20 or 25—constitute 1 to 2 percent of the mentally retarded population; mild cases (IQ 50–55 to approximately 70) make up 85 percent; moderate retardation (IQ 35–40 to 50–55), 10 percent; and severe retardation (IQ 20–25 to 35–40), 3 to 4 percent. The level of intellectual impairment of persons with no known cause (for example, *idiopathic intellectual impairment) is usually mild and associated with IQs between 50 and 70.* No specific biological cause of mental retardation can be found in 75 percent of cases. *Psychosocial* (social, linguistic, intellectual) *deprivation has been believed to contribute to idiopathic mental retardation. Rubella has surpassed syphilis as the major cause of congenital malformations and mental retardation attributable to maternal infection.*

37.14 The answer is E (*Synopsis VIII,* page 1140).
Fragile X syndrome *has a phenotype that includes a large*

Table 37.1
DSM-IV Diagnostic Criteria for Mental Retardation

A. Significantly subaverage intellectual functioning: an IQ of approximately 70 or below on an individually administered IQ test (for infants, a clinical judgment of significantly subaverage intellectual functioning).

B. Concurrent deficits or impairments in present adaptive functioning (ie, the person's effectiveness in meeting the standards expected for his or her age by his or her cultural group) in at least two of the following areas: communication, self-care, home living, social/interpersonal skills, use of community resources, self-direction, functional academic skills, work, leisure, health, and safety.

C. The onset is before age 18 years.

Code based on degree of severity reflecting level of intellectual impairment:

Mild mental retardation: IQ level 50–55 to approximately 70
Moderate mental retardation: IQ level 35–40 to 50–55
Severe mental retardation: IQ level 20–25 to 35–40
Profound mental retardation: IQ level below 20 or 25
Mental retardation, severity unspecified: when there is strong presumption of mental retardation but the person's intelligence is untestable by standard tests

head and large ears, long and narrow face, short stature, and *postpubertal macro-orchidism, not micro-orchidism.* The syndrome affects both males and females. Female carriers are usually less impaired than males but can manifest the typical physical characteristics and mild mental retardation. In males the syndrome usually causes *low average intelligence to severe mental retardation (not severe to profound mental retardation). The syndrome is associated with antisocial, not schizoid, personality disorder in adulthood.* Those affected by the syndrome may also have attention-deficit/hyperactivity disorder and learning disorders.

37.15 The answer is C (*Synopsis VIII,* pages 1140–1142).
Causative factors in mental retardation include genetic (chromosomal and inherited) conditions, prenatal exposure to infections and toxins, perinatal trauma (such as prematurity), acquired conditions, and sociocultural factors. The child in the photograph demonstrates the characteristic facial features (including slanted eyes, midface depression, and flat nose) and high degree of social responsivity characteristic of Down's syndrome. In the overwhelming majority of cases, the etiology of Down's syndrome is an *abnormality of chromosome number known as trisomy 21* (three of chromosome 21 instead of the usual two).

Autosomal dominant inheritance as the etiology of mental retardation is demonstrated in tuberous sclerosis, characterized by a progressive mental retardation in up to two-thirds of cases, as well as seizures and other abnormalities. *Prenatal substance exposure* as the etiology of mental retardation is demonstrated in fetal alcohol syndrome, which occurs in up to 15 percent of babies born to women who regularly ingest large amounts of alcohol. *Enzyme deficiency* as the etiology of mental retardation is demonstrated in phenylketonuria (PKU). The basic metabolic defect in PKU is an ability to convert phenylalanine, an essential amino acid, to paratyrosine because of absence or inactivity of the liver enzyme phenylalanine hydroxylase. *Abnormality in sex chromosomes* as the etiology of mental retardation is demonstrated in fragile X syndrome, the second most common cause of mental retardation, which results from a mutation on the X chromosome at what is known as the fragile site.

37.16 The answer is E (*Synopsis VIII,* page 1140).
The figure shows a normal karyotype of a male. The overwhelming majority of cases of Down's syndrome are the result of trisomy 21 (three of chromosome 21 instead of the usual two). *A nondisjunction during meiosis, not mitosis,* is responsible for trisomy 21, and the *mother's karyotypes are normal. A minority of cases of Down's syndrome are the result of nondisjunction occurring after fertilization in any cell division, resulting in mosaicism, or due to translocation involving fusion of two chromosomes, mostly 21 and 15.*

The overriding feature of Down's syndrome is mental retardation, which, according to the DSM-IV diagnostic criteria, is characterized by an IQ of approximately 70 or below. *The majority of patients with Down's syndrome belong to the moderately and severely retarded groups, with only a minority having an IQ above 50.* Down's syndrome has a characteristic physical phenotype, which may include such features as upward slanting palpebral fissures, midface depression, epincanthic folds and brachycephaly (a disproportionate shortness of the head), *not microcephaly.*

37.17 The answer is E (*Synopsis VIII,* pages 1140–1141).
The figure shows a young adult with fragile X syndrome, the second most common single cause of mental retardation after trisomy 21, the predominant form of Down's syndrome. Fragile X syndrome results from a mutation on the X chromosome at what is known as the fragile site. Both genetic and phenotypic expression vary widely. The typical phenotype includes a large, long head and short ears, short stature, hyperextensible joints, and postpubertal macro-orchidism. The degree of mental retardation ranges from mild to severe.

The physical phenotype of *Down's syndrome* includes oblique palpebral fissures, high cheekbones, protruding tongue, single palmar transversal crease, and a number of other associated features, such as congenital heart disease (40 percent) and gastrointestinal malformations (12 percent). *Prader-Willi syndrome,* postulated to be the result of a small deletion involving chromosome 15, is characterized by mental retardation, compulsive eating behavior, and often obesity, hypogonadism, small stature, hypotonia, and small hands and feet. *Fetal alcohol syndrome* consists of mental retardation and a typical phenotypic picture of facial dysmorphism that includes hypertelorism, microcephaly, short palpebral fissures, inner epicanthal folds and a short, turned-up nose. *Klinefelter's syndrome* is an intersex condition with XXY genotype, characterized by a male habitus with a small penis and rudimentary testes because of low androgen production. Some patients develop gynecomastia in adolescence and many patients have a wide variety of psychopathology, ranging from emotional instability to mental retardation.

Answers 37.18–37.22

37.18 The answer is B (*Synopsis VIII,* page 1141).

37.19 The answer is E (*Synopsis VIII,* page 1144).

37.20 The answer is D (*Synopsis VIII,* pages 1146–1147).

37.21 The answer is A (*Synopsis VIII,* pages 1140–1141).

37.22 The answer is C (*Synopsis VIII,* page 1140).
In *Prader-Willi syndrome, compulsive eating behavior, obesity,* and *hypogonadism* are common. *Small stature,* along with small hands and feet, usually accompanies the syndrome. Lesch-Nyhan syndrome is characterized by severe *compulsive self-mutilation by biting of the mouth and the fingers,* microcephaly, mental retardation, seizures, and choreoathetosis. Children with *fetal alcohol syndrome* exhibit a characteristic phenotype consisting of *microcephaly, hypertelorism, short palpebral fissures,* inner epicanthal folds, and a short, turned-up nose. Children with fetal alcohol syndrome are at risk for *attention-deficit/hyperactivity disorder and learning disorders.* Persons with *fragile X syndrome* typically have *long heads and ears, short stature, hyperextensible joints, postpubertal macro-orchidism, and a risk of pervasive developmental disorders,* including autistic disorder. *Down's syndrome* is characterized by *a marked deterioration in language, memory, self-care, and problem-solving abilities in the patient's 30s.*

Answers 37.23–37.27

37.23 The answer is E (*Synopsis VIII,* page 1146).

37.24 The answer is C (*Synopsis VIII,* page 1140).

37.25 The answer is B (*Synopsis VIII,* page 1144).

37.26 The answer is A (*Synopsis VIII,* pages 1141, 1144).

37.27 The answer is D (*Synopsis VIII,* page 1143).
Infants who are exposed to *cytomegalic inclusion disease* in utero may be stillborn; when they are born alive, they may have *mental retardation with intracerebral calcifications, jaundice, microcephaly, and hepatosplenomegaly.* Fetuses whose mothers have *acquired immune deficiency syndrome* (*AIDS*) often die in spontaneous abortions. Children born with AIDS often die within a few years, and up to half of them have *progressive encephalopathy and mental retardation. Rett's disorder* is believed to be *an X-linked* dominant *mental retardation syndrome that is degenerative and affects only females. Phenylketonuria (PKU)* is a recessive autosomal disease in which the patient is unable to metabolize phenylalanine. Children with PKU often present with *mental retardation, eczema, vomiting, and seizures. Rubella* in a pregnant woman is a serious risk factor for the fetus. The risk of fetal impairment is greatest when the exposure is early in the first trimester. *Mental retardation, microcephaly, microphthalmia, congenital heart disease, deafness, and cataracts* can result.

Answers 37.28–37.32

37.28 The answer is D (*Synopsis VIII,* pages 1142–1143).

37.29 The answer is A (*Synopsis VIII,* pages 1142–1143).

37.30 The answer is B (*Synopsis VIII,* pages 1142–1143).

37.31 The answer is E (*Synopsis VIII,* pages 1142–1143).

37.32 The answer is C (*Synopsis VIII,* pages 1142–1143).
Hyperglycinemia is an autosomal recessive inborn error of metabolism in which large amounts of glycine are found in body fluids. It appears in ketotic and nonketotic forms. The clinical picture includes severe mental retardation, seizures, spasticity, and failure to thrive. Ketotic hyperglycinemia is characterized by *severe ketosis* secondary to blood elevation of several amino acids. The clinical picture includes seizures, mental retardation, vomiting, dehydration, ketosis, and coma.

Histidinemia, which is characterized by a defect in the histidine metabolism, is transmitted by a single autosomal recessive gene and involves a block in the conversion of histidine to urocanic acid. The urine gives a *positive ferric chloride test result* (green). Mild mental retardation and sometimes speech defects are part of the clinical picture.

Homocystinuria comprises a group of inborn errors of metabolism, each of which may lead to the accumulation of homocysteine. The *patients* are mentally retarded and *resemble those with Marfan's syndrome* in outward appearance.

Oculocerebrorenal dystrophy (Lowe's syndrome), a sex-linked disorder, presents a varied clinical picture that includes buphthalmos, microphthalmos, *cataracts,* and corneal opacities. Renal ammonia production is decreased, and a generalized aminoaciduria is found.

Cystathioninuria is marked by a metabolic defect that consists of a block at the site of cleavage of cystathionine to cysteine and homoserine. Patients with this disease are mentally retarded. Prolonged *treatment with pyridoxine* may improve the patient's intellectual performance.

Answers 37.33–37.36

37.33 The answer is B (*Synopsis VIII,* page 1150).

37.34 The answer is D (*Synopsis VIII,* page 1150).

37.35 The answer is C (*Synopsis VIII,* page 1150).

37.36 The answer is A (*Synopsis VIII,* page 1150).
The diagnosis of *mental retardation* is based on a standardized measure of intellectual capacity in the below average range as well as concurrent impairments in present adaptive functioning. Adaptive functioning includes communication, self-care, home living, social and interpersonal skills, use of community resources, self-direction, academic skills, and work. Persons with *mild* mental retardation have an IQ of 50–55 to 70. Very young children with mild mental retardation are often difficult to distinguish from normal children, since social and communication skills can develop at variable rates within the normal population. As they get older, it becomes clearer that they are not keeping up with their peers in terms of academic and social skills. *Moderate* mental retardation ranges from IQ levels of 35–40 to 50–55. In this group, speech and social communication is developed but social awareness tends to be poor, and children in this category generally require self-help training. *Severe* mental retardation denotes an IQ level of 20–25 to 35–40. Children with severe mental retardation can learn to speak and communicate but continue to need additional help with self-help and safety skills. *Profound* mental retardation is associated with IQ levels below 20 or 25. Young children with profound mental retardation have some motor development and may develop some speech by the time they reach adulthood. These patients need constant supervision and some nursing care throughout life.

Answers 37.37–37.40

37.37 The answer is A (*Synopsis VIII,* page 1141).

37.38 The answer is D (*Synopsis VIII,* page 1141).

37.39 The answer is B (*Synopsis VIII,* page 1140).

37.40 The answer is C (*Synopsis VIII,* pages 1140–1141).
Prader-Willi syndrome, which appears to be the result of a small *deletion in chromosome 15,* usually occurs sporadically. Its prevalence is less than 1 in 10,000. It has predictable manifestations, including compulsive eating behaviors, obesity, often mental retardation, hypogonadism, hypotonia, and small stature. Disruptive behavior, including oppositional and defiant behavior and temper tantrums, are said to be common. Several chromosomal aberrations may result in Down's syndrome. *Trisomy* 21 is the most frequent chromosomal aberration, believed to occur due to a *nondisjunction during meiosis. Nondisjunction after fertilization* in any cell division results in mosaicism, in which both normal and trisomic cells can be found. In *translocation,* mostly of chromosomes 15 and 21, there is a fusion of 2 chromosomes, resulting in a total of 46 chromosomes,

despite the presence of an extra chromosome 21. *Fragile X syndrome* is the second most common single cause of mental retardation. It results from a *mutation on the X chromosome* at the fragile site (Xq27.3). The fragile site is expressed in only some cells, and it may be absent in asymptomatic males and female carriers. There is much variation in both the genetic and phenotypic expression. It occurs in about 1 per 1,000 males and 1 per 2,000 females. Behaviorally, those with fragile X syndrome often have attentional problems, pervasive developmental disorders, and other learning disorders. Intellectual function seems to deteriorate in adolescence in persons with fragile X syndrome. *Phenylketonuria,* which is transmitted as an autosomal recessive trait, occurs in approximately 1 per 10,000 births. The defect transmitted is an inability to convert phenylalanine, an essential amino acid, to paratyrosine due to absence or *inactivity of the liver enzyme* phenylalanine hydroxylase. The majority of patients with PKU are severely retarded, but some have borderline or normal intelligence. Eczema, vomiting, and seizures are present in about one third of cases. Early diagnosis is important, as a low-phenylalanine diet significantly improves both behavior and developmental progress.

38 

Learning Disorders

Learning disorders are academic skill deficiencies that consist of below-expected abilities in specific areas such as reading, arithmetic, and written expression. Reading disorder is a relatively common occurrence estimated to occur in approximately 4 percent of school children. It is 3 to 4 times as common in boys as in girls, but by adulthood, there seems to be an equal number of men and women who persist with reading disorder. Mathematics disorder is roughly estimated to occur in up to 6 percent of school children who are of normal intelligence. There is some evidence to suggest that children with mathematics disorder are likely to exhibit another learning disorder or language disorder. The sex ratio is not well documented, but mathematics disorder may be more common in females. Disorder of written expression is characterized by writing skills that are significantly below the expected level for a child's age and intellectual capacity. The prevalence is estimated to be 3 to 10 percent of school-age children. Written expression may partially depend on other skills, including those related to expressive language, receptive skills, and reading skills.

Reading disorder includes impaired ability to recognize words, poor comprehension, inaccurate reading, and low level of reading skill in the presence of normal intelligence. Prevalent studies have identified 2 to 8 percent of children with reading disorder, leading to an estimate of 4 percent of school-age children. Some 3 to 4 times as many boys as girls have reading disorder, which is diagnosed only when no sensory deficit or neurological condition accounts for the reading disability. In the past the term *dyslexia* was used for a syndrome including reading disability and speech and language deficits. When it became known that reading disorder often occurs along with other academic skill disorders, the term *learning disorders* began to be used.

Mathematics disorder is characterized by a disability in performing arithmetic skills that are expected for the child's age, given normal intelligence. According to the fourth edition of *Diagnostic and Statistical Manual of Mental Disorders* (DSM-IV), mathematics disorder interferes with school performance, and the impairment is in excess of any sensory deficit present. The prevalence of mathematics disorder is not known, but it is estimated to occur in 6 percent of school-age children with normal intelligence. Mathematics disorder often occurs in conjunction with other learning disorders, such as reading disorder and disorder of written expression, and with developmental coordination disorder.

Mathematics disorder includes impairment in a variety of related skills, including linguistic (converting written problems into mathematical symbols), perceptual (understanding mathematical symbols and ordering clusters of numbers), arithmetic (addition, subtraction, multiplication, and division), and attentional (copying figures and observing operational symbols correctly) skills. It is usually apparent by age 8 years, and remediation is most useful when offered immediately after diagnosis. Individual attention given to the child to strengthen the specific weaknesses is most useful.

Disorder of written expression, also known as developmental expressive writing disorder, is characterized by writing skills significantly below those expected for the person's age and intellectual capacity. The skills can be measured by a standardized test. This disorder includes poor spelling, errors in grammar and punctuation, and poor handwriting. In the past it was assumed that writing disabilities did not occur in the absence of a reading disorder, but it is now known that disorder of written expression can develop on its own.

Learning disorder not otherwise specified is for learning disorders that do not meet the diagnostic criteria for any of these specific disorders but that cause impairment in academic performance. For example, the diagnosis is made when spelling skills are markedly below the expected performance in a child of normal intelligence.

Students should study Chapter 38 in *Kaplan and Sadock's Synopsis VIII* for additional information on learning disorders and then turn to the questions and answers below.

HELPFUL HINTS

The student should define these terms related to learning disorders.

- ▶ academic skills disorders
- ▶ dyslexia
- ▶ hearing and vision screening
- ▶ phoneme
- ▶ right-left confusion
- ▶ spatial relations
- ▶ visual-perceptual deficits
- ▶ word additions
- ▶ word distortions
- ▶ word omissions

▲ QUESTIONS

DIRECTIONS: For each of the following numbered syndromes, choose the correct lettered choice. A lettered choice can be used once, more than once, or not at all.

Questions 38.1–38.4

A. Reading disorder
B. Disorder of written expression
C. Both of the above

38.1 This disorder tends to be more prevalent among family members of persons who have the disorder.
38.2 This disorder may result from the combined effects of several disorders.
38.3 Children with this disorder tend to have dyslexia.
38.4 There are 3 times as many boys as girls diagnosed with this disorder.

Questions 38.5–38.8

A. Reading disorder
B. Mathematics disorder
C. Both of the above

38.5 This disorder often coexists with other learning disorders.
38.6 This disorder is related to communication disorders.
38.7 When not remediated, this disorder is associated with poor self-concept and depression.
38.8 This disorder affects an estimated 4 percent of school-age children.

DIRECTIONS: Each of these questions or incomplete statements is followed by five suggested responses or completions. Select the *one* that is *best* in each case.

38.9 Reading disorder is characterized by all of the following *except*

A. impairment in recognizing words
B. poor reading comprehension
C. increased prevalence among family members
D. occurrence in 3 to 4 times as many girls as boys
E. omissions, additions, and distortions of words in oral reading

38.10 Which of the following does *not* characterize mathematics disorder?

A. More common in boys than in girls
B. Prevalence estimated to be about 6 percent in school-age children with normal intelligence
C. Includes impairment in addition, subtraction, multiplication, and division
D. Usually apparent by the time a child is 8 years old
E. Often found in children with reading disorder

38.11 Disorder of written expression

A. presents earlier than do reading disorder and communication disorders
B. occurs only in children with reading disorder
C. is not diagnosed until the teenage years
D. includes disability in spelling, grammar, and punctuation
E. is always self-limited

38.12 Janet, 13 years old, had a long history of school problems. She failed first grade, supposedly because her teacher was ''mean,'' and was removed from a special classroom because she kept getting into fights with the other children. Currently in a normal sixth-grade classroom, she was failing reading and barely passing English and spelling but doing satisfactory work in art and sports. Her teacher described Janet as a ''slow learner with a poor memory'' and stated that Janet did not learn in a group setting and required a great deal of individual attention.

Janet's medical history was unremarkable except for a tonsillectomy at age 5 years and an early history of chronic otitis. She sat up at 6 months, walked at 12 months, and began talking at 18 months. An examination revealed an open and friendly girl who was touchy about her academic problems. She stated that she was ''bossed around'' at school but had good friends in the neighborhood. Intelligence testing revealed a full-scale intelligence quotient of 97. Wide-range achievement testing produced grade-level scores of 4.8 for reading, 5.3 for spelling, and 6.3 for arithmetic.

The most likely diagnosis is

A. disorder of written expression
B. expressive language disorder
C. phonological disorder
D. reading disorder
E. none of the above

38.13 Disorder of written expression is often associated with

A. reading disorder
B. mixed expressive-receptive language disorder
C. developmental coordination disorder
D. mathematics disorder
E. all of the above

DIRECTIONS: The questions below consist of five lettered headings followed by a list of numbered statements. For each numbered statement, select the *one* lettered heading that is most closely associated with it. Each lettered heading may be selected once, more than once, or not at all.

Questions 38.14–38.17

A. Reading disorder
B. Mathematics disorder
C. Disorder of written expression
D. Learning disorder not otherwise specified

38.14 Used to be known as dyslexia
38.15 Spelling skills deficit an example
38.16 Usually diagnosed later than the other learning disorders
38.17 Reported to occur frequently in children born in May, June, and July

ANSWERS

Learning Disorders

38.1 The answer is C (*Synopsis VIII,* pages 1157, 1161).

38.2 The answer is B (*Synopsis VIII,* page 1161).

38.3 The answer is C (*Synopsis VIII,* pages 1155, 1160–1161).

38.4 The answer is A (*Synopsis VIII,* page 1157).
Reading disorder and disorder of written expression are both found to be more prevalent in family members of those who have these disorders. The disorder of written expression may include elements of reading disorder. Although a hereditary predisposition has been hypothesized, this relationship has not yet been documented by twin studies. *There seems to be a relationship between the disorder of written expression and several other deficiencies.* These additional deficits may occur in expressive language, mixed receptive-expressive deficits, reading disorder, and possibly deficits in short-term memory, attention, and freedom from distractibility. Many of these are components of communication disorders. *Dyslexia* originally denoted a syndrome that consisted of a disability in reading mixed with a number of other problems, such as speech and language deficits, and right-left confusion. *Dyslexia actually means a deficit in the ability to read, which is obviously the case in reading disorder, but it is also often the case in the disorder of written expression. Reading disorder has been found to be approximately 3 times as common in boys as in girls.* The disorder of written expression appears to be as common as reading disorder, although the actual male-to-female ratio is unknown.

38.5 The answer is C (*Synopsis VIII,* pages 1155, 1159).

38.6 The answer is C (*Synopsis VIII,* pages 1157, 1159).

38.7 The answer is C (*Synopsis VIII,* pages 1157–1158, 1159).

38.8 The answer is A (*Synopsis VIII,* page 1155).
Both reading disorder and mathematics disorder often coexist with other learning disorders. Among the common comorbid learning disorders with mathematics disorder are reading disorder, expressive writing deficits, coordination, spelling problems, and deficits in memory or attention. *Reading disorder seems to have an increased probability of coexisting with a communication disorder.* Thus, both mathematics disorder and the disorder of written expression appear to have a relationship with communication disorders. Both reading disorder and mathematics are basic building blocks on which rests academic success. When either of these skills is deficient and not remediated, it can affect a child's entire level of success in school. School is the main occupation and daily life of every child, and thus it is exceedingly common for children with reading disorder or the disorder of written communication to become demoralized and feel helpless and depressed. *When remediation is introduced, there is a greater sense of hope and the potential for success.* Self-esteem can be repaired when a child believes that his or her problem is not hopeless. *Reading disorder is estimated to affect approximately 4 percent of the school age population who are of normal intelligence.* The prevalence of mathematics disorder is not as well studied, and it can only be roughly estimated to be 6 percent.

38.9 The answer is D (*Synopsis VIII,* pages 1155–1156).
Reading disorder is reported to *occur in 3 to 4 times as many boys as girls.* The rate of reading disorder in boys may be inflated, since boys with reading disorder are more likely to have behavioral problems than are girls, and the boys may be identified initially for their behavioral problems. Reading disorder is characterized by *impairment in recognizing words,* slow and inaccurate reading, and *poor reading comprehension.* Reading achievement is below that expected for the person's age, as measured by standardized tests (Table 38.1). Although no unitary cause of reading disorder is known, it appears to have *increased prevalence among family members,* leading to the speculation that it has a genetic origin. Children with reading disorder make *omissions, additions, and distortions of words in oral reading.* The children may have difficulty in distinguishing printed letter characters and sizes, especially letters that differ only in spatial orientation and length of line.

38.10 The answer is A (*Synopsis VIII,* page 1159).
Unlike reading disorder, in which the rate in boys is reported to be 3 to 4 times the rate in girls, the sex ratio for mathematics disorder has yet to be determined. In fact, mathematics disorder may be *more common in girls than in boys.* The *prevalence* of mathematics disorder is *estimated to be about 6 percent* in school-age children with normal intelligence. Mathematics disorder *includes impairment in addition, subtraction, multiplication, and division.* Mathematics disorder is *usually apparent by the time a child is 8 years old,* although in some children it may present as early as 6 years of age or as late as 10 years of age. Mathematics disorder is *often found in children with reading disorder.* Table 38.2 lists the diagnostic criteria for mathematics disorder.

Table 38.1
DSM-IV Diagnostic Criteria for Reading Disorder

A. Reading achievement, as measured by individually administered standardized tests of reading accuracy or comprehension, is substantially below that expected given the person's chronological age, measured intelligence, and age-appropriate education.

B. The disturbance in criterion A significantly interferes with academic achievement or activities of daily living that require reading skills.

C. If a sensory deficit is present, the reading difficulties are in excess of those usually associated with it.

Coding note: If a general medical (eg, neurological) condition or sensory deficit is present, code the condition on Axis III.

Table 38.2
DSM-IV Diagnostic Criteria for Mathematics Disorder

A. Mathematical ability, as measured by individually administered standardized tests, is substantially below that expected given the person's chronological age, measured intelligence, and age-appropriate education.
B. The disturbance in criterion A significantly interferes with academic achievement or activities of daily living that require mathematical ability.
C. If a sensory deficit is present, the difficulties in mathematical ability are in excess of those usually associated with it.

Coding note: If a general medical (eg, neurological) condition or sensory deficit is present, code the condition on Axis III.

Reprinted with permission from American Psychiatric Association: *Diagnostic and Statistical Manual of Mental Disorders,* ed 4. Copyright, American Psychiatric Association, Washington, 1994.

Table 38.3
DSM-IV Diagnostic Criteria for Disorder of Written Expression

A. Writing skills, as measured by individually administered standardized tests (or functional assessments of writing skills), are substantially below those expected given the person's chronological age, measured intelligence, and age-appropriate education.
B. The disturbance in criterion A significantly interferes with academic achievement or activities of daily living that require the composition of written texts (eg, writing grammatically correct sentences and organized paragraphs).
C. If a sensory deficit is present, the difficulties in writing skills are in excess of those usually associated with it.

Coding note: If a general medical (eg, neurological) condition or sensory deficit is present, code the condition on Axis III.

Reprinted with permission from American Psychiatric Association: *Diagnostic and Statistical Manual of Mental Disorders,* ed 4. Copyright,

38.11 The answer is D (*Synopsis VIII,* page 1161).
Disorder of written expression *includes disability in spelling, grammar, and punctuation marks.* The disorder is characterized by writing skills that are significantly below the expected level for the child's age and intelligence, as measured by a standardized test (Table 38.3). Because a child normally speaks well before learning to read and reads well before learning to write, *disorder of written expression presents later than do reading disorder and communication disorders.* Disorder of written expression can occur in children without reading disorder. The disorder *is diagnosed in the early school years, not the teenage years,* and it *is not self-limited.*

38.12 The answer is D (*Synopsis VIII,* pages 1155–1159).
The most likely diagnosis for Janet is *reading disorder.* Reading disorder is characterized by marked impairment in the development of word recognition skills and reading comprehension that cannot be explained by mental retardation, inadequate schooling, visual or hearing defect, or a neurological disorder. Reading-disordered children make many errors in their oral reading, including omissions, additions, and distortions of words. Janet's difficulties were apparently limited to reading and spelling. She had average intelligence and normal scores on achievement tests of arithmetic but markedly low scores for spelling and reading.

Disorder of written expression is characterized by poor performance in writing and composition. *Expressive language disorder* is characterized by marked impairment in age-appropriate expressive language. *Phonological disorder* is characterized by frequent and recurrent misarticulations of speech sounds, resulting in abnormal speech. The case described does not meet the criteria for any of these disorders.

38.13 The answer is E (all) (*Synopsis VIII,* page 1161).
Reading disorder, mixed expressive-receptive language disorder, developmental coordination disorder, mathematics disorder, and disruptive behavior disorders are often associated with disorder of written expression. The ability to transfer one's thoughts into written words and sentences requires multimodal sensorimotor coordination and information processing. Disorder of written expression is an academic skills disorder that first occurs during childhood and is characterized by poor performance in writing and composition (spelling words and expressing thoughts).

Answers 38.14–38.17

38.14 The answer is A (*Synopsis VIII,* page 1155).

38.15 The answer is D (*Synopsis VIII,* pages 1162–1163).

38.16 The answer is C (*Synopsis VIII,* page 1161).

38.17 The answer is A (*Synopsis VIII,* page 1157).
Reading disorder used to be known as dyslexia. It is *reported to occur frequently in children born in May, June, and July,* suggesting that reading disorder is linked to maternal winter infectious disease. *Disorder of written expression is usually diagnosed later than the other learning disorders,* since writing skills are acquired at a later age than are language reading skills. *Learning disorder not otherwise specified* is a category of learning disorders that covers disorders in learning that do not meet the criteria for any specific learning disorder. *Spelling skills deficit is an example. Mathematics disorder* includes deficits in linguistic skills related to understanding mathematical terms and converting written problems into mathematical symbols and perceptual skills (the ability to recognize and understand symbols and to order clusters of numbers).

39 Motor Skills Disorder

Motor skills disorder is a developmental coordination disorder characterized by imprecise or clumsy gross motor skills. Children with this disorder may also have clumsy fine motor skills, but they do not have a pervasive impairment in the gross motor area. They have normal intellectual capacity, but their poor coordination does cause impairment in daily functioning, especially with regard to social and academic demands. A child with developmental coordination disorder may have delays in achieving motor milestones such as sitting up, crawling, and walking. Developmental coordination disorder may also affect activities such as writing and produce a propensity to drop things. Children with this disorder sometimes resemble younger children in the way they function physically. Clumsiness in childhood has been associated with learning disorders, communication disorders, and disruptive behavior disorders. Children with developmental coordination disorder are commonly poor in sports, and they may be socially rejected on this basis. The prevalence of developmental coordination disorder has not been well studied but has been estimated to affect 6 percent of school-age children of normal intelligence. Reports of the male-to-female ratio have ranged from 2 to 1 to as much as 4 to 1.

The causes of developmental coordination disorder are unknown, but its risk factors include prematurity, hypoxia, perinatal malnutrition, and low birth weight. Neurochemical abnormalities and parietal lobe lesions may contribute to the disorder. Developmental coordination disorder and communication disorders are associated; both seem to be prevalent in children with short attention spans and impulsive behavior.

The diagnosis of developmental coordination disorder can be made by getting a history of the child's impairment in early motor skills and by direct observation of the child's motor skills. Informal screening can be done by asking the child to perform some gross and fine motor tasks. Gross motor skills can be assessed by asking the child to hop, jump, and stand on one foot. Fine motor coordination can be screened with such tasks as finger tapping, shoelace tying, and writing. Eye-hand coordination is often impaired in developmental coordination disorder; children with the disorder may have trouble catching a ball or copying figures. Standardized tests of motor coordination include the Bender Visual Motor Gestalt test and the Frostig Movement Skills Test Battery.

Developmental coordination disorder may be evident in infancy when a child is impaired or delayed in resulting motor milestones, but generally the disorder is first noticed after age 2 years. Affected children seem to drop objects frequently, trip over their own feet, and bump into things. In older children, impaired motor coordination may interfere with the ability to do puzzles, use building blocks, and play ball. Since physical skills, especially those used in sports, are important in everyday life among school-age children, children with poor coordination may become socially ostracized and demoralized.

No reliable data are available regarding the prognosis of children with developmental coordination disorder. Some children with above-average intelligence compensate for their disability by pursuing other activities that do not require good motor coordination. Treatment for developmental coordination disorder includes perceptual motor training, neurophysiological techniques of exercise for motor dysfunctioning, and modified physical education. Since peer relationship problems may lead to low self-esteem, unhappiness, and withdrawal, counseling is needed. Students should study Chapter 39 in *Kaplan and Sadock's Synopsis VIII* and then turn to the questions and answers below.

HELPFUL HINTS

The student should know the terms listed here.

- attention-deficit/hyperactivity disorder
- Bender Visual Motor Gestalt test
- Bruininks-Oseretsky Test of Motor Development
- catching a ball
- cerebral palsy
- clumsiness
- conduct disorder
- deficits in handwriting
- delayed motor milestones
- expressive language disorder
- eye-hand coordination
- fine motor skills
- finger tapping
- Frostig Movement Skills Test Battery
- gross motor skills
- informal motor skills screening
- learning disorders
- perceptual motor training
- shoelace tying
- social ostracism
- unsteady gait

▲ QUESTIONS

DIRECTIONS: Each of the questions or incomplete statements below is followed by five suggested responses or completions. Select the *one* that is *best* in each case.

39.1 Children with developmental coordination disorder generally have impairment in all of the following *except*

A. jumping
B. hopping on one foot
C. tying shoelaces
D. reading
E. catching a ball

39.2 Developmental coordination disorder is commonly associated with

A. expressive language disorder
B. attention-deficit/hyperactivity disorder
C. conduct disorder
D. social ostracism
E. all of the above

39.3 Which of the following is a risk factor for developmental coordination disorder?

A. Birth in May, June, or July
B. Borderline intellectual functioning
C. Female gender
D. Prematurity
E. Dysfunctional family

39.4 Which of the following statements is *false*?

A. Children with developmental coordination disorder may motorically resemble younger children.
B. Developmental coordination disorder is frequently seen in conjunction with a communication disorder.
C. The male-to-female ratio in developmental coordination disorder is estimated to be 2 to 1.
D. Prematurity, low birth weight, perinatal malnutrition, and hypoxia are all risk factors for developmental coordination disorder.
E. Developmental coordination disorder is usually due to a lesion in the parietal lobe of the brain.

39.5 Which of following signs and symptoms is *not* part of developmental coordination disorder?

A. Poor handwriting
B. Inability to catch a ball
C. High-arched palate
D. Poor balance
E. Delayed motor milestones

39.6 Which of the following tests is *not* helpful in demonstrating developmental coordination disorder?

A. Bender Gestalt Visual Motor test
B. Below-normal scores on the verbal subtests of the Wechsler Intelligence Scale for Children
C. Bruininks-Oseretsky Test of Motor Development
D. Frostig Movement Skills Test Battery

39.7 Which of the following treatments is *not* appropriate for developmental coordination disorder?

A. Physical education
B. Parental counseling
C. Montessori technique
D. Practicing motor movements
E. Learning to use the typewriter

ANSWERS

Motor Skills Disorder

39.1 The answer is D (*Synopsis VIII,* pages 1164–1165).
Developmental coordination disorder is not particularly associated with *reading* impairment. Children with developmental coordination disorder have disability in gross motor tasks, fine motor tasks, and tasks requiring eye-hand coordination. Among the gross motor tasks that may be impaired are *jumping* and *hopping on one foot.* Fine motor tasks that may be impaired include *tying shoelaces.* Tasks involving eye-hand coordination that may be impaired include *catching a ball.* The diagnostic criteria for developmental coordination disorder are listed in Table 39.1.

39.2 The answer is E (all) (*Synopsis VIII,* pages 1164–1165).
Developmental coordination disorder and communication disorders, such as *expressive language disorder,* are often associated, although the specific causative agents for both disorders are not known. Developmental coordination disorder also seems to be frequent in children with *attention-deficit/hyperactivity disorder* and *conduct disorder.* Children with developmental coordination disorder who are clumsy and inept in a variety of sports often experience *social ostracism,* which can lead to demoralization, social withdrawal, and ultimately dysphoria or depression.

39.3 The answer is D (*Synopsis VIII,* page 1164).
Risk factors for developmental coordination disorder include *prematurity.* Reading disorder, not developmental coordination disorder, has been reported to be frequent in children *born in May, June, or July,* suggesting a link between winter maternal infectious illness and the development of reading disorder.

Table 39.1
DSM-IV Diagnostic Criteria for Developmental Coordination Disorder

A. Performance in daily activities that require motor coordination is substantially below that expected given the person's chronological age and measured intelligence. This may be manifested by marked delays in achieving motor milestones (eg, walking, crawling, sitting), dropping things, "clumsiness," poor performance in sports, or poor handwriting.

B. The disturbance in criterion A significantly interferes with academic achievement or activities of daily living.

C. The disturbance is not due to a general medical condition (eg, cerebral palsy, hemiplegia, or muscular dystrophy) and does not meet criteria for a pervasive developmental disorder.

D. If mental retardation is present, the motor difficulties are in excess of those usually associated with it.

Coding note: If a general medical (eg, neurological) condition or sensory deficit is present, code the condition on Axis III.

Borderline intellectual functioning, an intelligence quotient (IQ) between 70 and 90, is not identified specifically as a risk factor for developmental coordination disorder. *Female gender* is not a risk factor for developmental coordination disorder, which is reported to occur in at least twice as many males as females. A *dysfunctional family* is not known to be a risk factor for developmental coordination disorder.

39.4 The answer is E (*Synopsis VIII,* pages 1164–1165).
Developmental coordination disorder is not usually due to a lesion in the parietal lobe of the brain, although parietal lobe lesions have been suggested as causes of the disorder. *Children with developmental coordination disorder may motorically resemble younger children. Developmental coordination disorder is frequently seen in conjunction with a communication disorder. The male-to-female ratio in developmental coordination disorder is estimated to be 2 to 1* and is estimated to occur in approximately 6 percent of school-age children of normal intelligence. Prematurity, low birth weight, perinatal malnutrition, and hypoxia are all *risk factors for developmental coordination disorder.*

39.5 The answer is C (*Synopsis VIII,* pages 1164–1165).
High-arched palate is a minor physical anomaly but is not usually associated with a developmental coordination disorder. Poor handwriting; poor abilities in sports, such as *inability to catch a ball; poor balance;* and *delayed motor milestones* are all typical of developmental coordination disorder. Children with developmental coordination disorder often have delays in achieving motor milestones, although they eventually do attain the milestones.

39.6 The answer is B (*Synopsis VIII,* pages 1164–1165).
Children with developmental coordination disorder do not generally have below-normal scores on the verbal subtest of the *WISC-III,* but they sometimes have below-normal scores on the performance subtests of the WISC-III. *The Bender Gestalt Visual Motor test, the Bruininks-Oseretsky Test of Motor Development, and the Frostig Movement Skills Test Battery are all specialized batteries that pick up motor coordination difficulties.*

39.7 The answer is B (*Synopsis VIII,* page 1166).
Although *parental counseling* helps reduce parents' guilt about their child's impairment and helps increase their confidence in dealing with the child's problem, it does not directly treat a child with developmental coordination disorder. *Physical education, Montessori technique, practicing motor movements,* and *learning to use the typewriter or computer* are all treatments for the disorder. Although no studies have reported on the efficacy of any of these forms of treatment, appropriate exercise and training skills help children develop motor skills. Associated emotional and behavioral problems and communication disorders must be managed by appropriate treatment methods.

40

Communication Disorders

Communication disorders include disorders of expressive language, mixed receptive-expressive language, phonological disorder, and stuttering. The literature suggests that communication disorders are commonly developmental in nature, having a familial aggregation and affecting approximately 3 times as many males as females. Comorbidity of language disorders with each other and with other types of learning disorders is high. Although in significant numbers of children, communication skills do improve spontaneously over time, it appears that remedial interventions may enhance improvement. In the past, expressive and receptive language impairment were conceived of as separate entities, but it is now generally believed that receptive language impairment is always accompanied by some expressive deficits; hence the current classification of mixed receptive-expressive language disorder. Most communication disorders are considered developmental, and acquired childhood language disorders fall into two categories. The first subgroup of acquired language disorder is associated with a known cerebral injury or trauma, and the second category is characterized by a progressive loss of acquired language due to a neurological disorder. Expressive language disorder in a child consists of below-expected ability in vocabulary, in the correct use of tenses, in the production of complete sentences, and in the recall of words. The deficit in expressive language is confirmed by scores obtained from standardized measures of expressive language that are below the child's nonverbal intellectual capacity and by evaluation of the child's receptive language abilities. The prevalence of expressive language disorder ranges from 3 to 10 percent of all school-age children and is at least twice as common in boys as in girls.

Language disabilities can be secondary to neurologic trauma, but most occur developmentally, without a known etiology. It is suspected that expressive language disorder has genetic contributions, since relatives of children with a variety of learning disorders have a higher likelihood of expressive language disability.

As many as 50 percent of children with mild expressive language disorder appear to recover spontaneously without lasting impairment. In moderate and severe cases, language therapy, including practicing verbal expression of phonemes, is useful. Vocabulary remediation and exercises involving sentence construction are also important. The goal is to increase the number of age-appropriate phrases that the child can use in everyday speech.

Mixed receptive-expressive language disorder consists of functional impairment in the expression and comprehension of language. Mixed receptive-expressive language disorder is confirmed through lower than expected scores from standardized tests of both receptive (comprehension) and expressive language development for a child's age. Estimates of the prevalence of either expressive language disorder or mixed receptive-expressive language disorder range from 1 to 13 percent. Expressive language disorder is believed to be much more common than mixed receptive-expressive language disorder. Both disorders are more common in boys than in girls. The etiology of mixed receptive-expressive language disorder is not known, but some studies suggest that impairment of auditory discrimination may contribute to it. As with expressive language disorder, there is a higher risk of left-handedness and ambilaterality among people with mixed receptive-expressive language disorder.

Phonological disorder is characterized by frequent misarticulations, sound substitutions, and omissions of speech sounds for a child's age and intelligence, often giving the impression of baby talk. It is more common in boys than in girls and seems to run in families. Omission of sounds is thought to be the most serious type of misarticulation, substitutions the next serious, and distortion of sounds the least serious. Most children outgrow phonological disorder by the third grade, but children who persist in misarticulation into the fourth grade are in need of remediation. Other communication disorders are common in children with phonological disorder.

Stuttering is a disturbance in normal fluency and time patterning of speech that is inappropriate for the child's age. Stuttering includes sound repetitions, prolongations, interjections, pauses within words, word substitutions to avoid blocking, and audible or silent blocking. Stuttering is 4 times as common in boys as in girls and is more common in family members of affected children than in the general population.

Stuttering does not suddenly occur but tends to be episodic, with intervals of normal speech for weeks or months. Chronic stuttering does not usually set in until the middle elementary school years. Stutterers may avoid particular words or sounds in which stuttering is anticipated. Eye blinks or tremors of the lips and jaw may occur. Frustration, anxiety, and depression often accompany chronic stuttering. Stress and fear may exacerbate bouts of stuttering in children with the disorder. Most treatments for stuttering are based on the belief that stuttering is a learned behavior. Communication disorder not otherwise specified is the diagnosis of disorders that do not meet the criteria for any specific communication disorder. Students should review Chapter 40 of *Kaplan and Sadock's Synopsis VIII* and then study the questions and answers below to test their knowledge of the subject.

HELPFUL HINTS

These terms relate to communication disorders and should be known by the student.

- ambilaterality
- articulation problems
- audiogram
- baby talk
- comprehension
- decoding
- dysarthria
- encoding
- expressive language disorder
- fluency of speech
- language acquisition
- maturational lag
- misarticulation
- mixed receptive-expressive language disorder
- omissions
- phoneme
- phonological disorder
- semantogenic theory of stuttering
- sound distortion
- spastic dysphonia
- standardized language test
- stuttering
- substitution

▲QUESTIONS

DIRECTIONS: For the following numbered language disorders, select the most appropriate lettered description.

Questions 40.1–40.3

A. A child sings normally.
B. A child cannot understand language.
C. A child plays with toys appropriately.
D. A child has an abnormally loud voice.
E. A child substitutes and omits speech sounds.

40.1 Phonological disorder
40.2 Expressive language disorder
40.3 Mixed receptive-expressive language disorder

DIRECTIONS: Each of the incomplete statements below is followed by five suggested completions. Select the *one* that is *best* in each case.

40.4 In expressive language disorder

A. scores from standardized measures of expressive and receptive development are usually below intellectual capacity
B. the disorder is often diagnosed with a pervasive developmental disorder
C. the diagnosis cannot be made when mental retardation is present
D. there is limited vocabulary, poor word recall, confusion of tenses, and poor sentence construction for the child's age and intelligence
E. the disorder does not interfere with academic or occupational achievement

40.5 All of the following statements about mixed receptive-expressive language disorder are true *except*

A. scores from standardized measures of both receptive and expressive language disorder are substantially below measures of nonverbal intellectual capacity
B. the diagnosis cannot be made if a pervasive developmental disorder is present
C. children with the disorder may initially appear deaf
D. the disorder includes receptive disability in the absence of expressive deficits
E. children with the disorder have difficulty processing visual symbols and pictures

40.6 Phonological disorder

A. is more common in children over 8 years old than in children under 8 years old
B. has a low rate of spontaneous remission in children over 8 years old
C. is 2 to 3 times as common in girls as in boys
D. does not occur with other communication disorders
E. includes errors in sound production, substitutions of sounds, and sound omissions

40.7 Stuttering

A. is probably caused by conflicts, fears, or neurosis
B. has two peaks of onset: 2 to 3 years and 5 to 7 years
C. is associated with more psychiatric disorders than other communication disorders
D. usually presents as a chronic disorder
E. does not cause impairment in academic or occupational achievement

40.8 Phonological disorder is related to

A. maturational delay
B. genetic factors
C. twins
D. low socioeconomic status
E. all of the above

40.9 A phoneme is

A. a constellation of sounds
B. a genetic marker on a chromosome
C. a chemical mediator
D. the smallest sound unit
E. an artificial language device

DIRECTIONS: These lettered headings are followed by a list of numbered phrases. For each numbered phrase, select the *best* lettered heading. Each lettered heading may be used once, more than once, or not at all.

Questions 40.10–40.11

A. Expressive language disorder
B. Phonological disorder

40.10 May give the impression of baby talk

40.11 May forget old words as new words are learned, but comprehension is not affected

Questions 40.12–40.16

A. Expressive language disorder
B. Mixed receptive-expressive language disorder
C. Phonological disorder
D. Stuttering
E. All of the above

40.12 When this disorder results from a neurological impairment, it may include dysarthria and apraxia.

40.13 A child with this disorder may appear to be deaf.

40.14 This disorder is most commonly seen in males.

40.15 Cluttering, a dysrhythmic speech pattern with jerky spurts of words, is often an associated feature of this disorder.

40.16 This disorder has two peaks of onset: between 2 and 3½ years and between 5 and 7 years.

ANSWERS

Communication Disorders

40.1 The answer is E (*Synopsis VIII,* page 1173).
In *phonological disorder, a child substitutes and omits speech sounds.* The misarticulation of speech in this disorder may resemble baby talk. The omissions, substitutions, and distortions typically occur with late-learned phonemes.

40.2 The answer is C (*Synopsis VIII,* page 1169).
In *expressive disorder, a child plays with toys normally.* Although a child with this disorder has a markedly impaired use of language, his or her language understanding remains relatively intact.

40.3 The answer is B (*Synopsis VIII,* pages 1170–1171).
A child with *mixed receptive-expressive language disorder cannot understand language.* Although his or her nonverbal intellectual capacity is age appropriate, a child with this disorder neither speaks nor mimics others' sounds. *A child* who stutters may *sing normally. A child* who *has an abnormally loud voice* may have a communication disorder not otherwise specified. Other such disorders include severe abnormalities of pitch, quality, tone, or resonance.

40.4 The answer is D (*Synopsis VIII,* page 1169).
In expressive language disorder *there is limited vocabulary, poor word recall, confusion of tenses, and poor sentence construction for the child's age and intelligence.* The diagnosis is confirmed using scores of expressive language obtained from standardized measures that are shown to be below nonverbal intellectual capacity as well as receptive language development. The disorder does not include receptive language disability; *scores from standardized measures of expressive, but not receptive, language development are usually below intellectual capacity. The disorder cannot be diagnosed with a pervasive developmental disorder.* However, *the diagnosis can be made when mental retardation is present,* if the language difficulties are in excess of those usually associated with mental retardation. *The disorder does interfere with academic or occupational achievement* and social communication. The diagnostic criteria for expressive language disorder appear in Table 40.1.

40.5 The answer is D (*Synopsis VIII,* pages 1171–1172).
Mixed receptive-expressive language disorder is characterized by the child's impairment in both the understanding and expression of language. According to the fourth edition of *Diagnostic and Statistical Manual of Mental Disorders* (DSM-IV), *the disorder cannot include receptive language disability in the absence of expressive deficits* (Table 40.2). In mixed receptive-expressive language disorder *scores from standardized measures of both receptive and expressive language development are substantially below measures of nonverbal intellectual capacity. The diagnosis cannot be made if a pervasive developmental disorder is present. Children with the disorder may initially appear deaf* because they do not respond appropriately to simple commands, yet they are able to respond to nonlanguage sounds in the environment. In the disorder *children have difficulty processing visual symbols and pictures.*

40.6 The answer is E (*Synopsis VIII,* page 1173).
Phonological disorder consists of failure to use developmentally expected speech sounds appropriate for age. The disability *includes errors in sound production, substitutions of sounds, and sound omissions.* Phonological disorder *is more-*

Table 40.1
DSM-IV Diagnostic Criteria for Expressive Language Disorder

A. The scores obtained from standardized individually administered measures of expressive language development are substantially below those obtained from standardized measures of both nonverbal intellectual capacity and receptive language development. The disturbance may be manifest clinically by symptoms that include having a markedly limited vocabulary, making errors in tense, or having difficulty recalling words or producing sentences with developmentally appropriate length or complexity.
B. The difficulties with expressive language interfere with academic or occupational achievement or with social communication.
C. Criteria are not met for mixed receptive-expressive language disorder or a pervasive developmental disorder.
D. If mental retardation, a speech-motor or sensory deficit, or environmental deprivation is present, the language difficulties are in excess of those usually associated with these problems.

Coding note: If a speech-motor or sensory deficit or a neurological condition is present, code the condition on Axis III.

Reprinted with permission from American Psychiatric Association: *Diagnostic and Statistical Manual of Mental Disorders,* ed 4. Copyright, American Psychiatric Association, Washington, 1994.

Table 40.2
DSM-IV Diagnostic Criteria for Mixed Receptive-Expressive Language Disorder

A. The scores obtained from a battery of standarized individually administered measures of both receptive and expressive language development are substantially below those obtained from standardized measures of nonverbal intellectual capacity. Symptoms include those for expressive language disorder as well as difficulty understanding words, sentences, or specific types of words, such as spatial terms.
B. The difficulties with receptive and expressive language significantly interfere with academic or occupational achievement or with social communication.
C. Criteria are not met for a pervasive developmental disorder.
D. If mental retardation, a speech-motor or sensory deficit, or environmental deprivation is present, the language difficulties are in excess of those usually associated with these problems.

Coding note: if a speech-motor or sensory deficit or a neurological condition is present, code the condition on Axis III.

Reprinted with permission from American Psychiatric Association: *Diagnostic and Statistical Manual of Mental Disorders,* ed 4. Copyright, American Psychiatric Association, Washington, 1994.

common in children under 8 years old than in children over 8 years old. The disorder *has a high rate of spontaneous remission in children over 8 years old;* most children outgrow it by the third grade. Phonological disorder *is 2 to 3 times as common in boys as in girls.* Phonological disorder *commonly occurs with other communication disorders,* such as expressive language disorder, reading disorder, and developmental coordination disorder. Table 40.3 presents the diagnostic criteria for phonological disorder.

40.7 The answer is B (*Synopsis VIII,* page 1176).
Stuttering consists of sound repetitions, word prolongations, interjections, pauses within words, and word blocking. It *has two peaks of onset: 2 to 3 years and 5 to 7 years.* The precise cause of stuttering is not known, but the current consensus is that it *is not caused by conflicts, fears, or neurosis.* Children who do stutter, however, may have episodic exacerbations when they are under stress. Although children with any type of communication disorder are at higher risk than the general population for a variety of concurrent psychiatric disorders, there is no evidence that stuttering *is associated with more psychiatric disorders than other communication disorders.* Stuttering *usually presents as an episodic rather than a chronic disorder,* but it can become chronic within several years. Stuttering *causes impairment in academic or occupational achievement* and impairment in social communication. Table 40.4 lists the DSM-IV diagnostic criteria for stuttering.

40.8 The answer is E (all) (*Synopsis VIII,* page 1173).
The cause of phonological order is unknown. It is commonly believed that a *maturational delay* in the neurological processes underlying speech may be at fault. A disproportionately high number of children with phonological disorder are found to be second-borns, *twins,* or of *low socioeconomic* status. It is now believed that the children, rather than being at risk for the disorder, are the recipients of inadequate speech stimulation and reinforcement. Constitutional factors, rather than environmental factors, seem to be most important in determining whether a child has phonological disorder. The high proportion of children with developmental articulation disorder who have relatives with a similar disorder suggests that there is a *genetic component* to the disorder.

Table 40.3
DSM-IV Diagnostic Criteria for Phonological Disorder

A. Failure to use developmentally expected speech sounds that are appropriate for age and dialect (eg, errors in sound production, use, representation, or organization such as, but not limited to, substitutions of one sound for another [use of /t/ for target /k/ sound] or omissions of sounds such as final consonants).
B. The difficulties in speech sound production interfere with academic or occupational achievement or with social communication.
C. If mental retardation, a speech-motor or sensory deficit, or environmental deprivation is present, the speech difficulties are in excess of those usually associated with these problems.

Coding note: If a speech-motor or sensory deficit or a neurological condition is present, code the condition on Axis III.

Table 40.4
DSM-IV Diagnostic Criteria for Stuttering

A. Disturbance in the normal fluency and time patterning of speech (inappropriate for the individual's age), characterized by frequent occurrences of one or more of the following:
   (1) sound and syllable repetitions
   (2) sound prolongations
   (3) interjections
   (4) broken words (eg, pauses within a word)
   (5) audible or silent blocking (filled or unfilled pauses in speech)
   (6) circumlocutions (word substitutions to avoid problematic words)
   (7) words produced with an excess of physical tension
   (8) monosyllabic whole-word repetitions (eg, "I-I-I-I see him")
B. The disturbance in fluency interferes with academic or occupational achievement or with social communication.
C. If a speech-motor or sensory deficit is present, the speech difficulties are in excess of those usually associated with these problems.

Coding note: If a speech-motor or sensory deficit or a neurological condition is present, code the condition on Axis III.

40.9 The answer is D (*Synopsis VIII,* page 1170).
Phonological disorder cannot be accounted for by structural, physiological, or neurological abnormalities. Language is within normal limits. The term actually refers to a number of articulation problems that range in severity from mild to severe. Only one speech sound or phoneme (*the smallest sound unit*), may be affected, or many phonemes may be involved. The child may be completely intelligible, partially intelligible, or unintelligible.

A phoneme in linguistics is a speech sound that serves to distinguish words from one another (for example, the vowels in *tan, ten, tin, ton, tune*). There is a rigid sequence in the process of acquisition of new phonemes by a child learning to speak, and accordingly, this process is reversed in various types of aphasic speech disorders. A phoneme is not *a constellation of sounds, genetic marker on a chromosome, a chemical mediator,* or *an artificial language device.*

Answers 40.10–40.11

40.10 The answer is B (*Synopsis VIII,* page 1173).

40.11 The answer is A (*Synopsis VIII,* page 1173).
Phonological disorder is characterized by errors in sound production, substitutions of one sound for another, and omissions of sounds such as final consonants. The frequent misarticulations, word substitutions, and word omissions *may give the impression of baby talk.*

In expressive language disorder, the child is below expected ability in vocabulary, correct use of tenses, and production of complex sentences. In *expressive language disorder* children *may forget old words as new words are learned, but comprehension is not affected.*

Answers 40.12–40.16

40.12 The answer is C (*Synopsis VIII,* page 1173).

40.13 The answer is B (*Synopsis VIII,* page 1171).

40.14 The answer is E (*Synopsis VIII,* pages 1168, 1170, 1173, 1175).

40.15 The answer is A (*Synopsis VIII,* page 1169).

40.16 The answer is D (*Synopsis VIII,* page 1176).
Phonological disorders are characterized by poor sound or articulation. There can be substitutions of one sound for another, omissions of some sounds, or inability to reproduce a sound correctly. Often children with phonological disorder give the impression of speaking baby talk. *In certain neurological conditions dysarthria and apraxia (loss of movement) may occur.* Dysarthria results from impairment in the neural mechanisms regulating muscle control, whereas apraxia is an impairment in the muscles used for speech themselves. Mixed receptive-expressive language disorder is an impairment in both the understanding and the expression of language. It is generally believed that a deficit in receptive language always results in some impairment in expressive language. Children with mixed receptive-expressive language disorder show markedly delayed ability to comprehend verbal or sign language, despite normal intellectual capacity. A child with this disorder often appears to be deaf, since he or she does not respond normally to language sounds, except that such a child does respond to nonlanguage sounds in the environment. Usually when these children begin to use language, their speech contains numerous articulation errors and substitutions of phonemes. *All of the communication disorders seem to be 2 to 4 times as common in males as in females. This striking gender difference implies a genetic basis for the communication disorders. Cluttering is a disordered speech pattern in which speech is erratic, with bouts of rapid and jerky words or phrases.* Commonly, a child with this speech pattern is unaware that the production of speech is abnormal. This differs from stuttering in that the disturbance in fluency in stuttering is characterized by sound repetitions, pauses within words, prolongations, and audible or silent word blocking. Stutterers are generally aware of their stuttering and many experience anxiety in anticipation of speaking and stuttering. Cluttering is often an associated feature of an expressive language disorder. Stuttering usually appears before the age of 12 years. *There are two peaks for its onset, 2 to $3^1/_2$ years and 5 to 7 years.* In the preschool age group, children tend to stutter most often when they are excited or have a lot to say. Stuttering at this age may be a passing phase. In the elementary school years, stuttering may be more chronic and may characterize a child's everyday speech. Later in childhood stuttering is often an intermittent event that manifests itself in the course of specific situations. Stutterers often show fear, embarrassment, and anxious anticipation of speaking in public, or they avoid certain words or phrases that have become associated with their stuttering.

41

Pervasive Developmental Disorders

Pervasive developmental disorders include impairment in reciprocal social skills, language development and usage, and a limited set of interests and behavioral repertoire. Autistic disorder, the prototype of the pervasive developmental disorders, is characterized by sustained impairments in social interactions, communication deviance, and restricted, stereotyped behavioral patterns. In most cases, appropriate skills do not develop, but in some of the pervasive developmental disorders, such as Rett's disorder and childhood disintegrative disorder, there is development and then loss of skills. According to the fourth edition of *Diagnostic and Statistical Manual of Mental Disorders* (DSM-IV), aberrant functioning in one of the core areas must be present by age 3 years. More than two thirds of persons with autistic disorder have mental retardation.

The fourth edition of *Diagnostic and Statistical Manual of Mental Disorders* (DSM-IV) includes the following disorders within the category of pervasive developmental disorders: autistic disorder, Rett's disorder, childhood disintegrative disorder, Asperger's disorder, and pervasive developmental disorder not otherwise specified.

Autistic disorder is the best known of the pervasive developmental disorders. It is characterized by significant impairments in social interaction, marked qualitative impairments in communication, and restricted, repetitive, and stereotyped patterns of behavior. Autistic disorder was described by Leo Kanner in 1943, but not until 1980 was it recognized as a distinct clinical entity. Before 1980, children with any pervasive developmental disorder were classified as schizophrenic. Autistic disorder occurs in 2 to 5 per 10,000 children. It is reported to be at least 3 times as common in boys as in girls.

About half of all children with autistic disorder do not develop useful language skills, although they may acquire occasional words. Unlike normal young children, who have good receptive language skills and understand much before they speak, autistic children who do develop language say more than they understand. Their speech contains immediate and delayed echolalic words and phrases, and stereotyped phrases are often repeated out of context.

Stereotyped behavior and restricted repertoire constitute another dysfunction in autistic disorder. Children with autistic disorder show a markedly diminished ability to use imagination in play and to play symbolically. Children with autistic disorder may show a fascination with repetitive stereotyped behavior, such as spinning, banging, watching water flow, or lining up objects. They may exhibit bodily movements that are repetitive, such as flapping their hands or fingers or twisting their bodies. They may become attached to an inanimate object, such as a metal pipe or a table.

The cause of autistic disorder is not known, although it is generally believed to be a neurological or biological disorder. Reports comparing the parents of autistic children with the parents of normal children have not shown significant differences in child rearing. A biological cause of autism is supported by evidence that autistic disorder is frequent in conditions with known neurological lesions, such as congenital rubella, phenylketonuria (PKU), and tuberous sclerosis. Children with autistic disorder have significantly more minor physical anomalies than do normal children, suggesting that first-trimester insults may contribute to the disorder.

Autistic disorder has no specific treatment, although various medications have been used to control self-injurious and stereotyped motor behaviors. The prognosis is best in autistic children with intelligence quotients (IQs) above 70 who have communicative language skills by age 5 to 7 years. Rett's disorder appears to occur only in girls; it is estimated to have a prevalence of 6 to 7 cases per 100,000 girls. Rett's disorder is characterized by normal development for at least 5 months after birth, as manifested by normal social and motor milestones and normal head circumference at birth. The onset of the disorder, which occurs between 5 and 48 months after birth, consists of a deceleration of head growth, the loss of previously acquired purposeful hand movements, and the presentation of stereotyped hand motions, such as hand-wringing. In addition, the patient shows a loss of social engagement early in the course of the disorder, the appearance of poorly coordinated gait or trunk movements, and marked delay and impairment of expressive and receptive language and motor skills. Rett's disorder then proceeds as a progressive encephalopathy. Associated features include seizures in 75 percent of affected patients and irregular respiration with episodes of hyperventilation, apnea, and breath holding. As the disorder progresses, the patient's muscle tone seems to increase from initial hypotonia to spasticity to rigidity. Long-term receptive and expressive communication skills remain at a developmental level of less than 1 year.

Childhood disintegrative disorder, also known as Heller's syndrome, is a devastating deterioration of intellectual, social, and language functioning in 3- to 4-year-olds with previously normal functioning. After the deterioration, the patients resemble children with autistic disorder. Childhood disintegrative disorder is estimated to be at least one tenth as common as autistic disorder, occurring in one case in 100,000 children. It appears to be 4 to 8 times as common in boys as in girls. The cause is unknown, but the disorder has been reported to occur with other neurological conditions, including seizure disorders, tuberous sclerosis, and metabolic disorders.

Asperger's disorder has some similarities to autistic disorder and the other pervasive developmental disorders but is distinctive in that there is a lack of clinically significant delays in language and such cognitive development as adaptive behavior and self-help skills. However, the patient has a qualitative impairment in social interaction and restricted, repetitive, and stereotyped patterns of behavior. The cause of Asperger's disorder is unknown, but family studies suggest a relation to autistic disorder. The prevalence of Asperger's disorder has not yet been well studied. The course and the prognosis of patients with Asperger's disorder is not well known, but factors associated with good prognoses are normal intelligence and a high level of social skills. Students should study Chapter 41 in *Kaplan and Sadock's Synopsis VIII* and then address the following questions and answers to test their knowledge of the area.

HELPFUL HINTS

The student should know the following terms related to pervasive developmental disorders.

- abnormal relationship
- acquired aphasia
- Asperger's disorder
- attachment behavior
- autistic disorder
- childhood disintegrative disorder
- childhood schizophrenia
- communication disorder
- concordance rate
- congenital deafness
- congenital physical anomaly
- congenital rubella
- CT scan
- dermatoglyphics
- disintegrative (regressive) psychosis
- dread of change
- echolalia
- echolalic speech
- educational and behavioral treatments
- EEG abnormalities
- ego-educative approach
- encopresis
- enuresis
- extreme autistic aloneness
- eye contact
- failed cerebral lateralization
- grand mal seizure
- haloperidol (Haldol)
- Heller's syndrome
- hyperkinesis
- hyperuricosuria
- idiot savant
- insight-oriented psychotherapy
- islets of precocity
- Leo Kanner
- language deviance and delay
- low-purine diet
- mental retardation
- monotonous repetition
- organic abnormalities
- parental rage and rejection
- perinatal complications
- pervasive developmental disorder
- physical characteristics
- PKU
- play
- prevalence
- pronominal reversal
- psychodynamic and family causation
- Rett's disorder
- ritual
- rote memory
- self-injurious behavior
- separation anxiety
- sex distribution
- social class
- splinter function
- stereotypy
- tardive and withdrawal dyskinesias
- tuberous sclerosis
- vestibular stimulation
- voice quality and rhythm

▲ QUESTIONS

DIRECTIONS: Each of the questions or incomplete statements below is followed by five suggested responses or completions. Select the *one* that is *best* in each case.

41.1 Which of the following features does *not* distinguish autistic disorder from schizophrenia with childhood onset?

A. Auditory hallucinations
B. Mental retardation
C. Age of onset
D. Socioeconomic level
E. Prenatal and perinatal complications

41.2 Which of the following features does *not* distinguish autistic disorder from mixed receptive-expressive language disorder?

A. Echolalia
B. Stereotypies
C. Imaginative play
D. Associated deafness
E. Family history of speech delay

41.3 All of the following are characteristic of children with autistic disorder *except*

A. delayed functioning in social interaction, language, or symbolic or imaginative play
B. qualitative impairment in social interaction
C. impaired communication
D. stereotyped patterns of behavior
E. normal development during the first 2 to 3 years

41.4 Rett's disorder is hypothesized to have a genetic cause because

A. the onset of a deteriorating encephalopathy occurs between the ages of 5 and 48 months
B. some patients with the disorder have hyperammonemia
C. poor muscle coordination and ataxia occur in addition to irregular respiration
D. autistic disorder and Rett's disorder are similar
E. it appears to occur only in girls

41.5 Which of the following is *not* true of childhood disintegrative disorder?

A. It is also known as Heller's syndrome.
B. In most cases there is normal development for 3 to 4 years.
C. The onset may be gradual over several months or occur within days.
D. The disorder occurs only with another neurological condition.
E. Most children with the disorder are left with at least moderate mental retardation.

41.6 Asperger's disorder differs from autistic disorder in that Asperger's disorder does *not* include

A. impaired peer relationships
B. any clinically significant delay in language or impairment in cognitive development
C. impaired nonverbal communication
D. impaired social interaction
E. restricted, repetitive, and stereotyped patterns of behavior

41.7 Treatment of autistic disorder includes

A. insight-oriented individual psychotherapy
B. loosely structured training programs
C. phenobarbital (Luminal)
D. haloperidol (Haldol)
E. all of the above

41.8 Unusual or precocious abilities in some autistic children are called

A. Rett's syndrome
B. echolalia
C. splinter functions
D. stereotypies
E. hyperkinesis

41.9 Neurological-biochemical abnormalities associated with autistic disorder include

A. grand mal seizures
B. ventricular enlargement on computed tomography (CT) scans
C. electroencephalogram (EEC) abnormalities
D. elevated serum serotonin levels
E. all of the above

41.10 Characteristics thought to be associated with autistic children include all of the following *except*

A. intelligent and attractive appearance
B. increased sensitivity to pain
C. ambidexterity
D. abnormal dermatoglyphics
E. high incidence of upper respiratory infections

DIRECTIONS: The questions below consist of five lettered headings followed by a list of numbered statements. For each numbered word or statement, select the *one* lettered heading that is most closely associated with it. Each lettered heading may be selected once, more than once, or not at all.

Questions 41.11–41.15

A. Autistic disorder
B. Childhood disintegrative disorder
C. Pervasive developmental disorder not otherwise specified
D. Asperger's disorder
E. Rett's disorder

41.11 Normal development for the first 5 months, followed by a progressive encephalopathy

41.12 A better prognosis than other pervasive developmental disorders because of the lack of delay in language and cognitive development

41.13 Some but not all of the features of autistic disorder

41.14 Several years of normal development followed by a loss of communication skills, a loss of reciprocal social interaction, and a restricted pattern of behavior

41.15 Occurrence at a rate of 2 to 5 cases per 10,000 and characterization by impairment in social interaction, communicative language, or symbolic play before age 3

Questions 41.16–41.20

A. Risperidone
B. Haldol
C. Naltrexone
D. Fenfluramine
E. Serotonin-specific reuptake inhibitors

41.16 This opiate antagonist is being investigated in the treatment of autism.

41.17 This drug has both dopamine (D_2) and serotonin (5-HT) antagonist properties.

41.18 This drug has been shown to reduce lability and stereotypic behaviors and is associated with withdrawal dyskinesias.

41.19 This drug is used to decrease obsessive-compulsive and stereotypic behaviors.

41.20 This drug increases brain serotonin levels and has been used to treat autism.

Questions 41.21–41.24

A. Rett's disorder
B. Childhood disintegrative disorder
C. Both

41.21 This disorder is known to occur in females only.

41.22 Children with this disorder appear to be developmentally normal for at least 4 months.

41.23 Head growth decelerates after 5 months, and the patient eventually develops severe hand-wringing or hand-washing.

41.24 The patient develops normally for at least 2 years but has subsequent loss of language, social skills, play, or motor skills.

ANSWERS

Pervasive Developmental Disorders

41.1 The answer is B (*Synopsis VIII,* pages 1179–1186).
Auditory hallucinations are not features of autistic disorder and are common in schizophrenia. *Mental retardation* is present in up to 70 percent of autistic children and is not a feature of schizophrenia. *Seizures* have a prevalence of 4 to 32 percent among those with autistic disorder but are absent or have a lower prevalence in those with childhood schizophrenia. *Age of onset* for autistic disorder is before 36 months; for childhood schizophrenia, onset is not before 5 years of age. Those with autistic disorder are overrepresented in upper *socioeconomic levels,* whereas childhood schizophrenia occurs more commonly among those in lower *socioeconomic levels. Prenatal and perinatal complications* occur more commonly among those with autistic disorder and less commonly among those with childhood schizophrenia.

41.2 The answer is E (*Synopsis VIII,* page 1180).
A family history of speech delay or language problems occurs in about 25 percent of children with autistic disorder and of those with mixed receptive-expressive language disorder. *Echolalia* occurs more commonly in children with autistic disorder and less commonly in those with the language disorder. The presence or absence of *stereotypies* does not distinguish those with autistic disorder from those with mixed receptive-expressive language disorder. Stereotypies are more common and more severe among children with autistic disorder and absent or less severe among those with the language disorder. *Imaginative play* is absent or rudimentary in children with autistic disorder and usually present in those with the language disorder. *Associated deafness* is very infrequent in children with autistic disorder and not infrequent in those with the language disorder.

41.3 The answer is E (*Synopsis VIII,* pages 1179–1184).
Autistic disorder is believed to be a neurological disorder in which aberrant development is usually manifested in infancy; thus, *development during the first 2 to 3 years is not normal.* The diagnostic criteria for autistic disorder include abnormal or *delayed functioning in social interaction, language, or symbolic or imaginative play* (Table 41.1). Autistic disorder is also characterized by *qualitative impairment in social interaction, impaired communication,* and *stereotyped patterns of behavior.*

41.4 The answer is E (*Synopsis VIII,* page 1188).
Rett's disorder is hypothesized to have a genetic cause because *it appears to occur only in girls.* Although it is true that *the onset of a progressive encephalopathy occurs between the ages of 5 and 48 months,* that *some patients with the disorder have hyperammonemia,* that *poor muscle coordination and ataxia occur in addition to irregular respiration,* and that *autistic disorder and Rett's disorder are similar,* those factors could result from genetic, metabolic, or infectious causes. The diagnostic criteria for Rett's disorder are listed in Table 41.2.

Table 41.1
DSM-IV Diagnostic Criteria for Autistic Disorder

A. A total of six (or more) items from (1), (2), and (3), with at least two from (1), and one each from (2) and (3):
   (1) qualitative impairment in social interaction, as manifested by at least two of the following:
      (a) marked impairment in the use of multiple nonverbal behaviors such as eye-to-eye gaze, facial expression, body postures, and gestures to regulate social interaction
      (b) failure to develop peer relationships appropriate to developmental level
      (c) a lack of spontaneous seeking to share enjoyment, interests, or achievements with other people (eg, by a lack of showing, bringing, or pointing out objects of interest)
      (d) lack of social or emotional reciprocity
   (2) qualitative impairments in communication as manifested by at least one of the following:
      (a) delay in, or total lack of, development of spoken language (not accompanied by an attempt to compensate through alternative modes of communication such as gesture or mime)
      (b) in individuals with adequate speech, marked impairment in the ability to initiate or sustain a conversation with others
      (c) stereotyped and repetitive use of language or idiosyncratic language
      (d) lack of varied, spontaneous make-believe play or social imitative play appropriate to developmental level
   (3) restricted repetitive and stereotyped patterns of behavior, interests, and activities, as manifested by at least one of the following:
      (a) encompasing preoccupation with one or more stereotyped and restricted patterns of interest that is abnormal either in intensity or focus
      (b) apparently inflexible adherence to specific, nonfunctional routines or rituals
      (c) stereotyped and repetitive motor mannerisms (eg, hand or finger flapping or twisting, or complex whole-body movements)
      (d) persistent preoccupation with parts of objects

B. Delays or abnormal functioning in at least one of the following areas, with onset prior to age 3 years: (1) social interaction, (2) language as used in social communication, or (3) symbolic or imaginative play.

C. The disturbance is not better accounted for by Rett's disorder or childhood disintegrative disorder.

Reprinted with permission from American Psychiatric Association: *Diagnostic and Statistical Manual of Mental Disorders,* ed 4. Copyright, American Psychiatric Association, Washington, 1994.

41.5 The answer is D (*Synopsis VIII,* pages 1189–1190).
Childhood disintegrative disorder *sometimes occurs in the absence of another neurological condition,* and it has been reported to occur in children with metabolic disorders. Childhood disintegrative disorder *is also known as Heller's syndrome. In most cases there is normal development for 3 to*

Table 41.2
DSM-IV Diagnostic Criteria for Rett's Disorder

A. All of the following:
   (1) apparently normal prenatal and perinatal development
   (2) apparently normal psychomotor development through the first 5 months after birth
   (3) normal head circumference at birth

B. Onset of the following after the period of normal development:
   (1) deceleration of head growth between ages 5 and 48 months
   (2) loss of previously acquired purposeful hand skills between ages 5 and 30 months with the subsequent development of stereotyped hand movements (eg, hand-wringing or hand-washing)
   (3) loss of social engagement early in the course (although often social interaction develops later)
   (4) appearance of poorly coordinated gait or trunk movements
   (5) severely impaired expressive and receptive language development with severe psychomotor retardation

Reprinted with permission from American Psychiatric Association: *Diagnostic and Statistical Manual of Mental Disorders,* ed 4. Copyright, American Psychiatric Association, Washington, 1994.

Table 41.3
DSM-IV Diagnostic Criteria for Childhood Disintegrative Disorder

A. Apparently normal development for at least the first 2 years after birth as manifested by the presence of age-appropriate verbal and nonverbal communication, social relationships, play, and adaptive behavior.

B. Clinically significant loss of previously acquired skills (before age 10 years) in at least two of the following areas:
   (1) expressive or receptive language
   (2) social skills or adaptive behavior
   (3) bowel or bladder control
   (4) play
   (5) motor skills

C. Abnormalities of functioning in at least two of the following areas:
   (1) qualitative impairment in social interaction (eg, impairment in nonverbal behaviors, failure to develop peer relationships, lack of social or emotional reciprocity)
   (2) qualitative impairments in communication (eg, delay or lack of spoken language, inability to initiate or sustain a conversation, stereotyped and repetitive use of language, lack of varied make-believe play)
   (3) restricted, repetitive, and stereotyped patterns of behavior, interests, and activities, including motor stereotypies and mannerisms

D. The disturbance is not better accounted for by another specific pervasive developmental disorder or by schizophrenia.

Reprinted with permission from American Psychiatric Association: *Diagnostic and Statistical Manual of Mental Disorders,* ed 4. Copyright, American Psychiatric Association, Washington, 1994.

Table 41.4
DSM-IV Diagnostic Criteria for Asperger's Disorder

A. Qualitative impairment in social interaction, as manifested by at least two of the following:
   (1) marked impairment in the use of multiple nonverbal behaviors such as eye-to-eye gaze, facial expression, body postures, and gestures to regulate social interaction
   (2) failure to develop peer relationships appropriate to developmental level
   (3) a lack of spontaneous seeking to share enjoyment, interests, or achievements with other people (eg, by a lack of showing, bringing, or pointing out objects of interest to other people)
   (4) lack of social or emotional reciprocity

B. Restricted repetitive and stereotyped patterns of behavior, interests, and activities, as manifested by at least one of the following:
   (1) encompassing preoccupation with one or more stereotyped and restricted patterns of interest that is abnormal either in intensity or focus
   (2) apparently inflexible adherence to specific, nonfunctional routines or rituals
   (3) stereotyped and repetitive motor mannerisms (eg, hand or finger flapping or twisting, or complex whole-body movements)
   (4) persistent preoccupation with parts of objects

C. The disturbance causes clinically significant impairment in social, occupational, or other important areas of functioning.

D. There is no clinically significant general delay in language (e.g., single words used by age 2 years, communicative phrases used by age 3 years).

E. There is no clinically significant delay in cognitive development or in the development of age-appropriate self-help skills, adaptive behavior (other than in social interaction), and curiosity about the environment in childhood.

F. Criteria are not met for another specific pervasive developmental disorder or schizophrenia.

Reprinted with permission from American Psychiatric Association: *Diagnostic and Statistical Manual of Mental Disorders,* ed 4. Copyright, American Psychiatric Association, Washington, 1994.

4 years. The onset may be gradual over several months or occur within days. Most children with the disorder are left with at least moderate mental retardation. The diagnostic criteria for childhood disintegrative disorder appear in Table 41.3.

41.6 The answer is B (*Synopsis VIII,* page 1190). Asperger's disorder, unlike autistic disorder, lacks *any clinically significant delay in language or impairment in cognitive development,* as manifested by adaptive behaviors. Patients with Asperger's disorder, like patients with autistic disorder, have *impaired peer relationships, impaired nonverbal communication, impaired social interaction,* and *restricted, repetitive, and stereotyped patterns of behavior.* The diagnostic criteria for Asperger's disorder are listed in Table 41.4.

41.7 The answer is D (*Synopsis VIII,* page 1188). Pharmacological treatment of autistic disorder includes *haloperidol (Haldol).* The administration of haloperidol both reduces the behavioral symptoms of the disorder and accelerates learning. The drug decreases hyperactivity, stereotypies, withdrawal, fidgeting, abnormal object relations, irritability, and labile affect. *Insight-oriented individual psychotherapy* has proved ineffective as a treatment of autistic disorder. Educational and behavioral methods are currently considered the treatments of choice. Careful training and individual tutoring of parents in the concepts and the skills of behavior modification, within a problem-solving format, may yield considerable gains in the child's language, cognitive, and social areas of behavior. However, the *training programs are* rigorous, not *loosely structured,* and require a great deal of the parent's time. The autistic child requires as much structure as possible, and a daily program for as many hours as feasible is desirable. *Phenobarbital (Luminal)* is not an effective treatment of autistic disorder. Fenfluramine (Pondimin) was found to be useful in some cases of autistic disorder but was withdrawn from the U.S. market in 1997 because of heart valve damage as an adverse effect.

41.8 The answer is C (*Synopsis VIII,* page 1185).
Unusual or precocious cognitive or vasomotor abilities are present in some autistic children. Those abilities, which may exist even within the overall retarded functioning, are called *splinter functions,* or islets of precocity. Perhaps the most striking examples are idiot savants, who have prodigious rote memories or calculating abilities. Their specific abilities are usually beyond the capabilities of normal peers. Other precocious abilities in young autistic children include hyperlexia, early ability to read well (although they are not able to understand what they read), memorizing and reciting, and musical abilities (singing tunes or recognizing musical pieces).

Rett's syndrome, a disorder of progressive mental retardation accompanied by autistic-like and neurological symptoms, occurs only in girls. *Echolalia* is the immediate or delayed repetition of words or phrases said to the person. Often the speaker's tone and inflection are preserved. *Stereotypies* are repetitive behaviors, often performed rhythmically, that are not goal-directed. *Hyperkinesis,* overactivity, is a common behavior problem among young autistic children, as are aggressiveness and temper tantrums.

41.9 The answer is E (all) (*Synopsis VIII,* page 1182).
Current evidence indicates that significant neurological and biochemical abnormalities are usually associated with autistic disorder. *Grand mal seizures* develop at some time in 4 to 32 percent of autistic persons, and about 20 to 25 percent of autistic persons show *ventricular enlargement on computed tomography scans.* Various *electroencephalogram (EEG) abnormalities* are found in 10 to 83 percent of autistic children; although no EEG finding is specific in autistic disorder, there is some indication of failed cerebral lateralization. *Elevated serum serotonin levels* are found in about one third of autistic children; however, the levels are also raised in about one third of nonautistic children with severe mental retardation.

41.10 The answer is B (*Synopsis VIII,* pages 1182–1185).
Many autistic children have a *decreased (not increased) sensitivity to pain.* The children may injure themselves severely and not cry. They may not complain of pain either verbally or by gesture and may not show the malaise of an ill child. Leo Kanner was impressed by autistic children's *intelligent and attractive appearance.* Cerebral lateralization is not found in most autistic children; that is, they remain *ambidextrous* at an age when cerebral dominance is established in normal children. Autistic children also show a greater incidence of *abnormal dermatoglyphics* (for example, fingerprints) than does the general population. *A high incidence of upper respiratory infections* is found in young autistic children. Autistic children may not have elevated temperatures with infectious illness, and their behavior or relatedness may improve to a noticeable degree when they are ill.

Answers 41.11–41.15

41.11 The answer is E (*Synopsis VIII,* page 1188).

41.12 The answer is D (*Synopsis VIII,* page 1190).

41.13 The answer is C (*Synopsis VIII,* page 1191).

41.14 The answer is B (*Synopsis VIII,* pages 1189–1190).

41.15 The answer is A (*Synopsis VIII,* page 1182).
Rett's disorder is characterized by *normal development for the first 5 months followed by a progressive deterioration. Asperger's disorder* may have *a better prognosis than other pervasive developmental disorders because of the lack of delay in language and cognitive development. Pervasive developmental disorder not otherwise specified* (Table 41.5) includes atypical autism—presentations that include *some but not all of the features of autistic disorder. Childhood disintegrative disorder* is characterized by *several years of normal development followed by a loss of communication skills, a loss of reciprocal social interaction, and a restricted pattern of behavior. Autistic disorder occurs at a rate of 2 to 5 cases per 10,000 and is characterized by impairment in social interaction, communicative language, or symbolic play before age 3.*

Answers 41.16–41.20

41.16 The answer is C (*Synopsis VIII,* page 1188).

41.17 The answer is A (*Synopsis VIII,* page 1188).

41.18 The answer is B (*Synopsis VIII,* page 1188).

41.19 The answer is E (*Synopsis VIII,* page 1188).

Table 41.5
DSM-IV Diagnostic Criteria for Pervasive Developmental Disorder Not Otherwise Specified

This category should be used when there is a severe and pervasive impairment in the development of reciprocal social interaction or verbal and nonverbal communication skills, or when stereotyped behavior, interests, and activities are present, but the criteria are not met for a specific pervasive developmental disorder, schizophrenia, schizotypal personality disorder, or avoidant personality disorder. For example, this category includes "atypical autism"—presentations that do not meet the criteria for autistic disorder because of late age at onset, atypical symptomatology, or subthreshold symptomatology, or all of these.

Reprinted with permission from American Psychiatric Association: *Diagnostic and Statistical Manual of Mental Disorders,* ed 4. Copyright, American Psychiatric Association, Washington, 1994.

41.20 The answer is D (*Synopsis VIII,* page 1188).
Numerous drugs with various mechanisms are being investigated in the treatment of the pervasive developmental disorders. Symptoms being targeted include aggression, self-injurious behaviors, mood lability, irritability, obsessive-compulsive behaviors, hyperactivity, stereotypic behavior, and social withdrawal. Naltrexone, an opiate antagonist, has been tried in the hope that if endogenous opioids are blocked, there will be a decrease in stereotypic behaviors in *autistic disorder.* Risperidone, a high-potency antipsychotic with *both dopamine* (D_2) *and serotonin (5-HT) blockade,* appears to be somewhat efficacious in decreasing aggression and self-injurious behaviors. Haldol has been shown to *reduce behavioral symptoms, reduce irritability, and improve sociability* among autistic children. It has also been shown to promote learning of tasks. Approximately one quarter of autistic children develop *withdrawal dyskinesias,* however, when the Haldol is withdrawn. This syndrome generally remits. The serotonin-specific reuptake inhibitors have been shown to have positive effects on *obsessive-compulsive symptoms* among adults. They are now under investigation and sertraline (Zoloft) has been approved as effective drugs on the *obsessions, compulsions, and stereotypic symptoms* among autistic children and adolescents. Fenfluramine results in an *increase in serotonin level.* It has not been shown to ameliorate behavioral problems among autistic children. Fenfluramine was taken off the market in 1997 because of severe adverse effects, such as mitral and aortic valve damage.

Answers 41.21–41.24

41.21 The answer is A (*Synopsis VIII,* page 1188).

41.22 The answer is C (*Synopsis VIII,* pages 1188–1190).

41.23 The answer is A (*Synopsis VIII,* page 1188).

41.24 The answer is B (*Synopsis VIII,* page 1189).
Rett's disorder is postulated to be a genetically determined disorder in which there is normal development for at least 5 months, after which head growth decelerates between 5 and 48 months. When this deceleration occurs, there is a loss of skills, including social development and language skills. This disorder is known to occur only in females, and clinical features of this disorder include severe stereotypic hand movements such as hand-wringing or hand-washing. Other stereotypic movements that occur in this disorder include licking, biting, or tapping the fingers. Childhood disintegrative disorder is similar to Rett's disorder in that there is a period of apparently normal development with a subsequent loss of function. In the case of childhood disintegrative disorder, however, this period is for at least the first 2 years and may last even longer. This disorder is also known as Heller's syndrome. After the deterioration of language, social skills, bowel or bladder function, play skills, and motor skills, these children resemble those with autistic disorder. Childhood disintegrative disorder appears to be about one tenth as common as autistic disorder and to be much more common in boys than in girls.

42

Attention-Deficit Disorders

Attention-deficit/hyperactivity disorder (ADHD) is common in childhood, affecting up to 5 percent of school-aged children. According to the fourth edition of *Diagnostic and Statistical Manual of Mental Disorders* (DSM-IV), ADHD may be diagnosed if a child has multiple symptoms of inattention or hyperactivity-impulsivity compared with other children of the same age for at least 6 months. Symptoms of inattention include making frequent careless mistakes, failing to follow instructions or complete school tasks or chores at home, seeming to be unable to listen to what is being said, and high levels of distractibility. Symptoms of hyperactivity-impulsivity include fidgeting with hands or feet or squirming, inability to remain seated for the duration of a structured activity, running or climbing inappropriately, blurting out answers to questions before the questions are completed, and difficulty in waiting for a turn in a game or a group. DSM-IV requires that symptoms be present by 7 years of age and that the symptoms be exhibited in at least two settings, such as in school and at home. The three types of attention-deficit/hyperactivity disorder are ADHD, predominantly inattentive type; ADHD, predominantly hyperactive-impulsive type; and ADHD, combined type.

The most obvious sign of ADHD is hyperactivity. Children who have hyperactivity as the predominant feature are more likely to be referred for treatment than are children with inattention but without hyperactivity. Children with predominantly hyperactive-impulsive symptoms are likely to have an enduring disorder and may be the ones who are most vulnerable to concurrent conduct disorder. Children with ADHD are also at high risk for learning disorders, including mathematics disorder and reading disorder; communication disorders; and developmental coordination disorder. Since children with ADHD are commonly intrusive and impulsive, their peer relationships tend to be poor; over time, children with ADHD are often rejected by their peer group. Children with ADHD generally have normal intelligence and are aware of their social difficulties. Sometimes the children become frustrated, demoralized, or depressed in response to continually being in trouble at school and having difficulties with their schoolwork. Their frustration may take the form of irritability or aggressive outbursts.

The majority of children who have ADHD benefit from sympathomimetics. Methylphenidate (Ritalin), dextroamphetamine (Dexedrine), and pemoline (Cylert) are the stimulants used most often for children. Methylphenidate is effective in up to 75 percent of children with ADHD, and it has relatively few side effects. Methylphenidate is a short-acting drug that has its onset of action within an hour of ingestion, and the effects last for several hours. The most common side effects associated with methylphenidate are headaches, stomachaches, nausea, and insomnia. During periods of use, methylphenidate is associated with some growth suppression, but that effect is generally compensated for with a growth spurt when the children are taken off medication in the summer and on weekends. Some children experience a rebound effect when the medication wears off; then they become mildly irritable and transiently exhibit increased hyperactivity. Dextroamphetamine is approved by the Food and Drug Administration (FDA) for children over age 3 years, whereas methylphenidate is approved only for children over age 6 years. Dextroamphetamine has an effect similar to methylphenidate, although dextroamphetamine is a slightly longer acting drug.

The course of ADHD is variable; about half of the children with it are still symptomatic in early adolescence, and about one third are still symptomatic in adulthood. The hyperactivity symptoms are often the first ones to remit, and distractibility is the last to remit. Remission is not likely to occur before age 12 years. The outcome for patients with ADHD into young adulthood is more guarded than it is for children who are virtually asymptomatic by age 18. Adolescents with persistent ADHD are vulnerable to a number of other disorders, especially conduct disorder, substance abuse, and depressive disorders. Patients with ADHD and conduct disorder in adolescence have a 50 percent chance of having antisocial personality disorder as adults. Patients with adult manifestations of ADHD respond to sympathomimetics in the same manner as do children with the disorder and are often maintained on those medications.

Students should study Chapter 42 of *Kaplan and Sadock's Synopsis VIII* and then study the questions and answers in this chapter to enhance their knowledge of the area.

HELPFUL HINTS

The student should know these terms.

- adult manifestations
- ambidexterity
- antidepressant
- clonidine (Catapres)
- developmentally inappropriate attention
- disinhibition
- disorganized EEG pattern
- distractibility
- emotional lability
- growth suppression
- hyperactivity-impulsivity
- hyperkinesis
- impaired cognitive performance
- inattention
- learning disorders
- matching familiar faces
- nonfocal (soft) signs
- perceptual-motor problems
- PET scan
- poor motor coordination
- rebound effect
- right-left discrimination
- secondary depression
- soft neurologic signs
- sympathomimetic

▲ QUESTIONS

DIRECTIONS: Each of the questions or incomplete statements below is followed by five suggested responses or completions. Select the *one* that is *best* in each case.

42.1 Which of the following statements about attention-deficit/hyperactivity disorder (ADHD) is *false*?

A. Children with ADHD can have inattention with no hyperactivity or impulsivity.
B. Children with ADHD may have symptoms of hyperactivity but no inattention.
C. The disturbance must be present in at least two settings.
D. Children can meet the criteria for ADHD with impulsive symptoms only.
E. Many children with ADHD have many symptoms of inattention, hyperactivity, and impulsivity.

42.2 Which of the following medications used in the treatment of ADHD has been approved by the Food and Drug Administration (FDA) for children 3 years of age and older?

A. Dextroamphetamine (Dexedrine)
B. Methylphenidate (Ritalin)
C. Pemoline (Cylert)
D. Imipramine (Tofranil)
E. None of the above

42.3 All of the following disorders are associated with ADHD *except*

A. reading disorder
B. developmental coordination disorder
C. psychotic disorder not otherwise specified
D. oppositional defiant disorder
E. conduct disorder

42.4 Which of the following statements about ADHD is *false*?

A. Many children with ADHD have disorganized EEG patterns that are characteristic of younger children.
B. Some children with ADHD do not exhibit any signs of hyperactivity.
C. Borderline intellectual functioning is an associated feature of ADHD.
D. Children with ADHD into adolescence are at high risk for conduct disorder, substance-related disorders, and mood disorders.
E. Growth suppression associated with methylphenidate (Ritalin) is compensated for during drug holidays.

42.5 The most frequently cited characteristic among children with ADHD is

A. perceptual-motor impairment
B. emotional lability
C. disorders of memory and thinking
D. hyperactivity
E. disorders of speech and hearing

42.6 The first symptom of ADHD to remit is usually

A. hyperactivity
B. distractibility
C. decreased attention span
D. impulse-control problems
E. learning problems

42.7 The hyperactive child is often

A. accident prone
B. explosively irritable
C. fascinated by spinning objects
D. preoccupied with water play
E. all of the above

DIRECTIONS: These questions consist of lettered headings followed by numbered phrases or statements. For each numbered item, select the *one* lettered item that is most closely associated with it. Each lettered item may be used once, more than once, or not at all.

Questions 42.8–42.12

A. Methylphenidate (Ritalin)
B. Dextroamphetamine (Dexedrine)
C. Bupropion (Wellbutrin)
D. Clonidine (Catapres)

42.8 This may become the drug of choice for children with ADHD and a history of severe tic disorders or increased difficulties in the late afternoon or evenings.

42.9 This drug has the shortest half-life and has been shown to lead to improvement in about 75 percent of children with ADHD.

42.10 This drug may be the drug of choice in children who cannot tolerate stimulants because of severe rebound reactions.

42.11 This drug has a half-life of 8 to 12 hours.

42.12 It has been shown that growth suppression occurring with drug use can be compensated with drug holiday in the summer and weekends.

Questions 42.13–42.16

A. Psychosocial interventions
B. Medication treatment
C. Both of the above
D. None of the above

42.13 This treatment would be beneficial for the learning disorders that often accompany ADHD.

42.14 This treatment is important because many children with ADHD have poor social skills and are socially isolated.

42.15 This treatment best controls the core symptoms of ADHD.

42.16 This treatment may have an impact on aggressive behavior in children with ADHD.

ANSWERS

Attention-Deficit Disorders

42.1 The answer is D (*Synopsis VIII,* page 1193).
Children cannot meet the criteria for attention-deficit/hyperactivity disorder (ADHD) with impulsive symptoms only; hyperactivity or inattention symptoms are also needed. *Children with ADHD can have inattention with no hyperactivity or impulsivity* if they have at least six symptoms of inattention. *Children with ADHD may have symptoms of hyperactivity but no inattention,* but they must then have four symptoms of hyperactivity or at least four symptoms of a combination of hyperactivity and impulsivity. *The disturbance must be present in at least two settings. Many children with ADHD have many symptoms of inattention, hyperactivity, and impulsivity.* Persons with adult manifestations of the disorder are maintained on sympathomimetic drugs. Table 42.1 lists the diagnostic criteria for attention-deficit/hyperactivity disorder, and Table 42.2 lists the diagnostic criteria for attention-deficit/hyperactivity disorder not otherwise specified.

42.2 The answer is A (*Synopsis VIII,* page 1197).
The Food and Drug Administration (FDA) has approved the

Table 42.1
DSM-IV Diagnostic Criteria for Attention-Deficit/Hyperactivity Disorder

A. Either (1) or (2):
  (1) six (or more) of the following symptoms of **inattention** have persisted for at least 6 months to a degree that is maladaptive and inconsistent with developmental level:

  Inattention:
  (a) often fails to give close attention to details or makes careless mistakes in schoolwork, work, or other activities
  (b) often has difficulty sustaining attention in tasks or play activities
  (c) often does not seem to listen when spoken to directly
  (d) often does not follow through on instructions and fails to finish schoolwork, chores, or duties in the workplace (not due to oppositional behavior or failure to understand instructions)
  (e) often has difficulty organizing tasks and activities
  (f) often avoids, dislikes, or is reluctant to engage in tasks that require sustained mental effort (such as schoolwork or homework)
  (g) often loses things necessary for tasks or activities (eg, toys, school assignments, pencils, books, or tools)
  (h) is often easily distracted by extraneous stimuli
  (i) is often forgetful in daily activities

  (2) six (or more) of the following symptoms of **hyperactivity-impulsivity** have persisted for at least 6 months to a degree that is maladaptive and inconsistent with developmental level:

  Hyperactivity
  (a) often fidgets with hands or feet or squirms in seat
  (b) often leaves seat in classroom or in other situations in which remaining seated is expected
  (c) often runs about or climbs excessively in situations in which it is inappropriate (in adolescents or adults, may be limited to subjective feelings of restlessness)
  (d) often has difficulty playing or engaging in leisure activities quietly
  (e) is often "on the go" or often acts as if "driven by a motor"
  (f) often talks excessively

  Impulsivity
  (g) often blurts out answers before questions have been completed
  (h) often has difficulty awaiting turn
  (i) often interrupts or intrudes on others (eg, butts in on conversations or games)

B. Some hyperactive-impulsive or inattentive symptoms that caused impairment were present before age 7 years.

C. Some impairment from the symptoms is present in two or more settings (eg, at school [or work] and at home).

D. There must be clear evidence of clinically significant impairment in social, academic, or occupational functioning.

E. The symptoms do not occur exclusively during the course of a pervasive developmental disorder, schizophrenia, or other psychotic disorder and are not better accounted for by another mental disorder (eg, mood disorder, anxiety disorder, dissociative disorder, or a personality disorder).

Code based on type:
  Attention-deficit/hyperactivity disorder, combined type: if both criteria A1 and A2 are met for the past 6 months
  Attention-deficit/hyperactivity disorder, predominantly inattentive type: if criterion A1 is met but criterion A2 is not met for the past 6 months
  Attention-deficit/hyperactivity disorder, predominantly hyperactive-impulsive type: if criterion A2 is met but criterion A1 is not met for the past 6 months

Coding note: For individuals (especially adolescents and adults) who currently have symptoms that no longer meet full criteria, "in partial remission" should be specified.

Reprinted with permission from American Psychiatric Association: *Diagnostic and Statistical Manual of Mental Disorders,* ed 4. Copyright, American Psychiatric Association, Washington, 1994.

Table 42.2
DSM-IV Diagnostic Criteria for Attention-Deficit/Hyperactivity Disorder Not Otherwise Specified

This category is for disorders with prominent symptoms of inattention or hyperactivity-impulsivity that do not meet criteria for attention-deficit/hyperactivity disorder.

Reprinted with permission from American Psychiatric Association: *Diagnostic and Statistical Manual of Mental Disorders,* ed 4. Copyright, American Psychiatric Association, Washington, 1994.

use of *dextroamphetamine (Dexedrine)* for children of 3 years of age and older and the use of *methylphenidate (Ritalin)* and *pemoline (Cylert)* for children 6 years of age and older. *Imipramine (Tofranil)* has been approved by the FDA only for the treatment of nocturnal enuresis in children above age 6 years.

42.3 The answer is C (*Synopsis VIII,* pages 1193–1197). Children with ADHD are often described as concrete thinkers and may exhibit perseveration, but thought disorder consistent with *psychotic disorder not otherwise specified* is not a common associated disorder. Children with ADHD are at higher risk than the general population for a number of other psychiatric disorders. Learning disorders, including *reading disorder,* are common in children with ADHD. Children with ADHD are also often found to have neurological soft signs and *developmental coordination disorder.* Children with ADHD are likely to have difficulties with aggressive impulse control and are commonly found to have *oppositional defiant disorder.* Children with ADHD into adolescence are the ones at highest risk for *conduct disorder,* which is found in up to 50 percent of adolescents with ADHD.

42.4 The answer is C (*Synopsis VIII,* pages 1193–1197). *Borderline intellectual functioning is not an associated feature of ADHD.* Children with ADHD have a higher incidence of EEG abnormalities than do the general population. *Many children with ADHD have disorganized EEG patterns that are characteristic of younger children.* In some cases the EEG findings normalize over time. *Some children with ADHD do not exhibit any signs of hyperactivity* but do have multiple symptoms of inattention. *Children with ADHD into adolescence are at high risk for conduct disorder, substance-related disorders, and mood disorders.* Growth suppression is a recognized side effect of methylphenidate (Ritalin) treatment, but evidence indicates that *growth suppression associated with methylphenidate is compensated for during drug holidays*—the times when children are not taking the medication, such as weekends and summers.

42.5 The answer is D (*Synopsis VIII,* pages 1193, 1194). The most frequently cited characteristic among children with ADHD is *hyperactivity,* followed by *perceptual-motor impairment, emotional lability,* general coordination deficit, disorders of attention, impulsivity, *disorders of memory and thinking,* specific learning disabilities, *disorders of speech and hearing,* and equivocal neurological signs and electroencephalographic irregularities.

42.6 The answer is A (*Synopsis VIII,* pages 1193, 1194). *Hyperactivity* is usually the first symptom of ADHD to remit, and *distractibility* is the last. The course of the condition is highly variable: Symptoms may persist into adolescence or adult life, they may remit at puberty, or the hyperactivity may disappear but the *decreased attention span* and *impulse-control problems* persist. Remission is not likely before the age of 12. If remission does occur, it is usually between the ages of 12 and 20. Remission may be accompanied by a productive adolescence and adult life, satisfying interpersonal relationships, and few significant sequelae. The majority of patients with ADHD, however, undergo only partial remission and are vulnerable to antisocial and other personality disorders and mood disorders. *Learning problems* often continue.

42.7 The answer is E (all) (*Synopsis VIII,* pages 1196–1197). The hyperactive child is often *accident-prone, explosively irritable, fascinated by spinning objects,* and *preoccupied with water play.* In school, hyperactive children may rapidly attack a test but answer only the first two questions, or they may be unable to wait to be called on. At home, they cannot be put off for even a minute. Irritability may be set off by relatively minor stimuli, and they may seem puzzled and dismayed over that phenomenon. The children are frequently emotionally labile and easily inspired to laughter and to tears, and their moods and performances are apt to be variable and unpredictable.

Answers 42.8–42.12

42.8 The answer is D (*Synopsis VIII,* page 1198).

42.9 The answer is A (*Synopsis VIII,* page 1197).

42.10 The answer is C (*Synopsis VIII,* page 1197).

42.11 The answer is B (*Synopsis VIII,* page 1198).

42.12 The answer is A (*Synopsis VIII,* page 1197). The pharmacologic agents used most widely in the treatment of ADHD are the stimulants, including methylphenidate and dextroamphetamine. Cylert (pemoline) is also a stimulant and is used when methylphenidate or dextroamphetamine has not been effective, but it requires monitoring of liver function. Since tic disorders can be exacerbated by the use of the stimulants, in children with a history of troublesome tics, a drug from another category may be indicated. *Clonidine (Catapres)* has been chosen in some of these cases, since it is reported to *diminish tic behaviors* as well as control hyperactivity and short attention span. Clonidine is also an antihypertensive, so that monitoring of blood pressure is necessary with its use. Clonidine can cause significant sedation for some children, and this side effect may be beneficial for some children with ADHD who become very hyperaroused in the evening. *Methylphenidate* has its peak plasma level 1 to 2 hours after ingestion, and its half-life of 3 to 4 hours *is the shortest of the stimulant drugs.* Some children experience a rebound effect consisting of mild irritability and increased hyperactivity when the drug wears off. Studies with ADHD children have shown methylphenidate to have an efficacy rate of about 75 percent. Some children with ADHD cannot tolerate either methylphenidate or Dexedrine because of either severe rebound effects or an increased need for medication in the late afternoon and evening. Especially for children who are also exhibiting symptoms of depression, *bupropion (Wellbutrin)* may be used. This drug is a unicyclic antidepressant whose half-life is approximately12 hours. Thus, when it is given twice daily, a steady-state blood level can be achieved. Its efficacy for ADHD symptoms should be present throughout the day and evening evenly. *Dextroamphetamine* is approved by the Food and Drug Administration (FDA) for use in the treatment of ADHD in children 3 years and older. Its half-life is 8 to 12 hours, after which a rebound may sometimes be experienced. Dextroamphetamine is an efficacious treatment for ADHD and is not infrequently found to be a drug of abuse among adolescents and adults with substance use disorders. There has been concern over the years regarding the growth suppression that may occur in children during the course of *methylphenidate* use. While *growth may be suppressed* during the days that methylphenidate is being taken, there is evidence that final height of children who have taken *methylphenidate* is not affected as long as drug holidays are given on the weekends, summers, or during other periods.

Answers 42.13–42.16

42.13 The answer is D (*Synopsis VIII,* pages 1197–1198).

42.14 The answer is C (*Synopsis VIII,* pages 1197–1198).

42.15 The answer is B (*Synopsis VIII,* pages 1197–1198).

42.16 The answer is C (*Synopsis VIII,* pages 1197–1198). Learning disorders are seen with greater frequency in children with ADHD than in the general population. The treatment for the learning disorders, however, *is independent of the treatment for ADHD,* and the use of psychostimulants to control the ADHD does not automatically ameliorate the learning disorders. Learning disorders respond to remedial educational programs geared specifically to the affected subject. Neither psychosocial nor pharmacological treatment is useful. Both *psychosocial interventions* and medication treatment are important in improving *social skills* and self-esteem in children with ADHD. Social skills groups are effective in providing a supervised forum for ADHD children to practice appropriate interpersonal skills, and medications that can mediate impulsivity and hyperactivity also promote social acceptance. It is well known that *the core symptoms of ADHD are highly responsive to stimulant medications.* Conversely, it is also well known that psychosocial interventions alone are unlikely to influence core features of ADHD. Environmental interventions, such as small, structured educational settings, appropriate levels of stimulation in the home, and family education, are helpful in containing the symptoms of ADHD. Both *medication intervention* and psychosocial interventions may play a role in decreasing aggressive behavior in children with ADHD. Studies have shown that within the classroom setting, *ADHD children who are responsive to treatment with stimulant medication also exhibit less aggressive behavior.* Behavioral interventions focused on providing positive reinforcement for nonaggressive and prosocial behaviors are also helpful to children with ADHD who are aggressive.

43 

Disruptive Behavior Disorders

The fourth edition of *Diagnostic and Statistical Manual of Mental Disorders* (DSM-IV) includes three disruptive behavior disorders: oppositional defiant disorder, conduct disorder, and disruptive behavior disorder not otherwise specified.

Oppositional defiant disorder consists of a pattern of negativistic, hostile, and defiant behaviors aimed at authority figures. This disorder specifies a duration of these defiant and disobedient behaviors for at least 6 months and the frequent occurrence of at least four of the following: loss of temper, arguments with adults, refusal to comply with adults' requests, deliberately doing things to annoy people, blaming others for personal failings, touchiness, anger, resentment, and spite. The behavior must occur more frequently than is expected for developmental level and must cause impairment. Oppositional behavior and negativistic attitude are developmentally normal in very young children. Oppositional behaviors seem to peak in children between 18 and 24 months, when toddlers are striving toward greater autonomy. Some have characterized this period as the "terrible 2s." Epidemiologic surveys estimate that about 20 percent of school-age children exhibit negativistic traits. Oppositional defiant disorder is more prevalent among boys than girls and may manifest itself as early as 3 years, but it more commonly emerges at about 8 years of age.

No single cause of oppositional defiant disorder is accepted. A temperamental predisposition to a strong will or stubborn behavior may interact with family and environmental forces to result in a nonadaptive pattern of control and defiance.

Children with oppositional defiant disorder often have difficulty in school because of their lack of cooperation with their teachers' requests. In addition, such children are often rejected by their peer group and perceive friendships as unsatisfactory. Some children exhibit oppositional defiant behavior in their homes but do not manifest the same behaviors in school or in a clinical setting. Children with oppositional defiant disorder may be especially resistant to receiving help from adults; therefore, any problems they encounter may remain unsolved. Some children with oppositional defiant disorder recognize their difficulties and become demoralized or depressed.

Conduct disorder consists of an enduring pattern for at least 6 months of behaviors in which the basic rights of others or age-appropriate societal rules are violated. A pattern of only 3 of 15 symptoms is required for the diagnosis of conduct disorder. The symptoms of conduct disorder include the following: often bullies, threatens, or intimidates; often initiates physical fights; has used a weapon; has stolen with confrontation with a victim; has been physically cruel to people; has been physically cruel to animals; has forced someone into sexual activity; often lies or cons others; often stays out at night against parental rules; has set fires; has destroyed property; and is often truant from school. DSM-IV specifies a childhood-onset type (one conduct problem before age 10) and an adolescent-onset type (no conduct problems before age 10). The severity of the conduct disorder is also specified by DSM-IV as mild, moderate, or severe.

No single factor can account for the development of conduct disorder; a combination of parental, biological, and sociocultural factors contribute to its development. Harsh, punitive child-rearing styles and physical or sexual abuse can contribute to aggressive, cruel behaviors in children. Children raised in such harsh environments often have difficulty in verbalizing their feelings and may overreact to situations with anger and violence.

Conduct disorder does not develop overnight; instead, symptoms evolve over time until a consistent pattern is present. Very young children are unlikely to meet the diagnostic criteria for the disorder, since they are developmentally unable to exhibit many conduct disorder features, such as breaking into a home, stealing with confrontation, and forcing someone into sexual activity. The average age of onset of conduct disorder is 10 to 12 years for boys and 14 to 16 years for girls.

Students should study Chapter 43 in *Kaplan and Sadock's Synopsis VIII* and the questions and answers in this chapter to enhance their knowledge of the area.

HELPFUL HINTS

The student should be able to define the following terms.

- ADHD
- child abuse
- CNS dysfunction
- harsh child-rearing structure
- issues of control
- negativistic relationships
- poor peer relationships
- poor self-esteem
- socioeconomic deprivation
- terrible 2s
- truancy
- violation of rights

▲ QUESTIONS

DIRECTIONS: Each of the questions or incomplete statements below is followed by five suggested responses or completions. Select the *one* that is *best* in each case.

43.1 Which of the following statements about oppositional defiant disorder is *false*?

A. The most common symptoms include often losing one's temper, arguing with adults, and refusing to comply with adults' requests or rules.
B. It is characterized by a pattern of behavior that violates the rights of others.
C. Oppositional defiant disorder cannot be diagnosed if conduct disorder is present.
D. About 25 percent of children with oppositional defiant disorder no longer meet the diagnostic criteria after several years.
E. Oppositional defiant disorder is not diagnosed if symptoms occur exclusively during a mood disorder.

43.2 Conduct disorder

A. has the best prognosis when it has its onset at a young age
B. cannot be diagnosed in a child who has received a diagnosis of oppositional defiant disorder
C. usually includes cruelty to animals, enuresis, and fire setting
D. cannot occur concurrently with major depressive disorder
E. generally has its onset earlier in boys than in girls

43.3 All of the following may contribute to the development of conduct disorder *except*

A. harsh and punitive child rearing
B. parental sociopathy, alcohol dependence, and substance abuse
C. physical and sexual abuse
D. single-parent family
E. attention-deficit/hyperactivity disorder

43.4 Conduct disorder frequently coexists with all of the following *except*

A. learning disorders
B. major depression
C. attention-deficit/hyperactivity disorder
D. separation anxiety disorder
E. substance abuse disorders

DIRECTIONS: These lettered headings are followed by a list of numbered statements. For each numbered statement, select the lettered heading most closely associated with it. Each lettered heading may be used once, more than once, or not at all.

Questions 43.5–43.9

A. Oppositional defiant disorder
B. Conduct disorder

43.5 It may be diagnosed when symptoms occur exclusively with attention-deficit/hyperactivity disorder, learning disorders, and mood disorders.
43.6 It may be equally prevalent in adolescent boys and adolescent girls.
43.7 The patient often bullies, threatens, or intimidates others.
43.8 The patient often actively defies or refuses to comply with adults' requests or rules.
43.9 Beginning before 13 years of age, the patient often stays out at night despite parental prohibitions.

DIRECTIONS: Match the statements with the appropriate medication.

Questions 43.10–43.15

A. Antipsychotics
B. Lithium
C. Serotonin-specific reuptake inhibitors
D. Stimulants
E. Carbamazepine

43.10 This medication has recently been shown to work no better than placebo in decreasing aggression.
43.11 This medication has been shown to be efficacious in the treatment of a disorder that commonly occurs with conduct disorder.
43.12 This medication is under investigation as a treatment for irritability, mood disturbance, and mood lability among children with conduct disorder.
43.13 This medication has been shown to decrease explosive aggression and assaultive behavior in children with conduct disorder.
43.14 This medication is used to stabilize mood as well as to diminish overt aggression.
43.15 This medication is associated with withdrawal dyskinesias.

ANSWERS

Disruptive Behavior Disorders

43.1 The answer is B (*Synopsis VIII,* pages 1201–1202).
Conduct disorder, not oppositional defiant disorder, *is characterized by a pattern of behavior that violates the rights of others. The most common symptoms of oppositional defiant disorder include often losing one's temper, often arguing with adults, and refusing to comply with adults' requests or rules. Oppositional defiant disorder cannot be diagnosed if conduct disorder is present.* Oppositional defiant disorder is not a stable disorder, since *about 25 percent of children with it no longer meet the diagnostic criteria after several years.* Unlike conduct disorder, *oppositional defiant disorder is not diagnosed if symptoms occur exclusively during a mood disorder.* Table 43.1 lists the diagnostic criteria for oppositional defiant disorder.

43.2 The answer is E (*Synopsis VIII,* page 1205).
Conduct disorder *generally has its onset earlier in boys* (10 to 12 years) *than in girls* (14 to 16 years). It *has the worst prognosis when it has its onset at a young age* and when the child exhibits the greatest number and frequency of symptoms. A good prognosis is predicted by mild conduct disorder, onset at a late age, the absence of coexisting psychopathology, and normal intellectual functioning. Conduct disorder *cannot be diagnosed in a child who has received diagnosis of oppositional defiant disorder;* however, when conduct disorder is diagnosed, the oppositional defiant disorder diagnosis is preempted. Conduct disorder *does not usually include cruelty to animals, enuresis, and fire setting,* although in the past that triad was believed to be typical of children with conduct disorder. Enuresis is not a diagnostic criterion for conduct disorder, but cruelty to animals and fire setting are diagnostic criteria. Conduct disorder *can occur concurrently with major depressive disorder.* Conduct disorder can be diagnosed even when the conduct symptoms occur only during depressive episodes and resolve when the depression remits. The diagnostic criteria for conduct disorder are listed in Table 43.2.

Table 43.1
DSM-IV Diagnostic Criteria for Oppositional Defiant Disorder

A. A patter of negativistic, hostile, and defiant behavior lasting at least 6 months, during which four (or more) of the following are present:
   (1) often loses temper
   (2) often argues with adults
   (3) often actively defies or refuses to comply with adults' requests or rules
   (4) often deliberately annoys people
   (5) often blames others for his or her mistakes or misbehavior
   (6) is often touchy or easily annoyed by others
   (7) is often angry and resentful
   (8) is often spiteful or vindictive

   Note: Consider a criterion met only if the behavior occurs more frequently than is typically observed in individuals of comparable age and developmental level.

B. The disturbance in behavior causes significant impairment in social, academic, or occupational functioning.

C. Does not occur exclusively during the course of a psychotic or mood disorder.

D. Does not meet criteria for conduct disorder, and if the individual is age 18 or older, criteria are not met for antisocial personality disorder.

Reprinted with permission from American Psychiatric Association: *Diagnostic and Statistical Manual of Mental Disorders,* ed 4. Copyright, American Psychiatric Association, Washington, 1994.

43.3 The answer is D (*Synopsis VIII,* pages 1205–1206).
A *single-parent family* does not necessarily contribute to the development of conduct disorder; instead, the strife between parents is believed to promote conduct disorder. *Harsh and punitive child rearing* is thought to promote aggressive and violent behaviors in children. *Parental sociopathy, alcohol dependence, and substance abuse* are associated with conduct disorder in children. *Physical and sexual abuse,* especially when it is long-term abuse, contributes to violent and aggressive behaviors in children. Abused children are likely to violate the rights of others because of their life experiences of being terrorized and brutally treated. Persistent *attention-deficit/hyperactivity disorder* seems to be associated with a high risk for conduct disorder.

43.4 The answer is D (*Synopsis VIII,* pages 1206–1207).
It is becoming widely recognized that children who develop conduct disorder are likely to have a history of *attention-deficit/hyperactivity disorder, learning disorders,* and opposi-tional-defiant disorder. Approximately one third of prepubertal children develop full diagnostic criteria for conduct disorder during an episode of *major depression.* Shared risk factors including conflictual family relationships, early history of disruptive behaviors, poor parental supervision, and negative life events may partially explain the association of mood disorders and conduct disorders. Children with conduct disorder without mood disorders are also at high risk to develop a mood disorder in adolescence. Children with conduct disorder are also at high risk for developing *substance abuse disorders* as adolescents. There is an association between aggression toward peers as a child and the later development of substance abuse. *Separation anxiety disorder,* although associated with very high risk for mood disorder, is not correlated with conduct disorder.

Answers 43.5–43.9.

43.5 The answer is B (*Synopsis VIII,* pages 1206–1207).

43.6 The answer is A (*Synopsis VIII,* page 1201).

43.7 The answer is B (*Synopsis VIII,* page 1205).

43.8 The answer is A (*Synopsis VIII,* pages 1202–1203).

43.9 The answer is B (*Synopsis VIII,* page 1205).
Conduct disorder may be diagnosed when symptoms occur exclusively with attention-deficit/hyperactivity disorder, learning disorders, and mood disorders, whereas oppositional defiant

Table 43.2
DSM-IV Diagnostic Criteria for Conduct Disorder

A. A repetitive and persistent pattern of behavior in which the basic rights of others or major age-appropriate societal norms or rules are violated, as manifested by the presence of three (or more) of the following criteria in the past 12 months, with at least one criterion present in the past 6 months:

Aggression to people and animals

(1) often bullies, threatens, or intimidates others
(2) often initiates physical fights
(3) has used a weapon that can cause serious physical harm to others (eg, a bat, brick, broken bottle, knife, gun)
(4) has been physically cruel to people
(5) has been physically cruel to animals
(6) has stolen while confronting a victim (eg, mugging, purse snatching, extortion, armed robbery)
(7) has forced someone into sexual activity

Destruction of property

(8) has deliberately engaged in fire setting with the intention of causing serious damage
(9) has deliberately destroyed others' property (other than by fire setting)

Deceitfulness or theft

(10) has broken into someone else's house, building, or car
(11) often lies to obtain goods or favors or to avoid obligations (ie, "cons" others)
(12) has stolen items of nontrivial value without confronting a victim (eg, shoplifting, but without breaking and entering; forgery)

Serious violations of rules

(13) often stays out at night despite parental prohibitions, beginning before age 13 years
(14) has run away from home overnight at least twice while living in parental or parental surrogate home (or once without returning for a lengthy period)
(15) is often truant from school, beginning before age 13 years

B. The disturbance in behavior causes clinically significant impairment in social, academic, or occupational functioning.

C. If the individual is age 18 years or older, criteria are not met for antisocial personality disorder.

Specify type based on age at onset:

Childhood-onset type: onset of at least one criterion characteristic of conduct disorder prior to age 10 years

Adolescent-onset type: absence of any criteria characteristic of conduct disorder prior to age 10 years

Specify severity:

Mild: few if any conduct problems in excess of those required to make the diagnosis **and** conduct problems cause only minor harm to others

Moderate: number of conduct problems **and** effect on others intermediate between "mild" and "severe"

Severe: many conduct problems in excess of those required to make the diagnosis **or** conduct problems cause considerable harm to others

Reprinted with permission from American Psychiatric Association: *Diagnostic and Statistical Manual of Mental Disorders,* ed 4. Copyright, American Psychiatric Association, Washington, 1994.

disorder cannot be diagnosed when symptoms occur exclusively during a mood disorder. *Oppositional defiant disorder may be equally prevalent in adolescent boys and adolescent girls,* but conduct disorder is present more often in adolescent boys than adolescent girls. In conduct disorder the *patient often bullies, threatens, or intimidates others.* A typical core symptom of oppositional defiant disorder is that the *patient often actively defies or refuses to comply with adults' requests or rules.* And, *beginning before 13 years of age, the patient often stays out at night despite parental prohibitions* in conduct disorder.

Answers 43.10–43.15

43.10 The answer is E (*Synopsis VIII,* pages 1208–1209).

43.11 The answer is D (*Synopsis VIII,* pages 1208–1209).

43.12 The answer is C (*Synopsis VIII,* pages 1208–1209).

43.13 The answer is A (*Synopsis VIII,* pages 1208–1209).

43.14 The answer is B (*Synopsis VIII,* pages 1208–1209).

43.15 The answer is A (*Synopsis VIII,* pages 1208–1209).
In controlled studies, *carbamazepine* was shown to be no better than placebo in decreasing overt aggression among children with conduct disorders. *Stimulants* have been used widely among children with conduct disorder who also have attention-deficit/hyperactivity disorder. There is some evidence that in these children, the stimulant medication diminishes aggression within the classroom setting. *Serotonin-specific reuptake inhibitors,* for example, fluoxetine (Prozac), sertraline (Zoloft), and paroxetine (Paxil), are being investigated for treatment of the irritability, mood lability, and mood disorders among children with conduct disorder, with and without the full clinical picture of major depression. *Antipsychotics,* especially haloperidol (Haldol), has been shown in studies to decrease explosive outbursts and aggressive behavior in children with aggressive conduct disorders. Lithium has also been shown to diminish aggression in children with rage outbursts, assaultive behavior, and unstable mood. Haloperidol is known to produce withdrawal dyskinesias in approximately one fourth of children who have been treated with it for the control of aggressive behavior.

44

Feeding and Eating Disorders of Infancy or Early Childhood

The three disorders that are included in the feeding and eating disorders of infancy and early childhood include pica, rumination disorder, and feeding disorder of infancy or early childhood.

Pica has no single causal explanation, although it seems to run in families. It may consist of ingesting such substances as paint, plaster, string, hair, and cloth. Nutritional deficiencies may play a role in the development of pica in certain situations, such as cravings for ice and dirt associated with iron and zinc deficiencies. Pica is common in children with failure to thrive; hence, parental neglect and deprivation have also been associated with pica. Pica often has its onset in children less than 2 years old. Pica can result in morbidity or mortality, depending on what is ingested. Among the most serious complications are lead poisoning from lead-based paint; intestinal parasites from soil; anemia; zinc deficiency after eating clay; and iron deficiency after eating starch. In some cases, zinc and iron deficiencies may induce pica.

Rumination disorder is the repeated regurgitation and rechewing of food, usually in infants. Its onset typically occurs when the infant is 3 months of age, and it is diagnosed only when the pattern continues for at least 1 month after a period of normal functioning. Rumination disorder is not diagnosed when the regurgitation occurs in association with a gastrointestinal illness or a medical disorder, such as hiatal hernia, pyloric stenosis, or esophageal reflux. Rumination disorder is rare, is found equally in boys and girls, and is seen in up to 10 percent of adults with bulimia nervosa. Rumination disorder is also more common in mentally retarded children and adults than in the general population. Adults with rumination disorder maintain their normal weight.

The cause is not known, but several factors may contribute to the development of rumination disorder. In some babies it may begin as self-stimulatory behavior and be reinforced by the sensation and by the attention it attracts from adults. In other babies, a dysfunctional autonomic nervous systems may contribute to it. Some infants with rumination disorder are eventually found to have esophageal reflux or hiatal hernia. Overstimulation, tension, and a lack of proper nurturance and stimulation have been suggested as contributing factors in rumination disorder.

The course of rumination disorder is variable. It ranges from spontaneous remission in many babies who have remained healthy and well-nourished to failure to thrive in other babies. When failure to thrive, growth retardation, and developmental delays occur, the prognosis is significantly worsened. Demoralization and discouragement on the part of the mother may further impede feeding the infant.

Treatment includes improving the psychosocial environment and increasing the nurturant feeding by the infant's caregivers. In some cases, behavioral techniques—such as aversive conditioning, using a squirt of lemon juice each time the child ruminates—may be a rapid and effective way to diminish rumination disorder.

Feeding disorder of infancy or early childhood is characterized by persistent failure to eat adequately and a failure to gain weight or a significant loss of weight over a period of at least one month. The onset must occur before the child is 6 years old, and the disorder is not accounted for by a lack of appropriate food or by another mental disorder. Students should study Chapter 44 in *Kaplan and Sadock's Synopsis VIII* and then test their knowledge with the questions and answers in this chapter.

HELPFUL HINTS

The student should know the following terms.

- ► amylophagia
- ► anemia
- ► esophageal reflux
- ► failure to thrive
- ► geophagia
- ► hiatal hernia
- ► iron deficiency
- ► lead poisoning
- ► nutritional deficiencies
- ► overstimulation
- ► positive reinforcement
- ► psychosocial dwarfism
- ► regurgitation
- ► self-stimulation
- ► spontaneous remission
- ► zinc deficiency

▲ QUESTIONS

DIRECTIONS: Each of the questions or incomplete statements below is followed by five suggested responses or completions. Select the *one* that is *best* in each case.

44.1 Pica has been associated with all of the following *except*

A. pregnancy
B. lead poisoning
C. mercury poisoning
D. failure to thrive
E. zinc and iron deficiencies

44.2 Iron deficiency has been associated with a repeated pattern of ingesting

A. paint chips
B. clay
C. string
D. ice and dirt
E. paper

44.3 In children with pica, serum hemoglobin readings should be obtained because the children may have

A. zinc deficiency
B. lead poisoning
C. intestinal parasites
D. failure to thrive
E. iron deficiency

44.4 Which of the following statements about rumination disorder is *false*?

A. It is most commonly seen in infants between 3 months and 1 year of age.
B. Adults with rumination disorder are usually emaciated.
C. It occurs equally in boys and girls.
D. It is more prevalent in adults with bulimia nervosa than in the general population.
E. It is associated with overstimulation and understimulation.

44.5 Feeding disorder of infancy or early childhood

A. typically has its onset after the child is 6 years old
B. is diagnosed along with esophageal reflux
C. must be accompanied by a significant failure to gain weight or by significant weight loss
D. must be present for a minimum of 3 months
E. is diagnosed when food is not available

DIRECTIONS: The questions below consist of lettered headings followed by a list of numbered phrases. For each numbered phrase, select

A. if the item is associated with *A only*
B. if the item is associated with *B only*
C. if the item is associated with *both A and B*
D. if the item is associated with *neither A nor B*

Questions 44.6–44.10

A. Pica
B. Rumination disorder
C. Both
D. Neither

44.6 High rate of spontaneous remission
44.7 Reinforcement by pleasurable self-stimulation
44.8 Associated with failure to thrive
44.9 Associated with adult eating disorders
44.10 Associated with pregnant women

Questions 44.11–44.15

A. Pica
B. Rumination disorder
C. Feeding disorder of infancy or early childhood

44.11 This disorder is not diagnosed if it occurs exclusively during the course of anorexia nervosa or bulimia nervosa.
44.12 Repeated regurgitation may occur in this disorder but is not necessary for the diagnosis.
44.13 Symptoms of this disorder are considered developmentally normal in persons under 1 year of age.
44.14 Symptoms of this disorder appear pleasurable in some young children.
44.15 Kleine-Levin syndrome is part of the differential diagnosis of this disorder.

ANSWERS

Feeding and Eating Disorders of Infancy or Early Childhood

44.1 The answer is C (*Synopsis VIII,* pages 1210–1211).
Mercury poisoning has not been associated with pica. Pica is associated with *pregnancy,* particularly in certain cultures in which the ingestion of substances such as clay and starch is reported to be common. Pica is also associated with *lead poisoning,* since in some instances children with pica ingest lead-based paint chips. Pica is one of the symptoms seen in children with *failure to thrive* syndromes, particularly psychosocial dwarfism. *Zinc and iron deficiencies* may cause pica; in some children, when zinc and iron are replaced, pica resolves. The diagnostic criteria for pica are listed in Table 44.1.

44.2 The answer is D (*Synopsis VIII,* page 1210).
Iron deficiency has been associated with cravings for *ice and dirt.* The ingestion of *paint chips* has been associated with lead poisoning, since some paint used to be made with lead. The ingestion of *clay* has been linked to anemia and zinc deficiency. The ingestion of *string* and *paper* has not been linked to any nutritional deficiency.

44.3 The answer is E (*Synopsis VIII,* pages 1211–1212).
Children with pica should be tested for their hemoglobin count, since many such children may have *iron deficiency* and may be anemic. Children who have ingested large amounts of clay may also end up with *zinc deficiency* and anemia. Lead levels should also be obtained for children with pica, since they may have ingested paint chips that contain lead, resulting in *lead poisoning. Intestinal parasites* are sometimes found in children with pica who have ingested dirt. Children with pica should be screened for overall nutritional status, since in some cases pica is seen in conjunction with *failure to thrive.*

44.4 The answer is B (*Synopsis VIII,* pages 1212–1213).
Adults who have rumination disorder *are not usually emaciated.* Rumination disorder is most *commonly seen in infants between 3 months and 1 year of age* and in mentally retarded children and adults. It occurs *equally in boys and girls* and is more prevalent in adults *with bulimia nervosa than in the general population.* Rumination disorder *is associated with overstimulation and understimulation.* The diagnostic criteria for rumination disorder are listed in Table 44.2.

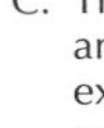

Table 44.2
DSM-IV Diagnostic Criteria for Rumination Disorder

A. Repeated regurgitation and rechewing of food for a period of at least 1 month following a period of normal functioning.
B. The behavior is not due to an associated gastrointestinal or other general medical condition (eg, esophageal reflux).
C. The behavior does not occur exclusively during the course of anorexia nervosa or bulimia nervosa. If the symptoms occur exclusively during the course of mental retardation or a pervasive developmental disorder, they are sufficiently severe to warrant independent clinical attention.

Reprinted with permission from American Psychiatric Association: *Diagnostic and Statistical Manual of Mental Disorders,* ed 4. Copyright, American Psychiatric Association, Washington, 1994.

44.5 The answer is C (*Synopsis VIII,* page 1214).
Feeding disorder of infancy or early childhood is characterized by a feeding disturbance that *must be accompanied by a significant failure to gain weight or by significant weight loss* (Table 44.3). The onset of the disorder must occur *before the child is 6 years old,* and it *is not diagnosed along with esophageal reflux* or when another medical condition accounts for it. Feeding disorder of infancy or early childhood *must be present for a minimum of 1 month, not 3 months,* and it *is not diagnosed when food is not available.*

Answers 44.6–44.10

44.6 The answer is C (*Synopsis VIII,* pages 1210–1211, 1213).

44.7 The answer is B (*Synopsis VIII,* page 1212).

44.8 The answer is C (*Synopsis VIII,* pages 1210, 1213).

44.9 The answer is C (*Synopsis VIII,* pages 1210, 1212).

Table 44.1
DSM-IV Diagnostic Criteria for Pica

A. Persistent eating of nonnutritive substances for at least 1 month.
B. The eating of nonnutritive substances is inappropriate to the developmental level.
C. The eating behavior is not part of a culturally sanctioned practice.
D. If the eating behavior occurs exclusively during the course of another mental disorder (eg, mental retardation, pervasive developmental disorder, schizophrenia), it is sufficiently severe to warrant independent clinical attention.

Reprinted with permission from American Psychiatric Association: *Diagnostic and Statistical Manual of Mental Disorders,* ed 4. Copyright, American Psychiatric Association, Washington, 1994.

Table 44.3
DSM-IV Diagnostic Criteria for Feeding Disorder of Infancy or Early Childhood

A. Feeding disturbance is manifested by persistent failure to eat adequately, with significant failure to gain weight or significant loss of weight over at least 1 month.
B. The disturbance is not due to an associated gastrointestinal or other general medical condition (eg, esophageal reflux).
C. The disturbance is not better accounted for by another mental disorder (eg, rumination disorder) or by lack of available food.
D. The onset is before age 6.

Reprinted with permission from American Psychiatric Association: *Diagnostic and Statistical Manual of Mental Disorders,* ed 4. Copyright, American Psychiatric Association, Washington, 1994.

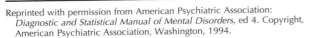

44.10 The answer is A (*Synopsis VIII,* page 1210).
Both rumination disorder and pica seem to have *high rates of spontaneous remission. Rumination disorder* seems to be *reinforced by pleasurable self-stimulation. Pica* is sometimes *associated with failure to thrive,* notably psychosocial dwarfism, in which children have been reported to eat garbage and to drink out of the toilet. *Rumination disorder* also has been *associated with failure to thrive,* and in some cases life-threatening malnutrition may accompany rumination disorder in infants. *Both* rumination disorder and pica are *associated with adult eating disorders. Pica* is *associated with pregnant women* and is reported to be especially prevalent in certain cultures, such as the Australian aborigines.

Answers 44.11–44.15

44.11 The answer is B (*Synopsis VIII,* page 1213).

44.12 The answer is C (*Synopsis VIII,* pages 1210–1211, 1212).

44.13 The answer is A (*Synopsis VIII,* pages 1210–1211).

44.14 The answer is B (*Synopsis VIII,* pages 1212–1213).

44.15 The answer is A (*Synopsis VIII,* page 1211).
The diagnosis of *rumination disorder* is not made if the repeated regurgitation symptoms occur exclusively within an episode of anorexia nervosa or bulimia nervosa. The onset of rumination disorder is typically after 3 months of age but is most common in infants and rare in children, adolescents, and adults. Thus it would be unusual for these symptoms to arise in older children or adolescents outside of the context or another eating disorder. The diagnosis of rumination disorder does not depend on whether or not an appropriate weight has been attained. Failure to thrive, however, is sometimes a sequela of rumination disorder. Repeated regurgitation may occur in feeding disorder of infancy or early childhood and is a core feature of rumination disorder. The core features of feeding disorder of infancy or early childhood relate to the refusal to eat, but *regurgitation may or may not occur.* In this disorder, inability to attain appropriate weight, or loss of significant weight is a necessary symptom. In infants less than 1 year of age, symptoms of pica, that is, eating of nonnutritive substances, *is considered within the range of developmentally normal behaviors.* Pica is much more commonly seen among young children than older children or adolescents, and the risk of developing pica appears to be increased among the mentally retarded. Pica has been reported to occur in 10 to 32 percent of children between 1 and 6 years old and is equal in both sexes. In rumination disorder, infants have been observed to strain in order to bring food back into the mouth after it has been swallowed. Once back in the mouth, it may be swallowed again or spit out. Infants who have been observed appear to *derive pleasure from this process.* Among the differential diagnoses for pica are iron and zinc deficiencies, lead intoxication, and *Kleine-Levin syndrome.* Kleine-Levin syndrome is a rare condition consisting of recurrent periods of prolonged sleep, irritability, voracious eating, and sometimes psychosis. It seems to have its onset after 10 years of age and is almost always self-limited.

45

Tic Disorders

It is becoming increasingly evident through twin studies, adoption studies, and genetic segregation analysis studies that tic disorders are genetic in origin. Tics range from simple involuntary sudden and recurrent stereotyped motor movements to complex sequences of ritualistic behaviors. Simple motor tics are composed of rapid contractions of similar muscle groups resulting in behaviors such as eye blinking, shoulder shrugging, and facial grimacing. Simple vocal tics include coughing, throat clearing, grunting , snorting, and barking sounds. The demarcation between complex tics and compulsive rituals is not clear. Complex motor tics may comprise grooming gestures, jumping, turning around, smelling of objects, echopraxia (imitating observed behaviors), and copropraxia (obscene gestures). Complex vocal tics may include palilalia (repeating one's own words), echolalia (repeating the words of others), and coprolalia (blurting out obscene words or phrases). There is an unusually high comorbidity of tic disorders with other psychiatric disorders, including attention-deficit/hyperactivity disorder and obsessive-compulsive disorder. All of the tic disorders may be characterized by waxing and waning of tics within the context of the particular disorder.

The fourth edition of *Diagnostic and Statistical Manual of Mental Disorders* (DSM-IV) includes four tic disorders: Tourette's disorder, chronic motor or vocal tic disorder, transient tic disorder, and tic disorder not otherwise specified. In all tic disorders, some patients can voluntarily suppress tics for minutes or hours; however, children often do not anticipate their tics or are unable to control them. Stress and anxiety commonly exacerbate tics. They often disappear during sleep, but not always..It is important to differentiate tics from other motor movement abnormalities such as those that occur in Sydenham's chorea, Huntington's disease, Wilson's disease, and Parkinson's disease.

In 1885, George Gilles de la Tourette first described what is now known as Tourette's disorder. Tourette's disorder is characterized by both multiple motor tics and at least one vocal tic that has been present at some time during the illness. The tics may occur many times during the day, nearly every day, or intermittently for at least a year. In Tourette's disorder, tics are never absent for more than 2 months at a time. Tourette's disorder is estimated to occur in 4 to 5 persons per 10,000. It is at least 3 times as common in male patients as in female patients. Motor tics usually emerge by 7 years of age, and vocal tics usually emerge by 11 years of age.

Increasing evidence suggests that genetic factors play a role in the development of Tourette's disorder and in chronic motor or vocal tic disorder, since these disorders run in the same families. There is a relation among Tourette's disorder, obsessive-compulsive disorder, and attention-deficit/hyperactivity disorder. First-degree relatives of people with Tourette's disorder are at risk for developing chronic motor or vocal tic disorder and obsessive-compulsive disorder. Tourette's disorder is a chronic illness that naturally waxes and wanes, but it is not degenerative. Some children with Tourette's disorder function well and lead normal lives without treatment.

Chronic motor or vocal tic disorder consists of either motor or vocal tics, but not both, that have been present intermittently or nearly every day for more than a year. The onset is before 18 years, and the diagnosis cannot be made if Tourette's disorder has previously been diagnosed. The prevalence of chronic motor or vocal tic disorder is estimated to be 100 to 1000 times greater than Tourette's disorder (approximately 1 to 2 percent). School-age boys are at highest risk for chronic motor of vocal tic disorder. Vocal tics are usually not loud or intense and may be caused by thoracic, abdominal, or diaphragmatic contractions. Tourette's disorder and chronic motor or vocal tic disorder aggregate within the same families. Twin studies have found a high concordance for either Tourette's disorder or chronic motor tics in monozygotic twins.

Transient tic disorder consists of single or multiple motor or vocal tics that occur many times a day for at least 4 weeks but for no longer than 12 consecutive months. Transient ticlike habits and muscular twitches are common in children with transient tic disorder. Some 5 to 24 percent of all school-age children have a history of tics, but the prevalence of transient tic disorder is unknown. The DSM-IV category of tic disorder not otherwise specified is used for tic disorders that do not meet the criteria for any other tic disorder. Students are referred to Chapter 45 of *Kaplan and Sadock's Synopsis VIII* for a more detailed discussion. Studying the questions and answers below will enhance their understanding of those problems.

HELPFUL HINTS

The terms that follow relate to tic disorders and should be known by the student.

- barking
- benztropine (Cogentin)
- Jean Charcot
- clonidine (Catapres)
- compulsions
- coprolalia
- dystonia
- Hallervorden-Spatz disease
- hemiballism
- Huntington's chorea
- hyperdopaminergia
- Lesch-Nyhan syndrome
- motor tic
- neck jerking
- palilalia
- Pelizaeus-Merzbacher disease
- echokinesis
- echolalia
- encephalitis lethargica
- eye blinking
- facial grimacing
- Gilles de la Tourette
- grunting
- pimozide (Orap)
- shoulder shrugging
- simple or complex tic
- stereotypy
- Sydenham's chorea
- tardive dyskinesia
- torsion dystonia
- Tourette's disorder
- transient tic disorder
- tremor
- vocal tic
- Wilson's disease

▲ QUESTIONS

DIRECTIONS: Each of the questions or incomplete statements below is followed by five suggested responses or completions. Select the *one* that is *best* in each case.

Questions 45.1–45.2

A 46-year-old married man was referred to a psychiatrist for evaluation because of unremitting tics. At age 13 he developed a persistent eye blink, soon followed by lip smacking, head shaking, and barking noises. Despite these symptoms, he functioned well academically and eventually graduated from high school with honors. He was drafted during World War II. While he was in the army his tics subsided significantly but were still troublesome, and they eventually resulted in a medical discharge. He married, had two children, and worked as a semiskilled laborer and foreman. By age 30 his symptoms included tics of the head, neck, and shoulders; hitting his forehead with his hand and various objects; repeated throat clearing; spitting; and shouting out "Hey, hey, hey; la, la, la." Six years later, noisy coprolalia started: he would emit a string of profanities in the middle of a sentence and then resume his conversation.

Various treatments, all without benefit, were tried: administration of various phenothiazines and antidepressants and electroconvulsive therapy. The patient's social life became increasingly constricted because of his symptoms. He was unable to go to church or to the movies because of the cursing and noises. He worked at night to avoid social embarrassment. His family and friends became increasingly intolerant of his symptoms, and his daughters refused to bring friends home. He was depressed because of his enforced isolation and the seeming hopelessness of finding effective treatment. At 46, he sought a prefrontal lobotomy, but after psychiatric evaluation, his request was denied.

45.1 In the case example, the diagnosis is made on the basis of

A. vocal tics
B. coprolalia
C. onset before age 21
D. no known central nervous system disease
E. all of the above

45.2 If the onset is after age 18, which of the following tic disorders may be diagnosed?

A. Transient tic disorder
B. Chronic motor or vocal tic disorder
C. Tourette's disorder
D. Tic disorder not otherwise specified
E. All of the above

Questions 45.3–45.5

45.3 The dopamine system has been hypothesized to be involved in the development of tic disorders because

A. haloperidol (Haldol) suppresses tics
B. pimozide (Orap) suppresses tics
C. methylphenidate (Ritalin) exacerbates tics
D. pemoline (Cylert) exacerbates tics
E. all of the above

45.4 Which of the following statements concerning evidence supporting genetic factors as likely to play a role in the development of Tourette's disorder is *false*?

A. Concordance for Tourette's disorder is significantly higher in monozygotic than dizygotic twins.
B. Tourette's disorder and chronic tic disorder are likely to occur in the same family.
C. First-degree relatives of probands with Tourette's disorder are at higher than average risk for developing Tourette's disorder, chronic tic disorder, and obsessive-compulsive disorder.
D. Sons of men with Tourette's disorder are at highest risk for developing the disorder.
E. Concordance for Tourette's disorder or chronic tic disorder is high in monozygotic twins.

45.5 Which of the following distinguishes transient tic disorder from chronic motor or vocal tic disorder and Tourette's disorder?

A. Age of onset
B. The presence of motor tics only
C. The presence of vocal tics only
D. The presence of both motor and vocal tics
E. Progression of the tic symptoms over time

DIRECTIONS: These lettered headings are followed by a list of numbered phrases. For each numbered phrase, select the lettered heading most associated with it. Each heading may be used once, more than once, or not at all.

Questions 45.6–45.9

A. Coprolalia
B. Palilalia
C. Echolalia
D. Echokinesis

45.6 Repetition of the last word, phrase, or sound
45.7 Repetition of socially unacceptable, commonly obscene words
45.8 Repetition of one's own words
45.9 Imitation of observed movements

Questions 45.10–45.14

A. Tourette's disorder
B. Sydenham's chorea
C. Both

45.10 This disorder may be due to an autoimmune reaction to a streptococcal infection.
45.11 Obsessive-compulsive symptoms are commonly seen in association with this disorder.
45.12 This disorder is generally self-limited.
45.13 Treatments include dopamine-blocking agents with some utility of serotonin-specific reuptake inhibitors.
45.14 In some families this disorder has been found to be transmitted as an autosomal dominant gene with variable penetrance.

Questions 45.15–45.19

A. Tourette's disorder
B. Huntington's disease
C. Tardive Tourette's disorder
D. Wilson's disease
E. Sydenham's chorea

45.15 This disorder, which is characterized by choreiform movements and transmitted via autosomal dominant gene, progresses to death within about 15 years.
45.16 This disorder, which consists of tics, choreoathetosis, and facial dyskinesias, occurs after use of antipsychotic medication.
45.17 This disorder is characterized by a motor movement known as St. Vitus' Dance.
45.18 This disorder, characterized by dystonia and a wing-beating tremor, is due to an inborn error of copper metabolism.
45.19 This disorder, usually genetically determined, is thought to be related to abnormalities in the basal ganglia.

ANSWERS

Tic Disorders

45.1 The answer is E (all) (*Synopsis VIII,* pages 1215–1216).
In the case of this patient, the correct diagnosis is Tourette's disorder. He has both chronic motor tics and *vocal tics,* including *coprolalia.* The tics have occurred for more than a year. The disorder started when the patient was under *age 18.* He also has *no known central nervous system disease.* Obsessions and compulsions are often seen in persons with Tourette's disorder. Table 45.1 lists the diagnostic criteria for Tourette's disorder.

45.2 The answer is D (*Synopsis VIII,* page 1222).
All tic disorders with onset after age 18 must be diagnosed as *tic disorder not otherwise specified,* a residual category for tics that do not meet the criteria for a specific tic disorder. *Transient tic disorder, chronic motor or vocal tic disorder,* and *Tourette's disorder* all specify onset before age 18. Table 45.2 lists the DSM-IV diagnostic criteria for tic disorder not otherwise specified.

45.3 The answer is E (all) (*Synopsis VIII,* pages 1219–1220).
Supportive evidence of dopamine system involvement in tic disorders includes the observations that pharmacologic agents that antagonize the dopamine system, such as *haloperidol (Haldol) and pimozide (Orap), suppress tics,* and observations that agents that increase central dopaminergic activity, such as cocaine, dextroamphetamine (Dexedrine), *methylphenidate (Ritalin), and pemoline (Cylert), exacerbate tics.*

45.4 The answer is D (*Synopsis VIII,* page 1215).
Evidence that genetic factors are likely to play a role in the development of Tourette's disorder include the findings that *sons of mothers, not sons of fathers, with Tourette's disorder are at highest risk for developing the disorder.* Twin studies reveal that *concordance for Tourette's disorder is significantly higher in monozygotic twins than in dizygotic twins.* In addition, the findings that *Tourette's disorder and chronic tic disorder are likely to occur in the same family* supports the view that both disorders are part of a genetically determined spectrum. *First-degree relatives of probands with Tourette's disorder are at higher than average risk for developing Tourette's disorder, chronic tic disorder, and obsessive-compulsive disorder,* implying a genetic relation among the three disorders. A genetic relation between Tourette's disorder and chronic tic disorder is also supported by findings that *concordance is high for Tourette's disorder or chronic tic disorder in monozygotic twins.*

45.5 The answer is E (*Synopsis VIII,* pages 1221–1222).
Transient tic disorder (Table 45.3) can be distinguished from chronic motor or vocal tic disorder (Table 45.4) and Tourette's disorder (Table 45.1) only by following the *progression of the tic symptoms over time.* DSM-IV emphasizes precise and specific symptom patterns, time framework, and age of onset in classifying the tic disorders. Transient tic disorder cannot be distinguished from chronic motor or vocal tic disorder and

Table 45.2
DSM-IV Diagnostic Criteria for Tic Disorder Not Otherwise Specified

This category is for disorders characterized by tics that do not meet criteria for a specific tic disorder. Examples include tics lasting less than 4 weeks or tics with an onset after age 18 years.

Table 45.1
DSM-IV Diagnostic Criteria for Tourette's Disorder

A. Both multiple motor and one or more vocal tics have been present at some time during the illness, although not necessarily concurrently. (A *tic* is a sudden, rapid, recurrent, nonrhythmic, stereotyped motor movement or vocalization.)

B. The tics occur many times a day (usually in bouts) nearly every day or intermittently throughout a period of more than 1 year, and during this period there was never a tic-free period of more than 3 consecutive months.

C. The disturbance causes marked distress or significant impairment in social, occupational, or other important areas of functioning.

D. The onset is before age 18 years.

E. The disturbance is not due to the direct physiological effects of a substance (eg, stimulants) or a general medical condition (eg, Huntington's disease or postviral encephalitis).

Table 45.3
DSM-IV Diagnostic Criteria for Transient Tic Disorder

A. Single or multiple motor and/or vocal tics (ie, sudden, rapid, recurrent, nonrhythmic, stereotyped motor movements or vocalizations)

B. The tics occur many times a day, nearly every day for at least 4 weeks, but for no longer than 12 consecutive months.

C. The disturbance causes marked distress or significant impairment in social, occupational, or other important areas of functioning.

D. The onset is before age 18 years.

E. The disturbance is not due to the direct physiological effects of a substance (eg, stimulants) or a general medical condition (eg, Huntington's disease or postviral encephalitis).

F. Criteria have never been met for Tourette's disorder or chronic motor or vocal tic disorder.

Specify if:
Single episode or **recurrent**

Table 45.4
DSM-IV Diagnostic Criteria for Chronic Motor or Vocal Tic Disorder

A. Single or multiple motor or vocal tics (ie, sudden, rapid, recurrent, nonrhythmic, stereotyped motor movements or vocalizations), but not both, have been present at some time during the illness.
B. The tics occur many times a day nearly every day or intermittently throughout a period of more than 1 year, and during this period there was never a tic-free period of more than 3 consecutive months.
C. The disturbance causes marked distress or significant impairment in social, occupational, or other important areas of functioning.
D. The onset is before age 18 years.
E. The disturbance is not due to the direct physiological effects of a substance (eg, stimulants) or a general medical condition (eg, Huntington's disease or postviral encephalitis).
F. Criteria have never been met for Tourette's disorder.

Tourette's disorder by *the age of onset, the presence of motor tics only, the presence of vocal tics only,* or *the presence of both motor and vocal tics.*

Answers 45.6–45.9

45.6 The answer is C (*Synopsis VIII,* page 1215).

45.7 The answer is A (*Synopsis VIII,* page 1215).

45.8 The answer is B (*Synopsis VIII,* page 1215).

45.9 The answer is D (*Synopsis VIII,* pages 479, 1215).
Vocal tics may be simple. For example, coughing and barking are simple vocal tics. Complex vocal tics consist of repeating words or phrases out of context. *Coprolalia* is the *repetition of socially unacceptable, commonly obscene words.* Palilalia is the *repetition of one's own words. Echolalia* is the *repetition of the last heard word, phrase, or sound* of another person. Echokinesis is a complex motor tic consisting of the *imitation of observed movements.*

Answers 45.10–45.14

45.10 The answer is C (*Synopsis VIII,* pages 1216, 1218).

45.11 The answer is C (*Synopsis VIII,* pages 1216–1218).

45.12 The answer is B (*Synopsis VIII,* pages 1217–1218).

45.13 The answer is A (*Synopsis VIII,* pages 1219–1220).

45.14 The answer is A (*Synopsis VIII,* pages 1215–1216).
Sydenham's chorea is a well-known self-limited syndrome consisting of a variety of abnormal motor movements that can include tics, choreiform movements, and compulsive behaviors caused by an autoimmune response to the streptococcal antigens. Autoimmune processes related to streptococcal bacteria have been proposed as etiological components of some cases of obsessive-compulsive disorder, as well as some cases of *Tourette's disorder.* Such an autoimmune process may act synergistically with a genetic vulnerability for these disorders, or it may act without a prior vulnerability. Elevated titers of circulating autoantibodies can sometimes be detected in these cases. The increased prevalence of *Tourette's disorder* and other tic disorders in males may be related to high levels of gender-related hormones in the developing male central nervous system. Obsessive-compulsive behaviors are associated with *Tourette's disorder* as well as with *Sydenham's chorea.* One main distinguishing feature between Tourette's disorder and Sydenham's chorea is that *Tourette's disorder* is a lifelong illness with a waxing and waning course, and *Sydenham's chorea* usually has a self-limited course. Treatment for *Tourette's disorder* includes the treatments for the core features of the disorder as well as for the associated syndromes. Dopamine blocking agents such as haloperidol (Haldol) and pimozide (Orap) have been shown to diminish tic behaviors. Conversely, agents that increase central dopaminergic activity, such as methylphenidate (Ritalin), may exacerbate tics. Serotonin-specific reuptake inhibitors such as fluoxetine (Prozac), sertraline (Zoloft), or paroxetine (Paxil) are sometimes used in patients with *Tourette's disorder* to treat associated obsessive-compulsive symptoms. *Tourette's disorder* appears to be transmitted via autosomal dominant genes in some family pedigrees. There seems to be variable penetrance, so that not every family member with the genetic contribution will exhibit the same number of symptoms or illness severity. Concordance for the disorder in monozygotic twins is significantly greater than in dizygotic twins. In other family pedigrees, Tourette's disorder may be transmitted in a bilinear mode, that is, a pattern that is intermediate between dominant and recessive.

Answers 45.15–45.19

45.15 The answer is B (*Synopsis VIII,* pages 1217–1218).

45.16 The answer is C (*Synopsis VIII,* pages 1215–1216, 1218).

45.17 The answer is E (*Synopsis VIII,* page 1218).

45.18 The answer is D (*Synopsis VIII,* page 1218).

45.19 The answer is A (*Synopsis VIII,* pages 1215–1216).
Huntington's disease is genetically transmitted via an autosomal dominant gene resulting in a fatal illness that is characterized by choreiform movements. It usually does not manifest itself until adulthood, although there have been childhood forms, and it progresses to death over 10 to 15 years after onset. Caudate atrophy has been shown on computed tomography scans. *Tardive* Tourette's disorder is a potential sequela of antipsychotic medication use, generally occurring when the medication is reduced or discontinued. It consists of orofacial dyskinesias, choreoathetosis, motor tics, and vocal tics. These symptoms may diminish over time without any treatment, and they have a variable response to either increasing or decreasing the medication. *Sydenham's chorea* is a self-limited childhood sequela to a streptococcus exposure that occurs more commonly in females; the motor movements, which are generally choreiform, have been characterized as St. Vitus' dance. Sydenham's chorea may be associated with rheumatic fever. *Wilson's disease* is transmitted via an autosomal recessive gene

and results in an inborn error of copper metabolism. Characteristic wing-beating tremor and dystonia are present. Kayser-Fleischer rings may be seen in the eyes, and liver dysfunction results. This disorder is fatal without chelating therapy. *Tourette's disorder* is believed to be the result of dysfunction in the basal ganglia and related structures in the midbrain and cortex. The basal ganglia have been recognized as central in the network of circuits related to motor control, sensorimotor integration, and some aspects of cognitive processing and emotional expression. These areas of the brain are rich in dopaminergic neurons. Tic disorders may be caused by alterations in the basal ganglia by dysfunctions in its major fiber pathways, or by lesions in proximal brain regions with prominent connections with the basal ganglia.

46 Elimination Disorders

Elimination disorders consist of bowel and bladder control disorders. These functions develop over time and are affected by a child's social and intellectual functions, family interactions, and toilet training methods. The two elimination disorders in the fourth edition of *Diagnostic and Statistical Manual of Mental Disorders* (DSM-IV) are encopresis and enuresis.

Encopresis consists of a pattern of a child with a developmental level of at least 4 years passing feces into inappropriate places either voluntarily or unintentionally. In Western culture, bowel control is established in more than 95 percent of children by their fourth birthday. After the age of 4 years, encopresis occurs 3 or 4 times as often in boys as in girls. The cause of encopresis is usually a combination of factors. In some cases, children are affected because of physiologically ineffective sphincter control. Inadequate toilet training or lack of appropriate supervision can also contribute to the development of encopresis. In other instances, children refuse to control their sphincter muscles because of an ongoing power struggle with parents. Sometimes encopresis occurs around the time of the birth of a sibling or a move to a new home. Children who are sexually abused, especially boys who are abused rectally, may be more vulnerable to the disorder.

Once encopresis is established, secondary behavioral and emotional problems are likely to develop, since the behavior is socially unacceptable. Children with encopresis often retain feces and become constipated, with resulting bowel distention. The chronic rectal distention may become a megacolon, and the hard fecal mass may cause loss of tone in the rectal wall. In that case, the child may not feel the fecal pressure and may not be aware of the need to defecate, and small amounts of soft stool leak out.

According to DSM-IV, the diagnosis of enuresis is not made until the child is chronologically or developmentally 5 years of age. Enuresis consists of repeated urination into clothes or bed, twice weekly, for at least 3 consecutive months, or the presence of clinically significant distress or functional impairment. Enuretic children at highest risk for concurrent psychiatric disorders include girls, day and night enuretics, and children who continue to have symptoms in later childhood. Children with enuresis are at higher risk for developmental delays than is the general population.

Genetic and psychosocial factors are involved in the etiology of enuresis. It does not appear to be related to a specific stage of sleep, since it can occur any time, or to deeper than normal sleep. Some studies indicate that enuretic children have bladders that are anatomically normal but that feel full when there is a small amount of urine, so that there is an increased urge to void. Other studies have suggested that children with nighttime enuresis have a lower than expected level of antidiuretic hormone, so that the bladder becomes full. Students should study Chapter 46 in *Kaplan and Sadock's Synopsis VIII* and then test their knowledge with the questions and answers that follow.

HELPFUL HINTS

The student should know the following terms.

- ► abnormal sphincter contractions
- ► aganglionic megacolon
- ► behavioral reinforcement
- ► bell (or buzzer) and pad
- ► diurnal bowel control
- ► ego-dystonic enuresis
- ► fluid restriction
- ► functionally small bladder
- ► Hirschsprung's disease
- ► imipramine
- ► intranasal desmopressin (DDAVP)
- ► low nocturnal antidiuretic hormone
- ► nocturnal bowel control
- ► obstructive urinary disorder abnormality
- ► overflow incontinence
- ► poor gastric mobility
- ► rectal distention
- ► thioridazine
- ► toilet training

▲ QUESTIONS

DIRECTIONS: Each of the questions or incomplete statements below is followed by five suggested responses or completions. Select the *one* that is *best* in each case.

46.1 Encopresis

A. always occurs voluntarily
B. must occur at least once per week for at least 3 months
C. always occurs with constipation and overflow incontinence
D. is diagnosed only in a child who is chronologically or developmentally at least 6 years old
E. may be due to decreased rectal tone and desensitization of rectal pressure

46.2 Children with encopresis

A. may engage in the behavior when they are angry with their parents
B. have high rates of abnormal sphincter contractions
C. may have a fear of using the toilet
D. are at risk for short attention span, poor frustration tolerance, and hyperactivity
E. all of the above

46.3 Enuresis

A. is more common in females than in males
B. must occur once a month for at least 3 consecutive months, according to DSM-IV
C. resolves spontaneously in most cases
D. is always intentional when it is diurnal
E. is not diagnosed until the child is chronologically or developmentally 3 years old

46.4 Risk factors for additional psychiatric disorders that coexist with enuresis include

A. being male
B. having symptoms both diurnally and nocturnally
C. having the symptoms in early childhood
D. having a family history of enuresis
E. having only nocturnal symptoms

46.5 Which of the following statements about enuresis (not due to a general medical condition) is *false*?

A. Psychiatric problems are present in about 20 percent of enuretic children.
B. Males are more frequently enuretic than females.
C. Diurnal enuresis is much less common than nocturnal enuresis.
D. Enuresis is usually self-limited.
E. Psychotherapy alone is an effective treatment of enuresis.

46.6 Enuresis can be defined as repeated voiding of urine into bed or clothes in children over the age of

A. 2 years
B. 3 years
C. 4 years
D. 5 years
E. 6 years

46.7 Children with encopresis are frequently found to have

A. excessive emphasis placed on bowel habits
B. depressed mothers
C. critical fathers
D. gastrointestinal lesions
E. all of the above

46.8 Organic causes of enuresis include

A. obstructive uropathy
B. urinary infection
C. diabetes mellitus
D. epilepsy
E. all of the above

46.9 The treatment of enuresis includes

A. desmopressin
B. imipramine (Tofranil)
C. a star chart
D. restricting fluids
E. all of the above

DIRECTIONS: The lettered headings below are followed by a list of numbered phrases. For each numbered phrase, select the *best* lettered heading. Each lettered heading may be used once, more than once, or not at all.

Questions 46.10–46.17

A. Encopresis
B. Enuresis
C. Both of the above
D. None of the above

46.10 This disorder is seen most frequently in females.
46.11 Psychopharmacological intervention for this disorder, such as desmopressin nasal spray (DDAVP), is limited in that relapse tends to occur as soon as medication is withdrawn.
46.12 Psychopharmacological intervention is not likely to be helpful in this disorder.
46.13 Physiological determinants are believed to be significantly contributory to this disorder, while structural abnormalities are rare.
46.14 At age 7 years, approximately 1.5 percent of boys have this disorder.
46.15 At age 5 years, approximately 7 percent of children have this disorder.
46.16 To be diagnosed with this disorder, a child must have a chronological or developmental age of 5 years.
46.17 To be diagnosed with this disorder, a child must have a chronological or developmental age of 4 years.

ANSWERS

Elimination Disorders

46.1 The answer is E (*Synopsis VIII,* page 1224).
Encopresis is the repeated passage of feces in inappropriate places. Encopresis *may be due to decreased rectal tone and desensitization to rectal pressure.* Encopresis *occurs either involuntarily or voluntarily.* Many children with encopresis retain feces and become constipated either voluntarily or secondary to painful defecation. Encopresis must occur at least *once a month, not once a week, for at least 3 months* (Table 46.1). Encopresis *occurs* both *with* and without *constipation and overflow incontinence.* It *is diagnosed only in a child who is chronologically or developmentally at least 4 years old, not 6 years old.*

46.2 The answer is E (all) (*Synopsis VIII,* pages 1224–1225).
Encopresis may be due to any or all of a variety of physiological and emotional factors. Some children with encopresis have control over their bowel function and *engage in the behavior when they are angry at their parents* or as a means of asserting control. Studies have also shown that children with encopresis who do not have gastrointestinal disorders *have high rates of abnormal sphincter contractions.* Abnormal sphincter contractions are especially prevalent in children with constipation and overflow incontinence. Those children have difficulty in relaxing their anal sphincters when trying to defecate and are not likely to respond well to laxative treatment. Although it is not common, some children with encopresis have a specific phobia or *have a fear of using the toilet.* Children with encopresis are at risk for *short attention span, poor frustration tolerance, and hyperactivity.*

46.3 The answer is C (*Synopsis VIII,* page 1227).
Enuresis is the repeated voiding of urine into bed or clothes, whether involuntarily or intentionally. Enuresis *resolves spontaneously in most cases* over time. It is *more common in males than in females.* Enuresis, *according to DSM-IV, must occur twice weekly, not once a month, for at least 3 consecutive months,* or manifest clear functional impairment due to enuresis (Table 46.2). Enuresis *is not always intentional when it is diurnal* or nocturnal, although most children find their symptoms ego-dystonic and have enhanced self-esteem and improved social confidence when they become continent. According to DSM-IV, enuresis is not diagnosed until the child is *chronologically or developmentally 5 years old, not 3 years old.*

46.4 The answer is B (*Synopsis VIII,* page 1226).
Psychiatric disorders are reported to occur in at least 20 percent of children with enuresis. Risk factors for additional psychiatric disorders include *having symptoms both diurnally and nocturnally* and being female, not male. *Children who have symptoms in late childhood* are also at higher risk for additional psychiatric disorders.

About 75 percent of children with enuresis have a first-degree relative with enuresis or who was enuretic, but no data suggest that *patients with a family history of enuresis* are at risk for additional psychiatric disorders. *Having only nocturnal symptoms* puts a child at less risk for additional psychiatric disorders than children who have it both at night and during the day.

46.5 The answer is E (*Synopsis VIII,* pages 1227–1228).
Controlled studies have found that *psychotherapy alone is not an effective treatment of enuresis.* However, psychotherapy is useful in dealing with emotional and family difficulties that arise because of enuresis or with coexisting psychiatric problems. *Psychiatric problems are present in about 20 percent of enuretic children,* and they are most common in enuretic girls and in children who wet both day and night. Classical conditioning with the bell or buzzer and pad apparatus is the most effective and generally safe treatment for enuresis. Dryness results in more than 50 percent of cases. *Males are more fre-*

Table 46.1
DSM-IV Diagnostic Criteria for Encopresis

A. Repeated passage of feces into inappropriate places (eg, clothing or floor) whether involuntary or intentional.
B. At least one such event a month for at least 3 months.
C. Chronological age is at least 4 years (or equivalent developmental level).
D. The behavior is not due exclusively to the direct physiological effects of a substance (eg, laxatives) or a general medical condition except through a mechanism involving constipation.

Code as follows:
With constipation and overflow incontinence
Without constipation and overflow incontinence

Table 46.2
DSM-IV Diagnostic Criteria for Enuresis

A. Repeated voiding of urine into bed or clothes (whether involuntary or intentional).
B. The behavior is clinically significant as manifested by either a frequency of twice a week for at least 3 consecutive months, or the presence of clinically significant distress or impairment in social, academic (occupational), or other important areas of functioning.
C. Chronological age is at least 5 years (or equivalent developmental level).
D. The behavior is not due exclusively to the direct physiological effect of a substance (eg, a diuretic) or a general medical condition (eg, diabetes, spina bifida, a seizure disorder).

Specify type:
Nocturnal only
Diurnal only
Nocturnal and diurnal

quently enuretic than females. Diurnal enuresis is much less common than nocturnal enuresis. Only about 2 percent of 5-year-olds have diurnal enuresis at least weekly. Unlike nocturnal enuresis, diurnal enuresis is more common in girls than in boys. Enuresis (not due to a general medical condition) *is usually self-limited.* The child can eventually remain dry with virtually no psychiatric sequelae. Although a medical cause precludes a diagnosis of enuresis (not due to a general medical condition), the correction of an anatomical defect or the cure of an infection does not always cure the enuresis, which suggests that the cause may be at least partially psychological in some cases.

46.6 The answer is D (*Synopsis VIII,* page 1226).
Enuresis is manifested as a repetitive, inappropriate, involuntary passage of urine. Operationally, enuresis can be defined as repeated voiding of urine into bed or clothes in children over the age of *5 years* (or equivalent developmental level) who fail to inhibit the reflex to pass urine when the impulse is felt during waking hours and in those who do not rouse from sleep of their own accord when the process is occurring during the sleeping state.

46.7 The answer is E (all) (*Synopsis VIII,* page 1226).
The child who fails to attain bowel control may soon suffer from hostile behavior by one or more family members. As the child associates with others outside the home, there is ridicule by peers and alienation from teachers. There appears to be *excessive emphasis placed on bowel habits,* and many persons with encopresis seem to lack the sensory cues as to when they need to defecate. Psychologically, the patient remains blunted to the effect of encopresis on other people. Nevertheless, the child comes to feel unwanted and to have a low self-concept. Dynamically, children with encopresis commonly have *depressed mothers,* often dissatisfied with marriage and maternal roles, compulsive, and emotionally unavailable. Such households may have *critical fathers* who are emotionally distant and often absent physically or psychologically or both. A rash of mechanical problems may result in *gastrointestinal lesions* as the condition continues. The sufferer may require treatment for fissures, rectal prolapse, rectal excoriations, or impaction.

46.8 The answer is E (all) (*Synopsis VIII,* page 1227).
The combination of nocturnal and diurnal enuresis, especially in the patient with frequency and urgency, should signal the high possibility of an organic basis for the complaint. Bed wetting may be the presenting symptom in children with *obstructive uropathy,* which is a physical blockage of the urinary tract. *Urinary infections* are often associated with enuresis. Many enuretics are sleepwalkers, and they attempt to urinate during somnambulism. Therefore, sleepwalking must be differentiated from both enuresis and epilepsy. In young children, the sudden development of enuresis is a common presentation of *diabetes mellitus,* which is characterized by polyuria (excessive output of urine), polydipsia (excessive intake of fluid), and polyphagia (excessive food intake). Diabetes mellitus is caused by insulin deficiency.

Another possibility to be ruled out is *epilepsy,* a neurological disorder resulting from a sudden excessive disorderly discharge of neurons in either a structurally normal or a diseased cerebral cortex. It is characterized by the paroxysmal recurrence of short-lived disturbances of consciousness, involuntary convulsive muscle movements, psychic or sensory disturbances, or some combination thereof. It is termed idiopathic epilepsy when there is no identifiable organic cause. The loss of urine or feces during the seizure is common.

Diagnoses to be considered when a child presents with enuresis include diabetes insipidus, spina bifida, lumbosacral myelodysplasia, sickle-cell anemia, foreign body, calculus, paraphimosis, vaginitis, mental retardation, intestinal parasites, and spinal tumors. Spinal tumors have a low incidence in childhood, but the loss of sphincter control in a child with progressive weakness, clumsiness, pain, and gait disturbance should alert the doctor to the possibility.

46.9 The answer is E (all) (*Synopsis VIII,* pages 1227–1228).
Desmopressin (DDAVP), an antidiuretic administered intranasally, has been shown in initial studies to be effective in reducing enuresis in some cases. Drugs should rarely be used in treating enuresis and then only as a last resort in intractable cases that cause serious socioemotional difficulties for the sufferer. *Imipramine (Tofranil)* is efficacious and has been approved for use, primarily on a short-term basis, in treating childhood enuresis. Initially, up to 30 percent of enuretics may stay dry, and up to 85 percent may wet less frequently than before taking the medication. This effect, however, does not often last. Tolerance often develops after 6 weeks of therapy; once the drug is discontinued, relapses and enuresis at former frequencies usually occur within a few months. A more serious problem is the drug's adverse effects, which include cardiotoxicity; therefore, the drug should not be used on a long-term basis. A *star chart,* a record-keeping device that rewards the child, is helpful in many cases. Other useful techniques include *restricting fluids* before bed and night lifting to toilet-train the child.

Answers 46.10–46.17

46.10 The answer is D (*Synopsis VIII,* pages 1227–1228).

46.11 The answer is B (*Synopsis VIII,* pages 1227–1228).

46.12 The answer is A (*Synopsis VIII,* page 1226).

46.13 The answer is C (*Synopsis VIII,* page 1227).

46.14 The answer is A (*Synopsis VIII,* page 1224).

46.15 The answer is B (*Synopsis VIII,* page 1226).

46.16 The answer is B (*Synopsis VIII,* page 1227).

46.17 The answer is A (*Synopsis VIII,* page 1227).
Bowel and bladder control appears to be more difficult for males than for females. *Both encopresis and enuresis are 3 to 4 times as common in males as in females.* At all ages, encopresis is 3 to 5 times as common in males as in females. Enuresis is also 3 to 5 times as common in males as in females. A variety of medications, such as imipramine and more recently desmopressin nasal spray, have been used with some success in the treatment of enuresis.

Imipramine has received FDA approval in the treatment of childhood enuresis on a short-term basis. Tolerance commonly develops, however, within 6 weeks of treatment, and relapse at former frequencies usually ensues when the drug is discontinued. *Desmopressin, an antidiuretic compound that is available as an intranasal spray, has been successful in some children while it is being used, but it does not seem to affect the condition after the medication is discontinued.* The primary treatment of encopresis is a sensitively developed behavioral and family intervention. In order to do this, an accurate evaluation and understanding of a child's encopresis pattern is necessary. It is important to determine whether the child has chronic constipation with overflow incontinence. It is also necessary to determine whether the child is well aware of the passage of feces when it occurs. Furthermore, if encopresis is a behavior developed by a child to express anger or attract negative parental attention, this is also pertinent to the design of treatment. *Psychopharmacological interventions are generally not a part of treatment of encopresis, although in cases of chronic constipation, medications are sometimes used to regulate fecal continence.* Children with constipation who have difficulty with sphincter relaxation are among the more difficult to treat. Physiological characteristics are believed to be important contributors to both encopresis and enuresis. Abnormal sphincter contractions are very common in children with constipation and overflow incontinence. Enuresis tends to run in families (three quarters of children with enuresis have a first-degree relative with enuresis), and children with enuresis are twice as likely to have concomitant developmental delay. Even when a structural anatomical defect is not obvious, evidence suggests that heritable physiological factors contribute to enuresis. Bowel control is established in 95 percent of the children by the fourth birthday and in 99 percent of children by the fifth birthday. At age 7 to 8 years, the *frequency of encopresis* is 1.5 percent in boys and 0.5 percent in girls. The *prevalence of enuresis* decreases with age; 82 percent of 2-year-olds, 49 percent of 3-year-olds, 26 percent of 4-year-olds, and 7 percent of 5-year-olds have enuresis on a regular basis. To be diagnosed as having encopresis, a child must have a chronological or developmental age of 4 years, whereas to be diagnosed as having enuresis, a child must have a chronological or developmental age of 5 years.

47

Other Disorders of Infancy, Childhood, or Adolescence

This chapter describes separation anxiety disorder, selective mutism, reactive attachment disorder of infancy and early childhood, stereotypic movement disorder, and disorder of infancy, childhood or adolescence not otherwise specified. In the fourth edition of *Diagnostic and Statistical Manual of Mental Disorders* (DSM-IV), separation anxiety disorder is the only anxiety disorder with specific criteria for onset in childhood included with disorders usually first diagnosed in infancy, childhood, or adolescence. It consists of developmentally inappropriate and excessive anxiety in a child upon separating from a major attachment figure, usually the mother, sometimes the father. The child often has a persistent worry that something resulting in permanent separation will happen to the major attachment figure. The child may refuse to go to school to avoid being separated from family members. Fears of catastrophic events and fears of going to sleep without being near a major attachment figure are common features. Anxiety may take the form of multiple somatic complaints, such as headaches and stomach pains, when separations are anticipated.

Some degree of anxiety on separation is developmentally normal. It does not reach pathological proportions until it causes impairment in usual activities for the child. Separation anxiety disorder is more common in young children than in adolescents, and it occurs equally in boys and girls. It occurs in 3 to 4 percent of school-age children and in up to 1 percent of adolescents. Many children with separation anxiety disorder have parents with anxiety disorders such as panic disorder or agoraphobia. Anxious parents often communicate their fear to the child, who learns that new situations or separations are to be feared. Separation anxiety disorder in adolescents is often more incapacitating than in a young child. A treatment approach that includes family education, family therapy, and individual cognitive-behavioral psychotherapy is helpful. In some cases, imipramine (Tofranil) may be used to reduce fear and panic related to separation.

Selective mutism is an uncommon childhood disorder in which a child who is fluent with language consistently refuses to speak in a specific situation, usually in school or elsewhere outside the home. Although most children are silent in the mute situations, they use communication in the form of eye contact, head nods, and other nonverbal communication. Some children whisper but do not speak out loud. Most children with selective mutism continue to speak fluently at home and in some familiar settings. Selective mutism is rare, found in fewer than 1 percent of individuals seen in mental health settings. It is more common in young children than in older children. The etiology of selective mutism is not clear. Some affected children have histories of delayed onset of speech, and most are shy. Selective mutism may be a manifestation of social phobia, since it is usually accompanied by social anxiety.

Reactive attachment disorder consists of markedly disturbed and developmentally inappropriate social behaviors characterized either as a failure to respond to social situations or indiscriminate sociability and excessive familiarity with relative strangers. It is not accounted for by developmental delay and is associated in all cases with pathogenic child rearing. Parental behavior characterized by chronic neglect or disregard of the child's emotional or physical needs is presumed to contribute to the child's inappropriate behavior. It is possible that the same social environment meets the social needs of one child satisfactorily but is markedly inappropriate and insensitive for another.

Stereotypic movement disorder is characterized by repetitive, nonfunctional behaviors such as rocking, head banging, self-biting, picking, or waving that occur over at least 4 weeks. The movements interfere with normal activities and in some cases result in injury if preventive measures are not used. Some repetitive behaviors such as nail biting, are very common, affecting up to half of all school-age children. Other stereotypic movements, such as thumb sucking and rocking, are normal in young children but may cause functional impairment if they continue repeatedly in older children. Mentally retarded children and adolescents have an increased rate of stereotypic behaviors, including self-injurious behaviors. Disorder of infancy, childhood, or adolescence not otherwise specified is a residual category for disorders that do not meet criteria for any other disorder but cause distress and impairment. After completing Chapter 47 of *Kaplan and Sadock's Synopsis VIII,* students should answer the questions herein. A review of the answers and the explanations will help them assess their knowledge in this area.

HELPFUL HINTS

The student should know the following terms.

- anticipatory anxiety
- delayed language acquisition
- desensitization
- driven, nonfunctional behavior
- dyskinetic movements
- emotional and physical neglect
- failure to respond socially
- failure to thrive
- generalized anxiety
- indiscriminate familiarity
- inhibition to speak
- lack of stable attachment
- Lesch-Nyhan syndrome
- major attachment figure
- nonverbal gestures
- panic disorder
- pathogenic caregiving
- ''psychosocial dwarfism''
- school phobia
- school refusal
- selective mutism
- self-injurious stereotypic acts
- sensory impairments
- separation anxiety
- shyness
- social anxiety
- social phobia
- specific phobia
- stereotypic movements
- stress anxiety

▲ QUESTIONS

DIRECTIONS: Each of the incomplete statements below is followed by five suggested completions. Select the *one* that is *best* in each case.

47.1 A 16-year-old high school junior was referred by a teacher to the mental health clinic with the complaint that she was unable to make any verbal contributions in her classes. Her inability to speak had begun 1 year previously, after the death of her mother. It took school personnel some time to realize that she did not speak in any of her classes. She had kept up with her assignments, handing in all her written work, and was receiving better than average grades on tests.

The patient's father was a janitor in a large apartment building. Because of his work, he usually came home late, and he was rather passive and indifferent toward the patient and her six younger siblings. He had never responded to school requests for visits to discuss his daughter's problems. Since her mother's death, the patient had assumed the mothering of the siblings: cooking the meals, cleaning, and listening to their requests and complaints.

When seen, the patient was a thin, neatly dressed girl who was alert but responded only with brief nods of her head at first. With reassurance, she began to whisper monosyllabic answers to questions. Her responses were rational and logical, but she denied that her failure to speak was much of a problem. A younger sibling reported that the patient had no difficulty in speaking at home.

As described, the patient's symptoms characteristic of selective mutism include all of the following *except*

A. no difficulty in speaking at home
B. difficulty speaking at school
C. communication by nodding
D. school performance
E. onset following an emotional trauma

47.2 At the suggestion of her pediatrician, Molly, aged 10 months, was taken by her mother for a consultation with a specialist in infant development. Her mother was most concerned because, as she said, "Molly is not responding to me. She often won't look at me. She looks in the opposite direction. She won't smile, won't play, and bangs her hand on the table, looking angry. She throws toys on the floor. When I talk to her, she closes her eyes." Her mother also reported that her little girl was waking up 3 or 4 times each night and refusing to go back to sleep unless the mother stayed with her in the room, either holding her or stroking her back.

The problems seemed to have begun 2 months earlier, when Molly's mother, a busy attorney, went back to work full-time. The father, also an attorney, was quite angry at her for returning to work; he wanted her to give up her career and stay at home. For the first month after she returned to work, Molly was cared for by a baby-sitter, who was fired after a neighbor reported that the baby-sitter was frequently drunk and left Molly in her crib, with a bottle of formula, ignoring her cries. Although Molly's mother had suspected that the baby-sitter was far from ideal, she did not realize how bad she was until she heard about it from the neighbor. For the past month, Molly's care had been arranged on a day-to-day basis, and she had had six baby-sitters.

During the past 2 months, because of sleepless nights and feeling overwhelmingly guilty about Molly's distress, yet at the same time feeling compelled to return to work or else "lose my status in my firm," Molly's mother had been "a nervous wreck." Now she blamed herself for all Molly's difficulties, saying, "I've done a terrible thing. Now, my husband doesn't love me, and Molly doesn't love me either."

Molly weighed 8 pounds at birth and was in good health. The pregnancy was unremarkable. The pediatrician's report revealed that Molly had slightly increased motor tone bilaterally, with no asymmetries, and tended to be oversensitive to touch. For example, her mother reported that when she tried to bathe Molly, the child would often scream and that she had to hold her with soft cotton blankets in order for her to feel comfortable. Molly was also very sensitive to loud noises, turning red and becoming rigid. She often cried if lights were too bright.

Molly had displayed social responsiveness by the fourth month but only if her parents worked hard and found just the right rhythm of sound and "funny faces." By age 6 months she was able to reach for objects, but her parents reported that if they handed her something, she would often try to knock it out of their hands, rather than grab it.

Molly had always been a fussy eater but nonetheless was gaining adequate weight and was in the 80th percentile for size and weight. Her pediatrician said that her overall physical health was good and that in terms of motor milestones she was doing fine.

During the evaluation, the impression of Molly as physically healthy was confirmed. Her gross and fine motor functioning were age appropriate. Observation of parent–infant interaction revealed an infant who held her body stiffly, looked away from her parents' eyes, and reacted to their vocalization by arching her back. When offered interesting objects, she would usually grab another object or knock the offered object away. Her facial expression was angry and tense. Her mother appeared depressed, and her interaction with Molly had a mechanical quality. Molly's father was impatient and abrupt with her.

The features of Molly's disorder include

A. excessive response to social stimulation
B. stranger anxiety
C. grossly pathogenic care
D. extreme interest in the environment
E. mental retardation

47.3 Separation anxiety disorder

A. is a developmental phase
B. accounts for most of the anxiety in childhood
C. has its most common onset at 1 to 2 years of age
D. is less serious when it occurs in adolescence
E. always involves refusal to go to school

47.4 Selective mutism

A. is a disorder in which a child who is not fluent in language consistently fails to speak in certain situations
B. is not associated with an increased risk of separation anxiety disorder
C. often occurs in children who are shy and show anxiety in social situations
D. is more common in boys than in girls
E. usually resolves by 5 years of age

47.5 All of the following may be characteristic of reactive attachment disorder of infancy or early childhood *except*

A. inhibited, withdrawn, and socially unresponsive behavior
B. excessive familiarity with relative strangers
C. chronically emotionally neglectful home environment
D. lack of stable attachment to the primary caregiver
E. a pervasive developmental disorder

47.6 In stereotypic movement disorder

A. the behaviors are always specified as intentional
B. the diagnosis can be made with mental retardation or a pervasive developmental disorder
C. hair pulling (trichotillomania) is the sole symptom
D. the diagnosis is made only if the symptoms are not better accounted for by a compulsion (as an obsessive-compulsive disorder) or a tic (as in tic disorder)
E. the age at onset is 7 years

47.7 Separation anxiety in children is characterized by

A. fears that a loved one will be hurt
B. fears about getting lost
C. irritability
D. animal and monster phobias
E. all of the above

47.8 Reactive attachment disorder of infancy or early childhood

A. may be reversed shortly after institution of adequate caregiving
B. includes a normal head circumference and a failure to gain weight disproportionately greater than the failure to gain length
C. is usually associated with gross emotional neglect or imposed social isolation in an institution
D. is indicated by a lack of developmentally appropriate signs of social responsivity
E. all of the above

47.9 Figure 47.1*A* shows a 3-month-old baby boy whose weight is 1 ounce over birth weight and who has a history of caretaking characterized by persistent disregard for his needs for comfort, stimulation, and affection. Figure 47.1*B* shows the same infant 3 weeks after hospitalization. Which of the following statements regarding this infant (prior to hospitalization) is *false*?

A. The infant's bone age is likely to be retarded.
B. The infant's head circumference is likely to be normal for his age.
C. The infant's growth hormone levels are low.
D. The infant is likely to exhibit paucity of spontaneous activity.
E. The infant suffers from reactive attachment disorder of infancy.

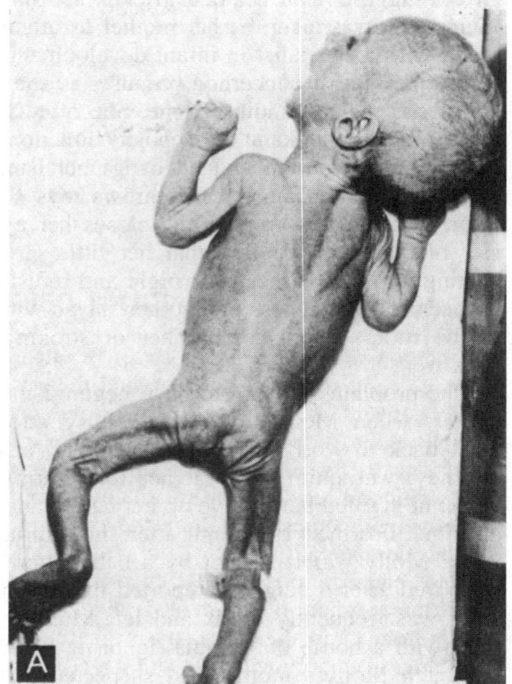

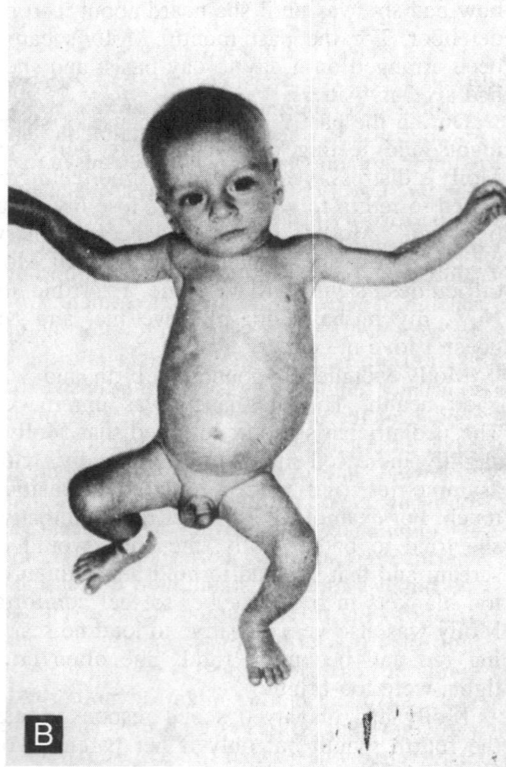

FIGURE 47.1A & B
Reprinted with permission from Barton Schmitt, M.D., Children's Hospital, Denver, CO.

DIRECTIONS: The lettered headings below are followed by a list of numbered phrases. For each numbered phrase, select the *best* lettered heading. Each heading may be used once, more than once, or not at all.

Questions 47.10–47.13

A. Separation anxiety disorder
B. Selective mutism
C. Reactive attachment disorder
D. Stereotypic movement disorder

47.10 Associated with grossly pathogenic caregiving

47.11 Difficult to treat when the major attachment figure also has the disorder

47.12 Often manifests only outside the home

47.13 Includes some symptoms, such as rocking or thumb sucking, that are considered developmentally normal, self-comforting behaviors in very young children

ANSWERS

Other Disorders of Infancy, Childhood, or Adolescence

47.1 The answer is D (*Synopsis VIII,* pages 1235–1236).
As described, the one symptom of the 16-year-old high school junior not typically characteristic of selective mutism is *her school performance.* She kept up with her assignments, handed in all of her written work, and received better than average grades. Children with selective mutism generally have *no difficulty in speaking at home,* but they do have difficulty elsewhere, especially *difficulty speaking at school.* Consequently, they often have significant academic difficulties and even failure. Some children with selective mutism *communicate by nodding* or saying ''um-hum,'' which may be their early responses to a therapist. In some children *the onset follows an emotional trauma* or a physical trauma. As in this case, the inability to speak can begin after the death of a parent. Table 47.1 lists the diagnostic criteria for selective mutism.

47.2 The answer is C (*Synopsis VIII,* page 1240).
Molly's disorder is reactive attachment disorder of infancy or early childhood. The disorder is characterized by *grossly pathogenic care,* persistent failure to initiate or respond to most social interactions, not *excessive response to social stimulation;* and indiscriminate sociability, not *stranger anxiety.* Children with this disorder often demonstrate listlessness and disinterest in the environment, not *extreme interest in the environment.*

The disturbance in relatedness in reactive attachment disorder of infancy or early childhood is not a symptom of *mental retardation* or a pervasive developmental disorder. Table 47.2 presents the diagnostic criteria for this disorder.

47.3 The answer is B (*Synopsis VIII,* page 1229).
Separation anxiety disorder *accounts for most of the anxiety in children,* affecting up to 4 percent of school-age boys and girls. Unlike many other childhood psychiatric disorders, it has been reported to occur in boys and girls equally. While separation anxiety is a developmentally appropriate response to various situations, especially in young children, separation anxiety disorder *is not a developmental stage.* It is characterized by impaired function and *has its most common onset at 7 to 8 years of age.* Separation anxiety disorder *is usually more serious in adolescence* than in childhood. Separation anxiety disorder consists of persistent worry about losing a parent or harm befalling a child's major attachment figure. Separation anxiety disorder *sometimes, but not always, involves refusal to go to school* to avoid separating from the parent, but not in all cases. The diagnostic criteria for separation anxiety disorder are presented in Table 47.3.

47.4 The answer is C (*Synopsis VIII,* page 1235).
Selective mutism *often occurs in children who are shy and show anxiety in social situations.* Some clinicians believe that selective mutism is a form of social phobia. Selective mutism

Table 47.2
DSM-IV Diagnostic Criteria for Reactive Attachment Disorder of Infancy or Early Childhood

A. Markedly disturbed and developmentally inappropriate social relatedness in most contexts, beginning before age 5 years, as evidenced by either (1) or (2):
   (1) persistent failure to initiate or respond in a developmentally appropriate fashion to most social interactions, as manifested by excessively inhibited, hypervigilant, or highly ambivalent and contradictory responses (eg, the child may respond to caregivers with a mixture of approach, avoidance, and resistance to comforting or may exhibit frozen watchfulness)
   (2) diffuse attachments as manifested by indiscriminate sociability with marked inability to exhibit appropriate selective attachments (eg, excessive familiarity with relative strangers or lack of selectivity in choice of attachment figures)

B. The disturbance in criterion A is not accounted for solely by developmental delay (as in mental retardation) and does not meet criteria for a pervasive developmental disorder.

C. Pathogenic care as evidenced by at least one of the following:
   (1) persistent disregard of the child's basic emotional needs for comfort, stimulation, and affection
   (2) persistent disregard of the child's basic physical needs
   (3) repeated changes of primary caregiver that prevent formation of stable attachments (eg, frequent changes in foster care)

D. There is a presumption that the care in criterion C is responsible for the disturbed behavior in criterion A (eg, the disturbances in criterion A began following the pathogenic care in criterion C).

Specify type:
Inhibited Type: if criterion A1 predominates in the clinical presentation
Disinhibited Type: if criterion A2 predominates in the clinical presentation

Table 47.1
DSM-IV Diagnostic Criteria for Selective Mutism

A. Consistent failure to speak in specific social situations (in which there is an expectation for speaking, eg, at school) despite speaking in other situations.

B. The disturbance interferes with educational or occupational achievement or with social communication.

C. The duration of the disturbance is at least 1 month (not limited to the first month of school).

D. The failure to speak is not due to a lack of knowledge of, or comfort with, the spoken language required in the social situation.

E. The disturbance is not better accounted for by a communication disorder (eg, stuttering) and does not occur exclusively during the course of a pervasive developmental disorder, schizophrenia, or other psychotic disorder.

Table 47.3
DSM-IV Diagnostic Criteria for Separation Anxiety Disorder

A. Developmentally inappropriate and excessive anxiety concerning separation from home or from those to whom the individual is attached, as evidenced by three (or more) of the following:
   (1) recurrent excessive distress when separation from home or major attachment figures occurs or is anticipated
   (2) persistent and excessive worry about losing, or about possible harm befalling, major attachment figures
   (3) persistent and excessive worry that an untoward event will lead to separation from a major attachment figure (eg, getting lost or being kidnapped)
   (4) persistent reluctance or refusal to go to school or elsewhere because of fear of separation
   (5) persistently and excessively fearful or reluctant to be alone or without major attachment figures at home or without significant adults in other settings
   (6) persistent reluctance or refusal to go to sleep without being near a major attachment figure or to sleep away from home
   (7) repeated nightmares involving the theme of separation
   (8) repeated complaints of physical symptoms (such as headaches, stomachaches, nausea, or vomiting) when separation from major attachment figures occurs or is anticipated

B. The duration of the disturbance is at least 4 weeks.

C. The onset is before age 18 years.

D. The disturbance causes clinically significant distress or impairment in social, academic (occupational), or other important areas of functioning.

E. The disturbance does not occur exclusively during the course of a pervasive developmental disorder, schizophrenia, or other psychotic disorder and, in adolescents and adults, is not better accounted for by panic disorder with agoraphobia.

Specify if:
Early onset: if onset occurs before age 6 years

is a disorder in which a child who is fluent with language consistently fails to speak in certain situations in which it is expected, such as in school. Selective mutism *is associated with an increased risk of separation anxiety disorder* and other anxiety symptoms. Selective mutism is rare, found in fewer than 1 percent of individuals seen in mental health settings. Young children are most vulnerable, and the disorder *is more common in girls than in boys.* Selective mutism has an onset usually before 5 years of age but *does not usually resolve by 5 years of age.* Half of children with this disorder show improvement by age 10.

47.5 The answer is E (*Synopsis VIII,* pages 1236–1241). Reactive attachment disorder of infancy or early childhood is a disturbance of social interaction and relatedness, based largely on grossly inappropriate caregiving, such as neglect of a child's basic physical or emotional needs. Reactive attachment disorder of infancy or early childhood cannot be accounted for by *a pervasive developmental disorder* (Table 47.2). Characteristics of reactive attachment disorder of infancy or early childhood include *inhibited, withdrawn, and socially unresponsive behavior, excessive familiarity with relative strangers, chronically emotionally neglectful home environment,* and *lack of stable attachment to the primary caregiver.*

47.6 The answer is D (*Synopsis VIII,* page 1241). In stereotypic movement disorder (Table 47.4) *the diagnosis is made only if the symptoms are not better accounted for by a compulsion (as in obsessive-compulsive disorder) or a tic (as in tic disorder).* Stereotypic movement disorder is defined by repetitive, seemingly driven, and nonfunctional motor behavior, such as rocking, head banging, self-biting, picking, and waving. Although the revised third edition of *Diagnostic and Statistical Manual of Mental Disorders* (DSM-III-R) specified the behaviors as being intentional, *the behaviors are not specified as intentional in the fourth edition (DSM-IV).* In stereotypic movement disorder, *the diagnosis can be made with mental retardation or a pervasive developmental disorder* as long as the stereotypic behavior is sufficiently severe to become a focus of treatment. Stereotypic movement disorder is not diagnosed when *hair pulling (trichotillomania) is the sole symptom.* Stereotypic movement disorder often contains self-injurious behaviors, and when self-injurious behavior is present, it must be specified, according to DSM-IV, whether the behavior would result in bodily damage if protective measures were not used. There is *no typical age of onset.* The onset may follow a stressful environmental event.

47.7 The answer is E (all) (*Synopsis VIII,* pages 1229–1230). Morbid fears, preoccupations, and ruminations are characteristic of separation anxiety in children. Children have *fears that a loved one will be hurt* or that something terrible will happen to them when they are away from important caring figures. Many children worry that accidents or illness will befall their

Table 47.4
DSM-IV Diagnostic Criteria for Stereotypic Movement Disorder

A. Repetitive, seemingly driven, and nonfunctional motor behavior (eg, hand shaking or waving, body rocking, head banging, mouthing of objects, self-biting, picking at skin or bodily orifices, hitting own body).

B. The behavior markedly interferes with normal activities or results in self-inflicted bodily injury that requires medical treatment (or would result in an injury if preventive measures were not used).

C. If mental retardation is present, the stereotypic or self-injurious behavior is of sufficient severity to become a focus of treatment.

D. The behavior is not better accounted for by a compulsion (as in obsessive-compulsive disorder), a tic (as in tic disorder), a stereotypy that is part of a pervasive developmental disorder, or hair pulling (as in trichotillomania).

E. The behavior is not due to the direct physiological effects of a substance or a general medical condition.

F. The behavior persists for 4 weeks or longer.

Specify if:
With self-injurious behavior: if the behavior results in bodily damage that requires specific treatment (or that would result in bodily damage if protective measures were not used)

parents or themselves. *Fears about getting lost* and about being kidnapped and never again finding their parents are common. Young children express less specific, more generalized concerns because their immature cognitive development precludes the formation of well-defined fears. In older children, fears of getting lost may include elaborate fantasies about kidnapping, being harmed, being raped, or being made slaves.

When separation from an important figure is imminent, children show many premonitory signs, such as *irritability,* difficulty in eating, and complaining and whining. Physical complaints, such as vomiting or headaches, are common when separation is anticipated or actually happens. These difficulties increase in intensity and organization with age because the older child is able to anticipate anxiety in a more structured fashion. Thus there is a continuum between mild anticipatory anxiety before a threatened separation and pervasive anxiety after the separation has occurred. *Animal and monster phobias* are common, as are concerns about dying. The child, when threatened with separation, may become fearful of events related to muggers, burglars, car accidents, or kidnapping.

47.8 The answer is E (all) (*Synopsis VIII,* pages 1236–1241). The essential features of reactive attachment disorder of infancy are signs of poor emotional and physical development, with onset before 8 months of age, and are due to a lack of adequate caretaking. Reactive attachment disorder of infancy or early childhood *may be reversed shortly after institution of adequate caregiving.* It is not due to a physical disorder, mental retardation, or autistic disorder. It *includes a normal head circumference and a failure to gain weight disproportionately greater than the failure to gain length, is usually associated with gross emotional neglect or imposed social isolation in an institution,* and *is indicated by a lack of developmentally appropriate signs of social responsivity.*

47.9 The answer is C (*Synopsis VIII,* pages 1238–1239). The infant suffers from *reactive attachment disorder of infancy,* presenting with the typical clinical picture of nonorganic failure to thrive. In such infants, hypokinesis, dullness, apathy, and *paucity of spontaneous activity* are usually seen. Most of the infants appear significantly malnourished and many have protruding abdomens, as seen in the photograph. Although many such infants' weight is below the third percentile and markedly below the appropriate weight for the infant's height, *head circumference is usually normal for the infant's age. Bone age is usually retarded. Growth hormone levels are usually normal or elevated,* suggesting that growth failure is secondary to caloric deprivation and malnutrition. The children improve physically and gain weight rapidly after they are hospitalized, as evident in Figure 47.1*B*.

Answers 47.10–47.13

47.10 The answer is C (*Synopsis VIII,* pages 1236–1241).

47.11 The answer is A (*Synopsis VIII,* pages 1229–1230).

47.12 The answer is B (*Synopsis VIII,* pages 1235–1236).

47.13 The answer is D (*Synopsis VIII,* pages 1241–1243). Reactive attachment disorder is a disorder of social relatedness that is *associated with grossly pathogenic caregiving,* in the form of emotional or physical neglect or multiple caretakers precluding the development of attachments. Separation anxiety disorder in children *becomes difficult to treat when the major attachment figure also has separation anxiety disorder.* In such a case the attachment figure (usually the mother) exposes the child to her own anxiety, reinforcing the child's discomfort. Treatment for separation anxiety includes the major attachment figure encouraging the child to separate and reinforcing a positive reunion after the separation. Selective mutism is a disorder *that often manifests only outside the home,* so that at home it is not apparent. In separation anxiety disorder, sometimes symptoms are also not evident at home when the major attachment figure is home, but symptoms would emerge in the home if the mother left and the separation occurred there. In stereotypic movement disorder *some symptoms, such as rocking or thumb sucking, are considered developmentally normal, self-comforting behaviors when they occur in very young children.* However, the symptoms can cause functional impairment if they continue into middle childhood and are manifested in socially unacceptable situations.

48 

Mood Disorders and Suicide

Mood disorders in children and adolescents have been recognized, and treatments for these disorders in the young have been given more attention over the past decade. The core features of major depression, dysthymic disorder, and bipolar I disorder are essentially the same at every age. Certain features, however, may be exhibited in a developmentally appropriate way. The diagnostic criteria in the fourth edition of *Diagnostic and Statistical Manual of Mental Disorders* (DSM-IV) for the mood disorders in children and adolescents is largely the same as they are for adults, with some minor developmental modifications. These modifications in the diagnostic criteria for major depression include the following: in children and adolescents, irritable mood may be the only expression of depressed mood. In children, instead of weight loss as a pertinent symptom of depression, failure to make expected weight gain is considered potentially symptomatic. In dysthymic disorder, the criteria are modified for children and adolescents in that irritability may be interpreted as depressed mood, and the symptoms must be present for a duration of 1 year, not 2 years, as it is for adults. The criteria for an episode of mania are identical for children, adolescents, and adults. Major depression is characterized by a constellation of at least five depressive symptoms, one of which must be irritable or depressed mood or loss of interest, and a duration of the symptoms for at least 2 weeks. Other symptoms include recurrent thoughts of suicide, feelings of guilt or worthlessness, psychomotor retardation, diminished ability to concentrate, sleep disturbance, and weight change. The criteria for dysthymic disorder include an irritable or depressed mood and at least two other symptoms, including appetite disturbance, sleep disturbance, low energy, poor self-esteem, difficulty making decisions, and feelings of hopelessness. Suicidal thoughts commonly accompany major depression in patients of any age.

Although the core features of mood disorders are the same regardless of age, some symptoms are more prevalent in very young children, and other symptoms predominate in adolescents or adults. For example, somatic complaints, mood-congruent hallucinations, and sad appearance are more commonly seen in young children than in adults, whereas the frequency of pervasive anhedonia, psychomotor retardation, delusions, and a sense of hopelessness increase with age. Depressed children often complain of a lack of friends and of being picked on by peers. Their complaints may continue even after the episode of depression resolves. Some features, such as suicidal ideation, depressed or irritable mood, insomnia, and diminished ability to concentrate, occur with equal frequency in patients of all ages.

Children's moods are particularly vulnerable to the influence of severe social stressors, such as family discord, abuse, neglect, and failure in school. Many young children with severe depression have endured harmful family and environmental conditions. Mood disorders increase in frequency with age. The rate of major depressive disorder in preschool children has been estimated to be about 0.3 percent. In school-age children, major depressive disorder is estimated to occur in up to 2 percent and affects more boys than girls. In adolescents, major depressive disorder is estimated to occur in up to 5 percent and is more common in girls than in boys. School-age children with dysthymic disorder have a very high rate of developing a major depressive episode after the year required to diagnose dysthymic disorder. In adolescents and adults, major depressive disorder is more common than dysthymic disorder. The rate of bipolar I disorder is extremely low in prepubertal children, and the diagnosis may not be made for years because usually no manic episode occurs until adolescence. The lifetime prevalence rate of bipolar I disorder in adolescents is estimated to be about 0.6 percent.

Suicidal ideation and attempts are frequently but not necessarily associated with mood disorders. Suicide attempts occur 3 times as often in adolescent girls than in adolescent boys, but completed suicide occurs 4 to 5 times as often in adolescent boys as in adolescent girls. The suicide rate is estimated to be less than 1 in 100,000 in children under 14 years of age. In adolescents aged 15 to 19 years, the suicide rate is estimated to be about 14 per 100,000 for boys and 3 per 100,000 for girls. The actual risk of suicide is low in children under 12 years of age, since their plans are often unrealistic. In the United States, the most common method of suicide among children and adolescents is the use of a firearm, which accounts for about 66 percent of suicides in adolescent boys and about 50 percent of suicides in girls. The second most common method of suicide in adolescent boys is hanging, whereas the second most common method in adolescent girls is the ingestion of toxic substances. Universal features of suicidal adolescents include inability to solve problems and lack of coping strategies. Risk factors for suicide in adolescents include a previous suicide attempt, being male, a history of violent or aggressive behavior, a history of substance abuse, a depressive disorder, and access to a gun. In girls, risk factors include a previous suicide attempt, pregnancy, a history of running away, and a mood disorder. Any child or adolescent must be hospitalized if there is persistent suicidal ideation or if the family is incapable of cooperating with outpatient treatment. Students should read Chapter 48 of *Kaplan and Sadock's Syn-*

opsis VIII and then test their knowledge of the area by studying the questions and answers herein.

HELPFUL HINTS

The student should study these terms.

- academic failure
- boredom
- cortisol hypersecretion
- developmental symptoms
- double depression
- environmental stressors
- family history
- hallucinations
- insidious onset
- irritable mood
- lethal methods
- poor concentration
- poor problem solving
- precipitants of suicide
- psychosocial deficits
- REM latency
- sad appearance
- social withdrawal
- somatic complaints
- temper tantrums

▲ QUESTIONS

DIRECTIONS: Each of these questions or incomplete statements is followed by five suggested responses or completions. Select the *one* that is *best* in each case.

48.1 Major depressive disorder in school-age children

A. may present as irritable mood rather than depressed mood
B. usually includes pervasive anhedonia
C. is more common than dysthymic disorder
D. includes mood-congruent auditory hallucinations less often than in adults with this disorder
E. occurs more often in girls than in boys

48.2 Which of the following symptoms of major depressive disorder are equally common in all age groups?

A. Suicidal ideation
B. Somatic complaints
C. Mood-congruent auditory hallucinations
D. Pervasive anhedonia
E. all of the above

48.3 Suicide in adolescents

A. decreases in frequency with increasing age
B. occurs more often in teenagers 12 to 14 years of age than in teenagers 14 to 16 years of age
C. is more common in girls than in boys
D. is almost always associated with a mood disorder
E. is often precipitated by arguments with family members, girlfriends, or boyfriends

48.4 Risk factors for adolescent suicide include all of the following *except*

A. being female
B. previous suicide attempts
C. a history of substance abuse
D. a history of aggressive behavior
E. being male

DIRECTIONS: Each set of lettered headings below is followed by a list of numbered words or phrases. For each numbered word or phrase, select

A. if the item is associated with *A only*
B. if the item is associated with *B only*
C. if the item is associated with *both A and B*
D. if the item is associated with *neither A nor B*

Questions 48.5–48.7

A. Major depressive disorder
B. Dysthymic disorder
C. Both
D. Neither

48.5 The disorder occurs first in double depression.
48.6 Mood-congruent auditory hallucinations are common.
48.7 The prevalence increases with age.

ANSWERS

Mood Disorders and Suicide

48.1 The answer is A (*Synopsis VIII,* pages 1246–1247).
Major depression in school-age children is essentially the same disorder that occurs in adolescents and adults. One modification in the fourth edition of *Diagnostic and Statistical Manual of Mental Disorders* (DSM-IV) criteria for major depressive disorder in children and adolescents is that it *may present as irritable mood rather than depressed mood.* Major depressive disorder in children *rarely includes pervasive anhedonia.* It is *less common than dysthymic disorder* in school-age children, but it is more common than dysthymic disorder in adolescence. Major depressive disorder in children includes *mood-congruent auditory hallucinations more often than in adults with this disorder.* It *occurs more often in boys than in girls in this age group.*

48.2 The answer is A (*Synopsis VIII,* page 1250).
Suicidal ideation occurs equally in patients with major depressive disorder in all age groups. Although the core features of major depressive disorder are essentially the same in children, adolescents, and adults, different specific symptoms predominate at different ages. In depressed school age children, *somatic complaints* and *mood-congruent auditory hallucinations* present more often than in depressed adolescents or adults. Mood congruent delusions and *pervasive anhedonia* increase with age and are more common in adolescents and adults than in young children.

48.3 The answer is E (*Synopsis VIII,* pages 1250–1257).
Suicide in adolescents *is often precipitated by arguments with family members, girlfriends, or boyfriends.* Completed suicide is almost nonexistent in children under 12 years of age and *increases in frequency with increasing age.* Thus suicide *occurs more often in teenagers 14 to 16 years of age than in teenagers 12 to 14 years of age.* Suicide attempts are about 3 times as common in adolescent girls as in boys, but completed suicide *is more common in boys than in girls.* That is primarily due to the greater lethality of the methods that adolescent boys use. The most common method of suicide in adolescent boys is the use of firearms, accounting for two thirds of male suicides. Firearms account for half of completed suicides among adolescent girls. The second most common method of suicide in adolescent boys is hanging. *Ingestions are a very uncommon method of completed suicides in males,* although they are common nonlethal methods used in suicide attempts by adolescent girls. Suicide *is not always associated with a mood disorder,* although the risk of suicide increases when there is a severe mood disorder.

48.4 The answer is A (*Synopsis VIII,* pages 1250–1251).
Being female is not a risk factor for adolescent suicide. Adolescent girls are more likely to attempt suicide by ingesting pills or a toxic substance, but the results are not often lethal. Risk factors for suicide in adolescents include *previous suicide attempts, a history of substance abuse,* and *a history of aggressive behavior.*

Answers 48.5–48.7

48.5 The answer is B (*Synopsis VIII,* pages 1247–1248).

48.6 The answer is A (*Synopsis VIII,* pages 1246–1247).

48.7 The answer is C (*Synopsis VIII,* pages 1246–1248).
Double depression is dysthymic disorder coupled with major depressive disorder. Usually *dysthymic disorder occurs first in double depression,* and then major depressive disorder begins some time after the first year of dysthymia. *Mood-congruent auditory hallucinations are not uncommon* in school-age children with *major depressive disorder.* In *both* dysthymic disorder and major depressive disorder, *the prevalence increases with age.*

49 

Schizophrenia with Childhood Onset

Schizophrenia with childhood onset is the same disorder as schizophrenia in adolescence or adulthood. The diagnostic criteria are identical to the adult form except that in children and adolescents a failure to achieve expected levels of social and academic functioning may take the place of a deterioration in functioning. Prior to the 1960s the term childhood psychosis was applied to a group of disturbed children who exhibited severe communication and language dysfunction, as well as to children who exhibited classic psychotic symptoms, such as auditory hallucinations and delusions. Over time, the children who exhibited pervasive impairment in reciprocal social interaction became identified in another diagnostic category, either autistic disorder or pervasive developmental disorder. The formal differentiation of schizophrenia, childhood onset, from autistic disorder occurred in the 1980s. Schizophrenia in general is easily distinguished from autistic disorder in that it is a set of symptoms that usually do not present prior to age 5, whereas the pervasive developmental disorders are usually obvious by age 3 years. In general, children with autism are impaired in all areas of adaptive functioning from early life. Schizophrenia in prepuberty is much rarer than autistic disorder, and it is approximately one fiftieth as common as schizophrenia in adolescence. According to the fourth edition of *Diagnostic and Statistical Manual of Mental Disorders* (DSM-IV), schizophrenia may be diagnosed in the presence of autistic disorder.

Family and genetic studies provide substantial evidence of a biological contribution to the development of schizophrenia, although no specific biological markers have been identified. The genetic transmission pattern in schizophrenia remains unknown, but it appears that there is more genetic loading for schizophrenia in relatives of probands who present with schizophrenia in childhood than in those who develop schizophrenia in adolescence or adulthood. There is no way, however, to identify vulnerable children at highest risk for the development of schizophrenia within a given family. Furthermore, environmental factors also influence the onset of schizophrenia in children and in adults. Children and adolescents who develop schizophrenia are more likely to have a premorbid history of social rejection; poor peer relationships; clingy, withdrawn behavior; and academic difficulties than patients with adult-onset schizophrenia. Some childhood schizophrenics have early histories of delayed motor milestones as well as delayed language acquisition.

The course and prognosis of childhood-onset schizophrenia depends on the child's premorbid level of functioning, the age of onset of the disorder, the degree of recompensation after the initial episode, the child's intellectual functioning, and the degree of support available from the family. Children with compromised premorbid functioning, including developmental delays and premorbid behavior disorders, seem to be at risk for poor medication response and guarded outcome.

In general, schizophrenia with childhood onset appears to be less responsive to medication than with onset in late adolescence or adulthood. The treatment of schizophrenia with childhood onset includes family education, family support, psychopharmacological intervention, and appropriate educational placement for the child. Readers are referred to Chapter 49 of *Kaplan and Sadock's Synopsis VIII* and should then study the questions and answers herein to assess their knowledge of the subject.

HELPFUL HINTS

The student should understand these terms.

- ▶ agranulocytosis
- ▶ autistic disorder
- ▶ childhood psychosis
- ▶ clozapine (Clozaril)
- ▶ delayed motor development
- ▶ disturbed communication
- ▶ expressed emotion
- ▶ family support
- ▶ haloperidol (Haldol)
- ▶ hypersalivation
- ▶ persecutory delusions
- ▶ premorbid disorders
- ▶ premorbid functioning
- ▶ schizotypal personality
- ▶ sedation
- ▶ social rejection
- ▶ tardive dyskinesia
- ▶ transient phobic hallucinations
- ▶ visual hallucinations

▲ QUESTIONS

DIRECTIONS: Each of the incomplete statements below is followed by five suggested completions. Select the *one* that is *best* in each case.

49.1 Predictors of poor prognosis in schizophrenia with childhood onset include all of the following *except*

A. misdiagnosed schizophrenia in a child with bipolar I disorder
B. onset before 10 years of age
C. premorbid diagnoses of attention-deficit/hyperactivity disorder and learning disorders
D. lack of family support
E. delayed motor milestones and delayed language acquisition

49.2 Which of the following statements about the difficulties of diagnosing schizophrenia in adolescents is *false*?

A. Patients may initially appear depressed.
B. Psychotic symptoms may be a normal feature of adolescence.
C. Substance abuse may cloud the clinical picture.
D. Adolescents tend to act out defenses.
E. All of the above statements are true.

49.3 Schizophrenia with childhood onset differs from schizophrenia with adult onset in that

A. schizophrenic children do not manifest command auditory hallucinations
B. parents of patients with childhood-onset schizophrenia are less likely than parents of patients with adult-onset schizophrenia to be schizophrenic
C. in children with schizophrenia there is often a premorbid history of behavior disorders, delayed motor milestones, and delayed language acquisition
D. childhood schizophrenics respond more to medication than do adult schizophrenics
E. childhood-onset schizophrenics are usually mildly mentally retarded

DIRECTIONS: The lettered headings below are followed by a list of numbered words or phrases. For each numbered word or phrase, select

A. if the item is associated with *A only*
B. if the item is associated with *B only*
C. if the item is associated with *both A and B*
D. if the item is associated with *neither A nor B*

Questions 49.4–49.6

A. Haloperidol
B. Clozapine
C. Both
D. Neither

49.4 Effective in diminishing positive symptoms in schizophrenia such as auditory hallucinations
49.5 Generally does not induce extrapyramidal side effects
49.6 Associated with agranulocytosis

ANSWERS

Schizophrenia with Childhood Onset

49.1 The answer is A (*Synopsis VIII,* pages 1254–1255).
Misdiagnosed schizophrenia in a child with bipolar I disorder is a factor in a good prognosis, not a poor prognosis. Although prospective studies are needed, factors that seem to predict poor prognosis in schizophrenia with childhood onset are *onset before age 10 years, premorbid diagnoses of attention-deficit/ hyperactivity disorder and learning disorders, lack of family support,* and an early history of *delayed motor milestones and delayed language acquisition.*

49.2 The answer is B (*Synopsis VIII,* pages 1253–1255).
Psychotic symptoms are never a normal feature of adolescence; there is no developmentally normal psychosis of adolescence. Diagnosing schizophrenia in adolescents may be difficult because *patients may initially appear depressed* and *substance abuse may cloud the clinical picture.* Schizophrenia in adolescence is not fundamentally different from that in other age groups. However, there are some variations. Patients who are actually schizophrenic may look depressed, and they become withdrawn and isolated and have impaired eating and sleeping habits. In addition, *adolescents tend to act out defenses,* that is, they externalize conflicts onto the environment to avoid the pain of loss or the feeling of being helpless and hopeless. This acting out may take the form of drug abuse, promiscuity, delinquency, or a combination of them.

49.3 The answer is C (*Synopsis VIII,* page 1254).
Schizophrenia with childhood onset is recognized as the same disorder as is seen in adolescents and adults. But *in children with schizophrenia there is often a premorbid history of behavior disorders, delayed motor milestones, and delayed language acquisition. Schizophrenic children manifest command auditory hallucinations* similar to those of adult schizophrenia patients. Yet there have been reports of increased genetic loading in childhood-onset schizophrenics. *Parents of patients with childhood-onset schizophrenia are more likely, not less likely, than parents of patients with adult-onset schizophrenia to be schizophrenic;* about 8 percent of first-degree relatives of childhood schizophrenics as opposed to 4 percent of adult-onset schizophrenics are affected. Although there have been no well-controlled studies, it appears that *childhood schizophrenics respond to medications less, not more, than do adult schizophrenics.* Epidemiological data indicate that *childhood-onset schizophrenics are usually not mildly mentally retarded* but rather function in the low average to average range of intelligence.

Answers 49.4–49.6

49.4 The answer is C (*Synopsis VIII,* page 1256).

49.5 The answer is B (*Synopsis VIII,* page 1256).

49.6 The answer is B (*Synopsis VIII,* page 1256).
Both haloperidol (Haldol) and clozapine (Clozaril) are *effective in diminishing positive symptoms of schizophrenia such as auditory hallucinations.* Clozapine has been used with some success in schizophrenic adults who are resistant to treatment with multiple conventional antipsychotics. Clozapine has the advantage that it *generally does not induce extrapyramidal side effects* and is not likely to cause tardive dyskinesia. However, *clozapine* has been *associated with agranulocytosis,* a potentially fatal side effect, so close monitoring is required when clozapine is used.

50 

Adolescent Substance Abuse

Adolescent substance abuse looms large as a serious disruption in the lives of many youths. It has been reported that the 1990s' downward trend in drug use among adolescents still prevails, yet a significant portion of adolescents regularly use alcohol, marijuana, and cocaine. Studies of alcohol use among adolescents in the United States report that by age 13 years, one third of boys and one fourth of girls have used alcohol. By age 18, some 92 percent of males and 73 percent of females drink alcohol.

Marijuana is the most widely used illicit drug among high school students. Marijuana has been described as a ''gateway drug,'' since the strongest predictor of future cocaine use is frequent marijuana use during adolescence. The highest rates of marijuana use are reported by Native American and white males and females and Mexican-American males. The lowest rates are reported by Latin-American and African-American females and Asian-American males and females.

The propensity to develop alcohol and drug abuse has multiple contributing factors. Alcoholism has been shown to run in families, and concordance for alcoholism is higher among monozygotic than dizygotic twins. Twin studies of rates of drug abuse appear to show similar results. Children of alcoholics raised outside of the biological home have a 25 percent chance of developing alcoholism. Psychosocial factors probably also play a role in the development of substance use disorders. Children identified as living in families with the lowest measures of parental supervision initiated alcohol, tobacco, and other drugs at an earlier age than children from more highly supervising parents. Greater monitoring of behaviors among middle school-age children by parents may diminish drug and alcohol sampling and ultimately reduce substance use.

There are high levels of comorbidity among various substance abuses and between substance use and other psychiatric disorders. Surveys of adolescents with alcoholism show rates of at least 50 percent for additional psychiatric disorders, especially mood disorders. Common concurrent psychiatric disorders include depressive disorders, disruptive behavior disorders, and other substance disorders. There seems to be a relationship between substance use and high-risk behaviors, such as use of weapons, fighting, suicidal behavior, early sexual experimentation, risky driving, and sometimes preoccupation with cults or satanic rituals. Adolescents with marginal social skills often enhance their sociability by using drugs or alcohol.

According to the fourth edition of *Diagnostic and Statistical Manual of Mental Disorders* (DSM-IV), the substance-related disorders include the disorders of dependence, abuse, intoxication, and withdrawal. Substance dependence is a cluster of cognitive, behavioral, and physiological symptoms indicating continued usage in the face of negative effects of the substance on functioning. Self-administration of the drug may result in tolerance, withdrawal, and compulsive substance use behavior. Dependence can be applied to every substance except caffeine. Dependence requires the presence of at least three symptoms of the maladaptive pattern occurring at any time in a 12-month period. Physiological dependence may or may not be present. Substance abuse is a maladaptive pattern of substance use leading to clinically significant impairment or distress, as manifested by one or more of the following symptoms within a 12-month period: physical danger to the user, obvious impairment in school or work, or legal problems. Substance intoxication is the development of a reversible, substance specific syndrome due to the use of the substance that manifests itself in maladaptive behavioral or psychological changes. Substance withdrawal is a substance-specific syndrome due to the cessation or reduction of use of the substance. Withdrawal syndrome causes clinically significant distress or impairment in social or occupational functioning.

Treatment for substance use disorders may occur in a variety of settings. These include inpatient units, residential treatment facilities, halfway houses, group homes, partial hospital programs, and outpatient settings. Basic components of adolescent alcohol or drug treatment include individual psychotherapy, drug-specific counseling, self-help groups (Alcoholics Anonymous, Narcotics Anonymous, Alateen, Al-Anon), substance abuse education, and relapse prevention programs. Behavioral interventions and structured programs that model themselves after Alcoholics Anonymous, such as the Minnesota Model, use an intensive 12-step program with self-help participation. Cognitive and behavioral approaches to psychotherapy and psychopharmacological interventions for comorbid psychiatric disorders may be helpful. The student should carefully read Chapter 50 in *Kaplan and Sadock's Synopsis VIII.* Once familiar with the material, the student will be able to address the questions and answers herein.

HELPFUL HINTS

The student should be able to define the following terms.

- aerosols
- Al-Anon
- Alateen
- Alcoholics Anonymous
- Antabuse
- comorbidity
- cocaine
- glue
- inhalants
- marijuana
- Narcotics Anonymous
- substance abuse
- substance dependence
- substance intoxication
- substance withdrawal
- 12-step program

▲ QUESTIONS

DIRECTIONS: These lettered headings are followed by a list of numbered phrases. For each numbered phrase, select the lettered heading most closely associated with it. Each lettered heading may be used once, more than once, or not at all.

Questions 50.1–50.5

A. Substance abuse
B. Substance dependence
C. Substance intoxication
D. Substance withdrawal

50.1 Only category in DSM-IV used for caffeine

50.2 A maladaptive pattern of substance use causing impairment manifested as tolerance, withdrawal, and inability to decrease substance use

50.3 The development of a reversible syndrome causing behavioral or psychological changes due to a substance

50.4 A maladaptive pattern of substance use causing impairment as manifested by diminished performance in school, legal problems, and continued use despite recurrent social and interpersonal problems

50.5 The development of a substance-specific syndrome due to the cessation of a substance that causes distress and impairment

Questions 50.6–50.12

A. Alcohol use
B. Marijuana use
C. Cocaine use
D. LSD use
E. Inhalant use

50.6 This causes a significant problem for 10 to 20 percent of adolescents.

50.7 This substance is the strongest predictor of future cocaine use in adolescents.

50.8 Approximately one in five students in 8th, 10th, and 12th grade has used this substance.

50.9 Prevalence rates for this substance appear to be decreasing.

50.10 Prevalence rates for this substance are highest among Native Americans and whites.

50.11 Children of abusers of this substance have a 25 percent chance of abusing this substance.

50.12 Approximately 0.1 percent of 12th graders use this substance daily.

DIRECTIONS: Each of these questions or incomplete statements is followed by five suggested responses or completions. Select the *one* that is *best* in each case.

50.13 The treatment for alcohol abuse in adolescents includes all of the following *except*

A. drug-specific counseling
B. self-help groups
C. relapse prevention programs
D. disulfiram (Antabuse) treatment
E. individual psychotherapy

50.14 Risk factors for the development of adolescent substance abuse include all of the following *except*

A. early onset of cigarette smoking
B. diminished parental supervision
C. high academic achievement
D. parental substance abuse
E. conduct disorder

50.15 Of adolescents who present to a pediatric trauma center, the number of cases that involve alcohol or drug use is approximately

A. 10 percent
B. 25 percent
C. 30 percent
D. 50 percent
E. 80 percent

ANSWERS

Adolescent Substance Abuse

Answers 50.1–50.5

50.1 The answer is C (*Synopsis VIII,* page 1258).

50.2 The answer is B (*Synopsis VIII,* page 1258).

50.3 The answer is C (*Synopsis VIII,* page 1258).

50.4 The answer is A (*Synopsis VIII,* page 1258).

50.5 The answer is D (*Synopsis VIII,* pages 1258–1259).
Substance dependence refers to a group of cognitive, behavioral, and sometimes physiological symptoms that accompany the continued use of a substance. (For a review of the diagnostic criteria for substance abuse, see Chapter 12.) There is a *pattern of repeated self-administration* that may result in tolerance, withdrawal, and compulsive drug taking. Caffeine (caffeinism) does not fall into any of the substance use disorders except intoxication, according to DSM-IV. Dependence requires the presence of at least three symptoms of the maladaptive pattern, all of which must occur within the same year. Substance abuse refers to a *maladaptive pattern of substance use* leading to a clinically significant amount of distress within a 12-month period. The impairment may take the form of decreased performance in school or work, or it may cause physical danger or legal problems. Substance intoxication is the development of a reversible substance-specific syndrome due to the use of the substance. Clinically significant maladaptive behavioral or psychological changes must be present. Substance withdrawal refers to a *substance-specific syndrome* related to the cessation or reduction of a substance that causes clinically significant distress or impairment.

Answers 50.6–50.12

50.6 The answer is A (*Synopsis VIII,* page 1257).

50.7 The answer is B (*Synopsis VIII,* page 1257).

50.8 The answer is E (*Synopsis VIII,* pages 1257–1258).

50.9 The answer is C (*Synopsis VIII,* page 1257).

50.10 The answer is B (*Synopsis VIII,* page 1257).

50.11 The answer is A (*Synopsis VIII,* page 1257).

50.12 The answer is D (*Synopsis VIII,* page 1257).
Alcoholism is a serious problem for *10 to 20 percent of the adolescent population.* Furthermore, 97 percent of adolescents who are substance abusers also use alcohol. Marijuana has been called a gateway drug, since it is the most widely used illicit drug among high school students, and it is the *strongest predictor of future cocaine use.* Inhalants are surprisingly widely used among younger adolescents. More than 17 percent of high school students *in the 8th grade and above* have experimented with inhalants, including glue, aerosols, and gasoline. The prevalence rate of cocaine use in adolescence appears to be decreasing. Marijuana use is reported to be highest among Native American males and females and is nearly as high in *Caucasian males and females. Children of alcoholics have a 25 percent chance* of also becoming alcoholics. Some 0.1 percent of high school seniors report using LSD daily. This is lower than the rates reported for LSD use over the past 2 decades.

50.13 The answer is D (*Synopsis VIII,* page 1259).
Treatment programs for alcoholic adolescents contain a number of basic components. *Disulfiram (Antabuse) medication* is not a current treatment of choice. Treatment components usually include some form of individual psychotherapy, a self-help group component, drug-specific counseling, and relapse prevention treatment. These may be combined in any of a number of inpatient or outpatient programs.

50.14 The answer is C (*Synopsis VIII,* page 1257).
Risk factors for the development of alcohol or drug abuse include decreased parental supervision, early onset of cigarette smoking, an underlying conduct disorder, and parental substance abuse. *High academic achievement is not* a risk factor for substance abuse, but academic difficulties may increase risk of developing substance abuse.

50.15 The answer is C (*Synopsis VIII,* page 1257).
One third of adolescents brought to a pediatric trauma center have evidence of involvement with drugs and alcohol. The four most common causes of death in young people between the ages of 10 and 24 years are motor vehicle accidents (37 percent), homicide (14 percent), suicide (12 percent), and other injuries or accidents (12 percent).

51

Child Psychiatry: Additional Conditions That May Be a Focus of Clinical Attention

Numerous conditions are identified as foci of clinical attention, although they are not clearly psychiatric disorders. These conditions are related to psychiatric disorders in a number of ways: (1) The problem is the main reason for treatment in someone who does not meet criteria for any psychiatric disorder. (2) The child or adolescent has a psychiatric disorder, but the particular problem requiring treatment is not a part of the disorder. (3) The child or adolescent has a psychiatric disorder that is related to the problem, but the problem is sufficiently severe to warrant independent clinical attention. The following such conditions are considered here: borderline intellectual functioning, academic problem, child or adolescent antisocial behavior, and identity problem.

Borderline intellectual functioning is defined by the presence of a full-scale intelligence quotient within the 71 to 84 range, along with a consistent level of adaptive functioning. If the level of adaptive functioning has deteriorated into the borderline range in conjunction with the onset of a major mental disorder, it is more difficult to make the diagnosis. In that case the clinician must evaluate the patient's history to determine whether the intellectual and adaptive functioning was compromised prior to the mental disorder. Persons with borderline intellectual functioning may be able to function well in some areas while being markedly deficient in others. Therapeutic interventions include helping patients to become more socially skilled and to accept their limitations while promoting autonomy and accepting challenges.

According to the fourth edition of *Diagnostic and Statistical Manual of Mental Disorders* (DSM-IV), academic problem is a condition that is not due to a mental disorder, such as a learning disorder or a communication disorder. Numerous factors may contribute to academic problem in children without related psychiatric disorders. Children who have problems with separation from parents, have anxieties, or are troubled by family problems or mood disturbances sometimes fail in school. Some children receive mixed messages from their parents about trusting teachers and may have difficulties accepting appropriate criticism of their work, which can lead to poor performance. Some children have unrealistically low expectations of the amount of studying necessary to succeed and become discouraged when they do not do as well as they had expected. Others are so preoccupied with interpersonal relationships or peer problems that they perform poorly.

Childhood or adolescent antisocial behavior covers a variety of acts that violate the rights of others. Acts of aggression, stealing, truancy, and running away from home fall into that category. The term ''juvenile delinquent'' is defined by the legal system as a youth who has violated the law, but it does not mean that the youth meets the criteria for a mental disorder. Estimates of antisocial behavior range from 5 to 15 percent of the general population, somewhat less among children and adolescents. Risk factors for antisocial behavior by children and adolescents include a harsh and physically abusive home environment, parental criminality, a past of impulsive and hyperactive behavior, low intellectual functioning, academic failure, minimal adult supervision, and a history of substance use.

Identity problem is related to distress about one's goals, friendships, moral values, career aspirations, sexual orientation, and group loyalties. In the revised third edition of *Diagnostic and Statistical Manual of Mental Disorders* (DSM-III-R) such a disturbance constituted a mental disorder. In DSM-IV, identity problem may cause severe distress and may become a focus of clinical intervention, but it is not classified as a mental disorder. The etiology of identity problem is multifactorial, and may in part reflect the pressures of a chaotic and unsupportive family life. Children with chronic difficulties in mastering the expected developmental tasks in synchrony with peers are likely to struggle with forming a well-defined identity in adolescence. Adolescents with identity problem are often consumed with doubts and lack confidence and are preoccupied with a sense of alienation. Identity problem must be differentiated from early signs of a psychiatric disorder (such as borderline personality disorder, schizophreniform disorder, or a mood disorder). Identity problem usually resolves by the mid-20s. Psychotherapeutic intervention may be helpful for some adolescents, who benefit from acknowledgment of their struggle, recognition of their conflicts, and support. Students should review Chapter 51 of *Kaplan and Sadock's Synopsis VIII* and then study the questions and answers provided.

HELPFUL HINTS

The student should be able to define the following terms.

- ▶ abulia
- ▶ academic failure
- ▶ achievement tests
- ▶ adaptive function
- ▶ comorbid disorders
- ▶ dysfunctional family
- ▶ irreconcilable conflicts
- ▶ juvenile delinquent
- ▶ learning disorder
- ▶ mental retardation
- ▶ performance anxiety
- ▶ physical abuse
- ▶ role diffusion
- ▶ sense of self
- ▶ sexual orientation
- ▶ substance use
- ▶ superego
- ▶ underachievement
- ▶ ''V'' code
- ▶ violation of rights

▲ QUESTIONS

DIRECTIONS: Each of the incomplete statements below is followed by five suggested completions. Select the *one* that is *best* in each case.

51.1 Identity problem

A. often includes doubts related to career choice and friendships
B. does not include uncertainty about sexual orientation
C. occurs when there is minor distress
D. is not classified as a mental disorder
E. rarely occurs with a concurrent mood disorder

51.2 The differential diagnosis of identity problem includes

A. borderline personality disorder
B. schizophreniform disorder
C. schizophrenia
D. mood disorders
E. all of the above

51.3 Which of the following is *not* associated with childhood or adolescent antisocial behavior?

A. Academic failure
B. Substance use
C. Physical abuse
D. Neglectful home life
E. Anticipatory anxiety

DIRECTIONS: Each set of lettered headings below is followed by a list of numbered statements. For each numbered statement, select the *best* lettered heading. Each heading can be used once, more than once, or not at all.

Questions 51.4–51.7

A. Academic problem
B. Childhood or adolescent antisocial behavior
C. Borderline intellectual functioning

51.4 Intelligence quotient (IQ) within the range of 71 to 84
51.5 Normal intelligence and no learning disorder or communication disorder but is failing in school
51.6 Covers many acts that violate the rights of others
51.7 Must be differentiated from conduct disorder

ANSWERS

Child Psychiatry: Additional Conditions That May Be a Focus of Clinical Attention

51.1 The answer is D (*Synopsis VIII,* pages 231, 1263–1264). Identity problem *occurs when there is severe distress, not minor distress,* regarding uncertainty about issues relating to identity. Identity problem *often includes doubts related to career choice and friendship,* and *does include uncertainty about sexual orientation.* Unlike identity disorder in the revised third edition of *Diagnostic and Statistical Manual of Mental Disorders* (DSM-III-R), in the fourth edition (DSM-IV) *identity problem is not classified as a mental disorder.* Identity problem *often occurs with a concurrent mood disorder* or psychotic disorder.

51.2 The answer is E (all) (*Synopsis VIII,* page 1263). Identity problem must be differentiated from a mental disorder (such as *borderline personality disorder, schizophreniform disorder, schizophrenia,* or a *mood disorder*). At times, what initially appears to be identity problem may be the prodromal manifestations of one of those disorders. Intense but normal conflicts associated with maturing, such as adolescent turmoil and midlife crisis, may be confusing, but they are usually not associated with marked deterioration in school, vocational, or social functioning or with severe subjective distress. However, considerable evidence indicates that adolescent turmoil is often not a phase that is outgrown but indicates true psychopathology.

51.3 The answer is E (*Synopsis VIII,* pages 582, 1261). *Anticipatory anxiety* is not a common associated feature of childhood and adolescent antisocial behavior. Associated features of childhood and adolescent antisocial behavior include theft, *academic failure,* impulsivity, oppositional behavior, lying, suicide attempts, *substance use,* truancy, *physical abuse,* sexual abuse, and *neglectful home life.*

Answers 51.4–51.7

51.4 The answer is C (*Synopsis VIII,* pages 147, 1261).

51.5 The answer is A (*Synopsis VIII,* page 1261).

51.6 The answer is B (*Synopsis VIII,* page 1167).

51.7 The answer is B (*Synopsis VIII,* page 1263). *Borderline intellectual functioning* is defined by the presence of an *intelligence quotient (IQ) within the range of 71 to 84.* According to the fourth edition of *Diagnostic and Statistical Manual of Mental Disorders* (DSM-IV), a diagnosis of borderline intellectual functioning is made when issues pertaining to that level of cognition become the focus of clinical attention.

In DSM-IV, *academic problem* is a condition that is not due to a mental disorder, such as a learning disorder or a communication disorder, or if it is due to a mental disorder, it is severe enough to warrant independent clinical attention. Thus a child or an adolescent who has *normal intelligence and no learning disorder or communication disorder but is failing in school* or doing poorly falls into this category.

Childhood and adolescent antisocial behavior covers many acts that violate the rights of others, including overt acts of aggression and violence and such covert acts as lying, stealing, truancy, and running away from home. However, it *must be differentiated from conduct disorder.* The DSM-IV criteria for conduct disorder require a repetitive pattern of at least three antisocial behaviors over at least 6 months. Childhood or adolescent antisocial behavior consists of isolated events that do not constitute a mental disorder but do become the focus of clinical attention.

52

Psychiatric Treatment of Children and Adolescents

Psychiatric treatments for children and adolescents include a wide range of therapeutic modalities as well as settings in which to apply them. Modalities comprise individual psychotherapy with a variety of techniques, including cognitive-behavioral strategies, psychodynamic constructs, interpersonal and supportive interventions, family psychotherapies, group therapy, and subspecialty groups such as social skills. Psychopharmacological interventions for children and adolescents have grown in number and specificity over the past few decades. Treatment venues include outpatient and inpatient settings, partial hospital setting, residential facilities, and special education sites. In most cases, a combination of treatments may best match the multifaceted problems that children and families present to clinicians.

There are many types of psychotherapy for children: intensive individual psychotherapy, brief psychotherapy, family therapy, behavior therapy, play therapy, and symptom-focused remediation, such as tutoring and speech therapy. The use of those approaches by themselves or in combination should stem not from the therapist's preferences but from the assessment of the patient and from a broad-based background of knowledge about available treatments.

In child psychiatry, clinicians function as advocates for their patients and are often called upon to make recommendations to schools, legal agencies, and community organizations. Unlike adults, children rarely seek treatment on their own. Thus, one of the first tasks of the clinician is to stimulate the child's motivation for treatment.

Children tend to have a limited capacity for self-observation, but they are likely to reenact their experiences in play and verbal conversations. Children should be encouraged to express feelings verbally and in play as long as they understand that the ground rules include not hurting anyone or destroying property. To maintain a therapeutic alliance with the child, the clinician has to educate the child and be positive and supportive.

Psychotherapy with children usually includes parental involvement, with confidentiality maintained in a way that is appropriate to the child's age and developmental level. The child may be encouraged to disclose certain information in sessions with the parents if it appears that this is in the best interest of the child. Issues of danger, suicide, and homicide obviously take precedence over confidentiality.

Certain elements in psychotherapy produce complications that militate against a particular type of psychotherapy for a given child. For instance, for many children, a form of exploratory-interpretive psychotherapy aimed at uncovering intrapsychic conflicts is indicated. But if the youngster's ego functioning, particularly in the area of reality testing, is borderline, such an approach calls for considerable caution. To treat a young patient effectively, a clinician should be firmly aware of the indications and contraindications for the various psychotherapies. Students must be familiar with the differences between psychiatric treatment of children and the treatment of adults.

Pharmacotherapy for psychiatric disorders in children and adolescents is aimed at increasing a child's functioning in school and at home. Specific issues that are pertinent in children are those related to cognitive function—that is, the clinician must always consider a medication's effect on memory and alertness, sedative effect, and any other adverse effect that might interfere with a child's education and learning. However, sometimes those cautions become secondary to the safety of the child or of others.

Pharmacokinetics must also be considered. Children have greater hepatic capacity, more glomerular filtration, and less fatty tissue than adults. Thus some medications, such as sympathomimetics, dopamine receptor antagonists, and tricyclic drugs, may be eliminated more rapidly in children than in adults. Medications that have been well studied for effectiveness include methylphenidate (Ritalin) for attention-deficit/hyperactivity disorder, antipsychotics for psychotic disorders and for aggressive behavior, and lithium for bipolar I disorder in adolescents and for aggressive behavior. Tricyclic drugs have been tried for a variety of psychiatric syndromes, including enuresis, major depressive disorder, panic disorders, separation anxiety disorder, and attention-deficit/hyperactivity disorder. However, tricyclic drugs have not been shown to be superior to a placebo in double-blind, placebo-controlled studies of children and adolescents with major depressive disorder. In children, developmental differences in neurotransmitters and neuroendocrine systems may be associated with responses to antidepressants. The potentially serious cardiovascular side effects of tricyclic drugs and the recent reports of a number of sudden deaths occurring in children treated with desipramine (Norpramin) for attention-deficit/hyperactivity disorder have increased the caution with which clinicians use tricyclic medications in children. Serotonin-specific reuptake inhibitors, such as fluoxetine (Prozac), sertraline (Zoloft), paroxetine (Paxil), and fluvoxamine (Luvox), are being used to treat depressive disorders, anxiety disorders, and obsessive-compulsive symptoms. After reading Chapter 52 of *Kaplan and Sadock's Synopsis VIII,* students should study the questions and answers to test their knowledge of the subject.

HELPFUL HINTS

These terms should be known and defined by the student.

- acting out
- action-oriented defenses
- activity group therapy
- ADHD
- anticonvulsants
- atypical puberty
- autistic disorder
- behavioral contracting
- bell-and-pad conditioning
- biological therapies
- cardiovascular effects
- child guidance clinics
- child psychoanalysis
- classical and operant conditioning
- cognitive therapy
- combined therapy
- communication disorders
- compliance
- conduct disorder
- confidentiality
- depressive equivalents
- developmental orientation
- dietary manipulation
- ECT
- enuresis
- externalization
- family systems theory
- filial therapy
- group living
- group selection criteria
- group therapy
- growth suppression
- haloperidol (Haldol)
- interview techniques
- learning-behavioral theories
- lithium
- liver-to-body-weight ratio
- MAOIs
- masked depression
- milieu therapy
- modeling theory
- mood disorders
- obsessive-compulsive disorder
- parent groups
- parental attitudes
- pharmacokinetics
- play group therapy
- psychoanalytic theories
- psychoanalytically oriented therapy
- puberty and adolescence (differentiation)
- regression
- relationship therapy
- release therapy
- remedial and educational psychotherapy
- renal clearance
- residential and day treatment
- same-sex groups
- schizophrenia
- self-observation
- sequential psychosocial capacities
- sleep terror disorder
- substance abuse
- suicide
- supportive therapy
- sympathomimetics
- tardive dyskinesia
- therapeutic playroom
- therapeutic interventions
- Tourette's disorder
- tricyclic drugs
- violence

▲ QUESTIONS

DIRECTIONS: Each of these questions or incomplete statements is followed by five suggested responses or completions. Select the *one* that is *best* in each case.

52.1 Traditional items in a therapeutic playroom include all of the following *except*

A. multigenerational doll families
B. blocks
C. crayons
D. a television set
E. rubber hammers

52.2 Group therapy is useful for all of the following childhood problems *except*

A. phobias
B. male effeminate behavior
C. withdrawal and social isolation
D. extreme aggression
E. primary behavior disturbances

52.3 The use of diazepam (Valium) in children has been well established for the treatment of

A. sleep terrors
B. enuresis
C. obsessive-compulsive disorder
D. attention-deficit/hyperactivity disorder
E. all of the above

52.4 Group therapy is

A. not useful for mentally ill children
B. generally unfocused with young children
C. useful in the treatment of substance-related disorders
D. more viable with adolescents when the group is composed of mixed-sex rather than same-sex members
E. most effective when parents oppose it

52.5 Childhood disorders in which medication is the mainstay of treatment include all of the following *except*

A. conduct disorder
B. attention-deficit/hyperactivity disorder
C. Tourette's disorder
D. schizophrenia
E. all of the above

52.6 Which of the following statements about children referred for residential treatment is *not* true?

A. Most children referred are between 5 and 15 years of age.
B. Boys are referred more frequently than girls.
C. Most referred children have severe learning disabilities.
D. Outpatient treatment often precedes residential treatment.
E. Suicidal behavior is among the most common referral diagnoses.

52.7 The side effects of tricyclic medications in children include

A. dry mouth
B. blurry vision
C. tachycardia
D. palpitations
E. all of the above

52.8 "Symptom bearer," "distractor," "scapegoat," and "rescuer" are terms used in

A. behavioral theories
B. supportive therapy
C. psychoanalytic psychotherapy
D. family systems therapy
E. relationship therapy

52.9 Pharmacological treatment of conduct disorder may include

A. haloperidol (Haldol)
B. lithium (Eskalith)
C. carbamazepine (Tegretol)
D. propranolol (Inderal)
E. all of the above

52.10 Which of the following statements about the treatment of mental retardation with antipsychotic medication is *true*?

A. About 12 percent of mentally retarded patients living in institutions are receiving antipsychotics.
B. The intelligence quotient deficits that define mental retardation respond dramatically to phenothiazines.
C. There is no risk of tardive dyskinesia.
D. Hyperactivity and stereotypies associated with mental retardation have been found to respond to antipsychotic medications.
E. All of the above statements are true.

52.11 Residential treatment centers for children and adolescents

A. are permanent out-of-home placements
B. generally have a psychoanalytically oriented program
C. accept patients with usually acute psychiatric decompensations
D. are only for children and adolescents who have been psychiatrically hospitalized
E. provide a highly structured and supervised behavior-based program

DIRECTIONS: Each set of lettered headings below is followed by a list of numbered statements. For each numbered statement, select the *best* lettered heading. Each heading can be used once, more than once, or not at all.

Questions 52.12–52.18

A. Interpersonal therapy plus fluoxetine (Prozac)
B. Response prevention plus paroxetine (Paxil)
C. Social skills group plus methylphenidate (Ritalin)
D. Desmopressin (DDAVP) nasal spray
E. Family therapy
F. Partial hospital plus risperidone
G. Inpatient unit with psychodynamic and behavioral interventions

52.12 A 12-year-old boy performs 3 hours of daily compulsive hand-washing and has extreme difficulty getting to school because of contamination fears.

52.13 A 10-year-old girl became oppositional and defiant shortly after her mother remarried a man with three children.

52.14 A 15-year-old girl has lost 25 percent of her body weight and cannot control her purging behaviors.

52.15 A 17-year-old girl has recently been discharged from an inpatient unit after a suicide attempt and severe depression.

52.16 A 14-year-old girl has not been in school for several weeks because her derogatory auditory hallucinations have been bothering her; she is not suicidal.

52.17 An 8-year-old boy will not attend sleep-over parties because of his bedwetting.

52.18 A 7-year-old boy is about to be suspended from school because of his inability to sit in his seat and stay on task and because of his provocative behavior toward his classmates.

ANSWERS

Psychiatric Treatment of Children and Adolescents

52.1 The answer is D (*Synopsis VIII,* page 1269).

Traditional items in a therapeutic playroom do not include *a television set.* The goal is not for the child to be entertained. Television puts the child in a passive, noninteractive mode and so is generally not considered useful therapeutically. The purpose of the therapeutic playroom is to create an environment in which the child feels comfortable enough to play freely and to express a wide range of feelings. The goal is for the child to engage in symbolic play—that is, play that expresses the child's unconscious feelings.

Multigenerational doll families include young children, parents, and grandparents. The child can use the dolls to express familial interactions. *Blocks* are therapeutically useful because they allow the child room to create and to project fantasies onto the creations. The use of blocks may also allow for the ventilation of aggressive impulses, as when a child builds a stack of blocks and then crashes it to the floor. Drawings with *crayons* allow the expression of creative impulses and provide access to the child's fantasy life when the child explains or tells a story about what is drawn. Play tools, such as *rubber hammers,* are also useful, enabling the child to demonstrate identification with a parental figure, to build, and to destroy.

52.2 The answer is D (*Synopsis VIII,* page 1271).

Group therapy is not useful for *extreme aggression.* In children, extreme aggression may indicate a diminished need or ability to be accepted by peers, and peer acceptance is thought by many therapists to be a prerequisite for group membership and treatment. Extremely aggressive children are also potentially disruptive to group functioning and intimidating to other group members, two features that severely impair their capacity for group involvement. Extremely aggressive children may engender such negative reactions from a group that group membership serves only to reinforce an already lowered self-esteem. Finally, extreme aggression in children may at least initially require the primary use of medication and limit setting as the essential therapeutic interventions. Indications for group therapy that have been investigated include *phobias, male effeminate behavior, withdrawal and social isolation,* and *primary behavior disturbances.*

52.3 The answer is A (*Synopsis VIII,* page 1281).

The use of diazepam (Valium) in children has been well established for the treatment of *sleep terror disorder.* It is not useful in the treatment of *enuresis, obsessive-compulsive disorder,* or *attention-deficit/hyperactivity disorder.* Diazepam is an anxiolytic from the general class of drugs called benzodiazepines. There are few indications for such drugs in the treatment of children, and they are frequently overprescribed. Sleep terror disorder consists of repeated episodes of abrupt awakening with intense anxiety marked by autonomic arousal. It occurs during stage IV sleep. Because diazepam interferes with stage IV sleep, the drug prevents the sleep terrors. Enuresis, or nocturnal bed wetting, is treated either behaviorally with bell-and-pad conditioning or with imipramine (Tofranil), a tricyclic antidepressant. Obsessive-compulsive disorder is rare in children and is marked by recurrent thoughts (obsessions) and ritualistic behaviors (compulsions) that if interfered with cause the patient tremendous anxiety. Clomipramine (Anafranil) and the serotonin-specific reuptake inhibitors have been found to be successful in several studies. Attention-deficit/hyperactivity disorder is generally treated with a sympathomimetic, such as methylphenidate (Ritalin). If sympathomimetics are not effective or if the adverse effects are severe, a second line of treatment is bupropion (Wellbutrin) or buspirone (BuSpar). Dopamine receptor antagonists, such as haloperidol (Haldol), have also been tried, but the risk of tardive dyskinesia must be considered.

52.4 The answer is C (*Synopsis VIII,* page 1272).

Group therapy has been found to be *useful in the treatment of substance-related disorders,* which are more commonly encountered in latency and pubertal-age children than in younger children. Group therapy is *useful for mentally ill children,* as well as healthier children. Group therapy is *generally focused with young children* (preschool and early school age), as they cannot provide that focus for themselves. Work with the group is usually structured by the therapist through the use of a particular technique, such as puppets or art. Play group therapy emphasizes the interactional qualities among the children and with the therapist in the permissive playroom setting. Group therapy is *more viable with adolescents if the group is composed of same-sex members, as opposed to mixed-sex members*—presumably because the upsurge of sexual energy and interest at this stage interferes, in a group setting, with the psychotherapeutic exploration necessary for psychotherapy. Group therapy is *not effective when parents oppose it;* no treatment is enhanced by opposition from significant family members, especially any therapy involving children.

52.5 The answer is A (*Synopsis VIII,* page 1277).

There is no specific or consistently effective medication for the treatment of *conduct disorder,* although lithium, carbamazepine (Tegretol), and propranolol (Inderal) have all been studied and have apparently yielded some benefits. Behavioral and verbal therapies have been the mainstay of treatment for conduct disorder, although in severe cases, when behavioral and verbal treatments fail, antipsychotic agents may be used to decrease the severity of aggression. Childhood disorders in which medication is the mainstay of treatment include *attention-deficit/hyperactivity disorder (ADHD), Tourette's disorder,* and *schizophrenia.*

ADHD provides the clearest indication for psychopharmacological treatment. The symptoms usually prompting therapy are developmentally inappropriate inattention and impulsivity that do not respond to social contact. The first choice among pharmacotherapies is a sympathomimetic. The sympathomimetics include methylphenidate (Ritalin), dextroamphetamine (Dexedrine), and pemoline (Cylert). Tourette's disorder, characterized by multiple motor and vocal tics, is also a clear indication for pharmacotherapy. Haloperidol (Haldol) is the standard treatment against which all proposed treatments are now measured. Serotonin-dopamine antagonists, such as risperidone (Risperdal) and olanzapine (Zyprexa), have shown early promise with fewer adverse effects than haloperidol. Schizophrenia in childhood is rare, but when symptoms such as hallucinations and delusions are present, antipsychotic medications are indicated. The same toxic side effects that adults experience—in particular, tardive dyskinesia—can also occur in children, so caution must be exercised. Table 52.1 covers psychiatric drugs in use with children.

52.6 The answer is E (*Synopsis VIII,* pages 1273–1274, 1285). *Suicidal behavior is not among the most common referral diagnoses;* in fact, among the reasons to exclude children are behaviors that are likely to be destructive to the children themselves or to others under the treatment conditions. Thus, some children who threaten to run away, set fires, hurt others, or attempt suicide may not be suitable for residential treatment.

Although the age range of children referred for residential treatment varies from institution to institution, *most children are between 5 and 15 years of age. Boys are referred more frequently than girls. Most children referred for residential treatment have severe learning disabilities* and have been seen previously by one or more professional persons, such as a school psychologist or a pediatrician, or by members of a child guidance clinic, juvenile court, or state welfare agency. Unsuccessful attempts at less drastic *outpatient treatment often precede residential treatment.*

52.7 The answer is E (all) (*Synopsis VIII,* page 1278).
The potential adverse effects of tricyclic medications in children are usually similar to the adverse effects in adults. They include *dry mouth, blurry vision* (loss of accommodation), *tachycardia* (rapid heart rate), *palpitations* (sensation of the heart's pounding in the chest), constipation, and sweating. The adverse effects result primarily from the anticholinergic properties of the tricyclic drugs.

52.8 The answer is D (*Synopsis VIII,* page 1267).
''Symptom bearer,'' ''distractor,'' ''scapegoat,'' and ''rescuer'' are terms used for roles that family members play in *family systems therapy.* In the therapy, the family system is viewed as a constantly evolving, self-regulating structure. The dynamic interactions between the family members are examined by family therapists to identify the roles the family members are assigned and to assess the boundaries and the subsystems within the family. Appreciation of the family system sometimes explains why a minute therapeutic input at a critical junction results in far-reaching changes, whereas in other situations huge quantities of therapeutic effort are absorbed with minimal evidence of change.

Behavioral theories, based on the concepts of classical conditioning (Pavlov) or operant conditioning (Skinner), hold that abnormal behavior is due to a failure to learn or is due to learning maladaptive behavior through conditioning. Appropriate behaviors are highlighted and rewarded in behaviorally oriented therapy.

Supportive therapy offers support by an authority figure. Supportive psychotherapy is particularly helpful in enabling a well-adjusted youngster to cope with the emotional turmoil engendered in a crisis. It is also used with those disturbed youngsters whose less-than-adequate ego functioning is seriously disrupted by an expressive-exploratory mode or by other forms of therapeutic intervention. At the beginning of most psychotherapy, regardless of the patient's age or the nature of the therapeutic interventions, the principal therapeutic elements perceived by the patient tend to be supportive ones, a consequence of therapists' universal efforts to be reliably and sensitively responsive. In fact, some therapy may never proceed beyond this supportive level, whereas other therapies develop an expressive-exploratory or behavioral modification flavor on top of the supportive foundation.

Psychoanalytic psychotherapy is a modified form of psychotherapy that is expressive and exploratory and that endeavors to reverse the evolution of the emotional disturbance through reenactment and desensitization of the traumatic events by the free expression of thoughts and feelings in an interview-play situation. Ultimately, the therapist helps the patient understand the warded-off feelings, fears, and wishes that have beset him or her.

In *relationship therapy* a positive, friendly, helpful relationship is viewed as the primary, if not the sole, therapeutic ingredient. One of the best examples of pure relationship therapy is found outside the clinical setting in the work of the Big Brother Organization.

52.9 The answer is E (all) (*Synopsis VIII,* pages 1276–1279). Behavioral and verbal therapies are the mainstays of treatment of conduct disorder. In severe cases, when these treatments have failed, medication may be used to decrease the severity of the aggression. For those children *haloperidol (Haldol)* and *lithium (Eskalith)* are the drugs of choice. Both have been effective in treating hospitalized children with assaultive conduct disorder. Recently, some researchers have claimed that *carbamazepine (Tegretol)* and *propranolol (Inderal)* are effective in decreasing the aggressivity of children with conduct disorder. The use of those medications necessitates further study, but they may be helpful in the treatment of some children with conduct disorder.

52.10 The answer is D (*Synopsis VIII,* page 1277).
Mental retardation in itself is not an indication for the use of psychiatric drugs, although some associated behaviors may respond to medication. *Hyperactivity and stereotypies associated with mental retardation have been found to respond to antipsychotic medications* and sympathomimetics. Approximately *50 percent of mentally retarded patients living in institutions are receiving antipsychotics,* despite the lack of any clear indications. *The intelligence quotient deficits that define mental retardation do not respond to phenothiazines* or to any pharmacological agent yet tested. *There is risk of tardive dyskinesia* in this population, and some studies show an increased risk compared with that of the general population, perhaps as a result of the underlying central nervous system impairment. Some psychotropic drugs may improve cognitive tests of learning functions. For example, amphetamine improves performance on a variety of tasks (Table 52.2).

52.11 The answer is E (*Synopsis VIII,* pages 1273–1274).
Residential treatment centers *provide a highly structured and*

Table 52.1
Common Psychoactive Drugs in Childhood and Adolescence

Drugs	Indications	Dosage	Adverse Reactions and Monitoring
Antipsychotics—also known as major tranquilizers, neuroleptics. Divided into (1) a high-potency, low-dosage, eg haloperidol (Haldol), trifluoperazine (Stelazine), thiothixene (Navane); (2) low-potency, high-dosage (more sedating), eg, chlorpromazine (Thorazine), thioridazine (Mellaril); and (3) Serotonin-dopamine antagonists, eg, risperidone (Risperdal), olanzapine (Zyprexa), clozapine (Clozaril)	In general, for agitated, aggressive, self-injurious behaviors in mental retardation (MR), pervasive developmental disorders (PDD), conduct disorder (CD), and schizophrenia Studies support following specific indications: Haloperidol—PDD, CD with severe aggression, Tourette's disorder Clozapine—refractory schizophrenia in adolescence Risperidone—PDD, Tourette's disorder	All can be given in two to four divided doses or combined into one dose after gradual buildup Haloperidol—child 0.5–6 mg a day, adolescent 0.5–16 mg a day Thiothixene—5–42 mg a day Chlorpromazine—child 10–200 mg a day, adolescent 50–600 mg a day, over 16 years of age 100–700 mg a day Clozapine—dosage not determined in children; <600 mg a day in adolescents Risperidone—1–3 mg a day	Sedation, weight gain, hypotension, lowered seizure threshold, constipation, extrapyramidal symptoms, jaundice, agranulocytosis, dystonic reaction, tardive dyskinesia; with clozapine, no extrapyramidal adverse effects Monitor: blood pressure, complete blood count (CBC), liver function tests (LFTs), electroencephalogram, if indicated; with thioridazine, pigmentary retinopathy is rare but dictates ceiling of 800 mg in adults and proportionately lower in children; with clozapine, weekly white blood counts (WBCs) for development of agranulocytosis
Stimulants Dextroamphetamine (Dexedrine) FDA-approved for children 3 years and older Methylphenidate (Ritalin) and pemoline (Cylert) FDA-approved for children 6 years and older; pemoline now second-line because of potential hepatotoxicity	In attention-deficit/hyperactivity disorder (ADHD) for hyperactivity, impulsivity, and inattentiveness	Dextroamphetamine and methylphenidate are generally given at 8 AM and noon (the usefulness of sustained-release preparations is not proved) Dextroamphetamine—2.5–40 mg a day up to 0.5 mg/kg a day Methylphenidate—10–60 mg a day or up to 1.0 mg/kg a day Pemoline—37.5–112.5 mg given at 8 AM	Insomnia, anorexia, weight loss (and possibly growth delay), headache, tachycardia, precipitation or exacerbation of tic disorders With pemoline, monitor LFTs, as hepatotoxicity is possible
Lithium—considered an antipsychotic drug, also has antiaggression properties	Studies support use in MR and CD for aggressive and self-injurious behaviors; can be used for same in PDD; also indicated for early-onset bipolar I disorder	600–2,100 mg in two or three divided doses; keep blood levels to 0.4–1.2 mEq/L	Nausea, vomiting, enuresis, headache, tremor, weight gain, hypothyroidism Experience with adults suggests renal function monitoring
Tricyclic drugs Imipramine (Tofranil) has been used in most child studies Nortriptyline (Pamelor) has been studied in children Clomipramine (Anafranil) is effective in child obsessive-compulsive disorder (OCD)	Major depressive disorder, separation anxiety disorder, bulimia nervosa, enuresis; sometimes used in ADHD, anorexia nervosa, sleepwalking disorder, and sleep terror disorder	Imipramine—start with dosage of about 1.5 mg/kg a day; can build up to not more than 5 mg/kg a day Start with two or three divided doses; eventually combine in one dose Not FDA-approved for children except for enuresis; dosage is usually 50–100 mg before sleep; clomipramine—start at 50 mg a day; can raise to not more than 3 mg/kg a day or 200 mg a day	Dry mouth, constipation, tachycardia, drowsiness, postural hypotension, hypertension, mania Electrocardiogram (ECG) monitoring is needed because of risk for cardiac conduction slowing; consider lowering dosage if PR interval >0.20 seconds or ORS interval >0.12 seconds; baseline EEG is advised, as it can lower seizure threshold; blood levels of drug are sometimes useful
Serotonin-specific reuptake inhibitors—fluoxetine (Prozac), sertraline (Zoloft) paroxetine (Paxil), and fluvoxamine (Luvox)	OCD, may be useful in major depressive disorder, anorexia, bulimia nervosa, repetitive behaviors in MR or PDD	Appears less than adult dosages	Nausea, headache, nervousness, insomnia, dry mouth, diarrhea, anorexia nervosa, drowsiness

Table 52.1 *(continued)*

Drugs	Indications	Dosage	Adverse Reactions and Monitoring
Carbamazepine (Tegretol)—an anticonvulsant	Aggression or dyscontrol in MR or CD	Start with 10 mg/kg a day; can build to 20–30 mg/kg a day; therapeutic blood level range appears to be 4–12 mg/L	Drowsiness, nausea, rash, vertigo, irritability Monitor: CBC and LFTs for possible blood dyscrasias and hepatotoxicity; blood levels are necessary
Benzodiazepines—have been insufficiently studied in childhood and adolescence	Sometimes effective in parasomnias; sleepwalking disorder or sleep terror disorder; can be tried in generalized anxiety disorder Clonazepam (Klonapin) can be tried in separation anxiety disorder Alprazolam (Xanax) can be tried in separation anxiety disorder	Parasomnias: diazepam (Valium) 2–10 mg before bedtime	Can cause drowsiness, ataxia, tremor, dyscontrol; can be abused
Propranolol (Inderal)—a β-adrenergic blocker	Aggression in MR, PDD, and cognitive disorder, awaits controlled studies	Effective dosage in children and adolescents is not yet established; range is probably 40–320 mg a day	Bradycardia, hypotension, nausea, hypoglycemia, depression; avoid in asthma
Clonidine (Catapres)—a presynaptic α-adrenergic blocking agent	Tourette's disorder; some success in ADHD	0.1–0.3 mg a day; 3–5.5 μg/kg a day	Orthostatic hypotension, nausea, vomiting, sedation, elevated blood glucose
Cyproheptadine (Periactin)	Anorexia nervosa	Dosages up to 8 mg four times a day	Antihistaminic side effects, including sedation and dryness of the mouth
Naltrexone (ReVia)	Self-injurious behaviors in MR and PDD; currently being studied in PDD	0.5–2 mg/kg a day	Sleepiness, aggressivity Monitor LFTs, as hepatotoxicity has been reported in adults at high dosages
Desmopressin (DDAVP)	Nocturnal enuresis	20–40 μg intranasally	Headache; hyponatremic seizures (rare)

Courtesy of Richard Perry, M.D.

supervised behavior-based program. Residential treatment centers are *temporary, not permanent, out-of-home placements* for children or adolescents with serious emotional and behavioral disorders who cannot be managed at home. They *do not usually accept patients with acute psychiatric decompensations,* for whom psychiatric hospitalization is usually necessary. *Residential treatment centers are not only for children and adolescents who have been psychiatrically hospitalized.* While a variety of individual psychotherapies may be employed for residents, residential treatment centers *do not generally have a psychoanalytically oriented program.*

Answers 52.12–52.18

52.12 The answer is B (*Synopsis VIII,* pages 1276–1277).

52.13 The answer is E (*Synopsis VIII,* page 1284).

52.14 The answer is G (*Synopsis VIII,* page 1276).

52.15 The answer is A (*Synopsis VIII,* page 895).

52.16 The answer is F (*Synopsis VIII,* pages 1276–1277).

52.17 The answer is D (*Synopsis VIII,* pages 1276–1277).

52.18 The answer is C (*Synopsis VIII,* page 1272).
The majority of children who present for psychiatric treatment are brought in by family members who are concerned about their functioning or who have followed up on suggestions from teachers or pediatricians. Often, children do not express a desire for treatment nor understand the degree to which they have caused others concern. Occasionally, an adolescent will ask a parent for help, but more often, distress is manifested through troubled behaviors. To synthesize a useful treatment approach, it is generally necessary to understand the views of both the child and the parents. In most cases, treatment consists of multiple modalities through which to manipulate the child's environment positively, as well as to influence the behaviors and feelings of the child. The following brief vignettes exemplify the combined approach to addressing children's and adolescents' psychological needs.

A boy of 12 years who presents with impairment due to compulsive hand-washing and obsessions regarding fears of becoming contaminated is a candidate for both medication and

Table 52.2
Effects of Psychotropic Drugs on Cognitive Tests of Learning Functions[a]

Drug Class	Continuous Performance Test (Attention)	Matching Familiar Figures (Impulsivity)	Test Function: Paired Associates (Verbal Learning)	Test Function: Porteus Maze (Planning Capacity)	Short-Term Memory[a]	WISC (Intelligence)
Stimulant	↑	↑	↑	↑	↑	↑
Antidepressants	↑	0		0	0	0
Antipsychotics	↑↓		↓	↓	↓	0

Adapted with permission from Aman MG: Drugs, learning, and the psychotherapies. In *Pediatric Psychopharmacology: The Use of Behavior Modifying Drugs in Children,* JS Werry, editor, p 355. Brunner/Mazel, New York, 1978.
↑, Improved; ↑↓, inconsistent; ↓, worse; and 0, no effect.
[a] Various tests: digit span, word recall, etc.

a behavioral intervention. Paroxetine (Paxil) is a serotonin-specific reuptake inhibitor that is being investigated as a medication of choice for obsessive-compulsive symptoms. The serotonin-specific reuptake inhibitor class of medications (fluoxetine [Prozac], sertraline [Zoloft], paroxetine [Paxil], and fluvoxamine [Luvox]) is known to have antiobsessional effects. The *response prevention technique* is a behavioral intervention that serves to diminish the hand-washing behavior by challenging the child to tolerate the feared situation (that his hands are contaminated and require washing). In this way, the child learns that the exposure to the feared situation does not have the feared negative effects, and anxiety gradually diminishes.

A 10-year-old girl who responds to a new family constellation with oppositional and defiant behaviors is expressing her discomfort about a major change in the family functioning. *Family therapy* is a useful modality to begin with, in order to understand the triggers, responses, and meaning of these behaviors to the family and to the child. It is likely that when the child is given a forum in which to express her discomfort, her oppositional behaviors will diminish.

A 15-year-old girl who has lost 25 percent of her body weight and cannot control her purging behaviors generally *requires an inpatient setting* in which to initiate treatment, to establish refeeding, and observe her to prevent vomiting. Given the complex effects of starvation, a malnourished adolescent is not a good candidate for outpatient treatment. The treatment approaches to the restricting and purging of anorexia nervosa are multimodality. A behavioral component is necessary to systematically address the nutritional needs and prevention of behaviors that further increase malnutrition, and a psychodynamic approach is beneficial to work with the adolescent regarding the meaning and psychological forces driving the disorder. Medications are sometimes used to treat concurrent anxiety and depression, and to mediate bingeing and purging when this is present.

A 17-year-old girl who has been discharged from an inpatient unit presumably is stable, not posing an imminent danger to herself, and is ready to engage in outpatient treatment. There is evidence from at least one double-blind, placebo-controlled study that fluoxetine is efficacious in the treatment of major depression in adolescents. Given the far-reaching social ramifications of a major depression and a suicide attempt and the longevity of lingering depressive constructs and symptoms, psychotherapy is indicated. *Interpersonal psychotherapy,* a mode of individual therapy that has been used in adults and adolescents, is aimed at improving interpersonal skills, as this is identified as pivotal in modifying depressive thoughts and feelings. Therapy addresses decreasing social isolation and is supportive around issues of furthering positive relationships.

A 14-year-old who has recently stopped attending school because of an increase in auditory hallucinations is in a crisis. Since she is not suicidal, she does not need the containment of an inpatient unit, but she is a candidate for a partial hospital program, in which she can receive daily monitoring of antipsychotic and antidepressant medication, as well as receive daily support from staff. School refusal in an adolescent is usually a sign of severe psychopathology and requires immediate evaluation and intervention.

Enuresis is much more common in boys than in girls, and it may occur in the absence of any psychological problems. It may cause social awkwardness and psychological stress for children who still have this condition in the mid-elementary years. Approximately 7 percent of 5-year-olds have enuresis on a regular basis, and about 3 percent of 10-year-olds have it. *Desmopressin* (DDAVP) nasal spray has been effective in some children with enuresis, and it can be used on an occasional basis if it is not needed every night.

A 7-year-old boy who cannot stay on task and who is hyperactive and socially provocative is exhibiting typical symptoms of attention-deficit/hyperactivity disorder. The main treatment for the core symptoms of this disorder is a stimulant medication such as *methylphenidate (Ritalin).* Most children with ADHD have social difficulties, and many are eventually rejected by peers. Thus it is often beneficial to include social skills groups as an additional therapeutic intervention.

53 

Forensic Issues in Child Psychiatry

Forensic evaluations in child and adolescent psychiatry often entail dilemmas of confidentiality, family law, civil law, and criminal law. Dilemmas of confidentiality with children and adolescents relate to disclosure of confidential information to family members; consent for treatment and consent to share information with agencies, including schools; and use of clinical information for research, education, and third-party payment. The most common forensic evaluations that fall within family law are child custody evaluations, necessitated when parents are in a dispute. Other proceedings in family law that may involve child and adolescent psychiatrists are issues related to foster-care placement, adoption, and termination of parental rights. In civil law, suits alleging psychological damage to a child or adolescent as a result of maltreatment, accidents, or other life events may require the evaluation of a child and adolescent psychiatrist. Child and adolescent psychiatrists may be asked to provide evaluations and recommendations relating to any phase of a juvenile criminal case. This may entail an evaluation in the preadjudication phase to assist in the determination of whether the adolescent will be tried in adult criminal court or to assess the need for immediate psychiatric intervention. Child and adolescent psychiatrists may also work with the defense or prosecuting attorney or be a neutral advisor to the court.

Dilemmas of confidentiality specifically deal with the decision by a clinician to share information that has been obtained from a patient in confidence. Breaches of confidentiality are necessary when any one of the following situations is present: indication that the patient is an imminent danger to himself or herself or to someone else; knowledge of physical or sexual abuse; or maltreatment to the patient. Other situations that may pose confidentiality dilemmas include scientific and research forums, in which presentations are used to demonstrate clinical issues and strategies. In these contexts, the clinicians must be careful to protect the confidentiality of the patient by omitting any data that might hint at the patient's identity.

Under family law, child custody decision making has increasingly used child and adolescent psychiatrists. Debate over what constitutes the best interests of the child and which parent is best suited to provide for those best interests has invited the wide involvement of psychiatrists in custody disputes. During bitter custody disputes, many allegations, such as true and false accusations of drug or alcohol abuse, of physical or sexual abuse, or of psychiatric disturbance, may be hurled at one parent by the other. The child and adolescent psychiatrist must be prepared to verify or invalidate allegations that have a bearing on custody and visitation.

The students should read Chapter 53 in *Kaplan and Sadock's Synopsis VIII* and answer the questions that follow.

HELPFUL HINTS

These terms should be known and defined by the student.

- adjudicated delinquent
- adjudication
- "best interests of the child"
- breach of confidentiality
- child custody evaluation
- confidentiality
- delinquent act
- disposition
- intake
- joint custody
- juvenile court
- mediation
- proof beyond a reasonable doubt
- rehabilitation
- status offenses
- "tender years doctrine"
- waiver of confidentiality

▲ QUESTIONS

DIRECTIONS: Each of these questions or incomplete statements is followed by five suggested responses or completions. Select the *one* that is *best* in each case.

53.1 Confidentiality refers to

A. promoting the best interests of a patient
B. withholding life-threatening information
C. becoming a confident therapist
D. the "entrustment of secrets"
E. protecting a patient against harm

53.2 Breach of confidentiality by a psychiatrist is indicated in all of the following situations *except*

A. a suicidal adolescent patient
B. a homicidal adolescent patient
C. disclosure of sexual abuse by a patient
D. a child custody evaluation
E. drug or alcohol use by an adolescent patient

53.3 The ''best interests of the child'' doctrine differs from the ''tender years'' doctrine in that

A. fathers are believed to be better providers than mothers
B. mothers usually do not get custody
C. school adjustment and comfort in the home take priority over which parent is suited for custody
D. mothers are not necessarily believed to be preferable in abilities to nurture and care for young children
E. children are allowed to make a choice about where they reside

DIRECTIONS: Each set of lettered headings below is followed by a list of numbered statements. For each numbered statement, select the *best* lettered heading. Each heading can be used once, more than once, or not at all.

Questions 53.4–53.10

A. Juvenile court system
B. Adult court system
C. Both of the above
D. Neither of the above

An alleged perpetrator has the following rights:

53.4 Legal counsel, Fifth Amendment privilege, and notice of charges
53.5 Pretrial hearing, trial, sentencing
53.6 Trial by jury
53.7 Intake, adjudication, disposition
53.8 Disposition right after confession
53.9 Mediation procedures
53.10 Trial by judge without a jury

Questions 53.11–53.15

A. Delinquent acts
B. Status offenses

53.11 Assault
53.12 Truancy
53.13 Theft
53.14 Running away from home
53.15 Consumption of alcohol

ANSWERS

Forensic Issues in Child Psychiatry

53.1 The answer is D (*Synopsis VIII,* page 1286).
Confidentiality, meaning intensive trust, refers in this case to the *''entrustment of secrets''* by a child or adolescent patient to a clinician. Confidentiality, according to the usual initial treatment contract, is limited by any situation that constitutes ''danger.'' Confidentiality does not refer to promoting life events that *are in the best interest* of the patient, and it does not refer to becoming a *confident therapist.* Contrary to withholding *life-threatening information,* confidentiality must be breached when it is determined that the patient's life is in danger and he or she must be *protected against harm.*

53.2 The answer is E (*Synopsis VIII,* page 1286).
Breaches of confidentiality occur in situations of danger to the life of a patient or information disclosed that leads the clinician to believe that the patient poses a danger to the life of another. *Patients who are suicidal or homicidal* and cases of *sexual abuse* automatically require breach of confidentiality. *Child custody* evaluations are also exempt from confidentiality. This is established through a written waiver of confidentiality at the beginning of a custody evaluation. Disclosure by an adolescent patient of *use of drugs or alcohol* does not necessarily fall into the category of required breach of confidentiality. The specific nature, situation, and type of drug and alcohol use allow the clinician to determine whether such behaviors constitute an imminent danger to the life of the patient. If so, the clinician is obligated to breach the confidentiality.

53.3 The answer is D (*Synopsis VIII,* pages 1286–1287).
The ''tender years'' doctrine made the assumption that mothers were the preferable parent in their abilities to provide the emotional nurturance necessary for growth and development of young children. Therefore, when this doctrine prevailed, mothers almost always were granted custody of their children. The ''best interest'' doctrine broadened the criteria for how custody is best determined in that it removed the assumption that a mother is always more able to provide nurturance. Furthermore, a child's adjustment in a number of areas including *school,* significant relationships, and home life must be factored into the decision about the custodial parent. The ''best interests'' notion *does not, however, assume that fathers are better providers* than mothers; it *does not imply that mothers do not usually get custody;* and it does not indicate that school and home adjustment take priority over parenting ability. A *child's choice* may be one consideration in the custody decision, but the determination by an evaluator is for the overall best interest of the child. The evaluator does not base a recommendation on what is fairest for the parents.

Answers 53.4–53.10

53.4 The answer is C (*Synopsis VIII,* pages 1286–1288).

53.5 The answer is B (*Synopsis VIII,* pages 1286–1287).

53.6 The answer is B (*Synopsis VIII,* pages 1286–1287).

53.7 The answer is A (*Synopsis VIII,* pages 1287–1288).

53.8 The answer is A (*Synopsis VIII,* pages 1287–1288).

53.9 The answer is D (*Synopsis VIII,* pages 1286–1288).

53.10 The answer is A (*Synopsis VIII,* pages 1287–1288).
Both the juvenile court and the adult court system must conform to the same rights of due process. These include the right to notice of charges, the right to legal counsel, the Fifth Amendment privilege against self-incrimination, and the right to confront witnesses. The adult court system uses the following process: the pretrial hearing, trial, and sentencing. The juvenile court, however, has a different procedure in that there is intake, adjudication, and disposition. If a juvenile defendant makes a confession, disposition may proceed without the trial. The adult court system uses jury decision making in its trials, whereas the juvenile court has trials decided by a judge. Mediation is a legal process that takes place outside of the judicial system, in child custody cases, for example, that generally use an attorney and an evaluator.

Answers 53.11–53.15

53.11 The answer is A (*Synopsis VIII,* page 1288).

53.12 The answer is B (*Synopsis VIII,* page 1288).

53.13 The answer is A (*Synopsis VIII,* page 1288).

53.14 The answer is B (*Synopsis VIII,* page 1288).

53.15 The answer is B (*Synopsis VIII,* page 1288).
Delinquent acts are ordinary crimes perpetrated by a juvenile. Status offenses are acts that are illegal for a juvenile but that would not be crimes if perpetrated by an adult. Thus, *assault* and *theft* are delinquent acts, whereas *running away* from home, *truancy,* and consumption of *alcohol* are status offenses.

54 Geriatric Psychiatry

Geriatric psychiatry, which is concerned with diagnosing, managing, and treating the mental disorders of old age, is one of the fastest growing fields in psychiatry. As with mental disorders at any age, those affecting older people result from a complex interplay of biological, psychological, and sociocultural factors. What distinguishes the mental disorders associated with the elderly from those observed in younger people are the specific biological, psychological, and sociocultural influences unique to the developmental phase of old age. For instance, dementing disorders such as Alzheimer's disease and vascular dementia are essentially mental disorders seen almost entirely among the elderly.

Elderly individuals are more likely to have experienced loss and to feel isolated than younger individuals. One of the most common mental disorders of old age is major depressive disorder. Suicide risk increases with age. Almost 20 percent of suicides are committed by people over 65 years of age. Other mental disorders common among the elderly include alcohol-related disorders, cognitive disorders, and phobias.

Delusional disorder and some somatoform disorders commonly have an age of onset late in life. Bipolar disorder I, anxiety disorders, sleep disorders, and substance-related disorders may have their onset or may worsen in elderly patients. In most instances, the onset of any mental disorder in a patient over age 40 years should alert the clinician to rule out an associated medical cause, such as a space-occupying lesion or side effects of a medication.

The psychopharmacological treatment of geriatric disorders is a major component of geriatric psychiatry. The basic tenet of treating elderly patients with medications is the individualization of dosage. Many physiological changes occur as a person ages, including decreased renal clearance, decreased hepatic metabolism, decreased cardiac output, and decreased gastric acid secretion, all of which affect the rate of clearance of drugs from the body. Changes in the lean-to-fat body mass ratio affect drug distribution in the elderly. In general, the lowest possible drug dose should be used to achieve therapeutic response.

Psychotherapy is another major component of geriatric psychiatry. Age-related issues specific to the developmental phase of old age include the need to adapt to recurrent loss, the need to assume new roles, and the need to confront one's own mortality. The institutionalization of elderly patients no longer able to live independently is a difficult and challenging issue.

The student should carefully read Chapter 54 in *Kaplan and Sadock's Synopsis VIII.* Once familiar with the material, the student will be able to address the questions and answers herein.

HELPFUL HINTS

Each of the following terms relating to geriatric issues should be defined.

- adaptational capacity
- agedness
- akathisia
- Alzheimer's disease
- anoxic confusion
- anxiety disorder
- cerebral anoxia
- cognitive functioning
- conversion disorder
- delirium
- dementia
- dementing disorder
- depression
- developmental phases
- diabetes
- disorders of awareness
- drug blood level
- emphysema
- fluoxetine (Prozac)
- FSH
- hepatic failure
- hypochondriasis
- hypomanic disorder
- ideational paucity
- insomnia
- L-dopa (Larodopa)
- late-onset schizophrenia
- LH
- lithium
- loss of mastery
- manic disorder
- mood disorder
- neurosis
- norepinephrine
- nutritional deficiencies
- obsessive-compulsive disorder
- organic mental disorder
- orientation
- overt behavior
- paradoxical reaction
- paraphrenia
- presbyopia
- psychotropic danger
- ranitidine
- remotivation techniques
- ritualistic behavior
- role of anxiety
- sensorium
- serotonin
- sleep disturbances
- social capacity
- theory of aging
- toxic confusional state
- toxins
- transdermal scopolamine
- trazodone (Desyrel)
- uremia

▲ QUESTIONS

DIRECTIONS: Each of the questions or incomplete statements below is followed by five suggested responses or completions. Select the *one* that is *best* in each case.

54.1 Of all patients with dementia, 50 to 60 percent have

A. vascular dementia
B. dementia of the Alzheimer's type
C. dementia due to Pick's disease
D. dementia due to Parkinson's disease
E. dementia due to Huntington's disease

54.2 Which of the following is a reason favoring the use of MAOIs in elderly patients?

A. Monoamine oxidase (MAO) decreases in the aging brain.
B. Orthostatic hypotension is common and severe with MAOIs.
C. Patients need to adhere to a tyramine-free diet.
D. MAOIs have the potential for serious drug interactions involving certain analgesics.
E. MAOIs exacerbate cognitive impairment.

54.3 One of the advantages in the use of serotonin-specific reuptake inhibitors (SSRIs) by the elderly is the absence of

A. nausea and other gastrointestinal symptoms
B. orthostatic hypotension
C. nervousness
D. headache
E. all of the above

54.4 Which of the following drugs has been implicated in producing psychiatric symptoms in the elderly?

A. Ibuprofen
B. Trazodone
C. Cimetidine
D. L-dopa
E. All of the above

54.5 Which of the following statements about the treatment of geriatric patients with psychotherapeutic drugs is *true*?

A. Elderly persons may be more susceptible than younger adults to adverse effects.
B. Elderly patients may metabolize drugs more slowly than do other adult patients.
C. Most psychotropic drugs should be given in equally divided doses.
D. The most reasonable practice is to begin with a small dose.
E. All of the above statements are true.

54.6 Elderly persons taking antipsychotics are especially susceptible to the following side effects *except*

A. tardive dyskinesia
B. akathisia
C. a toxic confusional state
D. paresthesias
E. dry mouth

54.7 Abnormalities of cognitive functioning in the aged are most often due to

A. depressive disturbances
B. schizophrenia
C. medication
D. cerebral dysfunctioning or deterioration
E. hypochondriasis

54.8 Which of the following statements about the biology of aging is *false*?

A. Each cell of the body has a genetically determined life span.
B. The optic lens thins.
C. T-cell response to antigens is altered.
D. Decrease in melanin occurs.
E. Brain weight decreases.

54.9 Which of the following statements about sleep disturbances in the elderly is *false*?

A. Complaints about sleeplessness are common.
B. Catnaps may interfere with a good night's sleep.
C. Frequent visits to the bathroom may lead to problems in resuming sleep.
D. Tricyclic drugs often induce sleep when insomnia is accompanied by a depressive reaction.
E. The elderly do not need as much sleep as they did in their earlier mature years.

54.10 Changes in the ratio of lean to fat body mass affect the distribution of all of the following *except*

A. imipramine
B. diazepam
C. chlorpromazine
D. lithium
E. fluoxetine

54.11 Which of the following statements about learning and memory in the elderly is *false*?

A. Complete learning of new material still occurs
B. On multiple choice tests, recognition of correct answers persists.
C. Simple recall remains intact.
D. IQ remains stable until age 80.
E. Memory-encoding ability diminishes.

54.12 In the physical assessment of the aged, which of the following statements is *false*?

A. Toxins of bacterial origin are common.
B. The most common metabolic intoxication causing mental symptoms is uremia.
C. Cerebral anoxia often precipitates mental syndromes.
D. Vitamin deficiencies are common
E. Nutritional deficiencies may cause mental symptoms.

54.13 Which of the following statements about the pharmacological treatment of the elderly is *false*?

A. The elderly use more medications than any other age group.
B. Some 25 percent of prescriptions are for those over age 65.
C. In the United States, 250,000 people a year are hospitalized because of adverse reactions to medication.
D. About 25 percent of hypnotics dispensed in the United States each year are to those over age 65.
E. About 70 percent of the elderly use over-the-counter medications.

54.14 Sexual activity in persons over age 60

A. occurs in fewer than 10 percent of women
B. occurs in fewer than 50 percent of men
C. is often accompanied by feelings of guilt
D. may increase compared with earlier levels of functioning
E. is characterized by all of the above

54.15 Elderly abuse by some caregiving children

A. is most likely to occur when the parent is bedridden
B. occurs most often when the elderly parent has a chronic medical illness
C. is likely to occur if the child was a victim of sexual or physical abuse
D. occurs more often toward women than toward men
E. is characterized by all of the above

ANSWERS

Geriatric Psychiatry

54.1 The answer is B (*Synopsis VIII,* pages 328, 1302).
Of all of the patients with dementia, 50 to 60 percent have *dementia of the Alzheimer's type,* the most common type of dementia. About 5 percent of all persons who reach age 65 have dementia of the Alzheimer's type, compared with 15 to 25 percent of all persons 85 or older.

Vascular dementia is the second most common type of dementia. Vascular dementia accounts for 10 to 20 percent of all cases of dementia. *Dementia due to Pick's disease, dementia due to Parkinson's disease,* and *dementia due to Huntington's disease* each account for 1 to 5 percent of all dementia cases.

54.2 The answer is A (*Synopsis VIII,* page 1301).
Monoamine oxidase inhibitors (MAOIs) are useful in treating depression because *monoamine oxidase (MAO) decreases in the aging brain.* MAOIs may be used with caution in elderly patients. *Orthostatic hypotension is common and severe with MAOIs. Patients need to adhere to a tyramine-free diet* to avoid hypertensive crises. *The potential for serious drug interactions* involving certain analgesics, such as meperidine (Demerol) and *sympathomimetics,* also requires that patients understand what food and drugs they may use. Tranylcypromine (Parnate) and phenelzine (Nardil) are examples of drugs that should be used cautiously in patients prone to hypertension. *Any kind of cognitive impairment* precludes MAOI therapy. Table 54.1 lists the geriatric dosages of the MAOIs.

54.3 The answer is B (*Synopsis VIII,* page 1300).
The serotonin-specific reuptake inhibitors (SSRIs) do not cause the characteristic side effects of the tricyclic agents. The absence of *orthostatic hypotension* is a clinically significant factor in the use of SSRIs by the elderly.

In general, the SSRIs—such as fluoxetine (Prozac), sertraline (Zoloft), and paroxetine (Paxil)—are safe and well tolerated by elderly patients. As a group, those drugs may cause *nausea and other gastrointestinal symptoms, nervousness,* agitation, *headache,* and insomnia, most often to mild degrees. Fluoxetine is the drug most likely to cause temporary nervousness, insomnia, and loss of appetite early in treatment. Sertraline is the drug most likely to produce nausea and diarrhea. Paroxetine causes some anticholinergic effects.

Table 54.1
Geriatric Dosages of Monoamine Oxidase Inhibitors (MAOIs)[a]

Generic Name	Trade Name	Geriatric Dosage Range
Isocarboxid	Marplan	10–30
Phenelzine	Nardil	15–45
Tranylcypromine[b]	Parnate	10–20

[a] Persons taking MAOIs should be on a tyramine-free diet.
[b] Not recommended in persons over 60 because of pressor effects.

54.4 The answer is E (all) (*Synopsis VIII,* pages 1298–1302).
Ibuprofen (Motrin, Advil), trazodone (Desyrel), cimetidine (Tagamet), and L*-dopa (Larodopa)* have been implicated in the production of psychiatric symptoms, such as depression, confusion, disorientation, and delirium, in the elderly. The symptoms usually cease after the drug is withdrawn, but the clinician must be alert to withdrawal reactions to a drug, especially if it is stopped abruptly.

Various drugs used in medicine can cause psychiatric symptoms in all classes of patients, especially among old patients. The symptoms may result if the drug is prescribed in too large a dose, if the patient is particularly sensitive to the medication, or if the patient does not follow instructions for its use.

54.5 The answer is E (all) (*Synopsis VIII,* pages 1298–1302).
Elderly persons may be more susceptible than younger adults to the adverse effects of psychotherapeutic drugs (particularly adverse cardiac effects), and *elderly patients may metabolize drugs more slowly than do other adults. Most psychotropic drugs should be given in equally divided doses* 3 or 4 times over a 24-hour period, because geriatric patients may not be able to tolerate the sudden rise in blood level of the drug that results from one large dose. *The most reasonable practice is to begin with a small dose,* increase it slowly, and watch for side effects. A common concern is that geriatric patients are often taking other medications, and thus psychiatrists must carefully consider the possible drug interactions.

54.6 The answer is D (*Synopsis VIII,* pages 1298–1302).
Paresthesias, which are spontaneous tingling sensations, are not a side effect of antipsychotics. Elderly persons, particularly if they have organic brain disease, are especially susceptible to the side effects of antipsychotics, including *tardive dyskinesia, akathisia,* and a *toxic confusional state.* Tardive dyskinesia is characterized by disfiguring and involuntary buccal and lingual masticatory movements; akathisia is a restlessness marked by a compelling need for constant motion. Choreiform body movements, which are spasmodic and involuntary movements of the limbs and the face, and rhythmic extension and flexion movements of the fingers may also be noticeable. Examination of the patient's protruded tongue for fine tremors and vermicular (wormlike) movements is a useful diagnostic procedure. A toxic confusional state, also called a central anticholinergic syndrome, is characterized by a marked disturbance in short-term memory, impaired attention, disorientation, anxiety, visual and auditory hallucinations, increased psychotic thinking, and peripheral anticholinergic side effects.

54.7 The answer is D (*Synopsis VIII,* page 1289).
Abnormalities of cognitive functioning in the elderly are most often due to some *cerebral dysfunctioning or deterioration,* although they may also be the result of *depressive disturbances, schizophrenia,* or the effects of *medication.* In many instances, intellectual difficulties are not obvious, and a searching evaluation is necessary to detect them. The elderly are sensitive to the effects of medication; in some instances, cog-

nitive impairment may result from overmedication. *Hypochondriasis,* the fear that one has a disease or preoccupation with one's health, is not the cause of an abnormality of cognitive functioning.

54.8 The answer is B (*Synopsis VIII,* pages 1302–1304).
As a person ages *the optic lens thickens (not thins)* in association with an inability to accommodate (presbyopia), and hearing loss is progressive, particularly at the high frequencies. The process of aging, known as senescence, results from a complex interaction of genetic, metabolic, hormonal, immunological, and structural factors acting on molecular, cellular, histological, and organ levels. The most commonly held theory is that *each cell of the body has a genetically determined life span* during which replication occurs a limited number of times before the cell dies. One study found 50 such replications in human cells. Structural changes in cells take place with age. In the central nervous system, for example, age-related cell changes occur in neurons, which show signs of degeneration.

Changes in the structure of deoxyribonucleic acid (DNA) and ribonucleic acid (RNA) are also found in aging cells; the cause has been attributed to genotypic programing, x-rays, chemicals, and food products, among others. Aging probably has no single cause. All areas of the body are affected to some degree, and changes vary from person to person.

A progressive decline in many bodily functions includes a *decrease in melanin* and decreases in cardiac output and stroke volume, glomerular filtration rate, oxygen consumption, cerebral blood flow, and vital capacity. Many immune mechanisms are altered, with impaired *T-cell response to antigens* and an increase in the formation of autoimmune antibodies. These altered immune responses probably play a role in aged persons' susceptibility to infection and possibly even to neoplastic disease. Some neoplasms, most notably cancers of the colon, prostate, stomach, and skin, show a steadily increasing incidence with age.

Variable changes in endocrine function are seen. For example, postmenopausal estrogen levels decrease, producing breast tissue evolution and vaginal epithelial atrophy. Testosterone levels begin to decline in the sixth decade; however, follicle-stimulating hormone and luteinizing hormone increase. In the central nervous system, there is a decrease in *brain weight,* ventricular enlargement, and neuronal loss of approximately 50,000 a day, with some reduction in cerebral blood flow and oxygenation.

54.9 The answer is E (*Synopsis VIII,* page 1298).
Contrary to the popular myth, *most elderly persons need as much sleep as they did in their earlier mature years.* However, *complaints about sleeplessness are common.* To some extent these complaints can be traced to sleep disturbances, rather than to sleeplessness. *Frequent visits to the bathroom* may lead to problems in falling asleep again. Furthermore, many of the elderly—retired, unemployed, inactive, and uninvolved—succumb to the practice of taking *catnaps that may interfere with a good night's sleep.*

When insomnia does occur and is unaccompanied by delirium or a psychotic disorder, it usually responds to standard hypnotics. *Tricyclic drugs often induce sleep when insomnia is accompanied by a depressive reaction.*

54.10 The answer is D (*Synopsis VIII,* pages 1299–1300).
Lithium, a hydrophilic drug, is excreted by the kidneys. The elderly person's decrease in renal clearance may cause an accumulation of lithium.

As a person ages, the ratio of lean to fat body mass changes. With normal aging, lean body mass decreases, and body fat increases. Because of that and because of decreases in plasma volume, total body water, and total plasma, the volume of distribution (V_d) for lipophilic drugs is increased. Increases in the V_d of the lipophilic drugs *imipramine, diazepam, chlorpromazine,* and *fluoxetine* may reduce their efficacy if the drugs are given in single or as-needed doses. The increased V_d also contributes to drug accumulation.

54.11 The answer is C (*Synopsis VIII,* pages 1289–1294).
In the elderly, *simple recall becomes difficult* and *memory-encoding ability diminishes.* Those functions decline with age. However, many cognitive abilities are retained in old age. Although the elderly take longer than young persons to learn new material, *complete learning of new material still occurs.* Old adults maintain their verbal abilities, and their *IQs remain stable until age 80. On multiple-choice tests, recognition of correct answers persists.*

54.12 The answer is D (*Synopsis VIII,* pages 1289–1298).
Vitamin deficiencies in the aged are uncommon. However, a number of conditions and deficiencies are typical and should be considered in the physical assessment of the aged. *Toxins of bacterial origin* and metabolic origins are common in old age. Bacterial toxins usually originate in occult or inconspicuous foci of infection, such as suspected pneumonic conditions and urinary infections. In the aged, the most common metabolic intoxication causing mental symptoms is *uremia,* which is an excess of urea and other nitrogenous waste products in the blood. Mild diabetes, hepatic failure, and gout are also known to cause mental symptoms in the aged and may easily be missed unless they are actively investigated. Alcohol and drug misuse may cause many mental disturbances in late life, but these abuses, with their characteristic effects, are usually easily determined by taking a history.

Cerebral anoxia often precipitates mental symptoms as a result of cardiac insufficiency or emphysema. Anoxic confusion may follow surgery, a cardiac infarct, gastrointestinal bleeding, or occlusion or stenosis of the carotid arteries. *Nutritional deficiencies may cause mental symptoms* or may be a symptom of a mental disorder.

54.13 The answer is D (*Synopsis VIII,* pages 1298–1302).
Psychotropic drugs are among those most commonly prescribed for the elderly; *40 (not 25) percent of all hypnotics dispensed in the United States each year are to those over age 65. The elderly use more medications than any other age group.* Indeed, *25 percent of all prescriptions are written for those over age 65.* Many old persons have adverse drug reactions, as evidenced by the fact that, *in the United States, 250,000 people a year are hospitalized because of adverse medication reactions.* The physician must remember that *70 percent of the elderly use over-the-counter* (OTC) *medications.* These preparations can interact with prescribed drugs and lead

to dangerous side effects. The physician should include the use of OTC medications when taking a patient's drug history.

54.14 The answer is D (*Synopsis VIII,* page 1290).
Sexual activity (for example, masturbation, coitus) *may increase, as compared with earlier levels of functioning* because as some persons get older, they *resolve feelings of guilt* about sex that may have existed when they were younger. Sexual activity continues well into old age, with William Masters and Virginia Johnson reporting sexual functioning of people in their 80s. Sexual activity in persons over age 60 *occurs in at least 20 percent (not fewer than 10 percent) of women* and *occurs in more than 70 percent (not fewer than 50 percent)* of men.

54.15 The answer is E (all) (*Synopsis VIII,* page 1288).
Abuse of the elderly by some caregiving children *is most likely to occur when the parent is bedridden* or *has a chronic medical illness* that requires constant nursing attention or when the abusing children have substance-related disorders, are under economic stress, and have no relief from their caretaking duties. Elderly abuse *is likely to occur if the child was a victim of sexual or physical abuse. Elderly abuse occurs more often toward women than toward men,* and most abuse occurs in the elderly over age 75.

55 

Forensic Psychiatry

At various stages in their historical development, psychiatry and law have converged. Both psychiatry and law are concerned with persons who have violated the rules of society and whose behavior presents a problem, not only because their deviance has diminished their ability to function effectively but because it adversely affects the functioning of the community. Traditionally, the psychiatrist's efforts are directed toward elucidation of the causes and through prevention and treatment, reduction of the self-destructive elements of harmful behavior. The lawyer, as the agent of society, is concerned with the fact that the social deviant presents a threat to the safety and security of other people in the environment. Both psychiatry and law seek to implement their respective goals through the application of pragmatic techniques based on empirical observations.

Forensic psychiatry is the branch of medicine that deals with disorders of the mind and their relation to legal principles. The word ''forensic'' means belonging to the courts of law. One of the most confusing aspects of forensic psychiatry is understanding the role of the psychiatrist as expert witness in criminal and other proceedings. Psychiatrists retained as experts for the defense in a criminal trial may declare a person not responsible, while opposing experts testify on behalf of the prosecution with equal conviction that the defendant was responsible for the acts.

There are several explanations of this phenomenon: (1) Honest differences of opinion are inevitable in any effort to formulate complex judgments. (2) Knowledge of the human personality in its normal and abnormal manifestations is imperfect at best. (3) The fact that complex problems must be resolved with imperfect tools and incomplete knowledge tends to enhance the unconscious bias and partisanship that are likely to arise. (4) Frequently, medical experts are not fully conversant with the language, practices, and objectives of the legal procedure in which they are participating. (5) There is common misapprehension among medical experts that in offering testimony they must use legal language as their own. (6) Finally, although it happens only very infrequently, venality may induce a medical expert to present testimony favorable to the individual or group that has retained him or her. Honest differences of opinion may be minimized, but they can never be eliminated entirely; however many workers in forensic psychiatry believe that the battle of the experts could be eliminated if the psychiatrists were appointed by and reported only to the court.

Students should read Chapter 55 of *Kaplan and Sadock's Synopsis VIII* and then answer the following questions to test their knowledge in this area.

HELPFUL HINTS

The student should be able to define each of these terms and know each of these cases.

- abandonment
- *actus reus*
- alliance threat
- antisocial behavior
- battery
- Judge David Bazelon
- civil commitment
- classical tort
- competence to inform
- competency
- confidentiality
- consent form
- conservator
- court-mandated evaluation
- credibility of witnesses
- culpability
- custody
- disclose to safeguard
- discriminate disclosure
- documentation
- Durham rule
- duty to warn
- emancipated minor
- emergency exception
- forced confinement
- the four Ds
- Gault decision
- going the extra mile
- *habeas corpus*
- hearsay
- informal admission
- informed consent
- insanity defense
- involuntary admission
- irresistible impulse
- judgment
- leading questions
- malpractice
- mature minor rule
- medical expert
- *mens rea*
- mental-health information service
- model penal code
- M'Naghten rule
- *O'Connor v. Donaldson*
- *parens patriae*
- peonage
- plea bargaining
- pretrial conference
- probationary status
- right to treatment
- right-wrong test
- rules of evidence
- seclusion and restraint
- state training school standards
- Thomas Szasz
- *Tarasoff v. Regents of University of California* (I and II)
- task-specific competence
- temporary admission
- testamentary capacity
- testator
- testimonial privilege
- voluntary admission
- *Wyatt v. Stickney*

▲ QUESTIONS

DIRECTIONS: Each of the questions or incomplete statements below is followed by five suggested responses or completions. Select the *one* that is *best* in each case.

55.1 The most frequent issue involving lawsuits against psychiatrists is

A. suicide
B. improper use of restraints
C. sexual involvement
D. drug reactions
E. violence

55.2 Involuntary termination of a patient by a therapist

A. may result in a malpractice claim of abandonment
B. cannot be done during an emergency
C. requires careful documentation
D. should include transfer of services to others
E. is characterized by all of the above

55.3 Pick the *one* best answer regarding *Dusky v. United States.*

A. Harmless mental patients cannot be confined against their will without treatment if they can survive outside.
B. An involuntary patient who is not receiving treatment has a constitutional right to be discharged.
C. A test of competence was approved to see if a criminal defendant can rationally consult with a lawyer and has a factual and rational understanding of the proceedings against him.
D. Civilly committed persons have a constitutional right to adequate treatment.
E. A clinician must notify the intended victim(s) when there is an imminent threat posed by his or her patient.

DIRECTIONS: Choose the *one* best answer.

55.4 If an attending psychiatrist is sued for the actions of a first-year resident, the principle applied is

A. mens rea
B. parens patriae
C. respondeat superior
D. habeas corpus
E. actus reus

55.5 Confidential communications can be shared with which of the following *without* the patient's consent?

A. A consultant
B. The patient's family
C. The patient's attorney
D. The patient's previous therapist
E. An insurer of the patient

55.6 Product rule is concerned with

A. testimonial privilege
B. involuntary admission
C. criminal responsibility
D. competency to stand trial
E. all of the above

55.7 The Gault decision applies to

A. minors
B. *habeas corpus*
C. informed consent
D. battery
E. none of the above

55.8 Situations in which there is an obligation on the part of the physician to report to authorities information that may be confidential include

A. suspected child abuse
B. the case of a patient who will probably commit murder and can only be stopped by notification of police
C. the case of a patient who will probably commit suicide and can only be stopped by notification of police
D. the case of a patient who has potentially life-threatening responsibilities (for example, airline pilot) and who shows marked impairment of judgment
E. all of the above

55.9 Of the following, which is the *least* common cause of malpractice claims against psychiatrists by patients?

A. Suicide attempts
B. Improper use of restraints
C. Failure to treat psychosis
D. Sexual involvement
E. Substance dependence

55.10 To reduce the risk of malpractice, preventive approaches include

A. documenting good care
B. providing only the kind of care the psychiatrist is qualified to deliver
C. acquiring informed consent
D. obtaining a second opinion
E. all of the above

DIRECTIONS: Each group of questions consists of lettered headings followed by a list of numbered phrases or statements. For each numbered phrase or statement, select the *one* lettered heading that is most closely associated with it. Each lettered heading may be selected once, more than once, or not at all.

Questions 55.11–55.12

A. *Tarasoff v. Regents of University of California* (Tarasoff I)
B. *Tarasoff v. Regents of University of California* (Tarasoff II)

55.11 Duty to protect
55.12 Duty to warn

Questions 55.13–55.14

A. One-physician certificate
B. Two-physician certificate

55.13 Temporary admission for 15 days
55.14 Involuntary admission for 60 days

Questions 55.15–55.19

A. *Rouse v. Cameron*
B. *Wyatt v. Stickney*
C. *O'Connor v. Donaldson*
D. *The Myth of Mental Illness*

55.15 Harmless mental patients cannot be confined against their will.
55.16 Standards were established for staffing, nutrition, physical facilities, and treatment.
55.17 The purpose of involuntary hospitalization is treatment.
55.18 A patient who is not receiving treatment has a constitutional right to be discharged.
55.19 All forced confinements because of mental illness are unjust.

Questions 55.20–55.28

A. Witness of fact
B. Expert witness
C. Direct examination
D. Cross-examination
E. Court-mandated evaluation
F. Privilege
G. Confidentiality

55.20 May draw conclusions from data and thereby render an opinion
55.21 The psychiatrist functioning no differently from laypersons generally
55.22 Most common role of a psychiatrist in a court proceeding
55.23 Loss of the confidential relationship between doctor and patient
55.24 Open-ended questions that require narrative type of answers
55.25 Right to maintain secrecy or confidentiality in the face of a subpoena
55.26 Does not exist in military courts
55.27 Right that can be waived by the patient
55.28 Binds the physician to hold secret all information given by a patient

Questions 55.29–55.35

A. Informal admission
B. Voluntary admission
C. Temporary admission
D. Involuntary admission
E. Habeas corpus
F. *Parens patriae*

55.29 Patient free to stay or leave at will
55.30 Patient applying in writing for admission
55.31 Need for admission that must be confirmed by a psychiatrist on the hospital staff
55.32 Application for admission to a hospital that may be made by relative or friend
55.33 Allows the patient to be hospitalized for 60 days
55.34 Casts the state as protector of patients from their own inability to survive unaided
55.35 Proclaimed by those who believe they have been illegally deprived of liberty

Questions 55.36–55.40

A. Irresistible impulse
B. M'Naghten rule
C. Model Penal Code
D. Durham rule
E. Diminished capacity

55.36 Known commonly as the right-wrong test
55.37 A person charged with a criminal offense is not responsible for an act if the act was committed under circumstances that the person was unable to resist because of mental disease.
55.38 An accused is not criminally responsible if his or her unlawful act was the product of mental disease or mental defect.
55.39 As a result of mental disease or defect, the defendant lacked substantial capacity either to appreciate the criminality of his or her conduct or to conform the conduct to the requirement of the law.
55.40 The defendant suffered some impairment (usually but not always because of mental illness) sufficient to interfere with the ability to formulate a specific element of the particular crime charged.

ANSWERS

Forensic Psychiatry

55.1 The answer is A (*Synopsis VIII,* page 1319).
Suicide and suicide attempts are the most frequent causes for lawsuits against psychiatrists; 50 percent of suicides lead to malpractice actions by relatives. The greatest degree of supervision (inpatient setting) is associated with the most culpability. The use of *restraints, drug reactions,* and patients committing *violence* are all potential causes of malpractice that can be forestalled with proper documentation of clinical decision making and informed consent. *Sexual involvement* with a patient is both illegal and unethical.

55.2 The answer is E (*Synopsis VIII,* page 1310).
A potential pitfall of involuntary discharge or termination is the charge of abandonment. *Malpractice litigation* is often associated with situations in which there are bad feelings and a bad outcome. Consultation and careful *documentation* are important safeguards. Charges of *abandonment* can be avoided by referring the patient to another hospital or therapist. Some authorities recommend giving a patient three names of therapists, clinics, or hospitals. A patient cannot be terminated while in a *state of emergency.* The emergency must be resolved (for example by hospitalization in cases of dangerousness) before the patient can be terminated and transferred.

55.3 The answer is C (*Synopsis VIII,* page 1314).
The Supreme Court, in *Dusky v. United States,* approved a test of competence that seeks to ascertain whether a criminal defendant "has sufficient present ability to *consult with his lawyer* with a reasonable degree of rational understanding and whether he has a rational as well as factual understanding of the proceedings against him." According to the 1976 case of *O'Connor v. Donaldson,* the U.S. Supreme Court ruled that *harmless mental patients* cannot be confined against their will without treatment if they can survive outside. In 1966, the District of Columbia Court of Appeals ruled in *Rouse v. Cameron* that an involuntary inpatient who is not receiving treatment has a constitutional *right to be discharged.* According to this decision, the purpose of involuntary hospitalization is treatment.

In *Wyatt v. Stickney* it was decided that civilly committed patients have a constitutional right to receive *adequate treatment.* In Tarasoff I (the case of *Tarasoff v. Regents of the University of California*), it was ruled that a psychotherapist or physician who has reason to believe that a patient may injure or kill someone *must notify* the potential victim, the patient's relatives or friends, or the authorities.

55.4 The answer is C (*Synopsis VIII,* page 1318).
Respondeat superior is a Latin phrase meaning "Let the master answer for the deed of the servant." A person high in the chain of command is responsible for the actions of those under his or her supervision. Some psychiatrists carry vicarious liability insurance, which protects them against liability for actions against clinicians they supervise directly or indirectly. Psychiatrists should remove themselves from situations in which they bear responsibility for clinicians whom they cannot control. *Mens rea* and *actus reus* are concepts that apply to criminal law. A criminal act has two components: (1) voluntary conduct (*actus reus*) and (2) evil intent (*mens rea*). The insanity defense deals with these principles in that there cannot be evil intent when an offender's mental status deprives him or her of the capacity of rational intent.

Parens patriae is the doctrine that allows the state to intervene and act as surrogate parent for those who are unable to care for themselves or may harm themselves. This principle originally referred to a monarch's duty to protect the people (literally meaning "father of his country"). In U.S. common law, this doctrine refers to paternalism in which the state acts for people who are mentally ill and for minors. A writ of *habeas corpus* is a legal procedure that asks a court to decide whether a patient has been hospitalized without due process of law. A writ of habeas corpus may be proclaimed by those who believe they have been illegally deprived of liberty.

55.5 The answer is A (*Synopsis VIII,* page 1307).
Confidentiality pertains to the premise that all information imparted to the physician by the patient be held secret. However, sharing information with other staff members treating the patient, clinical supervisors, and *a consultant* does not require the patient's permission. Sharing patient information with *the patient's family, the patient's attorney, the patient's previous therapist,* or *an insurer of the patient* does require the patient's permission. Courts may compel disclosure of confidential material (*subpoena duces tecum*). In emergencies, limited information may be released, but after the emergency, the clinician should inform the patient.

55.6 The answer is C (*Synopsis VIII,* page 1315).
In 1954, in the case of *Durham v. United States,* a decision was made by Judge David Bazelon, a pioneering jurist in forensic psychiatry in the District of Columbia Court of Appeals, that resulted in the product rule of *criminal responsibility.* An accused is not criminally responsible if his or her unlawful act was the product of mental disease or defect. Judge Bazelon stated that the purpose of the rule was to get good and complete psychiatric testimony. He sought to break the criminal law out of the theoretical straitjacket of the M'Naghten test.

Testimonial privilege is the right to maintain secrecy or confidentiality in the face of a subpoena. The privilege belongs to the patient, not to the physician, and it is waivable by the patient. *Involuntary admission* involves the question of whether or not the patient is a danger to self or others, such as in the suicidal or homicidal patient. Because those individuals do not recognize their need for hospital care, application for admission to a hospital may be made by a relative or friend and is involuntary. *Competency to stand trial* refers to defendants being able to understand the nature and the object of the proceedings against them, to consult with counsel, and to assist in preparing the defense.

55.7 The answer is A (*Synopsis VIII,* page 1312).
The Gault decision applies to *minors,* those under the care of

a parent or guardian and usually under age 18. In the case of minors, the parent or guardian is the person legally empowered to give consent to medical treatment. However, most states by statute list specific diseases or conditions that a minor can consent to have treated, such as venereal diseases, pregnancy, substance-related disorders, and contagious diseases. In an emergency, a physician can treat a minor without parental consent. The trend is to adopt the mature minor rule, allowing minors to consent to treatment under ordinary circumstances. As a result of the Gault decision, the juvenile must now be represented by counsel, be able to confront witnesses, and be given proper notice of any charges. Emancipated minors have the rights of adults when it can be demonstrated that they are living as adults with control over their own lives.

A writ of *habeas corpus* may be proclaimed on behalf of anyone who claims he or she is being deprived of liberty illegally. The legal procedure asks a court to decide whether hospitalization has been accomplished without due process of the law, and the petition must be heard by a court at once, regardless of the manner or form in which it is filed. Hospitals are obligated to submit those petitions to the court immediately. *Informed consent* is knowledge of the risks and alternatives of a treatment method and formal acceptance of treatment.

Under classical tort (a tort is a wrongful act) theory, an intentional touching to which one has given no consent is a *battery*. Thus, the administration of electroconvulsive therapy or chemotherapy, although it may be therapeutic, is a battery when done without consent. Indeed, any unauthorized touching outside of conventional social intercourse constitutes a battery. It is an offense to the dignity of the person, an invasion of the right of self-determination, for which punitive and actual damages may be imposed.

55.8 The answer is E (all) (*Synopsis VIII,* pages 1307–1308). In some situations—such as *suspected child abuse*—the physician must report to the authorities, as specifically required by law. According to the American Psychiatric Association, confidentiality may be broken when the patient will probably *commit murder* and the act can only be stopped by notification of police, when the patient will probably commit *suicide* and the act can only be stopped by notification of police, or when a patient who has potentially *life-threatening responsibilities* (for example, airline pilot) shows marked impairment of judgment.

55.9 The answer is D (*Synopsis VIII,* page 1318).
Sexual involvement with patients accounts for 6 percent of malpractice claims against psychiatrists and is the least common cause of malpractice litigation. This fact does not, however, minimize its importance as a problem. Sexual intimacy with patients is both illegal and unethical. There are also serious legal and ethical questions about a psychotherapist's dating or marrying a patient even after discharging the patient from therapy. Some psychiatrists believe in the adage "Once a patient, always a patient." Other psychiatrists hold the view that a period of 2 years after discharge is sufficient time to terminate prohibitions against personal involvement.

For other malpractice claims, the following figures are given: failure to manage *suicide attempts,* 21 percent; *improper use of restraints,* 7 percent; and *failure to treat psychosis,* 14 percent. *Substance dependence* accounts for about 10 percent of claims and refers to the patient's having developed a substance-related disorder as a result of a psychiatrist's not monitoring carefully the prescribing of potentially addicting drugs.

55.10 The answer is E (all) (*Synopsis VIII,* pages 1317–1318). Although it is impossible to eliminate malpractice, some preventive approaches have been invaluable in clinical practice. The *documentation of good care* is a strong deterrent to liability. Such documentation should include the decision-making process, the clinician's rationale for treatment, and an evaluation of costs and benefits. Psychiatrists should *provide only the kind of care that they are qualified to deliver.* They should never overload their practice or overstretch their abilities, and they should take reasonable care of themselves. The *informed consent* process refers to a discussion between doctor and patient of the treatment proposed, the side effects of drugs, and the uncertainty of psychiatric practice. Such a dialogue helps prevent a liability suit. A consultation affords protection against liability because it allows the clinician to obtain information about his or her peer group's standard of practice. It also provides *a second opinion,* enabling the clinician to submit his or her judgment to the scrutiny of the peer. The clinician who takes the trouble to obtain a consultation in a difficult and complex case is unlikely to be viewed by a jury as careless and negligent. The patient's acceptance of the proposed treatment should be documented.

Answers 55.11–55.12

55.11 The answer is B (*Synopsis VIII,* pages 1308–1309).

55.12 The answer is A (*Synopsis VIII,* page 1308).
In the case of *Tarasoff v. Regents of University of California (Tarasoff I),* in 1974, it was ruled that a physician or psychotherapist who has reason to believe that a patient may injure or kill someone must notify the potential victim, the patient's relatives or friends, or the authorities. The Tarasoff I ruling does not require therapists to report fantasies; rather, it means that when they are convinced that a homicide is likely, they have a *duty to warn.* The Tarasoff I decision has not drastically affected psychiatrists, as it has long been their practice to warn the appropriate persons or law enforcement authorities when a patient presents a distinct and immediate threat to someone.

In 1976 the California Supreme Court issued a second ruling in the case of *Tarasoff v. Regents of University of California (Tarasoff II).* It broadened its earlier ruling, the duty to warn, to include the *duty to protect.* The Tarasoff II ruling has stimulated perhaps the most intense debates in the medicolegal field. Lawyers, judges, and expert witnesses argue the definition of prevention, the nature of the relationship between therapist and patient, and the balance between public safety and individual privacy. Clinicians argue that the duty to protect may hinder treatment because the patient may not trust the doctor if confidentiality is not maintained. Furthermore, it is not always easy to determine whether a patient is dangerous enough to justify long-term incarceration because of defensive practices. As a result of such debates in the medicolegal field since 1976, state courts have not come up with a uniform interpretation of the Tarasoff II ruling, the concept of the duty to protect.

Answers 55.13–55.14

55.13 The answer is A (*Synopsis VIII,* page 1309).

55.14 The answer is B (*Synopsis VIII,* page 1309).
A *one-physician certificate,* also known as emergency or *temporary admission for 15 days,* is used for patients who are unable to make a decision on their own because they have a mental illness that impairs their judgment (for example Alzheimer's disease). Such patients may be admitted on an emergency basis to a psychiatric hospital on the written recommendation of one physician, provided the need for hospitalization is confirmed by a psychiatrist on the hospital staff.

A *two-physician certificate* is used for *involuntary admission for 60 days* when patients are a danger to themselves (suicidal patients) or to others (homicidal patients). Two physicians must make independent examinations of the patient, and the next of kin must be notified if a decision is made to hospitalize the patient. The patient may be hospitalized for up to 60 days; however, during that time the patient has a right to see a judge, who determines whether such involuntary hospitalization may continue. After 60 days, if the patient is to remain hospitalized, the case must be reviewed by a board consisting of psychiatrists, other physicians, lawyers, and other citizens not connected with the institution.

Answers 55.15–55.19

55.15 The answer is C (*Synopsis VIII,* page 1310).

55.16 The answer is B (*Synopsis VIII,* page 1310).

55.17 The answer is A (*Synopsis VIII,* page 1310).

55.18 The answer is A (*Synopsis VIII,* page 1310).

55.19 The answer is D (*Synopsis VIII,* page 1311).
Various landmark legal cases have affected psychiatry and the law over the years. In the 1976 case of *O'Connor v. Donaldson,* the U.S. Supreme Court ruled that *harmless mental patients cannot be confined against their will* without treatment if they can survive outside. According to the Court, a finding of mental illness alone cannot justify a state's confining persons in a hospital against their will; patients must be considered dangerous to themselves or others before they are confined against their will.

In 1971, in *Wyatt v. Stickney* in Alabama Federal District Court, it was decided that persons civilly committed to a mental institution have a constitutional right to receive adequate treatment, and *standards were established for staffing, nutrition, physical facilities, and treatment.* In 1966, the District of Columbia Court of Appeals in *Rouse v. Cameron* ruled that *the purpose of involuntary hospitalization is treatment* and that *a patient who is not receiving treatment has a constitutional right to be discharged* from the hospital.

In *The Myth of Mental Illness,* Thomas Szasz argued that the various psychiatric diagnoses are totally devoid of significance and that therefore *all forced confinements because of mental illness are unjust.* Szasz contended that psychiatrists have no place in the courts of law.

Answers 55.20–55.28

55.20 The answer is B (*Synopsis VIII,* page 1305).

55.21 The answer is A (*Synopsis VIII,* page 1305).

55.22 The answer is B (*Synopsis VIII,* page 1305).

55.23 The answer is E (*Synopsis VIII,* page 1306).

55.24 The answer is C (*Synopsis VIII,* page 1305).

55.25 The answer is F (*Synopsis VIII,* pages 1306–1307).

55.26 The answer is F (*Synopsis VIII,* pages 1306–1307).

55.27 The answer is F (*Synopsis VIII,* pages 1306–1307).

55.28 The answer is G (*Synopsis VIII,* page 1307).
One type of witness is the *witness of fact.* As a witness of fact, *the psychiatrist functions no differently from laypersons generally*—for example, as observers of an accident on the street. The witness's input—the facts—are direct observations and material from direct scrutiny. A witness of fact may be a psychiatrist who reads portions of the medical record aloud to bring it into the legal record and thus make it available for testimony. In theory, any psychiatrist at any level of training can fulfill that role.

In contrast, a psychiatrist under certain circumstances may be qualified as an expert. The qualifying process, however, consists not of popular recognition in one's clinical field but of being accepted by the court and both sides of the case as suitable to perform expert functions. Thus, the term ''expert'' has particular legal meaning and is independent of any actual or presumed expertise the clinician may have in a given area. The clinician's expertise is elucidated during direct examination and cross-examination of the clinician's education, publications, and certifications. In the context of the courtroom, an *expert witness* is one who *may draw conclusions from data and thereby render an opinion*—for example, that a patient meets the required criteria for commitment or for an insanity defense under the standards of a jurisdiction. Expert witnesses play a role in determining the standard of care and what constitutes the average practice of psychiatry.

The most common role of a psychiatrist in court proceedings is as an expert witness. When psychiatrists are asked to serve as experts, they are usually asked to do so for one of the sides in the case; rarely are clinicians independent examiners reporting directly to the court.

Direct examination is the first questioning of a witness by the attorney for the party on whose behalf the witness is called. Direct examination generally consists of *open-ended questions that require narrative-type answers.* It is a friendly interrogation that is routinely rehearsed with one's attorney before the trial.

Cross-examination is the questioning of a witness by the attorney for the opposing party. Cross-examination usually involves long, possibly leading questions that demand a yes or no answer. Few experiences can be as demoralizing for the clinician as cross-examination by an eager, aggressive, and sarcastic attorney for the opposing side. That segment of the experience, more than any other, makes many clinicians leery of appearing in the courtroom in any role.

In several legal situations the judge asks clinicians to be

consultants to the court, which raises the issue of for whom the clinicians work. In a *court-mandated evaluation* there is a *loss of the confidential relationship between doctor and patient* because clinical information may have to be revealed to the court. Clinicians who make such court-ordered evaluations are under an ethical obligation and in some states, a legal obligation to so inform the patients at the outset of the examinations and to make sure that the patients understand that condition.

Privilege is the *right to maintain secrecy or confidentiality in the face of a subpoena.* Privileged communications are statements made by certain persons within a relationship—such as husband–wife, priest–penitent, or doctor–patient—that the law protects from forced disclosure on the witness stand. Privilege is a right that belongs to the patient, not to the physician, and so *the right can be waived by the patient.* Psychiatrists, who are licensed to practice medicine, may claim medical privilege, but they have found that the privilege is so riddled with qualifications that it is practically meaningless. Purely federal cases have no psychotherapist–patient privilege. Moreover, the privilege *does not exist in military courts,* regardless of whether the physician is military or civilian and whether the privilege is recognized in the state where the court-martial takes place. The privilege has numerous exceptions, which are often viewed as implied waivers. In the most common exception, patients are said to waive the privilege by injecting their condition into the litigation, thereby making their condition an element of their claim or defense. In a number of contexts, clinicians may be ordered to give the court information that is ordinarily considered privileged.

A long-held premise of medical ethics *binds the physician to hold secret all information given by a patient.* That professional obligation is what is meant by *confidentiality.* Understanding confidentiality requires awareness that it applies to certain populations and not to others. That is, one can identify a group that is within the circle of confidentiality, meaning that sharing information with the members of that group does not require specific permission from the patient. As a rule, clinical information may be shared with the patient's permission—preferably written permission, although verbal permission suffices with proper documentation. Each release is good for only one bolus of information, and permission should be obtained separately for each subsequent release, even to the same party. Permission overcomes only the legal barrier, not the clinical one; the release is permission, not obligation. If the clinician believes that the information may be destructive, the matter should be discussed, and the release may be refused with some exceptions.

Answers 55.29–55.35

55.29 The answer is A (*Synopsis VIII,* page 1309).

55.30 The answer is B (*Synopsis VIII,* page 1309).

55.31 The answer is C (*Synopsis VIII,* page 1309).

55.32 The answer is D (*Synopsis VIII,* page 1309).

55.33 The answer is D (*Synopsis VIII,* page 1309).

55.34 The answer is F (*Synopsis VIII,* page 1309).

55.35 The answer is E (*Synopsis VIII,* page 1309).

Informal admission operates on the general hospital model, in which the patient is admitted to a psychiatric unit of a general hospital in the same way that a medical or surgical patient is admitted. Under such circumstances the ordinary doctor–patient relationship applies, with the *patient free to stay or leave at will,* even against medical advice.

In cases of *voluntary admission, patients apply in writing for admission* to a psychiatric hospital. They may come to the hospital on the advice of their personal physician, or they may seek help on their own. In either case the patients are examined by a psychiatrist on the hospital staff and are admitted if that examination reveals the need for hospital treatment.

Temporary admission is used for patients who are so senile or so confused that they require hospitalization and are not able to make decisions on their own and for patients who are so acutely disturbed that they must be immediately admitted to a psychiatric hospital on an emergency basis. Under the procedure a person is admitted to the hospital on the written recommendation of one physician. Once the patient has been admitted, the *need for hospitalization must be confirmed by a psychiatrist on the hospital staff.* The procedure is temporary because patients cannot be hospitalized against their will for more than 15 days.

Involuntary admission involves the question of whether the patients are a danger to themselves, such as suicidal patients, or a danger to others, such as homicidal patients. Because those persons do not recognize their need for hospital care, the *application for admission to a hospital may be made by a relative or a friend.* Once the application is made, the patients must be examined by two physicians, and if both physicians confirm the need for hospitalization, the patients can then be admitted.

Involuntary admission *allows the patient to be hospitalized for 60 days.* After that time, if the patient is to remain hospitalized, the case must be reviewed periodically by a board consisting of psychiatrists, nonpsychiatric physicians, lawyers, and other citizens not connected with the institution.

The powers of the state to commit mentally ill persons in need of care are known as *parens patriae* and the police power. The *parens patriae* principle *casts the state as the protector of patients from their own inability to survive unaided.* The police power casts the state as the protector of other citizens from patients.

Persons who have been hospitalized involuntarily and who believe that they should be released have the right to file a petition for a writ of *habeas corpus.* Under law, a writ of habeas corpus may be *proclaimed by those who believe that they have been illegally deprived of liberty.* The legal procedure asks a court to decide whether a patient has been hospitalized without due process of law. The case must be heard by a court at once. Hospitals are obligated to submit the petitions to the court immediately.

Answers 55.36–55.40

55.36 The answer is B (*Synopsis VIII,* pages 1314–1315).

55.37 The answer is A (*Synopsis VIII,* page 1315).

55.38 The answer is D (*Synopsis VIII,* page 1315).

55.39 The answer is E (*Synopsis VIII,* pages 1316–1317).

55.40 The answer is C (*Synopsis VIII,* pages 1315–1316).

The precedent for determining legal responsibility was established in the British courts in 1843. The *M'Naghten rule* is *known commonly as the right-wrong test.* In 1922 jurists in England reexamined the M'Naghten rule and suggested broadening the concept of insanity in criminal cases to include the concept of the *irresistible impulse*—that is *a person charged with a criminal offense is not responsible for an act if the act was committed under circumstances that the person was unable to resist because of mental disease.* To most psychiatrists the law is unsatisfactory because it covers only a small group of those who are mentally ill. However, it was used successfully in Virginia in the 1994 case of *Virginia v. Bobbitt,* in which the defendant was acquitted of malicious wounding. She had cut off her husband's penis after apparently enduring years of sexual, physical, and emotional abuse.

In 1954 in the case of *Durham v. United States,* a decision resulted in the product rule of criminal responsibility, or the *Durham rule,* which states that *an accused is not criminally responsible if his or her unlawful act was the product of mental disease or mental defect.* Bazelon stated that the purpose of the rule was to get good and complete psychiatric testimony. In 1972, the Court of Appeals for the District of Columbia in *United States v. Brawner* discarded the rule in favor of the American Law Institute's 1962 model penal code test of criminal responsibility.

In its *model penal code* the American Law Institute recommended the following test of criminal responsibility: (1) *Persons are not responsible* for *criminal conduct* if *at the time of such conduct, as the result of mental disease or defect, they lacked substantial capacity either to appreciate the criminality of their conduct or to conform their conduct to the requirement of the law.* (2) The term ''mental disease or defect'' in this test does not include an abnormality manifested only by repeated criminal or otherwise antisocial conduct.

Other attempts at reform have included the defense of *diminished capacity,* which is based on the claim that *the defendant suffered some impairment (usually but not always because of mental illness) sufficient to interfere with the ability to formulate a specific element of the particular crime charged.* Hence, the defense finds its most common use with so-called specific-intent crimes, such as first-degree murder.

56 Ethics in Psychiatry

The field of ethics is central to the practice of medicine; however, it is uniquely and particularly relevant to the practice of psychiatry. Psychiatric patients often suffer from disorders that interfere with their capacity to make informed decisions about their own care. Impairment of insight, judgment, and reality testing are often hallmarks of psychiatric disorders, making it extremely difficult for patients to know when they are gravely disabled or dangerous to others. Psychiatric practice has a long and not always illustrious history of treating patients against their will, with the underlying precept that it is for their own good. The evolution of ethical thinking in psychiatry associated with the increasingly intimate relations between the psychiatric and legal systems is a fascinating and essential component of current psychiatric practice.

The student needs to be aware of the major ethical theories underlying most ethical questions in psychiatry—in particular, utilitarian and autonomy theory—and how those theories view such fundamental concepts as paternalism and beneficence. Such issues as informed consent, the right to die, surrogate decision making, involuntary treatment and hospitalization, and sexual contact with patients must be conceptualized from the perspective of ethical theory. The benefits and limitations of professional codes of ethics, especially those specific to the practice of psychiatry, must be studied and understood.

The student should read Chapter 56 in *Kaplan and Sadock's Synopsis VIII* and then study the questions and answers that follow.

HELPFUL HINTS

The student should be able to define each of these terms and know each of these cases.

- autonomy theory
- best-interests principle
- confidentiality
- *Cruzan v. Missouri*
- decisional capacity
- duty of beneficence
- duty to protect
- individual paternalism
- informed consent
- *Planned Parenthood v. Casey*
- *Principles of Medical Ethics* with annotations especially applicable to psychiatry
- professional standards
- right to die
- right to health care
- *Roe v. Wade*
- state paternalism
- substituted-judgment principle
- surrogate decision making
- utilitarian theory

▲ QUESTIONS

DIRECTIONS: Each of the questions or incomplete statements below is followed by five suggested responses or completions. Select the *one* that is *best* in each case.

56.1 Which of the following statements regarding informed consent is *false*?

A. It is governed by autonomy theory.
B. It is governed by paternalism.
C. It requires the patient's knowledge of risks and benefits of a treatment.
D. It can be given by a patient who has a delusion.
E. It is not governed by beneficence.

56.2 Choose the *one* best answer about *Cruzan v. Missouri Board of Health.*

A. All patients have the right to have life support withdrawn.
B. Early-stage fetuses have no legal standing.
C. Only conscious patients can have life-sustaining treatment withdrawn.
D. All competent patients can refuse medical care.
E. Treatment can be withheld from a person in a persistent vegetative state who has not previously stated his or her wishes on the subject.

56.3 Confidentiality

A. is maintained under the principles of patient autonomy
B. can be broken under the principle of distributive justice
C. may be broken under the principle of beneficence
D. is an issue in the Tarasoff decision
E. is all of the above

56.4 Which of the following statements about *Roe v. Wade* is *incorrect*?

A. States can regulate early abortions under specific circumstances.
B. Early-stage fetuses have no legal rights.
C. States may regulate late-stage abortions.
D. Early-stage abortions cannot be regulated.
E. The Freedom of Choice Act supports many of the principles of *Roe v. Wade.*

56.5 Surrogate decision making

A. is for patients who have lost decisional capabilities
B. may require that a surrogate be designated by a court
C. is usually performed by the next of kin
D. often involves decisions about the costs of medical treatment
E. all of the above

56.6 A physician's obligation concerning an impaired physician colleague is to

A. inform patients
B. refer the impaired physician to a psychiatrist
C. report the impaired physician to the appropriate local medical authority
D. advise the spouse or next of kin about the problem
E. treat and monitor the impaired physician

56.7 The physician's obligation to refrain from sexual contact with a patient is based on which of the following principles?

A. A patient in the physician–patient relationship is generally too vulnerable to make fully voluntary choices.
B. The focus should be on the treatment of the patient.
C. Transference issues make voluntary choices about sexual contact almost impossible.
D. The physician has an obligation to uphold the standards and the reputation of the profession.
E. All of the above statements are true.

DIRECTIONS: These lettered headings are followed by a list of numbered phrases. For each numbered phrase, select the lettered heading most associated with it. Each lettered heading may be used once, more than once, or not at all.

Questions 56.8–56.11

A. Utilitarian theory
B. Paternalism
C. Autonomy theory

56.8 The basis for making decisions about the allocation of society's resources for treatment and medical research
56.9 The traditional model of the physician–patient relationship
56.10 The physician's duty of beneficence
56.11 The right to informed consent

DIRECTIONS: For each numbered question below, answer whether or not the situation described is ethical by selecting the appropriate lettered heading:

Questions 56.12–56.20

A. Yes
B. No

56.12 Confidentiality must be maintained after the death of a patient.
56.13 Suspicion of child abuse should be reported as soon as possible.
56.14 The psychiatrist can make a determination of suicide as a result of mental illness for insurance purposes from reading the records only.
56.15 A psychiatrist can pay another physician for a patient referral.
56.16 Moonlighting is illegal.
56.17 Dating a patient 1 year after discharge is ethical.
56.18 Having a patient do chores for the treating physician is permissible.
56.19 The psychiatrist can divulge information about the patient if the patient desires.
56.20 The psychiatrist can perform a physical examination of his or her patient.

ANSWERS

Ethics in Psychiatry

56.1 The answer is B (*Synopsis VIII,* pages 1323).
In *paternalism,* physicians make decisions for patients as a parent would for a child. This does not occur unless a patient is unable to make rational decisions regarding essential treatment. Paternalism may be court involved with a thorough assessment of the patient. Informed consent is the cornerstone of *autonomy theory.* Patients are assumed to be competent and able to make rational decisions on their own behalf. This assumption extends to the mentally ill. Informed consent requires that patients be given a thorough description of their treatment options, risks, and benefits. Patients must have a rational understanding of these issues. Also, they must be allowed to reach decisions without coercion. *Beneficence* is a feature of paternalism in which physicians act in what they perceive to be the best interests of a patient. *Informed consent* assumes patients can make their own decisions, right or wrong, unless proven incapacitated. A patient may have a delusional belief and still give informed consent if the delusion is unrelated to the issue.

56.2 The answer is D (*Synopsis VIII,* page 1326).
In *Cruzan v. Missouri Board of Health* the U.S. Supreme Court upheld the right of a competent person to have "a constitutionally protected liberty interest in refusing unwanted medical treatment." The Court applied this principle to all patients *conscious or unconscious* who have made their wishes clearly known, whether or not they ever regain consciousness. Life support can be refused provided that the patient made his or her wishes known. The legal standing of fetuses relates to *Roe v. Wade.* Cruzan applies to both *conscious* and unconscious patients, provided that the latter have already made their wishes known. The U.S. Supreme Court permits each state to decide the standards it wishes to apply when asked to withhold or withdraw treatment from a person in a *persistent vegetative state* who has not previously stated his or her wishes on the subject.

56.3 The answer is E (*Synopsis VIII,* pages 1326–1327).
Therapist–patient confidentiality is a broad right. Under normal conditions, patient autonomy mandates maintenance of confidentiality. The principle of *distributive justice* means that all members of society are allocated an equal share of public safety. Under this principle, confidentiality can be broken to protect members of society from harm. *The Tarasoff decision* mandates that third parties must be notified and protected when a therapist believes a patient to be an immediate threat to the third party. Confidentiality may be broken in certain circumstances by a physician's *beneficent action. Beneficence* is a feature of paternalism in which physicians act in the best interest of a patient. A therapist calling the authorities to hospitalize a suicidal patient is an example of a legal and beneficent breach of confidentiality.

56.4 The answer is D (*Synopsis VIII,* page 1328).
In *Roe v. Wade,* the United States Supreme Court ruled that there are no legal obligations toward early stage fetuses. Early abortions can be regulated only to ensure the safety of a pregnant woman. Common law precedents give limited legal rights to the fetus once it becomes viable; therefore, states may regulate late-stage abortions. Under *Roe v. Wade* states can regulate early abortions under specific circumstances. The U.S. Supreme Court has overruled many of the protections of *Roe v. Wade.* The Freedom of Choice Act would restore most of these protections.

56.5 The answer is E (all) (*Synopsis VIII,* page 1326).
Surrogate decision making *is for patients who have lost decisional capabilities.* The surrogate may be designated by the patient before losing capacity. Sometimes surrogate decision making *may require that a surrogate be chosen by a court* if the patient has not designated someone. In some cases, states allow surrogates to be designated by the hospital. Surrogate decision making *is usually performed by the next of kin,* although next of kin are not always the appropriate decision makers. Relatives may have psychological and other agendas that interfere with their ability to make just decisions. In the past, surrogates made decisions for patients on a best-interests principle. The surrogate is supposed to decide which treatments could be reasonably expected to be in the patient's best interests; therefore, surrogate decision making *often involves decisions about the costs of medical treatment.* Present autonomy-based legal approaches require surrogates to decide on the basis of what the patient would have wished, known as substituted judgment. The surrogate should be familiar with the patient's values and attitudes. Substituted judgments present problems because it may be difficult to determine whether a surrogate is able to determine what the patient would have wished. If a substituted judgment cannot be made, the surrogate is to use the best-interests approach.

56.6 The answer is C (*Synopsis VIII,* page 1327).
The first ethical obligation concerning an impaired physician is to *report the impaired physician to an appropriate local medical authority.* That authority may be the county or state medical society. It is best to start with the immediate authority (the hospital ethics committee). It is not the physician's responsibility to *inform patients* or to *refer the impaired physician to a psychiatrist,* although that may be done by the appropriate authority after all of the facts are determined. *Advising the spouse or next of kin about the problem* is also best left to the local authority to decide.

Impairment in a physician may occur as the result of psychiatric or medical disorders or the use of a substance (for example, alcohol). A number of organic illnesses may interfere with the cognitive and motor skills required to provide medical care competently.

Although the legal responsibility to report an impaired physician varies from state to state, the ethical responsibility remains universal. A physician should not *treat and monitor the impaired physician.* The physician who treats the impaired physician should not be required to monitor the physician's progress or fitness to return to work. The monitoring should be done by an independent physician or group of physicians who have no conflicts of interest.

56.7 The answer is E (all) (*Synopsis VIII,* page 1323).
Physicians have an obligation to refrain from sexual contact with their patients. A number of principles underlie this obligation. *A patient in the physician–patient relationship is generally too vulnerable to make fully voluntary choices* about sexual contact. The physician's *focus should be on the treatment of the patient.* A change in that focus to include sexual contact compromises the physician's ability to treat the patient appropriately. In the psychiatrist–patient relationship *transference issues make voluntary choices about sexual contact almost impossible* for the patient. In addition, *the physician has an obligation to uphold the standards and the reputation of the profession.*

Answers 56.8–56.11

56.8 The answer is A (*Synopsis VIII,* page 1321).

56.9 The answer is B (*Synopsis VIII,* page 1322).

56.10 The answer is B (*Synopsis VIII,* page 1322).

56.11 The answer is C (*Synopsis VIII,* page 1322).
Utilitarian theory holds that our fundamental obligation when making decisions is to try to produce the greatest possible happiness for the greatest number of people. Sometimes the choices available are dismal. In that case one should act in ways that produce the least pain. Utilitarian theory is still used as *the basis for making decisions about the allocation of society's resources for treatment and medical research.*

Paternalism may be defined as a system in which someone acts for another's benefit without that person's consent. The requirement that health care practitioners be licensed is an example of state paternalism. Individual paternalism was *the traditional model of the physician–patient relationship.* In this model the physician is supposed to treat the patient as a caring parent would treat a child. The parent is assumed to know what is best for the child and has no obligation to ask the child for permission to perform actions that may benefit the child. *The physician's duty of beneficence,* the principle of doing good and avoiding harm, is a paternalistic principle. The physician is presumed to have knowledge that the patient may not understand or in certain instances is better off not knowing.

Autonomy theory presumes that the normal adult patient has the ability and the right to make rational and responsible decisions. The patient is self-governing (autonomous) and has rights to self-determination. The relationship between physician and patient is perceived as a relationship between two responsible adults. The patient's right to refuse treatment, *the right to informed consent,* and the assumption of competence are examples of the person's right to self-determination.

56.12 The answer is A (yes) (*Synopsis VIII,* pages 1324–1325).
Ethically, confidences survive a patient's death. Exceptions include proper legal compulsions and protecting others from imminent harm.

56.13 The answer is B (no) (*Synopsis VIII,* pages 1324–1325).
A physician must make several assessments before deciding whether to report suspected abuse. One must consider whether abuse is ongoing, whether abuse is responsive to treatment, and whether reporting has the potential to cause harm. Make safety for potential victims the top priority.

56.14 The answer is A (yes) (*Synopsis VIII,* pages 1324–1328).
It is ethical to make a diagnosis of suicide secondary to mental illness on the basis of reviewing the patient's records. Sometimes called a psychological autopsy, interviews with friends, family, and others who knew the deceased may also be useful.

56.15 The answer is B (no) (*Synopsis VIII,* pages 1324–1328).
Fee splitting occurs when one physician pays another for a patient referral. This also applies to lawyers giving a forensic psychiatrist referrals in exchange for a percentage of the fee. Fee splitting may occur in an office setting if the psychiatrist takes a percentage of his or her office mate's fee for supervision or expenses. Costs for such items or services must be arranged separately. Otherwise, it would appear that the office owner could benefit from referring patients to a colleague in the office. Fee splitting is illegal.

56.16 The answer is B (no) (*Synopsis VIII,* pages 1324–1328).
Residents may work on the own time (moonlighting) if their duties are not beyond their ability, if they are properly supervised, and if the moonlighting does not interfere with their residency training.

56.17 The answer is B (no) (*Synopsis VIII,* pages 1324–1325).
Proponents of the view ''Once a patient, always a patient'' insist that any involvement with an ex-patient—even a date or one that leads to marriage—should be prohibited. They maintain that a transferential reaction always exists between the patient and the therapist and that it prevents a rational decision about their emotional or sexual union. Some psychiatrists maintain that a reasonable time should elapse before any such liaison. The length of the ''reasonable'' period remains controversial: some have suggested 2 years, not 1 year.

The *Principles of Medical Ethics and Annotations Especially Applicable to Psychiatry,* however, states: ''Sexual activity with a current or *former* patient is unethical.''

56.18 The answer is B (no) (*Synopsis VIII,* pages 1324–1325).
Exploitation occurs when the psychiatrist uses the therapeutic relationship for personal gain. This includes adopting or hiring a patient as well as sexual or financial relationships.

56.19. The answer is A (yes) (*Synopsis VIII,* pages 1324–1325).
The patient has the right (known as privilege) of insisting that information about his or her case be divulged to those who request it. Psychiatrists are allowed to contest that right if they believe that the patient will be harmed by reading such information. They can stipulate that a report sent to a third party not be shown to the patient; however, in complex cases proper disposition of records may have to be adjudicated.

56.20 The answer is A (yes) (*Synopsis VIII,* pages 1324–1325).
Psychiatrists may provide nonpsychiatric medical care and diagnostic tests (for example, blood pressure readings) if they are competent to do so and if the procedures do not preclude effective psychiatric treatment by distorting the transference. Pelvic and rectal examinations, for example, carry a high risk of distorting the transference and would be better performed by another clinician.

57 Case Studies

JOSHUA A.

Mr. A., a 56-year-old married man, was admitted to an inpatient psychiatric service with a chief complaint of ''I can't go on like this anymore.'' He had become depressed a year earlier and had got progressively worse, especially in the past 2 months. He reported a 40-pound weight loss over a year and said that he now had trouble concentrating and remembering; he could not recall how to write the word *eleven* as he was filling out a check. He had been sleeping much more than usual but still felt tired throughout the day. He insisted that he had no real plans for suicide but said it would be nice to fall asleep and never wake up.

Mr. A. had been running a business out of his home for the past 8 years. Initially the business did very well and brought in an income of up to $200,000 a year. Over the past 2 years, however, the business had been failing; last year it made only $20,000. He used up his savings and began to dip into retirement funds. He was ashamed that his wife, who is suffering from health problems, had to take a second job. He was finding it increasingly difficult to attend to financial and business matters.

Mr. A. had begun seeing an outpatient psychiatrist 6 months earlier. At different times he had taken fluoxetine, buspirone, alprazolam, and risperidone, but none for longer than 5 days. He would complain that the medication was not effective or that he felt too groggy. For the 5 days preceding admission, he had constantly been taking fluoxetine 20 mg per day, buspirone 10 mg 3 times daily, and risperidone 2 mg at night, and he stated that he wanted to give the medication a chance to work. He reluctantly agreed to be hospitalized at the urging of his psychiatrist, who wanted a more comprehensive neuropsychiatric assessment and the chance to conduct medication trials in a controlled setting in which noncompliance would be less likely. Mr. A. did not use alcohol, tobacco, or drugs of any kind. He had never seen a psychiatrist or counselor in the past and denied ever having had mood or other psychiatric symptoms before this episode. He was reported to be undergoing a workup for Alzheimer's disease, negative to date, with a head magnetic resonance imaging (MRI) remaining. His medical history was noncontributory. Mr. A.'s mother was diagnosed with Alzheimer's disease when she was 57 and died at age 79. His father died at age 72, reportedly of old age. There was no family history of psychiatric disorders.

He grew up in a large city, attended community college, and began working as a consultant for a major company, a job he held for 10 years. Eventually he moved to the suburbs with his wife and daughter and set up an independent consulting practice working out of their home. He was now preoccupied with the thought that he might be getting Alzheimer's disease, as he is 1 year away from the age when his mother was diagnosed.

A physical examination was within normal limits. Vital signs were stable, and there was no evidence of cardiopulmonary disease. A neurological examination that included all cranial nerves was normal. Laboratory studies including complete blood count, electrolytes, thyroid and renal studies, glucose, cardiogram, chest X-ray, and urinalysis were all normal.

Mr. A. was well groomed and neatly dressed in sweat pants and sweat shirt. He was cooperative and made good, appropriate eye contact but appeared anxious and fidgety throughout the interview. He described his mood as ''extremely depressed'' and said he could not go on living any more, although he denied any suicidal plans or real intent. He appeared profoundly depressed but without tearfulness. His mood was unvarying throughout the interview. His thinking was logical and goal directed. There was no evidence of delusions or hallucinations. He was awake, alert, and fully oriented. His concentration was good, and remote, recent, and immediate recall all appeared to be unimpaired. Fund of knowledge, abstract reasoning, calculations, and insight were all normal. His judgment was somewhat impaired because Mr. A. did not realize the seriousness of his condition.

1. The most characteristic age of onset for major depression in men is

A. late teens, early 20s
B. childhood
C. late middle age
D. late 20s, mid-30s
E. there is no characteristic age of onset for depression in men

2. Medical conditions that may present with depression include

A. hypothyroidism
B. occult malignancies
C. hepatitis
D. hypercalcemia
E. all of the above

3. The test most likely to confirm a diagnosis of Alzheimer's disease is

A. head computed tomography scan
B. head magnetic resonance imaging (MRI)
C. brain positron emission tomography (PET)
D. measures of cerebrospinal fluid acetylcholine metabolites
E. none of the above

4. Testing of which cranial nerve is most likely to reveal abnormalities early in the course of Alzheimer's disease?

A. I (olfactory)
B. II (optic)
C. V (trigeminal)
D. VIII (vestibulocochlear)
E. XII (hypoglossal)

5. Which of the following signs or symptoms cannot be explained by a diagnosis of major depression?

A. Weight gain
B. Weight loss
C. Auditory hallucinations
D. Dilated pupils
E. Memory impairment

6. Which of the following is required by the fourth edition of *Diagnostic and Statistical Manual of Mental Disorders* (DSM-IV) for a diagnosis of major depression?

A. Depressed mood
B. Impaired memory
C. A precipitating event
D. Weight loss
E. None of the above

Discussion and Answers

Unlike schizophrenia, there is no characteristic age of onset for depression. A first episode can occur in childhood or in advanced old age. Although this patient's age does not make major depression either more or less likely, it does increase the likelihood of underlying medical conditions that may appear as depression.

Among the most common medical conditions causing depression are endocrinopathies (hypothyroidism, Addison's disease), occult malignancies, and viral infections such as hepatitis, mononucleosis, and HIV infection. Furthermore, depression can be the initial presenting symptom, even before a disease is diagnosed, and not just a psychological reaction to hearing the diagnosis. Other possibilities are metabolic disturbances, such as hypercalcemia and hyperglycemia.

With his history (1 year of mood symptoms without physical symptoms) and his normal physical examination and laboratory studies, it is very unlikely that Mr. A.'s depression is caused by an undetected medical illness. Alzheimer's disease is a preoccupation of his, partly it seems because he is reaching the age when his mother was diagnosed with Alzheimer's. He is said to be undergoing an Alzheimer's workup, but this is somewhat misleading. There are no laboratory tests or neuroimaging studies that can confirm a diagnosis of Alzheimer's; the tests can only rule out other possible causes of dementia, such as hydrocephalus or space-occupying lesions. Alzheimer's disease is a purely clinical diagnosis that can be confirmed only with brain biopsy or postmortem microscopic examination.

Many people with neurodegenerative dementias lose their sense of smell early in the disease course. Testing the first cranial nerve (olfactory) may raise useful questions but by itself will not confirm or refute a diagnosis of Alzheimer's.

Cognitive changes in depression are common and may in fact be more prominent than the mood disturbance. They are referred to as "pseudodementia" and may make diagnosis in older people difficult. In fact, Mr. A. shows no cognitive impairment on mental status testing despite his subjective sense of difficulties. This finding can be followed up with more careful neuropsychological testing.

The diagnosis of depression does not require a precipitating factor. It seems that Mr. A.'s depression is in response to business reverses, but it should be kept in mind that the business troubles may be caused by a growing depression.

The presentation of major depression can be heterogeneous. Although most patients exhibit psychomotor retardation, a subset of patients are agitated. Typical vegetative symptoms include anorexia, weight loss, and insomnia—particularly early morning wakening. Some patients, however, have weight gain and hypersomnia. Psychotic symptoms such as delusions and hallucinations may occur in depression, and when they do, treatment with both an antidepressant and an antipsychotic is indicated. Dilated pupils cannot be explained by a diagnosis of depression.

Mr. A. had been treated with the antipsychotic drug risperidone, a questionable use of the drug, as he had no psychotic symptoms. Paradoxically, the diagnostic criteria of DSM-IV do not require a depressed mood for major depression. The diagnosis can be made if the person experiences marked anhedonia coupled with vegetative symptoms.

1–6. The answers are: 1, E; 2, E (all); 3, E (none); 4, A; 5, D; and 6, E (none).

ALLEN P.

Allen P., a 38-year-old married father of 4, was brought to the hospital emergency room in handcuffs by police after a struggle in front of his hotel. He and his wife had come to New York from his home in Western Europe 4 days earlier. He did not sleep at all the first night in their hotel and on subsequent nights slept only 1 to 2 hours. Despite this he was feeling extremely energetic. As time passed, he became increasingly suspicious, agitated, and euphoric and began to talk about communicating with God. On the day of admission he paid a street artist $7,000 in cash for all of his pictures; Mr. P. insisted that he could sell each one for $200,000 to $300,000 back in Europe. When he returned to his hotel, he and his wife began arguing in the lobby over this purchase. The argument became more heated; Mr. P. was belligerent and aggressive; and the hotel clerk called the police. When they arrived, several officers had to subdue Mr. P. The police report indicated that he was down on all fours on the sidewalk in front of the hotel barking like a dog, but Mr. P. stated that he was merely celebrating and was saying, "Wow, wow, wow!" because he felt so good at the time.

He had been in psychotherapy for 8 years because of episodes of euphoria, diminished need for sleep, pressured speech, spending sprees, and entry into irresponsible business arrangements. He had never been treated with psychotropic medication and had never before been hospitalized.

Mr. P. used neither drugs or alcohol. He was described as always being an energetic, youthful man who needed only 4 to 5 hours of sleep each night. He ran a real estate and construction business back home with his brother and on at least 2 previous occasions had had episodes of sleeplessness and excitement after completing lucrative business deals. He had never had episodes of depression and had never previously been involved with the police. A paternal uncle had been institutionalized for unknown reasons, but there was no other history of family psychiatric problems.

In the emergency room, Mr. P.'s physical examination was unremarkable except for a pulse of 92. He was agitated and in four-point restraints. His speech was pressured, and he was alternately threatening and euphoric. No visual or auditory hallucinations were elicited, but he described himself as "the million-dollar man" whom his clients would pay $20 million an hour. His thinking was marked by loosening of associations and flight of ideas. He was alert and fully oriented, but concentration and memory were poor. Complete blood count; electrolytes; and renal, liver, and thyroid function tests were all within normal limits. Creatine phosphokinase (CPK) was nearly 4,500 and a urine toxicology screen was negative.

Mr. P. was admitted to a psychiatric inpatient service, where he was treated with lithium and perphenazine. After 3 days he remained psychotic and agitated. The antipsychotic drug was switched to chlorpromazine in an effort to sedate him more heavily.

1. Mr. P. complains of persistent insomnia but not of daytime somnolence. The most likely explanation is

A. He is sleeping more than he realizes.
B. He is in the middle of a manic episode.
C. He is using stimulants during the day.
D. He is malingering.
E. None of the above statements are true.

2. The most likely diagnosis in this case is

A. bipolar I disorder
B. bipolar II disorder
C. schizoaffective disorder
D. psychosis due to substance abuse
E. adjustment disorder

3. Mr. P. has a monozygotic twin. The chances that he has the same disorder are

A. 0 percent
B. 5 to 10 percent
C. 10 to 25 percent
D. 25 to 50 percent
E. over 50 percent

Discussion and Answers

Mr. P. is easily diagnosed as being in the middle of a manic episode. With his history and medical evaluation, this disturbance is unlikely to result from drug use or an underlying medical condition. (The elevated CPK on admission to the emergency room was consistent with the physical trauma of his arrest, and indeed the levels had declined to normal by his fifth hospital day.) Manic episodes are distinguished from hypomanic episodes on the basis of severe impairment of social or occupational functioning, the need for hospitalization, or the presence of psychotic symptoms. Mr. P. qualifies on all three counts. Past episodes are less clear. Although he had had similar symptoms, he had never before been hospitalized or treated with medication, and it seems likely that the current episode is the most severe.

A manic episode in the context of a recurrent mood disorder establishes the diagnosis of bipolar I disorder. An episode of major depression is not required for the diagnosis. Bipolar II disorder is characterized by recurrent episodes of major depression and hypomania but never mania. A diagnosis of schizoaffective disorder requires prominent mood symptoms, as Mr. P. demonstrates, but also a period during which there are psychotic symptoms alone.

Lithium is a better prophylaxis against recurrent episodes than an acute treatment, but the prescription of lithium in this case was justified. After a single manic episode, 90 percent of bipolar patients go on to have further episodes.

There is a clear biogenetic substrate to bipolar I. Some 60 to 70 percent of monozygotic twins are concordant for it. Nevertheless, environmental events may trigger episodes. Among the most common are heavy alcohol intake, periods of sleep deprivation, and—as appears to have happened for this patient—rapid travel across several time zones.

1–3. The answers are: 1, B; 2, A; and 3, E.

ANGELA G.

Angela G., a 19-year-old single second-year college student, was brought to the psychiatric hospital by her mother, who stated that her daughter was threatening to jump out of the window of an apartment they shared on the fifth floor of a high-rise building in Manhattan. At age 17, during her last year of high school, the patient developed a nonmalignant tumor that required the removal of her left kidney. She was hospitalized for about 1 month and recalled a doctor telling her that she was going to "die at an early age because she had only one kidney left." She is the youngest of three daughters; the two older sisters have left the parental home and are married. Her mother obtained a divorce when the patient was 10 years old because of her father's alcoholism. At that time her mother returned to work as a teacher.

Until her kidney was removed, the patient described herself as being a happy person who had many friends and who did well at school. She never felt close to her father and was not upset by the divorce, but she did miss her mother when she went to work. After her kidney removal, she began to experience periods of sadness, bouts of crying, and feelings of being unable to enjoy herself. She became preoccupied with the idea that "I am going to die young." She would become upset during these periods and had thoughts of killing herself in her own time rather than waiting for kidney disease to do so. On the day of admission, she stated that the thought of her dying became most intense because she thought she heard her mother's voice telling her to jump out of the window to end her misery.

The major findings on mental status examination were a depressed mood and recurrent thoughts about her early death. She denied that she still wanted to kill herself. Aside from thinking that she heard her mother's voice on that one occasion, she denied hearing voices, seeing things, or having strange experiences that she could not explain.

1. In the DSM-IV scheme, the Axis III diagnosis would be

A. depression
B. schizoaffective disorder
C. psychological problems associated with physical disease
D. kidney disease (unspecified)
E. adjustment disorder

2. The repetitive return of the thought "I am going to die" is an example of

A. compulsion
B. obsession
C. delusion
D. disturbance of affect
E. autistic thinking

3. Which of the following was most predictive of Ms. G.'s developing a depression?

A. The loss of her father before age 12
B. Not feeling close to her father
C. Having a mother who worked
D. Having an alcoholic father
E. The removal of her kidney

Discussion and Answers

This patient is suffering from a major depressive disorder manifested by thoughts of suicide and anhedonia. The episodes began after a medical illness that necessitated the removal of the patient's kidney. Major depression is the preferred diagnosis rather than adjustment disorder with depressed mood because the depression has lasted for a long period.

In DSM-IV, Axis III refers to medical conditions (in this case kidney disease). Axis I includes all mental disorders, and Axis II covers personality disorders. She has an obsessive idea of dying young. Obsessions are repetitive thoughts, whereas compulsions are repetitive behaviors. Hearing her mother's voice telling her to jump out of the window is a psychotic symptom, and one cannot be sure whether it is a prodromal symptom of schizophrenia, which most often occurs at this age. Her relatively intact reality testing (for example, she is not sure that she heard her mother's voice) tends to rule out schizophrenia, although that diagnosis must be considered. The loss of a parent before the age of 12 has been associated with developing a depressive disorder as an adult.

1–3. The answers are: 1, D; 2, B; and 3, A.

ARNIE M.

Arnie M., a 38-year-old administrator, was referred by his internist for psychiatric evaluation. Mr. M. stated his reason for consultation thus: "I know I've got some emotional problems, but it's not all in my head. I can't get anyone to take me seriously."

A year earlier, he had been hospitalized with glomerulonephritis. During his recovery, he believed he heard a doctor say to another doctor just outside his door, "Be careful, he may have AIDS." He felt a sudden wave of great anxiety and began to feel physical sensations in his neck and back which he described as "like nerves being on fire." By the time of discharge, he was certain that he was suffering from a life-threatening illness and was terrified that it would not be discovered until after it had progressed to the point that it could not be treated. He alternately focused on the possibility of cancer or an HIV infection and pursued a series of medical consultations and investigations. He was evaluated by his own internist, an oncologist, a gastroenterologist, a urologist, an orthopedic surgeon, and a rheumatologist. He underwent multiple X-rays, computed tomography (CT) scans, sonograms, a colonoscopy, and a cystoscopy. Except for the finding of stress-related changes in his large bowel, there was no evidence of disease. His white blood cell count was at the low end of the normal range, and an HIV test was negative. Despite the multiple negative findings, he remained convinced that he had either cancer or a human immunodeficiency virus (HIV) infection. He began to have trouble concentrating and had difficulty falling asleep and staying asleep. His appetite declined and he began to lose weight, a fact that strengthened his suspicions that he had cancer. He withdrew from friends, took pleasure in virtually nothing, and contemplated suicide.

Mr. M. said that he had been depressed about 10 years earlier but did not seek treatment, and the depression had eventually lifted. His mother had been treated for major depressions. Throughout grade school and high school, Mr. M. was an unexceptional student, but he excelled in athletics and was popular. He had many girlfriends, and when he graduated, he married a girl he was seeing because he thought he should settle down and have a family. The marriage was troubled from its early days. They moved frequently, and he worked at a variety of jobs but never made as much money as his wife thought necessary. When their daughter was 3 years old, Mr. M. stopped working altogether and spent most of his day sleeping in bed and watching television. When his wife asked for a divorce and full custody of their child, he did not contest it. He moved back to the city where his parents lived and began a civil service job. Several years later, his father died of a coronary occlusion. Mr. M. had an occasional beer but did not use any other recreational drugs. He had been celibate for more than 5 years and had never received a blood transfusion.

He began psychotherapy and treatment with a tricyclic antidepressant. Although he was considerably distressed by the medication's side effects, his mood, appetite, sleep, and energy all improved, and he began going out with friends and playing tennis and basketball.

During the first year of therapy, his conviction that he had an undiagnosed fatal illness waxed and waned but never disappeared. He continued to pursue medical evaluations, including four more HIV tests. Each time, after blood was drawn, he experienced terrible anxiety, depression, and sleeplessness, with the certainty that this time the test would reveal what he suspected. A few days later, when the result was reported negative, he felt tremendous relief. As the weeks passed, however, he began to doubt the accuracy of the test. He would dwell on the possibility that blood samples could have been mixed up, that a laboratory technician could have made a mistake, or that the test itself might not be 100 percent accurate.

Mr. M. was remarkably vigilant about his own body. Minor changes or benign sensations were interpreted as evidence of disease. For example, small differences in skin pigmentation were seen as evidence of Kaposi's sarcoma and therefore acquired immune deficiency syndrome (AIDS). A short bout of diarrhea strengthened his conviction of having stomach cancer.

The tricyclic was eventually stopped because of side effects. In particular, the urinary hesitancy made him worry about prostate cancer. Several additional trials of antidepressants included sertraline, fluoxetine, nefazodone, and venlafaxine, but all either were ineffective or caused troublesome side effects. He agreed to a 6-month moratorium on any additional medical tests.

At the end of 2 years of therapy, Mr. M's appetite, sleep, and concentration were all good. His work was going well, and he had earned a promotion. He remained active in sports but was still convinced of the likelihood of an undiagnosed fatal disease despite the obvious lack of progression of symptoms or disease over the years. He was reluctant to begin dating and said it would be unfair to the woman to begin a relationship and then die shortly afterward. He refused to take medication and eventually dropped out of treatment.

1. The most likely diagnosis for Mr. M. is

A. somatization disorder
B. obsessive-compulsive disorder
C. conversion disorder
D. delusional disorder
E. hypochondriasis

2. The usual clinical course for Mr. M's disorder is

A. full recovery without residual symptoms by middle age
B. chronic, with periodic lessening or intensification of symptoms
C. chronic and episodic with clear functioning between discrete episodes
D. progressive psychosocial deterioration
E. gradual resolution of anxiety and depression but persistence of all physical symptoms

3. The mechanism of symptom production in somatoform disorders is believed to be

A. unconscious
B. conscious but for unconscious reasons (primary gain)
C. conscious and for clearly recognized reasons (secondary gain)
D. wholly biological
E. none of the above

4. Favorable prognostic features for hypochondriasis include

A. slow, insidious onset
B. the presence of secondary gain
C. the presence of a coexisting medical condition
D. the presence of an underlying personality disorder
E. none of the above

Discussion and Answers

Mr. M. is suffering from hypochondriasis, a preoccupation with having a serious undetected illness for which there is no medical justification. As is often described in people with hypochondriasis, he keeps close scrutiny over his body and body functions and has a tendency to misread minor signals as evidence of major disease (for example, diarrhea means stomach cancer). There is almost an obsessive quality to his thinking about illness and his requests for repeated medical workups resemble compulsive behavior. However, a diagnosis of obsessive-compulsive disorder is not made if a person's thoughts and behaviors are limited to health concerns. In somatization disorder, there is a preoccupation with symptoms more than with diagnosis. (There may be overlap between hypochondriasis and somatization disorder, but not for Mr. M.; his disorder easily meets diagnostic criteria for the former but does not have sufficient numbers of symptoms to be diagnosed as the latter.) In conversion disorder, the focus of attention is usually on a single symptom or deficit, and there is often "la belle indifférence," a curious lack of concern or anxiety about even major disabilities such as conversion blindness or paralysis. As is typical, Mr. M.'s conviction of having a fatal illness is not of delusional proportions. He is momentarily reassured by negative tests, only to have doubt recur with the passage of time. DSM-IV now calls for a modifier of hypochondriasis: with or without insight. Those with insight recognize the unreasonableness and irrationality of their worries. Mr. M. does not have insight.

The most common course of hypochondriasis appears to be chronic with periodic lessening or intensification of symptoms. There may be exacerbations of symptoms during times of stress or when friends or loved ones are diagnosed with major illnesses.

The etiology of hypochondriasis is unknown, but there is a general consensus, as with all somatoform disorders, that the symptoms are not consciously feigned or simulated. This fact distinguishes this group of disorders from malingering (conscious for secondary gain) and factitious disorders (conscious but for primary gain).

Mr. M. also appears to have a coexisting major depression. His mood and vegetative symptoms improved with antidepressant therapy, but his health preoccupations persisted. If his health concerns occurred only during periods of depression, he would not be given a diagnosis of hypochondriasis. Favorable prognostic indicators are acute onset, the presence of a coexisting medical condition, the absence of an underlying personality disorder, and the absence of secondary gain. Accordingly, the outlook for Mr. M. is mixed. There is not enough information to assess the presence or absence of a personality disorder, but the onset was acute and there is no obvious secondary gain. Paradoxically, the absence of what he fears most—coexisting medical morbidity—makes his future recovery less certain.

1–4. The answers are: 1, E; 2, B; 3, A; and 4, C.

CHARLES T.

Charles T., a 43-year-old white man, was admitted to a dual diagnosis unit from a residence for recovering substance abusers after 3 weeks of what he described as ''being out of control.'' He had been using increasing amounts of cocaine intranasally and heroin intravenously and had mood swings between depression and irritability. In the week before admission he was able to sleep only 2 to 3 hours each night and felt extreme fatigue and sleep hunger during the day. He had frequent crying spells, and in the days before admission his ability to care for himself had so deteriorated that he would urinate and defecate in his clothes.

He had been hospitalized once before in another city, about a year before the present admission, for mood lability and erratic behavior. He was given the diagnosis of bipolar disorder and dementia. The treatment at that time could not be ascertained, but more recently he had been receiving valproic acid and desipramine at his residence. He had undergone several drug rehabilitation programs in the past, including a period of methadone maintenance, but had returned to cocaine and heroin use shortly after each treatment. The longest period of abstinence in his adult life had been a 10-month stretch the preceding year, when he was living with his girlfriend. Because he did not get along with her family, he eventually had to move out and shortly afterward resumed heavy drug use. His elderly mother intervened and made arrangements for him to move into the therapeutic residence. Mr. T. was found to be HIV positive a year and a half before the present admission. He had had no opportunistic infections and had been compliant with a changing combination of antimicrobial and antiviral medications.

Mr. T. was born and raised in upstate New York. His father was an alcoholic who abused the patient, his mother, and his three sisters. When he was 10, his parents divorced and he had had no contact with his father since. He began using marijuana at age 14 and soon began to use LSD and heroin as well. He dropped out of high school and worked for 10 years as a manual laborer, during which time his drug use was virtually continuous. Eventually he was caught stealing money from his employer to buy drugs and at age 35 was incarcerated for a year. Mr. T. never married.

On admission to the dual diagnosis unit, Mr. T. was cachectic but afebrile. No skin lesions were noticed, and there was no lymphadenopathy. Although he was able to walk heel to toe, he complained of feeling off balance and would often use the wall for support. His speech was halting and at times garbled. He described his mood as ''bad,'' but in fact he appeared quite labile, shifting rapidly from excited optimism to tears and back. His thinking was slow but goal directed. There was no evidence of delusions or hallucinations. Mr. T. was alert and oriented. His immediate and recent recall were good, yet he had trouble remembering past events.

His complete blood count was remarkable for a hemoglobin of 13 and hematocrit of 36.8 but was otherwise normal. His CD4 count was 110. Urine was positive for opioids and cocaine. A computed tomography (CT) head scan revealed decreased attenuation without enhancement noted in the bifrontal white matter. He was given a trail-making test, which he completed slowly and haltingly, taking 3.5 minutes (normal is 2 minutes).

Mr. T. was treated with thioridazine, which quickly improved his sleep. Desipramine was stopped out of concern that anticholinergic side effects might be worsening his mental status. Valproic acid was increased to 1750 mg. Over the next 10 days, his mood lability decreased, but he remained intrusive and drug seeking and otherwise demonstrated poor judgment.

1. The findings that militate against a diagnosis of bipolar disorder are

A. dementia
B. HIV positivity
C. the presence of neurological signs
D. specific CT scan abnormalities
E. all of the above

2. Mr. T.'s mental changes are most likely the result of

A. opioid abuse
B. a manic episode
C. an episode of major depression
D. an adjustment disorder with mixed features
E. HIV encephalitis

3. All of the following are signs and symptoms of heroin intoxication *except*

A. euphoria
B. dilated pupils
C. decreased respiration
D. lethargy
E. decreased libido

Discussion and Answers

There is reason to suspect the earlier diagnosis of bipolar disorder. Mr. T. was also diagnosed as having dementia—an unusual concomitant to bipolar disorder and one that cannot be explained on the basis of that diagnosis. The presence of neurological signs (dysarthria and ataxia) can never be explained solely on the basis of a mood disorder. In addition, fecal incontinence is extremely unusual without neurological impairment. Structural brain abnormalities (as revealed by CT scan) have not been described for bipolar disorders.

In addition, he had already been found to be HIV positive. The most likely diagnosis then as now, based on the mood changes, cognitive impairment, and neurological signs, is HIV encephalitis. The virus is neurotropic as well as lymphotropic and can directly infect brain cells. This condition is not technically an AIDS dementia, as the mental changes are caused by the virus itself and not by opportunistic infections resulting from impaired immune function. Despite a lowered CD4 count, there was no evidence to suggest opportunistic brain infection, an observation supported by the CT scan abnormalities, which are characteristic for HIV encephalitis.

The typical dementia associated with HIV brain infection is subcortical, as opposed to a cortical dementia commonly seen in Alzheimer's disease. In subcortical dementias thinking is slowed but memory loss is often not prominent. In addition there are usually neurological signs, such as the dysarthria and ataxia experienced by Mr. T.

Mr. T. has also clearly established a long-standing pattern of polysubstance dependence. It is quite likely that his drug use exacerbated mood swings and may even have impaired cognitive abilities. The CT finding, however, cannot be explained on the basis of drug use. The course of HIV encephalitis is more rapid and progressive than is acquired immune deficiency syndrome (AIDS), and it often runs a fulminant course from first symptoms to death in 4 to 9 months. Mr. T. is somewhat unusual in surviving well over a year, but his prognosis remains grim.

The clinical picture is different from that of intoxication and withdrawal in heroin use. Intoxication is characterized by lethargy, euphoria, decreased libido, decreased blood pressure and heart rate, pinpoint pupils, and decreased respiration. Withdrawal is associated with arthralgia, malaise, dysphoria, intense drug craving, diarrhea and stomach cramps, dilated pupils, increased blood pressure, yawning, runny nose and eyes, and muscle fasciculations.

CD4 lymphocytes are predominantly helper-inducer cells of the immune system. A decrease in the absolute number of CD4 cells is the most characteristic immune deficit of HIV infection. In this case, the low CD4 count demonstrates HIV-associated immune dysfunction in addition to the encephalitis.

1–3. The answers are: 1, E (all); 2, E; and 3, B.

CHRIS

Chris, a 13-year-old Hispanic boy, was taken to an outpatient clinic because of increasingly disruptive behavior at home. He had been living with his father and stepmother for 5 months after being sent home for a trial period from a residence for emotionally disturbed children. Since his return home, Chris had been disobedient, lied to his parents, and frequently argued with his father. He was in trouble at school; he frequently did not complete homework, and he was receiving bad grades. His parents reported that he was obsessed with pornography and that he would inappropriately caress his stepmother's hair and face. The precipitating event occurred when Chris informed his uncle that he planned to set the living room on fire, using his sister's perfume as an accelerant.

Chris denied or minimized many of the incidents reported by his parents. He did acknowledge getting into trouble at school for not following instructions. He also admitted carrying a knife to school but claimed he only wanted to hold it, not to hurt anyone. He would feel like breaking things or running away from home after getting into arguments with his father. He had stolen from his sister and mother and from local shops. He did not, he stated, really plan to set fire to the living room, but was merely relating the plot of a movie to his uncle.

Chris further described having trouble sitting still, often starting tasks and not completing them. He had trouble concentrating and difficulty sleeping at night, both in falling asleep and staying asleep. He said he often felt sad because of the problems at home, but he denied crying spells, feelings of worthlessness, or suicidal thoughts.

Chris had been hospitalized at age 9 in a children's psychiatric service after he assaulted his infant niece and set a fire in his house. There was no reliable history of cruelty to animals or bed-wetting. Chris suffered asthma as a toddler, requiring multiple hospitalizations and at least three intubations. There was no history of surgery or trauma, and he was not known to be allergic to any drugs. At the time of his clinic visit, he was not taking any medication.

Chris was born at about 6 months' gestation and was in neonatal intensive care for more than 3 months. At the time he was born, his parents were not married. His father enlisted in the army, leaving him in the care of his 16-year-old mother. She developed a relationship with another man and smoked marijuana heavily. Her boyfriend eventually issued an ultimatum that resulted in Chris's being put into foster care at age 2. When his father returned from the army, Chris began living with him full time. His biological mother's maternal rights were terminated by court order.

He now lived with his father, who was a blue collar worker; his stepmother, who was a teacher; and a half-sister about his age. All his developmental milestones were said to be normal, but he was described as always being a restless, fidgety child. He had never been sexually active and had used no drugs, alcohol, or tobacco. He was enrolled in the eighth grade in normal-level classes.

A physical examination, including detailed neurological examination, was within normal limits. Complete blood count, electrolytes, glucose, and tests of thyroid, renal, and liver function were all within normal limits. Chris was well groomed and cooperative in the clinic. He looked younger than 13 and was restless throughout the interview, constantly moving his hands under the table. He exhibited poor eye contact. He said he felt sad and appeared so, although he was never tearful. His thinking was logical and goal directed, and there were no psychotic symptoms. He was alert, oriented, and able to concentrate. He demonstrated good memory and appeared remarkably well informed about current political events.

1. Based on only these data, the diagnosis that can definitively be excluded is

A. major depression
B. conduct disorder
C. antisocial personality disorder
D. bipolar disorder
E. attention-deficit/hyperactivity disorder

2. The main distinction between conduct disorder and oppositional defiant disorder is that conduct disorder

A. is more prevalent in boys than in girls
B. includes argumentativeness, defiance, and hostility
C. can be seen before the age of 10
D. always includes acts that violate fundamental rights of others
E. has a more benign prognosis

3. The most likely cause of the boy's restlessness, fidgeting, impulsivity, and lack of concentration is

A. premature birth
B. low birth weight
C. separation from mother before age 2
D. genetic endowment
E. inconsistent parenting

Discussion and Answers

At least two diagnoses seem warranted in this case. First, Chris's consistent violation of the rights of others justifies the diagnosis of conduct disorder. Because the behavior first occurred before age 10, it would be classified as childhood-onset type. Adolescents with the childhood-onset type are more likely to be physically aggressive and to have disturbed peer relationships than are those with adolescent-onset conduct disorder. They are also more likely to have persistent conduct problems and to have antisocial personality disorder as adults. (The diagnosis of antisocial personality disorder cannot be made before age 18 and is therefore excluded as a diagnosis in this case.) His argumentativeness, hostility, and defiance are typical of oppositional defiant disorder, but his behavior is more severe, including theft and destruction of property. A diagnosis of oppositional defiant disorder is not made if the individual, as in this case, also qualifies for a diagnosis of conduct disorder.

Chris's fidgeting, inattention, impulsivity, and difficulty in following through on tasks make a coexisting diagnosis of attention-deficit/hyperactivity disorder (ADHD) likely. ADHD often coexists with conduct disorder. Indeed, one risk of not treating ADHD is the development of conduct disorder and subsequent antisocial personality disorder.

Another important consideration for this boy's diagnosis is a mood disorder. He is certainly feeling demoralized, and his sadness comes through on the mental status examination. He is having trouble sleeping, which is an important symptom of mood disturbance in adolescents. In addition, the symptoms suggesting ADHD—irritability, talkativeness, hyperactivity, and distractibility—are the most common symptoms of bipolar disorder in very young people. The chronicity and absence of distinct episodes makes ADHD more likely than bipolar disorder, but the mood disorder cannot be ruled out and should be kept in mind, particularly if he does not respond well to standard therapies for ADHD.

The causes of ADHD are unknown and probably multiple. Although Chris had a most unstable early childhood, there is no evidence that this alone causes ADHD. He was also 3 months premature and kept in neonatal intensive care, which raises the possibility of perinatal neurological damage. There are no data from neuropsychological testing; however, the normal neurological examination, his remaining in normal classes at grade level, and evident intelligence on mental status examination suggest no brain damage. The most probable factor in the etiology of ADHD is genetic vulnerability.

1–3. The answers are: 1, C; 2, D; and 3, D.

ELAINE M.

Elaine M., a 55-year-old homeless white woman, was brought to the emergency room of a large city hospital by police after she approached them complaining that an "Aryan group" had placed a tattoo over her left buttock and had planted a device in her right ear that caused her to hear voices. Looking for safety from a "neighborhood watch" group that had been pursuing her for more than 2 years and that was sending her threatening messages through the listening device, she had left her home and had begun living in all-night coffee shops about 6 months earlier. For several years she had been changing residences every few months in an effort to find safety.

She had had a short period of outpatient counseling

24 years earlier, around the time of the breakup of her marriage. She had no previous psychiatric hospitalizations and had never been treated with psychotropic medications. When she was 40 years old she showed up at her father's funeral with a rifle, claiming the FBI was after her.

Ms. M.'s mother and 34-year-old daughter were both known to have received psychiatric treatment. Details of their symptoms or treatments were not available.

Ms M. had graduated from law school and worked as a corporate lawyer for a major national company on the East Coast, then abruptly left her job and moved to the Midwest, where she worked as an attorney for another 7 years before moving back East to take a job as a telemarketer. She claimed to be a moderate social drinker and to smoke 2 packs of cigarettes a day. She did not use any other drugs.

Her physical examination was unremarkable but did reveal a hyperpigmented circular area about a centimeter in diameter over her lower left sacral area. A urine toxicology screen was negative, and complete blood count, electrolytes, glucose, and liver and renal function tests were all within normal limits.

Ms. M. was well groomed and cooperative, and her speech was clear, articulate, and a bit pressured. She described her mood as ''OK'' and appeared euthymic. Although her thinking was generally logical and goal directed, at times she showed evidence of loose associations. During the interview she heard the voices of several people commenting on her actions. She again expressed the belief that she had been targeted by a neighborhood group. She was alert and fully oriented, and her recent and remote memory were unimpaired. Her sensorium was clear.

Ms. M. was treated with a high-potency antipsychotic, but her delusions and hallucinations persisted for several weeks. A biopsy of the sacral skin lesion revealed it to be a benign nevus.

1. The most likely diagnosis for this woman is
   - A. bipolar I disorder
   - B. paranoid personality disorder
   - C. paranoid schizophrenia
   - D. schizoaffective disorder
   - E. paranoid delusional disorder

2. The most typical age of onset for schizophrenia in women is
   - A. midteens
   - B. mid-20s
   - C. mid-30s
   - D. mid-40s
   - E. none, there being no typical age of onset for schizophrenia in women

3. The subtype of schizophrenia that is generally regarded as having the best prognosis is
   - A. paranoid
   - B. catatonic
   - C. disorganized
   - D. undifferentiated
   - E. hebephrenic

Discussion and Answers

In the absence of any suggestion of a medical or substance cause for her symptoms and with no evidence that the patient had significant mood symptoms, it is easy to make the diagnosis of schizophrenia. Similarly, because of her prominent delusions of persecution and threatening auditory hallucinations and because her thinking and behavior are not grossly disorganized, the diagnosis of paranoid subtype is appropriate. Her delusions are not bizarre: they do not violate the laws of the physical universe as we know them. Paranoid delusional disorder also is characterized by nonbizarre delusions, but the long-standing prominent auditory hallucinations preclude this diagnosis. Paranoid personality disorder is a diagnosis describing someone who is chronically suspicious and ready to believe in the malevolent intent of others, but without lasting delusions or hallucinations.

Ms. M. appears to have had a very good premorbid adjustment and a late onset of symptoms. The earliest clear indication of difficulties was at her father's funeral 14 years before her first admission. She would have been about 40 years old at the time—older than the usual age of onset for schizophrenia in woman (early to mid-20s)—but not inconsistent with the diagnosis.

Her declining function from well-paid corporate lawyer to unemployed homelessness is common in schizophrenia, although the paranoid subtype is usually thought to have a better prognosis than do other subtypes.

1–3. The answers are: 1, C; 2, B; and 3, A.

ERNIE F.

Ernie F., a 29-year-old man, was referred to an outpatient psychiatrist for reevaluation of medication. At the time, he was taking a combination of desipramine and thiothixene but continued to have episodic symptoms. Most recently, he had started to become fearful and suspicious and wanted to stay home from work but had been persuaded to continue by his social worker counselor. For the previous 3 weeks he had expressed worry that people at work were talking about him, although he acknowledged that he might be misreading the situation. Over the past week, he had begun to feel depressed and complained of having no appetite, feeling sluggish all of the time, and waking at about 4 or 5 A.M. and not being able to get back to sleep. He was also experiencing orthostatic hypotension and severe urinary retention and constipation following a recent increase in his desipramine.

He had first been hospitalized 4 years earlier for an episode characterized by the belief that other people could read his mind and that his coworkers were plotting to assassinate him. He was diagnosed as having atypical psychosis, treated effectively with an antipsychotic, and discharged.

A year later, several weeks after stopping medication at his doctor's request, he again began to fear going to work; he believed that people could read his mind and that when he walked down the street, people would make derogatory comments about him behind his back, just loud enough so that he could hear. Thiothixene was restarted, and over the next 2 weeks the dose was gradually increased. By the end of the third week, he no longer believed in mind reading but was convinced his coworkers wanted to hurt him (although he stated that they might not actually be plotting to assassinate him). He began to become withdrawn and depressed, with loss of appetite and early morning wakening. He started staying in bed most of the day and was frequently tearful. Four weeks after this episode began, over the Thanksgiving holidays, he attempted suicide by taking all of the thiothixene he had—roughly 60 mg. He was alone in his apartment at the time. When his family called and got no answer, his father went to his apartment and found Mr. F. unconscious. He was rushed to the nearest emergency room and later transferred to the psychiatric service of a teaching hospital. After a month-long stay, he was discharged on thiothixene and desipramine and began weekly counseling sessions with a social worker. In the ensuing month he worked steadily but continued to have mood swings. Because of what they saw as inadequate treatment, his family requested a second opinion for medication management.

Mr. F. grew up in a family with two older brothers. His father was a business executive, and his mother worked full time raising the children and looking after the house. A maternal aunt had made a suicide attempt and was being treated for major depression. A distant relative had been in psychiatric hospitals, but the diagnosis and nature of her illness were unknown.

Mr. F. had always been a shy boy, but he did well in school and graduated from a local college. He began work as a clerk for a small alternative publisher. At the time of evaluation, he was trying to decide whether to accept a promotion. He had a girlfriend whom he saw once or twice a week in a relationship that had been sexual for about a year. He had occasionally smoked marijuana in college, but denied using any drugs or alcohol for at least the past 5 years.

His physical health was good. Apart from urinary retention, constipation, and orthostatic hypotension, he had no physical symptoms. He had never been treated for a major medical illness and had never had surgery.

He appeared timid and apprehensive, and he avoided eye contact. His speech was soft, hesitant, but audible. He said he felt "low," and he looked very downcast; his eyes would frequently fill with tears. He expressed concern about the motives of people at work but said he thought he was wrong about any plot. He experienced no hallucinations. He was alert and fully oriented. His memory was good and sensorium clear. He appeared very insightful about his illness and was able to describe past episodes in detail. He wanted to know the name of his condition so that he could read up on it.

The antidepressant was switched to sertraline, and carbamazepine was added. Thiothixene was continued. Over the ensuing weeks, he experienced a gradual normalization of mood and an increased ability to work productively. About 3 months after the change in medication, he asked to know more about side effects. When told that sertraline could affect sexual functioning, he stated that sex had got better since starting the drug. Previously he had had trouble with reaching orgasm too quickly, sometimes within seconds of intromission. As a result, he had been feeling anxious about sex and often tried to avoid it. Now he described lasting much longer, to the increased satisfaction of both himself and his girlfriend.

1. The most likely diagnosis is

A. schizoaffective disorder
B. schizoid personality disorder
C. major depression with psychotic features
D. schizophrenia
E. delusional disorder

2. His now-treated sexual condition can best be described as

A. sexual aversion disorder
B. male erectile disorder
C. hypoactive sexual desire
D. premature ejaculation
E. male orgasmic disorder

3. The most likely consequence of an untreated overdose of 60 mg thiothixene is

A. sedation
B. neuroleptic malignant syndrome
C. brain damage
D. seizures
E. death

4. Drugs useful in the treatment of schizoaffective disorder include

A. haloperidol
B. valproic acid
C. fluoxetine
D. all of the above
E. none of the above

Discussion and Answers

It is fortunate to have so detailed and precise a history—something that is not always possible in clinical psychiatry. In this case, the history is very important in establishing a diagnosis. A previous episode clearly involved both mood symptoms and psychotic symptoms and at least a 2-week period in the same episode of psychotic symptoms alone. This situation defines schizoaffective disorder. The most recent episode is similar, although Mr. F.'s suspiciousness of coworkers is not delusional (he acknowledges that he may be wrong) and therefore not truly psychotic. Nevertheless, a schizoaffective disorder of the depressed type is the best diagnosis to account for his entire clinical course without postulating two separate, coexisting disorders. Major depression would not have the prominent delusions in the absence of mood symptoms, and conversely schizophrenia would not include such prominent and extended periods of mood symptoms. Schizoid personality disorder is an unlikely diagnosis in light of his social involvements and would not explain either mood or psychotic symptoms. Delusional disorder typically includes only ''nonbizarre'' delusions, that is, those that are physically possible, and also would not be sufficient to explain his depression.

It appears that Mr. F. had also been suffering from a sexual dysfunction, premature ejaculation, which came to light only after its successful—and inadvertent—treatment. Although Mr. F. said he had been avoiding sex, it was because of anxiety associated with premature ejaculation rather than because of loss of desire (hypoactive sexual desire) or disgust (sexual aversion disorder). Male orgasmic disorder describes an inability to achieve orgasm or reaching orgasm only after unacceptably prolonged stimulation. (Decreased desire and prolonged ejaculatory time are common side effects of sertraline and other SSRIs.)

An overdose of 60 mg of thiothixene is not medically serious and is unlikely to cause anything more than sedation and acute extrapyramidal symptoms. Neuroleptic malignant syndrome is a potentially fatal reaction to antipsychotic medication, but its appearance is idiosyncratic and not dose related.

Mr. F.'s previous suicide attempt must be regarded as serious, however. He took all of the medication he had, in a circumstance in which he might easily not have been discovered. There is no reason to suppose that he had sufficient medical knowledge to know the thiothixene overdose was nonlethal. Indeed, if he had taken an equivalent overdose of desipramine (30 pills) instead, he might well have succeeded in taking his life.

The usual pharmacological treatment of schizoaffective disorder is the combination of an antipsychotic, such as haloperidol, and a mood stabilizer, such as lithium, valproic acid, or carbamazepine. An antidepressant, such as fluoxetine, may be added for patients with depressive symptoms.

1–4. The answers are: 1, A; 2, D; 3, A; and 4, D (all).

GEORGE K.

George K., a 43-year-old white man, was admitted to a psychiatric inpatient service with this chief complaint: ''My doctor thought I should come in.'' Mr. K. had been seeing Dr. A. for 10 months for treatment of anxiety symptoms. He was seen twice a week for psychotherapy and was taking lorazepam 1 mg twice a day and 1.5 mg at bedtime with moderate but inconsistent relief. He described feeling grave apprehension in nearly all situations. The severe anxiety varied little in intensity throughout the day or from situation to situation, and it was accompanied by feelings of shortness of breath, heart palpitations, dry mouth, and tremors. Symptoms had been worsening over the previous 6 months. His sleep cycle had reversed so that he was staying up all night, falling asleep about 6:00 A.M., and sleeping until 2:30 P.M. His appetite had increased; his concentration was poor; and he found pleasure in virtually no activities. He had had fleeting suicidal thoughts but denied any current plans; however, he was hopeless about his future and ambivalent about being in the hospital.

Mr. K. had a long psychiatric history with 20 hospitalizations dating from age 18. His initial hospitalization was for panic symptoms resulting from experimentation with LSD. Over the years he was treated with a variety of medications including amitriptyline, phenelzine, protriptyline, lithium, valproic acid, chlorprothixene, molindone, thiothixene, tryptophan, clonazepam, haloperidol, fluphenazine, and risperidone. All medications either did not help or worsened his symptoms. He had also received a course of electroconvulsive therapy in the early 1970s but with no benefit.

Mr. K.'s parents divorced when he was 4 years old, and he was raised by his maternal grandmother. His mother was being treated for ''anxiety''; his father was a compulsive gambler who suffered from depression. Mr. K. had graduated from high school; however, at the time of his hospital admission he had been unemployed for more than 20 years and was living on disability payments. He had been married and divorced (his ex-wife had been hospitalized with a bipolar disorder), and he was now living with his girlfriend. He smoked a pack and a half to two packs of cigarettes a day but did not drink or use other recreational drugs. At the time of his admission, he was a tall, slender man with a regular heart rate of 88 and a blood pressure of 110/84. Deep tendon reflexes were brisk bilaterally. His physical examination was otherwise normal. All laboratory studies, including complete blood count, electrolytes, glucose, thyroid function studies, chest X-ray, and cardiogram, were within normal limits.

He appeared nervous and made poor eye contact. Throughout his initial intake interview he appeared restless and fidgety. His speech was soft, slow, and hesitant. He described his mood as ''terrible,'' and indeed he looked very anxious and uncomfortable. There were no hallucinations or delusions. He was alert and fully oriented. Concentration was impaired, but his memory was good and sensorium otherwise clear.

1. Each of the following medical conditions commonly causes anxiety symptoms *except*

A. hypercalcemia
B. hypoglycemia
C. pulmonary disease
D. hyperthyroidism
E. pheochromocytoma

2. The most likely diagnosis for Mr. K. is

A. agoraphobia
B. schizophrenia
C. panic disorder
D. social phobia
E. generalized anxiety disorder

3. Which of the following decreases the likelihood of a diagnosis of schizophrenia for Mr. K.'s disorder?

A. Age of onset
B. Long-term disability
C. Absence of positive symptoms
D. Presence of anxiety
E. Sleep reversal

4. Which feature of Mr. K's presentation is inconsistent with hyperthyroidism?

A. Anxiety
B. Tachycardia
C. Weight gain
D. Depression
E. Increased deep tendon reflexes

Discussion and Answers

Mr. K. presents a sobering diagnostic and therapeutic challenge. He is suffering from a chronic and disabling condition that has persisted for nearly 25 years and has not responded to medication that included drugs representing every major class of psychotropics: antipsychotics, mood stabilizers, antidepressants, and anxiolytics. Nevertheless, it is most helpful—as with all patients—to begin by attempting to make a diagnosis and to use the diagnosis as a guide to treatment strategy.

There is no evidence of an underlying medical condition causing his symptoms; however, because of the severity and intractability of his disorder, his medical evaluation must be thorough. In addition to hypoglycemia and hyperthyroidism, which have already been investigated, his workup should include all possible medical causes of anxiety, such as pheochromocytoma, hypocalcemia, hypomagnesemia, and pulmonary disease. Hypercalcemia tends to make people lethargic and obtunded. Hyperthyroidism usually results in weight loss rather than weight gain.

It is unlikely that his symptoms result from substance use. Even though he is a heavy smoker, his symptoms and disability cannot be explained on the basis of nicotine alone. Nicotine withdrawal can cause restlessness, dysphoria, insomnia, and weight gain, but Mr. K. has been smoking continuously, and his heart rate is rapid. The heart rate in nicotine withdrawal is usually slowed.

Although Mr. K. has symptoms of both anxiety and depression, the former appear to be much more pronounced. The fact that his anxiety is relatively constant and not situational makes panic disorder, agoraphobia, and specific phobia all unlikely. Although he avoids virtually all work and social situations, the fear of humiliation is not prominent, and avoidance gives no relief from symptoms. Therefore, a diagnosis of generalized anxiety disorder is more appropriate than one of a social phobia.

The age of onset, chronicity, and progressive impairment raise the possibility of schizophrenia, a possibility that may have occurred to other clinicians, as he had received trials of antipsychotics in the past. His withdrawal, anhedonia, and lack of drive motivation appear similar to negative symptoms of schizophrenia. He has never had positive symptoms, however, and DSM-IV does not permit a diagnosis of schizophrenia without positive symptoms at least some of the time. Some researchers have proposed inclusion of ''negative'' or ''deficit'' schizophrenia (marked negative symptoms, few or no positive symptoms), but his marriage and then later live-in girlfriend argue against that possibility.

Treatments for generalized anxiety disorders are remarkably heterogeneous. Because Mr. K. gets some relief from lorazepam, it is sensible to continue it, possibly at a higher dose. It is also worth considering trials of treatment approaches he seems not to have had: behavioral therapy, biofeedback, meditation, exercise.

1–4. The answers are: 1, A; 2, E; 3, C; and 4, C.

GORDON G.

Gordon G., a 48-year-old man, came to the emergency room of a Veterans Administration (VA) hospital and stated: ''I've been so depressed lately, I tried to jump in the East River last night.'' He described being depressed for at least 3 months, feeling empty and worthless, and crying several times each day. He said that he had no interest or pleasure in anything life had to offer. He reported a 10-pound weight loss over the past 3 months and trouble sleeping at night because of nightmares. The night before he came to the emergency room he had given away his bankbook and went to the East River with the intention of jumping in and holding his breath until he drowned. He was stopped by a homeless man, who noticed that Mr. G. was carrying a VA identification card and persuaded him to go to the emergency room for help.

The patient had served in Vietnam in the infantry. He reported having killed more than 200 men, women, and children while he was there. Ever since his return to the United States from Vietnam, he has had almost nightly nightmares consisting of various experiences about Vietnam and the people he killed. He also has had daytime flashbacks in which he saw Asian people or heard a helicopter overhead, and as much as possible he avoided situations in which he might be exposed to these experiences. He further described a constant hypervigilance, visually surveying a room before entering and keeping his eyes on everyone in the room. The nightmares, flashbacks, and vigilance have all worsened with time.

He first consulted a psychiatrist 4 years earlier. He had become estranged from his family because he feared that flashbacks and nightmares might lead him to hurt someone in his family. He was enrolled in group therapy and for a month his symptoms decreased; then he stopped going after 5 weeks, and claimed that listening to other people's stories was making him feel worse. After he left the group, his nightmares and hyperarousal worsened to the point that he was unable to sleep; 3 years ago he was admitted to a psychiatric hospital with anhedonia, depressed mood, and decreased sleep and appetite. He was treated with fluoxetine and discharged after 3 weeks with the depression lifted and the nightmares less frequent. A few weeks after discharge, however, the nightmares abruptly returned. He became discouraged, stopped seeing his psychiatrist, and threw away his medications. Leaving his apartment and all his possessions, he told friends he was going away for a long time. He moved to New York City, where he lived on the streets for 3 months. The week before he attempted to jump in the East River, he had bought and used $40 worth of cocaine in a suicide attempt, having heard that using that much cocaine would cause a heart attack.

Mr. G. smoked one to two packs of cigarettes each day and reported social alcohol drinking throughout his life. He had used heroin in Vietnam but not since his return to the United States. There was no family history of psychiatric illness. His father died in a fire in 1976. His mother and six sisters were all alive and well and living in another state.

Mr. G. recalled a warm, happy childhood. He had many friends, played baseball, was active in tutoring fellow students at high school, and worked part time as a cashier in a local department store. After graduating from high school, he was drafted into the army and served as a squadron leader in Vietnam. He did exceptionally well and was appointed a White House honor guard for 2 years. He then worked in the Office of Transportation in Washington and in a nuclear storage facility in Germany. When he heard of his father's death in 1976, he retired from the army with an honorable discharge. He then held a variety of jobs including security guard, short-order cook, and laborer for a moving company.

He met his wife and was married in 1969. He described their life as happy but stressful because of the constant nightmares. They had three boys and a girl. One son was killed in a drive-by shooting. Another died of human immunodeficiency virus (HIV) infection a few years before Mr. G.'s admission.

About 5 years ago Mr. G. woke up in the morning, left his family, and has not talked to them since. Embarrassed by his symptoms and worried for his family's safety, he felt that they would be better off without him. A physical examination and basic laboratory tests revealed no abnormalities.

During his admitting interview, Mr. G. sat very still and made no eye contact. He was cooperative and spoke slowly at low volume but clearly. He looked sad and said of himself, "I have nothing to live for. I don't remember the last time I was happy." His thinking was logical and goal oriented. He experienced no hallucinations and there was no suggestion of delusional thinking. He was alert without fluctuations and fully oriented. Concentration and memory appeared unimpaired.

1. The two most likely diagnoses for Mr. G. are major depression and

A. dissociative fugue
B. borderline personality disorder
C. adjustment disorder with mixed features
D. psychotic disorder not otherwise specified
E. posttraumatic stress disorder

2. A necessary precondition to the development of posttraumatic stress disorder as an adult after exposure to a trauma is

A. social isolation
B. a personality disorder
C. early childhood trauma
D. preexisting psychiatric disorder
E. nothing; there is no precondition to the development of posttraumatic stress disorder

3. A diagnosis of posttraumatic stress disorder cannot be made if the symptoms first occur

A. more than 3 months after the traumatic event
B. more than 1 year after the traumatic event
C. more than 5 years after the traumatic event
D. more than 10 years after the traumatic event
E. none of the above; there is no upper time limit

4. Each of the following medications may be useful in the treatment of Mr. G.'s disorder *except*

A. fluoxetine
B. propranolol
C. haloperidol
D. clonidine
E. alprazolam

Discussion and Answers

Mr. G. warrants two concurrent Axis I diagnoses: major depression (mood disturbance, anhedonia, weight loss, insomnia, and hopelessness) and posttraumatic stress disorder (nightmares, flashbacks, hypervigilance, and avoidance). By definition, posttraumatic stress disorder occurs in response to a severe trauma that presents the threat of death, physical injury, or a threat to physical integrity. In addition to military combat in war, as was the case for Mr. G., precipitants of posttraumatic stress disorder include natural disasters such as earthquakes, airline accidents, sexual assaults, attempted murder, and other equally severe traumas. (Individuals who suffer the symptoms of posttraumatic stress disorder in response to more benign events, such as being sharply criticized by one's boss, are diagnosed as having an adjustment disorder.)

Although workers formerly believed that the severity of symptoms of posttraumatic stress disorder varied directly with the severity of the traumatic event, empirical studies have now shown this not to be the case. Rather, symptom severity appears to be influenced by the meaning or psychological impact of the event. There is some evidence to suggest that the development of posttraumatic stress disorder is influenced by personality factors, an absence of social supports, adverse childhood experiences, or preexisting psychiatric disorders. None of these are necessary, however; there is no precondition to the development of posttraumatic stress disorder. Such appears to be the case with Mr. G., whose personal history describes a happy, well-integrated childhood. He was doing well enough in his career to be named a White House honor guard and was married with children. There was no evidence of a family psychiatric history.

Although Mr. G. used heroin in Vietnam, he stopped completely when he returned to the United States. This experience was commonly reported by combatants in the Vietnam War and is a helpful reminder that the addictiveness of a drug may be influenced as much by the setting in which it is used and the user's expectations as it is by the actual pharmacological properties of the drug.

The course of posttraumatic stress disorder is variable, as was true for Mr. G. The onset of symptoms commonly begins within 3 months of exposure to the trauma but may be delayed for many years. There is no upper time limit after which the diagnosis cannot be made. Symptoms may vary in intensity over a person's life and may be intensified by additional stressful events. Even though Mr. G. suffered nightmares and flashbacks almost immediately after leaving Vietnam, the impact of his symptoms was moderate and he was able to function very well until several years later. The death of his father in a fire and the loss of two sons—one in a drive-by shooting and the other from an HIV infection—coincided with his progressive inability to function. It is tempting to speculate that this succession of traumatic events progressively overwhelmed his capacity to adapt. His leaving his family, giving away his money, and attempting suicide are extreme but not unheard of reactions in posttraumatic stress disorder. Because he retained full memory of leaving his family and was aware throughout of the reasons for doing so, the episode cannot be considered a fugue state.

The core treatment for posttraumatic stress disorder is psychotherapy. Group therapy with some posttraumatic stress disorder patients has been shown to be particularly helpful, probably because it simultaneously provides a forum for talking about the trauma and a supportive social group. Adjunctive therapy with antidepressants, anxiolytics, or hypnotics may also be useful in selected individual cases. (Clonidine is an α_2 agonist. Because the α_2 receptor is a presynaptic autoreceptor, the net effect is to decrease α-adrenergic transmission. Propranolol is an α-adrenergic antagonist.) There are no controlled data to show the effectiveness of antipsychotic drugs, e.g., haloperidol, in posttraumatic stress disorder. Although the flashbacks of posttraumatic stress disorder may be vivid and emotionally intense, they are qualitatively different from hallucinations, and patients usually are able to recognize them for what they are.

Mr. G. had an abbreviated trial of group therapy and the SSRI fluoxetine. Despite some initial benefit, he became discouraged and stopped treatment prematurely. He might be helped with a determined pharmacological effort to control anxiety and depression. He might also be able to tolerate group therapy if he is taught some basic behavioral exercises to control anxiety, to decrease his intense response to flashbacks, to soften his hypervigilance, and to curtail his avoidant behavior. If a reconciliation with his family were possible, it might provide the emotional and social support to continue with treatment.

1–4. The answers are: 1, E; 2, E; 3, E, and 4, C.

GRACE M.

Grace M. is a 62-year-old woman whose daughter took her to the emergency room of a hospital because of her worsening depression and recent thoughts of suicide. About a month earlier she had begun feeling increasingly depressed and lonely. Around that time, her family noticed an increase in the amount of alcohol she drank; they reported it to be as high as five or six 22-oz. beers per day. Her daughter had found her drunk several times, and Mrs. M. had threatened to throw herself out of the window, although no attempt was reported. During this period, Mrs. M stated that she was sleeping less, but her sleep was not interrupted. She had experienced no loss of appetite or weight loss, but she did say that she was not able to enjoy things.

Her depression went back 20 years, to her divorce from her first and only husband. At the time of her divorce, she lost her house and stopped working. Since then she had not had a stable place to live but moved back and forth between her mother's house and each of her two daughters' houses. She began drinking about 5 years earlier, with an increase about a year ago and another increase over the past month. She was not known ever to have suffered seizures or withdrawal symptoms, and she was never arrested for driving while intoxicated. She did not use tobacco or any other recreational drugs. She had never seen a psychiatrist before or previously received any kind of psychiatric treatment.

About 5 months ago she began having nosebleeds, with about three episodes per week, each lasting 10 minutes. She had no other medical symptoms and was taking no medication.

The patient's immediate family consisted of her mother (91 years old) and her two daughters. She had five grandchildren and one great-grandchild. Her older daughter underwent detoxification for polysubstance abuse (alcohol and cocaine) 2 years ago. There was no other family psychiatric history.

The patient was born and grew up in the city in which she lived. She graduated from high school and worked for a time as a hairdresser. Since her divorce 20 years ago, she has not worked at all but supported herself on social security income and money given her by her daughters. Her daily routine consisted mostly of homebound activities. Although fully mobile, she did not go out of the house much. Her main enjoyment in life was spending time with her grandchildren. She stated that it was thoughts of her grandchildren that kept her from killing herself.

Physical examination revealed normal vital signs. She had a left-sided cataract. Her liver was not palpable and was percussed to an estimated length of 7 cm. All cranial nerves were intact. Motor tone and strength were normal in all groups. Sensory testing for two-point discrimination and sharp-dull distinction were normal. Her gait was unsteady, with short steps and arms stretched to either side for support. There was no asterixis.

Her hemogram showed a platelet count of 80 but was otherwise normal. Prothrombin time (PT) was elevated at 16.8. Aspartate aminotransferase (AST), lactate dehydrogenase (LDH), and total bilirubin were all elevated. Electrolyte, blood urea nitrogen (BUN), creatinine, random glucose, and amylase levels were all normal.

There was a distinct odor of alcohol on her breath.

She was judged to be acutely intoxicated and was admitted for detoxification with a chlordiazepoxide taper. A full mental status examination was performed at the end of the first week of hospitalization. She had no abnormal movements and her speech was not slurred. She described her mood as "tired," and she appeared depressed without lability. There were no delusions or hallucinations. She had no thoughts of suicide at the time of the interview, and in discussing past suicidal thoughts, she said, "It just happened." She was alert without fluctuations and fully oriented. Her concentration appeared impaired, and she was unable to spell simple five-letter words backward. She had difficulty performing simple calculations. Her memory of the past was intact, but both recent recall and immediate recall were impaired. Her fund of knowledge was adequate, but her ability to abstract was limited. She appeared to have little insight into the effects of alcohol on her symptoms and repeatedly dismissed her drinking as "not a problem."

1. Mrs. M's mood symptoms can best be explained by a diagnosis of

A. major depression, chronic
B. depressive personality disorder
C. alcohol-related mood disorder
D. dysthymia
E. mood disorder caused by a general medical condition (liver failure)

2. The primary distinction between alcohol abuse and alcohol dependence is

A. the amount of alcohol drunk
B. the degree of functional impairment at work or school
C. evidence of tolerance, withdrawal, or compulsive behavior related to alcohol use
D. the presence of alcohol-related medical problems
E. all of the above

3. The least likely explanation for her cognitive changes is

A. Alzheimer's disease
B. Wernicke's encephalopathy
C. Mood disorder
D. benzodiazepine intoxication
E. alcohol-induced dementia

4. Appropriate pharmacotherapy for this woman might include

A. sertraline
B. carbamazepine
C. lithium
D. haloperidol
E. phenelzine

Discussion and Answers

Mrs. M. has two separate but related problems: her mood disturbance and her drinking. Depression can be caused by chronic heavy drinking, but the reverse may also be true. Patients with an underlying depression may self-medicate with alcohol, and it is often difficult to distinguish the two. In the case of Mrs. M., it appears that her mood disturbance long preceded her drinking and that she is therefore likely to have an underlying depression not caused by alcohol. Although the physical examination and laboratory tests show evidence of liver disease, she does not appear to be in liver failure (no jaundice, no asterixis), and her 20-year history makes depression due to any general medical condition unlikely. The distinction between major depression and dysthymia may be difficult, particularly if the history is unreliable or inadequate. In general, dysthymia is chronic, with less-intense symptoms; major depression is more likely to be episodic with more-severe mood and vegetative symptoms. It is possible for major depression to be chronic. Ms. M. meets DSM-IV diagnostic criteria for dysthymia but not for chronic major depression. She still gets pleasure from her grandchildren, and she is not pervasively depressed and tearful. (There is no DSM-IV diagnosis of depressive personality disorder.)

The seriousness of Mrs. M's drinking is underscored by evidence of liver disease (elevated AST, LDH, and total bilirubin and decreased liver size as determined by percussion) and platelet dysfunction, both of which may be alcohol related. The epistaxis may be caused by platelet dysfunction. Both liver and platelets should be further evaluated. It is difficult to assess the impact of drinking on her life because she has been living so marginally. She was without work, a steady income, or fixed abode years before she is said to have begun drinking. The distinction between alcohol abuse and alcohol dependence is determined by the evidence of tolerance, withdrawal, or compulsive behavior related to alcohol, for example hiding full bottles around the house to protect against running out. Abuse and dependence are not distinguished by the amount of alcohol drunk, the seriousness of functional impairment, or alcohol-related medical problems. Although Ms. M's drinking history is sketchy, there is a likelihood of tolerance with her increase in drinking a year ago and then again a month ago. Accordingly, the diagnosis of alcohol dependence (in addition to dysthymia) is justified. It should be noted that a diagnosis of substance dependence can be made without tolerance or withdrawal, if there is compulsive behavior.

She was intoxicated on admission and was detoxified with progressively lower doses of chlordiazepoxide. Benzodiazepines are cross-tolerant with alcohol; they block signs and symptoms of withdrawal. In addition, chlordiazepoxide has a much longer half-life than does alcohol and serves to attenuate withdrawal symptoms. Not all clinicians or substance abuse units would immediately begin detoxification. Some would monitor vital signs and start the regimen only if evidence of instability occurs.

It is difficult with only the information at hand to know the cause or causes of her cognitive changes: impaired concentration and calculations, poor recent and immediate memory. Alcohol, depression, and benzodiazepine drugs (from her detoxification) can all cause some degree of cognitive impairment. Less likely but still possible is a separate, unrelated condition such as early Alzheimer's. The cause is most unlikely to be Wernicke's encephalopathy—a delirium that by definition must include an altered level of consciousness. She is fully alert without fluctuations.

Treatment must address both her drinking and her depression. Treatment of dysthymia may lessen the need to drink. Serotonin-specific reuptake inhibitors, such as sertraline (Zoloft), are recognized as effective in treating both dysthymia and major depression. Because they are metabolized in the liver, the dosage may have to be less than standard. There is nothing to suggest the need for either an antipsychotic or a mood stabilizer. Moreover, carbamazepine is potentially hepatotoxic and should be avoided for that reason. The addictive potential of benzodiazepines makes them a poor choice for this alcoholic woman. Buspirone is a nonaddictive alternative anxiolytic. Monoamine oxidase inhibitors are not indicated for people with cognitive impairments because of uncertain compliance with the necessary diet restrictions.

1–4. The answers are: 1, D; 2, C; 3, B; and 4, A.

HARRIET W.

Harriet W., a 42-year-old secretary, was brought to the emergency room of a large city hospital in handcuffs. The police had been called to her office after she became loud and argumentative and threatened a coworker. Ms. W. stated that the coworker was really someone in disguise who wanted to harm her. Other people in the office wore masks and pretended to be someone else, including one of her bosses, who harassed her in the office and followed her home. She described how she would say something out loud in her apartment and later have it repeated to her by a stranger on the street. She heard information about her private life projected from a hidden electronic device in the office where she worked. In addition, the device would sometimes announce, "We molest! We molest!" She had first noticed the broadcasts about 6 months earlier and had filed a report about them.

She denied any substance abuse or use of prescription medications. She did say, however, that she had had an alcohol problem in her 20s but that she had gone to Alcoholics Anonymous and been sober for the past 15 years. Appetite and sleep were both described as good, with no recent changes. She had never previously been hospitalized or had taken psychiatric medication.

Her physical examination was normal. There was no evidence of substance intoxication or withdrawal and no evidence of neurological disease. Laboratory tests, including a complete blood count, electrolytes, glucose, and renal, thyroid, and liver functions were all reported to be within normal limits.

Ms. W. was agitated when she was first brought to the emergency room, but after her handcuffs were removed, she quickly became calmer. She was wearing conservative business clothes and was well groomed. She appeared to be cooperative but became edgy when slightly stressed, for example when asked to clarify something she had said. Her speech was normal in rate and volume, and she was articulate. She described her mood as "fine" but appeared blunted. Her thinking was logical and goal directed. Delusions of doubles, thought broadcasting, and persecution were present. She denied any suicidal or homicidal thoughts and was not hallucinating at the time of the interview. She was fully oriented and alert, without fluctuations in consciousness. Cognitive functions were intact. Her vocabulary was large, and she seemed quite intelligent. Her insight and judgment were poor. She insisted that threatening her coworker was the right thing to do to make him reveal his true identity.

1. The symptom of believing that familiar people have been replaced by impostors is called

A. Cotard's syndrome
B. autoscopic psychosis
C. Capgras's syndrome
D. folie à deux
E. koro

2. This phenomenon may be seen in

A. schizophrenia
B. delusional disorder
C. brain lesions
D. all of the above
E. none of the above

3. The most likely diagnosis for Ms. W. is

A. paranoid schizophrenia
B. disorganized schizophrenia
C. delusional disorder
D. schizoid personality disorder
E. atypical psychotic disorder

Discussion and Answers

The belief that certain well-known individuals have been replaced by impostors is called Capgras's syndrome after the French psychiatrist Jean Marie Joseph Capgras, who first described it in 1923.

Capgras's syndrome is not listed as a separate diagnostic entity in DSM-IV, and it may occur in several different conditions, particularly schizophrenia, delusional disorder, and certain brain lesions. The delusion of doubles has been described in people with damage to the area of the association cortex in the brain which links perception with recognition. Patients who have this delusion and no other psychiatric symptoms should receive a thorough neurological workup, including appropriate imaging studies. If there is no evidence of brain disease or injury, the condition may be diagnosed as a delusional disorder.

In many patients, however, the delusion of impostors is part of a larger symptom complex. This is true of Ms. W., who also manifests paranoid delusions (being harassed by her coworker), thought broadcasting, and very probably auditory hallucinations (a hidden electronic device broadcasting "We molest"). This set of symptoms is best explained by a diagnosis of paranoid schizophrenia. From the information provided in the history, it is difficult to know the cause and duration of her illness. It appears to be at least several months old, and she may have had symptoms for many years. She has held her current position for only 2 years, and without details about her work history, it is impossible to know whether and to what extent her functioning over time may have been impaired. Paranoid schizophrenia is believed to have the best prognosis of all subtypes, and the long-term outcome of schizophrenia is usually more benign among women than men. As with other psychotic symptoms, Capgras's syndrome occurring in schizophrenia responds well to antipsychotic medication.

1–3. The answers are: 1, C; 2, D; and 3, A.

IRIS M.

Iris M., a 23-year-old woman, was taken by police to the emergency room of a large city hospital after she was arrested for shoplifting. She stated repeatedly that she was going to kill herself, and the police were concerned that she might not be well enough to face arraignment. She had been seen in the same emergency room under similar circumstances 3 weeks earlier. At that time, she gave a history of long-standing polysubstance abuse and asked for help with her drug habits. She was given a referral to a clinic but she never went and claimed to have lost the referral slip. There was no other known psychiatric history, and no information about her family or personal life was provided.

In the emergency room she complained of nausea, stomachaches, and diffuse muscle cramps. Her physical examination revealed a blood pressure of 145/95 and heart rate of 90. She was afebrile but diffusely diaphoretic. Her pupils were widely dilated; her eyes and nose were running, and she yawned repeatedly. On mental status examination, she complained of depression and anxiety, but hallucinations were not elicited, and she had no homicidal thoughts. There was no evidence of delusional thinking or of a formal thought disorder. She was alert and oriented to time, place, person, and situation. She was treated with 10 mg of methadone. Within half an hour her signs and most symptoms had subsided, although she was still threatening to kill herself. It was determined by the emergency room psychiatrist that she was able to face arraignment, and she was returned to police custody with an order to keep her on a one-to-one suicide watch.

1. What substance-related disorder is most likely to cause a clinical picture similar to the one seen in this young woman?

A. Heroin intoxication
B. Heroin withdrawal
C. Amphetamine intoxication
D. Amphetamine withdrawal
E. Phencyclidine intoxication

2. How useful would a urine toxicology screen be in this case?

A. A positive test would confirm the diagnosis; a negative test would rule it out.
B. A negative test would confirm the diagnosis; a positive test would rule it out.
C. A positive test would confirm the diagnosis; a negative test would neither confirm nor rule out the diagnosis.
D. A negative test would confirm the diagnosis; a positive test would neither confirm nor rule out the diagnosis.
E. None of the above statements are correct.

3. The most likely underlying psychiatric disorder is

A. major depression
B. histrionic personality disorder
C. antisocial personality disorder
D. dysthymia
E. none of the above

Discussion and Answers

This woman presents with classical features of opioid withdrawal: dilated pupils, rhinorrhea and lacrimation, increased blood pressure and heart rate, yawning, diffuse myalgias, nausea, and stomach cramps. No other medical or psychiatric condition causes this distinctive constellation of signs and symptoms. The diagnostic impression of opioid withdrawal was confirmed by her quick response to methadone. The clinical picture was so unambiguous that it is not necessary to request a urine toxicology screen. Moreover, the value of such a screen would be limited. By definition, her syndrome is the result of not having an opioid in her body after having become dependent. Depending on the time of her last use and the particular opioid, her urine might or might not be positive for opioid; a negative toxicology screen would not rule out opioid withdrawal.

Because of her substance use, it is impossible to assess her mood disturbance. Withdrawal often results in dysphoria, and her statements about wanting to kill herself may have been a reaction to having been arrested. Nevertheless, the treating psychiatrist was correct in taking her seriously and advising that she be kept on a suicide watch as she was returned to face arraignment. There is not sufficient information to make the diagnosis of a personality disorder or to exclude the possibility. The assessment of a personality disorder requires information about a person's functioning over an extended period of time and in a variety of circumstances.

1–3. The answers are: 1, B; 2, E; and 3, E.

JIMMIE K.

Jimmie K., a 38-year-old single African-American man, was taken to the medical emergency room of a large city hospital from the shelter where he had been staying with a complaint of "pain in my hand and my stomach." He had been in the city for only 3 weeks, having come by bus from a nearby city following his discharge from a psychiatric hospital. When asked the reasons for his move, he answered that he needed "food, toiletries, clothing, and a new environment." He was able to give only limited information about his health, but old hospital records revealed 6 hospitalizations over the past 11 years. He was diagnosed with atypical psychosis on the first admission and chronic undifferentiated schizophrenia on subsequent admissions. Each time he was treated with haloperidol, with marked reduction of psychotic symptoms. Noncompliance after discharge led to relapse and rehospitalization.

Mr. K. said he had a history of problems with his stomach but could not provide details of the illness or diagnosis. He had been encouraged to have surgery, but he had refused the procedure. He had also had swollen glands in his neck which his doctor wanted to biopsy, but he refused, and the swelling eventually subsided. He had undergone a biopsy for skin lesions but did not know the results or purpose of the biopsy.

Information from the old records indicated that his mother and half-brother (now deceased) were both diagnosed with schizophrenia. Mr. K. completed eleventh grade before leaving school to work. He eventually earned a high school equivalency diploma. His mother worked as a housekeeper. He worked as a janitor from age 19 to 27 and stopped because of what he said were sleep disturbances.

He was admitted to a medical–psychiatry service for management of psychiatric symptoms and workup of his stomach pains. All vital signs were stable. His physical examination revealed multiple scattered hyperpigmented macules with waxy tops, mainly on upper extremities, with lesser involvement of his thorax and lower extremities. No lymphadenopathy was detected. A fullness of his left flank was appreciated, and liver and spleen were both palpable below the costal margin. No abnormalities were detected on neurological examination. Thyroid function and renal function tests were normal, and rapid plasma reagin (RPR) was nonreactive. Abnormal test results included the following:

- Chest X-ray: bilateral hilar lymphadenopathy
- Echocardiogram: severe left ventricular hypokinesis, mild left atrial dilation, moderate left ventricular dilation
- Abdominal ultrasound: enlarged spleen; 2-cm periportal lymph node; no evidence of intrahepatic or extrahepatic biliary obstruction
- Liver function tests: markedly elevated alkaline phosphatase; mildly elevated total protein, total and direct bilirubin
- Complete blood count: low white blood cells (2.3) with eosinophilia (6 percent)
- Angiotensin converting enzyme (ACE): marked elevation (342)
- Erythrocyte sedimentation rate (ESR): mild elevation (11)
- Skin biopsy: noncaseating granulomas

On psychiatric examination, Jimmie K. appeared withdrawn, with a blunted emotional expression. Thoughts were incoherent, with few full sentences. There was marked derailment; answers seemed to come at random. He was vaguely paranoid but not clearly delusional. He denied hearing voices. He was awake, alert, and oriented to person and situation but not to place, time, day of week, date, or year. His concentration was poor, ability to think abstractly limited, and fund of knowledge appropriate. He could perform simple calculations, and recent and immediate recall were good.

Haloperidol was reinstated. After a week, he more easily engaged in conversation, and his mood became less constricted, with occasional smiles. His thinking was more rational, and he began to interact more with other patients.

1. The most likely medical diagnosis for Jimmie K. is

A. chronic active hepatitis
B. sarcoidosis
C. AIDS
D. sickle cell crisis
E. hepatic cirrhosis secondary to substance abuse

2. The most likely psychiatric diagnosis is

A. schizophrenia
B. HIV encephalitis
C. psychosis secondary to an underlying medical condition
D. polysubstance abuse
E. malingering

3. Complications of long-term corticosteroid therapy can include

A. paranoid delusions
B. emotional lability
C. hallucinations
D. disorientation
E. all of the above

Discussion and Answers

Jimmie K's physical symptoms and the findings on physical examination and laboratory testing are most consistent with a diagnosis of sarcoidosis, particularly because of the skin lesions and biopsy and the elevated ACE. His enlarged spleen, abnormalities seen on the echocardiogram, and liver abnormalities suggest multisystem involvement.

Psychiatric symptoms in a patient with multisystem sarcoidosis raise the prospect of central nervous system (CNS) involvement. Common manifestations of sarcoidosis of the nervous system include peripheral neuropathies, cranial nerve involvement (especially V), dementia, mood lability resembling rapid-cycling bipolar disorder, and psychotic symptoms. For Mr. K., with his long-standing history of psychotic symptoms responding to haloperidol, relapse when off medication, a family history of schizophrenia, social withdrawal, progressive functional deterioration, and current disorganized behavior, the most likely diagnosis is schizophrenia. The long clinical course, the absence of mood or memory disturbance, and a normal neurological examination argue against CNS sarcoidosis. Further investigations could include a computed tomography scan, magnetic resonance imaging, and lumbar puncture.

A finding of CSF pleocytosis with increased protein would suggest sarcoid meningitis.

The mainstay of treatment for sarcoidosis is corticosteroids. Management is complicated by the fact that steroids can cause psychiatric side effects resembling those caused by the underlying disease. Emotional lability and paranoid delusions are common consequences of long-term steroid treatment. Other possible side effects include hallucinations, increased aggressiveness, hypomania, and a confusional state with disorientation. Psychotic symptoms caused by steroids respond to standard antipsychotic medication.

1–3. The answers are: 1, B; 2, A; and 3, E (all).

JOHN S.

John S. is a 39-year-old self-employed businessperson who is married and has two children. He drove himself to the emergency room of a suburban hospital and complained in an agitated state: ''I can't put my wife and kids through this torture anymore! I've got to get help.''

Mr. S. has a 20-year history of symptoms. The course had been fluctuating, but over the past 2 years his symptoms became increasingly severe, intrusive, and time consuming. For example, 2 weeks ago, while drinking from a cup, he accidentally bit the edge of the cup. Feeling that he had to keep repeating the drinking gesture until he got it just right, he put the cup to his lips and then removed it for the next 10 hours. The doubt about drinking correctly and subsequent repetitive ritual persisted over the next 2 weeks. He developed other strange patterns of behavior that involved walking, crossing a threshold, sitting down, and hanging up the phone. He was occupied with the rituals virtually every waking hour of the day; in the past several years these rituals paralyzed him and his family and completely disrupted social and business life. He stated, ''I know it's absurd, but I just can't help it.'' Finally, on the day of his admission, he felt such anxiety that he drove himself to the emergency room of the nearest hospital, a 5-mile trip that took 3 hours because of his compulsive checking.

Mr. S. also experienced some fears of contamination, which he relieved with hand-washing (at least 30 minutes) and avoidance. Recurrent thoughts that some harm will come to his family were overcome by immediately thinking or saying aloud, ''Everything is all right.'' He also looked at or touched something that was a ''good color'' (white or gray—red and black were ''bad'') for relief. Counting (multiples of 3) also reduced his stress. He denied intrusive sexual thoughts. He described himself as being anxious or agitated all of the time, but insisted he was not depressed, merely sad.

Mr. S. no longer engaged in favorite hobbies such as working on cars because the rituals surrounding such activities were too time consuming and frustrating. He had lost 30 pounds during the previous 6 months because of rituals interfering with eating. He slept well but was restless and anxious when awake. He denied hopelessness or thoughts of suicide, saying, ''I have too much to live for—my family and my health.'' He had never had hallucinations or delusions, and he did not use alcohol or drugs of any kind.

Mr. S.'s first symptoms occurred in his early 20s, when after a near accident, he began to have the recurrent thought that he had run someone over. He began to check and recheck his tires as well as have his wife call the police to verify that no pedestrians had been hurt recently. For many years, he suffered in silence, but in 1986 he saw several television programs on mental disorders. He went to a local psychiatric clinic and began treatment with nefazodone and clomipramine. The nefazodone was discontinued after several months because of dizziness and sedation. He continued taking clomipramine for 2 years but with only mild (if any) relief of symptoms. He discontinued all medications and was relatively symptom free for a 2-year period, until his wife was injured in a serious car accident. He nursed her back to health, and after her recovery his symptoms slowly reappeared. He consulted a private psychiatrist and at various times was treated with fluoxetine, sertraline, paroxetine, fluvoxamine, bupropion, and risperidone. Only fluvoxamine at doses up to 300 mg/day for 6 months resulted in even moderate improvement of symptoms. Frustrated with the lack of complete relief, he had discontinued fluvoxamine a year earlier.

Mr. S. had no previous illnesses or surgery. His mother was hospitalized following a suicide attempt 25 years earlier. Over the previous few months his 13-year-old daughter had increasingly shown a need for symmetry and repetitive touching of objects.

Mr. S.'s childhood was uneventful. He had a number of friends, and he dropped out of school in the 12th grade to spend more time working on his car. When he was 22, he married his high school sweetheart. By age 28 he owned a successful carpet-cleaning business, but by his mid-30s repetitive rituals were interfering, and he eventually lost the business and went on disability. Mr. S. and his wife have a 13-year-old daughter and an 11-year-old son.

At the time of his admission his physical examination was normal, and laboratory investigations were all within normal limits except for a potassium of 2.9. He appeared somewhat disheveled and had not showered for a couple of days. He was friendly and cooperative but restless and anxious. He was intensively preoccupied with his obsessions, but there was no evidence of delusions or hallucinations. He was alert and fully oriented, memory was good, and sensorium clear. He stated, ''I know these rituals are absurd, but I can't help myself. I'll do anything to stop.''

1. The most likely diagnosis for Mr. S. is

A. schizophrenia
B. major depression
C. obsessive-compulsive disorder
D. obsessive-compulsive personality disorder
E. delusional disorder

2. The personality type most consistently associated with OCD is

A. schizoid
B. borderline
C. avoidant
D. obsessive-compulsive
E. none of the above

3. Mr. S.'s psychiatric diagnosis is seen in up to 50 percent of patients with which of the following neurological conditions?

A. temporal lobe epilepsy
B. petit mal epilepsy
C. multiple sclerosis
D. Tourette's disorder
E. Wilson's disease

4. Each of the following has been shown to be effective in the treatment of some cases of OCD *except*

A. psychoanalytic psychotherapy
B. behavioral therapy
C. clomipramine
D. fluvoxamine
E. psychosurgery

Discussion and Answers

Mr. S. presents with a fairly classic case of obsessive-compulsive disorder. His obsessions (primarily pathological doubt) are recurrent and anxiety provoking. He recognizes their absurdity and tries to relieve his anxiety with compulsions, which by this point have become all consuming and have crippled him occupationally and socially.

His problem is not obsessive-compulsive personality disorder, which, despite its similar-sounding name, does not include obsessions or compulsions. Rather, obsessive-compulsive personality disorder describes an individual who is emotionally cold and preoccupied with rules, order, tidiness, and punctuality. It was formerly thought that OCPD predisposed to the development of the axis I condition OCD. This is now recognized not to be the case; OCD is seen across all personality types. There is no personality disorder that puts a person at greater risk.

There is a high comorbidity between OCD and depression. Patients with major depression can ruminate about a particular subject, but it is usually about a more realistic concern and not associated with rituals. Mr. S. does admit to sadness, but his decrease in eating and his avoidance of hobbies are apparently secondary to his all-consuming rituals rather than to depression. He denies hopelessness and being suicidal.

A high comorbidity of OCD also exists with Tourette's disorder. Some 35 to 59 percent of patients with Tourette's also have OCD. (The incidence of Tourette's in OCD is lower: 5 to 7 percent.) Mr. S. has no history of muscle or vocal tics, and Tourette's is not likely.

The significant deterioration of functioning over the previous several years is typical of schizophrenia, but no other clinical features suggest that diagnosis. He had never had hallucinations or delusions, and he recognized and was extremely distressed by the absurdity of his compulsive rituals. (DSM-IV now allows for a diagnosis of OCD with poor insight, in which for most of the time during the current episode the person does not recognize the unreasonableness of obsessions or compulsions. If these reach psychotic proportions, an additional diagnosis of "delusional disorder" is warranted.)

Mr. S. did not respond well to multiple trials of antidepressants with serotonergic agonist properties, the mainstay of pharmacological treatment of OCD. The most effective and long-lasting treatments combine drugs and behavioral therapy. The basis of behavioral treatment for OCD is twofold: exposure to situations, such as contamination, that are likely to trigger obsessions and compulsions; and response prevention, in which the automatic performance of rituals is delayed or stopped. Some success has been reported with psychosurgery in relieving severe, intractable symptoms of OCD. There are no data to support the effectiveness of psychoanalytic psychotherapies of OCD.

The low potassium was likely secondary to transcellular shift due to β-adrenergic activity that comes with acute stress and/or low intake. Mr. S. had experienced no hypokalemic symptoms such as neuromuscular or gastrointestinal irritability.

1–4. The answers are: 1, C; 2, E; 3, D; and 4, A.

JOSE V.

Jose V., a 34-year-old divorced Hispanic man, was taken to the hospital complaining that he had been bitten by a rat that was under his bed. He had a long history of alcohol abuse, and he drank a liter of rum each day. He broke up with his girlfriend and moved back to his mother's house at her insistence 9 days before admission. For the next 8 days he had nothing to drink. On the day of admission he awoke early with tremors and heavy sweating. He reported seeing snakes and rats around his room and felt that flies were crawling on his arms. He and his family are followers of Santeria, a religion common in Caribbean island cultures, and his grandmother was called in to perform a cleansing ritual earlier on the day of admission. His agitation increased, however, until finally he believed that a rat had bitten his ankle. He jumped out of bed and started screaming. His mother called emergency medical services, and he was brought in by ambulance.

In the past, Mr. V. had had several episodes of blackouts. Until the week before admission, there had been no periods of abstinence from alcohol for more than 5 years. There was no other psychiatric history. He denied using tobacco or any other drugs.

Mr. V. was an only child. His parents had divorced when he was in his teens. He described his father and a fraternal uncle as alcoholics. Another uncle was diagnosed with bipolar disorder and well maintained on lithium.

Mr. V. graduated from high school and attended 1 year of community college. He left college to work and make money, and he married a high school girlfriend when he was 20. About 5 years ago they were divorced over allegations of her infidelities. He began drinking heavily at that time, and 3 years later he lost his job as a security guard. Some 9 months ago he began dating a woman whom he subsequently lived with until just prior to his admission, when she left because of his drinking.

By the time he arrived at the hospital, Mr. V. was agitated, tremulous, and profoundly diaphoretic. Blood pressure was 150/90, heart rate 110, and temperature 99.5°F. His pupils were dilated, and deep tendon reflexes were diffusely hyperactive.

He cooperated with the psychiatric examination but was shaky and very distracted. Speech was halting. He described his mood as ''depressed,'' but appeared frightened. He no longer had visual hallucinations but continued to feel bugs crawling on his arms. As the interview progressed, he seemed to doze off several times and awakened with a start. Concentration was impaired, and formal testing of cognitive functions was difficult. He was, however, able to perform calculations and easily remembered the details of recent sports events.

1. The most likely diagnosis to explain Mr. V's hallucinations is

A. alcohol-induced psychotic disorder
B. alcohol withdrawal delirium
C. alcohol abuse
D. alcohol-induced amnestic disorder
E. pathological alcohol intoxication

2. An appropriate treatment for his condition is

A. chlorpromazine
B. chlordiazepoxide
C. buspirone
D. all of the above
E. none of the above

3. The mortality associated with his condition when treated is

A. 1 percent
B. 5 percent
C. 10 percent
D. 20 percent
E. more than 50 percent

4. Alcohol-related blackouts are periods of

A. abstinence from alcohol
B. loss of consciousness because of heavy intoxication
C. alcohol-induced psychotic symptoms
D. grand-mal seizure activity
E. anterograde amnesia

Discussion and Answers

Mr. V.'s condition was a medical emergency. He was entering the most serious alcohol withdrawal syndrome, withdrawal delirium, also known as delirium tremens, or DTs. Withdrawal delirium tends to be a late-occurring phenomenon, often not appearing until several days after the last drink. It is a true delirium, with an altered, often fluctuating level of consciousness usually accompanied by autonomic instability, tremor (hence the name: delirium tremens), and diaphoresis. The syndrome may or may not be preceded by grand mal seizures. Mortality is high, estimated to be 10 percent among patients receiving appropriate treatment and higher for those who are left untreated.

The visual and tactile hallucinations (called ''formication'') experienced by Mr. V. are typical of DTs. Other alcohol disorders can cause psychotic symptoms, however. Hallucinations occurring in a clear sensorium during withdrawal have been called alcohol hallucinosis, labeled alcohol-induced psychotic disorder in DSM-IV. Psychotic symptoms can also occur during intoxication states. When delirium is present, as with Mr V., the diagnosis of alcohol withdrawal delirium preempts other diagnoses.

The principle for treatment of DTs is to replace the substance from which the patient is withdrawing. Alcohol itself would be effective in an emergency but is hepatotoxic. In practice, drugs that are cross-tolerant to alcohol are preferable and are used in hospital settings. Drugs with a long half-life such as chlordiazepoxide are preferred because withdrawal signs and symptoms are more attenuated as the drug is gradually tapered off. The antipsychotic drug chlorpromazine is contraindicated. It lowers the seizure threshold, increasing the risk of seizures, and its heavy sedative properties further cloud consciousness and complicate the clinical picture. Antipsychotics do not stop withdrawal. The nonbenzodiazepine anxiolytic buspirone is not cross-tolerant with alcohol and has no effect on withdrawal signs and symptoms.

The seriousness of Mr. V.'s drinking is supported by his history of multiple blackouts, periods of anterograde amnesia, in which new memories are not laid down (as opposed to retrograde amnesia, in which previously recorded memories are erased). When a person has blackouts, he does not pass out but rather cannot remember what he did or what happened while he was drunk.

1–4. The answers are: 1, B; 2, B; 3, C; and 4, E.

JOYCE G.

Joyce G., a 42-year-old white woman, was referred by her internist for an outpatient evaluation of ''emotional turmoil'' and ''trouble with my heart.'' She described a 6-month history of periods of intense anxiety and fear, accompanied by heart palpitations, tremulousness, sweating, and the feeling that she was suffocating. The episodes occurred in a variety of settings—at home, at work, while shopping, even when she felt completely relaxed. They were most likely to strike when she was crossing a bridge or riding on an escalator, and she tried to eliminate these activities altogether. The episodes typically lasted 10 to 15 minutes, but some lasted as long as half an hour, leaving her physically and emotionally exhausted. Twice she went to the emergency room of her local hospital thinking that she was having a heart attack. The first time she was met by her internist, who performed an electrocardiogram revealing a left bundle branch block but no evidence of infarction. Cardiac enzymes were tested and reported to be normal.

The second time she went to the emergency room her

internist again performed an EKG, which showed no changes from the earlier one. He recommended that she see a psychiatrist and helped arrange a consultation. She had no change in sleep or appetite but described "nervous eating," which resulted in a 20-pound weight gain over 6 months. She felt increasingly demoralized over the unpredictability of the attacks, her inability to plan activities, and the extent to which her life was becoming circumscribed.

She had similar episodes 10 years earlier. She started outpatient therapy twice a week and remembered her therapist telling her the attacks were the result of unresolved conflict with her mother and husband. She continued therapy for 2 years with no change in her condition before she dropped out. Over the next 2 years, the attacks gradually diminished in frequency and intensity until they disappeared altogether.

Her older brother, her only sibling, had suffered similar attacks for many years. He had been in psychotherapy for more than 5 years with no discernible benefit and was now essentially housebound. Her mother suffered from major depression and had been treated successfully with imipramine. Her father died of a heart attack almost 15 years earlier after a long history of coronary artery disease.

Mrs. G., a high school graduate, was married, with an 11-year-old son. Her relationship with her husband was cordial but distant. They had not had a sexual relationship for years. He seemed to be tired all of the time and spent most of his life at work or watching television. She was concerned about her son's growing rebelliousness and occasional truancy from school. She had been an office manager in a real estate company ever since her son started grade school. She enjoyed the work and the camaraderie of other people in her office. They went out together to movies, dinner, or bowling once or twice a week. Recently she had gone out less often out of fear that she might have an attack.

Her general physical health was good. Medical evaluations revealed nothing other than the left bundle branch block. A 24-hour urine collection for catecholamines was negative.

Mrs. G. came to her first appointment from work wearing a business suit. She was affable and forthcoming about her symptoms. Her speech was clear and articulate. She appeared worried about what was happening to her, but her mood overall seemed normal and flexible. She had no psychotic symptoms. She was alert and fully oriented. Concentration was mildly impaired but cognitive functions were otherwise intact.

1. The most likely diagnosis for Mrs. G.'s condition is

A. Somatization disorder
B. Specific phobia
C. Adjustment disorder with anxiety
D. Panic disorder
E. Major depression with psychotic symptoms

2. An appropriate treatment recommendation for Mrs. G. could include

A. psychodynamic psychotherapy
B. alprazolam
C. imipramine
D. buspirone
E. hypnosis

3. The patient's disorder is often comorbid with

A. agoraphobia
B. bulimia
C. histrionic personality disorder
D. sexual aversion disorder
E. mitral valve prolapse

4. The brain region most implicated in the etiology of Mrs. G.'s disorder is the

A. caudate nucleus
B. nucleus basalis of Meynert
C. limbic system
D. pituitary
E. locus ceruleus

Discussion and Answers

Mrs. G. is suffering from panic disorder: sudden, discrete attacks of intense anxiety or fear accompanied by physical symptoms such as palpitations or a feeling of suffocation. The attack may be so distressing that the person fears she is dying, and trips to an emergency room are not uncommon. Symptoms are usually not present between attacks, but wariness and demoralization may set in. Attacks may be triggered by specific events such as crossing a bridge, but for a diagnosis of panic disorder (and to distinguish it from a specific phobia) at least some of the attacks must occur without an environmental trigger. This is the case with Mrs. G., who has had attacks even while relaxing at home. Somatization disorder describes a condition of multiple symptoms and health seeking. Hypochondriasis is the preoccupation with having a serious illness. Both are chronic conditions that do not occur in discrete circumscribed bursts.

Although she is beginning to feel demoralized, her mood is not severe enough and there are not sufficient vegetative symptoms to warrant a diagnosis of depression. Diagnoses of adjustment disorders are tricky; most peoples' lives are eventful enough to find plausible antecedents to just about any set of psychiatric symptoms. For Mrs. G., however, there is no clear relation between symptoms and any external stressors. Moreover, her sudden, acute attacks of intense symptoms are not characteristic of the anxiety accompanying adjustment disorders, which is milder and nonepisodic.

The appropriate treatment for panic disorder is medication. Imipramine was the first drug to have demonstrated antipanic properties. Given at doses comparable with those used to treat depression (75 to 200 mg/day), imipramine is effective in preventing recurrent attacks. For Mrs. G., however, a tricyclic with its quinidine-like effect of slowing cardiac conduction is not appropriate because of her preexisting left bundle branch block. Alternative drugs for prophylaxis in panic attacks include SSRIs, MAOIs, and high-potency benzodiazepines, such as alprazolam. (Low-potency benzodiazepines, such as diazepam, are effective in stopping an acute attack but cannot be given in doses high enough to prevent recurrent attacks without oversedation.) Buspirone, a nonbenzodiazepine anxiolytic, is not an effective antipanic drug. Cognitive-behavioral therapy is often a useful adjunct to the medication treatment of panic disorder. Psychodynamic psychotherapy, as was consistent with Mrs. G's experience, has not been shown to be helpful.

Panic disorder often coexists with agoraphobia and may be a causative factor in its development. The intense distress of an attack may train people to gradually limit themselves to familiar environments that are perceived to be safe. This situation appears to be the case for Mrs. G's brother and now for her. She is already avoiding specific situations such as bridges and escalators and has begun to avoid more general situations such as going out with her friends. About 95 percent of patients diagnosed with agoraphobia also have panic disorder. Although early reports indicated a higher than normal prevalence of mitral valve prolapse in patients with panic disorder, this association has not been found in more recent studies.

The medical differential diagnosis of panic disorder includes conditions that cause anxiety: hypoglycemia, hyperthyroidism, pulmonary disease, stimulant intoxication, and sedative withdrawal. None of these is at all likely to occur with the characteristic sudden, short-lived attacks of panic disorder. Pheochromocytoma may be accompanied by bursts of anxiety, palpitations, flushing, and diarrhea. It is diagnosed on the finding of high catecholamine levels in a 24-hour urine collection, which for Mrs. G. was negative.

Abnormal firing from the locus ceruleus has been implicated in the neurobiology of panic attacks. The locus ceruleus, located at the base of the brain, is the origin of most brain noradrenergic pathways. It is sensitive to changing levels of carbon dioxide pressure (PCO_2). It is believed that the locus ceruleus may provide a protective mechanism by firing a burst of noradrenergic stimulation if breathing slows or stops. One appealing but as yet unproved theory about panic disorder is that the threshold for locus ceruleus firing may be set too low. This theory may explain the commonly reported sensation of suffocating by people who are having a panic attack.

1–4. The answers are: 1, D; 2, B; 3, A; and 4, E.

JUSTIN R.

Justin R., a 38-year-old black man, was transferred from the city jail, where he was serving a 1-year sentence for arson, to the prison ward of the city psychiatric service. The chief complaint was ''They thought I was setting fires.'' He denied having set the particular fire that resulted in the transfer, but he admitted to setting more than a hundred fires in his lifetime. His fire setting began at 4 years of age, when he set fire to a couch in the family living room. He had been incarcerated more than 20 times for arson for a total of 15 years in prison, in addition to a few arrests for robbery. He described his fire setting as impulsive: He would get an irresistible urge to start a fire. He always chose abandoned buildings and was proud that no one had ever been injured in his fires. ''If I ever hurt someone, I wouldn't be able to live with myself,'' he stated. In his teenage years, the fires became a sexual ritual for him: He would get erections and masturbate into the fires.

Mr. R. described having two voices inside his head. One of the voices belonged to Larry, a homosexual. Larry hated arson and called Mr. R. ''stupid'' when he set a fire; Larry sometimes tried to grope other men without warning. The other voice belonged to Justin (his own name), a boy who set fires. He acknowledged that both personalities were part of himself.

Mr. R. had been hospitalized in psychiatric facilities numerous times in the past and had been treated with medications, the names of which he could not remember. Nothing, however, had ever made any difference in his irresistible urge to set fires. About 2 months earlier he had been treated by the prison psychiatrist with fluoxetine and haloperidol but with no discernible benefit.

He began using marijuana when he was 18 and crack cocaine at age 28. He could not specify amounts but said he would sometimes steal money from his family to pay for drugs. He had been in a few residential drug treatment programs, but each time he had been kicked out for setting fires.

Mr. R. grew up in a large city. When he was a young child, he was beaten and sexually abused by his father and a male cousin. After his father left home when Mr. R. was 16, the youth continued living with his mother. He went to public high school, did average work, but remembered liking mathematics. Shortly after graduating from high school he was arrested for the first time. He worked at a city homeless shelter for 6 years—his longest job and one he enjoyed—but was dismissed for fire setting.

Some time earlier he had seen a television program about a boy who was severely scarred in a fire. He remembered feeling very sorry for the boy and hoping he would never cause harm to anyone. He regretted not getting psychiatric help earlier in his life and now said, ''Nothing can help. Nothing can change the way I am now.'' At the time of his most recent arrest he was living with and caring for his older brother, who was dying of cancer.

His physical examination revealed a pulse of 104 but was otherwise normal. Laboratory investigations were within normal limits, and urine toxicology screen was negative. He appeared neatly groomed and was friendly and forthcoming. He maintained eye contact throughout the interview and did not seem upset in any way. He exhibited a full range of emotions with good relatedness to the interviewer. When talking about happy moments in his life, he laughed, but he was visibly sad when discussing the abuse he suffered as a child. He was extremely serious when he described his fire setting. There was no evidence of delusional thinking, but he was preoccupied with the problem of fire setting. Mr. R. responded appropriately and logically to all questions. He was alert and fully oriented, and all cognitive functions were intact.

1. The most appropriate diagnosis for Mr. R. is

A. cocaine-induced psychotic disorder
B. dissociative identity disorder
C. antisocial personality disorder
D. schizophrenia
E. pyromania

2. Pyromania is distinguished from arson in that with the former

A. there are hallucinations or delusions
B. fire setting is usually well planned
C. there is no secondary gain
D. it is more common in men than in women
E. none of the above

3. Fire setting in adolescence is most commonly associated with

A. conduct disorder
B. attention-deficit/hyperactivity disorder
C. adjustment disorder
D. all of the above
E. none of the above

Discussion and Answers

The "two voices" Mr. R. mentions do not sound like hallucinations. He describes them as being in his head and acknowledges them as part of himself. Nor is there any suggestion of other psychotic symptoms. He does not have a formal thought disorder and he does not seem to be delusional. The absence of any substantial medical history, his overall good health, the absence of findings on physical examination, and the length of time he has experienced impulses to set fires make it most unlikely that his symptoms are caused by an underlying medical condition. (His tachycardia may represent anxiety at the time of admission.)

Despite a substantial history of cocaine and marijuana abuse, it is likewise difficult to relate his fire setting to his drug habits. The history does not fully describe the time relation between drug use and fire setting, but he began setting fires in early childhood, well before he began using drugs. By itself the negative toxicology screen does not rule out psychotic symptoms caused by cocaine or marijuana, as symptoms can persist after the drug has been cleared from a person's system. More important is the fact that there are no clear psychotic symptoms.

The presence of two personalities, Larry and Justin, raises the possibility of a dissociative identity disorder (formerly multiple personality disorder). Although he does describe two clearly distinct personalities, they seem to coexist. He reports no episodes of amnesia and maintains full awareness of both personalities. Thus a dissociative identity disorder is unlikely.

Superficially, his long-standing fire setting, drug use, theft, and arrest history may look like an antisocial personality disorder. He seems to have retained the capacity for remorse, however. He mentions the fact that no one has been hurt in his fires. He felt sympathy in seeing a badly burned boy on television and regrets that he had not got psychiatric help earlier. He has never committed crimes against people or animals. He was caring for his dying brother at the time of his arrest. For these reasons antisocial personality disorder does not seem to be the best diagnosis. Rather than a pervasive pattern of violation of and disregard for the rights of others, Mr. R.'s history is uniquely focused on fire setting. His behavior is best described by a diagnosis of pyromania, listed as one of the impulse-control disorders not otherwise classified in DSM-IV.

Pyromania appears to be quite rare. Early studies were contaminated by combining arsonists with pyromaniacs. Arsonists set fires for secondary gain: to obtain insurance money, to destroy criminal evidence, for crime-related retribution, for example. People with pyromania set fires because of the relief from tension or intrinsic pleasure it provides.

Among adolescents, fire setting is most commonly seen in the context of conduct disorder, attention-deficit/hyperactivity disorder, and adjustment disorders. It is much more common in men than in women.

There is not much information about Mr. R's social, romantic, or sexual life. If fire setting is the only means of sexual gratification, it qualifies as a paraphilia. His description of Larry and Justin suggests that he is struggling with homosexual impulses; this topic might be productive for psychotherapeutic discussion. He appears sincerely motivated, but his very long-standing history does not make the prognosis optimistic.

1–3. The answers are: 1, E; 2, C; and 3, D.

LAURA K.

Laura K. is a 42-year-old white divorced woman referred to a psychiatric unit by her internist for treatment of depression and suicidal thoughts. "I can't go on like this," she said. "I feel so empty. Like my life is nothing. I'm nothing." Ms. K. had moved to the city 6 months earlier to complete her MBA degree. At the time of her evaluation, she was finishing an internship with a small, local company. The internship was not going well because of frequent fights with coworkers and administration. She had been reprimanded several times by the woman who was her immediate superior and was threatened with dismissal. She was finally given an ultimatum: to get psychiatric treatment or to be fired. Ms. K. felt that her supervisor treated her with disrespect and condescension, that she "was on a power trip" and wanted things done her way just to prove that she could exercise control. Once or twice a week Ms. K. would become so enraged that she would bang furniture, throw papers, scream obscenities at her supervisor, and storm out of the office. The next day she would feel very sheepish about what had happened but still felt justified in her behavior. Over time, she came to believe that her supervisor was deliberately antagonizing her in the hopes of provoking her anger and making her lose control so as to be able to gain even more power over her.

Ms. K. also described chronic feelings of emptiness and loneliness, particularly on weekends and vacations. The feelings reached such intensity at times that she thought of suicide. Although she denied any specific plans or actions, she at various times had thoughts of taking an overdose; cutting her wrists, throat, or abdomen; or jumping in front of a subway car. She was troubled by nightmares (recurrent themes were being pursued or dismembered) and had difficulty both in falling asleep and staying asleep. Some nights she would force herself to stay awake as long as possible to avoid possible nightmares. She described her appetite as normal, but she dieted and exercised scrupulously to maintain the same weight she had in her 20s.

Ms. K. had one brief trial of psychotherapy. It lasted only a few months and ended because of fighting between her and the therapist. She had never taken psychiatric medication. She had never had hallucinations, but over the years had often felt that other people (especially boyfriends or employers) wanted to hurt her or humiliate her and that they would try to provoke her rage to make her look crazy and out of control.

Ms. K. was the youngest of three daughters born to a well-to-do family in the South. Both parents were alcoholics. Her father sexually abused her from age 8 until she left home for boarding school at age 16. He began having intercourse with her when she was in her early teens and would on occasion threaten her with a knife. The day after such episodes, he would deny that anything had happened. Her mother, usually in a constant state of alcoholic stupor, either ignored or was unaware of what was happening. Ms. K. once mentioned the abuse to an older sister, who told her she was crazy. In school, she had few close friends. She began experimenting with cocaine, marijuana, and heroin and spent most of her time with other girls who used drugs or engaged in petty criminal activity, such as shoplifting. She moved to another part of the country for college, where she did well academically and drastically curtailed her drug use. She developed a steady romantic relationship with a man in her class, and they were married shortly after graduation. Although her husband was not abusive, she began to feel taken for granted. She particularly chafed under the expectation that she would do housework while he worked in business. They stopped having sexual relations and began to live somewhat separate lives. She left him one night without warning while he was sleeping and moved to another city.

Over the years, her life was characterized by many brief, intense relationships, sometimes with alcoholic men who became physically abusive. She held a series of different jobs and had virtually no close, nonromantic friends. She joined the army for 2 years in an effort to force change in her life and relieve the nagging sense of emptiness.

Ms. K. had had 2 abortions during her 30s, with infection complicating the second. There was no other significant medical history, and at the time she came for psychiatric treatment she was not using drugs or alcohol at all. She lived alone and had no friends.

She was an attractive woman who wore no makeup. She was dressed in loose-fitting slacks and shirt. She appeared thin but not significantly underweight. Her speech was soft, and she often mumbled. She looked extremely anguished, with frequent tearfulness, and described her mood as horrible. Although suspicious of others' motives, she was not delusional and did not have hallucinations. Her thinking was logical and goal directed. She was alert and fully oriented, and her memory was good. Concentration was poor and statements were often interrupted by tears.

Ms. K. began psychotherapy and medication with an SSRI antidepressant. The early phase of therapy was marked by great turbulence. She was alternately enraged at the therapist for minor or imagined shortcomings or felt very dependent on him and fearful that he would leave or terminate her therapy. Once, when the therapist misremembered her age, she left a lengthy, obscene tirade on his office answering machine. After a year of treatment, thiothixene was added with considerable benefit. The nightmares stopped, she felt less fearful and suspicious of others, and she had much better control over her anger. She completed her graduate degree and began working for another company. Her mood became more stable, although she would usually experience a strong resurgence of depression during her psychiatrist's vacations. The chronic empty feeling persisted.

1. In addition to major depression, the most likely diagnosis for Ms. K. is

A. schizophrenia
B. borderline personality disorder
C. paranoid delusional disorder
D. schizoid personality disorder
E. schizotypal personality disorder

2. The main difference between Axis I disorders and personality disorders is

A. The defining features of personality disorders occur early and are long term, chronic, and unremitting.
B. Psychotic symptoms do not occur in personality disorders.
C. Symptoms of Axis I disorders are ego-dystonic, and those of Axis II disorders are ego-syntonic.
D. Personality disorders usually describe learned, nonadaptive behavior, while Axis I disorders are biologically predisposed.
E. Axis I disorders are treated primarily with medication and personality disorders with psychotherapy.

3. The most common natural course of borderline personality disorder appears to be

A. progressive chronic functional deterioration
B. increased frequency and severity of acute episodes
C. stable, unvarying symptoms throughout a person's lifetime
D. resolution of all symptoms by age 60
E. increased emotional stability and occupational functioning with decreased risk of suicide by middle age

Discussion and Answers

Ms. K. fits a fairly typical profile for borderline personality disorder. Particularly striking are her intense and unstable interpersonal relationships, her mood instability, sudden intense bursts of anger, and chronic feelings of emptiness. These personality features extend back at least into her early adulthood and possibly into adolescence. Although the information from her history is limited, it suggests that these features have been present throughout her life and have not been episodic or situational. (A possible exception is the period in college when she stopped using drugs, earned good grades, and entered a long-term relationship that led to marriage.) Schizophrenia is chronic but episodic. Acute psychotic episodes are followed by residual periods of negative symptoms. Ms. K.'s emotional turmoil would be unusual in schizophrenia, which more typically results in emotional flattening. Although Ms. K. lives alone and has no close friends, her social isolation seems to be in response to the painful emotional turbulence of close relationships. Her involvement in therapy shows strong emotional reactivity with others. Patients with a diagnosis of schizoid personality disorder seem indifferent to other people, neither desiring nor enjoying close relationships. They would not describe themselves as ''lonely'' or ''empty.'' Schizotypal personality describes people who are socially isolated by choice and who in addition have oddities of speech, thought, or behavior, which may make other people regard them as weird. Paranoid delusional disorder represents a fixed delusion of persecution with no other psychiatric symptoms. Ms. K. is suspicious of others, but her suspicion is not a fixed delusional belief. Moreover, her mood and anger are much more prominent symptoms.

Psychotic symptoms are possible in some personality disorders, including borderline, but they are usually transient and occur in response to stress, such as fear of abandonment. Psychotic symptoms in schizophrenia, on the other hand, are often well elaborated and may persist for weeks or months if untreated. Despite the absence of marked hallucinations, delusions, or formal thought disorders, many borderline patients benefit from small doses of antipsychotic medication, as has Ms. K. Major depression often coexists with borderline personality disorder, and antidepressants are also useful. It has sometimes been argued that the symptoms of Axis II disorders are ego-syntonic (the patient does not experience the defining features as symptomatic or undesirable), whereas symptoms of Axis I disorders are ego-dystonic. This generalization does not hold up to close scrutiny. Ms. K. may not fully understand the origins of her distress, but she is clearly unhappy and desires change.

The etiology of borderline personality disorder remains unclear, and several possibilities have been proposed. The fact that a higher than normal prevalence of mood disorders, alcoholism, and sociopathy have been found in the families of patients with borderline personality disorder suggests a biogenetic relationship with mood disorders. Because many borderline patients were sexually abused as children and adolescents, the possibility of psychological developmental abnormalities is raised. Finally, the natural history of the disorder—although varying widely from individual to individual—is a lessening of symptoms over time. To some observers this fact suggests an impairment of social learning: the affected individual takes much longer to understand social cues and to modify behavior appropriately. None of these theories has been proved, and they are not mutually exclusive. This observation is reflected in the fact that biological, psychodynamic, and behavioral therapies have all been attempted with some degree of success.

1–3. The answers are: 1, B; 2, A; and 3, E.

MARTIN D.

Martin D., a 76-year-old man, was referred by his social worker therapist for consideration of medication. The therapist had been working for the past 2 years with Mr. D's wife, who was diagnosed with Alzheimer's disease. Mrs. D. had been cared for at home by her husband and a home health worker until 3 months ago, when her condition deteriorated and she was placed in a nursing home. Since that time, Mr. D. had become more withdrawn. He failed to keep several appointments with the therapist and would spend most of his time in bed. His appetite had fallen off and he was eating every little; the therapist estimated that he had lost 10 to 15 pounds. He showered and shaved infrequently, and he did virtually nothing to look after the house, attend to bills, or shop for necessities. About 2 months earlier he was hospitalized and treated with 100 mg/day of sertraline, to which he quickly responded. His mood, appetite, and energy all improved; he began going out more often, meeting old friends, and visiting his wife 3 to 4 times a week in the nursing home. However, 2 weeks earlier he stopped medication, thinking it was no longer necessary, as he had fully recovered. In the ensuing weeks, his appetite declined, and he was becoming tearful and hopeless.

Mr. D. had been in and out of therapy much of his adult life. Many of his problems were centered on marital conflict, and he and his wife had been in couples therapy until the progression of her Alzheimer's disease made it impractical. He had once been prescribed diazepam but had never taken it or any other psychiatric medication.

Mr. D.'s physical health was good. He had an asymptomatic hiatal hernia, arthritis causing some limitation of movement in his right knee, and narrow-angle glaucoma that had been well treated for many years with β-blocking eye drops.

Mr. D's mother had died of Alzheimer's disease many years before. An older brother, his only sibling, was killed in World War II. Mr. D. attended college, graduated with a BA, and ran a successful accounting firm until 5 years earlier. He was fluent in three languages and enjoyed his solitude. A favorite pastime was staying home and reading history. He smoked a pipe and enjoyed an occasional social drink.

At the time of evaluation, he appeared healthy and much younger than his actual age of 76. Speech was clear and articulate. He described feeling blue most of the time, and he became tearful when speaking of his wife. There were no psychotic symptoms. Alertness, memory orientation, and concentration were all good.

Sertraline was restarted and gradually increased to a dose of 150 mg/day. He responded with improvement in mood and appetite. At a subsequent visit, he mentioned a problem that had been weighing heavily on his mind. He described getting violent during his sleep, pounding and throwing pillows, banging on furniture, and on several occasions while she was still living at home, hitting his wife. The violent episodes usually occurred in the early morning and often in the middle of a vivid dream. One time his wife shook him awake after he repeatedly hit her. He reported that he had been dreaming of walking through a park when he was attacked by a mugger whom he was attempting to fight off. Mr. D. was convinced that the violent episodes must mean that he did not love his wife.

1. The most likely diagnosis for Mr. D's mood disturbance is

A. major depression
B. bereavement
C. adjustment disorder with depressed mood
D. adjustment disorder with mixed disturbance of emotions and conduct
E. dysthymia

2. The most likely diagnosis for Mr. D.'s sleep disturbance is

A. adjustment disorder with mixed disturbance of emotions and conduct
B. sleepwalking disorder
C. sleep terror disorder
D. REM sleep behavior disorder
E. nightmare disorder

3. The most likely explanation for the cause of Mr. D.'s violent sleep episodes is

A. unresolved grief
B. latent hostility toward his wife
C. survivor guilt over his brother's death
D. unresolved sexual conflict
E. a neurological event without psychological meaning

4. Each of the following would be an acceptable treatment for his mood disturbance *except*

A. paroxetine
B. fluoxetine
C. psychotherapy
D. electroconvulsive therapy (ECT)
E. amitriptyline

Discussion and Answers

Mr. D. is suffering from an episode of major depression. Although the episode seems to have been triggered by his wife's nursing home placement, a diagnosis of an adjustment disorder is not made if the person meets criteria for another Axis I disorder, such as a mood disorder. Anticipatory grief can precede the expected death of a loved one, but the degree of his functional impairment is not consistent with bereavement. Although his mood was less disturbed at the time of his psychiatric evaluation, it was part of the same episode that began before his hospitalization. He had responded well to antidepressant medication but was beginning to suffer a relapse when he stopped the drug prematurely.

In addition to depression, he has symptoms characteristic of REM sleep behavior disorder, classified in DSM-IV as a parasomnia not otherwise specified. Parasomnias occur in the context of otherwise normal sleep (''para'' means ''alongside''). Nightmare disorder describes repeated awakenings with vivid recall of nightmares but does not include the violent behavioral disturbance experienced by Mr. D. During rapid eye movement sleep (REM sleep), cortical motor output is inhibited at the level of the spinal cord, and a flaccid paralysis results. For reasons not yet well understood, the motor inhibition sometimes fails, with the result that the individual appears to act out his or her dreams. This phenomenon is the REM sleep behavior disorder. It is believed to be a purely neurological event without psychological meaning (although the content of dreams themselves may be meaningful). The presence of easily recalled dreams and its occurrence late in the sleep cycle help to distinguish REM sleep behavior disorder from parasomnias such as sleepwalking and night terrors, which occur during stage IV sleep, when motor tone is normal, dreaming is minimal, and recall after waking is difficult.

Mr. D.'s depression has responded well to sertraline. Other SSRIs, such as fluoxetine and paroxetine, would be reasonable alternatives. ECT is an effective treatment for major depression and may be of particular benefit in treating older people because it has low morbidity and mortality compared with antidepressant drugs. ECT may be especially useful when a person's functioning is seriously impaired (as was true for Mr. D., who stopped eating) because of its relatively quick therapeutic effectiveness. Amitriptyline, one of the most anticholinergic psychiatric drugs in current use, should be avoided in someone with narrow-angle glaucoma.

Although Mr. D.'s depression is responding well to medication, the difficult adjustment he is facing to his wife's deteriorating condition, the conflicted relationship he has had with his wife over the years, and the memory of his mother's Alzheimer's disease all make it likely that psychotherapy would be a helpful adjunct to medication.

1–4. The answers are: 1, A; 2, D; 3, E; and 4, E.

RICKY J.

Ricky J., a 5-year-old Hispanic boy, was taken to a psychiatric clinic by his foster mother because of his increasingly disturbed behavior at home. Ricky himself said, ''I want to die. My mother died and I want to go where my mother is.''

About 8 months earlier, Ricky's mother died of AIDS. He had a chance to visit her in the hospital shortly before her death. He had not known she was infected with HIV, and to him her death was sudden and unexpected. He began to experience unremitting sadness and daily tearfulness. He had trouble sleeping, sometimes being able to sleep no more than an hour at night. His appetite was low and he had lost some weight, although his foster mother did not know how much. He became preoccupied with death, wanted to be near his mother's ashes at his aunt's house, and had frequent visions of his mother asking him to die and join her in heaven. He became convinced that his body was filled with worms. He talked openly about killing himself but did not discuss a plan. About 2 weeks before he was taken in for evaluation, he made vague threats against his foster mother and threatened to kill his 7-year-old foster brother with a knife.

Before his mother's death, there had been no reports of behavioral problems or any history of counseling or psychiatric interventions. He had not yet entered school but was described by an aunt as friendly and cooperative. He had not previously had any difficulty with sleeping or eating. His mother had used cocaine, heroin, and marijuana when she was pregnant with him, but his birth and first years of life were unremarkable. Developmental milestones all seem to have been reached on time. He had never suffered medical problems and was not known to have complained about physical symptoms.

When Ricky was born, his father was in jail. He had no brothers or sisters and was raised by his mother, who was living with her boyfriend. He was exposed to illegal firearms and drugs and recalled seeing his mother shoot one of the guns. About 9 months before the evaluation, their apartment was raided by police. The guns and drugs were confiscated, and Ricky's mother and her boyfriend were sent to jail. Ricky was put in the supervised custody of his aunt. A month later, his mother was transferred from jail to the hospital where she died. His aunt then took him to Puerto Rico, a move not authorized by child welfare, and when they returned, Ricky was removed from his aunt's custody and placed with a foster family.

Physical examination and laboratory testing revealed no abnormalities. Ricky was polite and cooperative, and he related well to the interviewer but avoided eye contact. His speech was slow and at low volume. He described himself as "very sad" and despite occasional smiles, looked unhappy. He repeated emphatically that his body was full of worms; he did not experience any hallucinations during the evaluation. He was awake and alert, did not know the date, but was otherwise oriented. His concentration and memory seemed normal for a 5-year-old. He was able to count to 10 in Spanish. When asked why he had been taken to the clinic, Ricky said, "Because I want to kill myself to be with my mother." Ricky was admitted to the children's unit of a psychiatric hospital.

After some time on the unit, Ricky responded well to reassurance and social contact. He interacted well with other children on the unit, laughed, loved to play, and enjoyed activities.

1. The most likely diagnosis is

A. childhood schizophrenia
B. conduct disorder
C. major depression
D. bereavement
E. adjustment disorder with mixed features

2. Each of the following may help distinguish major depression from bereavement *except*

A. length of time symptoms persist after the death of a loved one
B. auditory or visual hallucinations of the deceased
C. prolonged functional impairment
D. somatic delusions
E. all of the above

3. A difference between major depression in children and major depression in adults is

A. Anxiety is uncommon in children.
B. Childhood major depression never includes psychotic symptoms.
C. Children are unlikely to have vegetative symptoms.
D. Young children with major depression often look more oppositional than sad.
E. Children with major depression do not become suicidal.

4. Common drug treatments for major depression in children include each of the following *except*

A. phenelzine
B. fluoxetine
C. trazodone
D. imipramine
E. sertraline

Discussion and Answers

Ricky's distress goes beyond normal bereavement; a diagnosis of major depression is warranted. Although there are many common features between depression and grief, some features distinguish the two. The duration and intensity of normal grief vary a great deal from culture to culture, but generally a diagnosis of major depression would not be made until at least 2 months after the death of the loved one. Visual and auditory hallucinations of the deceased are not uncommon in bereavement. Other psychotic symptoms, however, such as Ricky's somatic delusion that his body was filled with worms, more strongly suggest major depression. In addition, major depression is more likely to include a morbid preoccupation with death and individual feelings of worthlessness or hopelessness. The diagnosis of an adjustment disorder specifically excludes bereavement.

Although it was thought at one time that major depression was uncommon in young children, it is now recognized to occur, although less frequently than among adolescents and adults. The clinical presentation may be different, however. Oppositional behavior and irritability may be more pronounced than a mood disturbance. Children with depression often have physical symptoms, such as headaches or stomachaches, and are more likely to suffer hypersomnia than insomnia. Ricky's presentation, typical of depression in adults, is actually atypical for young children. The reported absence of any behavioral problems before his mother's death makes a diagnosis of conduct disorder or oppositional defiant disorder very unlikely despite his aggressive, threatening behavior of the last few weeks. Unlike in adults, among whom the prevalence of major depression in women is 3 to 4 times that in men, the prevalence of depression in boys and girls is about equal. Suicide in children is not common, but it does occur and should be a major concern in dealing with depressed children. The rate is particularly high for children like Ricky, who talk about wanting to die, who have command auditory hallucinations, and who imagine that death will bring reunion with the loved one.

His mother's illness and death raise concern about the possibility of maternal transmission of an HIV infection. The absence of any opportunistic infections or evidence of neurological involvement and his steady health through the period of symptoms are inconsistent with either an immune deficiency syndrome or an HIV encephalitis.

Depression in children—as in adults—is best treated with a combination of psychotherapy and medication. SSRIs are often preferred because of their minimal side effects, but other cyclic drugs, including tricyclics, can be used with benefit. Because of the difficulty in controlling what young children eat, monoamine oxidase inhibitors (MAOIs) are usually not prescribed.

Despite the distressing circumstances of Ricky's early years, his good premorbid adjustment and his quick, happy social integration on the children's psychiatric service suggest an excellent prognosis. Terrible living circumstances themselves are not sufficient to cause psychiatric disability or to prevent recovery.

1–4. The answers are: 1, C; 2, B; 3, D; and 4, A.

58 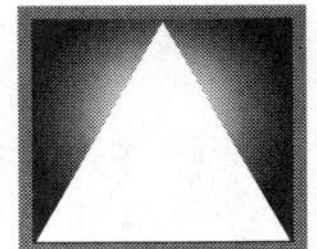

Objective Examinations in Psychiatry

There is a wide variety of objective multiple-choice question formats. They range from case histories followed by a series of questions relating to diagnosis, laboratory findings, treatment complications, and prognosis to the most widely used form, known as the one-best-response type, wherein a question or incomplete statement is followed by four or five suggested answers or completions, with the examinee being directed to select the one best answer. The multiple-choice questions are described as objective because the correct response is predetermined by a group of experts who compose the items, eliminating the observer bias seen in ratings of essay questions. The responses are entered on an answer sheet, which is scored by machine, giving a high degree of reliability. Two basic item types are used with the greatest frequency, one-best-response type (type A) and matching type (type B), which are detailed in Table 58.1.

The case history or situation type of item consists of an introductory statement that may be an abbreviated history, with or without the results of the physical examination or laboratory tests, followed by a series of questions, usually of the A type. In similar fashion, charts, electroencephalograms, pictures of gross or microscopic slides, or even patients' graphs may be presented, again followed by the one-best-response type or matching type.

Present testing procedures using objective multiple-choice items are highly effective in regard to reliability and validity in measuring the examinee's knowledge and its application. Experienced test constructors are able to develop items based on a given content and to word the answers in a neutral fashion. Thus, correct and incorrect responses are similar in style, length, and phrasing. However, no matter how well constructed a test is, with a high degree of reliability and validity for a large group of examinees, it is subject to inaccuracies about individual testees. Some examinees underscore, and others overscore, depending on their experience and test-taking skills, known as testmanship. In the final analysis, there is no substitute for knowledge, understanding, and clinical competence when a physician is being evaluated. However, some suggestions and clues inevitably appear in the most carefully composed and edited multiple-choice test. To improve one's testmanship, one should consider the following:

1. There is no penalty for a wrong response in the objective-type multiple-choice question. The testee has a 20 percent chance of guessing correctly when there are five options. Therefore, no question should be left unanswered.
2. In medicine it is rare for anything to be universally correct or wrong. Thus, options that imply "always" or "never" are more likely to be incorrect than otherwise.
3. Especially in psychiatry, many words are often needed to include the exceptions or qualifications in a correct statement. Thus, the longest option is likely to be the correct response. Test constructors who are also aware of this fact often try to lengthen the shorter incorrect responses by adding unnecessary phrases, but that tactic can readily be detected by experienced test takers.
4. The use of a word like "possibly," or "may," or "sometimes" in an option often suggests a true statement, whereas choices with universal negative or positive statements tend to be false.
5. Each distractor that can be ruled out increases the percentage chance of guessing correctly. In a five-choice situation, being able to discard three options increases the percentage from 20 percent to 50 percent and enables the examinee to focus on only the two remaining choices.
6. With questions in which one cannot rule out any of the distractors and these suggestions do not apply, the testee should always select the same lettered option. The examination constructors try to distribute the correct answers among the five options. In some tests the middle or C response is correct more often than the others.

Examinations are constructed for the most part by persons from the cultural background in which the test originates. Therefore, those who have been trained abroad and whose native languages are not English are often slower in reading the items and have less time to reflect on the options.

A significant contribution to the evaluation of clinical competence is the development of patient management problem tests. Those tests try to simulate an actual clinical situation, with emphasis on a functional problem-solving patient-oriented approach. From thousands of reported examples of outstandingly good or poor clinical performance, test designers defined the major areas of performance, such as history taking, physical examination, use of diagnostic procedures, laboratory tests, treatment, judgment, and continuing care. Armed with that information, the test designers evolved a type of test known as programmed testing. The test provides feedback of information to the examinee, who can use these data in the solution of additional problems about the same patient.

The format starts with general patient information, which gives historical data. The section may be followed by a summary of the physical examination and positive elements in the psychiatric status. Then the testees are presented with a series of problems, each with a variable number of options. If the examinees select an option, they receive the results of the laboratory test they requested, the patients' reaction to the med-

Table 58.1
Types of Items Used in Multiple-Choice Questions

Type A: One-best-response type

Each item consists of an introductory statement or question, known as the stem, followed by four or five suggested responses. The incorrect options are known as distractors, as differentiated from the correct response. Some of the distractors may be true in part, but the one *best* response of those offered must be selected to receive full credit.

DIRECTIONS: Each of the statements or questions below is followed by five suggested responses or completions. Select the *one* that is *best* in each case.

1. A 2-year-old boy occasionally plays with his older sister's doll, imitating her activities. This implies	Stem	
A. pathological problems with sibling rivalry B. undue identification with his mother C. future problems with heterosexual orientation D. development of problems with gender identity	Distractors	Choices or Options
E. natural exploration of his environment	Correct Response	
2. Children in the fourth grade in urban area schools who cannot read are most commonly	Stem	
A. isolated from peers B. mentally retarded	Distractors	Choices or Options
C. culturally disadvantaged	Correct Response	
D. brain damaged E. handicapped by a major perceptual deficiency	Distractors	

Type B: Matching type

DIRECTIONS: Each group of questions consists of five lettered headings, followed by a list of numbered words or phrases. For each numbered word or statement, select the one lettered heading or component that is most closely associated with it.

Questions 3–8

A. Mood disorder
B. Psychotic disorder
C. Chromosomal abnormality
D. Cognitive disorder
E. None of the above

	Correct responses
3. Delusional disorder	B
4. Conversion disorder	E
5. Down's syndrome	C
6. Bipolar I disorder	A
7. Obsessive-compulsive disorder	E
8. Wernicke's syndrome	D

The use of "None of the above" in a type A or type B question often makes the item more difficult and tends to lower the percentage of candidates giving correct responses. It should also be noted that the same response may be used more than once.

Type C:

A modified form of the matching type (type C) is also used. It necessitates the ability to compare and contrast two entities, such as diagnostic procedures, treatment modalities, or causes. The association is on an all-or-none basis. For instance, even if a treatment is only occasionally used or associated with a given disorder, it is to be included as a correct response.

DIRECTIONS: Each set of lettered headings below is followed by a list of numbered words or phrases. For each of the numbered words or phrases select

A. if the item is associated with A *only*
B. if the item is associated with B *only*
C. if the item is associated with *both* A and B
D. if the item is associated with *neither* A nor B

Questions 9–13

A. Down's syndrome (mongolism)
B. Tuberous sclerosis (epiloia)
C. Both
D. Neither

	Correct responses
9. Mental deficiency	C
10. Nodular type of skin rash	B
11. Higher than chance association with leukemia	A
12. Chromosomal nondisjunction	A
13. Specific disorder of amino acid metabolism	D

Adapted from Small SM: Role of examinations in psychiatry. In *Comprehensive Textbook of Psychiatry,* ed 6, HI Kaplan, BJ Sadock, editors, p 2734. Williams & Wilkins, Baltimore, 1995.

ication they ordered, or just a confirmation of the order. The examinees may select as few or as many options as befits good clinical judgment. The testees lose both credit and informational feedback if they do not select an important and necessary option. They may also lose credit by selecting unnecessary or dangerous options.

Having completed problem 1 about a patient, the testee is usually given some additional follow-up information, and the procedure is repeated for problems 2, 3, and so on. An oversimplified and much abbreviated example is as follows:

A young college student has been hyperactive, has slept poorly, and has lost weight during the past month. He has been known to use cannabis and possibly other substances on many occasions. Last night he became excited, thought he was going insane, and complained of a rapid pounding sensation over his heart. He was taken to the emergency room by his roommate. No history of prior psychiatric difficulty was obtained. Physical examination reveals a temperature of 99.5 degrees F, pulse rate of 108 per minute, respiration rate of 22 per minute, and a blood pressure of 142/80 mm Hg. His pupils are dilated but react to light, his mouth is dry, and the rest of the examination is noncontributory except for a generalized hyperreflexia. On psychiatric examination he is irritable, restless, and very suspicious. He states that people are after him and wish to harm him. He is well oriented.

1. At this time you would

A. order morphine sulfate 30 mg intramuscularly
B. inquire about drug usage
C. order an electrocardiogram
D. tell the patient that no one wants to harm him and that it is all his imagination
E. arrange for hospitalization plus many additional options

Of the choices given, the feedback on B could be ''Roommate states patient was taking amphetamines.'' D feedback: ''Patient becomes excited and refuses to answer questions.'' E feedback: ''Arrangements made.''

2. The following morning, after a restless sleep, the patient continues to express fears of being harmed. You would now order

F. chlorpromazine 100 mg 3 times daily
G. urine screen for drugs
H. projective psychological tests
I. imipramine 50 mg 4 times daily and other options

The feedback on F might be ''Patient quieter after a few hours.'' G feedback: ''Ordered.'' H feedback: ''Patient uncooperative.'' I feedback: ''Order noted.''

Although programmed testing differs from the real-life situation—in which the physician has to originate his orders or recommendations, rather than select them from a given set of options—it does simulate the clinical situation to a great extent. Examinees like this type of test and readily appreciate its clinical significance and relevance.

Various modifications of patient management problems have been introduced. It seems that the format, coupled with other forms of testing, is a favorable development in approaching the goal of a standardized reliable and valid means of evaluating some major components of clinical competence.

New methods of testing using computer-based systems for objective evaluation of clinical competence are being developed and tested. They are useful in patient management problems because they provide extensive and instantaneous feedback. They also provide contemporaneous scoring, so the testee knows the result of the test upon completion.

The National Board of Medical Examiners (NBME) has been exploring the use of interactive computerized clinical simulations (CBX) in the evaluation of clinical competence. Each CBX case is an interactive dynamic patient simulation. The student or physician interacting with CBX is presented with a brief description of the condition, circumstances, and chief complaints of the simulated patient. The CBX physician is then expected to diagnose, treat, and monitor the patient's condition as it changes over time and in response to treatment. As the case unfolds, patient information is provided only through uncued requests by the CBX physician for tests, therapies, procedures, or physical examination.

Index

Page numbers followed by *t* and *f* indicate tables and figures, respectively.

I

N

O

P